LET THE SEA MAKE A NOISE

LET THE SEA MAKE A NOISE

Four Hundred Years of Cataclysm, Conquest, War and Folly in the North Pacific

WALTER A. McDOUGALL

AVON BOOKS ◆ NEW YORK

The poetry in "The Fourth 'aha iki" is taken from *Ruling Chiefs of Hawaii* (revised edition) by Samuel M. Kamakau. Copyright © 1992 by Kamehameha Schools/Bishop Estate. Used by permission.

AVON BOOKS
A division of
The Hearst Corporation
1350 Avenue of the Americas
New York, New York 10019

Copyright © 1993 by BasicBooks, A Division of HarperCollins Publishers, Inc.
Published by arrangement with BasicBooks
Library of Congress Catalog Card Number: 92-56175
ISBN: 0-380-72467-7

The BasicBooks edition contains the following Library of Congress Cataloging in Publication Data:
McDougall, Walter A., 1946–
  Let the sea make a noise...: a history of the North Pacific from Magellan to MacArthur/ by Walter A. McDougall.
    p. cm.
  Includes bibliographical references and index.
  Pacific Area—History. 2. North Pacific Ocean—History.
I. Title
DU28.3.M39 1993   92-56175
909'.0982'3—dc20   CIP

First Avon Books Trade Printing: November 1994

AVON TRADEMARK REG. U.S. PAT. OFF. AND IN OTHER COUNTRIES, MARCA REGISTRADA, HECHO EN U.S.A.

Printed in the U.S.A.

ARC 10 9 8 7 6 5 4 3 2 1

To Jonna

Contents

II: Of Steam and Rails

III: Internal Combustion

Maps

Maps

Let the sea make a noise and all that is in it,
the lands and those who dwell therein.

—PSALM 98:8

Yet every place is duly allotted and judgment giv'n
Minos, as president, summons a jury of the dead.

—AENEID VI: 431–33

LET THE SEA MAKE A NOISE

The Summons

WordPerfect 5.0. *"Grabber." First Draft:* Japanese peasants, like those anywhere else, were accustomed to capricious taxation by the agents of castle or town. But Lord Matsukura, on the island of Kyushu, liked to embellish the business with occasional torture and rapine, and the fact that his tenants were mostly Christian converts seasoned the sport. But in the fall of 1637 crop yields were low and the countryside was seeded with samurai dispossessed by civil war. So when word spread that the tax men were confiscating the occasional daughter as well as rice, the peasants rose in revolt.

By early 1638, thirty-seven thousand insurgents had seized weapons and were holed up in a castle near Shimabara, defying an army one hundred thousand strong. Nearby Nagasaki, the center of European influence, watched in suspense as the rebel forces defended the walls with incongruous cries to "Jesu!" "Maria!" and "Santiago!" They felled thirteen thousand attackers and killed their general but failed to break the siege. Matsukura then named a new commander with close ties to the Great Shogun at Edo (Tokyo) and appealed for help to the Dutch based nearby. The local East India Company agent, Nicholaes Koeckebacker, faced an unhappy choice: defy Matsukura and possibly lose all rights to trade in Japan, or turn his cannon against Shimabara. Of course, the Christians involved were Japanese, not European, and Catholic, not Protestant. He sent in his ship, and the defenders—bombarded, starving, and short of ammunition—gradually lost their strength. A final, furious assault overran the castle in April. Not a man, woman, or child survived.

Decrees against Christianity had been intermittently enforced since 1587. But now the Shogun moved with the finality of a man who has made up his mind. All foreigners were banned from Japanese soil, and all Japanese suspected of being Christians were told to trample on the cross or face torture and death. Thousands were crucified. In 1640 the Shogun beheaded the last Portuguese emissaries and warned that the same greeting awaited their king or even their god if they dared approach the Japanese coast. As for the Dutch, they had escaped persecution by keeping a low profile—being Reformed churchmen, they had no priests in their midst and displayed no crucifixes. But when the head of the Shogun's anti-Christian commission noticed a Dutch warehouse marked "A.D. 1637," a decree went forth that all buildings dated by the Christian calendar be razed. The Dutch complied and won the right to remain—but only on an artificial island called Deshima, barely three acres large, in Nagasaki harbor. No white barbarians were allowed to cross the footbridge to shore, and no Japanese were allowed to travel abroad. For over two hundred years this *sakoku*, or policy of isolation, was the most important geopolitical fact in the North Pacific. For it meant that Russia, Spain, Britain, and the United States were free to contest for control of that still empty ocean, with all the sails and muscle and steam they could muster, while their greatest potential rival—Japan—sulked like Achilles in his tent.

Not bad. Enough blood and drama to serve as a "grabber," and enough cultural and geopolitical conflict to hint at the themes of the book. Of course, I'll have to do a flashback to the Spanish arrival in the North Pacific . . . and say something about technology. The Shogun's main motive for *sakoku*, after all, was to prevent his domestic rivals for power from getting their hands on European ships and guns. So the story begins with Japan purposely spurning Western technology, and it ends today with Western nations fretting over the invasion of Japanese technology. Nice symmetry, professor. Thanks to *sakoku* the North Pacific becomes a "white man's lake," but now, only 140 years after Japan's reemergence, the white man's day appears to be over in the Pacific.

Or is this too lugubrious an opening scene? May put off some readers. And there's no personal element, just nameless peasants and abstract geopolitics. I've got to personalize the saga from the get-go and advertise its humor as well as its drama. Alaska, maybe. The business about "Soapy" and Harriman's railroad reveries. So let's hit F7 to exit. Save document. Call it "Nagasaki" . . . whoops! Whoever said it's easy to use a portable computer on an airplane? Exit WordPerfect? No. Open new document, and . . .

Alaska "Grabber." First Draft: These days the luxury cruises put in all summer at the picturesque ports of the panhandle: Sitka, Ketchikan, Juneau, Wrangell, and Skagway. Their little populations seem to double, the Back Later signs disappear from the shops, and thousands of cameras record identical images of quaint wooden facades, totem poles and old sourdoughs, fjords and mountains whose verticality and ubiquity defeat the widest-angle lens. It was all just as thrilling, but far less familiar in June 1899 when the elegant steamer *George W. Elder* dropped a most extravagant party of 126 crewmen, scientists, guides, and tourists in a most unlikely place: Skagway. Presiding over the kingly procession was Edward H. Harriman, his wife and five children, four in-laws, and three servants. It was all ostensibly a holiday. But reporters wondered why the railroad magnate had wrapped his plans and route in secrecy if this were just a tycoon-sized version of a cruise up the Hudson?

John Muir, the California artist and conservationist, had been to Skagway two years before and likened its bustle to that of an anthill poked with a stick. The Klondike gold rush was cresting, and this was the jumping-off point for the Chilkoot Pass and Dawson City. But Skagway was a strange sort of anthill, filled not with communistic insects but with every sort of sharpster, whore, fortune hunter, and defiant individualist North America could debouch. Lord of them all was Soapy Smith, a black-bearded blackguard in a wide-brimmed hat whose agents as far away as Seattle told stampeders whom to see in Skagway for supplies and maps to the gold fields. When the pigeons arrived, the boys from Soapy's Reliable Packing Company accosted them with offers of guidebooks, rooms, maps, or tips for a single dollar, always a dollar. Then as soon as the tenderfoot pulled out his purse, the gangsters pinched his stake. Who would play benefactor to the now stranded lamb? Why, Soapy would hear tell of his misfortune and provide the fare back to Seattle . . . or something for his widow and orphans if he had dared make a ruckus. It was all in the public interest, said Soapy, for a man who couldn't look after himself had no business braving the Yukon!

But other routes to the Klondike competed for stampeders, and Skagway's merchants rued the town's reputation. When one well-liked veteran was robbed of his poke, a town meeting gathered to name vigilantes. Soapy was arrogant, visibly sloshed, and confronted the meeting Winchester in hand. When he jabbed the rifle at one of the guardians, Frank H. Reid, surveyor, pulled his revolver. At once each man fired, and Soapy fell dead. Reid, sad to say, also died of his wound. But just think if Soapy had reigned one more year, to greet E. H. Harriman on the wharfs of old Skagway. Guidebooks for all, Mr. Harriman, sir, and only a dollar, just one U.S. dollar!

But Harriman was on a different quest, just as reporters had suspected. He imagined himself proprietor of a 'round-the-world railroad. And why not? A bridge over the Bering Strait could not be all that different a matter than the new Brooklyn Bridge, or a tunnel beneath it more challenging than New York City's subway. Skagway's own little railroad proved that construction was possible even in subarctic conditions, while Russia's Trans-Siberian Railway was now nearly finished. A crazy but wonderful dream: Americans and Russians pooling their talents to restore the ancient land bridge that knit the continents together!

So the *George W. Elder* made its foggy crossing and deposited the Harrimans on the Siberian side. The two dozen Eskimos who clomped out to greet them looked diseased, and the stench from exposed remains of mammals and fish overpowered the white people's nostrils. Even the dogs, no woolly huskies eager for "mush," looked sickly and fled from the strangers. It was freezing in midsummer and the wind was outrageous. So Harriman traded for souvenirs, took some pictures, and fled for the boat with a silent promise never to think of the place again. In any event, railroading's swashbuckling era was ending, the whole age of steam was giving way to oil and electricity, and there was not much chance for Russo-American partnership. The Tsar had no interest in giving American capitalists the run of Siberia, while the United States was considering shutting down all trade with Russia because of its gross anti-Semitism. So Alaska and nearby Siberia remained, as it were, worlds apart, with only walrus and whales, Chukchi and Eskimos, passing between them as each season decreed.

It's fantastic, it's fun . . . it's flippant . . . and trivial. The opener has to convey a sense of majesty and tragedy, the North Pacific as a place of explosions. Racial explosions, the explosions of war, the explosiveness of the environment itself, the sense of a dangerous heaven. On the Pacific Rim people live life on the *rim,* waiting for the next typhoon or drought, or fire or volcanic eruption, or—F7 to exit! Save "Alaska." New document. Go!

Professor Omori of Tokyo Imperial University suspected that something extraordinary was building up on the other side of the ocean. His excellent Milne seismograph detected what looked to be foreshocks along the San Andreas Fault. But he could not predict an earthquake, much less where its epicenter might be, so he could only hope that San Franciscans had received some sort of warning of their own when the jagged line on his seismograph suddenly jumped off the scale.

The San Andreas temblor of April 18, 1906, is judged to have measured about 8.25 on the scale invented by Charles F. Richter in the 1930s. It lasted an interminable forty-five seconds, building from a dull to an overpowering roar, and left behind cracks in the earth twenty feet wide. Buildings and bridges collapsed, locomotives careened, and captive waters gushed free along a zone stretching from the wine country of Sonoma through Marin County and down the peninsula to Stanford, where halls crumbled and statues fell, and on to San Jose, Monterey, and Santa Cruz, where the beach sank ten feet, and finally to San Juan Bautista, where this "act of God" ruined the old Spanish mission. Smack in the middle was San Francisco, where a third of all Californians lived in closely packed structures perched on steep hills or the crumbly landfill engineered so proudly by the first generation of Yankees. Almost every chimney or tower toppled, and second or third stories descended on the first. Grand hotels buckled; flophouses disintegrated. Chinese, Italians, Irish, and Anglos ran shrieking into the streets in their nightgowns or less, women clutched rosaries and children, sailors and roughnecks bellowed half-remembered prayers, and crazed old men proclaimed Judgment Day. Dozens took mortal wounds at once, as did Dennis Sullivan when the California Hotel's gimcrack cupola toppled and fell through the roof of the firehouse on Bush Street, leaving him comatose until his death four days later. Sullivan was the Fire Chief, and by the time the aftershocks died at 5:25 A.M., the fires were already out of control.

This may have been the 418th earthquake recorded in 'Frisco since 1848. But it was the first of any magnitude to strike since the city had been rigged for gas heating and light. Broken mains and the odd stove or lamp ignited scores of minor fires and a dozen major ones among tenements and warehouses south of Market Street. Within minutes the sky looking south from downtown or the hills was a blaze of orange, touching off the usual range of human reactions. Some men panicked, some looted, some fled. Others formed up to rescue the injured, evacuate buildings, and combat the flames. Only there was no water to be had: the water mains had burst in the earthquake, rendering the reservoirs carefully husbanded in the city and in San Mateo utterly, pitifully useless. Acting Fire Chief John Dougherty did his damnedest, ordering men to tap into any source of moisture, including the sewers. But south of Market was doomed, and the merging fires generated enough heat to ignite the Financial District to the north and Mission District to the west. Dougherty gave up trying to extinguish the blaze and worked instead to contain it. That meant blowing up whole city blocks to form fire breaks, and that required massive evacuations, not to mention explosives. But telephone lines were down and the streets gorged with refugees.

By afternoon the fire had moved southward to consume the Southern Pacific terminal and jumped north across Market Street into downtown. One by one the landmarks succumbed: the old Post Office, Old St. Patrick's Church, the old Opera House where Caruso had sung the night before, Union Square, even the splendid Palace Hotel, built to be earthquake- and fireproof. Brigadier General Frederick Funston, hero of the

Philippine War and commander of the city's presidio, ordered his sap-
pers to blow up buildings on broad Montgomery Street. But the fire-
break failed, while the dry, still, and unseasonably warm weather—
"earthquake weather," it would later be called—was no help at all. Nor
were the winds sucked in by the flames, nor the perverse influx of people come from across the bay to save their possessions, find relatives, or
gawk. Funston shut down the ferries. Henceforth, no person could enter
San Francisco without written approval of the Army or the Mayor.

By Thursday morning, two hundred thousand people had lost or left
their homes, ten times the number Funston first estimated he would
have to feed at the Army's makeshift shelters in Golden Gate Park. And
still the fire spread, up California Street into the most exclusive quarter
of the city, and into Chinatown, the most despised. Nob Hill (so named
because the nabobs lived there) sported the $5 million Fairmont Hotel
and the homes of Stanford, Huntington, and Crocker, which were filled
with priceless art. The brownstone mansions would resist the fire for
hours until their walls grew so hot that the furnishings within burst
into flame. Chinatown was mere kindling, and its destruction brought a
new horror on that second day. As the fire advanced, great rats emerged
in waves from subterranean nests and tunnels, stopping only to feed off
the odd human corpse. The Chinese, too, fled into the neighboring districts, including Italian North Beach, and there, in the midst of the
inferno, a race riot broke out.

Yes, and even their common purgation did not move the city's ethnic
groups to reconcile. Instead, the whites made San Francisco's reconstruction the occasion to segregate Asians and ban new immigration,
thereby provoking the first Japanese-American war scare in 1907. Did
they suspect even then, even as they tried to legislate white supremacy,
that the white man's hold on the North Pacific was bound to slip in the
twentieth century? Homer Lea did, weird prophet that he was. And it's
not so shocking a thought when you realize how brief a time whites
have been here in any numbers. The California gold rush began in
1849. The Russians, on the other side, didn't even found Vladivostok
until 1860. The mid-nineteenth century was just a charmed moment—a
conjuncture, as we historians say—when the whites had all the technology, and the Chinese, Japanese, and Mexicans were immobilized:
huge human rookeries just staying put. So the North American coast,
Alaska, Hawaii, and Siberia were all up for grabs—and America,
Britain, and Russia grabbed 'em up. But sooner or later, Asia and Mexico were bound to spill over. The whites even hastened the process by
forcing open China and Japan and importing Asian and Hispanic
workers. The whites on Pacific shores have always been paranoid, as if

they knew they were interlopers, as if they knew their hold on the region was somehow artificial.

Now it's Japanese and Chinese who buy up Waikiki and Pebble Beach and Hollywood and the Seattle Mariners and millions of acres of farmland in the United States and Canada, while immigration will make the whites a minority in California within ten or fifteen years. The San Francisco Irish and Italians surely hate seeing their old neighborhoods go Asian. Still, I don't see anyone in the Sunset District turning down $400,000 for their row house just because the money's from Hong Kong. . . . I hope the Irish bars survive, at least.

You'd think Berkeley folks would celebrate the diversity. But Asian capitalists aren't *their* kind of "persons of color." Serves them right! The Yellow Peril become the Philistine Peril. Maybe in fifty years California's whites will be confined to ghettos of their own, surrounded by thirty or forty million Asians and Latin Americans. That's assuming the water holds out. And what of the poor blacks? The only neighborhoods many of them can afford are being bought up and rehabbed by Vietnamese and Koreans. Once Oakland and Watts and Sacramento are Asian/Hispanic, will the blacks just give up and head east? They say there are already three hundred thousand Chinese in Vancouver, British Columbia, for heaven's sake! And Hawaii's really interesting. There was a move in the eighties by Hawaiians, even of Japanese descent, to outlaw land sales to Japanese aliens. So now Asians, Mexicans, and blacks fight over Pacific turf with immigration and ownership laws—the same weapons used by whites against them a few generations ago.

Flying is so very *boring*. . . . So why do I feel guilty for not properly appreciating the miracle of zipping over the Pacific at five hundred miles per hour, jet stream at my back, on the way to Oahu, the gathering place of peoples? Shame on me. To think it was all so unreachable before Captain Cook. Now jet airplanes, not to mention orbiting satellites, whiz above the same weather and waves that destroyed Vitus Bering and countless other captains and sailors. Safe as houses, unless the pilot drifts over Kamchatka! Poor Russians—imagine staring at a radar screen all night in some windowless blockhouse in Siberia, guarding an empire that no longer exists against enemies you're hoping will bail out your country so that stranded military posts like yours can keep on getting their rations.

People ask how you get interested in things. With me it was maps. Always loved maps. And the North Pacific still seems exciting despite all the fads: Pacific Rim, Pacific Century, coming Pacific War, new Pacific Culture. To me the Pacific Ocean still suggests cleanliness, sweetness, and strangeness, even in California if you get out of L.A.

and the Bay Area. Is there anything more golden than the Gold Country in summertime, or spookier than the woods and legends of the Pacific Northwest? I wonder what the crows of the Alaskan panhandle think of all the cruise ships steaming up and down the Inland Passage. *Caw! Caw! Caw!* Perhaps they think the Tlingits went forth in their canoes to convert the white man to the raven cult, so that now we come in endless pilgrimage to sacrifice popcorn and sandwich crusts and leftover salmon to the feathered lords of Alaska.

It's odd—no, I suppose it isn't odd that the Vietnam War brought me to this ocean for the first time. Can't remember anything about the flight from Fort Sill, Oklahoma, to Oakland, but I sure remember being bused to the Army base down on the Bay and locked up in a warehouse lest we go AWOL. There were protesters outside, purporting to save us lambs from the slaughter. A year later they were still there for us, but now we were baby killers. How asinine the Army was to fly us over on a commercial jet, complete with stewardesses and Muzak. "I'm leavin' on a jet plane, don't know when I'll be back again." Great for morale. But the stopover at Clark Field in the Philippines—*that* was the point. To feel the moistness and smell Asia, and see jungle on the horizon and the Stars and Stripes above it. It seemed wrong, not for any political reason, just . . . wrong.

Then there was Fort Ross. Strange that I taught at Berkeley twelve years and never checked it out. Then a friend suggested I might like to see the old Russian fort. Did I! Imagine the flag of the Russian-American Trading Company flying over the California coast, an armory stocked with muskets and cannon forged in St. Petersburg in the early 1800s, biscuit barrels and samovars, and the little chapel and onion dome caked with the residue of rising incense. American flags in the Philippines, Russian flags in Sonoma County . . . now Japanese flags on buses at Pearl Harbor. The North Pacific got parceled and reparceled in a hurry.

Still four hours to Honolulu. They locked us up there, too, while the plane was refueling on the way to Vietnam. I wonder why they flew us the long way on the westbound flight—via Hawaii, Wake Island, and the Philippines—but flew us home on the Great Circle Route via Japan and—well, we were supposed to stop at Anchorage, but didn't. Major jet stream help, I guess. But did I sleep on that Freedom Bird! It would be great, *sublime* to sleep that well again. What was I thinking about? Oh, why I decided to write on the North Pacific. The third episode was that time on Waikiki when my wife and I had to share an elevator with a Japanese tour group. But crammed into the opposite corner, their heads likewise also protruding over the crush of people between us, was another American couple. In a split second—before any inhibition had time to kick in—the four of us raised our eyebrows toward one another, as if to say, Thank God for *you,* my fellow Americans. That other couple was black.

There must be two dozen books out now on the Japanese "threat" and no two agree on what it means. One says the Japanese are taking over because their "development" economy, based on government/industry collaboration, is better suited to today's marketplace than either free enterprise or communism, so we'd better get with the program through some kind of "industrial policy." No, says another, the Japanese are not taking over, and you can't extrapolate from current trends. Japan Incorporated is a myth, and anyway the conditions that made for the rise of Japan are on their way out. Its population is aging, and the young people want more leisure and consumption. The Japanese stock market and real estate bubbles have burst, and their savings rate will fall. In any case, says another, the Japanese system is so rooted in a communitarian, tribal culture that we couldn't copy it even if we wanted to. No, says another, Japanese economics is *not* culture-based. Rather, the one-party state, bureaucrats, businessmen, and media just perpetuate the myths of Japanese homogeneity, superiority, work ethic, hierarchy, consensus, and so on to maintain their grip on the overworked masses. So Japan cannot change, no matter how loudly Americans bitch. Ah so, says the wildest book of all, in that case the United States must turn protectionist and make Japan pay for its own defense, which will force Japan to rearm and seek markets in Asia, which will scare Americans with the specter of a new Coprosperity Sphere, which will make it 1941 all over again!

I've had it with this computer. Where's my pen? In my jacket. Where's my jacket? In the overhead bin. Ugh! Why do I always try to stand up before undoing the seat belt? . . . Look at all the happy Japanese. Four dollars for a cocktail must be pocket change to them. . . . OK, let's get down and didactic on the old legal pad. An epic history of the North Pacific *in tres partes divisa est:* the Era of Sail—no, "Sail and Muscle"; the era—let's call 'em ages—the Age of Steam and Rails; and the Age of what—Flight? The Internal Combustion Engine? How about just "Internal Combustion"? And I'll explain the politics and demographics of each age by the technological constraints of the time, in addition to geography, population shifts, wars. But what makes for the mastery of new technologies by one country or another? How about this: the rise and fall of empires in the North Pacific as a function of the relative strengths and weaknesses of market economies like the American, statist economies like the Russian, and the mixed, directed economy of the

Japanese? Only that's not so. The U.S. Transcontinental Railroad was hardly a product of free enterprise, while the Russian fur companies in Alaska were founded by entrepreneurs without government help. In any case, the United States didn't decline after 1950 for economic reasons alone: it spent its treasure, and built Japan up, for *political,* Cold War reasons. So maybe the biggest arena of all is still the geopolitical.

Karl Haushofer would be pleased, or maybe just smug, that the occasional scholar still checks his *Geopolitik des pazifischen Ozeans* out of the library. Impenetrable Teutonic sludge. I can't believe his stuff influenced the Nazis, because I'm sure none of them read it. But Haushofer saw that every great power on the Pacific Rim was tempted by the empty openness of the region to expand beyond its appointed sphere, and that each in turn suffered—how did he put it?—*"fühlbare, sichtbare Strafe"* (tangible, visible punishment). Thus Spain, Russia, Britain—and after Haushofer's time, Japan and the United States—overextended themselves and were forced to retreat. But that's just common sense. The interesting question is *where* those "appointed spheres" lie for each nation, and *why.*

Let's try a geopolitical outline. In the early days the North Pacific was a free-for-all among Spain, Russia, and Britain, then later the United States, all competing for claims and commerce. By the early twentieth century Spain is out and Britain fading, while Meiji Japan enters the fray. So it settles down into a triangle among the United States, Russia, and Japan, fighting for empire from California around the Pacific Rim to Manchuria and in the waters and islands in the middle. Whenever two nations clashed the third benefited, which allowed the loser of one round to recoup in the next round. Might work. But war and politics aren't the whole story either. Military power didn't do Russia much good in the nineteenth century, or Japan in the twentieth. So geopolitics has to make room for economics—thank you, Paul Kennedy—as well as technology and especially demography, the crests and troughs of the waves of migration. "The whites crawl in, the Indians crawl out, the Asians crawl in, the whites crawl out. . . ." I wonder if Alaska and Siberia are safe. Imagine if the *seventy* million Koreans should unite and start pouring out of their crowded little thumb of land? Settlers are mightier than guns in the end. The Yanks took Oregon with settlers. But how about Hawaii? It's filled up now with Japanese, Okinawans, Chinese, Filipinos, Portuguese and Mexican *paniolos,* African-Americans, Puerto Ricans, and just a smattering of more or less pure-blood Polynesians. And yet it's as American as the Beach Boys.

What would King Kamehameha I (Kah-MAY-ah-MAY-ah) say if you told him his land was populated by just about every race *except* Hawaiians? Kamehameha the Great, Napoleon of the Pacific. So in other words American culture, religion, government, and so on triumphed in Hawaii even though whites remained a small minority. Values and institutions have to figure in somehow. As the white man retreats from the North Pacific, he leaves behind a legacy of democracy, individualism, revealed religion, free enterprise, private property, equal protection under the law, and—late though it was in coming—racial equality. The North Pacific as Yankee cultural zone even though U.S. military and economic might is receding. But then, how Americanized is Japan? I guess we'll find out, now that the Rising Sun is rising again. I wonder if General MacArthur is up there watching, or Commodore Perry . . . or the Emperor Jimmu. *Banzai!*

Three and a half more hours to kill before we land in Honolulu. . . . Maybe I should open the book with a Hawaiian episode. The fate of Hawaii as somehow a metaphor for the whole ocean. Cook's death is too well known. Same with Pearl Harbor. But maybe Kamehameha founding the Hawaiian monarchy? Or the missionaries converting the Hawaiian queen, what's her name?, and establishing American influence? I could pair that with the rejection of Christianity in Japan. . . .

Or I could just go to sleep. Best way to fly: unconscious. If only I could sleep the way I did on the flight back from Vietnam.

Now *that* was sleep. . . .

"*Aloha, haole.* We have summoned you. You will *kokua.*"

The First 'aha iki

Ah yes, the familiar dream feeling. Like I'm watching a movie, only somehow *in* the movie at the same time. And obviously on location. What a splendid place this is, and yet in ruins. Some sort of temple complex—it seems to cover this whole peninsula. The ocean's phosphorescent. Curious, these long rows of volcanic stones. Must have been walls, or foundations of buildings, and all laid out so neatly. A *heiau*, a Polynesian holy place! Has to be. But ruined by something—a war or volcanic eruption. White sand, palms, a catamaran: Hawaii. The humidity here is so bearable, because of the breezes.

"*Haole!* We have summoned you. You will speak to us."

He's talking to *me*. Or *she* is. Heaven help me if she's a she, with that voice! But I can't . . . seem to . . . I'll have to . . . turn around . . . my God, she must be six foot four, and two hundred pounds. What a dress: a tartan print with gigantic sleeves, and a band of fur stitched in the hem, and that great hat with its halo of blossoms and feathers.

"How do you do, ma'am?"

I'm talking to her bodice! But what if she considers it impertinent to look her in the eye?

"Forgive me, but who are you?"
"You know who we are. The question is, Who are you?"

OK. This person, who scares the heck out of me, says she wants *kokua*. That's "help" if I remember my pocket dictionary. Good thing to have. Got me out of a speeding ticket once in Hilo. Yet she says she doesn't know who I am, but claims that *I* know *her*. What can that mean?

"I'm just a historian."

Blank stare.

"A teacher of the deeds of our ancestors. And I don't even know where I am, except somewhere in Hawaii."

"You are frightened. Do not be frightened. You are safe here, you are at Pu'uhonua O Honaunau, the Place of Refuge—"

"Place of refuge. . . . Near Kailua/Kona on the Big Island! I've been there, or here, rather!"

"And what we require will take no time at all."

Why is she laughing at that?

"You are a storyteller, a person of learning. We desire such a one, who knows all that has happened in our ocean after we departed from time. Tell me, please, what has become of my husband's kingdom, and of the doings of the *haoles?*"

First she uses a royal "we," then slips into the first person. And she talks as if she were dead. But I'm not dead, I'm—.

"I *do* know who you are! Your Highness, you speak of your husband's kingdom, and are dressed in the style of the eighteen-teens or twenties. You are Kaa—. . . . Forgive me, I can never pronounce your name."

"We are Kaahumanu (kah-ah-hu-MAHN-nu)—favorite consort of Kamehameha the Great and *kuhina nui* of the Sandwich Islands. Welcome to paradise."

She's laughing again, but this time beautifully. Do I kneel or bow to a sort-of queen? She seems pleased, fairly jiggling with mirth.

"Ma'am, this is a dream come true. But you cannot want—I can think of many historians, well, several, more qualified than I. Surely you do not mean to choose me!"

"Do I know aught of your scholarly pecking order? Do not invent excuses for denying *kokua.*"

"Of course not, your . . . ladyship. But you say you want to learn about the *whole* ocean? It's a very large ocean. . . ."

"I can see that the ocean is large, storyteller—the Englishman Vancouver marveled that our ancestors crossed it in our canoes. Yes, I want to know about *all* the peoples on its shores. . . . Why do you resist us?"

"It's just that you do me such honor. I don't know how well I can . . . perform. I would need help myself, I. . . . Tell me, Your Highness, is it possible to conjure up *other* people the way you did me? Imagine if we could consult with other great statesmen, chiefs, *alii,* from America or Japan, filled with the spirit, the *mana,* of the nations that shaped the history of the Pacific."

"Who are these *alii?* Did they come to Hawaii?"

"Depends on whom you summon, or I summon . . . or who answers our summons.

But *I* didn't hear any "summons." I haven't a clue how this works.

"Some of them will have come to Hawaii, perhaps. But they all would have visited your ocean, or had much to do with its history, even as *you* did, Elizabeth."

Oops, that slipped out. She's blushing the color of cooked lobster, as Hawaiians say.

"*Ae!* The man *does* know Kaahumanu—the old and the new."
"I do indeed, magnificent lady. I know of your marriage to a king, and your role in his wars, and in the coming of the *haoles*. You turned a whole culture on its head when you abolished the taboo, *kapu*, and freed the women and welcomed the missionaries. In a sense you *wrote* the history of your times."
"I only learned to write at the end of my life. . . ."
"Imagine if we could call others as important to their nations as you were to yours. I'm sure I can tell you all I know—at abominable length, no doubt—but I need you and others to correct what I say. Please, *kuhina nui*, if it is possible, summon others like yourself."
"Others. Yes. Then we may hold *'aha iki* (ah-ha-EE-kee), and sit together in judgment on what you are to say."
"*Haha icky!* What is—?"
"*'aha iki*, storyteller. It seems I am to teach you. As when a few important people, chiefs or *kāhuna*, met to discuss grave matters. Very secret. Like a council of war. But sometimes we would gather *after* the battle—"
"To do a postmortem. Yes, we must stage an *'aha iki*."
"So be it. Then wish, with me, for the others."

Why do I wish, or pray, with my eyes tightly shut? Is it St. Augustine's influence, or Peter Pan's? Maybe all cultures do it. But do I dare *open* my eyes? If she can do it . . . it would be heaven itself for an historian! But it's not working. Nothing's. . . . It *is* working: there's someone here! I see a man about five-and-a-half-feet tall—probably average height for his time—and what a mop of hair, glowing orange and gray. Ooooh, his neck's been scraped by a straight razor, and his high, stiff collar is rubbing against it. Almost hurts to look. Strong chin, long, bony nose, intelligent blue eyes, paternal brow—the sort of man you want for your lawyer. Black broadcloth suit. I've got to try to remember all this. And he's not the only one!

"Sir, allow me to introduce myself. William Henry Seward, Governor of the great state of New York, and Secretary of State during our Civil War. At your service, sir. But I perceive by your dress that you came later than I."

"How do you do, Your Excellency, and the pleasure's mine, I assure you. I am Saitō Hirosi (sigh-TOH hee-ROH-shee), and I've read much about you. In fact, I was friends with another New York Governor, Franklin Roosevelt. Of course, he became President."

"Did he, sir? A sly patroon from the Hudson, no doubt. As for me, I was cheated of the White House. Only time Thurlow Weed—my campaign chairman—ever let me down. To think we were outsmarted by the hayseed Lincoln and his weasel from Chicago. . . . Davis was his name."

"No need for regrets, Mr. Secretary, not anymore. Besides, why would *anyone* have wanted to become President in 1861? The war—"

"Damn me man, I might have *prevented* the War of Secession, whereas Lincoln's election condemned us to it."

"And condemned you to be remembered for nothing more than the purchase of Alaska. . . ."

"Nothing more! Alaska was the least of my achievements. . . . But forgive me, I speak of myself. You are—"

"I was Ambassador of His Majesty the Emperor of Japan to the United States. In the 1930s. My mission was also to prevent war, but the boys back in Tokyo double-crossed me. Then I kicked the bucket."

Saitō Hirosi! The charming diplomat who talked in American slang! He can't be more than five feet tall, and *maybe* a hundred pounds. Toothy grin, wire-rimmed spectacles, enormous ears, and the top hat, morning jacket, and striped pants of the diplomatic corps: like a prewar caricature of a Japanese dignitary. Seward and Saitō: it's a miracle. But do they look out of place in a *heiau*!

"Forgive me, Ambassador, but did you know that *I* was instrumental in the early relations between our peoples? Your revolution on behalf of the Mikado occurred in 1868, near the end of my term as Secretary of State, and I visited your country soon afterward."

He's talking about the Meiji Restoration and the beginning of Japan's crash modernization. I'd forgotten that Seward went to Japan.

"It was I who promoted American civilization in the Pacific, and you Japanese were receptive to our good help. . . . But you say there was later a danger of war between us? Surely you exaggerate. What could have gone so wrong—?"

"Your people turned their backs on us, Governor. And my people went mad."

"Indeed, Ambassador, went mad, you say? Uh, ah, and you, sir, whom do I have the honor of addressing?"

There's a third!

"I am *Count* Sergey Yulyevich Witte (VIT-teh), Prime Minister to His Majesty Nicholas II, Tsar of all the Russias, and I know what you mean about frustration at being smarter than your superior. Only, I would not denigrate the wisdom of Mr. Lincoln."

"Forgive me my informality, Count Witte. It was I who had to teach the President that one does not address titled foreigners as "sir"! You say you were Prime Minister? After my time, was it?"

Witte's a giant, at least compared with all of us but Kaahumanu. Tall and ursine, not fat, but clumsy-looking. I'd be afraid to see him sit for fear the chair would collapse. His head is large, too, and the forehead broader still, maybe to make room for more brains. He has striking eyes, set apart, and a full black beard. But his voice is high-pitched, whiny, frankly a bit irritating.

"I was Prime Minister after the 1905 revolution following our disastrous war with Japan. But my greatest influence was earlier. My calling, Mr. Secretary, was to modernize Russia—I believe this—and to save my Emperor and people from their own blasted Russianness. Gentlemen, *I built the Trans-Siberian Railway.* But my enemies—my Russian enemies—were bent on military expansion. They brought on the war with Japan, and that spoiled everything. So I suppose I, too, was a failure. But what more could I have done?"

"Do you detect a pattern, Count Witte? I tried to prevent an American civil war; you, Count Witte, a Russo-Japanese war; and you, Mr. Ambassador, a Japanese-American war, I take it. And we all had to fight against "madness." But who is this fellow, this little monk of some sort?"

"Little monk? Yes, and smaller still for being among such statesmen, doubtless wise in worldly things. My name is Junípero Serra (hu-NEEP-air-oh SER-rah), Order of St. Francis. I founded some missions once in Alta California. It was nothing."

Father Serra, by the grace of God! Let this not fade away. Don't figure this out, brain, and burst in to spoil everything. Let this be a deep sleep. I do hope it's sleep. Father Serra: he's taller than Saitō, but just barely. Hard to judge his frame beneath the cowl and robe, but there's no sign of a padre's paunch. His face is round, a bit effeminate, and see how he works his stubby fingers, always twisting his waistcord, never at rest. His skin is olive, and—oh—he's got an awful limp.

"Your missions were more than nothing, Father. You were the—well, one might say you were the *first Californian*. Except for the Indians, of course."

"Yes, Mr. Seward, except for the Indians. But I fear that we failed in California. By the time of my death, the Anglos and Russians were almost upon us, and New Spain was sick. I suspected that it was only a matter of time until we were driven from the Pacific, and the Indians killed or made into slaves."

"I don't know about the Indians, Father, but you all were driven out in our war with Mexico, well after your time. A foolish, unnecessary conflict—I opposed it, of course. But if you were alive when our republic was founded, you must have guessed that the continent itself could not hold it."

"Blessed are peacemakers, for they shall be called the children of God."

"I think you misunderstand me, Father. I believed in expansion, but only so long as it *was* peaceful. Still, it usually isn't, right, Count Witte?"

"One might as well say, '*Cursed* are peacemakers, for they shall be made to look foolish.'"

"Sometimes peacemakers *are* foolish, gentlemen. Much depends on their motives, and what sort of 'peace' they are trying to save."

"Perhaps to a holy man, Father, but in politics effects count more than motives. Don't you agree, Governor?"

"Indubitably. And meanwhile, gentlemen, I suspect some *purpose* behind this cozy caucus."

Caucus! There's a good translation for *'aha iki*. I think.

"All four of us sought to expand our country's dominion and culture; we all dipped our toes in the Pacific because we believed our national destinies lay there; and none of us thought violence the most lasting means of securing those destinies. We have much in common, we four. Hold on—how many are we?"

"All people have more in common than they will admit—even men and women. *Ae!* There is always a purpose to *'aha iki*. We are Kaahumanu, Queen of the Sandwich Islands, and we seek instruction in the story of our ocean. What can these *haole* chiefs, and this papal *kahuna*—and this brown gentleman (who looks something like us, but he is so small!)—what can they tell us of Hawaii, scholar?"

"I'll explain, Your Highness, but may I ask how it is that Count Witte and Father Serra speak English so fluently?"

Why is Witte winking at her?

"It only sounds like English to you, Professor, as it sounds like Russian to me. Babel appears to be reversed in this place, yet we preserve the charms of our own personalities. It would be good beyond hope—if we could only forget."

"Why, Count Witte, I think you may have missed your calling."

"Perhaps, little Father, but not in your church!"

"Enough! Sectarian rivalry is *kapu Kaahumanu!*"

She's roaring again. I understand already something of her power.

"You are summoned here to give help to this man. He is a—"

"Historian."

"—from America. Are you ready?"

"Your Highness, my whole life was a preparation!"

God knows I'm not ready. I'm pitifully unready. . . .

"O Musa, mihi causas memora!"

"Vergil's *Aeneid!* 'Muse, recall to me the reasons.' So the schools still taught the classics in your time? Good!"

"I'm afraid that's almost all I remember, Mr. Seward, and no, American schools have gone to pot. Maybe that's why Saitō's people now own Waikiki."

"The hell, you say?

"Hai! Banzai!"

"Hawaii could have been Russian once, were it not the nature of Russia to fail. Always tragically, always on the grand scale, but always to fail."

"Silence! I must know who "Saitō's people" are and how it is they own Waikiki. Listen now to the historian. He tells us tales of the North Pacific."

You're on! Now, don't choke. You always bragged you could do history lectures in your sleep. So just forget the audience. But, what an audience!

◆

Scholar: In the beginning of the modern era the North Pacific was like another planet, one-sixth the size of the earth. It was incomparably remote, dangerous to approach, and full of mystery. It was empty of people, full of resources, and full of crisp beauty. The lands stretching from Baja California around the semicircular coastline to Korea and China contained every sort of terrain and climate, from salty depressions two hundred feet below sea level to arctic peaks twenty thousand feet above it, high deserts, rich valleys and kingly redwood groves, glaciers and fjords, tundra, volcanic isles, and rain forests. In the end—as I guess one must call the present—much beauty remains, but the North Pacific is filling with people and losing resources, a marketplace linked to older human centers by instantaneous communications, and home to a society as racially mixed as any in history. What then of the middle? What made people from so many lands choose to fill the North Pacific vacuum, and how did their sailing ships, railroads, and airplanes help to shape their nations' Pacific careers? And how were the pioneers helped or hindered by government policies either foolish, wise, ignorant, or passive . . . ?

This is pretentious. I better get to the point.

For as this great slice of the earth became better known, patterns of settlement and conflict emerged. In time, the pioneers and their governments identified six great prizes in the North Pacific: the West Coast of North America, Father Serra's Alta California northward; Alaska, first discovered by Witte's people and purchased for America by Seward; eastern Siberia, which Witte struggled to develop with his great railroad; the Chinese province of Manchuria, which Saitō's countrymen risked all for, twice; the conveniently placed Hawaiian Islands, to which Kaahumanu welcomed the white man; and the sea lanes that tied them together. And the fates of these six North Pacific prizes have always been linked, because no nation could feel secure in its control of any *one* region unless it bid for control of one or more of the *others*. In time the imperial rivals for hegemony in the North Pacific whittled down to three—Russians, Americans, and Japanese— and the unstable triangle they formed still defines the geopolitical and cultural shape of the ocean.

What was the North Pacific like when Europeans first made its acquaintance? In 1866, 353 years after the Spaniard Balboa first spied the ocean, Mark Twain leveled a blast at "that infatuated old ass" who "looked down from the top of a high rock upon a broad sea as calm and peaceful as a sylvan lake, and went into an ecstasy of delight, like any other greaser"—

sorry, Father Serra—

"over any other trifle, and shouted in his foreign tongue and waved his country's banner, and named his great discovery 'Pacific.'" Mr. Clemens's voyage had not been entirely comfortable, and he opined that "if this foreign person had named the ocean the 'Four Months' Pacific,' he would have come nearer the mark." Twain was wrong about Balboa—when he first gasped at the new ocean from the Pana-

manian heights, he baptized it the South Sea. Magellan called it
Pacific. But Twain was right about the weather. In northern latitudes
especially, it is sometimes brutal, and never predictable.

Unless we have visited a place in person, our minds are trained to
imagine geographies in terms of maps. But flat maps obviously distort
the shapes and sizes of lands and seas, and they encourage us to measure distances with a ruler. A globe eliminates the first deficiency but
not the second, for the ocean and the air are no more uniform or fea-
tureless than land masses. A strong current or contrary prevailing
wind is at least as daunting a travel barrier as a mountain range, and
sometimes the old Yankee quip "You can't get there from here" is
simply so. That is why we need to picture the geography of the North
Pacific as it really was when sail and muscle were the only means of
human propulsion.

As our earth rotates on its axis the surface moves at speeds ranging
from almost zero near the poles to one thousand miles per hour at the
equator. At the same time, different portions of the earth receive
varying degrees of heat from the sun, depending on latitude, season,
and time of day. These differentials in motion and heat cause the vigorous circulation of the earth's gases and liquids known as weather.
Today, meteorologists and oceanographers understand the myriad
factors that make for weather, but the patterns of behavior of water
and air first became known to the practical captains and pilots of the
age of sail. The water of the Pacific describes two great circles, one in
each hemisphere. The north and south equatorial currents flow westward from America to Asia, curl northward and southward along the
coasts of Asia and Australia, then flow back toward America. The
Japanese named the warm northward current along their coast the
Kuroshio, or Black Current. Once out to sea these waters break on
the rugged coasts of the Aleutians and Alaska, creating secondary and
even reverse currents. Finally, the main flow turns south again,
where it is known as the California Current. The circulation means
that if you were caught in a lifeboat off San Diego, say, the only way
you'd be likely to get to Los Angeles is via *Japan.* Hawaiian history
tells of distressed Japanese fishing boats washing up on Hawaiian
shores. But a Hawaiian adrift might not reach Japan, by chance or
design, in a thousand years.

Of course, ocean currents (unlike rivers) get no boost from gravity
and rarely move at more than a few knots. Winds are more important
for the sailor. The Pacific trade winds generally blow east to west from
semipermanent high-pressure centers sitting off the American coast at
latitudes up to 30° north and south of the equator. In between the
trades lie the equatorial doldrums, while just north and south of the

30° parallels the trade winds peter out into little versions of the doldrums. These are the horse latitudes, said to be the region where becalmed sailors would throw horses overboard to save water. Beyond these zones, north and south, lie the "stormy forties," and here it is, finally, that the Pacific's prevailing winds turn around and return to the east. But the eastbound voyage in these latitudes is still far from easy, for the northern forties are unreliable and pregnant with storms. On the American side, the temperature difference between the sun-heated land and the cold offshore current makes for a smoke screen of fog, while on the Asian side monsoons blow and typhoons roil the waters from the Philippines to Japan in summer and fall.

By the sixteenth century European shipwrights acquired the art, and sailors the skill, to prod but not tame the Pacific. Their multi-masted, stern-ruddered, straight-keeled carracks, caravels, and galleons freed them from the coastal waters of the Mediterranean and the Baltic, and were of a size to make oceanic voyages economical. Clever deployment of sails and rudder also permitted a pilot to buck cross winds and currents up to a point. But sixteenth-century sails were still few and simple, and the hulls dragged in the wash and collected barnacles. Sometimes just getting out of port was impossible under bad conditions, and only the brave or foolish captain dared waters where winds and currents were unknown.

What this "real map" tells us is that at Renaissance levels of technology the North Pacific was all but closed on the Asian side up to 30° north latitude, unknown and perilous north of it; that the waters off Alaska and Siberia were tricky and the climate treacherous; that sailing north along the American coast was an ordeal; and that the elements guarded Hawaii against easy approach from any direction. It would be charitable to conclude that these facts are enough to explain why the first North Pacific imperialists, the Spaniards, missed the chance to seize the geopolitical prizes astride the ocean. But they are not enough, at least not by themselves.

Kaahumanu: Mahalo, thank you, scholar. But why did you say nothing of—

Scholar: I haven't started yet!

Kaahumanu: Then *start*, that you might finish!

Saitō: If I were you, Doc, I'd do as she says.

I

Of Sail and Muscle

32° North Latitude,
159° East Longitude, 1565

THE FIRST OF THE SIX geopolitical stakes of the North Pacific to come to the knowledge of intruders was the highway to the rest—the sea lanes. Ten days shy of the summer solstice in 1565 (June 1 under the ancient Julian calendar, which still had seventeen years to run), Fray Andres de Urdaneta ordered his speedy caravel, *San Pedro*, out of San Miguel in the Philippines. His destination of Acapulco, whence he had sailed fourteen months before, lay over 9,200 miles due east. Yet Urdaneta, once drawing clear of Leyte Gulf, set a course north by northeast in hopes of passing above the trade winds and horse latitudes and finding westerly breezes. Forty-five years had passed since Magellan made the first westward crossing of the Pacific on the southern trades, but since that time no one had found a way home except by circumnavigating the globe.

After a month of patient tacking, Urdaneta's lonely crew reached 32° north and—though they had no means to measure it—a longitude of about 159° east. This was the point of no return, where another captain had given up twenty-two years before. But Urdaneta prayed for the intercession of St. Peter, patron of his ship, that this might be a season when westerly monsoons this far to the north might carry them back to America. It was Magellan's dare in reverse—and all the more so, for Urdaneta *knew* how broad and empty this ocean was. When westerlies did fill his sails, Urdaneta ordered the *San Pedro* into unknown seas bereft of any land where water or food might be taken. The ship made uneven progress eastward until finally the California current appeared to buoy the mariners south to Mexico. Urdaneta made Acapulco on October 8 after sailing over twelve thousand miles in 130 days. Sixteen of the forty-four crewmen were dead, most from scurvy. Worse yet, the survivors learned that a rival had beaten them to it! Alonso de Arellano, in the patache *San Lucas*, had deserted the expedition on the outward voyage, coasted the Philippines, then set sail for home. He went as far as 43° north, where he claimed to spy porpoises "as big as cows," and anchored at Navidad in August. But where Arellano's log was so fantastic and vague no pilot would trust it, Urdaneta's was precise and professional. So it was the monk, not the freebooter, who truly opened the North Pacific. After the founding of Manila in 1571, the Spanish galleons followed "Urdaneta's route" back home, and his charts of winds and currents remained standard until the time of Captain Cook.

The discovery and conquest of a New World marked a continuum, not a break, in the Spanish experience. In 1492 the armies of Ferdinand and Isabella (whose crownlands of Castille and Aragon had merged to form the kingdom of Spain) overran Moorish Granada, completing the *reconquista* of the Iberian peninsula. In 1492, the royal government expelled the Jews and required Muslims to convert. And in 1492 the court financed the first voyage of Columbus. So when his successors fanned out in the Americas, they carried with them the courage, cruelty, and plundering eye of crusaders and a grudging deference to a jealous monarchy and church. New Spain displayed extremes of individualism and initiative, statism and paralysis. It would be easy to say that the former qualities, those of the *conquistadores*, made the Empire, while the latter ones, those of the bureaucrats, caused its demise. But without the rigid hand of state and church, the Spanish Empire might have disintegrated centuries before it did. The question before us is why neither the crown nor the Quixotic spirits who came to American shores succeeded in expanding the empire *farther* . . . into the North Pacific.

When Balboa, in 1513, claimed the South Sea and all its lands for the King of Castile, the Portuguese had already beaten the Spaniards to the original goal, the Spice Islands, by sailing east through the Indian Ocean. That is what prompted Spain to sponsor Magellan's bid to sail *around* the American continent to Asia in the same year Hernán Cortés set off on his storied march to Mexico. The rapid conquest of the Aztec Empire extended the grip of Spain to the West Coast of America, and by 1526 Cortés had begun shipbuilding on the Pacific and founded ports, notably at the excellent harbor of Acapulco. The California current hindered northbound explorations, but Cortés nevertheless sent several expeditions up the coast, one of which explored the Gulf of California (Sea of Cortés). In 1540 Juan Cabrillo fought his way up to what is now San Diego, discovered the Santa Barbara Islands, and landed about thirty miles north of San Francisco Bay. But California—a name derived from a fictional island that was close to Paradise but guarded by black Amazons—seemed not worth pursuing. The Indians were sparse and destitute, the river valleys few and arid. There were rumors of fabulous wealth in the interior—the Seven Cities of Cíbola—but Coronado's fruitless attempt from 1540 to 1541 to find them convinced sensible people that the lands north of Mexico were a waste. In any case, riches greater even than those of Mexico had just been found in the opposite direction, in Peru.

Spain's colonial government also failed to encourage North Pacific explorations, although its rigid centralization, bureaucracy, and uniformity are otherwise explicable. This was the first modern overseas empire, carved out by lusty soldiers of fortune with their own agendas and populated by every manner of mercenary and cutthroat. To permit self-government under such circumstances would only invite anarchy, local despotisms, and civil war, destroy any chance of the crown's getting its share of the profits, and expose the empire to the predations of European enemies. So the crown divided the Americas into viceroyalties and *audiencias* (roughly, provinces) under Spaniards acting in the name of the king. In exceptional cases they might set aside a royal decree as inappropriate to local conditions, but by and large they administered the Americas according to regulations great and petty, contrived by the king's Council of the Indies, most of whose members had never set foot in the New World. Such government from a distance was bound to provoke the *encomenderos*, the holders of colonial land grants, not least when the crown tried to halt their savage treatment of Indian laborers. The Church, moved by the Dominican Bartolemé de Las Casas (himself a penitent *encomendero*), argued that the Indians were souls beloved of God and equal subjects of the crown. But the colonials had no trouble finding ways around laws meant to protect Indians, and the crown's moral sanction was further undermined when the Peruvian Viceroy himself drafted thousands of Indians to work the silver mines of Potosí. So the Indians just died from European diseases, the wars of conquest, bondage, and demoralization. From a pre–Columbian population of between 5 and 17 million (a matter of much dispute), Mexico's Indian population fell by the year 1600 to just 1 million (and 100,000 Spaniards), while the Andean realms fell from perhaps 5 million to about 1.5 million Indians (and 70,000 Spaniards). This meant that even if California had been colonized during the time of Spain's Pacific monopoly, few colonists were available to fill that great void.

The Spanish crown's effort to control the colonial economy through the Casa de Contratación also impeded new Pacific initiatives. Now, the Casa was not a chartered company of the type founded by European kings after 1600 but a government agency that collected all colonial taxes and duties, approved all voyages of trade and exploration, guarded

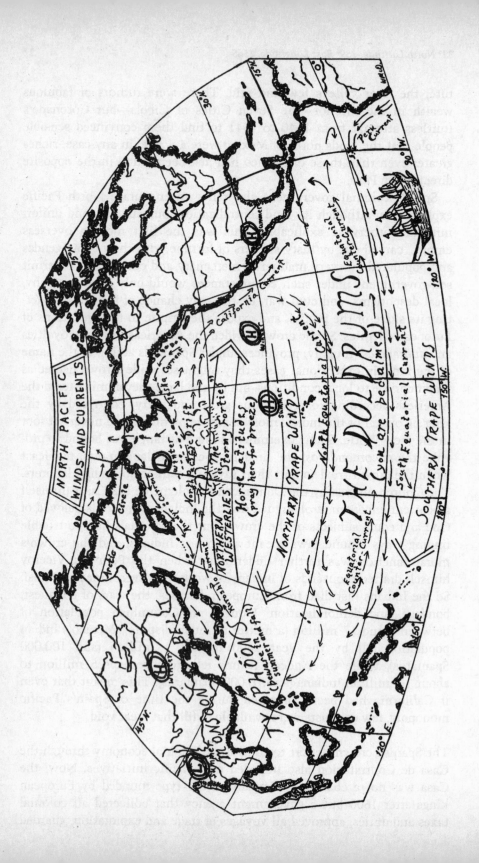

all intelligence about sea routes, administered all commercial law, licensed all pilots, and even delivered the mail. Theoretically, no Spanish subject was permitted to sail anywhere without the Casa's approval. Of course, a single agency based in Seville could not hope to control the deeds of thousands of profiteers spread halfway around the world. Corruption and smuggling and avoidance of dues were rife. But for the crown to give up and adopt a free-trade policy was simply unthinkable in this mercantilist age. Opening the ports of America to all comers would mean the loss of revenue for the crown and the supplanting of Spanish merchants altogether by the more dynamic and numerous Dutch, French, and English. By the lights of the sixteenth century, a state monopoly appeared the only rational means of making the colonies "pay."

Nor are planned economies like that of the Casa de Contratación necessarily stifling in every respect. An enlightened, visionary Casa endowed with the necessary capital might launch new voyages of discovery and encourage subcolonization on the part of New Spain. And for a while it did. But Spain's energies, while they lasted, were wasted on a series of expensive expeditions to the South Pacific. The only sizable Pacific colony founded was the Philippines, and even then the Casa restricted its commerce to the one annual voyage of the famous galleon from Acapulco to Manila and back. By the late seventeenth century the Casa succumbed in any case to bureaucratic sclerosis and such a shortage of capital that the royal share of American wealth was usually signed over to Spain's creditors long before it arrived in Seville. It is customary to say that Spain squandered the wealth of the Americas on vain and constant warfare. Constant it was, but not vain. For Charles V and Philip II, both pious, responsible rulers, could hardly have abandoned the Mediterranean and central Europe to the cresting empire of Ottoman Turks, or the Holy Roman Empire to the rebellious Lutheran princes, or their own possessions in Italy and the Low Countries to foreign invaders and internal rebels. The riches of the New World certainly encouraged Spain to try to roll back those threats, but the threats existed whether treasure ships sailed from America or not. Still, the chronic bankruptcy of the Spanish crown, plus the great inflation in Europe caused by the influx of American silver, gradually left Madrid and Seville bereft of the capital needed to expand their hold on the Pacific.

Finally, what resources could be scraped up had to go increasingly toward mere self-defense. In 1572 Francis Drake began raiding the Spanish Main. Four years later his compatriot John Oxenham slipped a ship through Caribbean waters to Panama, carted his guns and ammunition across the spiny isthmus, built a serviceable pinnace on the Pacific side, and captured the first prize ever in the Pacific Ocean—a coastal merchantman with thirty-eight thousand pesos aboard. By then a more serious expedition was at sea. Drake sailed from Plymouth in the *Pelican* (later rechristened *Golden Hinde*) in 1577 on what was arguably the greatest sea voyage in history. During his three-year circumnavigation Drake raided the Pacific ports of Spanish America, explored the North American coast, crossed the Pacific on the northern trades, and returned to Plymouth with captured treasure worth at least 600,000 pounds sterling. Drake and his imitators like Cavendish and Hawkins forced Spain to make defense of its existing possessions a higher priority than seizing new lands.

Did no Spaniard wonder what exciting new lands might lie astride "Urdaneta's route"? Yes, some did and considered that there were two possibilities. The first was the rumored Rica de Oro y de Plata (Land Rich with Gold and Silver), said by a Portuguese smuggler to lie in the seas east of Japan. The second was California. The first had the irresistible name and reputation, but of course did not exist. The second bore the name of a mockery, yet did exist and sparkled with gold. In 1587 Pedro de Unamuno set sail from Manila with the intention of veering off the galleon route in search of Rica de Oro. He found nothing in the Western Pacific but on the American side explored a fine harbor near present-day San Luis Obispo. The Mexican authorities showed an interest. In these days before scurvy prophylaxis the galleon rarely covered "Urdaneta's route" without disease and hunger afflicting the crew. Why not develop a port or two on the coast of Alta (Upper) California where the ships could put in for rest and refreshment? The viceroy obtained permission to instruct an eastbound Manila vessel under Sebastian Rodriguez Cermeño to seek out such ports, but the ship was lost off Cape Mendocino in 1595. The next viceroy, the Count de Monterey, decided to outfit an expedition from Mexico itself. His choice as captain, Sebastian Vizcaíno, knew Spain's vulnerability, having been aboard a galleon captured by Cavendish. But he was also a shameless self-promoter and fortune hunter, and he wasted his first venture in an effort to harvest a fortune in pearls from the waters of Baja California. In 1602, however, Vizcaíno not only discovered an excellent port (which he named Monterey to flatter the Viceroy), but also returned to Acapulco full of zeal for California. Unfortunately, Monterey chose that moment to resign, his successor showed no interest, and Vizcaíno was forced to appeal to the crown. Three years later—about the normal time to get a decision out of Madrid—a royal decree authorizing Vizcaíno to colonize California arrived in Mexico just after he had given up and sailed away to Japan. The California project was shelved in favor of another fool's quest for the Land Rich with Gold.

Vizcaíno's frustrations aside, one may ask whether the Spaniards were up to the task of colonizing California in the seventeenth century. More than a port of call was needed if California was to be kept out of foreign hands in the future. To be sure, once on the ground, the Spaniards might have come to appreciate the potential of the frontier province. But pioneers were not likely to pour in from Mexico, which was at its dreadful demographic nadir and suffered an appalling shortage of labor, or from Spain, whose population—a mere eight and a half million—was actually dropping from war and economic depression. It may be that even a vigorous policy could not have made up for its lack of a demographic impetus to imperial growth. So instead of discovering Alaska or Hawaii or supplying colonies in California, the galleons retraced "Urdaneta's route" year after year after year, and the officials forgot about the promising feints made up the American coast. Only when Spain was free, after blessed defeat, of responsibilities in Europe, and a progressive monarch mounted the throne, would the Mexican viceroyalty recover the inclination, money, and means to try again in California. And by then it was too little, too late.

Nagasaki 1638

AN OBSERVER FROM another planet around the year 1600 might have concluded that the Japanese, now that they were familiar with the maritime and military technology of Renaissance Europe, must be the inevitable masters of what, after all, was *their* ocean. Spanish America lacked the numbers, resources, and will to people the North Pacific, while Spain's Philippine outpost was hardly defensible. The rest of the North Pacific rim, from Alta California to Alaska and down the Siberian coast, contained only sparse communities of aborigines. Japan, on the other hand, was a nation of over twenty million, homogeneous, mobilized for military force, and experienced in seafaring and commerce. A Japanese "breakout" in the seventeenth century would surely have made the new shogunate an imperial player in the North Pacific, had it so willed. So why did it not? European scholars from Voltaire to Marx later assumed that Japan and China were inward-looking, self-sufficient, and stagnant civilizations bereft of the curiosity and restless creativity of Western peoples, and they explained this by reference to Buddhism, Oriental despotism, or the "Asian" (as opposed to capitalist) mode of production. But what Western observers could not understand was their own catalytic role in the self-imposed isolation of China and especially Japan.

The Japanese archipelago sits offshore of the Eurasian landmass like a mirror image of the British Isles. It consists of four main islands—Hokkaido, Honshu, Shikoku, and Kyushu—and two chains of lesser islands—the Kuriles, trailing off to the north toward Kamchatka, and the Ryukyus, trailing off to the south toward Taiwan. During the seventeenth century, chilly Hokkaido and the Kuriles were not part of the Japanese Empire, their only inhabitants being the primitive "hairy Ainu," whom Japanese migrations had pushed onto the margins in the dim past. The rest of Japan, warmed by the Kuroshio current, enjoyed moderate temperatures and ample rainfall. But since arable lowlands made up only 20 percent of the total land area, the densely packed Japanese people relied for sustenance on an unusually narrow agricultural base. No wonder that Japanese elites, and all urban folk, were at pains to ensure the docility of the peasants. Moreover, Japan is singularly unsettled. Its long chain of islands is an upwelling of the great fault line in the earth's crust that circles the Pacific Ocean. Over sixty active volcanoes have been recorded there, and seismic activity is, if such a thing can be, a normal hazard of life. Japan also sits astride the greatest typhoon belt, and its wooden and paper buildings were especially vulnerable to fire. One can only speculate to what degree recurring catastrophes contributed to the collective psychology of a people once described as teetering always on the edge of hysteria.

Every people lives in part by its myths. Americans had their Pilgrim fathers, who believed the American continent was a land set apart by Providence. Millions of Americans who were not Puritans imbibed the myth, which legitimated their exclusivism and isolationism. Japanese believed their land itself was holy, the Land of the Dawn where the sun god emerged from the eastern sea before deigning to bless the rest of the world. The Japanese emperor was descended from the sun, hence Japan was the Land of the Gods. The reality is that the Japanese came to Kyushu from the mainland around 200 B.C. armed with aspects of Han Chinese culture, and they continued to borrow, not from gods but from China, most notably Buddhism after A.D. 600. That was the era during which Japan's leading clan, based on the Yamato plain of Honshu, first united the islands. The Yamato overlord became an emperor housed at Kyoto and the government a hierarchical bureaucracy administering a complex system of provinces, districts, and villages. The primary functions of imperial government were to preserve unity and peace, promote virtue, and regulate distribution of farmland and rice. In the twelfth century the system broke down. Local lords and officials grew powerful enough to defy the central government and take arms against one another. So the conflict between feudal and imperial authority became rhythmic. In time, the court restored unity but at the cost of relinquishing real power to a military government acting in the name of the emperor and ruled by a *sei-i tai-shōgun* (great general who subdues the barbarians). Two hereditary shogunates then governed Japan from 1185 to 1467, at which time the cycle repeated itself. Local lieutenants grew too strong, rebelled against the shogun's authority, and heaved Japan into *sengoku,* an era of "warring states" lasting 125 years.

In the midst of this anarchy, in 1543, three shipwrecked Portuguese washed ashore on Tanegashima Island off Kyushu. The rude muskets they brought with them quickly became known among the warring fac-

tions as the "Tanegashima weapon." (Today, with poetic justice, Tanegashima is the site of the Japanese space launch center.) Europeans
could not have stumbled onto Japan at a more propitious moment: the
divided nation had no functioning central government, hence no foreign
policy. Great magnates, or *daimyō*, ruled their domains as autonomous
states, and far from banding together against the white-skinned barbarians, they competed to purchase European weapons, build European-
style armories, and profit from European trade. Within a few decades
European influences flowed up and down the Japanese social scale. St.
Francis Xavier brought the gospel in 1549, and such was the leverage of
the Portuguese that at times they could afford to boycott *daimyō* who
did *not* throw open their lands to missionaries. By 1571 the Portuguese
regularized the annual voyages of their famous Black Ships from Macao
to Nagasaki, which became the cathedral city for a Japanese church
numbering 150,000 souls. The Europeans also could not help meddling
in the civil war raging in Japan. It was to be their undoing.

For *sengoku* could not last forever. Sooner or later the conflict was
bound to throw up a warlord with the charisma, skill, and luck to subdue any combination of rivals, while wiser *daimyō* were sure to conclude that peace was worth the price of vassalage. The first such warlord, Oda Nobunaga of south central Honshu, inherited an "army" that
may have numbered only a few hundred. But he rallied his own kins-
men, seized a neighboring castle, then ambushed and routed a *daimyo*
army ten times the size of his own in a blinding rainstorm in 1560.
More lands changed hands, orphaned samurai shifted allegiance, and by
1568, when Oda occupied Kyoto, a third of Japan was under his sway.

Oda Nobunaga was a great general, but the key to his success was
employment of Western cannon and drilled musketeers. He also
cemented the loyalty of his growing force of retainers with grants of
property seized from defeated *daimyō*, and he revoked the peasantry's
right to bear arms so that *daimyō* could not forge instant armies out of
local levees. He also forbade all contact with foreigners, except at his
will, lest any potential rebel gain access to Western arms. But Oda was
undone by treachery when some of his own retainers fell upon him with
swords after a tea ceremony in his most secure castle.

The second unifier of Japan, Toyotomi Hideyoshi, was a peasant by
birth but took advantage of the revolutionary campaigns of Oda
Nobunaga to achieve high command. In the confusion following his
lord's death Hideyoshi rushed to Kyoto to take vengeance, and through
intimidation and diplomacy he won recognition as regent of Oda
Nobunaga's holdings. He also wasted no time launching new campaigns
that subdued the island of Shikoku in 1585, Kyushu in 1587, and north-

ern Honshu in 1590. But Hideyoshi's success in unifying Japan was due as much to politics as to war and so pointed the way to a reconciliation of the persistence of local feudal power and the need for strong central government. He left defeated *daimyō* in possession of their estates, completed the disarming of the peasantry through his infamous Sword Hunt, and froze Japanese society: farmers must remain on the land for life, samurai must not shift their loyalty or take up business or farming, and everyone was encouraged to inform on violators. In this way he made it difficult for would-be warlords to attract the manpower needed for revolt even as he conferred upon loyal *daimyō* local security and tax exemptions. Hideyoshi's reforms aimed to prevent, quite simply, the possibility that any other warlord might fashion a career like his own!

In unifying Japan, Hideyoshi also restored to it the capacity to exe-cute a genuine foreign policy. Not surprisingly, he promptly began to persecute Christians, contain the foreign presence, and project Japanese power overseas. Already in 1586 Hideyoshi envisioned the invasion of Korea and asked the Jesuit official Gaspar Coelho to provide his navy with two Portuguese carracks. Anxious to please the regent, Coelho agreed, but in so doing he only proved to Hideyoshi how dangerous these foreigners were. If they promised warships to him this year, they might arm some other *daimyo* next year, and civil war would erupt again. The following year, during his campaign on Kyushu, Hideyoshi had another encounter with Coelho. First they celebrated his victories with generous quantities of wine, then went to bed. But at midnight, samurai rousted out Coelho and dragged him before Hideyoshi. Why did the Portuguese force Japanese to become Christians or urge their follow-ers to destroy Buddhist temples? Why did they offend Japanese by eating meat? And who gave them authority to carry Japanese off as slaves to India? The befuddled Jesuit denied the charges, but Hideyoshi had already decided to order all Jesuits out of Japan. When they temporized, took to wearing disguises, or tried to persuade Christian *daimyō* to rebel, the persecutions began.

The Jesuits judged Japanese by the standards of their own religion and time, but it is still remarkable how durable their impressions proved to be. The famous report by Alessandro Valignano described the Japanese as "all white [the notion that Asians were 'yellow' came later], courte-ous and highly civilized, so much so that they surpass all the other known races of the world." They were "naturally very intelligent," and behaved with punctilious honor. And yet, Valignano observed the Japan-ese to be "the most warlike and bellicose race yet discovered on the earth." Fathers killed their sons or underlings, and brothers each other,

The map contains the following labels:

130° E. 140° E. 46° N.

Kurile Islands

Kunashiri

"Hairy Ainu" dwell here

Manchuria

Yalu River

EZO (Hokkaido)

Matsumae Hakodate

40° N.

Korea (tributary state of Ming China)

SEA OF JAPAN

Pyongyang

Seoul

Honshu

Battle of Sekigahara 1600

Edo

Pusan

Tokyo Bay

Kyoto

Inland Sea

Seki

34° N.

Yi-sun's Tortoise Boats

Invasion of Korea 1592

Hirado

Japan

Shikoku

GREAT EASTERN SEA (PACIFIC OCEAN)

Nagasaki

Shimabara Castle

Kyushu

THE SHOGUNS' JAPAN

|||| conquests of Oda Nobunaga 1560-1582
≡ conquests of Hideyoshi 1583-1590
⊞ original domains of Tokugawa 1599

W.McD.

Tanegashima Is.

30° N.

on the slightest pretext, and mothers thought nothing of stepping on the chests of their newborn to smother them. "Similarly many men kill themselves by cutting their intestines with a dagger." They never complained of betrayals, or grumbled about bad luck, and were ready themselves to violate any loyalty or oath to increase their own income or rank. Japanese were simply "the most false and treacherous people of any known in the world" and never spoke their true thoughts, face-to-face, about anything. But converted, the Jesuit expected, Japan would produce "the finest Christianity in all the East, as in fact it already has."

Instead, the Japanese only displayed techniques of torture that surpassed anything current in Europe. Rather than burning a victim at the stake with the wood piled about the feet, the Japanese placed the fuel in a circle to roast the victim slowly. Or they suspended the victim upside down in a bucket with his nostrils just below the water line so that spectators could enjoy watching the martyr squirm and slowly drown. Other martyrs were cut with swords, then dipped in sulfur water to maximize their pain, and still others were hung head-down in pits of human excrement. Thousands, mostly Japanese converts, were crucified, and some Jesuits and Franciscans also died on the stake or the cross. But the intermittent persecution was designed as a warning rather than a "final solution," and directed as well at dissident Buddhists who dared to dabble in politics.

In his later years Hideyoshi went mad. He exhibited sudden mood swings, executed imagined rivals on a whim, and spent his time producing and starring in elaborate court dramas. But his costliest caprice was the invasion of Korea in 1592. A Japanese army of 250,000 men sailed to Pusan and marched northward to Seoul. The Korean admiral Yi Sun-sin's fleet of "tortoise boats"—junks protected by metal plates and spikes—sank the whole Japanese fleet, but on land, the invaders pressed on beyond Pyongyang until, suddenly, Chinese forces crossed the Yalu River and forced the Japanese back to a perimeter around Pusan. Negotiations ensued on and off for three years, until the fighting ended in stalemate. When Hideyoshi died, and the Koreans won another naval victory (though Yi Sun-sin was killed), the Japanese gave up and went home in 1597.

What they found there was another brief and violent struggle over the succession. The victor, the third in the roster of Japan's unifiers, was the *daimyo* Tokugawa Ieyasu. In 1600, he and his allies defeated an opposing coalition and mastered all of Japan. Tokugawa took the title of Shogun in 1603 at the behest of the figurehead emperor and promptly institutionalized Hideyoshi's system of compromise between the central government and the *daimyō*. In so doing, he laid the foundation for 250 years of stable prosperity under the Tokugawa Shogunate. The shogun directly controlled a fourth of all Japanese land, regulated all commercial activity, and imposed an ingenious hostage arrangement to keep the *daimyō* in line. This *sankin kōtai* system required all *daimyō* to present themselves at Edo at least every other year, while their wives and children lived permanently in the capital under the shogun's guards. Just one more foundation stone remained to be laid: the extirpation of foreign influence.

In 1600, the same year as Tokugawa's triumph, the Dutch ship *Liefde* collided with the shoals of Japan. In a magnificent feat of seamanship, the Dutch sailors and their English pilot, Mr. Adams, found their way through the Straits of Magellan and across the Pacific to Asia. The

Jesuits warned Ieyasu against these newcomers, while the Dutch railed about the evils of Catholicism. At first Tokugawa Ieyasu was uncertain what to do about the barbarians. The Governor of Manila, Rodrigo de Vivero, shipwrecked near Edo, even persuaded the Shogun to let him command a Japanese ship (built for the Shogun by Adams) and transport Japanese merchants to Mexico, while Vizcaíno, after his California plans aborted, sailed to Mexico in 1613 with 150 merchants and samurai. One can only imagine how Pacific history might have evolved had this movement of people and goods been allowed to continue.

But in time, the Tokugawa *bakufu* (administration) grew tired and paranoid of the quarrelsome foreigners. A tougher anti-Christian edict went forth in 1614, then the restriction of all foreign shipping to Hirado and Nagasaki, then more tortures and executions, including a mass burning of fifty Christians in 1632 to celebrate the inauguration of a new shogun. The Shimabara rebellion of 1638, which ended with the slaughter of thousands of Japanese Christians at Hara Castle on Kyushu, seemed only to confirm the wisdom of total exclusion.

What can one make of the decision to purge from Japan's body politic all the influences of the so-called "Christian century"? Certainly the onset of *sakoku* (isolation) was not the result of sheer xenophobia. Japanese welcomed Buddhism when it came and showed receptivity to Christianity, too. Japan had had important contacts with the outer world, toyed with expansion, and was not in immediate danger of invasion. So the most likely explanation both for the progress of the Europeans before 1600 and for their expulsion afterward was the state of Japanese politics. The civil war gave the outsiders an opening without which there might never have been a "Christian century," while the emergence of a strong central government enabled Japan, for the first time, to close the door. The question remains why the *bakufu* chose to exercise that option, and the most immediate answer is that the Shogun—he who "subdues the barbarians"—could prove his legitimacy only by subduing the barbarians. That is, any government *in*capable or *un*willing to enforce obedience on foreigners could hardly expect Japanese to obey. Moreover, the only threat to the shogun could come from disaffected *daimyō in alliance with European powers.* So by cutting off access to foreigners, the *bakufu* removed from any would-be warlord the temptation to rebel.

Behind these exigencies of a crisis-prone era lay the blunt fact that the Japanese government derived its legitimacy from the otherwise figurehead emperor, and the emperor was a god. Christians denied this and insisted that even emperors were subject to the one God in Heaven. To the extent that Japanese converts believed this message—and the mar-

tyrdoms prove many did—how could the shogun permit them to live?
For whatever combination of causes, the story ended in Japan's isolation. And *that* meant that the great game for control of the still empty
North Pacific would proceed for two and a half centuries with Japan, its
greatest potential player, sulking like Achilles in his tent.

Peking 1644

SIX YEARS AFTER Japan closed its doors, China's were beaten in. The Last Emperor—last *Chinese* Emperor—knew a despondency beyond the ken of any Westerner. To be the Son of Heaven and rule a Celestial Kingdom to which all nations were theoretically subject, to be the model for all that is moral and just and the guardian of the people's peace and prosperity, to be charged with a birthright preserved for 276 years—then to be judged unworthy by Heaven and have all power and dignity torn from one's person—that is about as far as a mortal can fall.

That was the psychological burden of the Ch'ung-chen Emperor, last of the Ming dynasty to preside in the Forbidden City. His people were dying from plagues in the cities and famine in the countryside. Bandit warlords and peasant mobs ravaged whole provinces. Manchu armies threatened the capital from the north. His own armies were of dubious loyalty and impotent to resist all his enemies at once. His officials were corrupt and decadent. The treasury was empty. Soothsayers discerned the anger of heaven in the appearance of comets, freakish northern lights, ghostly groans of battle and woe in the quiet of night. In April 1644 astronomers reported that the Pole Star had "slipped" from its throne in the northern sky—a sure augury of the end of an age.

The Emperor's choices were few. Li Tzu-ch'eng, greatest of the rebel warlords, had crossed the Yellow River southwest of Peking. Some ministers urged the recall of General Wu San-Kuei from the northern frontier so that his army might drive off the bandits. But that meant leaving the north undefended against the Manchu barbarians. Others advised the Emperor to raise and lead a militia, trusting in the charisma of his person to rally the people. But the Emperor was no soldier and could not ride a horse. Still others urged him to flee Peking for southern provinces still loyal to the Ming. But the Emperor elected to remain, to tend the sacred altars of soil and grain, until Li's rebel army marched in a gloomy

April drizzle through the gates of Peking. That evening the Ch'ung-chen Emperor called his last council. As the court wept, he gave his ministers leave to commit suicide—thirteen of whom did so—and surrendered to his despair. The Emperor sent his male heirs into hiding, fortified himself with wine, then ran a sword through his consort and two princesses. The Empress, in shame and horror, committed suicide. After midnight the Emperor removed his royal robes and donned a blue silk robe and red trousers. Accompanied by his head eunuch, he walked to a pavilion on a nearby hill, wrote the character for "Son of Heaven" beside his chosen spot, and hanged himself.

When Li Tzu-ch'eng occupied the Forbidden City, the obsequious Ming officials offered to instruct him in the duties of emperorship. Li was not averse to the thought of founding a new dynasty, but he despised the imperial bureaucracy, whose moral depravity he blamed for China's ruin. So he put forty-six officials to death and levied punitive taxation on the rest, the better to pay off his soldiers. Still, his undisciplined troops sacked and raped until it was clear to all that whoever possessed the Mandate of Heaven, it was not Li Tzu-ch'eng. The crucial actor now was General Wu, whose army stood between the capital and the Manchus. Li made offers of alliance and bribes, which Wu decided, after long deliberation, to accept. But en route to Peking a hysterical refugee—one of his own father's concubines—stumbled into his camp with dolorous news. She reported that Li had grown weary of waiting, massacred the Wu family, and hung the head of Wu's father from the city walls.

General Wu was now bent on revenge, but his army was not strong enough to act alone. And so in May 1644, he "invited" the Manchus to invade China in hopes they would restore the Ming. Li's rebels soon learned that their days in the capital were numbered, multiplied their outrages, and set the city on fire. Now the residents of Peking rose up and hacked and burned as many as two thousand rebels. That is why, when the Manchu hosts entered Peking in June, they were greeted not as feared invaders, but as bearers of a heavenly mandate to restore tranquillity. Dorgon, their prince and commander, ensured that the Manchu soldiers did not break discipline. He also staged the appropriate liturgies for the dead Emperor, invited Ming officials to resume their posts, and—on behalf of his imperial nephew—founded a new Ch'ing dynasty on traditional models and mores. Thanks to Dorgon's wisdom, the Manchus ruled China into the twentieth century.

But how swiftly the mighty had fallen! For if the Japanese, by dint of location, population, and spirit, might have seemed favored protagonists in the emerging struggle for North Pacific power, then how much more favored might the Ming have seemed? Not only were Chinese the most numerous people in the world—one hundred million in 1500—they had invented gunpowder, developed iron smelting to a level unsurpassed before the Industrial Revolution, and possessed skills in shipbuilding and seamanship in advance of any other race. The great Ming treasure ships, under legendary admirals like Cheng Ho (d. 1431), were longer than a football field, plied the Indian Ocean as far west as Africa, and might well have rounded the Cape of Good Hope decades before the Portuguese.

We can guess at some of the reasons they did not. First, the voyages were expensive, designed less for trade than for collecting tribute that may not have covered the cost. Second, they were subject to an emperor's whim, and even brief neglect can bring a navy to rot and ruin. Third, the Chinese did not need oceangoing fleets to reach the nearby Spice Islands. Fourth, the court eunuchs who commanded the voyages aroused the envy of the Confucian bureaucracy. Fifth, foreign trade meant that impure foreign and mercantile influences would sully the hierarchical, agricultural, and by definition virtuous social order. By 1500, the Emperor forbade his own subjects to put to sea on pain of death and restricted foreigners to specified ports administered by the central bureaucracy. Sixth, and probably most important, the threats to China's security came almost exclusively from the landward frontier.

Moreover, the Chinese world view left no room for foreign relations as Westerners understood them. Having achieved a precocious political and cultural unity over lands embracing three million square miles, protected by deserts to the north and west and jungle and the world's highest mountains to the south, the Chinese had never encountered a people more refined or mightier than themselves. Chinese could thus not imagine a treaty between sovereign states. Rather, all non-Chinese were barbarians, all owed tribute and homage to the Emperor, and thus "foreign" relations were simply tributary relations. Ignorant and disharmonious barbarians were incapable of virtue, required rewards and punishments to keep them in line, and were undeserving of any consideration except insofar as they acknowledged their subservience. But what should happen if the barbarians proved the stronger? This problem became critical in 1279 with the Mongol conquest. Happily, the Chinese quickly "civilized" the Mongols, who embraced official ideology and themselves perpetuated the Chinese world view.

Invasions, when they came, were invariably from the north where the steppes of Mongolia and lower Siberia supported fluctuating populations of fierce mounted tribesmen. Whenever nomadic populations were sparse or divided, Peking exercised sway over them. But when their numbers reached a saturation point and they began to probe restlessly toward the North China Plain, whoever ruled China was obliged to meet that threat to the exclusion of all other concerns. But wait, one might object, how could invaders from the north get past the Great Wall? To which the answer is that there was no Great Wall. There never had been. Legend had it that Ch'in Shih-huang, first Emperor of a united China, built the Great Wall in the 200s B.C. But no documentary or archaeological evidence exists of any Great Wall at that time, or for sixteen hundred years thereafter. Fortified outposts of various lengths were built at various times and places, but those predating the Ming were small, earthen, and long gone. It was the Ming, beginning in the sixteenth century, who made the unimaginable investment to build what we know as the Great Wall of China. And it was a measure not of the wealth and power of their economy but of the bankruptcy of their policy.

How could China secure its fluid northern frontier at times of barbarian activity? Over the centuries three strategies had emerged. First, subdue the noxious tribes by force and make them tributaries; but war was risky and expensive. Second, set the barbarians against one another; but that required clever, sustained diplomacy. Third, give the barbarians a stake in Chinese power through commerce, bribes, or royal marriage; but that was humiliating. Only after devastating defeats at the hands of the Mongols in 1550, and the failure or rejection of the other options, did the Ming resort to the least imaginative solution: wallbuilding. The years 1572 to 1620 were its heyday, when hundreds of garrisoned towers and natural strong points were linked by 2,500 miles of bricked bastion at a cost that must have run to several million ounces of silver. Where did it come from? Some doubtless came from across the Pacific, for as much as a fifth of all the silver mined in Peru—1.8 million ounces in the first third of the seventeenth century—traveled with the galleon to Manila to pay for the silks and other luxuries originating in China. It would be interesting to know the degree to which the inflow of American metal regulated the pace of construction of the Great Wall of China!

But the Wall could not compensate for decadence within. Confucian bureaucrats exploited high office to amass fortunes and gave themselves over to hedonism, sartorial showmanship, and perverse sexuality. A long stretch of cold, wet weather and flooding spoiled harvests, diminished tax receipts, and drove impoverished peasants into the cities. Then in the 1630s, Philip IV limited the amount of silver that could be shipped from Acapulco, the Chinese merchant community in Manila was all but exterminated in strife with the Spanish authorities, and Dutch assaults on the Portuguese closed down the trade at Macao. Throughout its last decades the Ming treasury ran a deep deficit.

Sad to say for the beleaguered Chinese, those were also the times when a new and mightier tribal confederation appeared on the northern border. The land to which they gave their name, Manchuria, was never part of China proper and lay beyond the Great Wall. A region the size of France, Manchuria is separated from the Gobi Desert to the west by mountains and from Siberia to the north by the Amur River. Manchuria's central plain is well watered and fertile, its forests full of timber and fur-bearing animals, its hills rich with coal, iron, and gold. For all that, Manchuria was a rough frontier land of long winters and insect-ridden summers, a place to prosper but to be miserable doing it. In the late fourteenth century the Jurchen tribe settled in the southeastern corner of Manchuria. Their Korean neighbors taught them to farm and Chinese prisoners taught them to work iron. In 1583 a chief arose, Nurhachi, who united the Jurchen clans and organized their warriors, households, and slaves into self-contained legions. They rode into battle under huge banners of red, yellow, white, or blue, and plain or bordered. In 1616, at the behest of these bannermen, Nurhachi accepted the title of Khan, or Emperor. His son Abahai (one of sixteen) completed the evolution of the Jurchen state by subordinating the banners to a Chinese-style bureaucracy based at Mukden. He also renamed his people the Manchu and his dynasty Ch'ing (meaning "pure"). Manchu might was thus a synthesis of the ferocity and skill of the mounted steppe warrior and copious borrowings from Chinese civilization. That the Manchus were able to induce Chinese to collaborate is a measure not only of disgust with the Ming, but of Abahai's "nourishment policy" that welcomed defectors. He died in 1643, but the following year, as we know, his brother Dorgon succeeded in placing Abahai's little boy on the Peacock throne of China.

What had this dynastic change to do with the North Pacific? It certainly did not restore to China the maritime power it knew briefly under the Ming. For the very Manchurian origins of the new dynasty, the specific way they took power in China, and their natural bias toward land power all ensured that China would *not* project its power beyond, up, or down the Pacific coast. And that was a fact of surpassing importance. China, like Japan, was content to stay home during the climactic centuries of European exploration. Manchu energies were absorbed by forty years of tough campaigns to subdue the surviving Ming loyalists in the south. At the same time, the Manchus were vexed by a self-made pirate king who called himself Kuo Hsing-yeh (Coxinga, to European ears) and who exploited the chaos in China to seize long stretches of the coast and even lay siege to Nanking. Manchu bannermen eventually chased Coxinga offshore, but he fled to Taiwan with twenty-five thousand men, ousted the Dutch, and ruled until his death in 1662. Not until 1683 did the Ch'ing marshal the three hundred junks needed to reconquer Taiwan, but having done so, they sealed off the island to foreigners and turned their backs on the eastern sea.

Finally, the Ch'ing were obsessed with their northern frontier—it was, after all, their homeland. And just as Hideyoshi and the Tokugawa aimed at preventing any other Japanese warlord from repeating their own success, so did the Manchus adopt policies to ensure that no other northern tribe could repeat the manner of *their* own success. So they occupied Inner Mongolia, reduced Outer Mongolia to a tributary, and sent armies 2,500 miles to establish suzerainty over the Turkic tribes of Sinkiang. Manchuria, of course, was garrisoned in perpetuity by bannermen. But one thing the Manchus did not do, which could have had a great impact on the future of Northeast Asia, was to flood their homeland with settlers. Some Chinese pioneers moved into the southern Manchurian valleys after 1644, but China's own population was shrinking by 20 percent because of the famine, plagues, and wars of the late Ming. Then, in 1668, the Manchus declared their home province off-limits from fear of its being inundated with Han Chinese. The upshot was that vast and vulnerable Manchuria remained underpopulated during the very centuries when it might have been irreversibly melded into imperial China.

Of course, the Ch'ing could not anticipate that imperialists would buzz around Manchuria like flies around honey 230 years in the future. And for the time being it did not matter. The Europeans could be kept at arm's length, the Japanese were bent on staying at home, and the tribes to the north were under control . . . all the tribes but one, that is, a new and strange one from far away, who called themselves Russians.

Nerchinsk 1689

BEYOND THE WORLD of the Chinese, Manchus, and Mongols lay another world larger than the face of the moon. Stretching 4,500 miles from the Ural Mountains to the Bering Strait, this northeastern swath of the Asian landmass contained five million square miles. But in all that expanse lived a mere two hundred thousand primitive tribespeople divided among dozens of ethnic groups. They were scarce because they wandered in a singularly grim world, and they were helpless when the Russians came. The Russians! It was as if some mischievous deity had bestowed upon Ivan the Terrible a benefice worthy of his epithet. "O mighty Rus, I bear you good news: a road of conquest lined with golden fleece, from the gates of your empire to the shores of the Pacific! The bad news is that it is Siberia."

Lord Salisbury said that "politics should be studied with large maps." A map of Siberia must not only be large, but on a curved, polar projection inasmuch as it spans 120° of longitude, or one-third the way 'round the earth. Such a map should be large enough to show Siberia's relation not only to Russia, but to the caravan routes of central Asia, China, Korea, Japan, and the Pacific. For Siberia, empty and cold as it was, was the locus of the first war and treaty between China and the West and the route by which whites first colonized the North Pacific. The map should also show that Siberia is defined by lines running south to north—its great rivers that empty into the Arctic Sea—and by lines running west to east marking Siberia's five zones of vegetation: arid tundra along the Arctic Sea, populated by Eskimos, reindeer, and walrus; the taiga belt, carpeted with forests of hardy larch, pine, and cedar, and teeming with ermine, fox, sable, and beaver; the mixed forest belt of coniferous and deciduous trees harboring bands of hunter/gatherers; the wild grasslands of the steppe, where herders awaited each rainfall; and finally the desert.

Into this land Russians came in 1581. They were already foresters and steppe men inured to the cold, constrained by few niceties of habit or conscience, and above all, skilled rivermen. In all this they had much in common with the *coureurs* and mountain men of North America. For river-and-portage travel, the only means of traversing Siberia, was what made "Russia" (from, according to one theory, the Finnish *ruotsi,* those who rowed) in the first place. The Slavic tribes who settled the wooded regions of the Valdai Hills northwest of Moscow discovered that those modest highlands were the source of four great river systems—the Volga, Dnieper, Western Dvina, and Lovat/Neva—that gave access to four seas—the White, the Baltic, the Black, and the Caspian. By making only short portages over gentle watersheds, Russian boatmen could traverse an area as large as the rest of Europe combined. The legendary Rurik founded the first Russian state, at Kiev, in 862, and in 988 Kievan Rus was converted by missionaries from the Byzantine Empire. But Russia's sheer distance from central Europe and the schism between the Catholic and Orthodox churches curtailed Russian participation in the flourishing culture of medieval Europe. Then, in 1238, the Golden Horde arrived from Mongolia, and Russia lay under the Tatar yoke for almost two and a half centuries. The grand dukes of Moscow finally ousted the khans in 1480, and Ivan the Terrible (who first called himself Tsar, meaning caesar) learned to exploit Russia's riverine arteries for geopolitical advantage. By the end of his long reign (1533–84) he had extended the sway of Muscovy to the Caspian Sea and the Ural Mountains, making Russia an empire of forest *and* steppe, Slavs *and* Tatars. From this mix came the Cossacks, and from the Cossacks the conquest of Siberia.

Most Cossacks (from the Turkish *kazak,* a free man or wanderer) were Tatars, but others were fugitive Russian serfs, river pirates, luckless retainers of Ivan's enemies, or galley slaves escaped from Turkey. Whatever their origin, Cossacks were a rapacious, stateless element organized for plunder. Ivan always had to find something for them to do, and so, too, did the brothers Stroganov. Their entrepreneurial family had amassed an empire of salt works, mines, granaries, and furs that stretched from Novgorod to the Urals. When their assiduous trappers depleted the furbearing animals on the western slopes, they asked and received from the Tsar the right to look further afield. But Grigorii Stroganov hesitated to cross the mountains and risk war with the Tatars beyond until Ermak the Cossack appeared with his band, fresh from raids on the Volga. Anxious for them to plunder lands other than his own, Stroganov offered three hundred of his own men, outfitted the expedition with muskets and food, and in 1581 sent them off to Siberia.

Ermak's army sailed and rowed their heavily burdened flotilla up and

over the Urals. The going was hard, and not until spring did they
descend the eastern slopes to sack the town of Tiumen. At length (the
chronology is vague), Ermak reached the Khan's capital, called Sibir by
the Russians. His men were outnumbered ten or twenty to one, but
Ermak's musketry and mettle, and desertions by the Khan's allies, settled the issue. The defeat of the khanate incredibly cleared Russia's path
all the way to the Pacific Ocean. Tsar Ivan had rebuked the Stroganovs
for sending Cossacks on a treasonous adventure, but he changed his
mind when Ermak's messengers returned with tidings of victory and
furs. The excited Tsar pardoned all concerned and promised soldiers and
a *voevoda* (governor) for Siberia. As it happened, Ivan died suddenly in
1584, and the following year Ermak perished in a raid on his camp. It
was said he fell into the water and his heavy armor—a gift from the
Tsar—pulled him under. But Boris Godunov, regent for Ivan's incompetent heir, rushed three hundred more Cossacks and *streltsy* (the Tsar's
bodyguard) and two *voevody* to found an *ostrog* (fort) at Tiumen and
another at Tobolsk on the Ob River.

Ostrogi were square wooden stockades with four corner parapets. The
Russians built them at river junctions and portages to house governors'
quarters, barracks, courts, jails, churches, trading posts, granaries, and
above all customs offices to collect, assess, and tax all pelts. As early as
1586 the Tsar received 200,000 sables alone from Siberia, and estimates
for the first half of the seventeenth century put the income from furs at
10 percent of the entire state revenue. The *voevody* not only exacted fur
tribute from the natives but a tithe on all furs garnered by Russian subjects, and an option to purchase a trader's best pelts, while the state
claimed a monopoly of export. Thus, what the Russian crown lacked in
receipts from overseas commerce, it made up for with the sable's
"golden fleece." No less than the Spanish, the Russian Empire rose on
the plunder of natural resources and native populations.

In fact, the frantic extermination of wildlife provided the impetus for
continuous movement eastward. Even famines and civil wars in Russia's Time of Troubles (1605–13) could not reverse the momentum.
Instead, peasants and Cossacks fled to the frontier in search of a new
life, while *promyshlenniki* (fur hunters) pressed onward. In 1607 (the
year the English founded Jamestown) *promyshlenniki* reached the river
Yenisey, and by 1632 the Lena, where Yakutsk was founded. Butalsk
ostrog on the Aldan River followed, and from there, in 1639, petty officer Ivan Moskitin reached the Sea of Okhotsk, an arm of the North
Pacific. As a potential Pacific port, Okhotsk was a study in misery: the
harbor poor and tricky, the waters frozen from October through April,
and the summers foggy. Still, the intrepid *promyshlenniki* built an

ostrog there in 1648. It was the first European settlement on the Pacific north of Mexico.

It is hard to imagine the stamina and savvy that moved these men four thousand miles across frigid, foodless wastes. The perils of land exploration pale beside those faced by Magellan and his kind, but Russian colonization of the length of Siberia in just sixty years is one of the great enterprises in history. By the mid-seventeenth century perhaps fifty thousand Russians had moved to Siberia, and one hundred thousand by 1700. But that in itself posed the most enduring problem: how were the colonies to be fed and supplied? Russia's Asian/Pacific destiny hinged on finding an answer. Even the best lands in Siberia were too cold, dry, or infertile to support much more than subsistence farming. Already during the Time of Troubles, when grain shipments from Russia ceased, some Siberian communities verged on famine. A local source of calories had to be found, and the most logical place to look was China.

Russians had heard rumors of the Amur River as early as the 1620s. It was said—like all unknown lands—to be laden with silver and gold. So in 1644, the same year the bannermen entered Peking, Vasilii Poiarkov sailed up the Aldan River in search of it. His orders were to subdue the natives and build forts, and his supplies were sufficient only for a one-way trip. Poiarkov's portage crossed the watershed from the Arctic to the Pacific basins, and the Zeya River carried him to the Amur. But he found no gold, ran short of food, and antagonized the local Daur tribe with his demands. Poiarkov lost half his 130 men in fruitless battles, 40 more starved over the winter, and others survived only by cannibalism. In the spring, the battered band fled down the Amur to the Sea of Okhotsk, coasted northward, and returned to Yakutsk in 1646. It was a mighty but disastrous journey. For even though Poiarkov could report to the *voevoda* that the Amur offered arable land and a moderate climate, his own brutality ensured that future Russian parties would have to fight their way in.

The Amur was indeed a potential breadbasket. Called the Black Dragon River by the Chinese because of the volume of silt its swift waters carry down from the mountains, the Amur flows 2,700 miles through alpine valleys and plateaus. Lying far enough south to pick up the monsoon, the valley receives warm, damp winds from the ocean in summer, and the river itself bubbles with fish. So in 1649 the Yakutsk *voevoda* chose Erofei Khabarov, the man who organized the first farming community on the Yenisey, to pioneer the Amur. But once he learned that the Daur tribesmen were subject to the Emperor of China, Khabarov requested a

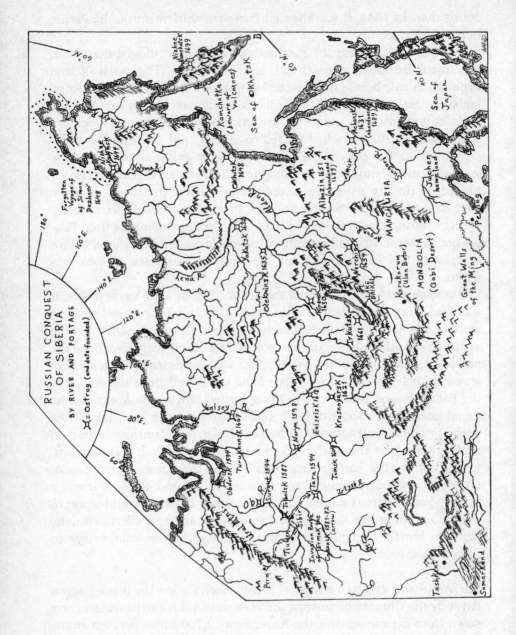

RUSSIAN CONQUEST
OF SIBERIA
BY RIVER AND PORTAGE

⋈ = Ostrog (and date founded)

60° N.

50° N.

40° N.

180°

160° E.

140° E.

120° E.

100° E.

80° E.

60

Nizhne Kamchatsk 1699

Kamchatka (beware of volcanoes)

Sea of Okhotsk

Sea of Japan

Anadyrsk

Nizhne Kolymsk 1644

Kolyma R.

Forgotten Voyage of Simon Dezhnev 1648

Okhotsk 1648

Aldan R.

Yakutsk 1632

Lena R.

Olekminsk 1635

Albazin 1651 (abandoned 1689)

Achansk (abandoned 1689)

Amur R.

Argun R.

Dzhugdzhur

MANCHURIA

Jülchen homeland

Peking

Great Walls of the Ming

MONGOLIA (Gobi Desert)

Karakorum (Ulan Bator)

LAKE BAIKAL

Nerchinsk 1654

Irkutsk 1661

Kirensk 1630

Krasnoyarsk 1621

Yenisey R.

Yeniseisk 1618

Narym 1598

Turukhansk 1607

Obdorsk 1594

Ob R.

Surgut 1594

Tara 1594

Tomsk 1604

U.-d. Ust-tym R.

Tiumen 1586

Tobolsk 1587

Sibir

Invasion route of Ermak the Cossack 1581-82 (arrow)

Irtysh R.

Perm

Tashkent

Samarkand

garrison of six thousand soldiers. In the meantime, he put his men to work planting fields and building *ostrogi* called Albazin and Achansk. But Khabarov was either persuaded or bullied by his *promyshlenniki*, for instead of lying low he began to raid and carry off women and goods back to Albazin. The Daur, not surprisingly, appealed to Peking.

Now, the Ch'ing had been in power only seven years and were busy trying to pacify China. But they could not ignore these new barbarians, whoever they were, without risking the loyalty of other border tribes. And so an army was sent. But rather than stand off and blow the *ostrogi* to bits with his cannon, the Manchu general gave orders to take the barbarians alive. The Cossacks sensed restraint in their adversaries, sallied forth, and routed the attackers. Khabarov claimed to have killed 676 of the enemy and captured two cannons, ample provisions, and over eight hundred horses. News of the victory and of the rich Amur basin spread all over Siberia, and more than a thousand fortune hunters and fugitives rushed there in search of plunder. Of course, physical occupation of the region by armed colonists was precisely what the Russians needed to hold on to the basin. But such was the lawlessness—and the depopulation of existing Siberian settlements—that the tsarist authorities garrisoned rivers to *stop* the land rush. Meanwhile, the Manchus left off making frontal assaults and burned the Russians' precious fields of grain.

What had become of the six thousand soldiers approved by the Tsar? They never left Russia, having been diverted instead to troubled borders with Poland. So the Tsar sent a lone ambassador. But when Fedor Baikov appeared at the gates of Peking in 1656, the Chinese did not connect this agent of a distant Emperor with the barbarians terrorizing the Amur! The latter, thought the Confucian scholars, must come from "beyond the great ocean" since they had white skin and traveled in boats. The ambassador, on the other hand, came overland and must therefore represent some khan of the steppe. In any case, Baikov's orders forbade him to negotiate with anyone but the Emperor, but he was not permitted an audience unless he performed the kowtow, implying that his Tsar was tributary to the Chinese Emperor. He refused and was dismissed after a matter of months.

Political wisdom is slow in coming when alien parties must start from scratch learning each other's interests, intentions, capabilities, customs, and categories of thought. Only after years of intelligence gathering, punctuated by the rare insight, did the Russian court learn that it had *two* interests at stake on the Amur: the victualing of Siberia, a proven source of wealth, and trade with China, a potentially greater source of wealth. Likewise the Chinese had to learn that to avoid constant war in the north they must grant something else these barbarians wanted in return for a Russian retreat. So the question hanging over the Amur was this: would Moscow risk an expensive war with China in hopes of rounding out its Siberian empire; or would Moscow relinquish the Amur and forever limit Siberia's future in hopes of making a killing through trade?

If the Cossacks had been less beastly, the crisis that opened everyone's eyes might have happened far sooner. As it was, only in the late 1660s, after another decade of intermittent massacres on the Amur and more failed embassies, did forty Daur tribesmen under one Gantimur walk into Nerchinsk *ostrog* and defect, pay tribute to the Tsar, and in time be baptized. *This*, above all else, was bound to alarm the Ch'ing, and their vigorous protest reached the *voevoda*. He in turn sent a courier to Peking demanding that the Emperor of China swear fealty to the Tsar. Suddenly it dawned on the Ch'ing court: the barbarians on the Amur were not pirates from the sea or an odd band off the steppe, but Europeans who had come across the continent! And that meant that the Tsar in Moscow must be great indeed. This recognition, in 1670, inspired a new and for the first time relevant Ch'ing policy. Peking responded with gifts for the Tsar, hints of trading rights, *and* a request that the "Great Lord" attend the fact that his subjects had a bad habit of raiding peoples on the frontier. The Tsar, too, reconsidered his options. Anglo-Dutch commercial wars were raging, Louis XIV had begun his lifetime of aggression, Europe's seaborne links to Asia were disrupted, and savants on the order of Leibniz were urging European monarchs to open a land route to China. The conflation of these events and ideas persuaded the Tsar to send his most learned official to Peking.

Nikolai Milescu (usually known as "Spathary" for having served as a *spathar* [officer] for the Ottoman Turks) was a renowned Moldavian scholar and humanist. But he was also arrogant and contemptuous—not the sort likely to ingratiate himself with the Chinese court. His painstakingly drafted instructions aimed at the achievement of full commercial rights in China and the Tsar loaded him down with gifts for the Emperor and a generous purse from which to make bribes. But on the rivers and caravan trails eastward, Milescu had time to study Siberia, with which he grew fascinated. He also gathered intelligence about China and concluded that the Manchus were frightened of the Cossacks and preoccupied by their internal troubles. So by the time he arrived in 1676, Milescu had decided not to yield on issues of protocol or substance. His opposite number, the Ch'ing bureaucrat Mala, was little better. An expert on "barbarian affairs," he insisted that Milescu behave like one, and not with the dignity of a scholar representing a Christian monarch. Most perplexing were Mala's repeated protests concerning Cossack raids and the defection of Gantimur. What had those trivialities to do with a commercial treaty? It took fifty days before Milescu was even permitted to enter Peking, whereupon more quarrels erupted over whether the Tsar's offerings were gifts or tribute, and whether Milescu would kowtow.

In the Ch'ing court resided Jesuits, who acted not only as translators but also as informers. Ferdinand Verbiest said he did it "for Christianity's sake"; Milescu thought he did it out of residual loyalty to the Ming. In any case, the Jesuits gave the Russians their first glimpse into the mind of the Ch'ing. They knew now that the Amur settlements were Russian, whispered Verbiest. They were enraged by the Cossacks and the threat to the loyalty of the northern tribes. So if the Russians refused to surrender Gantimur, the Chinese would surely make war. Their armies were very strong. Milescu shrugged off the advice and presented the Emperor with nothing but twelve demands concerning trade. The Chinese replied with three demands: the return of Gantimur, peace on the Amur, and the replacement of Milescu by a more "reasonable" ambassador. Seven more years passed, during which the Russians mistakenly thought their contempt justified and the Manchus prepared for war. Finally, in 1685, three thousand bannermen simply surrounded Albazin and set it afire. The Russians begged for clemency, and true to the Emperor's word, the Manchu general granted it, whereupon the Russians betrayed his trust, rebuilt Albazin, and were duly attacked again.

Moscow now dispatched Fedor Alekseevich Golovin, the gifted thirty-five-year-old son of the *voevoda* of Tobolsk, to parlay with Peking. His initial instructions were to demand the Amur and reparations and to threaten war if he were refused. But as news arrived of the military realities, two more packets reached Golovin en route authorizing a partial retreat. He was still forbidden to kowtow, however, and thus had to meet the Chinese on equal ground. That was why Nerchinsk *ostrog*, a rude frontier post, hosted Golovin, the mandarins, and their Jesuit interpreters, while ten thousand bannermen camped outside. Golovin effectively surrendered the whole of the Amur basin save Nerchinsk, which now had no purpose except as a trading station. All current fugitives were permitted to remain where they were, but all future defectors had to be returned—that disposed of Gantimur without loss of face. Finally, all properly licensed merchants were permitted to cross the border and trade—a concession to Russia that other Europeans could only envy. The Treaty of Nerchinsk, and the follow-up Treaty of Kiakhta (1728), governed Russo-Chinese relations for over 150 years.

The Russian conquest of Siberia, the clash on the Amur, and the final *modus vivendi* drip with paradox. The first white nation to reach the Pacific in force was not the most advanced, but the most backward. They did not come by sea over routes known for more than a century, but over four thousand miles of earth's most rugged terrain. Having reached the Pacific they realized that "people power"—that is, settlers and the loyalty of indigenous tribes—would decide their future in northeast Asia. Yet the Cossacks alienated the natives they met, and at one point the government choked off Russian immigration. Knowing that their Siberian empire depended on finding a fertile breadbasket, the tsarist government signed away its claims to the only one available in return for access to the China market. If the whole purpose of the drive to the east had been to reach China, then the retreat at Nerchinsk would have made sense. But it was not. The Russian drive to the east was borne of a lust for furs in particular and empire in general. Nor did the Russians repent of those lusts. Instead, they pushed still farther in quest of furs and empire, even though they lacked the economy to support what they already had. Tragic, if you are Russian, for the brave efforts still to come had already been rendered vain—in 1689—at Nerchinsk.

Petropavlovsk 1741

IT SHOULD HAVE BEEN so splendid, this panorama, especially on so fine a spring morning. Above and behind, the volcanic spine of the Kamchatka Peninsula stretched off far to the north. Beneath sparkled the deep waters of Avacha Bay, graced by two smart brigs, sails furled, like proud sons awaiting their father's orders. Their like had never been seen in these seas before. The wooden town numbered only a few scattered barracks, the scented chapel with its toy-sized onion dome, and a humble "captain's quarters." Still, considering its location, the scene bespoke the glory of Russia every bit as much as the new capital and navies the late Tsar had built on the Baltic. And just as Peter the Great had willed those into existence, so had he willed these and bestowed upon ships and port the blessed names of Peter and Paul. It could have been splendid, were Vitus Bering not so tired.

The old captain, now thirty-seven years in the service of Russia, descended the bluff to his shack. He had summoned Alexei Chirikov, his second-in-command, the French geographer Louis Delisle, the German naturalist Georg Wilhelm Steller, and his other lieutenants to counsel. They must weigh anchor soon, but St. Petersburg's instructions were an implausible wish list: sail southeast to search for Gamaland (another name for the legendary kingdom of silver and gold); sail south to search for Japan; sail north to chart the Siberian coast; sail east in search of America and claim all the lands beyond the reach of Spain! Chirikov argued for prudence. They should proceed northward to 65° on the course he and Bering had traced thirteen years before, then turn due east. There the American coast, if it existed, would lie closest to Siberia. Delisle's priority was Gamaland, potentially the richest prize. If it proved elusive the expedition could still turn north and hunt for America before bad weather closed in. Bering himself did not know what to do, or perhaps no longer cared. He had been eight years wrestling this expedition across the five thousand miles from Russia, fighting the terrain, the climate, contentious colleagues, rude Cossacks, and stupid, corrupt, and usually drunken Siberian officials. Every scrap of iron and canvas, not to mention all other necessities, had to be carted, rafted, sledged, and shipped from home—only to disappear through raids, theft, and mishap. By the time the expedition reached Yakutsk, it had already cost thirty times his sanguine estimate. They reached Okhotsk four *years* after departing St. Petersburg, felled and cut timber, and built their ships. Then two supply vessels sank off Kamchatka.

Bering's choice of Avacha Bay as base port seemed a brilliant stroke. The harbor was fine, the weather milder than on the mainland, the ocean nearer. But he had since found that Kamchatka was even less able to support a colony than the rest of Siberia. Cossacks had tried to cultivate its few coastal patches, but yields hardly returned the seed of even the hardiest grains. That meant that Petropavlovsk would have to be supplied from without. But Kamchatka could be reached only from Yakutsk through 2,800 miles of mountains and hostile Chukchi tribes, or by sea from wretched Okhotsk. In other words, European Russia would have to ship excess grain to central Siberia, so that the small Russian communities there could spare stores for Okhotsk, enabling it to serve as a tenuous way station to Petropavlovsk, so that it might in turn be a base for Pacific empire. No wonder Bering went down to the sea with a bitter insouciance. He might indeed become a Pacific Columbus. But what government could afford to repeat this venture—unless he really did find El Dorado out there in the fog? And what Russian government could hold it, if he did?

The turn of events that carried Vitus Bering to the far side of Kamchatka began when he was eight. That was the year when the Treaty of Nerchinsk deflected Russia's energies from the Amur to Siberia's northeastern extremities. It was also the year Peter the Great ascended the throne. It is customary to think of the reign of the red-headed giant as a watershed during which backward Russia underwent Westernization. But so did Russia retain its fundamentals of autocracy, serfdom, a state-dominated Orthodox church, and a court-directed economy. Peter's ambition was not to become *like* the West, but to endow Russia with the technology and knowledge necessary for it to *compete* with European powers. His foreign policy objectives were to push back the Swedes and Turks to gain outlets on the Baltic and Black seas. He never quite succeeded in the south, but in the Great Northern War (1699–1721) Peter conquered a coast on the Gulf of Finland and built a new port and capital to support Russia's destiny on the seas. To that end he hired foreign shipwrights and sailors, founded the Moscow Navigation School (and later the Russian Academy of Sciences), and financed a fleet of forty-eight capital ships. To command them Peter recruited nearly a thousand foreign officers. Most were Dutch, some were Danes, and one of the latter was Vitus Bering.

Bering apprenticed in the Dutch East India Company, took a lieu-tenancy in the Russian Navy in 1704, and in time achieved his cap-taincy, second class. But the personnel shakedown that followed the end of the Swedish war lost him the rank he thought he deserved, so Bering resigned and went home. The coming of peace also freed the Tsar's mind and resources for a project over which he had brooded. How far did his empire reach? What new provinces might lie beyond Siberia? When he visited Amsterdam in 1697 he had thought about the theories of Nicolas Witsen, a geographer with a special interest in northeast Tar-tary, as he labeled the Siberian extremities. Witsen believed in Gama-land (or Kompagnieland), a Dutch equivalent of the Land Rich with Gold and Silver said to lie near the Kurile Islands. He also urged Peter to send expeditions to learn whether Asia and America were joined. The Tsar needed little persuasion. He knew that the *promyshlenniki*, frus-trated on the Amur, were pursuing the sable and fox to the utter east, and he did not disapprove when the Yakutsk *voevoda* sent the Cossack Vladimir Atlasov off to conquer Kamchatka.

Peter received Atlasov personally in 1701 to hear his amazing report. The winters on that mysterious 1,500-mile-long peninsula, it happened, were milder than on the mainland. But Kamchatka's chain of volcanic peaks glowed red by night and smoked by day. The ground rumbled con-stantly. As for the native Kamchadalis, said Atlasov, they were a short, beardless people who dressed in quilted skins, built huts atop twenty-foot stilts, and lived off fish, especially a tasty pink variety that swam upriver and did not return (salmon!). Atlasov considered the Kam-chadalis primitive and foul-smelling—and if they seemed so to the Cos-sack, they must have been noisome indeed. Yet these Stone Age fisher-men possessed lacquered utensils acquired, they said, by trade with a "magnificent people" far to the south, one of whom they had held in captivity. He was a castaway, of course, slender, dark, with a small mus-tache. His name was Dembei and he said he was from "Uzaka" (Osaka). Dembei wept at the sight of the Russians and hoped they would let him go home. Instead, he became the first Japanese to visit Europe and sent Peter's imagination spinning.

So this Kamchatka was the back door to Japan, a secret, special Russ-ian advantage over all the maritime powers! In 1702 Peter issued a ukase (tsarist decree) commanding the pacification of Kamchatka *and* the gathering of intelligence about Japan. Neither task proved easy. Atlasov succumbed to his Cossack ways, plundered a caravan bound from China, and landed in prison. Then after the *voevoda* released him with orders to discipline the *promyshlenniki* in Kamchatka, his own men mutinied and killed him in his sleep. But the mutineers redeemed themselves by putting to sea in a few small boats and blundering into the Kurile Islands. They found no furs but learned from the "hairy Ainu" that these islands led indeed to Japan. So Peter dispatched geographers to Okhotsk with orders "to describe . . . whether Asia and America are joined by land." At least these were the public instructions. In fact, they sailed south, not north, and in 1721 reached the sixth Kurile island, about halfway down the chain. Three years later Peter went all out, financing what came to be known as the First Kamchatka Expedition and offering command, with full rank and double pay, to Bering. He could have had a comfortable retirement on his little estate at Vyborg. Instead, he left for Siberia.

Peter's orders, one of the final acts of his remarkable reign, instructed the captain to build one or two decked vessels on the Pacific, sail north, ascertain where (not "whether"!) Asia joined America, then proceed "to a settlement under European authority." Stripped of its scientific cover, Peter's intent would appear to be to get a foothold in America and find out where the Spaniards were. Three years after leaving St. Petersburg, in 1728, Bering's first expedition reached Kamchatka and built a sixty-foot ship. In July 1728, with Chirikov and Martin Spanberg as seconds, Bering sailed through the sea and strait that bear his name to 67° north in the Arctic Ocean. But the Alaskan coast, shrouded in fog, remained undiscovered. He returned with an excellent map of the Chukchi coast (East Cape), but nothing more. He got a cold greeting in St. Petersburg but deflected criticism with plans for a Second Kamchatka Expedition designed not only to explore the North Pacific, but to develop the Siberian littoral. Soon he had admirals and imperial senators chattering of lands filled with gold, a Russian empire in California, annexation of the Kuriles, and Okhotsk as an entrepot for Japanese trade. Of course, none of this was made public. Bering's official orders were to satisfy the curiosity of "the eternally famous Peter" and the French and Russian academies of science.

Martin Spanberg commanded the Japan expedition. After a hellacious and nearly fatal trek across Siberia, he supervised ship construction and sailed for the Kuriles in 1738—only to be forced back by ice and fog (in July!). The following year, Spanberg dipped down to 40° north, made landfall on the eastern coast of Honshu, and was amazed by the sight of rich farmland and populous villages. A second Russian ship sighted the southernmost coast of Honshu. But neither captain was bold enough to say "take me to your leader" and learn exactly where they were. They also managed to miss Hokkaido completely and so were uncertain whether they had reached Japan at all. These results were hardly encouraging, and Russians would not knock on the door of Japan again until the 1790s.

The hopes placed in the Second Kamchatka Expedition thus came to rest on the weary shoulders of Bering. His *Sviatoi Petr* and Chirikov's *Sviatoi Pavel*, eighty-foot brigs with fourteen cannon and seventy-five men, sailed from Petropavlovsk in June 1741 into the unknown waters of the North Pacific. After ten days Gamaland had still not appeared, and the captains, after some argument, changed course to the north. On June 19 a storm separated the ships and they wasted more valuable days in a vain hunt for each other. Bering turned south again for a last try at Gamaland, and by the time he made a nor'easterly course the *Sviatoi Petr* had to tack against adverse winds. But July 17 brought the sighting: the snowcapped peak of a mighty volcano over sixteen thousand feet high, the sentinel of a continent. The men cheered. Bering, in full sight of his crew, shrugged.

Steller the naturalist ached to go ashore, and the captain finally agreed to a landing at Kayak Island, sixty miles from Mount St. Elias. He gave Steller a sum total of ten hours ashore on the American coast after ten *years* of preparation. Bering was not interested in specimens and measurements. He wanted fresh water, and he wanted to go home. The season closed quickly in these latitudes. So after four days they raised anchor, found the latitude of Petropavlovsk, and endeavored to follow it westward to safety. Fogs, winds, and currents bedeviled them. A third of the crew came down with scurvy. Water ran low. Incessant storms collapsed the rigging. By November 5 both ship and crew were dying when land—Bering Island—appeared in the gloom. But its heavy surf ripped off their anchors and left them no choice but to winter over.

The shipwrecks gathered driftwood for fuel and lived off seal and manatee meat and the putrid corpses of two beached whales. Wild blue foxes by the hundreds attacked their makeshift shelters, dug up and consumed their dead, and mauled the enervated living. Bering himself, rotting with scurvy, lay in his lean-to, half-buried by shifting sand. "Leave it," he said, "for the warmth"—until December 8, when he died. The following spring the survivors patched together a boat from the remains of the *Sviatoi Petr*, put to sea in August, and discovered that Kamchatka lay only a hundred miles to the west. After all his labors, their captain had perished for want of one more good day under sail.

Chirikov, with better luck and judgment, had been a week ahead of Bering on the same northeasterly course. On July 15, 1741, he, too, sighted the coast at what is now Cape Addington on the Alaskan panhandle. He sent in a landing party on Chichagof Island. It did not return.

He sent a second boat. Indian canoes appeared instead, and Chirikov assumed the worst. Bereft of boats, he could make no more landings, which meant no fresh water. So he reluctantly sailed for home, sighting along the way the Kenai Peninsula, Kodiak Island, and several of the Aleutians. Scurvy did its work, taking the geographer Delisle among others, but Chirikov benefited from the last few weeks of tolerable weather and made safe haven at Petropavlovsk on October 10.

The Second Kamchatka Expedition exposed both the opportunities open to Russia in the North Pacific and the impossibility of its taking full advantage of them. The cost was so high—over 1.5 million rubles— that even Peter the Great might have lost interest. His successors certainly did. They also let Peter's navy decay through neglect and incompetence and fell again into wars that lasted on and off until 1762. Finally, the Bering expeditions so taxed the resources of Siberia that its *voevody* protested loudly *against* any repetition.

But to one group of Russians the expeditions were a success beyond hope—the *promyshlenniki.* For the crew of the *Sviatoi Pavel,* and even the survivors of the *Sviatoi Petr,* managed to limp back to port with over fifteen hundred sea otter pelts, which proved softer and glossier than any stroked or seen before, and brought forty times the price of Siberian sable from Chinese merchants. So the *promyshlenniki* pushed out on to the waters, to the Aleutian Islands, and finally to the mainland the Aleuts called "Alakshak." Siberian merchants outfitted them, and they ventured out in *shitiki* boats hewn from fresh timber and held together with leather string in lieu of iron. Such craft were good for two voyages at the most, but transportation and a handful of muskets was all they needed. The native Aleuts, reduced to slavery, did the rest.

Beginning in 1743 with Emelian Basov's maiden voyage, *promyshlenniki* sailed to the Aleutians a dozen or two to a boat. Having overawed an Aleut village and taken the women and children hostage, each Russian became a foreman on an Aleut kayak, forcing the skilled Indians to spear otters and seals. If the Aleuts resisted, they were slaughtered. Disease, as in Mexico, did the rest. Within two generations the Aleut population fell by 80 percent. So, of course, did the otter population, for those merry beasts, whom Steller named the "mildest of all marine mammals," bore only one pup per year. Yet the *promyshlenniki* were unlikely to retreat so long as a good voyage yielded 200,000 rubles and even a common hand's half-share seemed a fortune. By 1798 some forty-two companies had formed to sponsor expeditions that, in the course of things, also sketched out the first rough charts of the Aleutian and Alaskan coasts. As English scholar William Coxe wrote in 1780, "more important discoveries were made by these individuals at their own private cost than had hitherto been effected by all the expensive efforts of the crown."

But wait! Was this not just the sort of Russian migration that the food problem supposedly rendered impossible? No, because the *promyshlenniki* remained in Alaska for no more than one winter, made no permanent settlements until the 1780s, and needed little in the way of a base in Siberia. As late as 1770 only 550 Russians resided at Okhotsk and perhaps 1,500 on the entire Kamchatka Peninsula, while in the Aleutians, the Russians lived off their "hosts" or else gorged on Pacific manatee first described by Steller on Bering Island. These splendid sea cows could reach thirty-five feet in length and weigh three thousand pounds. Their mating swim, Steller observed, was a delightful tease ending in copulation face-to-face, like human beings . . . except that the male manatee's organ was six feet long. The meat of the beast looked and tasted like beef and seemed never to rot. Steller's sea cow was extinct within decades.

The rape of the Aleutians closed the curtain on the drama begun by Ermak. The fur hunters had gone as far as river boats and *shitiki* could take them, and they now faced two unpleasant options. One was to quit and scratch out a living by means fair or foul in Siberia. The other was to lay hands on genuine ships and press on down the American coast. Hence the government also faced an unpleasant choice. It could abandon the *promyshlenniki* and lose its claim to the North Pacific. Or it could sponsor a real colony in Alaska with expensive ships, food, officials, and forts to defend it. For thanks to the *promyshlenniki*, the Spaniards now awoke from their slumber.

Alta California 1769

IN THE YEAR 1731, when the Russian Admiralty was approving
Bering's second expedition, an eighteen-year-old youth on Majorca
made a decision equally momentous for the North Pacific. Kneeling
before the provincial at the Convent of Jesus, Miguel José Serra heard
the question "My sons, what is your petition?" and answered with his
fellow novices, "I desire to profess the rule of our Blessed Father Francis
. . . by living in obedience, without property, and in charity, in order to
serve God better and to save my soul." His vows acknowledged and
blessed, Miguel donned the tunic of undyed wool and the cowled frock
with white waist cord, and announced his desire to be known henceforth as Junípero—after the mirthful and commonsensical Brother
Juniper, "jester of the Lord" and companion to St. Francis of Assisi.

Majorca, the Balearic isle off the Mediterranean coast of Spain, had
only 140,000 residents in the early eighteenth century but boasted of
317 churches, five hundred priests, and fifteen monasteries. Protestants
would say it was "priest-ridden," but thanks to the church every town
had its houses for the sick, orphaned, and elderly. Young Serra was the
son of an illiterate hired hand, but thanks to the Franciscans education
was available even to one such as him. And when not at his studies, he
stood beneath the high altar, attending the monks' canonical hours or
chanting in the choir. Around and about him, arousing his fancy, were
dimly lit side chapels devoted to Santa Clara, Santa Barbara, Santa Rosa,
San Gabriel, San Rafael, San Diego de Alcalá, San Francisco, and other
saints revered by the Franciscans.

Miguel was a gifted pupil and singer. He was also a runt, and the good
fathers gently rejected his first application to take holy orders that he
might grow up a little. When after his vows he "sprang up" to five feet
two inches, he deemed it a miracle. Fray Junípero then completed a six-

year curriculum in language, philosophy, and theology. Following his ordination in 1737 he was kept on as a professor, and what a teacher he must have been. Philosophy, he said, was not mere manipulation of logic or airy speculation, but the pragmatic craft by which one diagnosed and cured the sick mind or soul: "Walk in that light worthily that you may be sons of Him who is Light itself and in Whom there is no darkness." Foster self-discipline, he urged, for where there is no will to say no, there also is no freedom. But when examination time arrived Serra quoted the pagan Vergil in puckish sympathy with his students: "To future good will Jove dispose/soon, our past and present woes!"

By all accounts, Serra had the gift of making complex points simple and simple ones profound. In 1743 the Lullian University gave him the honor of preaching at the Feast of Corpus Christi, the celebration of the body of Christ in the bread and wine, then named him to the Duns Scotus Chair of Sacred Theology. He might well have become rector of the university, even Bishop of Majorca. But in 1748 he gave it away, not to swim in some bigger pond—Salamanca or Madrid—but in smaller ponds, and more remote. He yearned "to revive in my soul those intense longings which I have had since my novitiate when I read the lives of the saints. These longings have become somewhat deadened because of the preoccupation I had with studies." And so, when a Mexican envoy arrived to recruit missionaries, a new calling burned its way into Serra's heart. He forsook parents, home, and career at almost a moment's notice, and took ship for America.

Like St. Paul, he faced three mortal perils at sea. In the Mediterranean, a "stiff-necked heretic" of an English captain insisted on arguing theology, cried "Recant, you petty monk of Satan!" and nearly strangled Serra. On the Atlantic crossing, the winds died and the water ration dwindled to eight ounces per day. "I have observed," Serra wrote, "that the best way of saving one's saliva is to eat little and talk less." On the Caribbean leg from San Juan, storms split the mainmast and battered the hull. The missionaries prayed to Santa Barbara, whose feast it was, and concluded that she had delivered them. But it was on land that Junípero suffered most. On the road to Mexico City he took what Serra's protégé, Francisco Palóu, thought to be the sting of a *zancudo*, a fearsome Mexican mosquito (it may have been a scorpion, chigger, or brown recluse spider). The infection spread upward from his foot and left Serra half-crippled and in pain for the rest of his life. "*No es cosa de cuidado*," he would tell the fussy: "It's a matter of no importance." Two days later he stumbled into the College of San Fernando and was immediately asked to join the faculty. But Serra had come to convert Indians. In 1750, he left with Palóu for the remote Sierra Madre, where he would stay for eight years, preaching and baptizing, until assigned to a still wilder post in a province called Texas. But before he could arrive Apaches massacred Spain's frontier guard, so Serra retreated to Mexico for another nine years of evangelizing. His zeal made him a celebrity. "Does the man ever sleep?" soldiers on guard duty would ask. Nor did he eat much: "What more do we want than a little tortilla and the herbs of the field"? And his method of reaching the Indians was through sensory display: the glories of the liturgy replete with incense, chant, and bells, the Stations of the Cross, and flagellation. Aroused by his own sermons, he would beat his breast with stones and burn himself with coals to reify hell. This from an esteemed college professor, traveling now across thousands of miles of wilderness on a pus-laden, abscessed foot. But none of that made Serra great in the world's eyes. What made him great was Carlos III.

Spain's languid decline from its sixteenth-century golden age reversed itself, with the chunk of changing gears, in 1700. That was when the Habsburg line died out and the throne passed to the grandson of Louis XIV. The first Bourbon rulers found conditions so bad as to justify Europe's sneers: chaotic administration, a fossilized economy, a culture that retained only the trappings of the passionate Catholic Reformation. So Philip V, Fernando VI, and Carlos III tried to recast the Spanish state after the model of Versailles. Proud Spaniards resented it ("They are like children who cry when their faces are washed," said Carlos), but the Bourbon kings and ministers set out to break the dead hand of church and nobility. Felipe broke relations with the Holy See, asserted royal authority over clerical appointments and income, put an end to autos-da-fé (burnings at the stake), and pulled the teeth of the Inquisition. Fernando turned Spain's provincial *corregidores* (governors) into French-style intendants and streamlined the bureaucracy and tax collection. The result was the sort of regime historians term "enlightened despotism."

The reign of Fernando VI ended in 1759, when the death of his beloved wife drove him to convulsive fits. His heir was his half-brother, Carlos, of whom it was said that one princess refused marriage upon spying his portrait and that he and his queen were "the ugliest couple on earth." Be that as it may, they had thirteen children, and so true was Carlos that after her death he walked barefoot at night on cold stones to kill his lust for others. He was also devoted to the state, keeping the same daily schedule of work, punctuated only by shooting game and attending mass, for thirty years. The reformers Carlos appointed set out to free markets and prices and abolish barriers to trade. The growth this encouraged helped support a population that more than doubled during the century. But Carlos III's most glorious, and problematical, legacy was undoubtedly California.

Historians used to think that Spain's Empire was as depressed as Spain itself during the last Habsburg century. But figures show this to be false. American mining, agriculture, and trade plugged along and even expanded. Colonial officials simply took advantage of Spain's lassitude to achieve more control over their own affairs. Viceroys sent from Spain had to relax their rules in exchange for obedience, losing revenue in the process. Meanwhile, Spain lost the naval power to enforce its monopoly so that American commerce fell into the hands of Dutch and English interlopers. Given that the crown relied on colonial receipts for as much as a quarter of its income, Carlos had a compelling motive for plugging leaks in "the Indies." So in 1765 he named José de Gálvez *visitador-general* and sent him off to Mexico.

A second motive was strategic. Spanish America had long been subject to piracy, but the growth of Britain's American colonies and the outcome of the Seven Years' War (1756–63) made Spanish America insecure as never before. In that war the British chased France—Spain's Bourbon ally—out of Canada and the Antilles and briefly occupied Spanish Florida. The American balance of power was upset in favor of the aggressive, Protestant English, and Carlos said it made his blood run cold. Last but not least was news of a threat to the north. In 1757 Miguel Venegas's *Noticia de la California* warned of the presence of Russians on the American coast, followed two years later by an Italian book, *I Muscoviti nella California*. Spain's ambassador at St. Petersburg confirmed the discoveries of Bering and Chirikov. It was enough to persuade Madrid to instruct Gálvez to see to it that the coastline of Alta California was explored and occupied.

So Gálvez arrived with a daunting agenda: put a stop to the comfortable corruption of Mexican *corregidores*, establish a network of royal intendants, raise taxes, enforce the crown's tobacco monopoly, stimulate mining and commerce . . . and colonize the huge and remote province called California. In so doing Gálvez angered every sector of the population except the Church, and he accomplished that in 1767, when he received orders to suppress the Jesuits, who were suspected of intrigue by the Bourbons and were the chief bogeymen of the Enlightenment. Gálvez confiscated their missions in Baja and gave them to the Franciscans, who gave them in turn to Serra by electing him *padre presidente*.

Gálvez had already inspected arid Baja and pronounced it deplorable. This could never be the supply base for Alta California. But the site he chose instead, the port of San Blas far down the coast, was no better. The harbor was treacherous, and the climate so fetid that stores rotted on the pier except in winter, which was the worst season for ships to brave California's winds and currents. In the long run success depended on a secure *land* route funneling people and supplies from Mexico to the north—on that, and on loyal colonial subjects. But where were colonists to be found? Gálvez and the Viceroy Count Antonio Maria Bucareli recruited only a handful of *gente de razon* (men of reason = Spaniards and Creoles). So the most likely "colonists" were the Indians already there. The colony could not be safe until the Indians were tamed in any case, so Gálvez wrote a message to Serra: "The king has need of you. Come at once. We are going to found new missions." Junípero, now fifty-five years old with eighteen years on the frontier, sang high mass in thanksgiving.

Gálvez and Serra considered what little was known of California's geography and imagined a "ladder" of a dozen or more "rungs"—missions spaced a day's journey apart along *el camino real* (the royal road) from San Diego to Vizcaíno's fabled port of Monterey. Five parties, three by sea and two by land, departed Mexico in 1769. One ship, the *San Antonio*, arrived in good order. The second was blown far out to sea and appeared two months late, its crew so scurvy-ridden that not a man had the strength to lower a boat. The third ship did not appear at all. The overland parties, with pack mules, cattle, and a guard of twenty-five soldiers, arrived intact. At their head rode Gaspar de Portolá, Governor of Baja, and Father Serra, so fever-ridden that he pronounced San Diego "very cold."

While the friars set about slapping adobe huts, nursing seamen, and founding a mission, Portolá took sixty-three healthy men—the last *conquistadores*—and plunged north in search of Monterey. Anyone who has driven even a stretch of the Coast Highway will recall the barren promontories, sand, and brush, twists and turns, and utter lack of food and water. After two and a half months Portolá in fact reached Monterey but spied no magnificent harbor such as described by Vizcaíno and embellished by a century's retelling. Thinking it must not be the place, he pressed on. At length they came upon great redwood trees and called the place Palo Alto (high tree). Then, to their greater surprise, they climbed a bluff on October 31 and "descried a large bay." San Francisco, hidden from sailors by fog and tricky waters, was finally discovered by land.

Portolá's starving men retraced their steps all the way to San Diego, devouring the scaly flesh of their emaciated mules. The *padres* they found were hardly better-off, having won no converts, garnered no harvest, and received no supplies. Portolá judged that if the *San Antonio* did not appear soon the colony must be abandoned. So Serra led the missionaries in a novena, a nine-day cycle of prayer, and on the last day the ship was sighted. Refreshed, Portolá and Serra led the servants of Spain and God in another hunt for Monterey. This time they found it, rendezvoused again with the ship, and established a second mission. Serra thought it "a pleasing stretch of land," and Portolá "proceeded to erect a fort to occupy and defend the port from the atrocities of the Russians [*sic*]." The mission was later moved to Carmel, a place, Serra said, where he would be content to live and die.

The new empire was now in the hands of some three score Spaniards with the most fragile of links to the world. The Indians were mostly tolerant of the newcomers, but they lived a naked, Stone Age existence, subsisting on crows, squirrels, rabbits, snakes, insects, worms, and a staple made from mashed acorns. So the Franciscans labored as preachers and teachers, agronomists and field hands, architects and carpenters, masons and weavers, shepherds and physicians. But they were fighting a vicious circle. The missions could not become a going concern without Indian labor. But the missions had already to be going concerns—with ample food, blankets, and tools—to attract Indians in the first place. The only way to prime the pump was to import more Spaniards, but the more lay settlers the more chance of violence between them and the Indians.

Serra rode, determined, up and down the coast to found missions called San Gabriel, San Buenaventura, San Luis Obispo, and San Antonio de Padua. But his exertions were stymied by Indian indifference, irregular supplies, and the depredations of Portolá's replacement, Pedro Fages, who turned out to be a sadist. So Junípero made the grueling trip back to Mexico—he arrived "in danger of death" and received last rites—to put his case to the Viceroy. First, a humane soldier must be appointed in place of Fages. Second, California needed a secure supply route and lay settlers of both sexes. At present there was not a single white woman in Alta California, and the Indians must be shown that Christians approved of marriage. Third, the crown should offer bounties to families, especially those of blacksmiths, tanners, carpenters—and a doctor. Single men should be encouraged to take Indian wives, but the Indians themselves must remain under the authority of the missions lest they be mistreated. The other great need was breeding stock. When Bucareli suggested closing San Blas as a bad bet, Serra protested that it was premature until a land route was established. There were not enough mules in all California to do the work of two ships.

The hagiography claims that Serra's appeal saved the colony. But geopolitics was at least as persuasive. Beginning in 1772 hysterical dispatches arrived in Madrid from the Condé de Lacy, the new ambassador at St. Petersburg. A tsarist ukase had ordered preparations for war in the

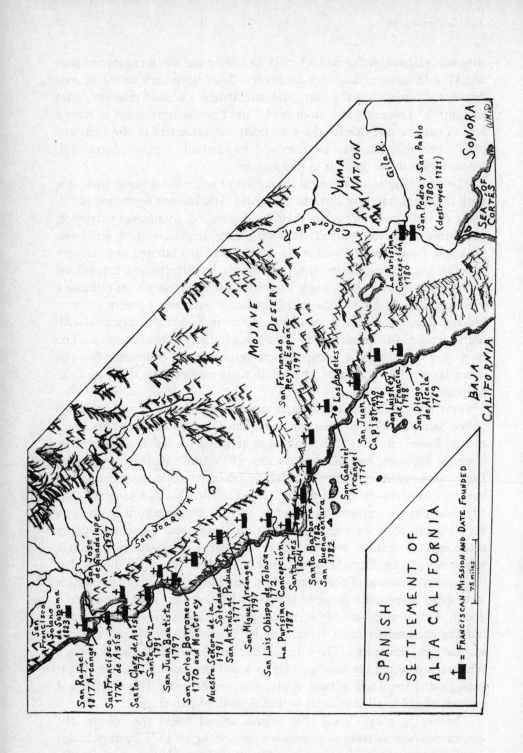

SPANISH
SETTLEMENT OF
ALTA CALIFORNIA

▮ = FRANCISCAN MISSION AND DATE FOUNDED

75 miles

SONORA

SEA OF CORTÉS

YUMA NATION

Gila R.

San Pedro y San Pablo
1780
(destroyed 1781)

La Purísima
Concepción
1780

Colorado R.

MOJAVE DESERT

BAJA CALIFORNIA

San Fernando
Rey de España
1797

San Luis Rey
de Francia
1798

San Diego
de Alcalá
1769

Los Angeles

San Juan
Capistrano
1776

San Gabriel
Arcángel
1771

San Buenaventura
1782

Santa Barbara
1782

Santa Inés
1804

La Purísima Concepción
1787

San Luis Obispo de Tolosa
1772

San Miguel Arcángel
1797

San Antonio de Padua
1771

Nuestra Señora de la
Soledad
1791

San Carlos Borromeo
1770 and Monterey

San Juan Bautista
1797

Santa Cruz
1791

Santa Clara de Asís
1776

San Francisco de Asís
1776

San Rafael
1817 Arcángel

San Francisco
Solano
de Sonoma
1823

San José
de Guadalupe
1797

San Joaquín R.

North Pacific! Russia was to send fifteen thousand men to Kamchatka and *cooperate* with any English ships that might appear (suggesting an alliance against Spain)! Russians planned to storm the Great Wall of China with twenty thousand men and send a navy to open Japan! That Russia was plotting an "aggression" in North America was all nonsense, of course, and the adroit Minister for the Indies, Julian de Arriaga, saw it as such. But when de Lacy reported accurately about "important [Russian] discoveries" on the American coast, Arriaga forwarded the letter to Bucareli with instructions to solidify Spain's hold on Alta California.

Bucareli shuddered at the "consequences of having other neighbors than the Indians." So he sent out two expeditions by sea to reconnoitre. The first, under Juan Pérez in 1774, was the first to sail through the Golden Gate, which the Viceroy recognized as "indispensable." The second reached the Alaskan panhandle but encountered no Russians. Addressing the supply problem, Bucareli authorized an ambitious overland wagon train to blaze a trail from Sonora to Monterey. The task fell to a veteran of the desert frontier, Juan Bautista de Anza, who set out from Mexico with 29 soldiers and their wives, 6 clergymen, 136 settlers, 695 horses and mules, and 355 cattle. Over 1,600 miles of mountains, high desert, and rugged coast, from Culiacán to Tubac (near present-day Tucson) through Yuma and the Imperial Valley to San Gabriel (detouring to suppress an Indian revolt at San Diego), then up to Monterey, de Anza led his Israelites. A sole person died in the exodus—a woman in childbirth—but three children were born en route. Having delivered his charges, de Anza proceeded to explore Portolá's bay and select sites for a presidio and a mission on the banks of a lagoon named Dolores. His chaplain described the site as "a marvel of nature" and "the harbor of harbors." Once it was settled "there would not be anything more beautiful in all the world." The mission was dedicated on June 28, 1776, and San Francisco was born.

The de Anza expedition was a tremendous boon, but Bucareli had still larger plans: discovery of a more direct route from Sonora to Monterey, plus new trails linking Sante Fe and Albuquerque on the upper Rio Grande with California and Sonora. Such a triangular system, buttressed by presidios, missions, and *pueblos* (towns) along the way, would integrate the territories into New Spain. To this end Gálvez created a virtual Viceroyalty of the northern frontier in 1776 and moved the governor's seat from Baja to Monterey—a symbol of faith in California's future.

Thanks to the leadership of Carlos III and Arriaga in Madrid, Gálvez and Bucareli in Mexico, and Portolá, Serra, and de Anza in California, Spain's last colony survived. In the years before his death in 1784, Serra went far toward completing his "Jacob's ladder" of missions at San Juan

Capistrano, Santa Clara, and Santa Barbara. His successor, Fray Lasuen, founded nine more. The Army placed presidios at San Diego, Santa Barbara, Monterey, and San Francisco, while de Anza's settlers built civil towns at San Luis Obispo, San Jose, Carmel, and, in 1781, at Nuestra Señora la Reina de Los Angeles del Río Portiúncula (a stream ten miles southwest of San Gabriel). The purpose of the whole enterprise was prophylactic, to make California a buffer between New Spain and the Russians or English to the north. But could it ever have served that purpose against a determined challenge? The missions did finally attract Chumash, Costanoan, and other tribespeople and baptized some 5,800 by the end of the century. They learned farming, handicrafts, and stock raising; hides and tallow quickly became California's chief exports. The missions pioneered irrigation, planted small orchards, and introduced wine grapes. On the other hand, European diseases checked their growth, while the Hispanic influx never rose above a trickle. As late as 1800 Alta California contained no more than two thousand colonists and only nineteen land grants were made.

Finally, the ability of colonists even to reach California depended on a secure overland route from Old Mexico. But the only possible one ran along the Gila River to its junction with the Colorado at Yuma. There two new missions, Purísima Concepción and San Pedro y San Pablo (an eerie echo of Petropavlovsk), were placed as havens to prepare travelers for the thirsty march to the coast. But the Colorado River was home to the untamed Yuma Indians. Men of the cloth and men of the sword quarreled over how to safeguard the missions and trail. Merciless soldiers like Fages were the only answer to warlike Apaches or Comanches, but they did nothing but damage among friendly or wavering Indians. That was why Serra had Bucareli replace Fages with the less belligerent Rivera y Moncado. So it was ironic that Rivera and his pacifist chaplain Father García entered Yuma in 1781 just in time to be massacred. The Indians burned the missions, tortured and killed the men, and carried off the women and children. Fages was recalled. He managed to ransom the hostages, but the missions were not rebuilt, and de Anza's route was closed.

To compare the Spanish breakout into California with the Russian breakout to Alaska might seem absurd, so antipodal were the climates and topographies and the motives of *promyshlenniki* and *padres*. Yet the dilemmas were identical. Alaska and California were distant outposts dependent on a flow of men and supplies from ports and bases not worthy of the name. Kamchatka and Okhotsk, Baja and San Blas were themselves underpopulated, undersupplied, and thousands of miles from their imperial centers. No amount of political vision on one end, or sheer guts on the other, could make up for the lack of supply lines across Siberia and Sonora. And that meant, despite the perceptions, that Russia and Spain posed no threat to each other at all, while both were mortally threatened by a new breed about to arrive. For even as the Yuma war party was shutting down de Anza's trail, the news of Captain Cook's third expedition was spreading around the world . . . and George Washington was plotting his victorious march to Yorktown. New sorts of empires were about to arise on Pacific shores.

The Second 'aha iki

Kaahumanu: I understand nothing of this. Your stories tread with thunder, Scholar, but no rain follows . . . and no light precedes.

Saitō: Ha! That leaves only the noise.

Scholar: What is it you don't understand?

Kaahumanu: I understand nothing. These heroes and nations you sing of, they had nothing to do with the ocean I knew. *Aohe!* Some Russians did come once, but my husband expelled them. Why don't you speak of the British, Americans, French?

Scholar: Wait, Your Highness, there's much more to come. But as for not understanding, well, we historians are a long-winded guild. Sometimes we lose track where we're going.

Kaahumanu: Like sermons I have heard.

Scholar: Precisely.

Kaahumanu: But a *good* sermon is like riding the surf, only with the soul, not the body. I should like to have heard Brother Serra preach—when he was still in Majorca, that is. The idolatry and whipping I do not understand.

Scholar: Perhaps Serra will explain. But let me try to make some sense of what I've been saying in a sentence or . . . twenty? My point is that from the sixteenth to the late eighteenth centuries the North Pacific was the habitable portion of the globe *most* remote from the centers of European population and power. Thanks to the Renaissance break-throughs in navigation and such, Spaniards were able to cross the ocean and discover a way back. But except for the Philippines they failed to colonize the North Pacific coastline until you, Father Serra, helped found California. The reasons for their tardiness were varied: demographic decline, wars in Europe, bureaucratic inertia, and not least, the winds and currents off the California coast. The Russians had similar handicaps. They found a land route to the Pacific early on, and plundered their empire for furs as the Spaniards had theirs for sil-ver and gold. But the Russians, too, could not overcome the harsh con-ditions they faced, their lack of supplies, and the sheer distances involved. *Meanwhile,* the Chinese and Japanese turned their backs on the ocean for reasons that had mostly to do with their quests for inter-nal stability. So, with China and Japan aloof, and Spain and Russia handicapped, the North Pacific remained up for grabs. What I meant to explain, I suppose, was why so little had happened in the North Pacific prior to the coming of the Anglo-Saxons.

Serra: I understand, Professor, and find you persuasive. What I fail to grasp is your purpose. Is the North Pacific an arbitrary convenience: "Let us set aside *this* portion of the globe and see what happened there"? Or do you mean to show how its history fits into some larger story? If so, what story is that, and what is the purpose of *it!*

Scholar: I'm sorry, Father, I don't—

Serra: I only wish to say that nothing is vainer than the glory of kings. Does it matter which state controlled which region, or had the most ships, or richest treasury, or wisest policies, or bravest soldiers? Your secular spirit prevents you from seeing more deeply into your history, or do you believe there is no more to it than the pursuit of power?

Scholar: I'm not sure I follow. . . . Of course, there is more to history. But power relations are crucial. They form the arena in which all else occurs—social, intellectual, economic—

Witte: I don't think those are what Serra has in mind, Professor.

Scholar: I'm sorry, I'm at a loss. . . . What more can creaturely schol-ars do but seek the connections between things, the patterns? It's a matter of method. As for some cosmic *purpose* . . . we're just people studying people. We're just—

Witte: Trapped in time, Professor.

Seward: Which *we* no longer are—here—so your "method" seems beside the point.

Witte: What *is* the point? That's all Father Serra is asking. And our professor is making rather a poor show of answering.

Saitō: History's bunk. That's what Henry Ford said!

Scholar: Maybe history has no point, but histor*ians* still need some criterion for *choosing* which facts to put in or leave out.

Saitō: I think you err on the side of "putting in."

Scholar: So ultimately, the meaning of a *work* of history, if not history itself, lies in the merits of the historians' choices. Where else can meaning come from? Oh, I get it. No, Father Serra, I expect you *can't* agree with secular scholarly method. You were even made a member of the Mexican Inquisition.

Serra: Peace, my son. I do agree that scholarship has intrinsic value. But knowledge exists for man, not man for knowledge. To be sure, falsehood is wicked, even if used in a good cause. That was the Jesuits' sin. But truth, or half-truth, marshaled for a bad cause is worse. The Devil kills bodies with his lies. But half-truth is the weapon by which he kills souls.

Scholar: Then, forgive me, but since you brought it up, let me ask you about the means your friars used to convert and keep the Indians at your missions. That is a topic much discussed these days, because—well, surely you know what I mean—they are trying to make you a saint, and some people are angry about it.

Serra: Who is a saint? Blessed Francis. But if the Church chooses to distill my virtues, such as they were, and venerate a myth composed only of them, so be it. What virtue I had was from God, *was* God within me. So in venerating the saints, the Church gives glory to God.

Scholar: Look, Father Serra, it's said that your friars flogged the Indians for minor offenses, that you lured them into the missions with bribes, exploited their labor, hunted down escapees and dragged them back. Your own records show that thousands died in your "care." . . .

Seward: Hold your horses, mister! I'm no Catholic, but if you're suggesting that Serra's missions were some kind of Andersonville, the Rebels' hell for our prisoners of war, then I'd say you're way out of line. I expect Serra *saved* Indians by the thousands, healed their sick, showed them how to plant crops, and stood between them and the soldiers. Quit being so blasted humble, Serra, and tell us what it was like in those days.

Serra: I have no desire to speak of my sins or those of others. Only that God brings good out of evil, or folly.

Kaahumanu: Then it is true? I do not understand. We expelled the papists when they came to Oahu, but I do not recall that they whipped anyone.

Serra: I was the worst of missionaries. But I confess I don't see the principle behind these accusations. Do you not spank your children when they are naughty? We punished only baptized neophytes who should have known better than to steal tools, or slaughter breeding stock for a private feast, or run off to the pagan dances in the gentiles' *pueblos*. We never punished the unbaptized, though they thieved and sometimes harmed us. And we never disciplined the neophytes more severely than we did ourselves.

Witte: But you took reprisals on backsliders and rebels?

Scholar: Who might only have craved their native freedom?

Serra: Not at my behest. As I wrote to Bucareli: "While the missionary is alive, let the soldiers guard him, and watch over him, like the pupils of God's own eyes. But after the missionary is killed, what can be gained by campaigns? Let us prepare the murderer, not for death, but for eternal life."

Scholar: That much is so. Under Spanish law unbaptized Indians— "gentiles," Serra calls them—were in a category called *personas miserables* that also included the destitute, orphaned, blind, lame, and leprous. Such people could not be expected to be responsible for their actions, and thus were placed under ecclesiastical rather than civil authority.

Witte: Our priests did the same, in Siberia and Alaska. What Christian would not?

Scholar: But the argument made, Father Serra, is that Indians were bonded servants of the missions. How did you reconcile that with Christian freedom?

Serra: I was the worst of missionaries. But we had to keep the gentiles near the missions. First, we could never instruct them in the faith without first attracting them with food and clothing. Second, even after instruction they were unlikely to give up pagan ways if they were exposed to temptation from without. Third, only through residency at the missions could the Indians be taught to read and write, plant and reap, spin and weave.

Saitō: And never leave.

Serra: Would you give your own son or daughter leave to run away to a brothel or a coven? In their villages they worshipped idols, starved, and raided each other. Women were property, lower than animals. In the missions they had the opportunity, at least, to choose to please God, to live in dignity and die in grace. And they worked no harder than we did. No doubt some of the brothers, in their zeal, sinned against the neophytes. But how can you suggest that we *meant* to destroy the lives of our wards? Our strategy in California depended on them.

Seward: You're a saint in my book, Serra—how many thousand miles on that bum foot? But what the dickens was your strategy for California? Surely you didn't envision armies of red savages fighting for the King of Spain against Russia—or the Royal Navy?

Serra: We did not teach our converts to fight, nor would we have let our soldiers do so. We occupied the land, which bestows certain rights. If only we had had more time. In Mexico the cruelty of the Aztecs and the cruelty of the *conquistadores* combined, by grace, to make a new and beautiful people. But it took two hundred years. In California we had only twenty. Perhaps you are right, Mr. Seward. Perhaps California was a quixotic quest. You know our Cervantes?

Seward: Indeed we do.

Serra: But spiritual warfare is never quixotic. For us Franciscans the comedy of competing states is like an ever-shifting storm. When it blows away from your destination, you drop anchor. When it blows toward your destination, you lay on sail and ride with it. Such a storm blew Holy Mother Church into California. Alas, it let up too soon.

Seward: You miss my point, *Padre.* What I'm suggesting is, however much Spanish policy advanced *your* cause, the missions proved useless to *Spain.* Worse than useless, because—how much of the good land was controlled by the missions?

Serra: At what date? I . . .

Scholar: I know. It was 80 percent around 1790.

Seward: Monopolized by celibate priests and Indians—

Saitō: Who died like flies.

Seward: —leaving no room for others to move in and build up agriculture and commerce. In our day we said that the Church's hold on the property and, I dare say, the minds of the Mexicans was what explained their stagnation. What you needed there in California was a dose of free enterprise. And that could only come from secularization, separation of church and state.

Scholar: The missions were secularized, by the Mexican Republic, in 1830. But as for encouraging development, Mexico did even worse than Spain.

Serra: Still, Mr. Seward is right about our queer position: we were attempting to found a church-run state at the behest of a state-run church. But I don't agree with your prescription. As I said at the time, "Unless our Catholic philosophy and way of life are taught religiously, our civilization will be founded on sand."

Seward: But it *was* founded on sand. History proves it.

Serra: Then I was the worst of missionaries. I did not do enough.

Saitō: Hold on, gents. I don't buy all this talk of success and failure. Are you implying that Tokugawa Japan "failed" because it chose not to conquer an empire?

Scholar: Far be it from me to render value judgments.

Saitō: I don't quarrel with political power as a measure of a nation's health. But you're throwin' us a curve with your talk of "seclusion." Don't you know, Professor, that *sakoku* is a myth?

Scholar: I beg your pardon?

Saitō: The word *sakoku*—it means "closed country"—was not even coined in Japan until 1801.

Scholar: Surely you're not suggesting that seclusion didn't occur? The expulsion edicts, Deshima, the prohibitions on travel and trade. . . .

Saitō: But Japanese continued to have relations with Korea and China, not to mention the Dutch. The *bakufu* was not even opposed to all contact with Russians.

Scholar: But you can't deny the essential isolationism.

Saitō: You historians are clever at making your job easy. You paint a picture from certain facts, give the picture a name, and the name becomes more real than the facts.

Scholar: I don't follow you, Mr. Ambassador.

Saitō: By calling Tokugawa policy *sakoku,* you leave the impression that Japan was isolationist. The *bakufu* did not seek to *eliminate* foreign influence, but rather to limit and control it.

Scholar: All right, but it also made no attempt to impose *its* influence overseas. That's my point. Because just imagine if they had, if Japan had adopted Western technology and ambitions in the seventeenth century instead of in the late nineteenth!

Kaahumanu: But you say they could not do so without risking their unity at home.

Saitō: In which case our scholar's just blowin' smoke with all his "just imagines" and "what ifs." If we had some ham, we could have some ham 'n' eggs, if we add some eggs!

Witte: This conversation deserves to die. Scholar, I also am unhappy with your treatment of Russia. I admire your erudition. You remind me of much I had forgotten, but you understand nothing of Russia.

Scholar: Thank you, Count Witte.

Witte: First you glorify tsars like Ivan and Peter, then explain the failure of Russia to consolidate its gains by reference to supply lines and such. You do not know that Ivan, Peter, and Catherine the Great were responsible for the *wreck* of Russia, not progress? Absolutism, serfdom, corrupt bureaucracy—these are what kept Russia from building a Pacific empire. Just as Siberia opened, the *muzhiki*—peasants—were bound to the soil. Just as English and Dutch and French were promoting enterprise, Peter crushed it in Russia. Siberia and Alaska were won by *promyshlenniki,* and all the tsars did was send a few hundred soldiers. Peter built a navy. It rotted after twenty years. Catherine swallowed half of Poland. What has Russia ever gotten from Poland but trouble? Meanwhile, the greatest empire in the world—Siberia—is left in the hands of stupid officials. What kind of official do you think got "sent to Siberia"? They only drank and lined their pockets.

Scholar: I said all that!

Witte: You glorify Stroganovs and entrepreneurial tradition. There was no such tradition. Jews and Old Believers, yes, but they were persecuted. Because of stupidity, Russia wasted two centuries. Then they asked me to make up for it all in twenty years.

Serra: An experience we share, Count.

Witte: Da! I've always thought Russia and Spain had much in common: so holy, so damned.

Scholar: Didn't I say exactly that? I would have thought you'd agree—

Seward: Well, I don't agree—not yet, anywise. Are you saying that Russia was somehow doomed to backwardness because of the way politics happened to break back in the sixteenth or seventeenth century? Couldn't Russia have reformed, modernized?

Scholar: Witte?

Witte: I thought so once. I thought a "good tsar"—like my Alexander III—with good advisers—like me—could make a difference. The essence of national power is a government that unlocks the energy of individuals, encourages virtue and hard work, and protects their creativity and labor from piracy. Government grows stronger because people are strong. But the Russian tendency is always to believe that people will grow stronger because government is strong. So the Russian government discourages work, and is the biggest pirate robbing the people.

Seward: Government's only as good as its people.

Witte: People did not choose to be serfs! You don't believe me when I say that Russian state is its own worst enemy? Scholar, are you going to tell us of Baranov?

Scholar: Soon, everybody, soon.

Kaahumanu: I do not understand something else. Why did your Spaniards not use their heads? They had an empire too large to defend. Why did they think the solution was to make it still larger? If they feared the advance of the Russians and the British, why did they not ally with one to hold off the other? If opening a land route to California was vital, why did they not send an army to Yuma?

Seward: Kaahumanu, you surprise me.

Kaahumanu: Mr. Seward, you disappoint me. I did not spend *all* my time as Kamehameha's consort combing my hair and making *ho'oipoipo.*

Scholar: I should have warned you, Governor. Her husband was a great war chief, and some say she not only learned from his campaigns, but helped plan them.

Kaahumanu: Let us say only that he needed me and loved me, though I can't say which he did more. When the wind and the current flow together, how much thanks does one give to each? I want to know why the Spaniards did not recapture Yuma!

Serra: I'm sure we must have tried. . . .

Scholar: They did try, soon after your death, Father. But even Fages could not pin down the hostiles, and in 1786 the search was called off until the Apache threat receded. Anyway, Gálvez had gone back to Spain, Bucareli was long dead, and the new *comandante,* Teodoro de Croix, was content to "tend shop" in Sonora.

Seward: Maybe no forces were available.

Scholar: That's another reason: Spain, as usual, was distracted by war. In 1778 it joined France in the coalition fighting for the thirteen colonies against Britain. Ironic, isn't it, that Spain turned away from California in order to help win independence for the very country that would seize California from it?

Seward: Poor judgment, I'd say. But I suppose there was no way out, not with the French Revolution about to shake things up . . . and the Brits and Yanks about to arrive in the Pacific. Say, shouldn't you be telling us about Captain Cook?

Scholar: I should indeed. And that, Kaahumanu, means Hawaii.

Kealakekua Bay 1779

IN ENGLISH HISTORY 1776 was a year akin to 1492 in Spanish history. In 1776 the thirteen colonies declared independence, Adam Smith published *The Wealth of Nations*, James Watt patented his steam engine, and Captain Cook sailed on his third voyage of discovery. These events—one political, one intellectual, one technological, one scientific—heralded the end of the age of mercantilism and the start of an age characterized by the spread of democracy, free trade, industrialization, and competition for wealth and power in the North Pacific.

The new year found the British cabinet muddled over its response to the fighting that had broken out at Lexington and Concord. One minister opposed to conciliation was First Lord of the Admiralty John Montagu, fourth earl of Sandwich. He believed the Royal Navy alone could bring the colonists to see London's version of common sense and deter France and Spain from interfering. He would, of course, fail of both objectives. But in his other project that spring he succeeded, and that was to persuade Cook to go to sea one last time.

There is no point in trying to summarize the five-thousand-odd treatises devoted to capturing Captain Cook. Given that the subject was a secular hero, as Serra was a religious one, much of it is hagiographic. He appears a paragon of duty, passionless about politics, religion, or anything else except precision. James Boswell illustrated the point with the following story. It seems a certain Scottish lord espoused the theory of an unbroken chain of being ranging from the lower animals to man, and reminded Cook that his South Seas journals mentioned a "nation of men like monkeys." Cook replied, "I did not say they were like monkeys. I said their faces put me in mind of monkeys." Here, Boswell concluded, was "a plain sensible man with an uncommon attention to veracity. . . . He seemed to have no desire to make people stare, and being a man of good steady moral principle, as I thought, did not try to make theories out of what he had seen to confound virtue and vice." In a Europe anxious to believe that the Pacific isles revealed earthly paradises, noble savages, and grist for "enlightened" theories about man and nature, Cook stands out as one of the more genuine men of the Age of Reason.

Pacific exploration reached a first peak with the Spanish and Dutch voyages to the southwest Pacific in the seventeeth century, then subsided for a hundred years. Spain and the Netherlands declined, while rising England and France directed their energies elsewhere until the end of the Seven Years' War in 1763. Around that same time a host of new technologies emerged that made the winds and currents, size and remoteness of the North Pacific less formidable barriers. More and better-designed sails, for instance, helped sailors capture the full energy of shifting winds. The high castles and deep keels of baroque ships gave way to flat decks, low poops, and shallow-draft hulls studded with nails or sheathed with copper, all of which reduced drag and discouraged barnacles. The horizontal tiller—which transmitted the whole force of the sea to the deck and required several men to lean on it with their whole body weight—finally gave way to a yoke-and-drum system that allowed a single helmsman to steer the rudder by means of a wheel. Not least was Benjamin Franklin's lightning rod of 1752, that all but eliminated the danger of storm-induced fire at sea.

A second category of advances was made in what we call life-support systems. Keeping fresh water potable was an age-old trial, for to put ashore for water on some unknown coast risked running aground, losing a boat to the surf, or encountering unfriendly natives. By the eighteeneth century stills were tested to desalinate sea water. But far and away the greatest biological defender of the Pacific Ocean's privacy was scurvy. When deprived of vitamin C for extended periods, just weeks in some cases, human skin develops ulcers and turns gray, gums bloat and erode, teeth fall out, long-healed wounds reopen, legs swell, energy departs and sooner or later the will to live. Susceptibility to scurvy is enhanced by filth, cold, dampness, stress, and fatigue—precisely the conditions faced by sailors rounding Cape Horn or daring the North Pacific. In the 1590s Richard Hawkins implored "some learned man" to do something about scurvy, but the curative virtues of fruits and vegetables were not scientifically demonstrated until naval surgeon James Lind's experiment of 1747. He isolated twelve stricken seaman and fed them identical diets except for one of six supplements. Those getting oranges and lemons recovered in a week. By Cook's time, fruit, "scurvy grass," malt, and sauerkraut were in use. Cook himself administered so many of them to his crew that he actually confused the search for the best prophylaxis. But by 1795 the British Admiralty had regularized shipboard issue of lemon juice.

A third set of enabling inventions was navigational. Quadrants for sighting the sun at midday and calculating latitude were refined and calibrated down to one minute of arc, while new sextants for sighting the moon and stars were accurate to ten seconds of arc. Charts, maps, almanacs, and tables of tides and currents improved as well. But these were incremental improvements: the revolutionary breakthrough was John Harrison's ship's chronometer of 1759. Figuring longitude is not a tricky matter so long as you know what time it is. But no one knew how to make a clock both accurate and impervious to the motion of a ship until Harrison crafted a spring-driven watch that bested the criteria of the British Board of Longitude.

All these inventions came together to make circumnavigations routine in the half-century after 1763. And they did so just as the French, having been chased out of North America and India, were looking for new colonial and commercial arenas in which to escape or outflank the British. The supremely maritime British were also alive to the possibilities in the Pacific and were determined not to leave that half of the earth's surface to the Bourbon powers. Armchair geographers imagined a great Southern Continent (Terra Australis Incognita) in the Pacific and a Northwest Passage somewhere between Siberia and California. A scientific motive also existed in the voyages undertaken after 1763, and academies of science shared in their planning. But when the Earl of Sandwich claimed that Cook's second voyage, for instance, was born of mere "curiosity," the *French* ambassador scoffed. In their scientific cover, strategic deception, and state funding, the Pacific voyages anticipated the space programs of a later time.

The first to sail was John Byron in 1764. His orders were to visit New Albion (as the British styled California, reserving their claims), but Byron judged his ships not up to the journey and crossed the South Pacific instead. So did Louis-Antoine de Bougainville (1766–69), Samuel Wallis (1766–68), Lt. James Cook (1768–71), and Comdr. James Cook (1772–75). These expeditions, especially Cook's second, dispelled Terra Australis, defined the limits of Australia and any possible Antarctica, and impressed Otaheite (Tahiti) on the Enlightened and Romantic alike. The North Pacific remained a mystery. What had the Russians found there? Why were the Spaniards lunging into California? Was the Northwest Passage discoverable only from the *western* side? Sandwich had reason to think so. That is why he invited Cook, his patron Sir Hugh Palliser, and an Admiralty official to an intimate dinner in late January 1776.

Cook's first biographer evidently based his description of the dinner on word of mouth, since no source has been found. But it must have been jolly fun for four lively, intelligent men gathered in a warm, paneled, candle-lit town house for a private repast well stocked with wine, and nothing to do but talk high strategy, make disparaging remarks about the French, and impress one another with nervy speculations. Another Pacific voyage must be made, announced Sandwich; only last year Parliament made naval personnel eligible for its standing prize of £20,000 to the discoverer of a Northwest Passage. To be sure, the peculiar demands of the voyage necessitated a careful choice of commander. Did Cook have any advice? He did; he rose and volunteered. Sandwich triumphantly informed the King and returned to his plans for suppressing the American rebellion.

Cook had been home a mere seven months after an absence of three years. He had two fine sons aged eleven and twelve and had promptly made his wife pregnant again. He was bored with the sinecure the Admiralty provided him, but he enjoyed a handsome income, Royal Society membership, a contract for his memoirs, and entreé to society. He might at least have taken a rest before setting out again. Beaglehole, his most exhaustive biographer, doubts the story of the sudden decision over dinner since Cook was not known to be impulsive. But his behavior also suggests that he might have been suffering from an ailment contracted on his second voyage, an intestinal infection that might have impaired his ability to metabolize vitamin B. If so, he would have become increasingly impulsive and irritable. Or perhaps even Cook's judgment was trumped by pride, and he begrudged a major mission to anyone else. Still, Boswell reacted to the news as we might today upon meeting an astronaut: "It was curious to see Cook, a grave, steady man, and his wife, a decent plump Englishwoman, and think that he was preparing to sail around the world."

Sandwich's instructions ordered Cook to proceed to 65° north latitude and search for the Northwest Passage. Behind that number lay a curious tale of two Russian maps. The first, produced by Gerhardt Müller in 1754, was widely known. Its outline of Kamchatka and Siberia was fairly true, as was the honest blank it contained for most of northwest North America. In 1774, however, the Russian Academy of Sciences published a second map drawn by Jacob von Stählin. Supposedly based on new discoveries, it depicted "Alaschka" as an island separated from America by a wide strait at 65° north, 140° west. The Russians were practiced in geographical deception, but why would they want to advertise potential "northwest passages" in their secret domain? Moreover, the idea had verisimilitude in light of prior theories about some sort of strait leading from the Pacific to Hudson's Bay, while the "Barrington-Engel theory" then current held that salt water did not freeze, so even a passage through the Arctic Sea would be navigable. All these fancies found place in the sealed orders delivered to Cook. He was to round the Cape of Good Hope, winter in Tahiti, make for New Albion at 45° north (thus avoiding San Francisco), then coast northward to 65° and look "very carefully" for Stählin's strait. Cook, now forty-seven and not well, sailed on July 12.

The *Resolution*, Cook's flagship, and the *Discovery* under Charles Clerke, had a near miss with a Cape Verde reef but otherwise made an uneventful passage to Tahiti, arriving in August 1777. A war was on among the chiefs from which Cook stayed aloof, but he did witness a human sacrifice, took violent reprisals for the theft of a sextant, and tried to persuade the crew to forgo their grog. His officers noted that he seemed irritable, pale, and unable to eat. But Cook also had reason to be edgy. He was attempting the first south-to-north Pacific crossing, over five thousand miles out of sight of land (as far as he knew), the first half through the doldrums and the second through wintry northern waters. Then the unexpected: on January 18, 1778, a great green island named Owahoo (Oahu), and further north, Kowhyhee (Kauai). There, at Waimea Bay, they became the first non-Polynesians (so far as anyone can prove) to visit the Sandwich Islands. The crewmen spent a month in serendipitous delight, though the captain insisted they not infect the *wahini* with gonorrhea and syphilis. They did anyway, and Cook gave one man twenty-four lashes. But they departed with every intention of returning. *This*, not Kamchatka, was the place to winter.

The expedition was twenty months out when it reached present-day Oregon at aptly named Cape Foulweather. Thanks to storms and coastal fog Cook missed Juan de Fuca Strait, the entrance to Puget Sound, so instead put in at Nootka on present-day Vancouver Island, visited by Juan Pérez four years before. It was another peaceful interlude, for the Moachat Indians welcomed the Europeans as neither superiors nor inferiors. Their technology was Stone Age and they smelled of the rotting remains of fish and sea mammals. But Nootka politics, commercial conventions, ceremony, and art commanded respect (if their cannibalism, noted by later voyagers, did not). They wanted metal, not junk, from the sailors and offered sea otter pelts in return. Cook remarked with a smile about one hard-bargaining native: "This is an American indeed!" So after two months Cook's men left behind some mutual friendships and no casualties.

The *Discovery* and *Resolution* proceeded northward to 65° and, needless to say, never found Stählin's strait. On earlier voyages Cook had enjoyed puncturing the bubbles of "theoretical geographers," but this time he grew impatient. A channel through the Aleutians appeared, and

Cook navigated Bering Strait as far north as 70° where he encountered walls of ice twelve feet tall in August. Still thinking sea water could not freeze, they wondered what great river had deposited all this ice. On the way south they stopped at Unalaska Island and found Russians who were equally perplexed by Stählin's map, whereupon Cook finally damned Stählin for a charlatan and gave up for the season. The ships cut straight south to the Sandwich Islands and put in at Kealakekua Bay (Kay-ah-lah-kee-ku-ah), on the southwest coast of the Big Island, Hawaii.

When Cook arrived, some quarter of a million Polynesians inhabited the eight main islands. Their ancestors came from the south in rugged twin-hulled outriggers sometime in the middle of the first millennium A.D., and wondered as much at the Englishmens' ships and iron as at their white faces and firearms. "They shook their spears at us, rolled their eyes about, and made a variety of wild uncouth gesticulations: But we had exchanged but few words with them before we found to our joy and surprize that with little variation their Language was the same as that of our acquaintances at the Southern Islands." It was a mellifluous, eco-nomical tongue of just eight consonants. The Europeans had trouble reproducing the sounds, hearing *T* for *K, B* for *P,* and *R* for *L,* hence their journals speak of King *T*amehameha, *t*aboo instead of *kapu,* and *eree* for *alii* (chiefs). And like Tahitians the Hawaiians possessed a subtle, self-confident culture. They lived well, except in times of overpopulation, on staples of poi (pounded taro root), yams, bananas, and coconuts. Pigs (for the chiefs) and mahi mahi, *amaama* (mullet), and other fish pro-vided protein. They lacked iron but worked beautifully in shell, bone, stone, and wood, plaited basketry, and *tapa,* the paperlike cloth beaten from tree bark and colored with vegetable dyes. The sailors gaped when the women swam naked, danced bare-breasted, composed lilting chants to gods or lovers, and apparently coupled at will.

But the *luau* and *hula* were deceptive if taken as proof of a culture given over to love of life and nature. For Hawaiian society was founded on universal, inescapable fear. War, slavery, infanticide, torture, human sacrifice, and ritual execution were not aberrations, and everyone, espe-cially women, lived in psychic cages constructed of *kapu.* At the top stood the chiefs, whose power derived from the *mana* that inhered in their spirit. *Mana* implied an essence of divinity, a closerness to the gods, hence a magic, prowess, and authority. *Mana* was hereditary and cumulative, hence the premium placed on noble matches and even on incest. Everything that had to do with a chief shared in his *mana,* be it a wife, canoe, tool, even a place he had stood. To have one's shadow fall on a major chief or to wander unawares into his presence might be a capital offense. For women to eat prized foods, and for the sexes to dine together at all, were *kapu.*

The chiefs inhabited a complicated hierarchy, but they enjoyed absolute authority over the persons and property of commoners and slaves. Above the chiefs stood only the gods, of which there were a plethora associated with phenomena (wind, surf) and activities (fishing, dancing). But four principal gods took precedence: Kane, god of life, sun, and fresh water; Lono, god of peace, fertility, and harvest; Ku, god of war; and Kanaloa, god of the lower regions. *Kāhuna* (priests) served the gods at *heiau* (temples), observing an annual cycle during which the gods came in and out of prominence. During *makahiki* season, for instance, the peaceful Lono was in ascendency and war was *kapu.* It was in such a season that the British dropped anchor in Kealakekua Bay.

The *Resolution* and *Discovery* had circled Hawaii in the precise direction and time as the procession of *kāhuna* honoring Lono. The ships arrived, on January 17, 1779, at the precise site of Lono's refuge. Hundreds of canoes welcomed the ships, two priests escorted Cook to the *heiau* and led him in liturgies, and a thousand or more onlookers worshipfully cried (as the English heard it), *"Orono, Orono!"* Food for the two hundred men appeared daily and a blissful week passed during which Cook was content in his apparent godhead. Then the temper changed, and the chiefs grew impatient. Unbeknownst to Cook, *makahiki* season was ending, and it was to everyone's satisfaction that the strangers sailed away on schedule. Cook planned to chart as much of the Sandwich Islands as time allowed before heading north again. Then a nasty squall sprung *Resolution*'s foremast and after only a week's absence they returned to "Karakakooa."

When we first meet strangers we "don't know what to think," but the second time, they are familiar. With the Hawaiians it was the other way around. The first time they "knew" this visitor as Lono; the second time they were utterly confused, for Lono's season had passed and his return was an impossibility. So instead of cheers and provisions, the Englishmen met with jeers and thievery. Cook's mood turned black; he went ashore with only a lieutenant and nine marines and attempted to make a hostage of King Kalaniopuu. The Hawaiians seemed docile at first, but when Kalaniopuu sat on the ground and refused to budge, his warriors donned their pleated war-mats. Cook retreated to the water's edge. Did he shout for the launch to approach, and either fire or rescue him? The lieutenant in charge later swore not and claimed he could have done nothing. The Hawaiians approached. Cook fired a ball. The Hawaiians charged, and the marines were overrun, stumbling in the surf as they tried to get away. Captain Cook did not.

The crew cried out for vengeance. But Commander Clerke, himself an ill man, did not need a battle: he needed his mast repaired. So he settled for the recovery of Cook's remains (the flesh boiled off in the Hawaiian manner), committed them to sea, and departed on February 22. The inexplicable Hawaiians waved a cheerful farewell. Even now Clerke hove to his duty of exploring the Arctic. He put in at ramshackle Petropavlovsk, where a hospitable Major Behm offered to send the English mail—including news of Cook's death—across Siberia to Europe. The ships then passed through the Bering Strait until ice again forced them back. Clerke died of consumption two days shy of Kamchatka. After repairs, the ships circled Asia and Africa and docked in the Thames in October 1780.

Their geographical work was unparalleled, but Cook was dead, the Northwest Passage elusive, and the voyage an apparent failure ... except for those otter skins so offhandedly acquired at Nootka two years before. On the way home the officers, under threat of mutiny, agreed to stop at Macao, where the crew's handful of pelts brought £2,000. The news kicked off a rush of private ships to the North Pacific, where they broke the Russians' monopoly in the fur trade and gave the Spaniards, too, good reason to fear. They could do it because "Cook's third" showed them the way and discovered Hawaii, the most perfectly placed port of call on the way to Nootka, Alaska, or the Far East. The North Pacific, almost at once, became a focus of great power politics.

Nootka Sound 1790

THE LIFE OF John Ledyard, first Yankee in the Pacific, was amazingly full for being so brief. Born in 1751 at Groton, Connecticut, he entered Dartmouth College to become a missionary to the Indians. It wasn't his calling. In 1773 he went to sea, volunteered for Cook's third expedition, and returned convinced that fortunes could be made in the Nootka fur trade. But the War of American Independence was on, so first Ledyard spent two years confined to barracks for refusing to serve in the Royal Navy, then another year in hiding after his desertion. He would not fight his fellow New Englanders. After the Peace of Paris of 1783 confirmed American independence, he finally had a chance to promote the fur trade, but no Boston merchants would back him. So he went to Paris, where American minister to France Thomas Jefferson encouraged him instead to journey overland across Siberia, sail to Russian America, then hike across North America to the Atlantic! Incredibly, Ledyard tried but made it only to Irkutsk before the tsarist authorities deported him as a spy. Ledyard then lit out for darkest Africa to locate the source of the Niger River, fell sick in Cairo, and died of a doctor's "treatment."

Unhappily for the rickety empires of Russia and Spain, the Atlantic ports of the United States and Britain brimmed with men of John Ledyard's pluck, vision, and maritime skill. The first private challenger to slip his moorings and make for Nootka was James Hanna, an Englishman, who sailed from Macao in 1785. He unwisely provoked an Indian attack (which he repelled "with considerable slaughter") by reacting with violence to the theft of a chisel but nonetheless made his peace with Chief Makweena at Nootka and made off with twenty thousand Spanish dollars' worth of furs. The following year, ten ships called at Nootka, a consortium of London merchants founded the King George's (Nootka) Sound Company, and Jean-François Galaup de La Pérouse explored the coast from Bering's Mount St. Elias all the way to Monterey. The La Pérouse expedition—a mighty bid to recoup French prestige in the wake of Cook—ended in mystery when his *Astrolabe* and *Boussole* disappeared in Melanesian seas in 1788.

Meanwhile, Americans began to act on Ledyard's clarion call when they discovered that independence meant that the British and Spanish Caribbean trade was off-limits to them. So New York merchants Daniel Parker and Robert Morris looked further afield. Their *Empress of China*, outfitted at the gigantic cost of $120,000 and provided with credentials from the Continental Congress, sailed in 1784, traded at Whampoa and Macao, and docked again in the East River in May 1785. The profits of 30 percent were not phenomenal, but the ease of the voyage encouraged imitators. Still, what were Americans—or any other outsider—to sell the Chinese in return for their porcelain and silks? The *Empress of China* had stowed 242 casks of ginseng, the aphrodisiac popular in China, and $20,000 in specie. But the former was hard to come by, while it galled any trader to give up precious metals. The obvious solution was to sail first to the Northwest coast, load up on sea otter pelts, winter in Hawaii, proceed to Canton to sell the pelts, and return home with a rich cargo of Chinese goods. The *Columbia* and *Lady Washington*, under John Kendrick and Robert Gray, inaugurated this circuit in 1787–88 and made the first American circumnavigation. Dozens of Yankees and Britons followed, and even the Spaniards—or more precisely, the Franciscan friars—entered the trade from California. The early fur trade reached its peak in 1792, when thirty-two ships, including thirteen British, eight Spanish, and five American, plied the Northwest coast.

What had become of the Russians? They were present, in greater numbers than ever, but increasingly outflanked by the enterprising Anglos. That Russia maintained its foothold in Alaskan waters at all was due to Grigorii Shelikhov, who had left Russia for Kamchatka, made a killing as a master of *promyshlenniki* in the Komandorskie Islands, and spent the rest of his life trying to impose structure on the Russian fur trade. The company that he founded in 1781 with Ivan Golikov accounted for over half the value of all furs taken in Pacific waters over the next sixteen years. Shelikhov also understood, as few before him, that Russia needed permanent settlements in Alaska, government support and capital, law and order, priests, an end to Aleut enslavement, development of Kamchatka, acquisition of trading rights in Canton, and exploration of the Kuriles and the California coast. In 1784, Shelikhov shepherded three vessels and 192 *promyshlenniki* to Kodiak Island and founded the first permanent Russian base in the New World. Still state support did not appear, so Shelikhov and Golikov trekked across Siberia in 1788 and petitioned the crown in person.

Catherine the Great, zealous expansionist, might be expected to sympathize. But politics, finance, and enlightened ideas stayed her hand. First, Russia was again on the verge of war with Turkey and Sweden, and the Tsarina was loath to court new conflicts and enemies so far from home. Second, the treasury, as always, was strapped, and Catherine turned away Shelikhov's bid for a 200,000-ruble loan and/or the opening of a branch of the state bank in Kamchatka. Third, she espoused the new spirit of free trade and thought chartered companies an anachronism. "It is for traders to traffic where they please. I will furnish no men, ships, or money." Catherine did abolish the tribute imposed on the Aleuts and the government's tithe on all furs, and she did dispatch a modest naval expedition to the Pacific. But the *Slava Rossii* (Glory of Russia), Cook-veteran Joseph Billings commanding, did no more than make a feeble, scurvy-ridden tour of the Alaskan coast in 1790–91. It was thanks almost entirely to Shelikhov, therefore, that the Russians made any response to the Anglo-American invasion.

The Spaniards, with even fewer resources, tried harder. In 1774 Pérez had spied Nootka Sound, and the following year Juan Francisco de Bodega y Quadra reached Alaska and discovered Bucareli Bay. In 1779, Bodega put to sea again and reached Alaska's Kenai Peninsula before scurvy forced retreat. Finally, in 1788, Estéban José Martínez and Gonzálo López de Haro landed on Kodiak Island. There, Shelikhov's factor, warmed by his own vodka, boasted of (nonexistent) plans to send two Russian frigates to lay claim to Nootka! Martínez estimated that as many as five hundred Russians now populated the northern coast, and he returned with the recommendation that Spain fortify Nootka at once. The Mexican Viceroy agreed, and Martínez sailed north in 1789 with orders to colonize Nootka Sound. He thought he would have to contend with Russians; instead he collided with Britain.

Pacific fur traders were, by and large, an unwholesome lot, and John Meares was the least scrupulous of all. A young lieutenant in the Royal Navy, he went out to India after 1783 and was caught up by news of the fur trade. Meares lacked money, judgment, seamanship, and even a license to trade in East India Company ports, but his fast talk netted him a stake and some mates and he sailed for America in 1786 with the intention of founding a base. Russians chased him from Cook Inlet, so he moved on to vacant Prince William Sound, where he decided stupidly to winter and to anchor his ship at the river's mouth, where it was sure to be iced in for months. The following May Capt. George Dixon, another Cook veteran, happened upon Meares's camp; just ten of his thirty-three men had survived. Showing no remorse or gratitude, Meares proceeded to sue Dixon for allegedly overcharging him for the supplies that saved his life. The following year Meares was back with false papers, and two ships tricked out in Portuguese flags. He purchased land from Makweena, the obliging chief at Nootka, and set his Chinese hands to work building a house and a sloop. He then returned to Macao, negotiated a merger with a respectable firm, and financed another voyage under Capt. James Colnett that arrived in April 1789. The Spaniards had gotten there first.

Captain Martínez was described (by the English) as bilious, proud, and belligerent. But he showed admirable restraint with the dubious "Portuguese" ship he found anchored at Nootka when he arrived in his warship. Lacking the manpower to sail it home as a prize, he let the ship and captain go and did the same with two subsequent Meares vessels. Only when Colnett appeared, waving forged papers, issuing threats, and making no secret of his contempt for the Spanish, did Martínez display his hot-bloodedness. The two captains quarreled until swordplay was threatened, whereupon Martínez barked at his soldiers to throw this pirate in irons, selected a prize crew to sail Colnett's ship to San Blas, and confiscated Meares's house at Nootka. News of the seizure reached Madrid and London in January 1790. A predictably sharp exchange of notes ensued, Foreign Minister Puerto de Floridablanca insisting on Spain's rightful possession of America's Pacific Coast, and Britain's Foreign Secretary, the Duke of Leeds, condemning the "illegal" seizures and upholding Britain's right to trade and settle north of California. The real stakes in the conflict were not Meares's house or even all Nootka, but rather the territorial rights to the entire region lying between the as yet undefined boundaries of California and Alaska, as well as the integrity of Spain's whole empire. Prime Minister William Pitt (the Younger) even saw how the crisis might be exploited to break the Bourbon Family Compact, isolate the vulnerable Spanish Empire overseas and volatile France in Europe, and recoup some of the damage done to Britain by its loss in the American war. But Pitt's intrigues were only begun when who should turn up in London but Meares! His wrathful, self-serving, and almost thoroughly false account of Spanish atrocities inflamed Parliament, which promptly voted funds for war. The alarmed Spaniards looked expectantly to France, Russia, and the United States for support against "perfidious Albion."

For the United States, whose Constitution had just gone into effect, Nootka was a dangerous nuisance. Jefferson was eager to help the Spaniards in gratitude for their recent help to the colonies, but Alexander Hamilton warned that America's real commercial interests were more in line with Britain's, while President Washington feared that in case of war the British might ask to march Canadian soldiers *across U.S. territory* to reach Spanish Louisiana. It was in response to the Nootka Sound Affair that Washington first formulated the doctrine of staying

neutral in Europe's quarrels. The Spaniards had no better luck elsewhere. Austria and Russia were busily engaged in partitioning Poland,
while France—well, who knew what France was about? For the day after
Colnett's arrest was the day the Parisians stormed the Bastille. As it
happened, the revolutionary National Assembly got bogged down in
1790 debating whether the King or the Assembly should have the power
to decide war and peace, no Frenchman was desirous of fighting Britain
on behalf of Spain's vague Pacific claims, and the revolutionaries certainly did not feel bound to honor a Bourbon Family Compact.

So Spain was isolated, and even though Floridablanca felt terribly
wronged, he had no choice but to swallow Britain's demands that Spain
renounce possession of Nootka and admit that the seizures were illegal.
Leeds also made immediate demands (lest Floridablanca be given "time
to breathe") that Spain pay reparations for the destruction of Meares's
property, renounce settlements north of 31° latitude (including all of
California!), and grant Britain's right to settle north of that line and
trade freely in the whole Spanish Empire. An influential junta in Madrid
preferred war to this humiliation, but events in Paris were again deter-
mining. For Spain's new king, Carlos IV, viewed the French Revolution
with "utmost horror and detestation," hoped to enlist Britain in a coun-
terrevolutionary coalition, and did not want colonial squabbles to interfere. Floridablanca did succeed in deleting the punitive boundary clause,
leaving vague the question of who could build settlements where, but
otherwise had to accept Britain's terms.

"We are not contending for a few miles but a large world," announced
one member of Parliament in the debate over Nootka. And Pitt moved
swiftly to make good on the convention by including a visit to Northwest America in the instructions for the next and last of the great explorations that began in 1764. Its commander was thirty-three-year-old
George Vancouver, a veteran of Cook's second and third, and an
explorer surpassed in his lifetime only by his mentor. Vancouver's *Discovery* sailed in April 1791 and arrived on the California coast near
Mendocino a year later. He explored northward, learned of a great river
(the Columbia) that the Yankee merchant Robert Gray (in the *Columbia*) would be the first to enter, penetrated the fabled Juan de Fuca
Strait, and dispatched Lieutenant Peter Puget to explore the Sound
within. "To describe the beauties of this region," wrote Vancouver,
"will on some future occasion be a very grateful task to the pen of some
panegyrist. The serenity of the climate, the innumerable pleasing landscapes, and the abundant fertility that unassisted nature puts forth,
require only to be enriched by the industry of man . . . to render it the
most lovely country that can be imagined. . . ." So it was that the smug
rivalry between Seattle and San Francisco—described in identical terms

by Portolá's chaplain—began before either site was adorned with a single cabin.

On August 28 the *Discovery* put in at Nootka, and what followed was one of the most unlikely feasts ever held in the North Pacific. For there to welcome the British was none other than Bodega, appointed head of an "Expedition of Limits" and given the task of deflecting the British from ousting Spain from Nootka. Vancouver, for his part, had virtually no diplomatic instructions. It was expected that he would merely accept the surrender of Meares's property, not face a negotiation *in situ* over the future of the North Pacific. But that is what he got—that and some fine hospitality. Bodega greeted the *Discovery* with a thirteen-gun salute, a courtesy he repeated over and over during its six weeks' layover. He invited the officers to dine with him that evening, and the next, and the next. Nootka, as we know, was an odiferous Indian village in a remote corner of the world. Yet Bodega's platoon of servants appeared with "a dinner of five courses, consisting of a superfluity of the best provisions . . . served with great elegance." The silver plate was changed five times during meals featuring stews and fricassees of whale, porpoise, and seal, marinated meats, fresh vegetables and fruits, salmon, olives, and chocolate, not to mention the wines. Hot rolls and milk appeared at the British ships every morning, as well as a large cask of rum. Poor Vancouver (who, his first mate whispered, "got quite fat") was embarrassed: his captain's table service was only pewter and brass, his galley stocked only with salt beef and pork, moldy biscuit and beer. But the crew was more than grateful to this Spanish gentleman. All voyages of discovery should hold such surprises.

Bodega's motives were political, of course. His orders from the Viceroy were to transfer Nootka to the British in hopes of winning British recognition of Spanish claims south of Juan de Fuca Strait. But Bodega was more ambitious: he told Vancouver that the surrender of Nootka was only temporary, and that Spanish sovereignty must be maintained. If he expected that Vancouver could be softened up by toothsome fare—or that London would recognize any deal he signed—then Bodega was sadly naive. If his goal was simply to buy time, then he succeeded, but at a terrible cost. For he not only spent his entire budget of 5,100 pesos, he took a year's advance on his own salary, spent that, and still plunged deeply into debt to support this entertainment in the wilderness. Back in Mexico, the poor man was repudiated, took sick, and died in poverty in 1794. All he had gotten out of Vancouver was a kind offer to name that place Quadra and Vancouver Island—and even that failed the test of time. Three years later England and Spain, now at war with the French Revolution, signed a final Nootka Convention providing for mutual evacuation of the site. In March 1795 Lt. John Pearce accompanied a Spanish commissioner to Nootka, ceremoniously raised and lowered a Union Jack over the Meares house, and gave the flag to King Makweena. Raise it, he said, whenever a ship enters the bay. Then they all went home.

So the Northwest coast, and much of the North Pacific, was still up for grabs. But Spain's career there ended in the Nootka Sound affair. Spanish ships ceased to take part in the fur trade to China. And in 1796 Spain was forced into alliance with the French Republic, which meant war with Britain and the loss even of the Atlantic to the Royal Navy. Cut off from the mother country, Mexico and the South American colonies began to mutter of revolt. When Napoleon occupied Spain and ousted the Bourbon king in 1808, mutterings became deeds. In 1815, after more than two centuries of regular transit, the appropriately named *Magallanes* left Acapulco for Manila. She was the last "Spanish galleon."

Hokkaido 1792

WE ARE NOT accustomed to thinking of insular Japan as having a frontier. But it always did, in the north, on the island then known as Ezo and now called Hokkaido. Not that Japanese never crossed the Tsugaru Strait over to Hokkaido; they did, obtaining fiefs on its southern coast and prompting ferocious rebellions among the hairy Ainu in the early 1500s. But the Kakizaki *daimyō,* aspiring lords of the northern island, pacified the frontier with promises not to challenge the aborigines' hold on the interior. Around 1590 Hideyoshi bestowed exclusive feudal rights to Hokkaido on the Kakizaki, who then took the name Lords of Matsumae. That was their town on the southern coast, and Hakodate was its port.

The Matsumae fief was really a march, the medieval term for a frontier province held by a margrave against barbarians in return for special privileges from his king or emperor. So it was that the Matsumae were exempted from the rice tribute and *sankin kōtai* (hostage system) under which *daimyō* families periodically had to reside at court under the watchful eye of the shogun. The Matsumae clan faithfully discharged its duty of keeping the frontier quiet, but the means employed—granting most of Hokkaido to the Ainu as a "reservation"—meant that Hokkaido and the Kuriles beyond it remained, like Manchuria, underpopulated and exposed when the Russians arrived on the scene. But so remote were these islands from their centers of power that when Russians and Japanese first came to collide, it was not a case of mighty fleets and armies, but of small ships and lonely squads groping for each other in a darkling, rugged island chain inhabited only by some strange and mysterious human relics, the Ainu. For unlike all other East Asians, they were not Mongoloid but proto-Caucasian. They had white skin, round eyes, short stature, and the most hirsute bodies of any people on earth. The Russians called them shaggy bears, and indeed the bear was the most sacred of all creatures to Ainu. They dressed in skins or bark cloth stained with geometric designs and lived by hunting, fishing, and trapping. The Ainu could be ferocious, but they lacked unity above the clan level and thus were helpless to resist encroachments.

Recall once again how precarious was the Russian position in the Pacific. The *promyshlenniki* began to found permanent bases in Alaska in 1785, but the Anglo-American traders and Anglo-Spanish tussle for Nootka limited Russia's ability to move south along the American coast, while the treaties with China closed off the Amur. So the population of eastern Siberia, perhaps a hundred thousand by 1790 (most in the interior around Yakutsk and Irkutsk), still lacked a secure source of food. Energetic merchants like Shelikhov, and *voevody* like Major Behm, imagined that Japan was their natural lifeline, if only it could be "opened." But since Spanberg's sterile exploration of 1738–39, Russians had done nothing more than creep down the Kurile chain in their little *bidarki* exacting tribute at gunpoint. The Ainu got occasional revenge, as when they speared a party of Russians in their sleep on Uruppu in 1771, but mostly the Ainu fled southward.

The Japanese *bakufu* (the shogun's bureaucracy) received its first warning of a Russian advance from a fantastic Pole, who had been exiled to Kamchatka as an escaped prisoner of war. Mauritius Augustus, Count of Benyovsky, organized a revolt among prisoners and sailors, murdered the governor, sacked the town of its provisions and furs, and put to sea in a government ship. In his fanciful journal Benyovsky laid claim to adventures worthy of Ulysses—he would later die trying to make himself emperor of Madagascar—but one actuality of his voyage back to Europe was a stop in Japan. He passed himself off as Dutch but upon his departure left a letter confessing that he was in fact a Russian spy sent to gather intelligence for an attack on Japan: a dirty trick to avenge himself against his late captors, perhaps. The Dutch factors who translated the letter told the Japanese it was rubbish, but such a frantic debate ensued in the *bakufu* that Japanese dubbed Benyovsky's letter their "first piece of national defense literature."

In almost no time Russians did arrive. Governor Behm himself took the initiative to make contact with Japan by enlisting the capital and services of local merchants. Pavel Lebedev-Lastoschkin of Yakutsk took the gamble, only to suffer total loss when the vessel carrying his stores sank in the Sea of Okhotsk. Behm persuaded him to try again, this time in partnership with Shelikhov, by granting them a temporary monopoly of trade in the Kuriles. Their plan was to sail to Uruppu with a navigator, Japanese translator, medic, a "sober" soldier, twenty-four Russian pioneers, and twenty-one native Kamchadalis. The expedition was to set up a base, then bribe or cajole some Ainu into leading them down to

Japan. They were then to assure the Japanese of their peaceful intentions, eschew trade in alcohol and guns, and learn what they could of Japan's defenses and commercial policies.

The ship made Uruppu in the summer of 1775 only to be wrecked in a storm. So Lebedev-Lastoschkin (throwing more good money after bad) reinforced the colony with two *bidarki*, and the Irkutsk *voevoda* contributed a brigantine. This time, in 1778, the expedition reached Hokkaido, bestowed gifts, and politely asked to trade. The official of the Lord of Matsumae regretted that he lacked authority to permit that and told the Russians to come back next year. The Russians misunderstood, thinking "come back next year" was a promise of trade, and when next year arrived, Russians and Matsumae officials returned punctually to the coasts of Hokkaido, looking for each other. Not until September did any connect, but when they did, the Japanese returned the Russians' gifts, forbade them ever to come again to the island, and advised them to inquire at Nagasaki if they wanted to trade. The Russians retreated again, this time dejectedly, to winter on Uruppu. In January 1780, violent earthquakes scared the Ainu and the beavers off the island, and a forty-two-foot high tidal wave lifted the Russian ship from its anchors and deposited it a quarter of a mile inland. Now even Lebedev-Lastoschkin gave up on opening Japan. If it were possible, let the government do it.

The task of piquing the government's interest, now that Siberian officials and merchants were demoralized, fell on the shoulders of a gentle professor. Eric Laxman was a Finn and a member of the Russian Academy of Sciences who happened to be doing research at Irkutsk in 1789 when some fascinating foreigners turned up. They were Japanese castaways found in the Aleutians, and though they pleaded to go home they were carted, like Dembei before them, across Siberia to St. Petersburg. Laxman accompanied them, for he had conjured up a plan to use their repatriation as an excuse to knock once more on the door of Japan. Catherine the Great bought the idea in 1791 and appointed Lt. Adam Laxman, the professor's own son, to command the voyage. He sailed within a year, which testifies to the regularization of Siberian transport since Bering's time, and put to shore on Hokkaido in October 1792. This time the Japanese were hospitable, permitted the Russians to winter over, and forwarded their papers up the bureaucracy. But Laxman, ostensibly on a mission of mercy, made an imprudent demand. He insisted on depositing the castaways in Edo (Tokyo) itself and threatened to sail there whether invited or not! The *bakufu*, understandably, reeled.

Japan's seclusion edicts had been in force for 150 years. But seclusion did not mean stagnation. The Tokugawa Shogunate was an era of rapid commercial development, exquisite cultural creativity, and of course political peace. It all rested on the backs of the peasantry, whose rice tax, the *koku*, grew ever more burdensome. Periodically, farmers deserted their land rather than work for so little reward, or died in famines, which helps to explain why the population remained stuck at twenty-five to thirty million. But the farmers' misery enabled higher strata of society to create or refine the culture that would confront and survive the later onslaught of the West. Traditional drama, the hypnotic tea ceremony, the sublime arts of flower arranging and gardening all approached perfection. Wood-block printing, copied from China, brought the delicate brushstrokes of Japanese landscapes to a larger market. The crafts of weaving and dyeing made the kimono one of the most graceful and colorful means ever devised to adorn the human body. The stylized Kabuki theater conquered audiences in Kyoto, Osaka, and Edo. Ihara Saikaku competed to write thousands of verses of poetry (from which the *haiku* developed) in a single day. His "tales of the floating world" replaced the traditional Japanese portrait of the human condition as heroic and tragic with one depicting man and woman as a "bundle of desire fitted out with arms and legs." Chikamatsu Monzaemon wrote over a hundred plays on the theme that duty is both our glory and shame insofar as our immorality prevents us from discharging it. In all, the Tokugawa was a golden age of art.

The audiences and customers for these arts and crafts included *daimyō*, samurai, and government officials but also the growing class of urban merchants. The seventeenth and eighteenth centuries witnessed a proliferation of markets and cities so great as to threaten the foundations of a feudal society. Castle towns became cities, and by 1700 Edo numbered one million people. All this meant a richer society and culture but placed tremendous strain on the rural base and its Confucian notion of a natural, ethical, and hierarchical order. As farmers deserted the soil, or defaulted on their taxes, or lost their lands to creditors, the samurai and others who lived off the farmers faced bankruptcy. In the eighteenth century, the *bakufu* serially tried to suppress the emerging capitalism, then to monopolize it, then just to tax it to maintain its own income. The *bakufu*'s troubles reached new heights in the 1780s when the volcano Mount Asama spread devastation, a four-year famine took tens of thousands of lives, and peasants rioted out of control, endangering Edo itself. The shogun's senior councillors, not surprisingly, turned over rapidly during these ordeals, and sometimes six months or a year would pass with no one clearly at the helm. Such was the state of Japanese government when the Russians appeared on the scene. No wonder they got mixed signals.

Internal criticism of the shogunate was a dangerous activity. But undercurrents of dissatisfaction had been discernible for decades, and over nothing so much as the policy of seclusion. One body of thought in Japan, the proponents of "Dutch" or "Western studies," wanted greater access to European ideas and technology than what trickled in through Deshima. Another, led by Kudo Seisuke, wanted to open the country to trade with Russia but to occupy and fortify all of Hokkaido to ensure that the trade remained peaceful. A third school of thought, that of Hayashi Shihei, insisted that seclusion could be maintained only by vigorous national defense, including militarization of Hokkaido and coastal fortifications. Honda Toshiaki criticized Japan for standing still and wanted to colonize Hokkaido, Sakhalin Island, and the Kuriles as well. "Guardians of Hakodate beware!" wrote a poet. "This is the kind of age when not only waves wash ashore!" The shogunate met such new thinking in paranoid fashion (Hayashi was imprisoned and his book suppressed) but still had to do *something* about the "Northern menace"— especially when the news came that Laxman's expedition intended to sail into Edo.

The senior councillor at the moment was Matsudaira Sadanobu. A "progressive" who had authored reforms following the peasant riots, he had plans drafted for a thoroughgoing coastal defense system fanning out from Tokyo Bay. He, too, would fall from power before the plan was in place, but in the meantime he tried to forestall the *aka-oni* (red-haired devils) by dispatching two envoys and five hundred men to Matsumae's port of Hakodate. They were to tell the Russians that they might come only to Matsumae, but only by land, not with their ship. Laxman and the others smelled a trap and finally persuaded the Japanese to let them sail into Hakodate accompanied by a Japanese ship. They dropped anchor in July 1793, set up a base on the shore, and prepared to march, in a Russo-Japanese parade 450 strong, to Matsumae castle. These were the first Westerners to view the stark beauty of Hokkaido, made known to the world thanks only to the televised Winter Olympic Games at Sapporo in 1972.

Once in Matsumae, Laxman's party was escorted by sixty armed guards to their guest house, done up as best the Japanese could in Western style and surrounded, for privacy's sake, with a blue-and-white curtain (did they know these were the colors of the tsarist ensign?). But in negotiations, the foreigners were expected to comport themselves as Japanese, removing their boots, kneeling, and bowing before the Shogun's envoys. Laxman refused, the Japanese relented, and Laxman's father later exulted: "My son did not have to deny his Christianity or to curse over the cross, he did not have to subject himself to ridicule or play the clown, as this happened with the Dutch." The envoys then bestowed upon Laxman three samurai swords and a hundred bags of rice more precious, to a Siberian, than gold. The Japanese then explained that the laws of their country could not be changed. Unarmed ships might enter Nagasaki, but all others of whatever type, origin, destination, *or number* (a heady bluff) were subject to seizure. Inasmuch as the Russians had come to return castaways, they would be pardoned this time and allowed to depart. Laxman protested that he would not surrender the castaways until his request for trade was answered. Three days passed, then the Japanese envoys returned with a document affixed with a seal, tore it in two, and gave half to Laxman. It translated: "Permission for entrance into Nagasaki harbor is granted to one vessel of the great Russian empire; as explained already, foreign vessels are forbidden to come to places other than Nagasaki, and we repeat that the Christian faith is not tolerated in our country." Back at Okhotsk, Laxman presented this "Nagasaki Permit" to the *voevoda*, and everyone craned their heads and turned it around, and wondered if it really meant what they hoped.

Then nothing happened, perhaps because Catherine's court was obsessed with European affairs. That is always the most likely explanation. Or perhaps court intrigues over who would glom the profits of Japanese trade delayed an official response. Or perhaps the bureaucracy just could not make a timely response. But not until 1796—three years after Laxman's return—did Catherine finally order the Siberian Governor-General to send another mission to Japan, and even then she hoped it could be privately financed. So more time was lost looking for "angels" who never appeared. Even Shelikhov could not help—he had just died. So Irkutsk referred the matter back to St. Petersburg, by which time Professor Laxman and Catherine were also dead, and Russia was at war with the French Revolution.

Did Russia miss a chance to "open" Japan some fifty-five years before Commodore Perry? Even Japanese historians are not agreed on whether the Nagasaki Permit was a dodge or an invitation. And given the confusion in the *bakufu*, perhaps Japanese at the time were not sure what it meant. What is certain is that the Russians waited too long. For when they next approached Japan, in 1804, all they managed to reap were misunderstandings and violence.

Kealakekua Bay 1794

THE SAME FALL and winter that Laxman was cooling his heels on rugged Hokkaido, hoping to extend Russia's sway down the Asian side of the ocean, Vancouver was buttressing Britain's claims on the American side. Departing Nootka in October 1792 the *Discovery* sailed south for California, dropping Lt. William R. Broughton en route to explore a hundred miles up the Columbia River, name Mount Hood (after a British admiral), and savor the firs and rich soils of what came to be known as Oregon. In San Francisco Bay Vancouver expected and received more Hispanic hospitality, pronounced himself moved by the sacrificial devotion of the missionaries, noted the Santa Clara mission's surplus of grain and beef, and marveled at the rodeo skills of the Spanish vaqueros. The mission Indians struck him as lazy, filthy, and no basis for a thriving colony. Most interesting of all was the presidio, which consisted of a modest adobe fort enclosing the thatched dwellings of some thirty-six soldiers and a single small cannon. The Spaniards were aware of the poor spectacle made by their defenses in Alta California, and the following year they issued strict orders forbidding foreigners to land except to fetch fresh water under the eyes of soldiers. But the truth was out: California was naked.

In January 1793 Vancouver sailed away for Cook's Sandwich Islands. He had put in there for a mere two weeks on his outward voyage and missed Kamehameha altogether. This time the would-be king of the Hawaiian islands rowed out to meet him. What Vancouver spied was a man about forty who looked ten years younger; who stood six feet six inches tall and was a prodigy of masculinity; who exercised physical and seemingly psychic control over all his people, including cohorts of fierce, feathered warriors; yet who teased and laughed with a child's spontaneity, gorged himself like a trencherman, and, when not playing or eating, looked down at you with what seemed the saddest eyes. He was there in Captain Cook's time, when Lieutenant King described "Maiha-Maiha, whose hair was now plaited over with a brown dirty sort of paste or powder, & which added to as savage a looking face as I ever saw, it however by no means seemed an emblem of his disposition, which was good natur'd & humorous, although his manner shewd somewhat of an overbearing spirit." Some sailors thought they saw him in the pack that killed Cook, and rumor had it that Kamehameha had claimed Cook's scalp, hoping to inherit its *mana*. He was a master of tactics, and his size and speed were unsurpassed: he could catch, deflect, or duck the spears of half a dozen young lions. If he had weak points, they were a volcanic temper, a puerile acquisitiveness, and a zealous patronage of the *kāhuna* and soothsayers. Or was the latter itself a calculated policy, the better to legitimize his rule in the eyes of his people and limit their exposure to Western ideas?

The *alii* system made war epidemic in Hawaiian society. All commoners and lands were in thrall to one or another chief, and the chiefs existed in a free-floating hierarchy based either on the ephemeral quality of their *mana* or their substantial fortunes in war. When a chief died, all his property and potentially that of his vassals was subject to redistribution. A great chief's death might throw a whole island or two up for grabs. Now, at the time of Cook's appearance, the islands of Kauai and Niihau, in the north, made up a single kingdom, and Oahu another. But the lord of Oahu disputed control of Molokai with the mighty Kahekili, who also ruled Lanai, Kahoolawe, and half of Maui. The rest of Maui was an offshore domain of Hawaii's King Kalaniopuu (whom Cook tried to take hostage). When Kalaniopuu died in 1782, his son Kiwalao and nephew Kamehameha contested the spoils. Alliances shifted rapidly as every chief calculated his best chance of survival and gain. Then during a lull in the fighting when Kamehameha went off to consult the oracles, his main ally, Keeaumoku, and enemy Kiwalao blundered into each other. With wild spear and club action spinning around him, Keeaumoku tripped and was set upon by two opponents. But he just would not die. Suddenly Kiwalao himself was felled by a stone from a slingshot. Keeaumoku, fending off his tormentors and dripping with gore, crawled over to the prostrate son of a king, drew his shark-toothed dagger, and sliced Kiwalao's throat. So Kamehameha was actually absent from the battle that established him as a power equal to the royal faction (now led by Kiwalao's younger brother). Meanwhile Kahakili, King of the middle islands, took advantage of Kalaniopuu's death to seize the rest of Maui and overrun Oahu as well. But he lacked the war canoes and numbers to risk invading the Big Island. By 1786 stalemate had set in and might have endured but for the eager intervention of white men.

For six years after the death of Cook no ship came to Hawaii. But by the late 1780s fur traders made a habit of calling there for rest, replenishment, and frantic fornication. Captains took to firing cannons at dawn and dusk to delineate the workday, lest the sailors abandon their duties entirely. The islanders in turn showed terrific interest in all the curiosities brought by the *haoles*, the most precious being iron, sailing vessels, and guns. And the chief most aggressive and lucky in the procurement of arms was Kamehameha. When an American skipper called on his coast in 1788, Kamehameha persuaded him to leave a carpenter behind to build a ship similar to his own. The following year he bargained for a light swivel cannon capable of being mounted on a double canoe. Then, in 1790, the Yankee trader *Eleanora*, Simon Metcalfe commanding, arrived off the coast of Maui. Metcalfe resembled our British friend Meares, being more pirate than merchant, while the Hawaiians, unencumbered by concepts of private property, likewise preferred theft to trade. When Metcalfe found a sailor and a boat missing, he turned his guns on a luckless canoe, then ordered the village and *heiaus* bombarded and burned. A neighboring chief offered to surrender the boat and sailor, but when that turned out to mean two stripped thighbones and a charred piece of keel, Metcalfe took a maniacal vengeance. Feigning satisfaction, he invited the trading canoes to approach the *Eleanora*, then raked them point-blank with broadsides of ball and shot. A hundred Mauians bled and drowned in the surf.

It was not Simon Metcalfe's first outrage. He had previously flogged a chief, prompting his village to swear retaliation on the next white men to come ashore. Those next were the crew of the *Fair American*, captained by none other than Thomas Metcalfe, Simon's son. The local chief ambushed the crew, seized the *Fair American*, and turned it over with its sole survivor, Isaac Davis, to his liege lord Kamehameha. When Simon Metcalfe then sent his boatswain, John Young, ashore to inquire about the fate of his son, Kamehameha seized him as well and chased the *Eleanora* away.

Thanks to these windfalls, Kamehameha now deployed not only a sizable Hawaiian army and canoe flotilla, but also a platoon of musketeers, a sloop, cannon, and two *haole* sailors versed in the use of firearms. When his war god "bristled its feathers"—a good omen—Kamehameha invaded Maui, pushed the defending army up a narrow inland defile, then watched with satisfaction while Davis and Young destroyed his enemies with a cannon removed from the *Fair American*. Predictably, Kamehameha's rival on Hawaii, Keoua, took advantage of his absence to renew the struggle there, forcing Kamehameha to withdraw from Maui and engage Keoua's forces, a third of which were destroyed in a volcanic eruption. Kamehameha finally crushed the rebellion by the simple expedient of inviting Keoua to a parlay, where-upon Keeaumoku ran a spear through his side.

Lord of Hawaii, Kamehameha had now only to wait for the aged Kahekili to die to bid for all the islands. So matters stood when Vancouver returned in 1793. But as impressive as Kamehameha was, the visitors were equally taken by his favorite consort, Kaahumanu, a daughter of Keeaumoku. Kamehameha had been smitten during an earlier raid on her home island of Maui. Now in her late teens, "Tahow-man-noo" struck Vancouver as "plump and jolly, very lively and good humored," and "one of the finest women we had yet seen on any of the islands." She must have been a Polynesian Venus and Minerva rolled into one. Her own people said that "of Kamehameha's two possessions, his wife and his kingdom, she was the more beautiful." She was an expert surfer, the equal of any man, and though eclipsed by her husband, a woman of mysterious depth and spirit. When Kamehameha proposed to cloister his females by making all canoes *kapu* for women, Kaahumanu reasoned that this did not apply to the *haoles'* ships and boldly rode out to visit the Englishmen. Kamehameha alternately loved and scolded her for her independence, defiance, and wit. She seemed the only person who exercised power over him.

Vancouver was a great seaman, surveyor, captain of men, and wise, though unprofessional, diplomat. His sojourns in Hawaii reveal that he was also a shrewd, humanitarian imperialist. If that seems oxymoronic, just reflect on the more hellish aspects of Hawaiian life under the *alii* and *kapu* systems. The obvious devastation and depopulation inflicted by the wars on villages he remembered from Cook's time troubled Vancouver deeply. Thus, he had no scruples about interfering in the Hawaiians' internal affairs. He sought rather to save them from themselves by brokering a peace and, if possible, placing the islands under a British protectorate. Kamehameha in turn had reason to befriend this British captain: he wanted Western arms and, if possible, intervention on his side in the war. So Kamehameha ordered a welcoming procession of eleven massive canoes in V formation with himself, resplendent with yellow feathers, in the van. On board the *Discovery*, Kamehameha opened the proceedings with a flamboyant welcoming speech and closed them by rubbing noses with Vancouver, a gesture of endearment. Vancouver presented him with cattle from California (Kamehameha called them "great hogs"), and the two traded entertainments. Once, on board the *Chatham*, Kamehameha quaffed an entire bottle of wine, then sent ashore "for a bite" that turned into an entire roasted canine, two raw fish, and a calabash of poi. "The quantity he consumed would have been a profusion for three moderate men," observed Thomas Manby. "He enquired particularly if King George lived as well as he did."

In important matters, Kamehameha parried Vancouver's demarches as adroitly as Vancouver had parried Bodega's. No, he could not consider discussing peace with Kahekili unless he enjoyed the protection and mediation of Vancouver himself. Nor could he contemplate a treaty placing Hawaii under British protection unless a British ship remained to protect his realm. For his part, Vancouver refused to hand over weapons; that, he said, was "taboo King George." But he did provide rigging and sails to transform a large war canoe into a schooner decked out with a Union Jack. Kamehameha was delighted to no end; it was a toy for the vain boy in him, a real addition to his fleet, and a symbol of British favor no other *alii* could match. Vancouver also stopped off at Maui to test his message of peace, but Kahekili scoffed at his suggestion that Kamehameha could be trusted.

Vancouver then sailed back to America to survey the coast from the Alaskan panhandle to the "country town of the Angels." While docked at Monterey, the Britons learned of macabre happenings in Europe: war between France and a coalition of powers in 1792, declaration of a French Republic in September, the execution of King Louis XIV on the guillotine in January 1793. Perhaps Vancouver, Puget, and the others guessed that the crash of the Old World rendered anodyne their efforts to open the New.

The expedition made its final visit to Hawaii in January 1794. This time Vancouver put in at Hilo, on the eastern coast of the Big Island—a port Kamehameha had recommended. The King was there and, after some arm twisting, sailed with Vancouver around to Kealakekua Bay. It was on that brief passage that Vancouver learned of strife in Kamehameha's household. The King believed that his beloved Kaahumanu had become too fond of Chief Kaiana and so had "discarded her." The charge was plausible inasmuch as Kaiana was handsome, a good deal younger than Kamehameha, and a man of mystery who had sailed with the white men to China and Nootka. Kaiana and Kaahumanu enjoyed surfing naked, in the Hawaiian fashion. Clearly Kamehameha's pride was hurt, and he honestly missed Kaahumanu, but he also could not overlook the possibility that Kaiana might betray him politically. So Vancouver played marriage counselor, arranging an "accidental" shipboard meeting between the royal couple that began in laughter and ended in hugs and tears. Even then Kaahumanu extracted a promise from Vancouver to accompany the couple home and ensure that the King did not beat her. Nor did the reconciliation dissuade the King from taking to wife Kaahumanu's own younger sister, heretofore married to *his* own younger brother, and seeking to produce an heir by her. For Kaahumanu had one failing as a royal wife: she was barren.

Vancouver also played matchmaker to beasts, adding another bull

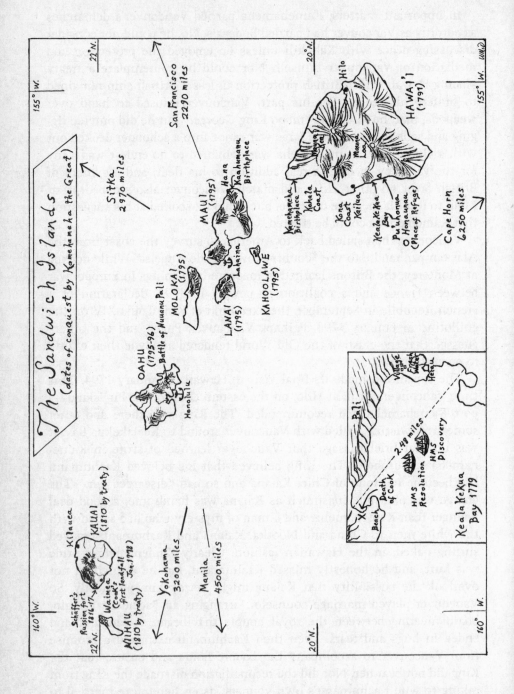

The Sandwich Islands
(dates of conquest by Kamehameha the Great)

155° W.

22° N.

San Francisco
2290 miles

Sitka
2970 miles

Cape Horn
6250 miles

155° W.

20° N.

HAWAI'I
(1791)

Hilo

Mauna Kea

Mauna Loa

Kamehameha
Birthplace

Kohala
Coast

Kona
Coast

Kailua

Kealakekua
Bay

Pu'uhonua
O Honaunau
(Place of Refuge)

MAUI
(1795)

Hana

Ka'ahumanu
Birthplace

Lahaina

MOLOKAI
(1795)

LANAI
(1795)

KAHOOLAWE
(1795)

OAHU
(1795-96)
Battle of Nuuanu Pali

Honolulu

160° W.

22° N.

KAUAI
(1810 by treaty)

Kilauea

Schäffer's
Russian fort
1816-17

Waimea
(Cook's
first landfall
Jan. 1778)

NIIHAU
(1810 by treaty)

Yokohama
3200 miles

Manila
4500 miles

160° W.

20° N.

Kealakekua
Bay 1779

Pali

Village

First
Fight

Heiau

Death
of Cook

2.49 miles

Beach

HMS
Resolution

HMS
Discovery

and two cows to those brought the previous years, and two pairs of sheep. He advised Kamehameha to *kapu* the herds for ten years to ensure their growth, and indeed within two generations the Hawaiian Islands would be a rancher's paradise. But what of Hawaii's human population? Could not killing people be taboo as well? A worthy question, but one based on ignorance. Kamehameha knew that the only way to end the war was for one side to win, and though he had to pay lip service to the Englishman's preachment of peace, his real goal was to acquire the guns with which to subdue his enemies. That, presumably, is why he finally took Vancouver's suggestion and solemnly ceded the Island of Owhyhee to his Britannic Majesty!

On February 25, 1794, Kamehameha gathered all the *alii* of the island on board the *Discovery* and announced that British protection would be a great boon inasmuch as the British were known to be well disposed and could ward off the depredations of other nations. Keeaumoku was more blunt: as soon as a British force arrived, he said, Maui could be conquered and held. In return for the cession, Vancouver promised that Britain would not interfere with the Hawaiian religion, government, and economy. Of course, no British force was forthcoming, but Vancouver did turn over rockets and grenades to John Young "for the sole purpose of Tamaahmaah's protection," and left behind the frame and keel, hardware and sails for a thirty-six-foot schooner. Kamehameha dubbed it *Britannia*.

After one last season of surveys of the American coast, Vancouver finally sailed for Cape Horn and home, arriving in October 1795. His expedition had been absent from Europe for five years, covered 74,500 miles—the longest on record—and performed almost flawlessly in the geographical and political arenas alike. Yet, Vancouver met with scorn and injury for having disciplined a crewman who just happened to be related to the Prime Minister and the Foreign Secretary. This "Camelford Affair" terminated his career and broke his health. He died in obscurity at age forty-one.

What was more, his momentous treaty with Kamehameha received the same treatment. But before critiquing Britain's Hawaiian policy (or lack of it), we must ask precisely what Vancouver and Kamehameha thought they were swearing to each other in 1794. First, Kamehameha was "ceding" the Big Island only—he was not yet master of the whole Hawaiian chain. Second, Vancouver's own account makes clear that the chief expected ships and guns in return for the "treaty"—and insofar as they were not delivered, he might consider the cession void. Third, Hawaiian historians argue that Kamehameha never intended to transfer sovereignty at all, that he was either trying to win British aid or was naively ignorant of Western law. For his part, Vancouver may not have expected that Britain would really take possession of the islands. His excuse for seeking a treaty with the lord of Hawaii, he wrote, was based on his experience at Nootka. In previous times, civilized nations made claims based on the right of discovery. "[But] in the case of Nootka a material alteration had taken place, and great stress had been laid on the cession that *Maquinna* [the Nootka chief] was stated to have made of the village and friendly cove to Senr Martinez." In other words, if in the eyes of Spain and others the agreement of *native rulers* was now necessary to stake a claim to a region, then Vancouver sought to bolster Britain's claims—and forestall those of others—through a treaty with Kamehameha.

Whatever the principals meant, London still showed no discernible interest. For the Pacific, including California as well as Hawaii, was just not all that strategic. The vast bulk of British commerce flowed to India and China by way of the Cape of Good Hope and the Indian Ocean, while the Nootka fur trade—for which Hawaii was extremely convenient—was not so profitable as to warrant the cost of formal empire. In any case, the fur traders themselves (men like Meares) were actually poaching on the East India and Hudson's Bay Company monopolies. Finally, vigorously to assert the protectorate that Vancouver supposedly achieved meant being sucked into the messy Hawaiian war, the dynamics of which escaped even Vancouver.

Or, the Pitt cabinet might not have given any thought at all to Vancouver's treaty. But if it did, any of these caveats would have sufficed to justify prudence. Of course, Britain had no desire to see Hawaii gobbled up by some *other* imperial power and would later act to prevent it. But so long as their ships were free to call and trade in Hawaii on equal terms, the British could reap Hawaii's geographical benefits without cost. That is why Britain's true self-interest lay in a united, independent, and friendly Hawaii. And that is just what it got.

For soon after Vancouver's final departure, Kahekili finally died, and his son and half-brother exhausted themselves contesting control of Oahu. That in turn allowed Kamehameha to overrun Maui and Molokai and plan an invasion of Oahu. He expected another rout, but while his fleet of canoes pulled for the beaches, Kamehameha was shocked to see a substantial portion veer off and separate from the fleet! Kaiana was betraying him after all. In the climactic battle for Oahu, fought in the Nuuanu Valley, Kamehameha's well-trained warriors and Western guns pushed the Oahuans and Kaiana's men up the slopes until their retreat was cut off by a thousand-foot precipice. Kaiana died fighting. Others leaped to their deaths. Most, including Kahekili's son, fled to the mountains and were tracked down and killed.

Kamehameha had won. Only the northern island of Kauai remained outside his grip when his invasion fleet was swamped by heavy seas in 1796. Otherwise, Kamehameha and his queens settled down to govern a united kingdom, deal with the *haoles* from a position of strength, and enjoy the blessings of power in peacetime. Kamehameha appointed governors for all the islands, set up a European-style court, and cajoled the *alii* to attend him there, not to mention the best craftsmen, advisers, dancers, *kāhuna*, and white retainers. In sum, he created a genuine state of the sort foreign powers were obliged to respect: the Kingdom of the Sandwich Islands.

The story resembles in a number of ways that of the three unifiers of Japan, who used Western arms to triumph, then strictly limited the Western presence. Vancouver himself advised Kamehameha to be careful about how many and what sort of white men to allow to settle in Hawaii. But he had in mind beachcombers and dishonest traders, whereas Kamehameha no doubt feared hostile navies and marines. Neither he nor Vancouver could imagine that the most powerful foreigners of all would be those who came, not with guns, but with Bibles.

Sitka 1799

OSTLY IT RAINED. Sometimes it snowed, or fog or mist obscured the world. But mostly it just rained. At least the winters here on Kodiak Island were milder than Kamchatka's, not to mention Siberia's, but the months of darkness, except for a few hours at noon, were just as depressing. No wonder Aleuts and Russians showed filial thankfulness to their gods or God for spring, when they no longer needed to hide from nature. Alexander Andreevich Baranov felt especially grateful for the spring of 1799, because his hopes of moving the main Russian base off of Kodiak were never so high or so justified. Not that the island was unalloyed misery. It offered wood, fish, and spectaclar vistas of snowcapped peaks, rugged inlets, and the blue-white Pacific. But hardly anything would grow there—just a few potatoes and turnips, and cranberries (from which the *promyshlenniki* distilled an alcoholic juice)—while the otters and other game were nearly exterminated. So Baranov dreamed of founding a more southern capital at Sitka that could serve in turn as a jumping-off point for Nootka and California.

For eight years as manager of Shelikhov's fur company, Baranov had been frustrated by the opposition of competing companies, lack of men, ships, and supplies, and pigheaded inertia. The four-thousand-odd Aleuts on Kodiak were not the problem; they were tame and well disposed toward Russians, in part because Baranov learned their lingo, paid them fairly (when inventories were up), and protected them from the *promyshlenniki*. Almost all Russians now took wives or (in Baranov's own case) mistresses among the Aleut women and were more or less faithful to them during the span of their contracts. Vancouver even remarked that the dress, diet, and domiciles of Russians and Aleuts were so similar that they could hardly be told apart. No, Baranov's problems were the very men Shelikhov sent out to help him. The priests did nothing but complain, the serfs and convicts were diseased and lawless, and the ship captains considered themselves above taking orders from a mere merchant. Gavriil Talin of the schooner *Eagle*, for instance, had nearly flunked out of the Naval Academy and, like so many others, was a drunkard. He simply refused to obey Baranov's orders, slipped out of port, and deserted.

Good riddance, thought the doughty manager. He still had one ship with a substantial hold, the *Ekaterina*, and the *Olga*, a sloop his own men had banged together on Kodiak, while the brig *Phoenix*, currently at Okhotsk, was expected to return with the season. Over 550 trusty *bidarki* were assembled to carry the Aleuts—three to a canoe. Supplies had come the previous year, and through careful rationing, Baranov's commissary still held flour, tea, sugar, and tobacco. There now seemed no reason why the hundred Russians and nine hundred Aleuts should not carry out the greatest North Pacific colonial project to date.

Then the sea spoke. As the armada attempted to exit the roiling waters of Prince William Sound, a squall swamped thirty canoes and forced the others to beach. Soaked and frigid, they made camp. Then the Kolosh spoke. About midnight, a raiding party from this fiercest tribe of the great Tlingit nation descended, their war whoops alone putting the Aleuts to flight. Moreover, the Tlingits had muskets sold them by British and Yankee traders in exchange for pelts. The Russians, with their Aleut wives clinging to their legs in terror, stood firm and returned the fire until the raiders retired. Depleted now by eighty-six deaths, Baranov's expedition limped out to sea and safely made Yakutat Redoubt, the most eastward of all Russian settlements. Expecting rest and refreshment, they found instead a demoralized remnant racked by scurvy and afraid to venture outside for fear of the Kolosh. Still Baranov pressed on until he sighted Mount Edgecumbe in mid-July and ordered the fleet ashore.

Baranov surveyed the island and chose a stony tor as the most likely site for a fort. The Tlingits had also seen the virtues of the spot and as the Russians unpacked their axes and adzes, twenty black-haired, bearded warriors, draped in wool blankets with single feathers on their heads, stared. The interpreter announced to Ska-out-lelt, their chief, that this man was the great "Nanook of the Russians" whose coming was foretold the previous year. His own master, the Tsar, was lord of all these regions, but Baranov wished only to build a village and was willing to pay for the site. Ska-out-lelt proved amenable, a deal was struck, and the nervous Russians went back to felling trees. It rained constantly, all fall and winter, but by Easter 1800 St. Michael Redoubt— kitchens, storehouses, and barracks—was done, and the finest in Russian America.

During the celebration, at which Baranov led prayers and saluted the

health of the Tsar, he learned that his interpreter had been kidnapped.
He could not imagine what this might mean; if the Kolosh were hostile
they would hardly have allowed the Russians to finish their fort. But
daring not to show weakness, he marched his men into the Kolosh camp
and confronted, in nervous silence, a warrior host twenty times the size
of his own and backed by row upon row of tall totem poles. Then Baranov gave his orders: when I lower my hand, discharge your muskets into
the air and quickly seize the two Indians guarding the chief's house. The
guns fired, everyone cringed, and in a flash the Russians held two
hostages of their own. When Ska-out-lelt appeared, he seemed
impressed by the Russians' grit, offered refreshment, and bargained over
the exchange of captives. A peace, of sorts, settled on Sitka. Baranov
then placed his best man in charge of a garrison, urged caution, and
sailed away to see to the needs of the rest of Russian America.

Alexander Baranov was born in 1747 at a latitude as far north as that
of Kodiak, in a town near the Finnish border. His father, a petty merchant, was as humble as the town. But this eldest son somehow
acquired the curiosity and gumption to run away to Moscow at age fifteen. He was good at numbers but had to teach himself to read. He was a
short man of round face, flaxen hair, and the temperament of a shop-
keeper. After apprenticing with a German firm, he returned to his home
province to set up as an importer of Siberian wares. Then, at age thirty-
three, he took off again, leaving behind a wife and daughter for whom he
provided from afar. A glass factory in Irkutsk, the first in Siberia, was a
success, but after eight years he moved again to Yakutsk to seek his fortune among the wild Chukchi tribes. There he encountered Shelikhov,
who urged him in 1788 to sail to America to manage the fur trade on
Kodiak. Baranov politely refused. Two years later, after Chukchi raiders
had swapped him a rich load of pelts in exchange for muskets, and then
used the muskets to rob him in the wilderness, Baranov changed his
mind. He would go to Alaska after all.

Baranov was forty-three and balding when he boarded a leaky galliot
and ventured onto the sea. The fresh water leaked out of rotten casks.
Headwinds stymied their progress. Scurvy broke out. Baranov, a land-
lubber, was seasick. In October, with the weather closing in, they put in
at the Aleutian island of Unalaska only to watch helplessly as a storm
flung the ship on the rocks. So repeating Bering's ordeal, the crew was
forced to winter there before proceeding in three makeshift *bidarki*.

That was why Kodiak looked positively verdant when the manager of
Russian America finally reached it in July 1791. But of animals and vegetables there were few. The cattle and sheep brought by Shelikhov
either failed to reproduce or turned into treats for Kodiak bears. Were it
not for the skills of the Aleuts the Russians might not have survived at

all. But the little trader with the big droopy eyes was weary of projects begun and abandoned. "My first steps into this country," he wrote Shelikhov, "were plagued with misfortune, but I am determined to change that luck or go down fighting." In 1792 an earthquake and tidal wave consumed Three Saints village, so Baranov set the colony to work rebuilding, and at a better site, he said cheerily. Then hostilities with the Kolosh disrupted the hunt, and Baranov had only two thousand skins to show for his first two years in Alaska. But a visit from the British ship *Phoenix* set him to thinking: he must build his own ships and cease to depend on chancy and inadequate supplies from Siberia. It meant scraping together all the available iron, finding substitutes for tar, pitch, and canvas, and deploying a large part of his labor force. But in September 1794 a seventy-nine-foot, three-masted, double-decked schooner, also called *Phoenix*, slipped into the bay. Her sails unfurled, caught the wind, then snapped, fluttered, and collapsed against the rigging. The sewn-up patches of cloth had been products of wishful thinking, and under the power of its one canvas sail the *Phoenix* crept over to Kodiak. Baranov was a prisoner of supplies from home after all.

That autumn the gloom lifted temporarily when a Russian ship, the *Three Saints*, appeared. But instead of replenishing Baranov's stocks, it only brought more mouths to feed: Archimandrate Iosaph with nine Russian Orthodox monks and seventy exiled convicts. Then the *Ekaterina* appeared with thirty serfs and their families, but the amenities listed on the manifest—vodka, brandy, tobacco, tea—had been consumed en route by the passengers. According to Shelikhov's letter, these reinforcements were to enable Baranov to found a true colonial capital that would "have the character of a city and not of a village" and ought to be named Slavorossiya (Glory of Russia). Instead, Baranov faced the worst winter yet as he struggled to feed and house his bloated colony of some three hundred Russians. They were crammed into barracks made for a fraction of their number, and with the windows sealed against the cold, the stench was indescribable. At night Russians lay with their Aleut women while the monks, a few feet away, chanted wrathful psalms. Accustomed as they were to monastic life, the priests refused to work, demanded that Baranov build a church, and terrorized the Indians with talk of sins that the Russians committed daily. "I fail to find one good thing," Father Iosaph wrote Shelikhov, "about the administration of Baranov."

Baranov himself pleaded only to be allowed to resign now that his five-year contract was up. But Shelikhov did not respond, the *Three Saints* was wrecked, and the *Phoenix*, dispatched finally to Okhotsk, did not return. Was the colony forgotten? Even the birth of a son to his Aleut mistress worried Baranov. He had already deserted one family;

must he now desert another? When a ship finally did arrive, in July 1797, it bore the news that Shelikhov was dead and his affairs were in turmoil, that Tsarina Catherine had also died, and in any case Russia was at war with the French Revolution. When the *Phoenix* returned in October, it bore a letter from Baranov's brother telling of family financial setbacks, lawsuits against Shelikhov's estate, and the illness of Baranov's wife. "I should get out of here," wrote the long-suffering manager. "But of course I cannot just get up and leave; the Company's interests are too closely involved with our country's affairs. . . . The place has made me old before my time." His depression was offset by the supplies on the *Phoenix*, a letter recalling Iosaph to Irkutsk (to be made a bishop), and the news that Shelikhov's widow had agreed to a merger known as the United American Company. "We only add," she wrote, "we want you to remain as our chief manager. In fact we beg you to remain." Several cases of vodka accompanied the plea.

The truth was that the merchants, officials, and royalty in Irkutsk and St. Petersburg had indeed been paying attention to Russian America, but their imperial fantasies, intrigues, and stockjobbing betrayed no understanding of the realities of Alaska. Shelikhov *had* understood. He had known every aspect of the trade from the taking of otters to the selling of the cured pelts at Kiakhta. He had known that the capricious Chinese might close down the trade, as they had in the early 1790s. He knew that the Anglo-American interlopers swelled the supply through their access to the Northwest coast and so drove the price of pelts down in China. And he knew that the cost of outfitting, feeding, and paying the hunters ate up half, sometimes all the receipts. To make matters worse, rival Russian firms, like the Lebedev-Lastoschkin Company, competed ruinously for the best hunting grounds, the loyalty of Aleuts, and Chinese buyers. That was why Shelikhov had gone to St. Petersburg to propose a single chartered fur company. But Catherine the Great sent him away with nothing but a ceremonial sword, a gold medallion of her majesty, and a promise to send priests and serfs to America.

Still, that mission planted a seed. For the man Catherine chose to shepherd the priests and serfs to America was Nikolai Rezanov. The son of a prominent lawyer and state official, he had spent five years as a guards officer and was appropriately dashing and fair. While crossing Siberia he met and married Shelikhov's daughter, received stock in his company as dowry, and carried his bride from her frontier town to the ballrooms of St. Petersburg. Six months later Shelikhov died, his Irkutsk rivals sued his widow, and her son-in-law Rezanov came to the rescue. It was doubtless on his advice that the widow agreed in 1797 to liquidate Shelikhov's assets and invest the proceeds in a merger of Irkutsk

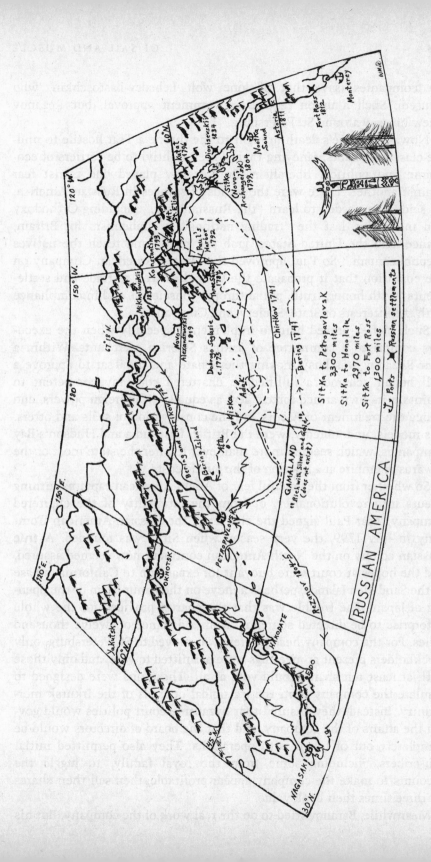

fur companies (save that of lone wolf Lebedev-Lastoschkin, who refused). Such a union required government approval, but Rezanov knew his way around St. Petersburg.

Now, Catherine's death brought to the throne a Tsar hostile to middle-class merchants, fancying them (often rightly) to be carriers of economic and political liberalism. So Rezanov played one tsarist fear against another. There were thousands of savages in Russian America, he said, who needed to learn "the Russian way," including Orthodoxy and monarchy, lest the "trading nations" (a euphemism for Britain, France, and the United States) grab the region and teach the natives "republicanism." So Paul approved the United American Company on the condition that it propagate the Gospel as well as trade and settlements "with honor, truth, philanthropy, conscience, and in compliance with the interests of State, Society, and Company."

Such pieties proved hard to implement, especially when the executors comprised a committee of jealous Siberian merchants. Within a year Rezanov was busy moving the Senate and the Tsar to approve a still bolder scheme: a full-fledged chartered company competent to maintain its own armed forces, deal as equals with foreign powers, and police the treatment of Aleuts and the conservation of seals and otters. His models, undoubtedly, were the British East India and Hudson's Bay companies, which seemed more than ever to offer the state most of the rewards of empire at a fraction of the public cost.

So whether from the fanciful fear of Anglo-American captains turning Aleuts into revolutionaries, or from the rationality of the chartered company, Tsar Paul signed the charter of the Russian-American Company in July 1799, the very season when Sitka was founded. A true Russian colony on the North American continent now seemed assured, and the hopes at court were buoyant for expansion to California, a base in the Sandwich Islands, perhaps a move on the Amur basin or the opening of Japan! The trouble was that the charter provided for the whole enterprise to be directed somehow from a distance of twelve thousand miles. For the company headquarters was moved to St. Petersburg, only stockholders present at meetings were permitted to vote, and only those with at least ten shares could vote at all. The terms were designed to insulate the company from the fratricidal quarrels of the Irkutsk merchantry. Instead, they ensured that byzantine court politics would govern the affairs of the company, and that the board of directors would be completely out of touch with operations. They also permitted initial subscribers, including some from the royal family, to juggle the accounts to make the company appear profitable, then sell their shares for three times their book value.

Meanwhile, Baranov tried to do the real work of the company. But his joy at the founding of Sitka did not last. One day out on his return voyage, his Aleuts gorged on mounds of mussels found on shore. Two hundred died, in gastric agony, from food poisoning. Later, at Constantine Redoubt, Baranov learned that the *Eagle* had sunk with eight of his sailors and twenty-two thousand rubles in furs. Worse still, boxes of tea and church candles washed ashore, and it was soon confirmed that Baranov's pride, the *Phoenix*, had gone down on its return voyage from Okhotsk. Bishop Iosaph had been on board, as well as the year's supplies. When Baranov finally reached Kodiak in November, he heard that the priests had so tormented his Aleut woman that she nearly killed their child. He put the priests under house arrest and closed the church.

By 1802 Baranov was again near despair. No Russian ship had called in four years, and only a friendly American, Joseph O'Cain of the *Enterprise*, kept the colony supplied. But there was nothing at all from home until a lone canoe entered St. Paul's harbor in May 1802 bearing a Dane in Russian service, Ivan Banner. He told of the founding of the Russian-American Company and Baranov's own generous share in it, of the assassination of Tsar Paul in a palace coup, and the new Tsar's conferral on Baranov of the Cross of St. Vladimir "for faithful services in hardship and want." A decade of repressed emotion burst forth in Baranov's tears. He could never repay such generosity, he said, but pledged a thousand rubles to the little school for orphans and Aleut children of Russian fathers, and proclaimed a feast. They would even slaughter a sheep.

Two months later Baranov was off inspecting outposts when a British ship, the *Unicorn* commanded by Henry Barber, dropped anchor off Kodiak. He had just come from Sitka, he said. The Russian fort no longer existed. Barber claimed he had put ashore at great peril but found only a charred ruin surrounded by heads of *promyshlenniki* impaled on stakes. As "an act of Christian charity" he rescued three Russians and twenty Aleuts and was now prepared to turn them over—for fifty thousand rubles' consideration. We can only imagine Baranov's anguish upon hearing the news and having to hasten back to Kodiak to engage the effrontery of this British captain. His ilk had armed the Kolosh in the first place, trading muskets for furs. Perhaps Barber himself goaded the Indians to attack, and now he wanted blood money. Baranov ransomed his men with furs worth some ten thousand rubles, then heard their account of the disaster.

It was June 20. The colonists had worked hard all spring and had just seen off ninety *bidarki* for the summer's otter hunt. Only twenty-six Russians and about forty Aleuts, male and female, stayed behind, looking forward to a Sunday feast. Then a cry sounded: "Kolosh!" Tlingits from several tribes had joined forces to overwhelm the depleted garrison. The Russians held off the attackers until they set fire to the fort,

forced the defenders outside, and cut them down one by one. When the
unsuspecting Aleut hunters returned to Sitka, they too were massacred.
Virtually no one, and nothing, was left.

If there was ever a moment for Baranov to quit, this was it. But driven
by hot vengeance, he willed the retaking of Sitka. He set his depleted
force to work on two more little sloops and prayed that somehow arms
and ammunition might come his way. They did, in 1803, when O'Cain
returned in his own ship with a full cargo. Alas, the Russians had just
sent away their inventories of furs and had no means of payment. But
the accommodating American devised an alternative: lend me your
Aleuts and I will transport them to the untapped otter herds off California. The Spaniards had no means of preventing it, so O'Cain could harvest his own fee. He returned with a full hold for himself and over six
hundred skins for the Russian company.

By September 1804 Baranov was ready to counterattack. So another
ragged flotilla coasted toward Sitka, wondering no doubt if they were on
a fool's errand. Then, on their approach to the harbor, the most beautiful
sight imaginable gradually took shape: a 370-ton, 14-cannoned Russian
man-of-war.

Rezanov had not been idle. He alone, back in St. Petersburg, seemed
to understand that the Russian-American Company's business, and
sheer existence in Alaska, depended on transport. With ships, the
colonists could import food and supplies from wherever, get their pelts
out, move men and matériel around as needed, defend themselves, and
even expand. Without shipping, they were at the mercy of their imperial
rivals—the British or Americans. So Rezanov lobbied incessantly for the
dispatch of first-class ships from Europe. He enlisted the Minister of
Commerce, Count N. P. Rumiantsev, and the two persuaded the Tsar
not only to approve, but to finance the enterprise through the Russian
state bank. Ships were bought in London: the *Leander*, renamed
Nadezhda, and the *Thames*, renamed *Neva*. Under the command of two
of Russia's finest captains, I. F. Kruzenstern and Iu. F. Lisianskii, they
sailed in July 1803. After a stop in the Sandwich Islands, where they
paid the Tsar's respects to King Kamehameha, the ships separated. The
Nadezhda, with Rezanov aboard, was bound eventually for Japan and
another attempt to open trade. The *Neva* made straight for Alaska.

For the first time in thirteen years Baranov enjoyed force majeure.
When the Tlingits defied his requests that they retire peacefully from
the fort, he led the attack himself, taking a musket ball in the arm. Still
the Tlingit warriors refused to retire. So Baranov turned the operation
over to Lisianskii, whose cannon battered the fort until the Kolosh fled.
Under the protection of the *Neva* the Russians went to work, and

within a year a new and larger fort, Novo Arkhangel'sk (New Archangel), was ready for business.

Sitka was secure. The company had begun to send capital ships to the Pacific. In need, American traders stood ready to supply the colony's wants. Finally, it seemed, Russian America was a going concern and ready to make the great leap southward to California. But what Baranov did not know, that autumn of 1805, was that another American, at that very moment, was carving his name in a yellow pine above the Columbia River and overlooking the Pacific Ocean. His name was William Clark; his companion, Meriwether Lewis. It was raining.

Paris 1803

WHEN THE PEACE terms ending the American Revolutionary War became known, London's *Morning Post* sounded an alarm. The peoples now clustered in thirteen states along the Atlantic littoral would never be content with mere independence. Rather, the "pride of empire will awaken and conquests will be multiplied on neighboring borders. Florida and all the Spanish possessions on the banks of the Mississippi will fall before them; and as they increase in power, that power will reach the limits of the Southern [Pacific] Ocean, and dispossess the Europeans of every hold upon the great continent of America." French diplomats agreed. Having obtained all the lands east of the Mississippi, the upstart Americans "are preparing for their remote posterity a communication with the Pacific." Most threatened of all was Spain, and within a year of the Peace of Paris the governor of Louisiana warned Madrid that the "unmeasured ambition" of this "new and vigorous people" posed a mortal threat to all Spanish possessions from the Mississippi to Mexico to the Pacific.

The geopolitical similarities in the Russian and American treks to the Pacific are striking. In each case a pioneering people skilled in the woodsman's arts looked from a secure political and economic base across a vast, empty expanse populated by only a million or so scattered aborigines. In the Russian and American cases alike the first attraction was furs. In each case great river systems connected by short and manageable portages provided routes across the continent. And in each case an old empire (China in the one case, New Spain in the other) loomed over the southern flank of the newcomers' advance but was unable to block their progress. In one sense, the Yankees had it even easier than the Cossacks. The American West, for all its rigors, was a kinder place than Siberia, and Americans did not suffer from the irrationalities of tsarist government or imperial distractions. In another sense the Americans faced a tougher task. For where Siberia had been virtually a political vacuum, North America was already partitioned, at least on the map, by Europe's great powers. Spain held Florida, Texas, New Mexico, and California and claimed all the lands north to Canada. France still cherished dreams of a comeback in Louisiana, founded under Louis XIV and stretching from New Orleans up the Mississippi and westward to the "Stony Mountains" (Rockies). Britain held Quebec and Ontario and claimed priority on the Northwest coast, while the Hudson's Bay and Northwest fur companies assumed proprietary rights over huge, undefined expanses of western Canada and the Rocky Mountains. Finally, Russians ruled in Alaska and meant to drive southward. Thus, American expansion westward, unlike the Russian drive eastward, took place through statecraft and war in the context of world politics. Had the European powers joined forces in a policy of "containment" against the United States, Americans might have found the gates to the West closed to them. But the Europeans were constantly at odds over what seemed, in the early nineteenth century, more important stakes and thus permitted the comparatively feeble United States to play them off against each other. That is why American expansion was (among other things) a by-product of European diplomatic history.

Surprisingly little was known of Louisiana in the late 1700s given that Coronado and De Soto had first penetrated it from the south in 1541 and La Salle, Marquette, and Joliet from the north in the 1670s, and that France had occupied New Orleans since 1718. It was known that the Mississippi Valley was fertile beyond a European's dreams, that the Missouri was a great river flowing out of a mighty mountain range, and that the wilderness in between was not the "great American desert" of later depictions but a veritable "garden." Otherwise ignorance held sway—and myths like that of a great salt mountain 180 miles long and whole ranges of flaming volcanoes. What knowledge existed of the American West found its way in these years into the hands of a curious Virginian named Jefferson. His library burned in 1769, but within four years he collected over a thousand books, including every one available on the exploration of North America, for his new home, Monticello. But not until American independence did Jefferson have the time and freedom to pursue his interest actively. In 1783 Jefferson remarked, in a letter to his friend George Rogers Clark, that the British fur companies seemed to be spending large amounts of money exploring the lands between the Mississippi and California: "They pretend it is only to promote knolege [sic]. Some of us have been talking here in a feeble way of making the attempt to search that country, but I doubt whether we have enough of that kind of spirit to raise the money."

Jefferson's vision of America itself was that of a southern agrarian

Republican (as opposed to the northern, commercial Federalists). Commerce and manufacturing were the enemies of freedom, for they obliged men to work for others, to be creatures of interest and faction, to fight for advantage and privilege, and ultimately to subvert the state in pursuit of money. Self-reliant farmers, on the other hand, knew how to improve their own land and derive freedom and virtue from the effort. Jefferson's rivals in the struggle for the soul of America were the urban businessmen of New England, New York, and Philadelphia, and those whose livelihoods depended on their trade. To their leaders, such as Alexander Hamilton, the United States could not survive at all in a world of power politics and economic competition without a strong central government willing and able to promote banking and trade, impose tariffs on foreign goods, and maintain an army and navy. They also envisioned a growing America but thought in terms of commercial, not territorial, expansion.

Transcending the tension between these two visions was the assumption of American exclusivity. Whether inspired by New England's Puritanism, with its notion of America as a City on a Hill, or by secular notions of Republican virtue, all Americans preferred to see their country as morally superior to the Old World with its tyranny, persecution, imperialism, and war. And the only way the United States could maintain its birthright of liberty was to stand aloof from Europe's quarrels. Exclusivism, therefore, implied isolationism. But how could isolationism be practiced when (1) those Yankee merchants relied so heavily on commerce with the wicked Europeans, and (2) those Jeffersonian farmers, multiplying yearly, found themselves blocked from virgin lands by the European imperialists? The only solution was to drive the empires off the continent and expand the United States and its virtues from sea to sea. European observers might not have perceived the cultural and social origins of American expansionism. But they knew them by their geopolitical fruits, and as far as they were concerned, the United States was just another rival all the more dangerous for being based in North America itself.

The wars of the French Revolution dragged on from 1792 to 1802 and were ruinous for impecunious Spain. By 1799 Napoleon was First Consul and a virtual military dictator. Two years later, his hold on half of Europe secure, Napoleon got the wild idea of snatching Louisiana back from Spain and fashioning a second empire in America.

What was Louisiana to Spain? If the Spaniards could not make a serious effort to settle California, how could they expect to defend the entire Great Plains? They could not, and Spanish Prime Minister Manuel de Godoy soon tired of Louisiana. It cost eight times more than it yielded in customs and trade, so if France wanted it back—for compensation, of course—Godoy was prepared to oblige. But Louisiana served another purpose. It was the buffer between the real source of Spanish wealth in America—the mines of Mexico—and the advancing Yankees. It was in Spain's interest, therefore, to yield Louisiana to France only if Napoleon promised never to relinquish it to any third party. That, of course, was a reference to the United States, and when rumors of the possible retrocession reached the United States, public opinion erupted. As Jefferson analyzed the situation from Paris: "Our confederacy must be viewed as the nest from which all America, North and South, is to be peopled. We should take care too not to think it for the interest of that great continent to press too soon on the Spaniards. Those countries cannot be in better hands." In other words, America's growing population would sooner or later swamp Spain's possessions with or without war. But having *Napoleon* as a neighbor on the Mississippi was another matter entirely. No American statesman, Federalist or Republican, could permit the retrocession of Louisiana. Napoleonic France in control of New Orleans would be able to choke American trade on the Mississippi, block U.S. expansion, perhaps even plot to "roll back" American borders *east* of the Mississippi by providing arms and support to Indians and restless frontiersmen. War fever spread along the eastern seaboard, and Americans openly spoke of an alliance with Britain and war with France.

Napoleon was undeterred. In 1800 he ordered Talleyrand, the perennial French Foreign Minister, to open talks with Madrid, and he even used the danger of an Anglo-American alliance to convince the Spaniards that their situation was hopeless. Better to trade Louisiana to France now than to lose it in war to the Anglo-Saxons. In the (second) Treaty of San Ildefonso he succeeded: Spain would cede all of Louisiana back to France in exchange for Napoleon's providing a member of the Spanish royal family with a kingdom carved out of his Italian conquests. The American position further deteriorated when Napoleon held out the olive branch to Britain, restoring a shaky peace to Europe in 1802. In October of that year, Carlos IV ordered his colonial officials to turn over New Orleans to the French.

Jefferson was the President stuck with the crisis. He had applauded the French Revolution in its early stages and was temperamentally anti-British. But the degeneration of the French Revolution into terror, aggression, and dictatorship—and the threat it now posed to the United States—changed his mind. The United States must somehow resist, but going to war with Napoleon was hardly the best solution. He must proceed gingerly, balancing overtures and threats in a diplomacy of brinkmanship, and grope for a safe resolution. So he outraged Federalist and western war hawks with "powder puff" references to the crisis in public, while behind the scenes Secretary of State James Madison threatened the French ambassador with an open break should the retrocession proceed. Between acquiescence and war lay a third possibility. In October 1801 Jefferson bade adieu to New York patrician Robert Livingston, appointed U.S. Minister to Paris, with instructions to spy out Napoleon's intentions and, if the retrocession were consummated, to offer to *buy* New Orleans and the Gulf Coast known as the Floridas. "There is on the globe one single spot," Jefferson wrote, "the possessor of which is our natural and habitual enemy. It is New Orleans, through which the produce of three-eighths of our territory must pass to market." But Livingston sent back discouraging news: the final retrocession agreement, the peace between Britain and France, and the outfitting of a French expedition to the West Indies. "There never was a government in which less could be done by negotiation than here," he lamented. "There is no people, no legislature, no counsellors. One man is everything. . . . Though the sense of every reflecting man about him is against this wild adventure, no one dares to tell him so." Even a personal embassy by Jefferson's Franco-American friend, Pierre Samuel DuPont de Nemours, failed to make an impression in the corrupt corridors of Napoleon's government. Nor was the news from New Orleans any better. The Spanish intendant Juan Ventura Morales, in one of his last acts before the transfer, suspended the "right of deposit" (of goods and capital) for American citizens, making it impossible for American citizens to do business. War hawks "whooped" again, insisting that Jefferson invade Louisiana before France had a chance to reinforce it.

Every manner of danger now confronted the young American union. Disgruntled Westerners might make common cause with the Federalists to wreck Jefferson's presidency, or provoke a war on their own, or even secede from the Union and cut their own deal with Napoleon. Or the French might send an army, incite the Indians, and try to drive the United States off the *eastern* banks of the Mississippi. The British posed a threat of their own. For it was also in 1802 that a certain book came into the hands of the inquisitive Jefferson. It was called *Voyages from Montreal . . . through the Continent of North America, to the Frozen and Pacific Oceans*, and its author, Alexander Mackenzie, had descended the river bearing his name to the Arctic, *and* found an overland route to the Pacific, arriving near Vancouver Island in 1793.

Jefferson could only be fascinated with the geographical results of the great journey and troubled by Mackenzie's call for Britain to colonize the American West, monopolize the fur trade, and open regular trade along the Columbia River. The next month, December 1802—and some months *prior* to his making any progress on Louisiana—Jefferson asked

Congress to fund an expedition to discover whether transcontinental communications might be possible with but a single portage from the Missouri to the Columbia river systems. "An intelligent officer with ten or twelve chosen men, fit for the enterprize [*sic*] and willing to undertake it ... might explore the whole line, even to the Western Ocean. ..." The bill became law in February 1803, and Jefferson had in mind a man to lead the party: his own secretary, the twenty-nine-year-old army captain and frontier veteran, Meriwether Lewis. Jefferson asked the Spanish minister in Washington if his government would mind a purely scientific expedition, indeed, a mere "literary pursuit" into the West! Carlos de Casa Irujo replied evasively and tried to discourage Jefferson. Spain certainly *did* mind greatly.

Meanwhile, Jefferson tried to resolve "this affair of Louisiana" by appointing yet another special emissary to Paris, his Virginia friend James Monroe. He also persuaded the Republican majority in Congress to defeat resolutions authorizing the President to raise the militia and seize New Orleans by force, but to pass an appropriation of $2 million in case Napoleon proved willing to sell New Orleans. In fact, the President's secret instructions authorized Monroe and Livingston to go as high as $9 million and to exercise their own discretion in setting the boundaries of the purchase. Monroe sailed in March 1803 with "the whole public hope," as Jefferson put it, resting on him. For if the mission failed, Jefferson's cabinet decided in April, the United States had no choice but war.

Then American luck changed. Napoleon did send a fleet to the Caribbean, but its first task—prior to occupying New Orleans—was to suppress the rebellious slaves who had overthrown French rule in Haiti. The black resistance led by Toussaint l'Ouverture and a yellow fever epidemic combined to decimate the French. What was more, the European peace broke down, and France and Britain moved swiftly toward a resumption of war. Suddenly the United States could not lose! Either Napoleon would unload Louisiana in exchange for American neutrality, or else the United States, in alliance with Britain, could walk into New Orleans at its leisure. Napoleon understood—his American dreams had aborted, and sometime in late March 1803 he decided to sell. On April 11, while Monroe was still riding the coach from Le Havre to Paris, Talleyrand sought out Livingston and asked whether he would like to have the whole of Louisiana. We want only New Orleans and the Floridas, replied Livingston. But without New Orleans, the rest of Louisiana would be useless to France, said Talleyrand. What would the Americans give for the whole of it? Twenty million francs, said Livingston. Not enough, said Talleyrand. Then Monroe arrived, and the two Americans judged they must strike while the iron was hot. They raised their bid to forty, then fifty, then sixty million francs and agreed to assume the claims of American citizens derived from France's wartime interference with Atlantic shipping. The total offer came to $15 million. When Livingston then inquired as to Louisiana's precise dimensions, Talleyrand shrugged: "You have made a noble bargain for yourselves, and I suppose you will make the most of it." In the event, the treaties of May 1803 transferred all the lands between the Mississippi River and the Rocky Mountains, doubling the size of the United States, at a cost of three cents an acre. All or part of thirteen states would someday be carved from the purchase. American territory now extended two-thirds of the way to the Pacific.

The news reached Washington on July 5, where the *National Intelligencer* boasted, "We have secured our rights by pacific means; truth and reason have been more powerful than the sword." But even now, Federalists were unhappy. They had wanted only to seize New Orleans. What they got was an expensive purchase (the entire federal budget in those years amounted to less than $15 million) of huge tracts of western lands that would inevitably fill up with frontier Republicans. Senator Samuel White of Delaware considered Louisiana "the greatest curse that could at present befall us," and Fisher Ames of Massachusetts warned, "We rush like a comet into infinite space." Besides, the Constitution made no provision for the acquisition of foreign territory, while Jefferson's imposition of federal rule over Louisiana violated the principle of representative government. But the Republicans had the votes and ratified the treaty in just two days.

Historian Henry Adams, descendant of the presidents, ranked the Louisiana Purchase below only the Declaration of Independence and the Constitution in its importance to the evolution of the United States. It placed the country on the path of expansion and showed how to achieve it through peaceful penetration and deft diplomacy. Jefferson, of course, was ecstatic over the reification of his "empire for liberty." It was at this time that he reread Thomas Malthus' treatise on population, which predicted inevitable famine as population expanded. Louisiana convinced Jefferson that Malthus was wrong: "Our food then may increase geometrically with our laborers, and our births, however multiplied, become effective."

The losers, of course, were the Spaniards, who had retroceded Louisiana on the promise that Napoleon would not turn it over to the grasping Americans. Now they would pour across the Mississippi, and how long would it be before they eyed Texas, New Mexico, the Rocky Mountains? That was the question the Viceroy in Mexico asked when Jefferson's two explorers set out to cross the continent with orders to report, with utmost precision, on everything. They were to take longitude and latitude readings at all river junctions or other notable points, describe the soil and face of the country, record all vegetation and animals (including the remains of possibly extinct ones!), measure temperatures and describe climates, and study the Indian tribes. Above all, Lewis and Clark were to ascend the Missouri, cross the mountains, and seek the Pacific, noting all furbearing animals and the best routes by which to carry their pelts to civilization. After all, Jefferson had conceived of the expedition as a direct riposte to that of Mackenzie.

Lewis and Clark "proceeded on under a jentle brease [*sic*] up the Missouri" in May 1804. They did not know that the highest-ranking officer in the American Army had already betrayed their mission to the Spanish authorities. Brigadier General James Wilkinson, like Benedict Arnold and Aaron Burr, was a man of brilliance, daring, and complete selfishness. He had conspired to remove George Washington from command of the Continental Army, would flirt with Burr's secessionist conspiracy, and had been for some time in the pay of the governor of New Orleans. And so he leaked to the Spaniards the fact, timing, and purpose of the Lewis and Clark expedition, recommending that the governors of Santa Fe and Chihuahua send out cavalry detachments to intercept and arrest the Yankee interlopers. Wilkinson pocketed $12,000 for his intelligence, waited a year and a half, then "patriotically" informed the War Department that he feared a Spanish attempt to capture Lewis and Clark.

They did try. Four times in the years 1804 to 1806 the commandant-general of New Spain sent out patrols in search of "Captain Merry" and attempted to enlist the Comanche and Pawnee in the hunt. The first three were under the command of Pedro Vial, a trader who had explored the Arkansas and Red rivers and was a chief blazer of the Sante Fe Trail. But Lewis and Clark were far up the Missouri by the time the first hunt got under way, a clash with marauding Indians spoiled the second sortie, and the third just disintegrated when New Mexican militia and their Indian escorts deserted. The fourth foray, however—a column six hundred strong under the able Lt. Facundo Melgares—left Sante Fe in June 1806, rode as far north as Nebraska's Republican River, and, on September 11, stopped just a few days' march from where the American heroes were making their way home down the Missouri.

When news of the return of Lewis and Clark reached the East, Jefferson celebrated and the Spanish minister fumed. In the short run, he reported, Lewis and Clark would bring the United States little but glory, but in the long run it "may encourage some attempts by individuals in this country, whose business spirit and mercantile sagacity are well known," to strike out in pursuit of furs and land. He urged Spain to settle the mouth of the Columbia River and forbid all foreigners to enter it by land or sea. But Spain had no stomach for another Nootka—and was about to be invaded by Napoleon. Nor did Yankees even wait "for the long run" before following Lewis and Clark. In the summer of 1806 Zebulon Pike was already on his way to Colorado, whence he made his way southward, in the teeth of the Spaniards, to Chihuahua, and home by way of vacant Texas. Expeditions up the Missouri followed in close succession. Nor did Americans with "mercantile sagacity" fail to see their new commercial opportunities. Foremost among them was the first Yankee to dream of an empire on the Pacific, John Jacob Astor.

Under Jefferson's aegis, the federal government had created the conditions under which American fur-trappers, merchants, and farmers might aspire to North Pacific power. It remained to be seen whether that same government had the power and the will to aid its own citizens in their efforts to outduel their state-backed competitors from Britain and Russia.

Sakhalin Island 1806

THE YEAR Lewis and Clark reached the Pacific was the year Baranov's men were rebuilding Sitka and dreaming of warm California, and the year Russians tried again to open Japan for the Tsar. Nine years had passed since Laxman brought back the so-called Nagasaki Permit, but finally Alexander I himself ordered the document brought to St. Petersburg and determined to cash it in. He chose, as his personal emissary, none other than Nikolai Rezanov. The latter at first was inclined to refuse; the death of his precious Anna, Shelikhov's daughter, had left him "estranged from everything in the world." But the Tsar persuaded him that a sea voyage was just what he needed and gave him command of the whole expedition. His wise instructions (the Russians had learned much while sniffing about the borders of Japan) admonished Rezanov to answer all questions put to him "simply and without pretense," even repeated questions and those to which the Japanese already knew the answer. But he was also to stress that Russia was a magnificent empire and the Tsar an absolute autocrat, facts Japanese would respect. He was to demand trading rights and spy out the Kuriles and Sakhalin Island with an eye to a Russian takeover.

Once at sea, however, the Russians as always fell to quarreling over their respective ranks. Captain Kruzenstern refused to accept the validity of the Tsar's own patent naming Rezanov commander and drove him to his cabin, where he remained, sick and suffering from the close air, for the final two months of the passage. The two English-made ships parted ways at Hawaii, the *Neva* bound for Sitka and *Nadezhda* (Hope) for Petropavlovsk. There Kruzenstern was forced to own up to his sovereign's will, and he apologized to Rezanov, whereupon the expedition put back to sea and reached the mysterious Japanese coast in October 1804. At first fog delayed their landing, then a North Pacific storm of such energy that "all nature appeared in commotion and uproar." At length the *Nadezhda* sailed into Nagasaki to be met by two polite Japanese officials. The Russians showed them the Nagasaki Permit. Why, the Japanese asked, had it taken them so long to use it?

Rezanov handed over Tsar Alexander's gracious letter and gifts for the Shogun, expecting speedy success for his mission. Instead, lengthy shipboard negotiations ensued, to no apparent purpose. But the Russians took care to make no outward sign of their Christianity and answered all inquiries faithfully. The Japanese were especially impressed by the news that Russia had colonies in "America"! After two months Rezanov was allowed on shore only to be isolated in a wooden house on a fenced-in peninsula fifty paces long. There they waited for another four and a half months before the *bakufu*'s emissaries arrived. They, too, asked why the Russians had not used the permit before, then read the Shogun's response:

> Already for a long time our country has no dealings with distant countries. We do not know neighborly friendship with foreign countries, nor do we have any ties with them, their characteristics and conditions being different. This is a hereditary law for the protection of our country's frontiers. . . . In the instance of commerce, we have concluded upon detailed deliberation of this that in exchange for unvaluable foreign things we would lose useful Japanese goods. All things considered, it is not to the good of the country as a whole. . . . Thus it is our government's will not to open this place; do not come again in vain. You must sail home quickly.

After all he had suffered in St. Petersburg, aboard ship, and throughout his patient wait in this "Russian Deshima," Rezanov erupted in rage. He cursed the officials, threatened them with the Tsar's revenge, and claimed for Russia all the islands north of Hokkaido. He also refused to take food until informed that the shame this caused his hosts must impel the local governor to commit suicide. So Rezanov reboarded the *Nadezhda*, its "hope" now extinguished, and left. He was also sick, this time with rheumatism and chest pains aggravated by the chill and humidity of the North Pacific. Yet after only a month at Petropavlovsk he boarded a Company ship and sailed to Alaska. On board he spent many hours with two young officers, Nikolai Khvostov and Gavriil Davydov, plotting revenge on Japan. From Kodiak Island Rezanov sent a letter to the Tsar insisting that the Japanese people wanted to trade in spite of their government, and requesting the Tsar's permission to *force* the opening of Japan. Clearly Rezanov was no longer the controlled statesman but bereft, ill, impatient, angry, and ashamed of the failure of his mission.

Rezanov sailed on to Sitka to meet Baranov and inspect New Archangel, which had sounded so grand from afar. Its humble reality appalled Rezanov, who thought of sacking Baranov on the spot. But after hearing the genial manager's account of his trials and the rigors of life in Alaska, Rezanov instead wrote the Company a paean to this "extraordinary person and a most original character." The winter of 1805–06 was another hard one: supplies were short, another ship went down, and the colony was saved again by the fortuitous appearance of the Yankee ship *Juno.* Begging Baranov never to resign, Rezanov promised to do what he could about feeding Russian America. He purchased the *Juno* outright and sailed to San Francisco in the spring.

California restored his health and made Rezanov feel like the dashing, forty-two-year-old widower he was. In just six weeks he wooed and won Commandant Arguello's teenage daughter Doña Concepción and promised to return in two years for the wedding. Romance no doubt aided business as well, for instead of expelling the Russians, Arguello loaded Rezanov down with supplies, heard his proposals for trade between Russian and Spanish America, and gave him leave to inspect the colony. It is intriguing to imagine how a Russian-Spanish colonial alliance might have altered the course of North Pacific history. But there is no evidence that Rezanov (much less Madrid or St. Petersburg) took the notion seriously. In his secret report he imagined a day when "all this country could be a corporal part of the Russian Empire," and he urged Baranov to leapfrog southward as soon as possible.

Then Rezanov turned his mind back to avenging himself on Japan. He had a second ship built in his absence to which he gave the curious name *Avos* (Perhaps), then recontacted Khvostov and Davydov in August 1806. Since he had received no reply to his letter to the Tsar, Rezanov then decided he must return to Russia at once, leaving his coconspirators with vague but broad instructions to proceed to Japanese waters and begin hostilities on their own! It was exceedingly poor judgment, but then, the North Pacific air had again attacked Rezanov's health. He set out across Siberia in the dead of winter and died at Krasnoyarsk in March 1807. A man whose career had begun with such achievements left behind a legacy of gratuitous violence, abortive schemes, and one very broken heart. Doña Concepción waited and waited, refusing to believe that her fiancé was dead, and then, in her grief, took holy orders. She was the first nun on the California coast.

Left to their own devices, Khvostov and Davydov sailed off to attack Japanese wherever they might be found. Davydov had to turn back in foul weather, but in October 1806 Khvostov landed on Sakhalin Island, only recently occupied by Japanese. His raiders took four hostages, ransacked a warehouse, burned every structure in sight, and stole sacred objects from the Japanese temple. They left behind a proclamation condemning the Japanese refusal to trade and threatening to lay waste all northern Japan. The following spring Khvostov and Davydov returned together in order to "liberate" the hairy Ainu and conquer the Kurile chain. On Etorofu Island their thirty sailors pillaged and burned a village, then challenged the island's small fort. Three hundred samurai and levies awaited within, but their commanders were absent by chance, and the Japanese officer in charge tried first to parlay with the intruders. The Russians answered with musket fire and, under cover of night, launched a surprise attack. The Japanese panicked, fled across the island, and took ship for Hokkaido, while the elated Russians, drunk on liberated sake, burned the settlement to the ground.

Khvostov and Davydov left behind on Etorofu another declaration "to the Governor of Matsumae." Had the Tsar's officers in Nagasaki been permitted to trade, they wrote, all would be well. But since the Japanese had sent them away, the Russian Emperor "commanded us to give you a specimen of his power. . . . If you comply with our wishes, we shall always be good friends with you; if not, we will come again with more ships and behave in the same way. . . ." If some members of the *bakufu* had favored trade with the Russians, the outrages of 1806–07 undercut their arguments and vindicated the advocates of "national defense." Responsibility for the northern territories was taken away from Matsumae and turned over to the Shogun himself, who sent reinforcements and awaited the chance to erase the shame inflicted by the "red devils." The chance came in 1811, when Lt. Comdr. Vasilii Golovnin, ordered by Tsar and Company to explore and chart the Kuriles, sailed the capital ship *Diana* into Japanese waters. Golovnin mistook an outcropping of the Hokkaido coast for one of the Kuriles, and his landing there in June alerted the Japanese. After another month of charting islands the Russians discovered that rats had been at their food barrels, and they also needed water. So Golovnin went ashore again, this time on Kunashiri, the twelfth and southernmost of the Kuriles, at a point known thereafter as the Bay of Deceit.

The Japanese on Kunashiri kept their distance, apologized after firing warning shots, and seemed to make the visitors welcome. Water casks appeared on shore, and food, and finally the Japanese beckoned the Russians to parlay by waving a flock of white fans. Five samurai approached in their pigtails and headbands, arms akimbo, their two swords dangling from their girdles, and their feet splayed so far apart that they appeared to be straddling a ditch. The Russians laughed and returned their bows. Refreshments were served, and the Russians learned that they must go to the fortress to discuss payment for the supplies with the local commander. On July 23 Golovnin, two officers, four sailors, and one Ainu entered a fort in which four hundred Japanese warriors lay in wait. Once seated inside, the Japanese commander unleashed a tirade concerning the Russians' prior atrocities. Golovnin's men bolted for the gate, but four were tripped up, while the other four made it to shore only to find that an ebb tide had grounded their boat. The Japanese bound and noosed their captives until their arms were immobile and they could barely breathe, then marched them in this state, for six hours, across the island. The Russians prayed to God for a swift death. That night they were herded into boats and transported to Hokkaido for another excruciating march to Hakodate. There they were twisted into tiny bamboo cages where they remained, except for interrogations and one failed escape, for twenty-six months.

The thunderstruck crew of the *Diana* was helpless. Shallow water prevented their approaching close enough to bombard the fort, and in any case hostilities might mean the slaughter of their imprisoned comrades. The ranking officer, Pyotr Rikord, had no option but to sail to Okhotsk and report to St. Petersburg. He stopped at Irkutsk when told that a request for a relief expedition had already been made. But the year was now 1812, and in June Napoleon's *grande armée* had invaded Russia. Clearly Rikord would be getting no help. By September he had returned to Okhotsk, sailed the *Diana* to the Bay of Deceit, and seized some hostages of his own. Luckily, one of them was a prominent merchant named Takadaya Kahei who opposed the shogunate's policy of exclusion. It took months for the two men to win each other's trust, but Takadaya finally agreed to serve as a go-between.

So the *Diana*, in June 1813, made its third visit to the Bay of Deceit. Takadaya said the Japanese wanted an affidavit to the effect that the raids of Khvostov and Davydov had not been approved by the Russian government, and the return of the articles stolen by them. He brought with him one released Russian sailor who bore a clandestine letter from Golovnin himself. Even after two years of confinement that noble captain had no words of hatred. Instead, he explained in measured tones the Japanese perception of events, offered advice on negotiating with them, and cautioned Rikord that on the wisdom of his actions

> depends not only our liberation, but also considerable benefit for the fatherland; I hope that our present misfortune may return to Russia that advantage which it lost because of the mad temper and recklessness of one man [Rezanov]. . . . I do not value my life a kopeck. . . . I greatly appreciate and thank you all for the great pains which you have taken for our liberation. Farewell, dear friend, . . . and all of you, dear friends! Perhaps this is my last letter to you; be healthy, in peace, and happy. Your devoted Vasilii Golovnin.

Rikord informed the Japanese that he would be back before winter. Despite heavy seas he returned, in October, armed with the required letter disavowing the raids of 1806–07. Within two weeks Golovnin was released, feted by the governor of Matsumae, and allowed to return home. He had learned and recorded much in captivity that contradicted the Russian perception of Japanese as treacherous and barbaric. Golovnin found them instead to be courteous, honorable, exceptionally clean, artistic, sensitive, and far more literate than any European people. Like the English, they were "a nation of shopkeepers," meticulous in weights and measures and prices. They were also fanatically devoted to their own land and tribe, which they considered to be of divine origin. On the other hand, the Japanese appeared to be overly fond of sexual and alcoholic diversions, and at present their government forbade them to learn about Western science and arms. But "if there will rule over this populous, intelligent, dexterous, imitative, and patient nation, which is capable of everything, a sovereign like our great Peter, he will enable Japan, with the resources and treasures which she has in her bosom, in a short number of years to lord over the whole Pacific Ocean."

Avos—perhaps—but when the Governor of Matsumae paid his leave, he reminded the Russians that foreign trade was illegal in Japan. They were not to send any more ships—ever.

The Third 'aha iki

Saitō: Time out!

Scholar: Not yet, I still need . . .

Saitō: You can't pitch, Lefty, I'm out of the batter's box.

Scholar: But I'm not finished with this part of the story.

Saitō: So sorry. I'm sure you'll think of something. It's easy to compose history when you get to ask and answer all the questions yourself. How about answering mine?

Witte: I too am ready for a break. Absence of time does not necessarily mean absence of boredom.

Scholar: You're a swell audience.

Saitō: You summoned us; we did not summon you. Tell me why you go into such detail about these early skirmishes between Japan and Russia.

Scholar: The Russian approaches to Japan? Because they're little known, and show how desperate the Russians were for a food supply in the Pacific. They also fix a pattern of conflict, especially over control of the Kurile Islands, that goes right down to the present day. They also raise the question: what if Russia had opened Japan before the United States, fifty years earlier?

Saitō: Very dramatic. So what if they *had* "opened" Japan? Do you know whether Japan had agricultural surplus to export?

Scholar: Good question . . . but we're not talking about great numbers of Russian mouths.

Saitō: Excuse, please, but so we are. Because *you* want to argue that Russia couldn't hold the North Pacific because of a lack of settlers, so access to Japanese rice would matter only if it *could* support "great numbers of Russian mouths." But let's say the Japanese *were* willing to export food. What would Russians trade in return?

Scholar: Furs, I suppose, like they exported to China.

Saitō: Did Japanese people want otter and sealskins?

Scholar: I don't know. We never found out, did we?

Saitō: No. But let's assume Japan *was* willing to import furs. Do you think Russians would be able to market them at a better price than Yankees or Brits?

Scholar: I suppose not. I suppose the Russian drive on Japan had little chance of doing what it was meant to do—unless Russia could somehow get monopoly rights in Japan, as the Dutch did, or else seize Hokkaido and settle it with Russian serfs. And the only way to do those things was to bully, and *that* was just the sort of behavior that would stiffen Japan's resistance. You were trained as a lawyer, weren't you, Saitō?

Saitō: Political science, Tokyo University, Class of 1911. I must also point out that it was never up to foreigners to "open" Japan. Only Japanese could open Japan. I hope you get that right when you tell about Commodore Perry . . . or won't you allow the Japanese to write their own history?

Scholar: With all due respect, Ambassador, the Japanese cannot always be trusted with their own history. They have a way of omitting unpleasantries.

Saitō: And I suppose Americans don't glorify their own history?

Scholar: We used to. . . . Now we stress the shame and leave the glory out.

Witte: Charity, gentlemen. Let us reflect on our histories with humility, and leave off accusing others. But there is something about our scholar's stories that troubles me as well: they are almost too exciting.

Scholar: But I thought you were bored.

Witte: I mean that by skipping from one episode to another, you leave out the time in between: endless winters in Siberia or Alaska; even Hawaii must have been tedious at times.

Seward: Ha! Would you care to address that, Ka-ah-ha—Your Highness?

Witte: I only mean that a Vancouver or Rezanov did not sail into port every week. And what about back in Europe? Years must have gone by without anyone of importance giving the least thought to the North Pacific.

Scholar: That's true, of course—an occupational hazard. It's only natural for historians to dwell on the turning points and moments of decision. Yet the "downtime"—let me rephrase that—"periods of inertia" are just as important in explaining why this country lost out and that country won. Depends on whose side *time* was on! Still, how do you document inactivity?

Serra: "Inactivity." You have Spain in mind again, do you not?

Scholar: I was speaking generally—anyway, who could accuse *you* of inactivity!

Serra: Just teasing, Doctor. But I'm not clear about the import of another episode: the Lewis and Clark affair. Do you mean to imply that the course of history would have been different had Lewis and Clark been captured? Is it not more likely that in return for the pleasure of incarcerating two most excellent explorers, Spain would have brought down on herself the wrath of the Anglos, provoked a war she could not win, and lost even more lands than she did? Britain might also have taken advantage—depending, of course, on the situation in Europe.

Witte: Why, Little Father, you are beginning to sound like a strategist.

Serra: A moment ago, Count Witte, I was struck by how much you were beginning to sound like a priest.

Scholar: Serra is probably right. It's not impossible that provoking a war was precisely what General Wilkinson had in mind. Maybe he wasn't a traitor, in so many words. Maybe he was trying to dupe the Spaniards into committing an "outrage" that would serve as *casus belli*. That's not what Jefferson wanted, but the war hawks were itching for a fight.

Seward: Goading your adversary to strike first is the best way to arouse a democracy. As for Wilkinson, we always thought him a hero, the man who foiled Aaron Burr.

Scholar: Maybe that's just what he was: the United States' first double agent.

Serra: Tell me, Doctor, how do you historians explain the "decline of New Spain"? I mean, its final inability to defend its claims to the American West. I would be interested to hear.

Scholar: I thought I'd covered that. To be sure, Spain revived somewhat under the Bourbon kings, but in terms of population, wealth, and technology it was still far behind countries like Britain and France. The cost of building and rebuilding navies sufficient to patrol the Atlantic and Pacific was far beyond Spain's means. Even the push into California was strictly defensive, and poor Bodega's mission to Nootka was a measure of how scanty Spain's resources had become. Imagine trying to deflect the Royal Navy and a rush of traders with double-talk and banquets! But remember, too, that when Napoleon invaded Spain in 1808 and ousted the Bourbons, the Spaniards were reduced to fighting for their own country and had nothing to spare for their colonies.

Saitō: The colonies were not loyal?

Scholar: Not very. In fact, in a strange way the rebellion of the South Americans and eventually the Mexicans from 1808 to 1820 was encouraged by Gálvez's reforms. He stiffened Spanish rule and taxation, just as the British did to the thirteen colonies after 1763, and prompted the same sort of resentment. When their chance arrived, the Latin Americans chose the same remedy: declarations of independence.

Seward: Rebellions or not, Spain could never have blocked the advance of the American people. Jefferson was right—in both senses of the word—about our westward expansion.

Saitō: "Right" because Americans were better than everyone else, and had God on their side? So when the U.S. expands, it's OK, but when other countries expand, they're wicked. Your idealism sounds more like chauvinism.

Seward: Not chauvinism, sir, patriotism.

Scholar: Or nationalism. They're all three different. Let's just say that the Americans, like the French after their Revolution, replaced veneration of monarchy with veneration of the nation. The U.S. could not have survived if its citizens had not felt a loyalty to the nation stronger than their loyalties to England or their own colonies.

Saitō: Which they did because they were chauvinistic. What's the difference between revolutionary France trying to conquer all Europe and a revolutionary U.S. trying to conquer all North America?

Seward: We did not conquer Louisiana, sir.

Saitō: You didn't have to, as it turned out. But you play hardball—always have—with anyone who gets in your way.

Scholar: And I suppose the Japanese are *not* chauvinistic—

Seward: Wait a minute! Where does he get these expressions like "hardball" and "throwin' us a curve"? Ambassador, you split my sides.

Scholar: That's right, the curveball wasn't invented until after your time, Mr. Seward. You know baseball, though?

Seward: Base Ball. Yes, the soldiers played it during the Rebellion. It became quite the sport. Went professional, didn't it?

Scholar: Well, be patient, and the phenomenon that is Saitō Hirosi will be fully revealed. Big Yankees fan, weren't you, Saitō?

Saitō: Lou Gehrig! He was my favorite.

Serra: Once again you gentlemen talk only of power. But power is not born only of guns and ships. Why not say instead that your North Pacific history is a story of philosophies in conflict?

Scholar: You mean Jeffersonian democracy and free enterprise versus tsarist autocracy versus Japanese, what, corporatism? And the system that best mobilizes its people for expansion wins out. The thought had occurred to me.

Witte: Too simple. You yourself argued for the value of chartered companies. Hardly free enterprise, but not wholly regulated either.

Saitō: Free enterprise and mercantilism are what Max Weber called "ideal types." They're just some more of those labels you historians like to invent. Take the British East India Company. Britain was supposedly the most "liberal" of all states, yet had the most successful chartered monopoly.

Scholar: I was just thinking out loud. Of course, the reality in any country, in any age, is a mixture of private initiative and public control. Freedom versus order, individual versus society, economic power versus political power, justice versus stability—it's never one or the other, but how you reconcile the two.

Saitō: Trade occurs in a political context. I could never get you Americans to admit it. But this business of chartered companies—interestin'.

Scholar: Very interesting. But you know, they could also be drags on expansion. The Russian-American Company stockholders, for instance, were more interested in short-term profits than real colonial development. And the Hudson's Bay Company was so jealous of its monopoly that it actually *hindered* British subjects from settling the Northwest coast. . . . I think there's a power greater than capital or government: it is people on the move in great numbers. You might say it's one of my "themes."

Seward: You've been awfully quiet there, ma'am. Methinks the queen is pouting! A lady's prerogative, of course.

Kaahumanu: It's a lady's prerogative to pout in silence, sir. Men usually pout with their tongues.

Scholar: Is something troubling you, *kuhina nui?*

Kaahumanu: I was remembering.

Scholar: Yes? Remembering. . . .

Kaahumanu: I was remembering all that I heard about Captain Cook. I was only a small child at Hana, on Maui, when the *haoles* first came to Hawaii. I do not think, Scholar, that you know all that happened, or why Cook was killed.

Scholar: Well, no outsider can know *exactly* what the Hawaiians were thinking. But surely the cycle of Lono, the apotheosis of Cook, and the Hawaiians' disillusionment when he returned—

Kaahumanu: Why do you say "what the *Hawaiians* were thinking"? Do you believe that we must all think alike?

Saitō: Take that, professor! So, Your Majesty, your leaders didn't really know *what* to make of Cook? A far more likely account.

Kaahumanu: I heard many tales, later, from many eyewitnesses: Kamehameha, of course, and my chiefesses. But all tales must be sifted and scrubbed, for the eye sometimes sees what it wants to see, and the memory nurtures what the heart tells it to. The *kāhuna* in the service of Lono naturally wanted to believe that Cook was their god. But the *kāhuna* in the service of other gods just as naturally did not. Nor were the *alii*, the chiefs, happy to imagine a visit from *any* god, lest the *kāhuna* eclipse their own authority. Other chiefs, like Kamehameha himself I believe, suspected that Cook was not a god at all, but a great chief from a distant island. They hoped to enlist his alliance, or trade, and so enhance their power and prestige over those of rival chiefs.

Scholar: But the liturgies performed over Cook at the *heiau:* they *were* religious?

Kaahumanu: Some were sacred, yes, but others were customary for a visitor of great *mana*, preparatory to negotiations over war or trade. No one doubted that Cook's *mana* was great.

Scholar: So the "Cook as Lono" theory—

Kaahumanu: Is only part of a great confusion. But the end of the story is simpler, I think. Captain Cook's return, and with a *broken* ship, dispelled the myth of Lono for those who had believed it, while his threatening behavior, especially toward King Kalaniopuu, enraged those who thought of him as a great chief and potential ally. He appeared instead as an aspiring conqueror who had come among us only to spy, then returned to despoil. There is also a tale that Kalaniopuu's warriors plotted to murder him on shore. But I believe they acted in anger.

Saitō: And self-defense.

Kaahumanu: Yes. But if so, such "defense" was foolish. My people were fortunate that the English captain—you say his name was Clerke?—elected not to avenge Captain Cook, or we might never have had peace with *haoles,* in which case. . . . Scholar! Why do you stop your story of Kamehameha in the middle?

Scholar: I didn't! Saitō stopped me. I was going to go on to the end of the Napoleonic Wars—1815. That would have been a better place to stop.

Kaahumanu: Kamehameha died in 1819.

Scholar: I know. But you must understand that Hawaii is part of the North Pacific, not the other way 'round!

Kaahumanu: Then tell me another thing. Why do you explain Kamehameha's victories as the fruit of Western arms and not his own strength and skill?

Scholar: I didn't mean to suggest that Western weapons alone explain Kamehameha's victories. He must have been one of the greatest warlords—sheer *personalities*—any country ever produced.

Saitō: "Warlords"—another term applied only to nonwhites. Why don't you call him a "general," as you would Wellington or Grant?

Scholar: All right, he was a great—no, he wasn't! And I won't take sensitivity lessons from a servant of imperial Japan. Kamehameha was not a "general" in some Western-style army. He was a warrior and a chief, according to his own culture. Now, if I may answer the question: the very fact that he saw the decisive potential of even a small amount of Western arms and knew how to use them to best effect was a measure of his genius. Not to mention that he was able to employ Western arms and advisers while upholding traditional Hawaiian beliefs and keeping the *haoles* at bay. "A great ruler"— how's that?

Kaahumanu: You are going to tell of Kamehameha's skill in peace, too?

Scholar: Yes, indeed, although there are two sides to that story too. On second thought, maybe 1810 or wherever we stopped *is* a watershed of sorts. First, Spain falls out of the game in the North Pacific. Second, the Russian pressure on Japan—meaningful or not—comes to an end until the era of Perry. And third, the period of real colonization—English, American, Russian—was about to begin. Let's say that around 1810 the Age of White Reconnaissance of the North Pacific began to merge into the Age of White Occupation. Come to think of it, 1810 was also the year Fulton launched his steamboat.

Saitō: White reconnaissance, *white* occupation. Hate to sound like a broken record, Prof, but all this occurred during a brief century or two during which your race had the upper hand. Your Age of the Whites will hit a "watershed" of its own someday; then you might learn something about the fullness of time.

Scholar: Funny you should say that, Ambassador. Sometimes I think maybe the Age of the Whites *has* come to an end—

Saitō: Aha! Well, in that case, Doc, let's get on with it. Batter up!

Astoria 1811

"H.B.C.—Here Before Christ"—was the joke made by settlers of British Columbia about the ubiquitous acronym of the Hudson's Bay Company. In the century after its founding in 1670 the Company's agents, clerks, factors, canoemen, and trappers fanned out from Hudson's Bay and stitched together a web of posts and forts, traveled by river, lake, and portage, befriended the Indians and enlisted them in the hunt, warded off the assaults of a frigid climate, and made war on beaver, otter, polecat, mink, and fox. English investors directed the empire from afar, but Montreal was its base of operations, and the frontiersmen themselves were overwhelmingly Highland Scots and French Quebecers, both peoples having been dispossessed by the advance of English power in the eighteenth century.

By the time of the American Revolution, however, the HBC ceased to be the driving force for Canadian expansion. So-called "free traders" or "winterers" went farther and farther afield in search of untapped beaver lands beyond the reach of the Company's monopoly. In 1785 the leading companies of free traders, like the merchants of Irkutsk, merged to form the unchartered but mighty Northwest Company to compete with the HBC. It was a Nor'wester named Peter Pond who pioneered the Athabasca country of present-day Saskatchewan and Alberta and first hypothesized that the rivers flowing out of it might carry a traveler to the Pacific. It was the Nor'westers who sponsored Mackenzie's land-ward crossing of North America. And it was two Nor'wester scouts, Duncan McGillivray and David Thompson, who first explored the Rocky Mountains of present-day Montana and Wyoming. But such was HBC influence that none could garner capital or government support for what Mackenzie called the "great Columbian enterprise." Finally, the "wintering partners," meeting at Fort William on Lake Superior, decided to act on their own. They rushed orders to Thompson, wearily making his way east, to turn and head west again, cross the Rockies at all costs, descend the Columbia River to the sea, and—if it turned out Americans had gotten there first—buy a one-third share in their enterprise. He braved the Blackfoot Indians, a winter crossing of the mountains, desertions, and cruel terrain but finally descended in July 1811 to the confluence of the Snake River and the Columbia. Selecting a prominent tree, he nailed up a note claiming "the country around" for Great Britain and the Nor'westers. He, his interpreter, and eight loyal Iroquois then rode their canoes down the fast-flowing Columbia. Just a few miles upriver from the ocean Thompson's heart leapt and sank. There, on the south shore, stood four rude cabins. The white man in charge was named Duncan McDougall, and he worked, he said, for John Jacob Astor.

Born near Heidelberg, Germany, in 1763, Astor had apprenticed in his uncle's musical instrument factory. He sailed to New York at the age of twenty with nothing but a cargo of flutes. But on the Atlantic crossing he met a fur merchant, and as soon as his flutes were sold he devoted himself to organizing the trappers on the Great Lakes. As his fortune grew, Astor took his place among New York's commercial elite, followed with interest the tales brought back by the first Pacific merchants, and conjured imaginary empires out of the lands crossed by Lewis and Clark. In 1807 he told DeWitt Clinton, Mayor of New York, of his plan to capture the entire North American fur trade. For he had the capital that Pond, Mackenzie, and the others lacked. He could act as he wished where they had to battle committees and partners. And he would gain government support while they, thanks to the HBC, could not.

The only problem was President Jefferson. Was there really a chance that a farmer/philosopher hostile to mercantilism would actually charter a company and provide it with armed protection? Astor's first letter to Jefferson was accordingly circumspect, asking only for "the countenance and good wishes of the executive of the United States." That he had: Jefferson was in fact hoping for "some enterprizing [sic] mercantile Americans to go on to the river Columbia and near the Pacific ocean, and settle the land there." But Jefferson also doubted "whether it would be prudent for the government of the United States to attempt such a project." All he would promise Astor was that "every reasonable patronage and facility" would be forthcoming. In hopes of pinning the President down, Astor rode the coach to Washington City in 1808 and explained to the President and cabinet that foreign concerns, aided by *their* governments, would surely destroy a private American venture. He later claimed that Jefferson gave him an oral promise of protection.

"That's as may be," as the Scots say, but Astor was wise to fear British hostility. The Royal Navy was blockading Napoleonic Europe, violating Americans' rights as neutrals, and impressing sailors into the Royal Navy. Beginning in 1806, Jefferson, then Madison tried to force Britain to relent through a series of embargoes and nonintercourse acts. War was not unlikely. And if the U.S. government would not or could not support him, then Astor felt fully justified in turning to foreigners, to Britain's other rival in the North Pacific, to Russia!

The Russian-American Company, as we know, had already settled into a love-hate relationship with the Boston merchants who invaded "its" waters. Unfriendly and unscrupulous profiteers skirted the Russian settlements and bought furs from the Tlingits in exchange for guns, powder, and ammunition. Friendly traders like O'Cain, on the other hand, were an invaluable source of food and supplies to Alaska. So in 1806, when the first American consul was appointed to St. Petersburg, the tsarist Minister of Foreign Affairs proposed a commercial treaty. Russia would grant the United States monopoly rights to supply the Russian colony in return for which the Americans would stop arming the Indians and transport Russia's furs to Canton. The U.S. Consul thought something could be arranged, and the hopeful Russians sent a chargé d'affaires, Andrei Dashkov, to Philadelphia.

Of course, Dashkov represented the Russian-American Company as well as his government, and his devious plan was not to let on how desperate the Russian colonies were. Moreover, the first article of his draft treaty included a clause to the effect that neither party was to provide arms to any third country with which the other was at war. A friendly enough gesture, except for the fact that the Russians intended to "declare war" on the Tlingits, whereupon Americans would be prohibited from running guns to them. What is striking about the episode is the *Russian* naivete about the way American government worked. Unlike the tsarist autocracy, the U.S. executive branch lacked both the will and the naval power to police the activities of its citizens on remote Pacific shores. Perhaps this fact sunk in. For after only a few months Dashkov gave up on a treaty and tried instead to make this "free enterprise" system work for him. He met with Astor, and Astor was eager to deal. He would agree to a three-year contract making him exclusive supplier of Russian America, the Russian-American Company would hire his ships to carry furs to Canton, whereupon Astor's would-be competitors—English and American alike—would have no incentive to ply the Northwest coast at all. Of course, St. Petersburg would have to approve, but in the meantime Astor prepared a maiden voyage. His *Enterprise*, under Capt. John Ebbets, crossed the bar out of New York harbor in November 1809, bound for Sitka.

While this private diplomacy was unfolding, Astor was founding his colony on the banks of the Columbia River. The seaborne expedition sailed in the sleek and spacious *Tonquin* in September 1810 under Capt. Jonathon Thorn. But the voyage was unhappy. Storms and doldrums, a water shortage, and Thorn's imperious decrees poisoned the passengers' mood. Everything seemed to get under the captain's hide, even the songs and dialects of the Scots and French Canadian furriers hired by Astor. In December 1810 the crew thankfully anchored off the Falkland Islands to water and hunt for game. When the landing party was tardy in returning to ship, Captain Thorn went into a fury, raised anchor, and sailed. The stranded Astorians leapt to their boat and pulled out to sea for all they were worth, but Thorn did not turn to retrieve them until the nephew of one of the stranded men put a pistol to the captain's head.

Thereafter the ship's company was divided into two surly factions. But the vessel rounded Cape Horn in style and fairly flew to Hawaii. Kealakekua Bay proved as delightful as ever, but the Big Island's governor, none other than John Young, the captured American in Kamehameha's service, advised them to go to Oahu if they wanted to stock up on supplies. The King had claimed for himself a monopoly on all foreign trade. Moreover, he would take no hardware or even guns in exchange, only money, and preferably Mexican silver. Still, when the *Tonquin* departed for America, the crew and company shared her decks with a hundred oinking pigs, pecking chickens, smelly goats, and a dozen Hawaiians who signed on to work for the company.

Spirits quickly fell to their pre-Hawaiian low when the ship entered northern waters. Squalls soaked all hands and carried overboard some of the livestock. Then the treacherous bar of the Columbia River wrecked an advance boat and nearly beached the *Tonquin*. Eight crewmen died, including one Hawaiian. Still, Astor's men had gotten there first, in April 1811, so by the time Thompson of the Nor'westers turned up, a warehouse, cabins, and little stockade were under construction, and the Astorians had begun to collect their two-year total of almost eighteen thousand beaver pelts.

Astor's overland party—sixteen men under Wilson Price Hunt—left Montreal in July 1810. They threaded their way through the Great Lakes in a thirty-six-foot canoe to Mackinac, where they were joined by the famous Philadelphia botanist, Thomas Nuttall, then down the Fox, Wisconsin, and Mississippi rivers to Saint Louis. Their presence aroused the suspicion of the jealous agents of the Missouri Fur Company, and so when the Astorians struck westward again in the spring of 1811, they elected to take a new southern route, hoping to elude the Missourian scouts, who hoped to incite Indians against the newcomers. But the new mountain man route via the Wind River of Wyoming and across the Tetons led them into craggy passes and white water accidents, hunger, thirst, and delicate negotiations with Sioux, Arikara, and Teton chiefs.

By the time this second American party to cross the continent did reach Astoria in February 1812, the men were exhausted and barely alive. If Astoria were going to flourish, it would have to be supplied and defended by sea. But the sea belonged to Britannia.

Astor viewed his enterprise as a business venture, not a patriotic service or geopolitical experiment. But in fact it was all these things, a fact made clear just four months after Hunt reached the Columbia, when the United States and Britain went to war. The immediate cause of the War of 1812 was the Royal Navy's continued interference with American shipping, but many Americans and Britons suspected that the real stake in the contest was nothing less than control of North America. Consider the vote in Congress. Members who hailed from the northeastern states voted thirty-three to eleven *against* the war resolution. In other words, the Yankee merchants opposed war in spite of the damage done by Britain to trade, while the southern and western Republicans, who had little stake in Atlantic shipping, voted sixty-eight to sixteen in *favor* of war. Judging from the newspapers and rhetoric of the day, they expected to conquer Canada and expel Britain once and for all from the continent.

All the war hawks got for their David versus Goliath act was an expensive stalemate fought on American soil. The U.S. invasion of Canada misfired, and the British scoured up enough ships and soldiers— even at the height of their war with Napoleon—to menace the American coast. Astor knew it was only a matter of time before the Royal Navy paid a visit to Astoria as well. What was more, Astoria was defenseless. One of Astor's ships in the Pacific had sailed for Canton, where the captain learned of the war and stayed put. The other, the *Tonquin*, no longer existed. In July 1811 Thorn took the ill-fated ship on a trading foray to Vancouver Island and predictably lost his temper with the hard-bargaining Nootka Indians. They in turn (in a poetic reversal of the trick Simon Metcalfe had played on Maui) feigned reconciliation in order to gain access to the *Tonquin*, then produced knives and hatchets from under their pelts and hacked the crew to death. All but one, that is, and he survived just long enough to rig the powder magazine and touch it off the next day when over two hundred Indians swarmed aboard to claim their booty. The *Tonquin* and all aboard were literally blown to bits.

Astor searched in vain for captains willing to run the British blockade. So he returned to Washington in 1813 and told any tall tale he could think of in hopes of goading the Navy to act. The entire future of the United States on the Pacific was at stake, he said. Many silent partners stood to lose their investment, he said. Jefferson had promised military support, he said. But all the Secretary of the Navy could do was to arrange for an armed privateer to accompany one of Astor's ships, and he even reneged on that. Astor's final gambit was to drape his *Enterprise* in

Russian colors and hope that Dashkov could trick the blockading British into letting it pass. Sorry, said the British duty officer, no ships could leave New York.

A continent away, the Astorians expected no help. When news of the war arrived in January 1813, McDougall prepared to abandon the site. Over the summer Hunt and his followers challenged the decision as hasty and defeatist, but its wisdom was confirmed in October when a party of Nor'westers under John McTavish arrived by river from Canada. The Royal Navy was on its way, they warned, so better to sell Astoria now for a fair price. So the two Scotsmen sat down to haggle over what value to attach to supplies, pelts, and buildings. On October 22, McDougall struck the Stars and Stripes and turned his keys over to McTavish.

The Royal Navy did arrive, in the form of Capt. William Black and his *Racoon*, in December. He was miffed to discover that he had been cheated of a battle, but he went through the motions of raising the Union Jack, smashing a bottle of port against the pole, and rechristening Astoria "Fort George." He scarcely imagined it to be an act of consequence. But when the war ended a year later in the Treaty of Ghent, the first article of peace held that all territories captured by either side would be restored. Of course, Astoria had been sold before being "captured," but Astor, still grasping for straws, argued that Black's bravado brought Astoria under the force of the treaty. For four years American and British negotiators disputed the issue of who had what rights in the vacuum called Astoria, New Albion, or Oregon. But in the Convention of 1818, Albert Gallatin and Richard Rush succeeded in fixing the U.S.-Canadian border at 49° north latitude *up to the Rocky Mountains*, while leaving the "Oregon country" west of the Rockies "free and open" to *both* British and American settlement for at least ten years.

Astor, though vindicated, no longer had the stomach for empire-building. "If I was a young man. . . ." he wrote. But in the United States dwelled many young men—and women—and their numbers were growing. One who understood their potential was British Foreign Secretary Lord Castlereagh. Pondering the implications of the Convention of 1818, he prophesied: "You [Americans] need not trouble yourselves about Oregon, you will conquer Oregon in your bedchambers."

California and Kauai 1815

A STOR DID NOT suffer from the collapse of his dream: he lived to
the age of eighty-four and left a fortune of $30 million to his son,
William, known as the Landlord of New York. But Astor's Russian "allies" continued to suffer. In August 1809, Baranov heard murmurs to the effect that a score of his own *promyshlenniki* were plotting
a coup. Perhaps they were seized by the spirit of revolution, carried to
this distant defile by a corporal from victimized Poland. Or perhaps they
had heard of the mutiny on the *Bounty* and longed for the South Seas. In
any case, their so-called Order of Ermak plotted to assassinate the manager, sack the warehouse, kidnap women, seize a ship, and live in bliss
on Easter Island. But one of their number lost his nerve and informed.
The incredulous Baranov raided their cabin, perhaps still hoping that
this could not be true, and captured the conspirators before they could
burn all their papers.

Thus began the last phase of Baranov's career. Fearing his own men,
he packed his Aleut family off to Kodiak, lived under guard, redoubled
his intake of alcohol, and seemed uncaring toward his health. This was
the state in which Astor's Captain Ebbets found him in 1810. Moreover,
the news of the bargain with Astor troubled Baranov. He suspected it
would not stop Yankee gunrunning to the Tlingits but would require
him to cease bartering with his friends among the good American captains. Baranov had again tendered his resignation and been promised a
replacement, Ivan Koch, that fall. But the Company brig put in with the
news that Koch had fallen sick and died in Kamchatka. Another
appointee, T. S. Bornovolokov, would arrive with the *Neva* in 1812.
Instead, in January 1813, a battered launch appeared and a salt-caked,
frozen lieutenant stuttered that a gale had wrecked the *Neva* on the
rocks beneath Mount Edgecumbe. Bornovolokov, too, was dead.

By now any normal man would have taken to cursing his luck, railing against fate, or hating God for His cruel injustice. But Baranov relied on his own sheer stubbornness buoyed in turn by a muscular faith. Long ago he had had his fill of priests. Now, he requested a new one be sent and built a church largely at his own expense. Nor was life at Sitka entirely grim. For Baranov had built there a merry haven by North Pacific standards. The Russian facilities for ship repair and refurbishment were the only ones north of Hawaii, and four or five brigs and schooners were now likely to be at anchor there. American and British captains looked forward to banquets at Baranov's "castle," made all the more jolly by the flow of grog and punch, conversation and music. Fiddles and flutes found their way to Alaska, and evenings ended with a raucous or sentimental rendition of "The Spirit of Russian Hunters," composed by the manager and known to Yankee captains as "Baranov's Song."

Still, the colony had to be fed. With the 200-odd Russians and their families, Creoles (offspring of mixed unions), and Aleuts, New Archangel numbered almost 700. Another 250 Russians dwelled at other Alaskan posts, each with its coterie of Aleut dependents. The colony required at least six thousand bushels of grain per year, which Baranov procured from Americans in return for furs or the use of Aleuts. But even this practical arrangement rankled Russian-American Company officials back in St. Petersburg, who periodically ordered Baranov to suspend trade with foreigners even though Russia failed to send ships on a regular basis. Why did St. Petersburg not make the effort to nurture its American colony? The Napoleonic Wars were surely one reason, but the Company shares the blame. From 1797 to 1821 Russian America shipped out pelts valued at 16.4 million rubles. The Russian state took 2 million rubles in duties, 3.6 million went to American traders for supplies, 4.2 million were paid out in dividends, and 3.3 million were added to the Company's capital. Only 3.8 million rubles (23 percent) went for ships, supplies, and salaries. Even then the directors preferred to borrow (which explains why the debits exceed 100 percent) rather than reduce their own dividends. In fact, exactly twice as much money was spent on the Company's headquarters in St. Petersburg as on all of Russian America. So it was always up to Baranov to make do in the wilds, and in his declining years he launched two new initiatives, either of which might allow him to present his successor with a secure source of food. He meant to break into California or Hawaii.

Baranov was not long in acting on Rezanov's idea of invading the Spanish preserve. His idea was to advance gradually, founding first a post on the Columbia River. But this plan aborted in 1808 when Nikolai Bulygin's ship was wrecked on the coast. Bulygin's wife, the first white woman in what is now Washington State, was taken hostage by the

Makah Indians, "went native" for a time, and finally committed suicide. Bulygin himself died of a fever before a ship could rescue the party.
Had his mission succeeded, Russians would have beaten everyone to the
Columbia River. Meanwhile Nikolai Kuskov, one of Baranov's best officers, scouted the coast north of San Francisco Bay, planting copper
markers inscribed Land of Russian Possession. In 1809 the Tsar
approved the Company's plan to found a colony in California, and two
years later Kuskov put ashore at a site eighteen miles north of Bodega
Bay (about sixty miles north of San Francisco). The nearby Rio San
Sebastian was known forever after as Russian River. A local chief sold
him a thousand acres in return for trinkets and medals. Kuskov then
reported to Sitka and returned in the spring with twenty-five Russians
and one hundred Aleuts. There, thirteen hundred miles south of Sitka,
they hammered together a sturdy, spiked, redwood stockade named
Ross—the last *ostrog*—mounted ten cannons, and solemnly saluted the
flag of the Russian-American Company.

No one knows what prompted Kuskov to choose this place rather
than the far superior Bodega Bay. Some say he wanted to be farther from
the Spaniards, but what would a few miles matter? A more likely guess
is that he purposely chose the poor anchorage of "Kuskov Bay," with its
currents and rocks, to frustrate British or American assault by sea.
Unfortunately, the Russian beachhead was just a vexation to Company
ships, while the sandy, forested bluff was poorly suited to agriculture.
Kuskov planted potatoes, but the yield was sufficient only to feed his
own men. The Russians also ate seal meat and birds and after 1817
acquired cattle, horses, and chickens from the *padres* of San Rafael mission. But the foggy coastal air discouraged farming, and the *promyshlenniki* in any case rebelled at the prospect of being turned into peasants.
Fort Ross's peak harvest, in 1829, was fewer than seven hundred
bushels. If the Russians were to send any surplus on to Sitka, they
would have to trade with, purchase, or seize existing *ranchos*.

When rumors of Russians first reached San Francisco, the authorities
raised their eyebrows in bemusement and suspicion. Why had Russians
come to this place? asked the first patrol up from the presidio. Kuskov
innocently mentioned the food problem, then moved on to talk of
Russo-Spanish trade. Governor Arillaga was not averse, but was also
soon dead, and his replacement arrived with orders to arrest all Russians. The crew of the *Ilmen* was seized while sealing off San Luis
Obispo and incarcerated at Monterey. A few Russians escaped back to
Ross, going four days without food or water, but (according to Kuskov)
one miserable Aleut was tortured to death by Franciscans who thought
him demonic because he insisted on making the sign of the cross *back-
wards* (which was the Russian Orthodox fashion!). If this story is not

just anti-Spanish propaganda, then northern California's first Christian martyr was killed by the missionaries themselves.

Baranov's riposte was to send a Company ship to Monterey in 1816. Under its guns, the Spanish governor agreed to free the captives and suffer the Russians to trade. Finally, Russian Foreign Minister Count Nesselrode defended his rights before the Spanish Ambassador in St. Petersburg, and the matter was settled in 1817. Henceforth the Russians at Fort Ross acquired and shipped to the north between one thousand and five thousand bushels per year, in addition to salt, meat, and wine. But once trade was established, Fort Ross was redundant. And Baranov could hardly aspire to a California empire without men, ships, and guns from Russia. So he flung Russia's last errant arrow in another direction, still hoping to conquer some sun.

American captains had told Baranov of Hawaii's beauty and richness, and even of Kamehameha's respect for Baranov himself. The curious King kept abreast of events in the north and knew of the Russian's trials. To him Baranov was a fellow Pacific monarch, and he had even offered to send warriors to help the Russians retake Sitka. Baranov, in turn, yearned to open direct trade to fill Alaskan bellies with tropical things and the Company's coffers with profits. But the bluster of a naval lieutenant had rendered it all problematical. Leontii Hagemeister, commander of the *Neva*'s second Pacific tour in 1806, grew impatient trying to trade with King "Tomeomeo," who monopolized commerce and let his taro, fruit, and sugar rot rather than accept a fair market price. So Hagemeister swore in the (probably boozy) company of a British officer to return with a fleet and annex Kamehameha's kingdom. Needless to add, the Englishman wasted no time warning the King.

So Baranov was on the lookout for a man of wit and judgment who could win back Kamehameha's confidence. The most likely candidate was Don Juan Eliot y Castro, a medical doctor of Brazilian origin, one of the first whites to settle in Honolulu, and Kamehameha's personal physician. But Don Juan sailed on the *Ilmen* with the crew that was captured by the Spaniards. So Baranov tried instead with an American, James Bennett, but a storm beached his ship, the *Bering*, on Kauai, whereupon it fell under the *kapu* of the local king. He eventually released the ship but kept its cargo. A third possibility marched into Baranov's castle after deserting his post as surgeon on the imperial ship *Suvorov*. He was a German in Russian service named Georg Anton Schäffer, and he had had enough of the *Suvorov*'s obstreperous commander, M. P. Lazarev. Since Baranov had his own problems with Lazarev, he and Schäffer became friends, and it soon struck him that this was the man for Hawaii. After all, Kamehameha would be grateful to him for sending along a new doctor. Schäffer sailed in 1815 with orders to ingratiate himself with the King, negotiate for the return of the *Bering's* cargo, and, if possible, conclude a treaty. Baranov promised back-up ships and gave Schäffer a blank check to draw on the Company account.

The Sandwich Islands had changed radically in the twenty years since their pacification. *Haole* ships stood constantly off Kealakekua or Honolulu, piers and grog shops arose, and Hawaii became the nerve center of the white community in the Pacific. Deals were struck there, news and gossip exchanged, friendships renewed, ships repaired, bodies soothed, all under the benevolent if covetous eye of Kamehameha. He built a Western-style house, dressed himself and his wives in European fashion, augmented his Western navy and artillery, and surrounded himself with white cronies or Hawaiians with nicknames like Jefferson, Bonaparte, or, in Prime Minister Kalanimoku's case, William Pitt. In the eyes of visiting sailors, Hawaii was a mad carnival.

On the other hand, much stayed the same. The King's word was still total and final. Hawaiian *kapu* still applied. Private property was still a fiction. And though the common people no longer suffered from war, their lot in some ways was worse. Whenever the foreigners showed an interest in a commodity, Kamehameha arrogated all supplies of it to himself and put his people to work producing it. After 1811 they wanted, above all, sandalwood. It seems the Chinese, after first disparaging this aromatic Pacific timber, could not get enough of it. So Kamehameha drafted forced labor to fell and cut sandalwood trees, while British and American traders vied for influence in hopes of controlling their export.

In foreign policy, Kamehameha had three broad aims. The first was to deflect any attempt by *haoles* to colonize the islands; he would fall back on his "British protectorate" if need be. Then he wished to ensure that no white visitors conspired with lesser *alii* to threaten his power. The royal trade monopoly, aside from enriching him, was a good means of doing that. Finally, he wanted to conquer Kauai. As we know, the winds and currents of the channel spoiled his first invasion. A second attempt in 1804 (launched at great expense and in defiance of the *kāhuna* oracles) succumbed to a typhus epidemic. Kamehameha then tried diplomacy, inviting Kauai's youthful King Kaumualii to parlay with him on Oahu. Remembering the fate of Kamehameha's rival on the Big Island, who had been murdered during a truce, Kaumualii resisted for five years and came only when Yankee merchant Nathan Winship promised protection and left a hostage of his own on Kauai. The meeting occurred in 1810 amid rumors of murderous plots, but Kaumualii simply agreed to recognize Kamehameha as overlord, and went home—quickly.

That was the setting when Schäffer disembarked in November 1815. Kamehameha proved gracious, anxious for news of Baranov, and willing to help oblige the Kauaians to compensate for the *Bering*'s lost cargo. Resident Americans (including Astoria veteran Wilson Hunt) whispered against the "Bavarian scientist." But when the King and Kaahumanu fell ill, Schäffer's remedies proved effective (at least, the royal couple got well). Kamehameha rewarded him with generous land grants on Oahu and even ordered a *heiau* constructed in honor of the Western *kāhuna* known as "physicians." The honeymoon did not last. When the two ships promised by Baranov, the *Otkrytie* and *Kadiak*, as well as the *Ilmen*, just freed by the Spaniards, all converged on Honolulu in 1816, Kamehameha grew anxious. Schäffer sensed the altered mood, decided a retreat would be prudent, and sailed for Kauai.

Now, given that Kauai's King was the one who had confiscated that Russian cargo, one might expect Schäffer to have gone in with guns lowered. Instead, he and King Kaumualii realized at once how much their interests dovetailed. Kaumualii wanted a guarantee of his autonomy vis-à-vis Kamehameha; Schäffer wanted a secure base in the islands. Baranov's instructions were to extract reparations from *this* man while negotiating a treaty with *Kamehameha*. But this was a target of opportunity Schäffer could not resist. Within days Kaumualii placed his "X" on documents making Kauai a tsarist protectorate, granting a commercial monopoly to the Russian-American Company, and approving construction of forts. The King, now sporting the uniform of a Russian naval officer, asked in return a ship of his own and began to dream of conquering Oahu and Maui from Kamehameha! He even promised to cede Russia half of Oahu and prohibit all trade with Americans.

Schäffer was in way over his head but chose to believe that all Hawaiians would leap at the chance to overthrow Kamehameha. "The people are so poor, however, so weakened, and so terrified by the present ruler of these islands that they have no idea of founding a new state, but wish all the more for some European power to take them under its more favorable protection." As soon as word spread of his alliance with Kaumualii, Kamehameha's men burned down his Oahuan posts. Then the *Otkrytie* sprung her masts in a storm, and Schäffer was obliged to purchase two American vessels, drawing on his "blank check" from Baranov. He also constructed a lava rock fortress at Waimea (where Cook had first landed), christened it Schäfferthal, and prepared to lord over it as Baranov did over Sitka: "The Sandwich Islands must be made a Russian West India and likewise a Gibraltar. Russia must have these islands at any cost!"

When the *Rurik*, a first-class brig sent by Tsar Alexander, appeared, all Schäffer's grandiose schemes seemed assured. Imagine his surprise when Capt. Otto von Kotzebue paid his respects to Kamehameha and in January 1817 disavowed all that Schäffer had done! A letter from Bara-

nov, carried by a Yankee trader, did the same. Schäffer was ordered to
Sitka at once to account for all he had done and spent. The doctor
ignored it all until March, when he returned to his fort from lovely
Hanalei to find the Russian flag struck and the warehouse raided. A
crowd of angry Kauaians forced Schäffer on to the *Kadiak* and drove him
from shore. What had happened was that as soon as Kotzebue disavowed
Schäffer, his Yankee competitors spread a rumor of war between Russia
and the United States and warned that an American fleet was en route
to slaughter every Hawaiian found supporting the enemy. Schäffer was
finished, but the *Kadiak* leaked and lacked provisions. So he and the
Russians and Aleuts aboard had no choice but to limp into Honolulu
and plead for help. It came in the form of Capt. Isaiah Lewis, an American whom the good doctor, in happier days, once had cured.

Lewis took Schäffer to Macao, whence he made his way back to
Europe. He first had the nerve to confront the Russian-American direc-
torate and demand that his losses be covered. He then lit out for Brazil,
took the title Count von Frankenthal, and lived in comfort until 1836.
His adventure cost the Russian-American Company 230,000 rubles and
any chance of making a commercial breakthrough in the Hawaiian
Islands. It also cost Baranov his credibility.

Perhaps it should have. The expedition was ill-conceived from the
start and suggests that Baranov, at long last, was losing his judgment. At
least, that is the way St. Petersburg saw it. Kotzebue served the Tsar
well when he disavowed the Russian protectorate over Kauai. Such an
outpost could never be maintained against the will of Kamehameha and
his British and American patrons, even if the Tsar were willing to risk
poisoning relations with all parties. So instead of erasing the damage
first done by Hagemeister, Schäffer magnified it tenfold. Still, we can
understand why those men dreamed the dreams they did. Just imagine:
a *Russian* colony on Kauai, the green and gracious Garden Isle, turned
into a plantation for the feeding of all Russian bases from Okhotsk to
New Archangel, and a monopoly of the sandalwood trade, judged by
Schäffer to be worth more than all the furs of America. But in fact no
part of Hawaii could be held without control of the sea lanes. And that
was something a backward, poor land power like Russia could never
achieve.

In November 1817 Hagemeister returned to Sitka with firm and final
orders from the Company: Baranov must go. But Hagemeister did not let
on as he quietly interrogated the colonists in hopes of turning up scandal. His second-in-command complicated matters by falling in love with
Baranov's half-Aleut daughter. So Hagemeister dissimulated some more
until Baranov had blessed and celebrated the union. Then he struck. All
furs must be removed from the warehouse to his ship; he would sail in

three days. What! asked Baranov, why was he not informed? Because, said Hagemeister, he was no longer Manager of the Russian-American Company—and must turn over all his books and accounts within twelve hours.

Baranov retreated, sobbing, to his quarters, and lay sick for the rest of the year while his own son-in-law redid old sums looking for evidence of graft. Not only did his books reveal no shortages, they proved that Baranov had given away most of his own earnings and shares to family, friends, and charities. Still, Hagemeister sailed in December to take Baranov back to Russia and refused him even the pleasure of seeing Hawaii en route. Nor would he ever see Russia. In April 1819, on the island of Java, Baranov died at age seventy-one.

"I cannot look upon this man without a certain respect," wrote Lieutenant Davydov in 1802,

> a man who has devoted his life to improving conditions in the field of trade ... surrounded by constant danger, struggling with the innate immorality of the local Russians, with endless work, faced by all the basic needs including hunger itself.... He seems to have been completely unaided, left on his own to seek his own survival and that of the institutions in America. All these tasks, obstacles, sorrows, needs, and failures have not weakened this splendid man's spirit, although they have naturally darkened his outlook a little.... It is not easy to know him well, but he will do anything for his friends. He loves to entertain foreigners, sharing everything he has, and always gladly helps the poor.... Even those living far away sometimes travel specially to see him, and they wonder that such great deeds should be accomplished by so small a man.

And Davydov knew only the half of it.

Washington City 1819

ONE BALMY BALTIC day in 1810 John Quincy Adams met the Tsar upon the quay along the river Neva. "I hear you have lately made an acquisition," said Alexander I. "I suppose you mean in Florida," the U.S. minister replied, referring to a strip of Gulf Coast in present-day Louisiana. "That is what I mean. But it appears to have been a spontaneous movement of the people themselves, who were desirous of joining themselves to the United States."

"So it appears from the accounts I've seen," replied the cautious Adams, "but I have no communication from my Government on the subject. . . . the people of that country have been left in a sort of abandonment by Spain, and must naturally be desirous of being annexed to the United States." The Tsar made a slight, crisp bow to the bespectacled agent of republicanism, and parted, with a hint of a smirk: "One keeps on growing bit by bit in this world."

Doubtless the Tsar recognized in the United States an empire akin to his own, one that would grow, bit by bit, until it *reached* his own somewhere on the Pacific. But the United States in 1810 in fact combined the strongest features of both Russia and Great Britain. Like the former, it was a continental polity with a huge open frontier—but without Russia's dangerous neighbors. Like the latter, it was a commercial nation cradled on the Atlantic Coast—but without Britain's European worries or insularity. What was more, Americans' relative freedom from proximate threats allowed them to make do with a small army and navy, a small central government and tax burden. Of course, natural advantages must still be exploited by people, but there, too, the United States possessed enormous strength. Its population was explosive, loyal, and self-motivated. Between 1700 and 1750 it doubled; between 1750 and 1800 it tripled; between 1800 and 1850 it quadrupled, to 24 million persons. The population in 1810—about 7.2 million—was already larger than that of Mexico and dwarfed Canada's eight hundred thousand. Given that the vast majority of Americans lived on the land and moved about as they willed, and that the votes of rural folk dominated politics, their government could not be other than expansionist.

We think of Manifest Destiny as a craze of the 1830s and 1840s, and certainly its articulation reached a crescendo at that time. But Jefferson stated virtually the whole case for it as early as the 1790s, and his torch-bearers in the next generation included people as otherwise incompatible as Andrew Jackson, the frontier rapscallion, and John Quincy Adams, the Puritan schooled at Harvard. It was Adams who wrote in 1812 of a "nation, coextensive with the North American continent, destined by God and nature to be the most populous and powerful people ever combined under one social compact." Jefferson had feared that Westerners might fashion their own republic across the Mississippi, but as it happened, their loyalty was not seriously in doubt *so long as* the federal government satisfied their needs for expansion, defense, removal of Indians, and internal improvements such as canals, roads, and levees. Even Frenchmen and Spaniards in Louisiana found cause to affirm their new citizenship. "I have suffered enough in person and property under a different government," wrote the St. Louis fur trader Manuel Lisa, "to know how to appreciate the one under which I now live." The loyalty of the people to American institutions was a national asset as mighty as their growing numbers.

Prospects for a new westward drive improved considerably after the final overthrow of Napoleon in 1815. The Bourbons returned to Spain, but Latin America was in rebellion, commanding the attention of what ships and soldiers still took their orders from Madrid. That made derelicts of Florida and Texas, and eroded Spain's leverage when it came to defining the boundary of the Louisiana Purchase. The man who inherited the futile task of defending Bourbon claims in Washington City was Luís de Onís y Gonzáles. To Americans he seemed almost a caricature of the Spanish grandee—proud, stubborn, devious, shifty, and royalist to the core. But Onís's haughtiness was well calculated. He realized that the American dream was to fix their southern border at the Rio Grande and thence westward to the Pacific, stealing Texas, New Mexico, and California from Spain: "This project will seem delirium to any rational person, but it certainly exists." And the man's only weapons were propaganda, procrastination, and the hope that Spain might find allies in its task of containing the Yankees.

Florida was the most pressing issue, since Indians, runaway slaves, and pirates raided American settlements and shipping from the refuge it provided. Americans argued that if Spain were unable to police Florida, it should turn it over to the United States. Madrid understood and in fact instructed Onís in 1817 to relinquish Florida if in return the United States would fix its boundary at the Mississippi River, thereby returning the entire Louisiana Purchase to Spain! This was an opening salvo, but Onís evidently expected to sucker the hayseed Americans into a settlement that bore little relation to the actual balance of power.

Now, Americans preferred to imagine that the ends and means of their foreign policy were high-minded by comparison to those of the duplicitous Old World monarchies. Europeans returned the favor either by underestimating American statesmen or disparaging their self-righteousness. The truth (it seems obvious in retrospect) is that the officials charged with formulating and executing U.S. foreign policy combined a belief in the purity of their goals with a shrewdness in their pursuit worthy of Talleyrand or Metternich. Never was the country so well served as by Franklin, Jefferson, Jay, Livingston, and John Quincy Adams. Son of the second President, Adams was reared, somewhat against his will, for politics and public service. His first devotion was to God—he began each morning by reading four or five chapters of the Bible—and his second was to his family. Those in turn supported his third devotion—statecraft. By the time of Monroe's election in 1816, Adams had already seen duty in the capitals of the Netherlands, Prussia, Russia, and Britain, and at the Ghent peace conference. Though a New Englander, he was the Virginian Monroe's obvious choice for Secretary of State and he sailed back from England determined to keep the peace but equally determined to assert American rights. Western expansionists would especially be watching for any sign of weakness from this last great Federalist.

Give up the Louisiana Purchase? Adams did not bother to acknowledge Onís's suggestion. Nor would he discuss his request that the United States refrain from recognizing the Latin American republics. This was no easy decision. American opinion cheered the Latin American revolutionaries and preferred to think they were following the example of 1776. But to recognize their independence at once might provoke war with the restored Bourbons of Spain and France. To delay too long, however, would encourage South Americans to look instead to Britain for political and economic support. As for the border dispute, Adams offered to take Florida off Spain's hands and accept a boundary between the United States and Mexico drawn along the Colorado River of Texas, then north to the source of the Missouri River, and from there to the Pacific Ocean. Onís protested that that would rob Spain of all its claims to the Northwest coast! True enough, Adams replied, but Britain and Russia had claims there as strong as Spain's, and so did the United States. Onís then suspended negotiations and secretly urged his government to send a naval force to the Columbia River. Madrid, in a flush of wishful thinking, so ordered the Viceroy in Mexico City, who quietly forgot about it. His Pacific "navy" consisted of one dilapidated brigantine. Onís also implored his government to seek British help in thwarting American expansion.

Britain's position was crucial indeed in light of scandalous doings in Florida. It seemed that Andrew Jackson, hero of the War of 1812, had exceeded his instructions to suppress the hostile Red Stick tribe and pursued them, in 1818, into Florida. In the course of things he also captured the small Spanish garrisons at St. Marks and Pensacola, and he tried and hanged two *British* subjects suspected of arming the Indians. Monroe was furious, but such was Jackson's popularity that Congress voted down, to the roars of the gallery, four resolutions condemning his actions. The President restored the forts and left it to Adams to handle the fallout. He did so masterfully in a lengthy note to the Spanish government that he then leaked to the press. Rather than try to defend Jackson, Adams indicted Spanish rule, described the mutilations of American men, women, and children by Indians skulking in Florida, and concluded with a demand that Spain either impose civil authority there or cede the province. Onís tried to rebut Adams in a series of pamphlets over the signature *Verus* (Truth-teller), but to no avail. When the British Parliament's own inquiry later found the two British subjects most probably guilty of arming the Seminoles, Adams was justified. This, plus the fact that Britain's economic interest lay in supporting Latin American independence, outweighed British concerns over U.S. expansion.

The Spaniards then looked to France. But while French Minister Hyde de Neuville condemned Jackson as a backwoods Napoleon, he would not risk war in defense of someone else's lost cause. And by the time Onís returned to the bargaining table in July 1818, Adams had upped his demands. Leaning over John Melish's recent (but inaccurate) map of North America, the Yankee and Spaniard haggled over rivers and latitudes, Adams gradually retreating in Texas in return for larger slices of the Northwest. Finally he lost his patience and delivered a final offer: the United States would stop at the Sabine River, leaving to Spain all of Texas, but insisted on a border of 41° to the Pacific. If Spain did *not* accept, well, then let there be no border at all! Onís was trapped. No clear boundary from the Missouri River to the Pacific meant no quarantine against mountain men, fur companies, coastal traders, even settlers. Meanwhile, Congress was itching to authorize a seizure of Florida if Spain did not relent. So Madrid just told poor Onís to do the best he could. It turned out to be 42° north. "It was near one in the morning," wrote Adams of February 22, 1819, "when I closed the day with ejaculations of fervent gratitude to the Giver of all Good. It was, perhaps, the most important day of my life. . . . The acknowledgement of a definite line of boundary to the South Sea forms a great *epocha* in our history."

John Quincy Adams was said to be a cold fish and an exact, unbending lawyer, while the Adams-Onís treaty has been called the greatest American diplomatic triumph. Neither reputation is entirely justified. Adams's chill was public and calculated, and his exactness did not save him from two blunders—misstating a river and misdating a clause limiting the validity of Spanish land grants. Far from being unbending, he compromised right down to the end (at Monroe's behest) and considered it humiliating. Finally, the treaty, while certainly a triumph, was not much more favorable than might be expected, given Spain's desperate weakness. No, Adams's great and personal contributions were in his nobility of aims—the extension of American law and liberty without war—and ignobility of means—the propaganda broadside devoid of even a twinge of regret over the enormities committed by Jackson. Let us say that to believe oneself the creature of a "superintending Providence" is a useful psychological habit for a statesman to cultivate.

Under the terms of the Transcontinental Treaty of 1819, Spain gave up Florida in return for the United States' dropping $5 million in damage claims and renouncing all title to Texas. Most important, the treaty drew a boundary between New Spain and the United States that ran from the Gulf of Mexico north along the Sabine River and east along the Red River, zigzagged north and west into present-day Wyoming, then extended due west to the Pacific along the forty-second parallel. That Adams-Onís line would later become part of the borders of the future states of Louisiana, Texas, Oklahoma, Utah, Nevada, Idaho, California, and Oregon. The Senate saw a good thing and approved the treaty unanimously in forty-eight hours. The only argument against it, made by the redoubtable Henry Clay, was that Adams had not gotten Texas, too.

Even now Ferdinand VII put off ratifying the treaty in anticipation of a final, furious counterrevolution in Latin America. But a mutiny in the ranks of the Spanish expeditionary force in 1820, followed by revolution at home, put an end to the story that had begun with Columbus. Except for Cuba, Puerto Rico, and a few smaller islands, Spain's American empire ceased to exist. And *that* made orphans of Texas and California. They were part of the new Mexican Republic, to be sure, and Mexico was quick to claim the American promise to respect the Adams-Onís frontier. But flat, arid Texas was nearly empty. So the Spanish Governor's last folly was to *invite* a Connecticut drifter named Moses Austin to lead colonists there, asking in return that they convert to Roman Catholicism and swear allegiance to the King of Spain. The Mexican government's first folly was to confirm the arrangement and transfer the land grants to Moses's son Stephen. The idea was that land-hungry Americans would steal across the Sabine River anyway, and this way they might at least become Mexican citizens. That was the idea.

California was another orphan, not only because it was remote and sparsely populated, but because the *californios* were decidedly unhappy about independence. The political culture of "the last *entrada*" was formed, after all, by priests, royal governors and soldiers, and favored rancheros, all of whom despised the antiroyalist, anticlerical revolutionaries to the south. So it was a wistful band in Monterey that lowered the flag of Spain in favor of Mexico's eagle and snake on red, white, and green. And in years to come *californios* prevented Mexico City from exercising control by the simple expedient of rioting whenever a new governor made himself obnoxious and chasing him out of the province. California was a vacuum inside a fragile glass bottle called the Adams-Onís Treaty.

That left Oregon. The United States did not acquire the Northwest coast in the treaty of 1819; it merely assumed Spain's *claims* to lands north of 42°. But those claims reinforced the American case and removed the threat of Anglo-Spanish collaboration, while Anglo-Russian collaboration was unlikely, given their imperial rivalries elsewhere. Tsar Alexander understood as well as Adams how much the Yankees' leverage had increased, and he was determined to make the first move.

St. Petersburg 1821

BE IT DECREED THAT: ... The whole of the north-west coast of America, beginning from the Bering Straits to the 51° of northern latitude, also from the Aleutian Islands to the eastern coast of Siberia, as well as along the Kurile islands ... is exclusively granted to Russian subjects. ... It is therefore prohibited to all foreign vessels not only to land on the coasts and islands belonging to Russia as stated above, but also, to approach them within less than 100 Italian miles [about 30 leagues or 92 English miles]. The transgressor's vessel is subject to confiscation along with the whole cargo.

(Signed) Alexander I.

This extraordinary ukase of September 1821 was the first sign of Russian alarm over the rise of the precocious United States, and a sign that Alexander understood, however many his distractions elsewhere, the stakes involved in the North Pacific. He had come to the throne in the midst of the Napoleonic Wars, led Russia to victory after the invasion of 1812, led all Europe back to monarchical legitimacy at the Congress of Vienna, inspired the Holy Alliance, and crusaded against revolutions wherever they arose. He had little time for the Pacific or for sea power generally and allowed the Russian Navy to decay once again. Admiral Vasilii Golovnin summed it up: "If rotten, poorly equipped vessels, aged, ailing, and ignorant admirals, inexperienced officers, and peasants masquerading as sailors can make a navy, then we have one." But in fairness to the Tsar, the Russian Army had first claim on resources, Russia was bereft of the expertise needed to stay abreast of naval technology, Russia was rural and lacked the commercial elite, merchant marine, and fishing industry needed to raise up skilled sailors, and finally, Russia was virtually landlocked.

These handicaps meant that the Russian-American Company's monopoly in Alaska was always a bit of a charade, however many capital ships the Tsar might dispatch on flashy circumnavigations. When foreigners resumed their poaching of furs and selling of guns to the Tlingits after 1815, Golovnin even warned that American captains would soon tire of the fiction of Russian control and simply seize Alaska for the United States. That was why he recommended, and the Company approved, bold action to assert Russia's rights. The result was the Tsar's ukase, which declared the entire North Pacific littoral a *mare clausum*, or "closed sea," from the Kuriles all the way around to just north of Vancouver Island. Six weeks later, Alexander rechartered the Russian-American Company for another twenty years, affirmed its monopoly, ordered the new manager at Sitka to enforce an embargo against all foreign ships, and promised to send him three additional warships.

> *Old Neptune one morning was seen on the rocks,*
> *Shedding tears by the pailful, and tearing his locks;*
> *He cried, a* Land Lubber *has stole, on this day,*
> *Full four thousand miles of my ocean away;*
> *He swallows the* earth, *(he exclaimed with emotion),*
> *And then, to quench appetite, slap goes the* ocean;
> *Brother Jove must look out for his skies, let me tell ye,*
> *Or the Russian will bury them all in his belly.*

Were the Russians bluffing, as this American bit of doggerel implied? Or did they really mean to treat all U.S. ships in their waters as pirates and seize the coast down to 51° north latitude? The administration of James Monroe dared not tolerate the Tsar's pretensions inasmuch as an expansionist lobby in Congress was beating the drums for annexation of the entire Pacific Coast. Senator Thomas Hart Benton of Missouri (who owed his election to Astor's campaign contributions) and Congressman John Floyd of Virginia (a friend of William Clark) sponsored a bill to authorize occupation of the Columbia River in advance of the British and Russians, "whose forts, magazines, towns, cities, and trade, seem to arise . . . as if by magic." So fierce was the campaign that Russian minister Pierre de Poletica pronounced himself amazed by the intensity of American feeling.

That intensity derived in part from the Panic of 1819, which reduced the cash available to U.S. merchants and made them even more dependent on the furs of the Northwest if they were to continue to trade in China. Floyd cried that the Northwest's potential exceeded "the hopes even of avarice itself," denounced John Quincy Adams for a weakling, and demanded that cannon be sent to the Columbia. Boston merchant

William Sturgis called for the United States to defend its rights up to 60°
north (including Sitka!) and build a fort on the Juan de Fuca Strait. He
considered the Tsar's ukase "little short of an actual declaration of hostilities."

It added up to a classic strategic triangle. Russia, Britain, and the
Unites States had overlapping claims, so whenever one made an aggressive move the other two were invited to make common cause. The agitation for *American* forts and cannon in lands claimed also by Britain
prompted the British minister in Washington to lodge a protest of his
own. Stratford Canning (George Canning's choleric and callow cousin)
hated what he considered his unworthy task of "keeping the schoolboy
Yankees quiet," and he asked Adams bluntly if the United States
intended to annex Canada as well. "Keep what is yours," replied Adams
coldly, "but leave the rest of the continent to us."

As we know, Adams was as firmly committed to acquisition of the
Pacific Coast as the congressional faction. He abhorred the pretended
restrictions on trade, believing that free trade among peoples contributed, more than anything else, to mutual "comfort and well-being."
But he saw no need to run risks and knew from his own experience that
the ukase eloquently expressed Russian weakness, not strength. His
note to Poletica rejected Russia's claims out of hand and advised the
Tsar to back down lest Americans be "molested in the prosecution of
their lawful commerce." The American minister in St. Petersburg,
Henry Middleton, was sterner still, blustering that unless the ukase
were repealed, war was inevitable.

So the Russians' bluff was called, and the three sloops sent by the
Tsar could now do little except provoke incidents. Foreign Minister
Nesselrode hardly needed a war halfway around the world, and Finance
Minister Guriev knew that attempts to enforce the ukase would burden
his treasury and ruin the commerce of Russian America. In July 1822
Guriev persuaded the Tsar to suspend interdiction of American ships
pending the outcome of a new embassy to the United States under
Baron Hendrik de Tuyll. But Adams refused to bargain with Tuyll when
he arrived in April 1823 and instead floated the idea of Anglo-American
cooperation to Stratford Canning. No good: Britain had already agreed to
negotiate in St. Petersburg about the border between Alaska and
Canada. So Adams gave Middleton powers to do the same lest a bilateral
Anglo-Russian accord leave the United States out in the cold. But what
terms should Middleton press for? Monroe's distinguished cabinet
debated that question and decided he should ask that the entire "Russian" coast be left open for trade and settlement for a period of years or
that he fix the southern limit of Russian America at 55° latitude. He
was certainly not to admit the tsarist ukase as a basis for negotiation.

In private, Adams went further. He spent several days poring over books on Captain Cook, the Russian explorations, Mackenzie, and Lewis and Clark, and he expressed his conclusions, in no uncertain terms, to an inquiring senator: "I do not see that the 100 Italian miles of close sea will form a stubborn knot in the negotiation. But what right has Russia to *any* colonial footing on the *continent* of North America? Has she any that we are bound to recognize? And is it not time for the American *Nations* to inform the sovereigns of Europe, that the American continents are no longer open to the settlement of new European colonies?" It was the first official enunciation of the principle to be made famous by the Monroe Doctrine.

It was also a pronunciamento every bit as arrogant as the Russian ukase! How was the young and weak American nation to police the entire Western Hemisphere, from Spain's rebellious South American colonies to the remote coast south of Alaska, and make good its defiance of every European great power with an interest in the Americas? The answer clearly was "nohow." As Adams wrote in his journal, "I find proof enough to put down the Russian argument, but how shall we answer the Russian cannon?" There was one military force on the globe capable of enforcing Adams's noncolonization doctrine, and that was the Royal Navy. Of course, the Americans might well enlist the British in their effort to contain the Russians—they, too, had an interest in bottling up the Tsar. But how then could the United States prevent the *British* from asserting colonial claims of their own in the Americas, whether on the Northwest coast or in vulnerable Spanish islands like Cuba and Puerto Rico? That was the question Adams pondered at his summer residence in Quincy, Massachusetts, when spectacular news arrived from London. It seemed that Prime Minister George Canning, hat and teacup in hand, had approached Richard Rush, the U.S. minister, asking for *American* help to forestall new European colonization! Canning followed up with a plan by which Britain and the United States would jointly warn Spain not to attempt reconquest of its Latin American empire and, at the same time, renounce possession of any portion of Spain's Empire for themselves. The flabbergasted Rush pleaded incompetence and sent for instructions. President Monroe then consulted his illustrious predecessors, Jefferson and Madison, each of whom urged acceptance of the proposition. Then he convened the cabinet.

The problem is to explain what happened next. Monroe, an amiable but impressionable man concerned mostly with avoiding any blunders that might harm his reputation, was inclined to accept the offer. But he had to wonder whether Canning was trying to dupe the Americans with that clause about renouncing possession of any portion of Spain's Empire. The United States might well wish someday to raise a claim to

Texas or Cuba, for instance. Yet Calhoun, the South Carolinian expansionist, curiously favored making the joint declaration even if it *did*
mean foreswearing future acquisitions, while Adams, the supposed
Anglophile, cautioned against the United States "[coming] in as a cock-
boat in the wake of the British man-of-war" and suspected that Canning's flattery was nothing more than a British move to contain the
United States in the New World, not Spain and its Holy Alliance partners. On the other hand, Adams reasoned, a noncolonization declaration
might indeed be effective if made *unilaterally* by the United States as an
effort, not to contain the King of Spain in Latin America, but precisely
to contain Britain *and* Russia on the Northwest coast!

In other words, the emerging doctrine we identify with Monroe was
at least as much a Pacific phenomenon as an Atlantic one and directed
in part against the very state that first proposed it: Britain. Nor was the
doctrine borne exclusively of foreign policy considerations, for Monroe's
cabinet members fashioned their otherwise uncharacteristic opinions
with one eye, at least, on the presidential election of 1824. The race to
succeed Monroe was a five-way scramble among Adams the Northerner,
Calhoun the Southerner, Crawford the heir to the Virginia dynasty, and
the Westerners Clay and Jackson. It was likely that none would receive
a majority in the electoral college; therefore, none could prevail without
reaching across sectional and philosophical lines to their rivals' supporters. It thus made *domestic* political sense for Calhoun to contradict his
image as a war hawk and seek to appease Britain, and it made sense for
the New Englander Adams to take a tough line.

While Monroe's cabinet debated its reponse, Canning went behind
the Americans' backs to extract a promise from the French Ambassador—the "Polignac memorandum" of October 9—not to support any
attempt by Spain to restore its Empire in the New World. He then kept
Rush in the dark until November 24, so it was mid-December before the
U.S. government learned that there was no danger of a royalist invasion
of Latin America after all. But in the meantime Monroe was at his wit's
end. "He'll recover from this in a few days," wrote Adams, and he did.
Monroe went on to deliver the presidential message drafted by Adams
on the basis of his memorandum to Russian Ambassador Tuyll, his
instructions to Middleton in St. Petersburg, his instructions to Rush
concerning Canning's proposal, and a warning he had planned to make
to the French—all "parts of a combined system of policy and adapted to
each other."

That speech, which came to be known thirty years later as the Monroe Doctrine, gave notice that the Western Hemisphere was henceforth
to be off-limits to new European colonization, that the United States did
not intend to interfere in the politics of monarchical Europe and

expected those powers not to seek to extend their system of government to the Americas, that any attempt to oppress the independent states of America would be considered an unfriendly act by the United States, and that the United States would oppose any attempt to transfer existing American colonies from one sovereignty to another. Monroe got his wish for historical stature—he is remembered more for this speech than anything else. Adams got his wish—the speech appeased the expansionist faction and established his credentials as a national candidate. But Europeans thought Monroe's message the squawk of a gamecock arrogating to himself the whole New World barnyard without the least right or power to back it up.

Indeed, Canning was so nonplussed by the unilateral U.S. declaration that he ordered his Ambassador in St. Petersburg to break off cooperation with his American counterpart and negotiate independently with the Russians on the boundaries in Northwest America. Adams was unruffled. He did not want to have to compromise with Britain anyway. As for the Russians, the Company manager at Sitka had learned by now how much he *needed* American ships to carry supplies and furs. He even wrote St. Petersburg threatening to disregard the ukase himself if it were not rescinded. So instead of ordering American captains arrested in Alaskan waters, the Tsar talked terms with Middleton. The result was the Russo-American treaty of April 1824, under which American sailors were permitted to navigate and trade freely in the coastal waters of Russian America for a period of ten years. Moreover, it fixed the southern boundary of Russian America at 54° 40′ north latitude. And while the Americans agreed to a prohibition on the sale of spirits, arms, and powder to Indians, the treaty forbade the Russians to detain any vessels suspected of violating the ban! What it meant was that in Alaska, as in Oregon, Americans had bought time to increase their commercial presence and settle the coast in advance of their competitors. And if commerce and settlement, rather than war, were to determine which nation eventually triumphed, Adams figured that the Americans could not lose.

The Russo-American treaty of 1824 was not a result of the Monroe Doctrine per se. But it applied the principles conceived by Adams and enunciated by Monroe to the Pacific coast. Russia was blocked from further expansion and forbidden to transfer its existing possessions to any third party, for instance, the Hudson's Bay Company. One may ask why the Russians agreed to all this. One reason was to get the Americans to recognize that everything *north* of 54° 40′ was indisputably Russian. Another was that the Russian-American Company had had to suspend dividends during the years of the ukase and was pleased to return to business as usual. Finally, the eyes of official Russia turned inward in search of surreptitious liberal and Masonic plots within the nobility, and indeed when Alexander died in 1825 even Russia had a taste of political revolt. But however much an accommodation with the Americans seemed like a good idea at the time, the treaty of 1824 nevertheless presaged the end of Russia's career in North America altogether. For now the Russians were blocked for good from Oregon and California as they had previously been blocked from the Amur, Japan, and Hawaii. All their efforts to reach and settle warmer lands had failed. St. Petersburg was not yet ready to admit that Russian America was a geopolitical orphan. But that was all right. The Americans could afford to be patient.

So it was two down—Spain and Russia—and one to go on the so-called Oregon coast that stretched from California to Sitka. It remained to be seen whether the "one to go" would be Britain or the United States. For however mighty and growing the American population and commerce, the Brits still had their navy and land power as well. In 1821, the Northwest Fur Company merged with the Hudson's Bay Company to form a continental conglomerate determined to build a network of posts all the way to the Columbia River. Its aim was the same as the Tsar's ukase: to drive all Americans out before it grew too late.

By the way, the 1824 election *was* thrown into the House of Representatives, where John Quincy Adams, who had finished second in the balloting, was elected sixth President of the United States over a justifiably furious Andrew Jackson. . . .

Honolulu 1825

IN 1818 A young Hawaiian died in Cornwall, Connecticut, with a prayer that the Christian gospel might soon be carried to his native islands. In Andover, Massachusetts, two graduating seminarians wrestled with their urge to answer that call. And in Boston, the American Board of Commissioners for Foreign Missions debated whether deploying scarce resources in the Sandwich Islands was, in fact, the will of God. Revival was in season again in New England, prompted by the atheism of the French Revolution and the shocking appointment of a Unitarian to the chair of theology at Harvard. But this time zeal expressed itself in the form of overseas missions. Cook and Vancouver had impressed on Protestant divines the image of thousands of darkling pagans, and the London Missionary Society, founded in 1795, financed an expedition to Tahiti. But it turned down a proposal for the Sandwich Islands. We can only imagine how the *political* history of Hawaii might have differed if Anglicans or Methodists had been the ones to remake the Hawaiian soul.

Instead, American Calvinists did the job. It began in 1809 when a youngster from the Kona Coast named Opukahaia ran away to sea on a Yankee trader. His parents had made the mistake of opposing Kamehameha and been speared before their son's eyes. Stranded in New Haven, Opukahaia wandered on to the Yale campus and begged for instruction. The Rev. E. W. Dwight took him into his household, bathed, dressed, and fed him, and taught him English. The Rev. Samuel J. Mills then arranged for Opukahaia to attend the newly formed school at Cornwall. Call it indoctrination or the fruit of love in action, but Opukahaia was soon a prize convert. He prayed and preached, translated Genesis, and was at work on a Hawaiian primer when he caught typhus. "My poor countrymen," he wrote, "who are yet living in the region and shadow of death, without knowledge of the true God. . . . May the Lord

Jesus dwell in my heart, and prepare me to go and spend the remaining part of my life with them. But not my will, O Lord, but thy will be done."

The American Board of Foreign Missions already had Hawaii in its sights. Opukahaia's perfect death forced its hand. In the summer of 1819 the Board allocated funds, hired a ship, and searched for other Hawaiian converts. Four were found, including none other than "George Sandwich," son of King Kaumualii of Kauai. The company mustered a farmer with his wife and five children, a printer, two teachers, a doctor, and two ordinands—Asa Thurston and Hiram Bingham—from Andover. Of course, the godly band dared not go among the tempting heathen alone (only the farmer was married), so the Board obligated them to find wives within eight weeks or stay home. A flurry of newly kindled or rekindled courtships ensued and no doubt some tense parlor scenes as parents learned of the suitors' intentions for their daughters. Yet all were betrothed, and "kits, cats, sacks, and wives" the party numbered twenty-three. It was also considered unseemly to oblige white women to live in grass huts. So a Boston firm donated the materials for a clapboard New England cottage. Still, for every such patron who admired the missionaries, there were ten scoffers who thought them "foolish or fanatical." How sad for them, thought Bingham, but to him the world's scorn was his own validation.

The Board's instructions revealed all that civilization meant to an early nineteenth-century Protestant. The ministers were sent to preach the gospel, but why had a printer been sent, and a farmer and doctor and wives? Because agriculture bestowed plenty *and* taught self-reliance; because medicine bestowed health *and* taught charity toward one's neighbor; because reading made accessible the Bible *and* all other tools of social progress; because family life bestowed health and virtue, *and* taught love and forbearance. Critics later accused the missionaries of terrifying the Hawaiians with preachments on sin and hellfire, making them sick and miserable. That was not their intention. To them, God's law was given in love to make people happy, and if they were not happy it was because they chose not to be.

Thus, the missionaries went forth to make a social, economic, and political revolution through the medium of evangelization. They were told not to become involved in politics, but how could one change any other important aspect of the people's lives without playing politics? For without a modicum of political freedom, the savages might not be *permitted* by their chiefs to learn religion. Without private property, they could never learn charity. And without education, even Christianity would be superstition to them. So the missionaries were instructed:

to aim at nothing short of covering those islands with fruitful fields and pleasant dwellings, and schools and churches; of raising up the whole people to an elevated state of Christian civilization...; to make them acquainted with letters; to give them the Bible with skill to read it; to turn them from their barbarous courses and habits; to introduce ... among them, the arts and institutions and usages of civilization and society.

And yet, Hawaiian paganism was not the missionaries' main enemy. Their main enemy was bound to be other white men, mostly American merchants and sailors, for whom Hawaiians were placed on earth to provide cheap labor or sexual receptacles for the randy offscouring of New England waterfronts.

Which is not to deny that the missionaries themselves were young, self-righteous Congregationalists prepared to interpret all they saw as the work of Satan's hand. They defined themselves as soldiers confident that "the whole armor of Christ" would shield them from their enemies. And if soldiers, then their self-appointed captain was Hiram Bingham. This thirty-one-year-old graduate of Middlebury College might have excelled in any profession he chose, such were his good looks, trenchant tone, and forceful personality. His eyes and bushy black eyebrows exuded will, and though his colleagues sometimes grumbled, Bingham established himself as the mission's leader not long after it sailed from Boston, on board the *Thaddeus*, in October 1819. They could not know that the revolution they dared to imagine had already begun.

Kamehameha the Great held to the old ways to the end and insisted that his subjects at least make a pretense of doing so, too. But forty-three years had passed since the coming of white men, and the *kapu* system, while still a sturdy prop for the monarchy, came under pressure as a religious system. The power, wealth, and knowledge of the *haoles* were enough to suggest that Hawaiian ways were, at most, of local relevance. Moreover, thousands of whites broke *kapu* wantonly and constantly, while Hawaiians under their influence did also. Those foolish or unlucky enough to be caught might be ritually strangled or clubbed, but at the hands of the *kāhuna*, not their silent gods. Perhaps the most stringent solvent of Hawaiian religion was the assertiveness displayed by women. They had, for obvious reasons, access to Western ships and prized Western goods. Women increasingly dared to eat with men and taste delicacies previously denied them. And their leader was none other than the King's favorite wife, Kaahumanu.

She, almost alone among her people, never walked in awe of Kamahemeha. She loved him, she feared his temper, but she just refused to stay put. Kaahumanu would run away for weeks at a time, find lovers willing to defy the *kapu* placed on *her*, and drink, gorge, and debauch on board Western ships. At the same time her big, round eyes and quizzical mind missed nothing, be it the customs and tools of the *haoles* or the political undercurrents in Kamehameha's kingdom. Someday he would die, and as to what would happen then—well, she kept her counsel to herself and a few well-placed, like-minded *alii*.

Kamehameha, now about seventy, fell fatally sick at Kailua/Kona near his own place of origin. The *kāhuna* tried their cures and called for human sacrifice (which the King forbade). A doctor was rushed down from Honolulu, but this time all ministrations proved vain. The Napoleon of the Pacific slipped away on May 8, 1819. Would Hawaiian unity survive him, or would rival *alii* toss the islands back into civil war? If so, would that give foreign powers the opportunity or excuse to colonize the islands? For all his native and acquired guile, Kamehameha had prepared badly for death. He never uttered a clear will and what he did communicate threatened to replicate the disastrous situation left by Kalaniopuu in 1782: he bequeathed his kingdom to one heir, the vacillating twenty-two-year-old Liholiho, and his personal war god to another, the ambitious warrior Kekuaokalani.

Kaahumanu may have seen the danger coming but still had to do some quick thinking when Kamehameha died with no one there but her. She emerged from the royal tent, looked at Liholiho from her queenly height, and pronounced what she purported to be the King's dying wish: "Here are the chiefs, here are the people of your ancestors, here are your lands. But we two shall rule over the land!" So Liholiho would be King, indeed he would be known as Kamehameha II, but Kaahumanu herself would rule with him as *kuhina nui*, coregent. The *kāhuna* then boiled the dead king's remains, buried the bones in secret lest their *mana* fall into unfriendly hands, and spirited Liholiho away lest he be defiled by the place of death. That left Kaahumanu in charge. How did she get away with it? Perhaps because other chiefs knew that a coregency really was Kamehameha's will. Or perhaps Kaahumanu had purchased their loyalty in advance. (One of the new regime's first acts was to abolish the royal sandalwood monopoly on behalf of local chiefs.) In any case, Kaahumanu's junta consisting of herself, Liholiho's supporters, the queen mother, Prime Minister Kalanimoku, and the chief *kāhuna* carried the day, while "war god" heir Kekuaokalani nursed his bitterness across the island.

Kaahumanu commenced at once the second phase of her coup d'état. Month after month she besieged Liholiho with envoys urging him to return to Kailua, assemble the chiefs, and declare *ai noa*—free eating. That would mean the abolition of the *kapu* system, which in turn would undermine much of Hawaiian religion. But the political implications were far from clear. Abolishing *kapu* might prove to be a popular act, but if conservatism held sway among the common people, then

Kekuaokalani would have just the weapon he needed to raise a revolt against the young King. It was not at all obvious that the prestige of the monarchy alone would sustain it in the absence of *kapu* and Kamehameha both. No wonder Liholiho remained paralyzed (and drunk) for months, until his own *kahuna* declared his unbelief. Let the old gods die, he advised.

So Liholiho allowed himself to be rowed into Kailua in November 1819 for the feast Kaahumanu desired. At first the sexes ate separately according to custom. Then the King rose, circled the tables in evident anxiety, suddenly sat down with the women, and conspicuously gorged himself. The *luau* sat stunned—then all clapped and shouted, "*Ai noa!* The *kapu* is broken!" Kaahumanu had to act swiftly, and, like Elijah purging the priests of Baal, she sent word to all the islands that the stone and wooden idols and temples must be pulled down. For the most part, the Hawaiian people celebrated their liberation, although sentiment for the cults, especially that of the volcano goddess Pele, lingered for decades. Kekuaokalani nevertheless marshaled an army out of motives religious or purely political and denounced Liholiho. But in the climactic battle of Kuamoo in December, Kekuaokalani and his wife were slain. So Kamehameha's realm survived, Liholiho reigning in tandem with Kaahumanu, and the islands no longer had an official religion.

The Hawaiian-born missionaries on board the *Thaddeus* were the first to spy their holy mountain—like a great shade on the western horizon—in the night of March 30, 1820. Then, by a yellow dawn, the white men and women awoke to share "a more impressive view of the stupendous pyramidal Mauna Kea, having a base of some thirty miles, and a height of nearly three miles. Its several terminal peaks rise so near each other, as scarcely to be distinguished at a distance. These, resting on the shoulders of this vast Atlas of the Pacific, prove their great elevation by having their bases environed with ice, and their summits covered with snow, in this tropical region, and heighten the grandeur of the scene." From the rail of the *Thaddeus* Hiram Bingham and his fellow New Englanders gazed upon "verdant hills, and deep ravines, the habitations of the islanders, the rising columns of smoke, the streams, cascades, trees, and vestiges of volcanic agency: then, with glasses, stretching our vision, we descried the objects of our solicitude, moving along the shore—immortal beings, purchased with redeeming blood, and here and there, the monuments of their superstition. Animated with the novel and changing scene, we longed to spring on shore, to shake hands with the people, and commence our work by telling them of the great salvation by Jesus Christ."

The missionaries' landing party at Kohala on the Big Island learned the amazing news of Kamehameha's death and the abolition of *kapu*.

"Nor could a doubt remain," wrote Bingham, "that he who created the light, and perfectly adapted to its properties the organization of the eye, had caused the movements in the two distant countries of Hawaii and the United States of America, to correspond for a benevolent end." After hymns of ardent thanksgiving, the mission went ashore to survey a panorama less comely to Puritan eyes: "The appearance of destitution, degradation, and barbarism, among the chattering and almost naked savages . . . was appalling. Some of our number, with gushing tears, turned away from the spectacle. . . . Can such beings be civilized? Can they be Christianized?" *Yes*, Bingham trumpeted, for had not Isaiah prophesied, "He shall not fail or be discouraged till he have set judgment in the earth, and *the isles shall wait for his law*"?

The Hawaiian people numbered about 130,000 in Bingham's estimate, a testimony to the demographic swath cut by Western diseases, Kamehameha's wars, and the widespread practice of infanticide. But they were not yet challenged in their dominion by immigrants or imperial powers. And the missionaries arrived, not as Americans, but as "ambassadors of the King of Heaven." The first two to greet them were a brother of Kaahumanu and the island's Governor, John Young. He did not say "How do you do?" to his fellow Caucasians, but "Aloha," and he warned that six months might pass before Liholiho, Kaahumanu, and the chiefs would reach a decision about whether to allow them to stay. The King in particular was troubled by the fondness white men showed for Oahu; he feared Americans aimed to take over that island. But Bingham dispensed gifts and assurances that they had no political aims, and after only twelve days he received permission to abide on probation. Asa Thurston would remain at Kailua to found the first mission while Bingham moved on to plant a second at Honolulu and a third on Kauai, where George Sandwich was reunited with his father, King Kaumualii. God, it seemed, was making straight their way.

In fact, the flotsam and jetsam of pagan survivals cluttered each step of their way. The *kapu* system might be dead, but "lewdness" lived on in the hula, polygamy, fornication, adultery, prostitution, incest, and drunkenness. How could a people so sensual be moved by a religion of "Thou shalt nots"? Should the missionaries take the gospel to the downtrodden and encourage them to resist their own pagan rulers? Or should they try to convert the chiefs and expect the rest to follow? When Liholiho and Kaahumanu moved their court to Honolulu, the latter ploy was irresistible.

Two years after Kamehameha's death the joint rule of Liholiho and Kaahumanu was secure but strained. The King was still a wastrel and wanderer unable to stay in one place for more than a few weeks. Kaahumanu still partook of her pleasures but was constrained by age and responsibility. The major chiefs, all tied by blood to her or the dynasty, remained loyal with the possible exception of Boki, the headstrong Governor of Oahu, and Kaumualii, the King of Kauai. In fact, within months of his son's return, Kaumualii (who dressed in a lavish velvet waistcoat and great golden watch chain) allowed the missionaries to open a school, and he made enough progress himself to write Bingham "a few lines to you to thank you for the good book you was so kind as to send by my son. I think it is a good book, one that God gave us to read." The coregents, fearing another Kauaian dalliance with foreigners, brought Kaumualii to Honolulu and placed him under virtual house arrest. Kaahumanu then married both him and, for good measure, one of his sons, thus merging the Kauaian royal family with that of Kamehameha.

The mission suffered another setback on the Big Island. The doctor and his wife took the first ship home, one of the Hawaiian evangelists succumbed to drink, and local resistance to Christianity forced the Reverend. Mr. Thurston to close down his mission for two years. But Bingham persevered on Oahu, holding Sabbath services and raising the first church (a thatched hut fifty-four feet long) in the summer of 1821. He also founded schools to teach English, while the missionaries transliterated the Hawaiian language and began printing primers and tracts. Bingham thought Hawaiian poetry and rhythms well suited to short "ascriptions of praise and adoration." Still, his services attracted only a few dozen gawkers more fixed on the curious skin, clothes, and behavior of the white women than the preacher's message. A few of the chiefs showed interest in *malamala* (writing), but Liholiho and Kaahumanu did not. Wrote Bingham:

> She was nearly fifty years of age. She was tall and portly . . . had black hair, a swarthy complexion, a dark, commanding eye, a deliberate enunciation, a dignified and measured step, an air of superiority, and a heathen queen-like hauteur; yet, sometimes, a full-length portrait of her dignity might have presented her stretched out prostrate on the same floor on which a large, black, pet hog was allowed, unmolested, to walk or lie and grunt, for the annoyance or amusement of the inmates. She would amuse herself for hours at cards, or in trimming and stringing the bright, yellow nuts of the Pandanus, for odiferous necklaces or rude coronets, listen to vile songs and foolish stories, and sometimes make interesting inquiries.

Kaahumanu was a wizard at cards and checkers. But she refused to look at a page of writing and deigned to offer the missionaries "her little finger" in lieu of a handshake. Bingham suspected that pride prevented her from admitting the importance of anything she could not do. His wife, Sybil, had to contend with the obvious disdain of the regent, yet sewed one dress after another for her in hopes of winning her favor. Yet Bing-

ham also observed how she went about the island destroying idols, and
he yearned to enlist her influence. In December 1821, Kaahumanu was
sick even unto "the borders of the grave," and Sybil nursed and prayed
over her. Once restored, however, she resumed her air of indifference.
"How can they believe the humbling doctrines of Christ who receive
honor one of another?"

So the Binghams waited patiently. They would call on Kaahumanu
and wait, sometimes for hours, for the Queen to look up from her
amusements. Then finally, one day in August 1822, Kaahumanu
deigned to accept a proffered pack of alphabet cards. For ten minutes she
shuffled through them and repeated—as the Binghams' hearts
pounded—"*a,e,i,o,u; a,e,i,o,u,*" and then: "*Ua loaa iau!*"—I've got it"!
With a boastful grin directed at her ladies-in-waiting, she accepted a
book from the Binghams, promised to learn *malamala*, and agreed to
attend services the next day. All at once the Binghams needed a new
church to hold the masses who now answered their bell. When reinforcements arrived from New Haven the following spring, the Hawaiian
mission was ready to soar.

Kaahumanu and her retinue were not yet Christian. They had only
begun to read, which the missionaries made a prerequisite even for pos-
tulant status. The only major figure that showed early signs of conversion was the Queen Mother, Keopuolani, who died in 1823 charging her
son to "obey God's word, that you may prosper and meet me in
heaven." But Liholiho preferred the company of sailors and beachcombers and more often than not could be found at Waikiki sleeping off
a binge beside his own pet pig and a nude wife or two cooling his brow
. . . until the autumn of 1823, when he decided to sail to England. "The
hearts of kings are deep," wrote Bingham, "and it is not easy to decide
what were the primary objects of this voyage." Perhaps he was bored, or
had got it in his head that George IV would send ships to expel the
killjoy Americans. For when Bingham urged him to include Boston on
his itinerary in order to see American morality at work, Liholiho
declined. The royal party sailed on the British whaler *L'Aigle* in November 1823. One other passenger talked his way aboard: a certain Jean
Rives. He, too, disliked the missionaries, and he coveted the islands for
France.

Liholiho's absence meant that Kaahumanu, and through her Hiram
Bingham, exercised total control. Within months decrees went forth
requiring Hawaiians to honor the Sabbath and abstain from gambling,
murder, theft, infanticide, and abortion. Kaahumanu progressed in her
studies to the point of taking an examination with the other adults and
children at school. She especially liked to memorize Scripture—not surprising given Hawaii's oral tradition—but could not understand why

Bingham denied her request for baptism. Indeed, the missionaries had so far baptized *no one* but George Sandwich, and he had fallen in with beachcombers after his father's removal to Oahu. That no doubt enhanced Bingham's determination to withhold baptism from Hawaiians pending proof of their capacity to comprehend what that step involved.

Kaumualii died in 1824. His own disgust with his wastrel son was such that he disinherited him and left his lands to Liholiho, in effect, giving up forever the old fight to maintain Kauai's autonomy. The Kauaian chiefs, egged on by George and his white cronies, staged a rebellion. What followed, under missionary inspiration, was a reenactment of Old Testament scenes: royalist chiefs praying for divine grace before battle, Kaahumanu declaring a fast, and—after victory was won—Hawaiian warriors bestowing mercy and pardon on the defeated rebels. Now Kaahumanu took to preaching herself and founding schools, but still Bingham refused to baptize her until she convinced him of her regeneration. She did, in March 1825, after learning that for King Liholiho, too, the wages of sin were death.

Liholiho's royal progress to the Court of St. James's was a shock and a farce to the British. George IV wanted no part of a reception to honor, as he put it, a "pair of damned cannibals," but he was spared the ordeal when the defenseless Hawaiians came down with measles soon after arriving. Within two months the King and his wife were dead. Foreign Secretary Canning judged that the wisest response to this unasked-for mess was to outfit a naval expedition under Lord George Byron to bear the remains home with full honors, and to appoint a consul, the merchant Richard Charlton, to ensure that Anglo-Hawaiian relations stayed friendly. So HMS *Blonde* sailed to Hawaii and gave the dead couple a grand Christian burial in June 1825. Before quitting the islands, Byron reaffirmed British goodwill and dedicated a monument to Cook at Kealakekua Bay. Consul Charlton then set up shop in Honolulu, having concluded already that Hawaii was "a feudal despotism" and that Americans had "engrossed" its trade. Soon he would have even worse to say.

For the following Sunday Kaahumanu, Prime Minister Kalanimoku, and a hundred other prominent Hawaiians presented themselves at the mission church, professed their faith in the Christian God, and asked to be baptized. They had to wait another six months as neophytes (and Kaahumanu had to sunder her polygamous and incestuous marriage to the Kauaian prince), but the great day arrived in December. The principal *alii* made their baptismal vows and bowed to Bingham's ministrations. Kaahumanu took the Christian name Elisabeta, after the barren woman who gave birth in old age to John the Baptist.

Hawaii was Bingham's, or, as he understood it, the Lord's. For

Liholiho's death made a King—Kamehameha III—of his ten-year-old brother, Kauikeaouli, and that made Kaahumanu sole regent. She took to the countryside herself to encourage Hawaiian pupils, and soon every major community had its own school. The printers labored on until, as an English visitor observed, "school-books and religious publications" might be seen "in every peasant's hut." Of course, Bingham was accused at once not only of playing politics but of turning the islands into a theocracy. In his defense it must be said that separation of church and state—or religious morality and civil law—was a concept alien to Hawaiians themselves. Kaahumanu had not abolished *kapu* because she had ceased to believe in moral laws but because she had ceased to believe the old laws were moral. Once convinced that the God of the Bible was real, that to obey his laws was salutary and to flaunt them fatal, she naturally used her authority to govern, as best she could, in their spirit. Nor were all her decrees aimed at personal morals. In 1826, Kaahumanu ordered that all sandalwood cutters, previously little more than slaves, might retain a portion of their produce as wages. For the first time, Hawaiian commoners reaped a reward from their own labor and began to learn the meaning of property, money, and the market.

So it was that all the suasion of the Hawaiian crown suddenly weighed in against nakedness, alcohol, crimes against persons and their property, and all violations of the Ten Commandments. (Kalanimoku was quick to observe that if people would honor the tenth commandment—thou shalt not covet—the other nine would be no problem.) Kaahumanu was especially rigid about adultery, taking care to enforce her edicts against *alii*, even Boki himself, and to levy a larger fine on *men* than on women, assuming them to be the seducers. Needless to say, the new laws aroused venomous hatred among white residents and visiting sailors who put in after months at sea only to learn that women and drink were *kapu*. When the first U.S. naval vessel to stop at Hawaii, the *Dolphin*, anchored off Honolulu, Capt. "Mad Jack" Percival found himself trapped between the appetites of his crew and the pieties of the missionaries. After a two-month standoff the sailors smashed all the church windows, pulled Bingham out of a service, and demanded women. "Put down your club if you wish me to talk with you," said Bingham. The sailor swung, a female *alii* deflected the blow, and the Hawaiian congregation drove the sailors away. But in the wake of this showdown Governor Boki resumed the traffic in women. He himself owned a dive in Honolulu where he sold booze, staged hulas, and pimped for the sailors. Henceforth, visiting crews learned the times and places where they could get what they wanted, preferring always the girls enrolled in the missionaries' own schools—they spoke some English and afforded a measure of prurient revenge. Spring and fall were the wildest times, when upwards of two hundred whaling ships stopped on their way to or from the Bering Sea.

In 1827 another form of resistance arrived. The mysterious Monsieur Rives had persuaded the French government of the value of Hawaii, and a party of Catholic missionaries under Alexis Bachelot came to contest for the islands. Bingham's people warned their congregations against the Catholics' "idolatry," wine, and brandy. Boki saved the French fathers from expulsion, but they made scant headway against the Protestant hegemony. Boki, meanwhile, grew more and more resentful of Kaahumanu. He drank to excess and shared his frustrations with American captains, the French Catholics, and British Consul Charlton. In 1829 he went so far as to plan a revolt, but Bingham, quite easily, talked him out of it. Poor Boki seemed incapable either of embracing the new reality or of mounting a serious challenge to it. And despite his considerable income, he borrowed heavily from his *haole* friends, then went further afield in search of money. In 1829, he sailed away with a private army to make himself king of a South Sea island said to be covered with sandalwood. One ship limped home in 1830, its crew decimated by malaria; the other, Boki's, was wrecked in the New Hebrides. The missionaries were quick to interpret his death as another divine judgment. Oahuans grieved for weeks.

Boki's destruction removed the final barrier to Kaahumanu's projects. At Bingham's urging she reaffirmed the morality laws and deported the French missionaries in 1831. But she now was over sixty, had given up carnality, put away her fancy dresses, and left her stone house for a modest hut. She took to visiting the sick and elderly among common people who might have been garroted for stepping on her shadow two decades before. Her health grew weak, and soon after celebrating the arrival of a fifth company of missionaries and a Hawaiian translation of the entire New Testament, she took to her bed for good in the restful valley of Manoa.

"Elisabeta, this perhaps is your departure," said Bingham. "We wish you to stay with us; that would be our joy; but we think the Lord will soon take you from us." In the wee hours of June 5, 1832, Kaahumanu opened her eyes for the last time and recited, in a voice once commanding but now barely audible: *"Eia no au, e Iesu, E, E nana oluolu mai."* [Lo, here am I, O Jesus, Grant me thy gracious smile.] Then the yellow sun arose from its liquid cradle far to the east, whence Bingham's brazen band first spied the islands on another dawn twelve years before.

The *kuhina nui* was dead and King Kauikeaouli, now eighteen, was of age. Under Boki's tutelage he had learned at least from puberty about drink, tobacco, gambling, and every sort of sexual union. He had, it was widely believed, slept with his sister for years. Now Kauikeaouli and his

ribald young protégés known as the Hulumanus let it be known by word
and example that Christian *kapu* was broken. The hula returned, alcohol and prostitution were legalized (the latter a state monopoly), and
drunken bands invaded schools to pressure the students to fornicate.
Many Hawaiians, perhaps a majority, followed their lead. Biblical law
was as yet a patina on traditional mores, and the missionaries had
attempted to banish the dress, dances, sports, and amusements that had
defined for centuries what it meant to be a happy, proud, or healthy
Hawaiian. Finally, it was Hawaiian tradition to mourn dead kings with
just such a season of freedom from *kapu*. It may be, therefore, that the
repressed Hawaiians were ready for a vacation from the dour regime of
the Calvinist *haoles*. Still, the teenage King was less a cultural hero
than a libertine and tyrant.

Kauikeaouli soon arrogated to himself all the prerogatives of pagan
Hawaiian kings. Private property was again abolished: all that Kamehameha the Great had owned was now to belong to him. Gradually the
chiefs recovered their nerve, reaffirmed the moral laws whenever the
King was absent, and waited for a chance to check him. Then, in June
1834, a messenger burst in on a doctor in Honolulu: the King had tried
to commit suicide when his sister refused his advances! By the time the
King recovered from his self-inflicted wounds, the Christian chiefs had
united in opposition. So Kauikeaouli gave up, retreated into sports and
idle amusements, and left the government to the new *kuhina nui*, his
Christian half-sister Kinau.

Kauikeaouli thus failed to undo the work of Bingham and Kaahumanu. And far from restoring absolutism, Kauikeaouli's pagan/royal
coup instead encouraged the missionaries to begin training the Hawaiians in the principles of limited, constitutional government. But the victory of the missionaries meant even more. For however lofty the Americans' motives, the British and French could not but view "the reign of
Hiram Bingham" as preliminary to a U.S. takeover of islands that Charlton described as the keys to the entire Pacific. A pagan Hawaii had
staved off foreign rule. Could a Christian Hawaii do as well?

The Fourth 'aha iki

Saitō: Why did you convert, Kaahumanu? A political move, right?

Seward: Rather a personal question, wouldn't you say, Saitō?

Saitō: Nothing about royalty is personal, and I bet Kaahumanu agrees.

Kaahumanu: A queen still has a soul of her own, Mr. Saitō. I converted because I believed.

Saitō: Sure. And why did you believe?

Scholar: Because Mrs. Bingham's prayers appeared to save her from death, while "sinners" like Boki and Liholiho were struck down. A logical conclusion under your circumstances. Anyway, you don't owe an explanation to—

Saitō: —the heathen Saitō? Surely not *all* the sick that Mrs. Bingham prayed over got well! And I'll wager even the old *kāhuna* had a few miraculous cures to boast of. No, it had to be politics.

Serra: Why not let the woman speak for herself?

Kaahumanu: Mahalo. Thank you. I converted because of sex.

Seward: Now that rings true! You were convicted of your sinfulness.

Kaahumanu: Sex is not sinful, sir, it is a gift from God. But it is the occasion for much that is sinful—the things we do to satisfy our wandering desires and the ways we exploit the desires of others. When I

heard the holy *palapala* about the pagans, and even Israelites who
worshipped idols of wood and stone and made their worship an
excuse to drink and dance naked and have whom they would, it
sounded so . . . familiar. And when the missionaries said that *all* men
and women partake of the *mana* of God, I understood that this was
true, *must* be true.

Serra: I thought you described her as proud, Brother Scholar.

Kaahumanu: I was very proud. I was even proud of being proud. But
Sybil Bingham was wrong to say that the pride of the chiefs was a barrier to conversion. It is easier, I think, to persuade the mighty that
their deeds are wicked than to persuade the weak that their thoughts
are wicked. Envy and resentment are perhaps greater barriers than
pride.

Scholar: But you were the one who abolished the *kapu.* How could
you turn around five years later and impose what one historian has
called "a new and more psychologically devastating set of prohibitions"?

Kaahumanu: Must Hawaii always be either a heaven or hell to you
haoles? Can you not see that even nudity and torchlights and feathers
do not reveal obsession with sex, but rather the lengths to which we
sometimes went just to summon the urge? Now the *white* women in
their modest dresses were mysterious, and I saw that our men
showed far more desire when the girls were clothed than when they
were not. Why do you think I loved Western clothing, even before the
missionaries came?

Saitō: "In olden days a glimpse of stocking was looked on as something shocking—now, heaven knows: Anything Goes!"

Seward: There he goes again.

Saitō: It's a sensual country where a mere flash of ankle can raise the
flagpole! Your Victorians understood, as do Japanese.

Scholar: But the point is that you suffered, especially as a woman,
under *kapu,* only to impose Calvinist taboos every bit as rigid.

Kaahumanu: I built schools and gave my people a choice they did not
have before.

Scholar: But you let your culture die!

Kaahumanu: The coming of Cook killed my culture. Our people liked what the *haoles* brought and wanted more. Unfortunately, the whites debased what we gave to them in return. The hula, for example, was not art to the *haoles*.

Scholar: But a striptease. Same with the luau, surfing, tapa cloth, big *kāhuna.* . . . So you're saying—

Kaahumanu: That my enemy was never my own people but the foreigners who corrupted them, used them, and infected them with disease. The Binghams were different. They taught us of a God who loved all people, Hawaiian and *haole.*

Saitō: Oh, please! As if your people could even *survive* Christianization!

Serra: There was a time when even *European* culture was not Christian, Mr. Saitō, and it may cease to be so again. But I must say to Elisabeta that while I bless your faith, I cannot bless Mr. Bingham and his laws. He did enslave your people as much as the old chiefs did.

Seward: Why Padre, what can you mean? Don't tell me *Catholics* are easygoing, while it's Protestants who peddle rules like Pharisees!

Scholar: To tell the truth, I always thought Catholics suffered from a double standard. When nuns and priests scold people for using birth control or missing mass, then Catholics are denounced as absurdly strict. But when adulterers or thieves receive absolution after mumbling to a priest inside a box, then Catholics are denounced as absurdly lax.

Serra: Son, it has always been so, because the sinner hates the forgiveness of God as much as he hates His laws. To the world, neither seems just. As for Hawaii, the Protestants did destroy the culture they found, where their job should have been to convert it. The *heiaus* could have been turned into churches, the seasonal feasts into saints' days, and their dress and diet left alone. Protestants preach justification by faith—and rightly so—but seem to place no faith in faith. And all those souls left unbaptized . . . a pity the French fathers were expelled.

Kaahumanu: They taught idolatry and sought to keep my people in ignorance. And they drank, just like the white beachcombers who made no pretense of religion at all.

Seward: Nothing in the Bible about being a teetotaler. Thank God.

Kaahumanu: I think it is *you* people who are obsessed with rules. What I learned was a religion of love. I know about love. Hear my poems.

Scholar: Kaahumanu, you don't have to prove anything.

Kaahumanu: You will hear my poems! This is one I composed for the death of my father:

My father and chief,
My beloved companion,
My loved one.
I am breathless with grieving for you,
I weep for my companion in the cold,
My companion of the chilly rain.
The chill encircles me,
The cold surrounds me,
Purple with cold not rejected,
Only two places to find warmth—
The bed mate at home,
The tapa covering is the second warmth,
Found in the bosom of a companion.
It is there, it is there, it is there.

Here is another:

Love to my mother who has gone,
Leaving me wandering on the mountainside.
You are the woman consumed by the wind,
Consumed by the trade wind,
Consumed, consumed, consumed with love.

Seward: Why, Father Serra, you're weeping.

Serra: Yes. I was thinking of Majorca, my parents. . . .

Kaahumanu: I also wrote songs for husbands and lovers. They all died. Some killed by Kamehameha, some dead in battle, and the last I had to put away, as you know. I knew much of love before the missionaries came, but my loves caused me pain and were never enough. Breaking *kapu* freed me of the old way between men and women, but I did not know the right way until I heard of the God who is the source of all love. For Him I could renounce my flirtations.

Scholar: You were also fifty-five years old by then.

Saitō: This is nonsense! If the Christian God is so loving, how do you explain the cruelty of Christians themselves, or the cruelty suffered by innocent people? Ha! Your insurance men call an earthquake an "act of God"—but your theologians *don't?* You give God all the credit and none of the blame!

Serra: I would say it is usually the other way 'round.

Kaahumanu: But God is just—

Seward: —by definition. What's just is God and what's godly is just. But let's come down to earth. Serra, I'd say your Counter-Reformation skirts are showing. If the Prots did tend to be legalistic about their behavior—a bit Baptist, we'd say in my time—it was in reaction to the decadence of the Catholic Church itself. Biggest spoils system outside of Albany. And the fact that the missionaries didn't go around baptizing thousands in the nearest creek has nothing to do with a lack of charity. Baptism without belief is empty. Perhaps the Yankee Puritans had a narrow aperture on an open-ended truth, but we mustn't reject the latter out of contempt for the former.

Serra: The Lord gave us a priesthood and told it to feed his lambs. He did not require all to become shepherds—

Witte: Thanks be to God that He spared Russia your Reformation! Why not just admit that religious obedience imposed by *man* is no obedience at all. Bingham was wrong to set himself up as the power behind the throne.

Kaahumanu: You speak wisely, sir. Sometimes a man from another island sees what one's own eyes cannot. But the scholar was right when he said I did not reject *kapu*, but only the old and bad ones. All people need *kapu* lest they swim like foolish children among the rocks . . . and drain the world of magic.

Scholar: Which reminds me, Kaahumanu, you never had a child. Is that why you married the Kauaian chiefs so late in life, and took the name Elisabeta?

Kaahumanu: I never stopped wanting a child, for personal *and* political reasons. But "it is written, rejoice, thou barren that bearest not; break forth and cry, thou that travailest not: for the desolate hath many more children than she which hath an husband."

Serra: Galatians.

Kaahumanu: My people became my children.

Saitō: 'Fess up, Old Girl, Bingham was a spellbinder, wasn't he?

Scholar: Right! Saitō, this time I've got *you.* Tell me, was Kaahumanu a . . . shrinking violet?

Saitō: Shrinking violet—good idiom, Doc! No, of course not.

Scholar: Was Kaahumanu the only person who could stand up to Kamehameha? And the shrewd and courageous revolutionary who seized the kingdom and then overthrew her entire religion?

Saitō: OK, I know the punch line.

Scholar: Do you really think it plausible that she of all people would fall under the "spell" of a *haole* with whom she could only imperfectly communicate, who came without armies, and who told her that everything she had ever done was evil?

Saitō: Point taken. And I suppose it didn't matter. If the chiefs and *kāhuna* and masses of people were so discontent with their own culture, then it was hardly worth trying to preserve. Now, Japan on the other hand—

Seward: "How oats peas beans and barley grows, nor you nor I—"

Witte: I beg to change the subject.

Saitō: Japanese culture, on the other hand—

Scholar: Wait. What were you just humming, Mr. Seward?

Seward: A child's rhyme. I learned it as a boy and heard it again years later in Scotland. "How oats peas beans and barley grows, nor you nor I nor anyone knows, how oats peas beans and barley grows."

Witte: May I change the subject? I want the scholar to tell us what difference Astor's failure made, since the United States won the right to occupy Oregon anyway. Another exciting tale that does not signify?

Seward: I would say rather that were it not for Mr. Astor, Quincy Adams would have carried a much thinner brief before the British bar. American claims to the Northwest coast hardly matched those established by Cook, Vancouver, and Mackenzie. And don't forget Nootka.

Witte: But remember our professor's quote from Castlereagh: that the Americans would win Oregon in the bedchambers of New England.

Seward: But only because Astor's boldness and Adams's deft diplomacy opened Oregon to Yankee settlement in the first place. Had the Hudson's Bay Company got there first, the U.S. might well have been "contained," as he put it.

Witte: But if it came to war, Americans must triumph on their own continent?

Seward: Not proven. In 1812 we took a licking. In any case, Adam's New Englanders did not want war. Did you know that the Hartford Convention in 1814–1815 considered seceding rather than going to war with Britain? 'Twas Napoleon that saved us in 1812—the Brits fought us with their little pinkie. Adams's genius, I believe, was in perceiving that in a world of open commerce and settlement the U.S. could not lose. In a world of monopolies and military frontiers, the U.S. could not win—or would cease to be a free country.

Scholar: So by negotiating regimes for free trade and settlement with Britain and Russia, he made the rules favorable to the peaceful expansion at which Americans excelled. In poker lingo, he was "betting on the come."

Witte: And Russians could only bluff monopolies and threats of force, because they could not compete in free settlements and business.

Seward: That is, ships and men.

Scholar: That is, sail and muscle.

Witte: Hence the Tsar's thunderous and vacuous ukase. Russia always thunders. But what the Tsar and Nesselrode overlooked was that another source of support for Alaska, another agricultural base, was available for taking the whole time. .

Scholar: You must mean—

Witte: The Amur basin. I shall listen closely when you come to talk of that. But I should also like to mention, regarding the "failure" of Russia in North Pacific, that we were first to pioneer the region, first to repent of cruel treatment of natives, first to establish law and order, and first to perceive the need for conservation of seals.

Scholar: I'm sure our ecologists will want to make icons of Shelikhov, and Rezanov.

Witte: I am serious, Doctor.

Scholar: So am I.

Serra: What became of Fort Ross after the Russo-American treaty?

Scholar: Witte, do you know the fate of Fort Ross?

Witte: It was abandoned, sold to an American, right?

Scholar: Right, but not before Kuskov's people made a real impression on northern California. Their numbers were small—perhaps two dozen Russians and a hundred Aleuts—and their efforts at agriculture and husbandry remained meager, but they left names on the land that survive to this day: Kuskov Bay, the Russian River, the town of Sebastopol, three Russian ranchos founded inland from Ross, and Mount St. Helena, the highest peak in Napa Valley. You might think all the Russians in Alaska would fight to get to California once a foothold was established, but the Company assigned only enough people there to seal the Farallon Islands and man the fort. A visiting officer, Zavalashin by name, hoped to conspire with local Hispanics to declare California independent of Mexico and associate it with Russia. He wrote the Tsar in 1826 that colonization of California

would "allow us to keep there an observation fleet which would give
to Russia mastery over the Pacific and control over the trade with
China, consolidate our possession of the other colonies, and serve to
restrain the influence of the United States and England." In 1834 the
Governor of Russian America, Baron Ferdinand Wrangell, tried again,
urging that Fort Ross expand eastward and even purchase the missions of San Rafael and Sonoma. But in return the Mexicans
demanded Russian recognition of their revolutionary regime, something Tsar Nicholas refused to consider. The failure to expand the
Russian colony into more fertile valleys meant that Fort Ross was a
loser. The average annual cost of upkeep was about 45,000 rubles
compared with an income of fewer than 13,000 rubles. Given the
mentality of the Company's directors, it is not surprising that they
asked permission to liquidate the colony. So the land, fort, livestock,
and supplies went on the block in 1839. The first prospective buyer
was the grandest ranchero of Old California, General Vallejo of
Sonoma, but he wouldn't meet the Russians' terms. So the Russians
sold out to a Swiss American, John Sutter, for $30,000, and sailed for
New Archangel on January 1, 1842, never to return.

Saitō: There were Yankees in California by then?

Scholar: Yes. The Mexicans could hardly keep them out.

Saitō: But you said the whole point of the Adams-Onís Treaty—from
the Spanish point of view—was to put a limit on American penetration of Mexican lands.

Scholar: That I did. But boundaries are creations of governments, sort
of reciprocal "quit claims." They affect real people only insofar as
they are enforced. But Mexico was a sieve and its government a joke.
It couldn't stop illegal American immigration. Ironic, when you think
of it.

Witte: Why so?

Scholar: Because now the shoe's on the other foot.

Witte: I see. Another similarity between the United States and Russia: interiors of great continents are like oceans, and peoples like the
tides. You cannot partition an ocean.

Washington-on-the-Brazos
1836

To the casual student of European history the years between 1815 and 1848 are a breathing space, a stable but repressive era dominated by the Holy Alliance and characterized by relative peace and balance of power. To the casual student of American history the years between 1836 and 1860 are likewise a pause of sorts, characterized by nondescript Presidents, between the Jacksonian Era and the Civil War. But if we take instead a global perspective, we discover that the decade from 1836 to 1846 was one of decision in the North Pacific Ocean when the initial struggles for occupation and empire reached climaxes in Texas, California, Oregon, Hawaii, and China all at the same time. What had Texas to do with the Pacific? Texas was the key that unlocked California. Texas and California both were Hispanic provinces of tremendous potential with long sea coasts and huge interiors. Both were orphaned provinces of a decrepit Mexico, and both were independent republics before they joined the United States. They were twin sisters from the beginning.

Of course, the Mexican revolutionaries did not consider their republic decrepit. Yes, it had suffered terribly in the wars of independence. But there seemed no reason why Mexico should not now repeat the success of the United States to the north. But unlike the Anglo-Saxon colonies, which enjoyed an essential consensus based on English principles of limited government, the Mexicans struggled with two conflicting traditions: that of the monarchy, church, and colonial administration, still supported by the landowners, merchants, and clergy; and that of republicanism, anticlericalism, and centralization inspired by the French and Spanish Revolutions and the Freemasonry to which almost all intellectuals adhered. In between sat the *Liberales*—democratic federalists who promoted pluralism and local government and placed their faith in constitutions and the rule of law. Unfortunately, each grouping had to rely on the army to keep the others in check, and that tempted its posturing generals to play Napoleon. Augustín de Iturbide, self-proclaimed emperor, was the first of this breed. But he so bankrupted Mexico that a junta of Liberal generals overthrew him and sponsored the Constitution of 1824. And that was why Stephen F. Austin (also a Mason, which aided his cause) was content to take Mexican citizenship in return for the right to settle three hundred families in Texas.

They were only the first in a flood of Americans fleeing hard times after the Panic of 1819 and attracted by the offer of land at twelve cents an acre. Those "G.T.T." (Gone to Texas) soon acquired the reputation of being frontier ruffians armed with sixteen-inch bowie knives ("Arkansas toothpicks"). But most planted cotton, farmed, or ranched and made Texas a prosperous province. Needless to say, not all took seriously the condition that they become Catholic, swear fealty to Mexico, or refrain from using slave labor. Trouble began in 1827—the so-called Fredonian Revolt—and prompted the Mexican Congress to ban American immigration, proscribe slavery, and place a high tariff on American or British imports. Still the Anglos came.

Meanwhile, Jackson succeeded Adams as President in 1829, and the Mexicans assumed that Old Hickory would try to grab Texas. Twice he offered to purchase Texas (for $5 million), and twice the Mexicans turned him down. But in the meantime Mexico collapsed again into chaos born of bankruptcy, strife between the two main Masonic lodges, conflict between the states and central government, and the ambitions of rival generals. By 1833 Antonio López de Santa Anna emerged as the champion of the "little people," defeated his enemies, and made himself dictator. A worried Mexican commissioner reported to him in 1834 that Texas contained 24,700 inhabitants, of whom 4,000 were Mexican, 1,000 were slaves, and the rest were Protestant, frontier Americans devoted to self-rule and slavery and dependent on free trade with the outside world. When Santa Anna then set aside the Constitution of 1824 and determined to rule by fiat, the Texans skirmished with his garrisons (an echo of Lexington and Concord), threw out his customs officials (an echo of the Boston Tea Party), convened a General Consultation (an echo of the Continental Congress), and finally, in January 1836, declared themselves free and sovereign (an echo of Philadelphia).

It happened at the town of Washington-on-the-Brazos, "laid out in the woods; about a dozen wretched cabins or shanties...; not a decent house in it, and only one well defined street, which consists of an opening out of the woods. The stumps still standing. A rare place to hold a national convention in." In this rude setting the founding fathers drafted a constitution, named Sam Houston commander of the army, authorized agents to solicit foreign loans, and approved a liberal land law to attract more Americans. Thousands of volunteers responded, especially from Tennessee, and just four days after the declaration of independence, on March 6, Davy Crockett, William Travis, Jim Bowie, and two hundred comrades perished at the Alamo. On the nineteenth Santa Anna surrounded another Texan force at Goliad and, citing his new "piracy" law against "foreigners" on Mexican soil, ordered three hundred prisoners shot. Anglo families made a ragtag retreat in hopes of reaching the U.S. detachment sent by Jackson to guard the Sabine River frontier.

Then Santa Anna blundered. He could have pushed his tired but superior army ahead to destroy the only Texan force left in the field, or he could have unified his forces in a defensive position to rest. Instead, he both stopped *and* split his army, affording Sam Houston's gritty militia a chance to regroup, sneak up, and fall upon the weary Mexicans during their afternoon siesta. The Battle of San Jacinto of April 21 cost the Texans eight men killed. The Mexicans lost 630 killed and 730 captured, one of whom was Santa Anna himself. Every man in Texas was ready to lynch him, but interim President David G. Burnet realized that "Santa Anna *dead* is no more than Tom, Dick, or Harry *dead*, but living he may avail Texas much." So the Texans forced him to sign a truce, evacuate Texas north of the Rio Grande, and promise to recognize its independence. Of course, Santa Anna reneged as soon as he was safely home, but no matter: the Texans were confident that they would soon be annexed to the United States.

It wasn't that simple. Northern abolitionists quickly organized to block Texas statehood on the grounds that it would expand the empire of slavery and undoubtedly mean war with Mexico. John Quincy Adams, now the most prestigious *congressman* in history, beat the drum for peace. Even Jackson wavered, lest the United States seem too eager for "aggrandizement," and only recognized the Republic of Texas on his last day in office. But the Senate tabled one resolution for statehood, and Adams, in 1838, filibustered another to death.

So Texas was now a rebellious province in Mexican eyes, an independent country in American eyes, and a no man's land in European eyes. Texan Secretary of State J. Pinckney Henderson sailed to Europe in search of recognition, commerce, and investment for what London and Paris disparagingly called the "buckskin republic." British Foreign Secretary Lord Palmerston—a militant liberal, imperialist, and geopolitician—ached for Mexico to reform itself and play the role of bulwark against the bumptious expansionist Yankees. He therefore urged the Mexicans either to reconquer Texas or, if that were impossible, to recognize Texan independence so as not to provoke American intervention.

But neither did Palmerston dare to anger the United States. For in 1837 a sizable rebellion broke out in Canada, and disaffected Quebecers and Ontarians and their American sympathizers repeatedly violated the U.S.-Canadian border. (William Mackenzie, the rebel leader, made the Eagle Tavern in Buffalo his headquarters.) President Van Buren and the cool young Governor of New York, William Henry Seward, worked to minimize incidents, but the war scare did not wholly subside until the early 1840s.

Henderson had better luck in Paris, which was engaged in its own tussle with Mexico over damage done to French property in the Mexican civil wars. So Prime Minister Guizot sent an agent to Galveston, who recommended that although Texas was an abysmal place and its people crude beyond description, France would do well to recognize it. The result was a treaty of friendship and commerce in September 1839. French recognition especially pleased Mirabeau Bonaparte Lamar, the poet-adventurer and second Texan President. Once inaugurated at the new capital of Austin, Lamar devised an imperial plan under which Texas would invade and conquer New Mexico and even gain a Pacific outlet on the shores of the Sea of Cortés! Unfortunately, his 270-man invasion force (disguised as a trading party) misjudged the distance, emerged from the desert at Sante Fe on the verge of starvation, and willingly surrendered to the Mexican *commandante*. But Mexico's vaunted invasions of Texas in 1842 fared no better and the war remained a stalemate. Meanwhile, a second Texan envoy, General James Hamilton, sailed for England in 1840.

He had to wait a year, but by then the Canadian business was sorting itself out and English agents had reported on the potential of Texas as a cotton producer. Hamilton's memo of September 1841 added ten well-crafted reasons why Britain should recognize Texas, including the "powerful check which Texas is destined to hold over the action of the American Union in relation to [Canada]." This was especially clever, because what Hamilton *said* was that if the northern states take over Canada, the slave states would insist on Texas, too, to preserve the balance, knowing that Palmerston would read the reverse: that if the southern states should succeed in annexing Texas, the North would be moved to take over Canada! Therefore, Mr. Englishman, if you want to hold on to Canada, much less contain the expansionist United States, you had better recognize Texas and help to preserve it!

Palmerston and Hamilton proceeded to draft treaties, ratified in 1842, that provided for recognition, commerce, and abolition of the slave trade (though not slavery) in Texas. Lord Aberdeen, Palmerston's successor, then ordered the British minister, Richard Pakenham, to implore the

Mexican government to end its foolish war with Texas and help Britain turn Texas into a buffer shielding the *rest* of Mexico from Yankee expansion. The "rest" of Mexico meant California.

Since Mexican independence American explorers, fur trappers, and settlers had found their way to California, though in tiny numbers compared with Texas. The three thousand whites were themselves divided into a northern faction grouped around San Francisco Bay and Monterey, and a southern community based at Los Angeles. The rancheros and missions did a lively trade in hides ("California bank notes"), tallow, and supplies for visiting whalers. Mexico City understood the need to reinforce the province and tried to do so by confiscating mission lands in favor of Indians and immigrants. But the tergiversations of Mexican politics, the *californios'* penchant for expelling governors, and the greed of rancheros all defeated the purpose of secularization of the missions. The rancheros ended up with the land, while most of the Indians ended up as abused peons. The *padres*, thoroughly demoralized by now, predicted as much.

This was the remote and underpopulated province given over to comic opera politics and petty local tyrannies that inspired the legend of Zorro. The real-life champion of the people, however, was a Northern Californian, not a Southerner; an official, not a bandit; and a failure, not a success. Juan Bautista Alvarado led a rebellion in 1836 against the centralizing policies of Santa Anna (not to mention his removal of the provincial capital to hated Los Angeles). He did so in league with a Tennessee whiskey distiller named Isaac Graham and his thirty marksmen, who captured Monterey and proclaimed California free and sovereign. Mexico City pacified the situation by the simple expedient of naming Alvarado governor, and for five years he battled the rancheros in a campaign for social reform.

Meanwhile, the United States became aware of this intriguing coast through the yarns of Yankee sailors and trappers. In 1826 the incomparable Jedediah Smith, the Calvinist mountain man who eschewed drink, smoke, and profanity, led seventeen men from the Great Salt Lake country down the Colorado River across the Mojave Desert to San Gabriel Mission. In San Diego the Mexican Governor judged him a spy and ordered him out. Instead, Smith traveled north up the San Joaquin Valley and made the first crossing of the Sierra Nevada and Great Basin back to Utah. On a second journey he explored the California coast north into Oregon. James Ohio Pattie, another bold trapper, entered California from Sante Fe along de Anza's old route. He, too, was imprisoned as an illegal alien and died in San Diego.

But Mexican efforts to expel Americans were hit-and-miss, while American immigrants who took Mexican citizenship were within the law. One such, Thomas Larkin of Massachusetts, sailed for the Pacific, met and married a widow stranded in Hawaii, and settled at Monterey in 1832. Mrs. Larkin—Rachel Hobson Holmes—was the first female Californian of American descent. John Marsh, a self-styled medical doctor, followed in 1836 and used his fees—fifty head of cattle in serious cases—to build up the first great inland rancho (in Diablo Valley, south of the Sacramento River). Then, in 1839, Johann August Sutter arrived. A Swiss ne'er-do-well, he abandoned his wife and five children, sailed to America, and tried his luck in St. Louis, Santa Fe, Honolulu, Sitka, and Monterey before befriending Governor Alvarado and winning a huge land grant on the Sacramento and American rivers. Using borrowed money, forced Indian labor, and the Russian cannon acquired in his purchase of Fort Ross, Capt. John Sutter built the famous fort where scores of American wagon trains recovered after crossing the High Sierra. The first of these was the Bidwell-Bartleson party of 1841. It was then that Governor Alvarado began to wonder if he had erred in patronizing Graham's Tennesseeans and in permitting Americans to settle at all. Some of them, he heard, were already whispering of a "Texas solution."

Frustrated, fearful, and fed up with rancheros and gringos alike, Alvarado resigned. His successor, Gen. Manuel Michaeltoreno, arrived at Los Angeles with three hundred toughs masquerading as soldiers. They were all that was keeping California Mexican when, in September 1842, the commander of the new Pacific squadron of the U.S. Navy received an alarm in Callao, Peru, that he could not ignore. The American Consul at Mazatlán sent Comdr. Thomas ap Catesby Jones two news clippings: one, three months old, claimed that Mexico and the United States had gone to war; the other, six months old, claimed that Britain had secretly purchased California from Mexico. Just the day before, Jones had been shocked to learn that the British Pacific squadron had sailed from Chile and Peru under sealed orders. What option did he have but to race them to California? Of course, the British were *not* bound for there, and when Jones strained his eyes toward Monterey on October 18, all he spied was a handful of soldiers and a fort not even worth guarding. Still, he raised the Stars and Stripes above the presidio only to haul it down two days later, apologize to the inhabitants, and sail down to Los Angeles to explain his mistake to Michaeltoreno.

But the cat was out of the bag. American settlers had overrun Texas and seemed bent on doing the same in California. Jackson had tried to purchase Texas and likewise offered Santa Anna $5 million for San Francisco Bay. American "volunteers" had fought Santa Anna; now the U.S. Navy turned up at Monterey. And if the Jones affair revealed how easy it would be to take California, the return of Lt. Charles Wilkes, also in

1842, revealed how fruitful it would be. He had been at sea three years in command of the first U.S. Navy exploratory mission in the Pacific. It was a brilliant scientific enterprise that made important discoveries in the South Seas and Antarctic waters. But Wilkes also pronounced San Francisco one of the "finest ports in the world" and thought California would "perhaps in time form a state that is destined to control the destinies of the Pacific."

None of this was lost on the Mexicans or on the lonely agents of Britain. In 1840, Pakenham even submitted a formal proposal from Mexico City that Britain establish a colony in California and keep it out of the hands of any other power. At first, London snubbed him; how curious, Aberdeen must have thought, that his envoy recommended partition of the very country he was instructed to help strengthen! But Pakenham understood that Mexico would never reform, at least not in the critical time frame. He appointed a vice-consul to Monterey, James Forbes, who promptly reported the danger of an American takeover: "I feel myself in duty bound to use all my influence to prevent this fine country from falling into the hands of any other foreign power than that of England. I repeat that it is impossible for Mexico to hold California for a much longer period."

Aberdeen finally realized what Palmerston knew all along and in June 1844 struck out in all directions in hopes of blocking Yankee expansion. First, he ordered the British Consul at Galveston to encourage the Texans to remain independent. Second, he implored his new minister in Mexico City (Pakenham having been promoted to Washington) to convince Santa Anna to recognize Texas. Third, he instructed his ambassador in Paris to enlist the French in the defense of Mexican territory. Guizot was amenable: he shared Britain's concern. But the Texans remained coy, while the Mexicans remained stubbornly and stupidly defiant. You must make *peace* with Texas, the British minister told Santa Anna, for only then can Britain and France render their good offices to see that you get favorable terms and block U.S. intervention. No, said Santa Anna, he would never treat with the Texans. He despised Houston and the others who had humiliated him, and anti-Yankee sentiment was a source of his popularity.

So Aberdeen's strategy foundered because Mexico refused to be helped. Its belligerence and brutality were sure to force U.S. intervention sooner or later, and once engaged the Yankees were not likely to stop at annexing Texas. What was more, the British could not threaten the United States with force without risking a war in which they might well lose Canada. Nor—most frustrating of all—could they even protest. For as Pakenham explained, after the U.S. Senate voted down a treaty for the annexation of Texas in June 1844:

It is scarcely necessary for us to remark that, by the rejection of the late Treaty the question of the annexation of Texas must not be considered as disposed of. On the contrary it must be looked upon as the question which at this moment most engages the attention of the American People, and which will form one of the most prominent Subjects of agitation and excitement during the approaching election to the Presidency. . . . Now I believe, My Lord, that one thing which greatly contributed to the rejection of the late Treaty, was the absence of all interference, at least open interference, in opposition to it on the part of England and France. Any demonstration of resistance on the part of those Govts would, I think, have the very opposite effect to that intended, and would probably have led to the ratification of the Treaty instead of its rejection."

Pakenham knew his American hosts. Left to their own devices they just might paralyze themselves over slavery and leave Texas alone. The upcoming election would be a critical indicator. But let it once appear as if the British lion were trying to intimidate them, then Yankees and Southerners would rise as one man to take Texas and California, too. Aberdeen saw the wisdom of Pakenham's advice and called off his diplomatic offensive. All he could do now was to renew his plea that the Mexicans see common sense . . . and wait anxiously for the results of the American election of 1844.

Canton 1839

THE CHINESE CALLED it *po-pi*, the British poppy, and their naturalists *Papaver somniferum*. Luxuriant crimson growths covered the valley of the Ganges River in the hot months between winter's rains and the summer monsoon. That was when hundreds of laborers employed by the British East India Company looked for the falling petals that signaled the poppy seed pods were ready to harvest. They used special curved blades to lance the skin of the pod and draw off its milky fluid. The field hand caught it in the palm and deposited it in vats. Then it was poured into pallets to dry, pressed into balls, wrapped in leaves, and packed for shipping. The laboriousness begs disbelief: eight acres of flowers with perhaps 144,000 pods lanced to make a single 160-pound chest. Yet trains ran weekly in autumn to carry the cargo to port. It was worth everyone's while, because those brown gummy balls were pure opium.

The East India Company prudently left the carrying and smuggling trade to non-Company ships and merchants. They sailed from Calcutta to Canton, then hung back in the Pearl River estuaries and waited for Chinese wholesalers to come to them in their swift armored craft called "smug boats" by the Brits and "fast crabs" or "scrambling dragons" by the Chinese. In no time papers changed hands to prove that the Chinese had paid the firm in advance in Canton, the opium chests moved from the East Indiaman to the smug boat, and the fierce rivermen were off to a dozen distribution points on the mainland. Upon reaching an opium den in a Chinese city, the drug was rehydrated by slow boiling and stirring in copper pots. It could then be pressed out as flat as pastry and left to seep overnight. Once filtered, boiled, and stirred again, the mix assumed the consistency of porridge and was sold by the glob. The addict, reclining on a cot in a dim and vaporous cell, speared a precious bit on the end of a wire, heated the opium over a lamp, placed it in the pipe, and sucked the vapor into his lungs. "The process is not like tobacco smoking but is an efficient mode of introducing morphine into the system."

Into the system of a human being . . . and of a whole society. By 1838 some forty thousand chests were smuggled into China each year. The scourge enervated workers and intellectuals, corrupted officials, fed crime and moral decay, bled the economy, and made the Ch'ing (Manchu) Empire a patsy of vicious barbarians. The Tao-kuang Emperor felt the shame and knew the danger. The self-evident hierarchy and sense of obligation of a Confucian society could withstand any assault except one directed at the self-consciousness, wakefulness, and presence of mind of the people themselves. As one imperial censor rued: "Fathers would no longer be able to admonish their wives; masters would no longer be able to restrain their servants; and teachers would no longer be able to train their pupils. . . . It would mean the end of the life of the people and the destruction of the soul of the nation."

Some imperial officials took a pragmatic line. To enforce the ban on opium would require the government to exercise an intrusiveness bordering on tyranny; better just to legalize the trade. Then China could grow its own poppies, stop the drain on silver, and enrich the state by taxing the drug. But a moralist faction argued that legalization amounted to surrender and would only condone and encourage addiction. To them opium was "a flowing poison; that it leads to extravagant expenditure is a small evil, but as it utterly ruins the minds and morals of people, it is a dreadful calamity." Moralists called for strict punishment of dealers and addicts combined with a vigorous campaign against the smugglers. Both lines of reasoning had merit, and the Tao-kuang Emperor did not make up his mind until a third problem was addressed: how to treat, humanely but without compromise, the addicts themselves. Legalizers had no answer. One moralizer did. He was Lin Tse-hsü, a fifty-three-year-old provincial governor, intellectual, and poet, with a reputation for brilliance and incorruptibility that earned him the epithet "Lin the Blue Sky." In 1838 he proposed a comprehensive program: search out and destroy all drug paraphernalia; behead all domestic drug dealers; close down foreign smugglers by threatening to suspend legitimate trade; and set up sanatoriums to help addicts break the habit. If after a year's treatment they failed, then the addicts, too, would be put to death.

The Emperor summoned Lin to Peking, consulted for many days, then appointed him Imperial Commissioner with instructions to "sever the trunk from its roots." He was to avoid war with the foreign barbarians but to shut down the supply and demand for opium. Now, Lin was an ambitious official who expected his moral crusade to earn him a lucrative governorship. So he left for Canton in January 1839, a little drunk on virtue and power alike.

A Chinese proverb holds that the rhythm of time brings a minor disturbance to society every thirty years or so and major disorder every one hundred. A new dynasty might infuse an ancient society with new blood and new dedication to the norms and truths of Confucian civilization. Over time, however, bureaucracies and armies always grew tired, stagnant, or decadent, losing the will to meet challenges and serve the people. By the end of the eighteenth century Mandarin officialdom was again bloated and venal, the tax burden on the peasantry huge and arbitrary, the imperial treasury strapped owing to waste and corruption, and even the vaunted bannermen more interested in profiteering and entertainment than the military arts. Men of integrity and wit could still rise, and a new intellectual movement, of which Lin was an exemplar, reinterpreted Confucianism as a reformist rather than conservative ethic. Still, protest was dangerous, while the insecure Manchus never forgot that they were outsiders ruling many times their number of Chinese.

The natural decay of Ch'ing institutions might have taken longer to provoke a crisis but for two singular events: a fantastic growth in population and the collision with the liberal, industrial British Empire. The first trend was an ironic consequence of the success of Ch'ing policy after its pacification of China in the late seventeenth century. Irrigation, the opening of new lands to cultivation, the spread of sweet potatoes, maize, and peanuts in addition to rice, and the growth of cities enriched by the Western demand for tea, silk, and porcelain: all these encouraged a prodigious display of fertility. During the eighteenth century China's population doubled to over 300 million people and reached 430 million by 1850, resulting in overcrowding, a declining standard of living, and insecurity for everyone from peasants and pettifoggers to poets and bureaucrats.

How did nineteenth-century Chinese release their anxieties? One means was through secret societies. The other was through opium. In the south, where overpopulation was greatest and resentment of the Manchu strongest, the so-called Triads flourished—secret undergrounds like the Three Harmonies Society, the Three Dots Society, and the Heaven and Earth Society—whose lodges (t'ang, hence the Tong) drew laborers and petty officials into piracy, banditry, and drug dealing. Though busy for the most part with local feuds and profits, the secret societies also pressed a political agenda: "Overthrow the Ch'ing and restore the Ming." One movement, the White Lotus Rebellion, fielded an army of one hundred thousand men before its defeat in 1805. Hence, the Emperor had three reasons to destroy the opium trade: moral, economic, and political.

The Manchus had begun their rule refreshingly receptive to foreign trade. But the death of the great Emperor K'ang-hsi in 1723 brought an abrupt change. Commerce was strictly regulated, and Chinese were forbidden to emigrate. The court withdrew its favor toward Jesuits and ceased to gather intelligence about foreign things. By 1760, imperial decrees closed all Chinese ports to Europeans with the exception of Canton, where (like the Japanese at Nagasaki) they attempted to isolate their people from the "red barbarians." The fact that Europeans came and went as they pleased with ships and guns the Chinese could not match was surely embarrassing. But insofar as the barbarians understandably craved the products of Chinese civilization, the imperial government judged that it still might control them simply by threatening to terminate trade. Moreover, the Europeans' refusal to kowtow and send tribute could be got around by the simple expedient of substituting merchant-to-merchant relations for state-to-state relations. Thus, the Canton system was organized around two sets of authorized monopolies: the thirteen Hong firms on the Chinese side and the thirteen foreign warehouses on the docks of Canton. The Emperor forbade Europeans to leave these Barbarian Houses, bring firearms or women into Canton, learn Chinese, or have any dealings other than with the Hong.

Equally irritating to the foreign community were the restrictions under which the Hong labored. They were subject to a customs superintendent, or Hoppo, and he to the provincial governors, who suspected as a matter of course that the Hong merchants were in cahoots with the barbarians. So European traders faced a gauntlet of officials, each demanding some tariff, tip, or bribe in the pidgin lingo of the China coast: "Just now have settee counter. Alla finishee; you go, you please, chop-chop." Thus, Peking garnered tariff income from the Canton trade even as it fulfilled its primary goal, which was to keep all foreigners under surveillance.

The primary goal of the English was to satisfy their own addiction to tea. The leaf had yet to be planted in India or Java; hence China was the sole supplier for a British habit that reached thirty million pounds per year by 1830. Unfortunately, this resulted in a trade deficit with China of £700,000 per year that had to be paid for with silver. For the Chinese simply had little interest in buying anything made in Europe since, as one Briton put it, they already had the best food (rice) and clothing (silk) in the world. It was the search for something Chinese *would* buy that drove British and Americans to poach in the Alaskan seal and otter preserves and to pay Kamehameha to shave Hawaii of sandalwood. But those commodities played out by 1830. Something new and expensive was needed, and that something was opium. It gave the East India Company new life and accounted for most of the £4 million profit it realized each year in India. It also vastly expanded the "country trade" of private merchants plying the waters between India and China. Dominated by Scotsmen and the occasional Farsi or Jew, the country trade reached a volume three times that of official East India Company trade. Finally, sales of opium more than covered the cost of tea, sucking silver from the Chinese economy and spewing it into the Bank of England.

Nor were the Brits the only ones to profit, for merchants of other nations, especially the United States, did well merely on the leftovers. Philadelphians competed with special vigor for the China trade. (The "Bucks County chicken" was an offshoot of birds bought in Shanghai.) Tea drinking had become a genteel affectation in the United States as well, while American tariffs stimulated the merchant marine by making tea carried in foreign bottoms prohibitively expensive. Still, American shippers had to find products to sell in Canton. Since the firms of Boston and Salem dominated the Russian-American and Hawaiian trades, Philadelphians turned readily to opium, found an alternative source in Turkey, and used it to pay for over twenty million pounds of tea per year. The Yankees were happy to collaborate with the British on the China Coast. As John Latimer said: "We will not oppose you. Gain all you can, we are sure to come in for the benefits."

To gain "all you can" meant opening more of China than merely Canton. In 1793, Viscount (later Earl) Macartney went to Peking with a train of three thousand coolies and ninety wagons filled with gifts for the Emperor. His goals were to interest the Chinese in British industrial products, open an embassy in Peking, and get China to open more ports. But the Chinese politely refused his requests: "We possess all things. I set no value on objects strange or ingenious, and have no use for your country's manufactures." A second try came up empty in 1816 when Lord Amherst offended the Emperor, and by the time a third was made, a change of consequence occurred in the British camp: the East India Company's monopoly no longer existed. The free trade economics of the Manchester School condemned it, while the country traders based in India and new English factory owners yearned to gain full access to the China market. So Parliament declared in 1834 that all British subjects were now free to trade on an equal basis anywhere between the Cape of Good Hope and the Strait of Magellan. That meant that henceforth the Hong merchants and Hoppo would not be dealing with a private company but with a British consul representing all the subjects of Her Britannic Majesty. Such an agent had no choice but to demand diplomatic equality.

The first Chief Superintendant of Trade, Lord William Napier, was instructed to be conciliatory, but Canton's Governor-General turned him away. The Emperor did not treat with barbarians as equals. The arrogant Napier not only refused to leave but engaged in the ludicrous practice of distributing propaganda broadsheets to Canton's clerks and coolies as if they were workers in London's East End. So the Governor-General blockaded the Pearl River with sixty-eight war junks, and Napier (now dying of malaria) backed down. In so doing he set the stage for war. For the Chinese now concluded that the British were weak and hostage to their own need for trade, while the British concluded that next time they must back up their agent with force. What was more, the debate over how to combat opium now raged in Peking, and Canton's Governor-General anticipated the Emperor's will. In 1838 his war junks destroyed the entire fleet of "fast crabs" and had opium dealers and addicts strangled daily in public. British merchants sat on priceless chests they could not unload and hoped the Emperor would opt for legalization. Instead, on March 10, 1839, "Lin the Blue Sky" arrived in Canton.

Lin's first move was to write Queen Victoria two letters translated by the American medical missionary Peter Parker, and sent to England via every ship in port. "There appear," he wrote, "among the crowd of barbarians both good persons and bad, unevenly. Consequently, there are those who smuggle opium to seduce the Chinese people and so cause the spread of the poison to all provinces. . . . Let us ask, where is their conscience? . . . May you, O Queen, check your wicked and sift your vicious people before they come to China." In his second letter, Lin confided his "towering rage" and reminded the queen that people "who only care to profit themselves, and disregard their harm to others, are not tolerated by the laws of heaven and are unanimously hated by human beings." The Queen did not respond, while Palmerston was not one to hear sermons from a Chinaman.

So Lin ordered, in March 1839, that all foreigners be confined to the Thirteen Factories until they surrendered their cargoes of opium and signed a pledge, on pain of death, not to trade in opium again. The new British superintendent, Capt. Charles Elliot, was on the spot. He would not have his people sign anything under a death threat, but after six weeks he advised them to turn over their opium. The crown, he said, would reimburse them. Lin triumphantly flushed over twenty thousand chests into the harbor, while British merchants retreated to a defensible base on the barren island of Hong Kong.

Palmerston was livid that Elliot had committed the crown to pay for $4 million of forfeited opium. But that act also "nationalized" the issue: henceforth, the British government, not private subjects, assumed the claim against the Chinese government for wanton destruction of property and could thus properly resort to military force. Palmerston judged the time propitious "to place Britain's relations with China on a proper footing" and sent a fleet to Canton. The Tories tried to bring the cabinet down over the fiasco, young William Ewart Gladstone (not yet a Liberal) naming it "a war more unjust in its origin, a war more calculated to cover this country with permanent disgrace" than any he could imagine. But Palmerston claimed that the conflict was over free trade, not opium, and survived by five votes.

Meanwhile, legitimate merchants began to take stock. Why should all trade be suspended because of the opium smugglers? Some British and most American merchants were prepared to sign Lin's pledge, and in December 1839 two captains did just that. But as they sailed into Canton in hopes of resuming trade, the angry captain of HMS *Volage* fired across the bow of one of the merchantmen. War junks came gallantly to her aid, so the *Volage* fired on the Chinese as well. The Opium War, though not yet declared, had begun.

Palmerston's fleet, commanded by Adm. George Elliot (Charles's cousin), arrived off Canton in June 1840. His strategy was to ignore Canton's fortifications and strike northward at points of his choosing. The British effortlessly humiliated the Chinese Navy, and the scapegoat, predictably, was Commissioner Lin. He had been sent to extirpate opium smuggling. Instead, he had blundered into a disastrous war. "When I think of this," wrote the Emperor, "how angry I become! Let me see what explanation you have to make!" Lin's explanation was that while "these barbarians were terrified of our celestial majesty" at first, which is why they turned over their opium, they were now encouraged by the lack of resolve shown by *other* Chinese officials and the government's failure to take Lin's own recommendations regarding military defenses. This only "whet[ted] their dog-like appetites, making them more insatiable than they had been before." The frustrated Emperor called it "all nonsense" and banished Lin to Sinkiang, China's equivalent of Siberia. His replacement, Ch'i-san, tried to appease the British with a settlement concerning the destroyed opium. But Elliot demanded equal diplomatic status, the opening of Canton without restrictions, and the cession of Hong Kong. Ch'i-san refused. Elliot bombarded Canton's forts. Ch'i-san gave in.

Only it wasn't enough for Palmerston and was far too much for the Tao-kuang Emperor. The former lambasted Elliot for accepting the lowest possible terms, while the latter had Ch'i-san returned in chains for proposing to cede Chinese territory. The war continued, and the Ch'ing expected to win. First, they assumed that their bannermen were invincible. Second, they nurtured queer notions to the effect that Europeans lost their eyesight when deprived of tea and could not move their bowels without Chinese rhubarb. But even if those myths had been true, China stood no chance at all.

In early 1841, Elliot's fleet reduced the Chinese gun emplacements at the mouth of the Pearl River and trapped an army inside the walls of Canton. The battle featured HMS *Nemesis*, the first iron-hulled steamship in the Pacific. She was admittedly experimental, but her 120-horsepower engine moved the 184-foot-long ship smartly through the swells, winds, and currents of three oceans en route to China. Even more impressive, her flat bottom allowed her to slide over sandbars and estuaries thought to be impassable, and her iron bulkheads and water-tight compartments contained any damage done to the hull. At Canton the *Nemesis* sneaked through uncharted channels, transported marines, took boats in tow, reduced hilltop forts with her guns, and sank eleven junks with Congreve rockets (a weapon invented by the Chinese six hundred years before). Proud sailors turned up their noses at this over-grown paddleboat choking in her own smoke. But in decades to come such shallow-draft gunboats would steam up rivers a thousand miles inland, overawe Asians and Africans, and serve as the picklock of European imperialism.

The second action occurred one hundred miles south of Shanghai. An expeditionary force under Sir Hugh Gough captured the mouth of the Yangtze River, then put ashore in strength. The Emperor leaped at the chance for a ground campaign and dispatched an army over four times the size of Gough's. But most of it was composed of raw militia, and even the bannermen, with their matchlock muskets and immobile tactics, stood no chance against British flanking movements and firepower. The Chinese chose their moment to strike by astrology, sending their troops into battle after an all-night march through a driving rainstorm. So thousands of Chinese ran into the bullets and shot of British regulars firing from cover and in perfect discipline. Another Chinese attack faltered because the chief-of-staff was lying prone, far behind the lines, dazed by opium. Gough occupied Shanghai and besieged the fort guarding the intersection of the Yangtze and the Grand Canal. The defenders fought bravely, but once defeat was certain hundreds of them strangled or cut the throats of their wives and children and set themselves afire. A preindustrial force of whatever size could no longer stand against a competent Western army or navy. The age of sail and muscle was nearing its end.

The Emperor sued for peace in August 1842, and the Treaty of Nanking reflected Palmerston's *strict* instructions. China paid an indemnity of $21 million, abolished the Hong's monopoly, opened five treaty ports (Amoy, Foochow, Ningpo, and Shanghai, in addition to Canton), ceded Hong Kong to Britain, and limited itself to a low tariff on imports. The Opium War also quickened Americans' consciousness of China. Some condemned the drug-dealing British bully (John Quincy Adams did not; he approved of forcing the Chinese to join the modern world), but most just wanted in. Lieutenant Lawrence Kearny brought the first U.S. Navy squadron to Chinese waters in 1842, while Yankee merchants made windfall profits along the coast during the Chinese embargo of Britain. After the peace, Caleb Cushing obtained the first Sino-American treaty, in July 1844. His Treaty of Wanghia granted the United States "most favored nation" status, and thus all the rights enjoyed by Britain.

So China was open! And the implications for the North Pacific rolled like a tidal wave against the shores of Japan, Hawaii, California, and the Atlantic ports of the great naval powers. The Japanese, still clinging to *sakoku*, saw an Asian power greater than themselves humiliated and exposed, and they wondered how to prevent the same from befalling them. The Russians, peering south from Siberia, noted the disappearance of the Manchu genius for war and supply that had blocked them at Nerchinsk so long ago. The British saw another milch-cow as rich as India and helpless before the Royal Navy. The Americans figured that whatever China was—a market, a labor force, a missionary zone—it was certainly the biggest in the world. Britain was the early leader in the race to penetrate the Middle Kingdom, but what if the United States should become a Pacific power, perhaps annex Hawaii or California? That would change everything, and that depended on the outcome of the election of 1844.

Honolulu 1843

CAPTAIN ROBERT BEWS dropped into a longboat from the deck of his British whaler and pulled for the piers of Honolulu. He customarily put in at Lahaina, the whalers' port on Maui, for a reason most everyone knew. But this time, in the autumn of 1833, he checked into a Honolulu hotel, seabag in hand, signed his own name to the register, and made at once for the bar. A merry hour or two went by. Then two men stormed into the bar and damned Bews's impudence for daring to set foot on Oahu. The first was a "bully boy" armed with a club. The second was Her Britannic Majesty's Consul to the Sandwich and Society Islands, Richard Charlton. Bews reminded him of his sworn duty to *defend* the rights of Englishmen like himself, but Charlton, his face crimson and veins stiff with ire, shoved him down and threatened to break his skull if he didn't get the hell out. Bews retreated cursing, but upon his return to England he wrote to Lord Palmerston naming Charlton a "disgrace to his country," "grossly immoral," and deserving of immediate recall.

The life of Consul Charlton, the merchant too casually screened by the Foreign Office in the days after Liholiho's death from measles, reads like the script for a film. And it was thanks to his apoplexy that British influence in Hawaii tumbled steadily downward for two decades to the point where Hawaii was nearly annexed in turn by France, Britain, and the United States, all within the space of a few years. But it was not all Charlton's fault. In some cases he was justifiably angry at American arrogance, Hawaiian credulity, and the incomprehensible passivity of his own superiors in London. After all, he was there. He saw the growing American danger. He understood the strategic and commercial importance of the islands, and he reported it over and over again. Yet his government did nothing. That is the refrain of "Charlton's song."

The verses, on the other hand, are comic. It seems, for instance, that

Charlton first sailed for Hawaii accompanied by his wife, her sister Mrs. Taylor, and Mrs. Taylor's fugitive husband. When the ship sprang a leak and had to return to Plymouth, Mr. Taylor was apprehended and eventually transported to Australia. Charlton and the ladies then reembarked on Captain Bews's ship. Over the course of the passage south to Cape Horn, Bews took to playing cards in the ladies' cabin and became quite their chum. One dark night in the South Atlantic, the wind shifted. Bews heard the rigging protest, threw his watch coat over his longjohns, and went on deck. He noticed a candle burning in the ladies' sleeping quarters. Fearing fire, he silently entered, extinguished the flame, but then, in the blackness, brushed against Mrs. Charlton, who screamed. The next day she wished to forget the incident, but her sister threatened to press charges until Bews signed an apology, which Mrs. Taylor brandished as "proof" of his impure motives.

Charlton, needless to say, acted the outraged cuckold and warned Bews never to enter his presence again—hence the incident on Oahu. Charlton's own account, laboriously prepared for Palmerston, made Bews's story out to be a fabric of lies. The voyage was en route *to* London, Mrs. Taylor was *his* sister, not his wife's, Bews could not have seen the candle through the Venetian blinds, and he had no need to enter the curtained-off bedchamber either to extinguish the candle or to leave the cabin. "I am certain that Your Lordship would despise any man who put up with such an insult." As for his own alleged immorality, Charlton did not know what Bews had in mind except that he had attended "native dances" on Tahiti and Hawaii in performance of his duties, whereas everyone knew that *Bews's* wife had given birth before marriage. Who knows the truth? Was it really Mrs. *Taylor*, the grass widow of a convict, who had perhaps flirted with the captain during those long days at sea, and who turned on him after his blunder to cover her own complicity? Palmerston let the matter drop but noted his lack of confidence in Mr. Charlton in light of his "violent temper."

Charlton's original instructions enjoined him to counteract efforts by any other power to gain influence over Hawaii. And inasmuch as he arrived just as Bingham was converting the chiefs and American whalers were visiting by the hundreds, how could he not conclude that the Yankees were a threat? All the British had to show was the vague protectorate granted Vancouver by a king now dead, and even that seemed defunct in 1826 when the USS *Peacock*, under Thomas ap Catesby Jones, forced a treaty on the Hawaiians at gunpoint, obliging them to respect American notions of private property and contracts.

Charlton probably imagined that as Britain's Consul he would be the most powerful man on Hawaii. Instead, he was stuck in paradise with his wife and sister and found himself outside a power structure dominated by Kaahumanu and her missionary friends. As a result, he claimed, Englishmen could not get standing in court no matter what outrage they suffered, while the Hawaiians did whatever the Americans told them. When one of Charlton's cows was shot while trampling on a neighbor's crops, his demands for satisfaction went unheard. When his dog bit a *haole* woman, he considered his five-dollar fine insufferable. He protested mightily against the laws banning alcohol, fornication, and gambling, to no avail. When he interceded on behalf of the French priests, Kaahumanu herself wrote, "Be quiet you; this is our bussiness [*sic*] of me and the king." There was no point appealing to the Hawaiian authorities since all their correspondence was translated and drafted by the missionaries.

Charlton urged his government to encourage British merchants to invest in Hawaii and to send naval squadrons to support British rights. As it was, 90 percent of the whalers and merchants were Yankees who did not hide their hostility to the small British community. Demographic trends disturbed him even more, as he wrote in 1836: "The native population is rapidly decreasing partly owing to the oppression of the chiefs and partly to the abominable (but common) practice of destroying the Infant in the womb—the decrease has been much more rapid in the districts where the Natives have had little or no communication with Foreigners."

This demographic decline is one of the most emotional issues in Hawaiian history. Some historians blame the *haoles*, in particular the missionaries, for so demoralizing the people that they just wasted away. Contemporaries were more apt to note that the Christian communities were the only ones still reproducing since their behavior minimized venereal disease, abortion, and infanticide. But the leading factors in the decline of the Hawaiians were undoubtedly Western infections of all kinds, miscegenation, and the departure of thousands of young Hawaiians who signed on to white men's ships. The question was who would replace them, and the answer, wrote Charlton, was Americans. If Britain were to retain even equal rights in Hawaii, it would have to counter these trends. Instead, when the first showdown occurred regarding foreign sovereignty over Hawaii, Britain was not even a party to it.

It began in 1836 when the Catholics came back. Unlike the Americans, the French considered missions an acceptable agency of political expansion, and the July Monarchy of Louis Philippe was especially aggressive in colonial affairs. In 1833 a Vicar Apostolic was named for the Pacific Ocean, and the Order of the Sacred Hearts tried again to break the Calvinist hold. Fathers Alexis Bachelot and Patrick Short, exiled by Kaahumanu six years before, arrived in April 1837, and Capt. Abel Du Petit-Thouars of the frigate *La Vénus* forced Kauikeaouli

(Kamehameha III) to sign a treaty permitting Frenchmen to "go and come freely" as citizens of a most favored nation. But then he sailed, and when two more priests arrived in the fall, Kauikeaouli outlawed their "idolatrous" religion again, as well as the import of wine and spirits, and he persecuted Hawaiian Catholics.

It would seem, therefore, that American missionary influence was as solid as ever. But the nature of that influence was changing. First, Bingham was no longer the patriarch. He had always been the target of attacks from American laymen and clergy, but his obvious success sustained his reputation with the American Board of Commissioners for Foreign Missions until Kauikeaouli's pagan revival. Bingham then had to confess that Christianity had not taken root as deeply as he had reported. The Board also rued his extreme reluctance to baptize and told him to lower his standards even as the growing number of missionaries diluted his authority.

Second, the reconversion of the Hawaiians began in 1837 under the auspices of new and younger spirits with whom Bingham was out of touch. The Rev. Titus Coan had been working in Hilo, on the windward coast of the Big Island, for two years. A disciple of Charles G. Finney, a New England revivalist of extraordinary power, Coan put more emphasis on the power of the Holy Ghost than on the laborious catechisms favored by Bingham. He prayed for God to reveal Himself to these "dead" people, as "hard as a nether millstone," and received his sign in the form of a freakishly powerful tidal wave that roared out of the sea "like a wail of doom," washed canoes, houses, and people up and inland, then sucked them back and down into the surf as the waters receded. Suddenly Mr. Coan's God seemed not only present, but angry and merciful (only thirteen died). It was the start of a great revival that drew thousands of Hawaiians back into the churches. Within five months Coan baptized 3,200 people and pastored the largest Protestant parish in the world. The corresponding increase in the number of indigenous clergy also spurred the development of a distinctively Hawaiian style of Christianity. In 1840, Bingham went home—for his wife's health, he said—and his day was done.

Third, the newer missionaries undertook to complete the sociopolitical revolution envisioned from the first by the American Board. That, too, began toward the end of 1837 as a direct response to the treaty forced on Hawaii by the French. Now the King, as we know, had no head for statecraft, so he and his chiefs asked William Richards to bring them back a teacher in "political economy." The American Board did not oblige, but Richards was moved, in 1838, to teach the King and chiefs himself, though it meant resigning as a missionary. What a scene it must have been when this earnest but hardly expert young preacher sat down with his noble Hawaiians each day to lecture on law, government, and economics—keeping one chapter ahead of his admiring students. In 1839 Boaz Mahune, a bright graduate of Richards's mission school, drafted the Hawaiian Bill of Rights, of which the preamble read:

> God hath made of one blood all nations of men, to dwell on the face of the earth in unity and blessedness. God has also bestowed certain rights alike on all men, and all chiefs, and people of all lands. These are some of the rights which he has given alike to every man, and every chief—life, limb, liberty, the labor of his hands, and productions of his mind.

Charlton predictably dismissed the King as "completely in the hands of the Reverend William Richards . . . who is a most bitter enemy of the English."

Nor did the Bill of Rights impress the French, who ordered Captain Cyrille Laplace in the frigate *L'Artémise* to sail to Hawaii for another go-'round on the matters of priests and brandy. She anchored in July 1839, and Laplace issued an ultimatum: revoke the prohibitions on Catholicism and alcohol or Honolulu would learn what life was like under a French cannonade. The quaking merchants chipped in a $20,000 bond to stay Laplace's hand until Kauikeaouli arrived. But Hawaii had no fortresses and few modern weapons, while the *alii* had forgotten the arts of war, thanks to Kamehameha's peace and the missionaries. So the French extracted another Treaty of Commerce and Friendship establishing equality for Catholics and Frenchmen.

How could the kingdom remain sovereign so long as each foreign ship that dropped anchor could force it to remake its laws? The first way was to fashion a rule of law that foreign powers would have to respect. So the King and chiefs promulgated the Constitution of 1840, providing for an elected legislature. The second way was to secure official recognition of Hawaiian independence. So Kauikeouli sent off letters to President John Tyler, King Louis Philippe, and Queen Victoria, inviting them all to guarantee Hawaiian independence and pledge to submit future claims to peaceful arbitration. He then appointed a blue ribbon delegation including Richards, Gov. Sir George Simpson of the Hudson's Bay Company, and a smart young chief, Timothy Haalilio, to sail to Europe and America in July 1842.

They were still at sea when Charlton's nerves snapped. As always, he paraded Britain's deteriorating position in the islands as the source of his despair. As always, personal concerns lurked in his brain. Charlton held what he claimed to be a 299-year lease, dating from 1826 and signed by Boki, to a plot of beachfront property. Why he waited until 1840 to produce it is a mystery, since Hawaiians (not least the King himself) had built and dwelled on the land in the intervening fourteen years. The King's advisers suspected a forgery but simply decided to declare it void insofar as Kaahumanu had been regent then and Boki had exceeded his authority.

Charlton ranted that he would summon British men-of-war, and in September 1842 he wrote the King a blistering note to the effect that it was his "bounden duty to repair immediately to Great Britain to lay statements before Her Majesty's Government. . . . Justice, though tardy, will reach you: and it is you, not your advisors, that will be punished." He then appointed one of his few friends, Alexander Simpson, to serve as deputy consul in his absence and booked ship for England. Simpson was as indiscreet as Charlton and had bragged of their intention to wreck Kauikeaouli's diplomacy and bring about British annexation. Not surprisingly, therefore, the King refused to receive Simpson's credentials, entertained a lawsuit against Charlton, and attached his property. Simpson sent an S.O.S. to the commander of Britain's Pacific squadron at San Blas, and Adm. Sir Richard Thomas ordered the *Carysfort*, Lord George Paulet commanding, to Honolulu. He put in on February 10, 1843, lowered his guns, and promised "immediate coercive steps" if the King did not remove every complaint lodged by British subjects. Kauikeaouli was prepared to submit until it became clear that Paulet and Simpson did not want concessions: they wanted the islands. So the King figuratively sat on the ground and even debated placing his realm under the joint protection of the United States and France. But finally, on February 25, 1843, Kamehameha III gave away, under protest, "the life of the land" to Great Britain. Paulet then governed like a tin god, even recruiting a Queen's Own Hawaiian Regiment. Charlton's fantasy had been realized.

In the meantime halfway around the world, Lord Aberdeen had finally heard Charlton's litany of woe and declared a new policy as of October 1842. Henceforth, warships should stop at Hawaii more frequently to counterbalance the efforts of other powers to establish dominance in the islands. However, he also insisted that captains show special solicitude to the rulers of all Pacific islands, strengthen their authority, and avoid interfering every time a foreign subject felt himself wronged. Two months later, in December 1842, the Hawaiian embassy arrived in Washington. They had trouble seeing Daniel Webster, Secretary of State, until the Reverend Mr. Richards hinted that he would sign the islands over to Britain if the Americans did not pay attention. Webster then prevailed upon President Tyler to mention the Sandwich Islands for the first time in a presidential address. The United States, said Tyler, had a greater interest in the fate of the islands than any other power. The government of those islands ought to be respected, and no power ought to take possession of them as a conquest or a colony, or seek to achieve undue control over the government. In effect, Tyler draped over Hawaii the mantle of the Monroe Doctrine, and Congress allocated funds for a resident commissioner.

By early 1843, therefore, a British Admiral had taken over Hawaii, the British and American governments had affirmed its sovereignty, and none of the parties knew what the others had done! That was where matters stood when Charlton himself arrived back in London, expecting to be received as a patriot. His first note to the Foreign Office listed the "arbitrary and unjust" actions against Britons by the Hawaiians and the Americans, "whose will is law" in Hawaii. Aberdeen snubbed him. Charlton's second letter took the form of a lengthy and ever so proper report describing conditions in the islands and making a strong case that even U.S. government recognition of the Hawaiian kingdom meant nothing so long as Americans were the power behind the throne. Aberdeen snubbed him again. Charlton's third and fourth letters were whiny, defensive, and plaintive. Aberdeen snubbed him for a month and then finally reprimanded him icily for having written the King to whom he was accredited a letter "so intemperate" and "ill-judged" that it could only do great mischief; for having deserted his post without permission; for having left before making sure his appointed deputy would be accepted. Then Aberdeen fired him. Charlton's last letter was a humble plea for mercy on the grounds that he had acted out of love of country, with no personal motive whatsoever.

When news of Paulet's seizure of Hawaii reached London, Aberdeen repudiated it as well and went on to sign a joint declaration with France that recognized the independence of the Sandwich Islands. Admiral Thomas himself sailed to Honolulu, dressed down Paulet, and presided over what became the national holiday of the Hawaiian kingdom. On July 31, 1843, the Hawaiian flag replaced the Union Jack, and Kaui-keaouli bestowed on his realm a motto drawn from a Psalm: *"Ua mau ke ea o ka aina i ka pono"* (The Life of the Land Is Preserved in Righteousness). Charlton, on the other hand, was pensioned off and replaced with "an experienced and impartial person." He returned to Hawaii in 1844 only to find that he was now under subpoena for calling an adversary a sodomite. When the jury found him guilty, Charlton pronounced them *all* sodomites and quit Hawaii for good. He died in England in 1852.

In the wake of these crises Hawaii entered a new and progressive era. The first legislature convened in 1845 and passed laws providing for a royal cabinet and land redistribution, the Great Māhele, begun in 1846. The whaling industry reached a peak that same year, and experimental sugar cultivation began on Kauai. But were Charlton still around, he would have noticed that the vaunted "Hawaiian" cabinet consisted of Richards as Minister of Education, Gerritt P. Judd as Minister of Justice, John Ricord as Attorney General, William Lee as Chief Justice, and Robert Wyllie as Minister of Foreign Affairs. And that much of the land freed from the hands of old *alii* ended up in the hands of Americans, who now monopolized the political and economic life of Hawaii as much as they did its religious life.

Prescient Americans cheered. Caleb Cushing saw control of Oregon, the opening of China, and the fate of Hawaii as all of a piece, and acting Secretary of State Hugh S. Legaré thought Hawaii so important that "it seems doubtful whether even the undisputed possession of the Oregon territory . . . or indeed anything short of the acquisition of California (if that were possible) would be sufficient indemnity to us for the loss of these harbors." But perhaps Americans would not have to choose. Perhaps they could have it all. Much depended on the outcome of the election of 1844.

Oregon 1844

THANKS TO THE War of 1812 the honor of becoming "father of Oregon" fell not to Astor's man McDougall but to a Hudson's Bay Company man John McLoughlin ... although some wondered if he were in fact a man, for he had the body and shaggy white visage of a polar bear, and judging from his twenty-year reign over a half-million square miles, he had the temper of a polar bear, too. McLoughlin was born in Rivière-du-Loup in 1784, apprenticed himself to a surgeon, and at the age of twenty earned a license to practice as a frontier doctor. By the time the Northwest Fur Company merged with the HBC in 1821, McLoughlin was already one of the most imposing men in the trans–Rocky Mountain fur trade, with a reputation for whipping into shape—or just whipping—unruly employees, Indians, or competitors whose behavior disturbed the tidy prosecution of the Company monopoly. Thus, when the Company needed someone to outmaneuver the Yankees for control of the empty empire known as Oregon, Gov. George Simpson chose McLoughlin: "He was such a figure as I should not like to meet in a dark Night."

Simpson himself was no mere bookkeeper. He not only knew every river and wood around the Company's "capital" on Hudson's Bay, he wore out horses and canoes inspecting for himself the expanse of western Canada. In 1824 Simpson made his first tour to the Columbia River and devised the strategy by which Britain might muscle aside Russians and Americans alike. The mammoth stakes embraced the entire region between the Pacific Ocean and the Rocky Mountains from 42° north latitude (the northern boundary of California as fixed by Adams and Onís) and 54°40′ north latitude (the southern boundary of Russian America as fixed by the treaties of 1824–25). Now, inasmuch as there was plenty of room for all, the logical solution would seem to be a partition. Why not, for instance, just extend the 49th parallel boundary, already the U.S.-

Canadian line up to the Rockies, all the way to the sea? In fact, Albert Gallatin proposed such a division in 1824, but the British offered to concede only the land south of the Columbia River. So the real bone of contention consisted of the lands *between* the Columbia River and the 49th parallel, the present-day state of Washington. But since the British wanted access to the Columbia, the "St. Lawrence of the West" as they styled it, and the Americans lusted after Puget Sound, no agreement was possible. When the ten years' "joint occupation" agreement was nearing an end, in 1827, the rival governments resigned themselves to a simple renewal of the arrangement for the indefinite future. Sooner or later, the Americans figured, their settlers would occupy the land and strengthen the U.S. claim. Sooner or later, the British figured, their Company would get a commercial grip on the land and strengthen the British claim. That was why Simpson's strategy was important.

Astoria was gone, but Yankee sea captains vexed the Canadian fur traders. If the HBC was to prevail, it must first cooperate with the Russians and Indians to destroy the American coastal trade, then reduce the Russians and Indians to helpless dependency. Now, the Americans' weakness was the very fact that they were individual entrepreneurs. They could make fine profits trading for furs with the coastal Indians or Russians. But their capital was limited, and most could not stand even a single failed voyage. So Simpson proposed that the HBC establish forts from the Columbia River to the Alaskan panhandle, and he turned McLoughlin loose to build them. Within a decade an elaborate network of posts stretched from Fort Vancouver and Fort Walla Walla on the Columbia, to Fort Nisqually (near present-day Tacoma) and Fort Langley on the Fraser River, all the way to Fort Simpson on the border of Russian America. At these strategic collection points HBC agents might gather in all the furs the Indians had to offer. *Only they did not treat them all alike.* At the inland posts, which the seaborne Americans could not reach, Company agents made the Indians turn in five pelts to get one standard blue-and-scarlet HBC blanket. At river posts or Puget Sound landings where American ships *might* venture, agents gave the Indians a better bargain, say, a blanket for only three pelts. And wherever the Americans were clearly present as competitors, the Company practically gave away its blankets at one per pelt! Of course, the interior tribes, like the Nez Percé, learned of the ploy and grew restless. But the Yankee merchants, in no position to win a price war with the great HBC, suddenly found no coastal Indians willing to deal with them at all. By 1830 the New Englanders were licked and their ships disappeared. One played-out captain, William H. McNeill, even sold his ship to McLoughlin in 1832 and went over to the Canadians.

Then McLoughlin turned to the Russians. Remember that the brouhaha following the Tsar's ukase ended in a treaty that granted Americans full trading rights in Alaska for ten years. But as that agreement neared its end, the Russian-American Gov. Ferdinand Wrangell was anxious to find an alternative, fearing American penetration of Alaska. So McLoughlin pursued a carrot-and-stick strategy, first trespassing across Russia's borders in threatening fashion, then offering to supply all of Sitka's needs for manufactures and foodstuffs. The Russians parried the "stick" when the *Chichagoff* drove a Hudson's Bay Company ship out of the Stikine River, causing a minor incident. But the carrot did the trick. When the HBC offered not only to supply the Russian Americans but to provide them with prime otter and beaver skins at good prices, St. Petersburg signed a deal in 1839. Now *American* traders were shut out along the entire Pacific coast, and time seemed to be on the side of the British.

Only, the fate of Britain was not in the hands of London, or even the HBC directors, but in the hands of notorious John McLoughlin, Principal Resident Superintendent of the Honourable Hudson's Bay Company's affairs for the west side of the *continent*. His boss, George Simpson, could only applaud McLoughlin's energetic construction of forts, elimination of competition, and foundation of an HBC subsidiary, the Puget's Sound Agricultural Company, in 1839, which cut Company costs and helped it fulfill its contract to supply the Russians. But on the other side of the ledger were accumulating complaints about McLoughlin's irascibility. When the simpering, priggish Anglican chaplain at Fort Vancouver complained of no carpets on the floor, or a proper place to hold Bible study, or a cook to prepare salmon the way his picky wife preferred, McLoughlin merely cussed him out. But when the Reverend Mr. Beaver went so far as to write the Company damning the fur traders' Indian marriages and naming McLoughlin's wife a tart, the White Eagle beat him bloody. More worrisome to Simpson was the big man's habit of setting aside Company policy whenever he doubted its wisdom. When Simpson ordered the HBC office at Yerba Buena (San Francisco) closed, McLoughlin kept it open. When Simpson sent him the HMS *Beaver*, first steam-powered ship on the Northwest coast, McLoughlin removed its engine to run a sawmill. Most important, when Simpson ordered him to discourage any American settlers who turned up in the Columbia basin, McLoughlin positively encouraged the settlers.

Why would he do that? Why did he tolerate the one trend that might in time undermine the British claim to the Northwest coast? One theory holds that McLoughlin had a sentimental side. Another judges him a secret republican, who turned against Britain after the redcoats suppressed the Canadian rebellion of 1837. The facts are that when the first settlers arrived in 1832—a pitiful band of ten under Nathaniel Wyeth of Boston (who hoped to start a smoked-salmon factory)—McLoughlin not only nursed them back to strength but entertained them for months. Two decided to stay and were granted leave to settle in the rich Willamette Valley. Wyeth returned in 1834 with another party including two Methodist missionaries. Once again McLoughlin gave them help, and the Rev. Peter Parker returned to the East to publicize both the fertility of Oregon and the kindness of Dr. McLoughlin. Simpson got wind of it, too, and recalled McLoughlin for consultation.

Now, Simpson was no weakling and would surely have sacked any underling he suspected of treason. But McLoughlin remained a fiery defender of the British fur monopoly, whatever insouciance he showed toward Yankee farmers south of the river. And the HBC, after all, was a business, not a political entity. So long as the settlers did not trouble the fur trade, there was no need to risk bloodshed and international incidents. In fact, making a great show of *banishing* all comers to Oregon and shrouding it in Spanish secrecy might only convince Americans all the more that Oregon was worth grabbing. So McLoughlin returned to the Pacific with orders not to encourage the Yankee settlers, to protect as always the fur monopoly, and to prepare a place for British settlers north of the Columbia. Unfortunately, British emigration just then was in a slow period that did not end until the Irish potato famine, and those who did go overseas preferred the enticements of the New Zealand Association. So the Puget's Sound Agricultural Company stagnated while the Willamette colony prospered.

In 1841 about five hundred American citizens resided or roamed in the country south of the Columbia, and about the same number of British subjects lived north of it. All that changed in 1842, when reports of Oregon inspired Dr. Elijah White to lead one hundred emigrants in the first organized wagon train to plod the Oregon Trail. Simpson disparaged them, as he did all Americans, as "worthless and lawless characters of every description." But most of those who cried, "Whoo ha! Go it boys! We're in a perfect *Oregon fever!*" were Midwestern farmers pulled down in the undertow of the Panic of 1837. Prices for grain, hogs, and cotton reached all-time lows, and farmers stuck with debt or marginal land went bust. So although there is no need to romanticize the pioneers of the Oregon Trail (they littered it so much that no one could ever get lost on it), neither is there cause to condemn the men who cried for Oregon as imperialistic. Anyone who has tried to clear even a small plot of virgin meadow or forest of the roots and rocks and roots and weeds and roots— without power tools—can imagine the heartbreak of those luckless set-

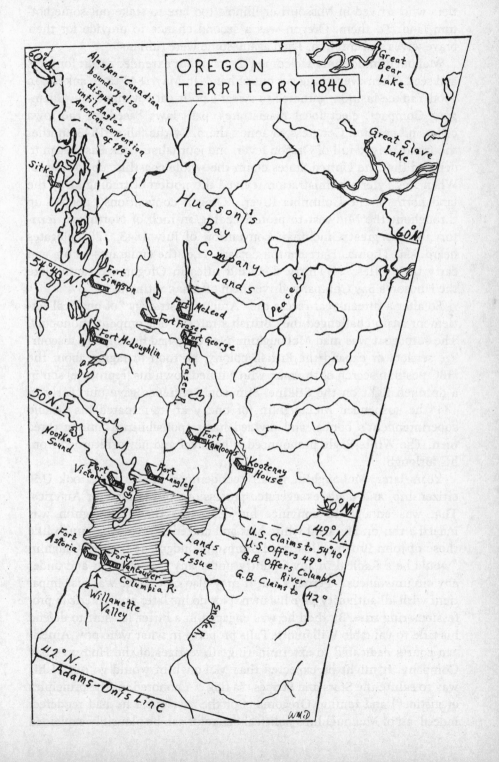

OREGON
TERRITORY 1846

Great Bear Lake

Great Slave Lake

Alaskan-Canadian
boundary also
disputed
until Anglo-
American convention
of 1903

Sitka

Hudson's
Bay
Company
Lands

Peace R.

60° N.

54°40' N.

Fort Simpson

Fort McLeod

Fort Fraser
Fort George

Fort McLoughlin

Fraser R.

50° N.

Nootka Sound

Fort Kamloops

Fort Victoria

Fort Langley

Kootenay House

50° N.

49° N.

U.S. Claims to 54°40'
U.S. Offers 49°
G.B. Offers Columbia River
G.B. Claims to 42°

Fort Astoria

Fort Vancouver

Columbia R.

Lands at Issue

Snake R.

Willamette Valley

42° N.

Adams-Onis Line

W.M.D.

tlers who arrived in Missouri or Illinois too late to stake out some bottom land. To them, Oregon was a second chance to provide for their brave wives and children. Then again, some were ruffians.

McLoughlin not only welcomed them all but extended credit for tools and seed. Then everything got out of hand. In May 1843 the Yankees, in good Yankee fashion, gathered to swear a political covenant, the Champoeg Compact, elect local magistrates, pass laws based on the Iowa code, and petition Congress to annex them. By the fall of 1843 another thousand arrived full of Oregon fever, and journalists back East began to demand that the United States claim the whole coastline up to Alaska. When the Tyler administration revived the notion of trading away the land *north* of the Columbia River, "Oregon conventions" popped up throughout the Midwest to protest ceding an inch of Northwest territory. In the great Cincinnati convention of July 1843, 120 delegates heard Sen. Thomas Hart Benton declare, "Let the emigrants go on; and carry their rifles. . . . Thirty thousand rifles in Oregon will annihilate the Hudson's Bay Company, drive them off our continent."

So after a fifteen-year recess the "American strategy" of physical settlement again challenged the "British strategy" of Company monopoly. The scapegoat was mad McLoughlin. Not only had he failed to discourage settlers or expand the British colony, he took to raging about the HBC posts in search of the men who gunned down his (reprobate) son in a drunken fight on the Stikine. Simpson's patience gave out. Early in 1844 he suspended McLoughlin for one year, terminated his sizable superintendent's bonus, and divided his responsibilities among three men. The White Eagle pronounced it betrayal and never returned from his furlough.

Years later, McLoughlin vocally condemned British rule, took U.S. citizenship, and made exaggerated professions of his love for America. That was enough to convince his detractors that McLoughlin was indeed a traitor. His wild white hair and crazed eyes, ever so much like those of John Brown, illustrated Simpson's judgment that McLoughlin "would be a Radical in any Country under any Government and under any circumstances." Perhaps, but it may also be that he was just impatient with all authority save his own. Nor do his later pro-American professions ring true. By then he was engaged in a bitter lawsuit to defend his title to valuable Willamette Falls property in what were now American courts dedicated to exterminating all vestiges of the Hudson's Bay Company. It might be expected that McLoughlin would go out of his way to salute the Stars and Stripes ("a flag . . . honored for the principles of justice") and remind Oregonians of the assistance he had rendered. Indeed, all of McLoughlin's political behavior can be plausibly explained

by his own financial interest, whether as regards the fur trade or the settlers . . . assuming, of course, that the big man was rational.

By 1844, Oregon fever elevated the Northwest controversy to the level
of the Texas dispute, and together they made expansionism one of the
most pressing issues in American politics. That is not to say that it was
not always an issue. As we know, the generation of Jefferson, Adams,
and Monroe already assumed that the American peoples would grow
and spread westward until they reached the Pacific. The 1820s and
1830s brought a pause in formal acquisitions while the country busied
itself with the Jacksonian reforms, removal of Indians east of the Mississippi, industrialization in the Northeast, farming in the Midwest, and
cotton in the deep South. But the trends feeding expansionism only
accelerated. The population surpassed seventeen million by 1840, the
good land was nearly filled up, and it took little imagination to project
how the railroad, steamship, and telegraph might ease the task of span-
ning the entire continent.

The trouble was that several contradictory expansionisms confused
the public and confounded politicians. John O'Sullivan, editor of the
Democratic Review and New York *Morning News*, for instance, was an
idealist. In his mind, democratic federalism was a secular faith to which
all peoples—Yankee settlers in the unorganized West, Canadians and
even Indians and Mexicans—would someday convert, and the United
States was a secular temple the converts would someday enter. But the
process would be peaceful and gradual. Illinois Congressman John Went-
worth likewise "did not believe the God of Heaven, when he crowned
the American arms with success, designed that the original States
should be the only abode of liberty on earth. On the contrary, he only
designed them as the great center from which civilization, religion, and
liberty should radiate and radiate until the whole continent shall bask
in their blessing."

Another theory of expansion was biological. As an Indiana congressman put it, "Go to the West and see a young man with his mate of eighteen; after the lapse of thirty years, visit him again, and instead of two,
you will find twenty-two. That is what I call the American multiplica-
tion table." Thus, the United States needed to do nothing but exercise
restraint and await results. As Senator Calhoun advised concerning the
acquisition of Oregon, "There is only one means by which it can be
done; but that, fortunately, is the most powerful of all—*time. Time* is
acting for us; and, if we shall have the wisdom to trust its operation, it
will assert and maintain our right with resistless force, without costing
a cent of money, or a drop of blood. . . . Our population is rolling toward

the shores of the Pacific with an impetus greater than what we realize."

These idealistic and biological expansionisms, therefore, saw force as not only unnecessary but a violation of the American spirit, while the justification for incorporating lands of others was moral. Mexico and Britain, for instance, claimed huge tracts of North America but displayed a deadening sloth (for example, in California) or the deadening hand of monopoly (for example, in Oregon). Americans, by contrast, were tireless ranchers, farmers, miners, trappers, investors, and promoters, and they used the good earth as God intended. But reveries such as these, popular among Northeastern Democrats, obscured the substantial wheres, whens, whys, and hows of what amounted to *annexation*. A third sort of expansionism prevalent among Midwesterners was characterized instead by impatience and unscrupulous realism. These self-proclaimed war hawks demanded all of the Oregon territory up to 54°40′ and were ready to fight Britain if necessary.

Finally, there was still another division between expansionists in the North and the South. The former were hot to seize Oregon but had no love for slave-holding Texas. Southern expansionists were hot to take Texas but had no interest in risking war against Britain—their best customer for cotton—on behalf of Oregon. Finally, Whig partisans North and South resisted expansionism altogether, advising prudence in Oregon and rejection of Texas. These divisions help to explain why the Oregon issue simmered so long, and why Texas remained for nine years a rejected supplicant on the steps of the American temple.

These contrary strands of expansionism might well have continued to stymie American policy were it not for a strange turn of the political wheel that put the Democrats, for a change, on the defensive. It began during the eight-year term of Andrew Jackson, whose hillbilly supporters and populist policies were anathema to Northeastern business, and whose courting of Southern votes enraged abolitionists. So a ragtag alliance of groups who had little in common but antipathy to King Andrew I came together to form the Whigs. To the extent they had a platform, it favored high tariffs, state support of internal improvements like roads and canals, and restrictions on the spread of slavery. In 1840 they managed to elect William Henry Harrison, but he died within weeks and his successor, Tyler, soon earned everyone's enmity. Four years later the Whigs turned unanimously to Henry Clay, the great parliamentarian from Kentucky, but The Democracy had no notion of whom to name or what issues to run on. Moreover, the party convention labored under a two-thirds rule, and no one was close to winning after eight ballots. Finally, three political operatives, including the Harvard historian George Bancroft, stage-managed the nomination of James Knox Polk. A loyal Jackson man, he was touted by Democrats as

"Young Hickory." Whigs laughed in return, asking, "Who is James K. Polk?" although he had already served as Speaker of the House and Governor of Tennessee. Concerning the platform, far more important in the days when only a handful of voters ever saw or heard the candidate, the Democrats took refuge in foreign policy. Since Clay opposed statehood for Texas, the Democrats would call for the "re-annexation of Texas!" (pleasing the slave states) *and* the "re-occupation of Oregon" (pleasing the Midwestern free soilers). The "re-" prefixes were understood by all to mean that the United States had these lands won until John Quincy Adams and Anglophile Whigs let them slip away. So The Democracy and its champion, James K. Polk, gambled that it could pull all the expansionist constituencies together and deflect Americans' passions from their internal rivals to foreign ones, England and Mexico. For whatever their region, party, stand on slavery, or economic interest, many Americans did understand that the Republic had a great but possibly fleeting opportunity. Texas beckoned, and California, and Oregon. China was open, with Hawaii along the way. Britain and France were passive or preoccupied. Mexico was contemptible and vulnerable. And the United States itself was united, though it might not remain so for long. This was America's moment, and the inchoate mood the moment conjured would find its expression in Polk, just as it had found its name in O'Sullivan's Manifest Destiny after the election of 1844.

Sonoma 1846

IF THE UNITED STATES decided to move against Mexico, the only power in the world able to do more than protest was Britain. But Englishmen could not recall a time when Parliament had been so unstable. The Chartist movement among industrial workers, the Canadian revolt, the Irish question, and budgetary troubles had toppled the Whig cabinet of Melbourne and Palmerston in 1841. Robert Peel was now in 10 Downing Street and the passive Aberdeen in the Foreign Office. A series of bad harvests and the first hint of the potato famine then forced the Tories to focus on repeal of the Corn Laws, which in turn tore their majority asunder. So with Parliament split and Palmerston on the sidelines, Britain was in no condition to stand up to its strapping American offspring.

To be sure, Aberdeen awoke in the summer of 1844 to the danger that the United States might gobble up Texas. But Pakenham, his minister in Washington, persuaded him to do nothing that might anger the touchy Americans and make a Polk victory more likely. His advice was too clever by half since the Democrats were eager to believe in nefarious British plots, whether they existed or not, and branded Henry Clay a dupe. Nor did Clay help his own cause by waffling on Texas. Nor did his stand against the extension of slavery avail, because the abolitionist Liberty Party siphoned off enough votes to throw New York and the election to the Democrats. A crestfallen Pakenham reported, with customary understatment: "The Election of Mr. Polk to the Presidency of the United States will, I fear, cause some disappointment to Her Majesty's Government."

It did indeed. Aberdeen fairly whined that "we have carefully abstained from any ostensible Act which could inflame the wild and dangerous spirit which, partly for national, but more for party purposes, has been roused and sustained by demagogues in the United States." But under no circumstances would Britain "risk a collision for the sake of Mexico alone." Now, we can sympathize with Aberdeen's prudence, but to state categorically that Britain would not risk a war was to throw away the leverage of the Royal Navy at the outset of a crisis that would determine the hegemony of North America! Palmerston fumed on the opposition benches.

The election of 1844 was a virtual tie—a 40,000-vote difference out of two million—but lame-duck President Tyler declared Polk's victory a mandate in favor of Texas statehood and invited Congress to admit it, not by treaty (which required a two-thirds majority) but by joint resolution (needing simple majorities). The constitutionality of such an arrangement was dubious and the ancillary problems immense: in American eyes Texas was an independent country with its own laws and a large national debt; in Mexican eyes it was a rebellious province whose very boundaries were a matter of dispute. But Congress passed the resolution and Tyler signed it on March 1, 1845, his last day in office. Its passage proved that a pro-Texas majority was always there if only electoral politics and the slavery issue could be drained off. The November elections achieved the former; a widely distributed campaign tract by Robert J. Walker helped to achieve the latter. A Mississippi slaveholder raised in the North, Walker promoted the tortured theory that as plantation soils wore out, cotton production would shift to Texas. When in time the soil there became exhausted, the slaves might cross the Rio Grande and begin new lives in Mexico. If, on the other hand, Texas abolished slavery and remained independent, then sooner or later unemployed Negroes would flood the North or provoke race war in the South.

Aberdeen made a last-ditch effort by offering the Texans a guarantee against Mexican aggression, a loan, and support for a liberal boundary settlement in return for resisting the offer of statehood. But American envoy Andrew J. Donelson could offer all that and more. On June 18, 1845, the Texan Congress rejected a Mexican peace offer that came years too late and voted unanimously to add the Lone Star to "the constellation of the Stars and Stripes." By then the expansionist mood in the States had turned maniacal. "Yes, more, more, more," cried John O'Sullivan, till "the whole boundless continent is ours." Oregon and California would be next, ruminated the London *Times*, unless "something" intervened to prevent it.

But the spirit of Palmerston was dormant in London and alive in President Polk. He was one of those statesmen who benefited from being consistently underestimated, probably because he doubted himself. Though raised a devout Presbyterian, he had been jilted at the baptismal font after a violent row between his father and the pastor, and he remained thereafter uncertain of his standing with the Lord. He was a frail child, a frenetic worker, and a survivor of ups and downs thanks in part to his excellent wife, Sarah Childress. His nomination and victory were a surprise to him, and his determination to achieve the expansion he promised was a surprise to everyone else. He upheld the Texans' claim to a southern boundary on the Rio Grande and American claims in Oregon up to 54°40'. His Secretary of the Navy George Bancroft, Secretary of War William Marcy, and Secretary of the Treasury Robert J. Walker were avid expansionists, while Secretary of State James Buchanan, who mostly just wanted to be President, was easily carried along. A veteran of Congress, Polk also knew the danger of conflict between the legislature and executive over control of foreign policy. But the Red Fox put into play a nervy strategy: he would use his executive power to manufacture faits accomplis that the Congress must either accept or seem unpatriotic. He was also persuaded by Andrew Jackson's example that the best means of getting one's way was to bluff first and talk later. That the British government was weak and preoccupied, and the Mexican chaotic, did not hurt.

But what sort of bluff, to what end? The prophets of Manifest Destiny held that expansion need not provoke conflict but ought to come naturally as in Texas. The Champoeg Compact suggested that peaceful settlement would soon deliver Oregon, too, and perhaps California. But Western war hawks had no use for vague "destinies." They wanted to conquer Canada and be done with borders altogether. A third technique for expansion was the filibuster. Though this word now connotes a parliamentary ploy, it originally described a coup whereby freebooters would infiltrate foreign territory, stage a "popular" uprising, then request annexation to the United States. Such a filibuster had succeeded in Baton Rouge in 1810 and seemed just the thing for empty California. A fourth means of expansion, and the one favored by Polk, was diplomacy in the spirit of Jefferson, Monroe, and John Quincy Adams. But even then Polk must take care that the crises with Britain and Mexico did not come to a head simultaneously, and that if war came, it would be with the weaker opponent.

Oregon flared first. In 1843, Aberdeen had reopened the long negotiation with an offer he knew to be hopeless. Britain would retain all the territory north of the Columbia River but create "free ports" on the Puget Sound open to American shipping. Polk renewed the old American offer to make the 49th parallel the border but neglected to offer Britain navigation rights on the Columbia. Pakenham, knowing this was unacceptable, rejected it without even informing the Foreign Office. Polk called this an arrogant affront in his annual message, reaffirmed U.S. rights to the whole Northwest coast, and invited Congress to suspend the old "joint occupation" agreement. "The only way to treat John Bull," said Polk, "was to look him straight in the eye."

Meanwhile, American relations with Mexico virtually ceased to exist. After the annexation of Texas the Mexican Ambassador in Washington requested his passport and Mexico expelled the U.S. mission, leaving Polk with no one to talk to. So in October, just as the Oregon negotiations were breaking down, Polk gave Mexico, too, a chance to insult the United States. Ignoring the fact that Mexico had broken diplomatic relations, he named John Slidell, a slick, Spanish-speaking Louisiana expansionist, minister plenipotentiary and sent him off to Mexico City with instructions to press for the Rio Grande and purchase California. If he succeeded, fine. If the Mexicans spurned Slidell, Polk would have another affront with which to rally Congress and public opinion.

Now, California was barely mentioned in the expansionist rhetoric of 1844, but after annexation of Texas it seized center stage in the United States and Britain alike. Several hundred American immigrants arrived in 1845, some via Oregon, some across the newly blazed trails of the High Sierra. That was the year when the naval explorer Wilkes published his breathtaking account of California's beauty and strategic importance, and the would-be filibuster Lansford W. Hastings published his halcyon *Emigrant's Guide to Oregon and California.* (One wagon train misled by Hastings's book was the luckless Donner party, of which forty died in the High Sierra and others resorted to cannibalism.) The newcomers settled in the Sacramento Valley, though their presence was also conspicuous at Monterey and Yerba Buena, where one disgusted Englishman asked, "Is there nothing but Yankees here?" The American responsible for his countrymen's acts was the Consul at Monterey, Thomas O. Larkin. Over thirteen years he had come to love the land and people, and his hope was that independence or annexation might come with the consent of the *californios* themselves—idealistic Manifest Destiny.

His fellow *americanos*, however, grew more impatient with each new rumor of British, French, even Prussian plots to buy or seize California. The London *Times* insisted that "England must think of her own interests, and secure the Bay of Francisco and Monterey," while Aberdeen himself warned that "were California to fall into the hands of the enemy, Mexico would thenceforward look in vain for external peace and security." And the assumption that Britain *would* act decisively to contain Yankee expansion was what inspired Polk to order a series of surreptitious missions meant to keep the California plum on the tree until the United States was ready to pick it. First, in February 1845, the War Department ordered Capt. John Charles Frémont into the border country between the United States and New Mexico. He had already made a

lengthy journey to California and Oregon, and his exquisitely written
journals had made him the darling of pioneers and armchair expansionists. He was also a self-seeking adventurer, and even though he followed
routes long known to mountain men, Frémont won fame as the
Pathfinder. Born on the wrong side of the sheets, the dashing officer had
both genuine talents and a knack for self-promotion that peaked with
his successful wooing of Jessie Benton, the sixteen-year-old daughter of
Thomas Hart Benton, chairman of the military affairs committee and
leading expansionist in the Senate. Now Frémont was ordered west
again on an ostensibly "topographical" expedition. Setting aside his
orders, he peeled off sixty armed men, signed on Kit Carson as scout,
and made straight for California, descending the Sierra just before the
snows.

The second surreptitious mission was that of Col. Stephen W.
Kearny, ordered by the Secretary of War to take five companies of crack
cavalry to scout out the borders with New Mexico and befriend the
Indian tribes. Third, in October 1845, Secretary of State Buchanan sent a
secret message to Monterey promoting Larkin to the post of "confidential agent" and ordering him to propagandize the *californios* against foreign powers and in favor of "that love of liberty and independence so
natural to the American Continent." Fourth, in December, Secretary of
the Navy Bancroft secretly ordered Pacific squadron commander, Commodore John D. Sloat, to patrol the California and Oregon coasts, keep
watch on his British counterpart, and discreetly distribute to Americans
in the Willamette Valley copies of Polk's message to Congress (a reaffir-
mation of the Monroe Doctrine) and "any rifles or other small arms on
board your ships which can be spared for the purpose."

Polk had no way of knowing what these covert preparations might
lead to, except that they played to American strengths and Anglo-
Mexican weaknesses. The Peel government was already teetering. It had
decided to stake its future on abolition of the Corn Laws, which provoked a revolt by landed Tories in Parliament. Peel would have fallen
already had the Whigs been able to muster an acceptable cabinet.
Instead, Peel and Aberdeen remained in office in exchange for a promise
that the Whigs would support a peaceful resolution in Oregon. So even
though the Royal Navy stationed three warships off Oregon (flagged by
an eighty-gun frigate boasting Aberdeen's brother as commander and
Peel's son as lieutenant), Pakenham admitted that London "would be
glad to get clear of the [Oregon] question on almost any terms." So
Aberdeen instructed Pakenham to surrender everything south of the
49th parallel, even though a mere dozen Americans occupied what
became the state of Washington.

Polk knew of the British cabinet crisis as early as the turn of 1846, which is what allowed him to increase his pressure on Mexico. For as expected, President Herrera judged Slidell's petitions insulting and knew that he would be overthrown at home if he compromised with the Yankee despoilers. He was overthrown anyway, whereupon Polk argued that he had tried to bargain with Mexico, but the Mexicans had no government capable of doing business. On January 13, 1846, Polk ordered Gen. Zachary Taylor to advance from the Nueces River and establish defenses on the Rio Grande opposite the Mexican town of Matamoros. Polk called it "defending American soil." The Mexicans called it an invasion.

If so, it was not the first. For far beyond the reach of communication Capt. Frémont's little band now rode free in California. Colonel José Castro finally rousted out two hundred Mexican militia and persuaded Frémont to leave. But he "slowly and growlingly" made his way *north*, not east—and waited. In mid-April Marine Lt. Archibald Gillespie arrived by sea in Monterey, claiming to be a sickly trader come to California for his health. His mission was to deliver to Larkin Buchanan's instructions to forestall foreign intrigues and encourage pro-American sympathies. Gillespie also found Frémont up at Klamath Lake, Oregon, handed him letters from Jessie and Senator Benton, and told him of Buchanan's instructions. Frémont concluded that Polk must want a filibuster. After taking time out to massacre an Indian village in retaliation for a raid on his camp, he hightailed it back to the Sacramento Valley, by which time (unbeknownst to him) the United States and Mexico were at war.

"Mexico is an ugly enemy," Daniel Webster had complained. "She will not fight—and will not treat." By ordering General Taylor to the Rio Grande Polk was hoping to force them to do one or the other. Did he want war? Certainly he was prepared to believe the dispatches of every U.S. envoy that the Mexicans would not cease denouncing the United States until they received a good drubbing. At the same time Polk found it hard to believe "that Mexico will be mad enough to declare war." But Mexican President Paredes matched Polk bluff for bluff, evidently expecting that Britain and the United States would come to blows over Oregon. On April 11, 1846, Gen. Pedro Ampudia rode into Matamoros with three thousand soldiers and demanded that Taylor withdraw. Charles Bankhead, the British minister in Mexico, sensed that the tragedy that was modern Mexico was about to enter its final act. Having lacked the civic virtue to govern "what might, under other hands, have become one of the most flourishing countries in the world," the Mexicans would now play right into American hands. He was right. On April 23, Paredes proclaimed a "defensive war" and the next day Mexican soldiers ambushed an American patrol.

News of the bloodshed was en route to Washington when Polk and his cabinet were debating whether to ask Congress for a declaration of war. Bancroft and Buchanan preferred to wait in hopes that Mexico would fire the first shot. On May 9 they learned that it had. The next day Polk relaxed his observance of the Sabbath to draft a war message. In light of the Mexicans' bad faith and bad debts, abominations against the Texans, refusal to negotiate over boundaries, public defamations of American honor, and dismissal of every diplomat sent to avoid hostilities, Polk pronounced his "cup of forbearance . . . exhausted." It was not a question of starting a war, since "war exists" and Mexicans had shed American blood on what Polk claimed to be American soil. Whigs were suspicious of the President's account and wanted time to peruse the documents. But the Democratic majority cut off debate, and the Whigs were trapped. They recalled how their Federalist forbears had voted against the War of 1812 and disappeared as a political force. So the House voted 174 to 14, and the Senate 40 to 2, to declare war on Mexico. On May 30, Polk revealed his war aims: the Rio Grande, New Mexico, and California.

Aberdeen spent that spring of 1846 preparing public opinion for his new, conciliatory offer on Oregon. Details of its contents reached the White House on June 3: Britain would accept a partition on the 49th parallel, asking only that the Columbia River be open to navigation by the Hudson's Bay Company. Polk was satisfied that the United States would gain both banks of the Columbia and the Puget Sound. The problem was to disarm his own constituents who cried "Fifty-four, Forty, or Fight!" So once again Polk contrived to trap Congress, this time by presenting Britain's terms to the Senate in advance of a treaty. That way, the legislative branch, not the President, would be on record as having "backed down" from the maximum American position. Once again, speed was imperative. For 'Peel had shepherded abolition of the Corn Laws through Parliament and promptly fallen from power. Palmerston might be in charge again soon. Pakenham presented the terms on June 6, and by the eighteenth a treaty had been drafted and ratified. For thirty years the United States and Britain had blustered over Oregon. Then they liquidated the whole affair in just twelve days.

That left Polk free to pursue a second and greater Pacific beachhead. On June 3 Secretary of War Marcy ordered General Kearny to occupy New Mexico and proceed to California. He captured Santa Fe without a fight, then struck southward in September on the old de Anza trail with three hundred cavalrymen and a band of Mormon volunteers. Still in New Mexico, he bumped into Kit Carson and heard wonderful news: California was in American hands! It seemed that Frémont had completed his ride back to the settlements on the Sacramento River early in

June. It was hot and breezy, the grassy California hills were already yellow, and the province was aflame. How many conspiracies competed to set the spark? There was Larkin's plan to induce the *californios* to declare independence, Hasting's plan to filibuster, Frémont and Gillespie's belief that Buchanan wanted them to stage a coup, and Polk and Marcy's plan for conquest in war. But the plot that preempted them all was that of a pack of desperadoes under Ezekiel Merritt, who captured a herd of horses meant for Castro's militia and laid siege, on June 14, to Gov. Mariano Guadalupe Vallejo's simple, stately rancho in the Sonoma wine country. Vallejo invited his captors to calm themselves and produced generous goblets of brandy. His hospitality had just about carried the day when the abstemious William B. Ide burst in to arrest Vallejo and cart him off to Sutter's Fort.

Ide then declared a California Republic, "which shall secure to us all Civil & religious liberty, which shall encourage virtue and literature, which shall leave unshackled by fetters Agriculture, Commerce, and Mechanism." (A Franciscan might well have made something out of the words that Ide capitalized and those he did not!) Ide also inspired the grizzly bear ensign on green, white, and red that gave the filibuster its name: the Bear Flag Revolt. Castro satisfied honor with a militia attack on Sonoma but retreated after a skirmish near San Rafael that left eight people dead. The fighting gave Frémont his chance for glory. He arrogated to himself command of the Republic and set about raising a California battalion. He also gave a name to the strait separating the Marin headlands from San Francisco. Thinking of Constantinople's Golden Horn, he called it the Golden Gate.

Legitimate American authority arrived in the person of Commodore Sloat, who raised the Stars and Stripes at Monterey on July 7. Not to be outdone, Frémont shed his role as protector of the Bear Flag and raised American flags at Yerba Buena, Sonoma, and Sutter's Fort. Late in July Sloat, for health reasons, turned over his command to Commodore Stockton, who competed for the role of California's proconsul with Frémont and Gillespie, who captured Los Angeles in August. But the martial law Gillespie imposed was so obnoxious to the *californios* that José Maria Flores led a revolt, captured Gillespie, and carted him off to San Pedro. The chance arrival of some U.S. Marines won his release, but Flores's plucky band, armed with a ceremonial cannon from the plaza in Los Angeles, remained at large for three months. Then Kearny's hundred-man column emerged from the hellish lava hills east of San Diego after a two-thousand-mile trek. But Andrés Pico's *californio* troop ("the very best riders in the world," said Kearny) lured the Americans into pursuit, then turned to attack, killing twenty-two Yankees and wounding sixteen (including Kearny). Still, the brave *californios* could not pre-

MANIFEST
DESTINY
OR
UNITED STATES
EXPANSION
TO THE
PACIFIC OCEAN

A.O. Line = the
Adams–Onis
boundary from
Transcontinental
Treaty of 1819

BRITISH NORTH AMERICA

Québec

UNITED STATES
OF AMERICA

by treaty
1783

FLORIDA
by
treaty
1819

New Orleans

West Florida
by filibuster
1810, 1813

Mississippi
A.O. Line
St. Louis
St. Joseph
Arkansas R.
Red R.
Sabine R.
A.O. Line
Battle of
San Jacinto
Brazos R.
Colorado R.
San Jacinto
San Antonio
Galveston

REPUBLIC OF TEXAS
1836–45

HUDSON'S BAY COMPANY LANDS

To Britain
To U.S.A.
by treaty

Saskatchewan R.

Lewis and Clark 1804

Missouri R.

Oregon Trail
Fort Leavenworth
Fort Laramie
Santa Fe Trail
Bent's Fort
Santa Fe Trail
Santa Fe
Pecos R.

LOUISIANA
PURCHASE
1803

Platte R.
Yellowstone R.
Snake R.

To U.S.A.
by treaty 1818

Matamoros

Rio Grande
El Paso
del Norte
Gila R.

MEXICO
independent
1821

GADSDEN
PURCHASE
1853

Vancouver
Island

Fort Victoria

San Juan Islands
boundary settlement
1872

BRITISH
COLUMBIA
1847

Astoria

Columbia R.

Willamette R.

OREGON
by treaty
1846

Klamath
Lake

Snake R.

Mormon
Settlement
Salt Lake

Fort Bridger

Spanish Trail

A.O. Line

California Trail

MEXICAN
CESSION
1848
by conquest

Sutter's
San Joaquin R.
Monterey

Los Angeles
San Diego

105° W.
120° W.
40° N.
30° N.
120° W.
115° W.
110° W.
90° W.
75° W.
40° N.
30° N.
90° W.
75° W.

vent the American soldiers from occupying the *pueblos* and ports, and after Los Angeles capitulated in January 1847, Pico turned himself in and resistance ceased.

The American forces in California consisted of nothing but a few hundred filibusters, Frémont's sixty "topographers," Kearny's surviving troopers, two frigates, four schooners, and 250 marines. But that was enough, thanks to the fact that the British did not intervene. The commander of Britain's Pacific squadron, Admiral Seymour, had begged in vain for instructions in case of revolution or war in California. He finally sailed to Monterey on his own authority, where the *californios* cried out for his help. But the disciplined admiral dared not risk provoking an Anglo-American war. So the Royal Navy remained aloof, and by the time Palmerston returned to Whitehall, it was too late. The United States had won California as a legitimate prize in war.

Another tortuous year passed before the Mexicans admitted defeat and Polk's envoy, Nicholas Trist, found a government with the authority to negotiate. Trist had survived a feud with Gen. Winfield Scott, a double-crossing by old Santa Anna, and even a recall from Polk, but he finally brought home the Treaty of Guadalupe Hidalgo, signed on February 2, 1848. Mexico ceded Texas, New Mexico, and California (almost half its entire land area) to the United States in return for $15 million and the dropping of $3.25 million in American claims. Amazingly, almost no one was happy with it. Whigs, abolitionists, and the antiwar movement condemned the treaty as predatory. Extreme expansionists— the "all Mexico movement"—thought it too mild. But Americans were sick of the war by then and uncertain of its justice, while the British were finally urging restraint on the United States. So Polk submitted the treaty to the Senate, which ratified it thirty-eight to fourteen in March.

Then Americans turned their backs on the most successful war in their history. Whigs had voted for it lest they seem unpatriotic. John Quincy Adams and Abraham Lincoln were among them. But they denounced it as "Jimmy Polk's war," suspected the whole thing of being a plot to create new slave states, and called the President's account of its origins a lie. New England abolitionists and Pennsylvania Quakers likewise denounced the war as conceived in sin. For all that, few suggested giving the Southwest back to Mexico.

Frémont was court-martialed and might have been shot, but Senator Benton got him off with the mere loss of his commission, and Polk even commuted that. The Pathfinder remained a public icon and with the support of his ambitious Jessie went on to be the Republican party's first candidate for the White House. After his death, Jessie reigned as the "beautiful and brilliant" grande dame of Los Angeles society until 1902. Trist, who achieved more in Mexico City than a parade of diplomats before him, was anathema to Polk and the Whigs alike. He had to wait twenty-two years for the government to reimburse his expenses and hire him to be postmaster of Alexandria, Virginia. As for Polk, he gained for the United States one-third of its total eventual land area, yet his own party did not complain when he kept a pledge to retire after one term. Just months after leaving office, he came home from a tour of the South suffering from acute stomach pains. He called for a minister, received his long-delayed baptism, and died on June 15, 1849.

Thanks to the Treaty of Guadalupe Hidalgo Americans now governed from Father Serra's San Diego all the way to Vancouver's Puget Sound. The balance of power in the New World had ceased to exist, and its requiem was written in 1846 when Pakenham reported to London the satisfaction with which Americans greeted the Oregon treaty. An icy Palmerston scribbled in the margin: "It would have been strange if the Americans had not been pleased with an arrangement which gives them everything which they ever really wanted."

Beneath it a clerk wrote: "Nothing to be done."

Panama and Cape Horn
1849

MOUNT DIABLO stands 3,850 feet above the "counter-coast"
(Contra Costa) of San Francisco Bay, one range in from the
Berkeley and Oakland hills. On especially chilly winter nights
Diablo is the region's most likely peak to sport a frosty crown, and on
especially clear days—once common, now rare—Diablo's summit offers
a vista reaching clear across the Central Valley to the Sierra Nevada.
There are several legends as to how it got its name. The one that ought
to be true was popularized by Bret Harte. It seems that a gentle Jesuit,
Father José Antonio Haro, hiked up the mountain in the year 1770 and
met *el Diablo* at the summit. "Look to the west," said the Evil One, and
showed him a vision of Spain's Catholic glory: the happy missions dot-
ting the California coast. Then Satan said, "Look to the east," and lo!
the valley was so filled with Conestoga wagons and grasping Anglos that
the very dust rose up to heaven in supplication. "Who are these swag-
gering Ishmaelites?" asked Haro, whereupon the Devil showed him a
vision of caverns and rivers glowing with gold. Father Haro might postpone all this if he would go back to Spain, with all his crosses and bells,
and leave California to the Devil. The good *padre* swooned, his crucifix
fell, and he wrestled with the Enemy there at the summit. His simple
muleteer found him unconscious the following day and carried him
down in a litter. He had seen, he said, his master's assailant. "What
mean you, Ignacio?" cried Father Haro. "Why, the bear, your Reverence
. . . who attacked your worshipful person while you were meditating on
the top of yonder mountain."

Whatever the truth of the legend, the vision came true in 1849. For
just a week before the signing of the Treaty of Guadalupe Hidalgo,
gold was found at Sutter's Mill. What resulted was the first sizable
white colony on the North Pacific coast, the first metropolis of any

kind there save in closed Japan, the first omniracial society there, save perhaps for Honolulu, and the last Pacific product of the age of sail and muscle.

What would have become of California had gold been discovered ten or twenty years before? The immigrants, mostly American, would still have come in their tens of thousands, but they would not be arriving on American soil. The Mexican generals, heirs to the gold-hungry Spaniards, might have judged defense of the mines more interesting than their internal feuds. Canning or Palmerston might have protected the region and the rights of Englishmen who went there. Or California might have emerged as an independent republic held in place, like Hawaii, by an equilibrium of outside powers. But it is dangerous for historians to let their imaginations run free—they just might, like Father Haro, be tempted to betray their profession.

Speaking of victims, consider John Sutter, the Swiss empire builder who had the excellent idea of becoming the Cattle King of California two decades too soon. He had befriended the Spanish grandees and been granted forty-nine thousand acres along the best stretch of the Sacramento River. He had bought Fort Ross from the Russians, made Sutter's Fort impregnable, and pioneered agriculture, viticulture, and stock raising in the Central Valley. But he had three mortal vulnerabilities: a mountain of debt, a faulty (or unlucky) political sense, and a problematical legal claim to his gargantuan holdings. The first weakness meant that he needed cash flow. New settlers helped to provide that, which is one reason he opened his arms to Yankee wagon trains. But the instability the newcomers caused, and their own hunger for land, exacerbated the second and third weaknesses. In 1845 he tried to position himself between rival *californios* and between the Mexicans and the "foreigners," earning for himself the distrust of all parties. When the Bear Flag flew, he fell out with Frémont (though mostly through the latter's ill temper). And when the United States moved in, Sutter had to defend his land grants before American law.

Still, Sutter was optimistic as late as 1847, which was when James W. Marshall, a carpenter from Lambertville, New Jersey, suggested he build a sawmill. Marshall was frustrated by the dearth of trees in the valley, so Sutter put him to work constructing a mill at a place called Coloma, in the wooded foothills on the south fork of the American River. On January 24, 1848, while supervising the dredging of the tailrace (lest his logs become snagged beneath the current), Marshall spied a glimmering nugget. It was yellow and pocked, as if by toothmarks, and it sure looked like gold. Sutter agreed and tried to hush it up. He had no reason to believe it presaged a big strike, and he feared his land being overrun by lawless fortune hunters. But conscious promotion by two men triggered a gold rush that covered Sutter's lands with thousands of miners and thousands of claims. As his creditors closed in, Sutter staked all he had on a development called Sutterville, designed to be the capital and river port of the gold country. Instead, the miners and suppliers flocked to its competitor, Sacramento, four miles away. In later years Sutter retired to the Pennsylvania Dutch country and died in Washington, D.C., in 1880, still fighting for a court judgment or pension in honor of having done as much as any man to Americanize California.

The first of the two men who sparked the gold rush was a shady speculator named Samuel Brannon, who came around the Horn with two hundred Mormons. He took to investing his people's tithes in private business ventures and was admonished by Brigham Young himself to return "the Lord's money." Brannon said he would gladly do so as soon as he got a receipt signed by the Lord. When he heard the rumor of gold at Coloma, Brannon bought up all the stores that miners might need, then roared into San Francisco in May 1848 shouting "Gold! Gold from the American River!" In the words of the vexed colonel in charge of the presidio, "Labourers of every trade left their workbenches, and tradesmen their shops. Sailors desert their ships as fast as they arrive on the coast, and several vessels have gone to sea with hardly enough hands to spread a sail. . . . labouring men at the mines can earn in one day more than double a soldier's pay and allowances for a month." Towns lost over half their population, then swelled anew as six thousand "forty-eighters" sailed in from Hawaii and South America to expand the non-Indian population of California by 40 percent. By the turn of the year the first of five thousand Mexicans arrived overland from Sonora—the very migration Gálvez and de Anza had tried so hard to promote seven decades before.

The second man who triggered the gold rush was outgoing President James K. Polk, who could not help but gloat, in his last message to Congress, "The accounts of the abundance of gold in that territory are of such an extraordinary character as would scarcely command belief, were they not corroborated by the authentic report of officers in the public service." California gold, he said, would cover the cost of the Mexican War a hundred times over. Polk's hope was to push statehood for California through Congress before he left office. The slavery issue prevented that until the Compromise of 1850, but by then the non-Indian population had sextupled again and would reach 260,000 by 1852.

I soon shall be in Francisco, and then I'll look around.
And when I see the gold lumps there I'll pick them off the ground . . .
Oh! California, that's the land for me,
I'm going to Sacramento with my washbowl on my knee.

The forty-niners had three routes by which to reach El Dorado—one if by land and two if by sea. The overland California trail was simplest for Midwesterners, and several hundred pioneers had set out before news of the gold strike reached St. Louis. Imagine their surprise when they cleared the Nevada wastes and descended South Pass into—mayhem. But where a total of 2,700 men and women journeyed overland to California from 1844 to 1848, some 30,000 did so in 1849 alone. Most were single men, middle class (because outfitting required some capital), and tenderfeet. Some of them knew it, and that was the angle seized upon by various entrepreneurs touting safe, fast, and predictable alternatives. The most fantastic was that of Rufus Porter, founder of *Scientific American* magazine. Anticipating the great Zeppelin airships of the next century, he designed a steam-powered balloon with propellers and a rudder on which passengers might soar to California in comfort for a mere fifty dollars. Before its maiden voyage Porter sensibly abandoned the project to devote himself to preparing for the Second Coming.

More practical was the attempt to achieve economies of scale through "passenger trains" in which wagons, mules, supplies, and savvy would be provided up front by the company. All the migrant had to do was buy a ticket. The first attempt at scheduled overland transportation was the Pioneer Line's party of 161 people and three hundred mules that left Independence, Missouri, in May 1849. For a $200 fare, two St. Louis promoters promised to deliver a passenger safe and sound in Sacramento in under two months. The trip was a horror. Everyone overloaded the wagons, including the company, which expected to boost profits by hauling freight and then drove the mules literally to death. Rain, sleet, and hail assaulted the party. The company divided over which route to take. Discipline broke down, scurvy broke out, and the survivors arrived in California with joints so tight not a man could stand up straight. The Sand Walking Company, a party of gullible greenhorns on the southern route, resisted the advice of their own hired scout and took a shortcut that put another name on the map: Death Valley. So the Pioneer Line and its imitators were pronounced a "humbug," and after the gold frenzy subsided, emigrants returned to the more relaxed and ad hoc "family system" of wagon trains. The brief history of the Pony Express (1858–61) taught the same lesson. Regular, predictable, and affordable communication with the Pacific coast would come, but by railroad and telegraph, not muscle power.

Plenty of gold, so I've been told. Heave away! Santy Anno!
Plenty of gold, so I've been told, way out in Californ-i-o!

So heave her up, and away we'll go. Heave away! Santy Anno!
Heave her up and away we'll go, way out to Californ-i-o!

If the overland route was most direct but most grueling, the traditional Yankee merchants' course about Cape Horn was the least direct but safest. Unfortunately for the Argonauts it also took the longest, as one might expect of a voyage starting in Boston, at about 42° north latitude, reaching about 58° south latitude, and ending back at 37° north latitude in San Francisco. Moreover, a map or globe will show that ships could not even begin to make westward progress without first sailing about two thousand miles *east,* since South America lies almost entirely east of North America. As Navy Lt. Matthew F. Maury warned: "The California passage is the longest and most tedious within the domains of Commerce; many are the vicissitudes that attend it."

Why then was the Cape Horn voyage so popular that somewhere between sixteen thousand (the San Francisco customs house figure) and forty thousand (probably closer to the truth) braved it in 1849 alone? The main reason was that news of the gold strike reached the East in December when the overland route was wintry, but the Southern Hemisphere was at the height of summer. So rather than ride the rails and coaches to Missouri, stock up on gear, and wait for spring, the gold bugs stormed the docks of Boston, Salem, New York, Philadelphia, or Baltimore and bought passage on any jerry-built craft prepared to leave at once. It is amazing that none of the five hundred forty-niner hulks sank.

By all accounts—and scores were written—it was a miserable trip. For the first few weeks spirits were generally high and even seasickness a source of humor. Crossing the equator was an occasion for horseplay and revelry, and the customary stop at Rio de Janiero a treat. But bleak Patagonian seas conjured repressed irritations, dread of Cape Horn, and second thoughts about the whole enterprise. Few captains dared the Strait of Magellan, with its craggy two-mile-wide passage, terrific tides, ghostly volcanoes, and legendary cannibals. But in broad Drake's Passage the prevailing west-sou'westerlies might block a ship's progress for a month or more before it managed to creep into the Pacific. No wonder sailors called it "Cape Stiff," and not a few landlubbers panicked over the prospect of being marooned on Antarctica's doorstep. Morale rose again in the South Pacific, and at Valparaiso, where scores of ships piled up waiting to take on water and fruit, the Chileans marveled that Yankees paid without haggling what street vendors asked. But the second-most hazardous, tedious leg of the trip was to come, for the doldrums and currents sometimes forced ships as far as 140° west longitude before winds rose to nudge them toward the perilous approach to the Golden Gate.

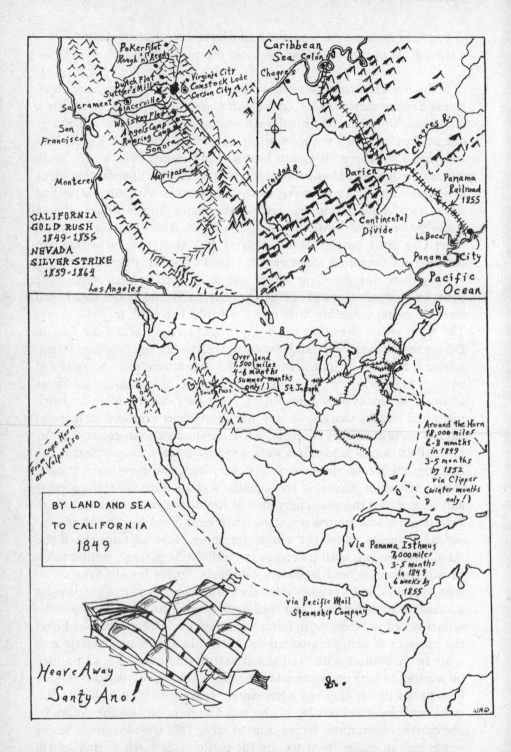

CALIFORNIA
GOLD RUSH
1849-1855
NEVADA
SILVER STRIKE
1859-1864

Poker Flat
Rough n' Ready
Dutch Flat
Sutter's Mill
Sacramento
Placerville
Whiskey Flat
Angels Camp
Roaring Camp
Sonora
San Francisco
Virginia City
Comstock Lode
Carson City
Monterey
Mariposa
Los Angeles

Caribbean
Sea Colón
Chagres
Chagres R.
N
Trinidad R.
Darien
Continental
Divide
Panama
Railroad
1855
La Boca
Panama City
Pacific
Ocean

BY LAND AND SEA
TO CALIFORNIA
1849

Over land
1,500 miles
4-6 months
(summer months
only!)
South Pass
St. Joseph

GOLD!

From Cape Horn
and Valparaiso

Around the Horn
18,000 miles
6-8 months
in 1849
3-5 months
by 1852
via Clipper
(winter months
only!)

Via Panama Isthmus
7,000 miles
3-5 months
in 1849
6 weeks by
1855

via Pacific Mail
Steamship Company

Heave Away
Santy Ano!

WM

Despite all that, the Cape Horn route flourished and shipowners got away with cargo rates of sixty dollars per ton and fares of $150 to $200. That meant that a single voyage could net more than $70,000, or the entire cost of building a sleek new vessel in eastern shipyards. Profits and the demand for speed combined to make the early 1850s the heyday of the U.S. shipping industry and the last and greatest era of sailing ship design.

Cliché or not, Americans have been in love with speed since Benjamin Franklin pledged two-day postal service and sailors in the War of 1812 celebrated the *flight* of Old Ironsides from five British pursuers as much as her *victory* over the *Guerrière*. The 1830s boom in the China trade was a special fillip to naval architects bent on speed. The most celebrated were Samuel H. Pook (of Civil War fame) and William H. Webb, designers, and Donald McKay, master shipwright. But what came to be known as the packet, the Baltimore clipper, and finally the "extreme clipper" were inventions of an industry rather than of discrete individuals. Suffice it to say that by gold rush days a clipper meant a "sharp built" ship, very heavily sparred, with a concave hull and pointed prow—in every way the opposite of the tubby galleons that first ruled the Pacific. The clipper's prow and hull minimized resistance and allowed it to "clip" through the wash, while the sparring allowed the captain to lay on as many as twelve sails, two forward, one aft, and three each on the masts. Of course, the pinched-in shape of the hull reduced the size of the hold considerably, but Chinese cargoes like tea and silks, and California cargoes like human beings and luxury items, were low-bulk/high-value commodities. Argonauts demanded speed, and so did the shippers, who had every incentive to squeeze in as many round-trips as possible. Shipyards, in turn, laid down clippers as quickly as capacity and capital allowed.

But the clipper ship was more than design; it was a system integrating scientific, technological, economic, and human factors. For even the sleekest clipper did not deserve the name unless skippered by a "driver" willing to throw every sheet to the wind and whip his crew into a sporting frenzy to coax the last knot out of the weather. The log of Capt. Josiah P. Cressy suggests the price of trying to harness, rather than sit out, a storm:

Heavy Gales, Close Reefed Topsails split fore Staysail & Main Topmast Staysail at 1 P.M. Discovered Main Masthead Sprung . . . sent down Royal & Topgallant Yards & Booms off Lower & Topsail Yard to releave the mast, very turbulent sea Running. Ship Laboring hard & shipping large quantities of Water over lee Rail. . . . Middle & Latter parts hard Gales & Harder squalls. No observations.

But even a "horse" of a captain could not do his ship honor without referring to the charts and instructions compiled by the U.S. Navy. For the clipper era succeeded a wave of reforms instituted in 1841 by Secretary of the Navy Abel P. Upshur and Lieutenant Maury. The latter, appointed Superintendent of the Naval Observatory after a stagecoach accident ended his career at sea, was a vigorous proponent of Pacific expansion and a disciple of science in the service of government and commerce. Thanks to him detailed studies of winds, currents, and tides on Pacific routes became available to clipper captains.

By 1851 the new-fangled steam frigates were "too expensive" and "too slow" to compete. Shipyards went back to building far more tonnage of pure sailing ships as clippers raced for records and cut the New York-to-San Francisco run from an average of over six months to about 120 days. The return trip was even faster, since the Cape Horn westerlies became a boost. Captain Freeman Hatch, in 1853, raced his *Northern Light* from San Francisco to Boston in seventy-six days. But that year was the floodtide, when 145 clippers plied the California route. By then the fleet was overbuilt, the gold rush was over, and freight rates were on their way down to $7.50 per ton. Clippers flew to the Pacific only to lie at anchor for weeks. In 1855 the Panama railroad and coastal steamers took what was left of the California trade. The Civil War was the final blow, and the Pacific became the plaything of iron and steam after all.

> *Now's the time to change your clime, give up work and tasking*
> *All who choose be rich as Jews, even without asking.*
> *California's precious earth turns the new world frantic:*
> *Sell your traps and a take a berth across the wild Atlantic....*
> *Yankee Doodle, keep it up.*

The third route to California was the gambler's choice, and since all Argonauts were risk takers by definition, it attracted 6,489 in 1849 and an average of twenty thousand per year throughout the 1850s. That was the Panama isthmus. An emigrant could take ship in anything, sail or steam, from the East Coast and reach Chagres on the isthmus in eight to twelve days. Then his troubles began. Chagres consisted of a thatched village populated by Indians, Africans, and a few officials from New Granada (or Colombia), of which Panama was then a province. A handful of miserable "hotels" sprang up to exploit the gold seekers, who were certain to "be sick part of the time. Most persons at Chagres become dissipated in a few weeks; and between drinking too much, running after women, or gambling, exhaust all their energies, and when they get sick, they have no vitality left in their systems to recover."

They were fortunate if they did, for thousands of whites caught tropical diseases and died there. But getting out was no easy task, despite advice on how to do it from dozens of guidebooks sold back in the States. To cross to the Pacific side one had to hire a canoe and native boatman, whose fares predictably soared to fifty dollars per trip. The thirty-nine-mile journey (in pouring rain from June to December) ended at the continental divide. From there travelers had to descend, on foot or rented mule, twenty-six miles to the Pacific, with all their baggage (if they hadn't sold or chucked it by now). One doughty American woman called it a "ride over a wild, inhuman country on the back of a wild, irresponsible mule driven by a wild, demoralized, irrepressible son of the tropics." The port of Panama was a good deal more pleasant than Chagres, but most grew to hate it as well. For there the Argonaut paced for a month or more waiting to find space on a California-bound vessel. Steamers dominated the Pacific coastal traffic because their freedom from winds and currents allowed them to plough up the Baja and Alta California coasts in about three weeks. All told, if you were grabbed by "the absurd notion that the whole [California] country would be appropriated before [you] had set foot on it," you just *might* reach it from New York in only six or seven weeks via Panama, but at high cost to health and pocketbook.

Those costs might be eliminated altogether by either of two methods. The first was to push a railroad through the mountainous jungle of Panama—a "transcontinental" railroad forty-eight miles long. New York investor William H. Aspinwall completed the task in 1855, after which time people and goods could move from the Atlantic seaboard to California entirely by steam power in less than two months. The second method of taming Panama was to cut a canal. Now, the Polk administration pulled off another diplomatic coup when it procured special transit rights from the government of New Granada. But no sooner did the Yanks begin to eye Panama than a threat arose to the north. The people of Yucatán, of all places, considered seceding from chaotic, defeated Mexico and placing their peninsula under British protection! Polk bluntly forbade the transfer in April 1848, and thus "Polk's Corollary" to the Monroe Doctrine held that no European power could colonize in the New World *even with* the consent of the people involved. Palmerston, needless to say, was outraged, and moved to reinforce Britain's existing protectorates over Belize and Nicaragua's Mosquito Coast. At length President Zachary Taylor and Secretary of State John M. Clayton negotiated a compromise. In the Clayton-Bulwer Treaty of April 1850, the United States and Britain pledged not to construct a canal without the other's approval, or fortify a canal once built, or even colonize or exercise dominion over any part of Central America. Given the balance of naval power at the time, it was a fair deal. But Democrats still called it a sellout and wryly nominated the Secretary of State for a British knighthood.

The California gold rush marked the end of the age when the North Pacific was accessible only within the limits of winds, currents, and sail, rivers, boats, and muscle. It also introduced a new sort of conflict to Pacific shores: enmity not only between Europeans and the people they found there but between competing races of immigrants. For if 70 percent of the forty-niners were Anglo-American, 30 percent were not. They included Irish, French, and German Catholics, German and Polish Jews, Hawaiians, Mexicans, South Americans, and Chinese. All might proudly claim to be Californians, or Americans. But what did it mean to be an American? A first hint of how difficult it would be to answer that question was the voyage of the steamer *California*, whose captain put in to Panama on the Pacific in January 1849 only to spy seven hundred American gold seekers clamoring to get on board. He had room for only 250, and 69 places were already occupied by Peruvians who boarded at Callao. So the furious Yankees pressured Gen. Persifor S. Smith, who was en route to command the California garrison, to order the ship's captain to oust the Peruvians. The general cited an American law (which he had just invented) to the effect that foreigners were not permitted to mine gold on U.S. territory. In the end, the Peruvians stayed aboard ship, but sure enough, within a year or two many thousands of Indians, Hispanics, Chinese, and others found themselves pushed to the fringes of the mining camps or put to work as laborers for those who owned the claims. American whites had not conquered a Pacific empire only to lose it, and its gold, to red, brown, or yellow hordes. So instead they posed that most uncomfortable of questions, and one that has haunted California ever since: just who is an American?

The Fifth 'aha iki

Saitō: So, your Jimmy Polk must be one of the most celebrated Presidents. Yet I don't recall hearin' tell of him.

Scholar: It doesn't surprise me. Polk is either forgotten or vilified.

Kaahumanu: But you said he was your people's greatest conqueror—

Witte:—except for Washington himself. Even democracies shame their best leaders. What they must do to succeed condemns them in their own peoples' eyes. But Seward, surely you cheered Polk's acquisitions?

Seward: I was glad of them later, but I abominated the means he employed.

Witte: He who wills the end must will the means.

Seward: Other means were available.

Scholar: I doubt it. Timing was everything.

Seward: I never believed in expansion for its own sake. Mr. Polk's war was "conceived in sin," as our paper in Albany put it, and it set us on course for civil war. Emerson said that the Mexican War was a dose of arsenic.

Scholar: Ralph Waldo Emerson?

Saitō: Excuse, please. Just how did Polk set a course for civil war?

Seward: Because, Ambassador, he—or his party (it really started with the Texas resolution) created for the first time the prospect of the *extension* of slavery to new lands. So long as slavery was contained in old Dixie, even wise Southerners believed it would eventually disappear. But the prospect of new slave states gave the institution a new lease on life, encouraged our Southern colleagues to make an issue of each new territory or state, and forced upon us a series of ever more tortured compromises until North and South alike grew ashamed of the pretense. Mind you, I don't believe we sinned against Mexico—at least, no worse than the Mexicans sinned against us. But we sinned against freedom and reaped the whirlwind in the Civil War.

Saitō: Then it was karma.

Seward: Yes, it was . . . what?

Saitō: Karma. The forces set in motion by one's deeds that determine the fate of the soul in its next incarnation. By dividing your nation, race against race, you doomed the nation itself to purgation.

Seward: Lincoln could not have said it better. Well, in fact he did: "A house divided against itself cannot stand."

Serra: If your Lincoln said that, he was only quoting the Lord.

Witte: If you mean that a nation's injustice to others comes back to haunt it, then I, too, believe. It is Russia's curse.

Scholar: I can't believe this! I expected you statesmen to help me *rationalize* history, and you turn out to be a bunch of mystics!

Saitō: Doctor, haven't you learned how little we understand even our own lives? How then can we claim to interpret the lives of nations? Our plans go awry, or we get what we want only to find it was not what we thought, or we prepare for dangers that never arise only to be attacked on unguarded flanks. Either history is random or its logic is imposed from without—karma.

Witte: Fate.

Seward: Providence.

Scholar: So you suggest that the Mexican War, by extending slavery, condemned the United States to four years of fratricide *even though* historians find no evidence that extending slavery was a motive for the war in the first place—?

Seward: I believe it *was* the motive.

Scholar: —and that nothing that might have happened *after* 1846 could have prevented the Civil War?

Saitō: You misunderstand *me*, Doc. I don't know whether your Civil War was inevitable. Nor do I judge slavery one way or another, except perhaps as evidence of hypocrisy. I mean that your folly was in building a nation on a mixture of races in the first place. That is an error Japan has never made.

Scholar: You leave me breathless.

Witte: Come, Professor. We do not mean to belittle your researches. You were about to make a point about Polk.

Scholar: Yes, for what it's worth. I was going to suggest to Seward that slavery and Southern political clout were facts of life. At least Polk can be credited with balancing Texas with the annexation of free states in Oregon and California. The Democrats overcame sectional rivalry in the interest of the whole nation—something the Whigs could never have done.

Seward: Do not call them Democrats—no slave party deserves that name. And if the Whigs proved weak it was by reason of folly, not principle! Texas, California, Oregon, perhaps Canada would have begged to join the Union, freely and without violence, if we had let time do its work and *set our own house in order*. Still, Polk would never have won were it not. . . . There's no point.

Serra: On the contrary, Mr. Seward, proceed.

Seward: Well, you know how close the election was in 1844, especially in New York State. Thurlow Weed and I prevailed upon Millard Fillmore to run for governor—he expected to be Clay's vice-presidential candidate and was damned mad at us for talking him out of it. We thought he would help the ticket, but frankly he proved a dud. Then

Clay himself ignored my advice to take a strong stand against Texas and the extension of slavery. His double-talk drove thousands to vote Liberty—

Serra: Could you have done nothing to turn the tide?

Seward: I campaigned for Clay, but . . .

Serra: Go on, Mr. Seward.

Seward: I didn't run myself. I'd been governor twice. I was tired, just wanted to practice law, thought it prideful to seek a third term. . . .

Serra: And?

Seward: And I thought I would lose, dammit! Anyway, my wife wanted me home for a change. And, well, I confess that half of me was glad Clay and Fillmore lost. I've never said that before. You see, the professor was right. What beat us wasn't the Democrats but the Liberty party—the abolitionists themselves—who helped throw the election to the slavers because we Whigs compromised our principles!

Scholar: I understand. But you're forgetting that New York is not the whole country, and all Whigs did not feel the same as you. Your party was a mishmash of all sorts of interests. You launched your own career under the anti-Masonic banner, and opposition to the Nativists' bigotry against the Irish and Jews. Moreover, Whigs in the West and South, even many in New York, were pretty nervous about the prospect of being swamped by freed slaves, or Irish Catholics for that matter. Anyway, Clay could hardly abolish slavery overnight, but he might *well* have lost Texas and Oregon for the U.S.!

Witte: How is that, Professor?

Scholar: I'm just saying that a Clay administration might have dithered until such time as the British got assertive about North America. At least Polk seized the moment. Seward seems to imply that the U.S. ought to have expanded, but only on the condition that all new territories were free-soil. Most likely that would have blocked expansion altogether, or provoked Southern secession fifteen years earlier than was the case. Polk did not act out of any slaveholder's plot; historians have proven that. He surveyed the *international* situation, saw it was ideal, and struck. God help the U.S. if it had fallen into Civil War *without* having already annexed the West.

Kaahumanu: Then it should have been British policy to *encourage* civil war. The word that divides one's enemies is mightier than the spears of an army.

Scholar: Eris—the goddess of Discord—mightier than Mars. No, not even Palmerston was that cynical. And Pakenham was right when he warned that the best way to *unite* the Americans was for Britain to seek to divide them. Come to think of it, even slavery in Texas helped the U.S. cause in the short run by preventing Aberdeen from embracing Texas too strongly.

Witte: You made Aberdeen out to be a weakling.

Scholar: Compared with Palmerston he was both a weakling and a man of principle. He sincerely hoped that Texas might renounce slavery as the price of British support, and that abolition might then spread to the American South.

Witte: Thereby setting up Texas as a barrier to U.S. expansion and abolishing slavery at the same time. But Aberdeen accomplished neither purpose.

Scholar: He accomplished neither. But Britain was trapped by the bloody-minded Mexicans, who wouldn't let Texas go and couldn't reconquer it. They just shot prisoners and multiplied their threats until Texas had no choice but to seek a protector. Failing Britain, that had to be the U.S.

Seward: Which is not to say the Texans weren't clever, especially General Hamilton. They played Tyler and the Brits like a brace of fiddles.

Witte: The solution was to persuade Mexico to reform itself, like Turkey.

Scholar: Exactly. Now that you mention it, the British pursued the same strategy in Mexico and the Ottoman Empire. Both were vast, crumbling empires preyed upon by Britain's rivals. So Britain set itself up as the champion of the weak while urging the Mexicans and Turks to reform and modernize. Of course, it didn't work. But at least

Palmerston proved willing to fight in Turkey's defense—you know, the Crimean War. Aberdeen did nothing for Mexico.

Kaahumanu: Perhaps the British were ashamed because of the Opium War. . . .

Witte: And the cabinet crisis stayed their hand. It did always strike me, however, that you Anglo-Saxons seem as ashamed of your victories as of your defeats. What other nations sheath their swords out of self-imposed guilt?

Seward: Other nations may judge themselves by their own lights. But in 1846 Americans did *not* sheath their swords. I blame myself, in part.

Scholar: Come, Governor, you did your best. We must take care that self-recrimination does not become a point of pride.

Serra: Bueno, Professor. When did you learn that?

Scholar: I guess when I realized how much I enjoyed it myself. . . . So, Witte thinks we Americans are ashamed of our power?

Seward: I'd say afraid. We founded our government on the assumption of human cupidity, hence the system of checks and balances. But checks and balances cannot function in foreign policy or else we leave ourselves impotent. That explains why we veer back and forth between bellicosity and shame. *And that is why assertion abroad must always be matched by reform at home.*

Scholar: But Seward, don't forget that "checks and balances" were what allowed slavery to persist for so long. The South was able to control Congress, or the White House, or the courts, for decades. Do you really think slavery would have "withered away"?

Kaahumanu: It did in Hawaii.

Witte: Your analogy between Mexico and Turkey intrigues me, Professor. You know that the British ended up partitioning the Ottoman Empire. Imagine if they had given up on Mexican reform in the 1840s: they could have forced a partition. Say, United States gets Texas, New Mexico, and Oregon in exchange for Britain's taking Yucatán, Baja, and California. Or California could have been divided—

Scholar: You're forgetting the Monroe Doctrine! And that British enthusiasm for free trade went hand-in-hand with a *resistance* to acquiring new colonies. Some call the Liberals' policy "informal empire," or an "imperialism of free trade," but the fact remains that the Brits, especially Aberdeen, showed remarkable restraint in the Western Hemisphere. The U.S. was just dumb lucky that it could make its bid for empire at the precise moment when its greatest rival was temporarily *soured* on empire. Or was that karma, too?

Seward: Sir, you are Anglophile!

Scholar: I like to root for the underdog.

Seward: But *we* were the underdogs vis-à-vis Britain.

Saitō: I *thought* I detected a certain remorse in your lecture. You wish Palmerston had been in power to keep Texas and Oregon out of the U.S.!

Scholar: Maybe. Or maybe I wish there *had* been war with Britain so that the U.S. could have annexed Canada, too.

Seward: Well, I cannot cry for Britain, or for Mexico.

Serra: I pity the Mexicans. I do not pity Mexico.

Kaahumanu: Do you know whom I pity: the Chinese people, and Commissioner Lin.

Scholar: Ah yes, the sainted Lin, drug tsar of the Ch'ing.

Witte: Ha! You have tsars in America?

Scholar: Ever so many, Count Witte.

Saitō: Well, if Lin was a frustrated "drug tsar," then the East India Company was the biggest "drug ring" in the world, and your dashing Palmerston the head "pusher"!

Scholar: No argument, but to the Manchester School of economists, free trade was a universal principle, the condition under which all nations might maximize their prosperity.

Saitō: How was Chinese prosperity maximized by the importation of opium?

Scholar: Of course, it wasn't. But the British could not be accountable for the manner in which Chinese abused their freedom. Obviously the merchants were hiding behind a principle, but the opposite principle—government dictation of private behavior, on pain of death in the Chinese case!—was far more repugnant to an Englishman.

Saitō: Ah, but the British government took the lead in abolishing the slave trade. Why not the opium trade?

Scholar: False analogy. No one enjoys a natural freedom to take away another's freedom.

Witte: But it *is* permitted to use one's freedom to impose freedom on others, as the British did in China?

Saitō: And does not addiction *take away* freedom and make one a slave to it?

Scholar: In a manner of speaking, but the addict still chooses to partake.

Saitō: How many chose to be enslaved, and how many were suckered into it by the enticements of profiteers?

Scholar: Look, I'm just trying to explain the British defense of free trade, not justify dope. I'm as sympathetic to Commissioner Lin as Kaahumanu.

Saitō: Then you believe in protecting people from self-destructive behavior?

Scholar: My beliefs are irrelevant. If you read Palmerston's speech—

Saitō: To hell with British lords! Can opium addiction be a *rational* choice?

Scholar: I suppose not.

Saitō: Then everyone who succumbs to addiction is *irrational*, and society is justified in curtailing their freedom.

Scholar: Where do you draw the line? The Southern planters argued that *slavery* was paternalistic because the slaves were thought incapable of caring for themselves. Would you have the state define what's irrational and *outlaw* it? You don't buy that, do you, Mr. Seward?

Seward: Of course not. But the issue is not the addicts, it's the dealers.

Saitō: That's not what Lin said! He held both responsible. Your "free trade" is only a conspiracy between the wretch and his supplier. If the Chinese understood shame their people would commit suicide before disgracing themselves, their family, their emperor. And *your* people would not shame themselves by profiting from the shame of others!

Witte: May we return to the point, Gentlemen? The point is the opening of China.

Scholar: Thank you, Count Witte. Weak, divided, despised, gigantic China—

Kaahumanu: Storyteller!

Scholar: Yes, Elizabeth. May I call you that?

Kaahumanu: In your sermon on the gold rush you made much—

Witte: Ho! ho! You accuse us of mysticism, and she thinks you're a preacher!

Kaahumanu: I did not mean to make a joke, but I think it was a good one. I want to say that at the end of your gold rush story you spoke of a new era of steam and rails. But you did not explain.

Scholar: I *want* to explain, if our friends will shut up about karma and opium.

Witte: Agreed.

Saitō: Speak for yourself, Count. Japan agrees.

Seward: Lay on, MacDuff.

Scholar: OK. My periodization is really simple. I merely suggest that the 1850s marked the beginning of the era in which industrial might came to determine the relative power that states could project into the North Pacific. It was America's good fortune that it boasted the enterprise, pioneering spirit, growing population, seamanship, and freedom from Old World rivalries sufficient to win a North Pacific empire even *before* its industrial era, and without any centrally planned imperial strategy—

Saitō: Stop right there, if you please.

Scholar: No karma.

Saitō: No karma, but how can you say Polk had no imperial strategy?

Scholar: I mean the U.S. had no long-term, coherent strategy.

Seward: I'm afraid I must agree with my Japanese colleague. If you mean that we pursued no tsarist plan for conquest or British imperial grand strategy, then I concur, but surely *government* propelled our expansion at every step. Our diplomats in Paris insisted on all the land east of the Mississippi River. Congress approved the admission of new states. Jefferson sent Lewis and Clark to explore and made the Louisiana Purchase. John Quincy Adams picked up the torch from Jefferson and promoted our Pacific destiny. Then he handed the torch to me. Monroe warned Europeans off the continent. Expansionism knew no parties, or rather all parties at different times. Pike, Frémont, Kearny—U.S. Army officers—and Wilkes, a Navy lieutenant. You mentioned Upshur and Lieutenant Maury, who marshaled government support for science. I may condemn Polk for reasons I need not repeat, but the record of government is long and honorable in support of national growth.

Scholar: Must a strategic *outcome* always be the result of a strategy? Against your litany, Mr. Seward, I would cite the pioneers who pushed west through the Appalachians despite government worries that they would make trouble with the Indians. Individual pioneers pressed against Louisiana and into Texas. The first Yankees in the Pacific were private merchants with no protection from government. Even Astor got no help in the end. Mountain men and settlers crossed the continent at their own risk. And Hawaii! No government agency sent missionaries there, or whalers to the Bering Sea, or clipper ships to China. The U.S. did not annex the North Pacific; Americans did.

Seward: Let us say that the federal government played a supportive, enabling role, though not a prescriptive, coercive one.

Saitō: The Mexican War?

Seward: An exception that proves my rule. The genius of American government is not in doctrinaire *laissez-faire,* or in centralized administration, but in policies that unleash, prudently, the energies of the people themselves.

Saitō: For good or ill?

Seward: For good or ill, perhaps. But I'll take American institutions over those of the shogun or tsar, or Santa Anna!

Scholar: Then I wonder when it was we lost that genius. Because nowadays—

Kaahumanu: Scholar! Steam and rails!

Scholar: Yes. Sorry, Kaahumanu. Steam and rails it is.

II

Of Steam and Rails

The Sixth 'aha iki

Scholar: Listen to this. "Without a prototype, a marvel not merely of American progress, but of all civilization. . . . As mercantile as Amsterdam or Liverpool, it has neither the hoarding avarice of the one nor the unscrupulous cupidity of the other. Just now grasping, with an iron arm, the broad and fertile shores of the North Pacific, how splendid seems the destiny of Chicago!"

Saitō: Chicago? On the North Pacific?

Scholar: *Grasping* the North Pacific, with an "iron arm."

Seward: It does sound familiar. . . . I wrote it! Why, Professor, you've read my *Travels.*

Scholar: Of course. You made my point for me about the impact of steam and rails. Remember that "real map" of the ocean I asked you to imagine, with its winds and currents? Well, the application of steam power to transportation changed the "real map" of the Pacific into the one that you and Witte will find most comfortable. To Saitō, a man of the 1930s, it will seem just a bit out of date. And to Father Serra and Kaahumanu I fear it will be futuristic. For in the age of steam engines, say, from 1850 to 1905, Western man broke the bonds of winds and currents and gained the power to travel the oceans in any direction. Steam navigation conquered the remoteness of Hawaii, the contrary currents off California and the Asian monsoons, not to mention the sheer distance that previously made the Pacific so daunting. Steam power opened the few great rivers of the North Pacific, like the Sacramento and the Amur, to oceangoing ships. Steam dredging conquered the sandbars that guarded the Columbia River, and

Pearl Harbor on Oahu. Steam ended that old trade-off between cargo space and speed and made possible the transport of hundreds of thousands of people to, or across, the Pacific.

Saitō: Chinese and Japanese in California.

Scholar: Precisely. In the age of steam the whites' technology forced open the ports of East Asia, then shipped their peoples abroad in such numbers that the whites began to fear for their own future. The railroad likewise revolutionized the North Pacific. Suddenly vast amounts of people and goods could be moved at a fraction of the time and cost across continents. But steamships, unlike sailing ships, required fuel depots and docks with spare parts and repair shops. Thus steam power created a new kind of dependency. Navies and merchant fleets needed coaling stations on coasts and islands astride their routes, a fact that helped to promote new forms of Pacific imperialism. Continental railroads needed points for taking on coal and water, and stations and yards across thousands of miles of wilderness, a fact that transformed the American and Canadian West and Siberia. Finally, the railroads carried with them the mammoth spools of telegraph wire that made communication with Pacific shores a matter of hours rather than months and made portions of the North Pacific susceptible to centralized imperial control. In all these ways the strategic environment changed after 1850, rewarding nations that adjusted quickly to the industrialization of transport.

Witte: And punishing those that don't. So Russia loses again.

Scholar: Now, Count Witte, no one knows better than you that Russia acquired strengths, too, in this period that even defeats in war could not expunge. So let's put out of our minds the way the story turned out and review the North Pacific struggle at the opening of the age of steam and rails. The United States would seem to hold every advantage in the short run. It possessed the West Coast and had Pacific-minded merchants, bankers, and industrialists and a free and growing population. It was speedily assimilating the industries pioneered in Britain and was beginning to demonstrate its own inventiveness. Moreover, the U.S. had a powerful balance in its business community between size (necessary for mobilizing capital) and competition (necessary for innovation). But most Americans still lived far from the Pacific, their energies were bound to be absorbed by the development of their own continent, and they ran the risk of being torn apart by the seething sectional crisis over slavery.

Looking back from 1900, one might conclude that the Pacific was bound to become an "American lake," another Manifest Destiny. But looking forward from 1850, one might just as well ask whether the country was already too large and divided to integrate the territory it had. Would a civil war tear the nation apart? If so, would California and Oregon go their own ways? Would foreign powers take advantage of American strife to revive their ambitions in North America and move in strength to the North Pacific? And even if the U.S. retained the West Coast, would Americans there be able to resolve the contradiction between a concept of citizenship and democracy open to all and a growing fear of being swamped by Asian immigrants?

Now consider Russia. As of 1850 it still held Alaska, though its five hundred residents there still relied on others, like the Hudson's Bay Company, for their daily bread. Of course, Russia was backward by comparison with the U.S. and preoccupied as always by imperial interests ranging from Europe to the Middle East to central Asia. Moreover, the tsarist government was the least adaptable to change. On the other hand, Russian control of eastern Siberia was uncontested, and the population east of the Urals had leapt from one million to 2.5 million over the previous fifty years. What if the tsarist government built a railroad to the Pacific and freed the youth from its thousands of crowded villages to emigrate to Siberia? Now that the Ch'ing dynasty was noticeably decrepit, would Russia make a new bid for the Amur and finally win a breadbasket for its North Pacific empire? If so, could it not then employ the new steamship technology to regularize communications and supplies to Alaska? Russia would probably never be capable of defending the North Pacific sea lanes, but perhaps the tsars could play Britain and the U.S. off against each other, buying time to build up its landward Pacific defenses. To statesmen like Witte and intellectuals like Dostoevsky, Russia's true mission lay in civilizing Siberia and reaching out to its pioneering twin, the U.S., across the waters of the North Pacific.

The third potential power in the theater would seem to have more short-run handicaps even than Russia. Japan had no access to modern technology and had a sociopolitical system designed to keep it that way. Though an island nation, it had no oceanic navy and thus was vulnerable to a determined thrust on its own shores. Even if the shogunate did open up to the world, as it must sooner or later, that might only conjure up the internal chaos that had led to its seclusion in the first place. Of the three possibilities attending an "opening of Japan"—civil war, a Chinese-style humiliation at the hands of the whites, or an internal revolution leading to rapid industrialization and North Pacific empire—the last seemed by far the most unlikely in 1850. But should that miracle occur, Japan had two advantages the Russians and Americans lacked: proximity and freedom from all other domestic and foreign ambitions. For Japan, foreign policy *was* North Pacific policy, and domestic development was identical to North Pacific development.

Of course, a modernizing, expansionist Japan would face terrible dangers. How could the Japanese obtain *from* the West the technology it needed to *compete* with the West without inspiring the *hostility* of the West? To remain passive was to choose national eclipse, but to become active was to choose unending struggle. No wonder Japan preferred for so long to sleep: the "rising sun" illuminated nothing but danger.

Saitō: Well said, Doc. This time you're off to a good start.

Kaahumanu: Why do you make it so complicated? Surely the nations that build the most steam engines will win. You make them sound so mighty.

Scholar: I have made Kaahumanu, of all people, a materialist! No, I only mean that the new technology created new rules for the game and a new range of possible outcomes. But it still mattered greatly not only how many steamships or railroads the nations could build, but how many they would decide to build, and how advanced they were, and when and where they were deployed. All that depended on human decisions.

Seward: Emerson said, "Machines are in the saddle and ride mankind," though I never really agreed with that.

Scholar: Neither do I, unless we put them in the saddle. I suppose that's possible. But getting back to Kaahumanu's point, none of this happened all of a sudden. New steamship construction, in fact, did not surpass that of pure sailing ship construction until the 1880s. Now, steam navigation began—

Seward: —when Robert Fulton—

Scholar: —in 1736, when a clock repairman from Chipping Camden, England, addressed the problem of how to get sailing ships out of port when the wind is against them. So he conceived of a tugboat with mechanical paddles! Alas, the primitive Newcomen engines of the day made the idea premature, and the man died in poverty. But even after much experimentation in France, England, and America culminated in Fulton's *Clermont*, steamships still faced a fight. Aside from their noisome qualities (one Hudson Valley yeoman, spying the *Clermont* from the bank, ran home to tell his wife he had spotted the devil paddling to Albany in a sawmill)—

Seward: Ha! I saw him there often, when the legislature was in session!

Scholar: —early steamboats were too slow and uneconomical for anything more than river transport. No steamship could carry enough fuel to make a long sea voyage, since their wooden hulls tended to "hog"—sag—amidships and at the ends if built too large, while steam-assisted sailing ships were much slower than full sail because of the drag caused by the paddle wheel. An auxiliary steam vessel, the *Savannah*, did cross the Atlantic in 1819 but used her engine only to get in and out of port. The problem of how to haul enough coal to cross an ocean seemed so intractable that one British scientist said a steam trip from New York to London was as likely as one to the moon. But as the price of iron fell, iron hulls won acceptance and expanded the size, hence the fuel capacity, of steamships. Second, the stern-mounted screw propellers of Sir Francis Pettit and John Ericsson (who later built the *Monitor*) created less friction and more propulsion than side-wheelers. To be sure, propellers required a higher engine speed and thus dangerously high boiler pressures. But the compound engine, first imagined by Jonathan Hornblower in 1781 and reintroduced in the 1850s, solved that by recirculating the hot steam and using it more than once. The compound engine increased power at a third less cost in fuel, without adding strain on the boiler.

These innovations made possible the first transatlantic steam lines and the beginnings of steam navigation in the Pacific, where coal was especially scarce and costly. Regular steam service in the Pacific was the brainchild of William Wheelwright, who began life as a printer's apprentice in Massachusetts, then ran away to South American seas. One of the few Yankees living "around the Cape," he won appointment as U.S. Consul in Guayaquil, then Valparaiso. It was there that he realized the newfangled steamships were the answer to the difficulties of sailing in the eastern Pacific Ocean. Wheelwright failed to find American backing, so his Pacific Steam Navigation Company of 1840 was British. Times were hard until the gold rush, but thereafter Wheelwright's compound-engine paddle steamers *Chili* and *Peru* showed tens of thousands of Argonauts the future. George Law, an American shipper, teamed with Aspinwall of the Panama Railroad to found the American Pacific Mail Line, their cash flow assured by a government contract to carry the mails to California. Within a decade twenty-nine steamers plied the Panama-to-San Francisco route and made their first appearance in Hawaii and East Asia.

The railroad was likewise the product of two ideas—steam power and rails—that had been applied for a century in Cornish mines and English collieries: steam engines to pump out water, and cars on wooden rails to roll out the ore. In 1767 the first iron rails were cast, and in 1814 George Stephenson constructed the first locomotive. Of course, horses could pull cars along rails, too, needed no fuel, didn't explode, and were ever so much more pleasant than the raucous, belching engines that left everyone caked in soot and gasping for air. But by the time Stephenson's Manchester-to-Liverpool line was completed in 1830 at the prodigious cost of $5 million, the locomotive's superior speed assured its future.

Three years earlier a group of Baltimore merchants met to launch the first American railroad despite the opposition of Congress, a skeptical public, and the entrenched interests of the Chesapeake and Ohio Canal. They had to raise all the capital themselves and import everything from England. But the gradual completion of the Baltimore and Ohio Railroad sparked a speculative boom in railroad construction that deepened and broadened the Industrial Revolution. The miles of track laid in the U.S. increased from 2,818 in 1840 to 9,021 in 1850, to 30,626 in 1860. And like the steamship, the railroad conquered on the strength of a series of incremental innovations. American engineer Robert L. Stevens's T-shaped rail and hooked spike greatly reduced derailments, while the wooden tie provided a flexible cushion. Boilers increased in size and drive mechanisms in efficiency and safety; the reverse gear, for instance, was a breakthrough in convenience on the mostly single-track lines of the day, and in safety, especially while braking. Americans also contributed to theoretical advances in the arts of tunneling, bridge building, curvatures, and grading.

Finally, the first generation of rail construction required novel techniques of corporate investment and political lobbying to obtain subsidies and rights-of-way. The building of railroads to the Pacific was a watershed in government-business relations. With their arrival, and that of the steamships, American expansionists had all the tools they needed to build on the advantages won during the age of sail and muscle and to dream of evangelizing Asia itself with the twin gospels of Christ and commerce.

Edo 1853

J OHN QUINCY ADAMS was eighty years old when he slumped from his chair to the floor of the Congress in February 1848. Virtually all Americans praised "Old Man Eloquent" but none more sincerely than Seward. His eulogy left the New York State legislature in tears, and his biography of Adams convinced tens of thousands of a fact to which Charles Francis Adams would later attest: that Seward was Adams's political heir. Throughout the tumultuous 1850s no public figure restated so often Adams's long-standing goals for America: peaceful emancipation at home, peaceful expansion abroad, and promotion of agriculture, science, and industry through education, internal improvements, and protection of trade. But the Democrats tolerated slavery, expanded through war, and resisted public works. To Seward, the great compromises over the extension of slavery made a mockery of God's "higher law" and postponed the day of true national unity. Americans, he believed, must hearken both to the gospel of Christ and the gospel of commerce, or else they would miss their destiny.

Freeman H. Hunt coined the term "gospel of commerce" in New York City in 1839. His *Hunt's Merchants' Magazine* extolled the power of trade to expand not only prosperity but Christianity, democracy, and science to the ends of the earth. To Hunt, businessmen were missionaries and commerce a "science . . . calculated to elevate the mind, and enlarge the understanding." To Hunt, "Commerce is now the lever of Archimedes; and the fulcrum . . . wanted to move the world is found in the intelligence, enterprise, and wealth of the merchants and bankers, who now determine the questions of peace and war, and decide the destinies of nations."

The 1850s seemed to prove him right, thanks in good part to the infusion of capital from the gold fields of California. American clippers and steamers sailed every ocean, and U.S. foreign trade grew 144 percent.

Most of the increase was in the Atlantic and Caribbean, but the region of greatest potential was the Pacific. As Seward said in the Senate, the world "contains no seat of empire so magnificent as this, which ... offers supplies on the Atlantic shores to the overcrowded nations of Europe, while on the Pacific coast it intercepts the commerce of the Indies. The nation thus situated ... must command the empire of the seas, which alone is real empire." By this Seward did not mean colonialism but an empire of free people, free soil, and free trade. For "one nation, race, or individual may not oppress or injure another, because the safety and welfare of each is essential to the common safety." Americans had the duty to "take up the cross of republicanism and bear it before the nations."

The geopolitical facts of steam were laid out by none other than Lieutenant Maury in the House Committee on Naval Affairs in 1848. Pointing to a Mercator projection map, he showed that the shortest distance between San Francisco and Shanghai would *seem* to be a straight line. But then he replaced the map with a globe, put one end of a string on San Francisco, and demonstrated that because of the curvature of the earth it was far shorter to sail north around the top of the Pacific to Shanghai than directly across the ocean. Of course, that route bucked both winds and currents, but thanks to steam those obstacles were overcome. All that was needed were coaling stations along the way. The Aleutian Islands were a possibility, but the weather and harbors were terrible there, and anyway they belonged to the Russians. The best forward base, and one known to be rich in coal, was Japan.

The first Yankees to touch on Japan were crewmen of John Kendrick, a pioneer fur trader, in 1791. During the Napoleonic Wars, when the Netherlands was part of the French Empire and feared the Royal Navy, the Dutch chartered eight Yankee vessels to trade for them at Deshima. Captain O'Cain, Baranov's friend, even tried to enter Nagasaki under Russian colors. After Pacific duty in the War of 1812, Capt. David Porter urged President Madison to send an expedition to open Japan, but the idea seemed fantastic to all but a few (like John Quincy Adams). What was more, the Shogun's *bakufu* ordered its coastal authorities in 1825 to "repel and destroy" all foreigners, and the "Mito School" of scholars applauded the decree. Its founder, Aizawa Seishisai, denounced all "alien barbarians of the West, the lowly organs of the legs and feet of the world ... dashing about across the seas, trampling other countries underfoot, and daring, with their squinting eyes and limping feet, to override the noble nations. What manner of arrogance is this!" Aizawa held that America in particular "occupies the hindmost region of the earth ... its people are stupid and simple, and incapable of doing great things." Still, Japan must take care, for now that the white nations were

at peace with each other, they would seek to ravage other lands, insinu-
ate themselves with pleas for trade, and "preach their alien religion to
captivate the peoples' hearts."

Americans knew nothing of the "repel and destroy" decree, only that
American whalers wrecked on Japanese shores were confined, tortured,
or forced to trample on the Christian cross. So New England congressmen insisted that the federal government do something to make Japan
treat shipwrecks humanely. The Opium War did it instead. The Japanese saw for themselves the power of Western ships and guns, and a new
decree of 1843 instructed authorities to provide shipwrecks with at least
a minimum of assistance before they were expelled. But even this gesture provoked resistance in court circles. At the same time, the Opium
War magnified Japan's attractiveness as a commercial target. President
Polk therefore authorized his deputation to China to try for a treaty
with Japan as well. But Comdr. James Biddle blundered into Edo Bay
(Tokyo) in 1846 without an interpreter or any foreknowledge. He
allowed his ships to be surrounded by war boats, allowed himself to be
put off by minor officials, and to his shame was even bumped by a common Japanese sailor. Biddle retreated, having convinced the Japanese
that the American barbarians were weaklings.

By the late 1840s curiosity, pride, vengeance, commerce, international rivalry, evangelism, the opening of China, and the acquisition of
California all fed a growing American interest in Japan. But the need for
coal was the clincher. After Maury's testimony, Committee Chairman
Thomas B. King recommended the immediate establishment of
steamship lines from California to Hawaii and to China by the northern
route. When augmented by a Panama canal or transcontinental railroad,
the steamers would "cause the balance of trade with all nations to run
in our favor." In 1850, the United States made arrangements for a coaling station in Honolulu, and a hero of the Mexican War, Comdr.
Matthew Calbraith Perry, began to promote an expedition to Japan.
Perry was aware of Japanese policy and suspicions, and he thought the
return of castaways might provide the opening wedge—the same tactic
tried repeatedly by the Russians. But "the real object of the expedition
should be concealed from public view." That, of course, was a coaling
station. Perry knew that the U.S. representative must arrive in force and
behave with the utmost reserve. He insisted on steamships, since they
were bound to produce "astonishment and consternation" among the
Japanese, moving "without sails, and without regard to wind and tide."
Steamships and cannon "would do more to command their fears, and
secure their friendship, than all that the diplomatic missions have
accomplished in the last one hundred years."

Perry's lobbying efforts supplemented those of New York merchant

Aaron Palmer, Navy Comdr. James Glynn, and a majority of the U.S. Senate led by Seward and Hannibal Hamlin of Maine. The facts of geography and technology in the new age of steam, and the beatitudes of the gospel of commerce, made for an incontestable brief, and Secretary of State Daniel Webster quickly concurred: "The moment is near when the last link in the chain of oceanic steam navigation is to be formed." All the United States required was that "gift of Providence, deposited, by the Creator of all things, in the depths of the Japanese islands for the benefit of the human family"—that is, coal. President Fillmore drafted a letter for the Emperor in 1851, sent the steam frigate *Susquehanna* to Asia, and gave command of the expedition to Capt. John H. Aulick.

He should have been the one to open Japan. Instead, Aulick fought with the *Susquehanna's* captain, then relieved him of duty. His own clerk jumped ship at Rio. He allowed his son to sail with him without authorization. He demanded payment from a Brazilian diplomat who had been promised passage home as a courtesy. It soon dawned on the Navy Department that this was not the man most likely to deal prudently with the Mikado, and news of his dismissal awaited him in China. To make matters worse, the Japanese castaways were afraid to go home lest the *bakufu* have them beheaded for traveling abroad. Three escaped to California, and the others sneaked into Japan on Chinese junks. In January 1852 Fillmore chose Aulick's replacement, and Commodore Perry was not pleased. He had hoped for command of the Mediterranean Squadron. But he used his reluctance to win three major concessions from the White House: an increase in the number of ships in the squadron to twelve, including three steamers; full discretionary powers for himself; and authorization to scout out suitable island bases. "I assume the responsibility," he said, "of establishing a foothold in this quarter of the globe."

Commodore Perry is called the "father of the steam navy." He was also the founder of American geopolitics in the Pacific. For Perry foresaw the press of Russia toward the coasts of China: "and thus the Saxon and the Cossack will meet once more, in strife or in friendship, on another field. Will it be in friendship? I fear not. The antagonistic exponents of freedom and absolutism must meet at last, and then will be fought that mighty battle on which the world will look with breathless interest; for on its issue will depend the freedom or slavery of the world." Perry did not foresee that a third party would interpose itself between America and Russia, the very nation Perry was instructed to arouse.

Japanese experts in "Dutch studies" had learned enough about the United States so that the hostile Mito School did not go unchallenged. A geography text of 1847 included an account of how a military official named Washington and civil official named Franklin had won the Americans their independence. "Since then the nation's strength has steadily increased, and its territory has expanded enormously." A *New Account of America*, published just prior to Perry's arrival, described the equality of habits, dress, and status among all classes of Americans, their (disgusting) fondness for beef and milk, and the simplicity of their religious observance: "on every seventh day all clasp hands and worship. That is all." In 1851, Manjiro Nakajima, a castaway rescued by an American, returned to tell the Shogun's officials that Americans "are perfect in body with white skins. They are naturally gentle and sympathetic and prize integrity. Above all, they are industrious and trade with countries in all directions." Manjiro praised Americans for their loving marriages but found them "lewd by nature." And in America "toilets are placed over holes in the ground. It is customary to read books in them."

But the most useful intelligence still came from China. Not only had the Ch'ing dynasty been humiliated and forced open to trade, opium, and Christianity, but afterwards the Chinese bureaucracy collapsed into factions advocating resistance to foreigners or assimilation of the foreigners' ways. Then, in 1851, the Taiping Rebellion broke out. Would the same course of events befall Japan? To resist the barbarians meant probable defeat and colonial status. But to bow to their demands would be humiliating and provoke domestic revolt. That was the conundrum presented to Abe Masahiro, Senior Councillor to the Shogun. What could he do but try to uphold the prudent 1843 decree, keep the foreigners at arm's length, and search for some policy that lay between war and surrender? Perry, in turn, knew something of the Japanese, but not much (he thought them "a weak and barbarous people"). It just so happened that his calculated arrogance, persistence, and veiled threats of force made just the right impression on the rulers of Edo at just the right time. The Russians had tried similar tactics but had come in insufficient strength and *before* the Opium War had softened up the Japanese.

"Old Matt," now sixty years old, set out to execute his comprehensive Pacific program. He stopped first at Okinawa in the Ryukyu (Lew Chew) Islands, for what amounted to a dress rehearsal. Refusing to leave his cabin for anyone but the island's regent, then riding to his palace in an elevated sedan chair, Perry lorded it over the island for two weeks. Next he put in at the Bonin Islands, where a small colony of Americans had settled. Perry appointed one of them chief magistrate, endowed him with a law code, and raised the Stars and Stripes. Washington, he hoped, would make it a colony.

Perry rightly figured that word of his mighty fleet and his own imperiousness would reach Japan before him. When his black ships

appeared off Edo Bay on July 8, 1853, the city of a million people panicked. Mothers grabbed their children and fled, priests prayed for tidal
waves to sweep away the barbarians, temple bells tolled, and soldiers
marched and countermarched. Perry just hovered. The Japanese surrounded his ships with menacing armed boats. Perry warned them
away. They tried to board the American ships. Perry refused access.
They sent low-ranking officials to open negotiations. Perry would not
receive them. They tried to deflect the Americans to Nagasaki. Perry
would not budge. When the local governor appeared, Perry obliged him
to talk with lesser American officers. In sum, he let the Japanese understand that the United States expected to be treated with equality, and to
back up his point, he permitted some Japanese officials to gawk at the
gundeck of the *Susquehanna*. He finally told the Japanese they had
three days to deliver his President's letter to the Emperor or he would
sail into the inner bay and bring the city under his guns.

The Senior Council, Abe Masahiro presiding, faced turned tables. In
the past the Japanese had kept barbarians waiting interminably and
maneuvered so that force was on their side. Now they were obliged to
act, out of weakness, and at once. In the middle of the night of the third
day, the Council decided to pass the buck to the unfortunate governor:
"Accept the letter.... Cope with the matter properly so that our
national honor will not be lost and no trouble will arise in the future."
On July 14, therefore, Perry, his officers, and 250 marines confronted the
Japanese officials and a host of robed, double-sworded samurai in a special pavilion of gauze and thatch. The Japanese accepted the letter, told
Perry to await a response at Nagasaki, and briskly invited him to leave.
Perry replied to them that he would return not to Nagasaki but to Edo,
the following spring, with a larger fleet. After just a half-hour, the Amer-
icans marched off to "Hail Columbia!" and "Yankee Doodle."

A month later four Russian warships under the command of Evfimii
Putiatin sailed into Nagasaki. After an interlude of some forty years, the
Tsar was trying again to open Japan. Putiatin told the Japanese he
wanted to fix the boundary on the island of Sakhalin and obtain the
right to trade in one or two of Japan's northern ports. After the usual
delay the Japanese replied, Sorry, our Shogun has just died and affairs are
so pressing just now that we cannot possibly discuss the issues you
raise; come back in four or five years. Putiatin dejectedly sailed for
Shanghai, where he met Perry and asked to merge their squadrons in a
joint mission to Japan. But Perry wanted no partners, and no interference, even from Washington. When new instructions arrived to the
effect that he was to await the arrival of a new U.S. minister to China
and provide him with one of the steamships, Perry wrote the Secretary

of the Navy that he could not comply without endangering his mission to Japan. Then he put every ship to sea and appeared again off Edo in February 1854.

The shogunate, meanwhile, had entered the first stage of its terminal crisis. Unable to chase the Americans away, unwilling to risk the consequences of opening the Empire to the barbarians, and aware of the weakness it had displayed, the Senior Council jettisoned its 250-year-old political monopoly and begged the *daimyō,* the great aristocracy, for advice. That way the lords most likely to defy the *bakufu* would be implicated in whatever course of action the government chose. Unfortunately, no consensus emerged. Within the *bakufu* opinions spanned the usual, obfuscatory range: offer the Americans a piece of the Nagasaki trade, or drag out negotiations for a decade while bolstering coastal defenses. Most *daimyō* considered seclusion and resistance the only honorable course, but some, led by Ii Naosuke, took a longer view. Let the Shogun's officials license merchants to trade abroad and learn how to build steam-powered warships of their own. Once Japan had obtained the weapons of the barbarians it would then be strong enough to revert to seclusion and make it stick! Of course, the difficult conditions that made this expedient necessary would have to be explained to the spirits of their ancestors.

The situation taxed even Abe's skill at building consensus, but the Council finally opted for a variety of responses meant to appease all factions. It would issue a Great Proclamation summoning all Japanese to gird themselves for war and initiate a crash program to upgrade Japan's defenses but at the same time to adopt a cooperative stance toward Perry. Perhaps everything would work out. For under the Japanese calendar the Era of Everlasting Happiness was about to give way to the Era of Peaceful Politics.

Since he had not waited for spring, but sailed in late winter, Perry approached Edo the second time through a fog so thick that even rain and gales failed to disperse it. One of his sailing ships ran aground and had to be taken in tow by a steamer. When the weather broke, Perry's nine vessels sailed magnificently into Edo Bay and after a few weeks of palaver he sat down on March 8 to negotiate near the little fishing village of Yokohama. After cakes and tea, the Japanese Commissioner Hayashi Daigaku (Rector of Edo University) surprised the Americans by coming right to the point. He could not alter the Empire's ancient laws, but inasmuch as the President of the United States requested friendly relations the Commissioner was prepared to fashion terms under which Japan would lend aid to shipwrecked sailors and make supplies, including coal, available to visiting vessels.

Perry, cheated of an occasion to deliver his blustery speech about Japanese inhumanity and American power, delivered it anyway. He explained how the United States and Japan were now neighbors, that their seas would soon roil with steamships, and he warned them of what had happened to Mexico when it insulted and defied the United States. Still Hayashi would not talk of trade, since Japan had no need of foreign things, and Perry did not insist. Thanks to that decision, as well as Abe's prior decision not to resist, Perry and Hayashi were able to conclude the Treaty of Kanagawa on March 31. Henceforth American ships might put in at Shimoda or Hakodate and purchase wood, water, provisions, and coal, and the United States might station a consul at Shimoda.

The rest was celebration. The Japanese gave the Americans lacquer ware, translucent silks and porcelain, samurai swords, and various customary tokens including four little dogs. The Americans gave the Japanese a scaled-down steam locomotive and telegraph set and serenaded them with a black-faced minstrel show. The technology fascinated the samurai, and the show reduced "even the saturnine Hayashi" to "general hilarity." When Perry rose to depart, a jovial Japanese official "threw his arms about the Commodore's neck, crushing, in his tipsy embrace, a pair of new epaulettes, and repeating with maudlin affection: 'Nippon and America, all the same heart.'"

Once back in Hong Kong, Perry resigned his command and booked passage on the British steamer *Hindostan* for home. Congress and the New York Chamber of Commerce hurled money and honors upon him. No one understood at first that he had *not* opened Japan to trade—that task remained for the American Consul, Townsend Harris. But he won the right to take on coal, which had always been his principal purpose. Indeed, had he asked for more, it is quite possible he would have gotten nothing. For large numbers of Japanese *daimyō* and intellectuals thought that Abe had already conceded too much.

As for Admiral Putiatin, he returned to Nagasaki and sent two ships to Sakhalin Island. But he won no concessions from the Japanese and had to evacuate Sakhalin in June. Terrible news had arrived. Russia was at war with Britain and France, Alaska was cut off, and Kamchatka was under attack.

Aikun-on-the-Amur 1858

Twenty-five years ago the Russian-American Company requested from the government the occupation of California, which at that time was still hardly controlled by anyone. . . . now it has already been over a year that California constitutes one of the North American States. One could not but foresee . . . that these States, once they had established themselves on the Pacific Ocean, would soon take precedence over all other naval powers there. . . . Besides now, with the development of railroads, one must become convinced, even more than before, that the North American States will without fail spread over all of North America, and *we cannot but bear in mind that sooner or later we shall have to yield to them our North American possessions.* However, neither could one but bear in mind something else in connection with this consideration, namely, that it is highly natural also for Russia, if not to possess all of Eastern Asia, so to rule over the whole Asian littoral of the Pacific Ocean.

So wrote Nikolai Nikolaevich Muraviev, appointed by Nicholas I to rule all eastern Siberia in 1848. Muraviev's rapid rise, the result of his gallant action in Turkey and Poland, earned him the hearty dislike of fellow officers, and the mustachioed, twice-wounded thirty-eight-year-old returned their sentiments. He had no patience for the court politics, paper pushing, and profiteering of St. Petersburg generally and the directors of the Russian-American Company in particular. But if Muraviev's prophecy concerning Alaska was right, the Russian-American colony itself continued to make heroic exertions of its own in the 1830s and 1840s. The contract with the Hudson's Bay Company regularized food supply. Expeditions like that of Lavrentii A. Zagoskin (1842–44) explored Alaska's interior. The Russian Academy sponsored biological, geological, and anthropological surveys. And education finally "took"

among Aleuts and some Tlingits, thanks mostly to Father Ioann Veni-
aminov. A native of Irkutsk, the muscular priest even awed George
Simpson: "The gentleness which characterized his every word and deed
insensibly molds reverence into love." At Gov. Ferdinand Wrangell's
behest he founded schools and taught the Aleuts their letters, numbers,
and catechism, and even trades such as carpentry and navigation. He
visited the California missions to observe their methods, communicating with his Franciscan colleagues in Latin. When the Holy Synod made
Russian America a diocese and Ioann's wife died (thus making him eligible), he was named Alaska's first bishop. Thanks in large part to Ioann,
now Bishop Innokenti, the Aleut population recovered by 25 percent in
these years. He went on to become Metropolitan of Moscow, highest
ranking cleric in Russia.

Yet efficient, humane administration could not make up for the
dearth of colonists and the decline of furbearing animals. When the
Opium War disrupted the China market, the Company was unable to
market the furs it had. Then the gold rush so inflated the price of food
and supplies in the North Pacific that the Company verged on bankruptcy. Muraviev was not alone in perceiving that Russia's career in
North America was nearing an end.

The reign of Nicholas I (1825–55) is rightly known as one of reaction.
The regal and handsome Tsar had come to the throne amid the Decem-
brist revolt and devoted himself to extirpating liberalism under Count
Uvarov's triptych, "Autocracy, Orthodoxy, Nationality." As late as
1841 the finance minister opposed railroads on the grounds that they
would drain off capital needed for agriculture, eat up Russia's forests,
and ruin the morals of the people. Only when a Viennese professor convinced the Tsar of the military value of railroads did he allow an experimental line to be built from St. Petersburg to his summer palace fourteen miles away, and finally a first trunk line from St. Petersburg to
Moscow. The fact that it ran perfectly straight, bypassing important
towns, gave rise to the legend that the ramrod-stiff Tsar had simply
placed a ruler on a map and drawn a line. In fact, he judged that the
lower cost of a straight route outweighed its drawbacks. As it was, the
state had to guarantee a 4 percent return on thirty-four million rubles
in bonds to raise the necessary capital. The Tsar did try to stimulate
industry by obliging the railroad to buy Russian iron. But the foundries
in the Urals charged twice the British price and in any case could
deliver only a tenth of the iron needed. The railroad was not finished
until 1851, cost seventy-five million rubles, and the fifty-thousand
serfs drafted for the task labored under such cruel conditions that the
poet Nekrasov wrote:

The way is straight, the embankment narrow
Telegraph poles, rails, bridges
And everywhere on both sides are Russian bones—
Vanechka, do you know how many?

Nicholas lived just long enough to see the military consequences of Russian backwardness vis-à-vis the West. But in Asia Russia still had the advantage over China, whose helplessness the Opium War laid bare. But now that China was open, new dangers loomed. The English and French might revitalize China with their technology, or move northward to the Amur themselves, or open Japan and station fleets in the northwest Pacific. Then not only would the Amur be lost, but Siberia itself would be outflanked. So Nicholas turned from his maps and summoned his ministers. Russia must probe the Amur and learn what China's defenses were there. The Kuriles and Sakhalin Island must be occupied. The entire Siberian military district must be placed in the hands of an empire builder. So it was that the Tsar overruled his timid or jealous ministers and named Muraviev governor of all lands from the Yenisey to the Bering Sea. "If any power should seize Kamchatka," joked the Tsar nervously, "you in Irkutsk will only learn of it six months later."

Muraviev knew the stakes. If "foreigners were to occupy the mouth of the Amur," he wrote, "it would be so detrimental to the Empire that we would instantly have to resort to the use of force to expel the new intruders, and thus declare war against the power to which they belong, be it America, France or England." What was more, "Neighboring China, very populous, is powerless now because of ignorance, but can easily become dangerous for us under the influence and leadership of the English and French. In such a case Siberia will cease to be Russian." So Muraviev sent a bold lieutenant in Russian-American Company employ, Gennadii I. Nevelskoi, to occupy the mouth of the Amur, while he took off on a tour of his domains. In Kamchatka he marveled as Bering had at Avacha Bay and ordered Russia's Pacific naval base moved lock, stock, and barrel to Petropavlovsk. The argument against that had always been that Kamchatka was impossible to supply. But Muraviev already foresaw the day when a swift, warm-water supply route might run from Siberia down the Amur and thence through Japanese waters to Kamchatka.

Foreign Minister Nesselrode's fear of war was justified when news reached St. Petersburg that Nevelskoi had founded a settlement on Chinese territory. But the Tsar kept his nerve (did it help that the base was named Nikolaevsk?) and replied, "Where the Russian flag has once been hoisted it must not be lowered." Then Muraviev heard rumors of a plan to force open Japan "in accordance with the project of Palmer" (Aaron Palmer, Commodore Perry's merchant friend), so he went to St. Petersburg in 1853 and won the Tsar over to the occupation of Sakhalin, reinforcement of Siberia, and a new expedition to Japan. And *that* was why Admiral Putiatin sailed into Nagasaki just as Perry was triumphing at Edo.

To be sure, the Tsar counseled prudence: "I want no smell of powder about this." But he also gave Muraviev full authority to negotiate with China. So as soon as he arrived back at Irkutsk in 1854 Muraviev sent off a dispatch to Peking inviting a delegation to meet him at Aikun. Then he loaded nine hundred Cossacks into ninety boats and barges and one steam-powered launch and floated, as brazen as you please, down the Amur past Nerchinsk and Albazin and the other sites where Russians and Manchus had clashed long ago. He founded a new town at the confluence of the Amur and Ussuri rivers and named it Khabarovsk after his seventeenth-century predecessor. Finally he reached Nikolaevsk . . . only to learn that Russia was at war with Britain and France.

The Crimean War, needless to say, had nothing to do with the Pacific. It had to do with ideological cleavages in Europe and the struggle for influence over the Ottoman Empire. But Russia was vulnerable *wherever* it could be reached by sea, including the remote North Pacific. So the British and French Pacific squadrons, based nine thousand miles away at Callao, Peru, and numbering twelve ships and five thousand men, sailed at once in hopes of intercepting any Russian frigates at large. They failed. The *Avrora* and *Dvina* eluded pursuit, put in at Petropavlovsk, and added their seven hundred sailors to its garrison. Muraviev had made Vasilii Zavoiko an admiral and put him in charge of the earthworks and batteries. But he had time to prepare a defense only because the aged Adm. David Price stood off Avacha Bay for two days, then opened a cannonade in which the Russians gave better than they got. Conscious of having blundered, Price put a pistol to his head. He botched even that, poor man, and suffered for hours before dying. On the second day the French admiral pressed the action and silenced most of the Russian guns. But then he, too, waited four days before deciding to make a landing. A sizable force of sailors scaled a spiny neck of land, broke into separate columns, got lost in the undergrowth, and finally stumbled down to Petropavlovsk. By this time the Russians waited in ambush, and their musket volleys and bayonet charge killed or wounded over 350 allied attackers. The rest pulled for their ships and beat a retreat to Chinese waters.

Why did the Anglo-French attack Petropavlovsk at all? The Russian frigates were Price's first responsibility, while a Kamchatkan village of two hundred wooden buildings was far less attractive than New

Archangel. Why didn't the allies head for Alaska? The answer lies in that contract, signed sixteen years before, by the Russian-American and Hudson's Bay companies! Though enemies in Europe and Asia, Britain and Russia were partners on the Northwest coast, and in January agents of the two companies had met in London to declare their North American possessions off-limits in case of war. Still, the Russians at Sitka did not entirely trust the British, so they drew up phony papers stating that they had sold the colony to a U.S. firm for the sum of $7 million. Any flummoxed British captain would thus be forced to sail away rather than fire on neutral "American property."

The bill of sale proved unnecessary. The Anglo-French squadrons remained in the western Pacific and returned in a vengeful mood to Petropavlovsk in 1855. But Muraviev figured they would and before he was recalled to command armies against Turkey he ordered Zavoiko to evacuate Petropavlovsk as soon as the ice broke. But the allied fleet reappeared too soon! Thankfully, their new commanders were just as hesitant as the old ones and delayed long enough to allow the Russians to slip six ships into the fog and past their attackers to safety. Allied marines charged in the next day to find Petropavlovsk vacant but for a handful of drunken American whalers. It was not the most glorious action in the annals of the British and French navies.

Still, the campaign persuaded Muraviev that the Russian Navy could never defend the Tsar's maritime Pacific possessions. So it was high time to liquidate the failed experiment called Russian America and concentrate on Russia's real Pacific mission on the banks of the Amur in Manchuria.

That Muraviev got his chance to redirect Russian imperial energies down the Asian side of the North Pacific was thanks in part to the mentally unbalanced third son of a Chinese peasant. Hung Hsiu-ch'üan was a Hakka ("guest settler") who spoke a central Chinese dialect and thus was considered a social inferior even by other peasants around Canton. But despite that, and despite the overpopulation, inflation, banditry, corruption, and hatred for the Manchu dynasty that all enraged his province, Hung was not a rebel. He just wanted to be a civil servant. But at age twenty-four he failed the Confucian examination for the third time, took to his bed, and dreamed strange dreams. A heavenly mother washed him in a river to make him fit to meet the father. Then he was raised to heaven, where an old bearded man exhorted him to slay demons, and his "older brother" taught him swordplay. It made no sense to him until 1843, when he flunked for a fourth time, and in his despair reread a half-baked missionary tract given him years before in Canton. Then he decoded his mysterious dreams: the old man was God the Father, and Hung himself was none other than the second Son of

God, Jesus' younger brother. His cousin believed it was true, then a neighbor, then thousands of peasants and malcontents. In 1851 Hung's worshippers proclaimed a Heavenly Kingdom of Great Peace, or *T'ai-p'ing t'ien-kuo*, to be founded on the wreckage of the demonic Ch'ing Empire. The next year brought a sign from heaven that a change of dynasties was indeed imminent: the mighty Yellow River burst its banks and cut an entirely new course to the sea three hundred miles to the north.

How many Chinese believed in Hung's cult is anyone's guess. But millions were moved to rebellion against the seemingly discredited policies and mores of the Ch'ing. Where coolies cut their hair short and wore a pigtail, the Taipings grew their hair long and free. Where traditional landlord-tenant relations produced great disparities in wealth, the Taipings preached communal ownership of land. Where Confucianism stressed natural hierarchies, the Taipings preached the equality of all in heaven's eyes. And where the Manchus were foreign, the Taipings were fiercely Chinese. They formed military units, allied with secret societies, and in 1852 burst northward to capture cities, weapons, treasuries, and two million recruits. It was the start of the bloodiest war of the nineteenth century.

Europeans and Americans based at the treaty ports did not know what to make of the Taiping Rebellion except that it threatened to play havoc with trade. So the British pronounced themselves neutral, and the other legations followed suit, until an incident in Canton forced them out of aloofness. It had to happen sooner or later, inasmuch as the Taipings and Imps (as the Ch'ing imperialists were called) both played to the popular hatred of the foreign presence. In October 1856 Imps boarded a British-registered lorcha, the *Arrow*, and hauled down its Union Jack. British Consul Harry Parkes demanded the return of the crew and respect for Britain's extraterritorial rights. The Chinese refused, the British shelled Canton, the Cantonese burned down the Barbarian Houses, and the *Arrow* War was on. Palmerston took advantage of his own nation's rage to call a parliamentary election and reinforce the China squadron. In December 1857 an Anglo-French force blasted its way into Canton. Now what was the Emperor to do? He could not defeat the Europeans and needed every spare soldier to fight the Taipings. On the other hand, to give in to the barbarians would advertise Ch'ing weakness and justify Taiping propaganda. So after its customary obfuscation, the desperate and ill-used regime made a show of giving in to Britain's demands.

The Treaties of Tientsin of 1858 required the Chinese to pay an indemnity, open ten more ports to Western trade, permit missionaries anywhere in China, and host legations in Peking itself. But when

Palmerston's envoy, Frederick Bruce, arrived in March 1859 to exchange ratifications, the mandarins refused him entry into the Forbidden City. Bruce then proceeded northward with a bodyguard of six hundred marines. At the Peiho River bridge the Chinese opened fire, inflicted 434 casualties on the British, and forced Bruce to retreat. So Gen. Sir Hope Grant returned in 1860 with forty-one warships and an Anglo-French force of 17,600 men. Come hell or high water, they would see to it that the inscrutable, mendacious Imps honored their treaties.

Now consider all these events from the point of view of the Russians. They had just been humiliated in the Crimean War (mostly because their lack of railroads prevented them from bringing their superior numbers to bear). The Peace of Paris of 1856 prohibited Russia from fortifying the Black Sea coast, eliminated Russian influence in the Ottoman Empire, and blocked Russian expansion in the Balkans. But now consolation arrived. The Taiping Rebellion and the Anglo-French tussle with Peking opened magnificent opportunities for Russia on the Amur, if only someone knew how to exploit them.

As it happened, not one but three men on the scene thought they knew how to exploit them. The first, Muraviev, returned to Siberia determined to press the advantage he had won two years before. The second, Admiral Putiatin, was still charged with authority to negotiate with Japan. The third, Count Nikolai Ignatiev, was a prestigious statesman and master of duplicity sent out to negotiate with Peking. These jealous three did nothing but get in one another's way but in the process so completely confused the Chinese that Russia ended up with all it desired and more!

Muraviev's first priority was to reinforce the Cossacks he had left strewn along the Amur, especially when he found they were dying. The supply barge of 1855 had run aground thirteen miles below Albazin, so the outposts on the lower river spent a winter without bread. A Cossack officer arrived to report:

> Below Albazin, near the stranded barge with flour, there were several corpses.... [T]he starving soldiers had gorged themselves on flour and died. Below this barge we saw heart-rending scenes: starving soldiers, wearing only overcoats and hats, walked through the bitter cold [–47° F.] half-dead, disfigured by the frost.... In spite of all this the soldiers dragged their rifles and packs. If one met soldiers who could barely move their legs and advised them to discard their ammunition, they replied that they would be court-martialed were they to lose government property.

Muraviev recouped by drafting eight thousand "volunteers" from Siberian towns and three hundred head of cattle. He oversaw the military colonies personally, shared his men's rude biscuits and complaints

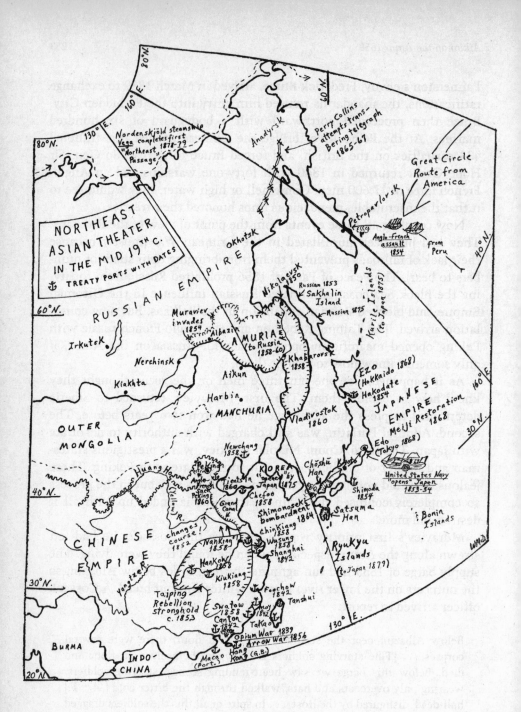

NORTHEAST
ASIAN THEATER
IN THE 19TH C.
⚓ TREATY PORTS WITH DATES

Nordenskjöld steamship
Vega completes first
"Northeast
1878-79
Passage"

Perry Collins
attempts trans-
Bering telegraph
1865-67

Anadyrsk

Petropavlorsk

Great Circle
Route from
America

Anglo-French
assault
1854

from
Peru

RUSSIAN EMPIRE

Okhotsk

Irkutsk

Muraviev
invades
1854

Albazin

Nerchinsk

Kiakhta

Aikun

Harbin
MANCHURIA

Nikolaevsk
1850

Russian 1853
Sakhalin
Island

Russian 1875

A MURIA
(to Russia
1858-60)

Khabarovsk
1858

Karile Islands
(to Japan 1875)

EZO
(Hokkaido 1868)

Hakodate
1854

JAPANESE

EMPIRE

Meiji Restoration
1868

OUTER
MONGOLIA

Vladivostok
1860

Edo
(Tokyo 1868)

Newchang
1858

Huang Ho

Peking
Anglo-
French
take
Peking
1860

Tientsin
1860

Grand Canal

KOREA
"opened"
by
Japan 1875

Chefoo
1858

Chöshū
Han

Kyoto

United States Navy
"opens" Japan
1853-54

CHINESE

EMPIRE

Huang Ho

changes
course!
1852

Nankiao
1858

Hankow
1858

Kiukiang
1858

Yangtze R.

Shimonoseki
bombardment
1864

Chinkiang
1858

Wusung
1858

Shanghai
1842

Shimoda
1854

Satsuma
Han

Ryukyu
Islands
(to Japan 1879)

Bonin
Islands

Taiping
Rebellion
stronghold
c. 1853

Swatow
1858

Canton
1842

Foochow
1842

Amoy
1842

Takao

Tamshui

Opium War 1839
Arrow War 1856

Macao
(Port.)

Hong
Kong (G.B.)

BURMA

INDO-
CHINA

about their officers, and established himself as a soldiers' general. Confident now of his strength, he invited the Chinese to Aikun to discuss the transfer to Russia of both banks of the Amur. The local Manchurian Governor, I-shan, refused to entertain such arrogance and damned Muraviev for a pirate.

Putiatin, meanwhile, had been in Japan, where the *bakufu* proved willing to entertain several foreign delegations after Perry's initial success in the hope of playing the barbarians off against one another. So Japan concluded a treaty with Britain in October 1854 and made Putiatin welcome in December. Then the North Pacific spoke: an earthquake and tidal wave washed the treaty port of Shimoda away, and a maelstrom spun Putiatin's flagship *Diana* around forty-two times in thirty minutes. The dizzy Russians got the frigate under sail, but she sank off the coast in January. Had the disaster occurred a decade before there is no telling what their fate might have been. But now the Japanese not only nursed the shipwrecks but gave Putiatin the Treaty of Shimoda, which opened three ports and permitted Russia a consul. In return, Putiatin gave up Russian claims to the southern Kuriles and made Sakhalin a "joint possession."

Putiatin then returned to the Amur, puffed up with proof that his methods had worked while Muraviev's had failed. St. Petersburg seemed to agree and in March 1857 requested that Peking receive Putiatin as envoy. That prompted Muraviev to write, "Putiatin is really not a bad man, but it is a pity that he has meddled in the Amur affairs, which he may damage. Now we prepare for the sacrament and keep the fast [the Lenten season], therefore any unrelated arguments will be inappropriate, but as soon as one kisses one another on Easter day . . . I shall be many-worded." The Chinese in fact refused to receive Putiatin, but the admiral would not go home. Instead, he sailed to Hong Kong and hinted to Chinese officials that Russia might mediate between Peking and the Anglo-French in exchange for territorial concessions on the Amur. The Ch'ing court, hopelessly confused now as to who spoke for Russia, told Putiatin to see I-shan if he wished to talk boundaries. At roughly the same time, Muraviev was telling I-shan that *he* had sole authority to discuss boundaries and that Putiatin's mission was only to help China settle its differences with the Anglo-French. The only sense the Chinese could make of all this was that *Putiatin* seemed willing to help them versus the sea powers so long as they conciliated *Muraviev* on land issues. So all of a sudden, in May 1858, Peking ordered I-shan to make a show, at least, of bargaining with Muraviev!

That put I-shan in an impossible position. Russian soldiers and steamboats continued to float down the Amur, while all but a thousand surly, ill-paid soldiers of his own garrison had gone south to fight the

Taipings. Thus, when Muraviev punctuated his demands with an all-night bombardment of the south bank of the Amur, I-shan had no choice but to sign. The Treaty of Aikun of 1858 ceded to Russia all the lands north of the Amur and guaranteed free navigation on the Amur, Ussuri, *and* Sungari rivers, the last of which ran smack through the middle of Manchuria. But the Ch'ing behaved true to form by refusing to ratify the Treaty of Aikun. It seems that the whole negotiation had been a ploy to buy time in hopes that the Western barbarians would fall to fighting each other. I-shan was sacked for signing the treaty at all, and Muraviev was informed that so far as China was concerned, the old treaties of Nerchinsk and Kiakhta were still in force.

Enter Count Ignatiev, sent from Russia to ratify the Treaty of Aikun and try to ask for the cession of the Ussuri Maritime Province on top of it. He arrived in Peking overland in June 1859 and quickly grasped that the Ch'ing court was consumed with hatred for foreigners and blind to the danger the Anglo-French posed. So Ignatiev took Putiatin's tactic one step further. First, he went to Shanghai to *urge* the Anglo-French to march on Peking with all the speed and fury they could muster (he even provided Grant with a map of the city), then hinted to the Chinese that Russia alone stood between them and disaster. Meet our territorial demands, he said in effect, and we Russians will make the sea barbarians go away. Thus, the Anglo-French expedition would accomplish *Russia's* goals without Muraviev's army having to fire a shot.

Lord Elgin, the British envoy, never suspected Ignatiev's motives. So the allied force landed in north China in August 1860 and began its nervous march to Peking. Ch'ing officials and hovering bannermen tried to arrest their progress, while the British learned of tortures inflicted on prisoners taken in the *Arrow* War. In a hot rage, Elgin ordered the armies to blast their way into the Forbidden City, where they proceeded to sack and burn the incomparable Summer Palace and gardens. Among the prizes they found were four trunks full of documents revealing Russia's ambitions. The British obligingly turned them over to Ignatiev without so much as an attempt to decipher them.

The Emperor had fled, leaving his brother Prince Kung the humiliating task of surrender. Then all Ignatiev's schemes fell into place. Kung pleaded for Russia's help in ridding the capital of the foreign armies. So Ignatiev advised Kung to ratify the Anglo-French treaties, which was done in October, then frightened Grant by conjuring images of Chinese hordes pouring out of the countryside to attack the allies should they attempt to stay the winter. The Anglo-French obediently evacuated Peking in November, after which a grateful Prince Kung not only ratified the Treaty of Aikun but agreed to cede all the lands between the Ussuri River and the sea—Siberia's Maritime Province.

Muraviev, Putiatin, and Ignatiev, working at times at cross-purposes but sustained by Chinese weakness and Anglo-French gullibility, thus added 350,000 square miles to the Russian Empire. In a sense they saved the rest of Siberia as well. For the comparatively warm, rich soils of Amuria finally gave Russia the capacity to support a sizable population on the Pacific, while the maritime coast freed Russian shipping from reliance on Okhotsk and Kamchatka. In the summer of 1860 Muraviev's settlers broke ground for a city, which they named Ruler of the East— Vladivostok. Finally, Siberia now curled around rich Manchuria from the north and east like a hand poised to scoop. All that was needed now to realize Russia's own manifest destiny, wrote Count Muraviev-Amurskii upon his retirement, was pioneers and railroads. Tsar Liberator Alexander II took a big step toward providing the first when he freed the serfs in 1861. The second task awaited Count Witte.

By the way, the denouement of the *Arrow* War presaged the collapse of the Taipings. Their Heavenly Kingdom had already fallen into the hands of jealous and decidedly earthly "kings" who squeezed taxes from supporters, slaughtered opponents, and indulged their own less than spiritual desires. Hung himself went thoroughly mad, stocked his inner sanctum in Nanking with nude girls, and proclaimed to sycophants the tidings of his daily ascensions to talk with Jesus. Meanwhile, the Imps encouraged the rise of regional warlords in exchange for their help against the rebels—a tactic that would come back to haunt the dynasty. Finally, the Europeans turned against the Taipings after 1860. After all, now that they had forced unequal treaties on the Manchus, they had a big stake in their survival. By 1864 the Taiping Rebellion was effectively dead, and the Ch'ing Empire survived as the object, not a subject, in the struggle for North Pacific power.

San Francisco 1860

TOWNSEND HARRIS PAID the price for Perry's priority in the opening of Japan. A son of Puritan New England (his grandmother Thankful Townsend taught him to "tell the truth, fear God, and hate the British"), he rose to the presidency of the New York Board of Trade. But in 1849 Harris, a bachelor, gave it all up for the Pacific. When the job of first American consul to Japan became available, Harris volunteered, and the frigate *San Jacinto* delivered him in August 1856. The Japanese tried to put him off, besides which Shimoda had just been devastated by that tidal wave. But Harris persisted and was housed in an abandoned, vermin-ridden Shinto temple. Even his sole American flag was shredded in a typhoon and he had to make do with one stitched up by a local Betsy Ross. There he sat, sick and frustrated, for over a year until allowed to present his credentials to the Shogun. But by July 1858 he secured a treaty granting the United States full trading rights.

The *bakufu*'s logic was less mysterious than it had seemed at first to Harris. The new Anglo-French assault on China and the Russian advance to the Amur reminded Japanese anew of the costs of resisting the barbarians, and of them all the Americans seemed the least menacing. So they not only honored the United States with a treaty but made it the destination of their own first embassy to the non-Asian world. Was a party of two hundred sufficient? they asked. Harris told them three was enough. They compromised on seventy-seven, to be carried by the American steam frigate *Powhatan* and Japanese steam corvette *Kanrin Maru*, built for the Shogun in the Netherlands. The seventy-seven samurai were to learn all they could about the power and the ways of the Americans, secure their good will against the day when their help might be needed, and presumably help to persuade the xenophobic *daimyō* of the correctness of the decision to open Japan. The *Powhatan* carried the ranking ambassadors, but the *Kanrin Maru* was first to pass through the Golden Gate, turn to starboard amid the dozens of ships speckling San Francisco Bay, and dock at the Vallejo Street wharf. It was St. Patrick's Day, 1860.

"We visited the ship yesterday," boasted the *Daily Alta California*. "When we entered [Admiral Kimura] was having his hair most artistically dressed with oils and pomatum by one of his servants—the Admiral being seated on the floor and evidently enjoying the luxury of his shampoo. Soon after he appeared on deck—in an unassuming but gentlemanly costume—his feet encased in snowy white sandals and stockings; a dark brown or olive frock, contrasting finely with a blue vest, which was laced in front with a heavy silver cord. At his side hung two swords. . . . We noticed in the Admiral's cabin a picture of President Buchanan hanging in a conspicuous place." The San Franciscans were amazed when their topknotted visitors acted like Japanese—elaborate etiquette, a reporter concluded, must be a kind of religion to them—and were amazed again when they acted like Americans—for instance, using knives and forks, or eating ice cream "with good Christian relish." The samurai were equally amazed to find California's Governor Downey dressed in a business suit no different from those of subordinates and to observe how Americans trod fully shod on a hotel carpet "made of such expensive material as the richest man in Japan would buy by the square inch."

All parties celebrated the beauty of the new city by the bay from atop its many hills. The *Kanrin Maru* and battery on Alcatraz traded twenty-one-gun salutes and raised the Stars and Stripes and Rising Sun. When the *Powhatan* finally pulled into view on the thirtieth, editors implored their readers to make a good impression, for "it is a prophecy that many of those now among us will live to see fulfilled—when we say that the day will come when the iron horse, lashed to the long train of railway carriages, shall take up the produce and manufactures of Japan from our docks and warehouses and set forth with the rich freight to the borders of the other great ocean." The state legislature agreed and appropriated the generous sum of $3,000 to entertain the seventy-seven samurai. When the *Powhatan* sailed for Panama, whence the delegation would make its way to Washington, Ambassador Norimasa Muragaki confided to his journal: "We are now leaving this prosperous and beautiful city and take with us most happy recollections of San Francisco—where we first set foot on United States soil and obtained our first experience of American life."

Prosperous and beautiful, and quintessentially American—in just ten years San Francisco had become all these things: an "instant city." But while its beauty was sui generis and its prosperity the effortless product of gold and greed, San Francisco's Americanness was in doubt from the

start. This city alone attracted thousands of "foreigners" *before* generations of Anglo-Saxon Protestants had a chance to establish their laws,
institutions, and taboos. Here, on the North Pacific, Anglos were as
much newcomers as Irish or Germans, Hispanics or Asians. Hence the
political and economic rules of the game must be *engineered* in their
favor lest their military conquest prove ephemeral. In the East and Midwest bountiful rains watered the soils to nourish a growing population.
Here, in California, the land was desert or nearly so. Hence the geography must be *engineered* if the state were to grow and thrive. Back East,
new communities sprang up on the edges of old ones, well connected to
centers of commerce by rivers, canals, and railroads. Here, the new community existed at far remove from the Union of which it was part.
Hence, transportation and communications must be *engineered*, and
swiftly.

Everything happened swiftly. As late as 1847 the very word San Francisco denoted a bay, a presidio, or a mission, but not a town. Then the
new Yankee *alcalde* (a sort of judge and sheriff in one, under Spanish
law), Washington A. Bartlett, decreed that the "miserable village of
Yerba Buena" with its few hundred inhabitants be renamed San Francisco. It was pure public relations: there was no compelling reason why
that location should become the hub of California. Its weather ran to fog
and chill, and its harbor was no better than others on the Bay. Since
most people and goods headed for the Mother Lode anyway, it made
sense to build an entrepôt in the Sacramento River delta. General
Vallejo did so, hoping that Benicia or a new town bearing his name
would attract forty-niners. But when Sen. William Gwin persuaded
Congress, in 1851, to name San Francisco the site of the U.S. mint and
customs house, its future was secure. Henceforth, all gold flowing out of
California, and all goods coming in, passed through the city. Benicia and
Vallejo languished while San Francisco's population exploded to 56,800
by 1860, making frontier California the most *urbanized* state in the
nation.

Immigrants came from everywhere, almost all young males whose
"human character crumbled and vanished like dead leaves." Gambling
and crime were incessant, and arson surely played a role in the fires that
consumed the town six times in three years. Lieutenant William
Tecumseh Sherman found such an absence of civility in San Francisco
that he took to doffing his cap to Negroes. "At a time when every white
man laughed at promises as something to be broken," he said, the black
servants were the only gentlemen to be found. Luck was the goddess of
this first white metropolis on the North Pacific. But for every person
who struck it rich in the gold country, five to ten did so in the city. Real
estate values and interest rates fluctuated wildly, and development

could not keep up with the influx. Thanks to the fires and steam exca-
vation, the downtown district moved eastward toward new deepwater
docks gouged out of the sands of the embarcadero. Brick replaced clapboard, gas lighting bathed the streets, and luxury offices and hotels
sprang up. Times were gaudy, fed by investments like that of the 1852
New York firm called Wells Fargo and by layers of credit based on the
expectation of next year's harvest of gold. In 1854, when the volume of
gold dropped suddenly, a spiral of bankruptcies reached major banks.
But local fortunes built on monopolies like the California Steam Navigation Company, California Stage Company, and California Telegraph
Company survived the lean years until the Nevada silver strike of 1859
kicked off a second boom. Speculation in land and commodities, the
respectable equivalent of the faro table, sucked up the savings of immigrants, investors, and miners and reconcentrated it in the hands of a
few. As entrepreneur John Dwinelle said of San Francisco, "My diggings
are here."

California was likewise an "instant state." After its occupation by
the U.S. Army in 1846 the territory had five different military governors
in four years, prompting *californios* to quip that American rule was no
more stable than Mexican. But Gwin inspired residents to call a constitutional convention at Monterey in 1849. Its first major decision was to
petition for statehood, though the southern California delegates (numbering eleven of forty-eight) preferred to organize as a territory. They
feared, rightly, that the northerners would dominate a state government
and tax ranchland rather than miners' pokes. The northern Anglo majority also decided to prohibit slavery lest they have to compete in the
mines with slave labor. The legislature later passed a twenty-dollar foreign miners' license tax that yielded almost a fourth of the state government's revenue. Even then, Chinese were permitted to glean only mining claims already abandoned by Americans. As for California's Indians,
150,000 of whom remained in 1848, the settlers waged what some
openly called a "war of extermination." Violence, hunger, and disease
reduced their numbers by four-fifths, to just thirty thousand by 1870.

There is a myth to the effect that white magnates imported the first
Chinese to California to build the Transcontinental Railroad. In fact,
Chinese middlemen organized transport of thousands of "Celestials" (as
the whites called them) or *k'u-li* ("bitter strength," as they called themselves) before the railroad was even begun. They came from the delta
around Canton, where the coolie trade with Southeast Asia was already
so profitable that secret societies fought to control it. But Chinese merchants no longer had to shanghai peasants to do overseas labor. The
poverty, crowding, and chaos of south China encouraged thousands to
indenture themselves in order to gain passage to the "golden moun-

tains." A Chinese broker bought tickets, at forty to fifty dollars apiece, for a boatload of Cantonese sojourners and crammed as many as 350 aboard a vacant eastbound clipper or steamer. The emigrants endured the sixty-day crossing with more or less suffering depending on the humanity of the captain. They arrived in San Francisco to bind themselves over to a broker in "Chinatown" (the name first appeared in 1853) who sold their labor to construction crews and mining camps until their wages covered the price of their tickets. Attempts by San Francisco police to bust the Tong foundered on their inability to find Chinese witnesses brave enough to testify. Chinese, being "neither free nor white," were ineligible to own property, plead in court, or become citizens. The alternative was unthinkable: the twenty-five thousand Chinese present in 1852 numbered a tenth of the population of the state.

Intimidation drove most Mexicans out. But what of the old *californios* whose American citizenship was guaranteed by the Treaty of Guadalupe Hidalgo? Many welcomed the American takeover and were looked upon by the Yankee settlers with a certain sentimentality. Moreover, the rancheros did brisk business for a time selling beef to the forty-niners. But soon the old Hispanic residents also got pushed aside. The Federal Land Act of 1851, though meant to do justice to the holders of Spanish land grants, only facilitated the concentration of land in the hands of cash-rich Anglos. A three-man commission sat for five years to adjudicate titles and reconcile as best it could the laws of Spain, Mexico, the United States, the state of California, and English common law. The process was so tedious that most small claimants went bankrupt from legal fees or chose to sell their claims and be done with it. Other *californios* went bankrupt in 1856 when the gold rush ended and beef prices collapsed, and the rest were ruined by drought in the early 1860s. So the original owners were eager to sell to the new American "cattle kings."

Only the greatest of them was not an American (who is an "American"?) but a German named Heinrich Kreiser. Born in 1827, he left his homeland in the hungry 1840s, first for England, then for New York, where he worked as a butcher until a friend named Henry Miller had second thoughts about joining the gold rush and put a ticket to California in his hands. The ticket was "non-transferrable," so Kreiser simply became "Henry Miller" in the New York docks where he boarded his ship, in Panama City where he butchered meat for his fellow Argonauts, and in San Francisco, where he arrived in 1850 with all of six dollars. The price of meat was climbing weekly, so the butcher had no trouble earning a stake. When the fire of 1851 burned down his employer's shop, Miller set up on his own and was soon supplying meat to the best people and hotels. But getting good meat was not easy; the ranchos were far away and the Mexican longhorn cattle, bred for their hides and tallow, were tough eating. New breeds began to arrive around 1852, and Miller reckoned that he could control the market of the whole burgeoning state if he could control those herds. And he could control the herds if he could control the land. In 1858 Miller entrusted his slaughterhouse to an employee, rode down El Camino Real to the Santa Clara Valley, then looked eastward beyond Pacheco Peak.

Stretched out before him was the San Joaquin Valley, two hundred miles long and fifty wide, with the Sierra Nevada adorning the horizon. Along the San Joaquin River at the bottom was a thin ribbon of green; the rest was an ugly brown. In fact, topographical engineer Lt. George Derby found the valley "exceedingly barren, and singularly destitute of resources . . . without timber and grass, and can never, in my estimation, be brought into requisition for agricultural purposes." But to Miller it seemed the Promised Land, and he was Joshua, set to conquer. He realized that California would never stop filling with people *so long as they could be fed*, and that the only way to support agriculture was to husband and distribute the precious spring runoff from the snowpack of the High Sierra. So Miller bought an option on the 8,835 acres of the Rancho Sanjon de Santa Rita (the patron saint of women about to give birth for the first time) and rode back home to raise more capital in partnership with his erstwhile competitor, Charles Lux.

The new firm of Miller and Lux acquired riparian property on the San Joaquin River and threw up crude boxes to divert a portion of its flow. Wherever the trickles reached to quench the hundred-degree heat of the valley, moist grass sprang up like the reeds of the Nile, and tasty new herds of cattle feasted. But Miller, too, was helped by the law—the Swamp Land Act of 1850. To encourage reclamation, Congress ceded to state governments all swampland on condition that the proceeds from its sale be used for drainage. California received title to two million acres of seasonal mud, and rather than pay the cost of engineering, the state government chose to deed land over (for $1.25 per acre) to any bidders willing to drain it themselves. Miller and Lux promptly acquired over one hundred miles along the San Joaquin River. Miller then decreed: "I wants a canal . . . for the land above the main canal." "That would run uphill," protested his chief engineer. "You builds me a canal!" said Miller, and turned on his heel and left the room. The canals were dug, and the valleys turned lush. Those who justified Manifest Destiny seemed vindicated: Yankee ingenuity could do in a decade what other indigent landlords would never have done. California the land, just as California the legal entity, was Americanized in an instant.

The third realm that begged to be engineered was California the destination. Steamships and the Panama railroad did much to link the new state to the east, but the Transcontinental Railroad remained a subject

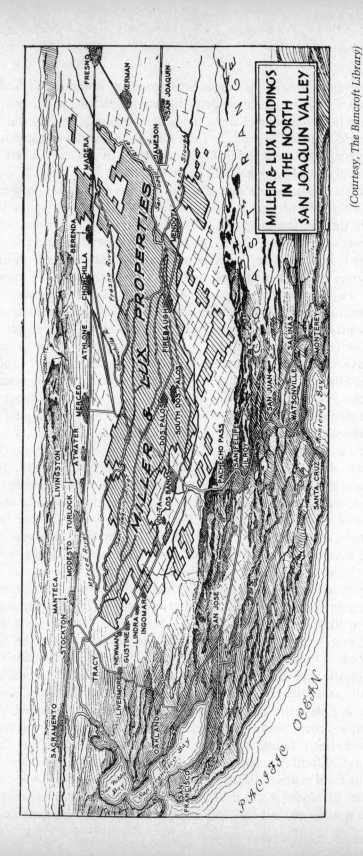

MILLER & LUX HOLDINGS IN THE NORTH SAN JOAQUIN VALLEY

of endless studies and sectional feuds. If eastern initiatives were barren, then let the initiative come from California, or rather, let those with initiative come to California. Theodore Dehone Judah, the son of an Episcopal minister, went to Rensselaer Polytechnic Institute and sailed via Panama in 1854 to supervise construction of the Sacramento Valley Railroad. Soon Judah was obsessed by the idea of a great Pacific railroad. Three times he went east to lobby Congress and returned persuaded that the federal government would never act unless presented with one thoroughly researched route and a privately funded project. That way, no sectional interest could veto it.

Judah found his route while surveying in the central Sierra Nevada in 1860, one year after the discovery of the Comstock Silver Lode on the Nevada side. Dr. Daniel W. Strong, from the mining camp of Dutch Flat, drew Judah's attention to the so-called Emigrant Trail over Donner Pass. It was like a gentle ramp that rose seven thousand feet above the valley over a seventy-mile stretch. Judah did the measurements and found it was true: the Sierra Nevada could be tracked with a grade of about a hundred feet per mile, well within current tolerances. The two men sat down in Strong's frontier apothecary to draw up papers of incorporation and a promotional pamphlet for the Central Pacific Railroad to California. Then Judah set out for the parlors of San Francisco, confident he could raise the $70,000 needed to incorporate. But the businessmen lampooned his fanaticism behind his back and said to his face that they preferred to wait for the federal government to make up its mind. Judah damned their smugness but also learned his lesson. From now on he would assure investors that the government was about to offer subsidies and thus guarantee them a quick, predictable return. That pitch worked, in an upper room above a hardware store in Sacramento, in October 1860 . . . and made four of his pigeons the richest men on the West Coast.

Collis P. Huntington was a farmer's son from Connecticut who went to New York at sixteen and prospered as a peddler. He sailed for California via the Isthmus in 1849. Charles Crocker, also a farmer's son, was born in New York and raised in Indiana. He worked for a time in a small iron forge until he discovered his own vein of ore. Then he sold his company and set out overland to California in 1849. Mark Hopkins was the son of a New York merchant and grew to manhood in Michigan. He studied law, clerked, and managed a firm back in New York until sailing to California via Cape Horn in 1849. Leland Stanford, another farmer's son from near Albany, New York, practiced law in Wisconsin before following his brother to California by sea in 1852. All four came to own prosperous stores in Sacramento, and all four liked Judah's plan. But even they would go no further than putting up money for surveys until the news reached California that the South Carolina secessionists had fired on Fort Sumter in April 1861. Sensing that civil war would mean big government transportation projects, the four associates filed to incorporate the Central Pacific Railroad Company.

Law and politics, economics and ethnic groups, land and railroads—there was one more way in which the forty-niners placed the American stamp on California. That was in foreign policy. For California (and Oregon) statehood not only meant that people with a Pacific perspective would now be represented in Washington, it also meant that California itself became a base for new filibusters, land rushes and gold rushes, and the engineering of new regions as far afield as Hawaii, Alaska, Hokkaido, and Manchuria. In the 1850s alone, Californians plotted or joined in four filibusters in Baja and two in Hawaii. When William Walker, alumnus of the University of Pennsylvania medical school and erstwhile dictator of Nicaragua, was caught in Mexico and returned to stand trial, a San Francisco jury gleefully acquitted him. Henry A. Crabb was not so lucky. The Mexicans tied him to a post and shot him in the back a hundred times—revenge, perhaps, for 1848. Sam Brannon's latest adventure was to sail off to Honolulu with 150 "restless young bloods" intent on "revolutionizing the government of his Kanaka Majesty," while a Committee of Thirteen in Hawaii tried to frighten Kamehameha III into selling the islands in 1853 by spreading rumors of an invasion from California. Hawaiian Foreign Minister Robert Wyllie cleverly stymied the filibusters by dangling a treaty of annexation before President Pierce, while securing reaffirmations from the British, French, and American consuls of their nations' commitments to Hawaiian independence.

Of far more moment was the influence California politicians and merchants might have on U.S. foreign policy. As early as 1851 Beverley C. Sanders, a nephew-in-law of Daniel Webster, founded the American-Russian Company. His first import was ice, shipped from Sitka at seventy-five dollars per ton to cool the drinks of San Francisco barkeeps. He also took advantage of Russian desperation during the Crimean War to win a twenty-year contract to procure ice, fish, timber, and coal in Alaska and provide the Russians with beef and wheat. Another San Franciscan, Perry M. Collins, dreamed bigger dreams. If Americans could win exclusive privileges to supply the Russians now on the Amur, the whole commerce of Siberia, which he estimated at $50 million a year, might lie within their grasp. Appointed U.S. commercial agent for the Amur, he set out in 1859 for encounters with Muraviev and the Tsar.

So within ten years of the American conquest, California had become a dynamic force for the continuing spread of American influence. Except that America's future in the western ocean depended on whether the folks back East could hold the nation together at all. For on the same day the seventy-seven samurai marched into the White House to be received by President Buchanan, the Republican Convention nominated Buchanan's successor, Abraham Lincoln.

Washington City and
Sitka 1867

ON APRIL 14, 1865—Good Friday, so it happened—William Henry
Seward lay in bed masticating his first solid food in over a week.
The sixty-three-year-old Secretary of State was convalescing
from a carriage accident that had left him with a broken jaw and arm to
go with his painful case of gout. At about ten in the evening the doorbell
rang and the black footman admitted a young man claiming to be the
physician's assistant. He had some new medicine, he said, and must
instruct Mr. Seward in its use. Once upstairs, the man pistol-whipped
Seward's son Fred and burst into the sickroom. His gun misfired, so he
plunged his bowie knife over and over again at the head and neck of the
invalid. Then he fled. Seward incredibly survived, and in days to come
received baskets of letters and cards from people praying lest the country fall into ruin, leaderless. For at the same hour that Seward's attacker
failed, John Wilkes Booth got his man at Ford's Theater.

Seward was an upper-class Huckleberry Finn: slight and towheaded,
sharp-witted and sensitive, stubborn. He grew up the invisible fourth of
six children in Orange County, New York, son of a Jeffersonian individualist who succeeded as a farmer, merchant, doctor, speculator, and
judge and who encouraged his boys, if necessary with the rod, to excel as
well. Henry, born in 1801, took refuge in the slave quarters—vestiges of
slavery could still be found in the North—and became quite the favorite
of the kitchen servants. He and some other white boys from the neighborhood, encouraged by their mothers, paid back the mammies for their
kindness and cookies by teaching their children to read. Seward went off
to Union College in 1816, but the teenager was ashamed of being a
bumpkin and blew his stipend on clothes. When his father sent back the
bills unpaid, Seward ran away to teach in a grammar school in Georgia.
He never forgot the contrast between the lives of the field hands he saw
there and those of the blacks below stairs in his father's house. The

pleas of his mother and sister lured him home in 1819, whereupon his rebellion metamorphosed into ambition. He went on to graduate Phi Beta Kappa, made a reputation as a coming lawyer in Auburn, New York, married his boss's daughter, and abandoned his father's politics for those of John Quincy Adams.

The principled reasons for the switch included Seward's enthusiasm for public education, internal improvements, and restriction of slavery. The personal reasons included his disillusionment with the "cunning and chicanery" of Van Buren's political regency. When Thurlow Weed, the editor of the Albany *Evening Journal* and behind-the-scenes politico, founded an Anti-Masonic party, he spied in Seward a promising candidate. By 1830 he was in the state senate and the next year made his first pilgrimage to Massachusetts to see Adams. Seward loved politics more than domestic life and left his wife, Frances, for much of each year in the company of her family and the Book of Common Prayer. Then, in 1834, Seward was beaten in his first race for governor. He lay awake in his lonely room in Albany, then dozed into "a long and feverish and almost fatal dream" that revealed to him how much he was hostage to fear, selfishness, and pride. The thought of becoming a "genuine Christian" filled him with doubts, but Frances told him not to be too hard on himself; just let God do His work. Three years later, after smallpox took their third child, Seward joined the Episcopal church. "I may as well be explicit with you," he wrote Weed. "I do not anticipate that it will make any considerable change in my habits of life, but I humbly trust that it will gradually elevate and refine my motives of action."

Few attributes of a politician are more valuable than a conviction of the righteousness of one's cause and the ability to distinguish that cause from one's own fortunes. The former drives a man to succeed; the latter lets him accept failure. Seward went on to win two terms as governor, during which he championed education for all, prison reform, humane treatment of Indians, and equal opportunity for Catholics and Jews, and he refused to extradite fugitive slaves. During the Canadian uprising Governor Seward maintained scrupulous neutrality even though partisans violated his state's long border with Canada. He thought the annexation of Texas "reckless folly," denounced the Mexican War, and counseled compromise over Oregon. And yet, Seward was a sincere exponent of Manifest Destiny. He simply believed that America did not deserve to expand until it lived up to its ideals at home. Weed blanched and warned Seward that he might never be elected again with such talk. But thanks to the reaction against the Mexican War, Whigs regained the state legislature, Seward wowed them with his eulogy to Adams, and Weed pulled the strings. In 1849 the legislature elected Seward to the U.S. Senate, where he remained until 1861.

Seward's combination of progressivism at home and expansionism abroad was not at all anomalous in that less self-hating time. For according to Manifest Destiny in its pure New York variety, freedom fed empire and empire freedom. "Commerce is the god of boundaries," said Seward, and as early as 1846 he proclaimed that the American people must inevitably "roll its resistless waves to the icy barriers of the North, and to encounter oriental civilization on the shores of the Pacific." In 1852 he named commerce "the great engine of movement" and predicted that the Pacific Ocean was bound to become "the chief theater in the events of the world's great hereafter." Seward supported the Perry mission to Japan and called for steamship subsidies, naval cartography in the Bering Sea, a reciprocity treaty with Hawaii, and acquisition of Russian America.

His strongest ally was California Sen. William Gwin, who was otherwise a proslavery Democrat hailing from Tennessee. In Seward's view, Gwin himself was helping to undermine slavery by promoting the spread of free soil, free people, and free trade. Gwin, in turn, had a stake in the American-Russian Commercial Company and Perry Collins's Siberian schemes. "Steam has worked wonders on our own Mississippi," he argued, "may not the Amoor, the 'Mississippi of Northern Asia,' find in the life-giving principle of steam advancement in commerce and industry?" In 1859 Gwin went so far as to bid for Alaska, offering Russian minister Edouard de Stoeckl $5 million.

As we know, the tsarist government was in the midst of an agonizing reappraisal of its North Pacific empire. The endemic causes were the long decline in revenues of the Russian-American Company. The proximate cause was the Crimean War, which revealed how indefensible the colony was. Muraviev favored redirecting Russia's limited energies to the Amur and Siberia. Grand Duke Constantine, brother of the Tsar and chief of the Navy, concluded that Russia stood in danger of losing *all* its Pacific extremities if it did not cut its losses in America. Wrangell, ex-Governor of Russian-America, wrote that "anticipatory prudence" suggested the wisdom of selling out. Finally, Stoeckl warned that Yankee merchants and settlers would poach on Russian trade and territory until Alaska was ripe for a filibuster. Conquest of California had given Americans "a control almost without limit" in the North Pacific.

Who spoke for optimism and defiance, for the legacy of Bering and Baranov? Almost no one in the 1850s. After the Crimean War Russia was whipped and defensive, and obsessed with railroad construction and the abolition of serfdom: one admiral even advocated appeasing the Americans with Alaska lest they lust for Siberia as well. So Foreign Minister Gorchakov referred Gwin's offer to the finance ministry, which simply advised: try to get more money, perhaps $12 million, but sell. It was too late—or, as events proved, too early. For by now the Americans were at war with themselves.

Seward came late to the Republican party, which burst into being across the North in the mid-1850s as an ingathering of Whigs, abolitionists, farmers, and business interests favoring tariffs and internal improvements. Seward was uncertain whether the new party would fly and resisted associating with its temperance leagues and Know Nothings. But after his reelection to the Senate in 1855 Seward sat with the Republicans, and after Frémont's defeat in 1856, he became front-runner for the party's 1860 nomination. But a more moderate Republican with handlers as clever as Weed came out of nowhere to grab Seward's prize at the boisterous Wigwam convention in Chicago. Horace Greeley, it turned out, had turned against Seward out of spite, while the Illinoisans outbid Weed for delegates and exploited the galleries on behalf of their favorite son. The telegrams read "Lincoln nominated third ballot," and the town of Auburn wept.

Seward's ego was sorely bruised, but once again he separated it from the cause he served and campaigned for Honest Abe. In Boston he shared the platform with Charles Francis Adams, who judged that Seward expected to be the real decision maker in a Republican administration. Out West Seward promoted expansion, promising a St. Paul audience that the transcontinental railroad would soon be built and Alaska would soon be American. Now, smart investors know that sometimes the best moment to buy a stock is on bad news. Reports of a loss or company shake-up not only drive down the price but suggest that the company may finally address long-festering deficiencies. So it was that for over a decade an apparently booming United States was paralyzed by the split over slavery. But the moment Southern senators walked out of Washington, political deadlock disappeared and many things became possible: the transcontinental railroad, the Morrill Act creating land grant colleges across the West, the Homestead Act to encourage western settlement, and federal support for ventures in Alaska and Siberia, to name only those relevant to the Pacific. The war's stimulus to industry and agriculture accelerated the growth of the economic base supporting a Pacific drive. That is not to say that the Civil War was somehow worth the cost, only that the rupture released energy previously trapped. Assuming the Union survived, it would emerge stronger across the continent, and do so far sooner, than if the Civil War had not happened.

The task of making sure that the Union did survive fell to Secretary of State Seward more than anyone else save Lincoln himself. For if Lincoln bore the incomparable weight of winning the war, Seward bore the less glorious responsibility of not losing it. It was up to him to isolate the battlefield so that the North's superior manpower and industry could wear the South down. That meant warning the Europeans off, preventing them from supporting the Confederacy with arms, money, or diplomatic support; but at the same time not so *angering* them that they would intervene anyway against the Union. His first act upon moving into the Old Executive Office Building in March 1861 was to purge the foreign service of all persons suspected of Southern sympathies. Next, he devoted himself to strategy in a situation growing bleaker by the day. The British, French, Russian, and Spanish governments all intended to protest a federal blockade of Southern ports. Nor did it take much imagination to conclude that certain circles in Britain and France would delight in the destruction of their North American rival. So Seward sent Lincoln "Some Thoughts for the President's Consideration" on April 1, advising him to remonstrate with the European powers and ask Congress to declare war on any that failed to give satisfaction! Ever since, historians have wondered whether Seward was really so contemptuous of Lincoln or perhaps "deluded" or "temporarily insane." Certainly his belligerence got the attention of Lord Lyons, who named Seward "the fiercest of the lot" and denounced his "high-handed conduct and violent language" toward Britain. But Palmerston was not one to be bullied. Just two days after news of the Union blockade reached London, he declared Britain neutral, implying that the Confederacy was a belligerent nation. Seward responded with what his minister in London, Charles Francis Adams, considered a "crazy dispatch." Adams, like Lincoln, toned down Seward's rhetoric.

There is no question that the fate of the United States hung on the policy of Britain. Imperial strategy seemed to require helping the Confederacy to splinter North America into two or more resentful republics locked in a balance of power that the Europeans might then manipulate. The North would become less of a commercial threat, and the Cotton South a virtual colony of the British textile industry. Indeed, Southern statesmen expected King Cotton alone to entice Britain into their camp. But Lincoln and Seward could take solace in three factors that worked against European intervention in the Civil War: the British animus toward slavery, the peripatetic ambitions of Napoleon III, and the unlikely friendship of tsarist Russia.

Southern slavery divided British counsels. If the aristocracy and some mill owners sympathized with the South, most middle- and working-class Britons, newspaper editors, and Queen Victoria herself shrank from lending aid and comfort to slaveholders. Thus, Jefferson Davis was wrong when he likened the South's situation to that of the thirteen colonies of 1776. It was really more like that of Texas in 1836, when slavery stayed Britain's hand despite its other interests in Texan independence. Nor did Britain's hunger for cotton trump its moralism, for

Dixie had in fact produced such a bumper crop in 1860 that England's mills began the war with a large surplus and soon cultivated new cotton fields in India and Egypt. Finally, recognition of the Confederacy would assuredly mean war with the Union and an invasion of Canada. Indeed, no sooner had Seward begun to bluster than Canada's Governor-General begged Palmerston to reinforce his garrisons with all speed.

Anglo-American tension came to a head after November 1861 when Captain Wilkes, the Pacific explorer, now skippering the same *San Jacinto* that had borne Townsend Harris to Japan, captured the British steamer *Trent*, and arrested two Confederate envoys. But Queen Victoria and her dear, dying Albert counselled peace, while the Lincoln Cabinet put prudence before public opinion and released the captives. War fever subsided for good when news reached Britain of the Union victory at Antietam and Lincoln's Emancipation Proclamation. Young Henry Adams, Charles Francis's son, reported from London that the proclamation "has done more for us here than all our former victories and all our diplomacy."

Still, no end to the war was in sight, and Napoleon III floated the notion of a joint European intervention and mediation. The Emperor claimed to want to help end the American bloodshed; in fact, he wanted to promote American disunity while he took over Mexico. But what is not generally known about the Emperor Maximilian Affair is that a powerful faction of Mexicans favored a royal restoration and had solicited French (and Spanish) help in overthrowing the chaotic republic. In 1861 Mexico was so in arrears on its debts that Britain, France, and Spain made a joint naval demonstration. The British and Spaniards withdrew, but a French expeditionary force pressed inland to Mexico City in June 1863, while French agents conspired with Mexican monarchists to invite Maximilian of Habsburg to assume the throne. A puppet monarchy in Mexico promised to revive French power in the Americas and the Pacific, and incidentally win the plaudits of nationalist and Catholic factions back in France. Of course, it all depended on the United States' remaining divided—and if Napoleon had pressed for a brokered settlement of the Civil War *before* tipping his hand in Mexico, he might have undone the work of Louis XVI, who had helped to create the United States in the first place. Instead, the British suspected Napoleon's intentions and declined his invitation to mediate the Civil War, while Seward was pleased to do nothing: better that France should gambol in Mexico than actively help the Confederacy.

The third factor that scotched Southern hopes for European intervention was the constant friendship of Russia for the Union cause. It was a strange dalliance, this embrace of the Great Democracy and the Great Autocracy. In 1849 Seward had denounced the Tsar's role in snuffing out Hungarian freedom, and Lincoln had referred to Russia in 1855 as a land "where despotism can be taken pure, and without the base alloy of hypocrisy." Ambassador Stoeckl returned their sentiments, asking what could be expected of America, "a country where men of humble origin are elevated to the highest positions, where honest men refuse to vote and dishonest ones cast their ballots at the bidding of shameless politicians?" Even Alexander II replied to those who equated his emancipation of serfs with Lincoln's freeing of slaves: "I did more for the Russian serf in giving him land as well as personal liberty. . . . I am at a loss to understand how you Americans could have been so blind as to leave the Negro slave without tools to work out his own salvation. . . . I believe the time must come when many will question the manner of American emancipation of the Negro slaves in 1863."

But for all their ideological differences, Russia and America had one thing in common—fear of the British Empire. Stoeckl and Prince Gorchakov viewed the United States as a counterweight to Britain, wanted the Union to survive, and resisted any suggestion that Europe should intervene on behalf of rebellions in other countries, be they in America or—as in 1863—Poland! So San Franciscans and New Yorkers were amazed to spy, not meddling diplomats, but the Tsar's Pacific and Baltic fleets arriving in their harbors in fall 1863. Grand Duke Constantine had put the ships to sea in case the British and French should sortie their fleets on behalf of the Poles. But Americans interpreted the visits as a demonstration of Russian sympathy for the Union. "God bless the Russians!" prayed Gideon Welles.

Seward knew the affair was overblown. But he also knew that Russian amity promised dividends in the Pacific. Indeed, the Civil War was another boon to West Coast development. Comstock silver poured into the Northern war chest (and won Nevada premature statehood in 1863). The transcontinental telegraph opened in December 1861, and the first message it carried from the people of California expressed "their loyalty to the Union and their determination to stand by its Government on this, its day of trial." Thousands of Californians volunteered to go back East and fight, and many more Easterners fled to the West, most notably Samuel Clemens. American expansion into the Pacific continued apace, aided more than ever by a Russian government unusually willing to cooperate with Americans.

In 1858 Perry Collins had returned from his tour of the Amur and gone East to regale congressmen and businessmen with the commercial potential of Siberia. But Collins's imagination was of Vernian proportions. Why not, he asked, extend an American telegraph line all the way north to Alaska, *across the Bering Strait* to Siberia, and southward to the Amur, where it might link up with a Russian line leading all the way to Europe? He was suggesting that survey and construction teams plod across five thousand miles of the coldest, most rugged wilderness in the world. But success would make the whole civilized world a neighborhood, and without any costly and probably futile experimentation with suboceanic cables. Hiram Sibley, the President of Western Union, signed on, and so did Seward as soon as he took over the State Department. Moreover, they could now count on an exclusively Northern Congress friendly to internal improvements. In 1862 Congress passed the first Pacific Railway Act and in 1863 agreed to subsidize telegraph lines on *both* sides of the Bering Strait. In May of that year the Russians sold Sibley a Siberian right-of-way for $100,000 and 10 percent of the stock. So the Collins Overland Telegraph Company hastily accumulated capital and materials, while Collins and Sibley took tea with the Tsar and planned their electric empire. The line would have to pass through British Columbia—what if Britain refused? In that case, said Sibley, he would simply buy the Hudson's Bay Company outright! Gorchakov replied that if he was willing to spend that kind of money, why not buy Alaska, too?

Gettysburg spoiled the Confederacy's chances of winning European recognition through battlefield triumphs. In 1864 the South's defenses were breached, and when Lincoln won reelection that November, Appomattox was just a matter of months. And by the time Seward returned to his desk, five weeks after the terrible attack by a would-be assassin, the United States had made tremendous leaps toward becoming a continental superstate. The Transcontinental Railroad was under construction, and the Collins Overland Telegraph was racing the greatest steamship in the world to link the New World to the Old. The first attempts to lay a transatlantic cable had failed. It was a devilish task to draw out the cable at a steady pace and, in rough seas, to keep from snapping the wire. But Cyrus Field, the Atlantic cable king, would not give up. In 1865 he leased the largest ship in the world—by a factor of five!—the iron steamer *Great Eastern*, in hopes of laying his line. At the same time Charles S. Bulkley, the chief engineer to Western Union, with Samuel Morse himself as consultant, oversaw survey and construction teams working northward from Vladivostok and Vancouver.

A forgotten epic battle against the elements, the Bering Strait telegraph project exposed hundreds of Americans to the Alaskan and Siberian interiors, including Smithsonian scientist George Kennan, father of the diplomat. On the Asian side, crews charted in fog and rain to Anadyrsk and the Arctic Circle. On the American side, a linesman griped: "Everything has been unfavorable for us this month. Weather bad, worse crowbars, dog feed scarce and poor of its kind, men living on two meals a day, one of which only can we afford to have salt meat. The ground as hard as a Pharaoh's heart." But the technological crusade suddenly ended in June 1867 when the message arrived in the camps: the transatlantic cable worked; the *Great Eastern* had won. So all Western Union had to show for two years and $3 million were hundreds of coils of insulated wire and thousands of telegraph poles left standing, like white men's totems, in a fairy ring around arctic seas.

Edouard de Stoeckl displayed a queer sort of pomposity. He styled himself a baron (though he wasn't one), yet bragged to the Tsar that his bride was "American, Protestant, without property." A notorious double-dealer, Stoeckl would ask "for any post anywhere" to escape Washington's appalling corruption. As for Seward, Stoeckl began by naming him "the man above all others who should be President of the United States," later sniffed that Seward knew nothing about foreign policy, and ended by becoming his close confidant. Certainly the garrulous, mutton-chopped Stoeckl preferred Seward's drawing room, well stocked with whiskey and sarcasm, to the White House entertainments awkwardly staged by the Lincolns.

With the American Civil War and Polish insurrection over, Gorchakov recalled Stoeckl and polled St. Petersburg again on the issue of what to do with Russian America. Constantine still said sell it before the Yankees steal it. Minister of Finance Michael de Reutern wanted to use the receipts from its sale to build railroads. The head of the Asian department in the foreign ministry, Baron von Osten-Saken, dissented. Once in possession of Alaska, he feared, the Americans would have a "sufficiently strong motive" for occupying the Kuriles and Sakhalin, too. Moreover, Alaska was not just a played-out fur rookery—gold had been found on the Stikine River. But Stoeckl thought that another reason to sell, since a gold rush was bound to fill up Alaska with sourdoughs and invite an American filibuster. So be it, concluded Gorchakov and the Tsar, Russian America would cease to be Russian.

Back in America, Stoeckl's first move was to get *Seward* to make the first move, the better to stick up the price. He dropped word in New York to "one of [Seward's] political friends who exercises great political influence over him" (presumably Thurlow Weed) that a bid for Russian America would be entertained. In March 1867, Seward offered $5 million, Stoeckl wanted ten, and they settled on $7.2 million. Andrew Johnson's cabinet approved, and late on the twenty-ninth a telegram arrived via transatlantic cable conveying the Tsar's consent. Seward insisted that not a moment be wasted. Congress was fixing to adjourn, and he wanted to push through a treaty before the administration's enemies had time to think. So they roused their clerks, repaired to the State Department, and sat down to scribble. Seward curiously insisted that the Company archives be included in the sale as they would henceforth be part of America's heritage. Stoeckl insisted that the Orthodox church and its Aleut converts be permitted to practice their religion, as they would be all that was left of *Russia's* heritage in America.

They signed the treaty at 4:00 A.M. By noon it was in the Senate, and by the next day journals friendly to Seward were touting the purchase as a brilliant coup. Senator Charles Sumner, chairman of the Foreign Relations Committee, found his desk covered with mail from dignitaries urging ratification, while Seward lobbied committee members and President Johnson urged the Senate not to adjourn. Sumner hated Johnson and was a long-standing rival of Seward. But he, too, was an exponent of peaceful expansion. So he researched, drafted, and delivered a three-hour speech remarkable for its mastery of the history, resources, ethnography, zoology, and potential of Russian America. The Senate ratified the treaty thirty-seven to two.

The $7.2 million, as well as the expense of transfer and administration, still had to be voted by the House of Representatives. By the time Congress reconvened, Radical Republicans led by Horace Greeley persuaded many that the "Esquimaux Acquisition Treaty" was but a ploy to distract attention from Johnson's appeasement of the reconquered South, or that "Walrussia" or "Seward's Icebox" was not worth buying even at two cents an acre. In any case, the House had more pressing business: the attempted impeachment of Andrew Johnson. Not until July 14, 1868, did the Alaska measure pass the House, and only then, it was rumored, because of some creative persuasion by Stoeckl. Investigations revealed that only $7,035,000 of the purchase price made it to Russia. The remaining $165,000 was deposited in the Russian ministry's account at Riggs National Bank. Robert J. Walker, a "lifelong annexationist in favor of annexation in any quarter," admitted receiving $26,000 to lobby recalcitrant congressmen, and another $4,000 was traced to newspapers. As to the rest, no proof has surfaced except a note scribbled by Johnson to the effect that Stoeckl told Seward "there was no chance of the appropriation passing the House of Reps without certain influence was brought to bear." How ironic, if true, that after 120 years of pitiful exertions, Russia not only flung Alaska at the Americans but then had to bribe them to take it. Perhaps Stoeckl was sincere in wanting to "breathe for a while a purer atmosphere than that of Washington."

Seward, too, left nothing to chance. Without waiting for the House to vote funds, he ordered the War Department to arrange for the formal transfer of Alaska. So Gen. Henry W. Halleck, now commander of the Military District of the Pacific, designated one battery of artillery and one company of infantry for occupation duty at Sitka. After a two-week cruise from San Francisco, troops and commissioners went ashore below Baranov's castle. A correspondent described the meager settlement of New Archangel in flat, contemptuous tones. The Army's inventory was worse: a bureaucratic list of batteries, barracks, warehouses, and two churches devoid of any sense of the role those modest structures had played in the history of the ocean the United States now claimed for its own. Prince Dmitry Maksutov, the last Governor, exchanged salutes and struck the Company flag. He was sullen but correct. At least it was not raining. The Yankees, on the other hand, greeted the raising of the Stars and Stripes with three hip-hip hoorays.

U.S. Commissioner Lovell Rousseau spent a pleasant week in Alaska. But putting out to sea, he reported to Seward, his steamer "encountered a storm, the severest known on that coast by anyone now there. It lasted about 20 hours and we very narrowly escaped being lost, nothing but the strength of our ship and the efficiency of the crew under Providence saving us." But the inland passage to Victoria and the Puget Sound, he assured the Secretary, was "a safe one, and amidst scenery as grand and beautiful as there is in the world." As for the resources of Russian America, Rousseau was amazed at how accurate Sumner's descriptions proved to be in light of his having no personal knowledge. As for the people, there were about five hundred Russians who, if treated properly, would likely choose to become American citizens. The Indians were another matter. A Tlingit chief was very angry. It was true "we allowed the Russians to possess [Baranov] Island," he told the American. "But we did not intend to give it to any and every fellow that came along."

Tokyo 1868

D EEP IN THE NIGHT of April 24, 1854, the watch on the steamer
Mississippi heard the gurgle of oars in Yokohama harbor's black
water below. "'Merikan! 'Merikan!" cried a Japanese boatman,
and a letter of some kind waved from his upthrust hand. After much
gesturing, the Americans deflected the mystery boat to Commodore
Perry's flagship, which was soon accepting aboard two damp and excited
young Japanese. The letter introduced them as earnest students who
wanted only to cross the seas and study in America, despite the
Shogun's laws prohibiting Japanese to travel. Perry feared they were not
so innocent, and he did not want to risk angering the *bakufu* lest his
diplomacy be undone. So Yoshida Shōin and his friend were spirited
ashore through the same murk in which they came.

Yoshida was twenty-four when he tried to flee a land he loved and a
regime he had grown to hate. He was an impecunious samurai from the
Chōshū domains of southwestern Honshu—one of thousands whose
military prowess was unneeded and whose economic fortunes had collapsed. His family perforce devoted itself to the other occupation of
noble caste, education, to be pursued with the same intensity and discipline as the martial arts. By the age of ten little Shōin had absorbed all
his tutors had to teach him and was himself lecturing on military strategy and composing poetry. Not surprisingly, the child savant was drawn
to "Dutch studies," that knowledge of the outer world that seeped in
through the islet of Deshima. Yoshida visited it in 1850, learned of the
Opium War, Western arms, and geography, and chose as his *sensei* (master) a leading educational reformist. The next year, again having soaked
up all there was to learn, he did the unthinkable and fled his *daimyo*'s
domains in search of new sources of knowledge. In so doing, he symboli-
cally left feudal Japan behind.

After failing to persuade Perry to take him aboard, Yoshida Shōin

turned himself in as a protest against the seclusion laws. He spent fourteen months in prison, but by the time he emerged (having sampled 618
more books) he had conceived a revolutionary program through which
Japan might adjust to the arrival of the white barbarians. He then established a private academy to transmit that program to a generation of
frustrated young samurai. It was, in a word, meritocracy. His tracts entitled "Modest Proposal," "Words of a Madman," and "Four Urgent
Tasks" insisted that preferment for every post from a *daimyo*'s household and schools to the national government and military be based on
skill rather than birth or influence. The *bakufu* should be replaced by a
modern bureaucracy staffed with "excellent persons" and loyal, not to a
shogun, but to the emperor at Kyoto. The new regime must found a
national university and Western-style army and navy and pursue every
contact with the West that might strengthen Japan. But Yoshida was
more than an intellectual. He fancied himself "Twenty-One Times a
Valiant Samurai," possessed of a divine calling to impress his ideas on
the nation even at the cost of his life.

Not just intellectuals but entire social classes nursed grievances
against the old order. Most *daimyō* were subject to *sankin kōtai*, consigning them and their families to hostage status at Edo, where they
were nonetheless excluded from national political life. Merchants and
tradesmen were socially ostracized and inhibited by the economic policies of the state, not least the prohibition on foreign trade. Exploited
peasants were ever prone to insurrection, while lesser samurai—educated and proud, but barred from advancement—were a stereotypical
"revolutionary class."

Still, the Tokugawa Shogunate might have stumbled on, or even
reformed and strengthened itself, were it not for the existential crisis
posed by the barbarians. The legitimacy of the Shogun was based on his
putative ability to protect Japan from internal disorder and foreign
incursion. But Perry and his successors forced upon the *bakufu* a no-win
situation: to resist the barbarians was to invite a defeat in war; to give in
to them was to invite rebellion at home. Perhaps there was no way out,
but two strategies presented themselves within the structure of Tokugawa politics. The inclusivist approach was to try to include in the
Shogun's councils the most powerful "outs" in the Empire, the great
daimyō. If they could be brought to see the necessity of giving in to the
outsiders for the time being, implicated in the decision to do so, and persuaded to lend their strength to that of the Shogun, then the *bakufu* just
might avoid losing face. The exclusivist approach was to tough it out:
pursue whatever policy the *bakufu* wanted vis-à-vis the foreigners and
crush any domestic resistance from *daimyō*, peasants, or intellectuals.
Each approach, needless to say, had its dangers.

At the time of Perry's visit Abe Masahiro had tried to be inclusive, consulting the *daimyō* and then bowing to their militancy by promising a buildup of coastal defenses. But Abe died in 1857, and his successor as the Shogun's adviser, Hotta Masayoshi, had to address Townsend Harris's demand for a commercial treaty that opened six ports, allowed foreigners to travel freely in Japan, and granted them extraterritorial rights. Hotta could see for himself, in the *Arrow* War, the consequences of refusing, but he knew the treaty was wildly unpopular. So breaking another precedent, he went to the Mikado to beg the Emperor's approval. But the imperial court refused to bless the Townsend Treaty without *daimyo* approval, and Hotta was overthrown.

His successor, Ii Naosuke, took the exclusivist path, ignoring criticism and jailing opponents. But the Townsend Treaty remained in force, and Japanese abroad, like the seventy-seven samurai of 1860, quickly learned that such things as extraterritorial rights were a patent of Japanese inferiority. Yoshida Shōin now drafted a refutation of the Shogun's right to govern at all, since "a man can only be called a ruler when he sustains his people." Clearly the *bakufu* had failed in its duty and it remained only for the Emperor to bestow his mandate on a new regime. To expedite that eventuality, he wrote, youth ought to take to the streets *in the name of the Emperor* and force the *bakufu* to reform or die. Yoshida was imprisoned and executed in November 1859 for thoughts and deeds that would soon be considered the height of patriotism.

The exclusivist crackdown and Townsend Treaty sparked a spontaneous fanatical protest led by masterless samurai who threatened to kill every foreigner in Japan under the slogan *sonnō-jōi* (Revere the Emperor; Expel the Barbarians). In 1860 they assassinated Ii Naosuke. In 1861 they ambushed Townsend's secretary and slashed his throat as he tried to bolt his horse away. Secretary of State Seward insisted on reparation and prosecution of the criminals. In September 1862, when an Englishman was hacked to bits by the swords of outraged samurai, Sir Rutherford Alcock demanded enormous indemnities from Edo and Satsuma (where the attack occurred), and the East India Squadron dropped a "scarlet regiment" on the docks of Yokohama. This was enough to intimidate the *bakufu*, but the Satsuma *daimyo* ordered his forts to fire on the British fleet at Kagoshima. The maddened tars fell to their guns and leveled a good portion of the city. When an American steamer was shelled by Chōshū cannon, Capt. David McDougal of the USS *Wyoming* sank two *daimyo* boats in the Shimonoseki Straits between Honshu and Kyushu, and in 1864 an international squadron forced open the strategic waterway. Those engagements proved to even the most zealous xenophobes of southern Honshu and Kyushu that the weapons of the barbarians could not be overcome by "fighting spirit." If Satsuma and Chōshū

were serious about resisting barbarian influence, they would first have
to Westernize their own armies, going so far as to create "democratic"
rifle batallions from samurai and peasants alike. They did, and so repli-
cated the situation that had obtained 280 years before, when local feu-
dalities in contact with Europeans were in a position to field armies
mightier than that of the Shogun himself.

At the same time, the radical street campaign, labeled *tenchū*
(Heaven's Revenge), assassinated conservative officials and spread chauvinistic hysteria. The Shogun's latest regent, Matsudaira Shungaku, was
another inclusivist, but his attempts to involve the *daimyō* in the government further weakened the *bakufu's* prestige. Lords threw off their
obligation to reside at Edo and ducked any responsibility for foreign policy. The regime neared collapse in spring 1863 when agitators pressured
the imperial court at Kyoto to issue *jōi* edicts calling for expulsion of all
foreigners. Needless to say, all the navies of the world would descend on
the poor *bakufu* if it had tried to carry out such a decree. So suddenly
there were two centers of authority—Edo and now Kyoto—and in the
political space between them Japanese found they could say and do
things forbidden for centuries.

Then the Emperor got cold feet about being made a figurehead for the
jōi campaign. (Perhaps he meditated on the fate of the Chinese
Emperor's palace at the hands of the Europeans three years before.)
Shifting allegiances in August 1863, he invited the soldiers of conservative *daimyō* to clear Kyoto's streets of agitators. The young radicals, led
by Yoshida Shōin protégés like Kusaka Genzui, repaired to Chōshū and
made common cause with its modernizing provincial government. In
July 1864 Chōshū's army returned to lay siege to the imperial city.
Kusaka called for patience: they must not force themselves on the
Emperor but go to every length to respect his dignity. But the fiery commander of Chōshū's largest, most Westernized corps persuaded the
council to attack. To refuse battle while evil surrounded the Emperor
was cowardly! The battle that resulted was a macabre farrago of
medieval and modern weapons and tactics. Much of the city was sadly
burned, Kusaka was mortally wounded, and the Chōshū army was
thrown back. As a result, the progressive faction (Justice) in the Chōshū
regime lost out to the conservative (Mundane Views) faction, the shogunate survived, and Western envoys cheered. As far as they knew, the
Shogun (or Tycoon, as they called him) was the real modernizer—he had
opened Japan and signed treaties—while these *daimyo* armies were
composed of murderous xenophobes.

The three years' interlude that followed seemed a respite for the
bakufu and the fearful Western community. But during those years the

conditions for revolution fell into place. First, the hated Westerners solidified their beachhead in Japan despite the threat of violence against them. Yokohama was their preferred base, and by the mid-1860s some one hundred and fifty permanent foreign residents lived in rough-hewn go-downs and bungalows along the piers, while several times that number of sailors were likely to be in port. They lived on credit, exchanging chits in lieu of hard currency and winning or losing big stakes in the random markets for living quarters, cargoes, and commodities. A pidgin language and lively trade in Japanese dictionaries permitted a modicum of communication. In 1862 the Catholic Chapel of the Sacred Heart opened, the first Japanese Christian church in almost three hundred years, but mostly the foreigners preferred Japan's prostitutes and ubiquitous, explicit erotica. Alcock echoed the opinion of most Japanese when he dismissed Yokohama's denizens as "the scum of Europe."

The presence of foreigners and the impotence of the *bakufu* before them continued to enrage Japan's provincial political classes. But the Shogun still governed in the Emperor's name, and the *bakufu* retained a firm grip on its own extensive lands and the domains of central and northern Honshu. Rebellion against the central government, if it came, must therefore originate in the mighty southern domains of Satsuma and Chōshū. For a year after the Battle of Kyoto, Chōshū remained in the hands of Mundane Views reactionaries. But by 1865 a new leader arose to woo the *daimyō* back to rebellion: a rowdy, besotted young samurai named Takasugi Shinsaku. He, too, was a disciple of Yoshida Shōin and swore to avenge his martyrdom: "While yearning for our instructor Shōin's shadow, morning and night, I have grieved deeply. . . . Practicing military arts in the morning and studying in the evening, tempering my mind and body, serving the spirit of my forbears, and accomplishing my own duty, all become merged in the task of destroying the enemy of our master, Shōin." Takasugi had observed the humiliation of China, done a stint as a Buddhist monk, and meditated on his mission in prison. In December 1864 he stepped into the leadership vacuum among Chōshū radicals caused by Kusaka's death and the purge of the Justice faction.

Gathering like-minded samurai about him, Takasugi launched a guerrilla war against the Mundane Views faction. His forces captured weapons and funds and set up a shadow government among the peasants. By February 1865 the *daimyo* invited the Justice faction back into power, and the radicals initiated pilot reforms that they hoped to impose someday on all Japan. The Chōshū military was organized on Western lines into separate but equal units of peasants and samurai, who even exchanged their swords for humble infantry rifles. They restaffed Chōshū's academy on the basis of merit and created Western-style departments for civil and political affairs. Above all, the Chōshū and Satsuma *daimyō* initiated secret alliance talks in anticipation of another passage of arms with the shogunate.

What had the *bakufu* been up to during the years from 1863 to 1866? Did it not also take steps to reimpose its authority? It did indeed and might have succeeded were it not for the continued perturbations caused by the foreign presence. For even though the *bakufu* cracked down on the assassins and suppressed political dissent in the cities of central Honshu, the traditional structure of society gave way beneath it. Foreign trade drained off gold and flooded markets with cheap English cotton. At the same time, silk exports boomed to such a degree that farmers took to planting mulberry rather than rice and grain, and *daimyō* held back rice to feed their own domains. Food shortages hit the cities and prices doubled or tripled, propelling the urban poor into the streets. The shogunate had no choice but to arm its forces with Western weapons, but it lacked the revenue to pay for them as *daimyō* stopped sending taxes to Edo and the *bakufu* had no means of disciplining them short of military expeditions. So whether the *bakufu* tried exclusivist or inclusivist policies, the result was the same: delegitimation of its own authority.

There was nothing left for Edo to do but to try to restore the Shogun's monopoly of force in Japan. Chōshū officials were expecting it, which is why they recalled Takasugi on the eve of a foreign trip and solidified their alliance with Satsuma. "Both our armies fling away the papers of conciliation," wrote Takasugi, "and grasp the iron whip." In the Summer War of 1866 Western tactics and arms finally prevailed, and the Shogun's demoralized levees were thrown back at the borders of the rebellious fiefs. When Shogun and Emperor both happened to die, the *bakufu* called off the war and declared the Keio Reform, a final, furious effort to stave off extinction. It belatedly moved to establish promotion by merit, streamline the bureaucracy, adopt economies, modernize the army and navy, halt inflation, and place foreign trade on an honest, equal footing. But even if the government could make good on such promises, the Chōshū revolutionaries saw no reason why they should allow the *bakufu* to profit from reforms they had made and fought for against the resistance of Edo itself.

The end came with a brief bang, then a whimper. When fighting resumed in late 1867, Satsuma/Chōshū forces overwhelmed the shogunal army on the outskirts of Kyoto and assumed possession of the new Emperor's divine person. A few diehards in Edo wanted to fight on. But the last Tokugawa Shogun surrendered in Osaka and abdicated in January 1868. The Emperor had abolished his office. An Englishman, Algernon Mitford, watched beneath a frigid, overcast sky: "There were some infantry armed with European rifles, but there were also warriors clad in the old armour of the country, carrying spears, bows and arrows, . . . sword and dirk, who looked as if they had stepped out of some old pictures of the Gempei wars in the Middle Ages. . . . Hideous masks of lacquer and iron, fringed with portentous whiskers and moustachios, crested helmets with wigs from which long streamers of horsehair floated to their waists, might strike terror into an enemy. They looked like the hobgoblins of a nightmare." The entire host stood at attention while the Shogun rode, alone, through the castle archway for the last time. "A wild and wonderful sight, and one of the saddest I have ever seen."

The restorationist armies—for their goal in overthrowing the shogunate was to restore the rule of the Emperor—occupied the castles of all Japan in a matter of months. The shogunal navy defiantly sailed off to Hokkaido but gave up the following year. By then the *daimyō* and their samurai intellectuals from the south and west had already begun a thorough transformation of Japanese state and society. They retained Edo as capital but renamed it Tokyo (Eastern Capital) and moved the Emperor into the Shogun's palace. The Emperor himself took the title Meiji (Enlightened Rule) and thus gave the revolution its name: the Meiji Restoration. The men of Chōshū and Satsuma then set out to restructure government according to the blueprint first sketched by the likes of Yoshida Shōin. The shogunal domains disappeared into prefectures governed by a centralized national bureaucracy. In return, *daimyō* received the governorships, compensation paid in government bonds and pensions, and in many cases high office in the new Western-style ministries staffed by the talented samurai of Chōshū and Satsuma. Less favored samurai rebelled against the abolition of their old status, at least until 1877. But the Japan they wanted no longer existed.

Or did it? How much of the old Japan survived the Meiji Restoration? The revolutionaries had begun under the slogan *sonnō-jōi* (Honor the Emperor; Expel the Barbarians). The first would seem to have taken on a deeper sacredness now that they were invoking an imperial tradition older by far than that of the shogunate. The Meiji government encouraged, too, a revival of Shinto, the ancient national religion based on reverence for the divinity of the land, people, and emperor. But in practice the emperor remained a figurehead. As for *jōi*, the Meiji leaders appeared to forget about expelling the barbarians as soon as they took control. We must "cast off the stupid opinion of the past to look down on foreigners as dogs, sheep, or barbarians," read an imperial decree, and instead, the Meiji regime invited hundreds of Western experts to advise Japan in military affairs, science and engineering, education, finance, and medicine. The slogan of the new era, *fukoku kyōhei* (Rich Country; Strong Military) could be realized only through intense contact with the West.

Still, what was the purpose of it all? What had been the source of the initial discontent with the *bakufu?* Its new policy, begun with Perry, was to open Japan to the West. Why was that bad? Because it stained traditional Japanese culture, shamed the Japanese state through unequal treaties, and colonized Japanese land and labor. Those facts had not changed; all that had changed were tactics. The purpose of Westernization was to make Japan strong enough to *resist* Westernization. And if that were not contradictory, then the modernizers obviously believed that much of traditional Japan remained to be saved. By becoming as strong as the West, Japan might overthrow the unequal treaties and compete with the West on equal terms, or, to put it the other way around, restore Japanese culture, pride, and independence.

Western consuls, merchants, missionaries, and sailors understood little of this. American minister R. B. Van Valkenburgh thought "there is not the remotest prospect of the people being benefited" by the overthrow of the Shogun, and Seward "little dreamed that the restored Mikado would excel the dethroned Tycoon in emulating western civilization." Nor did they ask, at this early stage, whether a modern, industrial Japan might someday pose a threat to the United States. After all, the Meiji leaders were just planning their first little railroad on the Pacific. Americans, by contrast, were completing their Pacific railroad . . . and theirs was three thousand miles long.

Utah and British Columbia
1869

I
F THE MEIJI LEADERS wanted to learn how Western nations got things
done in the age of steam and rails, they needed only to study the
building of the American Transcontinental Railroad. It had been
blocked for a decade by sectional disputes, but the House of Representatives finally passed a bill based on the obvious idea of building *two*
Pacific lines, one northern and one southern. Seward dared to hope that
this "great measure of conciliation, of pacification, of compromise, and
of union" might stave off a civil war. Alas, that very day—December 18,
1860—South Carolina voted to secede.

The cloud of civil war, however, had a silver lining—the silver of
Nevada, whose rapid transport to Union coffers made a western railroad
urgent. Some solons worried whether the government could afford the
project in light of the burden the war placed on capital markets. But
then, no one imagined just how much the line would cost, and by the
time they did, railroad appropriations were small potatoes in annual war
budgets that reached $1.3 billion. Others, who had no qualms about
risking tax dollars for public works, worried about the potential for corruption. But then, the only way to prevent windfall profits was not to
build the railroad at all. Finally, interests favoring Chicago and St. Louis
still disputed the route. But California Sen. James A. McDougall
appeased the Missourians by supporting a spur to St. Joseph. Most
important, the defection of Southern Democrats left the Congress free
to interpret the government's role in society pretty much as it wished,
so a railroad bill was only a matter of time.

The Big Four Associates—Stanford, Crocker, Huntington, and Hopkins—exploited the "silver lining" by sending Theodore Judah to Washington to lobby on behalf of the Central Pacific plan. He had an easy
time, for McDougall and California Congressman Aaron A. Sargent had
Judah appointed chief clerk to *both* the House and Senate committees

responsible for drafting a bill. That this was a gross conflict of interest troubled no one. Still, Congress was groping in the dark. It had not chartered a corporation since 1819 (the much despised Second United States Bank) and shrank from the perils of railroad financing. American rail mileage had tripled and tripled again to 30,626 in 1860. But small local companies dominated construction. Some ran out of funds before completing their lines; others went bankrupt in operation. Clearly the rational approach was interstate consolidation, a method pioneered by the New York Central in 1853, but that took a daunting amount of private capital. The other method was for state governments to build and operate railroads, but bureaucratic incompetence and corruption had already forced seven states to sell off their lines at a big loss to lenders and taxpayers. How could anyone, public or private, finance an additional eighteen hundred miles of track across the unsettled plains of Nebraska, the Rocky Mountains, the Great Salt desert, the Great Basin of Nevada, the Sierra Nevada, and California's Central Valley?

Congress hoped to answer that question in the Pacific Railroad Act, signed into law by President Lincoln on July 1, 1862. It chartered one new railroad, the Union Pacific, and subsidized another, the Central Pacific. They won rights-of-way across the lands separating Omaha from California and were granted U.S. government loans (thirty years at 6 percent) for the sum of $16,000 for each mile of track laid across the plains, $48,000 for each mile in the Rockies and High Sierra, and $32,000 for each mile in the basins in between. Finally, the railroad companies would receive government grants to half the land extending ten miles out from the railroad in alternating, checkerboard sections. What the act did not provide was start-up capital. Inasmuch as the Central Pacific Company began life with a bank account of $15,800 and the liquid assets of the Big Four amounted to $100,000, they had no choice but to go begging. The president of the California Bank took one look at what they intended to do and sent them away. The president of Wells Fargo thought the company "liable to great embarrassment and I very much doubted their ability to carry out their contracts." And given that San Francisco interest rates still hovered at 1.5 to 2 percent per *month*, the Central Pacific would be hard-pressed to service any loans they got.

Leland Stanford, by then Governor of California, opened the great work with a shovelful of dirt and a grandiloquent speech in January 1863. But construction halted just thirty-one miles out of Sacramento, and nine miles short of the length at which the government would reward the company with its first loan. To make matters worse, the California telegraph, stagecoach, and steamship companies made venomous attacks on the Central Pacific. Their anonymous pamphlet, *The Great Dutch Flat Swindle,* charged that the Big Four never intended to build a cross-country railroad but planned only to build a line to the silver fields and make a fortune at taxpayer expense. Finally, the Associates' unethical ploy of awarding their construction contracts to a dummy firm controlled by them alienated the honest Judah. So he sold his partners his interest in the Central Pacific for $100,000 and sailed again for the East in October 1863.

Legend has it that the Big Four drove Judah out of the company, then cheated him. In fact, $100,000 was not an inconsiderable sum for a one-fifth interest in a nearly bankrupt company dedicated to a proposition most businessmen found absurd and in which Judah had invested little. Nor was he forced out but departed with options to buy *all* the stock in the Central Pacific, if he could find New York investors willing to back him. Instead, he caught yellow fever in Panama and was dead by November. If the Big Four were going to make a killing on this railroad scheme, therefore, those reputedly ignoble men would actually have to realize what Horace Greeley called "the grandest and noblest enterprise of our age."

Politics was Stanford's business. Once inaugurated as governor in 1862, he set out to persuade the legislature to authorize California counties to float bonds for the purchase of Central Pacific stock. Some questioned the constitutionality of the scheme, so Stanford appointed the railroad's chief counsel (and Charles Crocker's brother) to the state supreme court. Bookkeeping was the task of Mark Hopkins, oldest (at forty-nine in 1862), thinnest (the others all weighed in at 220-plus), most desk-bound and cautious of the group. As treasurer, "Uncle Mark" played the foil to the three swashbucklers and kept the railroad afloat during its early financial crisis. Surmounting the crisis was Collis P. Huntington's task. He had gone east with Judah to work for the Act of 1862 and remained there for the duration of the struggle. His first triumph was to band together with Union Pacific lobbyists and persuade Congress to pass a second Pacific Railroad Act in 1864. Under its terms the railroads could issue first-mortgage bonds equal in value to the government's loans. Thus the taxpayers would be putting up the money to build the railroad, but in case of default ownership would pass, not to the people, but to the private investors the railroads now could attract. What was more, the government agreed to make payments upon the completion of every twenty miles, not forty, and doubled the land grants awarded for each mile of track. Said Huntington of Congress: "You cannot, in my opinion, legislate intelligently. . . . If you have to pay money to have the right thing done, it is only just and fair to do it." The Central Pacific also persuaded the feds, thanks to some impeccable but irrelevant geology, that the Sierra Nevada began a mere seven miles from Sacramento. A preoccupied Lincoln approved the claim, thereby authorizing the railroad to begin claiming costs of $48,000 per mile instead of $16,000 for most of the meager work it had already done.

Thanks to the 1864 Act, the Union and Central Pacific Railroads became solvent and construction began in earnest, westward from Omaha and eastward from Sacramento. When an amendment in 1866 gave the Central Pacific the right to build as far east as it could, the joint project turned into a race. One or the other railroad stood to gain about $3 million in bonds, a million acres of land, and a larger percentage of the eventual rates and fares for every hundred miles of track. And freight rates were already so lucrative that the Central Pacific realized over $5.6 million by 1869 from traffic on the portion of the line completed. But Huntington's work had only begun. He was also the railroad's procurement agent, purchasing iron rails, spikes, and locomotives and chartering ships to haul it all via Panama or around the Horn. The Civil War made this doubly hard and more than doubly expensive since he had to compete with the Army for matériel and pay wartime prices. Even insurance rates were four times normal, thanks to Confederate naval raiders, and the fee for a single locomotive shipped via the Isthmus was $8,100.

Once equipment arrived at the loading docks of Sacramento, it became the responsibility of Crocker, the fourth Associate and general of the construction army. By modern notions he was a cad, the central figure in the shadow Contract and Finance Company set up by the Associates to receive their construction contracts. Its stock was wholly owned by the Big Four themselves, so they essentially paid themselves all the monies borrowed to build the railroad or else loaned money to themselves by paying the construction company in railroad stock! One company or the other was bound to clear a tidy profit, while control of the railroad and land grants remained in their hands. In the end, the Central Pacific portion of the Transcontinental Railroad cost about $50 million, but the personal fortunes that resulted, from income and appreciation on the railroad and its land, exceeded $200 million.

That was the wage that American society paid the Big Four for performing an extraordinary public service. Take Crocker, for instance. While Governor Stanford inaugurated the railroad with carefully memorized bromides about linking the oceans with an iron band, Crocker shouted, "This is no idle ceremony. The pile driver is now, while I am talking, driving piles for the foundation of the bridge across the American River. . . . It is going right on, gentlemen, I assure you! All that I have— all of my own strength, intellect, and energy—are devoted to the building of this section which I have undertaken. Amen." Some of his underlings hated him, but no one questioned his will. When a spring flood washed out a bridge over a canyon, Crocker told his engineer to rebuild it in five days. "I don't believe it can be done," he replied, "but I'll try it." Crocker roared, "I don't want anyone to 'try' it. What I want is a man who will go out and do it!"

"They were a great army laying siege to Nature in her strongest citadel. The rugged mountains looked like stupendous ant hills. They swarmed with Celestials shoveling, heeling, carting, drilling, blasting rocks and earth, while their dull, moony eyes stared out from under immense basket hats like umbrellas. At several camps we saw hundreds sitting on the ground, eating soft boiled rice with chop sticks as fast as terrestrials could with soup ladles." So wrote Albert D. Richardson of the Chinese whom Crocker recruited. Now California's second Governor, John McDougal, had welcomed Chinese immigrants in the 1850s, but Stanford made a point of condemning Asians in his inaugural address. Moreover, Crocker's chief engineer, James Harvey Strobridge, laughed at the idea of using coolies. Why, they barely weighed a hundred pounds apiece! But white laborers were scarce and disdained the stoop work of the railroad. So Crocker hired an experimental gang of fifty Chinese that grew, by 1865, into a force of between ten and fifteen thousand. He assured the White House that Chinese were "quiet, peaceable, patient, industrious and economical . . . [and] contented with less wages." When it came to cutting rock, Crocker thought the Chinese "equal to the very best Cornish miners" and Strobridge thought them "the best in the world." At Summit Tunnel, a 1,659-foot granite cut, the Chinese hacked with picks for ten hours a day and hung suspended in baskets over cliffs to chip out ledges for the rails to follow. They moved small mountains of earth with shovels and wheelbarrows for a dollar a day without board, and died by the scores in explosions and avalanches. Seward so appreciated their worth that he wrote a clause into the Burlingame Treaty with China that guaranteed unrestricted immigration. It was a response to the needs of the railroad, to be sure, but also in line with his lifelong advocacy on behalf of immigrants.

Once upon a time, in schools and books, the four Associates were heroes and the Chinese forgotten. Nowadays the four are deemed "robber barons" and the uncomplaining Chinese the true authors of the railroad. But Bret Harte described the reality in *The Overland Monthly:*

> The woods of the Sierra and Rocky Mountains rang with the strokes of axemen and the click of steel in the quarries. The streams were bordered with camps of lumbermen and choked with floating logs. At one place on the Truckee River, twenty-five saw-mills went into sudden operation. Lumber, iron, and material of every description lined the road, and the wake of the advancing workmen was marked by the odd debris of deserted

camps. On the Central road alone from seventy to one hundred locomotives and several hundred cars were constantly passing to and fro with material, supplies, and laborers. The wharves at San Francisco and Sacramento were piled with iron bars. At one time thirty vessels were en route from New York via Cape Horn with iron and rolling stock for the road, and locomotives and rails were even ordered by the way of the Isthmus.

Without all that activity, organized by the four entrepreneurs and carried out by mills in Pittsburgh, boiler plants in Philadelphia, shippers in New York, engineers, railroad men, ironmongers, sailors, stevedores, loggers, carpenters, chemists, and more, the Chinese would not have been there at all.

Crocker, "the man of giant energies, the man of iron will," rode up and down the line encouraging and cussing. Though he admittedly learned his trade on the job, his construction techniques were state of the art. Alfred Nobel's nitroglycerine, patented in 1867, was being synthesized by the vatfull in Donner Pass. To cope with avalanches after two snowy winters, Crocker invested $2 million in fifty miles of buttressed snowsheds—an innovation that made possible Alpine and Siberian railroads. When graders and tracklayers descended the eastern slope and set out across bleak Nevada, Crocker's engineers laid hundreds of miles of pipe to supply their camps with water.

As every pupil used to know, the race ended on May 10, 1869, when a spike of California gold and a plate of Nevada silver (engraved with the names of the Associates) were embedded in a polished tie of California laurel. Stanford swiped at—and missed—the last spike, but the telegrapher tapped out a prearranged code, and within seconds people from New York to Sacramento were declaring Promontory Point, Utah, the "Appomattox" of the war between steam and distance.

In fact, the Central Pacific did not reach the Pacific. The Associates had to build or buy out local lines west of Sacramento and up the peninsula to San Francisco. (The San Francisco–Oakland Bay Bridge, originally a railroad link, still lay sixty-three years in the future.) Nor did the Pacific Railroad make for an immediate boom. San Francisco actually lost some business to Chicago as a result of the rail connection. The end of construction created unemployment, Nevada silver began to play out, and California sank into the "terrible seventies" along with the rest of the industrial world after the Panic of 1873. Nor did the Associates realize their greatest profits until the real estate market picked up and their shares rose in value. But in time the Big Four became founding fathers of California society, their Nob Hill mansions paragons of Victorian splendor, and their names preserved in Stanford University, the Huntington Library in San Marino, the Crocker Bank, and the Mark Hopkins Hotel.

But the most immediate effect of the Transcontinental Railroad was suggested, unknowingly, by a *Daily Alta California* reporter who wired in May 1869: "From the Railroad Front—Victory." He was on a train carrying "the Asiatic contingent of the Grand Army of Civilization. The cars contained 557 Chinese, all laughing and shouting in high glee at the approaching completion of their work. . . . These Chinese expect to be sent north to work on the Northern Pacific Road." A Northern Pacific Road? Yes, and one of the silliest aspects of the long debate over transcontinental routes is that traffic would surely bear at least three transcontinental lines. The 1860 bill granted that principle, and the Railroad Act of 1864 reified it by providing for rights-of-way from Lake Superior to Puget Sound. And by the end of the Civil War, that hoped-for link to the Pacific Northwest supported a campaign by Seward for nothing less than the annexation of British Columbia.

Since Polk's Oregon Treaty of 1846, the settlement on Vancouver Island had not prospered. The Hudson's Bay Company was a dying monopoly and about to lose its lease on western Canada. In the meantime, Company lands were liable to American filibusters aimed at achieving a "fifty-four forty" boundary after all. The danger did not come from Oregonians, who tilled their fields, hewed the region's unmatched forests, and won statehood in 1859. Nor did it come from the handful of Yankees exploring the prospects of the Puget Sound region. Rather, the threat came from California. In 1850 the rumor spread south of gold on Queen Charlotte Island, and in 1858 of a rich strike on the Fraser River. In the latter case some ten thousand sourdoughs rushed up the coast, doubling the population of the British territory. Governor James Douglas called for help and was rewarded when the Royal Navy ordered three steamships from China to the Northwest coast. In the same year Britain took all of Canada west of the Rockies away from the Hudson's Bay Company and made it a crown colony. Queen Victoria gave it a name: British Columbia.

The show of force quieted the American miners, most of whom drifted home when the gold was gone. But with the outbreak of the Civil War, Canadians feared that the militarized Yankees might strike north as well as south, and the Royal Navy despaired of defending British Columbia. "I would consider it would be greatly for the interest of England," reported one admiral, "to divest herself of these possessions." By 1865 the white population of British Columbia was one-fourth American, and its economic ties with Oregon and California were far greater than with Canada or Britain. It seemed that Manifest Destiny might yet include the entire West Coast, and Seward, for one, dared to dream of that destiny. So when the U.S. Consul at Victoria reported that "the people of Vancouver Island, and of British Columbia, are almost unanimous in their desire for annexation to the United States," Seward did all he could to fulfill their wish.

Two geopolitical earthquakes shook the contested colony in 1867. The purchase of Alaska meant that British Columbia was now squeezed north and south by American territory. But just one day before the signing of the Alaska treaty, Queen Victoria ratified the British North America Act creating the self-governing Dominion of Canada. It had been in gestation ever since the Canadian insurrection and Lord Durham's Report of 1839. But the new federation included only Quebec, Ontario, Nova Scotia, and New Brunswick—not British Columbia or the Hudson's Bay Company lands in between. So the few scattered thousands on Britain's Pacific coast had a choice—defect to the United States, or demand membership in the Dominion of Canada. In London, the cabinet was willing to let the little Victoria colony go but refused to do so under American pressure or threats. In Ottawa, Toronto, and Montreal, Canadians espoused their own version of Manifest Destiny. As Alexander Galt put it: "If the United States desires to outflank us on the west, we must . . . lay our hands on British Columbia and the Pacific Ocean. The country cannot be surrounded by the United States." While in Victoria, it was dawning on British Columbians that they might use their leverage to hasten the one development on which their future depended: a railroad connecting them with the east.

As early as July 1867, the *New York Times* cut to the heart of it: "Without the opening of a railroad connection . . . British Columbia finds no more natural attraction in Canada than in Denmark." Thus, the fate of British Columbia came to hinge on whether the United States or Canada could make the most convincing promise to build a northern transcontinental railroad. Now, Congress had chartered the Northern Pacific in 1864 but neglected to offer government loans. As a result its directors had even a harder time than the Associates in raising start-up capital. In 1866 Thomas H. Canfield tried to convince the president of the Chicago and Northwestern Railroad to go in with them. Canfield recalled:

> Long after midnight I felt that he was won for the cause. I can see him now as he paced the room, completely absorbed in the subject.
> "How much money will it take to put this enterprise on its feet and begin its work of construction?"
> "It will take a great deal of preliminary work and your experience teaches you that it will take a great deal of money."
> "And what are our chances of getting our money back?"
> "About one in fifty."
> "And what is your excuse for asking me to place money at such a risk?"
> "This enterprise is one of the greatest ever undertaken in the world."

The next day the Northern Pacific reorganized its management and launched one of the most intensive promotional campaigns in the history of American business. But so well did the Union and Central Pacific interests move to squelch their would-be competitors that Congress did not budge. Seward used all his authority and New York contacts trying to drum up investment in the Northern Pacific, and no less a mover-and-shaker than Jay Cooke, "the financier of the Civil War," agreed to push its bonds. But the Northern railroad was a "premature enterprise." Its survey teams could not even penetrate the Big Horn country until General Custer arrived to protect them.

In January 1868 the residents of Victoria expressed a preference for joining Canada on condition that they be granted immediate provincial status and the promise of a railroad. The Canadian government wasted no time forwarding the request to London, and in June 1868 Parliament voted to sponsor construction of what became the Canadian Pacific Railroad. Its motive, as Sir Harry Verney put it, was to preempt "depredatory measures on the part of our neighbors who might cast a wistful eye on countries whose value England seemed to ignore." In November 1870, the British Columbians' council finally voted to join with Canada.

That vote brought to a close the initial partition of the North Pacific. Exactly a century had passed since Portolá and Serra led the first expedition into Alta California. Now California, Oregon, Washington, and Alaska were American, and only the original "Nootka coast" in between remained, by a quirk of railroad finance, British. The Russians had retreated to Asia but showed a new vigor by advancing to the Amur and founding Vladivostok. Only Hawaii with its brave monarchy, Sakhalin and the Kuriles, and, of course, decrepit China remained contested. But how permanent would the partition be as the age of steam and rails matured . . . not least in Meiji Japan?

The Seventh 'aha iki

Scholar: Well, Mr. Saitō, I await your blistering attack.

Saitō: Ah, but if you are waiting for it, then it would not be a *surprise* attack, so I would not make it. Besides, what's my target?

Scholar: Why, whatever I said about the Meiji Restoration.

Saitō: No problem here.

Scholar: Really?

Seward: Well, I have a problem. I didn't understand the Tycoon-Mikado business back then, and I'm afraid I still don't.

Kaahumanu: Nor do I. The rebels fought against the Shogun because he opened the country to *haoles*—

Saitō: Gaijin. We call all foreigners *gaijin*.

Kaahumanu: —and then, after their victory, they opened up their country more than ever? It makes no sense.

Seward: Hold on! The oldest trick in politics is for the "outs" to stir up public fear against some measure proposed by the "ins" and then, after taking office, proceed to adopt the same policy. So the Emperor's party just exploited the hatred of foreigners to overthrow the Tycoon?

Saitō: Not quite *that* simple, Mr. Seward. In the beginning, the opponents of the *bakufu* were not united—samurai, intellectuals, the imperial court, *daimyō* like those in Satsuma and Chōshū who always resisted the central government. Many motives overlapped, but one had potential to bring them all together: opposition to the humiliating treaties with the barbarians. Only it was not clear for some years what Japan could do to resist them, to avoid becoming like China. A few, like Yoshida Shōin, already believed that Japan must learn the foreigners' ways. But most just wanted to expel them. Shimonoseki was the turning point. After the Western fleets bombarded the coasts of Satsuma and Chōshū, the *daimyō* realized that the radical reformers were right: Japan must become modern, and quickly, or become slaves of the *gaijin*. But the *bakufu* was rotten and incapable of reform, so it had to be replaced by the dynamic samurai intellectuals who knew what to do. Our professor said it well: Japan had to Westernize to avoid being Westernized.

Kaahumanu: That is what I do not understand.

Saitō: Let me put it another way. You recall the slogan *sonnō-jōi* (Honor the Emperor; Expel the Barbarians)? Those sentiments did not disappear after the Meiji Restoration but took on new meaning. Here is what one of the Meiji leaders wrote in their journal of "Japanese enlightenment." What, he asked, would have happened if our people had not been defeated at Shimonoseki but won victory after victory over the barbarians? "Then foreign states would have warned against approaching a country of tigers and wolves like Japan ... and our unparalleled emperor, representing an unbroken line, would be regarded as the chief of savage wolves. Could a man with the least degree of spirit permit his sovereign to be thus demeaned rather than honored? How splendid it was for the empire that you were fortunately defeated and pacified before we suffered great shame."

Scholar: Now *I'm* lost.

Saitō: Because this enlightened scholar—his name was Sakatani Shiroshi—explained the lessons of history. If Europeans were *i* (barbarians), so too were Japanese *i* once upon a time, and might become so again. To expel the Westerners out of blind ignorance was shameful— like defending the Emperor's name through drunken brawling instead of honorable combat. Rather, the enlightened way of honoring the Emperor was to "expel the barbarian" *within ourselves* and return to our ancient paths of virtue even as we opened up to enlightenment from abroad. That way Japanese would not succumb to foreign barbarism, nor resist it by their own barbarian methods, but bring foreign enlightenment in harmony with Japanese enlightenment. "To open the ports today," wrote Sakatani, "is both just and in conformity with the times, and this is why opening the ports is honoring the emperor."

Scholar: So the line between virtue and barbarism is drawn *through* nations and not *between* them? And by adopting what was enlightened from the whites the Japanese could better preserve what was virtuous in their own culture.

Saitō: You got it, Doc. *All* nations exhibit a mixture of barbarism and enlightenment ... except for Chinese and Koreans, who loved flattery and oppression, and shamed their emperors. Sakatani wasn't surprised to hear that Americans wanted to "expel the barbarians," too—the Chinese immigrants.

Witte: So Chinese were despicable because their "inner barbarism" prevented them from assimilating Western enlightenment? Can we not interpret this Taiping Rebellion as a modernizing movement similar to the Meiji Restoration in Japan?

Scholar: Some have tried. But it's hard to imagine the Taipings imposing peace, unity, centralized government, and rapid industrialization on the whole of China. Or anyone else doing it, for that matter, since the Westerners were already there in force and had a stake in Chinese weakness.

Witte: The only distinction being that Russia and Japan wanted China weak and *divided.* Sea powers wanted it weak and *united.*

Kaahumanu: Because Russia and Japan were neighbors and wanted to annex portions of China! Whereas the sea powers wanted only to impose their trade.

Scholar: Kaahumanu is very perceptive, but we're getting ahead of ourselves.

Serra: Thank you, Doctor. I was hoping to ask Mr. Seward a question.

Seward: Ha, the *padre* saw me pouting like a child ignored on Christmas morning. Is no one interested in the professor's biography of *me?*

Serra: I am. I wondered what you thought of his description of your Civil War policies, for instance, your "Thoughts for the President's Consideration."

Seward: Ah, yes. Now, I'm not a vain man, but am I to get no credit at all?

Scholar: I gave you plenty of credit.

Seward: You said that I urged Mr. Lincoln to wrap the world in flames.

Scholar: That's what you wrote, though it does seem incredible.

Seward: And you took it literally.

Scholar: How else was I to take it?

Seward: Do *you* believe that I was "temporarily deranged"? Tell me, sir, when I was Governor of New York did I exploit the Canadian Rebellion? You know I hoped the United States might annex Canada.

Scholar: No, you showed great forbearance.

Seward: Did I support the Mexican War? Did I not try every avenue to prevent the Civil War with plans to compensate slaveholders for emancipation, and build railroads to mesh the fortunes of North and South? After the Rebellion began, did I seize the opportunity to provoke a war with Britain over the *Trent* affair, with France over Mexico, or Spain over Hispaniola? You didn't mention that one. Is there any evidence that I was a warmonger?

Scholar: No—but the historians say that Lincoln and Charles Francis Adams in London had to tone down your dispatches and try to win British sympathy *despite* your belligerence.

Seward: Indeed, sir. And who appointed Adams to the Court of St. James's?

Scholar: I believe you did.

Seward: "Mr. Adams I take because you suggested him," that's what Lincoln wrote me, and he let Adams know, too. And as for the *Trent* affair, you said "the Cabinet" chose the prudent course, releasing Slidell and Mason—

Scholar: —the Confederate diplomats.

Seward: Do you know who wanted to *keep* Slidell and Mason in prison? Lincoln himself. I was the one who argued that they be released. Indeed, all my messages to London and Paris after May 1861 were like double helpings of warm porridge. Only a fool would have poked Palmerston in the ribs.

Scholar: Granted, and the historians all say that after Lincoln's rebuff of your initial memorandum, you showed skill.

Seward: Do they, now? So I became a worthy statesman *in spite of* my "temporary derangement" in 1861. Does no one grasp its purpose?

Saitō: It's obvious.

Witte: It is obvious.

Scholar: Then you *were* bluffing.

Saitō: He was *deterring* the British from intervening on the side of the South at the moment of maximum weakness and demoralization for the Union. But the threat was empty, for war with Britain would only ensure a Southern victory.

Seward: Yes, if Britain intervened the South would be lost to us, but *Canada* would be lost to Britain! My greatest handicap as Secretary of State was precisely that I *did* have a reputation as a man of peace, while Lincoln was an unknown quantity. Before Fort Sumter he had no policy at all; after Fort Sumter we had to establish our right to blockade thousands of miles of Rebel coast against the commerce of all the world. The Europeans needed to be warned off but not by direct challenges to which they would be compelled to respond. I had no intention of stirring up a foreign war, but I had to make the Europeans think I was daft enough to do it. In no time it was Britain that was running scared, sending troops to Canada. Once we survived 1861 without a European intervention, we could play on the differences among the European powers themselves, while removing *every* irritation in our relations with London and Paris. I muted my protests against British blockade-runners, I winked at Maximilian in Mexico and the Russian repression of Poland.

Scholar: So your belligerence at the start, and conciliation later on, were all part of a greater strategy. Why didn't you explain it to someone?

Seward: And have it leak out that "Seward doesn't really mean it"?

Scholar: After the fact, then?

Seward: And damage our postwar relations by gloating over past successes? The British Lion does not like to be reminded of the time you twisted his tail. No, the best diplomatic tactics are the ones that never come to light.

Scholar: So instead, the Radical Republicans excoriated you for remaining loyal to Andrew Johnson and made Lincoln the author of all glory. . . . Come to think of it, Charles Francis Adams did call you that rare man who was both a politician and a statesman, but that was a eulogy after your death.

Seward: Some people did know. In fact, I received a poem from Lincoln's secretary at the end of 1861. "To William H. Seward," it read:

And so a generous people, at the last
Will hail the power they did not comprehend,
Thy fame will broaden through the centuries;
As storm, and billowy tumult overpast,
The moon rules calmly o'er the conquered seas.

Scholar: Who was the author?

Seward: A youngster of some promise, I thought. His name was John Hay.

Witte: Since you are divulging secrets, tell us about Alaska. I am sure Stoeckl did use bribery. All Russian diplomats had "secret funds."

Saitō: All diplomats have secret funds.

Seward: I don't know all that Stoeckl did—

Saitō: Come on, Henry.

Seward: I truly don't know. He was a braggart. And he had no use for democracy. Perhaps he exaggerated his ability to corrupt Americans so as to mock our system. Or perhaps he pocketed the money himself while telling his superiors that he had spent it on bribes. Who could prove otherwise? I do know that Stoeckl skipped the country in a hurry after the Alaska bill went through, claiming that *we* were corrupting him.

Scholar: A classic case of "projection."

Seward: What?

Scholar: Seeing in others the sins you deny in yourself.

Kaahumanu: Mr. Witte, did you approve of the sale of Alaska?

Witte: I neither approved nor disapproved. I was eighteen years old.

Scholar: But later?

Witte: Later I thought it a tragedy. If only it could have been postponed.

Scholar: Until the Trans-Siberian Railway was finished?

Saitō: But then *Japan* would have conquered Alaska in the war of 1904!

Scholar: Wow! I never thought of that. But it's hard to imagine Russia holding on to Alaska for another generation.

Witte: Do you know what the $7 million was used for? To build railroads, including the ones that gave me my start.

Seward: As I always say, "It is characteristic of every good treaty that it confers great advantages upon one party without any serious cost or inconvenience to the other."

Witte: Especially when *your* country receives the "great advantages."

Seward: To be sure, but remember that not all my countrymen believed that was the case! That is why leadership is so important in a democracy.

Serra: Mr. Seward, do you affirm the methods of the men who built your Transcontinental Railroad?

Seward: Are you suggesting. . . ? I never made a *dime* off public service!

Witte: I admire your Associates. Whatever their manipulations, they *got the railroad built.* Would that we had such men in Russia.

Scholar: Russia did have such men, Count Witte: *you.*

Witte: I never made a *kopeck* off public service!

Scholar: No, but you said "they got the railroad built," implying that their public service excuses their methods and profits. Do you know what Huntington said at the congressional investigation of the Central Pacific's finances? "We have served California better than any other set of men have ever served any other state in the Union!"

Seward: Sounds like Collis. But the idea of congressmen sitting in judgment over the corruption of others—what a laugh! Still, I cannot condone the methods employed by the Big Four.

Serra: But do you condone democracy?

Seward: Of course.

Serra: Of the sort practiced by your Thurlow Weed?

Seward: Now, *Padre,* the world's not a pretty place. Let me say that the amazing thing about human beings is not their wickedness—that is universal and banal—but that occasionally they strive to do good. Perhaps Thurlow found it necessary to manipulate the baser instincts of man, but for a good cause—electing me to office.

Scholar: So the ends justify the means?

Seward: You may take that up with Serra. But before you decide, I suggest you try running for office, or fighting for something you believe in.

Witte: Seward is right. Trying to build Russian railroads, I had to fight *against* profiteers in corrupt government bureaus. American genius is to get profiteers and public interest on the same side.

Scholar: Sort of a "theory of creative corruption." We must take human nature and institutions as we find them, and cope with the realities—

Witte: To get things done!

Scholar: Whereas a society that bickers endlessly about the motives of all the people involved, or tinkers endlessly with its institutions—

Witte: —never gets around to doing anything at all.

Scholar: So in a weird way, Seward's Manifest Destiny is right, not because America was more virtuous, but because it was more "creatively corrupt" than, say, Mexico, where the creative people were not corrupt, and the corrupt were uncreative. What do you say to that, Father? We are called by God to be creative, but if to be creative we must be corrupt, how then can we serve God?

Serra: Does building a railroad serve God?

Seward: Absolutely.

Witte: Not necessarily.

Kaahumanu: I would say no.

Saitō: Such tender consciences you Christians have. You must always invent a divine calling to cover your greed and envy, and beatify even your corruption.

Scholar: Spoken like a *zen* master. And I thought you liked railroad trains, Saitō, especially the club car.

Saitō: Name your poison, Pardner! "Scotch and soda, bourbon and rye." Only, the ice on trains was always dirty.

Kaahumanu: I have another question. If Russia was shortsighted to sell Alaska, was not Japan shortsighted to welcome the Americans above all others?

Scholar: No, not really. The U.S. Navy was still small compared with the British, the Europeans had a much larger presence in China, and, of course, Russia was the biggest and nearest of all the powers. In

1875 Japan even had to surrender all of Sakhalin Island to Russia. By comparison, the U.S. seemed less predatory and potentially Japan's champion against the other powers.

Saitō:

New-hatched doves try out moist wings
Dawn is grayish yellow
Eyes pecked out by jays

Kaahumanu: Is that a poem? It is very sad.

Scholar: A *haiku*. Did you compose it, Ambassador?

Saitō: Just now. I was thinking of Japan in the first years of Meiji. Spring is a season of danger, a season of death.

Seward: I know what you mean. After my term of office was over, I took a trip around the world, 1870 and '71 it was. By rail to Chicago— what a city—and then by the Transcontinental to California, and steamer across the Pacific. I met Emperor Meiji and had a frank interview with his prime minister. He wanted to know everything: how we collect taxes, budget our government, conduct our census. But most of all he worried about Japanese weakness amid the great powers. Afterward I wrote that Japan has special reasons for prudence.

Scholar: "Especial." You wrote "especial reasons for prudence."

Seward: So I did: "Japan has especial reasons for prudence. The empire is a solitary planet, that has remained stationary for centuries, until now it is suddenly brought into contact with constellations that, while they shed a dazzling light, continually threaten destructive collisions."

Witte: And?

Seward: That's it. That's all I wrote.

Scholar: I wish you had said more.

Seward: I made it a point never to say more than I know.

Honolulu 1875

"IT IS A MATTER OF the utmost importance to the United States that her trade with these islands should be carefully fostered and augmented. Because—it pays." So wrote Mark Twain in 1866, on the last leg of the adventures recounted in *Roughing It* and *Letters From Hawaii*. Why, the Sandwich Islands merchants paid as much as $300,000 a year for the right to import sugar to San Francisco, and there were two ways, thought Twain, to cement this lucrative connection: "Let Congress moderate the high duties somewhat; secondly—let the Islands be populated with Americans. To accomplish the latter, a steamer is indispensable. . . . In California people are always pressed for time." Twain, the old riverboat pilot, was especially taken with the *Ajax*, "a two-thousand ton propellor, and one of the strongest vessels afloat." She could accommodate a hundred passengers and twelve hundred tons of freight, "and when a coal depot is established for her hereafter at Honolulu, so that she need carry only fuel enough for half the voyage, she can take two or three hundred tons more." Unfortunately, no coaling station yet existed on Oahu, and the Hawaiian kingdom lacked the funds to dredge Honolulu harbor. But no doubt those matters, too, would be set to rights as soon as American engineers were set loose on the place.

But American influence seemed less sure than during the long reign of Kauikeaouli (Kamehameha III). That prodigal King had been effectively tamed after his abortive coup and the government liberalized and staffed with foreigners. The Great Māhele land reform, completed in 1855 after nine years of legal muddle and slapdash surveys, granted the chiefs clear and alienable title to some 3.2 million acres, or 80 percent of the archipelago. That meant not only that they owned the land free from arbitrary seizure by feudal superiors, but also that they were free to *sell* it. The predictable result was that cash-rich foreigners proceeded to buy up huge tracts of arable land at bargain prices. The Parker Ranch, engulfing the vast grasslands from Kamehameha's Kohala Coast up the slopes of Mauna Kea volcano, established the cattle industry first envisioned by Vancouver and brought to the islands its first laborers: Mexican and Portuguese cowboys called *paniolos* (from *español*). Erstwhile missionaries and sons of missionaries founded cotton, silk, coffee, rice, and especially sugar plantations, while Yankee seamen continued to dominate whaling and commerce.

Hawaiians still outnumbered American residents perhaps sixty to one. But their numbers continued to fall. In 1853 smallpox carried off 10 percent of the entire population. Likewise, foreign ownership of Hawaiian land was now protected, while development was wholly the work of American capital. All the Yankees lacked was political and military control, so that imperial rivals like Britain or France or a hostile Hawaiian monarch could not challenge their cultural and economic hegemony. When Kauikeaouli died in 1854, that very nuisance arose. His nephew Alexander Liholiho (Kamehameha IV) was of a younger, gayer generation exposed to more worldly possibilities than the old "either-or" of Hawaiian tradition versus missionary rule. Moreover, his half-Hawaiian wife, the beloved Emma, was an Anglophile. Following an incident in which the King gunned down his own private secretary (an American accused of seducing the Queen), Alexander Liholiho sought forgiveness—and more—in the sacraments of the Church of England. The "more" was simply a religion he deemed more appropriate for a monarchy than evangelical Protestantism. By 1862 the royal couple secured Queen Victoria as godmother *in absentia* for their son Albert, donated a site for an Anglican cathedral down the street from Bingham's Kawaiahao church, and recruited Bishop Thomas Nettleship Staley. The man himself was a caricature out of Trollope: "a bishop out of very inferior material," wrote Twain, who "gossips habitually . . . and is vainer of being my Lord Bishop over a diocese of fifteen thousand men and women (albeit they belong to other people's churches) than some other men would be of wielding the power of the Pope." More to the point, a lei-sporting Bishop Staley presided over a syncretic cacophony of hula-hulas and high-church liturgies that the Hawaiians loved and the missionaries abominated. Dancing, drunkenness, and promiscuity became modish again, and Protestant power over Hawaiian royalty was broken forever. Henceforth the phrase "missionary faction" came to refer, not to American clergy, but to sugar planters.

Still, even Twain, as flinty a religious skeptic as ever dared offend his readership, pronounced an ambiguous verdict on that "band of stern, tenacious, unyielding, tireless, industrious, devoted old Puritan knights." Contemplating the remains of an old *heiau*, he meditated on the days before the missionaries came to tell the Hawaiians "how blissful a place heaven is, and how nearly impossible it is to get there" and "what rapture it is to work all day long for fifty cents to buy food" instead of "lolling in the shade through eternal summer." But those were also days when no one could call any property his own, when every vice and horror were encouraged, and men and women were disemboweled for breaking taboos. The missionaries, by contrast, "have clothed them, educated them, broken up the tyrannous authority of the chiefs, and given them freedom and the right to enjoy whatever the labor of their hands and brains produces, with equal laws for all and punishment for all alike who transgress them. . . . Their work speaks for itself."

Equal laws notwithstanding, Alexander Liholiho went unindicted for the cold-blooded shooting of his secretary. But then, the monarchy was the only major Hawaiian institution left, and one of the last two bulwarks against foreign domination—the other being the balance of naval power among Britain, France, and the United States. The royal flag symbolized this precarious condition. Designed with the aid of the foreign consuls, it combined a Union Jack in the upper left corner, a field of horizontal stripes like Old Glory (eight—the number of inhabited islands), and the hues of the French tricolor. Moreover, King Lot, who succeeded as Kamehameha V in 1863, moved at once to bolster the royal power by abrogating the missionary-inspired Constitution of 1840. He replaced universal manhood suffrage with a property qualification, packed the assembly with his nobles, made ministers responsible to the king rather than to a majority in the assembly, and arrogated veto power to himself.

The Americans, however, held a trump card. For the tax receipts of the crown still depended on the islands' prosperity, which in turn was a function of white economic activity. Tariffs and duties, port fees, and the money spent by visiting ships financed the Hawaiian monarchy. It had, therefore, to protect and encourage the very businesses that increased American population and power, and it ignored at its peril the political wishes of the *haoles* on whom it depended to fill the public purse. Lately the major source of income had been visiting whalers. But the Civil War killed the industry. Some whaling ships were converted for military use, others were captured or deterred from sailing by Confederate action. In 1865 Capt. James T. Waddell's *Shenandoah* carried the Civil War to the North Pacific, sinking ships and seizing cargoes worth millions. After the war San Francisco emerged as a competing port to Lahaina and Honolulu, then in 1871 an early winter crushed thirty-three whaling ships in the ice above the Bering Strait. Finally, whale oil was being replaced by that oozy new commodity first pumped commercially in Pennsylvania in 1859—petroleum.

At the same time, the Civil War cut off North American markets from their prior source of sugar in the Mississippi delta and so showed

Hawaiians a way to recoup. We have seen that farsighted Yankees identified Hawaii's future with agriculture as early as the 1830s, when Ladd and Company first domesticated the wild sugarcane that grew on Kauai. By 1850 enough modest plantations existed to export 740,000 pounds of the stuff. In that year the Act for Masters and Servants authorized Hawaiians and foreigners to contract for long-term service in the fields, with stiff penalties for desertion. The first Chinese coolies arrived two years later. In 1851 a new invention, David M. Weston's centrifugal machine, did for Hawaiian sugar what Whitney's gin had done for the cotton South: it separated and refined molasses from raw sugar in a matter of hours rather than weeks. Hawaii's future was engineered again in 1856 when William H. Rice risked $7,000 on a ten-mile irrigation ditch near Lihue on Kauai. Irrigation opened thousands of potentially lush acres to water-intensive cultivation—and an acre in Hawaii, with its volcanic soil and year-round growing season, yielded up to six times more sugar than an acre in Louisiana.

The planters and government also understood the need to persuade the United States to reduce its high tariffs on sugar. The first attempts to do so, in the mid-1850s, foundered on the opposition of Southern congressmen. But after 1861 Louisiana planters were blockaded, their plantations ruined, and after 1865 denied representation in Congress. Sugar prices rose sharply, while the number of Hawaiian plantations grew to thirty-two, with annual production of twenty-seven million pounds. Much of this boom was financed by Charles Bishop, the only indigenous banker and husband to the philanthropist granddaughter of Kamehameha the Great, Bernice Pauahi Bishop. The Hawaiian sugar was shipped to San Francisco, where a lively refinery industry sprang up, and it was a clash between the planters and the refiners that forced the *haole* sugar kings to look for relief to Washington.

For not only did the end of the Civil War bring falling prices, the very mechanization of the plantations made Hawaiian sugar too good for the San Francisco refineries! Now, there were two main sorts of wholesale sugar: low-grade yellow sugar in need of further refining, and "grocery grade" sugar suitable for immediate sale as a beverage sweetener. The Hawaiian plantations had built up their American market with low-grade product, which the San Franciscans were pleased to refine and distribute. But by the end of the war Hawaiian sugar was of such high quality that it could be shipped directly to hotel kitchens and grocers' shelves. So the San Francisco and Pacific Refineries proposed to buy a fixed amount of Hawaiian sugar at a premium price on condition that at least half the Hawaiian sugar be of *low* quality. After some hesitation the Planters Society pooh-poohed the offer, hoping for a full-scale commercial reciprocity treaty with the United States.

Secretary of State Seward was not the one to miss a chance for peaceful expansion and dreamed of annexing the Sandwich Islands. But when Hawaiian Chief Justice Elisha H. Allen petitioned him for a treaty in 1864, Seward advised him to wait. So long as the Civil War was on, he dared not risk annoying Britain, nor was Congress likely to entertain overseas diversions. Seward's judgment was sound, but by the time the Hawaiian negotiation began Congress was busy impeaching Andrew Johnson, while Lot Kamehameha, who succeeded as king in 1863, worried that a trade treaty might prove the first step toward annexation. The Hawaiians wanted to ensure the *economic* life of the islands, but not in such a way as to compromise their *political* life.

What was more, they had reason to fear. After the Civil War the United States Navy doubled its presence in Pacific waters and rotated as many as five warships into Hawaiian waters. The *Lackawanna's* Capt. William Reynolds was an especially obnoxious presence at Honolulu by dint of his vocal annexationism. In 1867 Reynolds sailed away to claim the Midway atoll for the United States as a possible coaling station. The island was inhabited by gooney birds, not people, but it still stoked Hawaiian resentment. Of course, the Planters Society pressed for the treaty on economic grounds, but the Hawaiian Legislative Assembly and King agreed to ratify it only if appeasing the Yankee economic interests served to *cool off* annexationist sentiment rather than encourage it. And that, ironically, was the reason the 1867 treaty failed in *Washington.* For Seward's secret fact-finder, Col. Zephaniah S. Spalding, reported to Congress that ratification of a solemn treaty with Hawaii's royal government would reinforce the sovereign status of that government and thus betray the long-term interests of the United States. So hard-core expansionists joined forces with other senators who argued that the treaty would reduce U.S. tariff revenues, or benefit only special interests, or encourage other nations to demand the same privileges. In the end the Senate voted only twenty to nineteen in favor, far short of a two-thirds majority.

Lot Kamehameha, who was forty years old but weighed 375 pounds, died without issue or heir in December 1872. Possible royal pretenders included his sister-in-law Emma, Princess Ruth, and Bernice Bishop—all justly famous for their intelligence and charity. But the women shunned the honor and unpleasantness that accompany power, leaving as candidates "Whiskey Bill" Lunalilo, who traced his lineage to a half-brother of Kamehameha, and David Kalakaua, the most energetic and aspiring chief outside the royal family. Kalakaua tried to smear his rival's claim through the employ of "skillful genealogists," but the Legislative Assembly chose Lunalilo in a landslide. "A splendid fellow," thought Mark Twain, "with talent, genius, education, gentlemanly manners, generous instincts, and an intellect that shines as radiantly through floods of whiskey as if that fluid but fed a calcium light in his head."

The following year, 1873, was a newsy one in the islands. First, the Belgian monk Joseph de Veuster, known as Father Damien, took up his mission in the recently established leper colony on Molokai. (Hawaiians believed the disease arrived with the coolies. At least they called it *mai pake*, "the Chinese sickness.") Second, the Household Troops, the King's sole military force, mutinied until Lunalilo, five miles away at Waikiki, granted them amnesty and met their demands. Outwardly, their grievances were internal—they hated their drillmaster—but beneath the surface was a growing racial antipathy to the *haoles* and any royal policies deemed to favor them. The affair only exposed the impotence of the monarch to command even his own lilliputian guard. Finally, 1873 was the year the Yankees made their first feint toward Pearl Harbor.

It began in January with a planter's well-crafted memorandum suggesting that Hawaii lease Pearl Harbor to the United States in exchange for a reciprocity treaty. Such an arrangement, he wrote, would not only place the sugar industry on a sound footing but attract American capital, speed the development of that excellent port at no expense to His Majesty, and "defeat and indefinitely postpone all projects for the annexation of these Islands to any foreign power." After all, no other country could threaten Hawaii so long as a U.S. naval base were present, while Americans and Hawaiians would enjoy all the benefits of annexation even as we "guarantee our national independence under our native rulers as long as the treaty may continue." The *Pacific Commercial Advertiser* floated the notion in February, insisting that a reciprocity treaty with the United States must be had even if it meant leasing "a position for a harbor and coaling station. . . . We refer, of course, to the Pearl River." The Honolulu Chamber of Commerce endorsed the idea, approached U.S. Minister (and sugar magnate) Henry A. Peirce, and persuaded the King to negotiate. At the same time, two more American agents, dispatched to investigate the value of Hawaii in time of war, urged the Grant administration to revive reciprocity. Generals John M. Schofield and B. S. Alexander shared the opinion of earlier visitors that Pearl Harbor would be the finest in the Pacific once $250,000 were spent dredging a channel through the coral barring its entrance. What was more, Peirce warned (falsely, as it turned out) that the planters were desperate enough to turn to the British Empire for markets and loans if negotiations with the United States should fail. But the mere hint of ceding Hawaiian soil to the *haoles* sufficed to provoke an outpouring of popular protest, which was orchestrated in good part by American "sympathizer" Walter Murray Gibson. His new Hawaiian-language newspaper identified Gibson as "a messenger forbidding you/To give away Puuloa (Pearl)/Be not deceived by the merchants/They are only enticing you/ . . . Desiring that *you should all die*/That the Kingdom may become theirs."

Then Lunalilo died of tuberculosis in February 1874, and the struggle for the succession became inseparable from the conflict over the treaty. David Kalakaua was quick to announce his availability, and the planters rallied to his support. But this time Queen Emma also put herself forward, and she was notoriously pro-British. The election in the Assembly was tense. Several thousand of Emma's devotees waited outside while foreign sailors went on alert in case of trouble. There is evidence that Kalakaua's men bribed the legislators; certainly the overwhelming and strangely sullen vote (thirty-nine to six) in his favor suggests a fix. The pro-Emma, antitreaty crowd, appalled by their unexpected defeat, burst into the Assembly to rough up Kalakaua's supporters and vandalize the building until American sailors arrived to restore order.

David Kalakaua, Hawaii's last King, is the most noted of all save Kamehameha the Great. He was a stocky, mustachioed man of elegant tastes, educated, clever, jealous of his prerogatives. He also proved popular with Hawaiians once he displayed his determination to deal with foreign governments on a plane of equality. Moreover, his plan to reconcile the needs of the national economy with Hawaiian independence proved surprisingly successful. In August 1874 Kalakaua became the first reigning monarch from anywhere to visit the United States. New Yorkers lavished five thousand dollars on royal entertainments, a joint session of Congress applauded him, and President Grant hosted a state dinner. All pronounced themselves charmed by the youthful but dignified sovereign. He also won the Americans over to a reciprocity treaty that established free trade in virtually all goods (except the highest grades of sugar) and left Hawaii in possession of Pearl Harbor on the promise that it would not cede land to any third party. Minister Peirce was disappointed, but he still thought time was on the side of the United States. Trade, he wrote, would grip the islands "with hooks of steel" and "result finally in their annexation." The Senate ratified the new treaty by a vote of fifty-one to twelve, and when the House (dawdling as usual) finally passed enabling legislation in August 1876, *haoles* and Hawaiians alike celebrated.

"Hurrah! For America and Hawaii! The Glorious News at Last! Hurrah!" cried the *Honolulu Advertiser*, and with good reason. Acreage planted to sugar multiplied tenfold during the course of the treaty's fifteen years, and sugar shipments to the United States exploded from 17 to 115 million pounds in just six years. By 1890 Hawaiian exports surpassed $13 million, 99 percent of which went to the United States. Private rail lines proliferated to carry sugar to port, and then public rail-roads, thanks to Kalakaua's Railway Act of 1878 and subsidies of $2,500 per mile of track laid. The telegraph appeared beginning in 1877, and four years later monthly steamship service to Honolulu began. Once a ramshackle village, Honolulu now numbered twenty-five thousand and began to expand inland across the flat coastal plain, hinting of its future as a modern, mid-Pacific metropolis.

The era of reciprocity was the most progressive and prosperous in the history of the Hawaiian monarchy. But the sugar empire needed more than land, capital, technology, and markets. It needed thousands of pli-ant, diligent field hands to plant and cut cane, work the mills, pack the product, load it on trains, and load it again on merchant steamers. Native Hawaiians, though sturdy workers, were diminishing in number, unused to the discipline of fixed hours, and uninterested in binding themselves to foreigners. The planters tried Portuguese, but they pre-ferred ranching and fishing, and wanted European wages. The planters tried Chinese, seventeen hundred of whom were imported during the 1860s. But they were an enterprising lot and invariably left the fields after their term of service to open shops in the towns. In 1868 the Amer-ican Eugene Van Reed, appointed Consul-General by Kamehameha V, succeeded in shipping 148 Japanese to Hawaii. But the Meiji govern-ment was so enraged by this commerce in people that it closed off emi-gration for seventeen years. So the planters turned again to Chinese, whose numbers tripled to almost eighteen thousand by 1885. By then native Hawaiians, their numbers down to forty thousand, were close to becoming a minority in their own land. Whites still numbered only a few thousand, but believed themselves destined to assume political leadership. As one planter wrote in 1886, the white race was given Europe to start with, the yellow race Asia, the red America, and the black Africa. But the white man alone sallied forth beyond the "bounds of his habitation" and carried his enterprise to the world, benefiting the colored races in the process.

Certainly Chinese Hawaiians were better-off than they were in Can-ton. But Mark Twain in turn appreciated the value of the Chinese to *white* civilization. "You will have coolie labor in California some day," he wrote. "The sooner California adopts coolie labor the better it will be for her." His economics were right. But for once—perhaps the only time—Twain held human nature in too high esteem. For at the same time Hawaii's whites were importing Chinese as fast as they could, Cal-ifornia's whites declared war on the Chinese already there.

Sacramento and Washington
1882

"UNLESS I GET some sleep, I shall break in some way," wrote Collis P. Huntington in March 1873. For "if something isn't done soon we shall all go to hell together." The something he hoped to do was unload his shares in the Central Pacific Railroad to anyone who would have them. Fewer than four years before, Stanford had driven the Golden Spike. But all it had earned Huntington was the task of shoring up and adding to a pyramid of debt that taxed even his skill, nerves, and health. The promoters of the Union Pacific were already buried: one was personally ruined, the others sold out for next to nothing in 1871. After all, ownership of a transcontinental railroad did not guarantee gilded grandeur, for the reason that its directors, like most venture capitalists, had also to manufacture customers who would "pay the freight" and cover interest on the debts incurred in construction. Imagine the sucker who bought Union Pacific bonds in the 1860s secured by the land grants awarded by the federal government. When the railroad defaulted, he could only ride the rails out to some arid, treeless knoll in western Nebraska, hold his hat against the wind, and claim it ruefully for his own (assuming the federal land office, or holder of a "first-mortgage" bond, didn't bump him aside). Chances are the sucker wouldn't bother.

In short, a railroad crossing a thousand miles of virgin land was a potential fortune maker but only *after* those miles were filled in by settlers and *assuming* all the while that the railroad enjoyed a monopoly. The Union Pacific directors failed to look ahead to the day after their line was complete; the Central Pacific's Big Four did, but even so were able to survive only by means that made their previous shenanigans look like a rehearsal. Already in the 1860s they bought up all the California short lines and seduced or bullied cities into granting rights-of-way. The village of Oakland ceded its entire waterfront to the railroad in return for becoming its main East Bay terminus. San Francisco stood in danger of being shunned altogether until it gave up sixty Bayside acres. The Big Four bought out the "Shasta Route" northward to the small but promising town of Portland (8,300 people in 1870) and projected the Southern Pacific Railroad so as to monopolize routes to southern California. The Associates even threatened to bypass Los Angeles (then a proud cowtown of five thousand people) until the city fathers handed over their little railroad running to San Pedro on the coast and subsidized the Southern Pacific to the sum of $600,000. Huntington's view of the matter was simple: "It is about as well to fight them on all the railroads in the state as on our road, as it is not much more fight and there is more to pay."

How did Huntington finance this overnight empire of West Coast rail construction? He borrowed, and borrowed some more, using *Central* Pacific stock as collateral for *Southern* Pacific construction. At times Wall Street suspected a shell game, but every time Central Pacific bonds took a dip or investors boasted of selling short (expecting the bonds to collapse), Huntington quietly raised the cash (by more borrowing) to buy his own Central Pacific notes and drive their price back up. At the same time, he had to defend the Central and Southern Pacific's erstwhile monopolies until they began to pay off in a big way. So he also borrowed to purchase the California Steam Navigation Company, pressured the Pacific Mail Steamship Company into offering his railroads low rates, then set up his own steamship line in 1874 to drive Pacific Mail out of business. Finally, Huntington kept a close eye on transcontinental competitors, bought out the struggling Texas and Pacific Railroad, and obtained the right-of-way to extend the Southern Pacific from Los Angeles to New Orleans. "Where the money came from nobody but the managers know," wrote a New York journalist. "All the public can realize is that the road is built—built of the best materials . . . and that too without any aid from State or Federal Treasury."

Still, the Big Four periodically despaired. During the Panic of 1873 Huntington and Mark Hopkins tried to sell out, and in 1878 Huntington threatened to quit and go home: "I am as near used up as I ever was in my life before. I am spending my last winter at Washington." His front man for the Southern Pacific, David D. Colton, urged him to "stand by the wreck to the last—we can at least die game," but pleaded "for Gods [sic] sake lets [sic] get out of debt before we talk about building any more roads." Now our image of the railroad kings of California places them in their splendiferous Nob Hill mansions, living as lords on fortunes gouged from poor farmers forced to pay exorbitant rail rates. But it

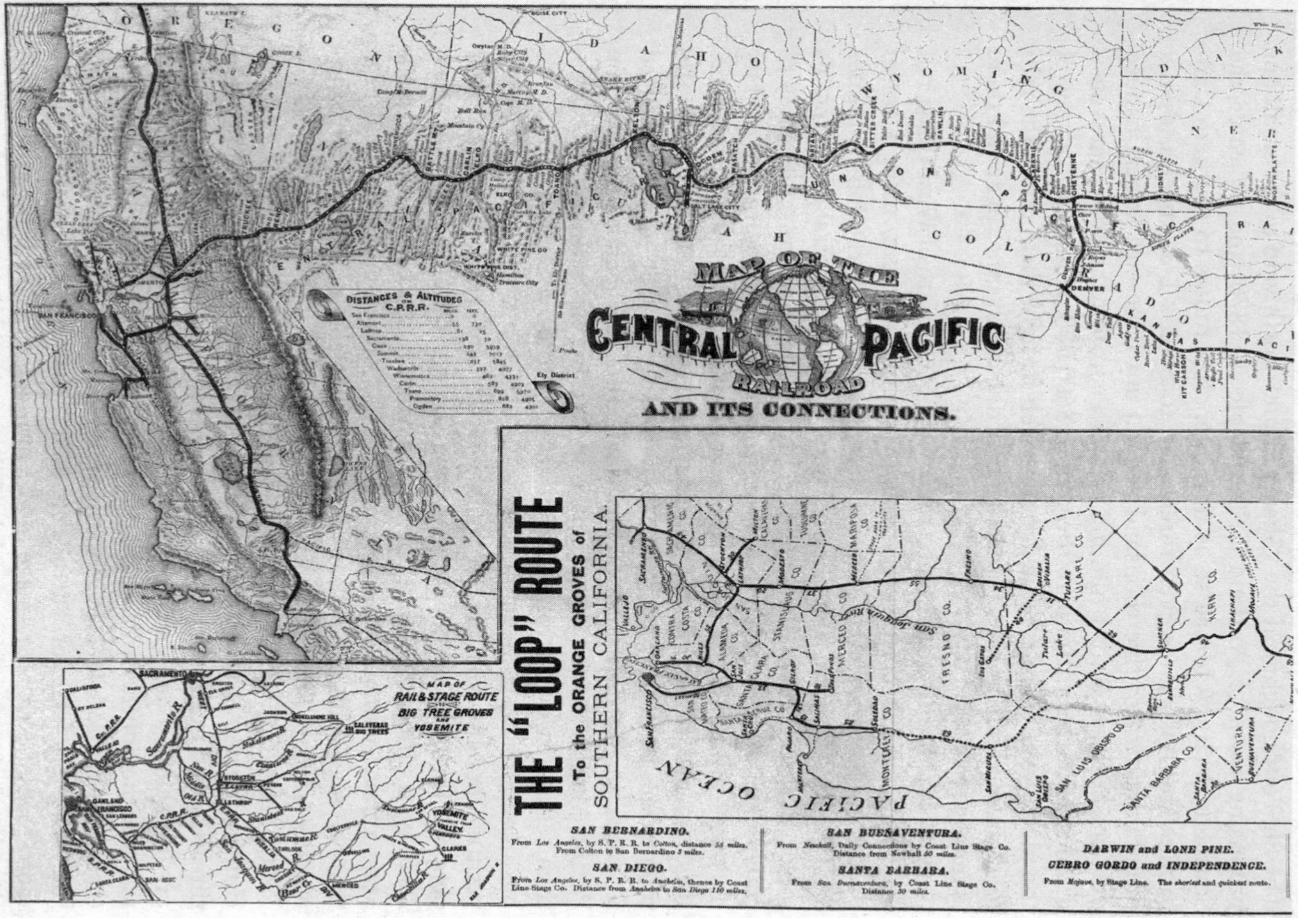

(Courtesy, The Bancroft Library)

is also true that Pacific railroads might have gone bankrupt, or not been built for decades, were it not for Huntington's stockjobbing and the monopoly forged in California.

Common folk, including hundreds of thousands who reached the West Coast via the railroad, hated its ubiquitous influence. For not only did the Central/Southern Pacific control all transport and manipulate governments, it was California's largest landlord. Much of the land that was left was owned by Henry Miller, the Cattle King (whose million acres allowed him to boast that he could ride from Mexico to Oregon and camp each night on his own property), or wheat kings like Hugh J. Glenn, who owned a twenty-mile stretch on the right bank of the Sacramento River. It was estimated, in the early 1870s, that one-fifth of one percent of the population owned over half the land in the state. Had California, the golden legend, been liberated from Mexico only to succumb to a new feudalism? That was the question that prompted philosopher Henry George to devise his scheme for a single tax on land to break the power of the robber barons.

So long as the flush times lasted, however, there were opportunities aplenty and no assaults on the various kings. Small farmers planted wheat in the valleys. Citrus growers broke ground for orchards along the Los Angeles and Santa Ana rivers. Vintners, drawing on Hungarian refugee Agoston Haraszthy's collection of cuttings from fourteen hundred varieties of European grape, realized the wine-making potential of Napa, Sonoma, and Santa Clara counties. Railroad construction employed thousands, and for the adventurous there was always mining. In *Roughing It*, Mark Twain tells of a telegrapher whose traffic consisted mostly of mining stock quotations from Virginia City, Nevada. He began to make trades on his own account and soon retired a millionaire. Finally, one could always find work in San Francisco, whose population passed 150,000 in 1870.

Then came the Panic of 1873, and the tremendous rates of economic growth that had prevailed in the 1850s and 1860s gave way to a worldwide stagnation that lasted until 1896. This first "great depression" of the industrial age stimulated business, labor, and farmers to organize, agitate, lobby, and collude in hopes of protecting their interests. The indebted West Coast was especially vulnerable, and when the Bank of California failed in 1875, hundreds of businesses went bankrupt. To make matters worse, Nevada silver began to play out, the phylloxera plague wiped out the grapevines, a drought blighted the wheat-growing regions, wages dropped up to 50 percent, and at least fifty thousand people had no work at all. These were the "terrible seventies" during which farmer and labor parties first arose on Pacific slopes to denounce the

Southern Pacific "octopus." Of course, the railroad men were also dodging creditors, but they unwound from their daily exertions by drinking whiskey in the easy chairs of clubs, not begging a pint of beer on credit from the bartender at the Irishman's local.

Denis Kearney is a natural for the novelist, not least because historians know so little about him. A native of County Cork, he left Ireland as a cabin boy and made first mate before trying his luck in San Francisco. Full of bite and blarney, too charming for his own good, he nonetheless displayed virtues thought to be Anglo-Saxon. He neither drank nor smoked, saved his money, and soon owned a likely fleet of wagons lading goods in San Francisco. Yet no sooner had thousands of unemployed or underpaid Irishmen taken to agitating in the sandlots around City Hall than Kearney placed himself at their head and flirted with insurrection. It began in 1877 when an embryonic Marxist movement, soon to be known as the Socialist Labor party, called for workers to rally in support of striking Pennsylvania miners. The Molly Maguires were in the vanguard of those strikers, so San Francisco Irish turned out eagerly. In the wake of the meeting, however, a band of rowdies fanned out to ransack Chinese laundries. Two days later another gang of toughs put the torch to the docks of the Pacific Mail Steamship Company, thought to be responsible for the influx of Chinese. A battle ensued with police and middle-class defenders of property armed with pick handles, and four people were killed. It was then that Kearney stepped forward to assume the presidency of a Workingmen's party dedicated to breaking the capitalist lock on economy and government. Symptomatic of Kearney's appeal was his use of the infamous "spite fence" raised by Charles Crocker around the home of a neighbor who had refused to sell out to make room for his mansion. Yet whatever the focus of his stirring and humorous Sunday speeches, they always ended, like Cato's in the Roman Senate, with the same refrain. As Kearney would say: "Whatever happens, the Chinese must go!"

In the words of a labor historian, the Chinese were "the indispensable enemy." For whatever splits might occur within the labor movement, California workers all agreed on one thing: coolies were an intolerable threat to the livelihood of "American" workers. The Chinese, it was said, stole away jobs, worked for slave wages, and *were* in fact slaves inasmuch as they were shipped in from overseas by big employers and put to work for years on a chain gang. Nor did they all go home to China but often stayed to open laundries and other businesses and work all night to outcompete whites who were fighting for the eight-hour day. The Chinese were reportedly filthy, addicted to drugs and prostitution, and impervious to American mores. So long as they remained, white workers would never be able to get a fair shake from employers.

Anti-Chinese sentiment had inspired a panoply of local laws: in the 1850s, the Foreign Miners' Tax and fifty-dollar Head Tax on "aliens not eligible for naturalization"; in 1860, a ban on Chinese in public schools and hospitals and a Chinese fishing tax; in the early 1870s, a ban on hiring Chinese for municipal public works, a tax on Chinese laundries, and prohibitions against gongs, firecrackers, and even the wearing of a queue (the Chinese pigtail). Moreover, Chinese had no right to vote or even defend themselves against sporadic violence such as the slaughter of twenty-two Chinese in Los Angeles in 1871. As the saying went, they didn't have a Chinaman's chance. The Anti-Chinese Union, the International Workingmen's Association, Knights of Labor, and Kearney's Workingmen's party all agitated for complete exclusion of Chinese. But to bring about such a result, organized labor had somehow to revoke international law as embodied in the treaty made under Seward between the United States and China.

As we know, the three constant themes in Seward's public life were civil rights, free immigration, and peaceful expansion. Anson Burlingame shared Seward's visions, and the resulting Burlingame Treaty of 1868 recognized "the inherent and inalienable right of man to change his home and allegiance and also the mutual advantage of the free migration and emigration of their citizens and subjects." The treaty granted Chinese in America equal rights to education and all the rights granted immigrants from other countries. The 14th Amendment with its "equal protection" clause and the Civil Rights Act of 1870, though passed for the benefit of Negroes, further strengthened the legal standing of Chinese, so that federal courts threw out as unconstitutional many of California's anti-Chinese laws. At the same time, Chinese immigration accelerated, with over twenty thousand arriving in 1873 alone and over one hundred thousand during the 1870s. Of course, large numbers of previous arrivals also sailed home, but by 1880 one in eleven Californians was Chinese—all of them males of working age. Moreover, they were only the first ripples of a yellow tide that could theoretically number in the millions.

In 1878 the Workingmen's party and the farmers of the Patrons of Husbandry forced the convocation of a state constitutional convention. The new Constitution of 1879 was an absurdly lengthy compendium of special pleadings directed against banks, railroads, landowners . . . and Chinese. Again, federal courts intervened, and in normal times the issue might have provoked another serious clash over the issue of states' rights. Instead, Chinese exclusion became a national issue, and within three years Californians got all they hoped for. That was because the electoral votes of the Pacific states, though modest, were enough to swing six consecutive presidential elections beginning in 1876, so evenly balanced were the major parties. Democrats and Republicans were also of equal numbers within California itself, so it behooved local and national politicians alike to cater to the fears and bigotries of West Coast voters. Nor were Easterners exempt from racial emotion. Thanks to the Transcontinental Railroad, factory owners imported Chinese strikebreakers to Beaver Falls, Pennsylvania, and North Adams, Massachusetts, Chinese replaced blacks in some Louisiana cane fields, and baby Chinatowns exposed New Yorkers, Philadelphians, and Bostonians to the sights, sounds, and odors of Asian culture. Democratic politicians and labor leaders like Samuel Gompers played on the fear that the "terrible scourge" would someday reach the shop floors of eastern cities. Republicans, eyeing the 1880 election, joined them in demanding revision of the Burlingame Treaty. The American minister in Peking was appalled—he was George F. Seward, nephew of the late Secretary of State, and he asked China only to revise the treaty so as to bar immigration of indentured laborers, criminals, prostitutes, and the diseased. So President Rutherford B. Hayes replaced Seward with James Angell, a University of Michigan professor, who demanded and got the right to "regulate, limit, or suspend" immigration whenever the influx of Chinese "affects or threatens to affect" the interests or "good order" of the United States.

The only groups to stand up for the Chinese were big business and the clergy. As the spokesmen for the gospels of commerce and Christ, they argued against restriction in the name of free enterprise (read also "cheap labor") and the brotherhood of man. But congressmen preferred the Californians' arguments to the effect that "coolie labor" was unfair competition, that Chinese were a menace to public health and morals and resisted assimilation. It was true that Chinese sojourners gambled incessantly, frequented brothels and opium dens, and formed tightly knit communities. But then, the white forty-niners had displayed the same vices. And it was true that the Chinese embraced a work ethic that Americans liked to claim for themselves. But then, so did the Italians and Jews of San Francisco, and no one advocated expelling them. At bottom, the sociological smokescreen hid a raw fear of Asians borne of their numbers and a hatred borne of their impenetrable "strangeness." For an Irishman to do poorly in life while other whites lived well was an aggravation. But for heathen to accept without complaint the capitalist power structure and *still* get ahead was a shame and a judgment. "One of my greatest objections to them," Sen. George Hearst candidly wrote, "is that they can do more work than our people and live on less, and for that reason . . . they could drive our laborers to the wall." In 1882 Congress passed, and President Chester A. Arthur signed, a total Exclusion Act that made Chinese ineligible for citizenship, forbade Chinese wives to join their husbands, and shut the door to new Chinese immigrants for a period of ten years. The expectation (borne out in 1892 and 1902) was that the door would never open again.

Meanwhile, California filled up with new waves of white settlers pulled in from the East. The Southern Pacific Railroad spearheaded a publicity campaign, tested first in the state of Iowa, depicting southern California as a land of healthy air, orange groves, and cheap land. The railroad hired popular authors like Charles Nordhoff and launched magazines like *Sunset* to extol the pleasures of the railroad journey and hyperbolize over the delights of California. Angelenos, who according to one visitor "believe their city and county to be the choicest part of the earth," cheerfully seconded the Southern Pacific prospectus. The Los Angeles Board of Trade's Immigration Association testified that "no happier paradise for the farmer can be found than Los Angeles County." So the population of the town doubled during the 1870s, then quintupled during the 1880s to surpass fifty thousand. The influx fed southern California's first real estate boom, during which property transfers rose from $10 million to $95 million in the space of three years. Since the Southern Pacific itself owned much of the choice land, the railroad made profits "coming and going." The bubble burst in 1887, but in that same year competition arrived on the tracks of the Atcheson, Topeka, and Santa Fe Railroad. The ensuing rate war drove the price of a Chicago-to-L.A. ticket to as low as fifteen dollars and thus sustained new emigration that boosted the state's population to 1.2 million by 1890.

Did the Chinese Exclusion Act buy time for the great migration that made California "safe" for white American civilization? Or would whites have continued to dominate anyway, albeit with a sizable Asian minority? The answer is probably the latter, but be that as it may, Californians won their battle to define American power on the Pacific in terms of race. Their campaign for exclusion first gave vent to the fear that everything whites had accomplished on the Pacific might be swept away in a flood of Asians, or—what seemed more unfair—that Asians might fall heir to all the blessings of America. And its lessons were not lost on the *Japanese*, who were, in the selfsame decade, grappling to learn American ways and wondering which of those ways to make their own.

Tokyo 1889

NATSUME SOSEKI owed all he was to the men of Meiji. Born in the year of the Shogun's overthrow, he became the first Japanese to hold Tokyo University's chair in English literature. But he also described the "enlightenment of contemporary Japan" as an endless bad dream. "Like a man fleeing helter-skelter, with a *tengu* (long-nosed goblin) hard on his heels, we ran and jumped for our lives, hardly conscious of how we did it. . . . We had to achieve in ten years something which took European countries a century." What made the Japanese so ambitious that in the space of twenty-two years they assimilated Western learning and technology, modernized their institutions, and prepared Japan to compete with the Western imperial powers? Was it their superiority complex born of a religion that made them a people divinely favored, or an inferiority complex born of their ignorance and isolation? Did they import Western ways out of earnest admiration, or just to get their hands on modern weapons so as to *expel* the foreign devils? Did they view their foreign relations as a conflict between races, or did their own imitative success prove that race was an irrevelant factor in the advancement of states? Or do all these "either-or" questions say more about how Westerners think than how Japanese might have been thinking back then?

One of the reasons the questions defy easy answer is that the Meiji leaders did not pursue their goal of "Rich Country, Strong Army" according to some ideology. They made it up as they went along. And their first task was to ensure that no *other* disaffected Japanese faction did to them what they had just done to the Shogun. Thus, they broke the power of the feudal *daimyō* , neutralized their fellow samurai, centralized the government, and identified it closely with the source of all legitimacy, the Emperor. But the whole point of their coup d'état was that the shogunate had yielded to the white imperialists and signed a series of "unequal treaties." So to establish its power at home, the Meiji oligarchy had to work for treaty revision. But that could not be achieved until Japan attained a level of law and commerce that Westerners respected. And to achieve that, the Japanese had to tolerate an influx of Western methods, machinery, and people on a scale far beyond that which had angered them so in the first place! So foreign and domestic policy were inseparable: to move too slowly in asserting Japanese power and pride entailed the risk of domestic revolt ("Why, this new government is even weaker than the old *bakufu!*"), while to move too swiftly increased the risk of foreign war ("These upstart Japs need to be taught a lesson!"). Springtime was indeed a dangerous season.

The first generation of Meiji leaders—including Ōkubo Toshimichi and Saigō Takamori of Satsuma, Kido Takayoshi and Itō Hirobumi of Chōshū, and Gotō Shōjirō of Tosa—constituted themselves a Council of State with central authority for the nation. The *daimyō* acquiesced in 1869: "[N]ow that the Imperial power is restored, how can we retain possession of land that belongs to the Emperor and govern people who are his subjects? We therefore reverently offer up all our feudal possessions. . . . Thus the country will be able to rank equally with the other nations of the world." The old domains became prefectures, the lords became governors subservient to Tokyo, and the samurai were pensioned off. When a free market in land was decreed in 1872, Japanese feudalism ceased to exist.

The more radical their policies, the more the Meiji men had to rely on the Emperor's sacred prestige. So the Council issued its reforms as *imperial* decrees and elevated Shinto to the status of an official cult. A peculiarly Japanese religion, Shinto is pantheistic—a form of nature worship. It has no word for God, recognizing only *kami*, superior entities, that might be identified with anything from Mount Fuji to the brooks and gardens that sedate the troubled soul. Shrines could be found in what Westerners thought the most unlikely places, for the very soil of Japan is infused with spirit. Mighty men, too, might partake of the divine, like the *mana* of a Hawaiian chief. But the Emperor—direct descendant of the Sun Goddess—was the apotheosis of *kami*, the center of purity, and potentially the focus of a nationalism all the more compelling for being sacred. The Meiji oligarchs took full advantage, imbuing the court with Shinto priestcraft and setting up shrines to the Emperor in schools and public buildings. At the same time, a new Ministry of Rites launched a nationwide campaign to shut down Buddhist temples, scatter their fifty-six thousand monks, and replace Buddhism's universal, transcendental, and pacifist message with that of state

Shinto's Three Injunctions: "Revere the *kami* and love the country; Clarify heavenly reason and the Way of humanity; Revere the Emperor and respect court directives."

All this would seem profoundly non-Western, but in fact the oligarchy's veneration of the Emperor enhanced its ability to carry out Westernization. The founding document of the Meiji era, the Charter Oath of 1868, announced "the seeking of knowledge throughout the world in order to strengthen the foundations of the Throne." So instead of forbidding Japanese to travel, the government paid the way for 350 students to study abroad beginning in 1871. The largest group, about 40 percent, went to America to study business, technology, and agriculture. Those chosen to learn engineering and foreign trade went mostly to Britain, law students to France, medical students and scientists to Germany. At the same time, the first of over four thousand *o-yatoi gaikokujin* (foreign employees) arrived in Japan to offer their expertise to the government and economy. British and American lawyers taught the foreign ministry how to draft documents and negotiate in the Western manner. British, German, and American engineers oversaw railroads, telegraph lines, docks, and factories built by the regime. British advisers instructed Japanese naval cadets, French and German officers drilled the army, and American businessmen taught production, marketing, and accounting.

Above all the Meiji leadership stressed education. They rousted out the old Confucian faculties and hired David Murray of Rutgers to design a system modeled on American public schools and land grant colleges. Its purpose, as described in the Japanese Education Code of 1872, was to help the future official, farmer, merchant, and artisan "raise himself, manage his property, and prosper in his business." By 1880, twenty-eight thousand primary schools were in operation and the nucleus of a university system inspired, and largely staffed, by *yatoi* professors like the chemist William Elliot Griffis, the physicist Thomas C. Mendenhall, the biologist Edward S. Morse, and the philosopher Ernest Fennelosa.

During the 1870s Japanese drank indiscriminately at the font of Western culture. They read Rousseau, John Stuart Mill, Herbert Spencer, and others—in no particular order. They went mad for Western art and architecture and all manner of "novel gadgets." It became fashionable to eat beef and bread, listen to Western music (preferably military marches), and exchange silk robes and topknots for broadcloth suits and Western haircuts. "This is one of the most remarkable events in history," wrote Henry M. Field. "In a word, it has, as it were, unmoored Japan from the coast of Asia, and towed it across the Pacific, to place it alongside of the New World, to have the same course of life and progress."

That was what Americans wanted to believe, of course, and during the honeymoon of the 1870s the Japanese gave them every reason. Evolutionary thought was all the vogue not only because of Darwin but because evolution seemed the fundamental idea of the West as opposed to the static East, and the obvious explanation for the uneven development of nations. The philosopher Fukuzawa Yukichi wrote in 1875: "Outside of the most stupid person in the world, no one would say that our learning or business is on a par with those of the Western countries. Who would compare our carts with their locomotives, or our swords with their pistols? We speak of the yin and the yang and the five elements; they have discovered 60 elements. . . . We think that our country is the most sacred, divine land; they travel about the world, opening lands and establishing countries. . . . In Japan's present condition there is nothing in which we may take pride vis-à-vis the West." Western philosophy taught that one natural law ruled *all* men and nations, hence Japan must become (as Foreign Minister Inoue Kaoru put it) "a newly Westernized country among the nations of Asia."

But what did it mean to be Westernized? Technically advanced, of course, but in the eyes of American *yatoi*, to be Western was also to be democratic and Christian. The Meiji regime obviously rejected Fukuzawa's suggestion that Christianity be made the official religion, but it did legalize Christian missions in 1873. Dr. Guido Verbeck, founding father of Tokyo University, never ceased to lead interested students in Bible study and prayer. Missionary J. C. Hepburn devised the best system of transliterating Japanese into the Roman alphabet. Catholic orders founded schools and what became Sophia University. Missionaries found a special calling in the education of women, whose subordination New York *Tribune* correspondent Edward H. House especially deplored since their intelligence was "relatively much above that of women in most Western countries." All told, some 140,000 Japanese converted by 1907, many from the most educated and powerful clans. Still, the government and almost all the people remained wedded to Shinto, and a Congregationalist missionary concluded after seven frustrating years that the Japanese, while "polished, intelligent, suave, apt, enterprising, eye-taking, and cheerful" were "none the less heathen from top to bottom." But Americans back home dutifully contributed to missionary societies and remained hopeful that the Japanese would open their hearts as well as their minds to enlightenment.

Nowhere did Americans so thoroughly shape the new Japan as on the northern frontier island renamed Hokkaido (Northern Sea Circuit) in 1869. Tokyo understood that should Japan fail to develop the island, the Russians might leap to it from their base at Vladivostok. So one of the first acts of the Meiji regime was to colonize Hokkaido and "check the power of Russian expansion southward." The official responsible was Kuroda Kiyotaka of Satsuma, but he and his underlings went dumb when asked to carve modern roads and farms and quarries and lumberyards out of virgin wilderness. So Kuroda left his first colonists the task of building a provincial capital at Sapporo and went himself to the United States. There he recruited President Grant's own Commissioner of Agriculture, Horace Capron, in return for $10,000 a year, free housing, and a free hand. Capron arrived in 1871 and immediately ordered his assistants, an engineer from the B & O Railroad and a Bureau of Agriculture chemist, to find the best locations to start lumbering, mining, and farming. In July 1873, when Capron himself turned the first furrow behind six prize bullocks imported from Illinois, the Japanese pioneers "were amazed to see one man ... doing the work of an hundred natives." Capron meant to grow grain, but the peasants resisted. To them the value of land was measured in its rice yield, and their word for *meal* was synonymous with *cooked rice.* Capron also had to convince Tokyo that Hokkaido was suitable for any agriculture, such was the disdain of Japanese for their little "Siberia."

The Colonial Agency was always a focus of controversy. Rivals in Tokyo charged that its budget was being misspent or siphoned off to favored merchants. So Capron had to defend the agency even as he fought the ignorance and corruption prevailing inside it. The way to develop Hokkaido, he insisted, was not to recruit pioneers for government projects but to permit free immigration and foreign investment. Tokyo would not hear of it; the purpose was to secure Hokkaido for Japan, not foreign "exploiters." Nor did Capron enjoy the free hand he was promised. "No sooner is anything started and fairly got underway," he complained, "than an important Jackanapes of a Yakunan [two-sworded man] makes his appearance and takes charge." It was a side of the Meiji Restoration little known except to *yatoi:* for all its meritocracy, the regime still had its share of supernumeraries untrained to run a modern economy and suspicious of the foreigners who were. Capron went home in disgust in 1875.

Almost immediately another American appeared on Hokkaido, the legendary William Smith Clark. A graduate of Amherst College and distinguished Civil War veteran, he was president of Massachusetts Agricultural College when the Japanese minister stopped by on a tour. When the Japanese saw the "aggie" students doing military drill on the Amherst green, he cried out: "This is the kind of institution Japan must have ... that shall teach young men to feed themselves and to defend themselves." In 1876 Clark contracted to establish an agricultural college at Sapporo. He stayed only a year, but the curriculum and model farm he founded taught the Japanese everything from the use of farm implements and fertilizers to what crops, houses, and even clothing were appropriate to the climate. Thanks to Clark, Hokkaido came to resemble the well-ordered valleys of western New England. He also left behind an entire class of "believers in Jesus." In the words of one convert, Clark's preaching was "so powerful that we felt as if the whole building were shaken by his energy," and his "practical religion" so captured his students that they continued to witness to incoming classes. It was more pleasing to Tokyo that Hokkaido's population zoomed from 58,000 to over 240,000 within a decade, thus Japanizing the frontier province for good.

Meanwhile, the foreign ministry labored to secure Japan's place in the world. On the suggestion of Western advisers, Japan opened full diplomatic relations with Russia and procured the Treaty of St. Petersburg in 1875. Japan withdrew its claims to Sakhalin in return for Russia's withdrawing from the Kurile Islands. Even more gratifying was Japan's intimidation of China. In 1871 Tokyo and Peking signed a treaty awarding each other equal status and providing for consultation against threats from third powers. But they politely ignored their two bones of contention: the Ryukyu island chain anchored by Okinawa; and the Chinese tributary, Korea. When fifty Okinawans were shipwrecked and slaughtered on the island of Taiwan, Tokyo felt compelled to retaliate. But for two years the Council was torn between fear of war and fear of appearing weak at home. Finally, in 1874, it ordered three thousand Japanese troops to Taiwan to punish the inhabitants. Five years later no less a personage than former President Ulysses S. Grant helped broker a Sino-Japanese treaty ceding the Ryukyus to Japan.

Korea was a far more dangerous problem. In 1869 the court at Seoul had turned away the Meiji embassy on the grounds that Korea could not recognize another emperor as being equal to the one in Peking. One faction in Tokyo demanded war, expecting it to "instantly change Japan's outmoded customs, set its objectives abroad, promote its industry and technology, and eliminate jealousy and rivalry among its people." But the Council doubted whether Japan was ready for war, whether the treasury could afford it, and whether the Western powers would stand aside. Saigō Takamori volunteered to head up a new delegation to Seoul, but his rivals in the Council vetoed the notion. If his mission *failed*, sullen samurai angry over their loss of status might use the national humiliation as an excuse to rebel. If his mission *succeeded*, Saigō would return a hero and perhaps brush aside his rivals in the Meiji oligarchy. As this *seikan ron* (Conquer Korea Question) simmered on, samurai took to assassinating officials, staging local revolts, and committing public suicides. Saigō, disgusted with the indecisiveness of his colleagues, finally offered to have himself murdered by the Koreans to provide *casus belli*, then resigned from the Council in protest. Dozens of high-ranking officials left with him and begged him to lead a revolt.

The Meiji Council, its grip on power slipping, finally ordered in gunboats to "open" Korea in 1875 and chose Kuroda, the Hokkaido Governor, to play the role of Commodore Perry. His Treaty of Kanghwa broke Korea's tributary tie to China, opened three ports to Japanese trade, and granted Japan the same special rights that the Western powers had imposed on Japan. But it failed to prevent a domestic revolt. Disaffected samurai enticed Saigō out of retirement and persuaded him to take up arms after a captured government agent confessed (under torture) that he had orders to assassinate Saigō. The resulting Satsuma Revolt of 1877 was a larger conflict in terms of combatants, deaths, and expense than the civil war that toppled the Shogun. But the Meiji military reforms enabled the central government to field a modern army capable of suppressing local rebellions. Saigō died on the battlefield, perhaps by his own hand.

Even now the Meiji oligarchy was not yet secure. For the final defeat of the old feudal orders in the Satsuma Revolt provoked new waves of protest of a national, populist character. Intellectuals and journalists cited the Meiji reformers' own promise to open up decision making to public discussion. English liberal doctrines were spreading in the schools. A People's Rights movement arose to demand representative government. Telegraphs and railroads drew rural commoners into national affairs, political societies sprang up in hundreds of villages, and a nondescript farmer launched a petition drive in 1879 that collected 101,161 signatures. What was more, the cost of samurai pensions, industrialization, and the Satsuma Revolt resulted in big budget deficits. Inflation drove up the price of rice and the mood in the cities turned ugly. That was the moment when the sturdy Kuroda embraced the idea first proposed by the *yatoi* Capron: why not turn over the expensive colonies on Hokkaido to private enterprise? A good idea, except that the only private offer forthcoming was for 387,000 yen, compared with 16 million yen already spent on the island. So a rival political faction condemned the sale as a sweetheart deal and leaked the "scandal" to the press. People's Rights journalists howled that the new regime was as secretive and corrupt as the old *bakufu*. Mobs in Tokyo cried that bureaucrats and businessmen swindled fortunes while the people's rice bowls were empty. The Council of State remained deadlocked over how to surmount this latest crisis and thus had no choice but to appeal to the throne for a decision.

Thirty-year-old Emperor Meiji was no decoration hidden away in perfumed chambers. He understood well the terrible costs of modernization and the strains it imposed on society. Someone—be it samurai, laborers, or peasants—had to sacrifice if Japan were to accumulate the capital it needed, and somehow the losers had to be appeased or repressed. So the Emperor issued an Imperial Rescript in October 1881 promising the nation a written constitution and popular representation within ten years. At the same time he approved the sale of the Hokkaido colonies and appointed Matsukata Masayoshi to oversee, as Minister of Finance, a radical program of austerity and private enterprise.

Matsukata ought to be the patron saint of development economists. That he is not may be because his reforms are distasteful to liberal Westerners. When he took over, paper yen were worth only 55 percent of face value, firms were starved for capital, and the urban masses were in distress. So Matsukata raised taxes, slashed government spending, empowered the new Bank of Japan to restrict the issue of paper currency, bought back millions of the depreciated yen, and promoted a national savings campaign. The result was a sudden and massive deflation. Most of all he announced a plan in 1882 to privatize *all* industrial enterprises except military plants, because government's proper role was confined to "education, armament, and the police." So the infant industries of Japan—coal mines, iron mills, textile plants, steamship lines, and the like—were sold off, usually at bargain prices, to the favored family firms that became known, pejoratively, as *zaibatsu*. Mitsui, for instance, began as a family saki brewery but by the 1890s was the coal giant of Japan. Mitsubishi shipping accumulated its cash reserve by transporting Meiji troops on the Taiwan and Satsuma expeditions and fell heir to the government steamship line. When the government announced its fire sale, *zaibatsu* acquired vast holdings, squeezed out smaller rivals, and came to dominate every major industry. They were Japanese octopuses akin to the Southern Pacific Railroad, but without them Japan, like California, would likely have developed at a far slower rate.

The peasants, as always, carried the load. But the government did one thing for them: it legalized emigration. Beginning in 1885 Japanese peasants began to depart for California and Hawaii, the land they called *tenjiku* (heaven).

Matsukata and the Meiji oligarchy got away with these radical adjustments because the Emperor's promise of a constitution deflected the energies of dissidents into the formation of modern political parties. The People's Rights intellectuals clustered in the *Jiyūtō* (Liberty party) and promoted social equality and human rights. Ōkuma founded the *Kaishintō* (Progressive party) to rally the *zaibatsu* and new middle class behind modernization. But the Emperor and oligarchy in fact used the ten-year interim to nudge the country toward more authoritarian institutions. In 1884 Meiji reconstituted an aristocracy, elevating *daimyō* and favored officials to the dignity of prince, marquis, count, viscount, or baron. In 1885 he turned the Council of State into an Imperial Cabinet under a prime minister, while his legal adviser, ItōHirobumi, crafted the bureaucracy into an efficient servant of the crown. Above all, Itō went abroad in 1882 in search of constitutional ideas and found them in Berlin, not London or Washington. Germany, too, was an authoritarian empire; Germany, too, had industrialized rapidly without disturbing traditional elites; and Germany had risen from weakness to strength, as proven by its victory over France in 1870–71. Itō was especially drawn to Lorenz von Stein's social monarchism by which the Emperor stood above the clash of interests and showed paternal care for all his subjects. The Germany of the Kaiser and Bismarck seemed the best model for Japan.

The drafting of a constitution coincided with a profound intellectual reaction against the unquestioning enthusiasm for Western things. As the seekers of enlightenment broadened their reading and meditated on what they had learned, they made some disturbing discoveries. Western societies, far from being perfect, displayed internal strains at least as bad as those in Japan. Western political philosophies contradicted one another. The spokesmen for spiritual and material knowledge—clergymen and scientists—seemed at war with one another. And although whites pronounced themselves civilized, their behavior often seemed barbaric. "There is no greater evil in the world than war," wrote Fukuzawa, ever the bellwether, "yet the countries of the West are constantly at war. . . . Within [the Western nations] factions are formed to struggle for power, and others, losing power, spread dissatisfaction." Someday, he imagined, the current state of the West would appear as backward as Japan seemed at present. "Civilization is unlimited; we must not be satisfied with the West of the present."

The 1880s also brought an explosion of European imperialism in Africa, Asia, and the Pacific. In 1882 the United States barred Chinese immigration. Japan's efforts to revise the "unequal treaties" continued to meet resistance. So Fukuzawa concluded: "[W]hether a treaty is honored or not, depends solely on the financial and military powers of the countries involved. . . . Day by day [the Western nations] increase their standing armies. This is truly useless, truly stupid. Yet if others work at being stupid, then I must respond in kind. If others are violent, then I must become violent."

No incident so disillusioned Japanese as the sinking of an English ship off their coast in 1886. The captain and crew commandeered the lifeboats while Japanese passengers drowned. So much for the moving tales of Western duty, heroism, and ethics as told by *yatoi* instructors! So much for "the captain always goes down with his ship" and "women and children first"! But they were even more enraged when a British consular court acquitted the captain of any wrongdoing. Clearly Japan was still "the scorn of white people" and would save itself and Asia only by breaking "the world-wide monopoly and . . . the special rights of the white races." Henceforth, wrote a coolly pragmatic spokesman for the younger generation, Western ideas "ought not to be adopted simply because they are Western [but] only if they can contribute to Japan's welfare."

The great constitution of 1889 that Meiji placed in the hands of Kuroda, now Prime Minister, was an amalgam of German authoritarianism and Shinto national piety. It described the Emperor as "sacred and inviolable" and the source of all legislative power, albeit "with the consent of the Imperial Diet." That body included a House of Representatives, but its electorate was limited to the wealthiest 1 percent of the population, its laws could be vetoed by the Emperor or House of Peers, and if it refused to approve a budget, last year's budget automatically remained in force. Cabinet ministers were responsible to the Emperor, not the Diet, and of course the Emperor was supreme commander of the Army and Navy. The constitution did grant some rights like freedom of speech, but only so long as their exercise did not threaten public order.

The 1890 Imperial Rescript on Education completed Japan's authoritarian reaction. Copies of it were posted alongside the Emperor's portrait in every school in Japan. Gone was the Meiji Charter Oath's admonition to seek knowledge in all the world. In its place was a Confucian call to piety, obedience, and willingness to give oneself "courageously to the State." Gone was the Charter Oath's appeal to "the just laws of Nature." In its place was a glorification of Japan's "national essence." Unquestioning love and obedience toward the Emperor were the highest duty of a Japanese, the measure of one's personal worth, the means by which the soul escaped the cares and vanities of earthly life and, in death, gained redemption.

Thus did the men of Meiji finally define their new Japan. It remained for them to define Japan's relationship to the world. The first tasks, in order to achieve full membership in the community of nations, were to establish clear boundaries by treaty with neighbors, to command respect for its interests abroad, and to recover full sovereignty at home by revising the "unequal treaties." But even before those goals were achieved, Japanese began to look beyond them. After all, the Japan of 1890 had laid the base for industrial power, overcome social protest, restored esteem in Japanese institutions, and modernized its military forces. It was ready now to step out into the world. But where, and for what? Nakae Chōmin, a radical politician and translator of Rousseau, addressed the problem in his *Discourse by Three Drunkards* in 1887.

The first man, still inebriated by Western ideas, argued against any military defense, believing that adherence to liberty, equality, and fraternity would shame the world into respect for Japan. The second, a nationalist, cried out for expansion: China in particular offered "nourishment for small nations like us to fill our bellies with." The third (presumably the author) endorsed prudent self-defense, playing the imperialists off against one another, and peaceful expansion on the continent. Foreign Minister Inoue, by contrast, spoke for realism: the Japanese must use the same methods as the Europeans if they hoped to get the same results. "To put it differently, we have to establish a new, European-style empire on the edge of Asia." But a spokesman for Japanese business preferred to look across the ocean to America, which he considered the most promising outlet for Japanese exports and emigrants. The nationalist Tokutomi Sohō merged all these projects into one ambitious vision: "Certainly our future history will be a history of the establishment by the Japanese of new Japans everywhere in the world."

Ambitious indeed, as the *yatoi* William Smith Clark had told his students on Hokkaido to be. "Boys, be ambitious like this old man," he exhorted. "Boys, be ambitious not for money or selfish aggrandizement, not for that evanescent thing which men call fame. . . . Boys, be ambitious for Christ. Boys, be ambitious for good." But soon after he went home to America, the Japanese edited Clark's parting speech to this: "Boys, be ambitious."

Vladivostok and Otsu 1891

EXCEPT FOR FAR Siberia, no spot in the Russian Empire was more remote from the centers of power and culture than Tiflis (Tbilisi), tucked against the frontiers of Turkey and Persia on the nether slopes of the Caucasus Mountains. But from that unlikely place emerged two cousins who changed the world. One became an embarrassment, then an outrage, then a horror to her family. She left her husband for a succession of lovers, fled to Turkey, Egypt, Europe, and the United States, and worked as a circus rider, singer, writer, and finally as a medium and hypnotist for the rich, bored, and gullible. She grew haggard and fat, wore shapeless housecoats, and eschewed cosmetics. "But her eyes were extraordinary. She had enormous, azure coloured eyes, and when she spoke with animation, they sparkled in a fashion which is altogether indescribable." Before her death in 1891, Yelena Petrovna Hahn, known by her married name, Madame Blavatsky, authored fourteen books on spiritualism, founded the Theosophical Society, and was one of the prophets of what came to be known as New Age religion.

The other cousin thought Madame Blavatsky a charlatan. Later on, having observed her intelligence and powers of persuasion, he changed his mind. She was not a fraud, she was demonic. He, on the other hand, grew up a devout Russian Orthodox, an emotional advocate of absolute monarchy, a mathematician, a leading railroad executive, and the individual most responsible for the industrialization of Russia and the development of Siberia. He was Sergey Yulyevich Witte, the builder of the Trans-Siberian Railway. But Witte shared one trait with his notorious cousin: self-will. When he failed to qualify for university because of his inattention to studies, Sergey enrolled in a provincial *gimnaziya* (secondary school) to escape the temptations of the city. "It was then that for the first time I gave evidence of that independence of judgment and sturdiness of will which have afterwards never deserted me."

Witte was admitted to university in Odessa in 1867. It was a turbulent decade. Alexander II had initiated reforms to eradicate what he
deemed to be the causes of Russia's defeat in the Crimean War: serfdom,
an antiquated military system, and a paucity of railroads. The shock was
terrific. Landed gentry, government officials, and the serfs themselves
damned the reforms for going either too far or not far enough, while the
radical *intelligentsiya*, composed of university men for whom no careers
were available in the backward economy, answered Chernyshevsky's
famous question "What Is to Be Done?" in various ways. Some radicals
so agitated the universities that the government shut them down for a
year. Others dreamed of expropriating the gentry and founding a Russian socialism on the strength of the traditional peasant commune. Still
others became anarchists after the fashion of Bakunin and formed secret
societies to plot violence against the autocracy.

Far more serious than the radical fringe, however, was the problem of
internal development. France, Germany, and the United States were
rapidly joining Britain in the age of steam and rails, while Russia was
barely ahead of Japan or Turkey. If Russia were to remain a great power,
it had to tap the three elements of economic growth: land, labor, and
capital. Russia had the first two in abundance, but who in the Empire
had accumulated capital? Not the commercial classes, which were
stunted by comparison with their western European equivalents, nor
the government, whose tax receipts disappeared into the Army. After
the Crimean War the treasury had to suspend convertibility of the ruble
into gold and print paper rubles to cover its deficits. That in turn ruined
the government's credit.

Nevertheless, the Tsar had issued a ukase in 1857 calling for rapid
construction of railroads: "In Our untiring concern for the welfare of our
fatherland which lies so close to Our heart, We have long recognized
that our fatherland, equipped by nature with abundant gifts but divided
by huge spaces, especially needs suitable communications." So the
Finance Ministry and Railway Commission granted concessions to private companies to build railroads at a cost of sixty-nine thousand rubles
per verst (about two-thirds of a mile). The companies were authorized to
issue 5 percent bonds backed by the government. But unscrupulous or
incompetent concessionaires only squandered their capital, spent as
much as ninety thousand rubles per verst on the lines they did build,
then defaulted on the loans.

Now, inefficiency and corruption accompanied the railroad booms of
other countries, but Russia's capital markets could not afford them. So
another tsarist commission recommended in 1865 that the state get out
of the railroad business and capitalize a new Railroad Fund from three
sources. The first was a 100-million-ruble loan from London (but Russ-

ian credit was so bad, and English commissions so high, that Russia received only 44.5 million rubles). The second was from the sale of railroad stocks already held by the government. The third was the cash from the sale of Alaska. Over the next decade some twelve thousand miles of track were laid covering all the more obvious routes in European Russia. It was in the midst of this boom that Sergey Witte graduated from university. He had discovered his affinity for mathematics, written a thesis on the theory of infinitesimal numbers, and decided to become a professor. His mother and his uncle, a distinguished army general, disapproved and persuaded him to take a government internship while "continuing [his] academic studies." There Witte met the Minister of Ways and Communications, who whispered to the youngster a magic word: railroads.

Witte began as a simple clerk in the ticket office. Within months he was a stationmaster, then head of a traffic bureau, and by 1875, director of traffic for the whole Odessa line. Then disaster appeared to strike. A military train was crossing the steppe in a blizzard when the rails disappeared beneath it: the maintenance bureau had removed a stretch for repair and neglected to inform local stationmasters or even post warnings. The train careened into a ravine and over a hundred soldiers were killed. Witte was one of the scapegoats and was sentenced to four months in prison. But those troops were heading to the Black Sea because of a danger of war with Turkey, and a grand duke offered clemency to Witte if he would transport his army in record time. Witte's solution was to institute the "American system" of traffic management. Dividing his labor force into rotating crews and imposing exact schedules for switching and rolling stock, Witte ran his meager fleet of locomotives twenty-four hours a day. He not only moved the Army, but by 1878 was named director of the Corporation of Southwestern Railroads.

In Russia, though, even victories are defeats. For the more the tsars did to industrialize Russia, the more they undermined the social basis of their own rule. Modern technology went hand in hand with education, urbanization, and enterprise, and called forth technocrats, entrepreneurs, and industrial workers who were sure to protest the autocratic rule of tsar, gentry, and church. When a radical conspiracy called the People's Will assassinated Alexander II in 1881, his son Alexander III determined to attempt the impossible: modernize Russian technology but at the same time crush all political opposition. Finally, it was always the same story in regard to geography. Russia needed to defend its hold on half a dozen corners of Eurasia. But a bold effort in one region, say, the Balkans, left no resources to develop another, say, Siberia. Following his brilliant campaign on the Amur, Muraviev had called for Siberian railroads and thousands of settlers. But the money was not there, while the initial measures to sponsor "official colonization" provoked frantic opposition from landlords. They rightly suspected that the youngest, hardest-working peasants would head for Siberia, leaving behind the aged, indolent, and drunken. Moreover, a labor shortage at home would drive wages up, while the cereals produced by Siberian farmers would compete with those of European Russia and drive down food prices and land values. So the government ended "official colonization" in 1874.

What Siberian industries did exist were moribund. The furbearing animals never recovered their old numbers, while efforts to conserve sea otters and seals died with the Russian-American Company. In 1871 the government franchised the Komandorskiye Islands to an American company that promptly killed all the animals it could find. In fact, the end of the Russian monopoly on the Alaskan and Siberian coasts kicked off such a frenzy of pelagic exploitation as to spark a diplomatic crisis between Britain and the United States. The timber industry told a similar story. When the government granted a concession in 1869 to harvest timber in western Siberia, the company's agents levelled the forests within easy access of the Ob and Yenisey rivers. Other industries, except for the mining of gold, languished for lack of mechanical power and transport. To be sure, several dozen steamships were in service on the subarctic rivers, and in 1879 A. E. Nordenskiöld fulfilled a dream three centuries old when his steamship *Vega* completed a Northeast passage to Asia via the Siberian coast. But what were a few dozen ships in a land so vast? Siberia needed the railroad.

Witte thrived as the manager of a privately owned rail network. His efficient management, innovative statistics, stimulation of new enterprises along the routes, and calculations of optimal freight rates all made the Southwestern a steady dividend payer. He would seem in every way a modern capitalist manager, even to the point of filling his staff with talented Jews and Poles at a time when Russification was official policy. And yet, when Witte prepared the second (1884) edition of his treatise on *Principles of Railway Freight Tariffs*, his essential Russianness reemerged. He granted the insights of every school of economics from Adam Smith to Karl Marx but thought them inapplicable to the unique reality that was Russia. Individualism might suit Britain, and secular socialism Germany, where Bismarck had nationalized the railroads and sponsored social security. But Russia was an Orthodox society and needed a Christian industrial policy. Witte was obscure, to put it kindly, about the implications of that fact for public policy, but he kept on searching for a third way.

One of Witte's earliest memories was of a roomful of wailing, stricken adults. They had just received word that Nicholas I was dead. He must have been a very dear friend, thought the six-year-old, for Mummy and the others to be crying so. Later, when Alexander II was carried off by a terrorist's bomb, he surrendered to rage rather than grief. In a letter to his father-in-law, the general, he berated the government for trying to combat radicals with clumsy police: "like trying to crush a grain of dust with a huge steam hammer." The state must fashion its own secret society and employ the terrorists' methods against them. Soon Witte himself was called to St. Petersburg and made a chief in the Holy Brotherhood. After one "preposterous incident," Witte repented of espionage. But his devotion to tsars remained. He granted that Alexander III was of limited education but denied that he was "incompetent and dull witted" simply because he patronized the church and suppressed the ideas that had inspired his father's murder. (In 1887 the Tsar's police hanged a terrorist named Alexander Ulyanov, whose younger brother, Vladimir, swearing vengeance of his own, would take the name Lenin.) In Witte's opinion, Alexander III was frugal, moral, hardworking, and farsighted. "He made an ideal treasurer for the Russian people, and his economical temperament was of incalculable assistance in the solution of Russia's financial problems." He kept Russia at peace and he genuinely cared for the peasants, "thus realizing the ideal of the Christian monarch." The Tsar also determined to drag Siberia into the age of steam and rails.

Alexander III's accession to the throne coincided with a new law encouraging emigration to Siberia. In 1883 the first railroad pushed across the Urals, a gold strike drew thousands to the Amur, and Siberian immigration boomed. In 1887, twenty-five thousand Russians crossed the Urals, then thirty-six thousand, then over forty thousand in 1889. Strategic considerations also suggested a new look at Siberia. Russian expansion in central Asia culminated in a renewal of border wars with British-backed Afghans in 1885. In the same year Russia tried to achieve the same rights Japan had acquired in Korea, only to be blocked by the meddling British fleet. On the other side of the Pacific, the completion of the Canadian Pacific in 1886 proved that a continental railroad could be built in cold northern latitudes, and the *voevody* at Irkutsk and Vladivostok called for a Trans-Siberian Railway.

Of course, the greatest naysayer was bound to be the Minister of Finance. But Alexander III presided over the most determined effort yet to balance the budget, stabilize the ruble, and improve Russia's credit abroad. The man he chose to accomplish all this was Ivan A. Vyshnegradskii. Like his contemporary Matsukata in Japan, Vyshnegradskii raised taxes sharply, slashed spending, and restructured government debt. An experienced bond trader, he borrowed heavily whenever interest rates dipped so as to pay off older loans and reduce the burden that interest placed on the annual budget. And like the Japanese, Vyshnegradskii understood that Russia could continue to borrow and invest only by selling abroad: "We must export though we die." The Japanese began earning foreign currency by flooding Western markets with silks. What did Russia have to sell abroad? Grain, when the harvests were good, and Vyshnegradskii was lucky that Russia enjoyed several good crops in a row. But the best way to boost grain production was to open new Siberian lands to cultivation.

Russian development policy did differ from that of the Meiji in one major respect: while the Japanese were busy divesting government of industrial enterprises to relieve the budget, the Russians were busy nationalizing them. Once again, war was the catalyst. For Witte's efficiency did not characterize the *rest* of the Russian rail network during the mobilization for the Turkish war of 1877. Tsarist bureaucrats preferred to blame that on profiteering entrepreneurs, especially Jews, in the private sector. So the Finance Ministry reversed the trend toward privatization, bought back private lines, and imposed uniform rates and regulations on the rest. So just as Japan was jettisoning "state capitalism," Russia jumped into it whole hog.

In 1888 Alexander III toured his southern provinces, and Witte, in his capacity as railroad director, ran his eye over the imperial schedule. Suddenly he flinched. The Tsar's train was expected to pass over a section of worn track at a far higher velocity than the roadbed and weight of the train would permit. Much to his relief, the train passed over it safely, but Witte told the Minister of Ways and Communications that he absolutely refused to assume responsibility should the party attempt to return at the same speed. The Tsar's schedule could not be changed, he was told, and the Tsar upbraided Witte: "I have travelled other roads with the same speed, and nothing ever happened. One cannot get any speed on your road, simply because it is a Jewish railway." Witte flushed, then barked at the Minister's back: "Your Excellency, let others do as they please, but I do not wish to endanger His Majesty's life. In the end you will break his neck."

The imperial train went off the rails at high speed at precisely the point Witte predicted. A score of people died, and twoscore more were wounded. The dining car's roof collapsed on the imperial family. Alexander III, a powerful man, hunched over forward and heaved upward with his back, supporting the roof until his companions escaped. Witte prepared his self-defense in a fever, but when he heard from St. Petersburg, it was Vyshnegradskii offering him the post of Director of Railway Affairs. Recalling Witte's warning and grit, he intended "to make good use of that man." It meant leaving private enterprise, in which Witte was his own boss and earned fifty thousand rubles per year, for the snake pit of court politics and a salary of eight thousand (plus another eight thousand from the Tsar's private purse). Witte went out of duty and affection for the Tsar, but also because he was now a convert to centralized economic management, at least so long as he was in charge.

For Witte had found the economic theory he was searching for in the 1840s writings of the German Friedrich List, who *is* credited with being the founder of development economics. In a pamphlet of 1889 Witte confessed himself a disciple of the neomercantilist List, who argued for protective tariffs to shelter infant industries from the competition of more advanced nations, as well as government policies to stimulate manufacturing, railroads, naval power, and colonies. List had especially stressed the power of railroads to knit Germany's thirty-odd states into a unified *Reich* and thought railroads would do the same for Russia in Asia. So this, it seemed to Witte, was a genuine third way by which Russia might modernize without succumbing to laissez-faire capitalism on the one hand or godless socialism on the other. The state itself would play the role of entrepreneur, modernizing Russia's economy while preserving its traditional politics, religion, and social order. As Witte was fond of saying in company, "I am neither a Liberal nor a Conservative. I am simply a man of culture."

Witte arrived in St. Petersburg just as the Trans-Siberian project finally won the government's full attention and the financial outlook was unusually hopeful. But still the ministries hung back. A Trans-Siberian Railway would stretch over some five thousand frigid *versts*. Thousands of workers would have to be moved, housed, and fed. All the matériel would have to be shipped, for the steppe offered no wood or stone. But the Tsar kept pushing for fear that Britain or some other power might win concessions from Peking to develop Manchuria and rob Russia of the main Pacific prize. So Asia was much on Alexander III's mind at the very moment when his son and heir, Crown Prince Nicholas, completed his formal schooling in May 1890. He was a slow student and conscious even at that age that he was unequipped to rule. Suffice it to say that he was still, in his late twenties, recording games of hide-and-seek in his diary. Nicholas vexed his stern father further by mooning over two women, one a dancer, the other a German princess of whom Alexander disapproved. So he sent the Crown Prince on a ten-month tour of Asia to foster his political education and cause him to forget his amours. The Tsarevich's retinue departed in November 1890.

The following month Alexander III summoned his ministers and demanded a decision. The Trans-Siberian Railway must be built, as fast and as cheaply as possible, along a route via Chelyabinsk, Omsk,

Novosibirsk, and Irkutsk. On March 17, 1891, the Tsar formally announced this most ambitious engineering project of the nineteenth century. Work was to begin at once and the Crown Prince himself would lay the foundation stone at Vladivostok. Nicholas, at that moment, was in India. There, and later in China, his official party paid special interest to inland regions as close to the Russian frontiers as they were allowed to go. The British and Chinese governments had no choice but to be courteous but began to put roadblocks in his way, citing the danger from cholera.

The Japanese, watching from afar, grew especially suspicious as the expedition approached their islands. Why did the Russian prince need nine capital naval vessels for a private tour? Why did the Tsarevich's itinerary begin on the Satsuma coast, source of the late rebellion, and not at Tokyo, where the Emperor awaited him? Why did the Russians plan to explore interior regions like Otsu, a town associated with ancient invasions? In March 1891, just as news of a Trans-Siberian Railway came out of St. Petersburg, the official Japanese newspaper published an editorial entitled "Suspicious Eyes Toward Nicholas' Visit." And in its wake an extraordinary rumor spread to the effect that the rebel Saigō Takamori had not died in the battle of 1877 but had *escaped to Siberia* and was now to return in the company of the Russians! Emperor Meiji joked that if that were true, he would have to revoke the medals he had given to Saigō's conquerors. But the Russian visit charged Japan with tension, stoked the growing rivalry between Satsuma and Chōshū factions, and obliged the cabinet to display alarm about the Russian "threat" without provoking a diplomatic crisis.

The crisis came anyway. On May 11, 1891, Nicholas inspected Otsu, five miles east of Kyoto on the banks of Lake Biwa. He rode in an open rickshaw but seemed safe enough insofar as the streets were lined on both sides with policemen ... until one of the policemen, Tsuda Sanzō, gave a staccato samurai shout and rushed forward to thrust his sword at the head of the heir to the throne of Russia. Nicholas flinched and took only a bleeding scalp wound before other policemen dragged Tsuda away. Emperor Meiji sent his sincerest apologies, but the Tsarevich retreated to his flagship, broke off his tour, and sailed to Vladivostok. Tsuda told the Japanese judge that the Russians' failure to pay their respects at Tokyo constituted an unforgivable insult to the Emperor, and that their real mission was to spy out Japan's military weakness. The prosecutor requested the death penalty, but the head of the Japanese supreme court—appointed for just this purpose—ruled that since Tsuda's crime was not directed against the *Japanese* royal family, capital punishment could not be exacted. Nevertheless Tsuda was imprisoned on Hokkaido and died of "illness" four months later.

Nicholas presided over the Vladivostok ceremony on schedule, inaugurating construction of the Pacific railroad twenty-eight years after Stanford had done the same in Sacramento. Back in St. Petersburg the Tsar named him Chairman of the Siberian Railway Committee and entrusted Nicholas to oversee "this Russian project of peace and enlightenment in the East. May the Almighty help You to achieve this enterprise so close to my heart, together with the proposals to facilitate the peopling and industrial development of Siberia." This solemn charge, and the experience gained on his tour, bestowed on the insecure Tsarevich a longed-for sense of expertise and a lasting patronage over Russia's Pacific career. Nor did he forget the scream of the samurai who tried to decapitate him before the first stone was laid.

Things got off to a wretched start when the Russian harvest failed in 1891 and laid waste all Vyshnegradskii's achievements. The Finance Minister urged that news of the famine and a cholera epidemic be censored, while he sought desperately for new credits. When a bond issue in Paris found no takers—in part, because Russia's anti-Semitic policies outraged the House of Rothschild—Vyshnegradskii was asked to step down. It was obvious by then to Alexander III and everyone else at court who alone might restore Russian credit and prosperity and get the Trans-Siberian built. He had already been promoted to the Ministry of Ways and Communications. Now, in August 1892, he was made Minister of Finance as well, and Sergey Witte became economic "tsar" of the entire Russian Empire.

Honolulu 1893

IN 1881 the Republic of Chile dealt the United States a considerable embarrassment. For three years it had waged the War of the Pacific (more contemptuously, the Guano War) against Peru and Bolivia for possession of a coast rich in nitrates. Washington backed Peru, but when the State Department dispatched a mission to Valparaiso with orders to force Chile to accept mediation, the Chileans told the *yanquis* to mind their own business or watch their Pacific squadron descend to Davy Jones's locker. Inasmuch as the Chilean Navy boasted two English-built armored battleships, while Adm. George B. Balch had only a few wooden cruisers, the United States did not press the point. The Chileans could even have bombarded San Francisco had they felt especially pepperish.

In the previous decade American industry sextupled coal production, more than doubled pig iron smelting, produced as much steel as Britain, and pioneered electric lighting and communications. By 1881 the United States was already the second industrial power on the globe, and its rate of growth was more rapid than any but Germany's. The same went for agriculture, thanks to the opening up of the Great Plains. By the late 1870s American farmers could export their grains via railroad and steamship all the way to Europe and *still* undersell local producers. How was it that this man-child of a nation lacked a navy sufficient to intimidate Chile?

To begin with, Americans lived through a fortunate generation between 1865 and 1895, during which no compelling threats or opportunities appeared from abroad. The acquisition of Alaska and the formation of Canada in 1867 brought to a close the struggle for North America, while Europe's renewed interest in African and Asian colonialism did not begin to pinch American interests until the late 1880s. Nor did Americans show an interest in stirring up trouble themselves. They had had enough conflict in the Civil War and were busy filling up their frontier. Congressmen in those dear, dead days had all the deportment and liberality of bulldogs when it came to the public purse. Naval vessels were expensive to build and maintain, and their value far from obvious. The two great political parties were passing through a transition during which neither promoted expansion. The era of Democratic land hunger —continental, military, and agrarian in nature—was over, and the era of Republican expansion—overseas, naval, and commercial—had not yet begun. In any case, the almost perfect balance of party and regional strength in Congress stymied any radical departure. So placid Americans let their Navy rot at a time when Europeans introduced iron and steel vessels, fully steam-powered and multiturreted engines, breech-loading then rifled naval artillery, and protective armor. The irony is that most Americans still had a grand chip on their shoulder regarding the British Empire, even though it was Britain's naval hegemony, restraint in its use, and commitment to free trade that permitted Americans to ignore their own maritime defense. They did, however, have to swallow British gall. "Never was there such a hopeless, broken-down, tattered, forlorn apology for a navy," wrote one journalist. And Rudyard Kipling quipped, "China's fleet today, if properly manned, could waft the entire American navy out of the water and into the blue. The big, fat Republic that is afraid of nothing . . . is as unprotected as a jellyfish."

President Garfield was murdered, like Alexander II, in 1881. But he initiated a naval renaissance by naming William H. Hunt, a Louisiana judge with a stylish goatee, his Secretary of the Navy. Thanks to him a new Naval Advisory Board made bold recommendations that President Arthur begged Congress to approve: "I cannot too strongly urge you my conviction that every consideration of national safety, economy and honor imperatively demands a thorough rehabilitation of our navy." But to move Congress meant educating public opinion, a labor of years. The Naval Appropriations Act of 1882 authorized the Navy only to junk wooden ships whose repair costs exceeded 30 percent of the price of new ships. Replacements were expected to be iron (modern, low-cost steelmaking was only a decade old), but no American mills were fitted to roll ship plating or cast gun mounts. Commander Robley D. Evans managed to persuade the board to trust in the skill of Pittsburgh's steelers. Congress authorized funds for four steel warships in 1883 and thirty more modern vessels of domestic manufacture by the end of the decade.

But what class of ships should they be, to execute what sort of strategy? Those were the questions that interested Rear Adm. Stephen B. Luce, who "taught the Navy to think, to think about the Navy as a whole." Luce had a distinguished career dating back to the Mexican

War, but on every tour of duty he found new cause to "gig" the Navy. Compared with foreign fleets, and even (horrors!) the U.S. Army, "we may be likened to the nomadic tribes of the East who are content with the vague tradition of the past." So as soon as Luce acquired a position of influence he devoted his life to educating officers and seamen in "the science of naval warfare under steam." It was he who extended the Morrill Act to include naval reserve officer training in colleges. But most of all he founded the Naval War College at Newport, Rhode Island, in 1885. Here officers might study naval strategy, tactics, and logistics and their relationship to foreign policy. He meant to draw on the best minds of Yale, Brown, and Harvard, but he also wanted officers who combined a theoretical bent with experience on the line. That was why he invited Capt. Alfred Thayer Mahan to join the War College faculty as soon as his ship returned from Central America.

"Now, there was a man," an older age might say of Mahan. In fact, it did, if one can imagine a time when Harvard granted an honorary degree to a naval propagandist, the American Historical Association elected a military officer its president, and Episcopal bishops eulogized an outspoken imperialist "for the beauty and charm of his Christian character." Mahan grew up at West Point, where his father was dean of faculty, an Army buff, and (being Irish) an Anglophobe. His parents were also strict Evangelicals, and Mahan learned the Bible almost by heart. His earliest surviving letter thanks his grandmother for religious tracts: "The story of Jonah teaches me that man cannot fly from God." But he could and did fly from his father, as when young Alfred pronounced himself an Anglophile and rejected his parents' extreme Protestantism for his uncle's High Church Anglo-Catholicism. (He later wrote a poem: "They make Religion be abhorred/That round with terror gulf her/And think no work can please the Lord/Unless it smell of sulphur.") Above all, Mahan bucked his father by choosing the Navy, and won appointment to Annapolis in 1856 by the simple means of walking into the office of Jefferson Davis, Secretary of the Navy, and asking for it. Like Sergey Witte, Mahan then made up for prior academic sloth; like Witte, he was on the outs with his fellows because of his piety; like Witte, he was thought of as conceited and a loner; and like Witte, he had some reason to be. On his cruises to Asia and South America Mahan remained celibate while his mates debauched in port, and he tried once to give up drink so the money might go to an Episcopal building fund. Mahan scorned imperfection in others and never forgave it in himself.

None of this personal detail would merit mention except that Mahan's view of history betrayed the same tension between God-centered and self-centered attitudes. For him, history was the working out of the divine will, and human beings were agents of that Omnipotence. He believed it was Providence, not stumbling luck, that had allowed the British to capture Gibraltar, and thus Anglican priests were right to say prayers of thanksgiving. But the danger in such faith is that public figures may slide into believing that everything *they* or their nation does has divine sanction as well. Like Bismarck, Mahan had the remarkable facility of believing in a God who never disagreed with him. And all that would be of no consequence if Luce had not called Mahan to the Naval War College and asked him to draft lectures on the principles of naval warfare. Mahan was delighted—he was prone to seasickness!—and soon discovered the purpose of this new calling through a revelation received at the English Club's library in Lima, Peru. He was wading through Theodor Mommsen's *The History of Rome* when it struck him that the Roman Army, mighty as it was, did not explain the rise of Rome: sea power did. Once installed at the War College, Mahan wrote furiously for four years, choosing the rise of naval powers in the seventeenth century as his laboratory. But his mind could not help but leap ahead to the present day, to the movement for a new steel navy, and the desperate need for a strategy to guide the construction program. For the United States had finally got embroiled in a dangerous overseas dispute. The Samoan archipelago was the scene of strife between rival Polynesian kings, and consuls and warships from the United States, Britain, and Germany arrived to back one or another candidate. Washington hosted a conference on Samoa in 1887, but the Europeans refused to budge—and why should they? The U.S. Navy was laughably weak. On the other hand, some good news arrived from Honolulu. A revolution of sorts had occurred . . . and Pearl Harbor was in American hands.

To late-twentieth-century Hawaiians and their white academic patrons, King Kalakaua is a hero. He refused to despair in the face of demographic decline but devoted his reign to preserving Hawaiian customs and independence, and to a precocious dream of uniting the Pacific peoples in the cause of peace and anticolonialism. But the *haoles* had a monopoly of money and guns, and so Kalakaua was tragically thwarted. The sugar planters and most of the foreign community in the islands saw matters rather differently. To them, Kalakaua was capricious, irresponsible, and a tyrant. Exploiting the royalist Constitution of 1864 for all it was worth, he made all ministerial appointments, packed the House of Nobles with his own supporters, and spent his precious tax receipts on royal displays instead of public works. Most appalling, in the eyes of the whites, was Iolani Palace, completed in 1882 at a cost of $300,000. Moreover, while the American Florentine residence was under construction, Kalakaua took an expensive world tour, and his visits to the courts of Japan, Siam, Italy, the Vatican, and England persuaded him all the more that kings should live well. When he returned home Kalakaua accordingly staged a grand coronation on the Iolani grounds, invested himself with the royal feathered cloak and pagan *puloulou* (or *kapu* stick) as symbols of Hawaiian sovereignty, and dedicated a statue of Kamehameha I at the courthouse across the street. The drinking, dancing, and (alleged) debauchery lasted a fortnight, and *haole* newspapers voiced their disgust at the recidivist display. Kalakaua did not care. He sponsored hulas, venerated the bones of his ancestors, restored the right of *kāhuna* to practice their cures, and presided over the rites of a Polynesian Masonic lodge dedicated to combining science and philanthropy with a "revival of Ancient Sciences of Hawaii."

The logical conclusion to Kalakaua's rejection of sixty years of missionary and planter influence was his appointment of Walter Murray Gibson to the prime ministry in 1882. Yet another of the fantastic characters who season the history of the North Pacific, Gibson had arrived in Honolulu in 1861, posing as an anthropologist from South Carolina. In fact, he was born in England, raised in Canada and New York, and went South only in his late teens. In 1844 his wife died and Gibson left his three children to go to sea. After a world cruise, Gibson went on the lecture circuit, describing his real and imagined adventures. In 1859 he traveled overland to Great Salt Lake City to offer his services to Brigham Young. He certainly had a swindler's gift, for once in Hawaii he presented himself to its struggling Mormon colony as the High Priest of Melchizedek come to found a Mormon kingdom in the East Indies. Nothing came of that, but Gibson did rule as priest-king of a community on Lanai until 1864, when Salt Lake City excommunicated him. It seems he had put the title to the church's ten thousand acres in his *own* name.

Gibson quickly found a new dodge as white advocate for the native Hawaiian people. To his credit he became fluent in Hawaiian, and many of his jeremiads against the planters were on the mark. He parlayed his popularity into a seat in the Assembly and finally the prime ministership. The white-bearded prophet was "an unquestionably eminent-looking veteran, of smooth address, silky manners, and a somewhat fascinating mode of speech . . . wise as a serpent, but hardly as harmless as a dove." Gibson's policy was to flatter Kalakaua in ways that served his own urge to build empires. He described the kingdom as holding "primacy in the family of Polynesian states" and conceived of a Polynesian Confederacy under Kalakaua's leadership. In 1883 he circulated a Hawaiian protest to foreign governments opposing new colonial acquisitions in the Pacific. The great powers ignored his pretensions. He then insinuated Hawaii into the Samoan conflict, sending an envoy extraordinary to invite Samoa and Tonga to form an alliance. In 1887 Gibson ordered the Hawaiian Navy to show its flag alongside British, German, and American cruisers. The "navy" consisted of a single converted guano tub, and its mission ended when the crew mutinied against the inebriated captain. When the Germans had to intervene to prevent the Hawaiians from scuttling their own ship, Gibson lost his taste for world politics.

But Hawaii's diplomatic offensive did have one success of tremendous importance. In 1882 Gibson petitioned the Mikado to revive Japanese emigration to Hawaii. To the planters it meant a ready supply of disciplined workers. To Gibson, it meant Japanese "recognition of His Majesty [Kalakaua] as one of the family of Asiatic Princes, and that to strengthen his hand is to elevate the sovereign of a cognate and friendly race." His first envoys were politely turned away, but as we know, peasant unrest in overpopulated Japan changed the mind of the Meiji oligarchy, and in January 1886 Meiji Foreign Minister Inouye Kaoru and Hawaiian Foreign Minister R. W. Irwin signed an emigration convention under which thirty thousand Japanese farmers would come to Hawaii in a single decade.

That was the year the American community, led by the planters, began what amounted to a taxpayers' revolt. The kingdom was nearly bankrupt, public works were neglected, and Kalakaua was himself in the pocket of Klaus Spreckels, a San Francisco sugar magnate who owned half the Hawaiian national debt and indulged the King's fancies for drinking and poker. So Sanford Dole and Lorrin A. Thurston, both sons of missionaries, did their Anglo-Saxon civic duty and founded a Reform party backed up by a white-dominated militia, the Honolulu Rifles. Gibson then asked the Assembly to approve a British loan sufficient to redeem the national debt, which it did after a tense debate, but only on condition that it be used to buy out Spreckels. The latter, beaten, went home to San Francisco.

Then a new threat appeared. For 1886 was the very year when the Hawaiian Reciprocity Treaty was up for renewal, and Southern senators, representing domestic sugar interests, tried to kill reciprocity by inserting an amendment *obliging* Hawaii to lease Pearl Harbor to the United States. That way, they figured, the *Hawaiians* would reject the treaty themselves.

Kalakaua was indeed hostile to the Pearl Harbor clause but was also at the end of his rope. The British syndicate skimmed 25 percent of its $1 million loan even before collecting its interest. So Gibson and Kalakaua took more desperate measures to raise cash, including the legalization of opium. This was shocking enough, but when it surfaced that Kalakaua had taken bribes from a Chinese merchant who wanted the opium concession, then sold it to another for more money, the Reform party sensed its moment had come. And it proved embarrassingly easy. The mere threat of public protest panicked Kalakaua into dismissing Gibson and promising a new cabinet. But Thurston bellowed out to a mass public meeting that the King must cease to interfere with the cabinet, the courts, or elections, and he ordered the Honolulu Rifles into the streets. Kalakaua had little choice but to accept their "Bayonet" Constitution of 1887. Henceforth even the Noble House was subject to election, with suffrage restricted to citizens of property and residents of the white race. Two-thirds of the Hawaiians were disenfranchised as well as all recent immigrants of Asian stock. The election gave the Reform party a landslide victory, and in December 1887 it ratified the Reciprocity Treaty, granting the United States the use of Pearl Harbor. The Reformers also wasted no time allocating $49,000 to purchase a steam dredger to deepen Honolulu harbor.

So American planters had finally regained the influence over the crown enjoyed by their missionary fathers. They faced one domestic challenge—an 1889 uprising of Hawaiians and Chinese under the free-booter Robert Wilcox—but suppressed the revolt at the cost of seven lives. A more serious challenge came from abroad when the Republican Congress in Washington passed the McKinley Tariff in October 1890. It placed all foreign producers of raw sugar on the same standing as the Hawaiians and compensated domestic American cane growers with a handsome subsidy. President Benjamin Harrison explained that hurting Hawaii was not the intent of the bill, but there it was. Hawaiian planters faced ruination unless they could get the act repealed or become "American" themselves—that is, get the United States to annex Hawaii.

The New Navy men had the same agenda. Mahan's *The Influence of Sea Power Upon History, 1660–1783* finally appeared in 1890 and (to employ an appropriate idiom) "made waves." Few reviewers bothered to read the dense narrative, but Mahan's recommendations seemed just what Americans needed to hear. Sea power, he wrote, was the decisive factor in geopolitical competition, and the United States had no choice but to pursue it. Moreover, the nation was well equipped to do so, given its security from invasion by land, long sea coasts, large population, and acquisitive spirit. The only thing holding back U.S. sea power was democracy: "Popular governments," wrote Mahan, "are not generally favorable to military expenditures." But Harrison and Secretary of the Navy Benjamin Tracy were favorable, within reason. And if the Republican Congress needed any reminders, Samoan events provided them. In 1889, at the height of the crisis there, a hurricane washed away the American squadron—their engines were too old and underpowered to flee. So Tracy's annual report challenged Congress to build twenty new battleships and sixty cruisers, to be divided between the Atlantic and Pacific. "The sea will be the future seat of empire," he said. "And we shall rule it as certainly as the sun doth rise." When Democrats from coastal states joined industrial-minded Republicans to approve the battleship program, they changed not only the size but also the shape and purpose of the U.S. Navy. For a high-seas fleet would need foreign bases. As Mahan explained, he was "imperialist simply because he was not isolationist."

There are two principal naval strategies. The first is to achieve command of the sea by destroying or bottling up the enemy's fleet and blockading its coast. Such a strategy requires that a navy possess decisive superiority or win it in a climactic battle. The second strategy, or *guerre de course*, relies on commerce raiding and blockade-running to harass the enemy and keep one's trade routes at least partially open. This is the poor nation's strategy and calls not for battleships but speedy cruisers. Tracy's fleet meant that the United States was now rejecting commerce raiding (an "insignificant kind of guerilla, bushwacking warfare") and bidding instead for command of the seas vital to American interests. Which seas were those? Mahan answered that question in the *Atlantic Monthly* of December 1890. The United States, he wrote, was a two-ocean nation, and its security required that it control its own coastal waters, the Caribbean Sea, and the eastern Pacific out to a radius of three thousand miles. Hawaii was vital, but its future, he acknowledged, was in doubt, owing to internal political strife.

That strife increased after January 1891, when Kalakaua died on a visit to California and his gritty fifty-two-year-old sister, Liliuokalani, ascended the throne. Let us just say that she was formidable and strange. A regular parishioner at Kawaiahao Church, she was also the thrall of a spirit-conjurer, Fräulein Wolf. A champion of Hawaiianness, she took her advice from an English/Tahitian favorite, Charles Wilson, who rivaled Kalakaua in forbidden appetites. A sentimental and talented musician, she demonstrated the touch of a blacksmith in her public life. For Liliuokalani's purpose, from which no counsel of prudence could move her, was to reverse the political trends once again and restore monarchical rule. And it seemed she might have a chance when the Reform party lost support, then split in two, rendering the Legislative Assembly a cacophony of choruses. Cabinets formed and fell within months, while the sugar industry languished under the McKinley Tariff. In 1892, the Queen's familiars came to the rescue. Fräulein Wolf conjured a prediction that a man would soon appear to solve all her money problems. Sure enough, who should come calling at Iolani Palace but a stranger peddling a plan for a government lottery. Next, Wilson revived the idea of a state-licensed opium trade. Lotteries and opium: a fine end to what began as a "missionary kingdom"! Finally, the Queen decided to stage a coup to impose yet another constitution. This one would grant only Hawaiians the right to vote and make the sovereign responsible to no one.

The Reformers now despaired of good government ever prevailing under the monarchy. Thurston and newly arrived California lawyer Henry E. Cooper founded an Annexation Club of which the U.S. Minister, John L. Stevens, heartily approved. Secretary of State James G. Blaine had advised the President that only three countries were so valuable to the United States as to warrant annexation—Hawaii, Puerto Rico, and Cuba—and his successor, John W. Foster, went even further. He instructed Stevens to conspire with the annexationists and keep him informed through secret channels. Liliuokalani gave them their opportunity in January 1893, when she showed herself on the balcony of Iolani Palace and spoke in her orotund way: "O, ye people who love the Chiefs, I hereby say unto you . . . go with good hope and do not be disturbed or troubled in your minds. Because, within the next few days now coming, I will proclaim the new constitution." Thurston at once formed a Committee of Safety, went to find Stevens, and sent an associate down to the docks to enlist Capt. G. C. Wiltse of the USS *Boston*. Assured of support, Thurston denounced the Queen before a crowd at the armory: "She wants us to sleep on a slumbering volcano, which one morning will spew out blood and destroy us all. . . . Has the tropic sun cooled and thinned our blood, or have we flowing in our veins the warm, rich blood that loves liberty and dies for it?" That afternoon 164 sailors from the *Boston* streamed into Honolulu while the Committee of Safety formed a provisional government, selected Sanford Dole as President, and demanded that the Queen abdicate. Within three days of her buoyant balcony speech Liliuokalani surrendered her government under protest and appealed to Washington for justice.

Thurston, with an annexation treaty in his briefcase, and the Queen's supporters, with their bill of particulars, now raced each other to Washington. The annexationists won the first round when Harrison snubbed the Queen's delegation and forwarded the treaty to the Senate. Most Republicans and all navalists were ecstatic. Mahan, now president of the Naval War College and a worldwide celebrity, wrote the *New York Times* that "it would be impossible to exaggerate the momentous issues dependent upon a firm hold of the Sandwich Islands by a great, civilized, maritime power." The alternative, he hinted darkly, was that Hawaii would be overrun by its Chinese immigrants. In "Hawaii and Our Future Sea Power," also written within weeks of the revolution, Mahan described annexation of Hawaii not only as a military and economic necessity but as the "first fruit and a token that the nation in its evolution has aroused itself to the necessity of carrying its life . . . beyond the borders which heretofore have sufficed."

But once again, Hawaiian and American politics were unsynchronized. For Grover Cleveland had just won the 1892 election and instructed Senate Democrats to block the treaty until he took office in March. Then he withdrew it and asked a personal agent to make a "confidential trip of great importance to the Pacific Ocean" and investigate the overthrow of the monarchy. The one he chose, Georgia planter James H. Blount, was not likely to favor annexation. Nor was the new Secretary of State, Walter Q. Gresham, who hated Benjamin Harrison and all his works, and took an ethical, legalistic approach to statecraft. Not surprisingly, Blount reported that the revolution was a fraud inspired by Stevens and sustained by the Navy, Gresham concluded that the provisional government did not represent the wishes of the Hawaiian people; and Cleveland asked Dole to put Liliuokalani back on her throne.

In the end, Cleveland got half of what he wanted. Annexation died, for the moment. But when Gresham hinted at a new U.S. intervention to *oust* the provisional government, Congress and the public cried no. Dole and Thurston had successfully spread their view that Liliuokalani was an ogre, and she hurt her own cause again by swearing vengeance (U.S. Minister Albert Willis thought he heard her threaten to "behead" the filibusters). So no one came out looking good, and the Senate washed its hands with a unanimous resolution against annexation, against the monarchy, and against interference in the islands' politics. For good measure, Congress then passed a new tariff schedule repealing the domestic sugar subsidy and restoring Hawaii's advantages.

Back to square one, except that now Hawaii had become another Texas, an independent republic dominated by Americans. But where in Texas Americans were a majority, in Hawaii they numbered two or three thousand against thirty thousand Hawaiians, almost twenty thousand Chinese, and twenty-five thousand Japanese. Perhaps Stevens was right when he said, "Hawaii has reached the parting of the ways. She must now take the road which leads to Asia, or the other which outlets her in America, gives her an American civilization and binds her to the care of American Destiny."

Korea 1895

TEN YEARS BEFORE, Kim Ok-kiun had been on the verge of taking over the government of Korea. He admired Japan's modernization and wanted the same for his small country. But Chinese troops foiled the coup d'état, and Kim had to flee to Japan. Now, in 1894, two fellow Koreans approached him and whispered that China was prepared to support him. Come with us to Shanghai, they said, where a bank account had been set up. Kim went, and as he relaxed on his futon in the Japanese hotel, one of the secret agents put a bullet in his head. The Chinese authorities made a great show of returning both culprit and victim to Korea aboard a warship. But Korean officials did not punish the murderer, they honored him. And they did not bury Kim's body, they carved it up and paraded the limbs all over the country as a sign of what happened to people who preferred Japan's influence to China's.

The assassination of Kim Ok-kiun infuriated the Japanese precisely because it was not the work of crazed fanatics but a calculated maneuver of Chinese foreign policy. By the 1890s the impotent Ch'ing Empire stood on the brink of partition. The French had occupied Vietnam and lusted after southern China. The Russians had begun their railroad and threatened China from the north. Japan was bidding to take over Korea. Even the British would be obliged to join the partition if China looked like it was falling apart. But the Ch'ing had one resource left, the venerable Governor-General of Peking's province, Li Hung-chang. For twenty-five years he had labored, with few resources but his own wits and patience, to protect Chinese sovereignty from the pushy Europeans while he borrowed, from the same Europeans, the money and machines needed to modernize. Compared with Japan's, his successes were modest, but by 1890 China did boast a steamship line, some railroads, a military academy, two naval bases, and a handful of students educated abroad. Unfortunately, most of his colleagues preferred the old ways and hampered Li's efforts to reform the Empire before it collapsed.

The status of Korea was a test case for the Ch'ing and Meiji empires alike, if only because each was the other's weakest potential opponent. If China could not even stare down *Japan* in its own sphere of influence, it could hardly hope to resist the inroads of European imperialists. And if Japan could not even intimidate *China*, it could hardly command respect as an equal of the white nations. So the old controversy over Korea was pushed to the limit.

Korea was a mountainous, primitive, and much despised country. According to George Kennan, the "first thing that strikes a traveler in going from Japan to Korea is the extraordinary contrast between the cleanness, good order, industry, and general prosperity of one country, and the filthiness, demoralization, laziness, and general rack and ruin of the other." The Korean ruler was as "unconscious as a child, stubborn as a Boer, ignorant as a Chinaman, and vain as a Hottentot. . . . He loves his sorceresses, witches, wise-women, and ground-doctors, and consults them constantly on the affairs of State." The Meiji oligarchs longed to take Korea in hand for reasons of strategy, economics, and pride, and the treaty they forced on Korea in 1876 was the vehicle by which to do so. It not only opened the ports of Pusan, Inchon, and Wonsan, whose trade Japan promptly monopolized, it also described the country as an independent state. But Li Hung-chang countered Japanese influence at Seoul through intrigue, bribes, and worse, while encouraging Korea to make additional treaties and set the barbarians against one another. The first beneficiary was the United States in 1882, followed by Britain, Germany, Russia, and others. But unfortunately for Li, the more contact young Koreans had with foreigners, the more they yearned to modernize. The Japanese exploited this by educating Koreans and drawing them into their orbit. One result was Kim Ok-kiun's abortive attempt to overthrow Korea's Confucian bureaucracy in imitation of Japan's Meiji Restoration. The Japanese government then salvaged what it could by diplomacy. In the Treaty of Tientsin of 1885, Itō Hirobumi and Li Hung-chang agreed not to station soldiers in Korea without prior consultation with each other.

But that only meant that the competition for influence took nonmilitary forms. Li appointed the promising soldier/official Yüan Shih-k'ai to be chief of the Chinese legation in Seoul, and over a decade Yüan succeeded in restoring Chinese prestige and breaking Japan's monopoly of trade. This was alarming to Tokyo, but the domestic and foreign events of 1890 made the Chinese recovery in Korea intolerable. That was the year when the Meiji Constitution went into effect, and though the elected Diet had little direct power, its angry opposition leaders could always enflame public opinion by pointing to any perceived weakness in foreign policy. At the same time, the Meiji government had to contend with pressure from the Army and Navy general staffs, which answered only to the Emperor. The Army staff, headed by Gen. Yamagata Aritomo, elaborated the first principle of Japanese geopolitics: Japan must control a "line of advantage" beyond its own shores, the most important point on which was Korea. Control of Korea would make the Sea of Japan a Japanese "lake," keep continental rivals at a distance, and provide a jumping-off point for expansion on the mainland. In enemy hands Korea would be a "dagger" pointing at Japan's home islands. Moreover, 1890 was the year Russia announced the Trans-Siberian Railway. If Korea were still up for grabs by the time the railroad was finished, Russia would doubtless seize the peninsula and enclose Japan in an icy grip. It was imperative that Korea remain under Japanese protection "for many future years or even forever."

Yet just as the Japanese were screwing themselves up to make a stand over Korea, their chronic political instability persuaded Li Hung-chang and Yüan Shih-k'ai that this was the moment to assert *Chinese* control over Korea. One ploy was to eliminate agitators like the unfortunate Kim. But China's main chance came when the feckless Korean government failed to suppress a peasant revolt, the Tonghak Rebellion, in 1894, and Yüan persuaded the court to send in a Chinese army. What was Japan to do? Foreign Minister Mutsu Munemitsu could never permit China to occupy Korea. But he worried about the international consequences of a conflict, especially on Japan's twenty-year effort to revise its "unequal treaties," then reaching a climax. If war *should* come, then at least China must appear the aggressor. So Mutsu cited the treaty of 1876 to challenge China's claim to Korea, then invoked the Treaty of Tientsin to justify sending Japanese soldiers to Korea as well. The Tonghaks were suppressed, but the two occupying armies remained in place with at least one of them—the Japanese—itching for a fight. Mutsu made a show of being conciliatory but held that "negotiating with the Chinese is no more productive than drawing well water with a bottomless bucket." The Chinese, for their part, looked upon Japan "as a tiny island of barbarians who have recklessly and impudently rushed forward in a mad effort to imitate the external trappings of Western civilization."

In fact, neither Li nor Mutsu dared to compromise, for to do so would seem to undermine their Empires' security, shame their Emperors, and undoubtedly cost themselves their posts. But *neither* could Mutsu allow war to break out until he heard the news from London about treaty revision. "I cannot now put into words the extent to which I was then subjected to anxiety and intense pressures from my official duties." When his negotiator finally reported success, "Viscount Aoki's auspicious telegram now made me forget all the accumulated tensions I had experienced." Then two days later: no, the British had refused to sign because of a report that Japanese in Seoul were pressing the Koreans to expel the British naval attaché! Mutsu did not even communicate with Seoul to learn if it were true—there was no time. He cabled London that the Japanese government would under no circumstances be "so foolish" as to offend a British subject. Finally, on the morning of July 17, Aoki cabled that "the recent problem has been overcome, and the new treaty was signed on July 16." Though it would not take full effect for five years, its signature meant that Britain and other Western powers would relinquish extraterritorial rights and restore Japan's control over its tariffs.

Mutsu's second item of pressing business was to make a last appeal to China so as to cast Japan and Korea in the role of hurt parties. He begged the Japanese commanders to stay put long enough for him to request simply that Japan receive most-favored-nation treatment in Korea, and that Korean modernization be allowed to proceed under foreign influence. That way, it would appear that Japan was the agent of progress and China the backward bully. Secretly, Mutsu admitted that the note's terms really implied future Japanese control of Korea, and that it was bound "to give provocation to China." It did. Li Hung-chang flung back Mutsu's ultimatum and ordered reinforcements, whereupon the Japanese Navy sank a Chinese troop ship on July 25, 1894, and the Army stormed the palace in Seoul to capture the royal family. On August 1, Japan *and* Korea declared war on China.

Few foreigners expected Japan to overcome China's huge manpower advantage. But Yamagata's army routed the Chinese in the Battle of Pyongyang, while the Japanese Navy destroyed the Chinese fleet in the Yellow Sea. In October, Yamagata crossed the Yalu River into Manchuria, and in November the Japanese land-sea attack against the Liaotung Peninsula ended in the capture of strategic Port Arthur. All Li Hung-chang could do now was beg the great powers to come to China's aid. Mutsu in turn knew that Japan "must be extremely cautious not to take any action which may substantially overstep the rules of international law either diplomatically or militarily." Accordingly, he declared at once that Japan stood for Korean independence, reform, and modernization—a program the Western powers could only applaud. But at the same time the glorious triumphs of Japanese arms undermined Mutsu's moderation by feeding the appetite of the public. Generals, politicians, and editors scorned the idea of a cease-fire, and some went so far as to demand "the conquest and absorption by Japan of the entire Chinese Empire." So Mutsu was still riding a dragon, only the dragon was now Japan, not China. His only choice was "to ride the wave of popular

Japanese antipathy toward China as far as we could, to gratify the people's wishes for a swift and far-reaching military offensive," after which "we might then turn to the formulation of a new foreign policy attuned to the international mood, which would stave off further threats to the nation." It seemed a wise solution, but it also ensured that (1) the "international mood" was bound to grow hostile as Japan grabbed for more; and (2) the Japanese public was bound to perceive Mutsu's subsequent willingness to bow to that mood as a betrayal and a humiliation.

The Russians understood sooner than anyone (except the Japanese themselves) what was at stake in the Korean war. As early as June 1894 St. Petersburg instructed its minister in Tokyo to warn the Japanese of serious consequences if they did not agree to a mutual withdrawal. When battle and conquest followed anyway, the Russians reinforced the Far East and Secretary of State Gresham became sufficiently alarmed to sponsor truce talks. They quickly broke up. China had sent only two minor envoys, which Mutsu took to be a sign that they weren't serious. Anyway, the Japanese wanted time to complete their triumphant campaigns. Talks resumed in April at Shimonoseki, and this time Li Hung-chang presided over the Chinese delegation. He wanted peace badly, and by now, so did Mutsu. The British had awakened to the danger to China and called for great power intervention. The Franco-Russian alliance and Germany balked at letting the British broker a peace, but some sort of intervention was imminent, especially after another Japanese fanatic wounded the seventy-two-year-old Li Hung-chang in the streets of Shimonoseki. So Mutsu and Prime Minister Itō leaned on Meiji to accept a cease-fire, and Mutsu visited his Chinese counterpart with the good news. "Li lay in bed with half of his face swathed in bandages; but in the eye which remained exposed to my view, there gleamed an expression of great joy."

The Europeans became alarmed anyway when the Treaty of Shimonoseki was published, on April 1. China was to cede to Japan the island of Taiwan, the Pescadores, and the Liaotung Peninsula with Port Arthur, recognize the independence of Korea, sign a commercial treaty granting Japan the same extraterritorial rights the Westerners enjoyed, and pay a substantial indemnity. Japan, at a blow, became a western Pacific power of the first rank. Of all these terms the one that frightened Europeans most was the cession of Port Arthur. It was Manchuria's outlet to the sea, and it controlled the Gulf of Chihli, leading to Peking. If the Japanese were not blocked from taking Port Arthur, said Witte, "the Mikado might become the Chinese Emperor and Russia would need hundreds of thousands of troops and a considerable increase of her fleet for defence of her possessions and Siberian Railway." Russia called at once for a joint European intervention to scale back the Japanese gains.

Why had the Europeans not intervened before? First, because it all happened so fast. Second, because Russia, France, and Germany saw no percentage in helping Britain uphold a status quo that benefited it most of all. Third, the other powers saw in the Sino-Japanese War a sweet opportunity to blackmail one side or the other. At various times the Russians and Germans posed as supporters of both Japan and China. But now this so-called Far Eastern Triplice (France, Russia, Germany) issued identical notes on April 23 to the effect that Japan must give back the Liaotung Peninsula. Now this sort of pressure was nothing more than what Mutsu had anticipated when he adopted his "conquer now, bargain later" strategy during the war. Nor did Japan have the financial or military might to defy the three powers. So Mutsu attended a conference and within two weeks agreed to retrocede Port Arthur.

In retrospect the Sino-Japanese War and the simultaneous revision of the "unequal treaties" got Japan off to a splendid beginning in world politics. And yet, the Triple Intervention and Mutsu's tactical retreat turned the Japanese public's euphoria into anger and shame. The Itō cabinet fell on account of its "weakness," and Mutsu's memoir justifying his policies was suppressed. Mutsu himself fell sick and died at fifty-three in 1897. Even more bitter was the astounding hypocrisy displayed by the Far Eastern Triplice in the wake of its intervention. The Russians, French, and Germans had styled themselves the protectors of China and opposed the Japanese conquest of Port Arthur because it threatened to disturb "the peace of the Far East." But the three powers did not even let a decent interval pass before proceeding to violate Chinese sovereignty themselves. Count Witte, armed with French capital, would win Li Hung-chang's approval for a Russo-Chinese bank to develop Manchuria. France won concessions in South China. Germany used the pretext of murdered missionaries to seize Kiaochow and Tsingtao (hence the excellent beer of that name) on the Shantung Peninsula. And Britain leased the so-called New Territories abutting Hong Kong, and Weihai directly across the gulf from the port *denied* Japan. This Scramble for Concessions in China discredited once and for all the moderate diplomacy of a Mutsu and made the hysterical militarism of a Yamagata appear the more "realistic." In 1896 the Japanese Army was doubled from six to twelve divisions, and in 1900 the Emperor decreed that all ministers of War and Navy must be generals and admirals on active duty. That meant the military chiefs had veto power over national policy and the power to topple a cabinet anytime they liked.

In his memoir Mutsu quoted an ancient poet who wrote that "the bones of ten thousand men rot for each general who becomes great." No wonder they banned his book. "But in an age like ours," he continued, "with complex and dynamic interactions among nations, the effects of war go far beyond the wretched spectacle of rotting skeletons, touching the entire fabric of national and international life. And woe be to the victor who errs in his efforts to capitalize on these effects, for he may then find himself in an even more precarious position than the vanquished." Well, Mutsu was wrong. Japan's position was not nearly as precarious as that of vanquished China. But he was certainly right to point out that war sets forces in motion one cannot even glimpse, much less control, and that victory creates ambitions at home and fears abroad where none existed before.

Lafcadio Hearn sensed the sea-change. An enthusiastic *yatoi* before 1895, he had told Americans of the sublime beauty of Japanese culture. After 1895, he confessed that Japan secretly hated the West and "will show its ugly side to us after a manner unexpected but irresistible."

Manila and Honolulu 1898

DOLE, THURSTON, and the *haole* planters had a lock on the economy of the Hawaiian Kingdom. After 1894 they had a lock on the politics of the Hawaiian republic. But locks do not need to be picked if the doors they guard can be smashed by sheer force. Ninety percent of Hawaii's population remained nonwhite and disenfranchised. So far the *haoles* could count on the passivity of the Hawaiians and Asian contract workers and on their own sturdy militia. A royalist uprising in 1895 aborted when Republican police sniffed out a weapons cache smuggled in from San Francisco and chased the plotters *mauka* (toward the mountains) until they surrendered. Arms were found in Liliuokalani's residence as well, and the Queen was incarcerated in what used to be her own palace. But how long could the whites sit atop what Thurston called a "slumbering volcano"?

A second conundrum derived from the planters' own need for labor. When the peripatetic sugar economy boomed again after repeal of the McKinley Tariff, broker R. W. Irwin imported 28,691 Japanese under the system approved by Tokyo in 1885. But even though Dole's government represented the planters, it grew so alarmed at the influx that it closed down Irwin's human pipeline and tried to discourage Japanese immigration by making saki prohibitively expensive. Still they kept on coming until Hawaii's foreign minister wrote, "We are in a great degree helpless. We cannot prevent the tide of Japanese immigration. Japanese property, trade, and interests are gaining ground all the time." Sooner or later the Asian majority would become self-confident enough to rebel or at least agitate for the right to vote. There was no alternative but for the Republic to abolish itself before that happened and to meld the Asians into the much larger *white* population of—the United States. "We must make a strong effort for annexation," wrote the Foreign Minister, "next spring."

Hawaiian annexation did not lack for Stateside advocates. Captain Mahan, who retired from active service in 1896 to become a full-time publicist for sea power, pronounced himself startled by Japan's performance in the war against China, and warned against the Yellow Peril. Had he been able to read Japanese literature, moreover, he would have found plenty of ammunition. For however much Korea, Taiwan, the Philippines, and the South Seas beckoned, no Japanese strategist could ignore the fact that 90 percent of Japan's émigrés lived in Hawaii. Nagasawa Setsu's book *Yankii* (Yankees) asked how Japanese might infiltrate Hawaii and the American West Coast without suffering the same fate as the Chinese. His answer was to pressure the United States to let Japanese vote. "Where else but in Hawaii can the Japanese race hope to compete truly and frontally with the white race?" Tokutomi Sohō looked forward to the day when "there will be established new Japans wherever the waves of the Pacific washed. . . ." And Inagaki Manjirō generalized: "If a nation wants to establish long-range plans and aim at achieving strength and prosperity, it must try to become the center of world commerce and industry, by implication becoming the focus of world politics."

Of course, it was the United States, not Japan, that was most likely to become the center of world commerce and industry. For in the thirty years since the Civil War the land, labor, and capital of the American democracy had undergone a decisive transformation. The Great Plains were settled, the Indian wars fought to their cruel conclusion, and not one but five transcontinental railroads spanned the continent. New waves of immigration from southern and eastern Europe changed the character of the population. The new immigrants settled mostly in the industrial cities of the East and Midwest and were joined there by hundreds of thousands of young men and women off the farms. In the mid-1890s the United States crossed a great threshold when more of its people came to live in cities and towns than in rural areas. And that meant that the politics and policies of big capital and big labor superseded those of agriculture. Predictably, the 1890s brought a last outburst of populist agitation on the part of small farmers. At the Democratic Convention of 1896 rural America shunted aside the party's eastern wing led by Grover Cleveland and found its spokesman in Nebraska's William Jennings Bryan. His platform called for farm price supports, easy credit, railroad regulation, and a sharp increase in the money supply based on silver. When Republicans countered with William McKinley and a platform endorsing the gold standard and high tariffs, the campaign became a showdown between the old and new Americas.

The nation also reached a crossroads in foreign policy. Bryan's Democrats hated the New Navy, endorsed Free Trade, and clung to Isolationism. Republicans supported naval power and commercial expansion. The "Hawaiian Islands," read the Republican platform, "should be controlled by the United States and no foreign power should be permitted to interfere with them." Jingoes like Theodore Roosevelt went further. "We should annex Hawaii immediately," he wrote in *Century* magazine. "It was a crime against the United States, it was a crime against white civilization, not to annex it two years and a half ago. The delay did damage that is perhaps irreparable; for it meant that at the critical period of the islands' growth the influx of population consisted, not of white Americans, but of low caste laborers from the yellow races."

Bryan swept the Solid South and Great Plains, but McKinley of Ohio carried the East and Midwest for 271 electoral votes to Bryan's 176. Republicans controlled both houses of Congress. In Honolulu it was extremely welcome news. Perhaps a new push for annexation "next spring" (1897) would succeed after all. But the quiet teetotaler McKinley was a sphinx. He proclaimed himself a man of peace, promised anti-imperialist Carl Schurz that there would "no jingo nonsense in my administration," and spoke cryptically of Hawaii: "I do not now say that I should consider annexation in all circumstances and at any time unwise." But the party wasted no time educating the new administration about the stakes involved in Hawaii. Senator Lodge especially leaned on John D. Long, Navy Secretary and fellow Bay Stater, to embrace annexation and to appoint Roosevelt his Assistant Secretary. Mahan advised Roosevelt on Hawaii: "Do nothing unrighteous, but as regards the problem, take the islands first and solve afterwards."

No sooner had McKinley taken office than the Hawaiian situation became critical. Japanese were entering the islands illegally at a rate of a thousand per month, aided by the steamship lines themselves. White newspapers screamed for Dole to act against this "insidious attempt to run in a horde of Asiatics." So beginning in February 1897 the Hawaiian Immigration Bureau began to prohibit new arrivals from debarking. Consul Shimamura was beside himself—the whites were sorely mistaken if they thought Japanese would sit still for the sort of treatment meted out to Chinese. But neither would the United States allow Hawaii to become the scene for the sort of gunboat diplomacy the Japanese had practiced in China. Secretary Long ordered the cruiser *Philadelphia* to Hawaiian waters, the Navy drafted its first contingency plan for war with Japan, and Congress considered legislation to begin construction of a naval base at Pearl Harbor. In April President Dole formally requested the United States to negotiate a treaty of annexation, and his government refused entry to five hundred more immigrants. Japanese Hawaiians organized public protests, and Japan's minister in Washing-

ton warned the United States against annexation. Then Consul Shimamura presented Hawaii with what amounted to an ultimatum: promise
equal rights to Japanese in the future, or else. The battle cruiser *Naniwa*
was en route from Yokohama.

O! The irony in the fact that *haoles* now suffered the same bullying
that their governments had practiced so often before. And like the
Hawaiian kings of old, they had no means of resisting the ships of one
great power except by placing themselves under the protection of
another. U.S. Minister to Hawaii, Francis M. Hatch, sent an S.O.S. to
Washington: "The conviction felt in Honolulu is that, failing annexation, it will become absolutely impossible to maintain an independent
existence." In other words, if the Republic of Hawaii were forced to
grant Japanese residents the vote, the Japanese would take over! McKinley now overcame his doubts and ordered the State Department to draft
an annexation treaty, which went to the Senate in June 1897. Japan
protested at once, and the United States rejected the protest on the
grounds that it had had a special relationship with Hawaii for seventy-
five years. "Under such circumstances," McKinley told the Senate,
"annexation is not a change. It is a consummation."

Senators did not necessarily agree. Certainly the thought of losing
Hawaii to Japan was repugnant, but to annex Hawaii was to make the
United States a colonial power in violation of its oldest traditions. So all
the pros and cons from the 1893 debate were dragged out again. The
Navy Department described Hawaii as the Crossroads of the Pacific, a
vital link in America's security perimeter and lifeline to the commerce
of Asia. George W. Melville, chief of naval engineering, and John R.
Proctor, chief of the U.S. Civil Service, explained that steam power had
the twin effect of reducing the importance of distance, while at the
same time enhancing the importance of secure coaling stations. "A
cruiser or battleship with a coal capacity necessary to carry her 5,000
miles, steaming at ten knots an hour, will exhaust her coal in less than
1,000 miles by doubling her speed. With a supply of coal well guarded at
Pearl Harbor, our war-ships and merchantmen can cross the Pacific at
maximum speed, or concentrate at distant points at high speed." An
enemy denied such an advantage could not reach much of the Pacific
Ocean, or do so only at a plodding, dangerous pace. In sum, control of
Hawaii meant absolute security for the eastern Pacific, whereas foreign
control of it meant substantial insecurity. Senator Schurz retorted that
the United States need not *annex* the islands to make use of Pearl Harbor. Wrong, said General Schofield, for then foreign powers would
demand that Hawaii award them bases in the islands as well. Japan,
Britain, and Germany were already making noises about a joint protectorate over Hawaii such as the one that finally settled the Samoan dis-

pute in 1889. So Pearl Harbor would be safe only if the entire chain was in American hands.

The liberal Schurz insisted that this amounted to colonialism, the very evil the thirteen colonies had rebelled against! Nor could one claim that Manifest Destiny extended to Hawaii, for according to Schurz history proved that Anglo-Saxon institutions could not be transplanted to the tropics: "No candid American could ever think of making a state of this Union out of such a group of islands with such a population." Worse still, imperialism would corrupt the United States at home and result in "a rapid deterioration in the character of the [American] people and their political institutions and to a future of turbulence, demoralization and final decay." Southerners played up the racial arguments against Hawaii, while the American Federation of Labor and the sugar lobby attacked annexation on economic grounds.

Lorrin Thurston was an effective lobbyist, too. He made sure every senator had a copy of his *Handbook on the Annexation of Hawaii* that refuted opponents' arguments. Perhaps his cleverest ploy was to suggest that annexation was not a scam perpetrated by the Hawaiian planters, since they stood to lose their cheap contract labor and tariff privileges if Hawaii became American. Yet he, in turn, was vexed by the reappearance in Washington of Liliuokalani and her graceful, enchanting niece, Princess Kaiulani.

The treaty never came to a vote. In December 1897 the Meiji cabinet blinked, declared itself satisfied with a small indemnity, and ordered the *Naniwa* home. The Japanese official on board, shamed by his government's weakness, attempted suicide. Then, on February 15, 1898, an issue of even greater moment wrenched away the attention of the White House and Capitol Hill. The USS *Maine*, one of the new battleships laid down in the late 1880s, blew up and sank in the harbor of Havana.

The Cuban revolution against Spanish rule was America's most intractable foreign policy problem in the 1890s. José Martí had organized the revolutionary movement on American soil, and most Americans could not help but romanticize his anti-colonial struggle. The war was not romantic. Cuban General Maximo Gómez employed guerrilla methods, burning fields and blowing up factories and railroads in a cynical effort to remove the Spaniards' incentive to stay. Spanish General Valeriano Weyler responded in kind, setting up concentration camps and earning the epithet Butcher of Cuba. The Cleveland Administration had remained aloof since the United States had no way to pressure Spain to grant independence or humane reforms to Cuba without threatening armed intervention. McKinley, on the other hand, was under intense pressure to act, especially after the *Maine* went down with 260 officers

and men. The gentle President was so unnerved by the war fever—
"Remember the *Maine!* To Hell with Spain!"—that he resorted to sleeping powders throughout the winter and spring of 1898.

Other administration figures relished the prospect of war or at least were prudent enough to prepare for it. One of Roosevelt's first acts as Assistant Secretary of the Navy had been to appoint Commodore George Dewey commander of the Asia Squadron. Mahan had told him that the Pacific command, given its remoteness, required an officer of the utmost skill and initiative. Ten days after the *Maine* incident, on February 25, 1898 (a day Secretary Long was home sick) Roosevelt sent his famous cable to Dewey: "Order the squadron, except the *Monocacy*, to Hong Kong. Keep full of coal. In the event of declaration of war [against] Spain, your duty will be to see that the Spanish squadron does not leave the Asiatic coast, and then offensive operations in Philippine Islands." Secretary Long was incredulous. Teddy "seems to be thoroughly loyal, but the very devil seemed to possess him yesterday afternoon. . . . He has gone at things like a bull in a china shop." Perhaps, but Long did not rescind the orders to Dewey, and later the War Board reviewed and signed off on them. Nor was the plan a Roosevelt concoction. Lieutenant William Wirt Kimball of naval intelligence had drafted an elaborate prospectus called "War With Spain—1896." Kimball recommended a rapid, decisive attack against Manila Bay to prevent Spain's Pacific fleet from reinforcing the Caribbean. It was a brilliant piece of staff work but one bursting with unexamined political consequences.

The first such consequence was a final push in Congress for annexation of Hawaii. On March 16 McKinley despaired of getting a two-thirds' majority for the Hawaiian treaty, withdrew it from the Senate, and allowed the friends of annexation to introduce a joint resolution instead. Once again, the history of Hawaii was to parallel that of the Republic of Texas, admitted to the Union by a joint resolution in 1845. The advantage was that a resolution needed only a simple majority in both houses, and both foreign affairs committees reported it out favorably on the grounds that annexation would forestall a Japanese takeover and be a military and commercial boon to the United States. But there was opposition in the House as well, led by Champ Clark. He damned the "unconquerable Anglo-Saxon lust for land" and denounced the annexationists' patriotism as "the specious plea of every robber and freebooter since the world began." With tongue in cheek, he added, "How can we endure our shame when a Chinese Senator from Hawaii, with his pigtail hanging down his back, with his pagan joss in his hand, shall rise from his curule chair and in pigeon English proceed to chop logic with George Frisbie Hoar or Henry Cabot Lodge?" But Hoar replied that the fate of the Pacific as between American and Asian civilizations had to be faced, and McKinley agreed: "We cannot let the islands go to Japan. . . . If something is not done, there will be before long another Revolution, and Japan will get control."

While the House chewed over the same old Hawaiian arguments, McKinley sent his final ultimatum to Spain calling for a truce, mediation, and Cuban reforms. Madrid made noises but promised little, and McKinley was persuaded that he had done "all that in honor could be done to avert war." On April 11 he asked Congress for authorization to end the Cuban war through use of force. The next day, Hawaiian President Dole gladly acceded to an American military request for extra dockside esplanades in Honolulu. On April 19 Congress voted to declare war on Spain. The next day, anticipating the news, Dole extended McKinley every assistance and even offered to conclude an alliance.

Commodore Dewey's flotilla left Chinese waters on the twenty-seventh and steamed into Manila before dawn on May 1, 1898—327 years after Legazpi had first raised the flag of Spain. Dewey had no battleships, but his six New Navy vessels were heavier, faster, and better armored than the enemy's. One sustained volley sank or disabled all but one of the Spanish ships, though Dewey did not know it until the smoke from his own guns blew away on the monsoon winds. He had also cut Spain's cable to the mainland, so it was not until May 5 that a cutter was dispatched to Hong Kong with the news that American forces could capture Manila anytime they liked, but needed additional men. When intelligence arrived that Spain's home fleet had left Cádiz for the Suez Canal, the War Board decided to reinforce Dewey and occupy Manila. It was the most important decision of the war.

McKinley's patience with Congress was now nearly exhausted. If there was to be a land campaign in the Philippines, then the United States needed Hawaii "just as much and a good deal more than we did California [in 1846]." He even considered annexation by an emergency executive act. But the Hawaiian republic's wartime assistance completed what the Japanese scare had begun. When it came to a vote on June 15, the House passed the joint resolution 209 to 91 (65 of the nays were from the South). The Senate concurred on July 6 by a vote of 42 to 21 (an exact two-thirds), with 26 not voting. So just short of eight decades after Hiram and Sybil Bingham first set foot there, the Hawaiian Islands became fully American. Was annexation a military measure taken in the heat of battle, or a prophylactic against Japanese expansion, or the first fruits of a new industrial imperialism, or a maritime necessity for a navy of steam and steel? It was all those things, and one more besides: the triumph of a small but clever, desperate, and sincere *haole* junta fighting in Honolulu for their wealth and way of life. What is surprising is not that the United States finally decided to accept their proffered paradise but that it resisted the temptation for so long.

The transfer ceremonies on August 12 were modest, dignified, and absent any gloating. Surrounded by U.S. Marines and Hawaii's National Guard (heirs to the Honolulu Rifles), U.S. Minister Harold M. Sewall mounted the steps of Iolani Palace and recited the joint resolution under which the U.S. government would take title to Hawaii's public lands, assume its national debt, and so forth. President Dole was then sworn in as temporary governor pending congressional action to organize Hawaii as a territory. The band played *Hawaii Ponoi* (Hawaii's Own) as the Hawaiian flag came down, limp. Native musicians, and the few Hawaiian onlookers, broke ranks and straggled off in tears, some to Kawaiahao Church, where women were chanting their mournful chants. Then the band struck up *The Star Spangled Banner*, and a special flag with an honorary forty-sixth star (there were forty-five states at the time) climbed the pole and caught the breeze wafting in from the western Pacific. Four days later the 1st New York Volunteers pitched their tents in Kapi'olani Park beneath Diamond Head and blew their bugles to inaugurate Camp McKinley. Up the coast naval engineers were deciding where to plant their steam dredgers, big as buildings, in the mouth of Pearl Harbor.

Hawaiian annexation made the United States supreme in the eastern Pacific. It did not necessarily mean that the nation was going to bid for empire in the western Pacific as well. Advocates of Hawaiian annexation had purposely presented Hawaii as a special case to allay fears that this was the first shot in an imperialist salvo. But it was. For the day of the Hawaiian transfer was also the day Spain's agony ceased and McKinley's began. The Spanish-American truce left U.S. forces occupying the Philippines and Guam, Cuba and Puerto Rico. What would become of these spoils of war? Congress had stipulated Cuban independence. Puerto Rico, the administration decided, would be retained by the United States in lieu of a cash indemnity from Spain. Guam was well placed to serve as a coaling station between Hawaii and Asia. The Philippines, a populous, primitive, distant country, were another matter entirely. Perhaps the United States could retain Manila as a naval base without annexing the entire archipelago, but that raised the same objections as the "Pearl Harbor only" idea. Other imperial powers would surely partition the Philippines and render Manila indefensible. A German squadron had already made itself obnoxious by shadowing Dewey's fleet. The U.S. could hardly give the Philippines back to Spain—the whole war was predicated on the cruelty of Spanish colonial rule. Nor were the Filipinos judged to be capable of self-rule or self-defense against the likes of Germany or Japan.

So McKinley worried and prayed, consulted public opinion, and (as he later told a Methodist audience) received a midnight epiphany. To give the islands back to Spain would be "cowardly and dishonorable"; to turn them over to our commercial rivals would be "bad business and discreditable"; to grant them independence would condemn them to "anarchy and misrule over there worse than Spain's"; and so "there was nothing left for us to do but to take them all, and to educate the Filipinos, and uplift and civilize and Christianize them, and by God's grace do the very best we could by them, as our fellow men for whom Christ also died. And then I went to bed and went to sleep and slept soundly." Given that the other three options seemed closed for hardheaded reasons, it was only human for McKinley to daub the fourth pill in the honey of American moralism. Nor was he alone. For if many otherwise moralistic *anti*-imperialists were in fact tinged with disgust at the prospect of annexing brown and Catholic peoples, the missionary lobby was eager to save the Filipinos from Spanish Jesuitry and superstition. And if commercial interests coincided with religious ones, well, said the head of the Presbyterian Board of Foreign Missions, they were both expressions "of the great outward impulse of civilization."

So McKinley appointed an expansionist peace delegation and sent them off to Paris to demand the Philippines. The Spaniards wailed but signed when the United States offered $20 million in conscience money. The struggle was now up to the American anti-imperialists, who mobilized to oppose the Treaty of Paris. It was a curious coalition, bringing together the likes of Andrew Carnegie of U.S. Steel, labor leader Samuel Gompers, rural populist William Jennings Bryan, the presidents of Harvard and Stanford, bleeding-heart authors like Jane Addams, and cynical ones like Mark Twain. Needless to say, they opposed colonies for contradictory reasons and sometimes bore out Roosevelt's remark that they were provincials from a bygone age. In McKinley's words, "[O]ur duty and destiny demanded that we undertake our own responsibilities and the people should not be alarmed or anxious about their ability to fulfill their obligations." Imperialism, in short, was an issue on which good humanitarians could disagree.

Henry Cabot Lodge led the fight for the Treaty of Paris and only just prevailed when the Senate ratified, fifty-seven to twenty-seven, on February 6, 1899. Now, for better or worse, the United States was a western Pacific power, too, with zones of control and supply lines that overlapped the already overlapping zones of Russia and Japan. The North Pacific triangle that would define the twentieth century was in place. Come to think of it, why did the testy Japanese, who made such a fuss over Hawaii, sit back like drowsy Buddhas while the Yanks grabbed the Philippines from under their noses? They were not nodding at all, but going over the same list of options as McKinley. If the United States set the islands free, a rivalry, possibly a war, would erupt among the East Asian imperial powers for influence in the Philippines. Japan was hardly capable of taking on the British fleet and was fearful and hateful toward the Russia/France/Germany Triplice that had just cheated it out of Port Arthur. If Germany took the Philippines, wrote one journal, "Japan would have a live volcano at her doors." Moreover, the Japanese agreed with their U.S. counterparts that the Filipinos were incapable of self-government. So American colonization seemed the lesser of evils. "On the whole," concluded the *Far East*, "the advent of the United States as a Far Eastern power is to be welcomed from a Japanese point of view, because our relation with her has been and is one of particular cordiality, and her interests in this part of the globe seem to be in general harmony with ours." Part of the credit goes to Commodore Dewey, who paid his respects to Emperor Meiji and reassured Japan of America's goodwill. But a lesser of evils was still an evil, for as Takayama Rinjirō wrote, 1898 had been a year of crimes now that "imperialism has conquered America."

The Eighth 'aha iki

Kaahumanu: So they stole my kingdom after all, and encamped their army under Kaimana Hila. The English killed our people when we stole from their boats. We did not know what stealing was. The Americans taught us "thou shalt not steal." Then they stole the entire kingdom. What evil did we do that God gave the sacred land to the *haoles?* Did we put our faith in the messengers of God, and not in God Himself? Did we worship His attributes like love and forbearance, instead of God Himself? Did the missionaries prepare our doom when they taught our warriors not to fight? Or perhaps it was Kamehameha and I who did our work too well. *We* tamed the people, and under our cloaks they forgot how to fight. . . . We thought of the *haoles* as a wave off the sea, and played with them in their zesty wetness. We did not see they were *kai'e'e,* a tidal wave that would sweep us away. No—if not for Kamehameha and me the end might have come far sooner. We built a dike that held off *kai'e'e* for many lifetimes. So many kings and queens, and all so . . . Hawaiian. I think I would have loved them. Kinau, my successor as *kuhina nui,* a good choice, a tough ruler. Kauikeaouli loved the old ways but gave his muscle to God and his people. He preserved the land in righteousness against that Charlton, the Beretanian Consul. Queen Bess and Bernice Pauahi—I would like to hear more of them. And King Kalakaua must have been fun. I never met a man who could beat me at drinking and cards. Though both are a waste of time in the end. The Christian *kapus* are wise. . . . But what changed my soul was when I learned about sins of omission. The things left undone, the precautions not taken and plans left unmade—they are what lose the battle. Yes, the kingdom was good, and the peace was good—we could never have beaten the *haoles* in war. But the Great Māhele, the Land Reform, was the blunder. To give the ignorant the power to dispossess themselves, the temptation to sell their birthright for a year's indulgence, that was a sin of omission. The people sold out to the whites and became wanderers in their own land, like Adam and Eve. Liliuokalani must have known, but it was too late, and her tactics were terrible. If only I had been there—no, she would not have listened. A Hawaiian chiefess follows her own counsel. So the Americans took my islands. Why do you say *Japanese* own Waikiki?

Scholar: There are tidal waves yet to come, Kaahumanu.

Seward: Excuse me, Your Highness, but Americans did not steal your kingdom. They settled it, made it prosper, and defended their just rights. In the end they arranged a peaceable transfer of sovereignty. No force involved. And I'll guess that *all* the people benefited from American law and commerce.

Scholar: But they did use force, Mr. Seward. The Honolulu Rifles stripped the monarchy of its power, sailors from the *Boston* helped overthrow it, and annexation proceeded under the guns of the U.S. Navy. As for the benefits, I suppose that's a matter of taste as much as dollars. The Army Corps of Engineers finally got its chance, and did some outstanding work on ports and roads—

Saitō: —to make Hawaii a military base and exclude the Chinese and Japanese?

Scholar: Chinese, yes, but not the Japanese. The fact is, they came in even greater numbers *after* the U.S. takeover. By 1900 there were sixty thousand Japanese in Hawaii—40 percent of the population! You see, once Hawaii was safely American the planters grew less paranoid about the Japanese, at least for a while.

Kaahumanu: But Chinese were banned.

Scholar: Yes, under the American law of 1882.

Kaahumanu: That makes no sense. Did China have nothing to say?

Saitō: Ha! The Chinese had nothing to say because China was decadent. Japanese were civilized enough to know that Americans would not honor their own principles unless they faced countervailing force.

Scholar: "Power comes out of a barrel of a gun," as one Chinese later put it.

Kaahumanu (1778?–1832), co-regent after the death of her husband Kamehameha the Great, revolutionized the politics and culture of the Hawaiian Islands. She was sketched by Louis Choris in 1822.
(Courtesy, The State Archives of Hawaii.)

William Henry Seward (1801–1872) believed that the United States had a grand destiny in the Pacific, but only if it lived up to its ideals of freedom at home. The lengthy exposure required in early photography accounts for the stiff poses of Seward and his daughter Fanny.
(Courtesy, Seward House, Auburn, N.Y.)

Ambassador Saitō Hirosi (1866–1939) had to use all his charm to deflect American anger over Japanese imperialism in China in the 1930s.
(Drawing by Covarrubias; © 1938, 1966. The New Yorker Magazine, Inc.)

Homer Lea (1876–1912), posing proudly in the uniform of the Imperial Chinese Reform Army, plotted to liberate China from the Manchu Dynasty and foreign imperialism. His extreme racial and militaristic theories were not so extraordinary then as they may seem today.
(Courtesy, The Joshua B. Powers Collection, Hoover Institution Archives, Stanford University.)

Sergey Yulievich Witte (1849–1915), Minister of Finance under Alexander III and Nicholas II, planned the Trans-Siberian Railway, but failed to persuade the Tsar to keep peace with Japan.

Junípero Serra (1713–1784), whose Franciscan missions were the first European settlements in California.
(Courtesy, The Serra Cause.)

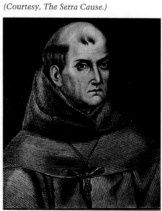

Spanish Galleons. The seventeenth-century vessels that made the annual commercial voyage from Acapulco to Manila, then home to Mexico along "Urdaneta's Route." The limits of Renaissance maritime technology inhibited the Spaniards from exploiting further their monopoly in North Pacific waters.
(Original in the Biblioteca Nacional, Madrid.)

Tokugawa Ieyasu (1543–1616), the last of Japan's three unifiers, founded the shogunate that isolated the islands from foreign contact for over two hundred years.

Public Persecution of a Japanese Convert. Fearful that foreign influence might perpetuate Japan's civil wars, the Tokugawa shogans and various *daimyō* attempted to crucify the church founded by the Jesuits and centered in Nagasaki.

A Siberian Ostrog.
Russian Cossacks, *promyshlenniki,* and
tsarist officials founded a vast network of
such fortresses from the Urals to the Pacific
Ocean. Trapping was a source of tremendous
wealth to the companies that controlled it
and, especially, to the crown.
(Woodcut from Robert J. Kerner, The Urge to the Sea, *New
York: Russell and Russell, 1942.)*

Russian Caravan Approaching the Great Wall of China.
This 1693 embassy illustrates the unique privilege obtained by Russia in the Treaty of
Nerchinsk to trade overland with the Ch'ing Empire. The same treaty, however,
barred Russians from the rich Amur Valley, dooming Siberians to a precarious exis-
tence.
(From E. Ysbrants Ides, Three Years Travels from Moscow Overland to China, *London: 1706.)*

The Founding of San Carlos Mission.
The sturdy ship lying at anchor belies the heartaches suffered by the Spanish while
trying to supply their new colony of Alta California. In this elegiac 1876 oil painting
by Troisset, Serra stands at the altar beneath the oak tree.
(Courtesy, The Serra Cause.)

Russians Skirmish with "Hairy Ainu," 1809. Lieutenants Kvostov and Davydov bungle into conflict with the aborigines of the Kurile Islands. Rezanov sent them on a mission of vengeance after his failure to "open" Japan a half-century before Commodore Perry. *(From S. I. Novakovskii,* Iaponiia i Rossiia, *Tokyo: 1918.)*

Visions of Paradise. The sketch of a tatooed teenage Queen Kaonee is just what a late eighteenth-century Enlightenment philosopher (or randy sailor) would imagine a child of paradise to be: innocent, healthy, trusting, and "natural." *(Courtesy, The State Archives of Hawaii.)*

The drawing of the missionary preaching at Kailua/Kona in 1826 likewise depicts all that a New England missionary society would want to imagine: tidy buildings thatched from coconut fronds and surrounded by attentive natives eager for useful knowledge. *(Rev. William Ellis Bishop Museum.)*

*John Quincy Adams
(1767–1848),*
as Ambassador, Secretary of
State, President, and finally
Congressman, was a shrewd
advocate for American expansion to the far Pacific.
(Brady Collection, National Archives.)

Nikolai P. Rezanov
(1764–1807),
a handsome and tragic visionary, persuaded Tsar Paul to
charter the Russian-American
Company and was among the
first to lobby for conservation
of seals and sea otters.
(Alaska State Library.)

Alexander Baranov (1747–1819) was a timid merchant who had never been to sea. But he founded New Archangel and almost single-handedly kept the Russian-American colony alive during its first two decades.
(Alaska State Library.)

Baranov's Castle.
A familiar sight to a generation of Yankee sea captains, the stockade and governor's residence at New Archangel were a caution to the hostile Tlingits and a delight to visitors, whom Baranov loved to entertain.

Kamehameha I ("the Great"),
1779–1819

Liholiho (Kamehameha II),
1819–1824

Kauikeaouli (Kamehameha III),
1824–1854

Alexander Liholiho
(Kamehameha IV), 1854–1863

Lot Kamehameha
(Kamehameha V), 1863–1872

William Lunalilo
("Whiskey Bill"), 1873–1874

David Kalakaua, 1874–1891

Queen Liliuokalani, 1891–1894
(deposed, 1893)

The Monarchs of the Sandwich Islands.
In order of dates of reigns.
(Courtesy, The State Archives of Hawaii.)

Sutter's Fort.
The first glimpse of
the trading post of
Johann August
Sutter (1803–1880)
on the Sacramento
River meant
"arrival" to
Americanos trekking
overland to
California before the
Gold Rush.
*(Courtesy, The Bancroft
Library.)*

The Red Jacket Amidst Ice Floes off Cape Horn.
Clippers like this one designed by Samuel Harte Pook cut the journey to the North
Pacific almost in half, and wrote a glorious final chapter to the Age of Sail and Muscle.
(From Carl C. Cutler, Greyhounds of the Sea, *Annapolis: Naval Institute Press, 1984; original from the Seaman's
Bank of New York.)*

San Francisco 1856.
This oil painting (artist unknown) depicts the first white metropolis on the North
Pacific. The wooden "instant city" burned repeatedly during the first decade of the
Gold Rush.
(Reproduced by permission of The Huntington Library, San Marino, Calif.)

Matthew Calbraith Perry (1794–1858),
though a vigorous proponent of steam navigation and Pacific expansion, did not want
command of the U.S. mission to "open" Japan.
(Photograph by Matthew Brady; Library of Congress.)

*Abe Masahiro
(1819–1857)*
was the luckless official
responsible for formu-
lating Japan's reaction
to the Perry mission.
(From Shujiro Watanabe, Abe
Masahiro Jiseki, *Tokyo: 1910.)*

Nikolai Muraviev
(1809—1881),
the Tsar's paladin on
the Pacific, knew that
Russia's destiny lay not
in Alaska, but in the fertile valley of the Amur.
(From Ivan Barsukov, Graf
Nikolai Nikolaevich Murav'ev-
Amurskii, *Moscow: 1891.)*

"The Curse of California."
An 1882 cartoon from the *Wasp* depicts the Southern Pacific Railroad as an octopus with Leland Stanford, Jr., and Collis P. Huntington for eyes, and tentacles gripping everything from the shipping industry, coaches, miners, farmers, land, and telegraphs to the state government in Sacramento.
(Courtesy, The Bancroft Library.)

Chinese Sojourners Below Decks on the S.S. Alaska.
This print from *Harper's Weekly* of 1876 depicts the Pacific crossing endured by Cantonese eager for work in Hawaii and California. Six years later, Chinese were banned from the United States.
(Courtesy, The Bancroft Library.)

Mutsuhito, the Emperor Meiji (1852–1912), was no mere figurehead, but made crucial decisions during Japan's swift, unsettling adjustment to modernity.
(Kyodo News Service.)

Prince Itō Hirobumi (1841–1909), the prudent draftsman of the Meiji Constitution, had a great affection for Theodore Roosevelt.

Li Hung-chang (1823–1901) undertook the thankless task of trying to preserve the decrepit Ch'ing Empire through diplomacy and reform.

Annexation Day, Honolulu.
The raising of Old Glory before the court house across the street from Iolani Palace on August 12, 1898. The United States acted in part to preempt growing Japanese influence in the islands, but native Hawaiians wept.
(Courtesy, The State Archives of Hawaii.)

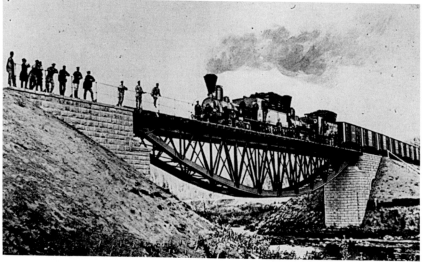

The Trans-Siberian Railway.
One of the hundreds of stone and iron bridges on the Trans-Siberian, built under frigid conditions by armies of workers in support on the Tsar's Pacific ambitions.
(The Hulton-Deutsch Collection.)

E. H. Harriman (1848–1909)
poses with Eskimos at Plover Bay, Siberia, in 1899. Only a few hours there sufficed to convince him that his scheme for a railroad across Bering Strait was fantastic.
(Courtesy, The Bancroft Library.)

Theodore Roosevelt (1858–1919)
takes the controls of a 95-ton Bucyrus steam shovel during his 1906 inspection of work on the Panama Canal. Bully!
(Library of Congress.)

Russo-Japanese War: Expectations.
Prior to 1904, the Russians had no doubt that they would make short work of the "little monkeys" from Japan, if the latter were so foolish as to provoke a naval war.

Russo-Japanese War: Realities.
In this British depiction of the Battle of Tsushima, Admiral Tōgō's battleships have already done their work and Japanese torpedo boats are finishing off the surviving Russian ships.

The Portsmouth Peace Conference.
A striking group portrait of some extraordinary statesmen: (*left to right*) Sergey Witte,
Russian Ambassador Baron Roman R. Rosen, President Theodore Roosevelt, Japanese
Foreign Minister Baron Komura Jutarō, and Ambassador Takahira Kogorō.
(*The Bettman Archive.*)

The Earthquake and Fire of 1906.
San Francisco burns, and in the aftermath California's white citizens ignited as well a racial conflict over Japanese immigration and segregation.
(Reproduced by permission of The Huntington Library, San Marino, Calif.)

The Great White Fleet Enters Yokohama.
In this Japanese post-card from 1908, a woman dressed in the traditional kimono gawks at the American battleship column. Rear Admiral Sperry, his flag lieutenant, and a Japanese attaché appear in the inset.
(Naval Historical Center.)

Doughboys Sent to Siberia.
Bleak and thankless duty for General Graves and his regi-ment, ordered in 1918 to guard the Trans-Siberian Railway—and to keep an eye on the Japanese.
(From William S. Graves, America's Siberian Adventure, 1918–1920, New York: Jonathan Cape and Harrison Smith, 1931.)

Beached for Repairs in Rugged Alaska.
The Douglas World Crusier *Seattle* fell behind its three sister planes in their 'round-the-world flight of 1924, and later crashed in Alaska while trying to catch up.
(Courtesy, National Air and Space Museum, Smithsonian Institution.)

The Los Angeles Aqueduct. The enormous Owens River aqueduct completed in 1913 allowed Los Angeles to surpass one million people. Today the metropolitan population is ten times that.
(Department of Water and Power, City of Los Angeles.)

The *China Clipper* buzzes the Golden Gate Bridge. Juan Trippe of Pan American Airways built the ocean-wide network of bases that allowed Capt. Ed Musick to pilot the Martin M-130 *China Clipper* from Alameda to Manila in 1935.
(Courtesy, National Air and Space Museum, Smithsonian Institution.)

Ishiwara Kanji (1889–1949) plotted the seizure of Manchuria, dreamed of enlisting China in a pan-Asian alliance, and prophesied an apocalyptic war against the United States.
(Kyodo News Service.)

The Young Officers' Rebellion, 1936.
Members of the Imperial Way faction of the Japanese Army occupy Tokoyo police headquarters in the February snow. The "moderate" Control faction that suppressed the revolt led Japan into war against China, Britian, and the United States.
(UPI/Bettmann.)

Saitō's Homecoming, 1939.
Ambassador and Mrs. Joseph Grew console the wife and children of Saitō Hirosi prior to the delivery of his ashes from the *U.S.S. Astoria.*
(UPI/Bettmann.)

Nomonhan: A Japanese Nightmare.
Japanese light tanks approach Soviet lines on the Mongolian steppe. Marshall Zukov dealt the cocky Kwantung Army a drubbing, and Japan was encouraged to strike south instead of north, even at the risk of war with the United States and Britain.
(Kyodo News Service.)

Adm. Yamamoto Isoroku (1884–1943)
conceived the carrier strike against
Pearl Harbor, but expected war against
the United States to end in disaster.
(Kyodo News Service.)

Japanese-American Internment.
Issei and *Nisei* who refused to surrender
their property and themselves upon reading notices such as this were deemed ipso
facto disloyal.
(Courtesy, The Franklin Delano Roosevelt Library.)

The Pearl Harbor Conference.
In July 1944, Franklin D. Roosevelt (1882–1945) kicked off his fourth presidential cam-
paign by seeming to adjudicate the quarrel over strategy between Gen. Douglas
MacArthur (1880–1964), seated to FDR's right, and Adm. Chester Nimitz (1885–1966),
standing with pointer.
(U.S. Navy, National Archives.)

Superpower.
A task force of U.S. Navy aircraft carriers led by the *U.S.S. Essex*. By 1943 the American capability to seize local air superiority at will made possible the successful amphibious invasions of Japanese-held islands.
(U.S. Navy, National Archives.)

The Strangest Bedfellows.
In November 1944, Gen. Patrick J. Hurley (1883–1963), an Oklahoma Republican, journeyed to Yenan in hopes of persuading the Chinese Communists to fight the Japanese more vigorously. Mao Tse-tung (1893–1976) is on the far left, Chou En-lai (1898–1976) on the far right.
(Courtesy, Western History Collections, University of Oklahoma Library.)

"The Enemy."
Marine Corps photograph of a rare Japanese taken prisoner on Saipan, July 1944. Fully 97 percent of his comrades died in dogged defensive action, *banzai* charges, or by suicide.
(U.S. Marine Corps, National Archives.)

"Hell Is Upon Us."
The battle for Marpi Airstrip on the north tip of Saipan. Once in U.S. hands, the
Marianas became home to B-29s built for the purpose of incinerating Japanese cities.
(U.S. Marine Corps, National Archives.)

The Profane and the Sacred.
B-29s overfly Mount Fuji on a bombing raid over Tokyo, 1945.
(UPI/Bettmann.)

The Sacred Defiled.
Emperor Hirohito
(1901–1989), direct
descendant of the
Shinto sun goddess,
inspects the ruins
of his sacred capital
in March 1945.
(AP/Wide World Photos.)

Valley of Dry Bones.
Nagasaki's Urakami Valley after the atomic bombing. In the distance stand the remains of "ground zero": the Catholic cathedral.
(Kyodo News Service.)

MacArthur and Yoshida Shigeru (1878–1967) support each other in old age as they supported each other's efforts to build a new Japan during the Occupation.
(AP/World Wide Photos.)

Heart of the New Pacific.
Waikiki's Royal Hawaiian Hotel, a pink art deco masterpiece photographed here in 1948, presaged the transformation of the Hawaiian Islands from colonial plantation and military base to bustling center of tourism and trans-Pacific business.
(Courtesy, The State Archives of Hawaii.)

Saitō: Who was that? Yüan Shih-k'ai?

Scholar: No, Mao Tse-tung, the Communist. But in a way, it was Japan that inaugurated China's education, in the war of 1894.

Saitō: Remember, Doc, you're talkin' to an expert at justifying Japanese wars against China. You yourself implied that Japan *had* to play the imperialist game in order to survive itself. Our security required control of Korea and the islands around Japan. Witte's Russians were coming, not to mention the other powers. And you admit that Japanese rule was more progressive than China's, just as American rule was more progressive than the Hawaiian monarchy's. But the war against China was more than strategy. It was a catharsis, a kind of Oedipal act.

Seward: A kind of what-in-blazes?

Scholar: I love this.

Saitō: Oedipus complex. Subconscious desire to kill your father. For Japan, defeating China was like killing the father of our old culture so we could fully realize the new Japan . . . and inherit the leadership of Asia.

Scholar: Saitō, you read Sophocles at Tokyo University?

Saitō: Nope, but I kept my ears open at the Hotel Pierre in New York. Freud was the cat's meow back in the twenties.

Seward: You're saying the Japanese considered China their "cultural father" and for that reason wanted to beat them in a war? What rubbish.

Saitō: Oh so? Then why did you Yanks declare war on the British in 1812, and when you didn't win, went on bearin' a grudge for a century?

Seward: And a Mister Freud, you say, dreamed this up? Sounds like the nonsense Witte's cousin was about. What was her name, Blavatsky? Anyway, if *Japan* wanted to slay China as its cultural father, tell me whom *China* goes about "slaying," eh?

Saitō: Itself, Mr. Seward. China slays itself.

Scholar: Then I think I know, Ambassador, what you will say to another episode I've been dying to mention. It happened in 1896, just after the Sino-Japanese War. The American *yatoi* had introduced baseball to Japanese education. It was the heyday of "muscular Christianity," physical fitness, the Boy Scouts, sports as a way to build character and teach teamwork. The Japanese schools founded teams and practiced to beat the band, but Americans refused to compete against them, or even let Japanese set foot on their fields. At length, a friendly *yatoi* managed to arrange a game for the Ichikō school team at the all-white Yokohama Athletic Club. The spectators greeted the Japanese with Bronx cheers, especially when the schoolboys showed some butterflies in the stomach in the first inning. But the club team was a pickup squad of paunchy Americans, and the young and fit Japanese went on to win by a score of twenty-nine to four. Ichikō received the boys home like a victorious army, shouting *banzai!* and thrusting saki into their hands. "This great victory is more than a victory for our school," said the student body president, "it is a victory for the Japanese people!" Their *shinki* (fighting spirit) and *wa* (sacrifice for the team) had overcome American size and experience, and *bēsubōru* became a vehicle for a reborn samurai spirit. "Ah, for the glory of our Baseball Club," wrote a poet. "Ah, for the glitter it has cast! Pray that our martial valor never turns submissive. And that our honor will always shine far across the Pacific." What do you make of that, Saitō?

Saitō: What do you want me to make of it? Baseball suits our psyche better than it does *yours.* Individual combat—pitcher versus batter, runner versus fielder—all within a collectivist competition in which teamwork and sacrifice are decisive. The bat is a sword, you know, a samurai sword.

Scholar: But we taught it to you.

Saitō: Yes, and you should have been proud of our teams. Instead, you viewed us with contempt. So we licked you!

Scholar: Only until *real* American teams came over. Then you got clobbered.

Saitō: So your people are bigger. How can Japanese players outslug Babe Ruth, or throw harder than Lefty Grove? But we will win again, someday. It's a matter of *wa.* Take my staff in the embassy. They worked sixteen hours a day and learned perfect English. I taught them every idiom, every pun. They even learned golf so they could banter with your big shots on the fairway. How many of your diplomats show such duty and discipline in their foreign posts?

Scholar: Point taken. But I think institutions were more important than "fighting spirit" in Japan's rise to power. At first, the Meiji oligarchy went the Russian route—state capitalism, state borrowing, state control. But when they nearly went bankrupt the state divested itself of its pilot industries. The *zaibatsu* then pooled the scarce capital of the country, worked with the government, and earned foreign currency through an aggressive export policy. Meanwhile, the emperor cult helped to quench any sparks of rebellion among the peasants and others who paid the price. It was touch and go for awhile, but Japan got most of the advantages of a state-controlled society *and* most of the advantages of a free-market society. Russia, by contrast, got neither.

Witte: Russia is Christian. We do not make gods of emperors.

Scholar: Uh, that's debatable. Your Procurator of the Holy Synod did everything he could to encourage the peasants to make an icon of their Little Father the tsar.

Witte: What do you know of the Orthodox faith?

Scholar: Please, let's not get into religion again. I'm trying to draw a comparison between Japanese modernization, based on a partnership between government and business, and Russian modernization, in which the state controlled everything. For all your talents, Count Witte, didn't you contribute to a futile trend when you left private industry for government?

Witte: What trend in Russia is not futile? Everyone mocks Russia for not keeping up. Who stops to pity Russia for the burdens it carries? The United States was free from foreign threats. Russia had huge burdens of defense and war. Japan was a small country, compact and unified. Russia was huge and had many sullen peoples to control. The United States drew on people and capital from the English middle classes. Russia had few merchants and little foreign trade. Japan broke its feudal nobility or turned them into capitalists. The gentry in Russia survived as a brake on capitalist development. I worked in private industry. I saw the difficulty it had getting capital, or paying back loans from meager receipts. Foreigners would not lend to us

unless the government backed up the loans. Anyway, Russia had no
time to wait for private investors to develop its economy. I knew
what had to be done; I was the best manager in Russia. You would
have me turn down my Tsar? I even took a huge cut in pay.

Serra: You were tempted by power.

Witte: I was moved by my duty—

Seward: Good man, Witte.

Witte: —and I accomplished more in ten years than all the petty capitalists and bureaucrats had done in fifty. If only—

Scholar: If only your selfsame government had not thrown it all away
in a vainglorious war? But that's the point. When the government
messed up, there was no private sector, no civil society, to pick up
the pieces.

Witte: Society would have emerged. Government railroads and industry were priming the pump. My job was to build the technology—and
once technology is in place, a new society springs into being.

Seward: I think you have it backward. A free society—inventors, scientists, entrepreneurs—makes new *technology* spring into being.

Scholar: I think it goes both ways. But perhaps Witte did too *well*. He
made it seem to Russians that the state alone *could* foster progess.

Witte: You all despise Russia, and your contempt blinds you to your
own histories. Where would Japan or the U.S. have been in this North
Pacific saga but for the leadership of their governments? Your New
American Navy, for instance—

Scholar: —was an expression of America's industrial *maturity*, not an
attempt by government to stimulate industry in the first place. In
fact, it's hard to find any clear economic motive for the imperialism
of 1898.

Saitō: Ah, then you don't buy Lenin's theory of imperialism? Neither
do I.

Witte: What is Lenin's theory?

Saitō: That imperialism is the highest stage of finance capitalism. When banks and businesses have developed the home economy to the point of saturation, their returns on investment begin to fall, and so they pressure their governments into overseas expansion in search of the high rates of return they're used to.

Witte: Absurd thesis. How does it account for the imperialism of Russia, which was still in the lowest stage of capitalism?

Saitō: Or Japan. Even the *zaibatsu* were nervous about expansion. Itō tried to get them to build railroads in Korea, but they preferred to invest at home.

Scholar: And American big business was split. Some stood to gain by war and annexations, and others to lose. To be sure, there was the mythical China market, but Carnegie, and McKinley's own "keeper," Mark Hanna—a big Ohio industrialist—hated war and colonies, thought them bad for business.

Saitō: So you figure God just told McKinley what to do? C-minus, Professor.

Serra: You mean, he *thought* God told him to. We're all experts on what God thinks.

Scholar: Why did McKinley change his mind? Yes, I think religious thought played an important role—religious thought updated to inform a nation now able and willing to intervene in world politics. Because whatever Americans' motives were for embracing imperialism—nationalism, jingoism, commerce, Social Darwinism, racialism, the China market, panic over European expansion—the fact was they did not even *need* a strong motive for colonial expansion! You see, steamships and machine guns and the whole technological advantage enjoyed by Western nations had made imperialism seem so cheap in terms of money and men that pretty much *any* excuse would do. If the price of empire had been high, you would have seen a lot more opposition. But to return to my point, *whatever* Americans' motives were, they couldn't embrace imperialism until they convinced themselves that it was right, moral, ethical. That is the great transition that the U.S. passed through in the 1890s, and that's why I stressed Mahan so much. He was a devout Christian, but he believed with all his heart that God meant for the U.S. to become a world power, to extend its influence around the world and challenge the hegemony of the other, more authoritarian imperial powers. And he wasn't alone. The church press was full of editorials supporting retention of the Spanish islands. Why? Because they were charity cases placed in American hands. Clearly Providence had blessed the U.S. with great power and wealth, but why? So Americans might feast in privacy and ignore the needs of others? So that they might hide their lamp under a bushel? No, if God had raised America from a scraggly string of colonies into a world power, it must be for some good purpose. So many church leaders persuaded themselves—and helped to persuade McKinley—that Americans were no longer called to be isolationist but to be *good* imperialists. Not too many years passed before the churches changed their minds. But that wasn't the mood of '98.

Kaahumanu: A religion that is always changing is not a religion at all.

Serra: Wise words, child. But every church bends in the breezes of time.

Seward: In my experience, the reverend clergy never got around to jumping *on* a bandwagon until everyone else was climbing *off.* When it comes to ideas, they buy dear and sell cheap.

Saitō: You remind me how much I hated American self-righteousness.

Scholar: Your mean streak is showing again, Saitō. I thought you liked Americans.

Saitā It is hard to rid oneself of a lifetime of canned politeness. Imagine having to operate always on three levels of consciousness, with one part of your mind thinking thoughts, a second screening each thought and twisting it into acceptable words, and a third reviewing each word for its possible interpretation by everyone present. That is the price a diplomat pays for his champagne and caviar. Maybe I did like Park Avenue, and the Twentieth Century Limited, and Bell Telephone, and western movies. But I hated your cant.

Seward: So according to you, any Christian who consults his conscience is a fool or a hypocrite? You're right about one thing: you Japanese are excellent at hiding your thoughts. God, was I taken in on my trip to Japan! Felt sorry for you, thought we could help civilize you. Don't you realize that all the things you admire about us are the *result* of our religious tradition? Our faith in freedom is secure in the knowledge that every personality is unique and loved, and made in the image of God. Our science derives from an understanding of *natural* law ordered by a *rational* God who made the world and saw that it was *good*. We don't shrug off the world as somehow unreal like your Buddhists, or make shrines of rocks and trees. We glorify the Creator who made them beautiful.

Saitō: Thank you, Governor. Your sermon proves my point. For you act on *none* of those beliefs, and so are hypocrites.

Seward: So we are to be condemned for our sins by people who don't even believe in sin? Who is the hypocrite? From what I'm hearing, you Japanese think yourselves a race of gods. Whatever enhances your power has heaven's own mandate. Whatever erodes your tribal unity is a capital offense. You're so damned holy you even act as your own judge and executioner. Suicide is the ultimate vanity.

Saitō: You accuse *Japanese* of worshipping themselves—you, with your world crusades that curiously seem to enhance your own power and wealth? What were Hawaii and the Philippines if not power grabs, whatever McKinley may have told himself in the interest of a good night's sleep? And you, historian: why don't you tell us the *real* fruits of your "moral" imperialism of 1898?

Seward: Damn your impudence, Saitō, you heard the man. The outrage in Cuba brought on the war, not some American plot—

Saitō: I refer to the war *after* the war.

Seward: What!

Scholar: In the Philippines, Mr. Seward, and can we please calm down? I'd read of your temper, but I knew nothing of Saitō's.

Saitō: Then I served my country well. Go ahead, tell him.

Scholar: It was ugly. When the U.S. occupied Manila there was already a revolt in progress against Spanish rule. Emilio Aguinaldo, a Filipino nationalist, was its leader. He'd been exiled to Hong Kong but returned with Dewey, expecting the Americans to grant the Philippines independence. When McKinley chose to colonize the islands instead, Aguinaldo's supporters declared independence, and the U.S. Army had a vicious war on its hands. Both sides committed atrocities—five thousand Americans died and maybe two hundred thousand Filipinos.

Seward: I see. I'm surprised our people had the stomach for it.

Scholar: And I'm surprised we won. It could well have been another Vietnam. . . . Well, you don't know about that. But the Filipino case was more fortunate for the U.S. First, the Americans had superior weapons, especially artillery. Second, no foreign powers were supporting the insurgents. Third, the Navy could isolate the war zone, since it consisted of islands. Fourth, the Filipinos were divided into dozens of antagonistic ethnic and linguistic groups and social classes. Aguinaldo and his lieutenants were mostly large landowners unloved by the peons. Finally, Aguinaldo made mistakes. He lost many of his veteran troops in conventional battles before resorting to guerrilla tactics. Then in 1901 he got himself captured, and the scattered insurgents were defeated or disbanded. The Americans immediately set out to justify the bloodshed by building schools and hospitals, roads and ports, and investing in the economy. But the Anti-Imperialist League in the U.S. declared itself vindicated, and Bryan ran again in 1900 on an anticolonial platform. He lost by a larger margin than in '96.

Saitō: And I suppose you called your victory in the Philippines "God's will"?

Seward: Why not? It apparently was not God's will that we should lose.

Witte: Then tell me, Gentlemen, to whom does it please God to grant victories? Does He hear the prayers of your presidents and missionaries? Does He play favorites with nations so long as they hearken, however deafly, to Him? If so, why did He not hear the prayers of Holy Russia, the number and volume of which drowned out those of Americans?

Serra: God uses nations as He pleases. Only the soul is immortal.

Scholar: And the meek shall inherit.

Saitō: Excuse please! That is so wrong even your own statesmen, your Teddy Roosevelts, would have none of it.

Serra: I take the beatitude to mean meek before *God.* We are not called to be meek before *men.*

Scholar: How about "turn the other cheek"?

Serra: A prescription for souls, not governments. The kingdom of God is not of this world.

Saitō: Not of this world? Then what in God's name gave Americans the right to set up *their* "kingdom of God" in the Pacific?

Seward: Quite obviously, *God* gave us that right, however we may have botched the job, for the simple reason, sir, that Christianity is true and your Shinto is not!

Saitō: So you violate the teachings of this religion you fervently believe is true in order to impose it on others—worse, in order to *use* it as a justification to grab power halfway around the world? Maybe you *are* white devils.

Witte: You forget who first drew the sword against China, and aspired to create "new Japans" all over the Pacific. You forget who sneak-attacked Port—

Kaahumanu: I condemn you all. All of you I condemn. I do not say we were happy in Hawaii before you came. We were cruel and ignorant and constantly at war. But so are you cruel and ignorant and constantly at war. I no longer care to hear the story of my ocean. Scholar, leave us now. Go away. Everyone.

Serra: Kaahumanu, we must continue.

Scholar: Yes, Kaahumanu, let me—

Kaahumanu: Silence! I will hear only the priest.

Serra: In your mercy you must let them finish, Your Highness.

Kaahumanu: But *your* people suffered from them, too—in Mexico, California, these "Philippines" of which I know nothing. Why must I listen?

Serra: Because you listen for him, and them. Just as they listen for you.

Scholar: Wait a minute, what do you mean?

Kaahumanu: I'm sorry. I do understand.

Seward: I'm sorry, too, Saitō. Perhaps we should lay off religion.

Saitō: And stick to politics. I reckon you're right.

Seward: So, what about Alaska, Professor? You ignored "Seward's folly" in this last go-'round.

Scholar: Yes, let's visit Alaska again. We could use some cooling off.

North, to Alaska 1899

T HESE DAYS THE luxury cruises put in all summer at the picturesque ports of the panhandle: Sitka, Ketchikan, Juneau, Wrangell, and Skagway. Their little populations seem to double, the Back Later signs disappear from the shops, and thousands of cameras record identical images of quaint wooden facades, totem poles and old sourdoughs, fjords and mountains whose verticality and ubiquity defeat the widest-angle lens. It was all just as thrilling but far less familiar in June 1899 when the elegant steamer *George W. Elder* dropped a most extravagant party of tourists in Skagway. Besides the crew of sixty-five, she carried twenty-three of the United States's most distinguished scientists, eleven wilderness guides and camp hands, a brace of taxidermists and a trio of artists, two doctors and a nurse, two photographers, two stenographers, and a chaplain. Presiding over the kingly procession was Edward H. Harriman, his wife and five children (including the seven-year-old Averell), four in-laws, and three servants. For the scientists it was an all-expenses-paid expedition to a huge, mysterious land. For the Harrimans it was ostensibly a holiday. But reporters doubted that the railroad magnate ever took his mind off business. Why had he wrapped his plans and route in secrecy if this were just a tycoon-sized version of a cruise up the Hudson?

John Muir, the California artist and conservationist, had been to Skagway two years before and found its people "a nest of ants taken into a strange country and stirred up by a stick." The Klondike gold rush was cresting, and this was the jumping-off point for the Chilkoot Pass and Dawson City. But Skagway was a strange sort of anthill—one block wide and four miles long—and filled not with communistic insects but with every sort of sharpster, whore, fortune hunter, and defiant individualist North America could debouch. Lord of them all was Soapy Smith, a black-bearded blackguard in a round, wide-brimmed hat whose agents

as far away as Seattle told stampeders whom to see in Skagway for supplies and maps to the gold fields. When the pigeons arrived, Soapy's men
accosted them with offers: guidebooks, or rooms, or tips on equipment
might be had for a dollar, always a dollar, from Soapy's Reliable Packing
Company. As soon as the tenderfoot pulled out his purse, more gangsters sidled up, created a ruckus and pinched the sucker's whole stake.
Who would play benefactor to the now stranded lamb? Why, Soapy
would "hear of his plight" and provide him the fare back to Seattle or
something for his widow and orphans.

Now, there was no law in Skagway, but there was economics. By
1898 other routes to the Klondike competed for stampeders, and Skagway's upright merchants rued their town's reputation. When a veteran
miner was robbed of his poke—everyone knew by whose men it was—a
town meeting gathered to name vigilantes. The arrogant Soapy, visibly
sloshed, confronted the meeting Winchester in hand. When he jabbed
the rifle at one of the guardians, Frank H. Reid, surveyor, pulled his
revolver. At once each man fired, and Soapy fell dead. Reid, sad to say,
also died of his wound. But just think if Soapy had reigned one more
year to greet E. H. Harriman on the wharfs of old Skagway. Guidebooks
for all, Mr. Harriman, sir, and only a dollar, just one U.S. dollar!

Harriman was a clergyman's son who went to work at fourteen as a
"runner" on the floor of the New York Stock Exchange. It was said he
had a "nose for money," and by his twenties he had made his first fortune. After a second brilliant career managing the Illinois Central Railroad, Harriman decided to raise the necessary capital (and squeeze the
necessary arms) to buy out the ailing Union Pacific. But the crude Harriman was an odd man out in Manhattan society, given his failure to
attend the right schools—or any schools at all. So when his doctor prescribed a long rest from his labors, Harriman chose the newest method
of translating wealth into prestige. Like Teddy Roosevelt, he would
become both a patron of science and a gentleman-adventurer, and the
result was the expedition to Alaska. After elaborate planning and purchase of the steamship, the party departed on his private train for
Chicago, and then over Union Pacific tracks to Cheyenne. Across Oregon and up the coast the private train rode Northern Pacific tracks gra-
ciously cleared of traffic by J. P. Morgan. The whole party rendezvoused
in Seattle, where a crowd turned out in the rain to see them off on the
George W. Elder.

The state of Washington, in 1899, was only ten years old. It had
lagged behind Oregon in its development, in part because the Hudson's
Bay Company had been so successful diverting Yankee farmers south of
the Columbia River. The rugged Cascades and Puget Sound region were
gorgeous but offered few ways to make a living at first, while the plains

of eastern Washington were so remote and arid that young Army Capt. George McClellan thought "no white man can ever make anything of this country." Still, a few hundred pioneers laid out streets on the eastern shore of the Sound, adopted the Indian names Tacoma and Seattle, and began to cut down trees. The mild and extremely damp climate supported a biomass so dense that an acre of Washington woodland yielded five times the lumber of an acre in the Midwest. Moreover, the timber was free for the taking until 1878, when Congress acted for the first time to protect a natural resource. The Timber and Stone Act made available tracts of forest in the Pacific Northwest to local residents for $2.50 per acre but limited each purchaser to 160 acres. It didn't work. Large sawmills, many run from San Francisco, used bogus front men to do their buying and within five years acquired over two hundred thousand acres. Free cutting, forest fires, and the conservation movement then combined to inspire the first federal system of timber management. In 1890 Congress set aside forest preserves, while still leaving plenty of room for lumber companies. By far the largest such company was founded in 1900 by German immigrant Frederick Weyerhauser. His purchase of almost a million acres of Northern Pacific Railroad woodland for $5.4 million was one of the largest real estate deals in Pacific history.

But the future of Washington, even more than that of California, was a function of railroad construction. The Northern Pacific's Jay Cooke aped the methods of the California Associates by playing the two candidates for western terminus off against each other. The tiny town of Seattle, a "veritable mudhole" according to one visitor, pledged $250,000 for the railroad and offered half its waterfront. But Tacoma bid even higher. As it happened, Cooke went bankrupt in 1873, and another decade passed before the rails reached the Puget Sound. But Seattle never forgave the railroad the slight, and its initial disadvantage vis-à-vis Tacoma helped create the "Seattle spirit," which a New Englander likened to the "dogged determination and energetic push . . . of Chicago." While Tacoma grew in population from 1,098 in 1880 to 36,026 in 1890, Seattle grew from 3,553 to 42,837 in the same decade on a diversified base of logging, shipping, small manufacturing, and service industries. Reconstruction after the great Seattle fire of 1889 further invigorated the city's trades. Then in 1893 Seattle got its own transcontinental connection via James J. Hill's Great Northern Railroad, and the Alaska gold rush provided a final stimulus. Seattle doubled to over 80,000 people by 1900 and tripled again to 237,000 by 1910, while complacent Tacoma, never more than a railroad town, leveled off at 40,000.

The railroad also made possible the settlement of eastern Washington, where all the northern lines came together at Spokane. But what made it blossom was irrigation. On his way across country on the Harriman train, wilderness writer John Burroughs had a vision: "Baptize the savage sagebrush plain with water and it becomes a Christian orchard." So it was in the yellow fields of eastern Washington. By 1890 the counties around Spokane, Yakima, and Walla Walla were already exporting over $28 million worth of hardy grain. But within a decade water ran short, and California-style conflicts over water rights tore at the new communities. So it was that another federal innovation came to pass, thanks to the lobbying of Republican Congressman Wesley L. Jones. Through the Reclamation Act of 1902 the federal government undertook to finance and engineer the dams, reservoirs, and irrigation systems needed to sustain the rich granary.

The Harriman party sailed first from Seattle to Victoria on Vancouver Island. Had he also put in at the city of Vancouver, Harriman would have seen more evidence of what railroads could do. In 1886 that westernmost settlement on the Canadian mainland was an old Hudson's Bay Company relic of a thousand souls. But the completion of the Canadian Pacific Railroad the following year, and the arrival of the first Canadian Pacific Company steamer from Yokohama, assured British Columbia's future. By 1900 the population of Vancouver reached 27,000, and one in twelve was Asian. Alaska, by contrast, was virtually deserted for three decades after the American purchase. There had been a sudden flurry of interest in 1867, and hundreds of scalawags streamed in to the old Russian capital of Sitka. But when no means of support presented itself, they went home. So did most of the five hundred Russians, and those that did not pushed off for San Francisco or Portland. For the next seventeen years, Gen. Jefferson C. Davis (no relation) and his small and scattered Army garrisons found themselves nearly alone but for the bitter Tlingits and orphaned Aleuts. The *Alta California* sneered that scarcely fifty white civilians lived in all of Alaska.

Besides Seward himself, who visited Sitka on his retirement tour, one of the few Americans to show an interest in the "icebox" was another German Californian, Charles Nordhoff. In *Harper's Monthly* in 1873 he asked why not make Alaska an American Botany Bay—a dumping ground for criminals and undesirables. The following year the California Senate endorsed the idea, but the penal reform movement did not: a Christian society should seek to rehabilitate criminals and not condemn them to exile. A decade later New Jersey revived the idea as being cheaper than penitentiaries. But it died for good in 1888 when *Century Magazine* serialized George Kennan's accounts of Russian convict labor camps. Better Alaska should remain vacant, said the critics, than become "another Siberia."

Alaska was also a candidate for maritime bases and coaling stations on the Northern Pacific Great Circle Route. But it just did not prove practical. Sail-assisted steamships needed no intermediate ports, while full steamers could now put in at Japan. Anyway, the rocks, cold, and fog chased ships away from the coast. Periodically coal could be had at Dutch Harbor in the Aleutians, but only for ships bound for the Bering Sea. Not until 1900 did the Navy Department plan an Alaskan base, and even then Arctic storms ruined its efforts. A permanent Aleutian coaling station was established only in 1911.

Didn't the Alaskan fur trade continue under American rule? Here the answer is an ironic yes. In 1870 the Alaska Commercial Company, a creature of Hutchinson and Kohl of San Francisco, purchased exclusive rights to hunt fur seals in the Pribilof Islands. It also obtained rights from Russia to seal the Komandorskie Islands and arrogated to itself a de facto monopoly around the rest of the Bering Sea. In 1880 its profits permitted a dividend of 100 percent. But just like the Russian-American Company of old, the American firm had a terrible time enforcing its claims against interlopers. Canadian and British ships took to pelagic (open-ocean) sealing to intercept the animals on their way to and from the Pribilofs, and a slaughter of such proportions ensued that the fur seal again faced extinction. Now, the U.S. government had never claimed jurisdiction in Alaskan waters beyond the usual three miles offshore. To do so would require it to argue that the Bering Sea was *mare clausum*, or a closed sea surrounded by American territory. Of course it wasn't. But the various rights obtained by the Alaska Commercial Company had made the Bering Sea a sort of *private* closed sea, and the Company begged for protection. In 1883 the U.S. revenue cutter *Corwin* seized three Canadian ships and shepherded them to Sitka for internment. The British took serious offense and reminded the State Department of *America's* protest when the Tsar, back in 1821, had tried to claim exclusive rights for *Russia*. The dispute dragged on through several administrations, more ship seizures occurred in 1887 and 1889, and in the latter year Mahan himself was sent to plan the defense of Puget Sound in case of war with Britain! In 1890 four British warships appeared in the Bering Sea to stand guard while Canadian hunters shot seals at will from their decks. Canadian anti-Americanism and the residual benefits of Britain-bashing in U.S. politics combined to drag out the crisis, and at one point a White House aide scribbled: "This may be the beginning of a 'War' diary." Finally, in March 1892 both sides accepted arbitration. The tribunal found against the U.S. claim but also gave rise to a new field of international law—environmental protection. In 1911, pelagic sealing was finally banned.

So what was Alaska good for? In the end, the same thing that built

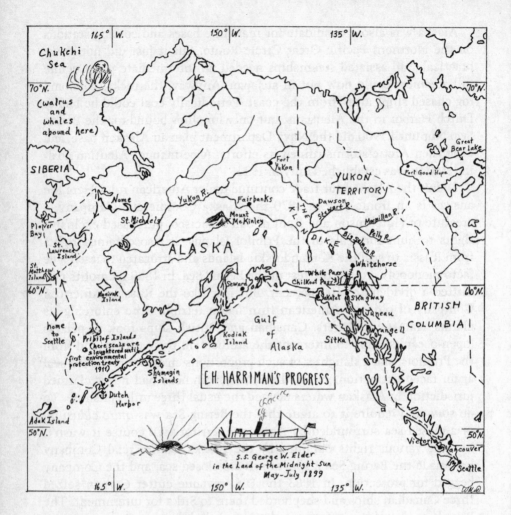

E.H. HARRIMAN'S PROGRESS

S.S. George W. Elder
in the Land of the Midnight Sun
May–July 1899

California—gold. The first big discovery was made by Fred Harris and
Joe Juneau in 1880. Several thousand transients followed them to the
panhandle, and (thanks to the advocacy of missionary Sheldon Jackson)
they were enough to persuade President Arthur to end military government. The Juneau fields were soon picked over, and so the miners
migrated across the coastal range to the Yukon. A few strikes were
made here and there, but the big one came in 1897. Tens of thousands of
young men and a smattering of doughty women made for the Klondike
via Skagway and the Chilkoot Pass. It was treacherous enough in summer, but many could not wait for summer and forty-three gold seekers
perished from just one avalanche. Other routes were even worse. An all-
Canadian trail touted by Edmonton boosters featured the nearest rail
terminus to the Klondike, but the promised "road" from there to Dawson was a figment of the imagination. Scores of others were enticed to

the port of Valdez only to die of exposure or scurvy in the Chugach and Wrangell mountains. The most up-to-date transport was by steamboat along the 1,800-mile Yukon River. But instead of watching the scenery, dining in luxury, or visiting the faro tables, chances were you would run aground, run out of fuel, or get iced in and spend winter like a Russian, in a lean-to at twenty degrees below. Skagway eventually won out, partly by ridding itself of Soapy Smith, but mostly because of the feature Harriman found most interesting: a twenty-one-mile railroad that wound back and forth up the rugged ridge and delivered its passengers and consignments to the summit. "The terrible and the sublime were on every hand," wrote Burroughs, gazing out from White Pass. "It was as appalling to look up as to look down; chaos and death below us, impending avalanches or hanging rocks above us. How elemental and cataclysmic it all looked!" This amazing piece of engineering cost the lives of thirty-two workers, but there is no telling how many lives it saved.

After Skagway, the Harrimans cruised on Glacier Bay and went ashore to bag a Kodiak bear. They did, after fighting off squadrons of bulbous flies and mosquitoes. Then the *George W. Elder* laid in a course for Harriman's ultimate destination: the Bering Strait. Here, too, the gold rush had left its mark, especially on the beach known as Nome. "Known as," because it never had a name. A clerk in the British Hydrographic Office was preparing a chart of Beringia when he encountered a blank. Assuming an error of omission, he penciled in "?Name"—which the printer, erring by commission, rendered as "Nome." Too bad he didn't choose "Nemo": the Bering Strait held a special fascination for M. Jules Verne.

Few whites had wandered the Seward Peninsula since the days of the Overland Telegraph project. But Daniel B. Libby and "the three lucky Swedes" wintered there in 1898. The following spring they found an amazing thing. Gold was just lying around in the fluvial sands at the mouth of Anvil Creek. All you had to do was hammer together a rocker of sorts and sift the sand for dust and nuggets. In the few warm months of 1899 some $2 million was made from Nome's golden sands, and by 1900 a tent-and-shanty town of twenty thousand people was pinned to the beach one hundred and fifty miles south of the Arctic Circle. "Wish I had my uncle Lem's pigsty up here to live in," joked one resident. "I would have better quarters than any in this country." At its height Nome supported a hundred saloons. Some amounted to little more than a hawker selling bottles right out of their crates. But others were permanent structures with pianos and barstools, dance hall girls and prize fights, like the one owned and operated by erstwhile peace officer Wyatt Earp.

When American law came to Nome in July 1900, it turned out to be worse than no law at all. Judge Arthur E. Noyes, appointed to end the chaos of claim jumping that prevailed on the beach, was the hand-picked agent of prominent Republican Alexander McKenzie. He in turn was an agent of the new Alaska Gold Mining Company set up by three swindlers from Nome. Their plan was to contest every claim in sight, whereupon Judge Noyes would place the claims in receivership pending litigation and grant McKenzie's company the right to work the claim in the meantime. The gold was then to be shipped to New York, where the Company's stock would soar and be sold. At length, some cheated miners filed suit in the Court of Appeals in San Francisco. But Noyes, perched at the top of the world, ignored the restraining order until two U.S. marshals sailed north and arrested him and McKenzie. Nome then returned to "every man for himself" until its gold petered out by 1903 and 90 percent of its people departed. Some headed for the interior, where Felix Pedro had made the strike that gave birth to the town of Fairbanks. In all, the Alaska gold rush produced $150 million.

Across the Bering Strait from Nome lay Siberia, and scientists and sourdoughs both reasoned that it must have the same geology as Alaska. One who acted on this belief was Washington B. Vanderlip, who sailed for Vladivostok in 1898. Some Russian merchants backed his venture and hired him to go north, first to Kamchatka and then to the north coast of the Gulf of Anadyr, the very tip of Siberia, in search of gold. After two miserable years he decided the geologists were wrong. But Harriman was on a different quest, just as reporters had suspected. He imagined himself proprietor of a 'round-the-world railroad, an updated version of the Bering Strait telegraph. And why not? A bridge over the strait would not be all that different from the recent Brooklyn Bridge, and a tunnel beneath it no more challenging than the New York City subway. The railroad at Skagway proved that construction was possible under Alaskan conditions, and the Trans-Siberian was nearly finished. It was a crazy but wonderful dream: imagine Harriman and Witte, capitalist and tsarist official, pooling their wills and talents to forge an artificial Bering land bridge and knit the continents together.

So the *George W. Elder* made the foggy crossing, nearly running aground en route, and deposited the Harrimans on the Siberian side. Two dozen Eskimos clomped out to greet them. They and their dogs, no almond-eyed huskies eager for "mush," looked diseased, and their campsite stank from the exposed remains of mammals and fish. It was freezing in midsummer and the wind was outrageous. C. Hart Merriam, the party's biologist, called it "the most barren and desolate place of its size I ever saw." So they traded for souvenirs, took some pictures, and made for the boats. The steamship then crossed to Port Clarence, a whaling haven on the Alaskan side. There Harriman discovered, after another exhausting visit ashore, that his wife and children had been left behind. He lowered a boat and fetched them himself, evidently making a silent promise never to think of the Bering Strait again.

Stories of a trans-Bering railroad continued to appear in the hopeful Nome *Nugget* until 1907. But the "swashbuckling" age of railroading was nearing its end, and the age of steam and rails was starting to give way to oil and electricity. Nor was there much of a chance for Russo-American cooperation since the Tsar's people had no interest in losing Siberia to American capitalists, while the U.S. government was even considering terminating its trade treaties with Russia in protest against its official anti-Semitism. So Alaska and northeast Siberia would go on evolving separately and unnaturally, as if a world apart, with only walrus and whales, Chukchi and Eskimos, passing between them as each season decreed.

Peking 1900

S ERGEY WITTE WAS a vigorous forty-two when named Minister of Finance. As such, he held primary responsibility for the budget, treasury, and currency of the Russian Empire. But that was only the beginning. Through his subdepartments he also administered foreign trade, tariff policy, and domestic trade and industry. He remained "tsar" of the entire railroad system. An avid patron of science and technical education, he founded schools and sponsored Arctic exploration. But Witte's special concern was the Trans-Siberian Railway, and he thus acquired a major voice over the development of Siberia and Russian foreign relations in Asia. Coming full circle, the Tsar's omnicompetent minister had much to say about all other branches of government by dint of his control over their budgets. That the Russian economy did not fly apart under one-man rule, but instead registered the highest growth rates in Europe, suggests that Witte was a sort of Huntington, Hopkins, Crocker, and Stanford rolled into one. As might be expected, his power aroused envy in others and arrogance in himself. "Witte despises us all," chided his colleague Prince Khilkov, "because he knows that he can buy any of us."

Capital, we must have more capital! was Witte's refrain. And he reached back to the methods of Vyshnegradskii to get it. First, he slashed state spending in every sphere not aimed at modernizing Russia. Second, he maximized revenues through higher tariffs, a government vodka monopoly, and indirect taxes. Third, he forced grain exports to their highest level yet. Fourth, he borrowed ceaselessly from Russia's ally France. Witte was even able to restore the ruble to the gold standard in 1897. To be sure, he was fortunate that capital was unusually plentiful in the money markets of the 1890s. In one gigantic operation Witte paid off the tsarist domestic debt with money borrowed at low interest rates from France, thereby freeing up a billion rubles for investment. But he also saved wherever he could, especially on the Trans-Siberian Railway.

It was decided from the start that speed and economy were its watchwords. Construction began in 1891 from five locations ranging from Chelyabinsk just beyond the Urals to Vladivostok. Wherever possible Witte used Russian iron and machinery, and he tried to contract out construction to private Russian firms. Few were up to the job, so the longest and most expensive stretches—around Irkutsk and along the Amur and Ussuri rivers—were entirely government-built. To his good fortune, Witte found a competent lieutenant in Khilkov, who had learned the railroad business in the United States and brought to his post as Minister of Communications a team of engineers and managers. Cheap labor was not a problem in Russia. Many workers were convicts, though Witte insisted that they be paid regular wages and promised reduced sentences. But the logistical burden of transporting, housing, and feeding up to thirty thousand men strung out over five thousand miles of wilderness was enormous. So Witte resigned himself to a single-tracked line and a route so direct that cities like Tomsk were bypassed. Lake Baikal, four hundred miles long and directly across the route, could not be spanned at all. So for the time being rolling stock would have to be detrained at Irkutsk and ferried across the lake to engines waiting on the other side.

Otherwise, the progress was extraordinary. The Pacific stretch up the Ussuri to Khabarovsk was done by 1894. The Chelyabinsk-Irkutsk line, a span longer than the Union Pacific/Central Pacific tracks, was in operation in 1898, two years ahead of schedule. But Witte's greatest worry was the middle portion, the fifteen-hundred-mile bow between Lake Baikal and Khabarovsk along the Shilka and Amur rivers. In winter the waters froze, and in spring they flooded, as in 1897, when sixty miles of track, bridges, and viaducts were washed away. A glance at the map suggested an easy solution: postpone the Amur line and build straight across Manchuria to Vladivostok. The terrain was friendlier, the climate milder, the country richer in food and raw minerals, and the route shorter by 340 miles.

The problem was getting China to agree. Had it not been Manchu policy for two hundred years to keep the northern barbarians out of their homeland of Manchuria? Had not Muraviev burst through anyway to despoil China of its provinces beyond the Amur and Ussuri? Were not the Russians revealing their true intentions even now by promoting mass immigration? They were indeed, for Witte knew that the Trans-Siberian would be profitable only if it served thriving communities of settlers. So under his administration over a million peasants—Ermaks of steam and rails—rode to Siberia. Most stopped to cultivate the valleys of the Irtysh and Ob, but the influx touched the borders of Manchuria as well. So why should threatened China agree to a railroad inside its own frontier?

Because the dragon needed friends so badly that even a bear would do. After all, Russia led the Triple Intervention that forced Japan to give back Port Arthur. Russia supplied the money (mostly French, of course) for China to pay off its indemnity to Japan. And Russia, at Witte's behest, promised to defend China against future assaults from Japan. So in 1896 Li Hung-chang traveled to St. Petersburg to discuss a permanent treaty. Witte took personal charge. He had studied the Chinese. He knew how to be patient while Li's minions ceremoniously prepared his tea or filled his pipe. He knew how to approach substantive matters through circumambulations spiced with proverbs both Chinese and Christian. He found Li "eminently sane" and flattered himself that the compliment was returned. In time they agreed on a treaty under which a Chinese Eastern Railroad Corporation received all rights and land needed to build the Manchurian line in return for a promise that Russia would never violate China's *political* sovereignty. The empires also pledged to defend each other against attacks by Japan. The bungling Russian Foreign Minister (or had Li bribed him?) left out the words "by Japan," thus committing Russia to defend China against *any* foreign power! Witte corrected the draft at the last minute, and Li, impassive as always, signed. He, too, had been bribed with five hundred thousand rubles from Witte's war chest.

The Russo-Chinese treaty seemed ideal. But Witte knew that it portended danger. In his view, the Sino-Japanese war of 1894 had been "the consequence of our starting to build the Trans-Siberian railway. It was waged against Russia, not against China." Moreover, completion of the railroad would shift the balance of North Pacific power in Russia's favor and thus "mark the beginning of a new epoch in the history of the nations." So Witte knew that *peaceful* development of Siberia and Manchuria could proceed only if Russia (1) achieved the cooperation of China, and (2) deterred Japan from interfering. His treaty with Li would seem to have accomplished both goals so long as Russia kept its side of the bargain and did not try to grab any Manchurian territory.

Unfortunately, politics cannot be engineered like a railroad, and Witte's plans were dealt four blunt blows. First, his beloved Alexander III died in 1894. His heir, Nicholas II, was imperial patron of the Trans-Siberian, but he was also an impressionable ruler who seized on the Far East as *one* arena in which he considered himself informed. The new Tsar listened readily to those at court who suggested that Witte was too frightened of the Japanese and too respectful of decadent China. The Russian Navy in particular was unhappy with Vladivostok (frozen four months each winter) and wanted a warm-water port on the Pacific. Its natural choice, now that Russia had penetrated Manchuria, was Port Arthur.

The second blow to Witte's peaceful project was Germany's seizure of the Shantung Peninsula during that Scramble for Concessions on the China coast. Li appealed to his Russian friends to persuade Germany to retreat. Witte sympathized, but the Russian Navy and foreign ministry did not. They saw the German move as an opportunity for Russia to claim Port Arthur as compensation. Witte protested that such a move would violate his treaty with Li and might provoke Peking to halt construction of the Chinese Eastern Railway. He appealed to the Tsar, who told him: "You know, Sergey Yulyevich, I have decided to occupy Port Arthur and Ta-lieng-wan. Our ships are already on their way there." It was Witte's first political defeat, and on his way out of the palace he muttered, "Remember this day: this fatal step will have disastrous results."

Witte offered to resign, but the Tsar would not let him. Instead, Witte had to instruct his agent in Peking to bribe Li once again to accept this Russian encroachment on Chinese sovereignty. The Chinese relented in March 1898, and the Russian Navy set up shop at the same strategic port that Russian diplomacy had denied to Japan. The third blow to Witte's hopes was the exile of Li in disgrace to the provinces. The Kuang-hsü Emperor had decided on a firm antiforeign policy combined, finally, with a program of modernization. It seemed that the depredations of the imperialists, reaching a peak in the Scramble for Concessions, might overcome Confucian inertia and inspire a Meiji-style imperial reform.

Now, Li Hung-chang was himself a modernizer, but his policies had clearly failed to contain the imperialists. Moreover, unrest was spreading in China, and when the Yellow River again burst its banks it seemed a warning of dynastic collapse. So the Emperor was shocked into rehabilitating radical reformers like K'ang Yu-wei, who was so bold as to write that he "could not bear to see such an event recur as when the last emperor of the Ming had to hang himself." Under their influence the Emperor eliminated wasteful offices, set up departments for industry and trade, secularized Buddhist monasteries, and replaced Confucian examinations with ones testing modern knowledge. But where the Meiji men had enjoyed military control of their country, the Kuang-hsü Emperor did not even control his own household. Within three months he fell victim of a reactionary coup d'état staged by the sixty-two-year-old Dowager Empress, T'zu-hsi, the Dragon Lady. In September 1898 she cornered her adopted son in the Forbidden City, spat venom on his reforming "churls," and explained that she alone stood between him and violent overthrow: "Stupid son! If I do not exist today, how can you exist tomorrow?" The Emperor meekly placed himself in the custody of her eunuchs and surrendered China to T'zu-hsi, who promptly purged the reformers.

Was there no popular outcry against the humiliation of China at the hands of the foreigners? There was, and that was the fourth blow against Witte's peaceful plans. It began among the followers of the I-ho ch'üan— the Righteous and Harmonious Fists—itself an offshoot of an offshoot of the undying White Lotus secret society. These new zealots, whose nickname of Boxers derived from their martial arts, had existed in the underground since at least 1808. Their sudden emergence in the 1890s was due to their adoption of a violently antiforeign program and the support they received from local officials. Though the Boxers considered themselves champions of traditional values, they in fact conjured up a mythological world of hero gods, magic, and witchcraft. A hundred days of Boxer training supposedly made one impervious to the white man's bullets, and four hundred days gave one the power of flight. Their enemies included all Chinese who adopted Western ways ("tertiary Hairy Men"), Chinese Christians ("secondary Hairy Men"), and foreigners ("primary Hairy Men"). One of their strongholds was Shantung, and it was in response to the German takeover there that the Boxer Rebellion began.

Some high-ranking officials, like the pragmatic Yüan Shih-k'ai, favored suppression of the Boxers. Their wild behavior and beliefs certainly recalled those of the Taipings of a generation before. But insofar as the Boxers seemed more antiforeign than anti-Ch'ing, the Dowager Empress cautiously encouraged them. So throughout 1899 and early 1900 Boxers attacked missionaries and foreign enterprises, sabotaged telegraphs and railroads, and massacred Chinese Christians. When T'zu-hsi herself pronounced the Boxers' magical powers "confirmed," Manchu bannermen went over to their side. By May 1900 the Western and Japanese legations feared for their lives, and a first international contingent of 340 soldiers, sailors, and marines reinforced the diplomatic community in Peking. The Boxers replied by cutting the railroad and telegraph to the coast, leaving foreign governments no means of communicating with their people. In June the Boxers turned back another relief force in stiff combat and went wild in their triumph. They burned Chinese Christians alive in Peking and killed any whites unlucky enough to get caught (including the German minister). Their long, ungroomed hair flailing about them, the Boxers adopted the walk and habit of Chinese witches, ransacked churches, pulled up the graves of seventeenth-century Jesuits, and desecrated their remains. The Dowager Empress dubbed them "righteous people," integrated thirty thousand Boxers into the imperial army, and then declared war on *all* foreign countries! The 3,200 whites, Japanese, and Chinese Christians holed up in the Peking legations could do nothing but barricade their buildings, husband their ammunition, and pray that help would come in time from abroad.

The Scramble for Concessions, the aborted Chinese reform movement, and now the Boxer Rebellion both united and divided the great powers. They had to assemble a force to march to Peking—their outraged publics demanded as much. But they all wondered what the *political* implications of these chaotic events would be. Would the Russians, Germans, French, British, or Japanese take advantage of the situation to expand their spheres of influence in China? If so, who would benefit the most, and who the least? These were the questions that prompted a new initiative on behalf of an old policy: the so-called Open Door. Like the Monroe Doctrine before it, the Open Door originated in Britain but was promulgated by the United States. In this instance, the agent of transmission was a British customs official named Alfred E. Hippisley. Passing through Baltimore in the early summer of 1899, he looked up his friend William W. Rockhill, the Assistant Secretary of State, and floated a notion. What if the United States circulated to all the powers an appeal to respect the integrity of China and the rights of all to trade there? The Open Door was familiar in London; a year before a member of Parliament called it "that famous phrase that has been quoted and requoted *ad nauseam.*" But Rockhill's boss, the new U.S. Secretary of State, saw it not only as new but as the answer to his own political problems.

That Secretary of State was John Hay. Since serving with Lincoln and Seward in the Civil War, he had gone to work for Horace Greeley, then returned to diplomacy under McKinley as Ambassador to Britain and Secretary of State. He had favored annexation of the Philippines but was not a jingo. If anything, he espoused Seward's philosophy of *peaceful* expansion and thought involvement on the mainland of Asia a bad idea. Anyway, the United States lacked the navy in the western Pacific to mix it up with the British, Russians, and Japanese, and its army was tied down by the Filipino insurgency.

For all that, Hay was under pressure to do something about China. Textile manufacturers had formed an American Asiatic Association to lobby for a strong policy in China. The Navy was anxious for a base on the China coast. Missionary groups were eager to have access to China. Even the *New York Times* complained that U.S. interests "had not been intelligently represented or adequately appreciated by the State Department." In sum, everyone wanted Hay to do something he did not want to do and that the United States was as yet incapable of doing: join the scramble on the Chinese mainland. No wonder the Hippisley/Rockhill suggestion of a hands-off policy toward China appealed to him. He could take the high road, stand forth as the protector of Chinese integrity, and shame the powers into respecting the Open Door. In August 1899 Hay wrote Rockhill that "I am fully awake to the great importance of what you say and am more than ready to act." Hay's first Open Door note was cabled to all the great powers on September 6.

It did exactly what Hay had intended. The American China lobby was pacified, and the press named Hay a capital diplomat. The British cheered the Open Door note, and the other powers grudgingly allowed as how they had no intention of carving up China. But then, what else *could* they say: "Sorry, Mr. Hay, but we have secret plans to annex half of China"? Moreover, the American military lacked the might (and the American public the will) to oblige any other power to behave itself. In sum, the Open Door was a rhetorical flourish masquerading as policy, and its toughest test came the following year when the Boxer horror reignited the danger of a free-for-all in China. An international force melding 8,000 Japanese, 4,800 Russians, 3,000 Britons, 2,100 Americans, 800 French, and a handful of Austrians and Italians assembled at Tientsin and set out for Peking on August 4. Who knew what "compensations" their governments might demand when it was over? So unless Hay was now prepared to demand Chinese colonies on his own account, he had no choice but to continue his pretense. The second Open Door note of July 3, 1900, thus explained that the *American* purpose in marching on Peking was solely to protect lives and property, and called on the others to endorse "equal and impartial trade" and preserve China as a "territorial and administrative entity."

For two months the legations had lived under siege. The periodic Boxer attacks killed 76 of their numbers and wounded 179. But the rest survived to cheer uproariously—or sob with pent-up emotion—when the Allied relief force broke through on August 14. The Emperor and Dowager Empress ducked out of Peking incognito and recalled—who else?—Li Hung-chang to save what could be saved. The Boxer Protocol of 1901 enjoined China to punish officials convicted of abetting the rebellion and to pay a gigantic indemnity ($337 million). Then everyone went home . . . except the Russians.

To Witte the Boxers were worse than a natural disaster. They were especially numerous in Manchuria, and in a few months they burned down stations and warehouses, killed Chinese workers and Christians, and ruined six hundred miles of track. But to Minister of War A. I. Kuropatkin the Boxer Rebellion was welcome: "I am very glad. This will give us an excuse for seizing Manchuria." Again Witte appealed to the Tsar, and again Nicholas sided with the military. So two hundred thousand Russian and Cossack troops fanned out over the province to defeat the Boxers and pillage. Witte managed to influence the ensuing negotiations enough so that Russia restored Chinese sovereignty to Manchuria on condition that Russian troops be allowed to remain as "railway guards." But it still amounted to a military protectorate. And just as Russia had previously organized a Triple Intervention to block Japanese expansion, so Japan, Britain, and the United States now pressured China to insist on complete Russian evacuation. That was where matters stood when seventy-eight-year-old Li Hung-chang, disgraced and ill used by all, died in November 1901.

For Britain the Russian threat to China was only one in a series of imperial crises. Within a decade Burma and Siam, Afghanistan and Tibet, Egypt, the Sudan, the Ottoman Empire, Venezuela, Samoa, and South Africa (where the Boer War was in progress) all hosted showdowns between Britain and one or more rivals. Under Lord Salisbury the overextended British Empire clung to splendid isolation, but by 1901 Lord Lansdowne, the new Foreign Secretary, was feeling his way toward a new strategy based on ententes and alliances. Nowhere was one more necessary than in Chinese waters, where the Royal Navy's once dominant squadron was now just one of many imperial fleets including the German and the Franco-Russian. Ergo, Britain needed to reduce the number of its possible enemies. Three times between 1899 and 1902 the British looked to Berlin for an understanding, but the cocky Kaiser asked too high a price. So instead Lansdowne looked to Japan.

The idea of an English alliance occurred to the Japanese as well. They always suspected the Russians would try to swallow Manchuria, and, as Foreign Minister Komura Jutarō put it, "if Manchuria becomes the property of Russia, Korea itself cannot remain independent." In fact, the leading expansionists in St. Petersburg, led by Witte's arch-rival, Alexander M. Bezobrazov, had already won a concession from Korea to fell timber along the Yalu River and were pressuring the Tsar to go further. But Japan dared not challenge the Russians so long as the threat of another Triple Intervention (Russia-France-Germany) loomed. If, on the other hand, Britain undertook to keep the other powers on the sidelines, then Japan might deter Russia from further advances. By January 1902 Lansdowne and the Japanese ambassador had worked up a draft. Britain and Japan, "actuated solely by a desire to maintain the status quo and general peace in the Extreme East," pledged to support the independence of China and Korea, and promised that if either Britain or Japan became involved in war, the other would work to keep third parties out of the conflict. Should other powers join in the war regardless, then they would come to each other's aid.

In retrospect, the Anglo-Japanese alliance of 1902 seems eminently rational, given the trends in the geopolitics of northeast Asia. Still, the fact that Britain had made a permanent peacetime alliance surprised everyone, and the fact that it chose as its high contracting partner the yellow Japanese was even more astounding. Within two months the jingo faction in St. Petersburg climbed down and promised to evacuate Manchuria after all by October 1903. Witte breathed a sigh of relief. The Trans-Siberian, always excepting Lake Baikal, was finished in 1901, and the Chinese Eastern Railway was due to open in 1903. If only peace could be maintained, Russian economic and cultural influence would surely grow, and the rail link to Europe might even draw Japan and Russia closer together.

But by now Witte had been in power ten years and was hated by nearly everyone around the Tsar. Some resented his power, others disputed his policies, still others hoped to profit from his removal. So Bezobrazov's camarilla began a whispering campaign. They claimed that Witte the Competent had built a poor railroad and that its service was awful; that Witte the Frugal had spent 800 million rubles, or 150 percent more than his original estimate; that Witte the Russian was not Russian at all, and that he chose "Jews and Poles . . . to be our color bearers in Manchuria." They said that Witte the Incorruptible had skimmed off a fortune for himself and had even darker dealings. Everyone knew he was cool toward his first wife: did he poison her? And so it went. By the time the first train made its historic journey, one-quarter of the way around the globe from Vladivostok to Moscow, Witte's stock was so low that the Tsar ordered no ceremony despite his own role as the railroad's patron.

"An armed clash with Japan in the near future would be a great disaster for us," wrote Witte in 1901, ". . . between the two evils, an armed conflict with Japan and the complete cession of Korea, I would unhesitatingly choose the latter." But as he wrote the same year, "He [the Tsar] does not talk to me any more. I say what I have to tell him and that's all. He is in an excited state; ideas of some kind or another are seething inside him." By 1903 the Tsar was thoroughly confused. Surely Witte could not be guilty of all that they said, but perhaps he was guilty of some of it. Perhaps there *had* been too much progress in too short a time. The landlords and peasants had suffered, and now the working class that grew up around Witte's infernal machines was engaging in strikes. As for Asia, Witte did not understand that Russia's true mission there was imperial and religious. All he cared about were timetables and peace treaties. In any case, it was beneath a tsar's dignity to negotiate with Japanese heathens as equals. Perhaps cousin Willy (the Kaiser) was right when he said Russia's destiny lay in the East. "Admiral of the Pacific," he had called the Tsar. So whose dupe was Nicholas II: the

Kaiser's, Bezobrazov's, or Witte's? Well, if a tsar must play the fool, then let him be a fool for Christ, and leave the results to God.

To escape the confusion, or find resolution, Nicholas took a lengthy retreat that summer of 1903 to the monastery of Sarov. There amid the thick forests lit with thousands of candles, he communed with the *real* Russian people and prayerfully made up his mind. In July the Tsar returned to St. Petersburg, relieved Witte of all Asian duties, and rebuffed a Japanese offer to yield Manchuria in return for Korea. In August the Tsar removed Witte from the Ministry of Finance. And in October the Tsar approved Bezobrazov's suggestion that Russia renege on its promise to China, and leave its army in Manchuria.

Panama City 1903

LOOKING BACK, we might conclude that the United States was already the leading Pacific power by 1900. But possessions that one is unable to defend, like the Philippines, only weaken one's strategic posture. For the past seventy years the United States had gotten by with one or two motley squadrons in the Pacific, numbering at most a single battleship. That was sufficient to show the flag in Hawaiian and Asian waters, and even defeat a third-rate power like Spain. But now that they had planted their flag in the western Pacific, Americans would need a fleet sufficient to deter the Japanese, Germans, or Franco-Russians. In fact, they needed two great fleets, since the U.S. Navy had no swift means of transferring ships between the Atlantic and Pacific. Nothing so illustrated that debility as the famous race of the *Oregon* at the start of the Spanish War. Ordered to the Caribbean from San Francisco, the battleship steamed thirteen thousand miles around the Horn in sixty-eight days. It arrived in time for the Battle of Santiago, but officials, the public, and Congress were all impressed by how much U.S. security would be enhanced by an isthmian canal. McKinley appointed a commission at once, and Rear Adm. John G. Walker reached the conclusion that "construction of such a maritime highway is now more than ever indispensable." Without it, as Mahan had said for years, American Pacific power was a pretense.

But if the need for an isthmian canal were so obvious, why had Americans not dug one decades before? We know that the United States and Britain jousted over the right to build a canal just after the California gold rush and agreed in the Clayton-Bulwer Treaty to proceed, if at all, in tandem. But after 1850 nothing happened, at least nothing American or British. The Grant administration did make studies of isthmian routes after the Civil War, but nothing came of them save a strong recommendation for Nicaragua as the most likely site. Cutting through the mountainous spine of Central America was a far different matter than, say, excavating the desert of Suez. But there was another reason why the titans of American industry snubbed the isthmus for so long: an all-sea route would compete with the transcontinental railroads. We have already seen how the Central and Southern Pacific stifled competition by absorbing the Pacific Mail Steamship Company. Our timeless force, Collis Huntington, then garnered monopoly rights to set rates across the Panama Railroad in return for a fee to its stockholders. Once in control of the Panama route, the Associates virtually shut it down. The volume of goods shipped via Panama fell from a peak of $70 million in 1869 to a low of $2.3 million in the mid-1880s. So the railroad magnates helped to block a canal even as Grant's experts testified that "it may be the future of our country is hidden in this problem."

Ferdinand De Lesseps was not an engineer and did not "build" the Suez Canal. But he was one of the most daring promoters of his era, and he maintained the confidence of nervous investors until that canal was opened in 1869. Six years later, his prestige at its height, the ebullient Frenchman with the bushy mustache turned to Panama. Three speculators—a Hungarian, a German Jew, and an illegitimate son of a niece of Napoleon I—formed a syndicate and purchased the rights, good for ninety-nine years, to build a canal in Panama, then a province of the country of Colombia. Grant's commission had just judged Nicaragua the better route, so the syndicate turned to De Lesseps to build confidence in the Panama plan. He convened a great international congress at the Société de Géographie in 1879 and won a majority to endorse "the French route" in Panama. De Lesseps proposed to blast, cut, and dredge down to sea level, as at Suez, and thus dispense with expensive locks and dams. It would cost a billion francs, he said, and be open by 1892.

De Lesseps then raised enough cash to buy out the syndicate, and his own first-share offering attracted over one hundred thousand investors. Americans, too, were enthusiastic once assured that this was not another French government assault on the Monroe Doctrine. De Lesseps even courted ex-President Grant to sign on as a front man, but Grant still believed in Nicaragua: "I was not willing to connect [my name] with a failure and one I believe subscribers would lose all they put in." Grant was no engineer either, but he was right and De Lesseps wrong. The Frenchmen soon doubled their estimate of the amount of earth that had to be moved, ignored problems of hygiene, and laid aside nothing for unforeseen difficulties. After digging began in 1882 De Lesseps granted that Panama would be ten times harder than Suez. By 1887 he admitted that the sea-level canal was impossible: there was too much rock to be cut. Panama stock prices plunged, and even the hiring of Alexandre Eiffel to fashion the locks and gates failed to restore public confidence. A new stock issue flopped, and the Company went under. Three years later a scandal was added when journalists, anticipating the Dreyfus affair, accused the canal's Jewish bankers of having bilked their small French investors. The parliament launched an inquiry, the government fell, and in the end De Lesseps was convicted of misusing funds and misleading the public. He died in disgrace in 1894, leaving the biggest pile of junk in the world behind him in Panama.

Three years later Mahan and his echoes were demanding that the United States take up the task, but along the "American route" through Nicaragua. Teddy Roosevelt agreed, writing Mahan in 1897 that the Nicaraguan Canal (and twelve new battleships to defend it) must be built "to see the United States the dominant power on the shores of the Pacific Ocean." After the *Oregon*'s voyage and the decision to annex the Philippines, McKinley asked Congress to commit the nation to a Nicaraguan canal in his annual message of December 1898. But before the United States could approach Nicaragua for concessions and land, it had to clear the project with London under the terms of the old Clayton-Bulwer treaty. So Hay persuaded British Ambassador Sir Julian Pauncefote to initial a treaty that removed British opposition to an American-built canal so long as it was "free and open . . . to vessels of commerce and of war of all nations." But Senator Lodge and Teddy Roosevelt exploded: "Better to have no canal at all than not give us the power to control it in time of war." Now, the tough old imperialist Lord Salisbury might have told Pauncefote to hang tough. But as we know, he had turned the Foreign Office over to Lansdowne, who was concerned above all with ending the British Empire's isolation and believed it was high time that Americans and Britons admitted their racial, cultural, and political affinities. Britannia could no longer rule *every* wave anymore, so if the canal was the price to be paid for American friendship, so be it. Thus, a second Hay-Pauncefote treaty of November 1901 gave the United States the right to build, operate, and implicitly defend an isthmian canal.

A route still had to be chosen and construction rights acquired. Enter Theodore Roosevelt. He had resigned from the Navy Department to lead the Rough Riders in Cuba and returned just in time to run for Governor. New York's Republican boss, Thomas C. Platt, did not trust the flamboyant Roosevelt, but agreed to slate him in return for his promise not to disturb the political machine. Teddy broke his promise, and in one restless year jailed a number of corrupt officials, and replaced the spoils system with a state civil service act. By then it was presidential election time. The Republicans convened in Philadelphia to renominate McKinley in June 1900, but his vice president had died in office and the President let the convention choose his successor. The popular choice was

Roosevelt, and when he appeared at the convention wearing his Rough Rider hat, a delegate beamed, "Gentlemen, that's an acceptance hat!" Mark Hanna and the eastern wing of the party generally thought Roosevelt a traitor to his patrician roots and dangerously out of control. "Don't any of you realize," Hanna cried, "that there's only one life between that mad man and the Presidency?" But Platt *wanted* Roosevelt to be vice president just to get him out of Albany. So Teddy was elected in the McKinley landslide, and ten months later an anarchist murdered McKinley in Buffalo. Mark Hanna's nightmare had come true.

Roosevelt was the consummate Progressive, who saw the remedy for big business and its abuses, as well as big labor and its crippling strikes, in big government intervention. Yet Roosevelt was also the consummate imperialist who wielded the "big stick," claimed police power in all the lands covered by the Monroe Doctrine, and believed that the ends justify the means in foreign policy. So late-twentieth-century categories of liberalism and conservatism, idealism and realism, just leave one confused about this boisterous, peripatetic doer. The fact is, his domestic and foreign policies were all of a piece. The same impulse to expand federal power at home inspired his interventionism abroad—and for the same purposes of reform, uplift, progress. Moreover, his successors (including Democrat Woodrow Wilson) displayed most of the same proclivities, including a belief in the efficacy of force, America's global mission, the demonstrated superiority of the white race, and the paternalistic responsibilities that went with it. Teddy Roosevelt was a Progressive imperialist, and most people loved him for it. Voters always love a leader who takes on powers bigger than themselves, gets things done, and flatters them with *his* successes.

Meanwhile, the Walker Commission had endorsed a Nicaraguan canal, very much pleasing Senator John Tyler Morgan (D., Ala.), chairman of the Committee on Interoceanic Canals. He hated Wall Street and railroads, and figured that a Nicaraguan canal would not only prosper his Gulf Coast constituents, it would bypass Huntington's Panama railroad! In any case, the French Company was demanding $109 million in exchange for its Panama concession. So congressmen, figuring this was the easiest vote they would ever cast, chose Nicaragua, 308 to 2, in January 1902. The following week President Roosevelt summoned the Walker Commission to the Oval Office. The commission held one last meeting and then announced its final, final opinion. It decided, unanimously, in favor of *Panama*.

A manipulation, a scandal! cried the press. Surely Mark Hanna was behind this, or the railroad lobby! But the leading historian on the subject suspects that Roosevelt just concluded that Panama was the better route, and that the man who persuaded him was commission member and fellow Harvard man, George S. Morison, who insisted that the great dams and locks required in Panama were indeed feasible, and that it would be folly to waste the equipment and earth already moved by the French. What was more, the French were now willing to sell out for the sensible sum of $40 million. Most important, perhaps, was Morison's observation that only in Panama could a canal be made deep and wide enough to accommodate the great battleships of the future. So Roosevelt asked Congress to change its mind, and pass the Spooner Bill specifying a Panama route.

That meant that the Frenchmen had a chance to pull off what the Panama *Star & Herald* called a *"manœuvre de la dernière heure"* (an eleventh-hour maneuver) and escape from Panama with a pretty purse after all. Maurice Bunau-Varilla, who oozed savoir faire, managed the blandishing promotional campaign in favor of the Spooner Bill. Panama was indeed the best route—De Lesseps had been a genius. The $40 million price was a bargain. Nicaragua was earthquake-prone and full of volcanoes. What was more, he hinted, a *German* company had been making overtures to buy the rights to Panama. But at least as important as Bunau-Varilla was William N. Cromwell, senior partner in the leading law firm on Wall Street and counsel to the French Company *and* Huntington's Panama Railroad. For five months Cromwell flooded Capitol Hill with depositions from engineers and shippers supporting the Panama route, while poor Senator Morgan fought to hold his votes. But the Spooner Bill passed in June, and the "Panamanians" won, by forty-two to thirty-four.

Now all Roosevelt needed was Colombia's approval. In the Hay-Herrán Convention of January 1903 the United States agreed to pay Colombia $10 million and $250,000 per year rent for a hundred-year option on a six-mile-wide zone in Panama. The Senate consented at once. The Colombian government did not. It had just emerged from a civil war of its own and had to appear to strike a hard bargain, given nationalist resistance in Bogotá to *any* deal with the hated Yanquis. So the Colombians first offered to approve the Hay-Herrán Convention on condition that the French Company kick in $10 million as a transfer fee. Cromwell refused. Next, Bogotá insisted that the United States raise its offer to $15 million. Roosevelt refused, damned "those contemptible little creatures in Bogotá," and barked that "you could no more make an agreement with the Colombian rulers than you could nail currant jelly to the wall." So the Colombian parliament, brash as you please, voted unanimously to reject the Hay-Herrán Convention.

Roosevelt now had three options: give up the whole idea of a canal, revert to Nicaragua after all, or arrange for Panama to cease *being* Colombian territory. When the French Company's agents, Cromwell included, held a secret meeting at the Waldorf Astoria to plot a revolution in Panama, Roosevelt chose option three. How dare those "foolish and homicidal corruptionists" stand in the way of a project that would be a blessing to all mankind? So Bunau-Varilla returned to Panama City, confident of White House support. (Roosevelt said later, "He would have been a very dull man had he not been able to make such a guess.") In a matter of months Bunau-Varilla recruited a band of patriots from resident Americans, railroad workers, and Colombian soldiers who loved a bribe. The U.S. Consul promised support, and the cruiser *Nashville* appeared on cue. We will "trust in the Lord," said Teddy, "and keep our powder dry."

It was a classic American filibuster, even if planned by a Frenchman and led by Panamanians such as Dr. Manuel Amador Guerrero, a railroad surgeon. For there was widespread support for independence among Panamanians, and Bogotá's rejection of the canal scheme spoiled their hopes for an economic boom. But all the world knew of the plot, so the very day the conspirators declared Panama's independence—November 3, 1903—Colombian soldiers debarked at Colón. It seemed that the coup might abort until Señora Ossa, Guerrero's wife, suggested a means of salvation. Let a Panamanian delegation ride the rails to Colón and, feigning loyalty, entice the Colombian colonel away. Sure enough, once in Panama City, the colonel accepted a bottle and $8,000 in gold, then ordered his regiment home. "Uprising occurred tonight at 6; no bloodshed," cabled the American consul. "Government will be organized tonight."

Hay recognized the republic at once, and within a week "Panamanian" Foreign Minister Bunau-Varilla arrived in Washington to conclude a treaty. He said later that he wrote it himself, but in fact an American draft was in existence by November 10. Bunau-Varilla tinkered with it, refusing for instance to include Colón and Panama City in the Canal Zone, but he did cede sovereignty over the zone to the United States, which the Hay-Herrán Convention had not. "[W]e have never had a concession so extraordinary in its character as this," concluded Sen. Hernando DeSoto Money (D., Miss.). "In fact, it sounds very much as if we wrote it ourselves." Hay and Bunau-Varilla signed on November 18. The Frenchmen got their $40 million, and the new nation of Panama, the $10 million that would have gone to Colombia. On the thirtieth a telegram arrived in Panama City: "Inform Municipal Council and Junta that I had the honor and pleasure of presenting to President Roosevelt the flag of the Republic forwarded through you. I remarked that the United States would never part with the Liberty Bell which rang out its first independence, yet, so profound was the gratitude and affection of the Republic of Panama to the President, that they gave to him their most precious treasure, the sacred and historic flag first raised upon the declaration of independence." The flag had been designed by Señora Ossa, the mother of her country. The telegram was signed by its godfather: WILLIAM NELSON CROMWELL.

Roosevelt had no qualms about Panama. Once he asked Elihu Root, "Have I answered the charges? Have I defended myself?" Root grinned: "You certainly have, Mr. President. You have shown that you were accused of seduction and you have conclusively proved that you were guilty of rape." When submitting the Hay–Bunau-Varilla treaty to the Senate, however, Roosevelt insisted that he "would have been guilty of folly and weakness, amounting in their sum to a crime against the nation, had it acted otherwise than it did when the revolution of November 3 last took place in Panama. . . . The course of events has shown that this canal can not be built by private enterprise, or by any other nation than our own; therefore it must be built by the United States."

Mahan had said he was imperialist simply because he was not isolationist. The world played by imperialist rules, and the United States was not so mighty that it could force others to change the rules. Perhaps someday it would be, but the only way of becoming that strong was to play the game by the rules it found, and play better than the others. "Honest collision," Mahan told his church audiences, "is evidently a law of progress, however we may explain its origin; whether it be in the ordinance of God, or in the imperfection of man." In any case, the canal was its own justification. "I no longer say, 'I will do this, God helping me.' I say only 'I will help God do this.'" Roosevelt could not have put better the spirit of Progressive imperialism.

But even if one grants that a Panama Canal was a gift to humanity, and forgives the methods used to enable it, such radical surgery on the face of the earth was bound not to please all nations. A Panama Canal meant a two-ocean American Navy, the Pacific contingent of which was inevitably aimed at Japan. And in the very year the canal was begun, 1904, Japan made unmistakably clear how it intended to deal with faraway powers that presumed to engineer routes to its neighborhood. For what was the Panama Canal but the watery equivalent of the Trans-Siberian Railway?

Port Arthur 1904

"THE RUSSIAN HAS ARRIVED on the Pacific. For decades, of course, the world has been dimly conscious of a gray-clad, militant figure standing on the frozen shores of that ocean. But while gigantic in its proportions, its outlines were vague and indefinite. Surrounded by arctic fogs, it was apparently nothing more than a maritime sentinel of the ice-imprisoned harbors of the Czar. . . . The world, and especially the American people, went on without a thought of the spectre which, after the first surprise at its appearance, became a mere commonplace, without meaning or interest." But Sen. Albert Beveridge (R., Ind.) had circled the world via the Trans-Siberian in 1901, and he meant to alert Americans, in the *Saturday Evening Post* and then in book form, to what Russia-on-the-Pacific meant.

The son of a small farmer, Beveridge worked his way through what is now De Pauw University, practiced law in Indianapolis, and became an enthusiastic exponent of Roosevelt's Progressive imperialism. During two terms in the Senate he fought for regulation of public utilities, child labor laws, meat inspection laws, conservation, and a foreign policy of "America first, and not only America *first*, but America *only*." But Americans seemed in danger of losing their future in the wide open Pacific because of the irresistible continental advance of Russia. So Beveridge went there to see for himself.

"If you will take Germany and France together, you will have a territory scarcely larger than the three great Chinese provinces combined under the general term Manchuria. . . . Pennsylvania, New York, New Jersey, and all New England are less than one-half the size of Manchuria, and no richer in resources." Beveridge judged it capable of supporting fifty million people, yet hardly fifteen million lived there at present, and "Russia, for all practical purposes, holds every foot of Manchuria in her firm, masterful, intelligent grasp." The Boxers had risen against her, but

it was a historical fact, noted the Senator, that once Russia inflicted punishment, rebellions did not recur. "Among all the defects of Russia's civilization, its virtues are striking and elemental, and one of the chief of
these is stability."

Beveridge taught Americans to recognize the Russians' virtues. Their
capacity for labor and patience in hardship allowed them to pioneer a
land from which other peoples recoiled. Nor was cupidity their sole
motivation. After a day of exhausting travel through a monsoon, he sat
conversing in the Russians' rude quarters. "Suddenly a bugle peals
across the night a few martial and not untuneful notes. . . . The talk
ceases. Every officer makes the sign of the cross, and the night is full of
the feeling and atmosphere of prayer. . . . Go, you doubter of the sincer-
ity of these bearded soldiers and behold the faces of these men as this
song-prayer is chanted. . . . And, however you reason it out, you cannot—resist it as you will—overcome the feeling that here is a vital element of Russian power and an efficient instrument of Russian policy."
Beveridge found Admiral Alexeiev, commander of Port Arthur, and General Grodekov at Mukden, to be "frank, very open, and astonishingly
independent in their opinions." Both were bachelors "too busy to
marry" and they ruled their empire with "an air of business curiously
American." To be sure, Russians were "not so expert in railway building
as Americans," but their numbers, discipline, and faith accorded them a
destiny. "Yes," one officer told Beveridge, "you may be stronger now,
richer now, than we are, but we shall be stronger tomorrow than you—
yes, and all the world; for the future abides with the Slav!"

"There is but one agency," wrote Beveridge, "which might dislodge
the Russians from Manchuria; that agency is the sword-like bayonets of
the soldiers of Japan, the war-ships of Japan, the siege guns of Japan, the
embattled frenzy of a nation stirred to its profoundest depths by the conviction that the Czar had deprived the Mikado of the greatest victory
and the richest prize in all the history of the Island Empire." But the
Russians were confident they could whip "those brown fellows" and so
control a commerce with China that would soon amount to a "thousand
million dollars a year." What moved this race of pioneers? Beveridge
explored that question along the length of the Trans-Siberian Railway.
He found Siberia unevenly developed, but by no means the vast slave
camp of American imagination. Children seemed everywhere, and a fellow traveler remarked, "How strong these people look! How ruddy their
faces! How broad their shoulders!" When an Englishman grumbled that
"they are nothing but so many human cattle," Beveridge asked some
Siberians if they wished they could vote for their government. "They
were dumbfounded," recorded the Senator, "they did not know what it
meant." Everything seemed to be controlled by the state, and "Indeed,

the Russian state may be said to be at the bottom communistic." For such were "the tendencies, conditions, and natural aptitudes of the Russian people."

What did a Russian hold dear, if not his own freedom? The answer to that hung in every railroad station and peasant cottage, in the offices of tsarist ministers, the boardrooms of factories, and the palaces of gentry, in vodka shops and "the basest places of sin"—everywhere hung an icon of the Savior, the Virgin, or some Russian saint. "It is the outward and visible emblem of a religious feeling instinctive, profound, racial—a religious *feeling*, more than the intelligent idea of any concrete faith. . . . Not that the Slav is not superstitious. He is superstitious, but he is genuinely religious, too." Where the American trusts in his own wits or luck, with the Russian it is always "here is my daily task. I am happy in it and I hope I am useful to my country and my Czar. What it will lead to is in God's hands." One could make no greater mistake, wrote Beveridge, than to dismiss Russia as priest-ridden: "It is nothing of the kind. The Russian priest is people-ridden, the Russian church is the people's church." To Russians, "God is a fact—the greatest fact in the universe."

But beneath it all Beveridge spied tribalism. "The only thing dominant, imperial, all-compelling in the mind of the Russian statesman is the nation. With Witte in the Finance Ministry, it is the Russian nation; with Pobyedonostseff in the Holy Synod, it is the Russian nation; with Grodekoff in Trans-Baikal Siberia, it is the Russian nation; with Alexieff on the seas, it is the Russian nation." That was why great Russian leaders like the novelist Leo Tolstoy, the technologist Witte, and the Minister of Religion, Konstantin Pobedonostsev, could disagree about politics, economics, and culture and still remain Russian to the core. Tolstoy, for instance, called on all Russians to imitate Christ, yet denied his divinity and espoused an historical determinism that belittled free will itself. Beveridge found the quirky nobleman clad in the trousers and boots of a peasant. His was a personality "to compel and repel. It is mentality which does not compromise or argue, but announces. . . . He talks about great things from the very first sentence and without any invitation." Tolstoy despised the church and denounced all rulers as murderers. But he also condemned American materialism and feared that the "Dutchman" Witte would destroy Russia's soul with machinery. But Tolstoy, it seemed, had no following. A noble woman told Beveridge: "It is said, you know, that Tolstoi is jealous of Christ. It will end with him trying to establish a religion of his own."

Witte, on the other hand, seemed to the Senator the "incarnation of the practical, the personification of the business and commercial spirit of Russia." He predicted that "Should Sergius Witte die [or] be the victim of court intrigue, and deprived of his power, Russia will have lost her ablest statesman." Yet Witte's "secret ambition," he judged, was to impel Russia toward mastery of the earth. The Russian who most resembled an American was thus the most dangerous Russian by far. Then there was Pobedonostsev, the inquisitor who was said to have locked the minds of the Russian masses in a religious prison. What Beveridge found, to his surprise, was a cosmopolitan intellectual who not only read but preferred the great authors of Western Europe and America. Emerson was his favorite. And what a personality! "He does not believe in democratic institutions. He does not apologize for Russian autocracy; he does not even defend it; he *asserts* that it is the only correct principle of government—asserts, asserts, asserts!" Americans, wrote Pobedonostsev, liked to think that they governed themselves. But democracy was a sham. A small oligarchy chose the candidates, purchased the people's votes, and manipulated policy in their own selfish interest. Should a man of integrity find his way into politics, he did not long survive, and in any case politicians spent all their time running for office. The free press was another sham. Journalists were as self-interested as the oligarchs, and readily bought. Americans claimed that the press reflected public opinion, but that was a lie. The press made public opinion, for "[e]xperience proves that money will attract talent under any conditions, and that talent is ready to write as its paymaster requires."

According to Pobedonostsev, the Tsar stood above petty interests and ruled as a father to his people. Of course, his authority must be unquestioned, and that is why the people must have a "fixed faith." Moreover, that faith must be Orthodox, for the Roman popes had surrendered to Western individualism and betrayed the ancient church, while the potpourri of barely distinguishable Protestant sects disgusted him. Are you not all Christians who believe in the Savior, he asked? Then why are there so many Methodists, Presbyterians, and Congregationalists? But for all his rejection of Western Enlightenment, Pobedonostsev believed Witte's technical programs necessary to strengthen Russia against foreign enemies. He did not, however, aspire to "mastery of the earth." Rather, Russia could preserve itself only by shutting out Western decadence and Eastern heathenism. "Russia," he said, "is no state; Russia is a world."

Who would capture the future of this "other-worldly" nation: the cultural idealist Tolstoy, the engineering statesman Witte, or the obscurantist authoritarian Pobedonostsev? Beveridge did not know, but it mattered mightily to Americans now that the Russian had "arrived at the Pacific and looks with dreamy eyes upon the world's waters." Nor did Beveridge know that Tolstoy's gloomy prediction of war, Pobedonostsev's of revolution, and Witte's of war *and* revolution were soon to

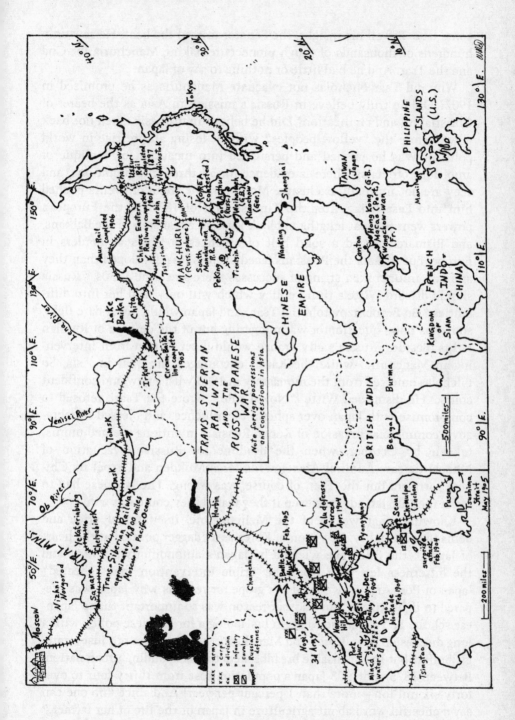

TRANS-SIBERIAN
RAILWAY
AND THE
RUSSO-JAPANESE
WAR
Note foreign possessions
and concessions in Asia.

Tokyo

PHILIPPINE
ISLANDS
(U.S.)

Manila

TAIWAN
(Japan)

KOREA
(contested)

Vladivostok

Ussuri
Rail
completed
1897

Khabarovsk

Amur Rail
completed
1916

Chinese Eastern
R. Railway completed

Chita

Lake
Baikal

Irkutsk

Circum-Baikal
line completed
1905

Tsitsihar

Harbin

MANCHURIA
(Russ. sphere)

South
Manchurian
R.R.

Mukden

Peking

Tientsin

Port
Arthur
(Russ.)

Weihaiwei
G.B.

Kiaochow
(Ger.)

Shanghai

Nanking

Hong Kong (G.B.)
Macao (Port.)
Kwangchow-Wan
(Fr.)

Canton

CHINESE
EMPIRE

FRENCH
INDO-
CHINA

KINGDOM
OF
SIAM

BRITISH INDIA

Burma

Bengal

Lena River

Yenisei River

Tomsk

Ob River

Omsk

Yekaterinburg

Chelyabinsk

Samara

Nizhni
Novgorod

Moscow

URAL MTNS.

Trans-Siberian Railway
approximately 4,800 miles
Moscow to Pacific Ocean

500 miles

Harbin

Changchun

Battle of
Mukden Feb. 1905

Yalu defenses
pierced
Apr. 1904

Seoul
Chemulpo
(Inchon)

Pyongyang

Pusan

Tsushima
Strait
May 1905

Nogi's
3rd Army

Port
Arthur

Mined
waters

Togo's
blockade
Feb. 1904

Siege
Dalny May-Dec.
1904

surprise
attack
Feb. 1904

Liaoyang
Hill

Mukden

Tsingtao

200 miles

xxxx = army
xxx = corps
xx = division
= infantry
= cavalry
= Russian
defenses

come true. For all his insight, the Senator missed the boat. He saw only hundreds of thousands of tough pioneers remaking Manchuria for God and the Tsar. And he had little or nothing to say of Japan.

Why did Tsar Nicholas not evacuate Manchuria as he promised in 1902? Did he truly believe in Russia's mission in Asia as the bearer of Christianity and civilization? Did he believe that Russia dared not back down before the "yellow peoples" without losing all prestige in world politics? Was he pushed and persuaded into incaution by a clique of ambitious officials? There is evidence for all three interpretations, and they are not mutually exclusive. Moreover, the trend of events pushed him into East Asia. After the Turkish War of 1877–78 the European powers went to great lengths to block Russian expansion in the Balkans, and Bismarck forged a solid belt of alliances on Russia's borders in Europe. But in Asia the Russians faced peoples less developed than they and had an unbroken string of successes there since the 1850s. "Russia should discard Witte's timid policy which will only lead her into difficulties." So Bezobrazov told the Tsar. And Japan would never dare fight, so it was not a question of warmongering but of the defense of Russian rights. Besides, Russia's ally France would deter Britain from intervening in Manchuria, while the Kaiser encouraged the Tsar in Asia. So Nicholas emerged from the monastery in 1903 with a new and confident course. He dismissed Witte ("Now I rule," wrote the Tsar), refused to compromise with Japan over spheres of influence, and blessed Bezobrazov's commercial invasion of Korea. Russia's intentions seemed unmistakable by October, when the deadline for Russian evacuation of Manchuria saw Admiral Alexeiev *reinforce* Mukden and expel its Chinese garrison. But the Tsar, of course, was wrong. The Japanese had to resist the Russian advance even if they feared they could not win.

Knowing what we do of the Meiji regime, its national pride and demand for equality, its vision of Korea as a "dagger pointed at the heart of Japan," the influence wielded by Japan's autonomous military, and the bitterness left over from the Triple Intervention that "cheated" Japan of Port Arthur, we need not grope for reasons why Japan was prepared to fight Russia. But another reason was so important that a Japanese scholar at Yale chose to begin his apologia for Japanese policy with a long discussion of it. Korea and Manchuria, he said, were not just strategic buffers but indispensable breadbaskets to an expanding urban nation. Between 1875 and 1903 Japan's population rose from thirty-four to over forty-six million—more than 1 percent per year! And since "no one can say a cheerful word about agriculture in Japan or the life of her farmer," feeding its mouths was the nation's greatest challenge. Should "the markets of East Asia be closed, Japan's national life would be paralyzed, as her growing population would be largely deprived of its food and occupation." Now, Russia had grabbed Manchuria in violation of treaties and the Open Door. The world must thus understand that Japan could not permit this.

The surprising fact is that Tokyo displayed forbearance for so long. But Prime Minister Katsura Tarō feared the consequences of war and adhered to the Japanese practice of waiting for consensus to emerge among the politicians, the *genrō* (elder statesmen), the military, and the public. Foreign Minister Komura, a brilliant graduate of Harvard Law School, likewise favored a strong policy but was careful to postpone conflict until it was clear in the eyes of the world that Russia, not Japan, was the aggressor. So throughout 1902 and 1903 the Japanese proposed the *Man-kan kōkan* policy (Manchuria to Russia, Korea to Japan) and establishment of a fifty-mile-wide demilitarized zone astride the Yalu River. What they failed to do, however, was to invite Britain and the United States, the Open Door advocates, to support their diplomatic initiatives. Such a combination of white powers *might* have persuaded the Tsar to back down since it would save him the humiliation of compromising with Japan alone. Instead, the Russians spurned Japan's offers, while the consensus sought by Katsura burst noisily to life.

The Japanese Army and Navy had warned for years that Russia was strengthening its hold on Manchuria, filtering troops into Korea, and reinforcing its Asian fleet. Time was not on Japan's side. In the last half of 1903, intelligence reported, thirty thousand more Russian troops had moved into eastern Siberia. By November, Russia's refusal to treat with Japan inflamed the public at large. Several major newspapers came out against agreement with Russia even if one could be had: "A peaceful solution of the Manchurian question through indecisive diplomatic measures and humiliating conditions is meaningless. This is not what our nation wants." Business leaders, usually cautious, also damned the stalemate. Japan needed economic access to Korea and Manchuria, and (as a Mitsubishi executive put it) people were "frightened without knowing what to do to restore their sense of security." Moreover, they had come to believe that a victorious war would spark an economic boom. Finally, politicians in the Diet were, as always, quick to criticize weakness in foreign policy. In December 1903 the opposition parties passed a resolution condemning the "misgovernment" of the cabinet as not in accord with the national will. These multiple demonstrations—military, journalistic, political—meant that Katsura and Komura now could and perhaps must lead the country into war.

On January 4, 1904, Tokyo received Russia's final offer. It asked Japan to recognize Manchuria as a Russian sphere of influence, in return for which Russia promised to respect the Open Door. It made no mention of Korea. The Japanese cabinet and *genrō* (even old Itō Hirobumi, who had hoped to avoid war) now concluded that Russia would not bargain in good faith, and that Japan had only two choices: acquiesce and see its military and economic position go to ruin, or drive the Russians out of Korea and Port Arthur by force. But could they do that? It seemed unlikely, given that the Russian standing army numbered 1.1 million men and Japan's but 180,000. To be sure, the Russians would not be able to deploy or supply anything like a million troops by the single-tracked Siberian railway. But then, all Japanese troops and supplies would have to be transported by sea in the teeth of Russia's Pacific fleet. Nor did the balance of naval power necessarily favor Japan. Counting two ships known to be en route through the Suez Canal, the Russian Pacific fleet would total nine battleships and five armored cruisers against the Imperial Japanese Navy's six battleships and six armored cruisers. The Japanese ships were newer and close to their home ports, and their crews were better trained. But the Russians might still manage to concentrate their fleet for a decisive action and win control of the Sea of Japan in a single afternoon. So the Japanese admirals begged for time and could not promise to land troops safely anywhere except on the southern tip of Korea. Whatever happened, said Adm. Tōgō Heihachirō, Japan *must* strike first and without warning. That was the only way to improve the naval odds.

The final Japanese demarche to Russia requesting a compromise went out on January 13, 1904. The Russians did not respond. Instead, they rushed three more battalions to the Yalu, mobilized Siberia, and ordered another battleship to the Pacific. On February 4, Emperor Meiji convened a war council. None of the ministers or *genrō* was prepared to assure him of victory. The Army figured it had an even chance of defeating the Russians; the Navy believed it might destroy the Russian fleet but at the cost of half of its own. Still, all agreed that what passed for peace had become intolerable. "We are bound to fight, even at the price of our national existence," mourned Itō. "I say frankly that I expect no success."

The next day Japan severed diplomatic relations with Russia and two Japanese fleets put to sea. One headed for Chemulpo (Inchon) on the Korean coast near Seoul, the other straight for Port Arthur. The Japanese ships crept into Chemulpo on the eighth, trapping the Russian gunboat *Koreetz* and cruiser *Varyag*. Rather than surrender, the Russian commanders chose to fight their way out. "May God help us! Let us cross ourselves and go boldly into this fight for our Faith, our Tsar, and for Holy Russia." English and American sailors in port cheered their courage as they sailed forth to meet the attackers. Three hours later—torn by shells, ablaze, and littered with corpses—the *Koreetz* and

Varyag limped back to port and were scuttled. "*Banzai* for His Imperial Majesty!" shouted the Japanese and landed the first companies of their Korean invasion force.

Port Arthur was ignorant that fighting had started—the Japanese had cut the telegraph lines. But such was the slovenliness of the Russians' training that even if they had known an attack was imminent, their dozen warships might still have been as the Japanese found them: "all mixed together in no sort of order." After torpedo attacks, Admiral Tōgō's five battleships steamed into the roadstead and recorded hits on four Russian ships. In addition, the prize battleship, *Tsarevich*, was beached. It was then that Alexeiev realized the consequences of having but a single drydock at Port Arthur, and that one too small to handle a battleship. So the Russian fleet, though intact and protected by mine-fields and shore batteries, was trapped in its precious warm-water port. "We shall know how to die," said a young lieutenant. "That is our specialty," replied a senior officer, "but it is a pity to do it without any object."

In fact, the Russian fleet was unready to carry out any mission at all. To begin with, it was divided between Port Arthur and Vladivostok, and neither squadron could reach the other without running a gauntlet through the Straits of Tsushima. Minister of War Kuropatkin, an Army man, thought the Navy a waste of money and believed that land power alone could hold Manchuria. Even Adm. Oscar Stark, the Pacific fleet commander, lacked a contingency plan to break a blockade. And *that* meant that Japan's main object—control of local waters to transport their troops—was conceded during the crucial first weeks of the war. So the Japanese called up their reserves, mobilized the merchant marine, and landed a half million men on the Manchurian mainland.

"This without a declaration of war," wrote Tsar Nicholas when the news came. "May God come to our aid." Instead, Adm. S. O. Makarov came to their aid when the Tsar, in his only good decision of the war, relieved Admiral Stark of command. Makarov was another Bering, Muraviev, or Witte, a man of talent and drive caught in an impossible system. He was a disciple of Mahan and a technical innovator who had overseen construction of the world's first icebreaker. He was also a leader. When Makarov arrived at Port Arthur, the sailors made the sign of the cross and hailed him as their "little grandfather." He went to work at once improving defenses and personally led a sortie to save a torpedoed destroyer. Spit and polish were replaced by ceaseless, meaningful drill, and the dispirited sailors believed once again they could whip the Japanese.

Admiral Tōgō knew of the change and that Japan's control of the sea was no longer assured. So he ordered increased mine laying outside Port

Arthur and kept his fleet at sea in case the Russians should try to break out. They did, on April 13, when a Russian destroyer got lost in the fog and joined by mistake a Japanese flotilla! Makarov led his flagship, *Petropavlovsk*, and four other battleships through the mined zones to the rescue. Then Tōgō appeared with his own battleships, and the Russians turned back, retracing their course through the mined waters. Two mighty explosions suddenly burst, a huge cloud appeared, and extending out of the cloud, at a sickening angle skyward, the stern of the *Petropavlovsk*. She went down in a minute, with 635 men, one of whom was Makarov. "We were astonished but at the same time unconsciously shouted *Banzai!*," wrote a Japanese captain. It was a queer emotion that followed a great victory won through no effort of one's own. As the Japanese contemplated the death of their enemy's chief, the *Banzais* gave way to "sympathetic murmurs" and then, in the embarrassed fashion of men, to stilted analysis of what had occurred.

Two weeks later the Japanese Army struck on the Yalu. The Siberian infantry occupied bluffs on the north bank and seemed untouchable. But they had suffered terribly in the winter's snows, immobile and short of rations. Japanese engineers built, under the Russians' noses, a great bridge across the water. But they never intended to use it. The Russians' frantic artillery fire at the decoy only revealed the position of their batteries, while the Japanese hauled 4.7-inch Krupp-built howitzers up seemingly impossible slopes. The Japanese then crossed the river in unexpected places, rained down shells on the Russians, and crushed their brave counterattack. The Japanese then streamed into the valleys behind the bluffs, blocking retreat. One of the few regiments that escaped, the Eleventh Siberian Rifles, was led by a priest in black robe and miter, holding his cross in the air. The Japanese Army now had a clear path along the coastal lowlands to the base of the Kwantung Peninsula and the railroad that led to Mukden and Russia.

The Russians won a victory of sorts in May, when two Japanese battleships were sunk by mines. But Port Arthur remained blockaded by sea, while the Japanese army advanced 150 miles from the Yalu to the neck of Port Arthur's peninsula. There, in late May, they assaulted Nanshan Hill, supported by gunboats and heavy artillery. In this one battle they spent more ammunition than was fired in the entire Sino-Japanese War. Human wave attacks finally overcame the long-suffering Russians, and by June the Japanese were streaming down the peninsula and laying siege to Port Arthur itself. That meant that the Russian fleet stood in danger of being shelled from behind, from the land, and Makarov's replacement, Adm. V. K. Vitheft, knew he must make a run for it. But his first sortie in late June had to sweep a path through the mines, which gave Tōgō time to react. When Japanese smokestacks appeared on the horizon, Vitheft gave up the attempt. In August the Port Arthur and Vladivostok squadrons both sallied forth in hopes of uniting their forces at sea. But Tōgō caught Vitheft with a superior force. The two lines then circled about each other for hours as the Russians tried to escape to the north. In this Battle of the China Sea the Japanese again fired the lucky shot, directly into the conning tower of the flagship *Tsarevich*. Vitheft was killed, the steering was jammed, and the rest of the Russian fleet fell into confusion. The cautious Tōgō (much to the shame of his lesser commanders) broke off the engagement and sent in his torpedo boats to finish the Russians. They failed. The *Tsarevich* crept at four knots to Kiao-chow to be interned by the Germans, and others reached the French at Saigon or the British at Shanghai. The rest returned to Port Arthur. The Vladivostok squadron had no better luck. Only one ship escaped, and her mutinous crew sailed her to San Francisco and internment.

The Battle of Port Arthur began on August 19. This time the Japanese commander was not an operational genius but a fanatical warlord named Nogi Maresuke, who incarnated the spirit of vengeance. His career dated back to the Satsuma Rebellion of 1877, when he tried to commit suicide after a defeat. Now he led his men into battle, invoking the souls of Japanese killed in the war against China. The Russians had stolen Port Arthur from them, and Nogi's forces would redeem their shame. Instead, he condemned fifty thousand of them to death or wounds in a four-months' siege marked by frontal attacks against entrenched and desperate Russians. But where Japanese losses could be made good by a short sea voyage, the Russians could expect no help. They were cut off by land and sea, and the Japanese were fortifying their own lines astride the Mukden railroad.

Finally, on November 27, Nogi identified "Hill 203" as the keystone of Port Arthur's defenses and concentrated every howitzer and gun on the heights. An unspeakably bloody week of attacks and counterattacks ensued until, on December 5, the Russians were spent. They scuttled their remaining ships in the harbor, opened parlays with the Japanese "monkeys," and on January 3, 1905, surrendered Port Arthur. For this "the Russian had arrived on the Pacific."

Portsmouth,
New Hampshire 1905

THE MOMENT Tōgō opened fire on the Russian fleet at Port Arthur, Theodore Roosevelt became the arbiter of the Pacific balance of power. Not that the United States might enter the war: Roosevelt had written the year before that "Russia knows as well as we do that we will not fight over Manchuria, for the simple reason that we cannot." Rather, the United States was arbiter because it alone among the powers was truly neutral. Wilhelm II had encouraged the Tsar in the policies that led to war and played the opportunist. If Russia triumphed, Germany might share in the partition of China. If Russia lost, then Germany might bully insecure France into making concessions in Africa. As for France and Britain, they were allied to Russia and Japan, respectively, and could hardly mediate the war.

Still, the Europeans could not escape involvement completely for the simple fact that Russia and Japan were both *dependent* belligerents. Neither could fight for long on its own meager resources and both needed sizable loans. The Russians could rely on France. But when the Japanese looked to Britain for money in December 1903, Prime Minister Arthur Balfour refused on the grounds that filling Japan's war chest would be morally "an act of war." He changed his moral theology after Japan's initial victories and the negotiation of an Anglo-French entente. London bankers then issued £10 million of Japanese war bonds in May 1904 and floated £12 million more in November. Thus, French and British capital underwrote the Russo-Japanese War even as the two governments clung to neutrality.

Roosevelt himself was pro-Japanese. The prevailing view in the Anglo-Saxon countries was of a brave little Japan ("pluck personified", wrote Teddy) standing up to the Russian bear. But he also peered into the future of the North Pacific and knew that "Japan is playing our game" by knocking out the Russians. The ideal outcome for the United States would be for Japan and Russia to fight to mutual exhaustion, whereupon "peace will come on terms which will not mean the creation of either a yellow peril or a Slav peril." Thus, while a Russian triumph "would have been a blow to civilization, her destruction as a Far Eastern power would also in my opinion be unfortunate. . . . It is best that she be left face to face with Japan so that each may have a moderative action on the other." It was up to America to see that such a balance of power emerged.

But there was no chance that either belligerent would consider peace talks so long as the fate of Port Arthur remained in doubt. It is a tiresome trait of warring powers that the initial victor becomes greedy for more, while the initial loser hopes to recoup. By New Year 1905 the Japanese had won victories beyond their most sanguine expectations, yet the Japanese military and press now thought it possible to destroy Russian power utterly. Even the realistic Prime Minister Katsura imagined a peace based on Japanese control of Korea, Port Arthur, and the southern Manchurian railroads; Russian withdrawal from all of Manchuria; cession of Sakhalin Island to Japan; and a large Russian indemnity. Tsar Nicholas, for his part, vowed "to proceed with the war to the bitter end" rather than parlay with "little monkeys." In February 1905 Witte advised him pointedly that if he made a bid for peace and was spurned by Japan, the Russian people would rally behind him. But if Russia refused to talk peace, the result would be defeat abroad and revolution at home. Strikes and peasant eruptions had already occurred. After the fall of Port Arthur over two hundred thousand people demonstrated before the Winter Palace until Cossacks and Guards shot hundreds dead on Bloody Sunday. But Witte's advice "had not the slightest effect on the tsar," and Roosevelt's first demarches came to naught. He hoped for better luck in the spring.

We know that Nicholas II saw Russian expansion in Asia as his personal mission and that he bore a special grudge against the samurai. His wife, Alexandra (who bore him his hemophiliac son in August 1904), and his uncles, the grand dukes, also urged him to fight on. And it was suicidal stubbornness only in retrospect. The war party argued that what the Tsar needed to counter unrest was battlefield victories, not diplomatic defeats; that Japan's initial advantages were nearly spent while Russia's manpower advantage was still to be felt; and that peace talks were premature so long as the naval war remained in doubt.

In June 1904 the Tsar had decided to order his Baltic Sea fleet to the Pacific. That decision, too, is often ridiculed as being four months tardy. But in truth, to sail a great battleship fleet over eighteen thousand miles would be enormously expensive if possible at all and would take many months. The admiral in charge even boasted that "[t]he Japanese will have capitulated long before then." The fact was that the Russians, like everyone else, expected a short war. So the delay was tragic *because* it was logical. What was *illogical* and therefore not tragic, was the failure to ready the fleet just in case. Instead, Adm. Z. P. Rozhdestvenskii had to plan from scratch the greatest fleet voyage in history. He was an energetic taskmaster, a big man with a beard identical to the Tsar's, and he sacked and promoted underlings on the slightest impulse. His second-in-command, Rear Adm. Dmitry von Fölkersam, he considered "a sack of manure." Little wonder that his officers both hated and obeyed him. Still, Russian supply services were so inadequate and corrupt that he was two months behind schedule when the fleet finally sailed on October 16.

Rozhdestvenskii's Baltic fleet, now the Second Pacific Fleet, numbered seven battleships plus cruisers and escorts, fifty ships all told and twelve thousand men. The admiral was to shepherd them around three continents on which Russia had not a single base or coaling station. As it was, the Russians made fools of themselves while still in the Baltic Sea. So paranoid had they become toward their devious enemy that sailors imagined every merchantman a Japanese torpedo boat. Off the Dogger Bank the repair ship *Kamchatka* gave way to mass hysteria, pumped 296 rounds at its alleged tormentors, and sank four English fishing boats. At Tangier the great fleet broke in two, Fölkersam taking one squadron toward the Suez Canal, Rozhdestvenskii continuing south around the Cape of Good Hope. They reunited off the French colony of Madagascar on December 28, just as Port Arthur was surrendering. For three months the ships sat at anchor until it was decided they would press on—destination now Vladivostok—and be reinforced by Russia's Black Sea fleet to make up for the ships lost at Port Arthur. So morale deteriorated, diseases spread, and hulls gathered barnacles while Rozhdestvenskii sent frantic cables begging for someone to bring him some coal. He finally purchased outright some fourteen loaded German colliers and put to sea again in March 1905.

Meanwhile, locomotives had been chugging their way through the Siberian fall and winter, pulling guns and soldiers (and crates of vodka) to Mukden, the last Russian stronghold in southern Manchuria. Kuropatkin, his hair turned white with worry, tried to make Mukden impregnable. His three-hundred-thousand-man army outnumbered the Japanese three to two, even after Nogi's forces joined Gen. Ōyama Iwao following their victory at Port Arthur. But the Japanese had no choice but to attack since their manpower reserves were nearly gone and time was now against them. Ōyama chose a flanking strategy similar to that which had worked on the Yalu. While his main armies feinted frontal assaults and sucked in Kuropatkin's reserves, the wild Nogi drove his

veteran infantry and cavalry thirty miles west and then north of Mukden. No sooner did the Russian commander on the exposed flank realize
his danger than the Japanese unleashed attacks on all fronts. For five
days in early March the gigantic armies clawed at each other until a
Japanese breakthrough on the eastern, mountainous flank threatened
the Russians with a double envelopment. The exhausted Russian soldiers broke, streaming to the rear, sharing rumors of catastrophe, and
staging "great scenes . . . round the vodka cases." Kuropatkin ordered a
general retreat just in time, and Ōyama occupied Mukden, having
killed, wounded, or captured ninety thousand Russians at a cost of seventy-five thousand of his own troops. The Russian Army then reassem-
bled forty miles up the railroad. Its survival was important, for it would
soon be the only bargaining chip left to the Tsar.

Whether Russia could fight on was now a matter of will. As news of
the latest defeat reached Russia, strikes, peasant revolts, and mutinies
intensified. As for world opinion, the Battle of Mukden destroyed the
illusion that Russia's land power would make up for its losses at sea.
Japan at once received a third £30-million loan, while Parisian bankers,
for the first time, turned the Russians away. The Tsar's last hopes now
rested on Rozhdestvenskii, whose fleet made its way by stages from
Malacca to Cam Ranh Bay in French Indochina, where it met up with
the Black Sea, now Third Pacific, Fleet. The Russians had made naval
history just by arriving, but their ships were covered with sea growth,
the crews were sullen and stricken, and the officers were depressed by
the report from Mukden. When Admiral Fölkersam died, Rozhdestvenskii suppressed the fact for days—his men could not stand any more bad
news.

The Russians knew that their assignment was hopeless. They had to
load their tenders to the brim with enough coal to reach Vladivostok,
but that would slow them down so much that they would never be able
to race past the waiting Japanese fleet. As one lieutenant put it, "Presumably Tōgō is no greater fool than we and knows that the only course
for us is the east side of the Gulf of Korea. I assume that he also knows
how to use a pair of compasses and is acquainted with the four rules of
arithmetic." In fact, the Japanese had been preparing for this since
November. Every available merchantman was armed and put on patrol
in a web 140 miles deep, while the main Japanese battle fleet was refit-
ted and retrained to a peak of efficiency. Still, when the Russians
steamed north along the China coast it seemed that heaven might be
with them: the weather closed in. "Look!" shouted Captain Semenov of
the battleship *Suvorov*, "you can't even see the rear of the fleet! It's
200,000 to 1 against any one running into us accidentally. . . . If it's the
same tomorrow, we'll give them the slip!"

But the fog lifted at 3:30 A.M. on May 27 to reveal the gray hull of the *Shinano Maru*. Her captain peered, counted all the ships he could see, and ordered the helmsman to flee. Then he employed a technology beyond the age of steam and rails—a Marconi device, a wireless radio—and within ninety minutes, four of Japan's finest battleships were on a course to intercept. When Tōgō's fleet fell into formation the following afternoon, it had a four-to-three advantage in tonnage and 127 heavy guns to the Russians' 92. More important, the Japanese guns could be fired faster and carried a greater charge. *Most* important, the Japanese ships were much faster, both by superior design and by virtue of carrying only enough coal for the battle. Tōgō was counting on that when he suddenly veered his fleet sharply to starboard, then to port in a left-hand circle and straight across the path of the enemy. His purpose was to "cross the T" so that his broadside guns could all fire at the Russian van, while only the first few ships in the Russian line would be able to fire at all, and then only from their forward turrets. Before completing the maneuver, however, the circling Japanese ships would themselves be exposed to broadside fire, and when Captain Semenov saw it, he could not believe his eyes. "My heart beat furiously, as it had never done before the six months at Port Arthur. If we succeeded! God grant it!"

The Russians opened fire, and fired and fired at the Japanese battleships. Hundreds of shells thumped into the sea, but the Russians could not find the range! For instead of regular fuses that went off on contact, they used delayed fuses on armor-piercing shells that exploded only when they struck metal. So they could not see their misses to know whether their aim was long, short, left, or right! Soon the swift Japanese completed the "Tōgō turn" and the roles were reversed. The Japanese poured shells into the Russian flagships and the battleships that followed. The Russians kept firing, madly, but one by one their guns were silenced and their crews torn apart, burned alive, or drowned. The *Suvorov* was the first to sink, then the *Osliabia*, leaving Admiral Fölkersam's coffin to bob pitifully amid the wreckage. By evening the *Alexander III* and *Borodino* went down, and Japanese destroyers and torpedo boats zoomed in to finish off the rest. In a few hours the Russian Navy lost thirty-five ships totaling two hundred thousand tons, and fell in rank from the world's third largest to number six. The Japanese lost three torpedo boats. "Neither Trafalgar nor the defeat of the Spanish Armada," said Roosevelt, "was as complete—as overwhelming." After the battle of Tsushima even the Kaiser urged peace. If it did not come, he feared, "they will kill the Tsar."

Japan was the first to respond to Roosevelt's renewed offer to mediate. "[S]ay to the President," Komura cabled his ambassador, that "it may be reasonably expected that the Government of St. Petersburg will turn now its attention to the question of peace." Roosevelt replied with a plea that the Japanese exercise restraint in their peace terms, and the Japanese assured him they would. In fact, Katsura's cabinet had already drafted its terms and received the Emperor's sanction. They included a free hand for Japan in Korea, Russian withdrawal from Manchuria, and Japanese control of Port Arthur and the railroad as far north as Harbin. Their "not absolutely necessary" terms included reparations and all of Sakhalin Island. In July Secretary of War William Howard Taft assured Japan in the Taft-Katsura Memorandum of American acquiescence in "the establishment by Japanese troops of a suzerainty over Korea."

Why did the Japanese government talk peace at a time when the military screamed betrayal at any mention of a truce and newspapers bandied such extreme aims as the annexation of Manchuria and Vladivostok? The reason was that the cabinet, unlike colonels and editors, bore the responsibility of deciding when Japanese leverage was maximal. The morning after Tsushima was that moment. For even if Russia appeared beaten and wracked by revolution, its Manchurian Army was still in the field and the Japanese Army was near the end of its offensive capacity. Besides, the treasury was low, and further belligerence risked losing Japan the sympathy of the "honest broker" Roosevelt.

Katsura's was a courageous decision. *Any* terms he got were bound to be judged insufficient in the superhot Japanese climate. He had anticipated this as early as December 1904 when he made an extraordinary secret deal with his political rivals. Support me in war and peacemaking, said Katsura, and I promise to resign as soon as peace is made and turn over the premiership to opposition leader Saionji Kimmochi! The deal was struck, and thanks to it Katsura felt free to accept Roosevelt's good offices on June 10, 1905. After some effort, Roosevelt won the Tsar over through a combination of threat and promise. The U.S. ambassador warned him that backing out of peace talks now risked losing him *eastern Siberia*, whereas if he made peace the United States would see to it that Russia remained a power on the Pacific coast. So the Tsar, struggling to contain the Russian Revolution of 1905, made the same decision that Lenin would make just twelve years later: make peace abroad to retain power at home.

Roosevelt considered Washington as the site of the conference, but it was too humid in August. Newport, Rhode Island, and Manchester, New Hampshire, were possibilities but too near the crowds of summer people. He chose instead the Portsmouth Navy Yard, where privacy, security, and an occasional breeze were available. In that unlikely spot the plenipotentiaries convened on August 9. Foreign Minister Komura, in Western top hat and tails, led the Japanese. At the head of the Russian delegation stood . . . Sergey Yulyevich Witte.

He was the best man for the job, said Russian Foreign Minister Vladimir N. Lambsdorff. "When a sewer has to be cleaned, they send Witte," said Witte himself. "Anyone but Witte," said Nicholas II. But when the Tsar's other choices took sick or begged off, he swallowed his knobby pride and asked him to take the assignment. Witte, the Li Hung-chang of the Romanov dynasty, was packed off to America to salvage the wreckage from a war he had fiercely opposed. But Witte had a plan. He sensed what the upshot of this conference must be. Russia, Japan, and the United States were a triangle. Russo-Japanese relations now would improve (they could hardly get worse), while American-Japanese relations would surely sour. The Japanese would resent whatever limits were placed on their victory, while Americans would swing around to fearing Japan as they had previously feared Russia. So Witte went to Portsmouth with the secret intention of negotiating not only peace but a Russo-Japanese entente based on joint exploitation of Manchuria. His vision inspired the next decade of Russian policy on the Pacific.

The President had no illusions about the task he took on. So determined were the Russians not to appear to be begging for peace, and so determined were the Japanese to be treated equally, that protocol had to be just so, and Teddy had to summon all his ebullience to break the ice. Far worse were the contrary instructions the two sides carried to Portsmouth. The Russians were ready to transfer Port Arthur and the southern railroad, accept a Japanese protectorate over Korea, and evacuate Manchuria so long as the Japanese did the same. But they were under the Tsar's strict orders not to cede Sakhalin, pay an indemnity, surrender their interned ships, or limit their armaments on the Pacific. The Japanese, as we know, wanted it all.

The initial crisis came at the end of the first week. After a plenary session in which the Japanese offered to drop their demand for Russian disarmament in return for Sakhalin and an indemnity, Witte staged a bit of theater. Feigning to draft a reply, he suddenly lifted his pen, stared at Komura, and suggested a private conference. Komura agreed at once. The room was cleared except for the six delegates, and four of them sat speechless while the scene played out. What would the Japanese say, asked Witte, to a partition of Sakhalin, the northern half remaining Russian, the southern going to Japan? Komura's brain did some swift calculations while his mouth motored on about Japan's battlefield victories and the expectations of the Japanese people. Then, his thinking done, he said a partition was possible, but inasmuch as Japan would be *restoring* half of the island to Russia, it would expect some payment in return. Witte asked how large. Komura answered 1.2 billion yen—the exact sum the war had cost Japan! Witte smiled inwardly. He had exposed the Japanese demand for Sakhalin as a fraud. They did not care about just claims to territory, or rights of conquest, or national pride: they cared only for money and were ready to resume the bloodshed for money alone. Roosevelt also saw at once that a payment for northern Sakhalin was nothing but a disguised indemnity.

St. Petersburg, of course, rejected this compromise and threatened to call Witte home. Then Roosevelt insinuated himself, instructing his ambassador to appeal to the Tsar to show *some* movement and save the conference. The Tsar agreed to part with southern Sakhalin, but he would not pay a ruble. Now the pressure weighed on Tokyo, where Witte's trap had its ultimate effect. The Katsura cabinet faced a choice of backing down or prolonging the war for cash alone. The cabinet and *genrō* deliberated all the next day, August 28. To drop the indemnity meant absorbing the entire cost of the war, which had vastly increased the national debt. But to bust up the peace conference and resume fighting would only plunge Japan deeper in debt. Finally, at the Imperial Palace, the cabinet admitted defeat. Its only face-saving instruction to Komura was to demand Sakhalin first, and if refused, to ask Roosevelt secretly to *request* Japan, in the interest of world peace, to make concessions. Witte's jujitsu had worked.

The Japanese delegates wept when they read their new instructions. But Komura dutifully obeyed, accepting half of Sakhalin and forgoing any indemnity. So it was peace after all, albeit a peace that left no one happy but Witte. When the Governor of New Hampshire threw a grand farewell party celebrating the Treaty of Portsmouth, the Japanese stayed in their quarters, packing their bags.

The Russian public heralded this end to half of their national agony. The other half, the Revolution of 1905, subsided only when the Tsar promised reforms that Witte and Peter Stolypin would fashion. Still, the patriotic press denounced the Treaty of Portsmouth as a sellout. The *Slovo* pledged "undying resentment against the regime that brought Russia so low." Other Russians at court blamed Witte for losing the peace and hinted that he had Jewish blood. But the greatest storms blew over Japan. "We are ashamed to report this," wrote one Osaka paper, and over a picture of a weeping skeleton begged the Emperor to reject the Treaty of Portsmouth. The Japanese also blamed Roosevelt. Mobs raged through the cities, attacked Japanese Christians, burned thirteen churches, and stoned the entourage of the visiting E. H. Harriman. Alice Roosevelt, the President's daughter, and George Kennan were both in Japan and did their best to downplay the anti-Americanism. But the change of mood was obvious.

Katsura nonetheless got the treaty ratified, thanks to that political deal struck a year before. Opposition leader Saionji kept his bargain, and when the Emperor gave his own imprimatur and issued an edict to silence the press, debate over the treaty ceased. Katsura then resigned the prime ministry in favor of Saionji.

Everything Witte predicted came about almost at once. The now harmless Russians enticed Japan with secret offers to partition Manchuria, the Japanese blamed the cynical Yankees for cheating them of the fruits of victory, and America's own unruly province, California, returned their hostility in kind. Such was the logic of the North Pacific triangle.

The Ninth 'aka iki

Seward: So you *were* a peacemaker, Count Witte, a great one.

Witte: Yes, but greatness is wasted in the service of littleness. The "Li Hung-chang" of the Romanovs: ho!

Seward: Were you grateful to America for helping you get out of the war?

Witte: One may be grateful to people, but not nations. Besides, you nearly poisoned us at Portsmouth with your platters of cold cuts and such! Yecch. You Americans prepare everything in advance, then put it away in the cooler for days. Very unhealthy. I warned Komura not to eat the shellfish, but he gorged himself daily at the buffet tables. And do you know? On the conference's last day he fell sick. I think that was why the Japanese missed the closing ceremonies! Americans eat anything so long as it's covered with seasoning and condiments. Nor did I like your President Roosevelt so well as I hoped. He behaved like a businessman on holiday, and I thought him quite "ignorant of international politics." He thought *our* conditions were blocking agreement and seemed not to appreciate the threat Japan had become.

Saitō: Perhaps the oysters weren't fresh, or did they feed you "Navy chow"?

Witte: Only good meals I had in America were on Mr. J. P. Morgan's yacht.

Saitō: So we can agree that Americans are uncivilized.

Witte: And grasping. Do you know what Morgan named his yacht? The *Corsair!* Only an American banker could get away with being so candid. I saw him in order to raise money for Russia. He was my liaison to the *quartier juif.* Americans uncivilized? Not completely. I visited Columbia University and was much impressed with its discipline. I asked if American students rioted like Russian students, and the professors said, "Should any student attempt to devote himself at the university to other activities than study, he would be immediately cast out of the school by his own comrades!"

Saitō: So it is with our students. We Japanese were right to copy America's educational system.

Witte: But I did not try to make friends with Americans. I knew they would clash with Japan on their own. I went to make friends with Komura.

Seward: Tell us what became of your reform movement after the Revolution of 1905.

Witte: I gave Russia its first constitution, and representative government, and first Bill of Rights! And Stolypin gave land to peasants.

Seward: So you *did* recover, and reform *was* possible?

Witte: Russia made a show of recovering. Russians always make shows—Potemkin villages, if you'll pardon the pun.

Seward: The pun being . . . ?

Scholar: Potemkin villages were model communities allegedly built by Potemkin to fool his lover, Catherine the Great, into thinking him a great administrator. The pun, I assume, refers to the fact that the battleship *Potemkin* staged the biggest mutiny of the Revolution of 1905.

Witte: Russian reforms all turn into Potemkin villages, sooner or later.

Kaahumanu: So what did happen to the reform movement?

Witte: Nicholas betrayed my constitution as soon as he could. The Duma, the parliament, was emasculated. And in 1911 Stolypin was shot. I never liked him much anyway. But then, no one liked me either. I, who industrialized Russia, founded the gold ruble, built the Trans-Siberian Railway, befriended China! Oh, the Tsar made me a count—he had to pretend that Russia had triumphed at Portsmouth—but he hated doing it. And those dogs in St. Petersburg, the ones with titles and the ear of the Tsar, were afraid. While I was at Portsmouth, they whispered—I know this for a fact—that I secretly sympathized with the revolution, that I wanted to be president of a Russian Republic, that I was too close to the Jews. "He must not be allowed to increase his popularity." That was their fear. . . . Do you know that the Jews still loved Russia, those in America? I saw them in New York, and again in Boston, at the railroad station, there were crowds of people of the Jewish type. Roosevelt's guards would not let me out of the car, but on the platform I spoke with some immigrants from Russia. They said they were free in America and could earn a living, but they missed their motherland, where the bones of their ancestors lay. "We do not love the Russian regime," they told me, "but we love Russia above all else." Those Jews promised to pray for our mission, and shouted "hurrah!" when we left, while my own government half-wished for my failure. My dream was to make Manchuria a new California, and Vladivostok a new San Francisco. We came to the Pacific with a cross in one hand—like Father Serra—and a theodolite in the other hand, to survey railroads. But the Tsar insisted we carry a sword. Russia has only two hands.

Scholar: But when the U.S. took its California, there was no "Japan" sitting one hundred miles offshore to contest the acquisition.

Seward: I still don't grasp why your reforms failed. Surely the Tsar understood that constitutional monarchy and prosperous farmers strengthened his country?

Witte: But they did not strengthen the *Tsar.* Once reforms were allowed, where would they stop? The liberal nobility wanted a parliament like England's, radical parties wanted to abolish monarchy and church, *soviets*—the workers' and soldiers' councils in 1905— wanted local self-government, Poles and Finns wanted independence. The Tsar himself would become expendable once politicians learned to govern without him. I thought my reforms would *save* the dynasty, but the imperial court saw reforms as a sop until autocracy could be reimposed. Perhaps Durnovo was right—a friend of mine, head of the Tsar's secret police. He thought autocracy was the only way for Russia, *providing* Russia remained at peace. Instead, the

Tsar engaged in his greatest folly of all, in 1914. You know that the
Great War—

Scholar: World War I.

Witte: —was an outgrowth of the Russo-Japanese War?

Kaahumanu: Then your "great powers" were not done with their
wars in my ocean?

Scholar: Well, World War I wasn't fought there, but it was sparked by
Pacific events. The balance of power in northeast Asia was the hinge
of world politics.

Saitō: Of course it was—that's where Japan is!

Scholar: Funny man. But in fact it was because *Russia* was there.

Kaahumanu: You will explain.

Scholar: I'll try. You see, Russia was a continental giant with one foot
in Asia and the other in Europe. It was a link between the old European balance of power and the emerging Pacific balance of power. So
long as the tsars sought to expand into the Balkans or Ottoman
Empire, Russia was a threat to the European balance. Bismarck's
nightmare was that Russia and France might join forces to encircle
Germany, and that "some damned fool thing in the Balkans" would
ignite general war. That was why he made alliances with the Aus-
trian Empire, Italy, and Romania, and tried to stay on good terms
with Russia itself. Of course, Wilhelm II let Bismarck go. Imperialism
was reaching its peak, and he thought navies and colonies more
important than old conflicts in Europe. But the 1890s were also the
years when Alexander III summoned Witte to St. Petersburg,
launched a crash program of industrialization, and made his alliance
with France. Now, Russia already dwarfed the other European states
in size and population. Imagine if Russia also acquired modern technology! It would become a superpower as threatening to Germany as
Germany was to France. But here is where Asia comes in. So long as
Russia was obsessed with Siberia and China, then the pressure was
off Germany and the Kaiser was free to challenge the British Empire
of his cousin Edward VII. But the Japanese spoiled everything by
blocking the Russian advance. So after 1905 the Russian Foreign Ministry faced a nasty choice: give up assertive policies altogether, which

in this heyday of imperialism was a sure sign of decadence; or turn *back to the Balkans* as a zone for expansion. And that placed Russia and her ally France on a collision course with Austria and her ally Germany. And to make matters worse, the British decided to encourage Russia because of their growing fear of Germany. So in a way Saitō is right: the rise of Japan was as disturbing to the structure of world politics as the rise of Germany.

Seward: How about the rise of China?

Saitō: Ha, ha. What rise?

Seward: I mean the *uprising*, the Boxer Rebellion. Until 1900 Witte's peaceful policy functioned fine—just what I would have done. But the Boxer revolt is what gave Russia the excuse to grab Manchuria, thus sparking the conflict with Japan. What ever happened to the Boxers anyway, after the siege of Peking?

Scholar: The Dowager disowned them and they melted back into that fertile mulch where secret societies take seed. And then the Ch'ing government lurched from xenophobia to the other extreme, pandering to the foreign legations and adopting Western reforms. Many Chinese students went abroad after 1901, and returned, predictably, full of Western theory and bent on overthrowing the dynasty. But the Russo-Japanese War also convinced Chinese, conservative or radical, that the Western imperialists were not invincible and might someday be driven from Asia.

Kaahumanu: Count Witte, do you bear no ill will toward the Japanese?

Witte: I do not, lady, though their sneak attack was abominable. I blame the Tsar and his cursed courtiers, and the mystics who convinced them they could fight Japanese bullets with the crosses of priests. They were fools, and the Tsar was their toy. When he blundered, ill-prepared, into war he thought he was trusting in God—

Serra: When in fact he was tempting Him.

Witte: I do have *one* sublime memory of the United States. It happened at an Anglican church. Our Orthodox priest had come up from New York, and clergy from many churches, and we gave thanks for peace. Never did I pray with more fire than at that moment. We seemed to have realized the unity of all Christians. And the hymn they played! It was the tsarist Russian anthem, but with English words. I cried like a penitent . . . "God the Omnipotent. . . ."

Seward:

God the Omnipotent! King who ordainest
Thunder thy clarion, and lightning thy sword;
Show forth thy pity on high where thou reignest
Give to us peace in our time, O Lord.

God the All-righteous One! man hath defied thee;
Yet to eternity standeth thy word;
Falsehood and wrong shall not tarry beside thee;
Give to us peace in our time, O Lord. . . .

There are several verses—

Witte: We all cried like penitents. . . . Could it really have been at Sarov, at the monastery, that the Tsar decided to sack me? No, Kaahumanu, I forgive the Japanese. But the Russians! Do you know what Durnovo said at the Tsar's coronation? "Mark my words, Nicholas II will prove a modernized version of Paul I."

Seward: Meaning?

Witte: "Mad Paul"—he allowed Napoleon to talk him into invading British India while the French dominated Europe. The parallel is exact, Kaiser Wilhelm playing the role of Napoleon. Only Nicholas got to act out his madness; Paul was assassinated. "That Witte is a hypnotist!" the Tsar said—like my cousin Blavatsky. But it was *there,* in the Winter Palace, that her spirit danced!

Serra: Can you blame the Tsar for doing no more than the other powers were doing? Did you expect Russia alone to show restraint?

Scholar: Yes, Father Serra, he did, and it had nothing to do with religion. You see, Russia was already a great land power. No one could prevent her from absorbing the Eurasian heartland, and no one expected to. But as soon as Russia bid for sea power as well, or tried to use land power to frustrate the sea powers, as in China, then Russia overstepped her bounds. Same with Germany. She had the great-

est military in Europe and the most advanced industry. That was
scary enough, especially to France. But when the Kaiser decreed that
Germany be a great sea power also, he frightened the British in the
same way that Russia frightened Japan. Call it unfair if you choose,
but Russia and Germany were *not* permitted to be as brazen and irresponsible in their imperialism, and when they were anyway, they
paid a terrible price. Let me put it another way. Thanks to its fortunate geography, the U.S. could seize Panama in an unabashed power
play without causing even a local stir. Thus the Panama coup was *not*
an irresponsible act. But for Russia to seize Manchuria or Korea *was* a
flagrant abuse of power. As I said, it may not be fair, but it's a geopolitical fact.

Saitō: And it is more important for a statesman to be factual than
fair—*which also explains* why I have no stomach for American moralism. I accept your seizure of Panama on power-political grounds. I cannot accept it on the "progressive" grounds you invent to comfort
yourselves.

Seward: As usual, Ambassador, you are right for the wrong reason.
Yes, the statesman must be a slave to the facts, but his reason must
serve something higher than facts. "Factually" speaking, the Southern senators were right about slavery. The Constitution did *not* forbid
it, nor did the federal government have the right to destroy it. But we
are called to serve truth, not facts. Roosevelt was justified in Panama
not just because he could "get away with it"—sorry, Professor—but
because his motives were higher than mere selfish interest.

Saitō: Oy, vay! as they say in Flatbush.

Scholar: Seward, surely *you're* not saying that ends justify means?

Seward: I am *suggesting* that when a nation is an instrument of Providence, means are made available. Japan, too, may be God's instrument; I do not rule it out.

Witte: But Russia, the Christ among nations, is not?

Scholar: I believe Poland is known as the "Christ among nations,"
Count Witte—

Witte: —which makes Russia Pontius Pilate? I know what you Americans really think of Russians. I felt your contempt at Portsmouth.

Seward: A low blow, Witte, against the nation that helped you out of a suicidal war. If you don't blame Japan for your debacle, how can you blame the U.S.?

Witte: What a vain man you are to think that all credit *or* all blame must always fall on America. You know whom I blame, I have said it enough.

Serra: You blame Russians.

Witte: I blame Russians.

Serra: Then perhaps you are as vain as Seward, Count Witte?

Witte: And you, Roman, for saying so.

Kaahumanu: Your vanities angered me. Now they just bore me. I will talk to Saitō.

Saitō: The lady wants to talk to *me!* "Meet me at the corner, in a half an hour. Meet me at the corner, in a half an hoooouur!" What kin I do fer ya, Sugar?

Kaahumanu: I want to know what is a "Marconi device." The historian said you put them on your ships, and they helped to win the battle.

Saitō: Ah, so. You want to buy good *Japanese* radio. Helps you win battles. And if so, then I'd say it was time we were leavin' the age of steam and rails.

III

Internal Combustion

The Tenth 'aha iki

Serra: With what will our dismal doctor follow his age of steam and rails? Do we dare hope for an age of charity, or just peace and quiet?

Scholar: Ah, sweet irony. You know, it's just about dead in my day.

Serra: Then so must paradox be dead, and if paradox, then truth.

Kaahumanu: What is the priest saying?

Witte: That irony is our only weapon against the idiocy of life.

Scholar: You're all too deep for me. I was just going to call the next age "internal combustion."

Saitō: Of course! Automobiles, airplanes, submarines.

Scholar: Yes, but internal combustion is also a metaphor for the racial explosions to come in the North Pacific.

Witte: I would think the Russo-Japanese War already qualifies.

Scholar: Yes, it was a racial war of sorts. But it was primarily an old-fashioned strategic war fought between governments. What I mean by internal combustion is racial conflict *within* societies, like California and Hawaii.

Saitō: Nothing new there either. Anti-Chinese agitation began in the 1870s.

Scholar: All right! No historical periodization is exact. But at least with technology I have a date to cling to . . . to which to cling. . . .

Saitō: Get on with it.

Scholar: 1903: Kitty Hawk, North Carolina, and the dawn of powered flight. And just a few months later—bet you don't know *this*, Saitō— the meaning of the new age was guessed in the halls of the Royal Geographical Society. Halford Mackinder had delivered a speech propounding his geopolitical theory to the effect that the heartland of Eurasia was "the pivot of history." He who controls the heartland must eventually control the entire "world island" of Eurasia, and he who controls the world island must eventually control the world. What he had in mind, of course, was the completion of the Trans-Siberian Railway. Mackinder believed that railroads and telegraphs made it possible for Russia to mobilize its continental resources and successfully challenge "island powers" like Britain or the U.S. Thus, Mackinder contradicted Captain Mahan and the navalists who thought sea power was always decisive.

Saitō: But Japan's victory proved Mackinder wrong.

Scholar: Not really. Russia's temporary loss only meant that the veracity of his theory would not yet be *tested.* But that's not my point. After Mackinder finished his lecture, a member of the Society, Amery by name, rose to dispute him. "Both the sea and the railway," he said, "are going in the future to be supplemented by the air as a means of locomotion, and when we come to that . . . a great deal of this geographical distribution must lose its importance."

Kaahumanu: The air? You mean flight, like the birds?

Scholar: I mean flight like the birds—by means of internal combustion.

Kaahumanu: Then feathers must lose their magic. . . .

Scholar: . . . and your exquisite feathered cloaks become dusty curiosities in Hawaiian museums. Of course, human flight dated back to the first hot air balloon ascensions in France in the 1780s, and its strategic implications were not hard to imagine. Remember that first Japanese embassy to the United States—the seventy-seven samurai who arrived in 1860? The most astounding thing they witnessed was a balloon demonstration in Philadelphia's Fairmount Park. As the Japanese bent their necks backward and gaped at the spectacle, a proud member of the ground crew told them that before long balloons equipped with steam power would be built, and Americans would be able to fly across the Pacific in six days. We do not know the private thoughts of the samurai, or the officials to whom they reported. But we know that by 1911, just eight years after Kitty Hawk, a visitor commented on the obsessive interest the *Japanese* showed in aviation. School children were taught the principles of aerodynamics and great crowds turned out for demonstrations even of model aeroplanes. The visitor, by the way, was a young Signal Corps officer named Billy Mitchell.

Saitō: Internal combustion, Professor?

Scholar: Yes, thank you. What made powered flight possible was not the attachment of steam engines to balloons, of course, but an entirely new method of energy conversion. By 1876 the development of petroleum and electricity, and the refinement of machine tooling, enabled the Germans Nikolaus Otto and Rudolf Diesel to design engines in which gasoline could be shot into a cylinder and ignited. The expansion of the exploding gases could then drive the piston. Gone were the tons of water and coal needed to fuel a steam engine. As gasoline engines improved (leading to the first automobiles), daring aviators were experimenting with gliders and learning aerodynamics. The Wright brothers' genius was to marry the technologies. They designed wings with greater lift, rudders and elevators for three-dimensional control, propellers to maximize the movement of air over the wings, and an engine both light and powerful enough to get pilot and machine into the air.

Powered flight meant that even remote regions of the earth might become accessible within a matter of days, if not hours. As steamships freed travelers from winds and currents, aeroplanes freed them from the ocean itself. As steamships placed a premium on bases and coaling stations along the world's sea lanes, aeroplanes placed a premium on islands that might serve as airstrips. Aeroplanes also collapsed the time envelope in the Pacific by another order of magnitude. As aviation matured during the first four decades of the twentieth century, the North Pacific, once the widest moat on earth, became a two-way invasion route by which Japan or the U.S. might project deadly force over thousands of miles.

That alone was enough to stoke paranoia. But at the same time that technology was shrinking the Pacific, so, too, was the more leisurely movement of people. Back in 1776, when Captain Cook appeared in those waters, Japan and China were closed and white people in the North Pacific consisted of a few hundred Russians and Spaniards. Let us review the matter again circa 1910. By then California contained 2,378,000 people (an increase of 60 percent in just one decade), Oregon 673,000 (a 62 percent increase since 1900), Washington 1,142,000, and British Columbia 392,000 (a 120 percent rise in both cases). The Alaskan population—including a raw estimate of the arctic peoples—totaled 64,000. The overwhelming majority of these 4,650,000 residents were white. The Mexican population of California remained small and invisible. Chinese Californians, banned from adding to their numbers through immigration, totaled just 36,248 in 1910, or 1.5 percent of the population. Another 10,000 Chinese lived in the Pacific Northwest. Japanese immigration, on the other hand, had boomed. But the 41,356 Japanese in California likewise made up a mere 1.7 percent of the state.

And yet, many white Pacific residents felt increasingly threatened at the dawn of the twentieth century. Some 30,000 of the Chinese, for instance, were concentrated in San Francisco, population 417,000, while Japanese numbers were growing by as much as ten thousand per year. Hawaii provided an example of what might happen on the West Coast itself. In 1910 the islands contained 192,000 people (an increase of 25 percent over the decade), of whom 80,000, or 42 percent, were Japanese. And on beyond lay the rookeries of Asia, free at last to export their excess labor around the Pacific Rim. Japan, as we know, exhibited the demographic boom that always accompanies industrialization, and tens of thousands of Japanese emigrated to Korea, Manchuria, Taiwan, Hawaii, and California. But as Japanese looked toward the Asian mainland they saw another swarm of *whites* heading toward them. Russian military power may have been blunted, but Russian settlers continued to come in waves until eastern Siberia counted 2.8 million people in 1910. And just as the advance guard of Asians frightened Americans, so the Siberian trends frightened Japanese. After all, the Russian Empire held 167 million people, and the Chinese Empire perhaps 345 million. Should those populations begin to move toward Manchuria, Japan would face a threat to its Pacific zone of control greater than that which panicky Americans imagined coming at them from Japan.

Political trends were equally unsettling. For Japan's defeat of Russia, and U.S. mediation of the peace, demonstrated how much a political triangle the North Pacific had become. Triangles in love or politics are inherently unstable, and this one was made more so by the overlapping security requirements of the six "geopolitical stakes" in the region. To secure Siberia, Russia needed Manchuria; to secure itself, Japan needed Korea, Manchuria, and control of the western Pacific; to secure its West Coast the U.S. needed Alaska and Hawaii; to secure them it needed the western Pacific; and so on. The once empty North Pacific was a volatile mix within a container that technology was making less roomy.

Witte: Like an internal combustion engine.

Saitō: Let us say, rather, that the fields of demography and power politics were as shifting and capricious as the geologic fault lines ringing the ocean.

Scholar: Excellent, Saitō-san! Clearly earthquakes are never far from the mind of a Japanese. And it so happened that the first explosion of racial antipathy between Americans and Japanese was occasioned by that original, elemental form of internal combustion: the one that reduced San Francisco to ashes just eight months after the Russo-Japanese War.

San Francisco 1906

ROFESSOR OMORI OF Tokyo Imperial University knew something extraordinary was building up across the ocean. He had been watching his excellent Milne seismograph, designed by three British *yatoi* in the 1880s, and had detected what seemed to be foreshocks along the San Andreas Fault. But he could not predict where the epicenter of an earthquake might be, and besides, to panic an entire population on the basis of rudimentary data was unthinkable. Still, he must have wondered whether San Francisco had its own Milne device when the jagged line on his seismograph suddenly jumped off the scale.

The entire Pacific Rim is an arc of fractures in the earth's crust running from the South American Andes north to the coast of Alaska, then down the western side of the ocean through Japan. Modern scientists estimate that 80 percent of all the seismic energy worldwide originates in this Pacific belt. The San Andreas fault, comprising the boundary between the North American and eastern Pacific tectonic plates, is not the sort of vertical fault that pushes up mountain ranges. It is a strike-slip fault along which plates scrape against each other on a *horizontal* axis until the earth's tortured skin gives in to the mounting pressure. Where it traverses dry land, for some 650 miles from the vicinity of Los Angeles to a point just south of San Francisco, the San Andreas is not always evident. It might hide beneath a friendly reservoir of cool water, or foliage rooted in soil strewn by wind and erosion. But it is always there—and at 5:13 A.M., Wednesday, April 18, 1906, all of California lying *west* of the fault abruptly shifted sixteen feet to the north.

The 1906 temblor is judged to have measured about 8.25 on the scale invented by Charles F. Richter in the 1930s. It lasted an interminable forty-five seconds, building from a dull to an overpowering roar, and left behind cracks in the earth twenty feet wide. A merchant captain thought his ship had run aground when the shock wave struck his steamer. On land, buildings and bridges collapsed, locomotives toppled over, and captive waters gushed free along a zone stretching from the wine country of Sonoma (where the Russian Fort Ross was wrecked) through Marin County and down the peninsula to Stanford (where university buildings crumbled and statues fell to the ground), and on to San Jose, Monterey, and Santa Cruz (where the beach sank ten feet), and finally to San Juan Bautista (where the Spanish mission was ruined by this "act of God"). Smack in the middle was San Francisco, where a third of all Californians lived in closely packed structures perched on steep hills or the crumbly landfill engineered so proudly by the first generation of Yankees. Almost every chimney or tower crumbled and fell. Second or third stories descended on the first. Grand hotels buckled and heaved; flophouses disintegrated. Chinese, Italians, Irish, and Anglos ran shrieking into the streets in their nightgowns or less, women clutched rosaries and children, sailors and roughnecks hurled half-remembered prayers at the skies, crazed old men proclaimed the end of the world. Dozens took mortal wounds at once, as did Dennis Sullivan when the California Hotel's gimcrack cupola toppled and fell through the roof of the firehouse on Bush Street, leaving him comatose until his death four days later. Sullivan was the Fire Chief, and by the time the aftershocks died at 5:25 A.M., the fires already blazed out of control.

This may have been the 418th earthquake recorded in 'Frisco since 1848. But none even a fraction of its magnitude had struck since the city was rigged for gas heating and light. Broken mains and the odd stove or lamp ignited scores of minor fires and over a dozen major ones, mostly among tenements and warehouses south of Market Street. Within minutes the sky looking south from downtown or the hills was a blaze of orange, touching off the usual range of human reactions. Some people panicked, some looted, some fled. Many spontaneously formed up to rescue the injured, evacuate buildings, and combat the flames. Only, there was no water to be had: the water mains had burst in the earthquake, rendering the reservoirs carefully husbanded in the city and San Mateo utterly, pitifully useless. Firemen cursed as they opened dry hydrants and wept as their firehouses went up in flames. The man who inherited the disaster, sixty-nine-year-old Acting Fire Chief John Dougherty, did his damnedest, ordering residents to tap into any source of moisture, including the sewers. But south of Market was doomed; the fires grew, merged, and generated enough heat to ignite the Financial District to the north and the Mission District to the west. Dougherty gave up trying to extinguish the blaze and concentrated instead on containing it. That meant blowing up whole city blocks to form fire breaks, and that required a massive evacuation effort, not to mention explosives. But telephone lines were down, and the streets were gorged with refugees. How could a citywide plan be executed?

The same question had already occurred to Brig. Gen. Frederick Funston, the commander of the garrison at the old Spanish Presidio. He was a 120-pound redheaded cliché—hot-tempered and hyperactive—and by his age of forty had already worked as a daredevil journalist, surveyed Death Valley, explored Alaska, planted coffee in Central America, commanded the Cuban artillery in the rebellion against Spain, and led a Kansas regiment in the war in the Philippines. It was he who had captured Aguinaldo, for which he won the Medal of Honor. When Funston awoke to the earthquake in his home on Nob Hill, he tried the telephone—nothing. He tried to hail a motorcar—the few he encountered refused to stop. He rushed downtown—the crowds of refugees forced him back. He asked about the fires—and learned there was no water. So on his own authority he grabbed a policeman and shouted: find the Mayor and tell him that every available soldier will be turned out to help in the rescue effort, prevent looting, and fight the fire. Back at the Presidio, two lieutenants bore Funston's orders to the colonel in charge. He rejected his general's order with an oath. "You two damned fools go back and tell that newspaperman that he had better look up his Army Regulations and there he will find that nobody but the President of the United States in person can order regular troops into a city!" The lieutenants retreated in confusion, until the bugler happened by, whereupon they ordered him to call out the garrison and, defying the colonel, marched 350 troopers downtown.

They were not enough, of course. But Funston's declaration of martial law (Gen. Philip Sheridan had done the same during the Chicago Fire of 1871) allowed him to reinforce the police and fire departments, combat panic and looting, and set up shelters in the safe reaches of Golden Gate Park. The corrupt Mayor, Eugene Schmitz, whined and hedged but accepted the Army's help. He also issued a "shoot to kill" order concerning looters, wired the Navy on Mare Island "EARTHQUAKE. TOWN ON FIRE. SEND MARINES AND TUGS," and pleaded for the Governor and the Mayor of Oakland to send firefighters, medicine, and dynamite. Funston, of course, wired Washington, where Secretary of War Taft promised all possible aid. Then, at 2:20 P.M., the fire reached the telegraph lines, and San Francisco was isolated.

By afternoon the fire had flown westward up Market and Mission streets, moved southward to consume the Southern Pacific terminal, and jumped Market Street into downtown. One by one the landmarks succumbed: the old Post Office, Old St. Patrick's Church, the Opera House where Caruso had sung the night before, Union Square, even the splendid Palace Hotel, built to be earthquake- and fireproof. Funston's engineers began blowing up buildings on broad Montgomery Street—the explosions, he said, made it sound like a battlefield—but failed to stop the blaze. Less professional demolition teams succeeded only in touching off the first fire in tindery Chinatown. The weather, dry, still, and unseasonably warm—"earthquake weather," it would later be called— was no help. Nor was the influx of people from across the Bay, come by ferry to find relatives or just gawk at the spectacle. Funston ordered the ferries shut down. Henceforth, no person could enter San Francisco without written approval of the Army or Mayor.

By Thursday morning, two hundred thousand people had lost or left their homes—ten times the number Funston first estimated he would have to feed. And still the fire spread, up California Street into the most exclusive quarter of the city, and into Chinatown, the most despised. Nob Hill (so named because the nabobs lived there) sported the $5 million Fairmont Hotel and the homes of Stanford, Huntington, and Crocker, filled with priceless art. Surely these fireproof brownstone mansions would resist the fire—and so they did, for hours—until their walls grew so hot that the furnishings within burst into flame. Chinatown was mere kindling, and its destruction brought a new horror on that second day. As the fire advanced, great rats emerged from their subterranean nests and tunnels and fled in waves into neighboring districts, stopping only to feed off the odd human corpse.

Funston ordered a strategic retreat. The loss of Nob Hill and Chinatown meant that North Beach was indefensible, and indeed all the neighborhoods east of broad Van Ness Avenue save perhaps Russian and Telegraph hills. In the south, the Mission District also appeared doomed, but there, too, a line might be drawn along Dolores Avenue— the site of the mission where San Francisco was founded in 1776. So Funston ordered evacuations and a furious campaign of dynamiting along Van Ness in hopes of saving the Western Addition beyond it. Meanwhile, the two hundred thousand refugees in Golden Gate Park, and another thirty-five thousand on the Presidio Golf Course, waited for whatever rations, tents, or latrines the Army and civilian volunteers could provide. The Mayor ordered all grocery stores subject to requisition, but even so the head of the food committee, Rabbi Voorsanger, had an empty larder more often than not. "FOR GOD'S SAKE SEND COOKED FOOD TO SAN FRANCISCO," wired the Governor to California cities—and they did, but never soon enough.

The battles of Van Ness and Mission Dolores seemed fought and won by Thursday evening, after a furious series of counterattacks. The fire jumped Van Ness in several spots, but the Army and firemen concentrated their dear reserves of water behind these fronts and managed to contain the breakthroughs. When flames appeared in the steeple of St. Mary's Cathedral, far above the range of hoses, two priests climbed the belfry with blankets and axes to suffocate or cut away the burning rafters. But Funston's sense of relief was premature: the fire swept down from another angle and jumped Van Ness again. The isolated and fire-proof mansion of Hawaiian sugar king Klaus Spreckels went up in flames (some suspected arson on the part of his enemies). This time old Acting Chief Dougherty, with what one reporter called Homeric hero-ism, tongue-lashed his exhausted men into training their sickly streams one last time into the flames, and saved the Western Addition.

Meanwhile, the fire had to be left to its own devices in the northeast corner of the city where the Italians of North Beach fought desperately for their homes and businesses. But on Friday the heat sucked in a gale-force wind from the northwest. It drove the flames back from Van Ness but also blew them with irresistible force to the waterfront warehouses and up Telegraph Hill. Mayor Schmitz wired the White House via the East Bay, promising to "RESTORE TO THE NATION ITS CHIEF PORT ON THE PACIFIC." But by Friday afternoon much of the Embarcadero and all of North Beach were gone. Only hose teams operating from the Bay itself were able to stop the fires before they reached the water's edge. By sunrise on Saturday, the fires finally ran out of fuel. It was over—and the refugees, both rich and poor, stood and stooped, and tried to find shelter from the mocking rain that now began to fall.

San Francisco in 1906 was a city of Mediterranean charms unlike any other in North America. Still free of skyscrapers, freeways or bridges, it presented the new arrival by sea with profuse vistas of pastel hills and vertical Victorian homes. To those who arrived by rail at the Southern Pacific terminal, it seemed a tawdry city of tenements, filthy docks, and bleak warehouses squatting in the morbid fog. It was a city of odors: of sea and fish and marine fuel, rotting vegetation behind street markets, and slaughterhouses; but also of tempting foods from the cookpots of half a dozen ethnic kitchens, flowering shrubs, and sweet, dank breezes from beyond the Golden Gate. It was a city of culture proud of its opera, art institute, and universities at Berkeley, Stanford, and Santa Clara. It was a city of churches, Roman Catholic especially, once the influx of Irish, Italians, and Germans overcame the Yankee bias against popery. It was a city of license, dubbed the Barbary Coast or Paris of the Pacific. In San Francisco a "French restaurant" meant one with a brothel upstairs, and Chinatown offered opium, gambling, and peep shows to whites clustered, for safety's sake, in tour groups. "Two-bittee lookee, flo-bittee feelee, six-bittee doee," cried the pimps. Preachers back east called it Sodom and Gomorrah, and regularly predicted its doom.

Above all, San Francisco was a city divided, a city that might otherwise have seemed the best laboratory in which to conduct a melting-pot experiment. Immigrants and children of immigrants were 75 percent of the population, with Irish and Germans about a quarter each. Ethnic neighborhoods were strictly segregated, and indeed, the first social product of the earthquake was a riot when fleeing Italians and Chinese collided with each other beneath Telegraph Hill. Class divisions were equally strict, with the "old money" perched atop Nob Hill and Pacific Heights. Bitter strikes racked the city around the turn of the century, and labor strife in turn permitted political bosses like Abraham Ruef to mobilize resentment of capitalist power and cheap Asian labor. His Union Labor party swept Schmitz into City Hall from 1901 to 1907, during which time Ruef and Schmitz conspired to keep peace on the labor front, while garnering a fortune in graft from city utilities.

Even the bluebloods knew division before 1906, when Stanford and Huntington fell to feuding. The latter had done most of the work to maintain their railroad empire, yet Stanford seemed to reap the glory, maneuvering himself into a U.S. Senate seat in 1885. Huntington assumed the presidency of the Southern Pacific and exposed his erstwhile friend's history of influence peddling. Stanford turned haggard and died in 1893. Huntington then returned to his own practices with a brazen scheme to escape having to pay back the federal loans issued to build the Central Pacific! Some $50 million were due in 1899, but Huntington promoted a bill in Congress to defer payment for another half-century. This time a united front, led by crusading young publisher William Randolph Hearst, rose up to protest. Huntington lost the crucial vote and was obliged to reimburse the American people by 1909. In the following year, the Progressive "Roosevelt League" of the Republican party won the state house and finally broke the Southern Pacific's stranglehold on local government.

A city of divisions—but now much of the city was gone. The earthquake and fire destroyed over five hundred blocks and twenty-eight thousand buildings at a cost of $450 million dollars and 452 lives. The survivors determined to rebuild, of course, and received a flood of offers for support from all over the United States and foreign countries as well. One offer came from Japan. But President Roosevelt refused it politely, as he did all offers of help from abroad. The San Franciscans then added injury to insult as they debated what to do, in the course of rebuilding, with the thirty thousand Asians in their midst.

The city's whites, especially the poorer ones, never had much use for Chinatown. It was a magnet for coolie labor and a noisome sink of filth and crime. In 1900 the bubonic plague turned up there, hence the fear of rats. In 1905, after Congress renewed the ban on Chinese immigration, Peking returned the rancor by sponsoring a boycott against American

goods in China. Now, in 1906, the destruction of Chinatown provided a
chance to do something about the Yellow Peril. Civic leaders planned to
relocate Chinatown somewhere south of Market. But the Chinese, like
everyone else, streamed back to their old neighborhood. At the very
least, thought the city fathers, a new school system might be designed
to segregate Asians from whites. So in October 1906 the school board
voted to establish an Oriental school that all Chinese, Koreans, and
Japanese must attend.

Now, there were not many Japanese in the city as yet, and only
ninety-three of their children were affected. But Japanese, unlike Chinese, were not officially designated as undesirables, their government
back home had won diplomatic equality with the white powers, and just
the year before Japan had vanquished the Russian Empire. Not surprisingly, Japanese refused to countenance this racial insult. Tokyo had
promised to restrict immigration to the United States, but that Gentlemen's Agreement had broken down thanks to the annexation of Hawaii.
Residents of the islands had every right to emigrate to the mainland,
and tens of thousands of Japanese did so. In February 1905, Michael
Harry deYoung's *San Francisco Chronicle* blew wind into the sails of a
Japanese Exclusion League, warning of the danger of "hordes" of
"immoral, intemperate, quarrelsome" Japanese overrunning the West
Coast. Japan's spectacular victories in war only frightened Californians
the more. Then, in July 1906, American agents fought a shooting war in
the Bering Sea against Japanese poachers who skinned seals alive and
left them in agony. When martial law was lifted after the earthquake, a
crime wave swept San Francisco in which Japanese were victimized.
Such was the atmosphere in which Boss Ruef, as one of his last acts,
presided over the school segregation act.

Local Japanese kept their children home and organized to resist.
Ambassador Aoki delivered a bill of grievances to the State Department.
But newspapers in Japan cried out, if necessary, for war. "The whole
world knows that the poorly equipped army and navy of the United
States are no match for our efficient army and navy," boasted the
Mainichi Shimbun. "It will be easy work to awake the United States
from her dream of obstinacy when one of our great Admirals appears on
the other side of the Pacific." That the Japanese were sensitive to racial
slights was well known. "A tenth of the insults visited upon China,"
said Secretary of State Elihu Root, would be enough to provoke hostilities from Japan. But it was inevitable that Japanese immigrants, like
Chinese before them, would meet resistance. The irony was that Hawaiian annexation, done in part to *stave off* a Japanese takeover there, was
the vehicle by which Japanese spilled into California.

Theodore Roosevelt presided over the mess. He knew that his role as honest broker at Portsmouth had soured America's image in Japanese eyes. The last thing he needed was a crisis born of gratuitous racial discrimination. "I am being horribly bothered by this Japanese business," wrote Roosevelt to his son Kermit. "The infernal fools in California . . . insult the Japanese recklessly and in the event of war it will be the Nation as a whole which will pay the consequences." The white Californians, said Roosevelt, were not asserting superiority but in fact making "a confession of inferiority in our civilization." So the crisis devolved into a struggle not between San Francisco and its Asian minority, or even between Tokyo and Washington, but rather between San Francisco and the federal government. When Roosevelt sent Secretary of Commerce and Labor Victor H. Metcalf to investigate, the *San Francisco Chronicle* told the "crawling degenerates" of the East Coast to mind their own business. The *Bulletin* was confident that "Japan is not going to fight about so small a matter unless that nation is spoiling for a fight, right or wrong." And if war came: "It might do them good."

The President's second move was to draft a bully rebuke in his annual message of December 1906. San Francisco's attempt at segregation, he said, was a "wicked absurdity" inasmuch as Americans had "as much to learn from Japan as Japan has to learn from us; and no nation is fit to teach unless it is also willing to learn." San Franciscans howled at this "tin soldier yawp" from "an unpatriotic President who united with aliens to break down the civilization of his own countrymen." And not a few congressmen sympathized: the prospect of federally imposed racial integration terrified Southerners. In February 1907 Mayor Schmitz led a delegation to Washington to put San Francisco's case before Roosevelt. The result of their closed door sessions was a horse trade: repeal of the school board decree in return for U.S. diplomatic action to stem the influx of Japanese.

Then the Californians spoke again. On February 28, 1907, the state legislature passed a law prohibiting Asians from owning land for a period longer than five years (threatening the property of prosperous Japanese farmers and Chinese shopkeepers). In May, white union men busted up a Japanese restaurant in San Francisco, and in June, San Francisco police rejected six Japanese petitions to open employment bureaus. Belligerent editorials appeared again in Japan, and this time Roosevelt barked that "the Japanese Jingoes are in their turn about as bad as ours." By the summer of 1907 even the *New York Times* acknowledged a full-scale war scare, and Roosevelt decided to order sixteen battleships on a "practice cruise" through the Strait of Magellan to the Pacific.

American military ruminations about Pacific defense began the day after Admiral Dewey steamed into Manila Bay. But genuine contingency planning began with this 1907 war scare. There was no question that the United States was the superior economic and naval power (with twenty-one battleships and armored cruisers to Japan's fourteen). But the American ships were stationed in the Atlantic, the Panama Canal would not be ready for years, and the Navy possessed but one inadequate Pacific drydock in Bremerton, Washington. Root's candid analysis was that a determined Japanese attack might overrun the Philippines and Hawaii and reach the West Coast before the United States could respond. Of course, the military was eager for Congress to fund a Pacific base, but the services could not decide where to put it. The Navy liked Subic Bay, in the Philippines, but the Army, citing the fate of Port Arthur, declared it indefensible on the landward flank. The Army favored Manila, but Dewey, citing his own victory in 1898, pronounced it indefensible from the sea. As Roosevelt admitted to Taft, "The Philippines form our heel of Achilles. They are all that makes the present situation with Japan dangerous."

The studies begun in 1907 eventuated in the famous War Plan Orange of 1914, which conceded Japanese strategic control of the western Pacific for at least sixty days after the start of a war. The fond hope was that the Army could hold out on Corregidor in Manila Bay until the Navy arrived. Otherwise, the best the United States could do was to launch a protracted counteroffensive supported from Hawaii, Midway, the Aleutians, and Guam. But no plan would mean anything if the United States did not begin at once to lay a logistical base in the Pacific. So Roosevelt approved the 1907 recommendations to begin fortifying Subic Bay, Guam, and Pearl Harbor, and to build a drydock in San Francisco capable of servicing the new dreadnought-class battleships. The following year the Army-Navy Board resolved the battle over bases: none in the Philippines would do, and Congress instead voted an initial $1.8 million to base the headquarters of Pacific defense at Pearl Harbor.

All this meant that for the time being the United States was helpless in case of war with Japan. How then could it silence the Japanese jingoes and deter their government from rash words or deeds? How else but by the grandest of bluffs, by imitating the Russian fleet's epic voyage, but in advance of hostilities? There had been talk of stationing ships in the Pacific ever since the school board vote, but Mahan feared that sending only a few ships would divide the fleet and send Japan a message of weakness rather than strength. Teddy replied not to worry: he would no more engage in such an "utter folly" than he would "[go] thither in a rowboat myself." He would send the *entire* fleet. The new

Navy needed a shakedown anyway, and a Pacific tour would quiet Californians and deter Japanese. Never was "speak softly and carry a big stick" more crisply applied than in Roosevelt's decision to send the Great White Fleet to the Pacific, then around the world in the year 1908.

It must have been wonderful fun: Teddy Roosevelt and his yacht, *Mayflower*, in the van of a great procession of battleships steaming out of Hampton Roads, then standing at anchor while the Great White Fleet, "Fighting Bob Evans" in command, passed in review! The fleet proceeded without a hitch to the Caribbean, then around South America in a balmy southern February. Its destination was San Francisco, and numerous calls had been heard from the military and the West Coast to leave the fleet there. General Leonard Wood, in the Philippines, even predicted the downfall of the white race in the Far East unless Japan was precipitously smashed. But in the very months when the war scare seemed to be peaking, Secretary Root and Ambassador Aoki were beginning to defuse the crisis. Aoki even suggested that they put to rest *all* the outstanding issues between them, including immigration, the Open Door, security, and the future of China. This was too much for Prime Minister Hayashi, who sacked Aoki lest he appear too weak. But he revived the Gentlemen's Agreement limiting immigration, and in March 1908 Roosevelt ordered the fleet home via the Philippines, Australia, and the Suez Canal. Five days later, Tokyo invited the fleet to visit Japan itself.

"You have in a peculiar sense the honor of the United States in your keeping, and therefore no body of men in the world enjoys at this moment a greater privilege or carries a heavier responsibility." So wired Roosevelt to Admiral Sperry, who had replaced the ailing Evans. The State Department was frantic over the possibility that American sailors would behave badly in Japan, or that Japanese fanatics would create an incident. Moreover, the fleet was scheduled to dock in Melbourne prior to sailing north, and the Australians predictably made much of "white solidarity" against the "yellow peril." But instead, the Great White Fleet's visit to Japan in October 1908 turned a military confrontation into a diplomatic love feast. Discipline held on both sides, the receptions were grand, and Japanese schoolchildren serenaded the Yankees with a phonetically memorized "Star-Spangled Banner." More to the point, within a month of the fleet's departure from Japan Secretary Root and new Ambassador Takahira Kogorō resolved the deeper issues on the very bases proposed the year before by Aoki. Under this Root-Takahira accord both nations pledged to respect the other's Pacific possessions, uphold the Open Door, and peacefully maintain "the independence and integrity of China." A cynical reading of the document would suggest that neither Japan nor the United States believed itself strong enough at the moment to challenge the status quo in the Pacific, and so both accepted it.

That might change, of course, should Russia or China collapse, leaving Japan a free hand in Asia. It might change when the United States completed its two-ocean Navy and Panama Canal. And it might change anytime Californians succumbed again to their fears. In the presidential election of 1908 California Democrats ran on the slogan "Labor's choice Bryan—Jap's choice Taft." Bryan lost, but in 1909 the legislature passed another law forbidding Japanese to own land in California.

Korea 1910

WHY *DID* THE Japanese relent? Why did they, of all people, not demand that Americans accord their emigrants the same rights as newcomers from other white nations? Why did patriotic *genrō* (elder statesmen) like Itō Hirobumi in fact plead that the government do nothing to provoke conflict with the United States?

Remember Itō? He was the constitutional genius of the Meiji Restoration, and although it is farfetched to compare samurai of Chōshū to a Founding Father of Virginia, Itō nonetheless played a role not unlike that of James Madison. To be sure, he was the one who admired the authoritarian constitution of Bismarck's Germany, but like Madison he believed that the principal danger to a new and vulnerable state was the unchecked play of *faction*. Moreover, nothing was more shameful to a Japanese man of courtesy than the public display of discord. So even as Itō abominated the rigid old *bakufu*, so too did he fear that the new regime might fall prey to political parties and interest groups always battling for majorities, denigrating opponents, and forcing their views on the losers. His constitution accordingly provided for a cabinet appointed by and responsible to the Emperor alone, and a bicameral legislature with restricted prerogatives. Such an arrangement, he hoped, might satisfy demands for popular representation while leaving real power in the hands of the Meiji oligarchy dedicated to achieving consensus.

Itō served as Prime Minister three more times after the promulgation of the constitution in 1889 and contributed to the abolition of the "unequal treaties" and the victory over China. But that same decade brought great disappointments. Party politics evolved anyway in the Diet, while factions *within* the oligarchy were increasingly tempted to align themselves with the parties and exploit the partisan press. Itō made one final attempt to dampen the play of faction by founding a broad and inclusive political party in 1900. And indeed his Seiyukai party held a majority in the Diet for two decades. But it did not bring consensus. Within a year new factional strife emerged, and Itō resigned as Prime Minister—the last of the original Meiji men to hold the post. Power then passed to a younger generation of ambitious civil and military officials that did not remember the overthrow of the shogunate and the long struggle for modernity, a generation that knew only victory, that looked only to the future, and was quick to exploit any perceived weakness in foreign policy on the part of their rivals.

So where Itō favored a relaxed foreign policy after 1905 in order that Japan might restore its finances and absorb its gains, the young bloods yearned for further expansion. After all, Japan needed outlets for its exploding population and industry, while the agitation in California only proved how persistent was anti-Japanese bigotry among whites. The most extreme expressions of expansionism came from the military, especially the new Kwantung Army based in Manchuria and the Black Dragon (or Amur) Society dedicated to Japan's "imperial mission." But similar sentiments echoed throughout the home islands. Politician Kaneko Kentarō warned of the war *after* the war—the economic struggle in which Japanese energies "should not be channeled only in the direction of Asia, but should cover the whole of mankind." Scholars like Tōgō Minoru observed that "Imperialism and colonialism are the great currents of the world today" and that "apart from the white races the Japanese are the only ones with an aptitude for colonization." He envisioned the day when "our country's predominance over the Pacific will have been assured" from ice-bound Siberia to North America. Japan had a special destiny to lead other Asian peoples out of the clutches of white imperialists. Finally, expansion was a necessity. "It is a great loss not to be able to export our surplus labor force and use it abroad," wrote the most popular antigovernment newspaper. "It is a great humiliation to have our laborers treated like Chinese." The operative phrase was "use it abroad," for Japanese viewed their emigrants as agents. A million Japanese in America might send back to Japan a *hundred* million yen per year and establish an economic foothold across the ocean. But that dream was spoiled by American bigotry as described in the inflammatory reports filed by journalist Kayahara Kazan. "China," he wrote, "now knows better and looks to Japan as its teacher. Europe, too, understands, and no European nation today wants to hurt Japanese feelings or injure Japanese interests. The only country that does not yet understand is the United States." Americans still viewed Japanese as children or worse, and the only response was to: "Struggle. Struggle like men. Endeavor. Endeavor like men. . . . Struggle, endeavor, and overwhelm the white race. . . . The struggle between races is not only a problem involving interests but is a problem of life and death."

So what should Japanese foreign policy be in the wake of the victory over Russia? At the height of the war scare of 1907–08 the official known as "Japan's Mahan," Satō Tetsutarō, berated the Americans for being "excessively nervous" since Japan was still inferior to the United States in overall naval strength. Satō urged that the Navy be built up even at the cost of shortchanging the Army. But his critics could just as easily reply: if we are to remain at peace with the United States, and thus renounce expansion in the Pacific, then it is all the more important for Japan to build up its Army on the mainland. So it was that the Japanese debate after 1905 reduced to the question: expand in the Pacific or expand in Asia?

The logic of the North Pacific triangle, from Japan's point of view, was this. To expand across the Pacific in the face of American resistance would require the Japanese to devote scarce resources to naval power, while making sure that Russia stayed friendly on their landward flank. To expand on the continent would require the Japanese to devote scarce resources to land power, while making sure that the United States stayed friendly on their watery flank. The worst scenario was for Russia and the United States to join forces against them, but that was unlikely. The Russians, in their temporary weakness, were eager to maintain their foothold in northern Manchuria by conciliating Japan. In sum, Japan could cast its eye on the Philippines, Hawaii, and California only by risking a do-or-die war with America and at the same time weakening its posture in Asia. Expansion on the continent, by contrast, was a low-risk, no-lose strategy.

Theodore Roosevelt understood all this. To the extent that the United States was now the odd man out in the North Pacific triangle, he had to decide which bad alternative he preferred: continued Japanese expansionism on the Asian mainland, or a war that would expose America's Pacific possessions to attack. Roosevelt may not have shared Archibald Coolidge's view that the question at hand was "Is the future population of the Pacific coast to be white or is it to be Oriental?" But he did favor barring immigration, if only to prevent *worse* racial conflicts on the West Coast. And the only way to compensate Japan was to give it a go-ahead to expand on the continent. Roosevelt had to pay lip service to the Open Door in Manchuria, but his renewal of the Gentlemen's Agreement paired with the Root-Takahira accord flashed a red light to Japanese immigrants and a green light to Japanese imperialists in Manchuria, thereby quietly abandoning an Open Door policy that was not enforceable anyway.

Finally, the Asian alternative was open as never before to the Japanese government after 1905. Under the terms of the Treaty of Portsmouth Japan now controlled southern Manchuria and assumed a protectorate over Korea. Not surprisingly, Japanese Army officials proceeded to close off the regions to foreign business and turn them into exclusive spheres of influence. Itō, now sixty-four years old and graced with a long white beard, intervened in a council of *genrō* to forestall the plan. Japan, he said, must proceed in friendly cooperation with China and not offend foreign powers by overstepping its bounds. But Itō's moderation was rejected by the Kwantung Army, which pressed its agenda heedless of Tokyo . . . while one callow American took it upon himself to resist. He raised the tallest flagpole in Manchuria and hoisted the Stars and Stripes high above the wondering Japanese officers patrolling the streets of Mukden.

According to Herbert Croly, the great American intellectual and founder of the *New Republic*, Willard Straight was a Quixote for capitalism: "Mounted though he appeared to be on a crazy little pony and armed with a lath for a sword and a reed for a lance, he was not afraid to enter the lists against the dragon of Japanese imperialism." Straight was Consul-General in Manchuria and imagined himself supplanting Japanese influence with that of American businessmen. Unfortunately, few U.S. investors showed an interest in the region, so Straight took it upon himself to negotiate with China behind the backs of the Japanese, organize a Manchurian Bank, and promote U.S.-financed railroads in Manchuria. In 1907 Straight intercepted Secretary of War Taft on his way home from a trip along the Trans-Siberian and regaled him with the benefits that would flow from breaking the Japanese monopoly. Straight returned to Washington in 1908, but the Japanese had already reacted to his threatening crusade by joining forces with Russia, as Witte foresaw, in a preliminary alliance against the Open Door.

Korea lay even more firmly in the Japanese grip. Foreign Minister Komura had urged that "Korea be made virtually our sovereign area," and the formula adopted after 1905 was that of "joint-government." So the corrupt (and now very old) Korean Emperor still reigned in Seoul, but real power rested with a Japanese Resident-General backed by an occupation force. "Joint-government" was a concession to diplomatic niceties and an expression of Japan's self-image as tutor to fellow Asians. Chief among the tutors was the man who agreed to assume the Residency-General: Itō himself. He was nothing if not earnest and did his best to conciliate or suppress Korean opinion while he tried to reform the country. But the Korean Emperor hated the reforms, whereas Korean patriots hated the occupiers. At the same time, Itō came under fire at home for coddling the barbaric Koreans. It was thus a thankless, hopeless task, especially for someone who deplored the venting of differences. But such was Itō's chosen fate. When the Korean Emperor sent a delegation abroad in 1907 to court foreign support, Tokyo decided to depose the Emperor, disband the Korean Army, and grant Itō full veto power over Korean law. This Japanese coup only provoked a Korean officer to commit public suicide, which in turn sparked a wave of riots against foreign rule. The Japanese Army then went on a rampage of torture and death that took almost twelve thousand lives. Itō was ashamed to report that Japanese troops had "sometimes resorted to burning a whole village because a few citizens were letting the rioters stay in their houses." So a consensus far different from that imagined by Itō began to build in Tokyo: if the Koreans hate us, but we dare not let go of the strategic peninsula, then perhaps annexation is best.

All these considerations—the American resistance to immigration, the arrival of the Great White Fleet, the opportunities and threats in Manchuria and Korea, and the marriage of convenience proposed by the Russians—found place in a long memorandum drafted by Komura Jutarō. It was he who negotiated the Treaty of Portsmouth, and he returned to the Foreign Ministry in July 1908 to explain what Japan really needed: peace and expansion. And since peaceful expansion could be had only in Asia, the cabinet endorsed Komura's views in September, and approved the Root-Takahira accord two months later. *That* was why Japan seemingly "capitulated" in the San Francisco school crisis of 1907–08.

One spring day in 1908 an American missionary visited Prince Itō at the Residency-General in Seoul. He noticed two photographs framed on the wall, one of the Emperor Meiji, the other of Theodore Roosevelt. When he expressed his surprise at the honor accorded the President, Itō replied: "President Roosevelt is a man I admire for he is an honest man. He always means just what he says. He is frank and straightforward and never leaves you in doubt. He gives every man a square deal." Unfortunately the straightforward Roosevelt chose to step down in 1908. To be sure, his protégé succeeded him, and wags even said that "TAFT" stood for "Take Advice From Theodore." But Taft preferred to take his advice from the youngster who had impressed him two years before on the train from Vladivostok to Harbin: Willard Straight. Now Acting Chief of Far Eastern Affairs at the State Department, he persuaded Taft that "one of the greatest commercial prizes of the world is the trade with 400,000,000 Chinese." Philander Knox, the Wall Street lawyer now Secretary of State, shared this conviction, as did Harriman and publicists such as Thomas F. Millard, who warned that "Japan's goal is commercial supremacy in the whole East." So Taft and his lieutenants, far from honoring the Root-Takahira accord, jettisoned what they considered to be Roosevelt's giveaway policy in favor of a new ploy they called Dollar

Diplomacy. It was true that the United States was militarily weak in East Asia, but it might substitute dollars for guns in a new campaign to contest for Manchuria.

The upshot was a radical shift in U.S. policy just a few months after the *Japanese* thought all was settled. Knox boasted that he would inject "American capital by diplomatic pressure into a region of the world where it could not go of its own accord," and "smoke out" the Japanese. First he promoted Harriman's latest plan to link his North American railroads by steamship with the Chinese Eastern Railway and Trans-Siberian. Next, he prodded a consortium of New York bankers to build railroads in China to compete with Japan's. When that failed, Knox enlisted European powers in a plan to buy out all the concessions issued to Japan and Russia, and internationalize the Manchurian railroads.

The result of such clumsiness, absent real force, was to invite Japan to huddle with Russia. In July 1910, they formalized their partition of Manchuria and agreed to shut the door to all outside investors. Knox's policy of "bluff and back down" proved worse than useless, and Roosevelt scolded Taft for his folly. "Japan is not rich," he wrote the new President, "her main interests are on the Continent of Asia, and especially in Manchuria and Korea; and she is obliged to keep in mind that Russia is a great military power, with rankling memories of injury. . . . I have reluctantly come to the conclusion that Japanese immigration must be kept out; but the way in which this shall be done is not only all-important in itself, but must be considered in connection with our entire Japanese policy." In Roosevelt's view, "Our vital interest is to keep the Japanese out of our country and at the same time to preserve the good will of Japan. The vital interest of the Japanese, on the other hand, is in Manchuria and Korea." But Taft refused to listen and Knox went on trying to muscle American capital into China. Of course, even Roosevelt would have had to ask himself sooner or later how far he could permit Japan to go. But if his policy had survived, at least that day might have found Japan and the United States negotiating on a basis of trust. The legacy of Taft's policy was apparent betrayal and abiding suspicion.

Conditions in Korea had now become intolerable. Korean secret societies devoted to independence and Japanese secret societies devoted to annexation vied for control of intrigue-drenched Seoul, while soldiers and rioters and soldiers-turned-rioters slaughtered one another and innocents in cities and villages. The only voice for moderation was Itō's, but he was snubbed by his own government, condemned as "weak-kneed" by the press, and finally obliged to resign. His heartbreaks ended in October 1909, when, on a trip to Manchuria, he was shot. As Itō lay dying he was told that his assassin was a Korean nationalist. "Then he is a fool!" choked Itō, for his death only convinced Tokyo to end the fiction of Korean independence once and for all. In August 1910, after another round of bloodletting, Japan imposed a treaty of annexation and full colonial government.

By then it was clear that the United States occupied the square that Roosevelt had always hopscotched to avoid: odd man out in the North Pacific triangle. Oh, the Americans may perform great feats of engineering in Panama and Pearl Harbor, but Manchuria and Korea were lost, the Philippines indefensible, and even Hawaii might fall in harm's way should the Japanese someday follow the navalist Satō's advice and build a fleet of Mahanesque proportions. Wise old heads remained cautious: "It was unprofitable," said Itō, "for any country to endeavor to go beyond the limits which appear to have been set by nature to its powers." But now Itō was dead and Komura retired, reading American poetry in the garden of his country estate. Japan's new generation of leaders saw no limits, especially in the world that Taft thought the greatest prize of all: China Proper. For in 1911 the celestial wheel turned again, and the Ch'ing dynasty, the Manchus of old, lost the Mandate of Heaven.

Peking 1912

SOMETIMES THE TRAGEDIES of private life weigh most heavily upon the mighty. They are used to having their way, and so shake their fists at heaven when they do not. Consider Leland Stanford, who waited eighteen years for a child, only to have the boy die at age fifteen. It was 1885, and Madame Blavatsky's theosophy was sweeping salons in San Francisco. So Stanford held a séance in which a ghostly voice instructed him to found a college in his son's memory. Such, at least, were the legendary origins of Leland Stanford Jr. University, situated on the capacious horse farm in Palo Alto. Frederick Law Olmsted, the landscape architect who laid out Central Park, designed this "Harvard of the West," famed biologist David Starr Jordan assumed its presidency, and Herbert Hoover was in its first class. But the queerest freshman to matriculate during Stanford's first decade was, without a doubt, Homer Lea. He was a hunchback, almost a dwarf, in his own way a genius, and he arrived in 1897.

Little for certain is known about Lea. His wife burned his papers for fear of becoming a target for spies, and Lea himself spun such tales as to leave a scholar reeling for want of a fact to lean on. He was not, as he claimed, a descendant of Robert E. Lee. He was not, as Sun Yat-sen later imagined, a confidant of that Chinese revolutionary since 1900. He was not, as Clare Boothe Luce believed, present at the relief of the Peking legations. Nor was "General Lea" in the army of any real government. But Lea's apparent militarism, fear of Japan, and sensitive quest to understand China made him California's unique contribution to American geopolitical thought and the personification of the now lucid, now fantastic American encounter with East Asia.

We do know that Homer's dad was sent west from Cleveland, Tennessee, so that he might escape from the ravages of the Civil War. He grew up in Denver, married, and sired Homer in 1876. The boy suffered from a curvature of the spine and limped badly. He stopped growing at five feet, except for his hump, which so overwhelmed the neck that Homer's head seemed simply to rest on his misshapen shoulders. His eyesight was so bad that young Homer could not even read and write without suffering headaches that forced him to recline in a darkened room. We can only wonder, therefore, at the willpower that made Homer Lea an authority on world history, military strategy, and the language and culture of China, and the author of two lengthy treatises, a novel, and a play. His classmates called him "Little Scrunch-Neck," but he deflected their teasing with cynical wit and eloquence. Within a year of his family's move to Los Angeles—he was seventeen—Lea was a leader of the local Lyceum League—a youth organization sponsored by Theodore Roosevelt. "His dramatic way of speaking," recalled a classmate, "his piercing eyes, the intonation of his voice, and his characteristic gesture of raising his hand with his long forefinger extended, brought home the point generated by his keen mind."

Lea dreamed of studying law at Harvard, but the plan miscarried owing to "unexpected financial difficulties" (or so he claimed—Lea was not one to admit rejection). So instead the dwarf wrote to David Starr Jordan himself, won acceptance to Stanford, and boarded the Southern Pacific en route to "the Farm." A classmate described him as "pathetically hunchbacked, his torso seem[ing] only a bulb fastened on to his legs and his face [having the] appearance of a wise child common among people with his affliction. For all that, he carried himself with a defiant dignity. He seemed to repel most advances toward intimacy, probably because he felt that pity prompted them." Lea was also the sort of class weirdo who swaggered about campus with a military air, lectured his pampered mates on strategy, and festooned his walls with flags and maps. *They* talked of football and girls and beer, he of Napoleon, Caesar, and Lee. When the Spanish-American War broke out, he actually drilled with a cavalry unit, albeit one of the "lame, halt, and blind." He also apparently argued with Jordan, for the pacifist prexy pronounced Lea "vulgar, loud-mouthed, and excessively warlike." In 1899 Lea's headaches became insufferable, and he had to drop out. What he did for the next eleven months is unknown, except that he spent a good deal of time in the City. Where did he go? classmates would ask. To Chinatown, always to Chinatown.

According to his biographer, Lea's fascination with China may have begun at Los Angeles High School, near to that city's Chinatown. Like himself, the Chinese were short and ugly in the eyes of the dominant society, and their Tong wars and underworld beckoned to a boy cut off from the normal excitements of youth. What was more, his parents knew the prominent Presbyterian pastor, Ng Poon Chew, in San Fran-

cisco. Ng was a leader in the Chinese Empire Reform Society and had
contacts with the Triad Society. Through him Lea observed the political
strains of émigré Chinese in the last years of the Ch'ing Empire. Some
were Christian, some Confucian, some secular. Some hoped to break
the dead hand of the Dowager Empress and stage Meiji-type reforms in
the name of the young Emperor. Others dreamed of overthrowing the
Manchus altogether. Lea joined their groups and relished the intrigue.
Defying the pain in his cranium, he read Chinese history, copied out
Chinese characters, and soon knew more about the mysterious Chinese
than any American save a handful of professors.

Then a story appeared in April 1900, in the Sunday supplement of the
San Francisco Call. It announced with bravura (Lea had penned it him-
self) that a "YOUNG CALIFORNIAN IS PLOTTING TO BECOME
COMMANDER-IN-CHIEF OF THE REBEL FORCES. HIS PLANS ARE
ALL LAID TO HELP THE CHINESE EMPEROR." The young man was
"Homer Lea of Stanford University," who was "well up in military
affairs." A student cried, "You'll get your head cut off in China!" To
which the hunchback replied, "Fortunately, they'll have a hard time
finding my neck." Bearing letters from San Francisco's Chinese leaders,
Lea sailed on the SS *China* in June. He was twenty-three.

Recall for a moment the state of Chinese politics. After China's
defeat in the war with Japan and the Scramble for Concessions that followed, the young Kuang-hsü Emperor presided over a "hundred days" of
reform, only to be foiled by the Dowager Empress, Tz'u-hsi. She suppressed the reforms, then encouraged the Boxers. So the thwarted
reformers fled abroad to seek support among overseas Chinese for their
Imperial Reform societies. Chief among them were K'ang Yu-wei and
Liang Ch'i-ch'ao—whose photographs appeared next to Lea's in the
Call—and a lesser known figure named Sun Yat-sen.

Sun was another child of the new, multicultural North Pacific. He
was born in Kwangtung Province in the south, always the center of
rebellion (his uncle had fought with the Taipings) and emigration (his
older brother left for Hawaii to work in the sugar fields). At thirteen Sun
also sailed to Honolulu and attended the Anglican Iolani School founded
in Queen Emma's time. He then studied medicine in Hong Kong, where
he was baptized in 1884 by a Congregationalist missionary. Yet the faith
Sun espoused was a syncretic, Pacific/Asian variety scarcely pleasing to
his pastors. He refused to renounce polygamy, grew to admire Lenin,
and dreamed of liberating Asia from white imperialism even as he
sought Western help for his campaign to overthrow the Ch'ing. In 1896
the Dragon Lady's spies waylaid Sun on his way to church one Sunday
in London. Only a letter secreted out to British authorities saved him
from extradition and torture.

In those early years Sun and K'ang looked to Japan as the model for Chinese renewal. In 1898 Sun and some Japanese friends went so far as to send arms to the Filipinos in their war against the Yankees. But Sun and K'ang parted ways over how to exploit the Boxer Rebellion. The former thought the chance had come to overthrow the Dowager Empress with Japanese aid. But the latter distrusted Japan and thought armed revolt premature. K'ang was right. Eight hundred rebels in the hills near Waichow (Hui-chou) did rise up against the Manchus in October 1900 and managed to hold off the soldiers sent to destroy them. Sun had promised them Japanese weapons. They never arrived, and the rebellion was crushed.

Homer Lea was reportedly everywhere and nowhere throughout this tumultuous year. One story has it that he commanded a division of the "Emperor's Army" in the relief of Peking and led a chase to capture the fleeing T'zu-hsi! Another puts him in the Waichow revolt, after which he disguised himself as a monk and left a local missionary (and fellow Stanford man) stupefied: "Not a word did he say what he was doing in our corner of the world and next morning he was gone. What the blazes?" At the other extreme is the account of Pastor Ng, who claimed that Lea never entered China at all but just hung about Hong Kong and Macao until his money gave out. But then, Ng was encouraged to discredit Lea by Jordan, who hated the fact that Lea's "militarism" sullied the image of Stanford.

Lea certainly went to Japan in January 1901. He not only met up there with Jordan, who was taking a scholarly leave, but obtained an interview with Count Ōkuma Shigenobu, former Prime Minister and a friend of K'ang. Ōkuma told Lea that the Meiji Restoration must be China's model for renewal, and that the foremost need of the reformers was a modern army. Lea praised the Japanese for their sympathy and warned that Russia was the main barrier to Chinese renewal. Lea returned to California in April and retreated into obscurity.

So the Boxer Rebellion would seem to have come up empty for K'ang and Sun and the would-be generalissimo Homer Lea. In fact, it triggered the trends that sent the Ch'ing Empire careening toward extinction a mere decade later. For after the Boxer Rebellion, the Dowager Empress herself agreed to reforms and railroad construction, reorganization of the Imperial Army, and foreign education (thousands of students went to Japan). The Ch'ing hoped that such "Self-Strengthening" would bolster, not undermine, the *political* status quo (thereby anticipating the Four Modernizations campaign of a later, Communist dynasty). But how could the exposure of masses of bright young Chinese to foreign ways *fail* to feed the movement for political change? So the empire's belated attempt at reform, like the *bakufu*'s opening of Japan after

Commodore Perry, proved to be the beginning of the end for the old regime.

Homer Lea surfaced again as manager of the visit of reform leader Liang to Los Angeles in 1903. Liang moved on to New York—where he froze in the presence of J. P. Morgan—and Washington—where he found his tongue before Secretary of State Hay and met with President Roosevelt. Of course, the U.S. government could not offer aid, but private citizens did. It was during Liang's tour that the first Imperial Chinese Reform school arose in Los Angeles to train young Chinese for a revolutionary army. Within a year, thirteen branches of the Chinese Imperial Reform Army existed in California alone and a score in other North American Chinatowns. A retired sergeant, "Captain" Ansel O'Banion, was the primary recruiter and drillmaster, about forty other paid officers, mostly Americans, commanded regiments numbering two thousand men, and at the top stood Lt. Gen. Homer Lea. No doubt Lea and his comrades could not have organized the Chinatowns without the imprimatur of Liang and K'ang. Still, the trust and respect shown these American friends was remarkable, as was the credulous expectation that someday they all would take ship for China and march on Peking.

In 1905 the *Los Angeles Examiner* reported that Lea "was on his way to London, travelling with His Excellency, Kang Yu Wei," and the *St. Louis Post-Dispatch* that an "American Hopes to be Lafayette of China—Leads Army." K'ang himself had come to America and reviewed the regiments of the volunteer army. Lea's relations with Jordan had also improved, for now the Stanford president gave him a letter of introduction to Roosevelt. So the President and the Secretary of State entertained a foreign revolutionary and an American citizen who were raising an army on American soil for the purpose of overthrowing a government with which the United States had treaty relations! K'ang wanted to use the interview to protest the Chinese exclusion acts, but Lea boasted of the army and claimed that Teddy's response was "Bully!" K'ang went on to tour New York, Chicago, San Francisco, and other cities where uniformed Chinese would march through the streets beneath dragon banners, led by K'ang in his silken robes and Lea in the outlandish costume of a Chinese field marshal. But this was the acme of Lea's Reform Army. Events in China soon rendered it superfluous, and it dissolved in 1911 when O'Banion was jailed for smuggling in illegal aliens.

Lea spent the years of 1906 and 1907 deep in research, judging by the 1908–10 publication dates of his novel and first tome on geopolitics. The novel, *The Vermilion Pencil*, told the story of a Chinese peasant girl whose voice wins the ardor of a traveling mandarin. She protests that her song is for "the birds and tea-pickers of the valley, not for the wolves and tigers" of the Manchu bureaucracy. But the provincial viceroy forces her to marry, and confides her education to a young French monk devoted less to evangelism than to relieving the suffering of rural Chinese. The girl and monk fall in love, flee, and are captured. The girl is sentenced to death. But the monk has been given a medallion of the secret Triad Society by a dying man he has comforted. Chinese will instantly obey anyone bearing the talisman, regardless of their fear of the Manchus. So at the last moment the monk displays the medallion, crowds of local Chinese overrun the place of execution, and the girl's life is saved.

Lea's allegory, called by one reviewer "the first real Chinese novel in English," is fascinating not for its idealization of Chinese virtue—that is expected—but for its problematical characterization of the West as represented by the monk. His Christianity is useless—he himself betrays his vows. Nor does he save the girl with superior technology or tactics—he is at a loss and does not even understand the power of the medallion. His role, in sum, is that of a catalyst, unleashing the undying spirit of the masses themselves. As Lea later wrote, "There is but one way to reform China, the way they themselves have done these six times in the past, the extirpation, root and branch, of official corruption. . . . The West has nothing whatever to do with the reformation of this nation." So much for the gospels of commerce and Christ, technology, the Open Door, and Dollar Diplomacy! The most an Occidental could do was what Lea meant to do: help the Chinese work out their own destiny, on their own terms, and then retreat across the Pacific where whites belonged.

Homer Lea was almost alone in his understanding that revolution in China must follow patterns traced by the Chinese themselves over millennia of cyclical history. Instead, the great powers hovered about the sickbed of Imperial China wondering whether or not to root for its death. They all had treaties with Peking and benefited from China's impotence. But if the regime were doomed in any case, then perhaps they should try to curry favor with the revolutionaries. But which revolutionaries would win out, and what policies would they pursue? Would they be protégés of Meiji Japan, or pro-Western, democratic, perhaps Christian? American policy, as we know, lurched from Hay's Open Door to Roosevelt's encouragement of Japanese expansion to Taft's Dollar Diplomacy, while the likes of Homer Lea and American missionaries sympathized with the Chinese reformers. Japanese policy was equally confused. Before the Russo-Japanese War the Meiji were sympathetic to Chinese radicalism, and private citizens like Miyazaki Torazo offered asylum and arms to Sun Yat-sen. But after 1905 Japan could no longer pose as simply an Asian brother: it had joined the ranks of the imperialists and had a stake in the survival of the Ch'ing. So when the Peking government protested in 1907 about the harboring of Chinese revolutionaries in Japan, Tokyo agreed to expel Sun but to give him a hero's send-off sweetened with a subsidy of seventy thousand yen. Japanese, too, were playing both sides in China.

Meanwhile, the Ch'ing were making a show of reform. The crux of the Self-Strengthening program was to reassert centralized government over the regional warlords that had grown up during the Taiping Rebellion. The Imperial Army was to be modernized and provincial warlords subordinated to a national command structure. It was a good idea, except that everyone knew that the Chinese were disloyal. So the court declared a revival of ethnic *Manchu* militarism, recalling the early days when bannermen ruled from the saddle and subdued all the provinces of China. Only now they no longer wore crude Mongol leathers but uniforms modeled on those of the Junker aristocracy of the Kaiser's Germany. Had military modernization occurred fifty years before, it might well have saved the dynasty. Instead, it magnified the resentment of Chinese officers and officials, who now had to bow directly to Manchu overlords and surrender what provincial autonomy they had enjoyed. For all that, the dynasty might still have rebounded had liberalization accompanied centralization, as the Kuang-hsü Emperor desired. But when the Dragon Lady finally died in 1908, the young Emperor also was gone, dead of illness the day before. At least, that was the story put out by the court. It did not take much imagination to suspect the old spider of murdering her heir as she saw her own death approaching. So the throne passed instead to her grandnephew, a child of three years, and that meant that the Manchu court was a vacuum. To overseas leaders like Sun, to radical students, Chinese merchants and land-owning gentry, angry young officers in the Chinese Army, and secret societies at home and abroad, there seemed no alternative now but to overthrow the Manchus. Still, the regime persisted with its policies of centralization and in May 1911 tried to nationalize regional railroads. To local Chinese this meant that the economy as well as the Army would fall into the hands of the corrupt Ch'ing bureaucracy and its foreign creditors. Rumors of revolt sped through the provinces.

Sun had traveled the world since his expulsion from Japan, and he made his third visit to the United States in 1909. Homer Lea's second book attracted Sun's interest, as did Lea's friendship with Charles B. Boothe, a Los Angeles businessman and would-be fund-raiser for Chinese reform. On Sun's initiative the three met in Los Angeles in early 1910 and formed a conspiracy. "President" Sun was to unify all disaffected Chinese and stage a final, national revolt. "Commanding General" Homer Lea was to plot military strategy for the defeat of the Manchus. "Financial Agent" Boothe would obtain loans to finance the revolt. But Boothe came up empty: Knox's Dollar Diplomacy was finally succeeding, and the loose change of Wall Street flowed to Peking. Lea himself could not even get an appointment at the State Department before having to sail to Germany to consult a famed oculist for his eyesight. Sun continued to tour American Chinatowns and was in Denver, in October 1911, when news reached him of another revolt back in China. This one was big, had Army support, and was spreading out of control.

The final agony of the Ch'ing began in Wuhan when some rebellious Chinese officers fumbled a bomb in their clandestine meeting house. Its detonation attracted police, who seized documents compromising the plotters. Rather than wait to be rounded up, the soldiers immediately mutinied, seized an arsenal, and made common cause with local reformers and secret societies. Soon the whole province flared up in revolt. Only one figure at court knew what to do—the mother of the baby Emperor—and she called out at once for Yüan Shih-k'ai. He had had a long career in Manchu service—we first met him in Korea with Li Hung-chang in 1882—and was now in disgrace and much feared by rivals at court. But Yüan's former generals and supporters rallied to him, and the Queen Mother gave him the task of handling this latest, most parlous insurgency.

Sun was hot to return and take charge of the Wuhan revolt. But his presence would mean little without funds and backing, so he took a train for Washington, where Knox snubbed him, too, then sailed for London to meet up with Lea. In hopes of attracting British support, Lea even promised that a Chinese Republic would make an "Anglo-Saxon Alliance," and he lied that Knox and Senator Root were on his side. All he could get was a promise of British support for any strong government that might emerge in China. So Lea contented himself with a new uniform sewn to his specifications by British tailors and took ship with Sun for China. The *Singapore Free Press* trumpeted that "General HOMER LEA, formerly of the American army, now retired, has undertaken to direct [a] Military Government." We know not what conversations passed between Sun and Lea on the long voyage from Europe, but when they arrived in Shanghai on Christmas Day, Lea stepped down the gangplank as Chief of the General Staff of the Chinese Republic.

Of course, there was no Chinese Republic yet, Lea had no army to command, and Sun's "government" in Nanking had more prestige than power. Yüan Shih-k'ai held the most power in China, but not enough to suppress the Wuhan rebellion. So the only way to avoid civil war was for Sun and Yüan to deal directly. That was what the Queen Mother had in mind: a truce to end the revolt but leave the regime intact. But why should Yüan save a decadent dynasty governed mostly by officials who hated and feared him? Why not translate his temporary power into lasting security by extorting eighty thousand ounces of gold from the Queen Mother and then betraying her by going over to the Republican side on condition that he, not Sun, become president? Sun was resigned: "Whether I am to be the titular head of all China, or to work in conjunction with another, and that other is Yüan Shih-k'ai, is of no importance to me. I have done my work." So Sun bowed out on condition that Yüan establish a republic; the liquidation of the Ch'ing Empire followed on February 12, 1912. The boy Emperor was pensioned off and permitted to reside as a virtual prisoner in the Summer Palace.

China was now a republic, and the foreign governments who had blithely bet on Manchu survival wondered what course it would take. Not the one Sun desired, for within a year Yüan made himself dictator, and Sun was forced to go into opposition as leader of the new Kuomintang (Nationalist) party. Homer Lea, the presumptive Lafayette of the Chinese Revolution, collapsed in a coma the day before the Manchu abdication, and when he came to, he was practically blind. Lea's wife took him home and nursed him in their Santa Monica cottage until a second stroke killed him on November 1 at the age of thirty-five.

Did Homer Lea influence China? Not really, nor did he believe any American could. Did he influence the United States? Perhaps, but not so soon, nor so much, as was necessary. He left behind *The Vermilion Pencil*, a few brief articles, and two works in the new science called geopolitics. But they scarcely affected the views of any American more important than the occasional colonel based in the Pacific—despite the fact that *The Valor of Ignorance* and *The Day of the Saxon* contained the most prescient analyses of the racial and military politics shaping the North Pacific. Perhaps it was because Lea prided himself on a ruthless objectivity, so ruthless in fact that he debunked all of Americans' favorite myths. The United States, he wrote, was *not* special but obeyed the same laws of rise and decline discernible in all history's empires. The United States did *not* enjoy isolation behind its Atlantic and Pacific moats, for modern technology now spanned the oceans. The fact that the United States was a white nation, or Christian, or democratic did *not* ensure its future. Rather, Americans' overweening pride in their various heritages only blinded them to their own defenselessness. Nor would their prosperity or pacifism preserve the United States, for "a nation that is rich, vain, and at the same time unprotected, provokes wars and hastens its own ruin." And Americans were *not* as patriotic as they liked to believe, for when "men postpone their patriotic activity to a time of war, their procrastination is only indicative of their worthlessness." The time to be patriotic, vigorous, martial, vigilant, and devoted to the tribe was in peacetime. Japanese understood, but American valor was the valor of ignorance—and that was why the United States would someday awake to find the Philippines, Guam, and Hawaii seized overnight by sneak attack.

Homer Lea counted ships. It was easy to see that the U.S. Pacific fleet was inferior to that of Japan. Less obvious was America's woeful inferiority in transport ships and garrisons. Lea pointed out the remarkable fact that Ulysses S. Grant's entire supply train for an army of 125,000 men could now be transported by giant steamship across the Pacific in less time than it took Grant to ride from the Rapidan River to the James. As of 1909, the Japanese military transport fleet boasted ninety-five ships capable of moving two hundred thousand soldiers across the Pacific in a week, while the Japanese Navy could concentrate 70 percent of its strength at any point west of Hawaii in ten days. With almost perfect precision Lea mapped out the invasion beaches and routes to Manila the Japanese would use and predicted that the Philippines would fall as easily as Cuba had in the Spanish-American War. He imagined the conquest of the Hawaiian Islands, made easier by the presence there of 133,000 Japanese immigrants. Alaska he considered of tremendous interest to Japan by dint of its size and "almost inexhaustible wealth." And once Japan seized the western Pacific she "would be placed in a naval and military position so invulnerable that no nation or coalition of them could attack her. Calmly, from this vast Gibraltar of the ocean, she could look down upon the world and smile at its rage and trepidation—this island tribe that owns no heaven and annoys no god."

Lea even catalogued what U.S. Navy planners only dared imagine as they labored over War Plan Orange. For once the Japanese controlled the western Pacific, their armada of transports could easily carry tens of thousands of fanatical soldiers—the sort the Russians met at Port Arthur—to the American West Coast. And what could the United States do to resist? The Columbia River forts had less firepower than a single Japanese battleship. Los Angeles was naked and San Francisco easily surrounded. He imagined Japanese landings at Monterey Bay to the south and Bodega Bay to the north, and the surrender of San Francisco as soon as the Japanese seized its vital reservoirs of water in San Mateo County. The only way Americans could counterattack was by training hundreds of thousands of raw recruits, shipping them west by transcontinental railroad, and advancing through narrow and dangerous mountain passes doubtless already in Japanese hands.

Lea did not think this apocalypse inevitable. But if war came, he wrote, it would be America's fault. For even as Japan knew "a production of wealth unequal to its political growth," so Americans displayed an atrophied political consciousness by comparison with their industrial growth. "The quotient of this equation has been, throughout the entire career of the human race, war." Why had Americans turned selfish and weak, even in the face of a potential enemy who was lean, hungry, martial and tribal? The cause, thought Lea, was America's most fatal myth, the melting pot. In his view, the mixing of races was slowly killing America. Anglo-Saxons had founded its institutions and won its empire. "When, however, the political and military power passes from [the ruling element] to racial elements that are dissimilar . . . then the ideal of national supremacy is lost in the endless controversies of internal legislation and petty ambitions." That prevented the United States from defending itself, which placed an irresistible temptation before the Japanese and made "the American people, and not Japan, responsible for this approaching conflict."

Curiously, Lea had donated the royalties on his Japanese editions to Sun Yat-sen, so that every Japanese who bought his books made an unconscious donation to the renewal of China. Sun repaid Lea after his death in a eulogy. "Unfortunately Mr. Lea was physically deformed," it began, "but he possessed a wonderful brain."

Panama and
Kiao-chow 1914

IN THE EARLY nineteenth century an engineer named John Stevens had helped inaugurate the age of steam and rails, vying with Robert Fulton for the first steamboat and winning the first railroad charter in the United States. In the early twentieth century another John Stevens capped that age in spectacular fashion. Like his namesake, he was an extreme Yankee—son of a farmer from Maine—and mastered his craft on the job. At age twenty, Stevens left home to help survey the new city of Minneapolis. He learned railroading as a track hand in New Mexico, helped explore the route of the Canadian Pacific, built the first railroad across Michigan's Upper Peninsula, and became chief engineer of the Great Northern Railroad. Stevens grew into a handsome, weathered warrior of technology, with short black hair, a bushy mustache, large ears, and a keen, mathematical gaze. His memoirs read like a pulp thriller, full of narrow escapes from wolf packs, torrents, and mountain passes choked with snow. He learned to survive "under the most primitive conditions" and "loved it!"

By age fifty-two, in 1905, Stevens had settled down to family life in the Chicago suburbs as an executive with the Chicago, Rock Island, and Pacific. But when Taft asked him to take over the Philippine railroads, he readily agreed. President Roosevelt was delighted: this Stevens was "a big fellow, a man of daring and good sense, and burly power"—rather like Teddy himself. But before Stevens could depart, his old boss on the Great Northern, James J. Hill, recommended him for a different post. "Mr. Hill told the President that he knew a man who could build the Panama Canal." Stevens hesitated, despite a princely salary of $30,000. But Cromwell, the lawyer for the Panama railroad, talked him into it, and Roosevelt hosted him at his home in Oyster Bay. Panama, he said, was a "devil of a mess"; but Stevens would be given authority to sort it out. He sailed in July 1905 and for the first weeks did nothing but ask questions, cigar between his teeth. Then he announced his conclusions: "There are three diseases in Panama. They are yellow fever, malaria, and cold feet; and the greatest of these is cold feet."

Panama was indeed a mess. For the political hurdles proved easy to leap by comparison with the technical, managerial, and natural ones. Roosevelt might bellow "Let the dirt fly!" but the Americans knew no more than the French how to protect workers from disease, whether to dig a sea-level canal or rely on gigantic locks, and how to manage logistics in that tropical, mountainous jungle. The Canal Commission had chosen as chief engineer another Chicago railroader named John Findley Wallace. But Wallace was demoralized by the rusting French equipment, the deplorable condition of the Panama Railroad, and the mud, vermin, insects, and disease. He made one excellent decision—selecting the ninety-five-ton Bucyrus steam shovel as the best tool for the job—then quit. Panama, he said, was a "God-forsaken country."

Now a great deal of progress had in fact been made, thanks to some brave, brilliant doctors. The Frenchman Eli Lazeran had found malaria cells in the stomach of an *Anopheles* mosquito. In 1897 the British scientist Ronald Ross found the same cells in a mosquito that had just sucked blood from a malaria patient, then located the salivary gland by which the insect transmitted the disease. In 1886, Cuban physician Carlos Finlay published evidence that yellow fever was transmitted by the *Stegomyia fasciata* mosquito, but few believed it until Finlay persuaded Dr. Walter Reed to experiment with the mosquito theory after the Yankees occupied Havana in 1898. Four volunteers slept in bedcloths soaked with the slimes of yellow fever victims—and showed no ill effects. But Dr. Jesse Lazear let a mosquito in the "yellow jack" ward feed on his blood—and died soon after in violent convulsions. Reed and Dr. William C. Gorgas then set out to rid Havana of mosquitoes by fumigation and elimination of the standing water in which they bred. Of course, Panama was a larger and less controllable battleground, but Gorgas was eager to tackle it. He had gone into medicine when West Point rejected him, and believed that God had planned his whole life for a humane war such as this.

Stevens understood that the real problem of Panama was not technical but human. If his workers perceived that every measure was being taken to combat disease, they might summon the heart to fight the more mundane battles against earth and water. So when Gorgas asked for men to drain swamps and nail screens and fumigate buildings, Stevens gave him a blank check and first call on labor in the Isthmus. By the end of 1906 yellow fever had disappeared and malaria was under control—which meant that the "grunt work" could begin in earnest. Stevens moved his headquarters to the Culebra Cut, put in twelve-hour days alongside his men, and willed the infrastructure needed to dig that canal. For after all the dam builders and hydraulics experts had their say, the fact remained that the rickety old Panama railroad must haul the machinery, supply the workers, and remove the mountains of dirt. So Stevens showed no interest in digging until his men had doubled the track and strengthened the rails and roadbed, built complex switching and siding systems, strung new telegraph and telephone lines, imported heavy locomotives and rolling stock, and drafted a freight schedule so complex as to awe the German General Staff. "There is no element of mystery involved in it," he said, "the problem is one of magnitude and not miracles."

True enough, but someone still needed to figure out *how* to lance the Isthmus. The canal's official motto, "The Land Divided—the World United," implied a sea-level canal, and the expert report commissioned by the White House recommended that solution in January 1906. It meant digging and hauling a great deal more earth but eliminated the need for an expensive and tricky system of locks. Then Stevens witnessed Panama's autumn floods firsthand. The Chagres River ran out of control, and the banks of the old French canal turned liquid and slid into the channel. He now feared that a sea-level canal would be "a narrow, tortuous ditch" at the mercy of the weather. So Stevens went to Washington to plead his case for a system of locks. Senator Philander C. Knox, whose constituents included the Pittsburgh steel firms that would cast the locks' giant gates, wholeheartedly agreed. But he was right nonetheless, and in June 1906 the Senate voted to abandon the sea-level plan.

Roosevelt showed his confidence in Stevens by shrinking and reorganizing the Canal Commission to make him the sole authority. Then Teddy showed his confidence in Dr. Gorgas by braving disease to inspect Panama himself, at the height of the wet season—the first overseas trip by a sitting President. Teddy slogged everywhere and saw everything, joyously mounted the controls of a Bucyrus steam shovel, and returned to describe Culebra Cut: "Now we have taken hold of the job. . . . With immense energy men and machines do their task, the white men supervising matters and handling the machines, while the tens of thousands of black men do the rough manual labor where it is not worthwhile to have machines do it. It is an epic feat, and one of immense significance."

It was, and nowhere more so than on the West Coast, where the city fathers of San Francisco and Los Angeles expected a shipping bonanza. Nor was San Francisco an automatic favorite in the competition for trade, since its earthquake and fire, racial unrest, and municipal corruption had soured its image considerably. The city rebuilt bravely after 1906, but the stream of newcomers shifted increasingly southward. And nothing so demonstrated Los Angeles's new clout like the fight over port facilities in anticipation of the Panama Canal.

The first step was to break the Southern Pacific Railroad's grip on the ports of San Pedro and Wilmington. So the Los Angeles Chamber of Commerce waged a three-year battle until, in 1909, a voter initiative condemned San Pedro property rights and created a municipal Harbor Commission. It began at once to float bonds for the rapid expansion of the waterfront. San Franciscans cried few tears for the Southern Pacific, but viewed with alarm their competitors' progress. Their own port had escaped railroad control, but its ownership was vested in the state of California. That meant that any upgrades on the Embarcadero had to be approved by a statewide electorate. San Francisco civic leaders conjured three solutions: make *all* ports in California state-owned, or restore San Francisco's port to municipal ownership, or consolidate all Bay Area docks under a single authority. The last scheme was a ploy to crush the upstart port of Oakland across the Bay. The *Los Angeles Times* pronounced judgment: "San Francisco never has failed and never will fail to advance its own interests at the expense of all other localities, and to do so without justice, without mercy, and without remorse." Councilmen in Oakland refused to consolidate, and legislators in Sacramento brooked no change of ownership, so San Francisco had to content itself with its share of $10 million in state bonds earmarked for docks and piers needed to handle the anticipated Panama boom.

But the Panama Canal meant more than expansion of commerce. It symbolized the full integration of the Pacific Coast into the world community. San Francisco's Panama-Pacific Exhibition of 1915 (for which it earned the epithet, The City That Knows How), was meant to celebrate the shrinking of the world, and the business community was eager to make it an occasion for expanded trade with Asia. Yet California legislators chose these very years to deny the right to own land to aliens ineligible for citizenship. Again the President (Woodrow Wilson this time) scolded the Governor. Again Californians told the East Coast to mind its own business. Again Japan's Ambassador protested this "grave reflection on her national honor and prestige." Again jingoes on both sides of the ocean predicted or rooted for war. Referring as well to the Mexican Revolution then causing Americans grief, the Hearst papers chanted:

> *Oh, say can you see by the dawn's early light*
> *Any possible way for avoiding a fight!*
> *The Star-Spangled Banner, oh, long may it flap,*
> *While we're kicked by the Greaser and slapped by the Jap!*

Eastern papers like the *Hartford Times* simply mused, "Of the two it might be cheaper to go to war with California than with Japan." This war scare of 1913 subsided when Secretary of State William Jennings

Bryan assured Tokyo of America's goodwill, but few dodges were more fatuous than his suggestion that the federal government could do nothing because the California law was an "economic problem," not a "racial" one. Japanese admirals wondered what future crises would hold in store once the U.S. Navy had quick access to the Pacific via the Panama Canal.

Nobody knows why John Stevens quit just as he had gotten everything in Panama under control—unless, of course, that *was* the reason. He was forever changing locales, jobs and employers and seeking new challenges. Perhaps he tired of Panama as soon as the railroad work was done. But even that does not explain the letter Stevens sent Roosevelt in January 1907: "The 'honor' which is continually being held up as an incentive for being connected with this work, appeals to me but slightly. To me the canal is only a big ditch, and its great utility when completed, has never been apparent to me, as it seems to be to others." Other jobs beckoned, he wrote, and "some of them, I would prefer to hold, if you will pardon my candor, than the Presidency of the United States." What had got into the man? Did his railroad executive friends turn him against the canal project as inimical to their interests? Did he have a falling out with someone? Were it not for Stevens's insult to the Presidency, Teddy might have called him home for a rest and sought to perk him up. As it was, he sent Taft the simplest of memos: "Stevens must get out at once."

So Gen. George Washington Goethals, an Army engineer of no mean talent, finished the job in Panama. In one sense, all he had to do was keep in motion the administrative and technological machines crafted by Stevens. Yet Goethals also coached a work force that peaked at almost fifty thousand people, and made some valuable contributions of his own, such as widening the Culebra Cut, deepening the locks to accommodate the latest battleships (and ocean liners like the *Titanic*), and adding a breakwater to shelter the outlet on the Pacific. Heartbreaks were also in store, such as explosions (one of which killed twenty-three men) and landslides (which undid months of work). But the crews worked on night and day: demolition men who touched off thirty tons of dynamite; steam-shovel crews and railroad men moving a hundred million square yards of dirt; cement mixers and pourers filling locks a thousand feet long and eighty feet high; electricians whose control systems allowed the whole isthmus to be turned on and off with a twist of a wrist. The canal cost $352 million and over 5,600 lives (mostly West Indians), but there was not a hint of corruption throughout—an achievement perhaps as great as the canal.

Everyone assumed that the opening celebration, scheduled for August 15, 1914, would be just as great. But Europe went to war two weeks before, and because of that war the United States was cheated of the acclaim it deserved, West Coast ports knew no shipping boom, and the western Pacific lay at the feet of those lucky, lucky Japanese.

But the Meiji era was over! The venerable Emperor had died in July 1912 and brought to a symbolic end modern Japan's adolescence. To be sure, he did not personally make policy, but the achievements of his reign were as brilliant as those of Elizabeth I or Peter the Great. And the piety of one of his lieutenants was so great that he honored the custom of *junshi* and buried his sword in his belly so that his spirit might accompany Meiji's to the afterlife. It was Nogi, the conqueror of Port Arthur, and he hoped that his sacrifice would inspire a nation that had forgotten samurai virtues in favor of Western materialism. For instance, socialist doctrines had reached Japan and attracted students and urban workers. One cell of anarchists went so far as to plot to kill the Emperor in 1911, and public horror was so intense that the police tried to drive all known socialists into jail, exile, or suicide. Respectable politics were also demoralizing, for no sooner had Meiji's feebleminded son passed through the elaborate liturgies of a Shinto coronation and taken the name *Taishō* (Great Righteousness) than scandal shattered the government. When the cabinet refused an Army request for two more divisions, the Minister of War resigned and no other officer would accept the post. So in the end the entire civilian cabinet had to resign in favor of a new one under a general. Liberal parliamentarians and rioting civilians then forced him to resign, and his successor, Adm. Yamamoto Gombei, was done in a few months later by revelations of corruption in naval procurement. After more recriminations the government lurched back into the civilian hands of old Ōkuma and Foreign Minister Katō Takaaki. But it was clear to all that the military held an informal veto over national policy, even though *civilian* ministers would be held accountable for any foreign policy setbacks. All this helps to explain the risky and opportunistic course of Japanese foreign policy.

No event opened so many choice opportunities to Japan as the outbreak of World War I. Suddenly Russia, its armies committed to a mortal fight against Germany, was a factor no longer in Asia. Britain and France were likewise engaged and eager to grant concessions in return for Japanese friendship. As for Germany, its Asian and Pacific colonies now lay defenseless. All Japan had to do was reach out and take them—in the name of the Anglo-Japanese alliance, of course. Sir Edward Grey understood and coyly told the Japanese that he did not expect them to trouble themselves on Britain's account. But when the German Asiatic squadron under Maximilian, Graf von Spee broke into the Pacific, Grey asked for help in tracking it down. The Japanese jumped, announced their intention of declaring war on Germany, and made ready to seize Kiao-chow on the Shantung Peninsula. Grey tried to retract his plea for help, but too late. A Japanese army laid siege to the orphaned German port with loud bugles and louder cannon until it surrendered in late October. There remained Germany's extensive island dependencies north of the equator, including the Marshalls and Carolines. Japanese merchants had done some business in the islands, and a romantic literature appeared in the 1880s about the possibilities of oceanic empire. Popular writers debated whether Japan's future lay in *hokushin* (continental expansion) or *nanshin* (oceanic expansion), and one member of the Diet believed "it is our great task as a people to turn the Pacific into a Japanese lake." Their chance came in September 1914 when two Japanese squadrons steamed deep into the Pacific with orders to search for Spee's squadron (which in fact was headed toward South America). The admirals in Tokyo browbeat the cabinet into authorizing "temporary occupations" of the German islands. So the Japanese Navy seized both archipelagoes, sealed them off from all foreign ships, and with scarcely a casualty doubled the size of Japan's overseas empire.

Still and all, the lodestone was China, and immediately upon news of the war in Europe the Japanese minister in Peking confronted Yüan Shih-k'ai with a shopping list of demands. It was all in the interest, he said, of solidarity among the yellow races in the face of the "more powerful white adversaries" sure to appear after the current war. In Tokyo, Foreign Minister Katō assembled all the ambitions of Japanese imperialists into a document known as the Twenty-One Demands, won the approval of cabinet, *genrō*, military, and Emperor, and dumped them on Yüan in January 1915. They were, to say the least, comprehensive. Groups One through Four required China to extend Japan's lease on Kwantung and all the southern Manchurian railroads, to grant Japan exclusive rights to mining and landholding in Manchuria, to grant Japan a veto over any loans or railroads proposed by third powers, to appoint Japanese to be China's military and economic advisers in Manchuria, to grant Japan extensive concessions elsewhere in China, "not to cede or lease to any other Power any harbour or bay or any island along the coast of China," and to recognize the transfer of Shantung to Japan. But Group Five—described by Katō as "highly desirable"—went beyond such traditional aims: it required China's central government to take its advice from Japanese political, financial, and military advisers, to place the police under Sino-Japanese joint command, to buy its weapons from Japan, and to allow Japanese schools, hospitals, and monasteries everywhere in China. Most presumptuous of all, Katō insisted that Yüan keep the demands secret.

Inasmuch as Britain, France, and Russia were otherwise engaged and technically allied to Japan, Yüan had nowhere to turn but to the United States. He told American Minister Paul S. Reinsch that Japan had "a definite and far-reaching plan for using the European crisis to further an attempt to lay the foundation of control over China," and proceeded to leak the Twenty-One Demands. He had every reason to expect sympathy. The United States had been the first nation to recognize the Chinese Republic, it stood for the Open Door, and nowhere was anti-Japanese feeling more intense than in California. But unfortunately for Yüan, U.S. policy was not in the hands of Taft and Knox, or even Roosevelt, but the pacifist Bryan. Woodrow Wilson had not yet formulated his vision of a new diplomacy based on democracy, the Open Door, disarmament, and collective security, and his instincts were to steer clear of Asian crusades so long as he was distracted by war in the Atlantic and revolution in Mexico. "I have had the feeling," he wrote Reinsch, "that any direct advice to China, or direct intervention on her behalf in the present negotiations, would really do her more harm than good, inasmuch as it would very likely provoke the jealousy and excite the hostility of Japan, which would first be manifested against China herself." When the Secretary of War suggested that the United States reinforce the Philippines as a precaution, Bryan "got red in the face and was very emphatic. He thundered out that the military could not be trusted to say what we should or should not do, till we actually got into war; that we were not discussing how to wage war, but how *not* to get into war."

The chief of the State Department's Far East division offered a more reasoned argument to do nothing. Japan was overpopulated, he said, and since we did not want its emigrants in California, better they should go to Manchuria. Robert Lansing, State Department counsel, agreed that the best solution was for Japan to drop its protests against California laws and U.S. immigration policy, and for the United States to acquiesce in some of Japan's Chinese ambitions. But this, too, seemed unworthy to Bryan, who merely instructed his diplomats to endorse the Open Door. That did nothing to help Yüan, who begged the Japanese to postpone Group Five but gave in to the rest of the Twenty-One Demands. After Yüan's death in 1916, China was even less able to resist: it fell into a decade of strife among warlords fighting to dominate the fiction called the Republic of China.

To make matters worse, Japanese diplomats spent the rest of the Great War negotiating secret pacts in which Britain, France, and Russia promised to recognize Japan's easy conquests at the peace conference to come. The Tsar's desperate ministers went so far as to conclude an alliance with Japan in 1916, in hopes that Japan would ship them munitions via the Trans-Siberian Railway. Finally, the British and French liquidated their foreign assets to pay for the war, and stood by helplessly as *zaibatsu* took over markets in Asia. World War I multiplied Japan's gold reserves one hundredfold and sparked tremendous industrial growth. The U.S. Navy noticed and hoped to neutralize the Marshalls and Carolines or, failing that, to persuade Japan not to fortify the islands. Otherwise, Pearl Harbor itself might be imperiled.

Bryan quit the State Department after charging that Wilson had abandoned strict neutrality and predicting that Wilson's pro-Allied tilt would drag the United States into war. On that, at least, he was right. In April 1917 the U.S. Congress declared war on Germany, and in so doing became an informal ally of Japan! There was much on which the two governments would have to cooperate in the war and peace to come, so they made a special effort to liquidate the affair of the Twenty-One Demands. Viscount Ishii Kikujirō traveled to Washington, and in the resulting Lansing-Ishii accord of November 1917, the United States recognized that "territorial propinquity creates special relations between countries" and therefore that Japan had "special interests" in China. Japan pledged again to honor the Open Door.

The Lansing-Ishii accord was only the latest in a series of vacuous "understandings" dating back to the Taft-Katsura memorandum, the Treaty of Portsmouth, the Gentlemen's Agreements, and the Root-Takahira accord. The real state of relations between the Pacific powers was better indicated by Ishii's statement that Japan expected to keep its island conquests and extend a Japanese Monroe Doctrine over the western Pacific. Lansing, in turn, defined Japan's "special interests" in China as only economic in nature. The bottom line was that World War I destroyed the fabric of European imperialism and left the United States (with its Panama Canal) and Japan (with its new conquests) as the only contenders for North Pacific hegemony. It also opened up three new corridors for Japanese expansion: Micronesia, northeastern China, . . . and Siberia.

For five days after the Lansing-Ishii accord the Bolsheviks seized power and Russia collapsed into civil war. Distant Siberia was orphaned. The key to Siberia was its railroad. And that meant that John Stevens was about to change jobs again.

Vladivostok and Paris 1919

THAT THE TSARIST regime survived thirty-one months of total war against the German-led alliance testifies to the endurance of the Russian peasant-soldier. But battlefield defeats, economic exhaustion, and official corruption finally destroyed the Romanovs' legitimacy. In March 1917 Nicholas II abdicated in favor of a provisional government. Woodrow Wilson applauded the fact that the Allied camp was now wholly democratic, but when Congress declared war on Germany the following month, the United States assumed much of the burden of sustaining the Russian war effort. The only way to do that was to ship supplies across the North Pacific and thence by the Trans-Siberian Railway to the eastern front. But the railroad was worn out, the authority of the provisional government barely extended beyond the Urals, and munitions collected on the docks of Vladivostok for want of transportation. So Wilson offered to send engineers to help maintain Russia's six-thousand-mile lifeline. Who was "the best-qualified man for the job"? John F. Stevens, of course. He reached Vladivostok in June, took a look around, and requested Wilson to send a whole *corps* of railroad workers. But by the time the three hundred engineers from the Great Northern and Northern Pacific arrived in Siberia in November, Lenin and Trotsky had toppled the provisional government, and Siberia fell into chaos. The engineers retreated to Japan and Stevens just fumed: "We should all go back shortly with men-of-war and 5,000 troops. Time is coming to put the fear of God into these people."

In fact, Russia was full of fear and about to be fought over by Communists, ex-tsarists, liberals, socialists, insurgent nationalities, and Cossacks, while German armies invaded from the west and Japanese militarists itched to do the same from the east. Britain and France wanted to intervene in order to deny the Germans Siberia's resources, protect the supplies in Russian ports, and perhaps revive an eastern front. But they had no troops or money to spare, so the Allies looked to the United States and Japan. Wilson feared that foreign intervention might alienate the Russians and make the Bolsheviks more popular. Nor did he trust the Japanese. So American policy must be to "Do Nothing." In his Fourteen Points speech of January 8, 1918, Wilson called for "evacuation of all Russian territory and such settlement of all questions affecting Russia as will secure the best and freest cooperation of the other nations of the world in obtaining for her an unhampered and unembarrassed opportunity for the independent determination of her own political development and national policy."

Unfortunately, a wait-and-see policy was unlikely to preserve Russia's territorial integrity or self-determination, much less defeat Germany. So the Allied chiefs leaned harder on Wilson, while the French Foreign Minister went so far as to warn of "some sort of alliance between Germany and Japan, providing for the division of Russia" if Japanese were allowed into Siberia alone. Americans in the field also urged that something be done. Stevens feared mounting German and Bolshevik influence in Siberia, and Reinsch, at Peking, believed that most Russians would welcome an Allied occupation so long as the Japanese did not go in alone. Lansing also came to favor intervention, if only to prevent a Bolshevik victory in the spreading Russian Civil War. He had foreseen that the communist revolution would "far surpass in brutality and destruction of life and property the Terror of the French Revolution." But intervention, Wilson insisted, would compromise the moral position on which the American war effort was based.

Then came the news of Brest-Litovsk. In March 1918 the Bolsheviks signed a treaty with the German High Command and took Russia out of the war. The purpose of Lenin's "peace offensive" was to free up the Bolsheviks to consolidate their power in Russia, but its effect was to turn over half the population and resources of European Russia to the Germans. Allied foreign ministers agreed at once "On the Urgency for Allied Intervention in East Russia." Japan expressed concern "over the chaotic conditions in Siberia," and landed units at Vladivostok in April. Within a month they were fanning out along the Chinese Eastern Railway. Wilson confessed that he was "sweating blood over the question of what is right and feasible to do in Russia." But the Japanese intervention, and some new intelligence from Siberia, finally forced him to act. Some seventy thousand Czech prisoners of war, formerly of the Habsburg armies, were stranded in Russia and trying to make their way out via the Trans-Siberian Railway. The Czechs' intention was to circle the globe and fight alongside the *Allies* in France to liberate their homeland.

At first the Bolsheviks aided this Czech Legion, but their attempts to disarm the formidable force soon led to friction and fighting. It would be "a serious mistake," wired Reinsch, "to remove the Czecho-Slovak troops from Siberia. With only slight countenance and support they could control all of Siberia against the Germans." Wilson was intrigued. The Czechs were "cousins of the Russians," and a small Allied force supplying the Czechs might save Siberia from Germans and Bolsheviks alike. Stevens cabled: "Quick effective Allied action Siberia against treacherous combination necessary . . . if Allies expect to save Siberia they should move."

Helping the brave Czecho-Slovaks was a pretext sufficient to satisfy even the scrupulous Wilson. On July 6 his cabinet sanctioned an occupation of the Trans-Siberian as far west as Irkutsk by a Japanese-American force, its sole purpose being to "cooperate" with the Czecho-Slovaks. Wilson made it clear that the troops were not to impair Russia's political or territorial sovereignty, and Tokyo solemnly agreed. Unfortunately, it was not clear who spoke for Japan, her cordial diplomats or the generals who pushed for the invasion. U.S. Army Chief of Staff Peyton C. March had no hope that Japan would forgo aggrandizement. "Well," replied Wilson, "we will have to take that chance."

Major General William S. Graves was eager to fight in France. He had never led large units in combat but was promised a command after four months' practice with a Stateside division. He was with the Eighth Infantry at Camp Frémont when a coded telegram came on August 2, 1918: "Take the first and fastest train out of San Francisco and proceed to Kansas City, go to the Baltimore Hotel, and ask for the Secretary of War." His train was late, so Newton D. Baker met him at the station and said "he was sorry he had to send me to Siberia." The Secretary of War then handed the general his orders, adding only: "This contains the policy of the United States in Russia which you are to follow. Watch your step; you will be walking on eggs loaded with dynamite. God bless you and good-bye."

Historians do not agree on why Wilson sent soldiers to Russia. There are just too many plausible reasons: to protect the war supplies in Russian ports; to aid nationalist Russians in resisting the Germans; to deny Japan a free hand in Siberia; to help extract the Czech Legion; to help *not* extract the Legion so it could secure the Trans-Siberian Railway; to help "White" Russians fight the "Reds"; to preserve the Open Door in Manchuria. But it is also plausible that Wilson gave in just to get his insistent aides and Allies off his back. For the secret orders given General Graves turned out to be nothing more than a State Department circular already sent to the Allied governments on July 17. It bespoke

America's desire "to cooperate in every practicable way with the allied governments, and to cooperate ungrudgingly; for it has no ends of its own to serve." It asserted that the proper place for the United States to contribute to victory was on the western front, and that intervention in Russia "would add to the present sad confusion in Russia rather than cure it; injure her rather than help her." The motives for intervention were only to help the Czecho-Slovaks, guard military stores, and "steady any efforts at self-government or self-defence in which the Russians themselves may be willing to accept assistance." Finally, the American note assured the Russian people that "none of the governments uniting in action either in Siberia or northern Russia contemplates any interference of any kind with the political sovereignty of Russia, any intervention in her internal affairs, or any impairment of her territorial integrity either now or hereafter."

Wilsonian words—and Wilson surely meant them. But the mere presence of American and Japanese troops on Siberia's lifeline endowed their governments with the power to tilt the politics of half a continent. So the caution to Graves not to interfere in Russian politics was absurd, and to the extent he honored it, good soldier that he was, he made himself absurd. Graves knew that soon enough and was bitter about it until the day he died.

The War Department cut orders on August 3: the twenty-seventh and thirty-first infantry regiments were to proceed to Vladivostok at once with whatever winter clothing was available. Given that those units were based in the Philippines, such clothing was hardly plentiful. The first contingents landed on August 16, and Graves arrived on September 1. He learned at once that the Japanese general was parading himself as "commander-in-chief" of the expedition. Graves told him that American boys served only under American officers, and the matter was never mentioned again. The second thing Graves learned was that there were not seven thousand Japanese in Siberia, as promised, but at least sixty thousand. The total reached seventy-two thousand, and their officers muscled their way into railroad matters, vexing Stevens and his men, and encroached on the American zone. Worst of all, the Japanese played favorites among the indigenous factions, especially the Ussuri Cossacks, who (in the absence of a Russian central government) had become lawless.

Graves was pleased to find Siberia no colder than North Dakota and relatively dry. Only in the interior were the snowpack and temperatures extreme. But the accommodations at Vladivostok and Khabarovsk, and on the railroad, were dismal. He commandeered tsarist barracks for his men and refused to share them, "although at the time it became embarrassing to justify the need of twice the air space considered necessary for a Japanese or Russian soldier." But bathing and sanitation facilities scarcely existed, and disease was endemic. The men in the field, the railroad guards, lived in boxcars. But then, during the Russian Civil War a Siberian boxcar was a sought-after billet obtainable only by a bribe or a gun. The railroad was a bloodstream, the only source of food, shelter, security, and mobility in a land otherwise careless of murder and famine. The Czechs lived in commodious boxcars insulated with layers of ash. Cossacks and Bolsheviks lived out of armored trains limned with steel plate and topped with sandbags and machine gun nests. Wealthy noblemen fleeing red terror, radicals fleeing white terror, young men fleeing conscription gangs, peasant girls and grandfathers fleeing this or that army—all sold whatever they had for passage a bit farther down the line toward the Pacific. And everyone wanted to know of everyone else "whose side are you on?" The Yanks weren't supposed to be on any-one's side, yet Graves "could not give a Russian a shirt without being subjected to the charge of trying to help the side to which the recipient of the shirt belonged."

If not to take sides, what was the expedition about? That question especially gripped Graves after November 11, 1918, when news of the armistice came by wire: Germany had quit, and the world war was over. He daily expected a recall, but no orders came. The armistice changed nothing in Siberia. Graves then concluded that his troops must be there to favor some side in the Civil War. But no orders came to that effect either, despite the fact that British agents, Japanese commanders, and the American Consul himself all urged him to oppose bolshevism. But where were the Bolsheviks? They had made a brief show of raising the red flag on the Pacific in 1917 until ex-tsarist officials and local Siberi-ans chased them away. Since then, a Siberian government of sorts had formed up at Omsk, and another at Ufa. When the two merged in November 1918 into an All-Russian Directory led by a minister of the former provisional government, it seemed that Siberia might have a "liberal" regime after all. But just two nights later a cabal of tsarist offi-cers in league with the British and French overthrew the Directory and made Adm. Alexander V. Kolchak "supreme ruler" of Siberia. Kolchak was a patriot but had contempt for the masses and no discernible savvy for politics or war. Under his aegis Siberia fell into the hands of corrupt reactionaries hiding behind lofty titles.

Graves hated the Omsk regime. Kolchak's officers rode up and down the railroad seizing taxes and impressing men for their army—an army unpaid and short of weapons because the officers themselves skimmed the payroll and sold off half the supplies. All who resisted were called Bolsheviks, beaten with the knout, or shot. And the worst of it was that

Kolchak's supplies were paid for by the old tsarist embassy's First National City account and shipped under the guns of the U.S. Army. Just by guarding the railroad Graves was helping Kolchak. Was that what Washington intended? Perhaps, because Ernest L. Harris, U.S. Consul at Omsk, supported Kolchak from the first. But Graves refused to favor anyone and so was denounced by Bolshevik propaganda as an agent of imperialism, *and* by Kolchak's propaganda as a Bolshevik sympathizer "most of [whose] troops were Jews from New York."

Nor was Kolchak the worst. The worst were Gregorii Semenov, Ivan Kalmikov, and their freebooting Cossacks, who plundered the railroad, razed villages, raped, thieved, and murdered at will, then fled for refuge to the Japanese zone. Semenov bragged of having to kill a man each day before he could sleep, and Kalmikov "was the worst scoundrel I ever saw or ever heard of and I seriously doubt . . . if a crime could be found that Kalmikoff had not committed." Why did the Japanese pay and protect them? Because, Graves surmised, they hoped that the chaos would drive the Yanks out, whereupon they could take over.

Graves wanted nothing more than to go home. Instead, on February 10, 1919, agreement was finally reached on formation of an Interallied Railroad Committee to manage the Trans-Siberian and Chinese Eastern railways. The Japanese had picked over every clause in hopes of expanding their rights, but so had Stevens—just as in Panama, he would brook no diluted authority. Now that agreement was reached, two months *after* the end of the war, Graves's regiments were stuck: someone had to guard Stevens's railroad men. To Graves and Consul Harris alike it was idiotic. If Washington really wanted to combat bolshevism, why did it not recognize Kolchak and rescind the nonintervention order? If, on the other hand, Washington did *not* care to fight Bolsheviks, why was the Army in Russia at all? But no decisions could be expected from Washington now. Wilson, Lansing, and Colonel House had departed for Paris.

The Paris Peace Conference opened on January 18, 1919. Its main business was peace with Germany, although the fate of Russia was a constant, ominous undercurrent. Moreover, the German settlement meant disposing of Germany's Asian and Pacific colonies, and that issue came as near to breaking up the conference as any of its bitter European disputes. For Baron Makino Nobuaki, the acting chief of the Japanese delegation, arrived in Paris with explicit instructions. On questions in which Japan had no direct interest, he was to "strive not to interfere"; on questions of general interest he was to "keep in step as far as possible with the Allied and Associated Powers"; but on questions of direct interest to Japan he was to demand the cession of all Germany's territorial and economic rights in China and the North Pacific islands. Britain and France had already granted Japan as much in wartime treaties, but Wilson was hostile to imperialism and secret diplomacy, and wanted Shantung returned to China.

Japan's effort to secure its share of the spoils of victory was no different from those of the other powers (save the United States, which asked for no territory or reparations). But rather than ranking Japan with Britain and France, whose wishes Wilson could hardly ignore, the President treated Japan on a par with Italy, whose ambitions he scorned with a hateful intensity. When the Italian delegation walked out in protest, the Japanese threatened to do likewise. More telling, Makino made it clear that Japan would not join the League of Nations unless Wilson acceded to his demands. Thus, the Peace Conference reduced itself to a clash between the victorious powers who expected to play politics according to pre-1914 rules and Wilson, who meant to enforce the new rules of diplomacy adumbrated in his Fourteen Points.

What did the Japanese think of Wilson's Fourteen Points? Makino's instructions on that score make for interesting reading, for nowhere else was the divergence between the Japanese and American views of the world more starkly revealed. In Point 1 Wilson called for "open covenants openly arrived at." The Japanese Foreign Ministry thought secret negotiations often appropriate, but "if there is a move to put an end to all secret diplomacy," then its delegates might "go along with the prevailing opinion." In Point 2 Wilson called for freedom of the seas. The Japanese wisely noted that "countries having superior sea power tend to interpret that freedom in a narrow sense," and so told their delegates "to keep in step with Britain." Point 3 called for the removal of economic barriers among nations. Here the Japanese found it "difficult to simply say yes or no" but insisted on retaining the right to discriminate in favor of their own firms and domestic market. Point 4 called for disarmament. Tokyo deemed that "inadvisable" but instructed its delegates not to appear "contrary to the spirit of peace and humanity." Point 5 called for adjustment of colonial claims in the interests of the inhabitants. The Japanese flatly refused to subordinate their colonial policy to the "interests" of Chinese or Micronesians. Points 6 through 13 dealt with Europe, in which the Japanese had no interest. But Point 14 called for a League of Nations, adjudication of international disputes, and collective security. "In the view of the present situation," read the Japanese instructions, "where racial prejudice among nations has not been eliminated at all, it is feared that the methods employed to achieve the objective of the League might bring disadvantages to our Empire." Japan preferred that the League Covenant be "remoulded into a statement of intention, leaving the methods for the implementation of the League system to be studied by each country." Still, if the League emerged, "our country cannot remain isolated outside of it."

Wilson made a host of tactical blunders in Paris, the most damaging of which was probably his decision to be there himself, rather than leave the dirty work to the State Department. But his insistence that the first order of business be the drafting of the League of Nations Covenant gave all the Allies the chance to blackmail him. The Japanese ploy was to insist that the Covenant include a racial equality clause under which all nations agreed not to "discriminate, either in law or in fact, against any person or persons on account of his or their race or nationality." Such a clause would prohibit white nations from restricting Asian immigration and was fiercely opposed in California, Canada, Australia, and New Zealand. When the League Commission approved the plank anyway, eleven to six, Wilson ruled that unanimity was required and threw it out. So his moral authority was punctured at once, and Japanese editorials damned him for a hypocrite, a "Kaiser" in sheep's clothing, worse yet, a "female despot."

Wilson's subsequent crusade against the Japanese demand for Kiao-chow never stood a chance. His credibility was shot, Britain and France were in Tokyo's camp, and Makino still held his trump card: refusal to join the League of Nations. So on April 30, after a sleepless night, Wilson surrendered, receiving in return only a promise that Japan would restore Kiao-chow to China sometime in the future. Now *American* editorials condemned Wilson for betraying his ideals and giving in to "wily, tricky, fight-thirsty Japan." Senator Hiram Johnson called it "the blackest day in all our history" and Henry Cabot Lodge, chairman of the Senate Foreign Relations Committee, warned that "Japan is steeped in German ideas and regards war as an industry." But this paled before the reaction in China. When news of the sellout leaked on May 4, student protesters raged in the streets against Japanese and Americans alike.

Finally, Japan demanded German Micronesia. The U.S. Navy had hoped that the Marshalls, Carolines, and Marianas might at least be neutralized, while clerks in the State Department, citing the danger to the Philippines and Guam, plotted to cheat Japan entirely. Breckinridge Long urged that the United States insist on returning the islands to Germany—with the secret intention of purchasing them from Berlin after a decent interval. "Of course," he added, "this could not be done morally while the Peace Conference sits." It could not be done at all. The Japanese would not budge, and Wilson finally handed them Micronesia under the fig leaf of a Class C mandate from the League of Nations. So the Paris Peace Conference was a clean sweep for Japan, while the United States gleaned nothing but ill will.

Nor did the Peace Conference make any progress on Russia. In January it invited Reds and Whites to parlay on the isle of Prinkipo, but the Whites refused to attend. In March, Wilson dispatched William Bullitt to Moscow, but by the time he returned with Lenin's terms for a truce, the Allies were no longer interested. Winston Churchill's plan for an invasion to overthrow Lenin broke on the war-weariness and labor opposition in Allied nations. In May Britain and France promised to aid Kolchak in return for a promise of liberal reforms, but Wilson clung to neutrality. So did General Graves. "Every Kolchak adherent I talk to asks the question if we do not intend to fight Bolsheviks why are we in their country. . . ?" But barring instructions to the contrary, he refused to engage his troops. As for the railroad, wrote Graves, the "noble sentiments" behind American policy might be to maintain traffic in the interests of the Siberian people, but the "value of the operation of these railways to the great mass of the Russian people was absolutely nil." They were in fact "Kolchak Railroads financed by the Allies." Graves wired the War Department that "We are squarely up against the proposition of using force or getting out."

So the Yanks were caught in a killing zone. Semenov multiplied his brutalities, as did his Japanese sponsors. In July, a Japanese firing squad summarily executed suspected Bolsheviks *inside* the American zone. "The five Russians were marched to some graves that had been dug in the vicinity of the railroad station; they were blindfolded and forced to kneel at the edge of the graves, bending forward with their hands tied behind them. Two Japanese officers, removing their coats and drawing their sabers, then proceeded to slash the victims on the back of the neck, while as each one fell forward into the grave, three to five Japanese soldiers bayonetted him several times with cries of pleasure." Graves protested but nothing changed. Nothing ever changed in Siberia.

In the summer of 1919 the U.S. Ambassador in Tokyo, Roland P. Morris, was ordered to evaluate Kolchak's prospects. He traveled with Graves over three thousand miles on a special train guarded by soldiers. Graves prayed they would encounter no Cossacks—he had no artillery sufficient to dent one of Semenov's steel-armored war trains. After safely arriving at Omsk, Graves then fought with Consul Harris for the Ambassador's mind. Morris agreed with the Consul that Kolchak was "an honest and courageous man" with "good intentions", but he agreed with the general that his regime was riddled with cruel reactionaries. More to the point, he learned that Kolchak's offensive against the Reds had collapsed, and his armies were in full retreat. Morris wired Washington that Kolchak might be saved, but only if the United States granted him recognition, $200 million, and twenty-five thousand American soldiers. Failing such help, "we will be forced to abandon eastern Siberia to Japanese domination."

Japanese domination, not Bolshevik domination! For as much as the Wilson administration feared the Communists, the sole consistent element in its policy had been to uphold Russian sovereignty on the Pacific seaboard. Wilson dreamed of a liberal, national, united Russia, but he also believed that it had to work out its own fate. He did not want—and could never persuade Congress to fight—a shooting war at the end of the earth. The most he could do was to hold the Siberian railroad in trust until some Russian government emerged to reclaim it. So the United States let Kolchak collapse, while warning *Japan* in the strongest terms yet not to exploit or remain in Siberia.

The Red Army occupied Omsk in November. Kolchak and his minions fled down the railroad in a convoy of trains, one of which carried $300 million in gold from the tsarist state bank. He surrendered to the Czech Legion and appealed to the Allies. But it was now a year since the end of the war, and the Czecho-Slovaks wanted only to escape. So they turned over Kolchak, gold and all, to the Communists, in return for safe passage out of Siberia. The Communists shot Kolchak on February 7, 1920. Down the railroad the refugees fled, starving and freezing in the Siberian winter, until "every station was a graveyard, with hundreds and in many places thousands of unburied dead." Those who survived to reach the Pacific brought with them their confusion over the role of the Yanks, who had not lifted a rifle to help them fight Lenin. In the Vladivostok terminal, one Russian officer accosted a drunken doughboy and called him a f—ing Bolshevik. The American made a fist and the Russian shot him dead. Nearby, some Japanese officers cheered.

Even Lansing knew it was over. "The truth of the matter," he wrote Wilson, "is the simple fact that the Kolchak Government has utterly collapsed. . . . [I]f we do not withdraw we shall have to wage war against the Bolsheviki." So the War Department ordered Graves to ship his men home as soon as the Czechs were safely out, thus fulfilling their ostensible mission. The last Yanks departed on April Fools' Day, 1920, marching to Stephen Foster's "Hard Times, Come Again No More" played by a Japanese band. Who stayed in Siberia? The Japanese did, and so did John Stevens, who reported with alarm the latest evidence that Japan intended to keep the Chinese Eastern Railway and establish hegemony over Manchuria.

Graves got no hero's welcome. In fact, Gen. Leonard Wood hoped he had kept his orders, else he would be "torn limb from limb" for refusing to fight the Bolsheviks. As the *Literary Digest* put it: "Some might have liked us more if we had intervened less, [and] some might have disliked us less if we had intervened more, but that, having concluded that we intended to intervene no more nor no less than we actually did, nobody had any use for us at all." But Stevens and Graves achieved one useful thing: they kept the Trans-Siberian out of the hands of Japan and the bloodthirsty Semenov. The irony is that they saved it for Stalin.

Wilson by now was an invalid. He had collapsed while barnstorming for the League of Nations, and when he refused to accept the Senate's reservations attached to the Treaty of Versailles, it failed of ratification on March 19, 1920. That meant that the United States would not join the League. It also meant that the United States did not formally recognize the gains made by Japan. So U.S.-Japanese relations were back to square one again, and the upshot could only be another war scare.

Washington, D.C. 1921

AMERICANS ALWAYS want to create new world orders. Japan's fate is to try to get by in whatever world order it finds. Following the Meiji Restoration the world was imperialist, and the Japanese learned how to play. Then Woodrow Wilson got it into his head to change the rules. And even though his own people rejected the League of Nations, they by and large shared Wilson's insistence that other nations repent of imperialism and war. But how could Japan's leadership embrace the new diplomacy without seeming to "knuckle under" to the white powers again? Moreover, the years after World War I were a time when representative government seemed to be winning out in Japan. Would a tough U.S. stance against colonies and armaments strengthen the Japanese liberals or just play into the hands of xenophobes? Americans did not ask that question, even though its answer was far more important to the future of the Pacific than which country had more battleships.

Hara Kei was not from Satsuma or Chōshū. He was born in "the sticks" of northeastern Honshu in 1856. Nor was he of noble birth but was called (like William Jennings Bryan) "The Great Commoner." Nor did Hara tether his ambition to the gunboats of Japanese expansion; rather, his upbringing prepared him for his role as modern Japan's first populist. He took a degree from Tokyo Imperial University, the conduit for Western ideas, then did a stint at journalism, which taught him the uses of public opinion. In 1882 he joined the diplomatic corps, where cosmopolitan, liberal ideas predominated. He prospered from the Meiji principle of promotion by merit and the patronage of Itō Hirobumi. Hara was a charter member of the Seiyukai party and served eight terms in the Diet and three times as minister in the Home Office. Finally, in 1914, he attained the Seiyukai party presidency. Of course, the old *genrō* still wielded tremendous influence, as did the military, while consensus

remained the watchword in Japanese politics. But Hara quietly fashioned a grass-roots organization based on patronage, the pork barrel,
kickbacks from business, and expansion of the franchise. Moreover,
Hara denounced socialism and unruly students, opposed the nascent
labor unions, quashed a bill favoring universal male suffrage, and
labored to appease the Army and Navy. In sum, he was just the sort of
leader needed to establish democratic government for the very fact that
he was skilled, authoritarian, and relatively nonthreatening to traditional elites.

Hara was especially skilled at taming the military. During the war,
the Army (stocked with Chōshū clansmen) and the Navy (dominated by
Satsuma men) had come to rely on Hara to broker agreements and shepherd their programs (and the taxes to pay for them) through the parliament. So when General Terauchi's cabinet had to resign in 1918 in the
face of inflation, rice riots, and strikes, the council of genrō made Hara
Prime Minister. Progressive newspapers hailed the advent of what they
called Taishō Democracy, the triumph of civilian, majority rule. Most
politicians still feared to give offense to the services, but Hara told his
finance minister to freeze the arms budget. The war would end soon,
after which he expected public opinion to shift in favor of arms control.
Then he might carry out his own agenda of education and public works.

Hara's instincts were right, but he failed to anticipate that events
abroad might weaken his hand and strengthen the military's. On March
1, 1919, over two million Korean patriots took to the streets in peaceful
protest against Japanese rule. The occupiers responded by killing 23,000
more people and arresting another 47,500. Korean nationalists, including the young Syngman Rhee, formed a government-in-exile in China,
while resisters and refugees fled north into chaotic Siberia. So an additional motive for Japan to occupy Siberia was to shut it down as a sanctuary for Korean rebels. But after the fall of Kolchak's regime the victorious Bolsheviks turned against the occupiers and in March 1920
slaughtered a hundred or more Japanese in the town of Nikolaevsk.
Ignoring Tokyo's pleas for prudence, the Japanese Army retaliated by
seizing the northern half of Sakhalin Island—the territory denied Japan
at the Portsmouth Peace Conference. Hara despised the Siberian expedition, not least because it cost 1.5 billion yen. But if he ordered the Army
home, it might refuse to obey, denounce civilian government, and possibly murder the Prime Minister himself. Needless to add, Japanese
excesses in Korea and Siberia only confirmed the American impression
that Japan was incorrigibly militaristic.

But so, it seemed, was the United States! For the Wilson administration, pacifist rhetoric notwithstanding, continued to promote naval
expansion right on past the armistice. The campaign had begun, for

unimpeachable reasons, in 1916. German U-boats plied the Atlantic and Wilson, arguing that preparedness was the best means of defending U.S neutrality, challenged Congress to fund "incomparably the greatest navy in the world." He later substituted the words "most adequate" for "greatest," but the 1916 program nonetheless authorized $588 million for 157 new ships. By the time the new keels were laid, America was in the war and committed to a two-ocean navy "second to none." The key to a strong Pacific fleet was the thousand-foot dry dock planned for Pearl Harbor. The San Francisco Bridge Company's first effort ended in spectacular failure. As soon as the water was removed from the dock, the viscous harbor bottom "sunk up," buckling the edifice. Alfred Noble, a famous New York engineer, solved the problem by designing an artificial sea bottom made of concrete boxes. (Hawaiians preferred to believe that the shark god was at fault, and an old enchantress inaugurated the new construction in 1913 with a sacrifice of cracker crumbs and a litany: "No more *pilikia* [nuisance] to this dock!") Six years later the dry dock was drained—and survived. The Navy now had a mid-Pacific port able to berth and service twenty-one capital ships—enough, it was thought, to frighten Japan.

All told, the U.S. buildup would yield a navy of six hundred ships totaling two million tons. The Royal Navy, by contrast, numbered seven hundred ships and 2.4 million tons. Still, the Navy asked for more, including twenty-eight battleships and battle cruisers. The British were not amused, but neither could they afford to race the United States after being bled dry by the Great War. The result was one of the lesser-known struggles at the Paris Peace Conference. In private conversations, Prime Minister David Lloyd George threatened to repudiate the Monroe Doctrine, refuse to share the surrendered German fleet, and boycott the League of Nations unless Wilson retreated on Freedom of the Seas and suspended his naval construction plan. On April 10, 1919, Colonel House and Lord Robert Cecil cut a deal. Wilson promised to forgo new naval construction in return for British cooperation on the League of Nations.

Back home, Wilson played his naval card again, warning senators that rejection of the League would condemn taxpayers to an expensive and dangerous arms race. But some senators thought naval supremacy a more reliable guarantee of peace than the League of Nations and attacked Wilson for making U.S. policy subject to the say-so of Britain. Others endorsed disarmament but saw no reason why a League was needed to implement it. Most senators were prepared to accept the Treaty of Versailles with reservations, but Wilson preferred political martyrdom to compromise. So the treaty failed of ratification, the Anglo-American deal became a dead letter, and American shipyards kept busy, while newspapers sounded alarms about Japanese expansion in China, Siberia, and the Pacific.

What were the Japanese to think? From their point of view it seemed that the United States was bent on Pacific naval hegemony. In 1918, Hara Kei had held the line on naval construction with the "eight-six program"—eight new battleships and six new battle cruisers. But by the spring of 1920 the Japanese Naval Ministry howled for more, and Hara had no arguments with which to resist. So he tabled his domestic programs, went back to the Diet, and won approval of an "eight-eight program" for capital ships and 103 new ships in all.

The reciprocal naval programs of the United States and Japan inspired a new round of war prophecies and war plans on both sides of the ocean. Imitators of Homer Lea published books entitled *The Menace of Japan*, *Must We Fight Japan?*, and *The Next War*, while Japanese debated "Shall Japan Fight America?" and condemned the United States as "a land of selfish devils" intent on extending its Monroe Doctrine to Asia. To the U.S. Office of Naval Intelligence it seemed that "Japan is preparing for any eventuality that may occur and that America is the country she has in mind." The Naval Plans Division confronted the contingency of a war against an alliance of Orange (Japan), Red (Britain), and possibly Green (Mexico). The Japanese Navy, in turn, identified the United States as its most likely assailant and justified the need "to make America think it is impossible to wage an unjust war against Japan, or even if she did, that she must expect very serious loss." The State Department badgered the British with inquiries about whether the Anglo-Japanese alliance might be renewed. Japan persistently clung to its British tie.

Charles Evans Hughes inherited the mess Wilson left in the Pacific. Named President Harding's Secretary of State following the Republican sweep in 1920, Hughes was the greatest statesman of his age never to become President. A native of Glens Falls, New York, he came of age at Brown University, where he delighted in cigarettes, poker, French novels, and baseball, and earned spending money by writing essays for classmates. Most shocking to his father, a Baptist minister, was his infatuation with Brown President Ezekiel Robinson and Professor J. Lewis Diman, both of whom rejected the Bible and taught an ethics of reason. By the time he graduated in 1881 Hughes had embraced Episcopal latitudinarianism and later wrote of Diman, "I came under his influence, and it was probably the most potent moulding factor in the formative days of my youth. That man woke me up."

After Columbia Law School, Hughes passed the bar with a near perfect score, married the daughter of his senior partner, and grew respectably rich. He worked long hours, played with his children, drank little, and quit smoking when he decided one day it was irrational: a puritan sans theology. Then, in 1905, scandal broke in New York City. That was hardly news—it was the heyday of Tammany Hall—but Hughes's "model inquiry" attracted the attention of Theodore Roosevelt, who all but ordered New York Republicans to run him for governor. His Democratic opponent, William Randolph Hearst, belittled Hughes as an "animated feather-duster" (a reference to his Edward VII whiskers), but Hughes warned that "the man who would corrupt public opinion is the most dangerous enemy of the state." He won in a squeaker and devoted his two terms to regulating utilities and railroads. In 1910, Taft appointed him to the Supreme Court, and in 1916 he seemed just the candidate to reunite the Republican party. When the convention chose him on the third ballot, Hughes wrote his opponent Wilson a laconic memo: "I hereby resign the office of Associate Justice of the Supreme Court of the United States."

Then Hughes's luck took a vacation. He made a high-profile visit to California at the very moment when Old Guard Republicans and Progressives were clawing for control of the state party. Hughes managed to offend both factions, while Teddy Roosevelt's bellicose interventionism toward the European war alienated California's German and Irish voters and reinforced Wilson's image as the peace candidate. Still, the November election was deathly close, and Wilson went to bed believing he had lost. But the early morning telegraph transmitted the California count: Hughes had lost its thirteen electoral votes by fewer than four thousand ballots—and the presidency by 254 electoral votes to 277 for Wilson. "I had done my best," Hughes wrote later. "While of course I did not enjoy being beaten, the fact that I did not have to assume the tasks of the Presidency in that critical time was an adequate consolation." But we can only imagine how history might have been different had Hughes, and not Wilson, presided over the end of World War I.

Four years later, President-elect Harding asked Hughes to suspend his $500,000-a-year law practice and take over the State Department. Hughes accepted for the usual reason: it was a "call no one could well refuse in justice to what he conceived to be his duty to his country." That duty was to head off a war with Japan, stop the naval arms race, replace the Anglo-Japanese alliance with some instrument of collective security, uphold the Open Door, and persuade the Japanese to leave Kiao-chow and Siberia.

Hughes was able to harness the widespread popular revulsion against armaments that followed the bloody Great War. "If peoples have really become convinced that war and preparation for war are poor *business*," he wrote, "we may hope for peace, provided a sense of security can be created and maintained and disputes find processes of peaceful adjustment." Not exactly a gripping applause line—he was always a bit stuffy—but in that sentence Hughes put his finger on the symbiosis between democracy and expert diplomacy, between idealism and realism. Wilson was right to denounce wasteful arms races, but it was up to the statesman to provide hardheaded structures for resolution of conflict and so inject reason into a world of emotion. The contrast between Wilson and Hughes emerges most clearly in their relationship to a third party, Sen. William Borah of Idaho. Borah hated armaments as much as Wilson did. But he was also isolationist, so the fixated Wilson could not employ him. Borah and Hughes had little in common. But the practical Hughes could exploit Borah's zeal to advance his own hardheaded diplomacy. When Borah's December 1920 resolution calling for arms talks with Britain passed the Senate unanimously, it lit a fire that leaped the oceans. Ozaki Yukio, a fiery democrat, preached to the Diet for two hours on behalf of an arms control conference and won the endorsement of 90 percent of Japan's newspapers. By mid-1921 the Japanese officer corps was on the defensive and began to discuss *how*, rather than *whether*, to go about limiting arms.

Lloyd George also cast about for ways to avoid a naval race, but to save face asked Hughes to make the first move. Hughes would make no move until the British and Japanese agreed to terminate their alliance. Both parties took pains to explain that their alliance was not anti-American. But Hughes politely protested to the British Ambassador that continuation of the alliance would oblige Britain to support "the special interests of Japan," which would only encourage the "militaristic party," which would necessitate American retaliation and so lead to a state of affairs "fraught with mischief." That same week, Canadian Prime Minister Arthur Meighen rallied the Dominions at an imperial conference to replace the Anglo-Japanese alliance with a security pact including the United States. Lloyd George was in a box: he feared offending Japan, a loyal ally of two decades, but he feared offending the United States and Canada more. That was the moment chosen by Hughes to throw a lifeline to London and Tokyo in the form of an invitation to a grand conference to discuss naval armaments and Far Eastern affairs.

But what exact form would the settlements take? The suspicious British dickered for weeks in hopes of manipulating the agenda. Hughes refused, and Lloyd George gave in. The Japanese, too, were suspicious— one editorialist predicted that Japan would be "drubbed and mauled by the Powers" if it went to Washington. But to *refuse* to attend once Britain accepted would ensure Japanese isolation. So even though Hughes refused to explain just what he meant by "Far Eastern affairs," Hara accepted his invitation anyway. He was able to pull it off for a number of reasons: the popular outcry led by Ozaki; Hara's carefully nurtured reputation as a friend to the military; his wisdom in choosing the respected Adm. Katō Tomosaburō as chief delegate; the Army's hopes of benefiting if the *Navy's* size was limited; and the fact that wise heads in the Navy began to appreciate the potential of arms limitation. At present, Japan enjoyed a tonnage ratio of about 6:10 versus the U.S. Navy. If the admirals sabotaged arms control talks and provoked an American buildup, Japan's ratio was bound to get worse. Moreover, "the fact that the Imperial Navy today is readily able to maintain the national defense against the United States Navy depends principally upon the fact that the United States has insufficient advanced bases in the Pacific and the Far East." Should the United States expand its facilities in the Philippines, Guam, and Hawaii, the "disadvantages [for] the Empire would most certainly be unendurable."

So just as Hughes rode the wave of American opinion and used his levers to move Britain, so did Hara manipulate the popular and elitist forces in Japanese politics into endorsing the Washington Conference. "Peace in the Pacific," he told the *New York World,* "is the insistent cry of the Japanese people." Nor was that a mere cream puff baked for American consumption. Hara's own instructions to Katō began: "The establishment of permanent world peace and the promotion of the welfare of mankind are fundamental principles of Japan's diplomacy." Katō was to refute the "misunderstandings or prejudices" about Japan's past policies and pursue "the maintenance of friendly and smooth relations with the United States." He was authorized to negotiate arms limitations and if necessary replace the Anglo-Japanese alliance with a "triple entente between Japan, Britain, and the United States." Still, no Japanese admiral expected a *reduction* of fleets, while the U.S. Naval Board endorsed, at most, a freeze.

The venue was Constitution Hall on Seventeenth Street, the home of the Daughters of the American Revolution. The hall's "white panels shone brilliantly, the more so because they were left unrelieved by colorful decoration," wrote Ichihashi Yamato. But breaking the whiteness were the black morning coats of the delegates and the green baize tabletops before them. Foreigners expressed wry shock at the bursting galleries. Was this what Americans meant by "open diplomacy"—that delicate talks should occur in the presence of journalists and assorted VIPs? H. G. Wells was there, and Justice William Brandeis, Alice Roosevelt Longworth, and William Jennings Bryan, who looked like an "Old Testament prophet, not quite sure, yet, whether to shed benevolence on the occasion or to thunder anathema if things should go wrong." They all expected a boring first day: an opening prayer, a welcoming address from the plodding Harding, the usual courtesies. Then Hughes mounted the rostrum with a text that had been locked in a vault. So fearful was he of leaks that he asked Harding for permission to deliver the speech at once. "Oh, that's alright," replied the uncomprehending President. "Go ahead." So Hughes proceeded to speak, not of principles, but of plans. The powers gathered here, he said, must declare to undertake no new construction of capital ships for at least ten years. Then, before the audience could catch its breath, Hughes pledged to scrap, within ninety days of an agreement, thirty capital ships from the U.S. Navy totaling 845,740 tons, instructed Britain to scrap nineteen and Japan seventeen— and not old tubs but many just launched or under construction. In a mere fifteen minutes, wrote a British observer, Hughes sank more battleships "than all the admirals of the world have sunk in a cycle of centuries." Nor need anyone fear the result, for the freeze and the cuts would leave the British, American, and Japanese fleets in roughly the 10:10:6 ratio they described at the time. "With the acceptance of this plan," promised Hughes, "the burden of meeting the demands of competition in naval armaments will be lifted. Enormous sums will be released to aid the progress of civilization. . . . Preparation for offensive naval war will stop now."

Hughes was gambling. The delegates—not to mention their naval attachés—might have howled in pain and been called home by their governments. But his calculation of the pressures on each was sure. The British blanched, the Japanese stared in confusion at the floor and one another, Bryan wept, and the galleries gave out a "tornado of cheering." Within days oceanic cables reported back the ecstatic reaction in London and Tokyo. Hughes's speech, thought Sen. Hiram Johnson of California, was "one of the most clever things that has ever been done in world politics" and would save Harding from "Wilson's fate."

What followed was one of the most efficient negotiations of arms control in modern history. Japanese Foreign Minister Uchida Yasuya ordered Katō to hold out for a naval tonnage ratio of 10:10:7 in the Five Power Treaty of February 1922, but authorized him to accept Hughes's 10:10:6 if the United States would forgo new Pacific fortifications. Inasmuch as the United States had broken the Japanese code and knew of these instructions, all Hughes had to do was stick to his ratio. But the Japanese also refused to scrap their mighty new dreadnought *Mutsu*, the pride of the fleet. So Hughes made allowance for the *Mutsu*, raising the tonnage allowed Britain and the United States proportionately, and so gave Katō a "victory" to boast of at home. A Four Power Treaty initialed in December already committed the United States, Britain, France, and Japan to recognize and respect one another's insular possessions in the Pacific. Moreover, Britain agreed not to fortify Hong Kong, nor the United States the Philippines, Guam, or the Aleutians. Japan, in turn, pledged to demilitarize its Micronesian possessions. Hawaii, of course, was exempt from the ban, as were Japan's home islands.

There remained Hughes's vague agenda entitled "Far Eastern Affairs." In practice this reduced, to no one's surprise, to an American formula for the Open Door in China. In one sense, it was the most important issue of all, since it bore on the political clashes of interest that inspired naval competition in the first place. Alas, it was also the one most resistant to clear and enforceable treaties. Hughes tried to do what no American had succeeded in doing before, that is, *define* the Open Door. In Article III of the Nine Power Treaty all governments with concessions in China promised not to seek or permit their nationals to seek "any arrangement which might purport to establish in favor of their interests any general superiority of rights with respect to commercial or economic development in any designated region of China." Hughes thus pinned down the Japanese to inclusive definition of the Open Door. Moreover, China was a party to this multilateral treaty ensuring its full sovereignty, and that in turn allowed Hughes to lean on Japan to promise to restore Kiao-chow. Finally, Hughes mentioned Siberia. The Japanese insisted again that their government had no territorial ambitions there but promised a timely evacuation.

Harding named the Washington Conference the "beginning of a new and better epoch in human progress." The whole world, he said, proclaimed "the odiousness of perfidy or infamy" and had learned "how alike, indeed, and how easily reconcilable, are our national aspirations; how sane and simple and satisfying the relationships of peace and security." The *New York Globe* agreed that this first great experiment in global disarmament was "the first gain from the World War, the first crop from the gigantic planting of dead men's bones and vast watering with blood." Katō "realized that a new spirit of moral consciousness had come over the world" and was sure "Japan is ready for the new order of thought—the spirit of international friendship and cooperation for the greater good of humanity—which the Conference has brought about."

Others read balance sheets, not spirits. Japanese nationalists denounced the Five Power naval agreement as another "unequal treaty" imposed by the West, and the Nine Power Treaty another case of white powers forcing Japan to relinquish the spoils of war. American nationalists fumed that the Japanese Navy, though inferior over all, now had permanent superiority in Asian waters. "Anybody can spit on the Philippines and you can't stop them," growled Adm. William S. Sims. "Our military prestige has received a blow," wrote Adm. H. S. Knapp. "The Treaty may well mark the beginning of a decreased influence in the Far East, with attendant loss to our proper, if selfish, trade interests, and to our altruistic purposes for China and Siberia." Captain D. W. Knox's judgment was a book entitled *The Eclipse of American Sea Power.*

Some contemporaries thought the China accords to be Hughes's greatest victory and Japan's greatest setback. If so, both victory and setback were largely ethereal. For the treaty ports, foreign quarters and legations, extraterritorial rights, leaseholds and railroad arrangements in China did not disappear, and nations were bound to exercise "superiority of rights" in whatever regions of China they chose to invest. Who was to judge the point at which contractual rights became "discriminatory"? So whether the Conference rolled back Japanese power or merely confirmed its local hegemony was ultimately a question of trust. And that trust rested on two shaky pillars.

The first pillar was American sensitivity to Japan's need for outlets for its growing population and economy. If the United States continued to deny Japan avenues of peaceful expansion, Japanese liberals would be discredited, the military party would press for aggression in Asia, the Open Door would close again, and the whole cycle of conflict would begin anew. That, wrote Professor Raymond L. Buell, was "the crux of the situation," and he urged Congress to loosen its restrictions on Japanese imports and immigration. The moment was ripe, for the Japanese delegates at Washington made a tremendous impression. They spoke excellent English and seemed to H. G. Wells "the most flexible minded of peoples." As a result, "the idea of them as of a people insanely patriotic, subtle and treacherous, mysterious and mentally inaccessible has been largely dispelled. . . . Our Western world, I am convinced, can work with the Japanese and understand and trust them." Instead, Congress passed the Fordney-McCumber Tariff, the highest in American history, in 1921, and the Supreme Court ruled that Japanese, like Chinese, were ineligible for American citizenship. Their timing could not have been worse.

The second pillar of Pacific trust was Taishō democracy. The Washington system was sound only so long as Japanese civilians succeeded in restraining their military. Unfortunately, Japanese liberalism was far from secure. For in November 1921, just before the Washington Conference convened, a fanatic lurking in a Tokyo railroad station rushed up with a knife and killed Hara Kei. Civilian government survived. But it would need all the help it could get.

Tokyo 1923

ACCORDING TO JAPANESE legend a giant catfish lurks in the waters beneath the islands, there to support the Land of the Gods so long as the Yamato race is true to its calling. But let the Japanese fall into decadence, and the catfish angrily arches his back, making calamitous earthquakes rock the people above. As recently as the 1850s an earthquake and fires left half of Tokyo in ruins, presaging the end of the shogunate. But under the Meiji Restoration the new imperial capital thrived, passing a million in population by the 1880s, doubling by the turn of the century, and doubling again to four million by 1923. The old Low City, comprising the arc of wards along Tokyo Bay, had the densest concentration of people and was the locus of the ancient trades and culture of Edo. The new High City rose in a concentric half-circle inland up the slopes of the hills overlooking the Bay. There the newly rich and powerful built their villas, temples, Shinto shrines, pleasure houses, and the new Waseda University, where baseball initially took root. But the new districts were all incorporated into a single prefecture overseen by the imperial government. City hall, in the Maranouchi quarter next to the palace, contained the offices of the mayor, prefect, and provincial governor, all of whom were usually named by the Home Ministry. For Tokyo was *Japan's* city, and its window on the Eastern Sea.

From Tokyo the railroads fanned out, first from the American-designed Shimbashi Station near the docks, and after 1914 from Tokyo Central Station at the end of the thoroughfare known as Mitsubishi Londontown for its brick pavement and buildings. Great department stores rose in the old commercial ward of Nihombashi, where the Bank of Japan and several *zaibatsu* were headquartered, then in the willow-lined Ginza. Tokyo was the sports center of Japan, and its monument to sumo wrestling, the Hall of National Accomplishment, was the largest arena in East Asia. Tokyo set national tastes in Kabuki theater, but by the twenties the Asakusa district sported Western-style movie palaces and risqué music halls where Western opera soon gave way to erotic revues, bloody criminal dramas, and freak shows. Much of Edo culture remained, but in what highbrows regarded as a debased fashion. Public sexuality, though prudish by later standards, was ubiquitous. Accomplished geishas, called "willows," lost business to bar or tearoom girls, called "flowers." Archery ranges and even Buddhist temples became fronts for prostitution. Country girls swarmed into town to work as clerks or telephone operators and adopted cheap Western styles and behavior, while residents of the High City seemed to indulge all the vices of the commercial class rather than the refined virtues of samurai. Tokyo still relished the seasonal festivals in honor of the cherry blossom, iris, or lotus, but pollution was stunting the trees and killing the clams in Tokyo Bay.

The Meiji modernizers had not imported Western technology only to see Japan sink into the scum of mass urban culture. But their successors could not turn back, if only because extreme population pressure and security needs necessitated rapid economic growth. Home Ministry planners had their dockets full just keeping Tokyo livable. After a great flood in 1910 and a typhoon in 1917 the government sponsored an engineering marvel reminiscent of the Chicago River: the dredging of fifty miles of new watercourse to handle the overflow from the Sumida River. City officials likewise fought fire by banning thatched roofs, fireproofing new buildings like Frank Lloyd Wright's Imperial Hotel, and training the fire brigades with military zeal. Still, what good was infrastructure if the people themselves tempted the catfish with their moneygrubbing, base eroticism, and Western conceits? Author Edward Seidensticker said it best: "The son of Edo knew a good geisha and an accomplished actor when he saw one. Less art and discrimination go into the making of a Ginza bar girl and a firstbaseman."

Otis Manchester Poole was down the coast in Yokohama on the day the catfish heaved. He was an American in the employ of an old British firm, and like the other 2,400 foreign residents had grown to love Old Yokohama. They had seen the fishing village, where Commodore Perry put in, grow to a city of half a million. They made good profits, built airy frame houses, clubs, and racecourses, and enjoyed the security of a U.S. Naval Hospital. Even their teenagers thought being sent abroad for prep school "the curse of the Far East" and often came back to Yokohama to work or marry.

September 1, 1923, was a Saturday, but Mr. Poole was at the office awaiting the noon break when he and the other foreign businessmen would rendezvous at the United Club for cocktails and gossip. "I had scarcely returned to my desk when, without warning, came the first rumbling jar of an earthquake, a sickening sway, the vicious grinding of timbers and, in a few seconds, a crescendo of turmoil as the floor began to heave and the building to lurch drunkenly. . . . Often before, we had hovered on the brink for a few perilous moments"—earthquakes were frequent—but this time "after the first seven seconds of subterranean thunder and creaking spasms, we shot right over the borderline. The ground could scarcely be said to shake; it heaved, tossed, and leapt under one. The walls bulged as if made of cardboard and the din became awful. . . . For perhaps half a minute the fabric of our surroundings held; then came disintegration."

Running outside after four minutes of shocks, Poole emerged into an awful silence, as if he and his office mates were the last people on earth. They skipped frantically through rubble-clogged streets, tripping when the dust and smoke obscured their vision. Poole heard a wounded Japanese wailing from the crotch of a tree, halfway up a cliff and beyond reach. He touched the shoulder of an elderly Japanese man seated, slumping, on a mound. The man rolled over, dead. But the living fled for the waterfront, for the fires were already spreading. Poole found that the Grand Hotel and others along the Bund were "vomiting red flames out over the water; and the old Pacific Mail coal sheds on the near side of the canal mouth had also caught fire from the French Consulate behind them, adding a new outburst to the spectacle of destruction." One by one, drums of marine fuel along the quay exploded, making the port appear to be under fire from great naval guns. And speaking of which, where was the Japanese Navy? Why didn't its ships from nearby Yokosuka steam over to pick up refugees and nurse the wounded? Because Yokosuka was flattened, its harbor clogged, and over seven hundred of its people dead. Other fantastic rumors spread, and most proved true. The brick and granite United Club had fallen in on itself, crushing the thirty or forty Westerners who were first to arrive at the Long Bar that noon. Two young Brits of the Hong Kong and Shanghai Bank arrived at the pier stark naked, their clothes slung over their shoulders and filled with the contents of the bank vault. With everything about them too hot to touch, there was nothing but their clothes to serve as knapsacks.

Poole found his wife and children and took refuge with hundreds of others on the decks of the *Empress of Australia*, which had been scheduled to raise anchor at noon. Now it was a floating sanctuary and a vantage point whence the survivors watched helplessly as Yokohama burned all night and into Sunday. Finally ships arrived, with four U.S. Navy destroyers in the van, to shuttle refugees down the coast to Kobe. Poole spent four days there but had to return to Yokohama to save what he could from his office. He found nothing left but "charred corpses, pathetic shrunken mummies." So he sailed on to Tokyo and was appalled: "the immense ocean of flattened, burned-out city beggared description."

What had happened was a massive wrenching of the fault that runs beneath Sagami Bay. The trough on the sea floor sank abruptly, as if the bottom had fallen out, while the sides of the fault heaved upward. Tokyo was farther from the epicenter than Yokohama, its newer buildings better made, and its ordinary dwellings mostly of resilient wood, all of which made for less immediate damage. The Imperial Palace and Imperial Hotel came through the quake, as did the city's most beloved Buddhist temple. But then the fires began. Some assume they were ignited by the thousands of gas jets and braziers alight for noontime cooking. But the biggest seem to have blown up from chemical plants and electric power lines. Again, the weather was sultry and breezy; again, one of the first neighborhoods consumed contained the fire department headquarters.

A dozen major blazes swept from all directions through Tokyo's teeming Low City. Hundreds of thousands of panicked people crammed into narrow streets and pushed, not to safety, but in whatever direction they could without being crushed by another human wave. One mob jammed into the park fronting on the Army Supply depot, only to have the fires converge on all four blocks around them. Flaming debris blew into their midst, bedding and bundles caught fire, and within minutes thirty-two thousand bodies fused into a single pyre of burning flesh. The fires rushed upward and inland through valleys and the Sumida River basin, gathering force from Tokyo's ocean of wood. Strange whirlwinds of flame and doughnut-shaped clouds appeared in the extreme conditions of heat and flux and oxygen depletion, as if demons from the deepest hell had been set loose for a holiday. Three-fourths of the Low City buildings were destroyed, and the death toll in Tokyo, Yokohama, and the towns swamped by the resulting tsunami surpassed one hundred thousand. Two thousand were Koreans lynched by Japanese "patriots" who accused them of plotting with Communists to overthrow the Emperor in the chaos.

The writer Tanizaki Junichirō, who despised the crass, new townspeople who had invaded and spoiled old Edo, did not mourn for his city. "When the earthquake struck," he wrote, "I feared for my wife and daughter, left behind in Yokohama. Almost simultaneously I felt a surge of happiness which I could not keep down. 'Tokyo will be better for this!' I said to myself." It was, but only in material ways. As early as September 12, the regent Hirohito reassured the people that Tokyo would remain the capital, and pledged "completely to transform the avenues and streets." The first chore was to feed and nurse the homeless host, and thousands of canvas barracks and outdoor rice kitchens, supplied in good part by the Red Cross, sprang up amid the desolation. But reconstruction began, too, under the restless sway of Home Minister Gotō Shimpei, ex-mayor of Tokyo and "the man with all the plans." A shortage of capital, the result in part of the postwar recession that had struck Japan, forced him to scale back his design, but Gotō eventually deployed five hundred million yen in a campaign reminiscent of Haussmann's in Paris. He widened boulevards and lined them with trees, laid out the grand Avenue Showa beside the Ginza and Nihombashi districts, planted new parks, and spanned the river so many times that Tokyo came to be known as a city of bridges. Private firms imitated the office buildings, department stores, and theaters of Western metropolises. In 1925 a new trunk railroad line made Tokyo Central "front door to the nation." Radio came to Japan that year, and in 1927 the Tokyo subway.

Cremation of old Edo also fed the growth of the High City and its taste for everything new and (in most cases) Western. Retailing and advertising, Western cosmetic and sartorial vanity, and the further degradation of Kabuki and geisha into peep shows inspired slang words like *Gimbura* (from Ginza and *burabura*, meaning roughly "hanging out at the mall") and *eroguro nansensu* (meaning "erotic, grotesque nonsense"). Of course, the twenties were years of emancipation, degradation, or both in all advanced countries, but to a Japan still largely rural, and only a generation removed from feudalism, Tokyo seemed as destructive of the nation's moral fiber as the Berlin of *Cabaret* seemed to early Nazis. "I am a bar flower that blooms by night," went a popular song. "Rouged lips, gauze sleeves, mad dancing by neon light. A flower watered by tears."

And unlike the other developed nations after 1924, Japan did not know an era of political stability and economic recovery. American tariffs and Chinese nationalism combined to close off two of Japan's largest markets. The earthquake sopped up much of the country's disposable capital. Then in 1927, two years before Wall Street, the Japanese banking system verged on collapse. Suicides in Tokyo doubled in just three years. It all seemed to prove that Japan's economy, society, and Taishō democracy rested on foundations as fragile as those of the land itself. One might say that the thirties began early in Japan.

Hughes was out of Washington when the Tokyo earthquake struck, and President Harding was dead—felled by a mysterious infection (or food poisoning?) while on a tour of Alaska. So it was laconic Calvin Coolidge who read the shocking telegrams from Japan. He asked where the Asiatic fleet was at present, and said to the Acting Secretary of State, "You might tell it to go right away to Yokohama." The Acting Secretary then spoke of a telegram of sympathy to the Emperor. "You might send such a message for me," replied Coolidge and then went to bed. So it was that the United States was the first foreign power to express its condolences. In coming days, Coolidge also admonished the American people to give for the Japanese victims, and of course the American people did.

How sad, then, that the Immigration Committee of the U.S. Senate was at that moment drafting legislation to ban Japanese immigration once and for all! The movement to restrict immigration began in the months after World War I but fed on fears and resentments dating from the 1890s, when millions of southern and eastern Europeans began to come to America. Most of these new immigrants were Catholic, many Jewish, and many Socialist in their politics. So when West Coast congressmen demanded total exclusion of Orientals, the East Coasters, for the first time, agreed, either because of the naval tension with Japan or because they, too, were now besieged by seemingly unassimilable aliens.

The "Keep California White" movement embraced all parties and classes, while all its old arguments seemed even more plausible in light of Japan's recent expansion. "A Jap was a Jap," said Sen. James Phelan; moreover, the Jap was so clever that he, unlike the Negro or Mexican, was truly "capable of taking the place of the White man." Nor did current legal barriers stop the invasion. Adult Japanese in California rose from 32,785 in 1910 to 47,566 in 1920, while the Japanese already there had children at an alarming rate. What was more disgusting, they got married to "picture brides" chosen from advertisements—who could then come to the United States in circumvention of the Gentlemen's Agreement. The California law prohibiting Japanese from leasing land likewise failed: Japanese landholdings had quadrupled since 1913. Was the Mikado plotting to buy up California? Did not a Japanese *zaibatsu* try to purchase a big chunk of Baja from Mexico (Magdalena Bay, in 1912)? According to Phelan, Japanese posed an economic, social, moral, and military menace to white civilization.

For once, contrary voices were heard as well, and none so loud as Sidney Gulick's. A missionary and Japanologist, he founded the National Committee for Constructive Immigration Legislation and wrote over two dozen tracts denouncing the exclusionists as hysterical and un-Christian. He granted that U.S. policy should provide "real protection for the Pacific coast States from the dangers of *excessive* Asiatic immigration [emphasis added]," but pleaded with Californians not gratuitously to insult Japan. If Congress wished to limit immigration, then let all peoples be admitted under quotas. But to discriminate against Japanese would be unjust, inflame U.S.-Japanese relations, and ruin the missionaries' chances of spreading Christianity in Asia. Chambers of

Commerce and the Japan Society of America seconded Gulick's appeals.

But such eloquent, organized opposition infuriated the exclusionists. Montaville Flowers damned the "Jap-lovers" in his *Japanese Conquest of American Public Opinion* in 1917, implying that the Japanese government was in league with East Coast business and bleeding hearts to dupe the American people. So the exclusionists organized in turn: the Native Sons of the Golden West with their magazine, *Grizzly Bear*, and slogan, "California—the White Man's Paradise," the American Legion and California Federation of Labor and the farmers' Grange, not to mention politicians, who drafted a manifesto in 1919. It proclaimed that "the immigration of the little brown men presents a very hard problem indeed—one full of menace not only to California but eventually to the United States." They demanded prohibition of "picture brides," exclusion of Japanese, barring of Asians from citizenship, and a constitutional amendment forbidding citizenship to Asian children born on American soil.

In 1920 an initiative barring Japanese ownership of land appeared on the California ballot. The Tokyo-based American-Japanese Relations Committee polled American opinion leaders in hopes of advancing the "friendship and goodwill of the two neighboring nations of the Pacific." The only result was that the initiative passed by a three-to-one margin instead of the ten-to-one predicted, and a Japanese Exclusion League arose under retired publisher V. S. McClatchy and Sen. Hiram Johnson. McClatchy's slogan was that Japan was the "Germany of Asia" and bent on world domination, and Wallace Irwin's 1920 novel, *Seed of the Sun*, spun out that scenario. When bills to restrict immigration from all nations on an equal basis came before Congress in 1920 and again in 1921, Johnson lashed out at them. "It is an incontrovertible fact that the Japanese continue ever Japanese, and that their allegiance is always to Tokyo." Whatever Congress did about other ethnic groups, he wanted Japanese banned, period. Then the Supreme Court upheld the notion that Japanese aliens could indeed be considered "ineligible for citizenship," and encouraged the exclusionists in the 1923 session of Congress. The Japanese, said McClatchy, "come here specifically and professedly for the purpose of colonizing and establishing here permanently the proud Yamato race. . . . California regards herself as a frontier State. She has been making for 20 years the fight of the nation against incoming of alien races whose peaceful penetration must in time with absolute certainty drive the white race to the wall."

Missionaries, businessmen, and academics did what they could to fight the trend. Professor Raymond Leslie Buell pointed out in *Foreign Affairs* the absurd contradictions of a movement that denies citizenship to parents even as the Constitution imposes it on their children; that rails against Japanese for not assimilating while it passes laws preventing them from mingling with whites in schools or the marketplace; that treats Japanese as inferior on the implicit grounds that they are superior in work habits and family values; that accuses them of disloyalty to America while it heaps abuse upon them in the name of America. Buell acknowledged that massive Japanese immigration would be damaging to the social fabric but warned against blatant discrimination lest Japan's polite silence become "the calm before the storm." Finally, Charles Evans Hughes urged Congress to leave the Japanese problem to the State Department, fearing that all the progress he had made at the Washington Conference might be undone.

It seemed, for a moment, that such pleas might resonate. When the final immigration bill went to the Senate in March 1924, the committee chairman and the floor manager both endorsed the Gentlemen's Agreement. No need, they said, to offend Tokyo needlessly. But what was this Gentlemen's Agreement, asked senators from the floor, this mysterious document that no one had ever seen, that the Senate had never ratified, and that West Coasters said was ineffective? Hughes figured he had to respond, and made a terrible mistake. He asked the Japanese Ambassador to write a letter describing the agreement and Japan's commitment to it. The letter was soothing enough, renouncing any desire on the part of Japan "to question the sovereign right of any country to regulate immigration" and appealing to the "high sense of justice and fairplay of the American Government and people." But it also lamented the bill's "stigmatizing [Japanese] as unworthy and undesirable" and referred to "the grave consequences" of exclusion for U.S.-Japanese relations. Hughes saw the problem in that last phrase but thought the friendly context was obvious.

Senator Lodge ignored the context. He called the reference to "grave consequences" a "veiled threat" against the United States and rallied the Senate not to surrender to it. He was not fond of Hughes, he was envious of Coolidge, and he, too, thought Japan "the Prussia of the East. Their culture is German, their ambitions are German." Now he threw his considerable weight beyond Johnson and the exclusionists. When the administration introduced an amendment replacing exclusion with one affirming the Gentlemen's Agreement, it lost by a vote of two to seventy-six. Coolidge personally intervened, threatening a veto. But Lodge scoffed: he had the votes to override. So Coolidge asked that exclusion be put on hold for two years, one year, even a few months. Again Lodge refused. So Coolidge had no choice but to sign the bill into law and hope that the Japanese government would forgive the "unnecessary and deplorable" *method* by which the result was achieved.

No single act wounded Japanese pride more than the Exclusion Act of 1924. Not that it made a huge difference in demography. But the utter closing off of American soil, combined with the relative closure of American markets and the bristling barrier rising up at Pearl Harbor, all made U.S. intentions clear: the eastern Pacific was off-limits to Japanese, even though the United States insisted that the *western* Pacific remain an Open Door zone. What's mine is mine; what's yours is negotiable—so American policy seemed in Japan.

The Eleventh 'aha iki

Saitō: You made a pun, Professor: You said Korea was Itō Hirobumi's "chosen fate."

Scholar: Chosen? Oh, *Cho-sen*—the Japanese name for Korea. Lame, Saitō.

Saitō: You said it, Prof, not I.

Kaahamanu: Is it customary to laugh about the peoples you kill? Did not the scholar say that your soldiers killed eleven thousand Koreans before annexation, and twenty-five thousand more in 1919?

Saitō: Regrettable. One of the prices of power, and the mixing of races.

Seward: Japanese and Koreans aren't of the same race?

Saitō: I shall ignore that insult, Mr. Seward, on account of your ignorance. Besides, even your historian understands that for us to let Korea go would be like handing a sword to our enemies. Surely you don't imagine that Korea could maintain itself as an independent state? Unfortunately, the Koreans were too stubborn to grasp reality, so they had to be taught. Same as you Yanks in the Philippines, or Kamehameha on the islands he conquered, or Russians everywhere.

Seward: I see. So allow me to recapitulate. You begin your wars with sneak attacks, on China and again on Russia. You did have the decency to declare war on Germany but gave as little warning as possible. Then you slaughter *unarmed* people who protest your rule. You complain of Yellow Peril hysteria but base your own policies on White Peril thinking. You complain that we ban immigration but welcome no—*gaijin*, was it?—into Japan. You complain about tariffs against your exports but plot to violate the Open Door. Then you pose as champions of racial equality in order to trip up Woodrow Wilson. That was smart, though. Damned smart. So what happens next, Professor, do they sneak attack *us?*

Scholar: Mr. Seward, you disappoint me. I thought the Washington Conference—

Seward: —which hasn't a chance—

Scholar: —would meet with your resounding approval. And Hughes! I thought you'd feel akin to a fellow Governor of New York who fought corruption, protected immigrants, just missed the White House, and became a great Secretary of State.

Seward: And so I do. But you say Hughes valued reason. I'd say he made an idol of it. You yourself hinted that his system was doomed.

Scholar: "Doomed" implies inevitability.

Seward: Look, each nation has a role to play, based on its geography and power. When a nation tries to be more than it is, it makes trouble for others and ruin for itself. But when a nation tries to be *less* than it is, it does almost as badly. Hughes left Britain and Japan more influence than they deserved and America far less. Well, what good is a treaty without the means to enforce it?

Saitō: You expected us to sign a treaty *leaving* you means to enforce it? I was at the Washington Conference. I thought we promised too much—after all, Japan made all the *political* sacrifices. But Katō Tomosaburō briefed us well. He explained the wisdom of getting the U.S. to decommission its fleet. So long as the U.S. remains an *eastern* Pacific power only, it cannot interfere in the western Pacific. Public opinion in both countries is happy, and Teddy's deal is renewed: we stay out of California and Hawaii, and you let us have our way in Asia.

Scholar: But you imply that balance of power and deterrence are the only reality. I wanted to suggest—such things can't be proven—that the most important variable was Japanese liberalism. The question was whether American policy on armaments or immigration would strengthen or undermine civilian government in Japan.

Saitō: Is that what Hughes thought, or just you? Taishō democracy *was* strong in the twenties. The military had made fools of themselves: Siberia was even more of a travesty than you said. The important question was whether *whoever* was in power managed to meet Japanese *needs.* Remember the rice riots and postwar depression. Japan had no choice but to export people and goods, and get raw materials. And Japan had to live—you said this well, Doc—in whatever world order *others* made for it. So we trusted that the Washington system was not just designed to frustrate Japan. That's the understanding I thought I had reached with Lodge.

Scholar: Understanding . . . that *you* reached?

Saitō: Ah, you historians. Always missin' second base in hopes the ump won't notice. Yes, my job at the Washington Conference was to get around Henry Cabot Lodge, the leader of the pro-Chinese faction. So I approached him during recesses and told him how much I admired him. Arranged to "bump into" him on the street. Pretty soon we were lunching together.

Scholar: But Japan *did* retrocede the German concession to China.

Saitō: The political concession—but Japan remained in economic control, just as it did in all southern Manchuria. Of course, Chinese delegates resisted, but without U.S. support, they had to accept our terms. Admiral Katō was very pleased with me, and I was rather pleased with myself!

Scholar: You mean Lodge privately compromised on the Open Door?

Saitō: Let us say he winked. But he got his revenge, with the Exclusion Act.

Scholar: For what it was worth. Lodge was old, had a prostate condition, and was dead by November 1924. Anyway, his policies on tariffs and exclusion all but invited Japan to resume its expansion in China.

Saitō: True, but how else could the Washington system function? If it was meant to give us no outlets at all, then it could never have worked—anymore than some treaty designed to contain *America* could have worked in the nineteenth century.

Seward: It could if it were backed with sufficient *force!* The trouble with those Washington treaties is that they deny the U.S. Navy the bases and ships needed to enforce the political settlement. And as for America in the nineteenth century, I think the British might well have contained us at the time of the Mexican War—

Saitō: Mexican War—*thank* you, Mr. Secretary. Once again I ask why it is that the U.S. gets to conquer its neighbors and declare Monroe Doctrines, but when Japan does the same it's condemned as uncivilized, imperialist?

Seward: Because there's a *difference* between a free country with opportunity for all and a militaristic *tribe* bent on enslaving. Your Homer Lea was wrong, Professor: the *strength* of America is its openness to all immigrants—

Saitō: Except Japanese!

Seward: —who truly *want* to be American.

Lea: I was not wrong. I was right.

Seward: Egad!

Witte: What have we here? Professor, did you. . . ?

Kaahamanu: I did! My little joke. This Homer Lea intrigued me, so I summoned him. And you will include him.

Scholar: With pleasure. Good grief, Homer Lea! So when did you and Sun Yat-sen first meet? Where were you during 1900? Were any of the stories true?

Lea: All and none. The martial dwarf charging Peking; the mysterious white monk hiding out with the Buddhists; the queer Stanford student who knows the secrets of Chinatown; the American agent plotting with secret societies; the genius behind Sun Yat-sen—they are the pipe dreams of the Occidental drugged by the Orient.

Scholar: Drugged! You mean . . . you were an opium addict? Your headaches—

Lea: I mean *you* are addicted to cultural myths. In the eyes of my countrymen I *was* America, China's brave friend. I let them believe it—it was useful for fund-raising. But I was not America gone to the East. I was China in the midst of America: brilliant, but stunted; ancient, but young; the giant who looks like a dwarf. But, of course, only Chinese understood.

Kaahamanu: Understood what, General Lea?

Lea: That the white man's role was not to change China, but to help China become China again.

Kaahamanu: I do not understand. The white men changed Hawaii and Alaska and California. How could China confront the whites and not change?

Lea: Let me ask you a question: how could *anyone* "change" China?

Kaahamanu: I do not know.

Witte: I think I know what Mr. Lea means. I, who negotiated with Li Hung-chang. China is a world, like Russia. Except Russia is of the West, while China is *not* of the East; the East is of China. China is the sun about which all else revolves. A sun cannot be a planet, nor a planet a sun. But when the imperialists arrived, it seemed to Chinese that planets had left their orbits and perturbed the universe. I never doubted that Li thought *me* inferior. An infuriating trait—it maddened the Tsar and complicated my work. In this regard I sympathize with you Japanese who had also to deal with China. But how does one move a center of gravity? So I suspect Mr. Lea is right. China cannot be changed from without anymore than a planet can capture the sun. All we "barbarians" can do is show, by our very unruliness, that China must right itself.

Lea: You are Count Witte? You are wiser than any American, except perhaps Roosevelt.

Scholar: Teddy Roosevelt.

Lea: Is there another?

Seward: But then, how badly we have misperceived China!

Lea: The profundity of our ignorance is beyond human measure. To think that the pundits of the Republic, and the Empire as well, regard China as an infinitely malleable lump of moist clay! They expect to make it a market, or a democracy, or Christian, or a replication of Meiji Japan! They think in terms of business or politics or population or religion, or the policies of imperial rivals *in* China, rather than of China itself. How few of our merchants come homeward to say, "Forget China, there is no bonanza there"? Instead we hear of the fortunes made, like the one Mr. Duke of Durham made pushing tobacco. How few missionaries return in despair, to tell us that Asia resists our faith? Instead we hear tales of mass conversions that will hasten the Second Coming. How few ambassadors cable reports that democracy as we know it is sterile in China? Some, perhaps, but their pessimism never penetrates the public's opinion. Verily, no people is more adaptable than Chinese *abroad.* But change China? And until China reforms and becomes strong again, then the perilous situation outlined by Mr. Seward must persist, whereby the Republic and the Empire are at loggerheads.

Seward: The Republic?

Scholar: The United States; and by the "Empire," Lea means Japan.

Lea: The world cannot be in balance until China regains her weight. Otherwise only the Republic can balance the Empire. And I fear the Republic must lose.

Scholar: Why must somebody lose? The Washington Conference—

Lea: —enshrined arbitration. I saw it coming, this American dream. I wrote that "the labors of arbitration are but human and inspired by human hope. They are the expedients of a single day." All diplomacy can do is lengthen the periods in which to prepare for war. Arbitration is vain even beyond the vanity of man, for it seeks to impose human laws over those of nature.

Saitō: Lea's right. Arbitration can't trump necessity. Under the Washington system Japan could expand only through commerce and emigration, but that was just what the Americans and British Dominions would not permit.

Lea: And should not have. The mixing of races weakens a people. As I wrote in my book, "Crime is an index to national character," and it expands "in direct ratio to increasing heterogeneity of population." Tell me I'm right, Professor.

Kaahamanu: I wish we Hawaiians had made immigration restrictions.

Saitō: And Japanese understood as well. We just hated being singled out as undesirable. But once you decided to keep us from *your* side of the ocean, you had to allow us our *own* side. Instead you asked us to compete in an Open Door world against an American economy ten times our size! Hardly a liberal system.

Seward: Face it, Saitō, your pride was hurt more than your trade. You people always have a chip on your shoulder.

Witte: I think it is the character of Japanese to be proud and ashamed at the same time. And the character of Russians is to be proud of their shame.

Scholar: And of Americans to be ashamed of their pride?

Seward: Just so. So are all these conflicts the result of national characters? Or are national characters the result of these conflicts?

Witte: I believe that nations have souls. But the stronger the soul the more suicidal it is in the face of superior technology. That is why Russian boys drowned at Tsushima and were mowed down like wheat by the Germans. And now you say Siberia is trapped between bolshevism on one side and Japan on the other!

Scholar: The devil and the deep blue sea.

Witte: But America should have supported us in Siberia. Remember Roosevelt's policy: maintain Russia as a Pacific presence in order to balance Japan. Instead, your American Consul wants to support Kolchak, while your General Graves does nothing at all. Have you no government in the United States?

Scholar: Ha! Good question, Count Witte. But it really wasn't so different from your quarreling bureaucracies whenever the tsar is a weakling. Remember, Wilson was obsessed with the Peace Confer-

ence in 1919 and by 1920 was disabled by a massive stroke. The War
Department could hardly topple Lenin with a single light regiment
and was dead set against sending more. So the State Department just
did what it could to support Kolchak in other ways. A bad business,
but Wilson was right when he said that the Russians had to work out
their own destiny.

Witte: Communism is destiny? And how many died?

Scholar: How many Russians? Tens of millions in the Great War and
Civil War, and maybe twenty million more in the thirties.

Kaahamanu: The price of power, Mr. Saitō calls it.

Lea: The material cost is the price of power, my sentimental friends.
The human cost is the price of impotence—and folly.

Seward: Speaking of material costs, Professor, when are you going to
get on with "internal combustion"? There was precious little about it
in your last chautauqua.

Scholar: Little about technology, but the San Francisco and Tokyo
earthquakes and the racial conflicts, too, are forms of internal combustion. But here's a technological fact for you. Everyone knows
about the Golden Spike, but do you know when the first motorway
reached the Pacific? The Lincoln Highway was complete—well, more
or less, it was hardly paved—in 1915, in time for that Panama Pacific
Exhibition in San Francisco. And believe it or not, the Lincoln Highway Association was privately funded.

Witte: But surely motorcars did not transform the North Pacific?

Scholar: Not just yet. But the Federal Highway Act of 1921 inaugurated construction of the U.S. Highway System, including the great
transcontinental Routes 30, 50, and 66 along which hundreds of thousands of internal migrants would head for "the Coast" in the thirties.
But you are quite right, Count Witte, the initial agents of internal
combustion were oil-fired ships and the airplane.

Witte: Petroleum. We had just begun to prospect for oil when the
Great War brought all to a halt. Siberia was rich in petroleum, we
believed.

Saitō: And Sakhalin Island—Japan's only source of oil, save for what you Americans and the British would sell us. And what of the Washington Conference talks? You neglected to mention air power at all.

Scholar: You anticipate me, as usual. But since Homer Lea is here, allow me to pose him a question. Will aviation become decisive in the Pacific, do you think?

Lea: You refer to my essay on "The Aeroplane in War." A *jeu d'esprit*—but when one acquires a certain reputation, one is asked to comment on everything. In 1909 I already saw clearly that the aeroplane—

Scholar: Wasn't it 1910?

Lea: The article appeared in 1910—I wrote it in 1909. There was already talk of aerial bombardment being decisive in future warfare. It can never be so, first, because war "has never been nor will it ever be mechanical. There is no such possibility as the combat of instruments. It is the soldier that brings about victory or defeat." Combat is a function of will, and to place one's reliance on the *machinery* of war is an admission that the will to fight is already absent. Count Witte should not blame Russia's defeats on inferior technology. Russia was beaten in spirit before she ever traded fire with Japan.

Witte: That, sir, is nonsense.

Lea: And aerial power is no use at all against underdeveloped countries like China. The bombs you may rain on the rice paddies will only seed the militancy you presume to destroy. No, gentlemen, the aeroplane will be a useful tool for observation, but the nation that thinks it can win wars is lost.

Scholar: And on that, Mr. Lea, you are finally wrong.

Seattle to Seattle 1924

EIGHT DAYS BEFORE the Senate's vote on Japanese exclusion, four Douglas S-WC biplanes, each one crammed with fuel, supplies, and a pair of daring pilots, sputtered into the air over the Puget Sound. The "WC" signature was not a manufacturer's code or airman's crude joke. It stood for World Cruiser, because Seattle was not only the point of departure for the eight Army pilots but their destination as well. Their orders were to fly around the world. General Mason Patrick, commander of the Army Air Service, paid for the mission out of his meager budget in hopes of alerting the penurious Coolidge and Congress to the skill of the Air Service staff, the daring of its pilots, and the reliability of its machines. The health of the service, American aviation, and quite possibly the national defense rode on the success of the mission. Or so General Patrick believed.

So, too, did his obstreperous underling, Billy Mitchell. Grandson of a Scottish curmudgeon who made a fortune on the Wisconsin frontier and *opposed* regulation of railroads in the teeth of public opinion, and son of a U.S. senator *opposed* to America's leap into imperialism, Billy learned early to stand up for what he believed in and damn the establishment if it refused to listen. But where his forbears valued money, politics, and education, young Billy liked "horses and guns." In 1898 he quit what became George Washington University to join the Army and began a professional odyssey that tossed him into every corner of the North Pacific. After duty in the Philippines and Alaska, he was introduced to flying in the Signal Corps School at Fort Leavenworth, where he wrote a treatise on ballooning. But the Aeronautical Division seemed a dead end—as late as 1914 it had but a half-dozen airplanes. After failing to win a transfer to the cavalry, Mitchell spent two more years spying out Japanese defenses in the Pescadores Islands.

World War I alerted the Army to the need to develop an air arm, and

Mitchell won a post at the Curtiss Aviation School in Newport News. In 1916 he learned to fly in his spare time—and at his own expense, since the Treasury judged his training not duty-related! But when the United States entered the war, he won appointment as Aviation Officer of the American Expeditionary Force. Brigadier General Billy Mitchell soon was convinced that air power was decisive over land and sea, but the armistice intervened before its potential was proven. In the postwar demobilization Mitchell landed as Third Assistant Chief of an Air Service slashed 95 percent. So he spent the years 1919 to 1921 stomping corridors and filing reports in hopes of persuading politicians and Colonel Blimps of the need to make the Air Service an independent branch, like Britain's Royal Air Force. He urged the opening of regular air transport to Panama and Alaska, and helped plan a 1920 Army flight from New York to Nome. But his campaign got nowhere. The Air Service budget shrank to $27 million, and the aviation industry was devastated by cancellation of $100 million worth of contracts and a drop in orders from 22,000 airplanes to a mere 328 in 1920. So the jut-jawed general with the impatient eyes decided to go public.

"Declares America Helpless in Air War," said the New York Times of Mitchell's first foray into public relations. He knew that external criticism of policy was a violation of military discipline of the sort that caused grief to Captain Mahan. But now Mitchell used the same tactics to fight the big-battleship fixation Mahan had inspired. Airplanes, said Mitchell, could sink the mightiest battleships—and for the cost of one dreadnought the nation could buy a thousand airplanes. The Navy cried for his head, but the public fascination with the idea of a gladiatorial duel between ships and planes moved the War and Navy departments to authorize a demonstration. Mitchell's career and cause were on the line in July 1921 when his air crews swooped down on the surrendered German battleship Ostfriesland off the Virginia capes. The Navy's rules required that the attack be halted after each hit so that damage might be assessed. But Mitchell told his pilots to press the assault à outrance and, by God, make their point. In twenty-one minutes the Ostfriesland heaved bow up and sank. "He was exalted," wrote Mitchell's sister. "They had done it. Now at last everyone, even the stupidest, must understand. And there would be no second world war."

No second world war, for the proof that a swarm of pesky mechanical insects could sting navies to death must surely deter the nations from the folly of war. After Mitchell's demonstration Congress authorized the first two U.S. aircraft carriers, the Lexington and the Saratoga, and the world's diplomats gathered at Washington to negotiate those gigantic cuts in their battleship navies. But what of air power at the Washington Conference? If naval aviation was the coming technology, should not *it* have been the first target of arms controllers? The answer is no, first because few admirals or statesmen were willing or able to predict the rapid advance of aviation, or guess its implications. Second, public opinion did not demand the curtailment of aviation, which in the Great War seemed a benign form of combat by comparison with the slaughter in the trenches. Third, if air war did prove to be devastating, for instance through the bombing of cities, then surely it would deter rather than cause war. Fourth, air forces were relatively cheap compared with navies and did not seem such a burden on government budgets. Fifth, there was simply no way to ban or control the spread of military aviation without stifling civil aviation as well. As Mitchell put it in the experts' report, "the only practicable limitation as to the numbers of aircraft that could be used for military purposes would be to abolish the use of aircraft for any purpose" and thus "shut the door on progress."

So Hughes presented no plan for limiting airplanes to the Washington Conference, though his low limits for naval tonnage would have restricted the United States to just three aircraft carriers and "one-and-a-half" for Japan. Baron Katō insisted that Japan's "geographical position and special circumstances" made seaborne aircraft a *sine qua non* of Japanese defense, so rather than lose his treaty Hughes granted Japan a tonnage allotment (still on a 10:10:6 ratio) permitting it two or three carriers. But since the treaties limited land-based air power by forbidding installations on Guam, Wake, and the Japanese-mandated islands, and placed strict limits on naval tonnage, the United States and Japan would presumably have trouble just "getting at" each other, and the mid-Pacific would function as the world's biggest buffer zone.

The Washington treaties frustrated the Army Air Service since they gave the impression that a Pacific war was impossible. When the Lassiter Board of seven General Staff officers recommended that the Service be expanded to thirty thousand men and twenty-five hundred airplanes—at a ten-year cost of $500 million—Congress frowned and voted only $12.7 million for 1923. Then Harding died, and General Patrick resorted to stunts in hopes of attracting the attention of Coolidge. But the 'round-the-world flight was a serious risk. The Army Air staff had to plot a route, devise navigation techniques, negotiate for rights of passage with foreign governments, arrange for landing sites, fuel, maintenance, and supplies every few hundred miles along the way, determine the payloads of the aircraft to the last pound and cubic foot, and the take-off weights from runways and seas under possibly extreme weather conditions. It also needed a top-drawer machine and, after rigorous testing of prototypes, chose the Douglas.

Few manufacturers of airframes and engines survived the armistice. The oldest were Curtiss of Buffalo and the Glenn L. Martin Company of

Los Angeles, to which Orville Wright had sold out in 1915. Two years later Martin relocated to Cleveland, near the Wright brothers' home in Dayton. There was also Boeing of Seattle, founded by a timber magnate who went into flight on a lark. Boeing's B-1 flying boat was used as early as 1919 to carry mail to British Columbia, the first international airmail service. But one of the few entrepreneurs willing to enter the industry after the war was Donald Douglas, who started up in the back room of a barber shop in 1920. With $40,000 borrowed from a Los Angeles flying buff, Douglas built a torpedo bomber for the Navy, borrowed some more, and rented a vacant film studio in Santa Monica. Douglas believed that southern California was the place to build and test airplanes for the same reasons it was the place to make movies: good weather year-round, lots of open country and coast, and a cheap, skilled work force. Still, one failed design and his company would go under. Douglas's entry for the World Cruiser was based on his torpedo plane and measured all of thirty-five feet, two inches, with a wingspan of fifty feet. It could carry up to 8,800 pounds at a maximum speed of 100 MPH and altitude of seven thousand feet. For reliability Douglas chose a tried-and-true Liberty liquid-cooled, twelve-cylinder engine that generated 420 horsepower. Built of wood and fabric on a tubular steel fuselage, it was a gritty machine by the standards of the day. But then, no one had flown around the world over ice and snow and seas and deserts.

The Air Service dubbed the four airplanes the *Seattle* (the flagship), the *Chicago*, the *Boston*, and the *New Orleans*, and chose Maj. Frederick Martin to command. All four pilots were accomplished veterans, of whom the oddest was surely the *Chicago*'s pilot, Lowell Smith. Born in Santa Monica in 1892, he fell in love with flying after the Wright brothers made it possible. In 1916 he served as a freebooting engineer in the "air force" of Mexican revolutionary Pancho Villa. He repatriated when the United States entered the Great War and served afterward as one of Patrick's endurance pilots. Still, Smith packed a rabbit's foot in his flight jacket like the other seven crewmen: skill alone could not see them through much of the world's roughest terrain without life rafts or even a rifle.

Mitchell was not with them. He had divorced and remarried, and was off to the Pacific on what was styled as his honeymoon. In fact, he was engaged in a strategic study of the North Pacific. His first stop was Hawaii, where the Army garrison made a fuss over him only to receive his stinging reprimand. Its maneuvers included no airplanes, whereas it was "obvious" to Mitchell that an attack on Oahu must come from above: "A modern boy fifteen years old, who knows about air power and had a simple military training in high school, could work out a better system." Mitchell wrote Patrick that "air power will certainly control the Pacific." Sailing westward, he meditated on Guam's vulnerability to Japanese airplanes based in the Marshalls. Guam, he predicted, would be "a dominant factor in the military future of the Western Pacific." The Philippines he also found indefensible in the absence of air power. Then, after a stop on the China coast, Mitchell apparently made a nonvisit to Japan; that is, he was not scheduled to go there until July, by which time he was ordered to avoid Japan in light of the ill feeling over the Exclusion Act. But his correspondence suggests he went to Kobe to negotiate landing rights for the World Cruisers, who were scheduled to depart on April 5.

As it happened, they left a day late because the *Seattle* failed to rise off the water and damaged its propeller. The *Boston* had the same problem on the sixth but finally caught up with the flock. As they waved good-bye to Seattle, Lieutenant Arnold recorded his view of Mount Rainier: "No wonder the Indians call it Iahuma—the mountain that is God. The memory of its grandeur will inspire us all the way around the world." The four planes then headed north to pioneer the Great Circle Route to Japan. But their lack of accurate weather forecasting cost them from the start. The waters off British Columbia roiled with storms, one plane nearly missed colliding with a steamer in a fog, and after eight hours the crews had to fix pontoons and put down in a snowstorm. It cost *Seattle* a wing strut and one rabbit's foot tossed overboard in anger. The mayor of Prince Rupert comforted them: "Gentlemen, you have arrived on the worst day in ten years."

The next morning the flight departed for the Alaskan town of Seward, 930 miles distant. The ill-starred *Seattle* began leaking oil and finally put down in the same coastal waters first glimpsed by Chirikov almost two centuries before. A Navy destroyer found the stranded flyers and towed the plane to Kanatak. After repairs, Martin learned that he was a week behind the other planes. So he and his engineer took off in haste and flew smack into another storm. Visibility dropped to zero, and the next thing they knew they were slumped in *Seattle*'s wreckage—frigid, sore, but alive—in a snowbank on the side of a mountain somewhere in coastal Alaska. Packing what they could salvage from the plane, the aviators braved forward into the dazzling whiteness of the glacier. Then they groped back. It was no use until the weather cleared. But the weather refused to clear. So on the fifth day, their food almost gone, they struck southward and found—O answer to prayer!—an abandoned hut with a store of food. After five more days of rest and warmth, they set out again, found a river, then a canoe, and blundered on to tiny Fort Moller.

By then the other planes had reached Japan. In the Kurile Islands and Hokkaido curious residents waded out to greet them. The weather was still awful, and they were stuck there a week. Devastated Tokyo received the Yankee heroes, but Japanese officers forbade photographs and warned them away from military bases. On June 4, the World Cruisers took off for China, and the weather, their progress, and their spirits improved. Shanghai and Hong Kong made a fuss over them, then Haiphong and Saigon, Bangkok, Rangoon, and Calcutta. Lowell Smith, the commander now, pressed on through the monsoon to Karachi and across the deserts to Baghdad and Aleppo. The crossing of Europe was easy, and familiar. Smith contrived to land in Paris on Bastille Day, escorted by the French Air Force decked in the colors of the Lafayette Escadrille. Britain put the Royal Navy at their disposal for the flight across the stormy Atlantic, and when the *Boston* lost oil pressure and went down at sea, a British trawler rescued the crew. But the remaining two planes survived the long stretches of sea to Iceland, Greenland, and Newfoundland. When they landed again on American soil the nation went berserk. Every town insisted they stop to be honored, so it was not until September 28 that the World Cruisers arrived back in Seattle, after 175 days and 26,345 miles, to the cheers of 250,000 people.

Captain Smith was becomingly modest. He praised the vision of General Patrick, the professionalism of the ground crews, his glorious *Chicago*, and Douglas Aircraft (whose future, and that of the southern California aviation industry, was now assured). Patrick gave thanks to an "allwise Creator that this little band we sent into the West has come safely out of the East," and President Coolidge thanked the airmen: "Your skill, your perseverance and your courage have brought great honour to our country. . . . I trust the appreciation of your countrymen will be sufficient so that in this field America will be kept first."

What were the strategic implications of this "'round-the-world" flight? Billy Mitchell thought he knew. He returned from Asia in July 1924 and was in New York to greet the world flyers. In October he filed a 325-page report on his tour of the Pacific. The mood in Japan was unremittingly hostile, he said, in light of the Exclusion Act. War was a certainty, and Mitchell deduced that Japan could only hope to defeat the United States with a surprise offensive based on air power. He drew triangles all over the North Pacific map, traced ranges, and predicted that the only way U.S. forces could fight their way back to the Philippines was by winning control of the air and island-hopping. U.S. air forces based in the Aleutians, he wrote, could deliver "decisive" destruction on Japan's "congested" cities built of "paper and wood." But the key to the U.S. position was Hawaii. If the Japanese neutralized Hawaii, they could outflank Alaska and jeopardize U.S. supply lines in any direction. Nor was Hawaii secure, for Japan might push a fleet to Midway, build airfields on Niihau, and batter Oahu at will. America's abiding need was a mighty air force in Hawaii, and Mitchell would risk his career again to see that America got it. Nor was Mitchell alone. For his ideas won booming support from an alcoholic Anglo-American journalist, spy, and strategic genius who published his own prophecy of a Pearl Harbor attack in the year 1925.

Hector Bywater was born in London but grew up in Massachusetts, New York, Canada, Germany, and everywhere else his peripatetic father alit (he even did a stint with the Pony Express). Hector was restless, too, but focused: he loved ships and strategy. As a youth he worked for the *New York Herald,* a pioneer in military reportage, and became a disciple of Frederick T. Jane, the publisher of *Jane's Fighting Ships* and foremost authority on the world's navies. Bywater spent World War I ferreting out data on the German Navy, and only in 1920 began to turn his attention to the Pacific. Given his knowledge of technology and geography, it was a straightforward matter to deduce the likely course of a Pacific war. The Japanese would undoubtedly launch a surprise attack to cripple the American fleet, after which they could expand at their leisure in the western Pacific. Bywater believed that the United States would eventually win but that its strategic dilemma would be "well-nigh insolvable."

No wonder Bywater's *Sea Power in the Pacific,* published in 1921, fascinated the Japanese admiralty. Prior to then the Japanese war plan, drafted by Satō Tetsutarō (the Japanese Mahan) and Akiyama Saneyuki in 1907, projected a defensive war in which they would fall upon the American fleet after its long voyage to Japanese waters, thus repeating 1905. But Bywater all but told the Japanese that their best ploy was to repeat 1904, to attack enemy installations already in the Pacific, and conquer an oceanic empire. The Washington Conference changed his mind. He reported on it brilliantly for the *Baltimore Sun,* predicting Hughes's proposal for "the ruthless scrapping" of battleships and Japan's demand that the United States not fortify its Pacific islands. But most of all, Bywater believed that the resulting restrictions on American ships and bases made Pacific war *more* likely, not less. "Japan may be innocent of imperialistic ambitions," he wrote, "but the temptation to exploit the unique strategic position in which she has been placed by the Washington Treaty may sooner or later prove irresistible." That judgment got him into a sharp debate with Franklin Delano Roosevelt, who followed the conference with care while undergoing treatment for the polio he contracted in 1921. In an article called "Shall We Trust Japan?" Roosevelt argued that the global revulsion toward war was for real, and that the Washington treaties would deter a Pacific war by ensuring that it could only result in "military deadlock."

So Bywater gathered his notes, got out the map again, and put to himself this question: would a Pacific war end in deadlock, or could the two

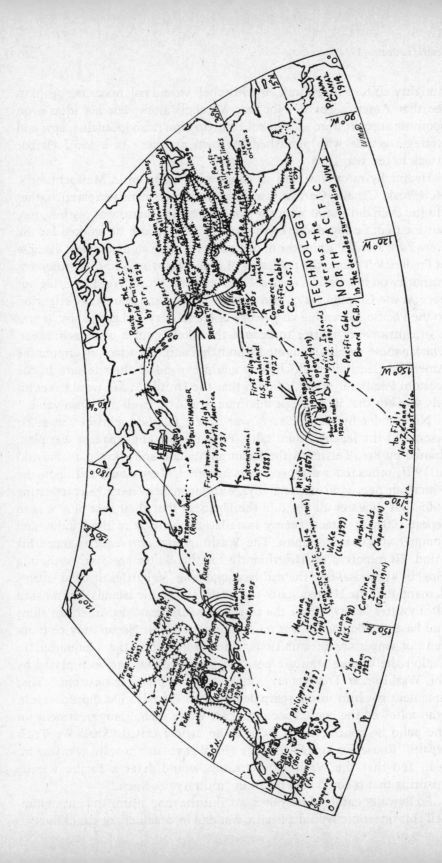

TECHNOLOGY
versus the
NORTH PACIFIC WWI
in the decades surrounding

navies find ways to cut across the mighty ocean and deliver decisive blows? He already knew that the Japanese answer was yes. But he agonized over how the Americans might counterattack. Finally, with a thrill of discovery, he hit on the solution. The Americans might leapfrog across the central Pacific through a series of amphibious assaults. Bywater was not the first to imagine that. Billy Mitchell, Admirals Alfred P. Niblack and William S. Sims and Marine Capt. Earl "Pete" Ellis had all imagined the islands as stepping-stones to the Philippines. But Bywater's numbers and charts gave the plan verisimilitude. In *The Great Pacific War* of 1925 he predicted that the Japanese attack would come "like a bolt from the blue" and shock the American people into "a stern resolve to see this struggle through to the bitter end." U.S. forces based in Hawaii would conduct their island leaps until they subjected Japan itself to blockade and withering bombardment. Bywater (like Homer Lea, whom he loved to belittle) still imagined the decisive battles as gunnery duels between battleships. But he did make room for aircraft carriers.

The Great Pacific War made an immediate splash. But it could not save Billy Mitchell. For Bywater was a civilian, and not even American, while Mitchell was a uniformed officer. Bywater criticized only implicitly, whereas Mitchell was as explicit as he could be. Where Bywater wrote about fact, but cast it as fiction, Mitchell spouted fantasy and insisted it was fact. In September 1925 he accused the War and Navy departments of "incompetency, criminal negligence, and almost treasonable administration," and was court-martialed, convicted, and moved to resign. Bywater's writings, by contrast, strengthened the hand of the Navy's forward-looking factions in their effort to revise War Plan Orange. In 1926, for the first time, the Navy shelved its fond contingencies for a fleet-sized dash to the Philippines and adopted the "marginally saner policy" of postponing any forays into the western Pacific until command of the sea was achieved. Moreover, command of the sea required air power, and in 1926 Congress finally acted to double the U.S. air arm over a five-year period. But Bywater influenced Japan even more. Saitō Hirosi, Consul General in New York, and his friend Yamamoto Isoroku, Naval Attaché in Washington, reported to Tokyo on Bywater's book and inspired a translation that was read and reread by Japanese officers. All that remained was for someone to marry Bywater's strategy to Mitchell's air power prophecies. That was Yamamoto, who two years later was back home lecturing that "Japan's only chance of victory would be to attack American forces at Hawaii," and with aircraft carriers, not battleships.

The mid-twenties were a turning point in American aviation. In 1925, Congress passed the Kelly Air Mail Act, authorizing the Postmaster General to contract out air mail to private firms, thus infusing the infant industry with much-needed cash. The Air Commerce Act of 1926 regulated safety and encouraged airport construction. The small but expert National Advisory Committee for Aeronautics expanded its wind tunnel research and consulted closely with airplane manufacturers. All that, plus the healthy economy, boosted production from fewer than 800 planes in 1925 to almost 6,200 in 1929 and midwifed the birth of scheduled airlines like Western Air Express (1926), Pan-American Airways (1927), and Transcontinental (1928), the forerunner of TWA. When Transcontinental's first eastbound flight left southern California in July 1929, over one hundred thousand people cheered. But then, the pilot was Charles Lindbergh.

Lucky Lindy's Atlantic solo of May 1927 proved it was high time someone inaugurated flight from the mainland to Hawaii. In 1925 a Navy crew had braved the 2,360 landless miles and died trying. Now the Kawanishi company, bent on making a Japanese pilot the Lindbergh of the Pacific, bought the only existing copy of Lindy's Ryan NYP and built its own version exactly 50 percent larger—on the reasoning that a Pacific pilot would have to fly 50 percent farther! It ended up as a factory display, above a sign reading How Not to Design a Special Purpose Aeroplane. Another idea that seemed good at the time was cabled to Hawaii's James D. Dole, the Pineapple King of Lanai, by two reporters in San Francisco:

IN VIEW LINDBERGH'S ATLANTIC FLIGHT PACIFIC REMAINS ONE GREAT AREA OF CONQUEST AVIATION STOP SITUATION THIS MOMENT RIPE SOMEONE OFFER SUITABLE PRIZE NON STOP FLIGHT HAWAII STOP FROM ANGLE ADVERTISING ISLANDS AND YOURSELF WE BELIEVE EXCEPTIONAL OPPORTUNITY YOUR OFFER TWENTY FIVE THOUSAND DOLLAR PRIZE.

Dole bought the notion of an air race to publicize himself, his business, and the islands for business and tourism. Unfortunately, he fixed the date of the race for three months' hence: August 12, Hawaii's Territory Day. That gave interlopers, including General Patrick's Army daredevils, a chance to steal Dole's thunder. On June 28 Army Lieutenants Lester Maitland and Albert Hegenberger took off from Oakland in a Fokker C-2 monoplane, the Bird of Paradise, and headed out over the Farallon Islands, the last land they would spy for twenty-six hours. Though shorter than Lindbergh's flight, theirs was in some ways more dangerous. For while Lindy could hardly have missed hitting Europe, the Army pilots might in fact fly right by the Hawaiian Islands through a navigational error of just 3 1/2 degrees. When their directional radio beacons quit, Maitland pushed on by dead reckoning and the next morning, sure enough, flew out of the sunrise to land on Oahu.

Dole did not cancel his Pineapple Derby, and between training accidents, amateurism, and disasters en route ten people died racing to do what had already been done. Stateside papers called it "an orgy of reckless sacrifice." But the *Honolulu Advertiser* hailed the new and lasting link to the mainland and trusted that "the tragedies attending the Dole flight will have their moral effect on those who now follow the others across the Pacific. Preparation, navigation, radio connection, a 100 percent expedition will be the result." Two years later an Australian crew spanned the ocean from Oakland to Brisbane, and in 1931 Clyde Pangborn, claiming a prize offered by a Tokyo newspaper, flew a Bellanca Skyrocket nonstop from Japan to Wenatchee, Washington.

Now it was just a matter of years before the U.S. and Japanese navies proved Bywater's and Mitchell's hypotheses. All they needed was aircraft carriers, island bases, and a reason to fight in the first place. Mizuno Hironori, a Japanese officer of liberal views, already knew what that reason would be. "Japanese militarists are treading in the footsteps of Germany," he wrote in 1923. Someday they would seize control of the government, attempt "the virtual enslavement of China," and provoke a war with the United States. If that happened, predicted British Vice Adm. G. A. Ballard, "that great expanse of blue water may become the highway to one of the most sanguinary racial conflicts that ever convulsed the world."

Shanghai 1927

THAT MILITARY FANATICS might take over in Tokyo and launch a war to enslave China might have seemed far-fetched in a decade when imperialism was considered passé, democracy held sway even in Japan, and the Washington treaties had broken the tyranny of geopolitics. The western Pacific was now a demilitarized buffer protecting the United States and Japan from each other, while Manchuria was understood to be part of China and subject to the Open Door. But Hughes's grand design suffered almost at once from the effects of the Japanese Exclusion Act, the Japanese economic slump, and the rapid recovery of China and Russia. Blocked from peaceful expansion, Japan was increasingly at risk of being forced backward even in Asia. In 1924 a liberal Japanese pleaded in *Foreign Affairs* for Americans to understand that the "vital question between America and Japan is not California, but China," and that U.S.-Japanese amity "will depend much on the rise or fall of the liberal movement in Japan." The implication should have been clear: if the United States sought to bolster civilian rule in Japan, then Americans must look with sympathy on Japan's efforts to defend its interests in China.

But that meant looking with less sympathy on the aspirations of China itself. Was it likely that Yankees would "tilt" toward the Japanese Empire, against which they conjured such animus, and away from a struggling Republic founded by the supposed Christian, Sun Yat-sen? Perhaps not, but the United States might well stand on the sidelines, given the miscarriage of Sun's revolution and the apparent disintegration of China itself. For after the death of Yüan Shih-k'ai, China reverted to a congeries of warlord satrapies. In Manchuria the Fengtien army of Chang Tso-lin ruled with erstwhile Japanese support. In Peking and north China a series of "presidents" backed by the Chihli army claimed to be the rightful heirs of Yüan. In the inland east, lesser warlords played the larger off against each other and battled each other for land and the taxes gouged from the populations. In May 1919 the great powers placed an embargo on the warring factions in China, but they managed to purchase modern arms, even airplanes, throughout the 1920s. Thus, when Hughes proposed at the Washington Conference to help China, French Premier Briand asked, with a Gallic sniff, "What is China?" *Foreign Affairs* likewise attested that "all the world knows, China is politically in a state little better than anarchy."

The most sophisticated answer to "what is China?" was that of Sun Yat-sen, who drafted an "Outline of National Reconstruction" and founded the *Chung-kuo kuo-min-tang,* or Nationalist party, on a syncretic mixture of American democracy, Leninism, and Meiji-style modernization. This was perhaps the greatest irony of the 1920s, for in the revolutionary era born of World War I the Americans, Japanese, and Soviet Russians all espoused anti-imperialist ideologies, even as they remained the chief competitors for power and influence in China—power and influence the Chinese vowed to expel in the name of those same ideologies. The Marxist heresy of Leninism was especially appealing to Chinese intellectuals, because it shifted the locus of Marxist revolution from the proletariats of industrial societies to the downtrodden victims of Western imperialism, and because Lenin had shown how a dedicated and disciplined party cadre might seize power, mobilize the masses, and win a civil war in a huge, underdeveloped country. No wonder a Chinese Communist party was founded in Shanghai in July 1921, and Sun himself courted Soviet aid. In January 1923 Adolf Joffe, an agent of Lenin's Communist International (Comintern), negotiated a deal with Sun, and by 1924 Mikhail Borodin and forty Soviet advisers were busy organizing the Kuomintang. Chinese Nationalists, including the promising Gen. Chiang Kai-shek, went in turn to Moscow to study the Soviet system.

The alliance seemed incontestable, for the Kuomintang and the Communists both favored centralization, modernization, and expulsion of the imperialists. Moreover, Joffe acknowledged that China was not ready for communism and therefore the proper Communist tactic was to promote the Nationalist movement. But Soviet policy was more complicated than mere "proletarian internationalism." For the new Union of Soviet Socialist Republics was not only the leader of world communism, it was also the successor to the Russian Empire. And geopolitics trumped ideology. By 1923 the USSR reclaimed the tsars' Asian empire, made a puppet of Outer Mongolia, and reclaimed all "Russia's legal and just rights in China." So much for Ambassador Karakhan's idealistic 1919 declaration in which the Soviets renounced all railroad, timber, and mining concessions and extraterritorial rights in northern Manchuria. So much for the Soviets' 1920 pledge of solidarity with Asia's "eight hundred millions of people" in their struggle against capitalism. The facts remained, as the Soviets soon discovered, that the Chinese Eastern Railway (CER) was still the most direct route to Vladivostok, that Manchuria was full of mineral wealth, and that tens of thousands of Russians still lived in Manchuria. It was also a fact that selfless renunciation would *not* mean the transfer of Russian rights to "China," but rather to the Peking and Manchurian warlords in cahoots with Japan. So the Soviets determined to stay.

During the U.S.-Japanese occupation of Siberia, the CER was in a sort of receivership. Its putative owner was the old Russo-Chinese Bank, but by 1922 the French stockholders were helpless to prevent the Soviets and the Peking regime from deciding the fate of the CER. Wellington Koo's opening ploy was to ask Moscow to "declare once more its intention of returning all its rights and interests in the said railway to China without compensation," but Karakhan denied he had ever made such a promise. American, British, and French diplomats warned Peking against Communist perfidy, Chinese newspapers depicted "the Soviets' aggressive policy as an echo of the Tsar's," while Communist propaganda denounced the Open Door as a smoke screen for world capitalism. All parties had a point. But the Peking regime, which lacked even the expertise to run the railroad, surrendered in 1924. Behind a fig leaf of Chinese sovereignty and joint management, a Soviet general manager was to enjoy "preponderant influence" over the railroad and all Russia's former economic concessions. Karakhan boasted that "the restoration of the Soviet Union's title [sic] to the Chinese Eastern Railway opens up broad vistas for economic and political collaboration with China. At present the Soviet Union is gaining a firm foothold in the Far East by *occupying one of the most important positions* of which its enemies were trying to deprive it." A frustrated Charles Evans Hughes could do nothing but present the railroad's new management with a bill for exactly $4,177,820.06 to cover the cost incurred by the Allies in keeping the CER running from 1918 to 1922. And all that accomplished was to provide sport for Soviet propagandists.

So Russia was back, exerting its rights on the North Pacific and competing for influence in China. But what of Soviet involvement in the *anti*-Peking Nationalist movement in South China? How could the USSR sign treaties with one Chinese government while supporting its overthrow by another? To sort that out we must meditate for a moment on the mysteries of Communist foreign policy. Karl Marx left no guidelines in his voluminous corpus to guide a would-be Marxist state, because he expected a world revolution to do away with national states altogether. Lenin did provide the ideological groundwork for a Marxist understanding of world politics but failed to anticipate the phenomenon of "socialism in one country." That is, the revolution succeeded in one great nation (Russia—the last one Marx expected) but failed to spread elsewhere. That meant the Bolsheviks had to lead a global millenarian conspiracy while at the same time conducting foreign policy as one great power among many. The agency Lenin created for the first task was the Comintern, through which Moscow orchestrated the subversive activities of Communist parties abroad while denying responsibility for their actions. The agency for the second task was the People's Commissariat for Foreign Affairs, through which the Kremlin petitioned foreign governments for the recognition, credits, and technology Russia needed to recover and "build socialism." So by the time Lenin died in 1924, the Soviets were pursuing a two-track strategy in China as in Europe: normal relations with the Peking regime to reestablish Russia's imperial sphere of influence, and collaboration with the anti-imperialist movement most likely to unify China, the Kuomintang. Matters grew more complex when Sun Yat-sen died in March 1925, and right-wing and left-wing factions vied for control of the party. Now the Chinese Communists and their Soviet patrons plotted to take over the Left Kuomintang in hopes of seizing control of the whole Kuomintang, in anticipation of its seizing control of all China.

A desperate game, and one that depended on perfect timing: when would the Communists be strong enough to prevail, and at what point should they show their hand? Trotsky and Stalin, rivals for power in the Politburo, were as ignorant of Chinese realities as all previous Western statesmen who had tried to "hustle the East," but they nonetheless made China policy a polemical battleground. In March 1926 Trotsky assailed Stalin's party line, urging that the Soviets needed a long "breathing spell" to recover and industrialize. So anxious was he to avoid blundering into a war with Japan that he not only insisted the Soviets refrain from premature Chinese adventures, but even suggested allowing Japanese emigrants to settle in Siberia! As for Manchuria, wrote Trotsky in early 1927, the USSR should simply back Chang Tso-lin and revive the Tsar's prewar agreements with Japan on spheres of influence. It was wise counsel but left Trotsky stupidly exposed in the byzantine politics of the Kremlin. By doing nothing, Stalin appeared the more zealous Communist, and should the day come when the Chinese Communists rose up and failed, he could always blame it on Trotsky's reticence.

The Soviets' four-pronged gambit began to come apart in 1926 when Chiang Kai-shek purged Left Kuomintang leaders in Canton, then launched his army on the long-awaited Northern Expedition toward Peking. Borodin, the Comintern agent, advised the Left Kuomintang to relocate in the Wuhan cities (Hankow region), where they would be out of Chiang's way until the time came to raise the masses and take over the party. As Stalin bragged in Moscow, the Kuomintang has "to be utilized to the end, squeezed out like a lemon, and then thrown away." But that was the very month—April 1927—that Chiang Kai-shek staged a preemptive strike. As his Nationalist soldiers approached Shanghai, the commercial capital of the China coast and locus of Leftist activity, the local Communists, true to the party line, helped paralyze the city's defenses. But once in control of Shanghai, Chiang's soldiers and agents swept down on Communist party cells, labor unions, and other bastions of the Left Kuomintang, shooting and arresting their members en masse. The Wuhan Communists and their Comintern advisers were stunned and fell into a nasty debate over what to do next. Borodin's counsel won out: launch their own Northern Expedition in alliance with inland warlords like Feng Yu-hsiang and race Chiang to Peking. But Feng doublecrossed the Communists and made his peace with Chiang. A desperate Stalin, reduced to moving imaginary armies across a board eight thousand miles away, ordered the Chinese Communists to field twenty thousand soldiers and raise the workers and peasants. Instead, the Left Kuomintang and Communist leaders in Wuhan spat recriminations at each other, and Borodin went home.

The scattered Communist cells still under discipline launched Stalin's belated revolution on August 1, 1927. By mid-1928 they themselves were reduced to a few strongholds and orphaned, wandering bands, one of them led by Mao Tse-tung. Meanwhile, Peking fell to the armies of Feng and Chiang Kai-shek, who declared his Kuomintang the first legitimate government of a unified China since 1911, and the only one truly dedicated to the expulsion of foreign imperialists.

So the Soviets made fools of themselves. But Stalin survived the Chinese debacle to consolidate his totalitarian power, send Trotsky into exile, and decree the massive industrialization and collectivization campaigns of the First Five-Year Plan. One of the ancillary goals of the plan was to take up where Witte left off in developing Siberia, and where Nicholas II left off in militarizing it. Moreover, the Soviets still controlled the CER and northern Manchuria, as well as the Mongolian People's Republic. So Chiang's victory simply meant that the Soviets shifted their strategy from the revolutionary track to the power political track until such time as the correlation of forces in China might shift. The Soviet Union, for all intents and purposes, was tsarist Russia reborn.

Now imagine how these dramatic events were perceived in the tearooms and barracks of Japan's Kwantung Army in southern Manchuria. Not only had Russia recovered to loom over the Japanese Empire from the north, but a strong and militant China had emerged to squeeze Japan's sphere from the south and demand an end to all foreign privilege. Japan was on the *defensive* and had to act boldly or risk losing its hold on the continent altogether. But the democratic cabinets in Tokyo, it seemed, were too weak or weak-willed to do so.

Chinese feeling against Japan had run high ever since the Paris Peace Conference. Nor were the Chinese fooled by the retrocession of Shantung after the Washington Conference: the peninsula was still dominated by Japanese capital. In 1925 Chinese workers struck a Japanese-owned cotton mill in Shanghai, protesting their paltry wages. In the ensuing demonstrations Japanese guards and British police killed at least a dozen unarmed Chinese, provoking nationwide protests and creating many more Chinese martyrs. That was the national mood when the Special Tariff Conference met in Peking from 1925 to 1926 to try to revise the old unequal treaties. This was the crucial test for the Open Door and the Washington Conference system, and China and the powers flunked it. Under civil war conditions the Chinese factions could not coordinate their policies. Indeed, on more than one occasion Western delegates had to shout to be heard over the Kuomintang and Communist mobs raging in the streets below. Nor could the foreigners present a united front. The United States and Britain agreed that China ought to regain control of its customs rates and receipts but haggled over the details, while the Japanese were reluctant even to grant the principle of Chinese equality. So the conference adjourned *sine die*.

Throughout the 1920s, the Japanese pursued a policy inspired by Foreign Minister Shidehara Kijūrō designed to promote bilateral relations with China. His syrupy "good neighbor" rhetoric extolling the possibilities of Sino-Japanese "co-existence and co-prosperity" went hand in hand with lower military spending and was popular with Japanese business. But so important were Chinese raw materials and markets, and the receipts from the South Manchurian Railway, that no one considered giving up Japan's concessionary rights. As a result, no one in China reciprocated. Of course, so long as China was in chaos, the Japanese could deflect the demands that they dismantle their informal empire. But that comfort, too, disappeared with Chiang's Northern Expedition. When his armies moved up the rails to Tsinan and threatened to occupy Shantung, Shidehara sent two thousand Japanese infantrymen for the "protection of Japanese nationals on the spot." Then that 1927 bank crisis toppled the Japanese cabinet. General Tanaka Giichi, the new Prime Minister, staged a highly publicized Eastern Regions Conference for the purpose of drafting a "strong" China policy as opposed to Shidehara's "weak" one. But all the ministers could reach consensus on was to recognize Chiang's government on a de facto basis and stick by their guns in Shantung and Manchuria. As Kuomintang armies neared Peking, Tanaka warned Chiang against initiating hostilities and ordered Manchurian warlord Chang Tso-lin to return to Mukden and stay put. The implication was clear: Japan would not interfere in China proper, if Chiang did not interfere in Manchuria. As Stanley Hornbeck of the State Department's Far Eastern desk put it: "Japan evidently intends to draw a dividing line in China with Manchuria on one side and the middle kingdom on the other."

When the United States and Britain proceeded in 1928 to recognize the Kuomintang as the legitimate government of China and to promise it tariff autonomy, Japan was in danger of isolation. Would Chiang continue his drive northward, oust Chang Tso-lin, and challenge the Japanese fief in Manchuria? And would Tokyo do anything to prevent it? Those were the questions asked over and over again by the fire-eating patriots of the Kwantung Army officer corps. Mostly of rural stock and trained in the spirit of the German Army, they were contemptuous of Tokyo's corrupt, cosmopolitan, and liberal politicians. Moreover, they had witnessed the power of Chinese nationalism firsthand, fighting against saboteurs, labor strikes, and mass demonstrations. They were keenly aware that Chinese immigration into Manchuria, driven by floods, poverty, and civil war, was exploding. A million arrived in 1927 and over two million more in 1928. Japanese colonists streamed in as well: 120,000 by 1927, another 100,000 by 1930, plus perhaps 800,000 Koreans. But what were they compared with twenty-five million Chinese? Anxious Japanese merchants and railroad officials staged an All Manchurian Convention to pressure Tokyo to defend Japan's rights, and in 1928 a Manchurian Youth League manifesto declared that "our sacred territory of Manchuria is on the verge of a crisis. We face a critical moment for the existence or destruction of this nation. The government has offered no counter-measure. . . . Should we sit by silently?"

Finally, the Kwantung Army, laced as it was with secret societies, spawned a conspiracy of "young officers" led by Col. Kōmoto Daisaku, who had sat through the Eastern Regions Conference and concluded that Japan's mission in Manchuria was doomed if it did not disarm Chang Tso-lin's army, and police Manchuria itself. So it was that his demolitions experts planted explosives on a bridge and, with perfect timing, blew up Chang Tso-lin's railroad carriage as he rode back to Mukden. The conspirators expected Tokyo to use the power vacuum as an excuse to invade Manchuria in full force. Instead, news of the assassination was censored from the Japanese press, while Emperor Hirohito, the cabinet, and genrō wrung their hands. "What fools! They behave like children," said Tanaka. "They have no idea what the parent has to go through." Tanaka's cabinet fell for failing to control the army, Kōmoto resigned for his "mistake in guarding the railway," and in Manchuria things only got worse. For the dead warlord's son—the "Young Marshal," Chang Hsueh-liang—murdered the Kwantung Army's prospective puppet and seized power himself, recognized the Kuomintang, and began to challenge Japan's railroad rights. Sino-Japanese tensions increased.

Sino-*Russian* tensions, on the other hand, boiled over. In 1926 Manchurian troops raided the Soviet legation, and Moscow fired off protests—in the wry words of a British diplomat—"quite as 'imperialistic' in tone as any that we should send." Then in 1929 the Young Marshal openly renounced the Soviets' presence in northern Manchuria on the grounds that they spread "propaganda directed against the political and social system of China." He then seized the CER telephone and telegraph system, arrested the Russian general manager, and began to expel Soviet officials. Ambassador Karakhan protested the Chinese bandits' "glaring violations" of the 1924 treaties, and Stalin ordered reinforcements to the Amur. But the Chinese refused to bend until October 1929, when Soviet planes, armored cars, gunboats, and infantry struck along the same terrain as Khabarov's Cossacks in the seventeenth century and Muraviev's Siberians in the nineteenth. Strafing from the air especially terrified the Manchurian soldiers, who broke ranks and looted a town "mainly to obtain civilian clothing, which they donned instead of their uniforms, and many of them appeared in women's clothing." The Young Marshal sued for peace, and the Khabarovsk Protocol restored Soviet management of the CER. Needless to say, this Sino-Soviet border war was a powerful example to the Japanese Army of how best to deal with Chinese arrogance.

So the Washington system was already dying. When it was signed there was no China to speak of, and the Soviet Union had not made itself felt. Now the China of Chiang and the Russia of Stalin weighed down on Japan's foothold in northeast Asia, while the Open Door was nowhere in evidence. If Japan were to avoid isolation, encirclement, and economic strangulation, its parliamentary government needed to show that it could command respect for Japanese rights and bring better economic times at home. Perhaps the 1930s would bring better times.

Mukden 1931

THE NEXT 'ROUND-the-world flight was not in an airplane at all but in the gigantic, hydrogen-filled, cigar-shaped airship *Graf Zeppelin*. Over 250 *yards* long, with a volume of over four million cubic feet, she was designed for transatlantic passenger and freight service. This greatest of Germany's zeps was luxurious and, to Capt. Hugo Eckener's eye, beautiful: a "silvery fish, floating quietly in the ocean of air and captivating the eye just like a fantastic, exotic fish seen in an aquarium. And this fairy-like apparition, which seemed to melt into the silvery blue background of sky, when it appeared far away, lighted by the sun, seemed to be coming from another world." The dapper and daring Eckener was not only designer, manufacturer, and pilot but promoter as well. And whom should he find to pay for the flight but William Randolph Hearst. The adventure began in New York on August 7, 1929, when the *Graf* circled the Statue of Liberty and set out across the Atlantic. A week later in Friedrichshafen, the crew of forty and eighteen passengers floated again up to cruising altitude and powered into the east. It was extraordinary that Stalin permitted the aeronauts in Soviet airspace, for they crossed the length of the USSR at fewer than three thousand feet, cameras at the ready.

The taiga and swamps of Siberia looked especially placid from above, though in a spooky sort of way. "Just imagine if we crash *here!*" passengers must have asked over drinks on the observation deck. In fact, communism had begun to turn Siberia into the land the elder George Kennan accused it of being in the nineteenth century—an empire of soldiers and slaves. Yet so monotonous was the forest below that Eckener groped like the Cossacks of old, from river to river, so as not to lose his bearings. At Yakutsk the crew dropped a wreath in honor of German prisoners of war who had died in Siberian camps. The original flight plan had the *Graf* turning south to follow the Amur to the sea. But Eckener chose instead to stay well to the north, perhaps to avoid the summer monsoons (as he claimed), or perhaps because that was the moment Chinese and Russians were shooting each other in Manchuria. The detour obliged the captain to pick out a pass through the Stanovoi Mountains, which proved to be a thousand feet higher than he thought. Eckener set his jaw, began casting ballast, and more ballast, and finally slid his giant gasbag over the top with just 150 feet of clearance.

The *Graf* had reached the Pacific from Europe in fewer than four days, and turned south over Sakhalin Island. The playwright Chekhov had visited bare Sakhalin and simply named it "hell." But geologists estimated that the northern, Russian half of the island held one hundred million tons of oil—oil "absolutely necessary" to Japan's national defense. No wonder the Japanese seized northern Sakhalin during their intervention in Siberia. The Soviets tried to recover their prize by signing a contract with Sinclair Oil in January 1922, hoping the Americans would force Japan out. But Hughes wanted no quarrels that might complicate his Washington Conference and did nothing when the Japanese arrested three Sinclair prospectors. So the frustrated Soviets had no choice but to deal with Japan. Former Secretary of State Lansing lambasted Hughes for "allowing to slip into Japanese hands the Sakhalin oil fields." But Hughes got his treaties, the Soviets got northern Sakhalin back, and the Japanese Navy got all the oil.

The Tokyo that the *Graf Zeppelin* gazed down upon was rather more cheerful than it had been in years. A grand festival was being planned to celebrate the reconstruction after the earthquake. New movie theaters and music halls in the Asakusa district and the Ginza department stores attracted young Japanese flappers with cosmetically whitened skin and rounded eyes, and swells in top hats and tails. Jazz and cocktails were in, and just about everything else Japanese traditionalists abhorred, that summer of 1929. Eckener and his passengers then looked forward to crossing the North Pacific in seventy-nine hours. But Eckener spent that leg doubled over with gastroenteritis, while the rest of the people were bored. Fog and clouds stuck to the *Graf* like cotton, and there was nothing to see anyway but water. It was probably the first trip in history in which passengers traveled with no sense at all of speed, distance, or danger. Like passengers on a jet today, they simply boarded a cabin in one part of the world and disembarked in another after some tedious but comfortable hours. As one of Hearst's scribblers put it, "On a plane you fly, but on the *Graf* you voyage."

The zeppelin floated south along California's coast to salute Hearst's castle at San Simeon, then moored at the U.S. Navy yard in Los Angeles, now the largest city in the eastern Pacific, having nudged out smug San Francisco in the 1920 census. Aviation, films, manufacturing, real estate, education, and especially agriculture all boomed in the twenties in southern California, thanks to the mass importation of water and electric power from the Owens River Project beneath the High Sierra, and the promise of more when the Boulder Dam project was approved in 1928. Over eight hundred thousand automobiles were registered in Los Angeles County by 1930, and traffic jams and foul air were already daily occurrences. But as the *Los Angeles Times* wrote in 1926: "how can one pursue happiness by any swifter and surer means . . . than by the use of the automobile?" Of course, Los Angeles did tend to get those temperature inversions that trapped the smog in the valleys. On August 26, 1929, one trapped the *Graf Zeppelin*, too. So Eckener tried a daring tactic: he churned the airship forward in hopes of generating enough aerodynamic lift to get airborne. Suddenly a high-tension power line loomed dead ahead! Their only chance was to highjump it. Eckener barked orders in commanding German to raise the elevators and get the nose over the wire, then reverse them to elevate the tail. The ship cleared the wire and cruised into the desert. But if one spark from that power line had reached the *Graf*'s hydrogen. . . .

Eckener chose a southern route to avoid the Rocky Mountains, then turned northeast across the Great Plains. Chicagoans poured out to gape at the apparition, lining the lakefront that an otherwise corrupt City Hall had turned into gorgeous parkland. Chicago never had it better than in 1929: the economy was strong, booze was easy to find, and the baseball Cubs were even winning a pennant. But the greatest celebration was New York's, where Eckener steered his ship once more about the Statue of Liberty to complete his circuit of the globe. Alas, it was the last gaudy show of a theatrical decade. For within weeks of the ticker tape parade for the zeppelin, Wall Street itself was in free fall. The Great Depression had arrived, and within a year the highest tariff in American history (Smoot-Hawley), the stock market crash, unemployment, bank and business failures, and massive deflation combined to destroy world trade.

That was especially bad news for Japan, living, as it always does, on the margin. Japanese exports plummeted 50 percent. Thousands of farmers whose livelihood rested on selling silk to merchants engaged in the export trade faced poverty by 1931 and starvation by 1932, when the rice crop failed. Americans would not or could not buy Japanese, while the Chinese boycotted Japanese goods altogether. To a country poor in raw materials and farmland, and dependent on exports to prosper, the collapse of world trade was the worst possible disaster. No wonder it seemed to more Japanese than ever that the whole 1920s world order— disarmament, the Open Door, arbitration—had brought them nothing but grief and shame. Even Europe, Britain, and the United States were verging on social collapse, and to think that the Japanese had, in weak moments, been eager to copy their ways! So why should Japan swallow more of the same from pro-Western civilians in Tokyo? Perhaps the righteous military critics were the saviors of the Yamato race after all.

But the Depression was only the occasion for the demise of Japanese democracy, not its cause. The possibility of Japan's succumbing to a mystical Shinto totalitarianism (resembling, in some respects, fascism) was implanted in its body politic by the Meiji Restorationists themselves. *They* launched a military campaign to overthrow the civil government and justified it by appeals to national security. *They* governed as a self-selecting oligarchy in the name of an Emperor who remained a figurehead. *They* crafted a constitution that made the Army and Navy responsible to the Emperor alone. *They* designed an educational system that prescribed universal, regimented, and hyperpatriotic schooling of youngsters. *They* elaborated and propagated the official Shinto myths concerning Japan's divine origin, nature, and destiny. *They* built a modern conscript army modeled after the German and imbued its officer corps with the samurai code of *bushidō*.

The Meiji men also opened Japan to liberal, cosmopolitan, and constitutional influences that seemed every bit as strong as the military, xenophobic ones. But liberals were elitist and urban and open to charges of decadence and effeminacy; the militarists seemed populist, rural, and pure. So where a Westerner might assume that the masses are always on the side of parliamentary government, the Japanese masses grew contemptuous of the corrupt politicians and the *zaibatsu* that funded them. So long as the politicians succeeded in managing Japan's economy and winning Western respect for Japan, their rule was tolerable. But there was nothing in Japan's history or constitution that made majority rule a matter of *principle*. The Meiji example only validated the military overthrow of civilian rule when it appeared to betray "Japan."

But what was "Japan"? Western observers might have assumed that Japan was the people they met and did business with: diplomats, bureaucrats, professors, merchants, hoteliers, and bar girls. They did not meet many army lieutenants, not to mention peasants. So the expectation that as Japan modernized it must become more like the West was a double conceit: first, because it assumed the universality of nineteenth-century liberal Western theories of progress and law; second, because liberalism and law had gone off the rails in the West itself, so an Asian who *wanted* to be Western and modern in the interwar years would more than likely be Fascist or Communist, not democratic. Instead of wondering why Taishō democracy failed, perhaps we should wonder that it lasted as long as it did. Meiji institutions, Japanese culture, and Japan's awful geopolitical and economic problems suggested instead a hierarchical, military, consensus-based politics, a politics of intuition, a politics of desperation.

The Yuzonsha, or Society for the Preservation of the National Essence, began to give form to Shinto expansionism in the years after World War I. Kita Ikki elaborated its goals in *An Outline for the Reconstruction of Japan:* Japan must launch domestic and international revolutions to be carried out under the auspices of the military, the protector of the *kokutai,* or national essence. For just as "multimillionaire" nations like Britain and America conspired to keep Japan down, so did the *zaibatsu* and their bought politicians conspire to oppress their own people. Only through revolution might Japan return to the principles of unity, sacrifice, duty, and piety, and so be worthy "to lift the virtuous banner of an Asian league" in a revolt against imperialism and Marxism alike. Here, in 1923, was national socialism in a Japanese idiom, anticapitalist and anti-Communist, nationalistic, militaristic, in revolt against the domestic and world orders alike. No less a personage than Prince Konoe Fumimaro anticipated Mussolini when he divided the world into "have" nations and "have nots" that must "destroy the status quo for the sake of self-preservation." Kita's ideas spread rapidly among military officers at a time when the civilian government cut their prestige along with their budgets. Nor was it difficult to justify revolt: all an idealistic soldier need do was contrast the purity of the Emperor with the filthiness of the place seekers and merchants of Tokyo. As the Meiji Restoration rescued Japan from the shogunate, so now a "Shōwa Restoration" was needed to save Japan from the parties. And if the generals were too craven to act, then colonels must act on their own. *Gekokujō*—direct action by subordinates in times of emergency—had a recognized place in Japanese history.

Finally, staff officers in the 1920s began planning for radical action at home and abroad for entirely down-to-earth reasons. A "preparedness" or "total war" faction coalesced among those whose business it was to plan Japan's war economics. They were not necessarily fanatical. Some were just bean counters who drew the obvious conclusion that Japan could not win a war of attrition. Just as Germany, the mightiest military state in the world, had lost because the Allied blockade had starved it into submission, so would Japan be strangled to death unless it were able to conquer the rice paddies and minerals it needed. Such thinking inspired the exploitation of Korea, the Army's campaign in Siberia and Sakhalin, and the effort to make the Pacific mandates "a new Japan." Where Germany had administered Micronesia with a mere two dozen officials, the Japanese Navy and Colonial Ministry sent 950, plus a tide of immigrants that would reach ninety-three thousand by 1941. But copra and the phosphate mines of Palau were not the stuff of industrial autarky. So in 1927 the new Cabinet Resources Bureau turned its attention to Manchuria. It was rich in iron and coal and already provided bountiful crops of soybeans, cereals, peanuts, ginseng, salt, timber, furs, and wool. The South Manchurian Railway turned annual profits of about 40 percent even during the Depression. But Japan might lose control of Manchuria unless the striped pants in Tokyo found the guts to defend it. "We were concerned," wrote a Resources Bureau member, "not only over the Manchuria-Mongolia problem but also over domestic reform. . . . We were fed up."

Lieutenant Colonel Ishiwara Kanji was the vessel that carried the ideology of autarky, expansion, and domestic purification into the arena of deeds. He was a brilliant outsider from a minor clan that had actually sided with the Shogun before 1868. And brilliant outsiders tend to conjure whole world views to justify their personal crusades. Ishiwara graduated from the Japanese Military Academy in 1907, did a tour in Korea, and then attended the Army Staff College, where he graduated with the Imperial Sword, an honor that usually placed an officer on the fast track to general. Instead, Ishiwara was passed over for promotions and finally ended up as a scholar. He spent three years in Germany reading history and returned to teach at the Staff College. But besides his lectures on Frederick the Great and Napoleon, Ishiwara prophesied Armageddon.

His inspiration was a curious mixture of Shinto, German idealism, and Nichiren (Sun Lotus) Buddhism. The last was founded by a thirteenth-century monk who divined that after three ages of history the world would fall into chaos and "a titanic world conflict, unprecedented in human history." The Japanese nation was destined to win and rule the earth in justice and peace. As a twentieth-century Nichiren priest put it, "Japan is the Truth of the World, Foundation of Human Salvation, and Finality of the World." The similarity to the Christian apocalypse and thousand-year reign of the saints is suggestive—except that in Nichiren Buddhism, the church is a *race*. Ishiwara superimposed this spiritual vision on his own narrative of military history and decided—no surprise—that "the Final War is fast approaching" and would pit the peoples of Asia led by Japan against the white nations led by America. But given his "grave doubts as to the political capacities of the Chinese race," it was necessary for Japan to organize Asia before turning to challenge America. "Truly, the Japanese armed forces are the guardian deity of that righteousness—the Japanese *kokutai*—which shall save the world." But victory was assured only if Japan seized the necessary raw materials in Asia and the Pacific according to the principle "war can maintain war." When the final showdown came, Japan must strike at the Philippines, Guam, and Hawaii, and defeat America quickly, or else lose horribly. For air power, he predicted, would wreak apocalyptic destruction.

Ishiwara was no crank. At least, he was no stranger than the quasi Hegelians and Social Darwinists brooding in Germany or the ubiquitous Communists with their hateful utopia. But Ishiwara, like Lenin, Hitler, and Sun Yat-sen, was also intent on making his dream come true. That is why he requested a transfer to Manchuria and set out to succeed where the murderers of Chang Tso-lin had failed. His intellectual prestige was enormous, as were his energy and zeal. The only qualities he lacked—the patience and mind for detail of the staff officer—arrived at Kwantung Army headquarters in the person of Lt. Col. Itagaki Seishirō in 1929. Together they drafted a plan to provoke a conflict at a time when the Young Marshal was absent, fall upon the Manchurian warlord's units by surprise, then fan out and occupy *all* of Manchuria. The Russians would not dare resist, and the Americans could not. The weaklings in Tokyo would then have no choice but to defend the fait accompli before world opinion. "We must lose no time in forcing our country to undertake foreign expansion," wrote Ishiwara, "in the course of which we can accomplish domestic renovation when conditions are ripe."

While Ishiwara and Itagaki identified officers they could trust, the politicians in Tokyo struggled with the effects of the Depression. As always, Japan had to live in a world others made for it, and this time that world was sick. One remedy touted by Hoover and British Prime Minister Ramsay MacDonald was more disarmament. So they reconvened the Washington Conference powers at London in 1930 and implored the delegates to set limits on all categories of vessel. After the usual bluff and bicker, the Japanese came away with parity in submarines and a better than 10:10:6 ratio in cruisers and destroyers. The Hearst papers and the *Chicago Tribune* scorned the treaty as a giveaway. Japanese nationalists had a different means of protest. In November 1930 a self-described patriot shot Prime Minister Hamaguchi Yūkō, the "Lion" of parliamentary government, at almost the same spot where Hara Kei had been killed during the last naval go-around. Parliamentary government was bleeding to death along with Hamaguchi, who finally succumbed to his injuries in August 1931.

Three weeks later an officer on the Army General Staff left Tokyo with an urgent message for the commander of the Kwantung Army, Gen. Honjō Shigeru. It was an order from the War Minister *not* to allow Japanese officers to take "direct action" in Manchuria. Why then did the courier leak the nature of his mission to certain colonels in Manchuria, but not to their commander himself? Why did he not fly to Port Arthur, where Honjō was based, but instead take a leisurely journey by rail through Korea? Why, upon arriving in Mukden, did he not even telephone headquarters but instead go out for saki and geishas? Why did he finally deliver the order forbidding "direct action" well *after* the action began? The reason, of course, is because the courier knew and approved of Ishiwara's plan, the War Minister knew that he knew and approved, and Ishiwara knew that the War Minister knew the courier knew and approved. The only man who did not know was General Honjō, who was relaxing in his bath when the telephone rang. It was a news agency wanting to know what he intended to do about the Chinese "provocation" and the fighting it had caused. It seems a bomb had gone off.

Now we think of the Kwantung Army as an *army*, and an elite one at that. And it became such over the course of the 1930s. But in 1931 its official purpose was to police the South Manchurian Railway, and it numbered just ten thousand men. The Young Marshal's Manchurian army, by contrast, numbered a quarter of a million. Although 110,000 Manchurians were deployed to the south in Jehol province, the Chinese still outnumbered the Japanese by about fourteen to one. Ishiwara and Itagaki nonetheless made the conquest of Manchuria seem almost easy. About 10:00 P.M. on September 18 their provocateurs detonated a bomb on the railroad near Mukden. That "sabotage" was the signal for prepositioned assault teams to strike at barracks and capture or kill the sleeping, drugged, or drunken Chinese soldiers. One fort yielded over seven thousand prisoners at the cost of two Japanese killed, as well as mounds of documents supposedly revealing a *Chinese* plot to strike first and claim that "the conflict originated in Japanese aggression."

With the Young Marshal away in Peking, the best Chinese garrisons neutralized, and the Japanese in control of the railroad, there was little that Manchurian units could do except surrender or fight where they stood. For all that, Ishiwara could only get the ball rolling; its momentum depended on General Honjō, who was at first disinclined to escalate. The crisis came on the night of September 20, when Ishiwara urged Honjō to strike north to Harbin on the Chinese Eastern Railway. Honjō dismissed his fiery underling but then listened as Itagawa calmly explained that the offensive would preempt Russo-Chinese cooperation, oblige Japanese units in Korea to cross the Yalu and link up with the Kwantung Army, and protect the flanks of both. At 3:00 A.M. Honjō relented, and the young officers waiting outside shouted "*banzai!*"

The zone of Japanese occupation expanded by leaps and bounds until it encompassed the whole of Manchuria. The northern campaign was most delicate, because of the danger of clashes with Russians, and the most grueling, because of temperatures reaching twenty below zero. But the War Minister assured the Soviets that so long as they acquiesced in Japan's operations, "we shall never encroach upon the rights of the

[CER] or break in upon Russian territory." Irregular Chinese resistance stiffened over the winter, especially when fighting broke out in Shanghai, and three Japanese divisions went ashore. But the Manchurian contest was over by summer. Ishiwara had done it. He had hurled his tiny army into a crazy war in all directions and obliged his superiors to throw in 140,000 reinforcements lest Japan lose face and an empire. No wonder he boasted in 1932, "Even if Japan has to face the entire world, she can't be beaten."

Of course, Japan did not have to face the entire world, because no one in the world did more than protest. It is customary to account for this by citing the economic crises in the Western powers and the Five-Year Plan in the Soviet Union. But it is equally valid to note that no other government had the means to resist the Kwantung Army. Stalin had at most a few divisions at the end of his Siberian supply line, while the U.S. Pacific fleet was incapable of bullying Japan in the latter's home waters. A third reason nobody acted is because few people cared. As the *Philadelphia Record* put it, the American people did not "give a hoot in a rain barrel who controls North China." Even would-be friends of China, like the State Department's Stanley Hornbeck, had groused that in China "there is today no guiding purpose or principle outside of the self-interest of certain militarists . . . here is China at its worst." The Soviets saw matters precisely the same way. "When the next Chinese general comes to Moscow and shouts 'Hail to the world revolution!'" sneered Borodin, "better send at once for the OGPU [secret police]. All that any of them want is rifles." Later, American hearts went out to the suffering Chinese, but not when it might have mattered most.

Secretary of State Henry Stimson wanted at least to "let the Japanese know we are watching them." So in January 1932 he circulated his famous note to the effect that the United States "does not intend to recognize any situation, treaty, or agreement" that either violated the Open Door in China or was brought about by means of force. The Stimson Doctrine did not deter the Kwantung Army from acting the following month to make its rule permanent. At the Mukden Conference China's Manchurian governors agreed (at swords' points) to the formation of a new state called Manchukuo, to be presided over by none other than the Manchu pretender, the "Last Emperor," Henry Pu-yi. This tragic and naive young man trusted the Japanese to allow him to govern. In fact, the Kwantung colonels were already boasting that Manchukuo would be run neither for Manchurians nor for the *zaibatsu* but according to national socialist principles. So the U.S. initiative was futile, and the *Honolulu Star-Bulletin* mocked, "After Stimson has got through invoking the Nine-Power Treaty, he might try for the Ten Commandments."

Chiang Kai-shek's appeal to the League of Nations was equally fruitless. The USSR and the United States were not even members, Communist propaganda vilified the League as an imperialist club, and Hoover thought imposing sanctions was like "sticking pins in tigers." "We can never," he said, "herd the world into the paths of righteousness with the dogs of war." The League did investigate (procedure and study being good substitutes for candor and action), but its Lytton Commission issued an equivocal finding: the Chinese did much to provoke the Mukden incident, but Japan had used excessive force and really ought to think about evacuating. Instead, the Japanese delegation evacuated the Geneva assembly in March 1933 and announced Japan's intention to withdraw from the League.

American moralism and League of Nations legalism were rather irrelevant in view of the principles that were guiding Japanese politics by the early 1930s. For during the same months of 1932 when the Kwantung Army was inventing Manchukuo, a League of Blood assassinated the Japanese Minister of Finance and the head of Mitsui corporation, while a squad of cadets murdered the Prime Minister in his own home. That May 15th Incident in turn marked the end of real civilian government, for the Army now refused to provide a minister of war to any cabinet associated with the parties in the Diet. Not that the Diet dissolved, or that elections ceased; they just ceased to exert any influence over the personnel and policies of the Japanese government.

What of the Soviet Union? Surely Stalin had to respond to the Japanese seizure of Manchuria by dint of Russia's interests in northern Manchuria. But Japanese War Minister Araki Sadao warned, "If the Soviet does not cease to annoy us, I shall have to purge Siberia as one cleans a room of flies." So Stalin's reflex now, as it would be later with Hitler, was to appease, all the while denouncing the policies of Japan, the United States, and the League in Marxian jargon that was as beside the point as the Stimson Doctrine. Throughout the crisis the Soviets hammered home two points: first, that they were prepared to stand aside while Japan gobbled Manchuria; second, that they would bloody any Japanese snout that poked across the Soviet or Mongolian boundary. Russians even transported Japanese units on the CER, while at the same time Stalin poured reinforcements into the Soviet Far Eastern command and held out an olive branch to the United States.

Was Soviet-American entente possible? Stalin's spokesman, Karl Radek, instructed the readers of *Foreign Affairs* in 1932 that it was bluntly indicated since "if Japan retains Manchuria this will represent a drastic defeat of the foreign policy of the United States." The Soviet minister in Lithuania dropped the same hint to the American chargé d'affaires: "the most salutary thing that could happen in the Far East right now was for Russia and the United States to join in a common

pressure upon Japan, if necessary breaking that country as between the
two arms of a nut cracker." When the new President Roosevelt sent a
secret message of his own asking how the Soviets would reply to an
invitation to establish diplomatic relations, they not only accepted, but
agreed "to waive any and all claims of whatsoever character arising out
of activities of military forces of the United States in Siberia."

Unfortunately, once the Americans and Soviets established relations
in November 1933, it soon became clear that neither party trusted the
other, that both were becoming more, not less, isolationist, and that
each hoped the *other* would stand up to Japan. So Stalin lurched back to
appeasement and, just to remove any source of friction, offered to *sell*
the Chinese Eastern Railway. Of course, the Kwantung Army was sitting on it, so the Japanese (acting on behalf of Manchukuo) shamelessly
bargained the Soviets down to a giveaway price of 170 million yen.

Witte's brainchild gone, given almost, to Japan in March 1935! But it
was an unavoidable strategic retreat. All Stalin could do was to order
more divisions, submarines, and bombers to Asia, commit to defend
Outer Mongolia, accelerate the double-tracking of the Trans-Siberian
Railway . . . and hope that Japan decided that some other target was
more tempting than Siberia.

Nanking 1937

IN DECEMBER 1933 the ocean liner *Berengaria* docked in New York harbor. Reporters crowded into her luxurious saloon in hopes of prodding some impromptu quotes from the new Japanese Ambassador to the United States. His aged predecessor was never good for much but the occasional Oriental proverb, but this new man was said to be different. His first words proved it: "May I swipe a cigarette from one of you fellows?" A reporter asked how he viewed his mission. "My chief purpose in coming here is to drink whiskey with good Americans." Whereupon Saitō Hirosi told the bartender to set up drinks for the house.

He grew up in the late Meiji era in a provincial town, son of a humble school teacher. But his father's subject was English, and he landed a job as translator in the Foreign Office. When Foreign Minister Komura took a liking to Hirosi, the boy's career was made. After attending the aristocratic Peers College and Tokyo University, Saitō joined the foreign service himself. He was a junior attaché in Washington and London, attended the Paris Peace Conference, and was a delegate to the Washington Conference. The happiest years of his life, 1923 to 1929, were spent as Consul General in New York. The gregarious Saitō served up cocktails to the elite of American banking, politics, and journalism at his residence on Park Avenue. He lounged and dined at the Century Club, frequented Yankee Stadium, took tea at Hyde Park with the Roosevelts, and worked on his golf game. He seemed living proof that Japan was Westernizing, and so long as the Washington treaties and Taishō democracy held sway, why should anyone doubt it?

By the time Saitō got his heart's desire, the Japanese embassy in Washington, times had rudely changed. The Depression was at its depth, the United States had thrown up towering tariffs, and the Kwantung Army had gobbled Manchuria. So the glad-handing little man with

the big ears and nose—who crooned Cole Porter, quoted Damon Run-
yon, twirled his putter at Burning Tree, and smoked three packs of
Lucky Strikes per day—had to serve as front man for Japanese militarism. Not that he wanted to be. The foreign service was always pro-
Western, and it is hard to imagine that Saitō believed his emperor was a
god or that Japan was destined to rule the world. His motto was
Thought Without Guile. But he had to defend the acts of mystical militarists who despised the Western hedonism to which Saitō himself was
addicted.

He performed that duty exceedingly well. What other ambassador
toured America speaking to ladies' luncheon clubs in places like Springfield, Illinois? What ambassador went on CBS Radio to plead his government's case? What ambassador published a book challenging the policies of the country to which he was accredited? Saitō did, trusting that
"one of the many admirable American traits [is] always to be ready and
even eager to listen to what the other side has to say." He dedicated the
book "To My Daughters Sakiko and Masako who . . . are destined to be
links in Japanese-American friendship." But friendship depended on
frankness. So Saitō disparaged the American tendency "to look down on
Japan as a bank of berserks who may amuck [sic] at any moment." How
did they think that made Japanese feel? "Another question that is frequently asked is whether we ourselves do not intend to take control of
China. To us Japanese that seems like asking 'Are you not likely to go
mad?'" To be sure, Japan had occupied Manchuria, but the "xenophobic
agitation of Chinese" had brought it about. China did not understand
that "with the progress of human civilization [antiforeign] sentiments
are fast losing their cogency and are being replaced by the realization of
the common interests of all humanity." The Japanese brought order and
progress to Manchuria, just as the United States did to Latin America.
As for trade, Japan's motives were pure: "We want all your ladies to
have as much silk as they want."

Americans needed to know, wrote Saitō, that the Japanese were "a
people who have striven hard to make good in this world." They were
not perfect, but then "even you Americans are not without blemish."
The important thing was to "turn a deaf ear when men tell you we want
war." For at bottom all men—and women, who "are the makers of
men"—are pilgrims on the same stormy road. He rejected Kipling's
verse to the effect that "East is East and West is West, and never the
twain shall meet," and asked Americans to share the sentiment of
James Russell Lowell: "For Mankind are one in spirit and an instinct
bears along / Round the earth's electric orbit, the quick flash of right
and wrong."

Saitō could leave the ladies in tears, then chuckle about it over a tumbler of Old Parr. Too bad that events in the mid-1930s gave the lie to all he said and seemed to confirm the rightness of Kipling and the wrongness of Lowell.

Saitō's opposite number, the U.S. Ambassador to Japan, shared his good will. Joseph C. Grew was a patrician of the old school with a highbrow, formal style. When Babe Ruth led a team of major leaguers on a tour of Japan in 1934, Grew envied the Bambino's earthy and bumptious charm: "He is a great deal more effective Ambassador than I could ever be." But Grew and his wife (a grandchild of Commodore Perry) loved Japanese culture. So it pained him no less than Saitō to serve during years of increasing hostility. In Grew's opinion the source of the tension lay in the fact that the "great majority of Japanese are astonishingly capable of really fooling themselves; they really believe that everything they have done was right. . . . Such a mentality is a great deal harder to deal with than a mentality which, however brazen, knows that it is in the wrong." The reason was that Japanese "mental processes and methods of reaching conclusions are radically different from ours; the more one associates with them the more one realizes it; this is one of the great cleavages between the East and the West. The Westerner believes that because the Japanese has adopted Western dress, language, and customs he must think like a Westerner. No greater error can be made."

By the end of 1934 Grew saw only two alternatives: either the United States pulled out of the Far East or insisted on its Open Door rights and built up its Pacific power. Grew favored the second, but other voices contended with his, and no one knew Roosevelt's mind. The Stimson Doctrine was worse than useless, for to make a great show of labeling something a crime while not even threatening to act as policeman only made the United States look foolish. But abandonment of China was morally, politically, and strategically distasteful. Pearl Buck's *The Good Earth* (1931), articles by American missionaries, and the skillful propaganda of Chiang and his Wellesley-educated wife inspired a wave of Sinophilia against which Saitō courageously struggled. But the second option was equally unpalatable. The public and Congress begrudged every dollar spent on arms and had fallen into the worst isolationist funk since the days of Grover Cleveland. In 1935 Sen. Gerald P. Nye chaired the famous "merchants of death" hearings and Congress passed the first Neutrality Act designed to prevent the President or private interests from doing anything that might suck the nation into war. So what could be done about Asia?

A retired China hand, the mousy, professorial John Van Antwerp MacMurray, thought he knew. At the behest of Stanley Hornbeck, director of Far Eastern affairs, MacMurray collected his thoughts on the sources of Japanese conduct in a long memorandum dated November 1,

1935. He began with a narrative of Asian affairs that blamed Chinese nationalism, hysteria, and disunity for the frustration of the Washington Conference system. He reminded his readers of the legality of Japan's rights in Manchuria, the flagrant attacks made on Japanese persons and property by Chinese bandits and warlords. He did not condone the Manchurian seizure but believed that China had "asked for it." So what was likely to happen next? That the Chinese might expel Japan on their own was "a possibility so remote" as to be irrelevant. The most probable future was that Japan would expand slowly in northern China, fashioning new Manchukuos. The United States could oppose Japan or acquiesce or continue to disapprove of Japanese policy without taking any steps that might lead to war. MacMurray favored the last, for *even if the United States beat Japan in a war*, that "would be no blessing to the Far East or to the world. It would merely create a new set of stresses, and substitute for Japan, the U.S.S.R., as the successor of Imperial Russia as a contestant (and at least an equally unscrupulous and dangerous one) for the mastery of the East. Nobody except perhaps Russia would gain from our victory in such a war."

This remarkable memorandum disappeared into the files. Hornbeck thought it too pessimistic, and in any case its recommendations differed little from what the United States was doing already, which was nothing. But where MacMurray advocated neutrality in East Asia for structural reasons born of the North Pacific triangle, the administration chose passivity for such contingent reasons as: let us wait to see if Japan respects the Open Door, or until China straightens itself out, or until the U.S. Navy is strong enough to make Japan think twice. And even if Roosevelt had thought Asia important enough to act upon, isolationists stood ready to block any initiative. So the United States had no policy at all during the years when Saitō was pleading that Americans not abandon Japan, Chiang was pleading that Americans not abandon China, and the odious Stalin was arguing (on the most solid grounds of all) that Japanese imperialism must be contained. The MacMurray memo resurfaced in 1937. Grew in particular pronounced it "masterly" and wished that "everyone from the President on down" could read it. But by then the Japanese Army had behaved so badly that MacMurray's advice seemed obscene. So far as Secretary of State Cordell Hull was concerned, Japan had shown itself to be another Germany, another vigorous, overpopulated country demanding *Lebensraum*, driving for autarky, crying about perfidious treaties and jealous enemies, claiming it was being encircled, and doomed by geography to rule or perish.

Three weeks after MacMurray submitted his report the notion that the Pacific Ocean was the world's largest buffer zone was erased. That was when marching bands and Boy Scouts and radio crews and giant flags and fireworks and a hundred thousand people serenaded Capt. Ed Musick as he flew *under* the uncompleted span of the Bay Bridge, over the uncompleted Golden Gate Bridge, and headed for Asia in a silver, four-engine seaplane named *The China Clipper.*

Juan Trippe of Pan American Airways was behind it all. Since beating out or buying up his early competitors (thanks in part to his manipulation of federal regulations), Trippe dreamed of transpacific service. In 1931 he hired Charles and Anne Morrow Lindbergh to reconnoitre the Great Circle Route from America to Japan. They reported that the weather precluded that route, but their mere presence in the Aleutians and Kuriles caused a Japanese admiral to alert his countrymen: "It is possible to say that they may have had in view the possibility of surrounding Japan in all directions with their warlike preparations. Soviet Russia is concentrating efficient bombing planes and making war preparations in the Far East. . . . they would surround Japan by air raids in three directions."

Trippe was not a front for the military, but he did lobby hard to get the government to place Wake and Midway islands under Navy jurisdiction, so that the Navy could turn around and grant him landing rights there, as well as on Oahu, Guam, and the Philippines. Beginning in March 1935 Trippe proceeded to do what the Four Power Treaty had banned: build airfields on the mid-Pacific isles. Trippe's engineers overcame the crazy problems involved in off-loading supplies and laying cement in sandy dunes, coral reefs, and atolls. And his radio ace, Hugo Leuteritz, solved the navigation problem by boosting the power of a big Adcock directional antenna and converting it to shortwave signals. That was how Musick was able to cover the 8,700 miles from Alameda to Manila safely and in just sixty hours. "I anticipate," speechified Postmaster General James Farley, "that our friendly relations and commerce with the countries of the Orient will be strengthened and stimulated by the transpacific mail." Instead, transoceanic aviation only heightened Japanese suspicions that the United States was planning an air war on Japan's defenseless cities, *and* American suspicions that the Japanese were fortifying Saipan, Yap, Truk, and Tinian behind a cloak of secrecy. When Amelia Earhart's Lockheed Electra disappeared near Howland Island in 1937 (well south of the Japanese mandate), many Americans suspected treachery.

Treachery had indeed become the reigning principle of Japanese politics. Not only had the military succeeded in subverting civilian rule but had itself divided into two jealous factions. The *Kōdō-ha* (Imperial Way) appealed to the fanatical young officers inspired by the likes of Kita Ikke. They believed in Japan's destiny to expand, especially into Mongolia and Siberia, but only in conjunction with a purgative revolution—the Shōwa Restoration—to rid Japan of democrats, capitalists, and Marxists. The rival *Tōsei-ha* (Control) Faction was content with existing institutions so long as they served the requirements of national defense as outlined by the "total war" officers. The Control Faction dreamed of molding Japan into a military command economy, then flinging the Kwantung Army southward to claim the resources of China and Southeast Asia.

In August 1935 the rivalry turned violent. The two most important military posts, war minister and inspector general of training, were both glommed by Control Faction men. So a young Imperial Way officer walked into the War Minister's office and ran him through with his sword. A rambunctious trial followed during which both factions hurled accusations of treason. When the War Ministry then took the precaution of reinforcing the Tokyo garrison, the Imperial Way hotheads knew they must strike now or never.

Ambassador Grew wired the news. "To: Secstate Washington RUSH 37 February 26, noon, 1936. It now appears fairly certain that former Premier Admiral Saitō [Makoto], former Lord Keeper of the Privy Seal Count Makino, Grand Chamberlain Admiral Suzuki, and General Watanabe, Inspector General of Military Education, have been assassinated. It is also reported that Finance Minister Takahashi and the Chief of the Metropolitan Police Board have been wounded. The military have established a cordon around the district containing the Government administration offices and the Imperial palace. . . . It is now reported that Premier Okada, Home Minister Goto, and former War Minister Hayashi were also assassinated and that Finance Minister Takahashi died of his wounds. The Embassy cannot confirm any of these rumors. . . . The uprising, as far as can be ascertained by the Embassy, is in the nature of a *coup d'etat* engineered by the young Fascist element in the Army and intended to destroy the entire group of elder statesmen who have been advisers to the Throne and thereby effect the so-called Shōwa Restoration."

It was snowing in Tokyo in the predawn hours of February 26. Some fifteen hundred Imperial Way zealots, none above the rank of captain, slipped out of their barracks and fanned out to hunt down every enemy of the "real" Japan: Control Faction officers, businessmen, the last of the *genrō*, cabinet ministers. Their incidental victims included the likes of Okada Keisuke's brother-in-law, killed in error, and wives who threw themselves on their husbands' bodies to intercept the saber blows and bullets. The mutineers then appealed to the whole Army to join their crusade and restore the Imperial Way, as their forefathers had in 1868.

Hirohito did not share the young officers' version of the Imperial

Way. General Honjō recorded that "His Majesty was extremely upset and said the incident must be quashed as quickly as possible and a way must be found to turn the disaster into a blessing." Within a day the General Staff had rushed in loyal units and closed off the blocks in downtown Tokyo occupied by rebels. For four days the soldiers of the two factions stared and shouted at each other in the cold. Gradually the enlisted men among the rebels, promised amnesty, crossed the barricades. Then the rebellious officers followed them into surrender, save one who committed *seppuku*. The Control Faction was victorious, and it knew how to drive home its victory. The Army condemned to death thirteen leaders of the mutiny, as well as Kita Ikki, the Imperial Way ideologue. The Control officers then purged Imperial Way sympathizers and pushed their own program through the cabinet and Diet. Military spending zoomed from 9 to 38 percent of the national budget, funding technical modernization, especially for aircraft and armor, and a new naval program. The government took special care to relieve the plight of Japanese farmers, the social support for "military fascism," and subjected *zaibatsu* to regulation, central planning, and ultimately a five-year plan. All people and property in Japan were now the playthings of the government. For as the new Principles of the National Polity of 1937 stated, individuals "are essentially not beings isolated from the state, but each has his allotted share as forming parts of the state." Japanese must thus expurgate Western influences, bow to reeducation according to the truths of State Shinto, and unite "under the emperor a body of people of one blood and one mind."

This was the irony of the "2/26 Revolt," as it came to be known: that a fanatical mutiny by military officers could be crushed and yet lead to more, not less, military control. For the struggle was not one between constitutional government and military dictatorship, but rather between two versions of military dictatorship of which the "total war" faction was the more *moderate*. Who breathed more easily in the wake of the mutiny? Stalin did, for the Control Faction preferred to expand southward. Japan shocked everyone but Hitler by joining the Nazi Anti-Comintern Pact in 1936, but the tactic was largely defensive. A Japanese entente with Germany would presumably deter *Stalin* from attacking Manchukuo and thus leave Japan free to strike elsewhere. Who was the big loser in the wake of the mutiny? Chiang Kai-skek was.

Perhaps a Sino-Japanese war was inevitable. For once the Kwantung Army had taken over Manchuria, it faced both the need and the temptation to invest the border provinces beyond and keep Chinese bandits, warlords, the Kuomintang, and the Communists at arm's length. But each step southward was bound to inflame Chinese nationalism, while each hostile incident was bound to inflame the Kwantung officers

586   INTERNAL COMBUSTION

accustomed to taking "direct action." Still, a full-scale war could occur
only if China were sufficiently united to say "Enough" and fight back.
And as of 1936 the question of who spoke for China was again very
much open. In 1934 and 1935 Mao led his exodus of one hundred thousand soldiers and cadre on the famous Long March to Yenan, just below
the Great Wall about five hundred miles southwest of Peking. After
1932 the Kwantung Army occupied Jehol Province, penetrated Peking's
Hopei Province, and exerted pressure on Inner Mongolia. Central and
southern China remained under Chiang's Nanking regime. And in
between these three rival forces Peking's local warlords revived, especially the Young Marshal, formerly of Manchuria.

Chiang hated the Japanese but was powerless to beat them and preferred to concentrate on the internal Communist threat. But the Communists did have an interest in embroiling China in war if it diverted
Chiang's army away from them and hastened China's readiness for
social revolution. Moreover, Stalin had awakened to the danger of fascism and ordered the Comintern to promote anti-Fascist Popular Fronts.
So in 1936 the Chinese Communists and northern warlords formed a
People's Anti-Japanese League. Chiang, thinking the Young Marshal
still an anti-Communist ally, landed at the latter's headquarters at Sian
and was shocked to be placed under arrest. Then Chou En-lai emerged
from the hills of Yenan to double-cross the Young Marshal and cut his
own deal with Chiang. He pledged to stop Communist propaganda, Chiang pledged to stop his anti-Communist offensive, and both pledged to
fight Japanese. Chiang then flew back to Nanking with the Young Marshal as *his* prisoner.

This sensational Sian incident alarmed the Japanese. If the Chinese
joined forces and allied with Russia, Japan would be hard-pressed to hold
even Manchuria. So advocates of a southern advance urged a preemptive
strike, while advocates of a northern advance, like Kwantung Army
Chief of Staff Tōjō Hideki, agreed that "if our military power permits it,
we should deliver a blow first of all upon the Nanking regime to get rid
of the menace at our back." The only high-ranking Japanese opposed to
a war against China was none other than Ishiwara Kanji. "The West's
greatest fear," he argued in 1936, "is a Japanese policy of 'benevolence'
toward China; its greatest hope is that through a Japanese policy that
promotes feelings of oppression in China there will be a racial conflict
between the two."

Just before midnight on July 7, 1937, someone fired on a Japanese
patrol as it rested near the Marco Polo Bridge outside Peking. It was a
delicate spot; the Japanese Army would need the bridges across the
Yunting River if it moved against Hopei Province. So the local commander demanded a Chinese withdrawal, more shots were fired, more units

moved in, and within days an undeclared war was on. Did Japanese conspirators stage the incident, as in 1931? Or did Chinese Nationalists, as
Japanese propaganda proclaimed? Or did Communists do it to embroil
the Nationalist army in a war with Japan, to take the pressure off themselves and the Soviet Union? Since no positive evidence has ever turned
up, chances are none ever will. But once fighting began neither Nanking
nor Tokyo tried very hard to stop it. Of course, Chiang was trapped by
his Sian pledges: to toady to the Japanese now would make a mockery of
his claim to be the leader of Chinese nationalism. But the General Staff
in Tokyo, expecting victory in a matter of weeks, *chose* to give the
Shantung army its head and when the weak Prime Minister, Prince
Konoe, went along, the Emperor had no cause to intervene. Perhaps
even Hirohito lived in fear of his Army, or judged that a foreign gallop
was just the thing to keep hotheads from mischief at home.

Only Ishiwara spoke up, warning that the China war would become
"the same sort of disaster which overtook Napoleon in Spain—a slow
sinking into the deepest sort of bog." But he could not persuade Konoe
to seek a truce. "Tell the Prime Minister that in two thousand years of
our history no man will have done more to destroy Japan than he has by
his indecisiveness in this crisis." But Ishiwara should have known that a
civilian minister could not rein in the Army. He himself had helped to
make that impossible by his success in Mukden six years before. In September Ishiwara was relieved of his post.

After the usual round of consensus-building, the Japanese command
judged that the way to win the war quickly (which meant getting Chiang to relinquish all of North China to Japanese puppet states) was to
capture the Yangtze valley from Shanghai to Nanking. So the Japanese
launched a blitzkrieg that proved to the world what amphibious landing
craft—and urban terror bombing—could achieve. "It was a frightening
thing to see," wrote an American resident of Shanghai, "a horrible, mad-
dening thing under which to dwell—tons of explosives hurtling down
from the skies, exploding in a cascade of bits of human flesh, dirt, stone
and mortar. Both night and day death rained upon the city from the circling, droning Japanese planes." Helpless civilians stormed the foreign
quarter in hopes of refuge from the collapsing buildings and raging fires,
a holocaust on the scale of the Tokyo earthquake. Tens of thousands of
men, women, and children died in agony while the foreigners behind the
fences, having done all they could, had to look on.

After the fall of Shanghai the generals delayed for a month, which
allowed Chiang to extricate his army. But when the Japanese commanders got the go-ahead to pursue, their armies reached the mammoth
stone walls of the old Nanking fortress in twelve days and plunged into
the most vicious battle their nation had known since Port Arthur. The

Japanese took over fifty thousand casualties, and nobody knows how many fleeing Chinese soldiers and civilians died in the crush of artillery and aerial bombs. But what followed the battle was worse.

"Friday, Dec. 17. Robbery, murder, rape continue unabated," wrote a foreign resident. "A rough estimate would be at least a thousand women raped last night and during the day. One poor woman was raped thirty-seven times. Another had her five months infant deliberately smothered by the brute to stop its crying while he raped her. Resistance means the bayonet. The hospital is rapidly filling up with the victims of Japanese cruelty and barbarity."

"It is now Christmas Eve," recorded an American in charge of a volunteer relief effort. "In these two short weeks we here in Nanking have been through a siege; the Chinese army has left defeated and the Japanese army has come in. On that day Nanking was still a beautiful city we were proud of, with law and order prevailing; today it is a city laid waste, ravaged, completely looted, much of it burned. Complete anarchy has reigned for ten days—it has been a hell on earth."

The terror started slowly after the entry of the enraged and bloodied Japanese Army. At first, officers and men did their duty, rousting out Chinese soldiers, securing supplies, and policing the streets. But in a matter of days Japanese officers began to show less regard for the identity of the Chinese they arrested and shot, and showed no interest in discipline. Their men, who gradually began to feel safe in the heart of the enemy's empire, drank heavily and formed up in mobs to loot and to rape. Still, who can explain the bayoneting of women and children, not once but seventeen times, or the execution of perhaps two hundred thousand Chinese beyond the city walls, most machine-gunned, but many decapitated, one by one and with obvious relish, by bare-chested, sword-wielding officers? Was it calculated terror to break the Chinese spirit? Was it the fear and ignorance of peasant recruits, thrust into a furious war after a few weeks of training? Or the years of racist indoctrination and the relativism of a state religion that taught no higher morality than obedient duty to the emperor, represented in situ by one's platoon sergeant? Or were Japanese, now armed and abroad, seeking release from the cultural restraints that penned up their emotions at home? Did the code that once gave samurai a capricious power of life and death over peasants now endow all Japanese with power over their inferiors, all foreigners and women? Even the whites in Nanking feared for their lives, and British merchants, American missionaries, and Nazi agents huddled together for mutual protection. Perhaps the Rape of Nanking, and all the Japanese atrocities to follow, were outbursts of frustration born of a crowded, dependent, contingent existence. Perhaps Japanese were mad with envy of peoples who owned *continents* in which to stretch their limbs.

Americans were torn. A majority of the public and Congress remained isolationist but were appalled by the newsreels and photographs of a crucified China. In his famous Chicago speech of October 5, 1937, Roosevelt condemned "international lawlessness," called for a quarantine of all gangster nations, and urged "positive measures to preserve peace." He also refused to invoke the Neutrality Act, leaving him the option of aiding China. Congress howled, but the President held firm, thereby winning the first battle in his campaign to regain foreign policy initiative for the executive branch.

During the battle of Nanking Japanese pilots purposely bombed foreign boats on the Yangtze. The USS *Panay* and three Standard Oil vessels went to the bottom, leaving two dead and thirty wounded. Saitō Hirosi begged America's pardon as abjectly as he knew how—"So sorry—excuse please" was the newspapers' caricature—and Japan paid over $2 million in reparations. But even Saitō's bonhomie could not overcome images of burning and bayoneted Chinese. After all, Saitō had scolded Americans for thinking that Japan meant to dominate China: "That seems like asking 'Are you not likely to go mad?'" Now Japan *had* gone mad. Saitō had chided the American tendency "to look down on Japan as a band of berserks who may amuck at any moment." Now the Japanese *had* run amok. And that meant that the Ambassador's credibility, and the credibility of the entire impotent liberal establishment in Japan, had ceased to exist. In American eyes Saitō was more than a "Diplomat in the Doghouse," as the *New Yorker* wrote. He was now either a fool or a liar, a cat's paw, a con man . . . a Jap.

Nomonhan 1939

GEORGY KONSTANTINOVICH ZHUKOV was one Army general whom Stalin did not completely mistrust. His Bolshevik pedigree dated back to 1918, but what attracted him to the Red Army was not the Bolsheviks' arcane ideology so much as their commitment to technological modernization. Zhukov served with distinction during the Civil War and over the next two decades became the leading Soviet theorist and practitioner of the new lightning warfare based on tanks, airplanes, and trucks. Starting in 1937, however, Stalin began to purge 70 percent of his general and field grade officers, so Zhukov could only shudder when a phone call summoned him from Minsk to Moscow on June 1, 1939. He *was* being sent to Siberia, but the reason, said the commissar, was "that the Japanese have started a major military adventure. At any rate it is only the beginning."

The beginning of what—a border skirmish, or a second Russo-Japanese war? For Manchukuo's 4,700 miles of unsurveyed or contested boundary described a gigantic salient pushing north into Siberia. To be sure, the Kwantung Army was now outnumbered by the Soviets' Far Eastern forces, but the Japanese enjoyed interior lines and a railroad network that allowed them to shift units easily. They might suddenly concentrate enough force to thrust northeast to the Pacific and cut off the Soviet Maritime Province. So the Siberian-Manchukuoan frontier was the longest, roughest, coldest, vaguest, and tensest in the world. In early 1937 Japanese and Soviet bombers and gunboats dueled for islands in the Amur. In July 1938 a division-sized battle erupted over a tactically valuable hill overlooking Changkufeng just seventy miles from Vladivostok. But the Japanese intention was only "to test or fish for the seriousness of Soviet intentions toward the China Incident," while Hirohito was so angry over the Kwantung Army's tendency to pick its own fights that he decreed, "Not even one man may be moved without Our order."

But now, in the spring of 1939, the latest skirmish not only showed signs of escalating, it called into question the entire Soviet strategic position. Consider that in 1904 Russia had seized all of Manchuria and penetrated Korea, forcing Japan to strike back. By 1939 Japan had seized all of Manchuria and threatened to penetrate Mongolia, forcing the Russians to strike back. So Zhukov's assignment was to bloody Japan's nose, keep Mongolia a Soviet satellite, secure the USSR's eastern flank in case of war with Hitler . . . and take some revenge for the humiliations of 1905.

Zhukov crossed a Siberia both scarred and developed by the Second Five-Year Plan. Entirely new cities sprang up on the steppes and taiga, while the population on the Soviet Pacific rim more than doubled. Khabarovsk now boasted 150,000 people, and Vladivostok 250,000. The double-tracking of the Trans-Siberian Railway was complete, thanks to forced savings and labor on a scale unimaginable under the Tsar. About 40 percent of all Soviet investment was targeted east of the Urals, and by 1937 an estimated 40 percent of all Soviet coal, iron, copper, and electric power originated in Siberia. Telegraphs and telephones, railroads and aviation linked Siberia to Moscow, while "the chain of Soviet radio stations in Asia, broadcasting in languages understood on both sides of the frontier, will not allow the border races to forget the growing power and prosperity of their cousins within the Union." The prosperity was a cruel myth, but the power was real. For the new infrastructure not only allowed Stalin to deploy far larger military forces in Asia, it (and the NKVD political police) gave Moscow the means to ensure the political correctness of Siberia's proconsuls. In 1937 three hundred were shot for alleged "wrecking" or pro-Japanese sympathies.

Still, Stalin had cause to worry. The Japanese were strong, aggressive, and prone to believe that his purges had crippled the Red Army, while the Outer Mongolians were restive. Japanese intelligence suspected that as many as two-thirds of them wanted to throw off communism. One Mongolian general said, "This scheme of ours could be realized at the very same time a war broke out between Japan and the Soviet Union." Thanks to Richard Sorge's Communist spy ring in Tokyo, Stalin knew that the Japanese were chary of hostilities with the USSR until the war in China was won. But what of the "direct action" hotheads of the Kwantung Army, led now by "the Razor" Tōjō Hideki? They, too, could read a map and perceive that if Mongolia were to throw off Soviet rule and ally instead with Japan, then the Trans-Siberian Railway would become indefensible. Mongolia was thus "the key to the whole Far East." The Communist rulers in Ulan Bator accordingly purged at least ten thousand people, including two thousand Buddhist monks, and invited a Soviet Army corps into their country to help guard the border with Manchukuo. It was there that fighting began in May 1939.

It was bleak and sandy steppe, save for the bluffs overlooking the Halha River. Were it not for geopolitics, nothing would have disturbed that back of beyond save the flocks of the nomads in their yurts and the wild chigetai flopping the flies with their enormous ears. But in 1939 that "insignificant little mound of sand would become the site of raging battles that made world headlines." At stake was a disputed wedge of turf fifty miles long and fifteen miles deep between the Halha and the village of Nomonhan. The trouble began when Mongolian cavalry waded across the stream and made a show of establishing a border post. Manchukuo's police and soldiers chased them away, but they returned, this time with Russians. So Japanese detachments were sent to throw them across the Halha again, whereupon Soviet fighter planes appeared in Manchurian skies. The Kwantung generals huddled and chose a typically aggressive response—a massive air offensive to reclaim the Manchurian airspace, then an infantry assault to clear out the enemy's staging areas. Their four regiments returned forty-eight hours later, "drenched with the blood of our comrades." So the gritty Russians crossed the river again and dug in on the bluffs. The frustrated Japanese replied with artillery barrages, nighttime tank assaults, and infantry charges that left the approaches to the river littered with corpses and gutted machinery. But their World War I tactics failed to dislodge the Soviet bridgehead. By the close of July the Japanese Twenty-Third Division gave up the assault and awaited reinforcements.

By then Zhukov's preparations were nearly complete. In a mere six weeks he had sized up the Manchurian theater and imported two and a half divisions of infantry, paratroopers, cavalry, and enough tanks to outnumber the Japanese armor four to one. Trucks transported eighteen thousand men and all their ammunition, fuel, food, even firewood across desert tracks from the Siberian railhead. Airfields sprang up on the Mongolian plateau. And Zhukov achieved all this without tipping off the enemy, thanks to Japanese smugness, Soviet air superiority, and *maskirovka*, or deceptive tactics. The Russians broadcast false radio traffic, faked the sound of tanks on the move until the Japanese ignored the real thing, flew squadrons on their planned attack routes until the Japanese considered them routine, and shielded their approach to the front with trenches and blinds. Zhukov's plan was to throw his cavalry, armored, and airborne units around and behind the Japanese flanks, then converge on Nomonhan while a frontal assault by Soviet infantry tempted the Japanese to counterattack, sucking them deeper into the trap. It was, in its way, a form of jujitsu.

Hundreds of bombers and fighter escorts opened the offensive on the clear, crisp dawn of August 20, striking Japanese gun emplacements and supply depots. Soviet artillery followed with a barrage "to the limit of their technical possibilities." Then ground support planes reappeared, and Soviet tanks went on the assault. The northern and southern pincers made stunning progress against the Manchukuoan forces to which the Japanese had blithely committed their flanks. The Japanese ordered all available aircraft into battle but were stunned to discover that Soviet planes and pilots were superior to their own. Russian tanks were also larger and better armored, and proud Kwantung infantrymen were reduced to throwing bottles of gasoline at their tormentors. Some Japanese units were ordered out of the pocket, but the Twenty-Third Division was hurled forward in a do-or-die attack across two miles of grassland raked by Soviet machine guns. One lieutenant risked shame by rushing to headquarters to question the order. He returned to tell his men that they were expected to succeed "because we are Japanese soldiers." His regiment plunged into the yellow, high-summer grass, exhorting each other forward until there was no one left to exhort. After a week of terrible combat Zhukov ordered his infantry to finish off the trapped Japanese. Some committed suicide; others accomplished the same result by charging the enemy guns. Two colonels burned their regimental colors, faced the Rising Sun, cried *"Tennō Heika Banzai!"* and shot themselves in the head. "Duty is weightier than a mountain," taught the Imperial Precepts to Soldiers and Sailors, but "Death is lighter than a feather."

The destruction of the Twenty-Third Division before Nomonhan was the first major defeat for Japanese arms in the modern era. But then, whom had the Japanese faced since 1905? Korean irregulars in 1910, some isolated German marines in 1914, Siberian bandits from 1918 to 1922, a Manchurian warlord in 1931, and backward, divided Chinese forces in 1937. Nomonhan was Japan's first encounter with modern weapons and combined arms tactics. So Tokyo denounced the battle as "the Kwantung Army's affair" and instructed Ambassador Tōgō Shigenori to press for a truce in Moscow. Stalin, satisfied that he had made the desired impression, granted it effective September 16. Zhukov's brilliant hammer-and-sickle offensive markedly reduced the chances that Japan would challenge the Red Army again, which in turn insured the USSR against a two-front war no matter what Hitler did back in Europe.

For Japan, on the other hand, the disaster at Nomonhan was but one of three that summer, all of which magnified the danger of war against the third member of the North Pacific triangle, the United States. On July 26, just before the Soviet offensive, the U.S. State Department

stunned Tokyo by reserving its right to suspend all trade with Japan
beginning in six months. Such was Americans' anger over Japan's
aggression in China. And then, on August 23, Nazi Germany—Japan's
partner in the Anti-Comintern Pact—signed a nonaggression pact with
the Soviet Union. Tokyo denounced it as "treacherous and unpardonable," but the fact remained that Japan was now horribly isolated. Citing "inexplicable new conditions" in Europe, the Prime Minister
resigned in disgrace.

The world was indeed inexplicable to the Japanese leadership, whose
policies and strategies now became increasingly confused, reactive, and
aimless. If from 1853 to 1931 the Japanese had been forced to live in a
world others made, then beginning with Manchuria they began to take a
hand in making a world for others to live in. Having disillusioned themselves of free trade and democracy, the Japanese next placed their faith
in a national socialism shrouded in lies, only to be disillusioned again
when power states more cynical still, like Hitler's and Stalin's, practiced the double cross and betrayed ideologies in their turn. By 1939 the
world was lawless, all states were slaves to geopolitics, and none was
more disadvantaged than Japan. Its Empire was supposed to release new
resources to strengthen Japan. Instead, the defense of Manchuria and
taming of China only drained the resources of a limited industrial base.
Japan was already mobilized for total war, its people reduced to a life of
labor on subsistence rations and sustained only by the carrots of religious and martial propaganda and the sticks of censorship and terror.
Now Japan was without a single reliable ally.

The China war was the source of it all. But the Japanese could not
just pull out without suffering an intolerable loss of face and inviting
rebellions in Manchukuo and Korea as well. But the alternative—to
prosecute the China war with greater vigor—risked exhausting the
nation and alienating the world. It seemed that Japan must expand or
die, but the act of expanding was killing it.

Since Chiang Kai-shek did not sue for peace after the fall of Nanking
but instead retreated to Hankow, the Japanese made it their target in
1938. But a Kuomintang offensive, the first major one of the war,
inflicted thirty thousand Japanese casualties. Then the Chinese did an
incredible thing: they blew the dikes on the Yellow River, flooding
thousands of square miles to inhibit the Japanese advance, but at the
sacrifice of as many as *one million* Chinese dead of drowning, starvation, or disease as a result of the torrent. But the Japanese grimly pressed
on until Hankow fell in the fall. Still Chiang refused to give up. Instead
he and millions of other Chinese fled farther inland, to remote Chungking, to establish a third capital. The Japanese made a show of ignoring
him and toyed with the idea of setting up another puppet regime under

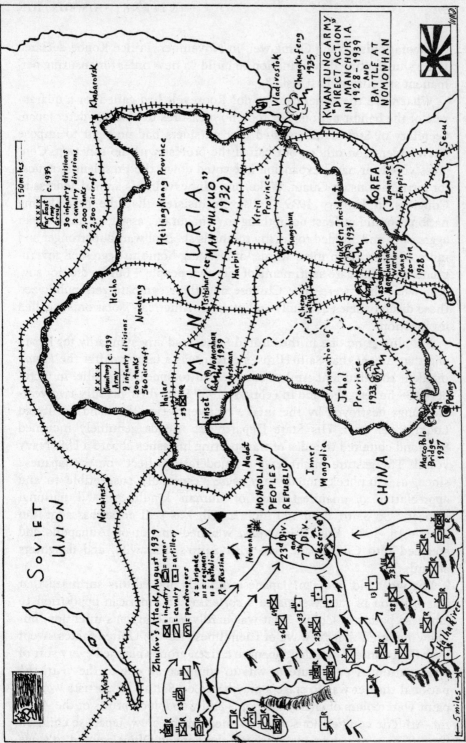

KWANTUNG ARMY
"DIRECT ACTION"
IN MANCHURIA
1928-1939
AND
BATTLE AT
NOMONHAN

SOVIET UNION

Khabarovsk

Vladivostok

Changk-Feng
1935

KOREA
(Japanese
Empire)

Seoul

150 miles

XXXX Far East
Army
Group c. 1939
30 infantry divisions
2 cavalry divisions
2,000 tanks
2,500 aircraft

Heilungkiang Province

MANCHURIA ("MANCHUKUO" 1932)

Heiho

Nencheng

Tsitsihar

Harbin

Changchun

Kirin
Province

Mukden Incident
1931

Assassination
of Manchurian
Warlord
Chang
Tso-lin
1928

Peking

XXXX Kwantung
Army c. 1939
9 infantry divisions
200 tanks
560 aircraft

Hailar

Cheng-
chiatun

Nomonhan
1939

Arshan

23 HQ

inset

Nerchinsk

Irkutsk

Nadat

MONGOLIAN
PEOPLES
REPUBLIC

Inner
Mongolia

Annexation of Jehol
Province
1933

CHINA

Marco Polo
Bridge
1937

Zhukov's Attack, August 1939

XX = infantry   ☐ = armor
X = cavalry   ☐ = artillery
X = brigade
III = regiment
II = battalion
R = Russian
☐ = paratroopers

Nomonhan

23rd Div.
and
7th Div.
Reserve

Halha River

5 miles

collaborationist Wang Ching-wei. In November, Prince Konoe declared
Japan's unshaking determination to build "a new order for ensuring permanent stability in East Asia."

What were the Americans to do? Roosevelt had called for a quarantine of the bandit nations but took no measures to block or deter Japan.
Secretary of State Hull insisted that outsiders had no right to impose
"new orders" on others, but paired the protest with no sanction. Congress voted for naval expansion but voted down the President's request
for fortifications on Guam, Wake, and Midway. In his annual address to
Congress in January 1939, Roosevelt insisted that the peace-loving
nations should at least do nothing to "encourage, assist, or build up an
aggressor" and alluded to "many methods short of war, but stronger and
more effective than mere words, of bringing home to aggressor governments the aggregate sentiments of our own people." But he did not suggest what they were. The Chinese and their sympathizers publicized
these discrepancies as loudly and often as American isolationists called
for inaction.

But almost no one in the United States had any sympathy for Japan,
and that meant that Saitō Hirosi's career was a failure. After the *Panay*
incident the ebullient Ambassador ceased to appear in public, in October 1938 he resigned, and in February 1939 Saitō died, his fifty-two-year-
old lungs destroyed by the intake of twenty-two thousand unfiltered
Luckies per year. His State Department friends genuinely mourned
Saitō and conjured the idea of transporting his ashes aboard a U.S. Navy
vessel. The gesture might have a "moderating effect" on the Japanese
since, as Hornbeck noted, they were "especially susceptible to and
appreciative of manifestations of human kindliness and national
respect." So Saitō, dead and incinerated, was still an ambassador. On
March 18, 1939, the USS *Astoria* weighed anchor off Annapolis and
steamed into Chesapeake Bay with Saitō's urn, wife, and daughters
aboard.

But what did it mean? Japanese officials and editors surmised that
this mission of mercy signaled a *softening* of American opposition to
Japanese policy in China! That was hardly Washington's intention, but
Grew reported that "a wave of friendliness for the United States swept
over the country" and that Japanese citizen groups planned every sort of
appreciation. A poet laureate was to compose an ode to the visit, the
national theater was to stage a play based on Saitō's life, artists were to
paint watercolors of cherry blossoms and woodblock prints of the *Astoria.* Athletic competitions were planned for the crew, Japanese children
were to present handmade gifts, and the Foreign Office wanted to stage
elaborate banquets and ceremonies. Indeed, the Japanese seemed to

behave like abused or lonely children who burst into tears whenever anyone shows gentleness toward them. But so long as the Japanese Army was cutting through China, Hornbeck and Grew agreed that too much "ballyhoo" would give the wrong impression. So all the while the *Astoria* was at sea and feted by the Japanese consuls in Panama and Honolulu, protocol experts haggled over what to do, or not to do, in Saitō's memory.

The *Astoria* arrived in Japan on April 17, 1939, and the toned-down obsequies proceeded without a hitch. Sailors bore the urn to a little shrine on the pier, and each member of the procession bowed while a Japanese band played Chopin's funeral march. A special train and hearse bore the ashes to the Saitō household in Tokyo, where Grew noted the three lit cigarettes and bottle of Old Parr placed in front of the urn—a comfort to the Shinto spirit hovering unseen overhead. The next day, Saitō's remains reached their final resting place in Hongwangji Temple, where an old friend eulogized, "With the spring coming, everything on earth is being refreshed. But you are no more."

You—the spirit of Japanese-American friendship—are no more. To be sure, the Emperor favored the American captain with "a brilliant smile," and at the final dinner on shore, the Navy minister assured Grew that the Fascist elements in Japan had been "suppressed." Japan would seek friendly relations with democracies and authoritarian states alike but "stand apart from either group, her own ideology being different from both of them." Be that as it may, suspicion and intimidation were never far from the surface. At the farewell banquet aboard the *Astoria*, the Americans made the diminutive Japanese delegates parade between honor guards composed of the *tallest* American sailors. On the way out of port, a photographer tried to shoot Yokosuka shipyard, but at the precise moment, two Japanese tugboats chugged in between, filling the sky with greasy smoke. The *Astoria* was ordered to visit China, then cross the Pacific straight through the waters of the Japanese mandate.

Nor did the heavy magazine coverage of the mission of mercy change the minds of Americans, 70 percent of whom favored the cutoff of war supplies to Japan. So even in their isolationism, it seemed, Americans discriminated against Japan. They opposed involvement in European affairs and approved of Britain's appeasement of Hitler but were ready to punish Japan from the start. Roosevelt's own predilection was to deter Japan by expanding U.S. ship and airplane construction, fortifying the Pacific islands, and basing the fleet in Hawaii. But Hull, Hornbeck, Henry Morgenthau, and Harold Ickes thought that economic sanctions alone might force the Japanese out of China. So in July, just as the Battle of Nomonhan was reaching its climax, the State Department announced its intention to abrogate its 1911 treaty of commerce with Japan, which relied on the United States for 80 percent of its oil, 75 percent of its scrap iron, and 60 percent of its machine tools.

What was Japan to do now? Bloodied on the Mongolian border, stunned by the Nazi-Soviet pact and outbreak of war in Europe, and facing a break with the United States, the Japanese had to rethink their strategy. The new cabinet, featuring the pro-Western Foreign Minister Adm. Nomura Kichisaburō, wanted to pursue détente with the United States before the six months' interim ran out. But the "total war" planners drafted even more ambitious imperial schemes in hopes of escaping economic dependency. In October 1939 the Cabinet Planning Board reported that Indochina, the Philippines, the East Indies, and Thailand might contribute from 50 to 70 percent of Japan's requirements for tin, rubber, bauxite, chromium, manganese, tungsten, nickel, copper, oil, and rice. The Navy favored the southern strategy since it would be largely a Navy show, while the Army, embarrassed at Nomonhan, was in no position to challenge it.

So Nomura had nothing of substance to offer the United States except the rational argument that American business had a far more profitable commercial relationship with *Japan* than it would ever have with China. For his part, Hull frankly wanted the trade treaty to expire. He surmised that once the President had his hands on the oil spigot, the Japanese would not dare overstep any bounds the United States laid out for them. In sum, *both* sides assumed that rational economic analysis would guide the policies of the other, whereas in fact the Japanese never considered getting out of China in order to save their trade with the United States, nor did the Americans consider abandoning China in order to save their trade with Japan. By January 1940 the "equal" trade treaty won at such effort by Meiji Japan was dead.

Then the world shook again. In May-June 1940 the German blitzkrieg occupied the Netherlands and France and chased the British off the continent. The democracies seemed doomed, while their colonies in Asia were orphaned. No one was more pleased than Matsuoka Yōsuke, as strange a man as ever presumed to play politics on a world scale. He was of Chōshū samurai origin but was raised in Seattle by an American dame. He was a baptized Catholic but burned incense at Shinto shrines. He was a cosmopolite but nurtured his bitterness born of childhood indignities suffered from whites in America. He was a successful administrator on the South Manchurian Railway but preferred intuition and metahistorical fantasy to analysis. A diplomat, he was nonetheless voluble and indiscreet, and lectured everyone from Grew to Stalin until they begged for mercy. People as disparate as Hitler, Roosevelt, and Prince Saionji thought him a madman.

It was Matsuoka in the van of the Japanese delegation that stormed out of the League of Nations, and Matsuoka who first predicted the Kwantung Army's strike into North China. "Most of the people of Japan," he said in 1935, "do not yet quite understand the great importance of these future operations. . . . The arrow has already left the bow. The progress of these operations will decide the destiny of the Yamato race." In May 1940 he went so far as to publish his belief that a U.S.-Japanese war for hegemony in the Pacific was "an historical inevitability" unless the United States respected Japan's sphere of influence in Asia. So when Prince Konoe returned as Prime Minister in July 1940, with Matsuoka as Foreign Minister and Tōjō as War Minister, Japan clearly had no intention of turning back in China. The cabinet's Outline of Fundamental National Policies declared the world to be "at a major turning point" in its evolution toward a system of regional blocs. Germany and Russia dominated Eurasia, Britain had its Empire, and the United States the Western Hemisphere. Now Japan, too, must carve out what Matsuoka dubbed the Greater East Asia Coprosperity Sphere.

Still the war in China dragged on, tying down almost a million Japanese troops and most of the Air Force, and costing money Japan could no longer afford. The plan for 1940 was to isolate the battlefield, deny Chiang's army all outside support, and pacify occupied China through the quisling regime of Wang Ching-wei. The Japanese successfully bullied defeated France and desperate Britain into halting shipments to China via the Hanoi railroad and Burma Road. It was then, in July 1940, the United States fired its first economic shot across Japan's bow by requiring licenses for all oil and scrap iron exports to Japan, and banning the sale of aviation fuel completely. In August Chiang rejected Konoe's final peace offer. In September the Japanese occupied northern Vietnam, the United States embargoed scrap iron, . . . and Matsuoka joined the Axis.

"It has been the great instruction bequeathed by Ameratsu [the Sun Goddess] that our grand moral obligation be extended in all directions and the world unified under one roof. This instruction is one we are faithfully observing day and night." So began the imperial rescript heralding the Tripartite Alliance of Germany, Italy, and Japan signed in Tokyo on September 27, 1940. It was "a source of great joy" to the Emperor, for by it all nations might "seek their proper places" and all Japanese subjects guard "the Imperial Throne coextensive with heaven and earth." Breaching all tradition, the Mikado then ordered Shinto priests to devise a special liturgy and shrine in the palace "to ask for the blessing of the Gods on his Tripartite Pact." The pact was aimed directly at the United States and its purpose was prophylactic. Berlin and Tokyo evidently believed that a formal alliance would deter the

Americans from interfering further with their respective New Orders. Instead, it proved beyond doubt the contention of American interventionists that Japan was implacably Fascist and had to be stopped. Only the 1940 electoral campaign, in which Roosevelt promised not to send American boys into foreign wars, stayed his hand from twisting the spigot another quarter turn.

To Matsuoka, however, the Axis was more than a tactical move. It was the first step in a global realignment to be engineered by him. Now that Japan was tied to Nazi Germany and Fascist Italy, and Germany was tied to the USSR, all that was needed to complete a vigorous authoritarian alliance was a link between Japan and Russia. A Japanese nonaggression pact with the Soviets would deprive the Chinese of their last source of outside supplies and secure the Manchukuoan flank while the Japanese struck south against the British, French, and Dutch colonies and carved out the Coprosperity Sphere. Japan would then be prepared if war with America did prove inevitable. So as early as August 1940 Matsuoka ordered Ambassador Tōgō to sound out Foreign Commissar Molotov. The Soviets were amenable but demanded the return of those oil concessions on Sakhalin Island—something Japan could not spare. In March 1941 Matsuoka himself flew to Moscow to ask for a nonaggression pact. No, said Molotov, but the USSR would consider a *neutrality* pact. The difference was subtle: nonaggression meant a promise not to attack each other; neutrality meant a promise to stay out of a war the other got into with some third party. The upshot was that the Russo-Japanese relationship would continue to rest on mutual deterrence and certainly not on trust. Matsuoka then met with Stalin in person and bored him with a dissertation on the natural communism of Japanese family life. Frustrated, Matsuoka moved on to Berlin to put his grand design before Hitler. How the Führer must have chuckled to Ribbentrop and his cronies about this ingenuous Japanese! No, said Hitler, Russo-German relations were not as good as they seemed, so the grand alliance would have to wait. Matsuoka then returned to Moscow, where he received the same treatment as before—a lot of niggling about Sakhalin and fishing rights and Outer Mongolia—until, on April 13, 1941, the day he was scheduled to leave, Stalin suddenly proposed a neutrality treaty based on recognition of the status quo in Manchukuo and Outer Mongolia. Matsuoka called it "lightning diplomacy" and boasted that "Providence put a Russian treaty in my pocket." Stalin gave him a "promiscuous" kiss and said, as they parted at the station, that Europe's problems could be solved by Soviet-Japanese cooperation. "Asia can also be solved," replied Matsuoka. "The whole world can be settled!" said Stalin.

For the Kremlin, the Japanese treaty was a hedge against a Nazi betrayal. For Matsuoka it was the realization of a grand Eurasian alliance aimed at the Anglo-Americans. His brilliance had seemingly saved Japan from isolation and parried the Sword of Damocles hanging over it since Nomonhan. Japan had adjusted to the world of the Nazi-Soviet Pact, the world of the dictators, the world of the future. Now even the Americans would have to show their respect.

Pearl Harbor 1941

"WILL THE POWER and prestige of the white man in the Far East be what it has been in the past?" If not, the white nations had only themselves to blame, wrote Pearl Buck, the missionary's daughter, in October 1940. They had acquired and used their power in Asia in un-Christian ways and began to lose it as soon as they turned on each other in 1914. The victorious Allies had talked of replacing imperialism with free trade and democracy, but China, where "even the Christian God has undergone change," was never a candidate for Western liberalism, while Japan "has always been Fascist in her soul." The United States especially lost face when it banned Japanese immigration, then did nothing about the theft of Manchuria. But the Japanese in turn misunderstood China! They thought they could win a short war while the whites were not looking, "but there is no such thing as a quick blow against anything so huge as China." And that mistake, made because Japan had embraced the *white man's* ways, gave the whites a second chance to come forward, like Androcles and the lion, and remove the thorn from China's paw. But Britain was wounded, France defeated, Italy foolish, and the United States isolationist. That left only Nazi Germany and Soviet Russia ("depend[ing] on how *white* Russia is, a point which has never been settled"). If only the Americans could show some "Far Eastern imagination" for once ... but as things stood, "their shadow upon the future of the Far East lies very light and indistinct, and will continue to do so as long as they do not make it a reality." Buck concluded her meditation with an appeal to "the simple and practical wisdom of peace and good will among men."

Ah, the missionaries, who seemed to know so much and so little! For after island-hopping triumphantly across the Pacific in the previous century, they hit a wall in Asia. Buck and other mission children grew up embarrassed for their parents, so resistant were Chinese and Japanese to

Christianity. But in China, the missionaries at least struggled bravely to maintain their schools and hospitals amid civil war and foreign invasion. In Japan they had to beg a totalitarian government just to be allowed to stay. By the later 1930s some Christian sects were outlawed completely, while even in foreign schools Japanese children were obliged to burn incense to the Emperor. By 1941 three-quarters of all Protestant pastors had given up, and one churchwoman said, boarding her ship, "I feel as if an iron jacket had been taken off my soul."

How might the missionaries still be of service to the Asians and their own people alike? Invariably, it seemed, by political advocacy. Some blamed America for not helping China, some blamed America for Japanese militarism, and Buck blamed America for both. "We may condemn Japan's actions in China," wrote one missionary, "but if Christianity can't demonstrate a better way to economic salvation, then our testimony is for naught." Another addressed his Japanese hosts: "Part of the present blood is on our hands—We taught you a dangerous game. Pardon us, we pray." That attitude was what inspired Father James M. Drought, his bishop, and two Japanese friends to form John Doe Associates in 1941.

Drought, like Maryknollers since, assumed that any foreign government that had a quarrel with the United States must be on the side of the angels. So he sought out and got Matsuoka's blessing—what did the pro-Axis Foreign Minister have to lose?—for a mission to Washington in March. Drought and his compatriots claimed to bear an official offer for a Japanese-American *modus vivendi*. Postmaster General Farley, a prominent Catholic, vouched for them. And inasmuch as Ambassador Nomura was considered a moderate, the State Department decided to receive the John Does. Then Hull discovered to his horror that Drought's alleged "peace offer" contained "all that the ardent Japanese imperialists could want." Hull was a country judge from Tennessee, had no use for Catholics or foreigners, and did not like being duped or diddled. So he called in Nomura and handed him his famous "four principles" regarding China. If Japan were serious about good relations with the United States, then let it pledge respect for the integrity and sovereignty of all nations; noninterference in the internal affairs of other nations; equality of commercial opportunity; and no changes in the Pacific status quo except by peaceful means. So where the Maryknollers asked the United States to accept Japan's New Order, the United States asked Japan to return to the terms of the Washington Conference. Nomura knew that Konoe and Matsuoka would reject Hull's four principles out of hand, so with good heart but weak judgment he delayed transmitting them and instead sent the Maryknoll document to Tokyo as if it were somehow an *American* offer. Months passed before both governments purged their confusion regarding the other's negotiating position. In the meantime, the Japanese erroneously concluded that their Axis and Soviet ties had softened up the Americans, while the Americans erroneously concluded that their economic sanctions had softened up the Japanese.

Yet the Maryknoll fiasco ought not to obscure Ambassador Grew's observation that there existed no language in which Japanese and Americans could fruitfully communicate. To Japan, such concepts as sovereignty, free trade, and liberalism had come to have negative connotations, while Japanese appeals to order and coprosperity filled Americans with disgust. No treaty relationships existed anymore between the two countries, since Japan had repudiated the political/military ones and the United States repudiated the commercial one. Hence the only basis for accord would have to be geopolitical, that is, some common security concern about a third power. But so long as Japan remained tied to the dictators and flaunted a Navy capable of bidding for Pacific hegemony, no geopolitical basis for accord existed either.

Cordell Hull has been criticized for being naively Wilsonian, self-righteous, unbending, and moralistic. Perhaps he was; his forty-odd conversations with Nomura in a Washington hotel suite were models of futility. But in fairness to him, what *realistic* basis existed for a Japanese-American détente? Barring an abrupt comeback by moderate elements in Japan, the answer was none, in which case peace in the Pacific could rest only on blunt deterrence. The U.S. Navy had responded to the emerging Axis alliance by melding its Plan Orange into the global Rainbow Plans 1 through 5 for simultaneous war in the Atlantic and Pacific. During the dark months of 1940 when Britain looked as if it might fall to the Nazi blitz, the admirals feared that the United States would have to stand on the defensive in the Pacific. And even after Britain's survival, Roosevelt and Churchill agreed on a "Europe First" strategy. The United States did finally fortify Wake, Midway, and Dutch Harbor, in the Aleutians, but Plans Dog and Rainbow-5 required the Navy to shift a quarter of the Pacific fleet to the Atlantic in spring 1941. At the same time Roosevelt labored to build the ABCD coalition (Americans, British, Chinese, and Dutch) in hopes of deterring a Japanese strike southward. But how could he deter an attack on Indochina or the Philippines without risking what remained of his Pacific fleet? "I simply haven't enough Navy to go around," mourned the President. But he did have the economic bludgeon: as late as 1941 the United States was still exporting $200 million worth of commodities to Japan compared with only $50 million worth of aid and trade to China.

During the Maryknoll affair Matsuoka was off in Moscow signing his neutrality pact. But he was a fool for thinking that he, Stalin, or even

Roosevelt held the key to the future. *Hitler* held the key to everyone's future. Would he invade the Middle East while Japan struck south, and so eviscerate the British Empire? Or would he invade Russia instead? If so, could the Soviets survive a blitz, especially if Japan struck Siberia in their rear? A Nazi victory meant a new Dark Age in whose shadows even the United States would shiver. But how could FDR help to prevent that in light of his people's continued opposition to war?

One suspenseful period ended and another began on June 22, when Nazi Germany attacked the Soviet Union. Churchill offered Stalin an immediate alliance, and Roosevelt promised lend-lease aid. But what would the Japanese do? Pearl Buck had written that what created the Yellow Peril was precisely the internecine wars of the *whites*, because only their disunity gave nations like Japan the leverage to move all of Asia. Now the devious Matsuoka went straight to the Emperor to urge that Japan repudiate his nine-weeks-old neutrality pact and order the Army back into Siberia. The Tennō, Hirohito, "was greatly astonished" by Matsuoka's suggestion, while Konoe shrank from taking on Russia, China, and perhaps Britain and the United States at the same time. The Navy opposed war with Russia, which would yield none of the raw materials needed by Japan, while the Army remembered Nomonhan. Grew reported the Japanese anxiety, and Roosevelt told Ickes, "The Japs are having a real drag-down and knock-out fight among themselves and have been for the past week—trying to decide which way they are going to jump—attack Russia, attack the South Seas (thus throwing in their lot definitely with Germany) or whether they will sit on the fence and be more friendly to us." He thought it imperative "for us to help keep peace in the Pacific."

The *hokushin/nanshin* (Go North, Go South) debate had the broadest of implications, for the more vigorous their military exertions in any direction, the sooner the Japanese would deplete their reserves of oil, requiring in turn secure relations with the United States and/or secure access to the oil of the Dutch East Indies. Nomura reported that the Americans were obsessed with the European war and wanted to find a basis for a Japanese-American accord. But it was hard to imagine what form an accord might take. Perhaps Japan could jettison its alliance with Hitler and refrain from attacking Russia, but it could never accept a loss of face in China. If the Americans agreed to *forget* about China in return for Japan's abandoning the *Axis*, all well and good. But if the Americans instead cut off oil to Japan in deference to China, then the Japanese *would* have to strike south, in which case they might as well cling to whatever benefits the Axis alliance offered. The alternatives were isolation or surrender.

The climax occurred on July 2, when the cabinet and military, in the presence of the Emperor, revised the Outlines of Fundamental National Policy. Konoe, with the support of the Navy and economic boards, prevailed. Japan would not attack the USSR at least until "the persimmon ripened," which meant that Russia was on the verge of defeat in Europe or had transferred so many divisions away from the Manchurian border as to insure that a Japanese attack would be a walkover. For that eventuality, 850,000 soldiers would be concentrated in Manchukuo. But the pacing element was the weather. An invasion of Siberia would take many months, and the Army command judged that it would have to be launched by early to mid-August or risk getting bogged down by winter. On the other hand, Japan should move south at once, occupy French Indochina, and "construct the Greater East Asia Co-Prosperity Sphere regardless of the changes in the world situation." Matsuoka resigned on July 18, and his more moderate successor, Adm. Toyoda Teijirō, was instructed to seek a *modus vivendi* with Washington.

The Americans had an accurate notion of Japanese thinking both from Grew and from MAGIC, the intelligence operation that succeeded in breaking the Japanese diplomatic code. But the contingent nature of the Japanese decisions ended up serving nobody's purposes. The removal of Matsuoka, Konoe's assurances, and the evidence that Japan was preparing to go south were all welcome, but they did not prove Japan's benign intentions toward Russia in light of the simultaneous buildup of the Kwantung Army and the knowledge that Japan planned to stab Russia in the back if Germany verged on winning. So the risks and probabilities all indicated that the United States should err on the side of protecting the Russians. Just prior to departing for Newfoundland to meet Churchill, Roosevelt issued a fateful decree apparently aimed at discouraging the Japanese from striking *north* even at the risk of encouraging them to strike *south:* he froze all Japanese assets in the United States. The President's directives were not worded so as to imply a total embargo, but under the aegis of Assistant Secretary of State Dean Acheson, the U.S. government approved no release of funds and issued no export licenses, so an embargo it became. After July 25, 1941, Japan got no more oil.

What Roosevelt intended, and when he intended it, are subjects of much debate. The actual regulations he approved implied that Japanese requests for oil would be judged on a case-by-case basis. It even made allowance for export of low-octane gasoline so the Japanese would not feel *forced* to invade the oil-rich East Indies. Roosevelt undoubtedly wanted to keep his options open and do nothing irreversible before consulting with Churchill. But that he did intend to deter Japan from new conquests is indicated by the fact that before his departure he ordered thirty-six B-17s to the Philippines and authorized Claire Chennault to form up his volunteer Flying Tigers in China. Finally, when Roosevelt learned in early September that a de facto oil embargo *had* been in effect, he backed up Acheson and let it stand.

This much seems clear. Roosevelt's *first* choice in mid-1941 was for the Japanese to strike nowhere until moderates somehow overthrew the hard-liners in Tokyo and bolted the Axis alliance. His *second* choice was for the Japanese, whatever else they did, to refrain from attacking Siberia. And Roosevelt's greatest *fear* was that Japan would fall on Russia's rear and help Hitler win World War II before the United States even found an excuse for getting in. *Stalin's* first choice was for the Japanese to spare Siberia and instead attack the United States, thereby saving the USSR from a war on two fronts and gaining for it a mighty ally. Stalin's *second* choice was that a neutral America might at least deter Japan from striking his rear. Stalin's greatest *fear*, of course, was the same as Roosevelt's.

In the end, Roosevelt got his second wish and Stalin his first. The Japanese learned to their aggravation that Stalin was slow to pull divisions off the Manchurian line—clearly he did not trust Japan. They also judged that their stockpile of oil was not sufficient to support a war of attrition in Siberia. So they would in all likelihood have to go south and grab the wells of the Dutch East Indies, whether or not they later struck north. Finally, a pause in the Nazi blitzkrieg from mid-July to mid-August meant that the USSR would survive beyond the August deadline the Japanese Army had set for a northern offensive. Even Tōjō ruefully granted, around August 9, that a Siberian invasion was no longer possible in 1941.

The Japanese were now in danger of missing the bus, as they put it. If they did not act soon to capitalize on their temporary military advantages, they would not only grow more thirsty for oil but face a stronger ABCD coalition led by a rapidly rearming United States. For the de facto U.S. oil embargo was itself a sneak attack in Japanese eyes and damaged Japan's military capacity more than any battle could ever do. And although Roosevelt had refused to promise to fight in defense of the British or Dutch colonies, he did promise Churchill that he would give the Japs a "mighty swat" and (according to Churchill) "would wage war, but not declare it." In any case, the Anglo-Americans' Atlantic Charter called for a postwar world of peace and disarmament, self-determination and free trade, and one in which Japan's Coprosperity Sphere clearly had no place. So the semiofficial *Asahi shimbun* denounced the Atlantic Charter as a blueprint for a "world domination on the basis of Anglo-American world views." Still, the Japanese Army command granted Konoe's request that diplomacy be given a chance. Throughout August he and Nomura, with Grew's avid backing, pleaded for a summit meeting between Roosevelt and Konoe, perhaps in Alaska or Hawaii. The idea appealed to FDR's sense of theater, but difficulties abounded. How could the President explain to the American people a willingness to talk turkey with Hitler's ally while at the same time trying to nudge the United States out of isolationism and do all he could to help Britain, Russia, and China? Hull just hated the idea. "Nothing will stop them except force," he believed, but if by some miracle the Japanese were ready to leave China and make other concessions, then a summit was not even necessary. On the Japanese side, how could Konoe make the concessions that Hull demanded and retain his office, or even his life? Finally, how could either party negotiate without betraying the alliances—Axis on one side, ABCD powers on the other—that were each one's main source of leverage? Not surprisingly, the Chinese lobbied hard against any summit, as did American Communists and fellow travelers like Harry Dexter White, Assistant Secretary of the Treasury. To sell out the Chinese, wrote White, would not only "weaken our national policy in Europe as well as in the Far East, but will dim the bright luster of America's world leadership in the great democratic fight against Fascism." This is not to say that the United States was sucked into World War II by a Communist plot, but rather that after June 22, the Soviets (and British) had every interest in getting the United States into the war, while Roosevelt had every interest in keeping Japan off the Soviets' backs.

American intransigence prompted another round of bargaining among the Army, Navy, civilian, and court politicians in Tokyo. It might be said that no government devoted such anguish and method to its strategic reviews, or got such abysmal results. For the resulting Guidelines for Implementing National Policies declared that war with the ABCD powers was inevitable unless the United States and Britain cut off all aid to China, stopped their military buildups in the Asian/Pacific theater, restored commercial relations with Japan, and persuaded the Dutch to sell Indonesian oil. Since they did not think Anglo-American acceptance very likely, the rest of the document stressed the urgency of preparing for war.

The Emperor noted that fact as he perused the Guidelines on September 5. He asked Army Chief of Staff Sugiyama Gen if he had any idea how long a war with the Anglo-Americans would last? The chief took refuge in animadversions about the southern campaign but finally mentioned the words "three months." The Emperor recalled the Army's earlier promise that the China incident would be over in a year. Sugiyama hung his head in shame, at which point "the Navy Chief of General Staff lent a helping hand to Sugiyama by saying that to his mind Japan was like a patient suffering from a serious illness. . . . He felt that the

Army General Staff was in favor of putting hope in diplomatic negotiations to the finish, but that in case of failure a decisive operation would have to be performed." The following day the same question was posed—did diplomacy still have priority over preparing for war?—and only the Navy minister said yes. A nervous silence followed, then the Voice of the Sacred Crane—the Emperor's own—croaked out a poem in a stylized whine: "Over the four sides of the sea all people are brothers/Why then are the waves so unsettled?" His grandfather Meiji had written it, but what did it mean? If the Emperor were *opposed* to war, could he not think of something more forceful to say than a sentimental Japanese echo of Pearl Buck's irrelevant plea? Could he not have intervened on Konoe's behalf and dared the Army to disobey or assassinate its Emperor? Or did his poem mean something different, for instance: if there is a natural order among nations, why do the *others* make waves? At length Adm. Nagano Osami assured Hirohito that the Navy minister spoke for all: war remained a last resort.

Amazingly, the ministers did try diplomacy. They even persuaded the Army to swallow an offer under which it would evacuate Indochina and pull back to garrisons in north China and Inner Mongolia, and broker a merger between Wang's puppet government and the Kuomintang. But Hull scotched the summit conference once and for all on October 2 and repeated his four principles like a mantra. That was enough for Tōjō. On the fourteenth he cried out that if Japan evacuated China and recognized the Open Door it would only encourage the Chinese to go for Manchukuo next and stir up a Korean rebellion. The result would be a "little Japan" that was merely an economic dependency of the United States and Britain. Therefore diplomacy was vain, therefore the U.S. embargo would stand, therefore Japan had to conquer its Coprosperity Sphere, therefore the southern advance must be made, therefore the only barriers to it—the U.S. Pacific fleet and Philippine bases—must be neutralized. Finally, if Japan did not initiate hostilities by a deadline of December 8 (Tokyo time), it might have to wait until spring, by which time Japan would have even less oil, and the United States would be much stronger. Moreover, the Navy was ready, having approved a new plan based on the Pearl Harbor assault sketched by Bywater, preached by Yamamoto, and published in a 1933 Japanese book called *When We Fight*.

Konoe resigned as Prime Minister for the third and last time on October 16. Tōjō, with the Emperor's approval, assumed the posts of Prime Minister, War Minister, and Interior Minister in charge of police. For whatever his private thoughts about war, Hirohito admired Tōjō. He was devoted to the Emperor, tireless, efficient, and honest—he was almost alone in not gouging a personal fortune out of his Manchurian command. Even Grew felt a flicker of hope that a Tōjō cabinet might better be able to rein in the Army. The alternative was too awful to contemplate: "If our peace efforts should fail, Japan may go all-out in a do-or-die effort to render herself invulnerable to foreign economic pressure . . . [and] war between Japan and the United States may come *with dangerous and dramatic suddenness.*" The Tōjō cabinet stuck to its deadline for war but consented to one final diplomatic mission. So Kurusu Saburō boarded a Pan-Am Clipper and flew to the United States, where he smiled for newsreels and spoke of "breaking through the line for a touchdown." But his Plan A, the minimum terms the military would accept, crashed on the dikes of Hull's four principles. So Kurusu and Nomura tried Plan B, a temporary understanding whereby Japanese forces would halt in place and the United States lift its embargo, pending an agreement on China. That had possibilities; the United States wanted to buy time for rearmament. So Hull drafted a three-month *modus vivendi* based on a withdrawal from southern Indochina in return for some oil. But China and Britain denounced any *modus vivendi* as a sellout, so all Hull could do was to present a lengthier version of his same old principles on November 26.

By then Yamamoto's Hawaii Task Force was a day out from the Kuriles and cutting through the North Pacific waters first navigated by Urdaneta 376 years before. Vice Admiral Nagumo Chūichi had briefed the flight crews of the six aircraft carriers the evening before. "This Empire," he told them, "is now going to war with an arrogant and predestined enemy." Their mission was to launch a surprise attack and "destroy the United States Fleet once and for all." It would not be easy, but he exhorted his men never to lose confidence, for "is there anything, no matter how difficult it may be, that cannot be done by an intrepid spirit and a burning loyalty?" His officers, airmen, and sailors had those in abundance, whatever else their Empire lacked. "AN AIR ATTACK ON HAWAII! A dream come true," wrote a sailor. "What will the people at home think when they hear the news. . . . We would teach the arrogant Anglo-Saxon scoundrels a lesson!"

By December 1, when Tōjō obtained the Emperor's final approval for war, the Americans knew that the game was up. The MAGIC decrypts of Japanese code words such as "East wind rain" and "things are automatically going to happen" proved that Japan meant to attack in the first week of December. On December 6, Roosevelt acted on a suggestion from the Japanese embassy and wired an appeal to the Emperor. The Japanese authorities delayed its transmission, and Grew received it pitifully too late. At the same time, the ten-part Japanese reply to Hull was also in transit, to be decoded, translated, typed, and delivered infamously too late. Finally, a world away on the front before Moscow, General Zhukov assembled the sturdy Siberian divisions finally released in October from the Manchurian border. On December 6 he counterattacked the exhausted Germans and saved the Soviet Union for the winter at least.

Yamamoto hated the Axis alliance Matsuoka had made and the American war that Tōjō had made. In 1940 he had prophesied that "in order to fight the United States we must fight with the intention of challenging practically the whole world. . . . I shall extend my utmost efforts and will probably die fighting on the battleship *Nagata*. During that time, Tokyo will probably be burnt to the ground." When queried by Konoe about the Navy's plans, Yamamoto replied, "If I am told to fight regardless of consequences, I shall run wild considerably for six months or a year. But I have utterly no confidence in the second or third years." He then begged Konoe to jettison the Axis and save the peace with America. But all the Japanese commanders were devoted to their Emperor, race, and service. Naval officers in particular swallowed their misgivings because an oceanic war at least assured them a bigger share of Japan's scarce steel and oil. Operational planning for the assaults on Malaya, the Philippines, and Hawaii was flawless. The questions they were afraid to answer before the Emperor were what it would all accomplish and how and when it would end.

"Will the power and prestige of the white man in the Far East be what it has been in the past?" asked Pearl Buck. Whatever motto one chose—Asia for the Asians, Coprosperity Sphere, Japanese Monroe Doctrine—it amounted in Japanese eyes to no more than what Americans arrogated to themselves on their side of the ocean. And yet, the best way for Japan to ensure that the white man *would* return in force as never before was to lash out and hit him Port Arthur–style, confirming his paranoia and stereotypes, and proving to him that to remain secure in the eastern Pacific, he, the white man, must control the western Pacific as well. That was hardly the motive of Admiral Nagumo's pilots when they cried *"Tora!"* (Tiger) and swept down on Battleship Row. Their motive was to achieve what a generation of Japanese statesmen had failed to achieve: just to get the Americans' attention. We exist, we Japanese! We are proud and strong and we have desperate problems. You whites ignore us, exclude us, constrain us, impose upon us vapid pieties and principles, turn your backs on your failures, then scold us when we try solutions of our own. Can't you see what a trap we're in, even if partly of our own making? If you will not help us, then at least leave us be!

Sidney Gulick, lifelong missionary-advocate for the Japanese cause, suspected something of the sort. He was retired and living in Honolulu when the dive bombers and torpedo planes appeared overhead. I'm unhurt, he wrote his children on December 7, so don't worry. Then he added, "I reckon the Japanese are desperate and prefer to be beaten by the U.S.A. than by China; when beaten she'll [sic] get better terms from us than from any other power. So much for this morning."

One of the agents of that severe mercy was Admiral Halsey, who returned to Pearl Harbor with the aircraft carriers that were fortunately at sea during the raid. Viewing the wreckage, Halsey snarled—and who wouldn't have?—"Before we're through with them the Japanese language will be spoken only in hell."

The Twelfth 'aha iki

Seward: So I was right. They struck without warning. What was it you said, Saitō, about the Japanese going crazy?

Saitō: Your people turned their backs on us, and my people went mad. Madder than I knew. I was thinking only of China. Could I have prevented this war? Perhaps not. I was merely spared the shame of Nomura and Kurusu, those good men.

Scholar: Scoundrels and pissants, that's what Cordell Hull called them. They finally delivered their war message over two hours *after* the Pearl Harbor attack.

Saitō: Betrayed by their own government, as all diplomats are. I know a lot of rubbish was talked back in Tokyo about Japan's destiny and "the world under one roof." Even Yamamoto and I joked about teaching Americans a lesson. But neither of us meant it. The madmen were all in the Army: provincials, primitives, barbarians within. I won't deny I was glad to be abroad in those years. . . . Funny they should transport my ashes in a U.S. Navy vessel.

Scholar: The cruiser *Astoria*—sunk in 1942 off Guadalcanal.

Saitō: And Yamamoto?

Scholar: Killed, on Roosevelt's orders. The Americans intercepted messages describing his flight plan and shot him down. "Pop goes the weasel."

Saitō: Yamamoto was no weasel. "How peas, oats, soybeans. . . ."

Seward: How oats, peas, beans, and barley grows . . . Nobody knows how oats, peas, beans, and barley grows.

Saitō: Yes. One should be careful about seeds carelessly strewn. Things have a way of growing. Meiji militarism, Yamato spirit, Ishiwara's "direct action," the revolt against corruption and decadence and Westernization—they were there all along but did not take over until after the fact, to justify what Japan had to do. If only you Americans had lived up to the spirit of your Washington principles, or been *tougher* on us, in 1931, when it all began to grow. . . . Perhaps we were not trapped by geopolitics and economics, as the professor implied. But *you* led us to believe that we were. You must understand that we are an insular people. In those days, few Japanese went abroad, and foreigners did seem like demons—some evil, some useful like teachers, like your myth of Prometheus. We also have a myth—a fairy tale you would call it—about the boy Momotarō, who was born from a miraculous peach found floating in a river. He grew up conscious of his mission as savior, to free Japan from the demons who lived on an island across the sea and periodically came to ravage. Sometimes it is said that the Peach Boy killed all the demons, and sometimes that he forced them to change their ways. I can imagine what our pilots were thinking when they flew down on Hawaii with their *hachimaki*—the white bands emblazoned with the Rising Sun—tied around their foreheads. A squadron of Peach Boys.

Seward: "The sun of heaven was loath to set, but stay'd, and made the western welkin blush. . . ."

Scholar: What's a welkin?

Seward: The sky, professor, the sky. You shouldn't attempt tragedy if you haven't read your Shakespeare. And did the Japanese achieve their surprise, or was it, like Fort Sumter, a mere kick in the shins to a sleeping giant?

Scholar: Funny, that's what Yamamoto said. But I forgot that none of you knows any of this. The Pearl Harbor story is so familiar to my generation. Yes, the Japanese achieved total surprise even though the Americans had broken their codes. You can imagine the sensational theories *that* has inspired.

Witte: Is there not a Scottish saying: fool me once, shame on you—

Scholar: —fool me twice, shame on me. Yes, but the question was not whether Japan would launch a surprise attack. The question was *where*, and strange as it seems, no one believed they would be so bold as to strike at Hawaii.

Witte: But your whole lecture leads up to it: rise of aviation, theories of Lea, Mitchell, Bywater, Yamamoto. You mean to say that the Japanese Navy maneuvered a great fleet across half the ocean, and were never detected?

Scholar: Your Russians at Port Arthur knew war was imminent and knew just where the Japanese fleet was based. You were still caught unawares.

Witte: But you said you had broken the Japanese codes.

Scholar: But none of the thousands of pages of decrypts said a word about Pearl Harbor. The evidence all pointed to a southern offensive, which made the most sense. Yamamoto's fleet sneaked out of port undetected and disappeared into the foggy North Pacific. And the Japanese apparently kept radio silence. We had reconnaissance planes, of course, but chances were slim that the Americans would crisscross the ocean south of Alaska unless they had reason to believe something was there. Some scholars argue that the MAGIC intercepts actually provided *so much* information on Japanese movements that the truth got lost amid the ambient "noise." Others insist that the truth was not there, for nowhere did the Japanese mention Hawaii or drop hints as to the whereabouts of their carriers. Of course, they also broadcast deceptive data just as Zhukov did at Nomonhan. Still, none of that excuses the War and Navy departments for not putting Pearl on full war alert.

Witte: Your bases were not on alert!

Scholar: Not the highest alert. And that's what allowed conspiracy theorists to speculate that FDR purposely tempted the Japanese to attack Pearl Harbor so that the U.S. could get into World War II "through the back door."

Witte: You believe this?

Scholar: Not for a second. Of course, Roosevelt did want to get into the war, but in Europe, not Asia. There was no guarantee that Congress would declare war on *Germany,* and FDR did not even ask it to do so. Happily, Hitler accommodated Tōjō and Roosevelt alike by declaring war on the United States, on December 10, for foolish reasons we can only guess at. Nor did Roosevelt need to lose half his battleship fleet to shock the nation into a war-fighting mood. The fact of an attack on Hawaii or, for that matter, just the Philippines would have sufficed. And even if FDR *had* wanted his battleships to be sitting ducks, he could not have prevented the Hawaii-based radar from picking up the Japanese planes, which it did, or caused the lieutenant on duty to ignore the blips on the assumption that they were a flight of B-17s. Nor could FDR have prevented the commanders on the spot, General Short and Admiral Kimmel, from ordering an alert on their own. Their defenders argue that if Short and Kimmel had been privy to the MAGIC data sitting in Washington, they might have deduced the Japanese plans. But the fact remains that they had been given a warning that war was imminent on November 27 and did not take all possible precautions. The bottom line was that nobody in Washington or Hawaii believed in Bywater's prophecies. When a congressional inquisitor asked Kimmel off the record why he did not at least order his battleships out to sea, the admiral blurted over the lunch table: "Alright, Morgan—I'll give you your answer. I never thought those little yellow sons-of-bitches could pull off such an attack, so far from Japan."

Witte: That is more like it. You *were* the same as the Russians in 1904.

Scholar: You mean blinded by pride and prejudice. But the Japanese were even blinder. They talked themselves into believing that Americans were a mongrel race, obsessed with material comforts, unwilling and unable to fight. They figured we'd give up after a few defeats, to the extent they figured at all.

Saitō: Takes one to know one, I guess. American material comforts *killed* me. But that's not the source of my shame. Now I know how I failed as ambassador. Instead of explaining to the Americans what the Japanese militarists really were like, I tried to excuse their behavior, put the best face on them. But the cormorant had slipped its noose.

Scholar: The cormorant. You mean the Kwantung Army?

Saitō: We fished with cormorants when I was a lad. Greedy birds, they'd fish whether they were hungry or not. Then you pulled the tethers around their necks and they'd choke up the catch. But the Army slipped its tether. I don't think I realized it myself until '37. And the worst of it was that I never told Tokyo what the Americans were really about. Gary Cooper, Jimmy Cagney. Maybe you Americans are softer than most, but you don't like to *think* yourselves soft, and your workers and farmers are as proud as samurai. But how could I explain to Tokyo how dangerous it was to provoke the U.S. when you did *nothing,* all through the thirties, even after we sank the *Panay?* You said one conspiracy theory involved getting America into the war through the "back door"?

Scholar: Yes, but I don't believe it.

Saitō: It doesn't matter whether it's true; the point is the very fact that the Pacific *was* the "back door" to you Americans, always the back door. Which made Japan what? A beggar, or a servant, or a thief, skulking at the *back door.* That is what we hated more than anything. I did try to communicate that through my embassy: that the Pacific was as vital to America as the Atlantic, and that we needed your attention. But I failed to describe the dangers. All I did was bow and smile and say "so sorry." I was a salesman, not a statesman.

Seward: Saitō, I know we've had some harsh words, but buck up, man. *You* didn't order the invasion of China. You did your duty like—

Saitō: Yamamoto? Perhaps. Who can stop an earthquake, even if his meters tell him it's coming? One of our "enlightened thinkers" from the early Meiji—he was already passé by the time I was in school—wrote that earthquakes were the means by which the Creator built up the earth. Without them the earth would be perfectly round, and covered with water. The existence of land and life and human beings therefore depended on earthquakes. He asked if the same were true of wars. All I remember of his answer is this: "Rivalry between the kingfisher and the clam brought profit to the fisherman. How do we not know that the struggle between the yellow dragons in the field will not benefit the sons of the white emperors?"

Lea: You have finally, my tiresome interlocutors, stumbled on the shed whence all your martial waters flow.

Kaahumanu: You sing when you speak, General Lea. We wish you to speak more often.

Seward: Speak for yourself, Your Highness. What the hell are "martial waters"?

Witte: Struggle between yellow dragons: Sino-Japanese War, perhaps?

Kaahumanu: It is as your missionary wrote, the Pearl lady: that the wars of the whites raise the Yellow Peril, and the wars of the yellows raise the White Peril. So the source of all discord is China—correct, General Lea?

Lea: China weak, not herself. The professor said much about the technology of flight, whose potential I may have underestimated, but he ignored the wisdom recorded by me in 1909: "Conditions permitting the voluntary self-segregation of the East and the West now no longer exist. Nations cannot in this age still hide themselves behind their mountain walls or their moats of space and sea. . . . Science, unlike God, has no chosen people. Those by the sunrise and those by its going down are one and the same. It has, in its impartial and relentless manner, crushed this once vast world into a little ball around which go, each day, the whisperings of a hundred tongues—"

Seward: Get to the point.

Lea: So long as China was weak, and the contenders for Manchuria were Russia and Japan, the latter could exploit the rivalries of the white powers elsewhere and expand its hold on the continent. But the Japanese were both victims and fools; victims of the very Asian nationalism their own success inflamed, and fools for thinking Japan an Asian image of Germany when it is in fact an Asian image of Britain. Japan was correct to keep Korea and Manchuria out of Russian hands, just as Britain always fought to save the Low Countries from France or Germany. But not since the Hundred Years' War had Britain attempted to seize lands for herself across the Channel. By seizing and holding the lands of the Manchu, Japan made China her enemy, divided the yellows, and forced the white nations to choose. That they were reluctant to do so hardly surprised me, but that Russia and the Republic both chose China was inevitable. Professor, you spoke of the "total war" faction that insisted on Japan's need for autarky.

Scholar: Yes?

Lea: Why did they liken Japan to Germany?

Scholar: Because they saw Germany as another superior military culture short of land and raw materials and strangled to death by an Allied blockade.

Lea: Why did they not rather see Japan as an impregnable island like Britain, which could never be beaten by a land power so long as it commanded the sea?

Scholar: Because they did not want Japan to *be* just an island empire.

Lea: Precisely. Japan's folly was in letting the *Army*, not the Navy, make foreign policy! A maritime-minded observer looks from the Japanese islands to the continent, sees two doddering, backward empires—China and Russia—and exploits the balance between them. Neither is a seagoing people, so as long as Japan is China's offshore protector *and controls its own seas with its Navy,* Japan need never lack for economic outlets. The seven seas are its living room.

Scholar: Lebensraum. But following up on your English analogy: *if* the Japanese were ever to expand on the continent, it had to have been in the seventeenth century, when Hideyoshi invaded Korea. For at that time Manchuria and what became the Russian Far East were still empty, not to mention Hokkaido, the Kuriles, and Alaska. But the Tokugawa exclusion took Japan out of the game until the 1890s, by which time the vacuums were filled and imperialism a matter of finance and commerce backed by armies and fleets. Japan might rule Korea or Manchuria as the British ruled India, but it could never hope to *supplant* the inhabitants already there short of a genocidal campaign of Nazi proportions. It was too late for Japan.

Saitō: So what would you have had Japan do? Sit back politely and hope that the nice white folks allow us to trade? Perhaps we overreached on the continent—we *did* overreach. But do you have any idea what *space* does to the Japanese soul, you Americans, and you Russian? Oh, you say we Japanese make a virtue of confinement with our little gardens and little poems and little flower arrangements and little apartments and even little dishes of food, all of which contain worlds by artful design. But it is still confinement. I saw *issei* get off the boat in America. San Francisco was familiar to them—a crowded seaport full of Asians and round eyes, maybe like Yokohama. But then they took the train to Stockton, or rode in pickup trucks to their relatives' farms in Napa, and their eyes got big, and they laughed and had to get out and stretch and look and laugh some more. All that land and sky! I bet the soldiers in China felt the same, and the colonizers of the Nan'yō—the South Seas. Why should Japanese alone not dream of Manifest Destiny? Why should they be the only vigorous, industrial, prolific, yes and martial people to lock itself in the closet? Well, maybe you're right, maybe because of Tokugawa we missed the boat, or bus, as they said in 1941.

Kaahumanu: Why did your people attack Hawaii if they wanted to conquer in China?

Scholar: I didn't make that clear?

Lea: Because the irresistible vectors of magnetic fields radiating outward in outrageous arcs from the lodestone of China thrust Da Nihon against the Republic no matter what compass point marked its intended target.

Seward: Let the professor explain, Mr. Lea.

Lea: You fancy me pompous, sir, while in truth you revel in ignorance. "Nothing is more difficult than to raise the eyelids of man. He loves his own dirt, and glories in the fact that God made him out of it."

Scholar: Kaahumanu, the Japanese high command concluded that Japan could not risk a major war unless it gained access to iron and oil and rice and the rest. And if it could not even *risk* a major war, then it would lack the leverage to defend its interests even through diplomacy. That fact was so obvious that Roosevelt's men assumed that embargoes would suffice to switch off the Japanese war machine. But by 1940 or so the economic planners in the Cabinet and General Staff had worked out a plan for seizing the French, Dutch, and British colonies of Southeast Asia that would yield the necessary supplies. Once the Coprosperity Sphere was secure, the Japanese figured that their Empire would be economically self-sufficient on the inside and impregnable from the outside. The only force in the world that might interfere with the plan was the U.S. Pacific fleet. So the Japanese determined to cripple it, and because it was based in Hawaii, that is where the Japanese had to attack it.

Kaahumanu: So the Japanese defeated the *haoles* at Pearl Harbor and conquered my islands . . . and *that* is why "Saitō's people" now own Waikiki!

Scholar: No, Your Highness, actually—

Kaahumanu: But they were already there! You said Japanese numbered almost half the population of the islands. Mostly young men, you said, who would have made strong warriors. Surely they wanted to fight for their country?

Scholar: No, Your Highness, actually—

Kaahumanu: Japanese on Hawaii did *not* want to fight for the Japanese from Japan? Perhaps they had all become Christians.

Scholar: No, Your Highness, actually few of them had. They set up their own schools, newspapers, and clubs, and celebrated Japan's victories in China. Hundreds went home to volunteer for the Imperial Army, and Japanese girls on Hawaii sewed the "thousand stitches"— ceremonial waistbands thought to protect their wearers against enemy bullets. Japanese-Hawaiians were pro-Japanese, but pro-American, too. If that makes any sense.

Kaahumanu: But if Japanese in American lands could learn to be pro-American, why could not Japanese in Japan? Is it because the *haoles* treated them kindly?

Scholar: No, Your Highness, actually—well, I'll be telling how they were treated. But you ask a powerful question: why were Japanese in Japan not friendlier toward America? They certainly wanted to be. Look at their response to the Babe Ruth tour and the *Astoria*'s visit. Despite the foreign policy disputes and all the propaganda Japanese received in their schools and press, they still wanted to be friends with America. But there was something deeper at work—a question of honor, wouldn't you say, Saitō?

Seward: So the Pearl Harbor attack was like throwing down the gauntlet, a gentlemen's duel? Hmmmm.

Saitō:

Isles of blessed Japan!
Should strangers seek to scan your Yamato spirit
Reply, "Scenting morn's sunlit air
Blows the cherry, wild and fair."

I remember now. A radio speech I gave in America, about honor. "Compare the Japanese cherry with its Western sister, the rose," I said. There is earnestness in the rose, animation in the cherry. The rose holds to life to the very last, while the cherry makes light of death and dances down in the breeze. The rose is self-assertive; each flower commands an appreciation of its own. The cherry glories in clusters, each flower losing its identity in the making of a beautiful whole. To the samurai, suicide is not to "end the thousand ills that flesh is heir to" but a solution to a problem in which his honor is involved. "Better to be dashed to pieces as a jewel than remain perfect as a tile." Honor does not permit Japanese to cling to life for its own sake, but rather to fall back to earth in the fullness of spring, like a cherry blossom. "'Tis a relief to die; death's but a sure retreat from infamy."

Scholar: Infamy!

Seward: So honor required the Japs to commit national suicide? So be it. *But why did you have to take Americans with you?*

Scholar: And Chinese, Mr. Seward, tens of millions of Chinese.

Tule Lake and
Midway Island 1942

"I REMEMBER THE FEELING of relief bubbling up inside me," wrote a Japanese intellectual on Pearl Harbor day. "There was a joy of having been given a direction clearly, a lightness of the whole being." Anxiety ended, and the frustrating war in China was transformed into a satisfying war against the whites. "I thought it was splendid," wrote a novelist. "No question of moaning that if there is war some of us must die. No lamentations, that was our mood."

By comparison, the commanders of the Hawaii task force brooded, even as their pilots exchanged congratulations on the decks of the Japanese carriers. Genda Minoru, the guru of Japanese naval aviation, urged Admiral Nagumo to resume the attack, find and sink the U.S. aircraft carriers that were absent from Pearl, and bomb the dry dock and oil depot on Oahu. That was tempting, Nagumo replied, but what if American planes found them first? The task force had completed its mission and was needed to support the conquest of Southeast Asia. It should hie for home without further risk. Yamamoto suspected Genda was right, but to overrule Nagumo would mean "a stinging loss of face before his whole command." So instead Yamamoto instructed his staff, on December 9, to begin planning a second offensive that would pave the way for a full-scale invasion of the Hawaiian Islands the following year.

Was the Pearl Harbor attack the "devastating blow" that Americans and Japanese both assumed it was at the time? Was it rather a tactical success but strategic failure, as most historians record? Or was it, as the boldest revisionists argue, a failure on every level? If the Japanese had blown up the fuel dumps and docks, they would have put the base itself, not just some ships, out of action and forced the U.S. Navy back to the West Coast. To be sure, their purpose was only to buy the time needed for Japan to conquer its Coprosperity Sphere. But U.S. offensive capacity depended far more on its carriers than on the obsolete battlewagons, all of which (thanks to the Washington Conference) were at least twenty years old. As one admiral suggested later, "the Japanese only destroyed a lot of old hardware." Even the fact that Pearl Harbor was taken by surprise was a blessing in disguise, for if Adm. Husband E. Kimmel had known the Japanese were coming and sent his ships out to meet them, they might all have met the same fate as the British *Repulse* and *Prince of Wales*, sunk by aircraft on the third day of war. As it was, the battleships settled in shallow water next door to the dry dock, and all but two returned to service. Admiral Chester W. Nimitz thought "it was God's mercy that our fleet was in Pearl Harbor on December 7, 1941."

But whether or not the attack was a tactical failure, it was surely a strategic folly. Not only did it transform the divided and doubt-ridden United States into a purposeful monster of vengeance, it failed to correspond to the geopolitics of the North Pacific. For the Japanese would never enjoy secure control of the western Pacific unless they occupied or neutralized Hawaii itself. They had done neither, and as a result heroic and around-the-clock efforts by American salvage crews, ironmongers, welders, electricians, and armorers restored Pearl Harbor to full operation in a matter of months, while the factories of the West Coast geared up to replace the three hundred aged airplanes destroyed in the raid with tens of thousands of the newest designs. Yamamoto had been skeptical of the chances of invading Oahu. Now he realized it was not only possible but mandatory. For the only way of winning the war was to convince the Americans that a long, bloody struggle to deny Japan an Asian empire was just not worth the effort. The best way to deliver such a "spiritual blow" was to invade Hawaii and force the U.S. fleet and air forces to defend California itself. Hawaii in Japanese hands meant a chance, at least, of a negotiated peace, while Hawaii in American hands meant a war of attrition against a country with ten times Japan's industrial capacity.

So it was that during the same months Japanese forces leapt from victory to victory at Guam, Wake, Hong Kong, Malaya, Singapore, the Philippines, and the East Indies, Yamamoto fretted over how to stave off *defeat*. He confided the planning of his second-phase Eastern Operation to Adm. Ugaki Matome, a dynamic, intelligent man with a round, bald head, a face like an angry toad, and a fierce devotion to the Emperor. As early as January 14, 1942, Ugaki recorded: "The conclusion is to take Midway, Johnston, and Palmyra [islands] after June, send our air strength to these islands, and after these steps are almost completed, mobilize all available strength to invade Hawaii, while attempting to destroy the enemy fleet in a decisive battle." But winning approval for such a bold scheme was as great a challenge as planning it. Naval strategists preferred to exploit Japan's stunning initial gains with a foray into the Indian Ocean and invasion of Burma and India, or a drive through New Guinea toward Australia, or a South Seas thrust to Fiji and Samoa, while the Army hoped for a chance to invade Siberia. Anyway, it seemed crazy to force a decisive fleet engagement in Hawaiian waters, where the Americans could make use of land-based air power. So an Army-Navy conference agreed in January 1942 to shelve the Eastern Operation. Nagumo's carriers instead supported the occupation of the Solomon Islands, bombed Darwin, Australia, and ran wild in the Indian Ocean.

Then the Americans came to Yamamoto's aid. On February 1 two U.S. carriers assigned to patrol the lifeline to Australia raided Japanese bases in the Marshall Islands. They did no serious damage but demonstrated that so long as the Americans held Hawaii they could venture out and attack at points and times of their choosing. The full implications of that became clear on April 18, when Adm. William F. "Bull" Halsey stealthily pushed the carrier *Hornet* within seven hundred miles of Japan and launched sixteen B-25 bombers under Jimmy Doolittle on a daredevil raid over Tokyo. That was the real "spiritual blow," for even though Japanese propaganda dubbed it the "do little" raid, it shamed the military and called into question the Emperor's safety. As Yamamoto's air officer, Miwa Yoshitake, put it, "Tokyo is our capital and the center of our divine country, so in this sense an enemy air raid on these cannot be allowed to take place under any circumstances." After the Doolittle raid, Miwa argued, "If this kind of enemy attempt is to be neutralized, there would be no other way but to make a landing on Hawaii. This makes landing on Midway a prerequisite." Even the Army bowed to his logic.

For the few Japanese who gave it much thought, Hawaii was an object of fascination. A Polynesian archipelago populated mostly by Asians, it had fallen to a coup d'état and then been annexed by the U.S. imperialists. Since then its large *issei* (first-generation) and *nisei* (second-generation) population was subject to the paranoid fears of the white minority. When Japanese workers went on strike, the mouthpieces of the sugar magnates cried that the real issue was "Is Hawaii to remain American or become Japanese?" When *nisei* began voting in large numbers, scaremongers predicted a Japanese takeover of local government. When a crazed Japanese kidnapped a white boy in 1928, the incident symbolized the racial threat. When the territorial legislature passed resolutions for statehood and bills went before Congress, opponents of statehood racebaited. How could Hawaii be made a state when it was 78 percent nonwhite and contained 160,000 Japanese of dubious loyalty? When Congress sent a fact-finding team in 1937, John F. G. Stokes, former curator of Polynesian culture at Honolulu's famous Bishop Museum, testified that Japanese were not only unassimilable but conspired to deliver Hawaii to the Mikado: "Unperceived by ourselves, the white population of Hawaii has become Japanese-minded, and this fact constitutes a strong argument against statehood. The technique has been that of the Japanese 'Gentle Divine Spirit' to which white people yield very readily—especially those of wealth and importance. It appeals to the white man's conceit and feeds his superiority complex to aid his 'little brown brother.'" *Nisei* could only reply, "If we Japanese in Hawaii are treated like 'Japs,' perhaps in time we shall come to feel like 'Japs'; but if our friends continue to treat us like Americans, we will feel and act like Americans."

Still, if white Americans feared that the *nisei* were disloyal, the Japanese in Japan hoped that they were! In official parlance all overseas Japanese were *dōhō*, a term not unlike the Nazi *Volksdeutsch*, and it was the fatherland's duty to reclaim them. After all, seventy-three thousand *nisei* held dual citizenship in 1940, Japanese Hawaiians bought 3 million yen in imperial war bonds, and fourteen thousand returned to Japan for school or military service. But at the same time, others attended American schools and the University of Hawaii, and formed the largest ethnic contingent in the Boy Scouts and Territorial Guard. The truth was that many *dōhō* did have mixed loyalties, and one youth, when asked what he would do if the United States and Japan went to war, answered: "I would kill myself."

The large, hardworking, but politically muted Japanese community in Hawaii could not fail to beckon to the architects of the Coprosperity Sphere. After Pearl Harbor, a tide of books and articles appeared in Japan describing the history of the *dōhō* struggle against white supremacy. "If one speaks of liberation of Hawaii's people," wrote an *issei* returnee to Japan in 1942, "then it is more logical to refer to the Japanese than to the Hawaiians." Hawaii was nothing but a colony, and tearing it away from America would be no different than liberating Hong Kong from Britain. Journalist Kanda Yoshi insisted that "Hawaii must belong to Japan," while Professor Komaki Sanashige simply wrote, "Hawaii *is* part of Japan." Scholars inside and outside of government expected their cousins in the islands to rise up in support of a Japanese invasion, and studied how Japan might reform Hawaiian government and society, and break up the Big Five sugar *zaibatsu!*

A soldier from Texas arrived in Hawaii in early 1942, looked around at the faces of the inhabitants, and joked, "My God, we got here too late. The Japs have already got the place." Considering that Japan had just killed or wounded 3,435 Americans in a sneak attack and that rumors spread to the effect that Japanese workers had cut "arrows" into cane fields to guide Japanese pilots, or blocked roads with their trucks, or signaled to submarines offshore, it is remarkable that lynchings did not occur. The Japanese consul had in fact photographed U.S. defenses, observed ship movements, and wired coded reports back to Tokyo. But his spies were Japanese nationals, not *issei* or *nisei*. So Lt. Gen. Delos C. Emmons, Walter C. Short's replacement, appealed to Hawaii's reputation as an "American outpost of friendliness and goodwill." Thanks to his statesmanship, the Aloha spirit, martial law, and the universal fear of race riots, a tense calm prevailed in the islands after December 7.

Roosevelt's cabinet took up the issue of potential fifth columnists on December 19 and recommended that Japanese Hawaiians be placed in concentration camps on Maui or Molokai. But Emmons dragged his feet, pleading a shortage of labor and shipping. He wanted no part of concentration camps. "While we have been subjected to a serious attack by a ruthless and treacherous enemy, we must remember that this is America and we must do things the American way." When the federal government's Roberts Report claimed (falsely) that civilian spies *had* functioned in Hawaii, the War and Navy departments directed that steps be taken toward "the removal of Japs from Oahu." But Emmons and FBI Special Agent Robert L. Shivers insisted that the *nisei* were not only loyal but made up an indispensable 40 percent of the islands' skilled work force. Indeed, every time Washington urged action on Emmons he dodged or delayed, until finally the issue was dropped. As a result, fewer than 2,000 Japanese Hawaiians were ever interned at all.

If the whites refrained from panicky acts in Hawaii, one would surely expect them to do so on the West Coast, where the military threat was less immediate. Again the rumors flew about after December 7: Japanese planes over San Francisco, saboteurs near war plants, submarines offshore, a Japanese pilot wearing a University of California class ring shot down over Pearl Harbor, even a poisoned vegetable scare. Again the federal authorities wanted action. And again local leaders like California Gov. Culbert L. Olsen and Congressman Leland Ford urged calm and fair play. Above all, the commander of the Pacific military district, Gen. John L. De Witt, reported that talk of removing the 117,000 Japanese within his command betrayed common sense. "An American citizen, after all, is an American citizen. And while they all may not be loyal, I think we can weed the disloyal out of the loyal and lock them up if necessary."

Yet within a month virtually all local leaders changed their minds in the face of a unanimous *national* cry for punitive action against Japanese Americans. It was almost as if the federal government, exaggerating the potential danger of Japanese espionage, positively encouraged white Californians to demand that the Golden State be rid of Japanese altogether. Navy Secretary Frank Knox, for instance, could have used his news conference in Los Angeles on December 15 to call for calm. Instead, he blamed Pearl Harbor on "the most effective fifth column work that's come out of this war, except in Norway." Roosevelt's private White House spies likewise warned that sabotage of power stations, harbors, and bridges could cripple the war effort: imagine if someone blew Hoover Dam or torched the Boeing factory! By mid-January Ford reversed himself, demanding that Japanese be removed to inland concentration camps on the theory that any who protested such treatment were ipso facto disloyal. "A viper is a viper, wherever the egg is hatched—" declared the Los Angeles Times, "so a Japanese-American, born of Japanese parents—grows up to be a Japanese, not an American." In early February, California Attorney General Earl Warren endorsed relocation, and Los Angeles Mayor Fletcher Bowron announced that "when the final test comes, who can say but that 'blood will tell'? We cannot run the risk of another Pearl Harbor episode in Southern California."

That, in truth, was the key to it all. For however much bigotry, fear, and vengeful spirit spewed forth in the terrible opening months of the war, only military necessity could justify the suspension of habeas corpus and only the military could carry it out. If the Army said no, as it did in Hawaii, Roosevelt might well have turned counterespionage over to the FBI and gotten on with the war. But General De Witt, a sixty-one-year-old cipher, shuddered to think of his fate should "another Pearl Harbor" occur on his watch. "I am not going to be a second General Short," he said. Meanwhile, no less a pundit than Walter Lippmann reported from San Francisco that "the Pacific Coast is in imminent danger of a combined attack from within and without," and the West Coast congressional caucus unanimously petitioned the President for "immediate evacuation of all persons of Japanese lineage." De Witt soon persuaded himself that internment was a "military necessity," and the War Department of Stimson and John J. McCloy concurred. FDR signed the executive order on February 19, 1942, with the sole admonition: "Be as reasonable as you can."

No genocide occurred, or slave labor, or Bataan death marches, or torture, or "medical experiments" such as the Japanese inflicted on prisoners. And if Americans could ever be excused for overreaction owing to a "Pearl Harbor complex," it was two months after Pearl Harbor itself. Still, the man appointed to run the War Relocation Authority, Milton S. Eisenhower, knew almost at once that "when this war is over and we consider calmly this unprecedented migration of 120,000 people, we as Americans are going to regret the avoidable injustices that may have been done." The roundup from Seattle to San Diego went quickly, and the Japanese went quietly (except perhaps third-generation sansei babies in their mothers' arms). So farmers left their farms, and Japantowns became ghost towns. By August 1942 the Army could report that the West Coast was "Jap-free," for the *nisei* now lived in tarpaper-and-canvas barracks in detention camps surrounded by barbed wire. They were put to work growing beets and such for the Army and did so with their usual vigor and teamwork. But not all agreed to sign loyalty oaths or volunteer to serve a country that did this to them. Some eighteen thousand "trouble-makers" were concentrated in the most infamous camp of all—Tule Lake, astride the lava beds near the Oregon border, where the extremes of temperature were brutal. Riots and strikes ensued, and in the end over seven thousand outraged Tule Lake inmates renounced U.S. citizenship and applied for postwar repatriation to Japan.

Meanwhile, during the same months when relocation went forward on the mainland, thousands of *nisei* employees of Pearl Harbor and Schofield Barracks, *nisei* Varsity Victory Volunteers from the university, *nisei* soldiers of the Territorial Guard, *nisei* civilians on Oahu's Morale Committee, and *nisei* translators in the employ of Naval Intelligence helped to prepare Oahu to resist new Japanese attacks. The Japanese in Japan, of course, had assumed that the whites would round up the *nisei*, which was why they smuggled a *German* spy into Hawaii before Pearl Harbor. But the German was caught in jig time, while *nisei* refused to betray the United States. So the only intelligence the Japanese got on U.S. maneuvers came from occasional overflight by seaplanes. The Americans, by contrast, were eavesdropping on Yamamoto and Ugaki even as they mobilized for the Midway offensive.

"The fate of the nation quite literally depended upon about a dozen men who had devoted their lives and their careers, in peace and war, to radio intelligence." So said Capt. Jasper Holmes of the Joint Intelligence Center, and Admiral Nimitz later agreed. By March 1942 Joseph Rochefort's Hypo office was in the process of breaking the latest Japanese naval code, termed JN25. By monitoring daily traffic the Hypo team learned the approximate location of almost every capital ship in the Imperial Navy. That permitted Rochefort and Capt. Edwin T. Layton, Pacific Fleet Intelligence Officer, to make an educated guess after the Doolittle raid that the Japanese intended to return to Hawaiian waters, with Midway as their probable first target. The intelligence people in Washington did not agree; they thought the "AF" target that appeared in the decrypts meant Pearl Harbor again, or possibly even the U.S. West Coast. It was vital that Nimitz know for sure: after all, he was responsible for defense not only of Hawaii, but Alaska, the approaches to the West Coast and the Panama Canal, and the sea-lanes to Australia. Presently two of his carriers were engaged off New Guinea to thwart a Japanese invasion of Port Moresby and possibly the Australian coast. In the Battle of the Coral Sea, from May 7 to 11, U.S. aviators sunk one Japanese flattop and damaged another, at the cost of the carrier *Lexington*. More important, Yamamoto elected after the battle to hold two of his carriers in port for repairs, reducing his Midway strike force from six to four. No matter, he figured; he would take the Americans again by surprise.

Instead, on May 10, Rochefort and Nimitz suckered the Japanese into revealing the identity of their target. Since Midway Island was a link in the suboceanic cable laid in 1903, Pearl Harbor could talk to it without fear of being overheard. So Rochefort cabled Midway to report back *by radio* that its water distillery was malfunctioning. That news would be significant enough for any listening Japanese ships to report home. Then Rochefort waited, and sure enough, two days later, Japanese on Kwajalein Atoll radioed Tokyo that "AF" had a water problem. Another bonanza buzzed off the airwaves on May 25, when Hypo decoded a message containing the entire Japanese order of battle and the probable day of attack, June 3. Of course, it could have been a false transmission meant to fool the Americans, but only if the Japanese suspected the United States had broken its code, and Nimitz was confident they did not. This time the Americans just might grab the advantage of surprise.

Yamamoto's plan showed all the signs of compromise and "victory disease," the overconfidence born of easy wins. His attack forces were huge but divided into four parts, each with obscure or multiple missions. Nagumo's four carriers and other ships were to soften up the defenses on Midway Island prior to the amphibious assault, as well as attack any U.S. carriers that wandered by. Yamamoto's main body, led by a mighty splay of seven battleships and shielded against submarines by twenty-one destroyers, was to support the Midway invasion but also destroy the remains of the U.S. Pacific fleet, should it dare to interfere. The invasion fleet itself, with its twelve transport ships full of soldiers, would approach from the Marshall Islands and wait to go in. Finally, a task force was to peel off from the main body and conduct a diversionary attack on the Aleutian Islands. The plan was needlessly complicated, but it seemed that the Japanese could not help but overwhelm the outgunned Americans, occupy Midway, and command the seas and skies around the ultimate goal, the Hawaiian Islands.

Nimitz had no choice but to defend Midway, Hawaii's sentry post. But he could not meet this armada head-on. His only chance, as he saw it, was for Adm. Raymond A. Spruance's three carriers to maneuver undetected on to the flank of the Japanese fleet, strike its carriers in hit-and-run style before the invasion began, and pray for a miracle. "I had some anxious and agonizing moments when the Japanese were on their way to Midway," he confessed, but when a U.S. patrol plane radioed at dawn on June 4—"many planes heading Midway"—anxiety dissolved in activity. Within an hour the Japanese carriers were spotted, and land-based bombers from Midway commenced an attack. But the Americans' low-altitude planes were chewed up by the Zeros over the course of a furious hour, while the high-altitude B-17s registered no hits. Then the Japanese squadrons that had been off bombing Midway returned to their ships. This time Genda was determined not to leave the chore half-done and wanted the planes refueled and rearmed for another strike at the island. But Rear Adm. Yamaguchi Tamon objected: it was imperative that planes be launched at once to find and attack the American carriers, even if the bombers returning from Midway had to ditch in the sea for lack of a deck to land on. Nagumo would not hear of that. He insisted on recovering his planes. And once again Nagumo was wrong. For while the Japanese deck crews madly worked to land planes, change their armament, pump fuel, and prepare for a new round of takeoffs, several squadrons of torpedo bombers from the *Enterprise, Hornet,* and *Yorktown* arrived to assault the Japanese carriers. They, too, fought frantically to penetrate the Zeros protecting the carriers, but their planes were inferior and their torpedoes old-fashioned. The American rookies took horrible losses and still could not record a hit. The exhausted Japanese just sighed in relief. They had taken the worst the Americans could give them, and won. Then a "glint in the sun appeared . . . like a beautiful silver waterfall."

An hour before, Lt. Comm. Wade McClusky had made a decision. His squadron of Douglas SBD Dauntless dive bombers from the *Enterprise* reached the point where they expected to find the Japanese fleet, but all they could see was ocean. His planes were low on fuel, so any guess he made now was the last one he was going to get. After a quick glance at his charts and some mental arithmetic he ordered the flight to proceed another thirty-five miles on a west-southwest course, then turn northwest along the reported course of the Japanese carriers. Seven minutes after this "most important decision of the entire action" McClusky spotted a Japanese ship steaming hell-bent for somewhere, probably the fleet from which it had been separated! So he followed, and in ten more minutes there was Japan's First Air Fleet looming below, the decks of its carriers covered with planes, armed and loaded with fuel. Best of all, the Zeros were so low over the water after fighting off the torpedo plane attacks that they had no chance of stopping the "silver waterfall" that dropped down on the Japanese carriers. "Splendid was their tactic," said the *Kaga*'s air officer, "of diving upon our force from the direction of the sun, taking advantage of intermittent clouds." But that was cool retrospection. What the Japanese cried at the time was "Dive bombers!" and "Hell divers!" and within minutes after 10:22 A.M. on June 4, 1942, three of the Japanese aircraft carriers were exploding. Yamaguchi, a Princeton graduate, launched an aerial counterstrike in vain, but a Japanese submarine sank the *Yorktown*. American pilots got their revenge the same afternoon when they found Yamaguchi's *Hiryu* and set her ablaze. Having sunk all four enemy carriers, Spruance ordered a prudent retreat. Yamamoto had no choice but to cancel the Midway invasion and withdraw his main body that had seen no action at all.

As their ships and planes and veteran pilots perished around them, Genda looked at Fuchida Mitsuo, who had led the first wave against Pearl Harbor, and simply said, "We goofed." Spruance said, "We were shot with luck." And between goofs and luck lie dozens of other variables, of which code breaking was probably the most important. Yamamoto wondered afterward if the Americans had known the Japanese plan, and the *Chicago Tribune* committed a terrible breach of security by screaming, "NAVY HAD WORD OF JAP PLAN TO STRIKE AT SEA—KNEW DUTCH HARBOR WAS A FEINT." But luckily for the United States, the cocky Japanese drew the wrong conclusion: a submarine must have stumbled upon them, they thought, and reported their location to Pearl.

The meaning of the Battle of Midway was clear even then. Japan's offensive might was broken, the war would be one of attrition after all, and the United States, its hold on Hawaii secure, could not lose. *Haoles* and *nisei* alike rejoiced.

Attu and Teheran 1943

L EGEND HAS it that even Yamamoto's diversionary attack on the Aleutians helped lose Japan the war. A pilot attacking the U.S. base at Dutch Harbor broke his neck in a crash landing, preventing him from burning his Mitsubishi Zero. The Americans soon located the prize and—so it's said—promptly designed the F6F Hellcat to reclaim the Pacific skies. The legend is false: the F6F was ready to enter production when test flights of the repaired Zero began in California. Still, what Navy pilots learned did much for their tactics and wonders for their morale.

Alaska remained a lodestone for strategists who had never been there. Even Churchill quizzed Roosevelt about why the Americans did not make use of the Aleutians as stepping stones to Japan. But anyone who tried to operate airplanes or warships off its rocky, windy, foggy coasts knew that at current levels of technology Alaska was a sideshow. So defenseless was it before the war that Billy Mitchell called it "the Achilles heel of American defense" and Territorial Gov. Ernest Gruening grumbled that "twenty parachuters could take Alaska." As late as 1939 Alaska's "home defense" consisted of "three hundred infantrymen in Chilkoot barracks, plus one antique cannon left by the Russians and now used as a flower pot." So Congress appropriated $11 million for airfields and bases at Dutch Harbor, Kodiak Island, Anchorage, Fairbanks, and Sitka. Canadians and Americans also surveyed, blasted, and dredged over a thousand miles of new road to complete the Alcan Highway through the Yukon to Fairbanks. By the time of Pearl Harbor, the United States was sending lend-lease aircraft to Russia across the Bering Strait. It was to defend that lifeline against Japanese interdiction that Gruening and Maj. Marvin Marston journeyed to Nome to appeal to the Eskimos—"the first time in history that these natives were regarded as bonafide citizens." Marston trekked around the Seward Peninsula by dog team in temperatures that reached forty-six degrees below zero, telling Eskimos that the Japanese wanted "to drive you out of your villages so they can take the fish, the whale, and the seal for their own people." So Eskimo guardsmen with World War I rifles kept their eyes peeled along the Bering Strait. Theirs was a cold but proud and quiet war.

Not so for the unfortunate Aleuts, who were evacuated once and for all during the battle for the Aleutians. Nimitz had made a slight show of contesting the Japanese invasion, and U.S. planes did succeed in sinking a Japanese transport. But by the end of July 1942 the enemy had 2,400 soldiers on Kiska and Attu. There they sat, waiting like Baranov's Russians for any supply ship Japan might remember to send. Meanwhile, the Americans bulldozed an airstrip out of a drained tidal basin on Adak and harassed Kiska with air raids that would have been laughable were they not so courageous. Engines had to be warmed up with blowtorches before they would turn over in the cold. Ice had to be scraped from wings prior to takeoff, and pilots had to hope for holes in the overcast to find their targets and even home base.

Alaskan defense was the responsibility of none other than General De Witt. Demonstrating the same case of "localitis" (overestimating the import of your own theater) that he displayed in the *nisei* removal, De Witt demanded reinforcements to clear the Japanese out of Alaska. But after August 1942 the Guadalcanal campaign absorbed everything Chief of Staff George Marshall could spare. So he told the Alaskan command to get by with what it had, and it did as soon as Rear Adm. Thomas Kinkaid took over in December. He immediately ordered his little fleet to blockade Attu and Kiska and intercept any supply ships. Tokyo ordered its garrisons to hang on to the Western Aleutians at all costs and in March 1943 dispatched Vice Adm. Hosagaya Moshirō with a swift fleet of cruisers, destroyers, and merchant ships to run Kinkaid's blockade.

The Japanese task force was cruising into the Bering Sea when it bumped into the flotilla of Rear Adm. Charles H. McMorris. He was outgunned almost two to one but ordered his cruisers *Salt Lake City* and *Richmond* to steam within range and bust up the show. An old-fashioned gunnery duel turned the pale subarctic seascape yellow and pink for three and a half hours. The Americans scored several times against the cruiser *Nachi* but could not get at the merchant ships. *Salt Lake City*'s turrets blasted so hard and long that their recoil threw off the ship's steering. Then she took a direct hit, listed to port, and lost power. McMorris had one chance left to save his flagship and the blockade: he ordered his destroyers to run a ten-mile gauntlet of incoming shells and launch torpedo attacks. If Hosagaya hung tough, he might sink the American cruisers and reach his Aleutian garrisons. But his ships were low on ammunition and fuel, and he was loath to risk his own damaged flagship. So the Japanese fleet suddenly retired, McMorris became a hero, and Hosagaya was relieved of command.

This recondite Battle of the Komandorskie Islands encouraged Kinkaid to retake the two Japanese-occupied Aleutians. Nimitz provided three old battleships and the Army Air Forces bombed the Japanese positions for weeks. Finally, on May 11, 1943, eleven thousand American soldiers waded ashore on Attu and tried out their footing in the crusty or spongy tundra of an Alaskan spring. The Japanese were outnumbered five to one, but they dug in on the heights between the U.S. landing points at Holtz Bay and Massacre Valley and rained fire down on the American draftees. The commander wailed it would take six months to dislodge the Japanese, so Kinkaid sacked him and after five terrible days the Yanks captured the heights. The Japanese held out for another ten days until Col. Yamasake Yasuyo ordered his wounded to commit suicide and his eight hundred remaining effectives to fix bayonets. "Only 33 years of living and I am to die here," he wrote. "I have no regrets. Banzai to the Emperor. . . . Goodbye Taeke, my beloved wife." Picking the darkest hour of a foggy night, he then led a suicide charge. The Americans resisted their terror and blasted away until the Japanese were dead or surrounded. The last five hundred held hand grenades to their bellies and pulled the pins.

The campaign ended on August 15 when a bloated force of thirty-five thousand Yanks and Canadians stormed Kiska. They took 313 casualties, but all from mines, accidents, friendly fire, and wild dog bites. For a Japanese task force had slipped in and spirited the garrison away. GI's sang, "O here's to mighty ComNorPac, whose kingdom lay at cold Adak, whose reign was known in fame for fog, and capture of two couple dog." All told, the casualty ratio on Attu was the worst Americans would know in the Pacific until Iwo Jima, while Kiska proved a farce. But the little battle on the roof of the ocean taught them much about amphibious assaults, boosted morale at home, and presaged the rollback of Japanese power.

"The year 1942 is going to pass tonight," wrote Admiral Ugaki in his diary. "How brilliant was the first-stage operation up to April! And what miserable setbacks since Midway in June! The invasion of Hawaii, Fiji, Samoa, and New Caledonia, liberation of India and destruction of the British Far Eastern Fleet have all scattered like dreams. . . . Looking back over all these, my mind was filled with deep feelings." They were not yet feelings of certain defeat but should have been. Just three weeks into the new year, Roosevelt declared at Casablanca that the Allies would fight until unconditional surrender by the Axis powers. That cancelled out the only strategy Japan ever had, which was to bludgeon the

Americans into settling for a negotiated peace. In February 1943, a German army surrendered at Stalingrad and the Japanese withdrew from Guadalcanal. In April Yamamoto was killed, in May the Aleutians fell, and in July Italy surrendered to the Allies.

Japan still occupied a Coprosperity Sphere some fifteen thousand miles in circumference. But the circular reasoning behind it was already exposed. In late 1941 the embargo imposed by the ABCD powers had denied Japan the matériel needed to bring the war in *China* to a satisfactory conclusion. So the Japanese struck south to conquer supplies that in many cases simply *replaced* what they were no longer getting through trade. But the conquest and defense of the new empire only multiplied several times over Japan's material needs. The equation could never be balanced unless China or the United States gave up. The Japanese made matters worse by leaving a million and a half soldiers in Manchuria and China, consigning the Aleutians, Solomons/New Guinea, and central Pacific theaters to small and scattered garrisons. But then, the Japanese Navy and Merchant Marine could not have supported hundreds of thousands of soldiers overseas anyway. As it was, the proud Japanese Navy had to spend half its time shepherding supply ships from the economic colonies to Japan, and from Japan to the island garrisons. Finally, the Japanese Navy ignored its vulnerability to submarine warfare, not even attempting a convoy system until late 1943. Japan *was* another Britain, wholly dependent on seaborne commerce, and the loss of 90 percent of its shipping would prove as crippling as its defeat in battle.

The Big Three—Roosevelt, Stalin, and Churchill—knew by fall 1943 that victory, while not yet imminent, was certain. But what did "victory" mean in a "World War II" that was in fact three or four separate wars that happened to overlap in time or space, and fought by "allies" with contradictory war aims? The Asian war, for instance, began in 1931 (with the Manchurian incident), the Mediterranean war in 1935 (when Italy invaded Abyssinia), the European war in 1939, the Soviet war in 1940 (if one counts the invasion of the Baltics and Finland), and the Pacific war in late 1941. Germany, Italy, and Japan claimed to make up a Tripartite Alliance, but Hitler rarely shared his intentions with his allies, Mussolini launched a "parallel war" in defiance of Hitler, and the Japanese failed to coordinate anything with the Germans. Nor was the Axis even bound by common enemies, thanks to the anomalous Soviet-Japanese Neutrality Treaty. The so-called United Nations were at least united by one common enemy, Germany, but the United States, the British Empire, and the Soviet Union existed in three different dimensions. Britain lived in a monarchical, imperial past, Russia in the totalitarian present, and America (in rhetoric, at least) in a democratic capitalist future. Churchill's goal was to defend the British Empire, but Roosevelt's goals included the dismantling of all colonial empires, while Stalin's were to expand in every direction in the security interests of the USSR, communism, and himself. Throw in the three-way contest in China among the Japanese, Nationalists, and Communists, and one must conclude that Asian/Pacific politics was never so tangled as in 1943.

"It will be a long, hard war," remarked Stanley Hornbeck, "but after it is over Uncle Sam will do the talking in this world." But what would Sam say? In the face of such global complexities the urge was to simplify, and that urge gave rise to four decisions by which Roosevelt meant to shape the postwar Pacific. The first was FDR's surprise announcement at Casablanca to the effect that the Allies would fight on until the unconditional surrender of all their Axis enemies. It was first and foremost a reassurance to Stalin that the Anglo-Americans were not contemplating a separate peace with Hitler. But in the Pacific it meant that the United States was setting aside the balance-of-power logic of MacMurray and Grew to the effect that the destruction of Japan would benefit only Russia. Grew himself even spent the war lecturing the American people on "the dangers of a false, treacherous peace." Japan's fanatical rulers, he said, dreamed of conquering the world even if it took a hundred years. No compromise was possible even if Tokyo made a "jujitsu feint in the realm of diplomacy." Rather, "Totalitarian aggression must be smashed first, and then its stump must be uprooted and burned."

But unconditional surrender raised the obvious question of who would fill the power vacuum that was once the Japanese Coprosperity Sphere? So the second American decision was that U.S. naval and air power must rule the Pacific Ocean after the war. As early as spring 1943 the State Department's Territorial and Security subcommittees concluded that the United States must take control of the Japanese island mandates and surround Japan with bases so that it could never rise again. The most extreme committee member, Capt. H. L. Pence, favored genocide: "They were international bandits and not safe on the face of the earth." Short of that, U.S. military power must embrace the whole ocean, with bases in Korea and Formosa as well as the Philippines and Micronesia. As Pence put it, the Pacific must be "our lake." Admiral Ernest King, Chief of Naval Operations, and Roosevelt himself concurred.

Still, control of the ocean would not allow the United States to reshape the Asian mainland. Indeed, the United States alone might be unable to force Japan into abject surrender without the intolerable bloodshed involved in joining the fighting in China and invading Japan itself. So Roosevelt was determined not only to keep the suffering Chi-

nese fighting until the end but to entice the Soviets to enter the Japanese war as soon as Germany was beaten. Stalin would inevitably
demand a price for such help, so how was the United States to prevent
Russia from replacing Japanese power in Manchuria, Korea, even China?
That question led to the third decision Roosevelt made, to wit, that
Nationalist China be initiated into the club of the great powers and,
with U.S. support and financial aid, made one of the "four policemen"
of the postwar world. In FDR's simplified view, China would join the
United States, USSR, and Britain in a condominium to remake the
world under the auspices of the United Nations. But that would require
Stalin's approval. So the fourth American decision was simply to
promise the Soviets that they could take their pickings of the Japanese
Empire in Russia's traditional spheres of influence *in return for* their
acceptance of Uncle Sam's points 1, 2, and 3: annihilation of Japanese
power with Soviet help; U.S. hegemony in the Pacific; and elevation of
Nationalist China to so-called equality, implying Moscow's abandonment of the Chinese Communists. That way, perhaps, the elimination
of Japanese power might *not* provoke new North Pacific conflicts but
result in a balance between China and Russia monitored by a hegemo-
nial America offshore.

Cordell Hull, seventy-two years old and ailing, had never before
flown in an airplane. But in October 1943 he strapped himself in and
flew to Moscow for a conference of foreign ministers. His mission was
to appease Stalin, who was piqued by the continued delay in the opening
of a second front in France, by the tawdry deal the Americans had cut
with French Fascists in North Africa, and by the Anglo-Americans'
denial of a Soviet role in the surrender and administration of Italy. So
Hull assured Foreign Commissar Molotov that the invasion of France
would occur no later than spring 1944. Their Four Power Declaration
reaffirmed the commitment to fight on until the unconditional surrender of the Axis and to establish "at the earliest practicable date a general
international organization, based on the principle of sovereign equality
of all peace-loving states." The fourth power in the Four Power Declaration was Nationalist China. Molotov was not happy about the elevation
of China to great power status, but Hull indicated how important it was
to Roosevelt when he warned of an interruption in lend-lease aid, "terrific repercussions, both political and military, in the Pacific area," and
"all sorts of readjustments by my government" in the event the USSR
refused to accept China into the club. So Stalin relented and promised to
enter the war against Japan after victory in Europe and to attend a summit meeting with Roosevelt and Churchill.

Still, China was a vexation to Roosevelt. On the one hand, the Chinese had a special claim on American sympathies since they had been

fighting Japan since 1937 and received little help from abroad. That was why the United States extended half a billion dollars' worth of credit and arms to the Nationalist regime and dispatched American airmen to fly supplies "over the hump" of the Himalayas to Chungking. In January 1943 the Roosevelt administration took the added, unprecedented steps of signing away all U.S. extraterritorial rights in China, replacing the 1882 ban on Chinese immigration with an annual (albeit tiny) quota and making Chinese eligible for citizenship. Meanwhile, U.S. war propaganda hailed the heroic efforts of the Chinese people and implored white Americans not to confuse Japanese with Chinese, Koreans, or Filipinos, all of whom "hate the Japs even more they we do." Indeed, the Chinese alliance was the only weapon Britain and America had against Japan's propaganda. The *Christian Science Monitor* wrote in July 1942, "Politically, China is the main bridge between western and eastern cultures. So long as 400,000,000 people of the yellow race belong to the United Nations, Tokyo cannot split the world on the basis of race hatreds, colored against white."

So the intangibles were all in favor of elevating China's postwar role. Unfortunately, the realities were all on the other side of the fulcrum. General Joseph Stilwell had nothing but contempt for the "Peanut" Chiang and his "Chinese cesspool. A gang of thugs with the one idea of perpetuating themselves and their machine." He and Ambassador Clarence Gauss agreed that Chiang preferred to husband his armies and American arms for the eventual showdown with Mao, that Kuomintang officials were corrupt and their soldiers ill-trained, and that a large Anglo-American effort on China's behalf would be wasteful and indecisive. On the other hand, it was imperative that Japanese armies continue to be bogged down in China. Roosevelt's solution to this conundrum was frankly to skimp on military aid but to shower Chiang with *political* gifts to enhance his prestige and give him every incentive to see the war through to the end.

The campaign began with Roosevelt's insistence on a tête-à-tête meeting with Chiang in advance of his summit with Stalin. The crippled and careworn President boarded the battleship *Iowa*, braved the U-boats across the Atlantic, debarked at Oran in Algeria, and flew on to Egypt to make the Generalissimo's acquaintance. Madame Chiang he already knew. She had toured the United States for the Chinese cause, addressed a joint session of Congress, and been received at the White House. Playing the sly and seductive China Doll, she appeared now in a black satin skirt slit up the thigh and proceeded to serve as her husband's interpreter. Roosevelt replied with his own famous charm. He had come to play Santa Claus and needed no prompting. Over dinner he shared his belief that China must rank among the Big Four and flattered

Chiang with an invitation to participate in the postwar occupation of Japan. Chiang declined that responsibility but got all he wanted and more. The Cairo Declaration of November 24, 1943, confirmed that the Allies would make no peace with Japan short of unconditional surrender, that all Pacific islands seized since 1914 would be stripped from Japan, that China would recover all the lands "stolen" since 1894, that Korea would become independent, and that Japan would "be expelled from all other territories which she has taken by violence and greed." The declaration did not say what would happen to these "other territories" (the French, British, and Dutch colonies), but whenever Churchill was absent, Roosevelt and Chiang outdid each other in denunciations of imperialism. FDR also hinted that the United States would doubtless retain a strong military presence in the western Pacific after the war, a prospect that pleased Chiang very much and sweetened the two pills Roosevelt asked him to swallow. First, the Kuomintang must compose its differences with the Communists and unify China. Second, Chiang must make concessions to Stalin in Manchuria in return for the USSR's entering the Japanese war and *not* assisting Mao Tse-tung.

"Stalin—I can handle that old buzzard," said FDR, grinning behind his cigarette holder. Indeed, he had boasted to Churchill, "I think I can handle Stalin better than your Foreign Office or my State Department." The President arrived at Teheran on November 27 with six objects in mind. The first was to allay Soviet suspicions through blatant snubbing of Churchill, thus demonstrating the absence of a bourgeois, Anglo-Saxon cabal. The second was to win Stalin's confidence with an absolute pledge to open the second front in France as early as possible. The third was to elicit Stalin's tacit approval for American offensives in the Pacific, where the United States was already deploying as many planes and more ships and men than in the Atlantic and Europe. The fourth was to secure Stalin's promise to enter the war against Japan. The fifth was to pin Stalin down as best he could on the payment he would want in the Far East. The sixth was to obtain Soviet cooperation in the formation of the United Nations.

Nor were these goals as divorced from reality as they later seemed after Yalta. After all, Japan *was* to be rendered impotent and the Soviet Union *would* emerge from the war as the major continental power in East Asia. That meant that Stalin would be free to grab all he wanted *unless* the United States persuaded him to pretend that China was more than it was, pinned him down to specific demands, and maintained a military presence in the western Pacific sufficient to keep him to his word. Stalin saw reality just as clearly. He indicated his approval of the Cairo Declaration and reportedly assured the President (in what must have been serpentine tones) that "respect for the sovereignty of other countries was a cardinal principle with him." But he also answered the President's question: Russia would indeed declare war against Japan soon after Germany surrendered, and expected in return its ancient rights on the Chinese Eastern Railway, a warm-water port on the Pacific, the southern half of Sakhalin Island, and the entire Kurile chain. Otherwise Stalin recognized Chinese sovereignty in Manchuria, accepted Korean independence "in due course," and implicitly disowned the Chinese Communists.

The Teheran Conference ended in boozy hugs and toasts, and Roosevelt went home to declare that he "got along fine with Marshal Stalin." But as prescient and prudent as the deals he had cut may have seemed at the time, they rested on two outrageous assumptions. The first was that the North Pacific triangle would cease to impose its logic after this war: that the total destruction of Japanese power somehow would *not* provoke a Russo-American rivalry. The other assumption— God bless FDR's optimism—was that China would behave in the way the white men expected.

Saipan 1944

"WE WERE HALFWAY in when word was radioed to land on Blue Beach Two, instead of Blue Beach One, as originally planned. Fire on Blue One was too heavy. . . . In a few minutes our tractor grumbled up onto the reef, lurching tipsily as we crawled over it, giving us the feeling, for that moment, that we were very naked and exposed. . . . Later, approaching the beach, a few more of us braved our heads over the side. Some of the amphtracs had been hit and were flopped over like pancakes on a griddle. . . . There were certainly no Japs. I think most of us would have felt better about it if there had been a few, preferably dead, just to reassure us that they had tried to stop us and hadn't succeeded. Our machine gunner, who had his weapon trained on trees that looked like good nesting places for snipers, turned to me and said, 'It gives me the creeps. Like fighting a bunch of ghosts.' It gave me the creeps, too, although I didn't tell him."

Sergeant Dempsey, a graduate of Yale's drama school, concealed his fear as his company padded single file into a little sugar mill town of brilliant bougainvillea and whitewashed concrete, now pocked and crumbling from naval bombardment. He noticed a baseball diamond the Japanese had laid out, and a Buddhist temple, and a clubhouse of some kind. "Then a shell crashed thunderously in the wooded area just ahead of us. Another came down. And another. There was no time to dig foxholes, so we flattened ourselves behind trees and in the shelter of buildings that were still standing. . . . Then one crashed very close by. There was an emphatic silence, until one of the lieutenants settled the argument in his familiar Harvard accent: 'Definitely hostile,' he announced."

In the waters facing Green Beach, war correspondent Robert Sherrod was still waiting to get ashore. Some landing craft had been lost in the confusion, but "after some of the most effective swearing I ever heard," a general preempted four amphtracs and the reporter reached the beach, then leapt into a tank trap a few yards inland: "We had arrived on Saipan, 1,500 miles from Japan." Shells exploded about them every three seconds for twenty minutes, though most were landing in the drink. Sherrod was deep in a seven-foot bunker dug by the defenders but now sheltering American flesh. Presently the incoming fire let up, like a rainstorm turning to drizzle. "I looked around to see what my corner of Saipan looked like. Along the beach, between the sand and the coral airstrip, there were many small trees which looked like pines and scrub oak. Occasionally there was a flame tree in brilliant orange. . . . I decided it might be a nice place if it were properly fixed up by the Seabees and the engineers." Some corpses started to stink, so the journalist and an artillery officer strolled up the beach. "We saw two dead marines lying on the sand, then two dead Japs. A third marine, a few feet farther north, had had the top of his head neatly carved out, evidently by a shell fragment, and his brains had run out on the sand. . . . In a big shellhole next to the airstrip the Japs had evidently registered a powerful direct hit, killing about six marines who had taken cover there. . . . They were terribly mangled; no more than half of any one man was left. One man's hand, ten feet from the hole, still held the trigger of his piece. Said Captain Swanson, 'That man loved his rifle.'"

June 15, 1944, was the D-day of the Pacific War. For the amphibious assault on Saipan, like the invasion of Normandy the previous week, was the opening blow of the decisive offensive. Once in possession of the Mariana chain—Saipan, Tinian, Guam—Americans could base their B-29 Superfortresses within range of Japan and bomb its cities, factories, and ports until the enemy's will or ability to resist gave out. Tōjō knew it, too. He named the Marianas a key sector in his Absolute National Security Perimeter, rushed thirty-two thousand troops to Saipan with orders to build defenses to "withstand assault by a million men for a hundred years," and got the Navy to promise to risk everything to save Saipan.

It was said of Admiral King, by contrast, that he wanted to fight the Pacific War without allies, in which category he included the U.S. Army. The Chief of Naval Operations did agree to support Gen. Douglas MacArthur's offensives in the Southwest Pacific, but his pet project was good old Plan Orange. King believed the quickest route to victory was directly across the Central Pacific to the Ryukyus and Japanese home islands. MacArthur, viewing the plan as a lever to pry resources away from his theater, called the Central Pacific campaign a pipe dream. Twenty-three hundred miles of open ocean separated Pearl Harbor from the next island chains to the west, the Marshalls and Gilberts. How could the Navy transport invasion forces over such a distance without land-based air cover? But this objection was answered by the dozen fast aircraft carriers armed with Hellcats that arrived at Pearl Harbor in 1943. The carriers, plus hundreds of Liberty ships, the amphibious LSTs and LVTs (landing vehicles tracked, or amphtracs), the Navy's mobile supply bases, and the Seabees' ability to carve out airfields just about anywhere, combined to realize the prophecies of Bywater, Ellis, and Mitchell. The Pacific fleet would span the ocean by degrees, establish air superiority wherever it went, pound selected islands with naval gunfire, disgorge Marines to capture them, and in a few weeks turn them into bases for the next offensive—all the while daring the Japanese fleet to come out and play.

At Casablanca King received Roosevelt's and Churchill's approval for the Central Pacific campaign and ordered a skeptical Nimitz to get cracking. Nimitz in turn put Spruance in charge of the newly created Fifth Fleet and selected Tarawa in the Gilberts as the first major target. The preparations were enormous, but so were the risks. Japanese submarines might intercept the fleet during its thousand-mile approach. The Japanese Combined Fleet might appear from the west in all its force. The landing craft might get hung up on reefs. The defenders might turn Tarawa into a death trap. They had crammed five thousand troops and two hundred coastal guns into a filament of coral and sand just eight hundred yards wide and gouged out such earthworks that Maj. Gen. Holland "Howlin' Mad" Smith said later the "Germans never built anything like this in France. No wonder those bastards were sitting back here laughing at us!" Some Americans hoped that Tarawa would be "another Kiska"—empty of Japanese troops—but instead it was another Attu. The Navy and Marines won Tarawa's 2.8 square miles at a cost of three thousand casualties. But they also learned to deploy landing craft, coordinate naval and air support, organize a beachhead, eject Japanese from their dugouts at least risk, combat snipers, and attack at high tide to avoid getting hung up on the reefs.

Tarawa fell on November 23, 1943, the second day of the Cairo Conference, and Spruance turned at once to the Marshalls. Kwajalein, Roi-Namur, and Eniwetok fell by February 1944, their garrisons resisting to virtually the last man. The next step was another long one—the Marianas lay a thousand miles to the west. But Nimitz and Spruance made the daring and life-saving decision to press on to Saipan without a pause. It was daring because of their proximity to the Philippines, where the undefeated Japanese fleet lurked, and because the admirals' staffs and men were exhausted. "When I came back from the Marshalls I was dead tired," said Kelly Turner, the master of amphibious operations. "I stayed dead tired for the rest of the war." But it was a life-saving decision because it denied the enemy time to prepare. The harried Japanese sol-

diers lacked heavy equipment and construction materials, lost supply
ships to U.S. submarines, and were only half-done with their labors
when Spruance's armada emerged from the ocean.

The American preparations could not have been better. Observation
planes took aerial photographs of Saipan's beaches and inland terrain,
while frogmen bravely searched for underwater obstructions, charted
the reef, and measured water just offshore from the enemy. Marines
rehearsed off Hawaiian beaches in seven hundred landing craft. The
command structures reflected all the lessons learned in the past, while
the supply services shipped several times more ammunition, food, medicine, and insect repellent than had sufficed in previous invasions. The
planes of fifteen aircraft carriers and the guns of fourteen battleships
then pounded Saipan's beaches and bunkers for four days in advance of
the 110 transport ships and 71,034 men of the Second and Fourth
Marine Divisions and Twenty-Seventh Infantry Division. The last leg of
the voyage covered the thousand miles from Eniwetok, and "after six
crowded days aboard an LST, many Marines were ready to fight anybody." Still, their trip to Saipan was not as uncomfortable as that of a
Japanese regiment, thousands of whom had to be pulled from the water
when two of their transports were torpedoed and sunk.

Would there be an enemy left on Saipan after such a preparatory bombardment? A Japanese observing from Tinian felt his heart sink: "The
planes which cover the sky are all the enemy's. They are far and away
more skillful than Japanese planes. Now begins our cave life." Another
on Saipan mourned, "At 0930, enemy naval guns began firing in addition to the aerial bombing. The enemy holds us in utter contempt. If
only we had a hundred planes or so." But the "cave life"—the network
of bunkers and volcanic and limestone caves that covered the heights on
Saipan—afforded the Japanese refuge, while the battleships had to fire
from such extreme range, owing to the fear of mined waters, that their
accuracy suffered. So a reporter was right to fear that "all this smoke
and noise does not mean many Japs killed." Finally, the ingenious plan
devised to spare the Marines the ordeal of being pinned down on
beaches did not work. Their specially designed amphtracs, meant to
blast a path inland before unloading the troops, were too thin-skinned to
resist Japanese shells. So the beaches were littered with the hulks
remarked on by the Yale drama student, and the marines had to fight for
a toehold. One regiment on Red Beach took 35 percent casualties in a
matter of hours, and before the day was done over two thousand Americans were hit.

Saipan was no atoll like Tarawa but an island fourteen miles long by
six and a half wide. The native Chamorros spoke a Spanish of sorts, a
reminder of their discovery by Magellan. After 1899 the Marianas were

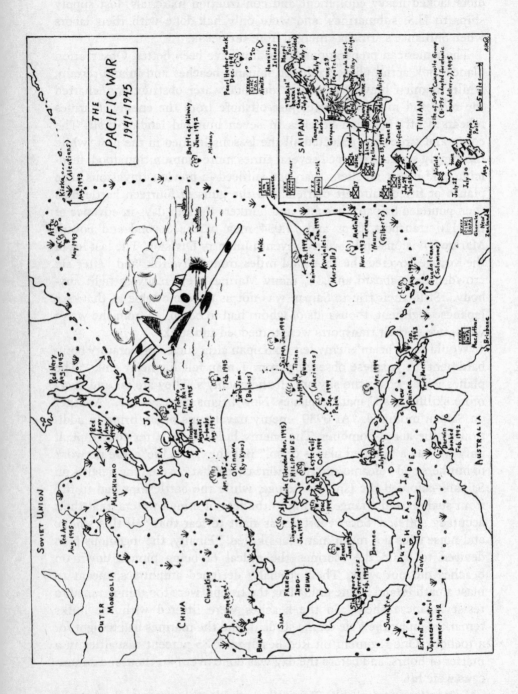

THE
PACIFIC WAR
1941–1945

ruled by Germany (save for American Guam), and after 1914 by Japan. Saipan's twelve thousand residents fished, grew tobacco, harvested copra, and mostly grew sugar (which they distilled into alcohol, much to the delight of visiting servicemen). But what made the island strategic was its location and airfields, and what made it hard to crack were the impenetrable cane fields and swamps and volcanic spine in the interior. For the first ten days Americans were fighting uphill against enemies they could not see except when they burst out to counterattack.

The ranking Japanese on Saipan was none other than Admiral Nagumo, who had come to Saipan to die in atonement for Midway. And since the Army commander for the Marianas was away on Palau when the Americans struck, it devolved upon the Forty-Third Division's Lt. Gen. Saitō Yoshitsugu to lead the 25,500 soldiers and 6,160 sailors on the island. Saitō knew from the start that he had only two chances: counterattack at once and win on the beaches, or drag the battle out until the Japanese Navy arrived to chase off the U.S. fleet. The first option vanished within forty-eight hours. Japanese infantry came screaming out of the swamps on the first night, sometimes shielding themselves with civilians. But the attacks were uncoordinated, as if colonels were trying on their own to obey some vague general order, and the sleepless Marines drove them off. The second night Saitō planned a combined infantry and tank assault, but again the attacks were piece-meal and inept. "The battle evolved itself into a madhouse of noise, tracers, and flashing light. As tanks were hit and set afire, they silhouet-ted other tanks coming out of the flickering shadows to the front or already on top of the squads." Marines fired furiously to their front, rear, and sides with bazookas and grenade launchers, while the tanks rolled about seemingly blind. "The Nips would halt, then jump out of their tanks. Then they would sing songs and wave swords. Finally, one of them would blow a bugle, jump back into their tanks, if they hadn't been hit already. Then we would let them have it with a bazooka."

On the third day Tōjō radioed Nagumo and Saitō that "because the fate of the Japanese Empire depends on the result of your operation, inspire the spirit of officers and men and to the very end continue to destroy the enemy gallantly and persistently; thus alleviate the anxiety of our Emperor." Later that day came a rather more truthful message: "If Saipan is lost, air raids on Tokyo will take place often; therefore you will hold Saipan." Of course, the beleaguered Japanese garrison had no chance of dislodging the Americans, and all the Japanese could do was to contest every acre in the hope that help was coming. It so happened it was. Two days before, an American submarine commander off the Philippine coast had spotted something beautiful through his peri-scope—the entire Japanese Combined Fleet headed toward the Marianas. "The Japs are coming after us," Spruance told Turner and asked if he could get his supply ships and landing craft out of the way. Turner said no: it was the critical point in the buildup onshore, and he would not leave his troops in the lurch. So be it, Spruance replied: "I will . . . try to keep the Japs off your neck."

Saipan thus accomplished what earlier offensives had not: it flushed the Japanese Navy. For as soon as Tokyo learned of the Saipan assault Vice Adm. Ozawa Jisaburō was ordered to execute Operation A-GO, the code name for the anticipated decisive fleet action. Ozawa's fleet was short on fuel so his pilots had little chance to train, and the American task force under Adm. Marc A. Mitscher had fifteen carriers to Ozawa's nine. But the Japanese were in friendly waters this time and hoped for land-based bomber support from Guam or Yap. Moreover, Ozawa contrived to get in the first blow, launching his planes at maximum range as soon as his scouts located the enemy early on June 19. His hope was to pull a "Midway" on the Americans. But just as his rookie pilots began to anticipate a glorious attack after their long approach flight, they were set upon by packs of Hellcats maneuvered by radar to intercept. Most of the Zeros got no further, and those that did ran into torrid antiaircraft fire from the battleships screening Mitscher's carriers. Over three hundred Japanese planes were felled in the "Great Marianas Turkey Shoot."

But the Japanese fleet remained undetected, all that day and the next, as Spruance grew more and more frustrated. Finally, late on the afternoon of June 20 Ozawa's task force was spotted at a range of 275 miles. To go after it now meant condemning the American pilots either to a ditch in the sea as they ran out of fuel on the way home or else to a dangerous nighttime carrier landing. But this was their last chance, and Mitscher said go. As dusk fell over the Philippine Sea, his pilots fought through the Japanese cover to sink one carrier and cripple three others. American submarines bagged two more carriers, for a total of six out of action. Combined with the losses of aircraft and pilots, it spelled the end of Japanese naval aviation. The rest of the fleet got away, provoking much criticism of Spruance. But he hung back for fear that part of Ozawa's fleet might slip into Saipan behind him. And that, after all, was the decisive objective.

"Howlin' Mad" Smith had more troops on Saipan than any Marine officer had ever commanded before. Unfortunately, as he saw it, they were not all Marines. The Twenty-Seventh Division was a National Guard unit out of New York, and he considered its officer corps a "silk stocking" outfit better at planning annual balls than frontal assaults. But he had no choice but to depend on them once the Japanese had been cleared from the south end of Saipan. The Marine divisions held down both flanks when the northern drive began on June 22. But one Army regiment got lost, and the Twenty-Seventh Division commander held back another. The Guardsmen finally got going but made little progress through the spiny, cave-pocked interior. The line bowed into a dangerous U, and "Howlin' Mad" sacked the New York general—a rash act that still raises the hackles of Army and Marine Corps advocates.

The Japanese defenders were painfully short of everything, as one of their generals reported: "The troops have been three days without drinking water but are hanging on by chewing leaves of trees and eating snails." Still, the Americans had to burn them out of their bunkers, trenches, and caves. On June 25 Marines finally scaled the fifteen-hundred-foot summit of Mt. Tapotcha, and by June 30, two weeks after D-day, the Twenty-Seventh Division fought its way through "Death Valley" and over "Purple Heart Ridge" and caught up with the flanks. Now the Americans held the high ground, while the defenders were confined to the northern peninsula. General Saitō radioed home: "Please apologize deeply to the Emperor that we cannot do better than we are doing." By July 6, his forces were compressed into a peninsula less than three miles on a side, save for a coastal strip reaching down to the town of Tanapag. Another few days and the Americans would push them over the cliffs. So Saitō squatted in his cave and dictated a final order: "Whether we attack or whether we stay where we are, there is only death. However, in death there is life. We must utilize this opportunity to exhalt true Japanese manhood. I will advance with those who remain to deliver still another blow to the American Devils, and leave my bones on Saipan as a bulwark of the Pacific."

He did not advance with the others. He ate a ritual last supper of tinned crabmeat and saki, after which he and Nagumo kneeled while officers fired bullets into the back of their skulls. The remaining three thousand Japanese, many in a fearless alcoholic daze, shrieked *"banzai!"* and *"Tennō haika!"* like devils themselves and hurdled into and over the Marines from Tanapag to Hara-kiri Gulch. "It reminded me of one of those old cattle stampede scenes of the movies," wrote a major. "The camera is in a hole in the ground and you see the herd coming and then they leap up and over you and are gone. Only the Japs kept coming and coming. I didn't think they'd ever stop." The marines had been warned that a suicide assault was coming and were prepared as well as one could be for people willing to die in exchange for a slim chance to kill. Gunners set their fuses almost for muzzle burst, fired until overrun, then the infantry fought with carbines, bayonets, and knives. The Japanese, some armed only with swords or "idiot sticks"—bamboo poles with a bayonet attached—died by the hundreds and finally the thousands until "the whole area seemed to be a mass of dead bodies, stinking guts and brains." But "The Raid," as it was evermore known, did pin two Marine battalions against the coast. A regiment of the Twenty-Seventh was ordered to rescue them, but its colonel hung back, fearing for his own flank. At that point "Howlin' Mad" put the whole division in reserve and swore he would never serve with it again. But his contempt was for the officers, not for soldiers like Medal of Honor winner Sgt. Thomas A. Baker. Wounded in "The Raid," he told his buddies just to prop him up against a tree and save themselves. The next day they found eight Japanese bodies piled in front of his own.

Incredibly, there was worse to come. When resistance ended on July 9, Japanese civilians began to hurl themselves over the cliffs—men, women, pregnant women, children, babies thrown by their parents, civilians thrown by soldiers, even as Americans with loudspeakers pleaded with them to stop. Many believed in suicide before surrender, others that the Americans would rape, enslave, disfigure, torture, murder, even eat them. So thousands of civilians joined the thirty-one thousand Japanese and thirty-one hundred American fighting men killed on Saipan. Japanese just seemed to insist on genocide or suicide, and so in their own way did Americans. For soon, the airfields of Saipan, Tinian, and Guam bristled with Boeing B-29s, designed and built for no other mission than to incinerate Japanese cities. "When we lost Saipan," said Hirohito's naval adviser, "Hell is on us."

It is now customary to refer to all this as a "race war." Some Japanese never considered it anything else. The whole plan had been to bully China into subservience, then lead all Asia in an antiwhite crusade. Once Pearl Harbor removed the last need for restraint, publications in Japan habitually referred to "the barbaric tribe of Americans [who] are devils in human skin" and interpreted Japanese history as one long struggle against the whites. The Yamato race, as children of gods, was the *shidō minzoku*, the superior race in the world. Japanese were pure, all other races were sullied, and whites in particular were *oni*, variously translated as "demon," "ogre," "devil," or "fiend." The initial victories won by Japan seemed to prove that whites were craven and lacked martial spirit. They were jealous of their miserable lives and surrendered rather than die like men. When Japan began to suffer defeats, its propaganda concentrated on American wickedness as was evidenced by the sinking of hospital ships, torture of captives, and gleeful bombing of civilians. Japanese cartoons depicted Roosevelt and Churchill with devil's horns and the Christian cross as a dagger. But FDR would be crucified in the end, for according to the tradition of *hakko ichiū* the eight corners of the world were destined to be covered by a Japanese roof, whereupon hedonism, individualism, and liberalism would be combed like dandruff from the heads of the liberated: "For the Japanese, the Greater East Asia War is a purifying exorcism, a cleansing ablution."

Nor were these only the fantasies of fanatical military officers. The Thought Bureau of the Japanese Ministry of Education issued the *Cardinal Principles of National Polity*, according to which Japanese were superior to other Asians by dint of a "national character that is cloudless, pure, and honest," and all Asians were superior to whites. The Ministry of Health and Welfare echoed the Mayor of Los Angeles to the effect that "blood told," inspired a National Eugenics Law, and encouraged Japanese to expand their population to one hundred million to colonize their Empire. The Kyoto School of philosophers argued that war is "eternal," the "creative and constructive" mechanism by which Japan's "unique racial power" would express itself and take away the sins of the world. A geography professor officially renamed America the "Eastern Asia Continent" and referred to all oceans as the "Great Sea of Japan." The Population and Race Section of the Ministry of Health drafted a four-thousand-page report entitled *An Investigation of Global Policy With the Yamato Race as Nucleus.*

But had not the military seized almost totalitarian control over the government, schools, and economy? Perhaps these expressions of a racist, expansionist ideology were born of fear and conformity more than conviction? To put it the other way around, no liberals, socialists, or Christians among the Japanese elite were likely to voice their dissent during the war. That is so, but the fact remains that little existed in Japanese mythology, official religion, political culture, or economic theory to throw up conceptual or moral *barriers* to a racist view of the world. The homogeneity and isolation of the Japanese people, the veneration of obedience, loyalty, hierarchy, community, and sacrifice, State Shinto's lack of an absolute moral code, the hatred of Western imperialism and resentment of unequal treatment, and the autarkic economics of the Coprosperity Sphere—there was much in Japan's culture and historical encounter with the West that complemented or could be exploited by the otherwise Nazified rhetoric of Japanese war propaganda.

By contrast, the racial content of the Pacific war for Americans was tortured, confused, and ultimately guilt-ridden. Americans were Judeo-Christian, democratic, individualist, and multiethnic. White Americans gave vent to their deepest dark urges during the war, in part because of white supremacist fantasies, in part because of Yellow Peril hysteria, but in part because the enemy invited them to. The Japanese, after all, had raped China, sneak-attacked Pearl Harbor, tortured and killed prisoners of war, blown up Marines after pretending to surrender, mutilated corpses, and staged bloodcurdling human-wave attacks. Let scholars concoct anthropological, sociological, or Freudian hypotheses to explain the behavior, the fact was that war in the Pacific was kill-or-be-killed. Just as Americans seemed to Japanese to be demons or animals—big, hairy, smelly, and brutish—so did Japanese appear to Americans to be monkeys with machine guns, insects on the swarm, reptiles slinking in tall grass, or an octopus with a million tentacles. They had, in any case, to be exterminated.

But something about it was ugly and wrong, and that is why American attitudes were more like a photographic negative than a mirror image of Japanese propaganda. To begin with, the official U.S. government line was that the war was about freedom and democracy, not race and conquest. And even when its propaganda contained "yellow peril" content, it was aimed at Japan, not Asians as a whole. U.S. propagandists went to extremes to extol Chinese heroism and solidarity, and to rebut propaganda to the effect that Japan was fighting for all colored peoples (including American blacks). That is not to say that the American public did not give vent to stereotypes and hatreds they had previously applied to the Chinese as well. Many white Americans nurtured hatreds and fears about the Oriental hordes, projected them onto the enemy of the moment, and did so with savage self-righteousness. The troops in the field likewise carried prejudices with them from civilian life and may have viewed the anti-Japanese, pro-Chinese propaganda as cynically as they viewed everything else the Army spoon-fed them. But American fighting men are an empirical lot. They are not prone to examine their consciences for unresolved racial anxieties before deciding whether to risk taking prisoners. The Pacific war began deceitful and brutal, and grew ever more so as reciprocal atrocities fed on each other. The Japanese soldier's embrace of death, the American soldier's love of life and gonads, and the utter contempt in which each held the other drove both to extremes in a cycle of violence that ironically gave credence to the propaganda of both.

The major difference between them, though, was that Japanese believed that their racial will to power was virtuous, validated by the cult of the nation and emperor. Most Americans knew deep down that racial hatred was wrong, tabooed by the Declaration of Independence and, somewhere in there, the Bible. Did that make Americans better, or worse, than the Japanese?

Nagasaki 1945

O N JULY 26, 1944, Pearl Harbor played host to the Commander-in-Chief, but General MacArthur, pulling up to the dock in a stretch limousine, received the loudest ovations. He had been lambasting Roosevelt for months and was rumored to want the Republican nomination. He also wanted to liberate the Philippines, an operation jeopardized by the Navy's success. Admiral Nimitz wanted to continue the Central Pacific drive and avoid a bloody and time-consuming war in the Philippines. But MacArthur hammered for three hours (he gave the President a headache) on the political dangers of abandoning "18 million Christian American citizens [sic] to wither in the Philippines under the conqueror's heel." That would confirm Japanese propaganda to the effect that whites would not shed blood for the sake of Asians, damage America's prestige in a part of the world destined to "determine the course of history . . . for the next ten thousand years," and (incidentally) harm FDR's reelection chances. MacArthur later claimed that Roosevelt approved his Philippine invasion in return for MacArthur's electoral support. The truth was that, inasmuch as the Army and Navy Chiefs, Marshall and King, did not accompany the President to Hawaii, no new strategies could have been made. In any case, Nimitz and MacArthur were both mistaken about how, and by whom, Japan would be beaten.

Long before Pearl Harbor, in fact on the day the Germans invaded Poland, the chief of the Air Corps Plans Division argued the probability that "sustained air attack alone would be sufficient to force Japanese acquiescence in our national policies." He was Lt. Col. Carl Spaatz, and he wanted to build the B-29, a gigantic four-engine bomber capable of flying the vast distances required for a Pacific war. General H. H. "Hap" Arnold approved the project in 1940, and three years later, after an expenditure comparable to that for the atomic Manhattan Project, Boeing rolled out the first operational Superfortress. It was the dreadnought of piston-engined aviation, designed for a range of 3,500 miles at cruising altitudes above 25,000 feet and a ground speed of 250 MPH. Crews had to wear oxygen masks and heated flight suits in a pressurized cabin. But what made the B-29 a complete weapons system was a new explosive, the M-69 incendiary. Each bomb contained thirty-eight canisters of jellied gasoline, or napalm, and each B-29 could carry forty such bombs. Testing suggested that under proper conditions firebombing might consume a medium-sized city. Arnold gave Roosevelt his "Air Plan for the Defeat of Japan" in August 1943. All he needed was bases within range.

The first available choice was China, where Chennault's Flying Tiger command developed into an elaborate air force flying cover for the Nationalist Army. But his bases could not handle B-29s, so three hundred thousand Chinese draftees set out with primitive tools to build runways and hangars. It reminded observers of the heroic construction of the Burma Road, or even "the building of the great pyramid of Cheops." On June 14, 1944, a day before the invasion of Saipan, sixty B-29s took off from China to bomb steel works on the island of Kyushu. It was the first air raid on the home islands since Doolittle, and the shame of it and the loss of Saipan made Japanese ask, "Why hasn't Tōjō committed suicide yet?" In fact, Tōjō resigned in disgrace on July 20, and the new cabinet and Supreme War Council set out to protect Japan from the monster B-29s. The Army's ICHI-GO ("Number One") Plan was an all-out offensive to knock China out of the war and overrun the B-29 bases, while the Navy's SHO-GO ("Victory") Plan was meant to destroy the American fleet in preparation for the reconquest of the Marianas. Instead, the Japanese Navy all but perished in the Battle of Leyte Gulf in October, but the Army drove relentlessly forward until the U.S. Army Air Forces pulled the B-29s out of China in January 1945 and transferred them to a new bomber command based in the Marianas.

General Curtis LeMay was a gruff, muttering, cigar-chomping thirty-nine-year-old apostle of air power from Columbus, Ohio. He had studied the air war in Europe, as Mitchell had done in World War I, and drawn the same conclusion: strategic bombardment was potentially decisive if the right tactics were devised and exploited. A B-29 raid on the docks at Hankow, one of the last launched from China, had shown the potential of napalm. As soon as he reached Saipan, LeMay put his crews on a schedule of training and experimental runs over Japanese targets, and learned that high-level precision bombing of military targets was no more effective there than in Germany. If Americans were not to waste their air power and needlessly prolong the war, they must give up their scruples about collateral damage and destroy the cities that housed Japan's war industry. Moreover, the first B-29s over Japan encountered what we call the jet stream, that rush of air above thirty thousand feet that sweeps eastward across the Pacific at speeds up to five hundred miles per hour. Fighting the jet stream drained fuel and made precision bombing impossible. There were even times when ground speed dipped below zero, and a plane simply backed off its target! So beginning on February 4, LeMay experimented with high-altitude precision bombing with incendiaries over Kobe, then high-altitude area bombing over Tokyo, and finally, low-altitude area bombing. He was searching for the exact mix that would allow him to ignite a city as one puts a match to a newspaper.

The day of the Kobe raid a dying Roosevelt arrived in the Crimea for his second summit with Stalin and Churchill. He and his colleagues and most critics since believed the encounter was crucial, the last chance to plan a good peace and save the wartime alliance. But the Yalta accords, on East Asia at least, were not new or surprising at all. Nor did FDR's concessions stem from his frailty or gullibility or deafness to Churchill's warnings or the influence of Communist agents. He *was* frail, *did* have a fatheaded belief in his ability to charm Uncle Joe, *did* snub Churchill, and *did* have spies in his camp. But far from selling out China in exchange for Soviet help that was no longer needed, Roosevelt just ratified American policy as laid down at Casablanca, Cairo, and Teheran, and it is hard to imagine his doing otherwise.

That was so, because in February 1945 the war with Japan was far from over, and growing more hideous week by week. Kamikaze planes had begun to torment the American fleet, and the battle for the Philippines was reaching its peak. Almost every major American commander was eager for the Red Army to pin down or destroy the Kwantung Army in Manchuria and Korea. LeMay's strategic campaign had barely begun, while the atomic bomb was still in gestation. Who could say if or when it would work, or whether its power would be so great as to end the war at a blow? But even if FDR *had* now preferred that the Soviets stay out of the war with Japan, there was nothing he could do to stop them. Japan was crumbling and China was weak and splintered, while Germany's defeat would free the Soviets to load dozens of divisions aboard the Trans-Siberian. Stalin was bound to inherit leverage in Asia and could use it in a number of ways. He could cut his own deal with Japan, receiving Manchuria in exchange for a promise *not* to enter the war. Or he could request the same spoils from the United States and China in exchange for joining the war. Or he could back Mao's Communists and hope to make all of China a client.

Roosevelt's task was clear: persuade Stalin to join the anti-Japanese alliance and then *pin him down* on the price he would ask in return. That was what Teheran had been about, and that was why Ambassador

Averell Harriman continued to press the matter. In December 1944, at Harriman's request, Stalin candidly named his terms: all of Sakhalin Island and the Kuriles, a lease on the Chinese Eastern Railway, access to Dairen and Port Arthur, and Outer Mongolian independence (viz., as a Communist satellite). At Yalta, Roosevelt was pleased when Stalin suggested putting his terms in writing. They agreed that their deal should remain secret until a time of Roosevelt's choosing, and that the United States would encourage Chiang to negotiate a treaty with the USSR. The incipient superpowers also agreed to set up a joint commission for Korea until it was ready for self-government. In every case, FDR gave Stalin nothing he could not have gotten from Japan or China through diplomacy or force. His aim was to *define* the limits of Russian Pacific power.

Meanwhile, LeMay's experiments came to an end when he told a pilot returning from Toyko, "I think we can do it." But what was "it"? Did he mean he could send waves of B-29s to Tokyo and back without major losses of airplanes and crews? Or burn Tokyo to the ground in a maelstrom of liquid fire? Or solve an intellectual puzzle about tactics and prove a point about air power? Or bring Japan to its knees in the shortest possible time and save hundreds of thousands of American lives? Or win for the Air Force a major role in the postwar defense establishment? "It" was all of those things, but absent from LeMay's priorities were the noncombatants doomed by "it." Americans had begun the war by denouncing enemies who coldly employed urban terror bombing. That was the Fascist way of war. They now proposed to end it by perfecting the enemy's methods. But LeMay would say that that was tendentious. "Actually, I think it's more immoral to use *less* force than necessary, than it is to use *more.* If you use less force, you kill off more of humanity in the long run because you are merely protracting the struggle." The Marines suffering twenty-seven thousand casualties in the battle for Iwo Jima no doubt agreed, as did the families of servicemen and almost all Americans in 1945 with the exception of some Quakers and Roman Catholic prelates.

General Lauris Norstad feared no moral rebuke when he briefed reporters on Guam: "If over three hundred aircraft take off you should release that number. . . . In order to establish foundation for what may be an outstanding show, you should leave no doubt that this is an important operation." Norstad went to sleep, but LeMay could not. He stayed up drinking Cokes and worrying while his B-29s were on their seven-hour flight to Tokyo. If this raid works, he said, "I don't think [the enemy] can keep his cities from being burned down—wiped right off the map."

"Bombs Away" crackled in on the radio soon after midnight on March 9, and 325 Superfortresses with names like *Texas Doll, South-*

ern Belle, God's Will, and *Sting Shift* began to unload their M-69 napalm. It took two and a half hours, during which time the canisters (in the words of a French reporter) "scattered a kind of flaming dew that skittered along the roofs, setting fire to everything it splashed and spreading a wash of dancing flames everywhere." The Asakusa ward west of the Sumida River and the working-class wards east of the river were especially chosen for their flammability, and LeMay's experiment was favored by a nocturnal wind "almost as violent as a spring typhoon." Soon thousands of fires merged into two conflagrations, walls of flame pushing before them air so hot that whole blocks ignited with a whoosh. The infernos leaped forward to grab any fleeing people whose padded hoods and leggings, issued as protection, had not already burst into flame, turning them into staggering torches. Others looked down to find their shoes and trousers on fire from the heat of the street until their feet turned to char and they fell to roast on the pavement. Thousands leaped from high bridges into the river's late-winter waters, with the result that by next morning, as a Japanese doctor described, "countless bodies were floating, clothed bodies, naked bodies, all as black as charcoal."

The capital was still burning when the last B-29s landed in the Marianas after noon the next day, and continued to burn until the flames gave out at the wide canals of the city's east end. Over 250,000 buildings were destroyed, about a quarter of the city, leaving over a million homeless and 83,793 dead, according to the punctilious statisticians of the Tokyo police. The *New York Times* reported: "CENTER OF TOKYO DEVASTATED BY FIRE BOMBS," called it a holocaust, but did not condemn it. LeMay noted in his diary that "the heart of the city is completely gutted by fire," called it the "most devastating raid in the history of aerial warfare," and went to work planning attacks on other industrial cities.

The Japanese military authorities had systematically lied to their people from the Battle of Midway onward. Only grudgingly, and in allusive language, did they report any setbacks for Japanese arms, and only then as a goad to greater sacrifice, greater obedience. But General LeMay broke their spell. Nagoye, Osaka, Kobe, and dozens of other cities burned under B-29s. Their voices are drowned out now by those of Hiroshima and Nagasaki, but at the time they were an eloquent national witness against the bad advisers surrounding the Emperor. City dwellers fled to the countryside, where smug peasants said it only served them right. Social unrest began to appear, and challenges to propaganda. When Germany surrendered on May 8, Foreign Minister Tōgō Shigenori went before the Supreme War Council to suggest a stunning new policy: Japan should offer the Soviet Union southern Sakhalin, the

CER, Port Arthur, Mongolia, if necessary even the Kuriles in return for help in getting Japan an acceptable peace. "If a ship is doomed," an official explained, "what matter its cargo, however precious? Jettison the cargo as fast as possible, if only doing so may save the ship."

Hirota Koki was sent to beseech Soviet Ambassador Iakov A. Malik at his mountain retreat from the American bombers. The Soviets had already given notice that they considered the 1941 neutrality treaty defunct, and Hirota's job was to revive it. In retrospect this may seem like grasping at straws, but it was not so farfetched in the context of the North Pacific triangle. As Russia had accepted U.S. mediation in 1905 lest Japan grow too mighty through war, so now Japan was seeking Russian mediation lest the United States win too complete a victory. But there was no percentage in Stalin's playing the honest broker. The Soviets could get what they wanted *with U.S. and Chinese approval,* so why should they tie their kite to a dying Japan and incur the wrath of the Americans? Now, a three-way balance *could* have been restored in 1945, but only if the *United States* chose to pull out of the war and let Japan remain a military power in Manchuria. Needless to say, that was unthinkable to U.S. officials and public opinion; hence the Japanese Empire was doomed, hence the Soviets had no reason to parlay. Over and over again Hirota assured Malik of Japan's "passionate desire" for friendship. But Malik delayed skillfully until, on July 1, 1945, the *real* negotiations on postwar Asia began. That was when the Chinese Foreign Minister arrived in Moscow to negotiate a Sino-Soviet treaty.

Ending the war on Allied terms was the new Truman administration's obsession as well. But what could be done to induce the Japanese to surrender? The first way was to invade the home islands and dictate peace terms on the steps of the Imperial Palace. Operation OLYMPIC called for an amphibious invasion of Kyushu and preparations for it were ordered on May 25. But the Chiefs of Staff shuddered to imagine the casualties that would involve. The battle of Okinawa was another hellish scene of flamethrowers and volcanic caves, *banzai* charges, mass suicides, and kamikazes crashing on the decks of American ships. Anything was preferable to another year of that. A second means of ending the war was to jettison the unconditional surrender conceit and offer Japan terms it could swallow. That was why a wizened group led by Grew, Stimson, and Navy Secretary James Forestall began urging Truman to make an appeal to the Japanese, assuring them that surrender did not mean extinction but only "the termination of the influence of the military leaders who have brought Japan to the present brink of disaster." But Tokyo dismissed Truman's first such appeal as propaganda. A State/War/Navy committee then went to work on a new declaration to be issued by the Allies from the Potsdam Conference. Just before it convened on July 17, Hirohito declared his "wishes that peace be restored as quickly as possible for the benefit of the human race." But "so long as the United States and England insist on unconditional surrender in the Greater East Asia War, Japan cannot but fight to the last with everyone joining hands for the sake of honor and the existence of the fatherland."

The new Secretary of State, James Byrnes, carried with him to Potsdam a draft declaration inviting Japan to surrender *and* indicating, as Grew had suggested, that Japan might retain a "constitutional monarchy under the present dynasty." Why was this phrase so important? First, because for Japanese to lose the Emperor would be tantamount to national death anyway, so they might as well go down fighting. Second, no one else in Japan had the authority to make the people lay down their arms. Third, Hirohito was unlikely to buck his die-hard militarists unless he were assured of his postwar dignity. He did not want to abdicate. But now look at it from the American side. How could the Allies guarantee the survival of a political system many deemed the root cause of Japanese militarism, or profess to try war criminals while pardoning the man most responsible for their deeds? But the telling arguments were those of the military. Admiral Leahy informed Truman at Potsdam that in the opinion of the Joint Chiefs the reference to the monarchy was problematical. If the Allies promised a "constitutional" monarchy, Japanese zealots might take it as a repudiation of the current Emperor and reject it, while others might see it as a promise that emperor worship might continue as it had in the past. Above all, it was "inadvisable to make any statement or take any action at the present time that would make it difficult or impossible to utilize the authority of the Emperor to direct a surrender of the Japanese forces." That is, the Americans *needed* a divine, almighty emperor to help them persuade the Japanese to quit! But at the same time, they dared not imply that a god-emperor could reign as in the past *after* the surrender. It just seemed better to say nothing.

The Potsdam Declaration of July 26 warned that Japan's forces would meet "inevitable and complete destruction" and Japan's homeland "utter devastation" if it did not make an unconditional surrender. It made no mention of the Emperor. So Japanese Premier Adm. Suzuki Kantarō called it "a rehash of the Cairo Declaration, and the government therefore does not consider it of great importance. We must *mokusatsu* it" (kill it with silence). The next day, Tōgō urged his ambassador to make another appeal to the Soviets. "Since the loss of one day relative to this present matter may result in a thousand years of regret, it is requested that you immediately have a talk with Molotov." But Molotov was at Potsdam with Stalin, who casually told his allies that he had another offer from Tokyo. "The document does not contain anything new. We intend to reply in the same spirit as the last time." Japan was helpless and utterly alone.

The third way to induce a Japanese surrender was through ever more terrible aerial bombardment to demonstrate that national extinction was a real possibility. The Army Air Force in the Marianas believed it was on the verge of achieving just that. How long would the war last, General Arnold asked LeMay in June 1945? "Give me thirty minutes and I'll give you a date," LeMay replied, then came up with September 1, for by then his bombers would have run out of targets. But the Japanese had absorbed firebombing for months and refused to give up. That was why the atomic bomb seemed a godsend. The Alamogordo test occurred during the Potsdam Conference, and the materials for the two existing bombs were shipped out through the Golden Gate to the Marianas on Spruance's old flagship, the *Indianapolis*. Truman said he never lost any sleep over the decision: "I regarded the bomb as a military weapon and never had any doubt that it should be used." In fact Truman never had to sign an authorization. The orders simply passed down the military chain of command from War Secretary Stimson to Col. Paul Tibbets on Tinian. His top secret 509th Composite Group had completed rigorous training to learn how to deliver a single very heavy bomb with pinpoint accuracy, then bank the hell out of the way. (The 509th was located at the corner of Eighth Avenue and 125th Street, off Riverside Drive, homesick airmen having laid out the island like Manhattan.) On August 3 LeMay arrived with orders naming Hiroshima primary target, and when no subsequent orders arrived to countermand them, the *Enola Gay* and its chase plane, both adapted B-29s, took off at 2:45 A.M. on August 6. The chaplain committed their crews to Almighty God in the prayer that peace on earth might soon be restored.

Americans believe queer things about the atomic bombings. Some think that members of the crews later committed suicide. One did, years later, but he was a manic depressive. Some believe that the bomb ushered in the age of apocalypse, as if World War I, Hitler, Stalin, and the Rape of Nanking had not already happened, or for that matter Britain's bombing of Germany or LeMay's fire raids on Japan. Some believe that the United States dropped the bomb on Japan rather than Germany out of racism. But Germany had surrendered before the bomb was even tested, and an A-bomb on Berlin could not have done more damage than the firebombings of Hamburg and Dresden. Some believe that the real reason for dropping the bomb was to intimidate the Russians, and Stimson and Byrnes did speculate that the bomb would be useful in dealing with Stalin. But if the Americans *were* already thinking in Cold War terms and were bent on containing Soviet power in

Asia, then why did they not do the sensible thing and negotiate a compromise peace with *Japan* any time after May 8, 1945? *That* would have been the way to block the Soviets. Instead, Truman honored the Yalta accords to the letter. Finally, some people believe that one or both of the atomic bombs were unnecessary. Perhaps they were. But the main rationale for their use was to help the peace faction in Tokyo win out at court and save countless American *and* Japanese lives.

The peace faction did not triumph at once. Suzuki and Tōgō told the Emperor the truth about the implications of the "new-type bomb" employed at Hiroshima and urged an immediate offer of peace. But the military blocked a surrender by refusing to attend the cabinet meeting. The same day, crews on Tinian loaded up the second atomic bomb and prepared to take off for Japan. In between time, on August 8, Molotov invited the Japanese Ambassador to the Kremlin. "Loyal to its Allied duty," he said, "the Soviet Government . . . has joined in the [Potsdam] declaration of the Allied Powers of July 26. The Soviet Government considers that this policy is the only means able to bring peace nearer. . . . In view of the above, the Soviet Government declares that from tomorrow, that is August 9, the Soviet Government will consider itself to be at war with Japan." It was three months to the day since the German surrender: Stalin, too, honored his promise at Yalta. He then encouraged his soldiers "to efface the shame of forty years before" as Red Army divisions sliced through the depleted and demoralized Kwantung units. By August 25 the Russians reached Port Arthur and Manchuria changed hands again, while the Red Navy took over the Kuriles.

Meanwhile the Chinese negotiators had been delaying and bargaining in Moscow just as Li Hung-chang, agent of an earlier weak Chinese regime, had done over fifty years before. On August 14 they signed a Sino-Soviet Treaty of Friendship and Alliance. Nationalist China acquiesced in a Russian concession at Dairen, a Russian naval base at Port Arthur, joint operation of *all* Manchurian railroads, and an independent Outer Mongolia. The Soviets recognized China's sovereignty over Manchuria and Sinkiang and promised to send military aid to the Nationalist government, implicitly abandoning China's Communists. Chiang Kai-shek allowed as how he was "generally satisfied with the treaty." It seemed to ensure him all China proper and the friendship of the United States and the USSR both.

The Japanese War Council convened on August 9 in the presence of the Emperor to discuss the disastrous news from Moscow. It was still in session when the report arrived that a second atomic bomb had been dropped. Even now the military brass refused to accept terms that would subject Japan to the pollution of a foreign occupation. All day and night the debate dragged on until, at 2:00 A.M. in the bomb shelter of the

Imperial Palace, the Emperor spoke. The war, he noted bitterly, had not progressed exactly as the military had led him to expect. The only way now to save the nation was to accept the Potsdam Declaration on condition "that the said declaration does not comprise any demand which prejudices the prerogatives of His Majesty as Sovereign Ruler." The Truman administration hurriedly huddled and wired a reply: "The ultimate form of government of Japan shall, in accordance with the Potsdam Declaration, be established by the freely expressed will of the Japanese people." Then the Americans waited a day, another day, and another day, while the hard-liners in Tokyo protested the ambiguous language. On August 14 Marquis Kido Kōichi, Keeper of the Privy Seal, convinced the Emperor to make his will known in Imperial Council. The air raid shelter of the palace was the stage on which Hirohito read his famous lines: "I fear that the national polity will be destroyed, and the nation annihilated. It is therefore my wish that we bear the unbearable and accept the Allied reply." He later recorded a message to be aired over national radio. A cabal of young officers, in a final fanatical spasm, invaded the palace bent on smashing the disk containing the Voice of the Sacred Crane before it could air at noon the next day. General Tanaka Shinichi turned them away. "Follow the Imperial Will," he said, "and stop this foolishness."

Dr. Nagai Takashi, a nuclear physicist who lost his wife to the second atomic bomb, gave thanks that it tipped the political balance against the militarists. He believed that Providence had steered the B-29 to its secondary target of Nagasaki, the city where the Shogun had crucified Christianity in the seventeenth century, and had steered the bomb away from its target above a munitions plant so it exploded instead above the Catholic Urakami Cathedral: "Nagasaki, the only holy place in all Japan—was it not chosen as a victim, a pure lamb, to be slaughtered and burned on the altar of sacrifice to expiate the sins committed by humanity in the Second World War?" Recovering from his radiation sickness, Dr. Nagai believed he had stood at the foot of a cross, and devoted his life to life.

A hundred miles to the east, on the other coast of Kyushu, Admiral Ugaki strained to hear the Emperor's broadcast, for his radio's reception was bad. Then he drove out to an airfield and asked to board a kamikaze. Every pilot shouted for the honor of joining him in death. "I am going to proceed to Okinawa, where our men lost their lives like cherry blossoms, and ram into the arrogant American ships, displaying the real spirit of the Japanese warrior. All units under my command shall keep my will in mind, overcome every conceivable difficulty, rebuild a strong armed force, and make our empire last forever. The emperor *Banzai!*"

Tokyo 1948

THE WHITE STAR painted on the sides of American warplanes was more "luminous with hope and joy and peace and good will for man than was the star which heralded the birth of Jesus Christ in Bethlehem." So wrote the aviation editor for the *New York Herald Tribune* in 1945. Religion and ideology had both failed the world, but power now lay in the hands of a people devoted to peace and goodwill, while the Air Force star was a "a symbol of undefeated idealism to isolated millions . . . who will find God in the throb of an engine." The Catholic magazine *Commonweal* protested the sacrilege and feared lest the "demons of vainglory and pride" possess the national soul. Still, Americans were rather pleased with themselves for having saved the world and considered their augmented power a just reward. Thanks to the devastation of Europe, Russia, and Japan, the United States flaunted almost half the world's industrial production, the only healthy currency, a globe-girdling network of sea, land, and air forces, and a technological hegemony symbolized by the atomic bomb.

The West Coast especially felt the rush of omnipotence. World War II had been good to it, boosting population another 30 percent and tripling its total economy on the strength of military contracts. It was fitting that San Francisco hosted the conference that founded the United Nations, for the American Century now dawning was also to be the Pacific Century, and the Pacific Ocean was an American lake. To be sure, the Philippines had been promised independence, and received it in 1946. But Filipinos loved Americans, MacArthur most of all, and were pleased to play host to American military bases. As for the rest of the central Pacific, the new Pentagon expected to swallow it all. Had "these atolls, these island harbors," said Admiral King, not "been paid for by the sacrifice of American blood"? So the State Department insisted that the UN transform the old Japanese mandates into U.S.

trust territories, and got its way (over Soviet and Australian demurrals) in 1947. Finally, the Pentagon wanted the Ryukyu Islands. Secretary of State Byrnes feared the United States might be "stepping outside the zone of its legitimate political and regional interests," but plans for an Okinawa base went ahead, pending a Japanese peace conference.

What it meant, California editorials were pleased to report, was that the frontier of white civilization now lay at the doorstep of Asia. And far from fearing another attack from that quarter, Americans could now set about realizing their dream of remaking Asia in their image. Only two counterweights to American power existed. The first was the third member of the old North Pacific triangle, Russia. And as if to warn of the rivalry that must now break out between the two survivors, Siberia remained the only Pacific shore in which Yanks were still off-limits. Even during the war Stalin refused to grant the United States landing rights there and only at Potsdam permitted ninety Americans to set up "radio stations and weather controls at Khabarovsk and Petropavlovsk." They did not arrive before the Japanese surrender, were set upon by NKVD agents demanding their ciphers and codes, and were expelled in December, taking with them whatever equipment was "not frozen to the ground." Needless to say, they saw no evidence of the slave camps that by then contained over four hundred thousand Japanese prisoners seized in Manchuria.

Stalin and Molotov asked several times for a role in the occupation of Japan, perhaps even a Soviet zone on Hokkaido. Truman refused, and Stalin did not press. Perhaps he figured a gracious retreat on Japan would inspire the Americans to leave him alone to sack and communize east Germany and Poland. But even the exclusion of the Russians did not leave the United States utterly free to remake Japan. For the second counterweight to American power was the Japanese themselves.

Throughout all the years of dictatorship the old Japanese establishment—call them liberals by comparison with the Tōjō regime—had lain low awaiting a time when they might steer Japan back to sanity. Like resisters in Nazi Germany, these Japanese noblemen, businessmen, politicians, and officials formed circles, and one such, the Yohansen group under Prince Konoe and Yoshida Shigeru, sneaked a message to the Emperor in spring 1945 warning of the "communist revolution which may accompany defeat." They argued that only by surrendering to the Americans did Japan stand a chance of saving the imperial system and recovering under something resembling Taishō democracy. When the Emperor finally leaped through that bolt-hole in August, these pre-Fascist elites came out of hiding, ready to welcome and sway the Americans.

Yoshida was stout and a mere five feet tall, son of a Yokohama businessman and a *geisha*, and raised as an adopted child. He took a degree from Tokyo University, married into the nobility, and joined the diplomatic corps. In 1928 the military got him removed as Consul in Mukden for opposing "direct action" in Manchuria, but he went on to serve as Ambassador in Rome and in 1932 was offered Washington. Yoshida thought "[t]he national character of the United States is such as to make it basically not very dependable in diplomacy," and turned it down. That was what cleared the way for Saitō Hirosi. In 1936, after the 2/26 bloodbath, Yoshida also had a shot at the Foreign Ministry, but the Army said no. So instead of presiding over the China incident in 1937, Yoshida was sent to London and became an Anglophile. His friendship with Grew, ouster by the military in 1939, and arrest by the thought police in 1945 completed the making of his liberal image. Yoshida was obviously a "good" Japanese, and like those of Adenauer in Germany, his postwar plans were to humor the victors, frustrate their more radical efforts to transform society, and exploit their quarrel with Russia to restore Japanese prosperity and sovereignty. And since Yoshida could count on thousands of like-minded civil servants and businessmen, no ephemeral occupation would be entirely free to remake Japan. Not even Douglas MacArthur's.

"Mr. Prima Donna, Brass Hat, Five Star MacArthur," growled Truman in June 1945. "He's worse than the Cabots and the Lodges—they at least talked with one another before they told God what to do. Mac tells God right off." But such were MacArthur's popularity and prestige in Asia that Truman had no choice but to make him the SCAP (Supreme Commander for the Allied Powers) in Japan. And who is to say he was not an inspired selection? When he flew into Japan on August 30 and descended unarmed into a country still filled with hundreds of thousands of brainwashed soldiers, MacArthur earned his mandate to rule. Churchill thought it one of the bravest acts in history, and a Japanese editor called it "a gesture of trust in the good faith of the Japanese. It was a masterpiece of psychology which completely disarmed Japanese apprehensions." From that moment on, Japanese veneration of the blue-eyed shogun was a byword. A *New Yorker* cartoon depicted a Japanese couple showing off their new baby: "We've decided to name him Douglas." A Japanese journalist wrote a best-selling biography that portrayed MacArthur as a "living god." One of his most beloved acts was to order Japanese baseball leagues to resume play at once in any stadia that were not bombed out. Nor was MacArthur the only American to make a good impression. Yoshida told the story of being waved over on a country road soon after the surrender and approached by two GI's. His fears disappeared when they simply asked for a ride to Tokyo and forced chocolates, gum, and cigarettes upon him and his driver. The "inherent good nature of the average American," he concluded, was what "enabled the Occupation of Japan to be completed without a shot being fired." A cliché perhaps, but one spread as much by foreigners as by the Yanks themselves.

Above all, the Japanese image of the white devil flip-flopped to what it had been in the early Meiji era: the foreign teacher from whom we must learn. Did that mean Japanese wanted to be like Americans, or accepted inferior status? On the contrary, they recruited lower-caste women to volunteer for prostitution lest GI's sully Yamato bloodlines indiscriminately. Rather, the Occupation was another mountain to be climbed, but a time, like the early Meiji, during which Japan would acquire the Western skills needed to compete with the West. Consider that nowhere in Hirohito's radio address to his subjects did he suggest that Japan had lost. "How odd that proclamation was," wrote a French journalist, "and how Japanese in spirit! How prudently it dealt with the future, how careful not to tarnish the book of Japanese history with the forbidden word 'surrender.'" The Japanese elites instead invoked the bamboo that "bent with the breeze but did not break. With the passing of the breeze, the bamboo straightened again."

Official American attitudes also lurched back to what they had been before the turn of the century. The military pulled Frank Capra's classic film *Know Your Enemy—Japan* only weeks after its release in 1945 because it depicted the Japanese as crazed worker and soldier ants. Instead, the War Department began to phase in an image of the Japanese as childlike people misled by wicked rulers. Above all, committees of experts in Washington prepared agendas by which the Occupation might deliver Japan (as Stimson put it) back to its "liberal leaders" and make it a "useful member of the future Pacific community." The first was the surrender instrument itself that subjected the Emperor and the cabinet to the orders of SCAP (as the whole Occupation came to be known) and directed that Japan be disarmed and democratized. The State Department's Initial United States Post-Surrender Policy called for a purge of militarists and their exponents in government, democratization of industry and agriculture, and reversal of Japan's "feudal or authoritarian tendencies."

According to Theodore Cohen, a veteran of SCAP, the instructions MacArthur took most seriously were those contained in his *military* orders, because they stated that "in addition to the conventional powers of a military occupant of enemy territory, you have the power to take any steps deemed advisable and proper by you to effectuate . . . the provisions of the Potsdam Declaration." The sum of these directives was a virtual invitation to MacArthur to make the Occupation the occasion for a social, political, economic, and cultural revolution. In a master-work of verbal economy, the general summarized them as follows:

> First, destroy the military power. Punish war criminals. Build the struc-ture of representative government. Modernize the constitution. Hold free elections. Enfranchise the women. Release the political prisoners. Liberate the farmers. Establish a free labor movement. Encourage a free economy. Abolish police oppression. Develop a free and responsible press. Liberalize education. Decentralize political power. Separate the church from state.

All this was very American, but the program also reflected scholarly opinion as to how militarism had permeated just about every aspect of Japanese society.

MacArthur, like God, "did not choose to expose himself," wrote a journalist of his life in Japan. Each morning he was driven from the U.S. embassy to the SCAP headquarters in the Dai Ichi Insurance Building in downtown Tokyo. There he presided over a bureaucracy that included some exceptionally skilled linguists, lawyers, economists, educators, social scientists, and soldiers mixed in with military and civil service deadbeats and carpetbaggers happy to join in a victory party in which cocktails cost a dime, servants came by the half-dozen, and geisha and single men abounded. But even the most brilliant administrators were uninitiated into the secrets of Japanese social and business life, and were far too few to administer a nation of seventy millions. So SCAP's first decision was to employ indirect rule and trust Japanese civil servants to execute its decrees.

That, in turn, would be impossible without the Emperor's assent. But happily, Hirohito needed MacArthur, too, for he alone stood between the Tennō and the loss of the throne, perhaps even a war crimes trial. Hirohito took the first step by humbling himself before the Supreme Commander at the U.S. embassy on September 27. MacArthur buoyed him up, praised his decision to end the war, and asked for his help in carrying out the directives of SCAP. They met every six months there-after, signaling that MacArthur intended to shelter the Emperor and that the Emperor blessed the Occupation. Thanks to this alliance, MacArthur could boast by October that seven million armed men had stacked their weapons, and that the Japanese Army and Navy "are now completely abolished."

A tsunami of reform filled the next two hundred days. SCAP ordered all political prisoners released from jail, disbanded the thought police, and began the purge of militarists. In the end, 210,288 people were banned from public life (at least until the Americans ceased checking up on them, changed their minds about the purge, or went home). Japanese schools were made to remove their shrines that housed the Emperor's portrait and Meiji Rescript on Education, while American pedagogues revised courses and textbooks just as the *yatoi* did in the 1870s. But the deepest revolution was in politics. MacArthur's lawyers set aside Itō Hirobumi's Meiji constitution and drafted a new charter that began, "We the Japanese People." The Emperor reigned on as the "symbol of the state", but his personal estates and other magnificent holdings were nationalized in the name of popular sovereignty. Even Hirohito's desk became "property of the state."

SCAP's constitution made the Japanese cabinet responsible to the majority in a Diet elected by universal male *and* female suffrage. The famous Article 9 renounced for Japan the establishment of armed forces or resort to war, meaning that Japan must depend on some other nation for its defense, obviously the United States. This and other disagreeable features of the constitution provoked resistance even from the moderate, obsequious postwar ministers, so "good cop" MacArthur deputized "bad cop," Gen. Courtney Whitney, to persuade them. Meeting with the Japanese in Yoshida's garden, Whitney breezily said, "We are out here enjoying the warmth of atomic energy," which line he considered a "psychological shaft." Reminding his hosts that MacArthur was the Emperor's protector, he added, "General MacArthur feels that this is the last opportunity for the conservative group considered by many to be reactionary, to remain in power. . . . I cannot emphasize too strongly that the acceptance of the draft Constitution is your only hope of survival." Yoshida's face was "dark and grim and his expression did not change." But on March 6, MacArthur expressed "deep satisfaction that I am today able to announce a decision of the Emperor and Government of Japan to submit to the Japanese people a new and enlightened constitution which has my full approval."

MacArthur was obsessed with Japan's religious life. He misread the docility of the people as a sign of anomie and was eager that Christianity fill the void left behind by Hirohito's magnificent renunciation. On January 1, 1946, the Emperor admonished his subjects to cease considering him of divine ancestry. In the same message he also warned against all "radical tendencies." MacArthur was ecstatic, advised Washington of his plan "to increase greatly Christian influence in Japan" (Truman scribbled: "I approve"), and wrote an open letter to the Southern Baptist convention to apprise them of "an opportunity without counterpart since the birth of Christ for the spread of Christianity among the peoples of the Far East." He called for eleven million Bibles and imagined Japanese Christians spearheading a spiritual offensive that would sweep across Asia, carry democracy and Christianity to the "billion of these Oriental people on the shores of the Pacific," and "fundamentally alter the course of world history." SCAP did introduce freedom of religion, but Japanese remained stubbornly resistant to the blandishments of missionaries.

Two million Japanese died in the war and 8.5 million were homeless. Sixty-six cities had burned and $26 billion in property was destroyed. A fifth of Japan's industrial plant was in ruins, and the rest was worn out or obsolete. Japan lost its Empire and access to materials and markets everywhere. The yen was in free-fall, inflation was rife, and the average working-class family earned less than half of a subsistence wage. The Potsdam Declaration called on Japan to pay reparations, for instance, to Chinese and Filipinos, but instead American taxpayers had to pay $350 to $400 million per year just to keep Japanese from starving. One lasting reform was in agriculture. SCAP distributed the land of estates among the tenant farmers, who then became a large, conservative force in Japanese politics. But in industry SCAP built up the Left by promoting unionization. Within a year four million workers were organized, the Socialist Party won their votes, Communists agitated, and the unions tried out their new liberties in a wave of strikes. SCAP reformers also explored the secret passages of the *zaibatsu* financial pyramids. At the top, as MacArthur put it, were "about ten Japanese families who practiced a kind of private socialism." The old family firms and more modern "concerns" controlled the stock of lesser banks and holding companies that in turn owned dozens of firms that in turn owned scores of subsidiaries. Nor did these vertically integrated colossi compete with one another, for corporate directors habitually met in their private dining rooms and gardens to coordinate prices and market shares in collaboration with government ministries. No wonder a SCAP wag wrote: "There's something rather fishy / About the Mitsubishi / And the rest of the *zaibatsu* / Are also not so hot-su."

No SCAP policies were more controversial than the industrial, for here the tasks of reform and recovery competed with each other. Politics added to the confusion insofar as MacArthur spied in any order from Washington a plot to curtail his authority, while conservatives and liberals in Tokyo and Washington accused each other of nefarious agendas. When SCAP moved against the *zaibatsu*, conservatives cried out that SCAP was in thrall to left-wing New Dealers. When the impulse for reform originated at home, MacArthur railed against the Reds in Washington. The result was that the otherwise free-market policy of trust-busting came to be seen as communistic, while policies friendly to Japan's traditional oligarchies came to be seen as good capitalism. MacArthur's ego and political ambitions also contributed to the confusion, but its root cause was this: insofar as reform delayed Japan's economic recovery, it played into the hands of Communists agitating among the working classes. So as time passed, American policy shifted from one of attacking big business to one of working with the elites to boost productivity. And that gave the old Japanese liberals the chance to fashion the Japan they wanted.

During the war *zaibatsu* and concerns put up with the militarists, but the Japanese war economy was, in retrospect, surprisingly inefficient. Japanese businessmen always preferred civilian government to Tōjō-type warmongers, not least because they bankrolled the parliamentary parties and had the politicians in their pockets. The militarists, by comparison, were statist, puritanical risk takers. Now the old business/parliamentarian alliance reemerged to deflect SCAP policy into desired channels. As Yoshida recalled, "Being a good loser does not mean saying yes to everything the other party says. . . . It was obviously important to co-operate with the Occupation authorities to the best of one's power. But it seemed to me that where the men within GHQ were mistaken, through their ignorance of the actual facts concerned with my country, it was my duty to explain it to them; and should their decision nevertheless be carried through, to abide by it until they themselves came to see that they had made a mistake." In time the Americans would need Japan, whereupon "the business world will be improved not only by the advancement of science but also by inviting in American capital."

SCAP experts did in fact shatter Mitsui and Mitsubishi into hundreds of supposedly independent firms. But as always they had to work through Japanese intermediaries whose own future careers would doubtless depend on the patronage of the businessmen they were called on to punish. Nor could a handful of Americans prevent the executives of each spinoff company from collaborating in the same old ways, or recombining after the Americans turned their backs. Anyway, Yoshida pleaded that "it would be a great mistake to regard Japan's financial leaders as a bunch of criminals," and that "modern Japan owed her prosperity largely to their endeavours." In 1947, Americans began to listen. Japan was still in ruins, a drain on the American treasury, and the scene of violent labor agitation. MacArthur acknowledged this in his message on the anniversary of the surrender: "Over all things and all men in this sphere of the universe hangs the dread uncertainty arising from impinging ideologies." Whether freedom or communism would prevail was "the great issue which confronts our task in the problem of Japan—a problem which profoundly affects the destiny of all men and the future course of all civilization." On January 31, 1947, he was compelled to suppress a general strike, and in April the Socialists emerged as the largest party in the Diet. Meanwhile, the old American Japan lobby began to denounce SCAP for trying to do too much too fast, and urged accommodation with Japanese institutions and elites. In January 1947 Harry F. Kern and Averell Harriman inspired a story in *Newsweek* that charged SCAP with purging thirty thousand of "the most active, efficient, cultured, and cosmopolitan" leaders in Japan instead of employing them to help fight the Communist menace. James L. Kauffmann, an expert on Japanese business, accused SCAP of making Japan go "under the knife of the economic quack" in pursuit of a "socialistic ideal," while Japanese labor ran "hog wild." He recommended a high-level mission to rein in SCAP's wild-eyed reformers.

MacArthur responded in the usual way: he called a press conference and lambasted his critics without regard for the chain of command. Thanks to SCAP, he said, Japan had undergone a "spiritual revolution" at little cost to the American taxpayer. If there were still economic problems, Washington was to blame. His purpose, he assured reporters, was not to keep Japan down, but rather "to keep Japan up." Perhaps, but the Japan lobby caught the ear of the administration at the critical moment in the early Cold War. The Truman Doctrine was announced in March 1947, the Marshall Plan in June, and the bill creating the National Security Council, Central Intelligence Agency, and independent Air Force passed Congress in July. George F. Kennan had outlined the new strategy of containment in the spring, and his emphasis on economic and political action to thwart communism had obvious implications for Japan. In a high-profile speech in May 1947, Dean Acheson— the same official who cut off oil to Japan in 1941—blamed the world's distress on the wreck of the "greatest workshops of Europe and Asia— Germany and Japan," and called for emergency aid to both former enemies. In September, Kennan told the War College that the United States must restore the prosperity of Europe and Japan, lest they be tempted by communism.

The scouts Truman chose in February 1948 to sniff out MacArthur's defenses were Kennan and Army Undersecretary William H. Draper, Jr., a Wall Street mover and shaker. George Marshall briefed Kennan on MacArthur's personality, so he was prepared when the general subjected him to an endless tirade late on the night of his arrival in Tokyo. The weary diplomat said not a word, then collapsed into bed. In their second meeting, however, Kennan led off by sharing viewpoints he knew they had in common, won the general's confidence, then sat back to let him discredit himself. Soon MacArthur was railing against those who criticized the purge and anti-*zaibatsu* legislation. The businessmen ousted were "elderly incompetents" that reminded him of "the most effete New York club men"; any hint of socialism was the work of leftists sent him by Washington; the real achievement was the conversion of Asia to Christianity, which, thanks to him, was proceeding apace. Kennan professed to be shocked by the "fragile psychic quality" at MacArthur's court and the philistinism of the Americans, obsessed as they were with cocktail parties, servants, and ski trips to Hokkaido. Most of all, he thought SCAP's economics "unintelligible to most Japanese" and put his own staff to work on a comprehensive new program.

Kennan considered his reversal of Japanese Occupation policy second only to the Marshall Plan as "the most significant contribution I was ever able to make in government." He might have ranked the two equally since the "reverse course" in Japan was the functional equivalent of Marshall aid in Europe. Completed in June 1948, it made economic recovery the centerpiece of Occupation policy, called for an end to disruptive reforms and reparations, a rollback of labor union prerogatives, and cooperation with business and government to boost Japanese exports and earn foreign currency. Draper agreed that Japan under SCAP was a "morgue" and a hotbed of socialism. He and the economist Ralph W. Reid recommended that the Tokyo government allocate raw materials, balance its budget, fix the exchange rate of the yen, and favor exports over domestic consumption (which is why labor unions had to be disciplined).

Truman approved the "reverse course" in December—his first imposition on MacArthur's fiefdom—and sent the Detroit banker Joseph Dodge to Tokyo to implement it. MacArthur growled like a dog protecting a bone, and one cannot help feeling a certain sympathy for him. But MacArthur's heart was no longer in the battle. He was tired of the job as resident god and lost interest in everything after the Wisconsin primary killed his chances for the 1948 Republican nomination. Anyway, he agreed with much of the new course. So, too, did the Japanese leadership. In March 1948 the two center-right parties merged to form the Liberal Democrats. An updated version of the Seiyukai party, it covered most of the political spectrum and relegated the Left to permanent minority status. After elections in October the Liberal Democrats formed the first of a succession of cabinets that was still unbroken after forty-five years. Yoshida returned as Prime Minister, the purges and war crimes trials came to abrupt ends, big business reconnected, and the Ministry of International Trade and Investment (MITI) emerged to coordinate the drive for overseas markets. American business, responding to the call of the Japan lobby, undertook joint ventures and infused Japan with American capital and technology.

The new Japan was not all that new. In many ways it resembled the Japan of the 1920s minus the military influence. But that was no mean accomplishment, and one for which MacArthur deserves credit. Moreover, said Kaufmann, Japan was "still the leading nation in ability, respect for law and order, and desire to work," and it was important that it emerge as "the buffer against Soviet Russia on our Pacific side." But what would a prosperous and secure Japan require? First, it would need access to markets and raw materials, either in the United States itself or in East Asia. So four years after Hiroshima, Kennan worried how the "Japanese are going to get along unless they again reopen some sort of empire to the South," and a SCAP economist confessed: "We have got to get Japan back into, I am afraid, the old Co-Prosperity Sphere." The second thing Japan would need was protection. Now, all the wonderful Occupation reforms were supposed to have vetted Japanese society of militaristic tendencies, but the SCAP constitution nevertheless implied that the United States must now assume the burden of defending not only Japan but its former Co-Prosperity Sphere from Korea to Southeast Asia. No wonder Richard Nixon, in 1953, referred to the demilitarization of Japan as "an honest mistake."

Perhaps it was, for by then the United States had already been at war for three more years in the North Pacific.

Korea 1950

THERE NEVER REALLY WAS a Cold War in Asia but rather a succession of hot wars lasting for thirty years. Nor did the Chinese civil war fit Cold War categories, for the Soviets were not sure they wanted the Communists to win, the Americans were convinced that the Nationalists could not win, and both the USSR and the United States lost in the end. How droll that it all redounded to the benefit of Japan. But such is the logic of the North Pacific triangle.

The first big stake in the postwar melee was the right to inherit the turf and the weapons of surrendering Japanese. MacArthur thus ordered Japanese units in China to surrender to Nationalists only and sent fifty thousand U.S. Marines to Shantung, while General Wedemeyer put planes at Chiang's disposal to rush troops to northern China. Such intervention might seem provocative, but as Acheson put the problem: "If you told the Japs to throw down their arms on the ground and march to the seaboard, that entire country [northern China] would be taken over by the Communists." Much of it was in any case. The Red Army did not turn Manchuria over to Chiang's officials until May 1946, by which time the Soviets had stripped the region of industrial plant and armed tens of thousands of Communists with Japanese weapons. Chiang was foolish to occupy Manchuria, but against American advice he deployed five hundred thousand of his best soldiers there in the very months that Mao's cadres fanned out to organize peasants and slaughter their landlords. Both sides prepared to resume the civil war interrupted by Japan eight years before.

We cannot now know Stalin's mind, but his thinking must have run something like this. It was splendid that Russia had now recouped all the privileges in Manchuria enjoyed by the tsar before 1904, and faced a China weak and likely to remain divided. The Chinese Communists were like a David facing a Kuomintang Goliath, and if they ever looked like winning the Americans would surely intervene to prevent it. The only apparent danger was that Chiang's forces might receive enough U.S. aid to crush the Communists and create a strong, unified, pro-Western China. Hence the USSR must give the Maoists enough support to ensure their survival, but not so much or so openly as to provoke U.S. intervention. That way the Russians might enjoy their informal empire in rich Manchuria while posing as a loyal anti-imperialist. Civil strife in China was always good for Russia.

For the United States, by contrast, China's civil war was disastrous. Either the Communists would topple Chiang's corrupt regime, or else the Americans would have to prop it up for who knew how long. So Truman, like Roosevelt, sent high-ranking mediators in an attempt to broker a "democratic and united China." Now, multiplying two negatives yields a positive product in mathematics but never in politics. General Hurley did manage to get Mao to come to Chungking, but Chiang refused to compromise. Hurley quit and Truman replaced him with General Marshall. Wedemeyer greeted America's top soldier in Shanghai and told him, "Sir, the Nationalists, the Kuomintang, have all the power here, and I can assure you they are not going to relinquish one iota. And the Communists are determined to get all the power here, and they have an alien supporter—Moscow. . . . You have come here on an impossible mission." Marshall vowed to prove him wrong.

Chiang and Mao were both reluctant to snub an American of such stature, so under Marshall's whip they agreed to a cease-fire and a preliminary plan to merge their armies. Mao and Chou En-lai pandered shamelessly, claiming that "we Chinese Communists . . . do not mean, nor deem it possible, to carry [socialism] into effect in the immediate future. . . . we mean to acquire U.S. styled democracy and science." They also assured Marshall that the Communist party was not a front for the Soviet Union. The second claim was largely true, the first was a lie. But a gratified Marshall flew home in March 1946 to secure for China $500 million in credits. In his absence fierce battles broke out in Manchuria. So Marshall crossed the ocean again and arranged another truce. But in July Chiang went back on the attack, confident of U.S. support. Did not the Americans themselves joke that their policy in China was to be "neutral against the Communists"?

Marshall went home for good in January 1947, bemoaning "irreconcilable groups" that held China under "feudal control." He expected that administrative rot, inflation, and overextension of the Nationalist armies would sooner or later produce a disaster from which the United States would be wise to remain aloof. In fact, Nationalist armies overran Yenan, the Communist stronghold, in March 1947, but it was Chiang's last victory, and he should have known it was an empty one. After all, the Japanese had chased him out of *two* capitals, and occupied cities and rail lines, and victory still eluded them. What was more, his army was not disciplined and fanatical and had few strengths other than the American weapons that his own officers hawked on the black market. But the greatest Nationalist handicap was that the Communists knew how to mobilize the countryside, while the Kuomintang cared nothing for peasants. China was an empire of peasants.

For a year and a half the Communists quietly trained and armed their rural recruits until their armies numbered 2 million against the Kuomintang's 3.7 million. In the summer and fall of 1947 Lin Piao's units launched a conventional offensive against exposed Nationalist garrisons, knocked 150,000 enemy soldiers out of the war in Manchuria alone, and purged whole districts of landlords and Kuomintang sympathizers. Said one Red cadre, "There were not a few persons beaten to death." Cut off from all outside help, Nationalist garrisons died on the vine of hunger, despair, and bullets. By mid-1948 only a huge American intervention could have saved the Nationalists in the north. But Truman and Marshall would not consider intervention until the Kuomintang made reforms. MacArthur's comment on this pious requirement was that it was like trying to "alter the structural design of a house while the same was being consumed by flames." He wanted to whip the Communists and worry about reform afterward. Truman finally proposed another $570 million for Chiang, but by the time it went into effect in late 1948 the game in China was over. Manchurian garrisons numbering 470,000 capitulated one after another, and the Communists took over Mukden on November 2. It was only a matter of months before they drove into Peking from the north. The U.S. ambassador cabled home: "We reluctantly reach conclusion that early fall present Nationalist Government is inevitable."

Chiang's last hope was for a Republican victory in the election of 1948. The GOP had been out of power for sixteen years, and it spied in the Communist menace a winning electoral issue. Truman's upset victory killed that hope. After Tientsin and Peking fell to the Communists in January 1949 and Nanking in April, Acheson drafted a white paper to preempt or deflect charges that the Democrats had somehow "lost" China: "The unfortunate but inescapable fact is that the ominous result of the civil war in China was beyond the control of the government of the United States. Nothing that this country did or could have done within the reasonable limits of its capabilities could have changed the result."

It was a bold admission but a weak defense. For if the Communists were the threat Truman said they were, how could his administration have stood by while the world's most populous nation went Communist? Putting emotions and politics aside (which at the time no American could do), one can offer a fourfold answer. First, the United States could allow it to happen because China was not a strategic priority of the same rank as the industrial zones of Japan and Europe. Second, the government could allow it to happen because the American people—especially the frugal Republicans—demanded that Washington bring the boys home, cut the defense budget, and convert to a peacetime economy. Third, it could happen because, as Acheson documented, all money and arms delivered to Chiang seemed to go down a rathole. Fourth, the United States could stand seeing the Communists win because their victory was *not necessarily in the Soviet interest.* Acheson expressed the hope that "ultimately the profound civilization and the democratic individualism of China will reassert themselves and she will throw off the foreign yoke." A Sino-Soviet split was inevitable, and if Mao did succeed in making China strong and united, then so much the worse for Russia.

Did Stalin suspect that a Communist triumph in China was the worst thing that could happen to the Soviet Union? Perhaps not, but then he was probably banking on the United States to support Chiang to the end. Then the civil war would drag on and on, leaving Russia secure in Manchuria and making Mao dependent on Moscow. Instead, the United States proved to be the "paper tiger" Mao said it was, "outwardly strong but inwardly weak." We do know that when Mao's armies rolled over southern China and he proclaimed a People's Republic in October 1949, Stalin was silent. There were no headlines or boastful editorials in *Pravda,* no celebration at all of the glorious triumph of a fraternal Communist party. No wonder, for now Stalin would have to play the good Marxist and *stop* playing Russian imperialist.

On December 16, 1949, Mao arrived in Moscow by train. Chou En-lai joined him in January, and the two did not leave until the middle of February 1950. Would that the transcripts of *those* negotiations fall into the hands of scholars someday! By the time they were over, the 1945 sweetheart treaty the Soviets signed with China was gone. Gone were their dreams of a base at Port Arthur and commercial rights at Dairen. Gone was Russian management of *any* Manchurian railroads. But worst of all for Stalin was this: the Maoist victory, and this first equal treaty between China and Russia, meant that now there were *two* world Communist leaders, and if two, then none.

But that was not the reality Stalin and Mao displayed to the world. Rather, to Acheson's embarrassment, the world saw the leaders of the largest and most populous countries signing a treaty of friendship and assistance, and a solemn alliance for mutual aid in case of aggression by Japan or "any other state which should unite with Japan, directly or indirectly, in acts of aggression." Acheson had said, in a phrase he regretted, that he would "wait until the dust settles" before fashioning a new China policy. Now it *had* seemingly settled, the whole Asian coast from Siberia to South Vietnam was either communist or contested by Communists, and the only Western foothold was beleaguered South Korea.

In Korean eyes, the United States deserted their country in 1910 and left them to suffer unrelieved exploitation under the guns of a self-described master race. Not until 1942, when Korean exiles came begging for recognition and a chance to help in the Allied cause, did the United States take official notice of the Hermit Kingdom. Nationalist leader-in-exile Synghman Rhee tried to persuade Cordell Hull of the "war potential of twenty-three million Koreans," and warned that another American failure to act would result in "the creation of a communist state" in Korea following the defeat of Japan. Hornbeck, the old China hand, reported that Korea's future would "be of paramount importance to Soviet Russia and to China," and that Korean Communists were being trained in Siberia. A State Department memo went further, describing Korea as a "tempting opportunity" for the Soviet Union to "occupy a dominating strategic position in relation to both China and to Japan." Roosevelt's solution, as we know, was an international trusteeship pending Korean independence. Under no circumstances must it fall united into hostile hands.

Yet that was the danger on August 10, 1945, after the USSR declared war on Japan. Colonel Charles H. Bonesteel and Maj. Dean Rusk of the State/War/Navy Coordinating Committee met long into the night pondering John J. McCloy's assignment that they "come up with a proposal which could harmonize the political desire to have U.S. forces receive the surrender as far north as possible and the obvious limitations on the ability of the U.S. forces to reach the area." Bonesteel and Rusk chose the thirty-eighth parallel, by coincidence the same line of partition Russia and Japan discussed before 1904. It cut Korea almost in half and left Seoul in the American zone. To their amazement, Stalin accepted.

The convoy bearing the American corps of occupation reached the port of Inchon on September 8, 1945. General John R. Hodge, a country boy from Illinois, was in command, and MacArthur gave open instructions of the sort he relished himself: "You will take such action on this matter in southern Korea as future events may justify." Now, Korean political activists were arming themselves and reducing the country to anarchy. The Yanks knew almost nothing of Korea, its language, or the identity of its Communists. As a result, Hodge enlisted the aid of Japan's colonial bureaucrats in setting up his military government. He then proceeded to stage his own "two hundred days" of reform, only his targets were indigenous leftists, not Fascists or collaborators. "All groups seemed to have the common ideas," reported a State Department adviser, "of seizing Japanese property, ejecting the Japanese from Korea, and achieving immediate independence. Beyond this they have few ideas. . . . Korea is completely ripe for agitators."

There is much to ponder in those short sentences. First, how were the Yanks to interpret such seizures: as an understandable outburst of hatred for the defeated colonial masters, or as a Communist-inspired assault on private property? Even if the former, one could not permit the disposition of property to become the business of mobs. Second, ejecting the Japanese from Korea was most assuredly the job of the occupying armies. One could not have Japanese weapons pilfered by revolutionary factions eager to use them on each other. Third, the independence that "all groups" demanded ran contrary to Allied policy. The great powers had judged that Korea was not ready for self-government, and its current anarchy seemed only to prove it. Fourth, if Korea were ripe for agitators, then the U.S. Army had all the more cause to clamp down.

One can debate how justified, ethical, prudent, astute, or in line with Allied directives Hodge's actions were. But their upshot was that the Occupation in South Korea practiced something like Cold War containment eighteen months before it became American policy. Hodge detained radicals, put collaborationist Korean police back on the job, created a South Korean self-defense force, and arranged for the return of nationalist leaders. The story in the north was roughly the same. By October 1946 Kim Il-sung, the thirty-three-year-old Stalinist guerrilla, established his own dictatorial regime at Pyongyang, a sort of Red Fascist stew of Stalinist and Maoist ingredients cooked up in a Korean pot.

The Moscow Conference on Foreign Ministers reaffirmed the policy of joint trusteeship, but so divergent had the politics of North and South Korea become that the diplomats could not patch together a coalition. By the end of 1946 the Soviet Union suspended the talks. In North Korea, communization proceeded apace, but the economy of South Korea, tied so intimately to that of Japan, verged on collapse, and radical movements became active again. Now these were the months of the Truman Doctrine and first hints of a "reverse course" in Japan. Not surprisingly, therefore, Korea became the "single most urgent problem now facing the War Department," and the Joint Chiefs of Staff named Korea "the one country within which we alone have for almost two years carried out ideological warfare in direct contact with our opponents, so that to lose this battle would be gravely detrimental to U.S. prestige, and therefore security, throughout the world." Finally, Acheson told Congress that Korea was "another place where the line has been clearly drawn between the Russians and ourselves."

Marshall made one last effort to unify Korea at the April 1947 Foreign Ministers Conference. But Stalin was evidently content to keep his North Korean buffer state, while the State Department was deep into planning for the setup of a South Korean state. Its policy statement of August 1947 declared that the United States could not "withdraw from Korea under circumstances which would inevitably lead to Communist domination of the entire country," and recommended the United Nations as a possible fig leaf for a partition. The UN obliged by sponsoring elections for a Korean National Assembly in May 1948. North Korea refused to participate, the South voted overwhelmingly for Synghman Rhee, the United States transferred sovereignty to the new Republic of Korea on August 15, and fewer than three weeks later Kim Il-sung founded a People's Republic in the North. Each claimed to be the legitimate government of all Korea, and each intended to assert its claims by force.

The United States dared not wash it hands, sticky mess though Korea became. Truman told Congress that Rhee's regime, by "demonstrating the success and tenacity of democracy in resisting communism, will stand as a beacon to the people of northern Asia." More to the point, it stood as a buffer. For the Americans had realized what the men of Meiji knew from the start: that Japan could never be safe if a hostile power controlled Korea. But between the will and the way there lay a great gap. In 1949 the United States had not yet remobilized to sustain global commitments, while the Sino-Soviet pact and the Russian test of an atomic bomb had raised the stakes. A Korean conflict might well trigger a global showdown with communism—the World War III scenario. Hence the United States must not allow itself to be sucked into a Korean war by its enemies *or by its friends.*

The puppets, in other words, must not be permitted to take hold of their strings and pull. But tensions in Korea only got worse. In October 1949 leftist opponents of Rhee launched a rebellion in the South that left three thousand dead, and along the thirty-eighth parallel hundreds of clashes occurred between South and North Korean Army patrols. Both regimes ached for the opportunity to cross the frontier in force. Would the United States fight to defend South Korea or not? Would it fight even if its own client started the war? Would it carry a war to the North? Would a Korean war escalate into a much wider conflict? Acheson sought to dispel the confusion in his famous speech of January 12, 1950, to the National Press Club in Washington. America's defensive perimeter, he said, "runs along the Aleutians to Japan and then goes to

the Ryukyus . . . and from the Ryukyus to the Philippine Islands."
(MacArthur had drawn the identical line while celebrating the fact that
"the Pacific has become on Anglo-Saxon lake.") Needless to say, South
Korea was absent, and Acheson himself called it an oversight born of
inexperience, or an example of the danger of speaking off the cuff.
Republican opponents saw in it a symptom of the Democrats' defeat-
ism. Radicals called it a ploy to *provoke* a North Korean invasion so that
the United States might counterattack and roll back communism in
Asia.

But a fine historian has now proven that the shrewd Acheson labored
over that speech for weeks and revised every sentence with care. In any
case he *did not exclude South Korea.* For Acheson went on to say, "So
far as the military security of other areas in the Pacific is concerned, it
must be clear that no person can guarantee these areas against military
attack. . . . Should such an attack occur . . . the initial reliance must be
on the people attacked to resist it and then upon the commitments of
the entire civilized world under the Charter of the United Nations,
which so far has not proved a weak reed." If Acheson erred, it was in
assuming that Kim Il-sung would grasp his subtlety, or that Stalin had
Kim under firm control. But Acheson surely meant what he said, which
was this: The U.S. defense perimeter ran thus and so, meaning that
those were the places where the United States had or planned permanent bases. But U.S. forces had left South Korea, so Acheson was making it clear *to Rhee* that they were not going to come back in support of
any aggressive designs of his own. If, on the other hand, the North Koreans attacked south and the South Koreans proved unable to resist, then
the whole *world* would rush to his aid.

So Acheson was not uncognizant of the danger of Korea exploding;
indeed, he was trying to defuse the bomb. Perhaps he failed because the
Communists really misunderstood, or decided to call his bluff. Perhaps
Stalin knew that the Americans *would* fight for South Korea and wanted
to see them bogged down there. Nikita Khrushchev's memoirs claim
that Kim initiated the idea of attacking the South, and that Stalin gave
him the go-ahead. Another theory holds that Acheson was trying to rein
in the roll-back faction in *Washington* that was itching for an excuse to
fight communism and persuade Congress to vote for the defense buildup
recommended by the National Security Council in NSC-68. But there is
no hard evidence of an American conspiracy to provoke a Korean war,
and as yet none of a Kremlin conspiracy. The Korean War, therefore,
appears to have started in Korea.

It seems that Asian wars are never declared but simply mature out of
border incidents. Of those there were plenty in 1949. But intelligence

also poured in of North Korean tanks and infantry massing behind the thirty-eighth parallel. Were they there for maneuvers, or to blunt an expected assault from the South, or to stage an invasion of their own? Whatever the truth, both Korean armies were primed for battle on the eve of the incident at Ongjin, a peninsula cut off by a protruding bay from the rest of South Korea. It was there in the dark of June 25 that reciprocal border attacks "happened." All night long the skirmishes spread until finally, at dawn, Communist spearheads turned south in unison and drove hard toward Seoul.

Ever since FDR committed the United States to the destruction of Japanese power, this sort of storm had been brewing. It broke on June 25, 1950. Within days Truman moved the UN to condemn the attack as an unprovoked aggression, announced that his containment doctrine applied to the Pacific, ordered MacArthur to support South Korea with air and sea forces, interposed the Seventh Fleet between Taiwan and mainland China, and promised France support in its war against the Communist Viet Minh. On June 30, he authorized MacArthur to ship ground forces to Pusan.

In October 1949, Kennan had written to Rusk that "the day will come, and possibly sooner than we think, when realism will call upon us not to oppose the re-entry of Japanese influence and activity into Korea and Manchuria. This is, in fact, the only realistic prospect for countering and moderating Soviet influence in the area." Instead, the United States not only inherited Japan's geopolitical burdens but desperately needed Japan itself as a military and economic base for the war in Korea. Yoshida had been pushing for a final peace treaty for years, and now he skillfully played hard to get. On September 2, 1951, delegates from Japan, the United States, and fifty other nations convened in the San Francisco Opera House to put a formal end to the Pacific War. In exchange for military use of Japan and Okinawa, the United States recognized Japan as a friend and an equal, restored Japanese sovereignty, and concluded a security treaty. The United States went on to deliver Japan $2 billion in economic aid and $4 billion in military spending, in addition to private investment. Japan's economic miracle, though prepared by the "reverse course" in Occupation policy, really began with the Korean War.

To General MacArthur, who took personal command in Korea and routed the North Korean offensive, the war was "Mars' last gift to an old warrior." To the Governor of the Bank of Japan it was "divine aid" for Japan, and to Yoshida "a gift from the gods." Japan was in effect a military colony of the American empire, but Yoshida predicted that "if Japan becomes a colony of the United States, it will also eventually become the stronger."

Kennan, as usual, understood. "It is an ironic fact," he wrote, "that today our past objectives in Asia are ostensibly in large measure achieved. . . . we have fallen heir to the problems and responsibilities the Japanese had faced and borne in the Korean-Manchurian area for nearly half a century, and there is a certain perverse justice in the pain we are suffering from a burden which, when it was borne by others, we held in such low esteem."

The Thirteenth 'aha iki

Scholar: Hasn't anyone anything to say? No questions or misunderstandings? Saitō? Kaahumanu?

Kaahumanu: We have heard enough of your North Pacific triangle and its endless cycle of wars. I no longer care how it is that Japanese now own Waikiki. After another war, no doubt, or the next after that. Go away now. The lessons are over.

Seward: Lord, have mercy upon us.

Witte: Christ, have mercy upon us.

Seward: Lord, I'm sorry for your people, Saitō. I know they started it—Pearl Harbor and all—but what a horrible judgment. I hope your people have forgiven us. And we them. . . . It seems that each war is worse than the last.

Lea: So the Republic won after all. I shall have to revise my formulations. Of course, the folly of the Japanese was to think they could break China like a horse, and force a bit in its mouth! The folly of the Russians was to think they could bully China in the old way, as if I, and Sun Yat-sen, had not lived! The folly of the Americans was to think they could keep the Empire down, however many cities they burned. The wars of the races do not end. How do you reform a race?

Saitō: Go to hell, General Homer Lea—and take with you all the wonderful Yanks who say *Asians* place no value on human life, then burn them alive with liquid fire? *Real* war is a sacrament performed by fighters as pure as priests, but you Americans don't fight wars. You overwhelm all possibility of combat, call your enemies ants, then stamp on the anthill as if even ants have no right to be ants.

Seward: Damn it, Saitō, you're not kidding.

Saitō: There's something monstrous in you Americans. In peace you're like goldfish, but at war you are dragons, breathing fire on all that you see, then stinking up the lands you lay waste with a noisome, reptilian stench. . . . Roosevelt, you were my friend!

Seward: Seems your people got what they asked for, and reaped what they sowed ten times over. Did they expect the Americans would fight the war with samurai swords, pairing off with your braves one-on-one? You can't blame us for wanting to win, and doing so at the least human cost.

Saitō: Oh no, Mr. Seward, it seems Japanese did not reap ten times what they sowed, but ten thousand times. Yamamoto bombed warships and killed a few thousand combatants. Your people burned dozens of cities and killed a million civilians. Where is the proportion in that?

Seward: Ah, "proportionality of force," a Christian concept, Mr. Ambassador. I'll thank you again not to judge Americans by standards you don't believe in yourself. I haven't the faintest idea whether the bombs, especially those atomic ones, were needed to force your zanies to give up. But they cannot be measured against the destruction done at Pearl Harbor, or even all the carnage and cruelty wrought by your armies. The cost of the bombing must be measured against the destruction that would have occurred had the bombing not taken place. That's a more humbling and meaningful query. Did Mr. Lincoln regret the campaigns of Sherman and Grant? Not for a moment. He gave thanks for generals who knew how to escalate violence in order to end it once and for all. Anyway, how can a nation that declares war on China, Britain, and the United States all at once have the cheek to accuse *others* of lacking a sense of proportion?

Saitō: Hypocrites. You did not ask yourselves whether such bombing was necessary, you just did it as soon as you could. And why? Hatred and the humiliating demand for unconditional surrender. I don't defend Tōjō. He was a fool. But the burning of Tokyo, women and children. . . . Did you bomb Kyoto, too?

Scholar: No, the Americans had enough sense not to bomb the ancient imperial capital with its sacred temples. When Secretary of War Robert Patterson toured Japan after the surrender, the road to Kyoto was lined with Japanese *cheering* him! The mayor explained that it was gratitude: "They all knew that your soldiers and airmen wanted to drop the atomic bomb on Kyoto and you did not allow them to do so." In fact, they had the wrong man—Stimson, Patterson's predecessor, made the decision. But do you know, the Japanese tried to firebomb the forests of California, Oregon, and Washington! They loaded over nine thousand balloons with hydrogen and set them loose into the prevailing westerly winds. Pitiful, when you think of it.

Seward: Seems to me we showed the Japanese a lot more mercy than they showed the peoples they conquered.

Saitō: Surely you don't mean the Chinese?

Lea: Dwarf bandit! What allowed you people to imagine even in your deepest Shinto trance that China would bow its neck to your swords?

Seward: Besides, the American way of war is to get it over with. We fight with all our might, we fight with every weapon we can invent, and we fight with righteous zeal. But it is never our *policy* to kill even one noncombatant for the perverted fun of it, as your people apparently do.

Scholar: But that's what's not clear. Would the Japanese have surrendered *anyway*, just from the blockade and loss of their Empire? Or would they have resisted an invasion with the same gritty determination we *admired* in the British in 1940, while hurtling thousands of kamikazes into our ships? They certainly prepared for invasion, and were mobilizing women and children.

Seward: But we do know who started the bombing of cities, who tortured their captives, killed and enslaved the peoples they claimed to be liberating, and browbeat their own people into jumping off cliffs instead of letting our soldiers give them food, shelter, medicine.

Saitō: "Onward Christian soldiers" is it?

Seward: If you insist, *yes.*

Saitō: That is what I cannot accept. I cannot accept that your violence only made you Americans more sanctimonious, not less.

Kaahumanu: Saitō is right. But it was no Christian soldier who elevated the star on American airplanes above the star of Bethlehem. I do not know whose pride is the greater, but it is obvious God meant the Japanese to lose. The loyalty of the American *nisei* proves by itself the superiority of the American cause. Did Japan command such loyalty from any other people, white or yellow?

Lea: Nations win loyalty from others through victory, not mercy or tolerance. Besides, the Americans threw the *nisei* into camps with every justification. Should never have let them in the country to begin with.

Kaahumanu: But most of them wanted to remain American—*even* those thrown in the camps. Evidently the *haoles* offered the peoples of my ocean more hope than their rivals did. How many people fled to Japan or Russia to live? I believe the American victory was Providence. Consider the Battle of Midway.

Lea: Christian sentimentality from a Polynesian chiefess! Tell me why it is necessary to postulate a Cosmic Admiralty to explain the outcome of a war in which one side had ten times the strength, and the other blundered at every pass?

Witte: Perhaps it is not. I cannot myself understand how God could permit Holy Russia to lose to the Germans, then allow Stalin's slave empire to beat them. Were tsars more wicked than Communists?

Scholar: No, but Hitler was more wicked than the Kaiser.

Lea: Your fancies disgust me. For the Empire to defeat the Republic everything had to go right for it. The Japanese needed to establish such tactical superiority—by surprise, superior weaponry, and training—that they achieved breakthroughs in the operational realm, conquests so sweeping that they in turn finally yielded a strategic advantage. The only way of doing this, as I proved in 1908, was to conquer Hawaii at the outset of a war. But Japan waited too long.

Kaahumanu: But even that—

Lea: Even that would not guarantee victory. As your Bywater described —he stole my ideas—the Americans might still island-hop across the Pacific. That is because the Japanese conquests, while adding to Japan's economic base, did not weaken their enemy's economic base.

Scholar: Unlike Germany's blitzkrieg, which added to Nazi resources at the same time it subtracted resources from its enemies. The only way Japan could win was if American resources had to be deployed overwhelmingly in Europe. Which means that Japan lost, not at Midway, but at the battles of Moscow and Stalingrad.

Witte: Of course. Russia always dies so that others might live and grow richer.

Lea: The Japanese plan took for granted a Nazi victory whereas your Matsuoka and Tōjō should have bet on an *Allied* victory, encouraged the Americans to deploy their forces in Europe, while secretly rooting for the Germans to hold out for years. Japan would then be in a position to profit from the Second World War as it did from the First. That might have required a partial pullback in China in deference to American opinion, but deescalation in China would also have strengthened, not weakened, the Empire.

Saitō: Instead, Tōjō clamored aboard the bus for fear of missing it, just as it ran out of gas.

Scholar: But the real folly was Roosevelt's, to think he could manipulate China, and elevate it to great power status, right, Mr. Lea?

Lea: No, pedant. You patronize me, as Americans patronized China. Your *Franklin* Roosevelt had his eyes on Moscow in all his dealings with China. That much is clear from your own confused account. His only alternative to pretending that China was a buttress of postwar Asia was to cut a deal with Japan so as to leave *it* the barrier to postwar Russian power—*Theodore* Roosevelt's strategy. But Teddy could afford to be neutral between Russia and Japan, whereas Franklin could not. He had to keep Russia *and* China in their respective wars, for those giants tied down the main enemy armies. For the U.S. to hint at a deal with Japan in the interest of a postwar balance of power would only have encouraged Stalin to seek *his* own separate peace with the Germans, and Chiang and Mao to give up all pretense of fighting Japan. So Roosevelt pledged that America would remain true to its allies and fight until unconditional surrender. But the utter destruction of Japanese power ensured that no balance of power would exist in East Asia after the war—*unless* the U.S. itself assumed the role previously played by Japan.

Scholar: All right, I *was* patronizing you. In any case, Americans were in a fury after Pearl Harbor, and later, the notion of compromising with the Japanese while Iwo Jima and Okinawa were raging—well, it was unthinkable.

Kaahumanu: Your Pacific war was horrible. But why do you all imply that the outcome was horrible? Did you not say that the defeat of Japan, then of the Kuomintang, made it possible at last for China to unify? And was not the discrediting of the militarists the best thing to happen to Japan? The Americans proved that their Shinto gods did not possess so much *mana* after all. I admire your General MacArthur for that and expect that the Japanese people would honor him.

Scholar: They did. But it's a severe mercy that costs millions of lives. And as for Chinese "unity," well, some twenty million more Chinese died in the Communist purges and famines.

Lea: China's civil wars are like world wars. Remember the Taiping Rebellion.

Saitō: An empire of peasants, like the prof said. All the Chinese want is to guard their pigsty, or steal their neighbor's if they can.

Lea: Then it served the Nipponese right to retreat from China covered in pig dung.

Scholar: On the contrary, Chinese are the most skilled traders, brilliant scientists, and disciplined workers in the world—

Saitō: Once they get out of the pigsty.

Scholar: But however vain U.S. policy may have been in China—and it was no worse than Soviet policy!—one must judge the American Occupation of Japan a success—

Saitō: One must judge, must one? So says the so-called historian, who lectures on people he never knew, from times and places he's never been, according to theories probably bogus, and which he hasn't thought through in any case?

Scholar: Enough, damn it! Kaahumanu, you want to stop? Fine. I quit. When you asked for my help, and I asked for theirs, I didn't expect constant abuse. This is a nightmare, not a—

Saitō: Then why did you summon us? To ratify a scholarly masquerade?

Scholar: So it's all a charade, is it? Everything I've spent decades trying to understand? You know what, Saitō, you're schizophrenic!

Kaahumanu: Peace, Scholar. Mr. Saitō pokes in order that you might learn from your squeals where your armor is weak.

Scholar: I think he pokes for the sake of poking. Maybe because he had to spend so many years sucking up to Americans. As I was going to say, the Japanese were damned lucky to be occupied by us, and not by the Russians.

Witte: Communists.

Scholar: Sorry, Witte. Communists, of course. MacArthur's army did not enter Japan to kill, enslave, remove, or destroy, but only to rid Japan of the militarists who *did* kill, enslave, and destroy. The Americans allowed the Emperor to remain, governed through the Japanese authorities, fed the people until they could get by on their own, poured in billions to help your economy recover, and signed a generous peace treaty. You would spit that back in our faces?

Saitō: I would do just what my buddy Yoshida did. I would say, "Thank you very much, United States. I appreciate your friendship and look forward to cooperating with you long into the future." Then I would exploit America's military exertions to recover the *real* freedom your Occupation denied us, like the freedom to choose our own leaders regardless of what they did in the war, the freedom to teach what we wish in our schools, to arrange relations between men and women according to our culture and tradition, to venerate the Emperor or not as *we* prefer and not as some Christian general says we must, to organize our economy as we think best for Japan and not according to some American blueprint, to trade with whomever we want, to rearm or not as we decide, to fashion a foreign policy without clearing it with Washington first. The treaties of 1951 lifted the burden of occupation but not the burden of defeat. They sound to me like unequal treaties that put Japan back where it was before 1894.

Nor did MacArthur expunge Japanese militarism with his SCAP constitution. If anyone destroyed Japanese militarism, it was Tōjō himself, with some help from your Curtis LeMay. But Japan will not need
military might so long as America is at odds with Russia. Tell me,
how long does that last?

Witte: Oh, so having saved the Allied cause in the war, Russia then
saves Japan after the war simply by posing a threat? Always Russia is
the bogeyman of the world. When we are enemies of China, everyone
hates us. When we make friends with China, everyone hates and fears
us still more. Will you be satisfied if we give back Siberia to the
tribesmen and return to the Russia of Ivan the Terrible? I can think of
no one more loathsome than Stalin, but I must say I feel for his
plight. He double-tracked my railroad and signed a friendly treaty
with China to recover rights in Manchuria—just what I would have
done. But he blundered in helping Communists at all. Revolution is
everyone's enemy, including other revolutionary regimes. When he
began to doubt Chiang Kai-shek, he should have expelled the Communists from Manchuria and upheld his 1945 treaty. Instead, he
assumed that Americans would do his dirty work for him. Americans
pulled out of the Chinese civil war, the Communists won, and Russians took the blame, even though the outcome cost them Manchuria. I believe Stalin *did* encourage this war in Korea you speak of,
if only to draw American power *back in* to East Asia, humble the
Chinese Communists, and make them dependent on Russia. Still,
this is an unnatural alliance—a strong Russia and a strong China. I
predict it will not last.

Scholar: Old treaties never die, they just fade away.

Saitō: Good line, Doc. You see, I'm not so hostile.

Lea: Stalin's *greatest* fear must have been a rearmed Japan. Imagine,
the Empire and the Republic in league with each other! Who could
stand before them?

Witte: For Russia, an American military presence in the Far East was
preferable to having America rearm *Japan.* So this Cold War you
speak of was mostly a pose!

Scholar: Let us say that the ideological conflict and strategic conflict
were not in all places identical. But wait 'til you hear about the
Korean War—

Kaahumanu: No! No more tales of war! I shall dismiss you all.

Witte: Not yet, Your Highness. He has yet to learn—

Saitō: Hush, Witte!

Witte: I meant to say, he has yet to bring us up to the present. Kaahumanu, you know you really *do* want to hear what happened to Waikiki.

Kaahumanu: I would like to know more of Dr. Nagai, who saw Nagasaki's destruction akin to a cross.

Scholar: Some Japanese *were* converted by their war experience, including the pilot who led the first wave against Pearl Harbor.

Saitō: So what if all Japan had converted? It is a peculiarly Christian conceit to believe that conversion will change a nation's behavior.

Seward: I'm not sure now that religion and policy have much to do with each other in the end. The latter's a matter of power, and the former's a matter of love.

Kaahumanu: Love and power can intersect to form a cross. Nagasaki was *not* like a cross until the moment Dr. Nagai looked up—

Scholar: —from the radioactive rubble—

Kaahumanu: —and loved. Why do you not tell the story of love in my ocean, instead of the story of power?

Seward: Confess, Your Highness, you enjoy the lore of politics as much as I.

Kaahumanu: Part of me does. But it is like the checkers I used to play with the sailors—diverting, but not for real. The time has come to make an end! I think the scholar is ready.

Saitō: You're sure, Kaahumanu?

Kaahumanu: He's telling me so, and I think he is right.

Scholar: What do you mean, "ready"? Who is "he"? Don't wink, Saitō!

Witte: Just continue, my good man, and leave the rest to us. You were going to pick up your story in 1950, I believe, and tell us of—how did Mr. Kennan put it—"a certain perverse justice."

Scholar: Yes, of course. The *rest* of the story.

Americans' Burden

C ALL IT THE AMERICANS' BURDEN. In forty years of Cold War the United States and Russia competed directly for North Pacific power for the first time since the 1820s, when Alexander I issued his famous ukase. The Cold War was much else besides but was surely the latest expression of the triangular logic that governs that part of the world. Just as Japan and Russia clashed at the turn of the century, during which time the *United States* rose to Pacific prominence, and just as the United States and Japan clashed from 1907 to 1945, during which time *Russia* regained Pacific prominence, so after 1950 the United States and Russia clashed, during which time *Japan* recouped in spectacular fashion. For long-suffering Russians the Cold War was a brave fight. However deadly the hand of their government, they stood alone for four decades against every other major power on earth. It was also a brave fight for Americans, who gave and gave of themselves and their treasure so that some Asians, at least, might not fall into the Communist maw. Thanks to the burden Americans bore, Pacific peoples emerged freer and wealthier than ever before, and more at peace than at any time since the eighteenth century.

The Korean War was the catalyst. The Truman administration quickly rearmed as prescribed by NSC-68, pushed for a hydrogen bomb and transcontinental bombers, and began to construct a global network of alliances. But Korea also revealed the limitations of American might. Truman's decision to "roll back" communism by ordering United Nations forces into North Korea provoked massive Chinese intervention. So only five years after Iwo Jima and Okinawa, American soldiers again faced a war to the death against suicidal, brainwashed armies drafted from Asian peasantry. Fearful that war with mainland China or the use of atomic weapons might provoke World War III, Truman and Eisenhower settled for a limited war—a stalemate in Korea and everywhere else. So far from fulfilling the fantasies of Perry, Seward, or Mahan, U.S. hegemony in the North Pacific only meant burdens without commensurate boons. The Korean War ended in a nervous truce in 1953, but the retreat of Dutch and French colonialism meant that by 1954, U.S. forces were pledged to defend virtually all of the old Coprosperity Sphere not already controlled by Communists.

The Japanese made out handsomely, and who can blame them? Not only did the Korean War inspire the treaties that restored their sovereignty and offered them free defense, it made Japan's industrial resurgence an explicit American goal. So the United States encouraged Japan to pursue the materials and markets of Southeast Asia and opened up the *American* market to Japanese exports. Finally, the Korean stalemate pleased Japanese (though they were too prudent to say it out loud). For if Japan were no longer able to rule Korea, then the next-best outcome was a divided country in which rival powers balanced each other. What was more, a unified Korea might itself become an economic rival to Japan, its former colonial master. So the truce that left two Korean regimes and the United States, Russia, and China all frustrated there suited the Japanese book.

Stalin died in 1953, Khrushchev denounced him in 1956, and President Dwight D. Eisenhower had reason to hope for a détente to retard the nuclear arms race. Instead, the technological and geopolitical trends of the latter half of the 1950s broadened the Cold War. Sputnik 1, the first artificial earth satellite, gave the Russians reason to boast that communism was indeed the best means for rapid modernization and proved their ability to threaten North America with nuclear destruction. Rapid decolonization expanded the arena of bipolar conflict until it embraced the whole world. Finally, the Cold War blocs began to rattle as Gaullist France, then Maoist China, then even Japan protested subservience to Washington or Moscow. The Sino-Soviet split, as it developed between 1956 and 1960, was expressed in sectarian Communist polemics but would likely have occurred even if emperors still reigned in Peking and St. Petersburg. The Chinese demanded that Russia provide them with nuclear weapons and rockets, help them reconquer Taiwan, and otherwise treat China as an equal. No prudent Russian was about to make China a military equal or permit the Maoists to drag the USSR into a nuclear confrontation. So by the 1960s the Communist giants were denouncing each other in vile terms even as each claimed leadership of the revolution against imperialism.

The Japanese government likewise protested its subordinate status. Almost no Japanese leaders took seriously the notion that the USSR might invade Japan. Furthermore, they cared little whether a given regime in Hanoi, Peking, Jakarta, or Pyongyang called itself Communist. From Yoshida onward Japan was eager to recognize Asian regimes so long as they granted economic access on acceptable terms. But the Americans refused to let Japan do so and insisted that it support the Cold War, to the consternation of Japanese leftists and rightists alike. Third, Japanese were mightily unhappy about having to play host to military bases and stockpiles of nuclear weapons. When John Foster Dulles requested that Japan rearm, Yoshida refused. After all, the Americans had insisted that Japan become impotent; let them live with the consequences. Washington sought to mollify Japanese opinion by renegotiating the 1952 security treaty. In exchange for a modest expansion of Japan's Self-Defense Forces, the United States promised not to use Japan as a base for military operations without consulting Tokyo. Still, Japanese anger exploded in riots so large and so violent as to force Eisenhower to cancel his visit in 1960. The revised treaty was ratified, but the disturbances put the United States on notice that Japan would exact an ever-higher price in return for its subservience.

Nothing shook the chessboard in the western Pacific so much as the Vietnam War. Another American attempt to hold a beachhead on the Asian mainland, it damaged the U.S. economy, shattered American social cohesion, and gave Russia and Japan a chance to fly past the United States in the military and economic races. Extraordinary damage control by President Nixon and Henry Kissinger prevented the American retreat from becoming a rout. But in the course of trying to turn an operational calamity into a strategic draw, Nixon inspired a new Japanese word—*shokku*—and made Japan more determined than ever to recover its full independence. After drafting all the rules for the postwar economy, the U.S. Treasury pulled the dollar off the gold standard without warning. It seemed prudent for various reasons but meant that foreigners saw the dollars they held fall in value by 12 to 30 percent. The second Nixon *shokku* was the opening to Red China. After forbidding Japan to consort with Asian Communists for two decades, the United States suddenly decided to do so itself without tipping Tokyo off in advance. It meant that the United States was finally prepared to profit from the Sino-Soviet split, the reality of which could no longer be doubted in 1968 and 1969 when battles broke out again on the Soviet-Manchurian border. But nothing so impressed upon *Japan* the degree to which its foreign policies were made in Washington, and Tokyo immediately established political and commercial relations with Peking. Nixon's third *shokku*, a freeze on soybean sales to Japan in the interest of fighting inflation at home, was hardly as portentous as the oil and iron embargoes before Pearl Harbor but demonstrated Japan's vulnerability to American whim. Finally, the Nixon Doctrine proclaimed that

Asian countries threatened with aggression must no longer assume that American boys would fight their battles for them.

So American military, economic, and technological might were limited after all. But the opening to China also meant that for the first time since 1941 the United States was talking to Russia, Japan, and China at the same time. So even though Nixon fell from power and Vietnam fell to the Communists, U.S. diplomatic flexibility was greatly enhanced. When the Soviets took advantage of Americans' post-Vietnam malaise to equal or surpass the United States in categories of nuclear weapons and score wins in Third World conflicts, President Jimmy Carter made the link to Peking an unspoken alliance and completed the apparent encirclement of the USSR. Leonid Brezhnev then redoubled his efforts to exploit the Soviets' military assets in the Pacific theater. They completed the Baikal-Amur Railroad, a tremendous project that freed Soviet forces from sole dependence on the Trans-Siberian Railway and opened another swath of Siberia to development. In the crescent that stretches from Outer Mongolia to Vladivostok the Red Army positioned a monstrous army of fifty-five divisions, fourteen thousand tanks, 2,400 airplanes, 160 SS-20 triple-warhead missiles, a huge air defense complex, and a portion of the Strategic Rocket Forces' intercontinental missiles. Under Adm. Sergey Gorshkov's inspiration, the Soviet Pacific Fleet became the empire's largest, including eighty-two surface ships, seventy-seven attack submarines, and twenty-five strategic nuclear missile submarines. The Red Navy spent billions of rubles upgrading its ports in the Sea of Okhotsk and Kamchatka, inherited the Vietnamese harbor in Cam Ranh Bay, and quietly obtained transit rights in a number of Micronesian islands. Should war break out, the U.S. Navy could no longer assure its communications with Japan and East Asia in the teeth of the Soviet submarines and Backfire bombers.

Then the Soviet Union collapsed. For at least the fourth time in modern history—the first three being the Crimean War, the Russo-Japanese War, and World War I—Russia proved unable to sustain intense competition with more advanced powers. By the late 1980s it was exhausted and rent by internal contradictions. Mikhail Gorbachev's *perestroika* failed, the subject peoples bravely stood up, and the USSR laid down and died. Suddenly the United States was supreme in the North Pacific to a degree never before attained by any empire. And yet, the end of the Cold War and the economic troubles within the United States suggested that American might must also wane. As early as the 1970s Carter spoke of withdrawing from South Korea. The Japanese had demanded and won the return of Okinawa to full Japanese sovereignty. Then the Filipinos (plus a volcanic eruption) expelled the United States from its famous old bases. Without a Soviet Union to counter-balance, Americans had every temptation to see Japan once again as their major rival for power and wealth.

But far from seeking out ways to overawe Japan in the wake of the Soviet collapse, Americans began to call for Japan to pay its fair share of defense and defend the sea-lanes in its vicinity. By the 1990s a supposedly disarmed Japan was supporting the world's fourth-largest defense budget. The Sino-Soviet border remained the most fortified anywhere, while both Russia and China struggled to maintain central authority. China may or may not make a safe escape from communism, may or may not crack up again into warlordism. Russia may or may not succeed in keeping the loyalty of the Yakuts, Chukchi, and Koriaks. To be sure, U.S. military power can help to patrol the Asian coast, cow North Korea until it collapses, and share the seas with Japan. But Americans are unlikely to wade into Siberia or China, or flatten Japan again out of spite. It would seem rather that the United States will never again wield the power to *control* North Pacific events to which it always aspired, and briefly attained.

Still, the U.S. military retreat is trivial by comparison with its economic decline. Throughout history American dreamers touted the markets of Asia and denounced the protectionism of Asian regimes even as they imposed high tariffs themselves. Well, the Open Door finally triumphed, and the result as time went by was a mighty flood of Asian imports on to the *American* market. The Roosevelt administration embraced free trade out of its conviction that the neomercantilism of the 1930s prolonged the Depression and led to fascism, imperialism, and war. So the General Agreement on Tariffs and Trade and the World Bank were to be the economic equivalents of the United Nations and promote universal access to materials and markets. The Truman and Eisenhower administrations opened American markets still more to help Europe and Asia recover, reward their allies for supporting the fight against communism, and prove the superiority of capitalism to the uncommitted world. Free Asians, led by Japan, jumped at the chance and within a few decades all but shut down U.S. shipyards and steel mills, and made gigantic inroads in automobiles, electronics, and many other industries. The United States did not *have* to open its markets anymore than it *had* to fight wars in Korea and Vietnam. It chose to do so out of a sense of responsibility, gratitude for its own prosperity, and more than a tinge of overconfidence. So while the United States spent trillions on defense in the half-century after World War II, and even more on domestic programs after the mid-1960s, the Asian "tigers" concentrated on industrial investment and ran up huge surpluses in their trade with America.

Japan was the biggest success. Its real growth rates peaked at almost 15 percent per annum in the late 1960s and remained at least 50 percent higher than American rates throughout the 1970s and 1980s. By now everyone knows how the Japanese redirected their national virtues from martial to peaceful expansion. Yoshida's Liberal Democratic party continued the tradition of one-party government by consensus. The powerful bureaucracy continued to plan and execute national strategy. The MITI was a postwar version of the economic bureaus founded by the "total war" faction in the 1930s. *Keiretsu*, or interlocking conglomerates of industries and banks, updated the structures of the old *zaibatsu* and interwar concerns. The hard work, discipline, and group loyalty of corporate executives, salarymen, and workers, the willingness of the people to accept a reduced standard of living and save a large portion of income, and the dedication of Japanese students all recall the zeal of soldiers and sailors in previous times.

In sum, the Japanese economy is a third type, a corporatist developmental economy combining some virtues of free enterprise with some advantages of central planning. So long as Japan operates in a free international environment, it enjoys the best of both worlds. Japan's gross national product, once one-tenth of America's, was over one-half by 1990 and the second greatest in the world. Once nine of the world's top ten banks were American; now eight of ten are Japanese. And the *keiretsu*—rolling in cash, free to tap Japan's huge savings at low interest rates, buoyed by the exploding values of Japanese stocks and real estate, and tempted by the weakness of the dollar—went on a shopping spree across the Pacific. Suddenly everything from U.S. Treasury bonds to great office buildings, Hollywood studios, golf resorts, hotels, residential real estate, and rich North American farmland seemed to be owned by Japanese. Hawaii was a favored vacation spot for prosperous Japanese, and so by the mid-1980s the strip of hotels along Waikiki was heavily Japanese-owned.

Some say the Japanese are guilty of dumping products at prices below cost to capture market share and ruin American competitors. But no one forces American consumers to buy from Toyota or Sony. The Japanese have earned their success, as have the South Koreans, Taiwanese, and fifty-five million overseas Chinese from Singapore to San Francisco, while Asian competition forced American firms to improve their own products markedly. What is more, Japanese actually spend as much per capita on U.S. goods as Americans spend on Japanese goods. Nor must the trends of the last generation continue. In some respects, Japan's exceptional growth was as artificial as U.S. hegemony in 1950 and has now slowed to the level of other advanced nations. If Japan is becoming a "normal" nation again, so has the U.S. economy merely returned to the position it had in the interwar years: about 22 percent of world production. Meanwhile, Japan's real estate and equity bubbles reached such absurd heights that downtown Tokyo was "worth" more than the entire country of Canada, and the issues on the *Nikkei* stock exchange were "worth" more than all those traded on Wall Street. The bubbles burst in the early 1990s as real estate went without buyers, stocks fell 60 percent, and Japanese began to unload high-profile overseas purchases. Their strategy of covering pyramids of corporate debt with ever-increasing foreign sales also reached limits as the American market showed signs of being unable or unwilling to absorb any more Japanese imports. So perhaps the great postwar reversal—"trading places," one author called it—is over. But to hundreds of thousands of American workers the damage was done, and certainly the United States will never again enjoy the Pacific economic supremacy that it pursued for so long, and briefly attained.

It was the Americans' burden to fight against communism in Asia for the ultimate benefit of Asians. It was the Americans' burden to honor their liberal economic ideals for the ultimate benefit of Asians. And it was the Americans' burden—espousing as they did a humanist world view over against the ideologies of their geopolitical opponents—to treat peoples of all races the same. The Fascists were a pushover in the war of philosophies since they were overtly racist and appealed to no one but their own compatriots. The Communists were a subtler enemy, claiming as they did to be champions of national liberation. So when the Cold War spread to the Third World, the United States seemed obliged to prove its moral as well as material superiority. And to win that competition for the hearts and minds of colored peoples abroad, Americans had perforce to prove that their society was color-blind at home. So it was that the Cold War completed a revolution in U.S. immigration policy.

It began in 1943 when Congress repealed the Chinese Exclusion Act in order (as one congressman put it) "to dull the edge of this Jap propaganda against us and our allies." In 1946 Americans repented of their spasmodic internment of Japanese when the War Relocation Authority appealed to the "strong and stubborn potential for fair-mindedness among the American people—a potential which should be carefully studied, fostered, and brought to the highest degree of assertiveness in the interest of greater racial tolerance and a richer realization of democratic values." In 1948 Congress voted token reparations to the internees, and the McCarren-Walter Act four years later repealed the ban on citizenship for eighty thousand Japanese-Americans. Thousands more Asians became eligible under the War Brides Act, while the California Supreme Court threw out the Alien Land Laws in 1952. World War II also occasioned the first big migration of blacks to the West

Coast, and by 1960 over one in twenty Californians was black. Farmers and ranchers, riding the agricultural boom born of irrigation, the war, and population growth, imported Mexicans to pick crops. Fear and prejudice remained high: in 1942 and 1943 white servicemen in Los Angeles beat up young Mexicans in the so-called "zoot suit riots," and in the 1950s the federal government's Operation Wetback attempted to stop illegal immigrants. But such was the demand for farm labor that legal *braceros* crossed the border in numbers that peaked at 445,197 in 1956. By 1970 over three million Mexicans lived permanently in California.

But nothing established the trend toward equality for immigrants of all races more than Hawaiian statehood. Island leaders had petitioned for it since 1903, and Hawaii and Alaska were both "incorporated" territories (implying their candidacy for eventual statehood). In World War II, Hawaiians and Alaskans of all races proved their patriotism, and the war boosted their populations and economies by more than 50 percent. Residents voted in large majorities in favor of statehood (Japanese Hawaiians most of all), Truman endorsed it in 1945, the national parties paid lip service to it in their platforms, and polls showed the American public in favor of admitting Alaska and Hawaii by three or four to one.

Still, statehooders were frustrated as one bill after another died in committee. The Pentagon worried that it would lose its free hand in a fully sovereign Hawaii or Alaska. Economic interests both local and Stateside feared the effects of federal laws and taxes in the Pacific possessions. The Democratic Congress feared that statehood for Hawaii would mean two more Republican senators, given the GOP's long ascendancy there, while the Eisenhower administration feared Democratic domination in Alaska. (Ironically, almost the reverse proved true in both cases.) An issue was made of Communist influence in the Hawaiian labor unions, while a Georgia representative spoke for many Southerners when he said that "the crosscurrents of racial feeling create political and administrative whirlpools too dangerous to yet be allowed the authoritative voice in the American government that goes with full statehood." Hawaii was a colored society of Asian/Pacific culture, and its admission seemed a terrible precedent. "Do we want to put a couple of Japs in the Senate of the United States?" asked the *Tulsa Tribune*. More to the point, both Alaska and Hawaii were sure to send senators favorable to civil rights legislation.

Year after year the debate was renewed until 1957, when the administration mustered the votes to pass a modest civil rights bill. Opposition to new states according to how their representatives might vote on racial issues thus became gratuitous, and the Democratic leadership acquiesced in Alaskan statehood. When news of the final Senate vote of

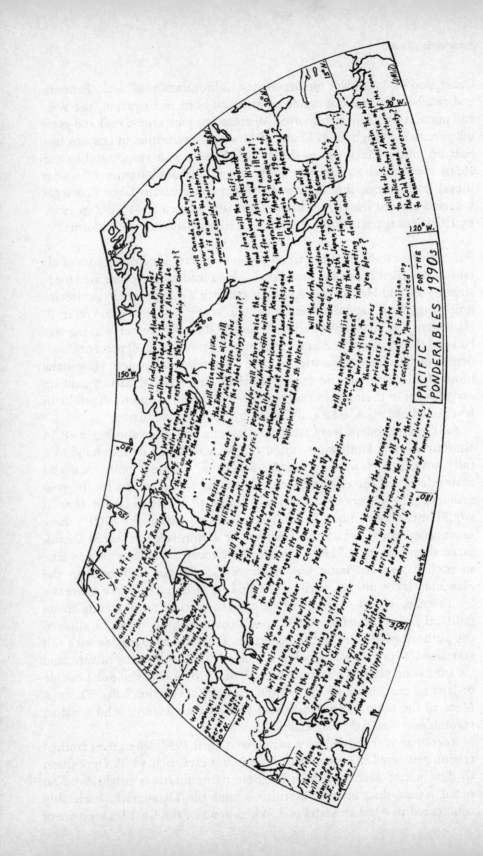

PACIFIC PONDERABLES 1990s

Will Canada crack over the Quebecois issue, and if so may its western provinces consider the U.S.?

How long will the Pacific southwestern states tolerate the flood of Asian and illegal immigration—regal conquest or "reconquista" of the 1990s—prove with the 190· conquest of California in the sphere?

Will the U.S. maintain its role to police Central America after the canal return to Cold War and sovereignty? the Pacific rim and sovereignty to Panamanian control?

Will "border" become an "electronic" curtain

Will the North American FreeTrade Association trade increase U.S. leverage in trade talks with Japan? Or crack the Pacific rim and dollar and competing into yen blocs?

Will indigenous Alaskan peoples follow the lead of the Canadian Inuits and demand that most of Alaska be restored to their ownership and control?

Will the native people of Bering Straits their coastline heritage in the wake of the Cold War?

Will disasters like the Exxon Valdez oil spill inspire North Pacific peoples to lead the global ecology movement?

...and/or will Nature punish the peoples of the North Pacific with drought as in California, hurricanes on Kauai, earthquakes as at Anchorage, Los Angeles, and San Francisco, and volcanic eruptions as in the Philippines and Mt. St. Helens?

Will the native Hawaiian "sovereignty" movement wrest title to thousands of acres of priceless land from the federal and state governments? Is Hawaiian Society truly "Americanized"?

Chukotsky

Kamchatka

Will Russia pay the cost to maintain its massive Military and naval Power in the northwest?

Will Russia reabsorbed the 4 Southernmost Kurile Islands for economic assistance?

Yakutia can a disintegrating Russia empire hold on to these autonomous Siberian provinces?

Will Japan choose— or be pressured— to complete its rearmament? Will its economy regain its habitual growth rates? Will One-party rule finally cease, and domestic consumption take priority over exports?

What will become of the Micronesians once the imperial powers have all gone home—will they recover the best of their heritage, or sink into poverty and violence, or be swamped by new waves of immigrants from Asia?

Will Japan escape to Japan in return to complete its rearmament? or go nuclear?

Will North Korea merge with Communism or will Taiwan merge with Mainland China after Hong Kong reverts to China in 1997? will the burgeoning capitalism of Guangdong (Kwantung) Province spread to all China?

Will the U.S. find new sites for Western Pacific military bases after the Philippines?

Will China's Communist gerontocracy permit economic pluralism or politic reform?

Will Japan objectively contest the U.S. or seek Asian economic competition?

Will Vietnam liberalize? Will Japan dominate the S.E. Asian economy?

June 30, 1958, reached Anchorage, "Alaska's largest city rocked and rolled as the air was split by the sounds of sirens, horns, bells, firecrackers, guns—and everything else that could be used to make a noise." Alaskan statehood followed on January 3, 1959, whereupon no sound argument remained against adding a fiftieth star to the flag. Lorrin P. Thurston, son of the man who had come to Washington to beg for annexation of Hawaii in the 1890s, led the lobby on Capitol Hill and triumphed in the vote of March 12. Hawaiian statehood followed on August 21, and the U.S. Information Agency was quick to interpret its Cold War significance:

> America will gain strength and reassurance at a time when forces of intolerance threaten the free peoples of the world. . . . As the only State in the Union with a striking Asian heritage, the example of Hawaii can have a profound effect on the so-called uncommitted nations of Asia. . . . It proves to others that, far from crushing minorities, we are glad to have them.

President John F. Kennedy opened the last act in 1963 when he asked Congress to reform immigration law. The most controversial proposal was elimination of all national quotas in favor of criteria for entry based on family status, economic skills, and status as a political refugee. That meant that Asians, Latin Americans, and indeed all aliens could apply for permits to live, work, study, and become citizens in the United States on an equal footing. And *that* meant that the United States would officially cease to be European or white. Proponents of the Immigration Act of 1965 promised that it would *not* open the floodgates to Third World immigration. In fact, it did. The family clauses meant that if one person got in, his or her entire family might follow, while the number of political refugees, especially from Southeast Asia, grew ever larger. By the late 1970s only 15 percent of new arrivals were European, over 40 percent were Asian, and the single greatest country of origin was Mexico. In the decade ending in 1980 over two million aliens settled in Los Angeles alone, by which time *whites* were often the ones living in walled-off neighborhoods. The demographic change in California was such that even while the state's population more than *tripled* between 1945 and 1990 to over thirty millions, the Caucasian percentage fell from three-quarters to barely half. An estimated quarter of a million legal and illegal immigrants continue to enter each year. Oregon, Washington, and British Columbia remain largely white, but the influx of Asian people and capital is unmistakable there as well.

So what transpired in the generation after the outbreak of war in Korea was the military, economic, and demographic retreat of (1) the United States, (2) American business, and (3) white people. And it happened not because the United States lost a war, or had a revolution, or because whites ceased to go West. It happened because the United States *won* World War II so thoroughly, dominated the entire Pacific, took upon itself the burden of defending the Free World's rimlands, and opened its markets and lands to the enterprise and immigrants of Asia and Mexico—all in the name of ideals of freedom, enterprise, equality, and human dignity introduced to the North Pacific by whites. To be sure, they made a poor show of living up to those ideals for two centuries, in part out of fear that their hold was tenuous. But after 1945 the United States (and Canada) reified those ideals, and so went into retreat.

The Dismissal

Saitō: Feelin' a bit sorry for ourselves, aren't we, Professor?

Seward: Sounds to me like our principles prevailed, even for Asians and Mexicans. Why don't you speak of Americans' triumph, rather than burden?

Witte: The burden was real. America sacrificed to overcome communism and helped to free even the Russians—but at a terrible cost to itself. It was America's finest hour, and if you are weaker for it, you should wear your weakness as a badge of honor.

Kaahumanu: You made Hawaii a state and ceased to consider the other states a preserve for *haoles* alone. Do your people now regret their charity?

Seward: Remember, Professor, why Yankees came to the North Pacific. It was to settle new lands, develop their resources, extend American law and commerce and religion to the great ocean of futurity. It would seem we succeeded, and if in the course of events we learned to respect the land and sea and animals and people we found there, so much the greater is our national glory. American principles do not exist just to serve the United States, nor do these United States exist just to serve white people. I would think our Civil War settled all that.

Kaahumanu: Who is an American? You asked that yourself, Scholar, when you spoke of the California gold rush. Does it matter that whites no longer dominate here, or there, if the peoples of other bloods embrace what they stood for?

Seward: Nor am I surprised that people of European stock are retreating a bit on Pacific shores. During my retirement tour I sensed a bit of what time held in store. "Unless the human race differs from all the other works of the Creator," I wrote, "He must have had some general plan for it, involving some unity of interest. Yet in all history, travel, and politics, any such design seems ignored, and mankind seems split up into diverse communities, warring against each other, or careless of each other's existence." It was to study the possibilities for human fraternity that I made my pilgrimage to the Pacific.

Saitō: And did you find your answer?

Seward: I found beauty beyond the imagining of Auburn, New York. I planned a Pacific library and had wood shipped back for beams and panels: Alaskan cedar, Vancouver laurel, Oregon pine, and redwood, of course, from California.

Scholar: I never heard of your Pacific library.

Seward: Never built it. Died first.

Saitō: But did you find your answer?

Seward: To the mystery of history? Only that—how did I put it?—"civilization has not been the prerogative, or the inheritance, or the work of any one race. One race takes it up and carries it to a certain point, then lapses into stagnation." See, I foresaw that Anglo-Saxon energies might flag. Then "another takes it up and carries civilization a step further. It marches on through one continent, at one time, through another, in a succeeding era. Different nations in turn become its leaders and exponents. Mankind, as a whole, profits by it, but only one portion, at a time, seems capable of assisting its progress."

Lea: Hegelian rubbish! Oh yes, nations and races rise and fall in their turn. That much is natural law. But to the profit of all mankind? Who is "mankind"? Even our sentimental sap of a professor careened into truth when he left off employing his inadequate brain and listened to what shrieked from his gut. The history of mankind is the history of race—blood and genetics trump "ideals" every time. That is why the "melting pot" nonsense verily *is* the American's burden. He talks himself into selling his birthright to assuage misplaced guilt. He ushers into his culture the aliens who would tear down his culture. He fools himself into thinking that peace and war are antonyms. "International war has no beginning or end, so long as mankind brings himself together in political and individual contention. Whether it is for good or for evil, this everlasting struggle forms the necessary motif of human aspiration. . . . Between a nest of ants by the roadside and a tribe of men upon a greater way, there is no difference. Individual strife is the epitome of selfishness; war a gigantic altruism."

Saitō: You know what, General Lea, you're beginnin' to bore me. Blood may be thicker than water, but even tribes learn when they get their fingers burned. The Russians overstepped their geopolitical limits when they tried to make a go in Alaska, or Manchuria. We Japanese overstepped when we tried to subdue China. Perhaps the Americans overstepped their natural bounds when they tried to police all of East Asia. But now that we've learned where our boundaries lie—

Lea: We'll all just bow and smile and exchange *alohas?* Envoy of the Mikado, you do your work well. Speak peace to the Saxon, the Slav, and Chinese. Espouse their ideals and lull them to sleep. Then *strike!* The Republic ignored my warnings. Open immigration for Asians and Mexicans! California less than half-white! I suppose Palo Alto now looks like Hong Kong.

Scholar: Hardly, Mr. Lea. Now, Berkeley—

Lea: America is already finished. Whatever superiority existed in the Saxon race is slain by its failure to grasp "the ephemeral character of national and racial existence in contrast to the inexorability of those external forces that control the progression and dissolution of political entities."

Scholar: Dissolution. . . ? You mean the United States itself will crack up?

Lea: As the British Empire before it. Tell me, is Canada still united?

Scholar: Good question. Barely.

Lea: So politics becomes a melee of breeds that rips the Republic apart from within. A mongrelized nation soon loses the will to defend its own city streets, or its borders against aliens, or its markets against commercial invasion. The *Empire,* by contrast, neither dies nor rests, for Japanese understand that the spirits of their ancestors and those of their children yet unborn are ever present about them, that a lifetime's toil is a small enough offering to place on the altar of the Yamato race. And that signifies that even the defeats of *six* generations cannot ruin Japan. But Americans have no contract with generations past or to come and are slaves to their wandering wants. And that signifies that the selfishness of *one* generation may suffice to spoil all that its forbears built up. It appears that is happening now, and if I hear any more I shall vomit. . . . Natter on, blind mice. By your leave, Kaahumanu, I am gone.

Scholar: He *is* gone.

Witte: Rude little man.

Seward: A Know-Nothing, and smeared by the Darwinist brush, I'd guess.

Scholar: But great in his way. Homer Lea! I just pray he's not right.

Seward: There are other sorts of power than those he imagines. Napoleon said that the spirit is to the sword as three is to one. And the craving for liberty is the greatest power of all. Seems to me that the races that share American soil will hang together so long as they cherish liberty more than resentments and fears.

Saitō: So what happens next, in the next North Pacific cycle? Do Americans resent Japanese success, or have we finally won their respect?

Scholar: Of course they resent it, but trends come and go. In a few years all the scaremongering over Japan may seem rather silly.

Seward: And do not underestimate the resilience of the American people. Remember, I lived through the greatest crisis of all, but the country was never so strong as when I departed. Problems are for solving, that's what I taught my children.

Scholar: But are the people still strong? Those same two or three generations of Americans that made such great sacrifices *abroad* to save the world from fascism and communism indulged themselves at home in the most—

Seward: Education's the ticket. So long as the schools and colleges are sound—

Scholar: But they're not, especially in black neighborhoods.

Seward: You don't say? I used to teach colored children their letters. Did fine, most of 'em. After the Rebellion we founded schools for them down South. Teach children their three R's, deportment, and civics, and the future takes care of itself. And sound money—got to have sound money—and partnership between government and business, internal improvements—the Republican party's genius. And immigrants! Every great burst of American growth was fed by immigration. These Asians—hard workers, I'll warrant. And Mexicans—get them thinking the American way and we might just lift up Mexico, too!

Scholar: That's the theory. There's a North American Free Trade Association in the works. U.S., Canada, and Mexico as one big economic bloc.

Seward: So my dream of a united North America wasn't so dotty after all! But what about the Pacific? Do you think Lea's right about another Japanese war?

Saitō: Not a chance, Guv. The Yanks won't turn their backs on us again—and my people wouldn't go crazy again even if they did.

Scholar: I tend to agree. But some authors have it that Japan is so dependent on exports that it can never satisfy U.S. demands for restraint. That will tempt the U.S. to go protectionist and quit paying for Japan's defense. That will force Japan to rearm and look for markets and materials in Asia, and it will be—

Witte: 1941 all over again. . . . Only it wouldn't be.

Scholar: How's that?

Witte: In 1941 the Germans were on the verge of conquering Europe, distracting Russia—

Scholar: —and distracting the U.S., which is what allowed the Japanese to think they could get away with grabbing their Coprosperity Sphere.

Kaahumanu: Recall the wisdom of Pearl Buck: only wars among *whites* raise the Yellow Peril. But you tell me that now even Russia is a friend.

Saitō: Nor can a new White Peril arise so long as Japan, China, and Korea remain at peace. But then where's the logic of your North Pacific triangle, Doc? If the last go-around led to Russia's defeat and Japan's revival, the next should lead to a Japanese-American conflict and *Russia's* revival.

Witte: A comforting thought. But let us pray first for Russia's *survival.* The professor sends chills down my spine with his talk of Siberian peoples seceding from Russia. But while I agree that Japanese-American tensions must doubtless recur, it does not follow that they must lead to war. Did Russia seek revenge against Japan after the calamity of 1905? No, tsars and Soviets lived in terror of another war with Japan. Even Nomonhan, when the brilliant Zhukov attacked, was meant to deter a war—an invasion of Siberia—not provoke one. I expect that Japan, in similar fashion, will be loath to repeat its experience of 1941–45.

Saitō: I concur. But how then will we two balance *American* power? Can't let the Yanks get too high and mighty, or they'll dream up some new world order and force us to play ball. How about a Russo-Japanese alliance, Count Witte? You game?

Scholar: That's a scary thought. Russia frees Japan from reliance on the U.S. and opens Siberia to Japanese capital. . . . And *that* would force China, Russia's rival on land, into alliance with the U.S., Japan's rival at sea. No, it can't happen. All of Siberia isn't worth half as much to Japan as access to the American market, while alliance with Russia would lose for Japan any hope of economic penetration of China. In any case, Moscow *still* won't give back those four Kurile islands, and the Japanese won't give the Russians the time of day until they do.

Witte: Oh yes, you said the Red Navy seized all the Kuriles north of Hokkaido. No, I suppose it is hard for Russia to disgorge them. They have been contested for so long and are so important to Russian control of the Sea of Okhotsk. I also imagine, after the loss of the Soviet empire, that Russians cannot bear to retreat any further. But imagine if the U.S. and Japan *did* confront each other again? Russia could sell its support for some price!

Seward: It therefore behooves the Yanks and the Japanese not to fall out but to help each other, and Russia as well. Perhaps that is the progress I looked for, the unity of interest, the march of civilization.

Every era of history presents civilization with challenges that call for a particular genius or virtue, and so it is that first one nation then another makes a gift of its genius to mankind. Americans offered their federalist system and reconciliation of law and liberty, their enterprise and technology, and suspicion of elites. Japanese can offer their example of discipline and consensus, love of nature and a dozen delicate arts, courage and sacrifice, and above all, adaptability. Perhaps it is time for Japanese to leave off living in worlds others make for them and take a hand in designing a better world for all.

Witte: Russia, Mr. Seward. What has Russia given the world, except musicians and novelists to record its pain?

Kaahumanu: Perhaps that *is* its gift, dear Count. Russia offers its pain so that others will not take their own blessings lightly. I can think of no greater gift.

Scholar: But if you insist on collective virtues, Mr. Seward, mustn't you also admit collective vices? Japanese say Americans are lazy, ignorant, shortsighted, hedonistic, selfish. There's some truth to it, isn't there? How about the American critique of Japan as a corporate hive of repressed, brainwashed, exploited, hysterical bees who read violent pornography on the subway and—what did the Frenchwoman say?—spend their nights thinking up ways to screw Europe and America. And remember Pobedonostsev's biting critique of the hypocrisies of the "democracy" of which Americans are so proud? I don't know how Russians and Japanese view each other. Maybe just with honest fear.

Serra: Perfect love casteth out all fear.

Scholar: Father Serra! I thought you had left.

Kaahumanu: The Serras of the world are never absent, Scholar.

Serra: We just know when to recede for a time. The habit—it puts people off. But I think it is time to dismiss you.

Scholar: Dismiss! And what do you . . . you mean it was *you* all along that—

Serra: Kaahumanu takes orders from no one, my son.

Kaahumanu: Father Serra means *we* judge it is time to dismiss you.

Serra: Tell us, Scholar, what have you learned from meeting us all?

Scholar: Plenty, and I'm looking forward to—. But isn't it more to the point to ask Kaahumanu what she learned from me? *She* was the one who . . . wasn't she?

Serra: Let me ask it another way. How would you describe us, in light of our histories?

Scholar: You mean you, Saitō, Seward, Kaahumanu, and Witte? Well, one thing I'd say is that you all represent your nations' best traditions of statesmanship.

Serra: A worthy reply, especially for one who "doesn't make value judgments."

Seward: I'm sure we appreciate the compliment, and it's certainly just so far as Witte and the others are concerned.

Witte: Mr. Seward, you're too modest.

Serra: Yet each of us knew failure—we have all admitted as much—

Saitō: Who thinks we're in for a sermon? Are heathens excused?

Serra: —and all of us had faults, and all of our policies had unintended consequences and nefarious side effects. So if we *are* among the best our nations produced, then how much more flawed must our compatriots have been? Why is it, doctor, that Saitō's common sense, savvy, and charm have rarely guided the statecraft of the Japanese Empire? Why have Seward's vision, integrity, and shrewd use of power in the service of justice not defined American statecraft as a matter of course? Why have Russian leaders so seldom displayed the qualities Witte was sacked for? Why do your nations hide their lamps under bushels?

Scholar: Great statesmen come along only so often.

Serra: Why? Just think if Americans, Japanese, and Russians—and Chinese and Koreans and Mexicans—radiated their genius instead of their fears?

Scholar: Because they've had reason. Fear inspired by real threats is healthy.

Serra: True enough, but geopolitics, economic competition, and cultural conflict are as much an excuse for your fears as the cause. How many of our fears and hatreds are born of our inability to face up to harm we have done others, not the harm that they have done us?

Scholar: Let me see if I understand. So I'm to forgive Saitō for bombing Pearl Harbor, or rather, I forgive *myself,* no, *he* forgives Japan for bombing Pearl Harbor and cornering the microchip market . . . while I forgive America for nuking Hiroshima—

Kaahumanu: And Nagasaki. Don't forget—

Scholar: —and we all live happily ever after. A counsel of perfection, Father Serra, or some kind of New Age . . . say, you *are* the founder of California. But *states,* governments, cannot "let go" of their fear—

Serra: I quite agree. Woe to the country that is *first* to lay down its fear. But it is not your own fears you need worry about, but those of the others. It is up to you to put *their* fears at rest, as they put to rest yours. Tame each other, learn from your failures, and your Pacific century may still come about.

Witte: No one has failed so often as Russians. Why haven't we learned the most?

Scholar: Perhaps you have. It was a Russian, Count Witte, imprisoned by the Communists, who told us that the line between good and evil does not run along national boundaries, or between races, classes, or genders, but straight through the middle of each human heart. Solzhenitsyn.

Witte: But Little Father, *our* days in the world are done. What does it profit Russia, Japan, or the United States if Witte, Saitō, and Seward meditate on how to *minimize* the fears of other nations . . . or is that where the scholar comes in?

Scholar: O no! Don't expect *me* to carry the wisdom of the ages to three great nations and tell them I heard it all from a Franciscan friar who's been dead for two hundred years!

Saitō: We've given up waiting for wisdom from *you*, Doc. Just tell our stories. And remember to leave 'em beggin' for more, just like in Vaudeville.

Scholar: What do you mean, stories?

Serra: You believe in history, correct? And that there is no one truth to be learned from it?

Scholar: That's right.

Serra: Then spread our stories like seed, and trust they may fall on some fertile ground. Remember, when Kaahumanu summoned you to this Place of Refuge, she did not call for a prophet or sage, or even historian. She asked for a storyteller.

Kaahumanu: And I always get what I ask for. Now, good man, is the time to go.

Scholar: But I don't want to go! I want to stay here with you.

Kaahumanu: You cannot stay in Pu'uhonua O Honaunau forever.

Saitō: It takes forever just to say it!

Kaahumanu: I tried to stay once, but my dog's bark betrayed me to Kamehameha.

Scholar: Please, Kaahumanu, don't send me away. I . . . I've—

Kaahumanu: You have fallen in love with me. All men do.

Scholar: But I love you all, even Saitō. Historians aren't supposed to fall in love with their characters.

Kaahumanu: But storytellers *must.* So which would you rather be? It is time, my Scholar. We give you our thanks . . . and our love. Now do what the lady is asking of you, and return your seatback to its full, upright position.

Acknowledgments

ONSIDERATIONS OF LENGTH and expense preclude a bibliography listing the six or seven hundred books, articles, and primary sources consulted over the five years I spent making *Noise* (the obvious in-house shorthand for this manuscript!). But those desirous of reading further on the history of the North Pacific will do well to begin with the following classics and recent masterpieces: O. H. K. Spate, *The Spanish Lake, Monopolists and Freebooters,* and *Paradise Found and Lost* (Minneapolis, 1979, 1983, and 1988), and J. C. Beaglehole, *The Life of Captain James Cook* (Stanford, 1974), on exploration in the age of sail; C. R. Boxer, *The Christian Century in Japan, 1549–1650* (Berkeley, 1951), and Mary Elizabeth Berry, *Hideyoshi* (Cambridge, Mass., 1982), on the founding of the Tokugawa Shogunate; Frederic Wakeman, Jr., *The Great Enterprise,* 2 vols. (Berkeley, 1985), and *The Fall of Imperial China* (New York, 1975), on the rise and fall of the Ch'ing dynasty; Marc Mancall, *Russia and China: Their Diplomatic Relations to 1728* (Cambridge, Mass., 1971), on the Russians in Siberia and on the Treaty of Nerchinsk; George A. Lensen, *The Russian Push Toward Japan* (Princeton, 1959), on tsarist ambitions in the North Pacific; P. A. Tikhmenev, *A History of the Russian America Company* (Seattle, 1978 [1861–63]), and S. B. Okun, *The Russian American Company* (New York, 1979 [1951]), on Alaska under the tsars; Hector Chevigny, *Lord of Alaska* (New York, 1942), on Baranov; Herbert E. Bolton, *An Outpost of Empire* (New York, 1966 [1930]), on Serra and the founding of Alta California; Warren L. Cook, *Flood Tide of Empire* (New Haven, 1973), on the Spanish and British in northwest America; Ralph C. Kuykendall, *The Hawaiian Kingdom,* 3 vols. (Honolulu, 1938–67), and Gavan Daws, *The Shoal of Time* (Honolulu, 1968), on Hawaiian history generally; William H. Goetzmann, *Exploration and Empire* (New York, 1966), on the early American West; Howard I. Kushner, *Conflict on the Northwest Coast*

(Westport, 1975), on U.S.-Russian rivalry in Alaska; Walton Bean and James J. Rawls, *California: An Interpretive History*, 4th ed. (Englewood Cliffs, 1983), and Robert Glass Cleland, *From Wilderness to Empire* and *California in Our Time* (New York, 1944 and 1947), on California history generally; John King Fairbank, *Trade and Diplomacy on the China Coast* (Stanford, 1969 [1953]), on the opium wars; Immanuel C. Y. Hsü, *The Rise of Modern China*, 4th ed. (New York, 1990), on nineteenth- and twentieth-century Chinese history; E. E. Rich, *Hudson's Bay Company*, 2 vols. (London, 1959), and John S. Galbraith, *The Hudson's Bay Company as an Imperial Factor* (Berkeley, 1957), on the settlement of western Canada and Oregon; Frederick Merk, *Manifest Destiny and Mission in American History* (New York, 1963), on U.S. expansion to the Pacific; David M. Pletcher, *The Diplomacy of Annexation* (Columbia, Mo., 1973), on Texas, Polk, and the Mexican War; Peter Booth Wiley, *Yankees in the Land of the Gods* (New York, 1990), on Commodore Perry; Thomas M. Huber, *The Revolutionary Origins of Modern Japan* (Stanford, 1981), and Conrad Totman, *The Collapse of the Tokugawa Bakufu* (Honolulu, 1980), on the origins of the Meiji Restoration; Norman E. Saul, *Distant Friends: The United States and Russia* (Lawrence, 1991), on the sale of Alaska, and William R. Hunt, *Arctic Passage* (New York, 1975), for Bering Sea history generally; Merze Tate, *The United States and the Hawaiian Kingdom: A Political History* (New Haven, 1965) and *Hawaii: Reciprocity or Annexation?* (East Lansing, 1968), on the American takeover; Richard Storry, *A History of Modern Japan* (New York, 1960), and W. G. Beasley, *The Rise of Modern Japan* (London, 1990), on Japan since the Meiji Restoration; Akira Iriye, *Across the Pacific* (New York, 1967), *Pacific Estrangement* (Cambridge, Mass., 1972), *After Imperialism* (Cambridge, Mass., 1965), and *The Origins of the Second World War in Asia and the Pacific* (London, 1987), on U.S.-Japanese relations generally; Harold and Margaret Sprout, *The Rise of American Naval Power* (Annapolis, 1966 [1939]) and *Toward a New Order of Sea Power* (New York, 1943), William R. Braisted, *The United States Navy in the Pacific*, 2 vols. (Austin, 1958 and 1971), and Roger Dingman, *Power in the Pacific* (Chicago, 1976), on American naval power before and after World War I; William Goetzmann and Kay Sloan, *Looking Far North* (Princeton, 1982), on the Harrimans in Alaska; David McCullough, *Path Between the Seas* (New York, 1977), on the Panama Canal; Ian Nish, *The Anglo-Japanese Alliance* (London, 1966) and *The Origins of the Russo-Japanese War* (London, 1985), and Denis and Peggy Warner, *The Tide at Sunrise* (New York, 1974), on the Russo-Japanese War; Raymond A. Esthus, *Theodore Roosevelt and Japan* (Seattle, 1966) and *Double Eagle and Rising Sun* (Durham, 1988), on the Treaty of Portsmouth; Mark R. Peattie, *The Japanese Colonial Empire* (Princeton,

1984), *Nan'yo: The Rise and Fall of the Japanese in Micronesia* (Honolulu, 1988), and *Ishiwara Kanji and Japan's Confrontation With the West* (Princeton, 1975), on the ideology of Japanese expansion; Gordon Thomas and Max Witts, *The San Francisco Earthquake* (New York, 1971), and Edward Seidensticker, *Low City, High City* and *Tokyo Rising* (New York, 1983 and 1990), on the San Francisco and Tokyo calamities; Roger Daniels, *The Politics of Prejudice* (New York, 1972), on the movement for Japanese exclusion; William H. Honan, *Visions of Infamy* (New York, 1991), on Hector Bywater, and Edward S. Miller, *War Plan Orange* (Annapolis, 1991), on U.S. war plans for Japan; Alvin D. Coox, *The Anatomy of a Small War* (Westport, 1977) and *Nomonhan*, 2 vols. (Stanford, 1985), on Russo-Japanese clashes in Manchuria; Michael Barnhart, *Japan Prepares for Total War* (Ithaca, 1987), and Meirion and Susan Harries, *Soldiers of the Sun* (New York, 1991), on the Japanese Army; Robert A. Divine, *The Reluctant Belligerent*, 2nd ed. (New York, 1979), and Gordon W. Prange, *At Dawn We Slept* and *Pearl Harbor: The Verdict of History* (New York, 1981 and 1986), on the origins of the Pearl Harbor attack; Ronald H. Spector, *Eagle Against the Sun* (New York, 1985), Prange, *Miracle at Midway* (New York, 1982), S. E. Smith, ed., *The United States Marine Corps in World War II* (New York, 1969), John W. Dower, *War Without Mercy* (New York, 1986), and Michael S. Sherry, *The Rise of American Air Power* (New Haven, 1987), on the conduct of the Pacific War; Richard B. Finn, *Winners in Peace* (Berkeley, 1992), Theodore Cohen, *Remaking Japan* (New York, 1987), Michael Schaller, *The American Occupation of Japan* (New York, 1985), Harries and Harries, *Sheathing the Sword* (New York, 1987), Marc S. Gallicchio, *The Cold War Begins in Asia* (New York, 1988), and Bruce Cumings, *The Origins of the Korean War*, 2 vols. (Princeton, 1981 and 1990), on the postwar period.

Readers will also benefit, as I did, from punching up the following names on a library computer. *On California:* Hubert Howe Bancroft, John Francis Bannon, Gunther Barth, Richard Batman, Charles E. Chapman, Richard Dillon, Robert M. Fogelson, J. S. Holliday, William Issel (and Robert W. Cherny), Judd Kahn, John H. Kemble, John C. Kennedy, Robert E. Levinson, Oscar Lewis, Roger Lotchin, Stanford M. Lyman, Doris Muscatine, Doyce B. Nunis, Spencer Olin, Herbert I. Priestley, Kevin Starr, George R. Stewart, Edward F. Treadwell. *On the Pacific Northwest:* G. P. V. and Helen Akrigg, Bern Anderson, Jean Barman, George Bryce, Malcolm Clark, Gordon B. Dodds, Robert E. Ficken (and Charles Le Ware), Gabriel Franchere, Peter Gerhard, George Godwin, Barry M. Gough, Herbert Hunt, Dorothy O. Johanson (and Charles M. Gates), Norbert MacDonald, James S. Marshall, Murray Morgan, Arthur S. Morton, Margaret A. Ormsby, Derek Pethick, James P. Ronda, Roger

Sale. *On Alaska:* Raymond H. Fisher, Brian Garfield, James R. Gibson, Frank A. Golder, P. N. Golovin, Ted C. Hinckley, K. T. Khlebnikov, Peter Lauridsen, Roy Minter, Claus-M. Naske (and Herman E. Slotnick), Morgan Sherwood, S. Frederick Starr, David Wharton. *On the Hawaiian Islands:* Jacob Adler (and Robert M. Kamins), Edward D. Beechert, Roger Bell, Harold W. Bradley, Joseph Brennan, George Cooper, A. Grove Day, Lawrence H. Fuchs, Dorothy O. Hazama (and Jane O. Komeiji), Paul F. Hooper, Edward Joesting, Donald D. Johnson, Alfons L. Korn, Andrew W. Lind, Gananath Obeyesekere, Thomas J. Osborne, Richard A. Pierce, Stanley D. Porteus, John J. Stephan, S. K. Stevens, Ruth Tabrah, Richard Tregaskis, Richard A. Wisniewski, Paul T. Yardley. *On Siberia and Russia:* Terence E. Armstrong, Glynn Barratt, William G. Bray, Francis Carr, O. Edmund Clubb, John S. Curtiss, Paul Dotsenko, Dietrich Geyer, William E. Griffith, G. M. Hamburg, Richard A. Hough, Taras Hunczak, Robert J. Kerner, George V. Lantzeff, Ivo J. Lederer, D. C. B. Lieven, W. Bruce Lincoln, William O. McCagg, Jr., Robert J. Maddox, Raisa V. Makarova, Janet Martin, Robert K. Massie, Vojtech Mastny, Donald W. Mitchell, Mairin Mitchell, James Morley, William Henry Parker, R. I. Quested, Nicholas V. Riasanovsky, Boris A. Romanov, Yuri Semyonov, Russell E. Snow, Peter S. H. Tang, Eugene P. Trani, Donald W. Treadgold, Adam Ulam, Betty Miller Unterberger, George Vernadsky, Robert Wesson, Alan Wood (and R. A. French), Donald Zagoria. *On Japan:* Pat Barr, Gordon Mark Berger, Delmer M. Brown, Lewis Bush, Albert M. Craig, Peter Duus, Edwin A. Falk, Carol Gluck, Roger F. Hackett, John A. Harrison, Edwin P. Hoyt, Saburo Ienaga, Marius B. Jansen, Chalmers Johnson, E. Morinosuke Kajima, Bartlett Kerr, Arthur J. Marder, Joseph L. Marx, Tetsuo Najita, Sharon H. Nolte, Sadako N. Ogata, Shumpei Okamoto, Kenneth B. Pyle, Edwin O. Reischauer, Gilbert Rozman, George Sansom, Robert Scalapino, Irwin Scheiner, Richard J. Smethurst, Thomas C. Smith, John Toland, Robert E. Ward, Ki-Baik Yee, Akira Yoshimura. *On Manchuria, China, and overseas Chinese:* Jack Beeching, Anthony B. Chan, Jack Chen, Peter W. Fay, Wolfgang Franke, Edmund S. K. Fung, Clarence E. Glick, Gerald S. Graham, Edgar Holt, Michael H. Hunt, Key-Hiuk Kim, Chong-Sik Lee, Robert H. G. Lee, Steven I. Levine, Li Tien-lu, Delber L. McKee, James M. Polachek, Alexander P. Saxton, Harold Z. Schiffrin, James Claude Thomson, Henry Tsai, Paul A. Varg, Charles Vivier, Arthur Waldron. *On U.S. westward expansion:* John Logan Allen, Ray Billington, Kenneth Bourne, Albert Britt, Alexander DeConde, Jonathan Goldstein, Norman A. Graebner, Thomas R. Hietala, Donald D. Jackson, John Keats, Robert R. Kirsch (and William Murphy), Gerald D. Nash, Stuart Nixon, Joseph W. Schmitz, Stanley Siegel, Marshall Sprague, Reginald C. Stuart, Richard W. Van Alstyne, Albert K. Weinberg, David J.

Wishart, Donald Worster. *On U.S. war and diplomacy:* Robert G. Albion, Steven E. Ambrose, Thomas A. Bailey, Glen Barclay, Harold K. Beale, Samuel Flagg Bemis, Dorothy Borg, James C. Bradford, David Calleo, Ian Cameron, Diane Shaver Clemens, Alan B. Cole, Richard Collier, Ernest Dodge, Arthur P. Dudden, Foster Rhea Dulles, Thomas G. Dyer, John Eisenhower, Keith Eubank, Herbert Feis, Robert Ferrell, John Lewis Gaddis, Lloyd Gardner, Betty Glad, Charles T. Gregg, A. Whitney Griswold, Robert A. Hart, Daniel R. Headrick, Waldo Heinrichs, Michael J. Hogan, D. Clayton James, Paul Johnson, Robert E. Johnson, Manfred Jonas, Stanley Karnow, George F. Kennan, Paul Kennedy, Walter LaFeber, Edwin T. Layton, N. Gordon Levin, David F. Long, Wm. Roger Louis, John Lukacs, William H. McNeill, Ernest R. May, Charles L. Mee, H. Wayne Morgan, Gerald D. Nash, Richard O'Connor, Thomas J. Osborne, Thomas G. Paterson, Julius W. Pratt, Merlo J. Pusey, James R. Reckner, David M. Reimers, William A. Renzi (and Mark D. Doehrs), Stephen Roskill, Keith Sainsbury, John Schroeder, Robert Seager II, Charles G. Sellers, Gaddis Smith, Philip V. Stern, Christopher Thorne, Pauline Tompkins, Robert F. Wesser, William A. Williams, Roberta Wohlstetter, Albert A. Woldman. *On sailing technology:* Kenneth J. Carpenter, H. I. Chappelle, Carl C. Cutler, Robin Fisher (and Hugh Johnson), Herman R. Friis, Clara I. Judson, David Mackay, Samuel Eliot Morison, John H. Parry, E. G. R. Taylor. *On railroads, steamships, and aviation:* George B. Abdill, Charles Edgar Ames, Pierre Berton, Gerald M. Best, Basil Collier, Ronald E. Coon, Burke Davis, R. E. G. Davis, Edwin M. Fitch, R. A. Fletcher, John Debo Galloway, Robert L. Gandt, Julius Grodinsky, Terry Gwynn-Jones, R. M. Haywood, James B. Hedges, Robin Higham, William J. Horvatt, Alfred F. Hurley, G. G. Jackson, Maury Klein, W. K. Lamb, Mary S. Lovell, Robert A. Lovett, Stephen G. Marks, Albro Martin, Jacob Metzer, Glenn Quiett, John Bell Rae, Doris L. Rich, Douglas H. Robinson, K. T. Rowland, Robert R. Russell, Robert H. Scheppler, William A. Schoneberger, George Rogers Taylor, Harmon Tupper, J. N. Westwood, Charles and Dorothy Wood. *On Kaahumanu:* Kathleen D. Mellen, Jane L. Silverman. *On Seward:* G. E. Baker, Frederic Bancroft, Earl Conrad, Norman B. Ferris, Thornton K. Lathrop, Ernest N. Paolino, Frederick W. Seward, Glyndon G. Van Deusen. *On Witte:* Vladimir Brenner, Theodore Von Laue, Abraham Yarmolinsky. *On Saitō:* No biography exists. *On Serra:* Katherine and Edward M. Ainsworth, Don DeNevi, Omer Englebert, Maynard J. Geiger, Noel Francis Moholy, James M. Sandos, Winifred E. Wise. *On Lea:* Eugene Anschel, Clare Boothe Luce. *On the Pacific Rim today:* Daniel Burstein, Thurston Clarke, William S. Dietrich, Bill Emmott, James Fallows, George Friedman (and Meredith Lebard), Frank Gibney, William J. Holstein, Robert L. Kearns, Michael Lewis, Clyde Prestowitz,

Gerald Segal, Jared Taylor, Ezra Vogel, Simon Winchester, Karel van Wolferen, Robert Zielinski (and Nigel Holloway).

For better or worse I drafted the maps myself. Their sources of data were: Spate, *The Spanish Lake*, vi–vii, 166, *Paradise Found and Lost*, 111, 140, and *Monopolists and Freebooters*, 238; *Encyclopaedia Britannica*, 15th ed. (1989), 25: 139; Berry, *Hideyoshi*, 28, 210; Lensen, *The Russian Push Toward Japan*, 16; Kerner, *The Urge to the Sea* (New York, 1942), 70, 74, 76, 80; Lantzeff and Pierce, *Eastward to Empire* (Montreal, 1973), 9–11; Mancall, *Russia and China*, 112–13; Bean and Rawls, *California*, 45, 118; Bradley, *The American Frontier in Hawaii: The Pioneers 1789–1843* (Stanford, 1942), frontispiece; Tikhmenev, *History of the Russian-American Company*, 2; R. R. Palmer, ed., *Historical Atlas of the World* (Chicago, 1965), 21; Goetzmann, *Exploration and Empire*, 23; Barman, *The West Beyond the West: A History of British Columbia* (Toronto, 1991), xvi; Cutler, *Greyhounds of the Sea* (Annapolis, 1984 [1930]), frontispiece; McCullough, *Path Between the Seas*, 131; Hsü, *Rise of Modern China*, 262, 266, 280; Totman, *Collapse of the Tokugawa Bakufu*, 230; Wiley, *Yankees in the Land of the Gods*, 236; Vladimir, *Russia on the Pacific* (London, 1899), 176, 216; Goetzmann and Sloan, *Looking Far North*, 7; Wharton, *The Alaska Gold Rush* (Bloomington, 1972), frontispiece; Warner and Warner, *The Tide at Sunrise*, 259, 293, 318, 468; Grodinsky, *Transcontinental Railway Strategy, 1869–1893* (Philadelphia, 1962), 39, 176, 310; *Atlas of the World and Gazetteer* (New York, 1924), 44, 50–55; Headrick, *The Invisible Weapon: Telecommunications and International Politics, 1851–1945* (New York, 1991), 95; Gwynn-Jones, *The Air Racers: Aviation's Golden Era* (London, 1984), 146; Coox, *Nomonhan*, frontispiece, 184–85, 588; Thomas E. Griess, ed., *Campaign Atlas to the Second World War* (Wayne Point, N.J., 1989), Part Two; Carl W. Hoffman, *Saipan: The Beginning of the End* (U.S. Marine Corps Historical Division, 1950).

It was rather silly of me, I suppose, to undertake this history of the North Pacific in the very year I *left* the University of California, Berkeley, for the East Coast. But the University of Pennsylvania has been a supportive home, thanks above all to Martin K. Alloy and Lawrence Ansin, whose endowment of a chair and research budget in International Relations helped to finance my research. I also thank former Provost Michael Aiken and former Dean Hugo Sonnenschein of the School of Arts and Sciences, who granted me a semester's sabbatical and another semester of leave to work on the book. I thank my excellent Associate Director and Administrative Assistant in the International Relations program, Frank Plantan and Donna Shuler, for loyal and tireless labors in our office while I stole time to work instead on this book. I also thank my colleagues at Penn, especially Thomas Childers, Hilary Conroy (who made available to me his extensive personal library on Japanese history), Bruce Kuklick, Susan Naquin (who read portions of the manuscript), Alfred Rieber, Alvin Rubinstein, and Marc Trachtenberg.

I am extremely grateful to the Earhart Foundation for a generous stipend during my semester of unpaid leave. I am indebted to the Hoover Institution on War, Revolution, and Peace, especially Director John Raisian, Associate Director Thomas Henriksen, and Senior Fellow Dennis Bark, for hosting me as a Visiting Scholar in 1991. The Hoover Institution is an excellent place to research and write for many reasons, not the least being its efficient and courteous staff. I thank Deborah Ventura in particular. But the Hoover is also a place of unusual liveliness, diversity, and sheer brainpower, and I thank Director Emeritus W. Glenn Campbell, Angelo Codevilla, and David Gress for allowing me to bounce ideas off them. I also thank the staffs of the Hoover and Stanford libraries, Doe and Bancroft libraries at the University of California, Berkeley, the Hawaii State Archives and Bishop Museum in Honolulu, the National Archives in Washington, D.C., and the Public Record Office at Kew Gardens, England.

A large portion of my research and some of the early writing was accomplished at the Library of Congress. I thank the Librarian of Congress, James H. Billington, for his support and counsel, and the excellent staff of the Library, including Ronald Morse, the Japan specialist. I also had the privilege of picking the considerable brain of Librarian of Congress Emeritus, Daniel Boorstin. In Philadelphia I welcomed the support of the Foreign Policy Research Institute, its former Director Daniel Pipes, and Associate Director Alan Luxenberg.

Many individuals contributed ideas, sources, and leads that enriched the final text. A great scholar and gentleman, the late Paul Seabury, encouraged and aided my study of the North Pacific. Christopher Gray, a living card catalog, alerted me to whole areas of inquiry I might otherwise have missed, then rattled off the three or four books I must consult about each. Thank you, Chris, and thanks, too, to Sara Baase, Daniel Bigelow, Gavan Daws, David Eisenhower, Drs. George and Myrl Hermann, Richard Herr (who encouraged me to indulge my imagination at a critical point in my life), Lance Izumi, Donald Johnson, Noel Francis Moholy, Robert S. and Nancy Morse, William A. Rusher, Peter Yongshik Shin, James Shinn, John Tanaka, and Arthur Waldron. Needless to say, I am deeply grateful to my editor Steven Fraser, who allowed me to sell him the notion, not of an historical novel, but of a novelistic history written, though it be serious nonfiction, in a spirit of magic. Steve saw what I saw and helped me to make the book match my vision. We in turn were expertly aided at Basic Books by Edward Cone, William Davis, Kermit Hummel, Michael Mueller, Gary Murphy, Mark Pensavalle, Julia Petrakis, Randall Pink, Gay Salisbury, Lois Shapiro, Akiko Takano, and Craig Winer.

Last of all I thank my wife, Jonna Van Zanten McDougall. A native Californian who never lets anyone forget it, she agreed to marry me in 1988 even *after* I told her of my decision to move to Philadelphia. So she and I and Penn and *Noise* have all been together these past five years. I know she'll be glad to be rid of one of those four. I refer, of course, to the book. . . .

Speaking of "noise," I take responsibility for the errors that have crept into the manuscript like rats that board a ship, hide out in the hold, and mock all efforts at extermination. So I ask my readers to join with Kaahumanu, Serra, Saitō, Seward, Witte, and Lea—who never shrank from noting my shortcomings—and to inform Basic Books of any errors found. It's a long book, after all, that tells many stories, and I composed it, remember, from memory, on an airplane, sound asleep.

Walter A. McDougall
Bryn Mawr, Pennsylvania
September 1993

Sources of Quotations

Epigraphs

"Let the sea make a noise": Psalm 98:8 according to the translation of *The Book of Common Prayer* (1979), 728.

"Yet every place is duly allotted": C. Day Lewis, ed. and trans., *The Aeneid of Virgil* (New York: Doubleday Anchor, 1952), 142.

The Summons

"Jesu, Maria, and Santiago": see George Sansom, *A History of Japan, 1334–1615*, 3 vols. (Stanford: Stanford University Press, 1961), 1:298.

"fühlbare, sichtbare Strafe": Karl Haushofer, *Geopolitik des pazifischen Ozeans* (Berlin-Grunewald: Kurt Vowinckel Verlag, 1924), 234.

The First 'aha iki

"That infatuated old ass" and "if this foreign person": A. Grove Day, ed., *Mark Twain's Letters From Hawaii* (Honolulu: University of Hawaii Press, 1966), 10.

32° North Latitude, 159° East Longitude, 1565

"as big as cows" and "Urdaneta's route": O. H. K. Spate, *The Spanish Lake* (Minneapolis: University of Minnesota Press, 1979), 105.

Nagasaki 1638

"great general who subdues the barbarians": Mary Elizabeth Berry, *Hideyoshi* (Cambridge: Harvard University Press, 1989), 12.

"Tanegashima weapon": Spate, *Spanish Lake*, 154.

"all white . . . courteous" and "naturally very intelligent" and "the most warlike and bellicose race" and "Similarly many men kill themselves" and "the most false and treacherous people" and "the finest Christianity in all the East": C. R. Boxer, *The Christian Century in Japan, 1549–1650* (Berkeley: University of California Press, 1951), 74–76.

Peking 1644

Pole Star had "slipped": Frederic Wakeman, Jr., *The Great Enterprise: The Manchu Reconstruction of Imperial Order in Seventeenth Century China*, 2 vols. (Berkeley: University of California Press, 1985), 1:258.
"Son of Heaven": ibid., 1:266.
"nourishment policy": ibid., 1:180.

Nerchinsk 1689

"politics should be studied with large maps": in House of Lords (June 11, 1877); Robert Taylor, *Lord Salisbury* (London: Allen Lane, 1975), 53.
"*ruotsi*, those who rowed": Jesse D. Clarkson, *A History of Russia* (New York: Random House, 1962), 28.
"beyond the great ocean.": Mark Mancall, *Russia and China: Their Diplomatic Relations to 1728* (Cambridge: Harvard University Press, 1971), 34.
"for Christianity's sake": ibid., 99.

Petropavlovsk 1741

"magnificent people": George A. Lensen, *The Russian Push Toward Japan* (Princeton: Princeton University Press, 1959), 26.
"to describe . . . whether Asia and America are joined": O. H. K. Spate, *Monopolists and Freebooters* (Minneapolis: University of Minnesota Press, 1983), 229.
"to a settlement under European authority": Frank A. Golder, *Russian Expansion on the Pacific, 1641–1850* (Gloucester, Mass.: Peter Smith, 1960), 134.
"the eternally famous Peter": F. A. Golder, ed., *Bering's Voyages*, 2 vols. (American Geographical Society, 1922–25), 1:31.
"Leave it, for the warmth": Sven Waxell, *The American Expedition*, M. A. Michael, trans. (London: W. Hodge, 1952), cited in George Wilhelm Steller, *Journal of a Voyage with Bering, 1741–1742* (Stanford: Stanford University Press, 1988), 215.
"mildest of all marine mammals": Stepan P. Krashennikov, *Explorations of Kamchatka, 1735–1741* (Portland: Oregon Historical Society, 1972), 156; cited by William R. Hunt, *Arctic Passage: The Turbulent History of the Land and People of the Bering Sea, 1697–1975* (New York: Scribner's, 1975), 33.
"More important discoveries were made": William Coxe, *Account of the Russian Discoveries between Asia and America* (Ann Arbor: University of Michigan Press, 1966 [1787]), 21.

Alta California 1769

"My sons, what is your petition?" and "I desire to profess": Don DeNevi and Noel Francis Moholy, *Junípero Serra* (San Francisco: Harper & Row, 1985), 17.
"jester of the Lord": ibid., 17.
"Walk in that light": ibid., 22.
"To future good will Jove dispose": ibid., 22.
"to revive in my soul": Maynard Geiger, ed. and trans., *Palou's Life of Fray Junípero Serra* (Washington, D.C.: Academy of American Franciscan History, 1955), 5.

"stiff-necked heretic": ibid., 13.

"Recant, you petty monk of Satan!": Omer Englebert, *The Last of the Conquistadors*, Katherine Woods, trans. (New York: Harcourt, Brace, 1956), 13.

"I have observed": DeNevi & Moholy, *Junípero Serra*, 36.

"No es cosa de cuidado": Englebert, *Last of the Conquistadors*, 23.

"What more do we want": DeNevi & Moholy, *Junípero Serra*, 13.

"They are like children": John D. Bergamini, *The Spanish Bourbons: The History of a Tenacious Dynasty* (New York: Putnam, 1974), 95.

"the ugliest couple on earth": (a British envoy, 1753), ibid., 84.

"The king has need of you": Englebert, *Last of the Conquistadors*, 59.

San Diego "very cold": DeNevi & Moholy, *Junípero Serra*, 92.

"descried a large bay": Alan K. Brown, trans., *Gaynor de Portolá: Explorer and Founder of California* (Lorida, Spain: F. Boneu, 1983), 241–42.

"a pleasing stretch of land": DeNevi & Moholy, *Junípero Serra*, 102.

"proceeded to erect a fort": Charles E. Chapman, *A History of California: The Spanish Period* (New York: Macmillan, 1921), 227.

"in danger of death": DeNevi & Moholy, *Junípero Serra*, 123.

"aggression" and "important discoveries": Charles E. Chapman, *The Founding of Spanish California: The Northwestward Expansion of New Spain* (Berkeley: University of California Press, 1916), 220–21, 226–27.

"consequences of having other neighbors" and "indispensable": Chapman, *History of California*, 272, 278.

"marvel of nature" and "harbor of harbors" and "there would not be anything more beautiful": Herbert E. Bolton, *An Outpost of Empire* (New York: Russell & Russell, 1966 [1930]), 506.

The Second 'aha iki

"While the missionary is alive": DeNevi & Moholy, *Junípero Serra*, 155.

"Unless our Catholic philosophy": ibid., 10.

Kealakekua Bay 1779

"nation of men like monkeys" and "I did not say" and "a plain sensible man": J. C. Beaglehole, *The Life of Captain James Cook* (Stanford: Stanford University Press, 1974), 451.

mere "curiosity": O. H. K. Spate, *Paradise Found and Lost* (Minneapolis: University of Minnesota Press, 1988), 81.

"It was curious to see Cook": Beaglehole, *Life of Cook*, 475.

Cook to look "very carefully": ibid., 490–91.

"This is an American indeed!": John Ledyard, *Journal of Captain Cook's Last Voyage*, James K. Munford, ed. (Corvallis: Oregon State University Press, 1963), 72.

"theoretical geographers": G. Williams, "Myth and Reality: Cook and the Theoretical Geography of Northwest America," in Robin A. Fisher and Hugh Johnston, eds., *Captain James Cook and His Times* (Seattle: University of Washington Press, 1979).

"They shook their spears at us": Ledyard, *Journal*, 66–67.

"Orono! Orono!": (Lt. James King journal), Gavan Daws, *Shoal of Time: A History of the Hawaiian Islands* (Honolulu: University of Hawaii Press, 1968), 11.

Nootka Sound 1790

"with considerable slaughter": London *World* (Oct. 6 and 13, 1788), cited by Derek Pethick, *First Approaches to the North-West Coast* (Vancouver: J. J. Douglas, 1976), 79.

"It is for traders to traffic": (1769), Hector Chevigny, *Russian America: The Great Alaskan Venture 1741–1867* (New York: Viking, 1965), 50.

"time to breathe": Leeds to Pitt (June 2, 1790), Public Record Office (hereafter PRO) 30/8/151, nos. 51–52, cited by Howard V. Evans, "The Nootka Sound Controversy in Anglo-French Diplomacy—1790," *Journal of Modern History* 46, no. 4 (Dec. 1974): 609–40 (615).

"utmost horror and detestation": Fitzherbert to Leeds (Sept. 16, 1790), PRO Foreign Office (hereafter FO) 72/19, nos. 26–32; cited by ibid., 623.

"We are not contending": Spate, *Paradise Found and Lost*, 318.

"To describe the beauties of this region": George Vancouver, *A Voyage of Discovery to the North Pacific Ocean and around the World,* 3 vols. (London: C. J. Robinson and J. Edwards, 1798), 1:259.

"a dinner of five courses": ibid., 1:385.

"got quite fat": Thomas Manby journal (Jan. 9, 1793), cited by Janet R. Fireman, "The Seduction of George Vancouver: A Nootka Affair," *Pacific Historical Review* 56, no. 3 (Aug. 1987): 427–43 (439).

Hokkaido 1792

"first piece of national defense literature": Lensen, *Russian Push Toward Japan,* 83.

"sober" soldier: ibid, 87.

"tales of the floating world" and "bundle of desire": "Japan," *Encyclopedia Britannica,* 15 ed. (Chicago, 1989), 22:319.

"Guardians of Hakodate beware!": Lensen, *Russian Push Toward Japan,* 181.

"My son did not have to deny": ibid., 118–19.

"Permission for entrance into Nagasaki Harbor": ibid., 114.

Kealakekua Bay 1794

"Maiha-Maiha, whose hair was now plaisted": Lt. King's Journal (Jan. 26, 1779), cited by Ralph S. Kuykendall, *The Hawaiian Kingdom,* 3 vols.; Volume 1, *Foundation and Transformation, 1778–1854* (Honolulu: University of Hawaii Press, 1947), 31.

"bristled its feathers": Richard Tregaskis, *The Warrior King: Kamehameha the Great* (New York: Macmillan, 1973), 177.

"plump and jolly, very lively" and "of Kamehameha's two possessions": Jane L. Silverman, *Kaahumanu, Molder of Change* (Honolulu: Judiciary History Center, 1987), 1, 13.

"for a bite" and "the quantity he consumed": Thomas Manby, "Journal of Vancouver's Journey to the Pacific Ocean (1791–1793)," cited by James Stirral Marshall and Carrie Marshall, *Vancouver's Voyage,* 2d ed. (Vancouver: Mitchell Press, 1967), 163.

"taboo King George": Ben Anderson, *The Life and Voyages of Captain George Vancouver* (Toronto: University of Toronto Press, 1960), 144.

"country town of the Angels": George Vancouver, *A Voyage of Discovery to the North Pacific Ocean and Round the World, 1791–1795*, 4 vols. (London: The Hakluyt Society, 1984 [London: John Stockdale, 1798]), 4:1104.

"discarded her": Silverman, *Kaahumanu*, 27.

"for the sole purpose of Tamaahmaah's protection": Vancouver, *Voyage of Discovery*, 3:836.

"[But] in the case of Nootka": ibid. 3: 31., Hakluyt, ed.

Sitka 1799

"Nanook of the Russians": Hector Chevigny, *Lord of Alaska. Baranov and the Russian Adventure* (New York: Viking, 1942), 164.

"My first steps into this country": ibid., 55.

"have the character of a city": Shelikhov to Baranov (Aug. 9, 1794), cited by S. B. Okun, *The Russian-American Company*, Carl Ginsburg, trans. (New York: Octagon Books, 1979 [1951]), 32.

"I fail to find one good thing": Chevigny, *Lord of Alaska*, 124.

"I should get out of here": ibid., 145.

"We only add": ibid., 144.

"the Russian way" and "trading nations" and "republicanism": Okun, *Russian-American Company*, 42.

"with honor, truth, philanthropy": Chevigny, *Russian America*, 73.

"for faithful services in hardship and want": Chevigny, *Lord of Alaska*, 189.

"an act of Christian charity": ibid., 200.

Paris 1803

"pride of empire will awaken": Eunice Wead, "British Public Opinion of the Peace with America in 1782," *American Historical Review* 34 (April 1929): 520, 522.

"are preparing for their remote posterity": Justin Winsor, *The Westward Movement, 1763–1798* (Boston: Houghton Mifflin, 1897), 216.

"unmeasured ambition" and "new and vigorous people": Carondelet's *Report on Louisiana* (Nov. 24, 1794), cited by Alexander DeConde, *This Affair of Louisiana* (New York: Scribner's, 1976), 59.

"they pretend it is only to promote": Jefferson to Clark (Dec. 4, 1783), cited by John Logan Allen, *Passage Through the Garden: Lewis and Clark and the Image of the American Northwest* (Urbana: University of Illinois Press, 1975), 64–65.

"Our confederacy must be viewed": Jefferson to Archibald Stuart (Jan. 25, 1786), *Jefferson Papers* 9: 218, cited by DeConde, *This Affair of Louisiana*, 49.

"There is on the globe one single spot": Jefferson to Livingston (Apr. 18, 1802), *The Writings of Thomas Jefferson*, Paul L. Ford, ed., 10 vols. (New York, 1892–99), 9: 363–68, cited by ibid., 113–14.

"There never was a government": Livingston to Madison (Sep. 1, 1802), *American State Papers: Foreign Relations*, 2: 525.

"An intelligent officer": Jefferson Papers, Library of Congress, cited by Donald Jackson, *Thomas Jefferson and the Stony Mountains: Exploring the West From Monticello* (Urbana: University of Illinois Press, 1981), 127.

"literary pursuit": Warren L. Cook, *Flood Tide of Empire: Spain and the Pacific Northwest, 1543–1819* (New Haven: Yale University Press), 449.

"the whole public hope": Jefferson to Monroe (Jan. 10, 1803), *Writings of*

Thomas Jefferson, 9: 416, cited by DeConde, *This Affair of Louisiana*, 134.

"you have made a noble bargain": Livingston to Madison (May 20, 1803), *American State Papers: Foreign Relations*, 2: 561.

"We have secured our rights by pacific means": (July 8, 1803), DeConde, *This Affair of Louisiana*, 178.

"the greatest curse": Rebecca Brooks Gruver, *American Nationalism, 1783–1830: A Self Portrait* (New York: Putnam's 1970), 163.

"We rush like a comet": *Works of Fisher Ames*, Seth Ames, ed., 2 vols. (Boston: Little, Brown, 1854), 1: 323–324, cited by DeConde, *This Affair of Louisiana*, 186.

"Our food then may increase": Merrill D. Peterson, *Thomas Jefferson and the New Nation: A Biography* (New York: Oxford University Press, 1970), 772.

"proceeded on under a jentle brease": Jackson, *Jefferson and the Stony Mountains*, 156.

"may encourage some attempts": Irujo to Viceroy José de Iturrigaray (Nov. 3, 1803), cited by Cook, *Flood-Tide of Empire*, 483–84.

Sakhalin Island 1806

"estranged from everything": Rezanov to I. I. Dmitriev (April 1803), cited by Lensen, *Russian Push Toward Japan*, 127.

"simply and without pretense": ibid., 131.

"all nature appeared in commotion and uproar": Georg Heinrich von Langsdorff, *Bemerkungen auf einer Reise um die Welt* (Frankfurt am Main: F. Williams, 1812), cited by ibid., 139–40.

"Already for a long time": Tokutomi Iichiro, *Kinsei Nihon Kokumin-shi* [History of the Japanese People in Modern Times], vol. 25 (Tokyo, 1936), cited by ibid., 155.

"extraordinary person": Rezanov to Board of Directors, Russian-American Company (Nov. 6, 1805), cited by Chevigny, *Lord of Alaska*, 224.

"all this country could be a corporal part": Cook, *Flood Tide of Empire*, 499.

"commanded us to give you a specimen": Lensen, *Russian Push Toward Japan*, 171–72.

"depends not only our liberation": Journal of Captain Pyotr I. Rikord, cited by ibid., 235–36.

"a nation of shopkeepers": ibid., 250.

"if there will rule": Golovnin's Report of 1818, cited by ibid., 252–53.

Astoria 1811

"H. B. C.—Here Before Christ": G. P. V. Akrigg and Helen Akrigg, *British Columbia Chronicle, 1778–1846: Adventurers by Sea and Land* (Vancouver: Discovery Press, 1975), 180.

"great Columbian enterprise": James P. Ronda, *Astoria and Empire* (Lincoln: University of Nebraska Press, 1990), 16.

"wintering partners": John S. Galbraith, *The Hudson's Bay Company as an Imperial Factor, 1821–1869* (Berkeley: University of California Press, 1957), 5.

"the countenance and good wishes": Thomas Jefferson Papers, Library of Congress, cited by Ronda, *Astoria and Empire*, 40.

"some enterprizing mercantile Americans" and "whether it would be prudent" and "every reasonable patronage": [Sen.] *William Plumer's Memorandum* of *Proceedings in the United States Senate, 1803–1807*, Everett S. Brown, ed. (New York: Macmillan, 1923), 520, cited by Ronda, *Astoria and Empire*, 44.

"Oregon country . . . free and open": Thomas A. Bailey, *A Diplomatic History of the American People*, 10th ed. (Englewood Cliffs, N.J.: Prentice-Hall, 1970), 160.

"If I was a young man": Astor to Albert Gallatin (Dec. 30, 1818), Gallatin Papers, New York Historical Society, cited by Ronda, *Astoria and Empire*, 315.

"You need not trouble yourselves": David M. Pletcher, *The Diplomacy of Annexation: Texas, Oregon, and the Mexican War* (Columbia: University of Missouri Press, 1973), 103.

California and Kauai 1815

"The Spirit of Russian Hunters" and "Baranov's Song": Chevigny, *Lord of Alaska*, 214.

"Bavarian scientist": Richard A. Pierce, "Georg Anton Schäffer, Russia's Man in Hawaii, 1815–1817," *Pacific Historical Review* 32, no. 4 (Nov. 1963): 397–405.

"The people are so poor": Egor Sheffer [Georg Schäffer], Journal entries (May 10, 1816, and Jan. 1, 1817): Richard A. Pierce, ed., *Russia's Hawaiian Adventure* (Berkeley: University of California Press, 1965), 170–71.

"The Sandwich Islands must be made": ibid., 197.

"I cannot look upon this man": Davydov's memorial of his voyages, cited by K. T. Khlebnikov, *Baranov: Chief Manager of the Russian Colonies in America*, Colin Bearne, trans. (Kingston, Ontario: Limestone Press, 1973), 109–10.

Washington City 1819

"I hear you have lately made an acquisition?" et seq.: *Memoirs of John Quincy Adams, Comprising Portions of His Diary From 1795 to 1848*, Charles Francis Adams, ed., 12 vols. (Philadelphia: Lippincott, 1874–77), 2: 261 (May 6, 1811), cited by Samuel Flagg Bemis, *John Quincy Adams and the Foundations of American Foreign Policy* (New York: Knopf, 1949), 301–2.

"nation, coextensive with the North American continent": *Writings of John Quincy Adams*, Worthington C. Ford, ed., 7 vols. (New York: Macmillan, 1913–17), 4: 128 (June 30, 1811), cited by ibid., 182.

"I have suffered enough in person": Walter B. Douglas, "Manuel Lisa," Missouri Historical Society *Collections*, vol. 3 (1911): 382, cited by William H. Goetzmann, *Exploration and Empire: The Scientist in the Winning of the American West* (New York: Norton, 1966), 28.

"This project will seem delirium": Pletcher, *The Diplomacy of Annexation*, 64.

"It was near one in the morning": *Memoirs of John Quincy Adams*, 4: 275, cited by George Dangerfield, *The Era of Good Feelings* (London: Methuen, 1953), 152.

"superintending Providence": From Adams's Diary, cited by Marie B. Hecht, *John Quincy Adams: A Personal History of an Independent Man* (New York: Macmillan 1972), 297.

"the last *entrada*": Spate, *Monopolists and Freebooters*, 290.

St. Petersburg 1821

"BE IT DECREED THAT": Tsar's *Ukase* (Sep. 16, 1821), in Alaskan Boundary Tribunal, *Proceedings* (Washington: GPO, 1904), 2: 25.

"If rotten, poorly equipped vessels": Donald W. Mitchell, *A History of Russian and Soviet Sea Power* (New York: Macmillan, 1974), 136.

"Old Neptune one morning was seen on the rocks": *Niles Weekly Register* (May 10, 1823), cited by Bailey, *A Diplomatic History*, 180.

"whose forts, magazines, towns": *Annals of Congress*, 16th Congress, 2d Session (Jan. 1821), 955–56, cited by Howard I. Kushner, *Conflict on the Northwest Coast: American-Russian Rivalry in the Pacific Northwest, 1790–1867* (Westport, Conn.: Greenwood Press, 1975), 30.

"the hopes even of avarice itself": *Annals of Congress*, 17th Congress, 1st Session (Dec. 17, 1822), 396–409, cited by ibid., 36.

"little short of an actual declaration": "Examination of the Russian Claims to the Northwest Coast of America," *North American Review* 15 (Oct. 1822): 370–401, cited by ibid., 40.

"keeping the schoolboy Yankees quiet": cited by Hecht, *John Quincy Adams: A Personal History*, 350.

"Keep what is yours": (Jan. 26, 1821), *Memoirs of John Quincy Adams*, 5: 252.

"comfort and well-being": Walter La Feber, *John Quincy Adams and American Continental Empire* (Chicago: Quadrangle Books, 1965), 48–50.

"molested in the prosecution": *American State Papers, Foreign Relations* (Mar. 30, 1822), 4: 863.

"I do not see": Adams to James Lloyd (July 15, 1823), cited by Bemis, *John Quincy Adams*, 515.

"I find proof enough": *Memoirs of John Quincy Adams*, 6: 159.

"[coming] in as a cock-boat": ibid., 6: 179.

"He'll recover from this": ibid., 7: 185.

"parts of a combined policy": (Nov. 7, 1823), ibid., 6: 177–80.

Honolulu 1825

"My poor countrymen": "Memoir of Obookiah" in Hiram Bingham, *A Residence of Twenty-One Years in the Sandwich Islands; or the Civil, Religious, and Political History of Those Islands* (Hartford: Hezekiah Huntington [and New York: Sherman Converse], 1847), 59.

"foolish or fanatical": ibid., 62.

"to aim at nothing short of": *Instructions of the Prudential Committee of the American Board of Commissioners for Foreign Missions to the Sandwich Islands Missions* (Lahainaluna, 1838), cited by Kuykendall, *Hawaiian Kingdom*, 1: 101–2.

"Here are the chiefs": Daws, *Shoal of Time*, 55.

"*Ai noa!* The *kapu* is broken!": ibid., 57.

"a more impressive view" and "verdant hills": Bingham, *A Residence of Twenty-One Years in the Sandwich Islands*, 69.

"Nor could a doubt remain": ibid., 79.

"The appearance of destitution": ibid., 81.

"He shall not fail": ibid., 85.

"ambassadors of the King of Heaven": ibid., 86.

"a few lines to you": ibid., 113.

"ascriptions of praise and adoration": ibid., 163.

"She was nearly fifty years of age": ibid., 164.

"her little finger": ibid.

"the borders of the grave": ibid., 148.

"How can they believe": ibid., 151.

"*Ua loaa iau!*": ibid., 164–65.

"obey God's word": ibid., 195.

"The hearts of kings are deep": ibid., 202.

"pair of damned cannibals": cited by Daws, *Shoal of Time*, 73.

"a feudal despotism" and "engrossed": Charlton to Canning (June 10, 1825): PRO FO 58/4, 21–23, 25–27.

"school-books and religious publications ... in every peasant's hut": F. D. Bennett, *Whaling Voyage Round the Globe* (London, 1840), 1:226, cited by Harold Whitman Bradley, *The American Frontier in Hawaii: The Pioneers, 1789–1843* (Stanford: Stanford University Press, 1942), 154–55.

"Put down your club": Bingham, *A Residency of Twenty-one Years in the Sandwich Islands*, 287.

"Elisabeta, this perhaps is your departure": ibid., 433.

"*Eia no au*": ibid. (Hawaiian text in Silverman, *Kaahumanu*, 145).

"the reign of Hiram Bingham": Ruth M. Tabrah, *Hawaii: A History* (New York: Norton, 1980), 34.

The Fourth 'aha iki

"a new and more psychologically devastating": Tabrah, *Hawaii: A History*, 37.

"In olden days a glimpse of stocking": Cole Porter, "Anything Goes."

"My father and chief, my beloved companion": Silverman, *Kaahumanu*, 43–44.

"Love to my mother who is gone": ibid., 55.

"it is written, rejoice, thou barren": Galatians 4:27 (Authorized [King James] Version).

"How oats peas beans and barley": Earl Conrad, *The Governor and His Lady: The Story of William Henry Seward and His Wife Frances* (New York: Putnam, 1960), 137.

"allow us to keep there an observation fleet": Okun, *Russian-American Company*, 136.

Washington-on-the-Brazos 1836

"G.T.T.": Bailey, *A Diplomatic History*, 239.

"Arkansas toothpicks": Francis C. Sheridan to Sir Evan Bark (June 23, 1840): PRO FO 75/1: 58–78.

"laid out in the woods": William Fairfax Gray, *From Virginia to Texas, 1835* (Houston: Gray, Dillaye, 1909), 108, cited by Stanley Siegel, *A Political History of the Texas Republic, 1836–1845* (Austin: University of Texas Press, 1956), 31–32.

"Santa Anna *dead*": Stanley Siegel, *The Poet President of Texas: The Life of Mirabeau B. Lamar* (Austin: Pemberton Press, 1977), 22.

"aggrandizement": Joseph William Schmitz, *Texan Statecraft, 1836–1845* (San Antonio: Naylor, 1941), 39.

"powerful check which Texas is destined": Memorandum on Project of New

Commercial Convention with England (Nov. 4, 1841): PRO FO 75/2: 41–71.

"California bank notes": Robert Glass Cleland, *From Wilderness to Empire: A History of California, 1542–1900* (New York: Knopf, 1944), 136.

"finest ports in the world" and "perhaps in time form a state": Richard W. Van Alstyne, *The Rising American Empire* (New York: Oxford University Press, 1960), 126–27.

"I feel myself in duty bound": Ephraim Douglass Adams, *British Interests and Activities in Texas, 1838–1846* (Baltimore: Johns Hopkins Press, 1910), 243.

"It is scarcely necessary": ibid., 178–79.

Canton 1839

"The process is not like tobacco smoking": John King Fairbank, *Trade and Diplomacy on the China Coast: The Opening of the Treaty Ports, 1842–1854* (Stanford: Stanford University Press, 1969 [1953]), 65.

"Fathers would no longer be able": Frederic Wakeman, Jr., "The Canton Trade and the Opium War," *The Cambridge History of China* (Cambridge, 1978), 10: 179.

"a flowing poison": Mark Mancall, *China at the Center: 300 Years of Foreign Policy* (New York: Free Press, 1984), 106.

"sever the trunk from its roots: Wakeman, "The Canton Trade," 185.

"overthrow the Ch'ing and restore the Ming": Susan Mann Jones and Philip A. Kuhn, "Dynastic Decline and Roots of Rebellion," *Cambridge History of China,* 10: 134.

"Just now have settee counter": Immanuel C. Y. Hsü, *The Rise of Modern China,* 4th ed. (New York: Oxford University Press, 1990), 152.

"We will not oppose you": (Sep. 30, 1821), Jonathan Goldstein, *Philadelphia and the China Trade, 1682–1846: Commercial, Cultural, and Attitudinal Effects* (University Park: Pennsylvania State University, 1978), 61.

"We possess all things": Hsü, *Rise of Modern China,* 161.

"There appear among the crowd of barbarians": ibid., 180.

"towering rage" and "who only care to profit themselves": Mancall, *China at the Center,* 111.

"to place Britain's relations": ibid., 113.

"a war more unjust in its origin": Edgar Holt, *The Opium Wars in China* (London: Putnam, 1964), 99–100.

"When I think of this": Hsü, *Rise of Modern China,* 185.

"these barbarians were terrified" and "whet[ted] their dog-like appetites": James M. Polachek, *The Inner Opium War* (Cambridge: Harvard University Press, 1992), 182–83.

"all nonsense": Hsü, *Rise of Modern China,* 186.

Honolulu 1843

"disgrace to his country" and "grossly immoral": Bews to Palmerston (Sep. 23 and Nov. 25, 1835): PRO FO 58/8: 41–44, 48–53.

"I am certain that your Lordship": Charlton to Palmerston (Dec. 28, 1837), with enclosed testimony from the ladies: PRO FO 58/9: 57–112.

"violent temper": Minute (Sep. 20, 1836), PRO FO 58/8: 147.

"be quiet you": Kaahumanu to Charlton (Dec. 16, 1831), PRO FO 58/6: 23.

"the native population is rapidly decreasing": Charlton to Palmerston (Nov. 23, 1836), PRO FO 58/8: 103–4.

"go and come freely": Kuykendall, *Hawaiian Kingdom*, 1: 150.

"dead" and "hard as a nether millstone": Daws, *Shoal of Time*, 99.

"like a wail of doom": Titus Coan, *Life in Hawaii* (New York: Putnam, 1882), 51–53, cited by ibid., 99–100.

"God hath made of one blood": *Hawaiian Spectator* (July 1839), cited by Kuykendall, *Hawaiian Kingdom*, 1: 160–61.

"completely in the hands": Charlton to James Bantenell (May 24, 1840): PRO FO 58/12: 7–8.

"bounden duty to repair immediately": Charlton to Tamehameha (*sic*) (Sept. 26, 1840), PRO FO 58/13: 44.

"immediate coercive steps": Kuykendall, *Hawaiian Kingdom*, 1: 214.

"the life of the land": Tabrah, *Hawaii: A History*, 56–57.

"arbitrary and unjust" and "whose will is law": Charlton to Aberdeen (Feb. 10, 1843), PRO FO 58/17: 1–2.

"so intemperate" and "ill-judged": Aberdeen to Charlton (Mar. 9, 1843), PRO FO 58/17: 49–51.

"*Ua mau ke ea o ka aina i ka pono*": Tabrah, *Hawaii: A History*, 57.

"an experienced and impartial person": Canning to Alex Simpson (Aug. 9, 1843), PRO FO 58/17: 215–19.

"it seems doubtful": Legaré to Everett (June 13, 1843), Senate Executive Documents, 52d Congress., 2d Session., No. 57, 7–8, cited by Kuykendall, *Hawaiian Kingdom*, 1: 200.

Oregon 1844

"He was such a figure": E. E. Rich, *Hudson's Bay Company, 1670–1870*, 2 vols. (London, Hudson's Bay Record Society, 1959), 2: 577.

"St. Lawrence of the West": Frederick Merk, *History of the Westward Movement* (New York: Knopf, 1978), 311.

"worthless and lawless characters": Akrigg and Akrigg, *British Columbia Chronicle*, 361.

"Whoo ha! Go It boys!": *Niles Weekly Register* (May 31, 1845), cited by Bailey, *A Diplomatic History*, 223.

"Let the emigrants go on": *Congressional Globe*, 28th Congress, 1st Session (June 3, 1844), 678, cited by ibid., 224.

"would be a Radical": Akrigg and Akrigg, *British Columbia Chronicle*, 269.

"a flag . . . honored for the principles of justice": *Oregon Statesman* (June 8, 1852); cited by ibid., 270.

"did not believe the God of Heaven": *Congressional Globe*, 28th Congress, 2d Session (Jan. 27, 1845), 200; cited by Frederick Merk, *Manifest Destiny and Mission in American History* (New York: Random House, 1963), 28.

"Go to the West": Indiana Congressman Andrew Kennedy, *Congressional Globe*, 29th Congress, 1st Session (Jan. 10, 1846); cited by ibid., 29.

"There is only one means": *Congressional Globe*, 27th Congress, 3d Session (Jan. 24, 1843), Appendix 139; cited by ibid., 64.

"re-annexation of Texas" and "re-occupation of Oregon": Paul F. Boller, Jr., *Presidential Campaigns* (New York: Oxford University Press, 1984), 78–79.

Sonoma 1846

"The Election of Mr. Polk": Pakenham to Aberdeen (Nov. 13, 1844), PRO FO 75/20: 98–103.

"we have carefully abstained": Aberdeen to Elliott et al. (Dec. 31, 1844), PRO FO 75/20: 77–81.

"risk a collision": Aberdeen to Bankhead (Dec. 31, 1844), PRO FO 75/20: 114–21.

"the constellation of the Stars and Stripes": Bailey, *A Diplomatic History*, 247.

"Yes, more, more, more": *New York Morning News* (Feb. 7, 1845), cited by Merk, *Manifest Destiny*, 46.

"something": London *Times* (Oct. 1, 1845), cited by ibid., 48.

"The only way to treat John Bull": Milo Milton Quaife, ed., *The Diary of James K. Polk* (Chicago: McClung, 1910), 1: 155, cited by Bailey, *A Diplomatic History*, 229.

"Is there nothing but Yankees here?": G. P. Hammond, ed., *The Larkin Papers* (Berkeley: University of California Press, 1951), 4: 369, cited by John A. Hawgood, "The Pattern of Yankee Infiltration in Mexican Alta California, 1821–1846," *Pacific Historical Review* 27, no. 1 (Feb. 1958): 27–37 (27).

"England must think of her own interests": London *Times*, cited by Norman Graebner, "American Interest in California, 1845", *Pacific Historical Review* 22, no. 1 (Feb. 1953), 13–27 (19).

"were California to fall": Aberdeen to Bankhead (Oct. 1, 1845), cited by ibid., 19.

"that love of liberty": Buchanan to Larkin (Oct. 17, 1845), William R. Manning, ed., *Diplomatic Correspondence of the United States. Inter-American Affairs, 1831–1860*, 12 vols. (Washington, D.C., 1932–39), 8: 169–71; cited by Pletcher, *The Diplomacy of Annexation*, 283–84.

"any rifles or other small arms": Bancroft to Sloat (Dec. 5, 1845), Navy Department Confidential Letters, 1: 163; cited by Merk, *Manifest Destiny*, 66.

"would be glad to get clear": J. S. Reeves, *American Diplomacy Under Tyler and Polk* (Baltimore: Johns Hopkins University Press, 1907), 260.

"slowly and growlingly": Frémont letter to his wife, cited by Walton Bean and James J. Rawls, *California: An Interpretive History*, 4th ed. (New York: McGraw-Hill, 1983), 75.

"Mexico is an ugly enemy": John H. Schroeder, *Shaping a Maritime Empire: The Commercial and Diplomatic Role of the American Navy, 1829–1861* (Westport, Conn.: Greenwood Press, 1985), 86.

"that Mexico will be mad enough": Quaife, ed., *Polk Diary*, 1: 33, cited by Norman A. Graebner, "The Mexican War: A Study in Causation," *Pacific Historical Review* 49, no. 4 (Nov. 1980): 405–26 (411).

"what might, under other hands": ibid., 424.

"defensive war": ibid., 425

"cup of forbearance . . . exhausted" and "war exists": J. D. Richardson, ed., *Messages and Papers of the Presidents* (Washington, D.C.: GPO, 1897), 4: 442.

"which shall secure to us all Civil": (June 15, 1846), Cleland, *From Wilderness to Empire*, 220.

"the very best riders": Bean and Rawls, *California*, 80.

"beautiful and brilliant": *Los Angeles Times* (Dec. 28, 1902); cited by Robert Kirsch and William S. Murphy, *West of the West* (New York: Dutton, 1967), 237.

"It would have been strange" and "Nothing to be done": (Oct. 16, 1846), FO 5/450, cited by John S. Galbraith, *The Hudson's Bay Company as an Imperial Factor, 1821–1869* (Berkeley: University of California Press, 1957), 250.

Panama and Cape Horn 1849

"Look to the west" and "Look to the east" *et seq.*: Bret Harte, *The Writings of Bret Harte*, 12 vols. (Boston: Houghton-Mifflin, 1906), vol. 1, *The Luck of Roaring Camp and Other Tales*, 382–97 ("The Legend of Monte del Diablo").

"the Lord's money" and "Gold from the American River!": Bean and Rawls, *California*, 86–87.

"Labourers of every trade": Kirsch and Murphy, *West of the West*, 296–97.

"The accounts of the abundance of gold": Donald Dale Jackson, *Gold Dust* (New York: Knopf, 1980), 64.

"I soon shall be in Francisco": ibid., 69.

"passenger trains" and "humbug" and "family system": Mary McDougall Gordon, "Overland to California in 1849: A Neglected Commercial Enterprise," *Pacific Historical Review* 52, no. 1 (Feb. 1983): 17–36.

"Plenty of gold, so I've been told": "Aweigh, Santy Anno" (traditional), Sanga Music, Inc. © 1958.

"The California passage": Matthew F. Maury, *Explanations and Sailing Directions*, 7th ed. (Philadelphia: Biddle, 1855), 321; cited by Raymond A. Rydell, "The Cape Horn Route to California, 1849," *Pacific Historical Review* 17, no. 2 (May 1948): 149–63 (150).

"extreme clipper" and "sharp built" and "driver" and "horse": Carl C. Cutler, *Greyhounds of the Sea* (Annapolis: Naval Institute Press, 1984 [1930]), 44–45.

"Heavy Gales, Close Reefed Topsails": (in Argentine waters, July 11, 1851), Raymond A. Rydell, "The California Clippers," *Pacific Historical Review* 18, no. 1 (Feb. 1949): 70–83 (76–77).

"too expensive" and "too slow": J. G. Bennett (1851), cited by Cutler, *Greyhounds of the Sea*, 173.

"Now's the time to change your clime": Jackson, *Gold Dust*, 74.

"be sick part of the time": Henry Tracy (Feb. 24, 1851), cited by John Haskell Kemble, "The Gold Rush by Panama, 1848–1851", *Pacific Historical Review* 18, no. 1 (Feb. 1949): 45–56 (50).

"ride over a wild, inhuman country": Mallie Stafford, *The March of Empire Through the Decades* (San Francisco, 1884), 39; cited by Glenda Riley, "Women on the Panama Trail to California, 1849–1869," *Pacific Historical Review* 55, no. 4 (Nov. 1986): 531–48 (547–48).

"the absurd notion": Jackson, *Gold Dust*, 95.

The Sixth 'aha iki

"Without a prototype, a marvel": Seward, *William H. Seward's Travels Around the World* (New York: Appleton, 1873), 6.

Edo 1853

God's "higher law": Senate speech (Mar. 11, 1849), cited by Glyndon G. Van Deusen, *William Henry Seward* (New York: Oxford University Press, 1967), 123.

"gospel of commerce" and "science . . . calculated to elevate" and "Commerce is now the lever": *Hunt's Merchants' Magazine* (1839), cited by John H. Schroeder, *Shaping a Maritime Empire* (Westport, Conn.: Greenwood Press, 1985), 82.

"contains no seat of empire": *Congressional Globe*, 31st Congress, 1st Session (1849–50), Appendix, 262; cited by ibid., 91.

"one nation, race, or individual" and "take up the cross": Van Deusen, *Seward*, 206–7.

"repel and destroy": Peter Booth Wiley, *Yankees in the Land of the Gods: Commodore Perry and the Opening of Japan* (New York: Viking, 1990), 265.

"alien barbarians of the west" and "occupies the hindmost region" and "preach their alien religion": William Theodore de Bary et al., eds, *Sources of Japanese Tradition* (New York: Columbia University Press, 1958), 2: 88–89, 95, cited by Wiley, *Yankees in the Land of the Gods*, 266.

"cause the balance of trade": *House of Representatives Report No. 596*, 30th Congress, 1st Session (1847–48); cited by Schroeder, *Maritime Empire*, 93.

"the real object of the expedition" and "astonishment and consternation" and "would do more to command their fears": (January 1851), Wiley, *Yankees in the Land of the Gods*, 79.

"The moment is near when the last link" and "gift of Providence": *The Writings and Speeches of Daniel Webster*, 18 vols. (Boston: Little Brown, 1903), 14: 427–29, cited by Helen Humeston, *Origins of America's Japan Policy, 1790–1854* (Ann Arbor: University Microfilms, 1981), 210.

"I assume the responsibility": U.S. Senate Executive Doc. No. 34, 33rd Congress, 2d Session, 81, cited by ibid., 217.

"and thus the Saxon and the Cossack": Samuel Eliot Morison, *"Old Bruin": Commodore Matthew Calbraith Perry, 1794–1858* (Boston: Little Brown, 1967), 429.

"Since then the nation's strength" and "on every seventh day": Foster Rhea Dulles, *Yankees and Samurai: America's Role in the Emergence of Modern Japan, 1791–1900* (New York: Harper & Row, 1965), 43–44.

"are perfect in body" and "lewd by nature" and "toilets are placed": ibid., 48–49.

"a weak and barbarous people": ibid., 57.

"Accept the letter": Wiley, *Yankees in the Land of the Gods*, 308.

"even the saturnine Hayashi": Francis L. Hawks, *Narrative of the Expedition . . . to Japan*, 3 vols. (Washington: B. Tucker, 1856); cited by Dulles, *Yankees and Samurai*, 77.

Aikun-on-the-Amur 1858

"Twenty-five years ago": Note to Crown Prince Alexander (Mar. 1853), Ivan Barsukov, *Graf Nikolai Nikolaevich Murav'ev-Amurskii* (Moscow, 1891), 1: 322–23; cited by Lensen, *Russian Push Toward Japan*, 300–301.

"the gentleness which characterized": Chevigny, *Russian America*, 197.

"The way is straight": Nekrasov, *Sochineniya* (Works), 3 vols. (Moscow,: Goslitizdat, 1959), 2: 7–9; cited by J. N. Westwood, *A History of Russian Railways* (London: Allen & Unwin, 1964), 33.

"If any power should seize Kamchatka": A. Lobanov-Rostovsky, *Russia and Asia* (Ann Arbor: George Wahr, 1965 [1933]), 135.

"foreigners were to occupy the mouth": Muraviev to Menshikov (Jan. 1, 1850), in Basil Dmytryshyn et al., eds., *The Russian American Colonies: A Documentary Record, 1798–1867*, 3 vols. (Oregon Historical Society, 1989), 3: 487.

"Neighboring China, very populous": Muraviev to Grand Duke Constantine (undated), in ibid., 493.

"Where the Russian flag has once been hoisted": Lobanov-Rostovsky, *Russia and Asia*, 138.

"in accordance with the project of Palmer": Lensen, *Russian Push Toward Japan*, 286.

"I want no smell of powder": Chevigny, *Russian America*, 218.

"Below Albazin": Roman K. Bogdanov, "Vospominaniia amurskago kazaka," (Recollections of an Amur Cossack), in George A. Lensen, ed. and trans., *Russia's Eastward Expansion* (Englewood Cliffs, N.J.: Prentice-Hall, 1964), 99.

"Putiatin is really not a bad man": Muraviev to Mikhail Korsakov (Apr. 2, 1857), in Barsukov, *Murav'ev-Amurskii* 1: 493; cited by Lensen, *Russian Push Toward Japan*, 308.

San Francisco 1860

"tell the truth": Pat Barr, *The Coming of the Barbarians: The Opening of Japan to the West, 1853–1870* (New York: Dutton, 1967), 44.

"We visited the ship yesterday": Lewis Bush, *77 Samurai: Japan's First Embassy to America* (Tokyo and Palo Alto: Kodansha International, 1968), 113–14.

"with good Christian relish": ibid., 115.

"made of such expensive material": ibid., 116.

"it is a prophecy": ibid., 126–27.

"We are now leaving": ibid., 139.

"instant city": Gunther Barth, *Instant Cities: Urbanization and the Rise of San Francisco and Denver* (New York: Oxford University Press, 1975), ix.

"miserable village of Yerba Buena": (John Marsh, 1845), Cleland, *From Wilderness to Empire*, 139.

"human character crumbled": ibid., 137.

"At a time when every white man": Barth, *Instant Cities*, 120.

"My diggings are here": *Quarterly of the Society of California Pioneers* 8, no. 3 (Sept. 1931), 174; cited by Roger W. Lotchin, *San Francisco 1846–1856: From Hamlet to City* (Lincoln: University of Nebraska Press, 1979), 5.

"war of extermination": Bean and Rawls, *California*, 166.

"bitter strength": Gunther Barth, *Bitter Strength: A History of the Chinese in the United States, 1850–1870* (Cambridge: Harvard University Press, 1964), 3.

"golden mountains": Bean and Rawls, *California*, 134.

"neither free nor white": Barth, *Bitter Strength*, 180.

"exceedingly barren, and singularly destitute.": Francis Farquhar, ed., "The Topographical Reports of Lieutenant George H. Derby," *California Historical Society Quarterly* 2 (1932); cited by Donald Worster, *Rivers of Empire: Water, Aridity, and the Growth of the American West* (New York: Pantheon, 1985), 9.

"I wants a canal" *et seq.*: Edward F. Treadwell, *The Cattle King* (Santa Cruz: Western Tanager Press, 1981), 76.

"restless young bloods" and "revolutionizing the government": Daws, *Shoal of Time*, 137

Washington City and Sitka 1867

"cunning and chicanery": Van Deusen, *Seward*, 11.

"a long and feverish and almost fatal dream": ibid., 33.

"I may as well be explicit": (Mar. 26, 1837), ibid., 37–38.

"reckless folly": Seward to E. A. Stansbury (Sept. 2, 1844), ibid., 103.

"Commerce is the god of boundaries": G. E. Baker, ed., *The Works of William H. Seward*, 5 vols. (New York: AMS Press, 1972 [Boston, 1884]), 1:60.

"roll its resistless waves": Albert A. Woldman, *Lincoln and the Russians* (Cleveland: World, 1952), 279–80.

"the great engine of movement" and "the chief theater in the events": Seward, *Works*, 1:248–50.

"Steam has worked wonders": (June 4, 1858), Kushner, *Conflict on the Northwest Coast*, 112.

"anticipatory prudence": Wrangell, "Concerning the Cession of the American Colonies" (Apr. 9, 1857), cited by ibid., 136.

"a control almost without limit": Stoeckl to Gorchakov (Jan. 4, 1860), cited by ibid., 137.

"Lincoln nominated third ballot": Van Deusen, *Seward*, 225.

"deluded" and "temporarily insane": See Van Deusen, *Seward*, 283; Bailey, *A Diplomatic History*, 318; and Philip Van Doren Stern, *When the Guns Roared: World Aspects of the American Civil War* (Garden City: Doubleday, 1965), 39.

"the fiercest of the lot" and "high-handed conduct": Norman B. Ferris, *Desperate Diplomat: William H. Seward's Foreign Policy, 1861* (Knoxville: University of Tennessee Press, 1976), 13.

"crazy dispatch": Bailey, *A Diplomatic History*, 318.

"has done more for us here": W. C. Ford, ed., *A Cycle of Adams Letters, 1861–1865* (Boston, 1920), 1:243, cited by ibid., 342.

"where despotism can be taken pure": (Aug. 1855), Woldman, *Lincoln and the Russians*, 13.

"a country where men": Frank A. Golder, "The American Civil War Through the Eyes of a Russian Diplomat," *American Historical Review* 26 (1920–21): 457.

"I did more for the Russian serf": Wharton Barker, "The Secret of Russian Friendship," *The Independent* 56 (Mar. 1904): 645–49; cited by Woldman, *Lincoln and the Russians*, 188.

"God bless the Russians!": John T. Morse, ed., *Diary of Gideon Welles*, 3 vols. (Boston: Houghton Mifflin, 1911), 1:443.

"their loyalty to the Union": Robert L. Thompson, *Wiring a Continent* (Princeton: Princeton University Press, 1947), 368.

"everything has been unfavorable": *Esquimaux* (Nov. 4, 1866), the company camp's newspaper in Alaska; cited by Hunt, *Arctic Passage*, 166–67.

"American, Protestant, without property": Woldman, *Lincoln and the Russians*, 15.

"for any post anywhere": ibid., 290.

"the man above all others": ibid., 23, and Golder, "American Civil War," 456.

"sufficiently strong motive": Osten-Saken to Gorchakov (Dec. 16, 1866), cited by Kushner, *Conflict on the Northwest Coast*, 140.

"one of [Seward's] political friends": Stoeckl to Gorchakov (Apr. 19, 1867), ibid., 141.

"Esquimaux Acquisition Treaty" and "Walrussia" and "Seward's Icebox": Virginia H. Reid, *The Purchase of Alaska: Contemporary Opinion* (Long Beach: Press-Telegram, 1939).

"lifelong annexationist": F. A. Golder, "The Purchase of Alaska," *American Historical Review* 25 (1919–20): 415–16.

"there was no chance of the appropriation": William A. Dunning, "Paying for Alaska," *Political Science Quarterly* 27 (1912): 385–98 (385–86); cited by Woldman, *Lincoln and the Russians*, 288–89.

"breathe for a while": Bailey, *A Diplomatic History*, 370.

"encountered a storm" and "a safe one" and "we allowed the Russians": Archie W. Shiels, ed., *The Purchase of Alaska* (College: University of Alaska Press, 1967), 165–73.

Tokyo 1868

"'Merikan! 'Merikan!'": Wiley, *Yankees in the Land of the Gods*, 427.

"Modest Proposal," etc.: cited by Thomas M. Huber, *The Revolutionary Origins of Modern Japan* (Stanford: Stanford University Press, 1981), 48–59.

"excellent persons": ibid., 48.

"Twenty-one Times a Valiant Samurai": ibid., 57.

"a man can only be called a ruler": ibid., 60.

"scarlet regiment": Dulles, *Yankees and Samurai*, 129.

"the scum of Europe": Barr, *Coming of the Barbarians*, 148.

"While yearning for our instructor": Huber, *Revolutionary Origins*, 148.

"Both our armies fling away": ibid., 203.

"There were some infantry" and "A wild and wonderful sight": Barr, *Coming of the Barbarians*, 205.

"cast off the stupid opinion": Dulles, *Yankees and Samurai*, 147.

"there is not the remotest prospect": ibid., 145.

"little dreamed that the restored Mikado": ibid.

Utah and British Columbia 1869

"great measure of conciliation": *Congressional Globe*, 36th Congress, 2d Session (1860–61), 250–51; cited by Robert R. Russel, *Improvement of Communication with the Pacific Coast as an Issue in American Politics, 1783–1864* (Cedar Rapids, Mich.: Torch Press, 1948), 288.

"liable to great embarrassment": John Debo Galloway, *The First Transcontinental Railroad* (New York: Dorset, 1989 [1920]), 98.

"the grandest and noblest enterprise": Maury Klein, *Union Pacific: Birth of a Railroad, 1862–1893* (Garden City: Doubleday, 1987), 18.

"You cannot, in my opinion, legislate": Glenn Chesney Quiett, *They Built the West: An Epic of Rails and Cities* (New York: Appleton-Century, 1934), 216.

"This is no idle ceremony": Galloway, *First Transcontinental*, 155.

"I don't believe it can be done," etc.: Quiett, *They Built the West*, 198.

"They were a great army": ibid., 199.

"quiet, peaceable, patient": Stanford to Andrew Johnson (Oct. 10, 1865), cited by Kirsch and Murphy, *West of the West*, 391–92.

"equal to the very best": George F. Seward, *Chinese Immigration* (New York Times and Arno Press Reprint, 1970 [1873]), 22–23.

"The woods of the Sierra and Rocky Mountains": *The Overland Monthly*, cited by Kirsch and Murphy, *West of the West*, 394–95.

"the man of giant energies": By "a Sacramento pioneer" (1888), cited by Quiett, *They Built the West*, 201.

"From the Railroad Front—Victory" and "the Asiatic contingent": (May 8, 1869), cited by Kirsch and Murphy, *West of the West*, 400.

"I would consider it would be greatly for the interest of England": Rear Adm. Joseph Denman in Margaret A. Ormsby, *British Columbia: A History* (Toronto: Macmillan, 1958), 218.

"the people of Vancouver Island": Allen Francis to Seward (Sept. 1866), cited by David E. Shi, "Seward's Attempt to Annex British Columbia, 1865–1869," *Pacific Historical Review* 47, no. 2 (1978): 217–38 (222).

"If the United States desires to outflank": *Montreal Gazette* (May 24, 1867), cited by ibid., 227.

"without the opening of a railroad connection": (July 17, 1867), ibid., 230.

"Long after midnight I felt that he was won" *et seq.*: Herbert Hunt, *Tacoma: Its History and Its Builders* (Chicago: S. J. Clarke, 1916); cited by Quiett, *They Built the West*, 406.

"financier of the Civil War" and "premature enterprise": Goetzmann, *Exploration and Empire*, 412 and 418.

"depredatory measures on the part of our neighbors": *Hansard Parliamentary Debates* (June 9, 1868), cited by Shi, "Seward's Attempt to Annex," 234.

The Seventh 'aha iki

"Then foreign states would have warned" and "To open the ports today": William R. Braisted, ed., *Meiroku Zasshi: Journal of Japanese Enlightenment* (Cambridge: Harvard University Press, 1976), 525–27.

"Mr. Adams I take because you suggested him": Lincoln to Seward (Mar. 18, 1861): Frederick W. Seward, *Seward at Washington*, 3 vols. (New York: Derby and Miller, 1891), 2: 525.

"And so a generous people": Ferriss, *Desperate Diplomacy*, 207.

"It is characteristic of every good treaty": Van Deusen, *Seward*, 515.

"We have served California better": Cleland, *From Wilderness to Empire*, 175.

"New-hatched doves": author's composition.

"Japan has especial reasons for prudence": Seward, *Travels Around the World*, 85.

Honolulu 1875

"It is a matter of the utmost importance": Day, ed., *Twain's Letters from Hawaii*, 20.

"Let Congress moderate": ibid., 21.

"a two-thousand ton propellor" and "and when a coal depot": ibid., 18.

"a bishop out of very inferior material" and "gossips habitually": ibid., 170–71.

"band of stern, tenacious": ibid., 171.

"how blissful a place heaven is" *et seq.* and "have clothed them, educated them": ibid., 53–55.

"skillful genealogists": Daws, *Shoal of Time*, 191.

"A splendid fellow": *Paradise of the Pacific* (July, 1910), cited by Edward Joesting, *Hawaii: An Uncommon History* (New York: Norton, 1972), 199.

"the Chinese sickness": ibid, 202.

"defeat and indefinitely postpone" and "guarantee our national independence": Henry M. Whitney, "Reciprocity and How To Secure It" (Jan. 27, 1873), cited by Merze Tate, *Hawaii: Reciprocity or Annexation?* (East Lansing: Michigan State University, 1968), 83.

"a position for a harbor": *Pacific Commercial Advertiser* (Feb. 8, 1873), cited by Tate, *Reciprocity or Annexation*, 84.

"a messenger forbidding you": (Nov. 4, 1873), cited by ibid., 98–99.

"with hooks of steel" and "result finally": Peirce to Secretary of State Hamilton Fish (May 26, 1873), cited by Merze Tate, *The U.S. and the Hawaiian Kingdom: A Political History* (New Haven: Yale University Press, 1965), 33.

"Hurrah! For America and Hawaii": *Honolulu Advertiser* (Aug. 30, 1876), cited by Daws, *Shoal of Time*, 205.

"bounds of his habitation": *Planters' Monthly* (Nov. 1886), cited by Daws, *Shoal of Time*, 213.

"You will have coolie labor": Day, ed., *Twain's Letters from Hawaii*, 271–73.

Sacramento and Washington 1882

"Unless I get some sleep" and "if something isn't done": Neill C. Wilson and Frank J. Taylor, *Southern Pacific* (New York: McGraw-Hill, 1952); cited by Julius Grodinsky, *Transcontinental Railway Strategy, 1869–1893: A Study of Businessmen* (Philadelphia: University of Pennsylvania Press, 1962), 31.

"It is about as well to fight": Cerinda W. Evans, *Collis Potter Huntington* (Newport News: Mariner's Museum, 1954); cited by ibid., 4.

"Where the money came from": *New York World* (Apr. 20, 1877), cited by ibid., 60.

"I am as near used up" and "stand by the wreck": (Feb. 9 and Mar. 5, 1878), Huntington papers in Mariner's Museum, Newport News, cited by ibid., 67.

"octopus": epithet made famous by Benjamin Franklin Morris, Jr., *The Octopus: A Story of California* (New York: Doubleday, 1901).

"Whatever happens, the Chinese must go!": Bean and Rawls, *California*, 238.

"the indispensable enemy": Alexander P. Saxton, *The Indispensable Enemy: Labor and the Anti-Chinese Movement in California* (Berkeley: University of California Press, 1971).

"the inherent and inalienable right": Li Tien-lu, *Congressional Policy on Chinese Immigration* (New York: Arno Press, 1978), 120.

"regulate, limit, or suspend" and "affects or threatens": Shih-Shau Henry Tsai, *China and the Overseas Chinese in the U.S., 1868–1911* (Fayetteville: University of Arkansas Press, 1983), 58–59.

"One of my greatest objections": Jack Chen, *The Chinese of America* (San Francisco: Harper & Row, 1980), 153.

"believe their city": *Los Angeles Star* (Apr. 25, 1874), cited by Robert M. Fogelson, *The Fragmented Metropolis: Los Angeles, 1850–1930* (Cambridge: Harvard University Press, 1967), 21.

"no happier paradise": ibid., 63.

Tokyo 1889

"enlightenment of contemporary Japan" and "Like a man fleeing": Noda Yoshiyuki, *Law in Japan* (1975), 32; cited by Hazel J. Jones in Edward R. Beauchamp and Akira Iriye, eds., *Foreign Employees in Nineteenth Century Japan* (Boulder: Westview Press, 1990), 26–27.

"[N]ow that the Imperial power is restored": Richard Storry, *A History of Modern Japan* (New York: Viking Penguin, 1960), 105.

"Revere the *kami* and love the country": Martin Collcutt in Marius B. Jansen and Gilbert Rozman, eds., *Japan in Transition* (Princeton: Princeton University Press, 1986), 155.

"the seeking of knowledge": Gilbert Rozman, "Social Change," in *The Cambridge History of Japan*, vol. 5, *The Nineteenth Century* (New York: Cambridge University Press, 1989), 561.

"raise himself, manage his property": Kikuchi Dairoku, *Japanese Education* (London: Murray, 1909), 68–69; cited by W. G. Beasley, *The Rise of Modern Japan* (London: Weidenfeld & Nicolson, 1990), 94.

"novel gadgets": ibid., 85.

"This is one of the most remarkable events": Akira Iriye, *Across the Pacific: An Inner History of American–East Asian Relations* (New York: Harcourt, Brace, & World, 1967), 26.

"Outside of the most stupid person": *Fukuzawa Zenshu* (Tokyo, 1926), 4: 125–26; cited by Albert M. Craig and Robert E. Ward, eds., *Political Development in Modern Japan* (Princeton: Princeton University Press, 1968), 121.

"a newly Westernized country": Watanabe Ikujirō (1938), in Marius B. Jansen, ed., *Changing Japanese Attitudes Towards Modernization* (Princeton: Princeton University Press, 1965), 69.

"relatively much above": *Tokio Times* (Mar. 2, 1878), cited by James L. Huffman, "Edward Howard House: In the Service of Meiji Japan," *Pacific Historical Review* 56, no. 2 (May 1987): 241.

"polished, intelligent, suave": Iriye, *Across the Pacific*, 19.

"check the power of Russian expansion": John A. Harrison, *Japan's Northern Frontier* (Gainesville: University of Florida Press, 1953), 65.

"were amazed to see one man": ibid., 88.

"cooked rice": Edwin O. Reischauer, *The United States and Japan* (Cambridge: Harvard University Press, 1965), 56.

"No sooner is anything started": Memoirs of Horace Capron, Department of Agriculture Library, cited by Harrison, *Japan's Northern Frontier*, 116.

"This is the kind of institution": *Springfield Republican* (July 18, 1872), cited by John M. Maki in Beauchamp and Iriye, eds., *Foreign Employees*, 72–73.

"so powerful that we felt as if": Oshima Shōken, "Reminiscences of Dr. W. S. Clark," *The Japan Christian Intelligencer* (Apr. 5, 1926), in ibid., 81.

"instantly change Japan's outmoded customs": Key-Hiuk Kim, *The Last Phase of the East Asian World Order: Korea, Japan, and The Chinese Empire, 1860–1882* (Berkeley: University of California Press, 1980), 125.

"education, armament, and the police": Thomas C. Smith, *Political Change and Industrial Development in Japan: Government Enterprise, 1868–1880* (Stanford: Stanford University Press, 1955), 95.

"There is no greater evil in the world than war": *Fukuzawa Zenshu*, 4:12; cited in Craig and Ward, eds., *Political Development of Modern Japan*, 124.

"[W]hether a treaty is honored or not": *Fukuzawa Zenshu*, 5: 254–56; cited in ibid., 128.

"the captain always goes down with his ship" et seq.: Hirakawa Sukehiro, "Japan's Turn to the West," in *Cambridge History of Japan*, 5: 488.

"the scorn of white people" and "the world-wide monopoly": John D. Pierson, *Tokutomi Sohō, 1863–1957* (Princeton: Princeton University Press, 1980), 229–35; cited by Beasley, *Rise of Modern Japan*, 99.

"ought not to be adopted": Kenneth B. Pyle, *The New Generation in Meiji Japan, 1885–1895* (Stanford: Stanford University Press, 1969), 94.

"sacred and inviolable" and "with the consent": Storry, *History of Modern Japan*, 116–17.

"courageously to the State" and "national essence": Hirakawa Sukehirō, "Japan's Turn to the West," in *Cambridge History of Japan*, 5: 497.

"nourishment for small nations": *A Discourse by Three Drunkards on Government* (New York and Tokyo: Weatherhill, 1984); cited by Beasley, *Rise of Modern Japan*, 100.

"To put it differently, we have to establish": Jansen in Craig and Ward, eds., *Political Development in Modern Japan*, 175.

"Certainly our future history": Akira Iriye, *Pacific Estrangement: Japanese and American Expansion, 1897–1911* (Cambridge: Harvard University Press, 1972), 44.

"Boys, be ambitious": versions described by Maki in Beauchamp and Iriye, eds., *Foreign Employees*, 83.

Vladivostok and Otsu 1891

"But her eyes were extraordinary": *The Memoirs of Count Witte*, Abraham Yarmolinsky, trans. (Garden City: Doubleday, 1921), 6.

"It was then that for the first time": ibid., 12.

"In Our untiring concern for the welfare": Theodore H. Von Laue, *Sergei Witte and the Industrialization of Russia* (New York: Columbia University Press, 1963), 6–7.

"continuing [his] academic studies": *Memoirs of Count Witte*, 15.

"like trying to crush a grain of dust" and "preposterous incident": ibid., 22, 24.

"incompetent and dull witted": ibid., 41.

"He made an ideal treasurer" and "thus realizing the ideal": ibid., 39, 43.

"We must export though we die": Von Laue, *Sergei Witte*, 27.

"I have travelled other roads" and "Your Excellency, let others do as they please": *Memoirs of Count Witte*, 28.

"to make good use of that man": ibid., 30.

"I am neither a Liberal nor a Conservative": Madame Witte in Preface to *Memoirs of Count Witte*, viii.

"Suspicious Eyes": Peter Yong-Shik Shiu, "The Otsu Incident," Ph.D. dissertation, University of Pennsylvania, 1989, 71.

"this Russian project of peace and enlightenment": Westwood, *History of Russian Railways*, 110.

Honolulu 1893

"Never was there such a hopeless": Foster Rhea Dulles, *Prelude to World Power: American Diplomatic History, 1860–1900* (New York: Macmillan, 1965), 124.

"China's fleet today": ibid.

"I cannot too strongly urge": James D. Richardson, ed., *A Compilation of the Messages and Papers of the Presidents*, 10 vols. (New York: Bureau of National Literature and Art, 1903), 8: 51; cited by Robert Greenhalgh Albion, *Makers of Naval Policy, 1798–1947* (Annapolis: Naval Institute Press, 1980), 207.

"taught the Navy to think": B. A. Fiske, "Stephen B. Luce, An Appreciation," cited by John B. Hattendorf, "Stephen B. Luce: Intellectual Leader of the New

Navy," in James C. Bradford, ed., *Admirals of the New Steel Navy* (Annapolis: Naval Institute Press, 1990), 3.

"we may be likened to the nomadic tribes": (Feb. 26, 1861), Luce Papers, cited by ibid., 8.

"for the beauty and charm": Letter to Ellen Evans Mahan, cited by William Edmund Livezey, *Mahan on Sea Power* (Norman: University of Oklahoma Press, 1947), 21–22.

"the story of Jonah": Letter to Mary Jay Okill (Nov. 10, 1847), cited by Robert Seager II, *Alfred Thayer Mahan: The Man and His Letters* (Annapolis: Naval Institute, 1977), 6.

"They make Religion be abhorred": ibid., 16.

"revival of Ancient Sciences of Hawaii": Daws, *Shoal of Time*, 220.

"an unquestionably eminent-looking veteran": description by the American David Graham Adee, in ibid., 225.

"primacy in the family of Polynesian states": ibid., 235.

"recognition of His Majesty [Kalakaua] as one of the family": Gibson to Kapena (Sept. 22, 1883), cited by F. Hilary Conroy, *The Japanese Expansion into Hawaii, 1868–1898* (San Francisco: R & E Associates, 1973 [Ph.D. diss., University of California, Berkeley, 1949]), 84.

"popular governments are not generally favorable": Alfred Thayer Mahan, *The Influence of Sea Power Upon History, 1660–1783* (Boston: Little Brown, 1890), 57–58.

"The sea will be the future seat of empire": Walter LaFeber, *The New Empire* (Ithaca: Cornell University Press, 1963), 127.

"imperialist simply because he was not isolationist": Seager in Bradford, ed., *Admirals of the New Steel Navy*, 42.

"insignificant kind of guerilla, bushwacking warfare": Harold and Margaret Sprout, *The Rise of American Naval Power, 1776–1918* (Annapolis: Naval Institute Press, 1966 [1939]), 233.

"O, ye people who love the Chiefs": Daws, *Shoal of Time*, 271–72.

"She wants us to sleep on a slumbering volcano": ibid., 273–74.

"it would be impossible to exaggerate": *New York Times* (Jan. 31, 1893), cited by Livezey, *Mahan on Sea Power*, 161.

"first fruit and a token": *Forum* (Mar. 1893), cited by ibid., 163.

"confidential trip of great importance": Tennant S. McWilliams, "James H. Blount, the South, and Hawaiian Annexation," *Pacific Historical Review* 57, no. 1 (Feb. 1988): 24–46.

"behead": *Foreign Relations of the United States* (hereafter FRUS) 1894, Appendix 2, cited by Charles W. Calhoun, "Morality and Spite: Walter Q. Gresham and U.S. Relations with Hawaii," *Pacific Historical Review* 52, no. 3 (Aug. 1983): 292–311 (301).

"Hawaii has reached the parting of the ways": Stevens to Foster (Nov. 20, 1892), cited by Michael J. Devine, "John W. Foster and the Struggle for Annexation of Hawaii," *Pacific Historical Review* 46, no. 1 (Feb. 1977): 29–50 (33).

Korea 1895

"first thing that strikes a traveler" and "unconscious as a child": George Kennan, "Korea: A Degenerate State", *Outlook* 81 (Oct. 7, 1905): 307–8; cited by John Edward Wilz, "Did the United States Betray Korea in 1905?" *Pacific Historical Review* 54, no. 3 (Aug. 1985): 243–70 (256).

"line of advantage": Roger F. Hackett, *Yamagata Aritomo in the Rise of Modern Japan, 1838–1922* (Cambridge: Harvard University Press, 1971): 138–39.

"dagger": Iriye, *Across the Pacific*, 66.

"for many future years or even forever": Mutsu to Itō (Aug. 17, 1894) in Kajima Morinosuke, ed., *The Diplomacy of Japan, 1894–1922*, 3 vols. (Tokyo: Kajima Institute, 1976), 1: 108.

"negotiating with the Chinese": Mutsu Munemitsu, *Kenkenroku: A Diplomatic Record of the Sino-Japanese War, 1894–1895*, Gordon Mark Berger, ed. and trans. (Princeton and Tokyo: Japan Foundation, 1982), 13. He borrowed the phrase from Sir Harry Parkes.

"as a tiny island of barbarians": ibid., 28.

"I cannot now put into words" and "Viscount Aoki's auspicious telegram": ibid., 71–72.

"so foolish" and "the recent problem has been overcome": ibid., 73.

"to give provocation to China": Mutsu to Ōtori (Seoul) (July 11, 1894), cited by W. G. Beasley, *Japanese Imperialism, 1894–1945* (Oxford: Clarendon, 1987), 48.

"must be extremely cautious": Mutsu to Ōtori (Aug. 23, 1894), Kajima, ed., *Diplomacy of Japan*, 1: 112.

"the conquest and absorption by Japan": Observation by British Minister in Tokyo (Nov. 16, 1894), cited by Beasley, *Japanese Imperialism*, 55.

"to ride the wave of popular Japanese antipathy": Mutsu, *Kenkenroku*, 112.

"Li lay in bed with half of his face swathed": ibid., 178.

"the Mikado might become the Chinese Emperor": F. Hilary Conroy, *The Japanese Seizure of Korea, 1868–1910* (Philadelphia: University of Pennsylvania Press, 1960), 294–95.

"the peace of the Far East": Storry, *History of Modern Japan*, 127.

"the bones of ten thousand": Mutsu, *Kenkenroku*, 106.

"will show its ugly side to us": Dulles, *Prelude to World Power*, 93–94.

Manila and Honolulu 1898

"slumbering volcano": Daws, *Shoal of Time*, 273.

"we are in a great degree helpless" and "We must make a strong effort": *Pacific Commercial Advertiser* (Dec. 1, 1896), cited by Conroy, *Japanese Expansion*, 166.

"Where else but in Hawaii": Iriye, *Pacific Estrangement*, 43.

"there will be established new Japans": *Dai-Nihon bochoran* (On the Expansion of Japan, Tokyo, 1894), cited by ibid., 44.

"If a nation wants to establish": *Japan and the Pacific: A Japanese View of the Eastern Question* (London, 1890), cited by ibid., 35.

"Hawaiian Islands should be controlled": Tate, *U.S. and the Hawaiian Kingdom*, 264.

"We should annex Hawaii immediately": "The Issues of 1896," *Century* 51 (1895), cited by ibid., 264.

"no jingo nonsense": McKinley to Schurz, cited by Foster Rhea Dulles, *The Imperial Years* (New York: Crowell, 1956), 109.

"I do not now say": *Speeches, Correspondence, and Political Papers of Carl Schurz*, 6 vols. (New York: Putnam, 1913), 5: 133–34; cited by H. Wayne Morgan, *America's Road to Empire: The War With Spain and Overseas Expansion* (New York: Knopf, 1965), 22.

"Do nothing unrighteous": Mahan to Roosevelt (May 1, 1897), cited by Harold K. Beale, *Theodore Roosevelt and the Rise of America to World Power* (Baltimore: Johns Hopkins University Press, 1954), 57.

"insidious attempt to run in a horde of Asiatics": William A. Russ, *The Hawaiian Republic and Its Struggle to Win Annexation, 1894–1898* (Selinsgrove, Pa., 1961), 134.

"The conviction felt in Honolulu": Hatch to State Department (May 22, 1897), cited by William Michael Morgan, "The Anti-Japanese Origins of the Hawaiian Annexation Treaty of 1897," *Diplomatic History* 6, no. 1 (Winter 1982): 23–44 (37).

"Under such circumstances annexation": Senate Reports, 55th Congress, 2d Session., no. 681, 66; cited by Tate, *U.S. and the Hawaiian Kingdom*, 273.

"A cruiser or battleship": "Hawaii and the Changing Front of the World," *Forum* 24 (1897): 34–45; cited by ibid., 279.

"No candid American" and "a rapid deterioration in the character": "Manifest Destiny," *Harper's* 87 (1897): 737–46; cited by Julius W. Pratt, *The Expansionists of 1898: The Acquisition of Hawaii and the Spanish Islands* (Baltimore: Johns Hopkins University Press, 1936), 154.

"Remember the *Maine!* To Hell with Spain!": Bailey, *A Diplomatic History*, 458.

"Order the squadron": Albion, *Makers of Naval Policy*, 326.

"seems to be thoroughly loyal": ibid., 325.

"War with Spain—1896": William R. Braisted, *The United States Navy in the Pacific, 1897–1909* (Austin: University of Texas Press, 1958), 21–22.

"unconquerable Anglo-Saxon lust for land" and "the specious plea": Dulles, *America in the Pacific*, 194.

"How can we endure our shame": *Congressional Record, U.S. Senate 1898*, 5790, cited by Tabrah, *Hawaii*, 108–9.

"We cannot let the islands go": George Frisbie Hoar, *Autobiography of Seventy Years*, 2 vols. (New York, 1903), 2: 307–8; cited by Morgan, "Anti-Japanese Origins," 41.

"all that in honor could be done": Dulles, *Prelude to World Power*, 176.

"just as much and a good deal more": Charles Sumner Olcott, *The Life of William McKinley*, 2 vols. (Boston: Houghton Mifflin, 1916), 1: 379.

"cowardly and dishonorable" and "bad business and discreditable" et seq.: James F. Rusling, "Interview with President McKinley," *Christian Advocate* 78 (Jan. 22, 1903): 137–138; cited by Ephraim K. Smith, "'A Question From Which We Could Not Escape': William McKinley and the Decision to Acquire the Philippine Islands," *Diplomatic History* 9, no. 4 (Fall 1985): 363–75 (364).

"of the great outward impulse of civilization": Dulles, *Prelude to World Power*, 190.

"[O]ur duty and destiny": Chandler P. Anderson memorandum of an interview with President McKinley (Nov. 18, 1898), cited by Smith, "'A Question From Which We Could Not Escape,'" 369.

"Japan would have a live volcano": James K. Eyre, Jr., "Japan and the American Annexation of the Philippines," *Pacific Historical Review* 11, no. 1 (Mar. 1942): 55–72 (61).

"On the whole, the advent of the United States": (July 20, 1898), ibid., 60–61.

"imperialism has conquered America": Iriye, *Pacific Estrangement*, 61.

The Eighth 'aha iki

"This great victory is more": Donald Roden, "Baseball and the Quest for National Dignity in Meiji Japan," *American Historical Review* 85, no. 3 (June 1980): 511–34 (524).

"Ah, for the glory of our Baseball Club": ibid., 534.

North, to Alaska 1899

"a nest of ants": William H. Goetzmann and Kay Sloan, *Looking Far North: The Harriman Expedition to Alaska, 1899* (Princeton: Princeton University Press, 1982), 56.

"hear of his plight": David Wharton, *The Alaska Gold Rush* (Bloomington: Indiana University Press, 1972), 26.

"nose for money": Robert A. Lovett, *Forty Years After: An Appreciation of the Genius of Edward Henry Harriman* (Princeton: Princeton University Press, 1949), 12.

"no white man can ever make anything": Robert E. Ficken and Charles P. LeWare, *Washington: A Centennial History* (Seattle: University of Washington Press, 1988), 51.

"veritable mudhole": ibid., 33.

"dogged determination and energetic push . . . of Chicago": Kirk Munroe, "The Cities of the Sound," *Harpers Weekly* (Jan. 1894); cited by Norbert MacDonald, *Distant Neighbors: A Comparative History of Seattle and Vancouver* (Lincoln: University of Nebraska Press, 1987), 41.

"Baptize the savage sagebrush": Goetzmann and Sloan, *Looking Far North*, 23.

"another Siberia": Edmund Noble, "No American Siberia," *North American Review* (Sept. 1882); cited by Ted C. Hinckley, "Alaska as an American Botany Bay," *Pacific Historical Review* 42, no. 1 (Feb. 1973): 1–19 (15).

"This may be the beginning": White House aide Everard F. Tibbott (Mar. 27, 1892), cited by Charles S. Campbell, Jr., "The Bering Sea Settlements of 1892," *Pacific Historical Review* 32, no. 4 (Nov. 1963): 347–67 (362).

"The terrible and the sublime": Goetzmann and Sloan, *Looking Far North*, 63.

"Known as" and "?Name": Hunt, *Arctic Passage*, 188–89.

"the three lucky Swedes": Wharton, *Alaska Gold Rush*, 187.

"Wish I had my Uncle Lem's pigsty": ibid., 182.

"the most barren and desolate place": Goetzmann and Sloan, *Looking Far North*, 137.

Peking 1900

"Witte despises us all": Yuri Semyonov, *Siberia, Its Conquest and Development*, J. R. Foster, trans. (London: Hollis & Carter, 1963), 331.

"eminently sane": *Memoirs of Count Witte*, 96.

"the consequence of our starting to build": Semyonov, *Siberia*, 334.

"mark the beginning of a new epoch": ibid., 330.

"You know, Sergei Iulievich": *Memoirs of Count Witte*, 100.

"remember this day": ibid., 101.

"could not bear to see such an event": Frederic Wakeman, Jr., *The Fall of Imperial China* (New York: Free Press, 1975), 212.

"churls" and "Stupid son!": ibid., 215.

"tertiary Hairy Men" et seq.: Hsü, *Rise of Modern China*, 466.

"confirmed": ibid., 470.

"righteous people": ibid., 473.

"that famous phrase that has been quoted": (Aug. 1898), Dulles, *The Imperial Years*, 202.

"had not been intelligently represented": Dulles, *Prelude to World Power*, 209–10.

"I am fully awake to the great importance": Hay to Rockhill (Aug. 7, 1899), cited by ibid., 210–11.

"equal and impartial trade" and "territorial and administrative entity": Foreign Relations of the United States (Hereafter FRUS) 1901, Appendix (Washington: GPO, 1902), 12.

"I am very glad": *Memoirs of Count Witte*, 107–8.

"if Manchuria becomes the property of Russia": Beasley, *Japanese Imperialism*, 77.

"actuated solely by a desire": Kajima, ed., *Diplomacy of Japan*, 2: 65–66.

"Jews and Poles . . . to be our color bearers in Manchuria": Von Laue, *Sergei Witte*, 245.

"An armed clash with Japan": *Memoirs of Witte*, 117.

"He does not talk to me any more": Semyonov, *Siberia*, 347.

"Admiral of the Pacific": Von Laue, *Sergei Witte*, 246.

Panama City 1903

"construction of such a maritime highway": Dulles, *The Imperial Years*, 244.

"it may be the future of our country": Robert Schufeldt (1870), cited by David McCullough, *The Path Between the Seas: The Creation of The Panama Canal, 1870–1914* (New York: Simon & Schuster, 1977), 27.

"I was not willing to connect": ibid., 127.

"to see the United States the dominant power": Beale, *Theodore Roosevelt*, 81.

"Gentlemen, that's an acceptance hat!": H. Wayne Morgan, *William McKinley and His America* (New York: Syracuse University Press, 1963), 494.

"Don't any of you realize": Boller, *Presidential Campaigns*, 180.

"*manœuvre de la dernière heure*": Jean Gilbreath Niemeyer, *The Panama Story* (Portland, Oreg.: Metropolitan Press, 1968), 116.

"those contemptible little creatures": Thomas G. Paterson et al., *American Foreign Policy: A History* (Lexington, Mass.: Heath, 1977), 221.

"you could no more make an agreement": Beale, *Theodore Roosevelt*, 33.

"foolish and homicidal corruptionists": Paterson, *American Foreign Policy*, 221.

"he would have been a very dull man": ibid., 222.

"trust in the Lord": speech to Naval Academy alumni reported in the Panama *Star & Herald* (Mar. 12, 1903); cited by Niemeyer, *The Panama Story*, 121.

"Uprising occurred tonight": McCullough, *Path Between the Seas*, 371.

"[W]e have never had a concession": John Major, "Who Wrote the Hay–Bunau-Varilla Convention?" *Diplomatic History* 8, no. 2 (Spring 1984): 115–23 (123).

"Inform Municipal Council": Panama *Star & Herald* (Nov. 30, 1903); cited by Niemeyer, *The Panama Story*, 154.

"Have I answered the charges?" and "You certainly have": Dulles, *Imperial Years*, 252–53.

"would have been guilty of folly and weakness": Message of the President (Dec. 7, 1903), FRUS 1903, xl–xli.

"Honest collision": Speech to Episcopal parish (Nov. 1900), Seager, *Mahan: The Man and His Letters*, 454–55.

"I no longer say": Speech to Episcopal parish (Mar. 1899), ibid., 449.

Port Arthur 1904

"The Russian has arrived": Albert J. Beveridge, *The Russian Advance* (New York: Harper & Brothers, 1904), 1.

"America first": ibid (Praeger ed., 1970), vii.

"If you will take Germany and France together": ibid. (1904 ed.), 8.

"Russia, for all practical purposes": ibid., 9.

"Among all the defects": ibid., 31.

"Suddenly a bugle peals": ibid., 39.

"frank, very open" and "too busy to marry" and "an air of business": ibid., 57–58.

"not so expert in railway building": ibid, 84.

"Yes, you may be stronger now": ibid., 109.

"There is but one agency": ibid., 122.

"those brown fellows": ibid., 131.

"thousand million dollars a year": ibid., 171.

"How strong these people look" and "they are nothing but so many human cattle" and "They were dumbfounded": ibid., 221–22.

"Indeed, the Russian state may be said": ibid., 332.

"the basest places of sin" and "It is the outward and visible emblem": ibid., 338–39.

"here is my daily task": ibid., 64.

"It is nothing of the kind" and "God is a fact": ibid., 350, 342.

"The only thing dominant": ibid., 265.

"to compel and repel": ibid., 429.

"It is said, you know": ibid., 437.

"incarnation of the practical" and "Should Sergius Witte die" and "secret ambition": ibid., 438, 450.

"He does not believe in democratic institutions": ibid., 455.

"[e]xperience proves that money will attract": ibid., 457 (quoting Pobedonostsev's *Reflections of a Russian Statesman*).

"Russia is no state": ibid., 461.

"arrived at the Pacific and looks with dreamy eyes": ibid., 337.

"Russia should discard Witte's timid policy": Ian Nish, *The Origins of the Russo-Japanese War* (London: Longman, 1985), 166.

"Now I rule": Tsar's diary, cited by Denis and Peggy Warner, *The Tide at Sunrise: A History of the Russo-Japanese War, 1904–1905* (New York: Charterhouse, 1974), 153.

"dagger pointed at the heart of Japan": Nish, *Origins*, 159.

"no one can say a cheerful word": K. Asakawa, *The Russo-Japanese Conflict: Its Causes and Issues* (Ft. Washington, N.Y.: Kennikat Press, 1970 [1904]), 5.

"the markets of East Asia be closed": ibid., 9.

"A peaceful solution of the Manchurian question": Shumpei Okamoto, *The Japanese Oligarchy and the Russo-Japanese War* (New York: Columbia University Press, 1970), 87.

"frightened without knowing": ibid., 92.

"misgovernment": Nish, *Origins*, 194–95.

"We are bound to fight": Warner and Warner, *The Tide at Sunrise*, 175.

"May God help us!": ibid., 192.

"*Banzai* for His Imperial Majesty!": ibid., 195.

"all mixed together in no sort of order": ibid., 198.

"We shall know how to die": ibid., 202.

"This without a declaration a war": ibid., 207.

"little grandfather": Mitchell, *Russian and Soviet Sea Power*, 219.

"We were astonished" and "sympathetic murmurs": Warner and Warner, *Tide at Sunrise*, 242.

Portsmouth, New Hampshire 1905

"Russia knows as well as we": Raymond A. Esthus, *Theodore Roosevelt and Japan* (Seattle: University of Washington Press, 1966), 9.

"an act of war": Ian H. Nish, *The Anglo-Japanese Alliance: The Diplomacy of Two Island Empires, 1894–1907* (London: Athlone, 1966), 278.

"pluck personified": Esthus, *Theodore Roosevelt and Japan*, 21.

"Japan is playing our game": Raymond A. Esthus, *Double Eagle and Rising Sun: The Russians and Japanese at Portsmouth in 1905* (Durham: Duke University Press, 1988), 16.

"peace will come on terms": Esthus, *Theodore Roosevelt and Japan*, 37.

"would have been a blow to civilization": ibid., 76.

"to proceed with the war to the bitter end" and "little monkeys": Esthus, *Double Eagle and Rising Sun*, 8, 7.

"had not the slightest effect on the tsar": Emile Dillon, *The Eclipse of Russia* (New York: Doran, 1918), 295.

"[t]he Japanese will have capitulated": Richard Hough, *The Fleet That Had to Die* (New York: Viking, 1958), 18–19.

"a sack of manure": Mitchell, *Russian and Soviet Sea Power*, 236.

"great scenes . . . round the vodka cases": Warner and Warner, *The Tide at Sunrise*, 471.

"Presumably Togo is no greater fool": Hough, *Fleet That Had to Die*, 150.

"Look! you can't even see the rear of the fleet": Vladimir Semenov, *The Battle of Tsushima* (London: John Murray, 1910), 36.

"My heart beat furiously": ibid., 52.

"Neither Trafalgar nor the defeat of the Spanish Armada": Esthus, *Double Eagle and Rising Sun*, 38.

"they will kill the tsar": ibid., 46.

"[S]ay to the President": Kajima, ed., *Diplomacy of Japan*, 2: 218–19.

"not absolutely necessary": ibid., 232–33.

"the establishment by Japanese troops": Wilz, "Did the United States Betray Korea?" 252.

"When a sewer has to be cleaned": Vladimir N. Kokovstsov, *Out of My Past: The Memoirs of Count Kokovstsov* (Stanford: Stanford University Press, 1935), 53.

"Anyone but Witte": Vladimir Brenner, *Count Witte: Scenes From His Life and Times, 1902–1915* (Hicksville, N.Y.: Exposition Press, 1979), 120.

"undying resentment against the regime": Esthus, *Double Eagle and Rising Sun*, 166–67.

"We are ashamed to report this": cited by Okamoto, *The Japanese Oligarchy and the Russo-Japanese War*, 169–70.

The Ninth 'aha iki

"ignorant of international politics": *Memoirs of Count Witte*, 162.

"Should any student attempt to devote himself": ibid., 171.

"He must not be allowed to increase his popularity": ibid., 165.

"We do not love the Russian regime": ibid., 149.

"some damned fool thing in the Balkans": Winston Churchill, *The World Crisis*, 2 vols. (New York: Scribner's, 1928), 1: 207.

"God the Omnipotent": Hymn 523, "Russia": *The Hymns of the Protestant Episcopal Church in the U.S.A.* (New York: Church Pension Fund, 1940).

"Mark my words": *Memoirs of Count Witte*, 179.

"That Witte is a hypnotist": ibid., 165.

The Tenth 'aha iki

"the geographical pivot of history" and "world island": Halford Mackinder, "The Geographical Pivot of History," *Geographical Journal* 23 (1904), and *Democratic Ideals and Realities: A Study in the Politics of Reconstruction* (London: Constable, 1919).

"Both the sea and the railway": Robert Strausz-Hupé, *Geopolitics: The Struggle for Space* (New York: Putnam, 1942), 166.

San Francisco 1906

"You two damned fools": John C. Kennedy, *The Great Earthquake and Fire: San Francisco, 1906* (New York: Morrow, 1963), 34–35.

"EARTHQUAKE. TOWN ON FIRE": Gordon Thomas and Max Morgan Witts, *The San Francisco Earthquake* (New York: Stein and Day, 1971), 103.

"FOR GOD'S SAKE SEND COOKED FOOD": Kennedy, *Great Earthquake*, 134.

"RESTORE TO THE NATION": ibid., 160.

"Two-bittee lookee": ibid., 81.

"hordes" of "immoral, intemperate, quarrelsome": Thomas A. Bailey, *Theodore Roosevelt and the Japanese-American Crisis* (Gloucester, Mass.: Peter Smith, 1964), 11.

"The whole world knows": *Mainichi Shimbun* (Oct. 22, 1906), cited by ibid., 50.

"A tenth of the insults": Root to Metcalf (Oct. 27, 1906), cited by Esthus, *Theodore Roosevelt and Japan*, 138–39.

"I am being horribly bothered": (Oct. 26, 1906), Elting E. Morison, ed., *The Letters of Theodore Roosevelt*, 8 vols. (Cambridge: Harvard University Press, 1951–54), 5: 475–76.

"a confession of inferiority": *Compilation of the Messages and Papers of the Presidents*, 15: 7055, cited by Esthus, *Theodore Roosevelt and Japan*, 147.

"crawling degenerates": (Jan. 3, 1907), Bailey, *Theodore Roosevelt and the Japanese-American Crisis*, 69.

"Japan is not going to fight" and "It might do them good": *San Francisco Bulletin* and *Call* (Dec. 3 and 6, 1906), cited by ibid., 74.

"wicked absurdity" and "as much to learn from Japan": *Congressional Record*, 59th Congress, 2d Session, 31.

"tin soldier yawp" and "an unpatriotic President": *San Francisco Examiner* and *Chronicle* (Dec. 21 and 10, 1906), cited by Bailey, *Theodore Roosevelt and the Japanese-American Crisis*, 97.

"the Japanese Jingoes": (July 1, 1907), Morison, ed., *Roosevelt Letters*, 5: 698–99.

"The Philippines form our heel of Achilles": (Aug. 21, 1907), ibid., 5: 761–62.

"utter folly" and "thither in a rowboat": (Jan. 10, 1907), ibid., 5: 550–51.

"You have in a peculiar sense": (July 7, 1907), RG 42, Bureau of Navigation, File 6072, cited by Braisted, *U.S. Navy in the Pacific, 1897–1909*, 229.

"white solidarity" and "yellow peril": Bailey, *Theodore Roosevelt and the Japanese-American Crisis*, 282–85; Braisted, *U.S. Navy in the Pacific, 1897–1909*, 229.

"the independence and integrity of China": FRUS 1908, 511–12.

"Labor's choice Bryan—Jap's choice Taft": Roger Daniels and Spencer C. Olin, Jr., eds., *Racism in California* (New York: Macmillan, 1972), 117.

Korea 1910

"imperial mission": Beasley, *Rise of Modern Japan*, 152.

"should not be channeled": Iriye, *Pacific Estrangement*, 129.

"Imperialism and colonialism are the great currents" and "apart from the white races" and "our country's predominance": ibid., 131–32.

"It is a great loss": ibid., 136–37.

"China now knows better" and "Struggle. Struggle like men": ibid., 139–41.

"excessively nervous": ibid., 147.

"Is the future population of the Pacific coast": A. C. Coolidge, *The United States as a World Power* (New York: Macmillan, 1909), cited by ibid., 154.

"mounted though he appeared to be": Croly, *Willard Straight* (New York: 1924), cited by Esthus, *Theodore Roosevelt and Japan*, 232.

"Korea be made virtually our sovereign area": (July 1904), Iriye, *Pacific Estrangement*, 93.

"sometimes resorted to burning a whole village": Itō to Hayashi (Nov. 29, 1907), cited by Conroy, *Japanese Seizure of Korea*, 366–67.

"President Roosevelt is a man I admire": George H. Jones (June 1, 1908), cited by Esthus, *Theodore Roosevelt and Japan*, 299.

"Take Advice From Theodore": Judith I. Anderson, *William Howard Taft: An Intimate History* (New York: Norton, 1981), 109.

"one of the greatest commercial prizes": Iriye, *Across the Pacific*, 109.

"Japan's goal is commercial supremacy": Thomas F. Millard, *America and the Far Eastern Question* (New York: Scribner's, 1909); cited by Iriye, *Pacific Estrangement*, 186.

"American capital by diplomatic pressure" and "smoke out": Bailey, *A Diplomatic History*, 531–32.

"bluff and back down": ibid., 533.

"Japan is not rich" and "Our vital interest is to keep the Japanese out": Roosevelt to Taft (Dec. 8 and 22, 1910), Morison, ed., *Roosevelt Letters*, 7: 180–81 and 189–90.

"Then he is a fool!": "Itō Hirobumi," *Encyclopedia Britannica*, 15th ed. (1989), 6: 436.

"It was unprofitable for any country": *British Documents on the Origin of the War, 1898–1914*, 11 vols. (London: HMSO, 1926–38), 4: 64–66; cited by Esthus, *Double Eagle and Rising Sun*, 196.

Peking 1912

"Harvard of the West": Bean and Rawls, *California*, 268.

"Little Scrunch-Neck": Clare Boothe's introduction to Homer Lea, *The Valor of Ignorance* (New York: Harper and Bros., 1942 [1909]), 9.

"His dramatic way of speaking": Eugene Anschel, *Homer Lea, Sun Yat-sen, and the Chinese Revolution* (New York: Praeger, 1984), 3.

"unexpected financial difficulties" and "pathetically hunchbacked": ibid., 4.

"lame, halt, and blind" and "vulgar, loud-mouthed, and excessively warlike": Boothe's introduction to *Valor of Ignorance*, 12.

"YOUNG CALIFORNIAN IS PLOTTING" and "well up in military affairs": *San Francisco Call* (Apr. 22, 1900), cited by Anschel, *Homer Lea*, 9.

"you'll get your head cut off in China" and "Fortunately, they'll have a hard time": Boothe's introduction to *Valor of Ignorance*, 12–13.

"Not a word did he say": Anschel, *Homer Lea*, 26.

"Self-Strengthening": Wakeman, *Fall of Imperial China*, 229.

"was on his way to London" and "American Hopes to be Lafayette": Anschel, *Homer Lea*, 71–73.

"Bully": Carl Glick, *Double Ten: Captain O'Banion's Story of the Chinese Revolution* (New York: McGraw Hill, 1945), 133.

"the birds and tea-pickers of the valley": Homer Lea, *The Vermilion Pencil* (New York: Harper and Bros., 1908), 32.

"the first real Chinese novel in English" and "There is but one way to reform China": Anschel, *Homer Lea*, 92.

"Anglo-Saxon Alliance": ibid., 161.

"General HOMER LEA, formerly of the American army": *Singapore Free Press* (Nov. 20, 1911), cited by ibid., 164–65.

"Whether I am to be the titular head": Sun Yat-sen, "My Reminiscences," *Strand Magazine* (Mar. 1912), cited by ibid., 172.

"a nation that is rich, vain, and at the same time": Homer Lea, *Valor of Ignorance*, 58.

"men postpone their patriotic activity": ibid., 6.

"almost inexhaustible wealth": ibid., 197.

"would be placed in a naval and military position": ibid., 205.

"a production of wealth unequal": ibid., 152–53.

"When, however, the political and military power": ibid., 124–25.

"the American people, and not Japan, responsible": ibid., 153.

"Unfortunately Mr. Lea was physically deformed: *China Press* (Nov. 6, 1912), cited by Anschel, *Homer Lea*, 178.

Panama and Kiao-chow 1914

"under the most primitive conditions": McCullough, *Path Between the Seas*, 461.

"a big fellow, a man of daring": ibid., 460.

"Mr. Hill told the President": ibid., 459.

"devil of a mess": ibid., 462.

"There are three diseases in Panama": ibid., 464.

"Let the dirt fly!": Bailey, *A Diplomatic History*, 496.

"God-forsaken country": McCullough, *Path Between the Seas*, 447.

"There is no element of mystery": ibid., 479.

"The Land Divided—the World United": ibid., 481.

"a narrow, tortuous ditch": ibid., 485.

"Now we have taken hold of the job": ibid., 498.

"San Francisco never has failed": (Feb. 10, 1911), G. Allen Greb, "Opening a New Frontier: San Francisco, Los Angeles, and the Panama Canal, 1900–1914," *Pacific Historical Review* 47, no. 3 (Aug. 1978): 405–24 (408–9).

"grave reflection on her national honor and prestige": Kamikawa Hikomatsu, *Japan-American Diplomatic Relations in the Meiji-Taisho Era* (Tokyo: Pan-Pacific Press, 1958), 305.

"Oh, say can you see": (Mar. 13, 1914), Bailey, *A Diplomatic History*, 557.

"Of the two it might be cheaper": ibid., 548.

"economic problem" not "racial": Kamikawa, *Japan-American Relations*, 303.

"The 'honor' which is continually being held up": McCullough, *Path Between the Seas*, 504.

"Stevens must get out at once": ibid., 504.

"it is our great task as a people": Mark R. Peattie, ed., *The Japanese Colonial Empire, 1895–1945* (Princeton: Princeton University Press, 1984), 179.

"temporary occupations": Mark R. Peattie, *Nan'yo: The Rise and Fall of the Japanese in Micronesia, 1885–1945* (Honolulu: University of Hawaii Press, 1988), 43.

"more powerful white adversaries": Kajima, ed., *Diplomacy of Japan*, 3: 128.

"not to cede or lease": Beasley, *Japanese Imperialism*, 113.

"highly desirable": ibid., 114.

"a definite and far-reaching plan": Foster Rhea Dulles, *Forty Years of American-Japanese Relations* (New York: Appleton-Century, 1937), 103.

"I have had the feeling": Tien-yi Li, *Woodrow Wilson's China Policy, 1913–1917* (New York: Octagon, 1969 [1952]), 112.

"got red in the face": Dulles, *Forty Years*, 105–6.

"territorial propinquity creates special relations": FRUS 1917, 264.

Vladivostok and Paris 1919

"the best-qualified man": Secretary of the Interior Franklyn K. Lane, cited by Betty Miller Unterberger, *America's Siberian Expedition, 1918–1920* (Durham: Duke University Press, 1956), 9.

"We should all go back shortly": (Dec. 20, 1918), FRUS 1918, Russia, 3: 213.

"Do Nothing": (Dec. 17, 1917), Eugene Trani, "Woodrow Wilson and the Decision to Intervene in Russia: A Reconsideration," *Journal of Modern History* 48, no. 3 (Sept. 1976): 440–461 (447).

"evacuation of all Russian territory": Unterberger, *Siberian Expedition*, 12–13.

"some sort of alliance": Stephen Pichon (Feb. 28, 1919), FRUS 1918, Russia, 2: 58.

"far surpass in brutality and destruction": (Dec. 7, 1917), Trani, "Decision to Intervene," 449.

"On the Urgency for Allied Intervention in East Russia": Hikomatsu, *Japan-American Relations*, 353.

"over the chaotic conditions in Siberia": (Mar. 19, 1918), ibid., 352.

"sweating blood": Trani, "Decision to Intervene," 458–59.

"a serious mistake to remove the Czecho-Slovak troops": (June 13, 1918), FRUS 1918, Russia, 2: 206–7.

"cousins of the Russians": N. Gordon Levin, *Woodrow Wilson and World Politics: America's Response to War and Revolution* (New York: Oxford University Press, 1968), 99.

"Quick effective Allied action Siberia": (July 6, 1918), FRUS 1918, Russia, 2: 262–63.

"Well, we will have to take that chance": Unterberger, *Siberian Expedition*, 70.

"take the first and fastest train" and "he was sorry" and "This contains the policy": William S. Graves, *America's Siberian Adventure, 1918–1920* (New York: Jonathan Cape & Harrison Smith, 1931), 3–4.

"to cooperate in every practicable way" and "would add to the present sad confusion" and "steady any efforts" and "none of the governments": ibid., 5–10; also FRUS 1918, Russia, 2: 287–90.

"although at the time it became embarrassing": Graves, *Siberian Adventure*, 77.

"could not give a Russian a shirt": ibid., 79–80.

"most of [whose] troops were Jews": ibid., 111.

"was the worst scoundrel I ever saw": ibid., 90.

"strive not to interfere" and "keep in step as far as possible" and "if there is a move" and "go along with the prevailing opinion" *et seq.*: Makino's Instructions Concerning Wilson's 14 Points (Dec. 9, 1918), Kajima, ed., *Diplomacy of Japan*, 3: 344–50.

"discriminate, either in law or in fact": ibid., 3: 396.

"Kaiser" and "female despot": Dulles, *Forty Years*, 124.

"wily, tricky, fight-thirsty Japan": Bailey, *A Diplomatic History*, 636.

"the blackest day" and "Japan is steeped in German ideas": Dulles, *Forty Years*, 131.

"Of course, this could not be done morally": FRUS, Paris Peace Conference 1919, 2: 512–15 (514).

"Every Kolchak adherent I talk to": (May 11, 1919), Pauline Tompkins, *American-Russian Relations in the Far East* (New York: Macmillan, 1949), 110.

"noble sentiments" and "value of the operation of these railways": Graves, *Siberian Adventure*, 179–80.

"Kolchak Railroads financed by the Allies": ibid., 187.

"We are squarely up against the proposition": (May 4, 1919), FRUS 1919, Russia, 491–93 (492).

"The five Russians were marched to some graves": Graves, *Siberian Adventure*, 253–54.

"an honest and courageous man" and "good intentions": (Aug. 4, 1919), FRUS 1919, Russia, 403–5 (403).

"we will be forced to abandon eastern Siberia": (Aug. 11, 1919), FRUS 1919, Russia, 408–10 (410).

"every station was a graveyard": Harmon Tupper, *To the Great Ocean:*

Siberia and the Trans-Siberian Railway (Boston: Little, Brown, 1965), 401–2.

"The truth of the matter": Unterberger, *Siberian Expedition*, 177.

"torn limb from limb": Graves, *Siberian Adventure*, 93.

"some might have liked us more": Unterberger, *Siberian Expedition*, 183

Washington, D.C. 1921

"The Great Commoner": Storry, *History of Modern Japan*, 160.

"incomparably the greatest navy" and "most adequate": Roger Dingman, *Power in the Pacific: The Origins of Naval Arms Limitation, 1914–1922* (Chicago: University of Chicago Press, 1976), 34.

"second to none": Harold and Margaret Sprout, *Toward a New Order of Sea Power: American Naval Policy and the World Scene, 1918–1922* (New York: Greenwood Press, 1943), 51.

"sunk up" and "No more *pilikia*": William R. Braisted, *The United States Navy in the Pacific, 1909–1922* (Austin: University of Texas Press, 1971), 210, 233.

"eight-six program" and "eight-eight program": Dingman, *Power in the Pacific*, 55, 122.

"Shall Japan Fight America?" and "a land of selfish devils": Dulles, *Forty Years*, 151.

"Japan is preparing for any eventuality": Braisted, *U.S. Navy in the Pacific, 1909–1922*, 545.

"to make America think it is impossible": Dingman, *Power in the Pacific*, 135.

"I came under his influence": Betty Glad, *Charles Evans Hughes and the Illusions of Innocence* (Urbana: University of Illinois Press, 1966), 30–32.

"model inquiry": ibid., 63–65.

"animated feather-duster" and "the man who would corrupt public opinion": Merlo J. Pusey, *Charles Evans Hughes*, 2 vols. (New York: Macmillan, 1931), 1: 175–76.

"I hereby resign the office": ibid., 330.

"I had done my best": ibid., 364.

"call no one could well refuse": Glad, *Hughes and the Illusions*, 133.

"If peoples have really become convinced": ibid., 158.

"the special interests of Japan" and "militaristic party" and "fraught with mischief": Hughes to Geddes (June 23, 1921), FRUS 1921, 2: 314–16.

"drubbed and mauled by the Powers": Dingman, *Power in the Pacific*, 187.

"the fact that the Imperial Navy today" and "disadvantages [for] the Empire": ibid., 188.

"Peace in the Pacific": Dulles, *Forty Years*, 160.

"The establishment of permanent world peace" and "misunderstandings or prejudices" and "the maintenance of friendly and smooth relations" and "triple entente": Kajima, ed., *Diplomacy of Japan*, 3: 459–62.

"white panels shone brilliantly": Ichihashi Yamato, *The Washington Conference and After: A Historical Survey* (Stanford: Stanford University Press, 1928), 34.

"Old Testament prophet": Mark Sullivan, *The Great Adventure at Washington* (Garden City: Doubleday, Page, 1922), 3–4.

"Oh, that's alright. Go ahead": Pusey, *Charles Evans Hughes*, 2: 465.

"than all the admirals of the world have sunk": Bailey, *A Diplomatic History*, 640.

"With the acceptance of this plan": Sprout and Sprout, *New Order of Sea Power*, 156–57.

"tornado of cheering": William Allen White, *Autobiography* (New York: Macmillan, 1946), 600.

"one of the most clever things" and "Wilson's fate": Dingman, *Power in the Pacific*, 197–98.

"any arrangement which might purport": A. Whitney Griswold, *The Far Eastern Policy of the United States* (New Haven: Yale University Press, 1962), 325.

"beginning of a new and better epoch" and "the odiousness of perfidy or infamy" and "how alike, indeed" and "the first gain from the World War": Dulles, *Forty Years*, 180–81.

"realized that a new spirit" and "Japan is ready for the new order": ibid., 177.

"Anybody can spit on the Philippines": Bailey, *A Diplomatic History*, 647.

"Our military prestige has received a blow": Sprout and Sprout, *New Order of Sea Power*, 267–68.

"the crux of the situation": Raymond Leslie Buell, *The Washington Conference* (New York: Russell & Russell, 1922), 364ff.

"the most flexible minded of peoples" and "the idea of them as of a people": H. G. Wells, *Washington and the Riddle of Peace* (New York: Macmillan, 1922), 283–84.

Tokyo 1923

"willows" and "flowers": Edward Seidensticker, *Tokyo Rising: The City Since the Great Earthquake* (New York: Knopf, 1990), 54.

"The son of Edo knew a good geisha": Edward Seidensticker, *Low City, High City: Tokyo From Edo to the Earthquake* (New York: Knopf, 1983), 184.

"the curse of the Far East": Otis Manchester Poole, *The Death of Old Yokohama in the Great Japanese Earthquake of September 1, 1923* (London: Allen and Unwin, 1968), 27.

"I had scarcely returned to my desk": ibid., 31.

"vomiting red flames out over the water": ibid., 66.

"charred corpses, pathetic shrunken mummies": ibid., 117.

"the immense ocean of flattened, burned-out city": ibid., 119.

"patriots": Storry, *History of Modern Japan*, 168.

"When the earthquake struck": Seidensticker, *Low City, High City*, 15.

"completely to transform the avenues and streets" and "the man with all the plans": Seidensticker, *Tokyo Rising*, 7–8.

"front door to the nation": ibid., 49.

Gimbura and *eroguru nansensu:* ibid., 46, 59.

"I am a bar flower that blooms by night": ibid., 61.

"You might tell it to go right away to Yokohama" and "You might send such a message for me:" Donald R. McCoy, *Calvin Coolidge: The Quiet President* (New York: Macmillan, 1967), 179.

"Keep California White": Raymond Leslie Buell, "Again the Yellow Peril," *Foreign Affairs* 2, no. 2 (Dec. 1923): 295–309 (303).

"A Jap was a Jap": Roger Daniels, *The Politics of Prejudice: The Anti-Japanese Movement in California and the Struggle for Japanese Exclusion* (New York: Atheneum, 1972), 83.

"capable of taking the place of the White man": ibid.

"real protection for the Pacific coast States": Sidney L. Gulick, *American Democracy and Asiatic Citizenship* (New York: Scribner's, 1918), ix.

"California—the White Man's Paradise": Carey McWilliams, "The Postwar Campaign Against Japanese Americans," in Daniels and Olin, *Racism in California*, 136–37.

"the immigration of the little brown men": Daniels, *Politics of Prejudice*, 84.

"friendship and goodwill of the two neighboring nations": Tasuku Harada, ed., *The Japanese Problem in California* (San Francisco: n.p., 1922), 5.

"Germany of Asia": Daniels, *Politics of Prejudice*, 92.

"It is an incontrovertible fact that the Japanese": ibid., 96.

"come here specifically and professedly for the purpose": ibid., 99.

"the calm before the storm": Buell, "Again the Yellow Peril," 304.

"to question the sovereign right" and "high sense of justice and fair-play" and "stigmatizing" and "the grave consequences": FRUS 1924, 372–73.

"veiled threat": McCoy, *Calvin Coolidge*, 230.

"the Prussia of the East": John A. Garraty, *Henry Cabot Lodge: A Biography* (New York: Knopf, 1965), 374.

"unnecessary and deplorable": McCoy, *Calvin Coolidge*, 232.

The Eleventh 'aha iki

"the labors of arbitration": Lea, *Valor of Ignorance*, 83–84.

"Crime is an index of national character" and "in direct ratio": ibid., 128–29.

"has never been nor will it ever be mechanical": Homer Lea, "The Aeroplane in War," *Harper's Weekly* 54 (Aug. 20 and 27, 1910), cited by Anschel, *Homer Lea*, 186–87.

Seattle to Seattle 1924

"horses and guns": Alfred F. Hurley, *Billy Mitchell: Crusader for Air Power* (Bloomington: Indiana University Press, 1975), 3.

"Declares America Helpless in Air War": *New York Times* (May 4, 1920), cited by ibid., 60.

"He was exalted": Burke Davis, *The Billy Mitchell Affair* (New York: Random House, 1967), 112.

"the only practicable limitation" and "shut the door on progress": Sprout and Sprout, *Toward a New Order of Sea Power*, 229.

"one-and-a-half" and "geographical position and special circumstances": FRUS 1922, 69, 676–78.

"A modern boy fifteen years old" and "Air power will certainly control the Pacific" and "a dominant factor in the military future": Davis, *Billy Mitchell Affair*, 160–64.

"No wonder the Indians call it Iahuma": Terry Gwynn-Jones, *The Air Racers: Aviation's Golden Era, 1909–1936* (London: Pelham Books, 1984), 149.

"Gentlemen, you have arrived on the worst day": ibid., 146.

"allwise Creator that this little band": ibid., 159–60.

"your skill, your perseverance and your courage": Terry Gwynn-Jones, *Farther and Faster: Aviation's Adventuring Years, 1909–1939* (Washington, D.C.: Smithsonian Institution Press, 1991), 202.

"decisive" and "congested" and "paper and wood": Michael S. Sherry, *The*

Rise of American Air Power: The Creation of Armageddon (New Haven: Yale University Press, 1987), 31.

"well-nigh insolvable": William H. Honan, *Visions of Infamy: The Untold Story of How Hector C. Bywater Devised the Plans That Led to Pearl Harbor* (New York: St. Martin's Press, 1991), 73.

"the ruthless scrapping": ibid., 85.

"Japan may be innocent of imperialistic ambitions": ibid., 97.

"military deadlock": ibid., 100.

"like a bolt from the blue" and "a stern resolve to see this struggle through": ibid., 143.

"incompetency, criminal negligence, and almost treasonable administration": Hurley, *Crusader for Air Power*, 101.

"marginally saner policy": Edward S. Miller, *War Plan Orange: The U.S. Strategy to Defeat Japan, 1897–1945* (Annapolis: Naval Institute Press, 1991), 139–40.

"Japan's only chance of victory": Honan, *Visions of Infamy*, 185.

"How Not to Design a Special Purpose Aeroplane": Gwynn-Jones, *Farther and Faster*, 218.

"IN VIEW LINDBERGH'S ATLANTIC FLIGHT": Robert H. Scheppler, *Pacific Air Race* (Washington, D.C.: Smithsonian Institution Press, 1988), 6–7.

"an orgy of reckless sacrifice": ibid., 119.

"the tragedies attending the Dole flight": *Honolulu Advertiser* (Aug. 28, 1927), cited by Gwynn-Jones, *The Air Racers*, 178.

"Japanese militarists are treading in the footsteps of Germany" and "the virtual enslavement of China": Honan, *Visions of Infamy*, 135.

"that great expanse of blue water may become the highway": G. A. Ballard, *The Influence of the Sea on the Political History of Japan* (London: John Murray, 1921), 296.

Shanghai 1927

"vital question between America and Japan" and "will depend much": Yusuke Tsurumi, "The Difficulties and Hopes of Japan," *Foreign Affairs* 3, no. 2 (Dec. 1924): 253–65 (265).

"What is China?": Stanley K. Hornbeck, "Principles and Policies in Regard to China," *Foreign Affairs* 1, no. 2 (Dec. 1922): 120–35 (128).

"all the world knows, China is politically": Kenneth Scott Latourette, "Books on the Far East Since the Washington Conference," *Foreign Affairs* 1, no. 2 (Dec. 1922): 162–68 (166).

"Russia's legal and just rights in China": Peter S. H. Tang, *Russian and Soviet Policy in Manchuria and Outer Mongolia 1911–1931* (Durham: Duke University Press, 1959), 142.

"eight hundred millions of people": Tompkins, *American-Russian Relations*, 191.

"declare once more its intention of returning": Tang, *Russian and Soviet Policy*, 142.

"the Soviets' aggressive policy as an echo of the Tsar's": ibid., 145.

"preponderant influence": Tompkins, *American-Russian Relations*, 208.

"the restoration of the Soviet Union's title": Tang, *Russian and Soviet Policy*, 154.

"breathing spell": Adam Ulam, *Expansion and Coexistence: The History of Soviet Foreign Policy, 1917–1967* (New York: Praeger, 1968), 175.

"to be utilized to the end, squeezed out like a lemon": ibid., 177.

"good neighbor": Storry, *History of Modern Japan*, 170.

"co-existence and co-prosperity": Akira Iriye, *After Imperialism: The Search for a New Order in the Far East* (Cambridge: Harvard University Press, 1965), 110.

"protection of Japanese nationals on the spot": ibid., 146.

"strong" and "weak" China policy: Sadako N. Ogata, *Defiance in Manchuria: The Making of Japanese Foreign Policy, 1931–1932* (Berkeley: University of California Press, 1964), 10.

"Japan evidently intends to draw a dividing line": Iriye, *After Imperialism*, 220.

"our sacred territory of Manchuria is on the verge of a crisis": Joshua A. Fogel, trans., *Life Along the South Manchurian Railway: The Memoirs of Ito Takeo* (Armonk: M. E. Sharpe, 1988), 137.

"young officers": Ramon H. Myers, "Japanese Imperialism in Manchuria: The South Manchurian Railway Company, 1906–1933," in Peter Duus et al., eds., *The Japanese Informal Empire in China, 1895–1937* (Princeton: Princeton University Press, 1989), 128.

"What fools! They behave like children" and "mistake in guarding the railway": Alvin D. Coox, *Nomonhan: Japan Against Russia, 1939*, 2 vols. (Stanford: Stanford University Press, 1985), 1: 15.

"quite as 'imperialistic' in tone": George Alexander Lensen, *The Damned Inheritance: The Soviet Union and the Manchurian Crises, 1924–1935* (Tallahassee: Diplomatic Press, 1974), 24.

"propaganda directed against the political and social system of China": ibid., 39.

"glaring violations": ibid., 41.

"mainly to obtain civilian clothing, which they donned": ibid., 71.

Mukden 1931

"a silvery fish, floating quietly in the ocean of air": Douglas H. Robinson, *Giants in the Sky: A History of the Rigid Airship* (Seattle: University of Washington Press, 1973), xxvii–xxix.

"hell": John J. Stephan, *Sakhalin: A History* (Oxford: Clarendon Press, 1971), xiv.

"absolutely necessary": ibid., 98.

"allowing to slip into Japanese hands the Sakhalin oil fields": Floyd J. Fithian, "Dollars Without the Flag: The Case of Sinclair and Sakhalin Oil," *Pacific Historical Review* 39, no. 2 (May 1970): 205–22 (221).

"On a plane you fly, but on the *Graf* you voyage": John T. Greenwood, ed., *Milestones of Aviation* (New York: Hugh Lauder Levin Associates, 1989), 157.

"multimillionaire" and "to lift the virtuous banner of an Asian league": Beasley, *Japanese Imperialism*, 178.

"have" and "have nots" and "destroy the status quo": ibid., 179.

"Showa Restoration": Beasley, *Rise of Modern Japan*, 168.

"preparedness" and "total war": Michael A. Barnhart, *Japan Prepares for Total War: The Search for Economic Security, 1919–1941* (Ithaca: Cornell University Press, 1987), 9 et seq.

"a new Japan": Peattie, *Nan'yō*, 65.

"We were concerned not only over the Manchuria-Mongolia problem": Barnhart, *Japan Prepares for Total War*, 31.

"a titanic world conflict, unprecedented in human history": Mark R. Peattie, *Ishiwara Kanji and Japan's Confrontation with the West* (Princeton: Princeton University Press, 1975), 46.

"Japan is the Truth of the World": ibid., 42.

"the Final War is fast approaching": ibid., 48.

"grave doubts as to the political capacities": ibid., 35.

"Truly, the Japanese armed forces are the guardian deity": ibid., 54–55.

"war can maintain war": ibid., 68.

"We must lose no time in forcing our country": ibid., 101.

"direct action": Storry, *History of Modern Japan*, 180, 187.

"the conflict originated in Japanese aggression": Coox, *Nomonhan*, 1: 31.

"we shall never encroach upon the rights of the [CER]": ibid., 44.

"Even if Japan has to face the entire world" Peattie, *Ishiwara Kanji*, 136.

"give a hoot in a rain barrel": Bailey, *A Diplomatic History*, 697.

"there is today no guiding purpose or principle": Iriye, *After Imperialism*, 217.

"When the next Chinese general comes to Moscow": Ulam, *Expansion and Coexistence*, 179.

"let the Japanese know we are watching them": Christopher Thorne, *The Limits of Foreign Policy: The West, the League, and the Far Eastern Crisis of 1931–1933* (New York: Capricorn, 1973), 158.

"does not intend to recognize any situation, treaty, or agreement": Griswold, *Far Eastern Policy of the United States*, 424.

"after Stimson has got through invoking": ibid., 699.

"sticking pins in tigers" and "We can never herd the world": Paterson, *American Foreign Policy*, 337, 339.

"If the Soviet does not cease to annoy us": Coox, *Nomonhan*, 77.

"if Japan retains Manchuria this will represent": Karl Radek, "The War in the Far East: A Soviet View," *Foreign Affairs* 10, no. 4 (July 1932): 541–57 (553).

"the most salutary thing that could happen in the Far East": Tompkins, *American-Russian Relations*, 256.

"to waive any and all claims of whatsoever character": ibid., 261.

Nanking 1937

"May I swipe a cigarette" and "My chief purpose in coming here": Jack Alexander, "PROFILES: Diplomat in the Doghouse," *New Yorker* (Apr. 30, 1938): 22–27 (22).

"one of the many admirable American traits" and "To My Daughters": Saitō Hirosi, *Japan's Policies and Purposes: Selections from Recent Addresses and Writings* (Boston: Marshall Jones, 1935), vii, v.

"to look down on Japan": ibid., 13.

"Another question that is frequently asked": ibid., 24.

"xenophobic agitation of Chinese" and "with the progress of human civilization": ibid., 33–34.

"We want all your ladies to have as much silk as they want": ibid., 78.

"a people who have striven hard" and "even you Americans are not without blemish": ibid., 83.

"turn a deaf ear when men tell you we want war": ibid., 86–87.

"are the makers of men": ibid., 157.

"East is East and West and West" and "For Mankind are one in spirit": ibid., 160, 203.

"He is a great deal more effective Ambassador": Joseph C. Grew, *Ten Years in Japan* (New York: Simon and Schuster, 1944), 144.

"great majority of Japanese are astonishingly capable" and "mental processes and methods of reaching conclusions": ibid., 84.

"asked for it": Arthur Waldron, ed., *How the Peace Was Lost: The 1935 Memorandum "Developments Affecting American Policy in the Far East" by John Van Antwerp MacMurray* (Stanford: Hoover Institution Press, 1992). Consulted in MS, 64 of Memo.

"a possibility so remote": ibid., MS 66.

"would be no blessing to the Far East or to the world": ibid., MS 70–71.

"masterly" and "everyone from the President on down": Grew Diary, Houghton Library, Harvard University, 3574, cited by Waldron, ed., *How the Peace Was Lost*, MS 3–4.

"it is possible to say that they may have had in view the possibility of surrounding Japan": Grew, *Ten Years in Japan*, 112.

"I anticipate that our friendly relations and commerce": Robert L. Gandt, *China Clipper: The Age of the Great Flying Boats* (Annapolis: Naval Institute Press, 1991), 101.

"To: Secstate Washington RUSH": Grew, *Ten Years in Japan*, 169–70.

"His Majesty was extremely upset": Edward Behr, *Hirohito: Behind the Myth* (New York: Villard, 1989), 132.

"military fascism": Peattie, *Ishiwara Kanji*, 254.

"are essentially not beings isolated from the state" and "under the emperor a body of people": J. O. Gauntlett, trans., *Kokutai no Hongi: Cardinal Principles of the National Entity of Japan* (Cambridge: Harvard University Press, 1949); cited by Beasley, *Rise of Modern Japan*, 187.

"if our military power permits it, we should deliver a blow": Meirion and Susan Harries, *Soldiers of the Sun: The Rise and Fall of the Imperial Japanese Army* (New York: Random House, 1991), 207.

"The West's greatest fear is a Japanese policy of 'benevolence'": Peattie, *Ishiwara Kanji*, 276.

"the same sort of disaster which overtook Napoleon" and "Tell the Prime Minister that in two thousand years": ibid., 301–2.

"It was a frightening thing to see": H. J. Timperley, ed., *Japanese Terror in China* (New York: Modern Age Books, 1938), 74.

"Friday, Dec. 17. Robbery, murder, rape continue": ibid., 33.

"It is now Christmas Eve. In these two short weeks": Harries and Harries, *Soldiers of the Sun*, 222–23.

"international lawlessness" and "positive measures to preserve peace": Bailey, *A Diplomatic History*, 704.

"So sorry—excuse please": ibid., 705.

"that seems like asking": Saitō, *Japan's Policies and Purposes*, 24.

"to look down on Japan as a band of berserks": ibid., 13.

"Diplomat in the Doghouse": Alexander, *New Yorker* (Apr. 30, 1938), 22.

Nomonhan 1939

"that the Japanese have started a major military adventure": Georgy K. Zhukov, *Memoirs of Marshal Zhukov* (New York: Delacorte, 1971), 147–48.

"to test or fish for the seriousness": Coox, *Nomonhan*, 1: 124.

"Not even one man may be moved": Alvin D. Coox, *The Anatomy of a Small War: The Soviet-Japanese Struggle for Changkufeng/Khasan, 1938* (Westport: Greenwood Press, 1977), 63.

"the chain of Soviet radio stations in Asia": Bruce Hopper, "Eastward the Course of Soviet Empire," *Foreign Affairs* 14, no. 1 (Oct. 1935): 37–50 (50).

"This scheme of ours could be realized": Coox, *Nomonhan*, 1: 162–63.

"the key to the whole Far East": ibid., 1: 148.

"insignificant little mound of sand": Kwantung Army senior operations officer in ibid., 1: 192.

"drenched with the blood of our comrades": ibid., 1: 342.

"to the limit of their technical possibilities": ibid., 2: 663.

"because we are Japanese soldiers": ibid., 2: 707.

"*Tennō Haika Banzai!*": ibid., 2: 811.

"Duty is weightier than a mountain. Death is lighter than a feather": Harries and Harries, *Soldiers of the Sun*, 25.

"the Kwantung Army's affair": Coox, *Nomonhan*, 2: 886.

"treacherous and unpardonable": ibid., 2: 898.

"inexplicable new conditions": Akira Iriye, *The Origins of the Second World War in Asia and the Pacific* (London: Longman, 1987), 81.

"a new order for ensuring permanent stability in East Asia": ibid., 67.

"encourage, assist, or build up an aggressor" and "many methods short of war": Robert A. Divine, *The Reluctant Belligerent: American Entry into World War II*, 2d ed. (New York: Wiley, 1979), 60.

"moderating effect" and "especially susceptible": Roger Dingman, "Farewell to Friendship: The U.S.S. *Astoria*'s Visit to Japan, April 1939," *Diplomatic History* 10, no. 2 (Spring 1986): 121–39 (125).

"a wave of friendliness for the United States": Grew, *Ten Years in Japan*, 275.

"ballyhoo": ibid., 277.

"With the spring coming, everything on earth": ibid., 279.

"a brilliant smile": Dingman, "Farewell to Friendship," 135.

"suppressed" and "stand apart from either group": Grew, *Ten Years in Japan*, 281.

"Most of the people of Japan do not yet quite understand": Harries and Harries, *Soldiers of the Sun*, 196.

"an historical inevitability" and "at a major turning point": Iriye, *Origins of the Second World War*, 106–7.

"It has been the great instruction bequeathed by Ameratsu": Behr, *Hirohito*, 187.

"a source of great joy" and "seek their proper places" and "the Imperial Throne coextensive" and "to ask for the blessing of the Gods": ibid., 187–88.

"lightning diplomacy" and "Providence put a Russian treaty in my pocket" and "promiscuous": George Alexander Lensen, *The Strange Neutrality: Soviet-Japanese Relations During the Second World War* (Tallahassee: Diplomatic Press, 1972), 14–15, 19.

"Asia can also be solved" and "The whole world can be settled!": ibid., 20.

Pearl Harbor 1941

"Will the power and prestige of the white man": Pearl S. Buck, "The Future of the White Man in the Far East," *Foreign Affairs* 19, no. 1 (Oct. 1940): 23–33 (23).

"even the Christian God has undergone change"; "has always been Fascist in her soul"; "but there is no such thing as a quick blow"; "depend[ing] on how *white* Russia is"; "Far Eastern imagination"; "their shadow upon the future of the Far East"; and "the simple and practical wisdom of peace": ibid., 26, 26, 30, 32, 31, 33, and 33.

"I feel as if an iron jacket had been taken off my soul": Paul A. Varg, *Missionaries, Chinese, and Diplomats: The American Protestant Missionary Movement in China, 1890–1952* (New York: Octagon Books, 1977), 265.

"We may condemn Japan's actions in China": Sandra C. Taylor, "The Ineffectual Voice: Japan Missionaries and American Foreign Policy, 1870–1941," *Pacific Historical Review* 53, no. 1 (Feb. 1984): 20–38 (34).

"Part of the present blood is on our hands": ibid., 35.

"peace offer" and "all that the ardent Japanese imperialists": Gordon W. Prange, *At Dawn We Slept: The Untold Story of Pearl Harbor* (New York: McGraw-Hill, 1981), 117.

"I simply haven't enough Navy to go around": Elliot Roosevelt, ed., *F.D.R.: His Personal Letters, 1928–1945*, 2 vols. (New York: Duell, Sloan, & Pearce, 1950), 2: 1173–74.

"was greatly astonished": Konoe diary, cited by Prange, *At Dawn We Slept*, 143.

"The Japs are having a real drag-down and knock-out fight": Harold L. Ickes, *The Secret Diary of Harold L. Ickes*, 3 vols. (New York: Simon and Schuster, 1953), 3: 567.

"the persimmon ripened": Iriye, *Origins of the Second World War*, 142.

"construct the Greater East Asia Co-Prosperity Sphere": Konoe diary, cited by Herbert Feis, *The Road to Pearl Harbor* (Princeton: Princeton University Press, 1950), 215–16.

"mighty swat": Paterson, *American Foreign Policy*, 375.

"would wage war, but not declare it": Divine, *Reluctant Belligerent*, 141.

"world domination on the basis of Anglo-American world views": Iriye, *Origins of the Second World War*, 156.

"Nothing will stop them except force": Feis, *Road to Pearl Harbor*, 248–49.

"weaken our national policy in Europe as well as in the Far East": Iriye, *Across the Pacific*, 220.

"the Navy Chief of General Staff lent a helping hand": Feis, *Road to Pearl Harbor*, 266–67.

"Over the four sides of the sea all people are brothers": Behr, *Hirohito*, 223; Prange, *At Dawn We Slept*, 211; Harries and Harries, *Soldiers of the Sun*, 292; Feis, *Road to Pearl Harbor*, 267 (variously translated).

"little Japan": Iriye, *Origins of the Second World War*, 165.

"if our peace efforts should fail": Grew, *Ten Years in Japan*, 470.

"breaking through the line for a touchdown": Divine, *Reluctant Belligerent*, 155.

"This Empire is now going to war with an arrogant and predestined enemy" and "destroy the United States Fleet" and "is there anything, no matter how difficult it may be": Prange, *At Dawn We Slept*, 387.

"AN AIR ATTACK ON HAWAII! A dream come true": ibid., 388.

"East wind rain" and "things are automatically going to happen": Gordon W. Prange, *Pearl Harbor: The Verdict of History* (New York: McGraw-Hill, 1986), 312–13; Feis, *Road to Pearl Harbor*, 313.

"in order to fight the United States": Behr, *Hirohito*, 174.

"If I am told to fight regardless": Prange, *At Dawn We Slept*, 10.

"Will the power and prestige of the white man": Buck, "Future of the White Man in the Far East," 22.

"I reckon the Japanese are desperate": Sandra C. Taylor, "Japan's Missionary to the Americans: Sidney L. Gulick and America's Interwar Relationship with the Japanese," *Diplomatic History* 4, no. 4 (Fall 1980): 387–407 (405).

"Before we're through with them the Japanese language": Edwin T. Layton, *And I Was There* (New York: William Morrow, 1985), 318.

The Twelfth 'aha iki

"The sun of heaven was loath to set": *The Life and Death of King John*, 5:v:1.

"Alright Morgan—I'll give you your answer": Prange, *Pearl Harbor: The Verdict of History*, 460.

"Rivalry between the kingfisher and the clam": Tsuda Mamichi (1874) in Braisted, ed., *Meiroku Zasshi*, 221.

"Conditions permitting the voluntary self-segregation of the East": Homer Lea, *The Day of the Saxon* (New York: Harper and Brothers, 1942 [1912]), 100–1.

"Nothing is more difficult than to raise the eyelids of man": ibid., 237.

"Isles of blessed Japan!/Should strangers seek" *et seq.*: quotations and paraphrase of Saitō, *Japan's Policies and Purposes*, 202–3.

Tule Lake and Midway Island 1942

"I remember the feeling of relief bubbling" and "I thought it was splendid": Louis Allen, "The Campaigns in Asia and the Pacific," *The Journal of Strategic Studies* 13, no. 1 (March 1990): 162–92 (162–63).

"a stinging loss of face before his whole command": Ronald H. Spector, *Eagle Against the Sun: The American War With Japan* (New York: Free Press, 1985), 84.

"the Japanese only destroyed a lot of old hardware": John Mueller, "Pearl Harbor: Military Inconvenience, Political Disaster," *International Security* 16, no. 3 (Winter 1991/92): 172–203 (176).

"it was God's mercy that our fleet was in Pearl Harbor": ibid.

"spiritual blow": John J. Stephan, *Hawaii Under the Rising Sun: Japan's Plans for Conquest After Pearl Harbor* (Honolulu: University of Hawaii Press, 1984), 93.

"The conclusion is to take Midway": Masataka Chiyaha, trans., *Fading Victory: The Diary of Admiral Matome Ugaki, 1941–1945* (Pittsburgh: University of Pittsburgh Press, 1991), 75.

"do little": Stephan, *Hawaii Under the Rising Sun*, 113.

"Tokyo is our capital and the center of our divine country": Gordon W. Prange, *Miracle At Midway* (New York: McGraw-Hill, 1982), 24.

"If this kind of enemy attempt is to be neutralized": ibid., 26.

"Is Hawaii to remain American or become Japanese?": Daws, *Shoal of Time*, 305.

"Unperceived by ourselves, the white population of Hawaii": Dorothy O.

Hazama and Jane O. Komeiji, *Okage Sama De: The Japanese in Hawaii, 1885–1985* (Honolulu: Bess Press, 1986), 116.

"If we Japanese in Hawaii are treated like 'Japs'": Stephan, *Hawaii Under the Rising Sun*, 26.

"I would kill myself": George H. Blakeslee, "Hawaii: Racial Problem and Naval Base," *Foreign Affairs* 17, no. 1 (Oct. 1938): 90–99 (96).

"If one speaks of liberation of Hawaii's people" and "Hawaii must belong to Japan" and "Hawaii *is* part of Japan": Stephan, *Hawaii Under the Rising Sun*, 156, 131.

"My God, we got here too late": Andrew W. Lind, *Hawaii's Japanese: An Experiment in Democracy* (Princeton: Princeton University Press, 1946), 88.

"American outpost of friendliness and goodwill" and "While we have been subjected to a serious attack": ibid., 70.

"the removal of Japs from Oahu": Roger Daniels, *The Decision to Relocate the Japanese Americans* (Philadelphia: Lippincott, 1975), 28.

"An American citizen, after all, is an American citizen": Roger Daniels, *Concentration Camps USA: Japanese Americans and World War II* (New York: Holt, Rinehart and Winston, 1972), 40.

"the most effective fifth column work": ibid., 35.

"A viper is a viper": ibid., 62

"when the final test comes, who can say": ibid., 61–62.

"I am not going to be a second General Short": Bean and Rawls, *California*, 432.

"the Pacific Coast is in imminent danger of a combined attack": Daniels, *Decision to Relocate*, 47.

"immediate evacuation of all persons of Japanese lineage": Daniels, *Concentration Camps USA*, 70.

"military necessity" and "Be as reasonable as you can": ibid., 72.

"when this war is over" and "Jap-free": ibid., 98, 91, 88.

"The fate of the nation quite literally depended": Layton, *And I Was There*, 470.

"victory disease": Prange, *Miracle At Midway*, 370.

"I had some anxious and agonizing moments": ibid., 143.

"many planes heading Midway": William A. Renzi and Mark D. Doehrs, *Never Look Back: A History of World War II in the Pacific* (Armonk: M. E. Sharpe, 1991), 73.

"glint in the sun appeared . . . like a beautiful silver waterfall": Spector, *Eagle Against the Sun*, 174.

"most important decision": Prange, *Miracle At Midway*, 260.

"Splendid was their tactic" and "Dive bombers!" and "Hell divers!": ibid., 262–63.

"We goofed" and "We were shot with luck": ibid., 265, 388.

"NAVY HAD WORD OF JAP PLAN": ibid., 367.

Attu and Teheran 1943

"the Achilles heel of American defense" and "twenty parachuters could take Alaska" and "home defense" and "three hundred infantrymen": William M. Franklin, "Alaska, Outpost of American Defense," *Foreign Affairs* 19, no. 1 (Oct. 1940): 245–50 (245, 247).

"the first time in history that these natives" and "to drive you out of your villages": Charles Hendricks, "The Eskimos and the Defense of Alaska," *Pacific Historical Review* 54, no. 3 (Aug. 1985): 271–95 (278).

"Only 33 years of living and I am to die": Hunt, *Arctic Passage*, 323.

"O here's to mighty ComNorPac": ibid., 326.

"The year 1942 is going to pass tonight": *Diary of Admiral Ugaki*, 319.

"parallel war": see MacGregor Knox, *Mussolini Unleashed, 1939–1941* (Cambridge: Cambridge University Press, 1982).

"It will be a long, hard war, but after it is over": Christopher Thorne, *The Issue of War: States, Societies, and the Far Eastern Conflict of 1941–1945* (New York: Oxford University Press, 1985), 25.

"the dangers of a false, treacherous peace" and "jujitsu feint in the realm of diplomacy" and "Totalitarian aggression must be smashed": Joseph C. Grew, *Turbulent Era: A Diplomatic Record of Forty Years, 1904–1945,* 2 vols. (Boston: Houghton Mifflin, 1952), 2: 1391–97.

"They were international bandits" and "our lake": Wm. Roger Louis, *Imperialism At Bay, 1941–1945: The United States and the Decolonization of the British Empire* (Oxford: Clarendon Press, 1977), 73, 75.

"four policemen": Keith Eubank, *Summit at Teheran* (New York: William Morrow, 1985), 298–99.

"at the earliest practicable date a general international organization": Keith Sainsbury, *The Turning Point* (New York: Oxford University Press, 1986), 315.

"terrific repercussions, both political and military" and "all sorts of readjustments by my government": Herbert Feis, *Churchill, Roosevelt, Stalin: The War They Waged and the Peace They Sought* (Princeton: Princeton University Press, 1957), 211.

"hate the Japs even more than we do": Daniels, *Concentration Camps U.S.A.*, 33.

"Politically, China is the main bridge": Christopher Thorne, *Allies of a Kind: The United States, Britain, and the War Against Japan, 1941–1945* (New York: Oxford University Press, 1978), 173.

"Peanut" and "Chinese cesspool": ibid., 181.

"stolen" and "be expelled from all other territories": Sainsbury, *The Turning Point*, 321.

"Stalin—I can handle that old buzzard": Bailey, *A Diplomatic History*, 760.

"I think I can handle Stalin better": Sainsbury, *The Turning Point*, 149.

"respect for the sovereignty of other countries": ibid., 241.

"in due course": ibid., 321.

"got along fine with Marshal Stalin": Paterson, *American Foreign Policy*, 395.

Saipan 1944

"We were halfway in when word was radioed": David Dempsey, "Saipan's Blue Beach," in S. E. Smith, ed., *The United States Marine Corps in World War II* (New York: Random House, 1969), 581–82.

"Then a shell crashed thunderously": ibid., 582–83.

"after some of the most effective swearing" and "We had arrived on Saipan" and "I looked around to see" and "We saw two dead marines": Robert Sherrod, "Green Beach Landings," in ibid., 584–88.

"withstand assault by a million men for a hundred years": Harries and Harries, *Soldiers of the Sun*, 429.

"Germans never built anything like this in France": Charles T. Gregg, *Tarawa* (New York: Stein and Day, 1984), 162.

"another Kiska": Spector, *Eagle Against the Sun*, 262.

"When I came back from the Marshalls I was dead tired": ibid., 302.

"after six crowded days aboard an LST": Henry I. Shaw, Jr., et al., *History of U.S. Marine Corps Operations in World War II*, vol. 3, *Central Pacific Drive* (Washington, D.C.: GPO, 1966), 253.

"The planes which cover the sky are all the enemy's" and "At 0930, enemy naval guns began firing": Carl W. Hoffman, *Saipan: The Beginning of the End* (USMC Historical Division, 1950), 36.

"all this smoke and noise": Robert Sherrod, *On to Westward: War in the Central Pacific* (New York: Duell, Sloan, & Pearce, 1945), 47.

"The battle evolved itself into a madhouse of noise": Shaw, *Central Pacific Drive*, 285.

"The Nips would halt, then jump out of their tanks": Sherrod, "Green Beach Landings," in Smith, ed., *Marine Corps in World War II*, 590.

"Because the fate of the Japanese Empire depends": Hoffman, *Saipan*, 101.

"if Saipan is lost, air raids on Tokyo will take place often": Shaw, *Central Pacific Drive*, 295.

"The Japs are coming after us" and "I will ... try to keep the Japs off your neck": Spector, *Eagle Against the Sun*, 305.

"silk stocking": Holland M. Smith, "The Relief of Major General Ralph Smith," in Smith, ed., *Marine Corps in World War II*, 599.

"the troops have been three days without drinking water": Hoffman, *Saipan*, 179.

"Please apologize deeply to the Emperor": ibid., 157.

"Whether we attack or whether we stay where we are": ibid., 222.

"It reminded me of one of those old cattle stampede scenes": ibid., 223.

"the whole area seemed to be a mass of dead bodies": John A. Magruder, "Epitaph," in Smith, ed., *Marine Corps in World War II*, 604.

"When we lost Saipan, Hell is on us": Hoffman, *Saipan*, 260.

"race war": John W. Dower, *War Without Mercy: Race and Power in the Pacific War* (New York: Pantheon, 1986), 4.

"the barbaric tribe of Americans [who] are devils": ibid., 247.

"demon," "ogre," "devil," or "fiend": ibid., 250.

"For the Japanese, the Greater East Asia War is a purifying exorcism": ibid., 225.

"national character that is cloudless, pure, and honest": ibid., 221.

"blood told": ibid., 268.

"eternal" and "creative and constructive" and "unique racial power": ibid., 216.

"Eastern Asia Continent" and "Great Sea of Japan": ibid., 273.

Nagasaki 1945

"18 million Christian American citizens" and "determine the course of history": Michael Schaller, *Douglas MacArthur: The Far Eastern General* (New York: Oxford University Press, 1989), 87, 90.

"sustained air attack alone": Sherry, *Rise of American Air Power*, 90.

"Air Plan for the Defeat of Japan": E. Bartlett Kerr, *Flames Over Tokyo: The U.S. Army Air Force's Incendiary Campaign Against Japan, 1944–1945* (New York: Donald I. Fine, 1991), 34.

"the building of the great pyramid of Cheops": Sherry, *Rise of American Air Power*, 167.

"Why hasn't Tōjō committed suicide yet": Renzi and Roehrs, *Never Look Back*, 104.

"I think we can do it": Spector, *Eagle Against the Sun*, 504.

"Actually, I think it's more immoral": Sherry, *Rise of American Air Power*, 288.

"If over three hundred aircraft take off": Kerr, *Flames Over Tokyo*, 165–66.

"I don't think [the enemy] can keep his cities from being burned": ibid., 173.

"scattered a kind of flaming dew": Robert Gullain, *I Saw Tokyo Burning: An Eyewitness Narrative From Pearl Harbor to Hiroshima* (Garden City: Doubleday, 1981), 184.

"almost as violent as a spring typhoon": Sherry, *Rise of American Air Power*, 276.

"countless bodies were floating": Kerr, *Flames Over Tokyo*, 202.

"CENTER OF TOKYO DEVASTATED BY FIRE BOMBS": ibid., 213.

"The heart of the city is completely gutted" and "most devastating raid in the history of aerial warfare": Sherry, *Rise of American Air Power*, 288.

"If a ship is doomed, what matter its cargo": Lensen, *Strange Neutrality*, 134–35.

"passionate desire": ibid., 138.

"the termination of the influence of the military leaders": Herbert Feis, *The Atomic Bomb and the End of World War II* (Princeton: Princeton University Press, 1961), 16.

"wishes that peace be restored" and "so long as the United States and England": Lensen, *Strange Neutrality*, 145.

"constitutional monarchy under the present dynasty": Feis, *Atomic Bomb*, 26.

"inadvisable to make any statement or take any action": ibid., 81.

"inevitable and complete destruction" and "utter devastation": Charles L. Mee, Jr., *Meeting at Potsdam* (New York: M. Evans & Co., 1975), 313–15.

"a rehash of the Cairo Declaration": ibid., 247.

"Since the loss of one day relative to this present matter": Feis, *Atomic Bomb*, 116.

"The document does not contain anything new": Mee, *Meeting at Potsdam*, 252.

"Give me thirty minutes and I'll give you a date": Sherry, *Rise of American Air Power*, 300.

"I regarded the bomb as a military weapon": Harry S Truman, *Year of Decisions* (Garden City: Doubleday, 1955), 419.

"new-type bomb": Feis, *Atomic Bomb*, 125.

"Loyal to its Allied duty, the Soviet Government": Lensen, *Strange Neutrality*, 151–52.

"to efface the shame of forty years before": John Lukacs, *1945: Year Zero* (Garden City: Doubleday, 1978), 127.

"generally satisfied with the treaty": William H. McNeill, *America, Britain, and Russia: Their Cooperation and Conflict, 1941–1946* (New York: Oxford University Press, 1953), 648.

"that the said declaration does not comprise": ibid., 636.

"The ultimate form of government of Japan": Feis, *Atomic Bomb*, 134.

"I fear that the national polity will be destroyed": ibid., 143.

"Follow the Imperial Will, and stop this foolishness": Edwin Hoyt, *Japan's*

War: The Great Pacific Conflict, 1853–1952 (New York: McGraw-Hill, 1986), 411.

"Nagasaki, the only holy place in all Japan": Takashi Nagai, *The Bells of Nagasaki* (Tokyo: Kodansha International, 1984 [1949]), 107.

"I am going to proceed to Okinawa": *Diary of Admiral Ugaki,* 665–66.

Tokyo 1948

"luminous with hope and joy and peace" and "a symbol of undefeated idealism to isolated millions" and "demons of vainglory and pride": *Commonweal* (Jan. 12, 1945), cited by Lukacs, *1945: Year Zero,* 208–9.

"these atolls, these island harbors": Louis, *Imperialism At Bay,* 84.

"stepping outside the zone of its legitimate": Lester J. Foltos, "The New Pacific Barrier: America's Search for Security in the Pacific, 1945–1947," *Diplomatic History* 13, no. 3 (Summer 1989): 317–42 (331).

"radio stations and weather controls" and "not frozen to the ground": G. Patrick March, "Yanks in Siberia: U.S. Navy Weather Stations in Soviet East Asia, 1945," *Pacific Historical Review* 57, no. 3 (Aug. 1988): 327–42 (331, 340).

"communist revolution which may accompany defeat": John W. Dower, *Empire and Aftermath: Yoshida Shigeru and the Japanese Experience, 1878–1954* (Cambridge: Harvard University Press, 1979), 259.

"[t]he national character of the United States": Richard B. Finn, *Winners in Peace: MacArthur, Yoshida, and Postwar Japan* (Berkeley: University of California Press, 1992), 20.

"Mr. Prima Donna, Brass Hat, Five Star MacArthur": Robert Ferrell, ed., *Off the Record: The Private Papers of Harry S Truman* (New York: Harper and Row, 1980), 61.

"a gesture of trust in the good faith": Finn, *Winners in Peace,* 8.

"We've decided to name him Douglas": Lukacs, *1945: Year Zero,* 213.

"living god": D. Clayton James, *The Years of MacArthur,* vol. 3, *Triumph and Disaster, 1945–1964* (Boston: Houghton Mifflin, 1985), 302–3.

"inherent good nature of the average American": Shigeru Yoshida, *The Yoshida Memoirs,* Kenichi Yoshida, trans. (Boston: Houghton Mifflin, 1961), 63.

"How odd that proclamation was and how Japanese": Behr, *Hirohito,* 319.

"bent with the breeze but did not break": James, *Triumph and Disaster,* 7.

"liberal leaders" and "useful member of the future Pacific community": Michael Schaller, *The American Occupation of Japan: The Origins of the Cold War in Asia* (New York: Oxford University Press, 1985), 11.

"feudal or authoritarian tendencies": Finn, *Winners in Peace,* 30–31.

"in addition to the conventional powers": Theodore Cohen, *Remaking Japan: The American Occupation as New Deal* (New York: Free Press, 1987), 11–12.

"First, destroy the military power": Finn, *Winners in Peace,* 29.

"did not choose to expose himself": Schaller, *Occupation of Japan,* 23.

"are now completely abolished": Finn, *Winners in Peace,* 35.

"We the Japanese People" and "symbol of the state": ibid., 95.

"property of the state": Meirion and Susie Harries, *Sheathing the Sword: The Demilitarization of Japan* (New York: Macmillan, 1987), 82.

"We are out here enjoying the warmth of atomic energy" and "psychological shaft" and "General MacArthur feels that this is the last opportunity" and "dark and grim and his expression did not change": ibid., 92–93.

"deep satisfaction that I am today": James, *Triumph and Disaster*, 132.

"radical tendencies": Schaller, *Occupation of Japan*, 42.

"to increase greatly Christian influence in Japan" and "I approve": Finn, *Winners in Peace*, 62.

"an opportunity without counterpart since the birth of Christ": Schaller, *Douglas MacArthur*, 127.

"billion of these Oriental people" and "fundamentally alter the course of world history": Schaller, *Occupation of Japan*, 70–71.

"about ten Japanese families who practiced": Finn, *Winners in Peace*, 57.

"There's something rather fishy / About the Mitsubishi": Cohen, *Remaking Japan*, 353.

"Being a good loser does not mean saying yes": Yoshida, *Memoirs*, 58.

"[t]he business world will be improved": Finn, *Winners in Peace*, 34.

"it would be a great mistake": ibid., 150.

"Over all things and all men in this sphere of the universe" and "the great issue which confronts": Schaller, *Occupation of Japan*, 50.

"the most active, efficient, cultured, and cosmopolitan": Howard Schonberger, "The Japan Lobby in American Diplomacy, 1947–1952," *Pacific Historical Review* 46, no. 3 (Aug. 1977): 327–59 (329–30).

"under the knife" and "socialistic ideal" and "hog wild": ibid., 332.

"spiritual revolution" and "to keep Japan up": Schaller, *Occupation of Japan*, 96.

"greatest workshops of Europe and Asia": Dean Acheson, *Present at the Creation* (New York: Norton, 1969), 229.

"elderly incompetents" and "the most effete New York club men" and "fragile psychic quality" and "unintelligible to most Japanese": Schaller, *Douglas MacArthur*, 151.

"the most significant contribution": George F. Kennan, *Memoirs, 1925–1950* (Boston: Houghton Mifflin, 1967), 393.

"morgue": Schaller, *Douglas MacArthur,*145.

"still the leading nation" and "the buffer against Soviet Russia": Schaller, *Occupation of Japan*, 112.

"Japanese are going to get along unless" and "we have got to get Japan back into, I am afraid": ibid., 179.

"an honest mistake": Harries and Harries, *Sheathing the Sword*, xxiv.

Korea 1950

"if you told the Japs to throw down their arms": Marc S. Gallicchio, *The Cold War Begins in Asia: American East Asian Policy and the Fall of the Japanese Empire* (New York: Columbia University Press, 1988), 188.

"democratic and united China": Ulam, *Expansion and Coexistence*, 480.

"Sir, the Nationalists, the Kuomintang": Leonard Mosley, *Marshall: Hero For Our Times* (New York: Hearst Books, 1982), 367.

"we Chinese Communists": Steven I. Levine, *Anvil of Victory: The Communist Revolution in Manchuria, 1945–1948* (New York: Columbia University Press, 1987), 62.

"neutral against the Communists": Ulam, *Expansion and Coexistence*, 480.

"irreconcilable groups" and "feudal control": State Department White

Paper, *U.S. Relations With China With Special Reference to 1944–1949* (Washington, D.C.: G.P.O., 1949), 686–89.

"there were not a few persons beaten to death": Levine, *Anvil of Victory*, 225.

"alter the structural design of a house": Hsü, *Rise of Modern China*, 732.

"We reluctantly reach conclusion that early fall": FRUS 1948, 7: 543.

"The unfortunate but inescapable fact": Acheson, *Present at the Creation*, 303.

"ultimately the profound civilization": *U.S. Relations With China*, xvi.

"paper tiger . . . outwardly strong but inwardly weak": Ulam, *Expansion and Coexistence*, 491.

"any other state which should unite with Japan": ibid., 494.

"wait until the dust settles": Acheson, *Present at the Creation*, 306.

"war potential of twenty-three million Koreans" and "the creation of a communist state": Hong-Kyu Park, "From Pearl Harbor to Cairo: America's Korean Diplomacy," *Diplomatic History* 13, no. 3 (Summer 1989): 343–58 (354–55).

"be of paramount importance to Soviet Russia and to China": James I. Matray, "An End to Indifference: America's Korean Policy During World War II," *Diplomatic History* 2, no. 2 (Spring 1978): 181–96 (188).

"tempting opportunity" and "occupy a dominating strategic position in relation": Bruce Cumings, "Introduction: The Course of Korean-American Relations, 1943–1953," in Cumings, ed., *Child of Conflict: The Korean-American Relationship, 1943–1953* (Seattle: University of Washington Press, 1983), 13.

"come up with a proposal": Bruce Cumings, *The Origins of the Korean War*, 2 vols. (Princeton: Princeton University Press, 1981, 1990), 1: 121.

"You will take such action on this matter: ibid., 1: 127.

"All groups seemed to have the common ideas": ibid., 1: 143.

"single most urgent problem now facing": James I. Matray, "The Case for Containment," in Cumings, ed., *Child of Conflict*, 172.

"the one country within which we alone": Thomas Etzold and John Lewis Gaddis, eds., *Containment: Documents on American Policy and Strategy, 1946–1950* (New York: Columbia University Press, 1978), 71–83.

"another place where the line has been clearly drawn": Lloyd Gardner, "Commentary," in Cumings, ed., *Child of Conflict*, 61.

"withdraw from Korea under circumstances which": FRUS 1947, 6: 738–41.

"demonstrating the success and tenacity": Matray, "Case for Containment," 193.

"runs along the Aleutians to Japan" and "the Pacific has become an Anglo-Saxon lake": Acheson, *Present at the Creation*, 357.

"So far as the military security of other areas": ibid.

"The day will come, and possibly sooner": Cumings, "Introduction," in *Child of Conflict*, 23.

"Mars' last gift to an old warrior": Schaller, *Douglas MacArthur*, 181.

"divine aid": Schaller, *Occupation of Japan*, 289.

"a gift from the gods": Dower, *Empire and Aftermath*, 316.

"if Japan becomes a colony": Schaller, *Occupation of Japan*, 257.

"It is an ironic fact that today": George Kennan, *American Diplomacy, 1900–1950* (Chicago: University of Chicago Press, 1951), 51–52.

The Thirteenth 'aha iki

"They all knew that your soldiers and airmen": Feis, *Atomic Bomb*, 85.

Americans' Burden

"trading places": Clyde Prestowitz, Jr., *Trading Places: How We Allowed Japan to Take the Lead* (New York: Basic Books, 1988).

"to dull the edge of this Jap propaganda": David M. Reimers, *Still the Golden Door: The Third World Comes to America* (New York: Columbia University Press, 1985), 15.

"strong and stubborn potential": Bean and Rawls, *California*, 513.

"the crosscurrents of racial feeling create": Claus-M. Naske, *A History of Alaska Statehood* (Lanham, Md.: University Press of America, 1985 [1973]), 236.

"Do we want to put a couple of Japs": Roger Bell, *Last Among Equals: Hawaiian Statehood and American Politics* (Honolulu: University of Hawaii Press, 1984), 253.

"Alaska's largest city rocked and rolled": Naske, *Alaska Statehood*, 271.

"America will gain strength and reassurance": Bell, *Last Among Equals*, 289.

The Dismissal

"Unless the human race differs" and "civilization has not been the prerogative" and "another takes it up and carries": Frederick W. Seward, *Seward at Washington: A Memoir of His Life With Selections From His Letters*, 2 vols. (New York: Derby and Miller, 1891), 2: 504.

"International war has no beginning or end": Lea, *Day of the Saxon*, 218.

"the ephemeral character of national and racial existence": ibid., 230.

Glossary

'aha iki	Hawaiian council, caucus, or "post-mortem"
alii	Hawaiian chiefs
bakufu	Japanese shogun's bureaucracy
bidarka (-i)	seagoing Russian open boats, wooden
bushido	premodern Japanese warrior's code
californios	Hispanic residents of California, prior to U.S. annexation
corrigedores	Spanish governors
daimyo (-ō)	Japanese land magnate(s), pre-Meiji period
doho	overseas Japanese
encomienderos	Spanish land-grant holders, magnates in New World
genro	Japanese elder statesmen, Meiji period
haoles	white foreigners or residents (Hawaii)
heiau	Hawaiian temple, pre-Christian
issei	Japanese immigrant, first generation
kahuna (-ā)	priest(s) of pre-Christian Hawaiian cults
kami	Shinto spirits of a divine quality
kamikaze	"divine wind"; Japanese suicide plane in World War II
kapu	taboo (Hawaiian)
kokua	help (Hawaiian)
kuhina-nui	female regent, under Hawaiian monarchy
mahalo	thank you (Hawaiian)
malamala	the white man's writing (Hawaiian)
mana	divine spirit in pagan Hawaii
muzhik	Russian peasant or serf
nisei	Japanese immigrant, second generation
ostrog(i)	Russian fort(s) in Siberia; fur-trading base
paniolo	Hawaiian cowboy
presidio	Spanish fort
promyshlenniki	Russian or Cossack fur trapper
pueblo	Spanish (or American) town
ranchero	Spanish or Mexican rancher
sakoku	national seclusion under Tokugawa Shogunate
sengoku	era of warring states in Japan

shitiki	ocean-going boats of the *promyshlenniki*
shogun	military regent ruling in name of Japanese emperor
tenno	Japanese emperor
ukase	Russian tsarist decree
verst	Russian unit, about 0.65 miles
voevoda (-y)	tsarist governor(s) in Siberia
yatoi	foreign advisors in Meiji Japan
zaibatsu	family-owned business conglomerates dating from Meiji period

Index

Walter A. McDougall is a professor at the University of Pennsylvania and winner of the Pulitzer Prize for ... *The Heavens and the Earth: A Political History of the Space Age.* He resides in Bryn Mawr, Pennsylvania.